WORKING WOMEN AND CHILDREN

WORKING WOMEN AND CHILDREN

Volume - 1

Working Women in India

Editor-in-Chief

C. P. RAI

LAXMI SHIKSHAN SANSTHAN
LUCKNOW

&

ANMOL PUBLICATIONS PVT. LTD.
NEW DELHI - 110 002 (INDIA)

ANMOL PUBLICATIONS PVT. LTD.
4374/4B, Ansari Road, Daryaganj
New Delhi - 110 002

Working Women and Children

First Edition, 2000

ISBN 81-261-0658-1 (Set)

PRINTED IN INDIA

Published by J.L. Kumar for Anmol Publications Pvt. Ltd., New Delhi -110 002 and Printed at Mehra Offset Press, Delhi.

CONTENTS

PREFACE

The women's and children's employment has brought mixed reaction both from professional and lay persons. It is common knowledge that social changes evoke sometimes more negative than positive emotions. However, in one of the ILO studies dealing with women's employment it was presumed that motive differed with marital status both objectively and subjectively. Not only the economic needs but the motivational reasons also varied with marital status. They broadly mentioned two reasons: (i) Women's economic need, and (ii) national necessity for increased production. Since the work conditions have important bearing on the employment of women some of the papers of this work deal with this issue. It has been found that most of the working women did not have any difficulty in securing a job. If there was any hurdle, it was the initial opposition by the family members. With regard to the attitude of women towards employment, it was found that both the working and the non-working women approved the idea of women's employment. A very large number of both the working and the non-working women felt that in the name of giving freedom to women, men had over-burdened them with various types of work.

Women have always made a very significant contribution to their societies, but a partriarchal conspiracy has prevented women's contribution from receiving its due recognition. Women and their problems have acquired growing importance in our social milieu. Hence, after realising the significant role of women it is desirable that a greater emphasis should be given for her all round development as such providing employment to this vast segment of population becomes prime need of the hour. It has been observed that Indian studies on women, by and large, suffer from a crucial lacuna such as, lack of an integrated approach, which takes into consideration both the micro and the macro level region. The present work is an attempt towards this direction.

It identifies a number of major issues and combines empirical material with theoretical insight and discuss the actual employment position of women in society. The study covers diverse aspects of the subject and discusses complexity of problems faced by women. This is a multi-disciplinary investigation into various aspects of the pressing socio-economic problems facing Indian women. It also provides an overall view on issues and problems related to women contribution. Hence, it is hoped that this work will be of immense importance and interest to all.

— C. P. Rai

1

Working Women: Status and Attitude

The employment of women has brought mixed reaction both from professional and lay persons. It is common knowledge that social changes evoke sometimes more negative than positive emotions. In regard to the employment of women, even social scientists, for the most part, took a negative view. Psychatrists gave negative comments. Lundberg and Farnham expressed a particularly pessimistic evaluation.[1] Some sociologists also tended to lump the increased employment of women along with other trends, such as higher divorce rates, more crime and delinquency. Others, such as Bossard took a strong negative position contending that such employment was gravely detrimental to children.[2] Many a people alert for a simple explanation of the numerous and complex social problems, speculated that the employment of women was the principal cause of current social problems. It was proposed that women should be forced out of employment. A very small number of sociologists such as Komarovsky[3] and Landis[4] favoured changes.

In the absence of sufficient empirical data, it is, however, difficult to say anything definitely. Only recently there have been some serious efforts to examine empirically the attitude and related aspects about women's employment. The enquiry described in these pages is designed to elicit the opinion of working women about some aspects of their life, their attitude towards working and related matters and also to assess the attitudes of their family members, relatives and neighbours to their employment in terms of the perception of the working women themselves. The question that comes up is: what is, on the whole, women's reaction to their dual role? Do they feel harrassed or not? The study commences with the understanding of the position of working women in their families.

Position in the Family

In this investigation, women respondents were asked about their position in two respects; namely, (a) their status in the family and (b) in matters of finance. The first question asked, therefore, was: "what would you say are the main differences your job has made to you in your family?"

The answers to this question are largely in favour of the status quo (fifty-seven per cent). A very large percentage (eighty-two per cent) of the semi-skilled working women felt that there was no change in their status, smallest being the percentage of the low-professionals

(46.5%). It is presumably because of their low income that, on the whole, no change was perceived. Klein mentioned that in her study, only twenty-seven per cent of the women reported that job made no difference.[5] A little more than two-fifths of them mentioned improvement in status in the family (42.5%). In addition to the women employed in N.C.C., a relatively larger section of the low-professionals closely followed by professionals reported improvement in their status. Those who reported improvement in their status, frequently mentioned that they enjoyed more power in family decision-making than before and husbands paid more attention to them. In Klein's study fifty-nine per cent of the married working women mentioned advantages.[6] A very negligible section (0.5% only) reported a decline in their status in the family. They were the semi-skilled workers. Both of them said that when they were not working, their husbands gave for expenses whatsoever they required but after their employment they refused to give a single penny and their requirements were not covered by the income they earned. That is why they felt that there was some decline in their status. Five per cent of them stated disadvantages in Klein's study.[7]

Employment and Change in the Financial Position

Nest, it was to be examined if the employment brought any change in the family finances of the working women. Since most of the women were in employment because of economic pressures, it was worthwhile to elicit information about this aspect.

On the basis of the responses. It was observed that only one-third of the working women were of the opinion that the employment made great change in their financial position (thirty three per cent) and almost the same number reported (32.5%) that it made only some change. In the British study, sixty-four per cent of the respondents mentioned that employment raised their standard of living.[8] Those reporting change in this study, frequently mentioned that they were in a position to fulfil their needs easily and that they were not to depend on others. They also mentioned that they were in a position now to provide better facilities to their family members. A little more than one third of them said that it did not make any difference in their economic condition (34.5%). They were still depending on their parents/ husbands as usual.

In order to make the study of working women regarding their employment adequate, it was necessary to ascertain from them as to what extent did they receive support from the members of their families. Did family members, on the whole, approve of their going to work? The working women were asked to indicate their assessment about the attitude of their family members and neighbours and relatives to their employment. These questions were asked since it was hoped that the attitude of the family, neighbours and relatives might operate as facilitators or barriers to their employment.

Attitude of Family Members

Since, women started entering a variety of occupations, the traditional notion of women's role as being exclusively concerned with house-keeping is likely to change.

Considering the many objections that could be anticipated to the idea of women working out-side the home, it is surprising that the percentage of respondents whose family members had been reported by them to have objected to their employment is less than over one-tenth (8.5%). As against this, there were as many as three-fourths of them who reported that the family members accepted the idea without qualification (seventy-five per cent). Slightly more than one-tenth remained netural (twelve per cent). Ross also found in her study that two-thirds of the men interviewed favoured the idea of women planning careers.[9] Kapadia found that 44.2% of the teachers interviewed favoured the idea.[10] Nye also found that husbands of working women generally approved women's employment.[11] In Detroit sample, sixteen per cent of the working mothers reported that their husbands gave unqualified approval to their working and nineteen per cent reported that their husbands were opposed to the idea.[12] In Klein's study, sixty per cent of the working women reported that their husbands approved of it, six per cent approved conditionally and, five per cent were indifferent.[13] In Gore's study of Delhi Aggarwal families, forty-three per cent of them totally rejected the idea, twenty-four per cent accepted it without qualification and thirty-three per cent conceded that women might work under special circumstances.[14]

An examination of data according to the occupations reveals that irrespective of their occupations, working women reported that their family members approved their working. The highest number was that of petty traders, the lowest being that of the semi-skilled. Some of the women (16.9%) employed in clerical and low-professional jobs reported that their family members totally disliked their employment. Their percentage was the highest of all other working women whose family members did not like the idea of employment at all. Similarly, 15.4% of the semi-skilled workers said that their family members had some objections. Their percentage closely followed by that of the skilled workers (11.8%) was the highest in relation to working women of others occupations. As many as 22.2% of the professionals said that their family members were neutral and this number was comparatively higher than that of other working women giving similar response. The response distribution is presented in Table 1.1.

Initial Opposition

The working women were also asked to indicate whether there was any initial opposition from the side of their family when they began earning.

Most of the working women, seven-tenths of them, gave out that they did not face opposition from their family members (70.5%) whereas less than three-tenths of them said that they faced initial opposition (28.5%). The question was not applicable on one per cent of the working women. Responses enumerating the reasons of initial opposition to their employment by family members indicate that as many as 68.4% of the working women reported that their husbands/parents felt ashamed of the idea of women going to work; 21.9% of them said that in their opinion it would interfere with domestic work and according to 2.5% of them, it might have bad effect on children. Seven per cent of them were of the opinion that family members were afraid of the criticism likely to be made by other people. Some of those working women who reported other reasons (twenty-one per cent) said that their parents wanted them to complete their study first and then get married. They did not prefer that their daughters would run after low paid jobs.

TABLE 1.1

Occupation and Attitude of Family Members (400)

(in Per Cent)

Occupation	*Approved*	*Neutral*	*Dis-Approved*	*Not Applicable*	*Total*
Petty trades (25)	80.0	12.0	—	8.0	100.0
Unskilled work (158)	78.5	11.4	4.4	5.7	100.0
Semi-skilled work (39)	64.1	10.2	18.0	7.7	100.0
Skilled work (34)	76.5	02.9	14.7	5.9	100.0
N.C.C. and armed forces (1)	—	100.0	—	—	100.0
Clerical and low professions (116)	74.2	12.9	11.2	1.7	100.0
Professions (27)	70.4	22.2	07.4	—	100.0

About one-third of the working women engaged in skilled occupations mostly the nurses affirmed that their husbands/parents felt embarrassed and opposed their employment. Their family members were not favourably disposed to their job. In some cases the objection was partly because nurses violated caste rules by handling bed pans, and in other cases, partly because nurses went out for night work, or lived out-side the family premises which was considered indecent in many Indian families. Cormack also pointed out this fact.[15] It may be noted here that prejudice against nursing prevailed in several other Asian countries. In Pakistan, as in India, there was the same feeling.[16] Burmese girls avoided nursing leaving this profession to girls from Karen tribe.[17] In Malaya too, nursing is frowned upon.[18]

One-tenth of those in semi-skilled occupations reported that their family members felt that it would interfere with the domestic chores, another 10.2% of them felt adverse effects on children; and 5.1% of them apprehended the adverse remarks of the neighbours, relatives and others. Thus, the initial objections varied widely and involved considerations of family status, concept of appropriateness of certain roles for women because of innate qualities and disabilities attributed to them, fear of neglect of home and children, and the fear of being unconventional. Table 1.2 gives the details.

TABLE 1.2

Occupation and Initial Opposition (114)*

(in Per Cent)

Occupation	*Felt Ashamed*	*Interfe-rence with Domestic work*	*Bad Effects on Children*	*Criticism from Community*	*Other Reasons*
Petty trades (1)	100.0	100.0	—	—	—
Unskilled work (42)	73.8	19.0	16.7	04.8	4.8
Semi-skilled work (13)	69.2	30.8	30.8	15.4	15.4
Skilled work (19)	57.9	10.5	—	—	52.6
N.C.C. and armed force (–)					
Clerical and low profession (38)	68.4	26.3	02.6	10.5	23.7
Professions (1)	—	—	—	—	100.0

* It is a multi-response Table.

Attitude of Neighbours and Relatives

When the working women were asked to indicate the attitude of their relatives and neighbours towards their employment, 57.5% of them told that relatives and neighbours very much appreciated their working for they were making use of their training and talents and supporting their families instead of sitting idle at home and wasting their time and energy unnecessarily. Twenty-four per cent of the working women were of the view that relatives and neighbours were generally neutral in this regard. Only 6.5% respondents mentioned about neighbour's and relatives criticism. Twelve per cents of the working women did not know as what were the attitudes of their neighbours and relatives towards their employment.

Attitude of neigbours and relatives on the basis of occupation of working women reveals that in addition the N.C.C. instructor, the largest proportion of the semi-skilled working women reported that their relatives and neighbours appreciated their working and only 7.7% of them said that they were critical. Unmarried girls working in family planning and drama division of AIR reported that since their jobs involved touring for several days and they had to stay at different places at night, their relatives and neighbours criticised their parents for allowing their daughters to remain out-side home for many days. Similarly if some male colleagues came to their residence, neighbours started making adverse comments. The detailed analysis has been given in Table 1.3.

TABLE 1.3

Occupation and Attitude of Neighbours and Relatives (400)

(in Per Cent)

Occupation	*Appreciate*	*Neutral*	*Criticise*	*Do not know*	*Total*
Petty trades (25)	48.0	32.0	04.0	16.0	100.0
Unskilled work (158)	57.0	25.9	03.8	13.3	100.0
Semi-skilled work (39)	69.2	20.5	07.7	02.6	100.0
Skilled work (34)	41.2	44.1	—	14.7	100.0
N.C.C. and armed force (1)	100.0	—	—	—	100.0
Clerical and low professions (116)	58.6	18.1	12.1	11.2	100.0
Professions (27)	66.7	11.1	07.4	14.8	100.0

Women's Own Attitude Towards Employment

According to the traditional notion, women are expected to perform household duties and it is for men to take care of other out-side work. It is just as undesirable for a woman to work out side home in other to earn money as it is for the man to do the domestic work. That this view is held by the women or not was examined. A comparison was made of the views of working as well as of non-working women.

It is seen that the percentage of working women disapproving the idea was only 10.5% and that of non-working women is 20.3%. Almost an equal percentage of both the working and the non-working women (34.5% and thirty-five per cent respectively) conceded that women could work under special circumstances. Frequent responses favouring women's employment conditionally were as follows:—Women should work if husband/father was unable to earn due to illness, unemployment and old age; the income of the husband/father was so meager that it was difficult to make two ends meet; children were adult and there was no adverse effect on them; she could work for a change; if a woman was widowed or separated and had to support her family. Gore found that forty-three per cent of women rejected the idea totally and twenty-three per cent of them accepted the idea of women's employment under special circumstances.[19]

More than one-half of the working women responded favourably (53.5%) whereas less than one-half of non-working women agreed to it (43.5%). Some working women (1.3%) and non-working women (1.2%) were not sure about their own views in this regard. The frequent responses of those who favoured the idea were. In the present days of spiralling prices a woman should work to contribute to her family income; it was necessary for a woman to make use of her talents and training; a women should work in order to compete with men in every field; women should work so that she might become economically independent.

Those who rejected the idea, their main fears were:

It would affect children adversely; community would be critical; working against the will of husband/parents lead to marital/family tensions; one should not work if husband was well paid because it would otherwise amount to depriving an equally qualified male worker of the employment he needed to support the family as it sole bread winner.

Service as an Interim between Education and Marriage

It is a prevalent view that women do not take their employment seriously. They consider it as a temporary arrangement. In order to while away their time before marriage, they should do something and one way of filling the gap was to do gainful work readily available to them. For the educated girls, service was just a stop-gap measure between their education and marriage. This attitude towards employment was likely to affect employment opportunity for women and also their performance. It is, therefore, essential to study the views of woman whether they considered service as an interim between education and marriage.

The opinion of the working women seemed to be sharply divided on the question of whether service for women was an interim between education and marriage. They were almost equally divided, 42.2% of them reporting as an interim and 43.3% said it was not more than one-half of the non-working women considered employment of girls to be only an interim arrangement (fifty-three per cent) whereas this view was held by less than half of the working women. Among those who did not consider it as an interim arrangement the percentage of the working and the non-working women. Among those who did not consider it as an interim arrangement the percentage of the working and the non-working women was almost equal (42.8%). Some 14.5% of working women and 4.2% of non-working women did not know whether service was an interim between education and marriage.

Should Young Girls Work and Remain Unmarried?

There is a tendency among some employed girls not to marry and lead an independent life. The respondents were asked to give their opinion whether they approved of their attitude of young girls who did not wish to marry but continued in employment because they thought that after marriage they might not been a position to lead a free and independent life. The question asked was: "A tendency is observed among some employed girls that they want to live an independent life and that they do not want to marry. Do you approve this idea?"

An overwhelming majority of both the working (74.3%) and the non-working women (74.0%) did not like the idea of young working girls remaining unmarried. Only a small number of women approved the idea, 16.5% of working and 20.5% non-working. Some 9.2%) working women and 5.5% non-working women were not sure about their views.

The main objections stated by both the working and the non-working women against this view of remaining unmarried are as follows:—

Marriage is a necessity of life. One needs life partner; unmarried girl is a burden on parents; one must marry because times are bad; community will raise an accusing finger; girl would lose her character; in old age who would help if the girl does not marry? Parents can not live for ever.

Those who approved the idea were generally of the view that if a girl did not want to marry, parents should not insist on her getting married. After all she has to lead her own life. Some considered marriage as a gamble. Some considered it an unnecessary hurdle in the way of free and independent life of a woman.

In the light of these remarks, it seemed worthwhile to enquire about the attitude of the unmarried working women regarding their future plan.

Plan for Continuity of Employment after Marriage

There were eighty-one unmarried working women and their responses were analysed to show the inclination of the unmarried working women towards their future career, *i.e.* whether they wished to continue their work even after they were married. A question was asked. "Supposing you were married, do you think you would want to continue in a job?"

Slightly more than one-fourth of the unmarried working women expressed their desire to continue work (twenty-six per cent). Slightly more than one-fifth of the unmarried working women said outright that they wished to give up employment on marriage (twenty-one per cent). In Klein's study twenty-eight per cent of the single women were for giving-up employment and only fifteen per cent of them said that they proposed to continue indefinitely.[20] A relatively larger proportion of the working women of this study, seemed to have an open mind on the question. Whether or not to continue in employment after marriage would depend on their husbands or family members' consent (thirty-seven per cent). In Klein's study only four per cent of them mentioned that it depended on their future husbands' financial position.[21] As many as 11.1% of the working women of Jodhpur said that they were not certain as to what they would do in future and 4.9% of them stated that they had decided not to marry in future but to continue in their job.

Working Girls Get More Chances for Mate Selection

It has been remarked that work place is the best possible marriage market because there the unmarried working women will meet a high concentration of her mental equals. To ascertain the views of women about this, the respondents were asked to tell whether in their view working girls were able to get more chances for mate selection. Table 1.4 is designed to show the distribution of responses.

More than one-half of the working women and only two-fifths of the non-working women were of the opinion that it was not necessary that working girls would get more chances to select mate at their work-place. Compared to working women, relatively a large section of the non-working women felt that working girls got more chances for mate selection. A very small number of both the working and the non-working women considered that working girls did not get more chances for mate selection.

TABLE 1.4

Working Girls Get More Chances for Mate Selection (400)

(in Per Cent)

Opinion	*Working Women*	*Non-Working Women*
Get more chances	35.8	44.5
Do not get more chances	09.2	14.8
Not necessarily	55.0	40.7
Total	100.0	100.0

Balance of Domestic Work and Employment

One of the problems for the employed home makers was the difficulty of combining the two roles-home making and employment. In order to sind out reaction of the working women about the question whether it was possible to carry on two roles, Table 1.5 has been designed to show their opinion on this question.

TABLE 1.5

Balance of Domestic Work and Employment (400)

(in Per Cent)

Opinion	*Working Women*	*Non Working Women*
Yes, possible	52.0	43.0
No, not possible	44.8	50.2
Do not know	03.2	06.8
Total	100.0	100.0

Over one-half of the working women felt that employment and domestic work both could be carried simultaneously. But non-working women did not feel so sure. As against working women, a relatively small section of them said that home making and employment could be balanced. Only 44.8% of working women thought that it would be difficult to do both home and outside work and one-half of the non-working women observed that it was not possible to do so. In Japan also sixty-five per cent of the wives reported incompatibility between occupational work and home.[22] It is possible that those working women who held that it was possible to do both might have approached the domestic work differently. They must have re-scheduled their domestic chores. They also expressed the view that a woman could do both if she got the co-operation of husband, adult children and other family members and also by getting-up early in the morning, she could finish her household duties easily.

The responses of those who expressed contrary opinion etc.

Working women cannot look after her family and children properly; the husband gets annoyed if the wife does not pay due attention to him; one does not get time for leisure; leaving home under the supervision of servant means double expenditure and less gain; work-load on children increases.

Should Married Women be Given Less Burden of Work?

The information were gathered whether the married working women should be given lesser burden of work than the unmarried working women in the same occupation.

Only a small percentage of the working (39.8%) and the non-working women (37.5%) said that married women should be given less burdensome work whereas a little more than half of working (52.5% and non-working women (51.5%) did not consider it proper to do so. Some working women (7.7%) and non-working women (eleven per cent) did not give their opinion.

Those who were in favour, frequently mentioned that married women had also to bear the burden of household tasks and the care of children. In their comparison, unmarried girls had to shoulder less responsibilities, so less work should be taken from married working women. Those who did not favour the idea, their most frequent responses were that one should be ready to do everything that was required to be done at work place and there should be no discrimination. If married women had responsibilities, the unmarried working women were not devoid of home responsibilities; that only the nature of responsibility might be different which did not call for discrimination.

Surprisingly, some women maintained that unmarried girls should be given less burdensome work as they were inexperienced, immature and less attentive than the married working women. It is clear from the emphatic way in which many informants replied that it would be wrong to differentiate between the married and single woman.

The Unemployment Scare

Some social scientists, more particularly economists[23] have pointed out the need for higher participation of women in economic activities specially in developing countries. But an equally strong opinion has been expressed against this view. It is argued that the advantages to some families by employment of women would be offset by a corresponding loss for other families whose bread-winner would lose his job if more women were given employment.

This question became part of serious consideration in many international gatherings of ILO since 1964. A delegate to ILO Conference of 1964 described a draft resolution from the women's committee as "the result of excited and often stormy verbal exchanges in the Committee." He continued by saying: "I firmly believe that it is a serious error of judgment for developing countries to ascribe high action priority to plan for encouraging women to enter the market, especially women with family responsibilities, when those same countries do not have or cannot create sufficient jobs for their male populations." The discussions at various other meetings showed considerable disagreement. They recommended that women's employment should be very carefully considered, and suggested that there might be need for giving priority to men in employment market, while other delegates thought that development in all spheres required the contribution of its women power as well as it men power.[24]

With this debate in view, an attempt is made here to understand the attitude of women towards this issue and hence a question was asked whether employment of women lead to unemployment among men. The responses given by women are presented in Table 1.6.

TABLE 1.6

Unemployment Among Men (400)

(in Per Cent)

Opinion	*Working Women*	*Non-Working Women*
Agree	29.8	32.3
Disagree	52.0	47.0
Do not know	18.2	20.7
Total	100.0	100.0

The data indicate that more than one-half of the working women considered that their employment would not create unemployment for men whereas similar view was expressed by less than one-half of the non-working women (forty-seven per cent) Approximately three-tenths of the working women reported that their employment would create unemployment among men and as against this opinion about one-third of non-working women said that women's employment created unemployment among men. One-third of them were unaware of the consequences.

Rights to Women

The constitution of free India guarantees all its citizens equal rights and it goes a step further and makes a special provision for safeguarding the interest of women. Women enjoy the same right of franchise as men, they get equal pay and equal opportunities for selection and appointment in various services of the country. They also enjoy the right to inherit property and the right to divorce. Legally speaking they enjoy equal rights in all aspects of the social, economic and political set-up of the country. It is maintain that they are in a very favourable position. In some cases they enjoy greater freedom than even those enjoyed by their counterparts in some of the Western countries, hence, it was considered appropriate to assess the views of women about the extent of the right they have been constitutionally provided. Whether they are adequate for them. The detailed analysis of their responses has been given in the Table 1.7

TABLE 1.7

Rights of Women (400)

(in Per Cent)

Opinion	*Working Women*	*Non-Working Women*
More than needed	06.8	09.0
Adequate	59.0	69.8
Less than needed	13.2	07.5
Not certain	14.2	07.2
Do not know	06.8	06.5
Total	100.0	100.0

A large percentage of both the working women (fifty-nine per cent) and the non-working women (69.8%) felt that it was almost adequate, but compared to working women (6.8%) a larger section of non-working women (nine per cent) considered it more than needed, and the percentage of the working women was more (13.2%) than that of the non-working women (7.5%) among those who considered it less than required.

Independence or Over-Burdened

After having examined the various factors of opinion and attitude of working women, an attempt is made to present in the end, their own assessment about the fact whether in the name of giving freedom to women, the men-folk had actually over-burdened them with variety of tasks and responsibilities such as making household purchases, arranging admission and education of children, going to banks and post offices when required and doing other odd jobs. The were asked to give their own assessment about this question.

As many as 73.8% of working women agreed with the view that in the name of giving freedom, men-folk had over-burdened them. Only 17.7% of them did not agree with this contention and 8.5% said that they were not quite certain about it. Among the non-working women 67.3% had agreed, 27.5% did not and 5.2% were not certain.

Conclusions

In this chapter an attempt has been made to show if employment had brought any change in the life of the working women and also to assess their attitude towards employment and some related issues. In the case of majority of working women there was no change in their status in family, but there had taken place some change in their financial position.

An overwhelming majority of working women reported that the members of their families approved their employment. But there was some initial opposition in some of the cases. The main reason of the initial opposition was the feeling of embarrassment among parents. Neighbours and relatives generally appreciated their employment. With regard to the attitude of women towards employment, it was found that both the working and the non-working women approved the idea of women's employment and the percentage of working women in this category was more than that of the non-working women.

A majority of the non-working women considered employment as an interim arrangement between education and marriage but most of the working women did not think so. However, a large selection of both the working and the non-working women were of the opinion that the unmarried young girls must also marry and they should not remain unmarried even if they were in employment. More than one-fourth of the unmarried working women expressed their desire to continue work after marriage. A large number of working women did not consider that working girl necessarily got more chances for mate selection whereas most of the non-working women were of the opinion that they did get more chances for marriage.

Contrary to the view expressed by non-working women, a majority of the working women held that it was possible to carry on domestic work and employment simultaneously. There was no difference of opinion among the employed and the non-employed women with regard to the differential treatment to be accorded to women on the basis of marital status. An equal percentage of both the working and the non-working women was of the view that the married women should not be given any special treatment. A relatively large number of working women considered that unemployment among men was not created on account of the employment of women.

A majority of both the working and the non-working women was of the view that adequate rights had been given to women and the percentage of the non-working women was higher than that of the working women.

A very large number of both the working and the non-working women felt that in the name of giving freedom to women, men had over-burdened them with various types of work.

REFERENCES

1. Lundberg, Ferdinand, and Marynia F. Farnham, *Modern Women: The Lost Sex*, New York: Harper, 1947 as quoted in *The Employed Mother*, p. 7.
2. Bossard, James H.S., *The Sociology of Child Development*, New York: Harper, 1954, pp. 282-86.
3. Komarovsky, Mirra, *Women in the Modern World*, Boston: Little Brown, 1953, as quoted in *The Employed Mother*, p. 7.
4. Landis, Paul, H., *Making the Most of Marriages*, New York: Appleton-Century-Crofts, 1955, as quoted in *The Employed Mother*, p. 273.
5. Klein, Viola, *Britain's Married Women Workers*, p. 59.
6. *Ibid.*
7. *Ibid.*
8. *Ibid.*
9. Ross, Aileen D., *The Hindu Family in its Urban Setting*, 1961, p. 201.
10. Kapadia, K.M., "Changing Pattern of Hindu Marriage and Family," Part II, *Sociological Bulletin*, 3 (September, 1954), p. 153.

11. Nye, F. Ivan, *The Employed Mothers*, p. 279.
12. Hoffman, L.W., 'The Decision to Work," *The Employed Mother*, p. 36.
13. Klein, Viola, *op. cit.*, pp. 64-65.
14. Gore, M.S., *Urbanisation and Family Change*, Bombay: Popular Prakashan, 1968, p. 159.
15. Cormack, Margaret, *The Hindu Women*, London, pp. 5,160.
16. Husain, A.F.A., *Employment of Middle Class Muslim Women in Dacca*. Dacca, 1958, pp. 60, 65.
17. Audrus, J. Russel, *Burmese Economic Life*, Stanford, 1948, p. 291.
18. Wee, Ann, E., "Some Aspects of the Status of Chinese Women in Malya," In Appadorai, A. (ed.), *The Status of Women in South Asia*, Bombay, 1954, p. 162.
19. Gore, M.S., *op. cit.*, p. 159.
20. Klein, Viola, *op. cit.*, p. 50.
21. *Ibid.*
22. National Public Opinion Research Institute, Japan, "Research Reports on the Occupational Life of Working Women," 1954, as quoted in Koyam, Takashi, *The Changing Social Position of Women in Japan*, 1961, p. 126.
23. Lewis, W.A., *The Theory of Economic Growth*, London, 1957, pp. 16-17; Nath, Kamla, "Urban Women Workers—A Preliminary Study," *The Economic Weekly*, 37 (September 11, 1965), p. 1412.
24. International Labour Organisation, *African Conference Report*, 1964, pp. 82-83.

2

Why do Women Seek Employment?

Causes that prompt women to enter into employment are as complex as those influencing other choices that affect their way of life. It is generally believe that socio-cultural changes play a very important role in creating a situation in which women would like to seek employment. While one would not deny the importance of socio-cultural changes, there are several other factors which lead one to take individual decision to work or not to work. It might be that in a particular cultural context, one was in a position to get employment but her desire might not be translated into action, if she was not in a position to go out of home. Examples can be multiplied and we could see that actual decision involved several underlying consideration requiring careful examination in any study dealing with motivating factors that impel women to seek employment. It is possible that one may have one's own reasons but scrutiny of data collected is likely to show some pattern which might throw light on these underlying considerations. It is, therefore, appropriate to know those factors which pull and push women to enter the working force. The analysis of individual's decision to work give insight about the processes inducing women to take to employment. Such an analysis also helps in making prediction abut the future impact of the employment of women, i.e., whether it would increase or decrease? This is why the study of the factors inducing women to join the working force deserves serious consideration. The present chapter therefore, deals with the factors that explain as to why women go to work.

WHY WOMEN WORK?

In one of the ILO studies dealing with women's employment it was presumed that motives *differed* with marital status both objectively and subjectively. Not only the economic needs but the motivational reasons also vary with marital status. They broadly mentioned two reasons: (a) Women's economic need, and (b) national necessity for increased production.[1]

Some other studies have brought to light the fact that loneliness is a powerful motive for women to seek employment outside their homes.[2] The Ministry of Labour, Government of India has pointed out that whatsoever the stage of economic or social development of a country, four factors prevail which lead women to join working force. They are: (a) the inadequate income of the principal earner which forces a women to work and supplement the income; (b) mishaps, such as incapacity of the bread winner; (c) death of the bread-winner; and (d) a women's desire for economic independence or for securing higher standard of living. There is also the desire on the part of the women to give expression to their own talents and skills.[3]

In view of these observations the per cent distribution of the sample of working women accounting to the motives and the board classification of responses are given in Table 2.1.

TABLE 2.1

Main Reasons for Employment (400)

Main Reasons for Work		*Per cent*
1. Financial Reasons		
(a)	Economic Pressures	58.5
(b)	Other economic needs	14.8
(c)	Higher Standard of living	04.2
	Sub-Total	77.5
2. Non-Financial Reasons		
(a)	Personality traits	15.8
(b)	To utilise time	03.7
(c)	Traditional occupation	03.0
	Sub-Total	22.5
	Grand Total	100.0

The percentage distribution of responses given by the employed women stating reasons of employment shows that women, essentially worked for financial motives. Like Klein's study, where she found that seventy-three per cent women worked for money,[4] more than three-fourths of the working women (77.5%) of this study mentioned financial reasons while less than one-fourth of them (22.5%) reported non-financial reasons. Delhi and Bombay studies also mentioned that a large proportion of working women worked for economic reasons (sixty-nine per cent and sixty-five per cent respectively).[6]

Financial Reasons

Among various reasons which have been termed as financial, three sub-categories are noted: (a) economic pressures which pertain to the fulfilment of basic minimum needs of life, (b) other economic needs—money required to help relatives, (c) higher standard of living some of the women reported that they worked for financial reasons. They desired to have better education of children and a supply of objects of comfort.

On the basis of the criteria used to identify financial reasons, it was found that economic pressures accounted for 58.5%. Of these, some women were working so as to satisfy the basic minimum (27.8%), to support dependents (25.7%) because of the death of the principal bread-winner in the family, and 4.5% of them reported that rapid increase in the cost of living had brought the family income to a difficult situation and it was imperative for them to work to provide for the family requirements. Two of them (0.5%) reported that they were working to repay the debts incurred due to necessities such as prolonged illness in the family and marriage of sons and daughters.

Besides economic pressures, they mentioned other economic needs. 14.3% of them said that they worked to support their relative while 0.5% worked to bear the expenses of medicines that they required to keep them fit.

Higher standard of living was mentioned by a very small number of women. Only 1.5% of working women reported that they wanted to make provisions for higher education of their children as well as for their own education and 2.7% of them maintained that they worked to live decently.

Non-Financial Reasons

The non-financial reasons for working have been classified into three categories.

(a) Personality Traits

There are several personality factors which are involved in the motivation for employment. For instance, in this study 10.8% working women who had deliberately chosen careers reported that they wanted to fill a need for accomplishment and 1.8% of them said that they worked because they wanted to attain recognition by proving themselves able to compete successfully with men in activities for which they were once debarred. Some (1.8%) considered it as a national duty, 1.2% of them worked for personal independence and only one women said that she was working because of the uncertainty of the future. On the whole, 15.8% of working women have mentioned one or the other type of personality traits to be the factor inducting them to work.

(b) To Occupy Time

3.7% of working women reported that they felt boredom with the continuous routine of household tasks and felt lonely and isolated in the home. They want an escape into the work day world to utilise time meaningfully.

(c) Traditional Occupation

Three per cent of working women reported that they worked because of the tradition of the family in a specific occupation. It also helped them to earn their living.

The financial reasons, thus, seem to be the most important reasons for women's seeking employment. However, it is possible that reasons for work differ among women themselves. Possibly, easily measurable demographic characteristics such as age, education etc. might be useful to explain the variations. To understand this, we shall compare these demographic variables to reasons for work.

Age

Table 2.2 classifies working women into reason-for-work categories on the basis of major reasons they have offered for working. From this table an attempt has been made to understand the association of these variables with the reason of their work. This might also explain the characteristics of women who offer each reason.

The percentage distribution of the response indicates that irrespective of their age, the working women reported that financial reasons were more important for them than the non-financial reasons.

Though the percentage of working women seemed to be increasing with the increase in age, it was found that there were no significant differences in the percentage accounted for by financial reasons. The old as well as the middle and the young working women were pressed almost equally by financial factors. But within the broad group of financial reasons, there were significant differences in the number of those working on account of one particular financial reason. Thus, more than three-fourths of the old aged working women (78.2%), more than three-fifths of the middle aged working women (63.8% and even less than one-half of the young working women (48.8%) worked due to economic pressures. There was, however, a decrease in the percentage of the working women accounting for other economic needs with increase in age. The young and the middle aged were almost equally distributed (15.9% and 15.2% respectively) while the working women of old age in this category were only 4.4%. Young working women's percentage accounting for standard of living is much higher than that of middle aged working women.

Of those who worked because of personality traits or to avoid domestic responsibilities the number of young working women was more than that of the women of other age groups. Old working women 8.8%) who stated non-financial reasons as factors in their employment held to traditional occupations.

TABLE 2.2

Main Reasons for Employment by Age

(in Per Cent)

	Financial				*Non-Financial*				
Age Groups	*Economic pressures*	*Other economic needs*	*Higher standard of living*	*Total*	*Personality traits*	*To utilise time*	*Traditional occupation*	*Total*	*Grand Total*
Young (170)	48.8	15.9	07.0	71.7	20.6	05.3	02.4	28.3	100.0
Middle (205)	63.8	15.2	02.5	81.5	13.2	02.3	03.0	18.5	100.0
Old (23)	78.2	04.4	—	82.6	04.3	04.3	08.0	17.4	100.0
Age not specified (2)	100.0	—	—	100.0	—	—	—	—	100.0

In short, it may be inferred that though economic pressures accounted for a sizable number of young working women, they were less than even one-half of all the working women of young age group. Some of them would like to live a life which gave them some compensation. For middle and old aged working women, and especially for the latter economic pressures were the most dominant factors.

Economic pressures, therefore, were the dominating factors with the working women irrespective of age. They became much pressing as the age increased. The old working women were continuing largely in the working force not to rise their standard of living or to occupy their surplus time, or for some self-compensation. They worked to provide for the necessities of life. The middle aged working women were working on account of economic pressures. Though young working women also worked largely on account of economic pressures yet some of them were motivated by self-expression and actualisation. Therefore, with the increase in age, the continuance in the working force was mainly determined by economic considerations and self-expression as determinant lost its significance. Standard of living was not found to be a motivating factor in this study.

Caste

In Table 2.3 details regarding caste status and main reasons of work have been discussed.

TABLE 2.3

Main Reasons for Employment by Caste (400)

(in Per Cent)

Reason for Work

	Financial				*Non-Financial*				
Age Groups	*Economic pressures*	*Other economic needs*	*Higher standard of living*	*Total*	*Personality traits*	*To occupy time*	*Traditional occupation*	*Total*	*Grand Total*
Upper (63)	41.3	17.4	09.5	67.2	27.0	04.8	—	31.8	100.00
Middle (104)	51.9	14.5	05.8	72.2	20.2	06.7	00.9	27.8	100.0
Lower and Scheduled Castes and Tribes (173)	76.9	12.7	01.1	90.7	04.6	01.7	03.0	09.3	100.0
Others (60)	35.0	18.3	05.0	58.3	28.3	03.4	10.0	41.7	100.0

It is evident from the table that with the rise in the status of the caste, the number of those working women reporting financial reasons declined whereas the number of those reporting non financial reasons increased. It is to be noted that economic pressures accounted for the largest number of lower and Scheduled Castes/Tribes. Three-fourths of them reported this whereas only one-half of the working women of middle castes and less than half of the upper caste women stated that they worked because of economic pressures. Though the number of working women reporting other reasons was small, there was a reverse trend with the rise in the status of caste. There was a decline in the number of working women reporting other economic needs, higher standard of living or personality traits. Only a very negligible section of working women of lower and Scheduled Castes/Tribes mentioned standard of living and personality trait as reason for employment. The number of upper caste working women was higher than that of lower and Scheduled Castes/Tribes and middle castes.

Thus, economic pressure was the compelling reason for employment irrespective of caste differentiation. But it is also evident that it was comparatively more dominant among lower and Scheduled Castes/Tribes. Standard of living and personality traits were not dominant. However, motive of actualisation accounted for more than one-fourth of the upper caste working women and some of them had also the desire for higher standard of living. Somewhat more than one-fourth of other-castes-working women also reported personality traits as factor in their employment.

Marital Status

Table 2.4 presents the distribution of the sample in terms of the marital status and cause of work.

TABLE 2.4

Main Reasons for Employment by Marital Status

(in Per Cent)

Reason for Work

	Financial				*Non-Financial*				
Marital Status	*Economic pressures*	*Other economic needs*	*Higher standard of living*	*Total*	*Personality traits*	*To occupy time*	*Traditional occupation*	*Total*	*Grand Total*
Unmarried (81)	33.3	14.8	11.1	59.2	34.6	06.2	—	40.8	100.0
Married (225)	53.3	19.5	03.6	76.4	14.8	04.4	04.4	23.6	100.0
Widowed and Separated (94)	92.6	03.2	—	95.8	02.1	—	02.1	04.2	100.0

The data with respect to marital status and reasons of employment indicate that a substantially large number of the working women irrespective of their marital status were in employment due to financial reasons. But a difference in response was perceptible among those reporting economic pressures. Only one-third of the unmarried working women (33.3%) reported that they were in working force because of economic pressures and almost the same number of them (34.6%) asserted that they worked because they wanted to attain recognition in the community. Only a small percentage of them (11.1%) talked of higher standard of living, but their percentage was higher than that of other respondents in this study. Contrary to this findings, Ferdinand Zweig who has made a study into the attitudes and habits of Lancashire working women, estimates that "among married wives no more than about one in three goes out to work under economic pressure..."[6]. In this study slightly more than half of the married working women worked due to economic pressures. It is the widowed and the separated women whose largest number, slightly more than nine-tenths of them (92.6%), reported their being in labour force because of economic pressures. It is in conformity with the findings of a study by the Women's Bureau, U.S.A. Of 8,300 women workers in 100 Trade Union Locals which showed that ninety-eight per cent of those without husbands (widowed, separated and divorced) were working to support themselves and others.[7] None of them has said that they worked to raise standard of living and only 2.1% of them attributed this working to personality traits.

It can be inferred that though the economic pressures was dominant as a factor of employment of the women, it was not much dominant among the unmarried. Their main consideration was to live a life which might give them compensation. Standard of living was not a motivating factors. Was perceptible only in some of the unmarried working women (11.1%). Among married women its percentage was negligible (3.6%). Almost all the widowed and the separated women were working because of economic pressures. It was clear then that marital status played an important role in creating difference in the responses related to reasons for work.

Nature of Family

The working women lived in various types of families. The composition of the family in which a working woman lived helped or hindered her entrance into employment.

TABLE 2.5

Main Reasons for Employment by Nature of Family (400)

(in Per Cent)

	Financial				*Non-Financial*				
Age Groups	*Economic pressures*	*Other economic needs*	*Higher standard of living*	*Total*	*Personality traits*	*To utilise time*	*Traditional occupation*	*Total*	*Grand Total*
Single Member (18)	72.2	05.6	—	77.8	16.7	—	05.5	22.3	100.0
Nuclear (209)	56.0	14.8	04.3	75.1	17.7	04.8	02.4	24.9	100.0
Joint (173)	60.1	15.6	04.6	80.3	13.3	02.9	03.5	19.7	100.0

As Table 2.5 indicates the financial reasons seemed to be equally important to all the working women irrespective of the nature of their families. However, it may be seen that the percentage of working women with joint families is the highest (80.3%) when compared to the working women belonging to a single member family or nuclear family. But the differences are not much. Economic pressures have been most important for 72.2% of the single member family and 60.1% to the joint family working women as against 56.0% of the nuclear family working women. Other economic needs were mentioned by 15.6% of working women of the joint families, 14.8% of nuclear and only 5.6% of single member families. Higher standard of living was mentioned by working women of joint and nuclear families (4.6% and 4.3% respectively). The working women of nuclear and joint families went to work to occupy their time. Their percentage distribution is 4.8% and 2.9% respectively.

Size of Family and Cause of Work

A large number of the working women irrespective of the size of their families mentioned that they worked for financial reason. The percentage of those with larger families is the highest and of those with small-size families is the lowest. Single member family working women worked for economic pressures whereas the number of those belonging to large families, where others are to support is the lowest in this respect. The percentage of working women with large families mentioning other economic needs and higher standards of living was more than that of others. Some (8.1%) of the working women with small families mentioned that they worked to while away time and 16.4% of large family women reported that they worked to carry on the traditional occupation. As many as 16.7% single member of 16.1% small families' women mentioned personality traits as cause for their taking to work. The distribution of detailed responses can be seen in Table 2.6.

TABLE 2.6

Main Reasons for Employment by Size of Family

(in Per Cent)

Reason for Work

	Financial				*Non-Financial*				
Size of Family	*Economic pressures*	*Other economic needs*	*Higher standard of living*	*Total*	*Personality traits*	*To occupy time*	*Traditional occupation*	*Total*	*Grand Total*
Single Member (18)	72.4	05.6	—	77.8	16.7	—	05.5	22.2	100.0
Small (62)	59.7	12.9	03.2	75.8	16.1	08.1	—	24.2	100.0
Intermediate (179)	62.0	13.4	04.0	79.4	15.1	02.2	03.3	20.6	100.0
Large (141)	52.5	18.4	05.7	76.6	03.5	03.5	16.4	23.4	100.0

Number of Children

A very large number of working women, irrespective of the number of children worked because of financial reasons; the highest being the percentage of working women with medium number of children. Though the percentage of working women who worked to occupy time was very small yet of those working women who had no children (9.8%) worked to avoid boredom. Their percentage was three times more than that of working women with small and medium number of children giving boredom as reason for their employment.

Number of Dependents

The data show that those working women on whom depended larger number of persons, were more likely to work because of financial reasons than those who had no dependents or small or medium number of dependents.

Earners

With the increase in the number of earners in the working women's families, the percentage of those who mentioned financial reasons decreased; the highest being only when one was earning i.e. working woman herself. A reverse trend was noted among those who mentioned non-financial reasons. The percentage was also decreasing with increase in number of earners in the category of those who worked under economic pressures. There was only one working woman with more than six earning members and she said that she worked to avoid boredom. The detailed distribution of responses is shown in Table 3.7.

It is also seen that with the increase in number of earners upto six, there was an increase in the percentage of working women who were in employment because of personality traits or of those who wanted to carry on their family occupation.

TABLE 2.7

Main Reasons for Employment by Number of Earners in the Family

(in Per Cent)

Reason for Work

	Financial Reason				*Non-Financial Reason*				
Number of Earners in Family	*Economic pressures*	*Other economic needs*	*Higher standard of living*	*Total*	*Personality traits*	*To occupy time*	*Traditional occupation*	*Total*	*Grand Total*
1 Earner (67)	80.5	06.0	—	86.5	10.5	01.5	01.5	13.5	100.0
2-3 Earners (285)	55.0	15.8	5.3	76.1	16.9	4.2	2.8	23.9	100.0
4-6 Earners (47)	48.9	21.3	4.3	74.5	17.6	2.1	6.4	25.5	100.0
7 + Earners (1)	—	—	—	—	—	100.0	—	100.0	100.0

Educational

The distribution of Responses of working women reporting the reasons impelling them to join labour force in terms of education is given in Table 2.8.

An analysis of the cause of employment by the educational standard of the employed women brings out the fact that with the increase in the level of education, the number of the working women reporting financial reasons was declining and increasing where non-financial reasons were in operation. More than three-fourths of the unlettered working women and slightly more than a half of low educated and also a little more than one-third of the highly educated working women reported that they worked due to economic pressures. Contrary to this, the number of working women who reported higher standard of living or non-financial reasons increased with the increase in education. It may be noted that more than three-fourths of non-lettered working women (78.0%) mentioned economic pressures whereas only one of them reported higher standard of living, and only two mentioned personality traits to be the cause of their going to work. Contrary to this only slightly more than one-third of highly educated working women reported economic pressures, one-third of them reported personality traits and eight per cent mentioned higher standard of living. In short, non-lettered women worked mainly because of economic pressures. Among highly educated, slightly more than one-third worked on account of economic pressures and one-third worked because they preferred attainment and recognition. One-tenth of them reported higher standard of living as the main cause of their work. The finding of this study in regard to educated women is more or less comparable to that of Kapoor who has reported that educate women take up jobs not only out of sheer economic necessity but also out of various other socio-psycho situational reasons.[8]

TABLE 2.8

Main Reasons for Employment by Education (400)

(in Per Cent)

Reason for Work

	Financial				*Non-Financial*				
Education	*Economic pressures*	*Other economic needs*	*Higher standard of living*	*Total*	*Personality traits*	*To occupy time*	*Traditional occupation*	*Total*	*Grand Total*
Non-lettered (192)	78.0	13.6	00.5	92.1	01.1	02.1	04.7	07.9	100.0
Low Educated (42)	54.7	14.3	04.8	73.8	14.3	04.8	07.1	26.2	100.0
Highly educated (166)	36.8	16.3	08.4	61.5	33.1	05.4	—	38.5	100.0

Occupation

A very large section of the working women employed in unskilled occupations described their work to financial reasons. Their percentage was the highest (94.2%) compared to that of the working women employed in various occupations. The lowest was the percentage in this category of the working women engaged in professions (29.6%). Similarly, the percentage of unskilled working women mentioning economic pressures as cause was the highest. They formed 82.8% of all the unskilled working women closely followed by those employed in petty trades. In this response category, the lowest percentage was again of the professionals (7.0%). Those who mention other economic needs, the percentage of working women engaged in semi-skilled occupations is the highest (30.8%) compared to women employed elsewhere; the lowest being that of the professionals (3.7%) . The higher standard of living accounted for 18.5% of the professionals which was the highest percentage of the other categories of working women; the lowest being that of the unskilled.

The percentage of the professionals is the highest (11.1%) who take to work to occupy time. The semi-skilled workers (20.5%) banked upon traditional occupation. Only one working women was engaged in N.C.C. and she considered it as a national duty. Like her, 59.3% of the professionals and fifty per cent of the skilled workers reported personality trait as cause of employment.

The occupationwise distribution shows that economic pressures were dominant among unskilled and petty-traders, whereas among those employed in N.C.C., professionals and skilled workers, personality traits seemed to be dominating. It was apparent then that the occupation of working women distinguished the factors making for employment. It may, thus, be inferred that working women of prestigious occupations were not working because of economic pressures but mostly because of the desire of attainment and recongition; and those in non-prestigeous occupations worked because of economic pressures (Table 2.9).

TABLE 2.9

Main Reasons for Employment by Occupation

(in Per Cent)

Reason for Work

	Financial				*Non-Financial*				
Occupation	*Economic pressures*	*Other economic needs*	*Higher standard of living*	*Total*	*Personality traits*	*To occupy time*	*Traditional occupation*	*Total*	*Grand Total*
Petty-Trades (25)	80.0	08.0	—	88.0	—	—	12.0	12.0	100.0
Unskilled work (158)	82.8	10.7	00.7	94.2	02.6	02.6	00.6	05.8	100.0
Semi-skilled work (39)	43.6	30.8	—	74.4	—	05.1	20.5	25.6	100.0
Skilled work (34)	23.5	20.5	03.0	47.0	50.0	03.0	—	53.0	100.0
N.C.C. and Armed forces (1)	—	—	—	—	100.0	—	—	100.0	100.0
Clerical and low professions (116)	48.3	17.2	08.6	74.1	21.6	04.3	—	25.9	100.0
Professions (27)	07.4	03.7	18.5	29.6	59.3	11.1	—	70.4	100.0

Family Income

The percentage distribution of the sample of working women according to their average family income is presented in Table 2.10.

TABLE 2.10

Main Reasons for Employment by Average Family Income (400)

(in Per Cent)

Reason for Work

	Financial				*Non-Financial*				
Family Income of Working Women	*Economic pressures*	*Other economic needs*	*Higher standard of living*	*Total*	*Personality traits*	*To occupy time*	*Traditional occupation*	*Total*	*Grand Total*
Lower (201)	75.7	14.4	01.0	91.1	01.5	01.9	05.5	08.9	100.0
Lower Middle (162)	46.9	17.3	05.5	69.7	26.0	03.7	00.6	30.3	100.0
Upper middle (31)	19.3	06.4	13.0	38.7	48.3	13.0	—	61.3	100.0
Upper (6)	—	—	33.3	33.3	50.0	16.7	—	66.7	100.0

The number of working women reporting financial reasons went on declining with the increase in the average income of their family whereas a reverse trend was perceptible among those mentioning non-financial reasons. Three-fourths of the working women of the Family of the lower income group, less than half of the working women of lower middle income family and even less than one-fifth of the upper middle income family relied on economic pressure compelling them to work. None of the upper-income family working women considered economic pressures as imperative for employment. However, one-third of the working women of the family of the upper income group said that they worked to raise their standard of living. The working women of the lower income families did not consider personality trait as any major cause of their employment. Slightly less than half of the working women of the families of the upper-middle and upper income group considered that they worked because of personality traits.

It is apparent that the family income and the reasons of employment were very significantly related to each other. As the family income increased the percentage of the women working because of economic pressures declined to the extent that no working women belonging to the family of the upper income groups reported that she worked because of economic pressures. Instead, one-third of them reported higher standard of living, approximately one half of them and also slightly less than half of the upper-middle income group families mentioned personality traits, attainment and recognition as cause of employment.

Income of Husband

After this, in order to make things a little more concrete, the analysis was further made to show the income of husband and ratio of working wife in terms of the responses given as reason of their employment (Table 2.11).

TABLE 2.11

Main Reasons for Employment by Income of Husbands (225)*

(in Per Cent)

Reason for Work

Age Groups	*Financial*				*Non-Financial*				
	Economic pressures	*Other economic needs*	*Higher standard of living*	*Total*	*Personality traits*	*To occupy time*	*Traditional occupation*	*Total*	*Grand Total*
No Income (21)	71.4	19.0	—	90.4	04.8	04.8	—	09.6	100.0
Lower (84)	70.2	16.7	01.2	88.1	01.2	04.8	05.9	11.9	100.0
Lower middle (92)	43. 5	23.9	03.3	70.7	19.6	04.3	05.4	29.3	100.0
Upper Middle (18)	27.8	22.2	05.6	55.6	44.4	—	—	44.4	100.0
Upper (10)	—	10.0	30.0	40.0	50.0	10.0	—	60.0	100.0

* Out of 400 working women, only 225 are living with their husbands.

From the responses one could note that with the increase in the income of husbands there was likelihood of substantial decrease in the number of working women who worked because of economic pressures. However, they would work for recognition and higher standard of living. This is also the finding of a study conducted by Kapoor of Delhi educated working women.[9] Similar results were obtained by Durand also.[10]

CONCLUSIONS

In this Chapter we emphasised the importance of studying the factors involved in women's decision to work. The flow of women into the labour market can be considered as directly related to their general economic conditions. Financial reasons, especially the economic pressures, were the major factors to draw women into the working force. This was more than evident from the responses given by approximately three-fifths of them. There were others who did not work just to keep the wolf away from the door but because of the desire for achievement and self-compensation. Some of these were professionally trained and considered it a duty to utilise their capacities in the interest of the community. A few of them felt social isolation because they had nothing to do in their homes and therefore, they went to work to avoid the boredom. It may, however, be kept in view that the number of women who stated non-financial reasons was small, less than one-fourth of all the working women.

It has been found that with the increase in the age of working women, there was an increase in the percentage of those stating financial reasons and there was a corresponding decrease among those stating non-financial reasons. With the increase in age the continuity in employment seemed to be determined by economic pressures and considerations such as actualisation and self-expression lost their significance. Higher standard of living was not an important motivational force. Irrespective of caste status, financial reasons were stated as the most important; but with the increase in the status of caste there was a decline in the percentage of those stating these reasons. The working women of lower, Scheduled Castes and Tribes worked mostly because of economic pressures whereas it was not so with the majority of upper caste working women. Practically all the widowed and the separated women worked on account of financial reasons, under economic pressures; married working women took to work for the same reasons. A larger section of unmarried working women worked on account of personality traits. Economic pressures had been the main reasons for employment irrespective of the nature of the family, (the percentage of single member family being the highest). The working women with single member family were mostly in employment because of economic pressures.

The working women with medium number of children, a large number of dependents and less number of earners were mostly working on account of dire economic needs economic pressure was most felt by non-lettered working women. A sizable section of highly educated women worked to eke out their personality traits. Unskilled working women closely followed by petty traders joined the working force due to economic pressures, but a large majority of the professionals worked to give out personality traits. It was observed that the larger the income of the family, the lesser was the chance of women joining the labour force on account of financial reasons and economic pressures, so much so that not a single working woman of upper income group was found in the working force because of economic pressures. Approximately one-half of them worked because of personality traits and one-third of them took to work for higher standard of living.

There existed an inverse relation between the percentage of wives in employment and the income of their husbands. The working women whose husbands had no earnings of their own or had low earnings, worked mainly on account of economic pressures whereas a small percentage of working women whose husband's income was higher, worked because of this reason. Not a single working woman whose husband's earnings is very high worked due to economic pressures. They were working mostly either because of personality traits or for higher standard of living.

REFERENCES

1. An International Survey of the Conditions of Working Women with Home and Family Responsibilities, carried out by the International Labour Office, as quoted in Myrdal, Alva and Viola Klein, *Women's Two Roles*, London, Routledge and Kegan Paul, 1962, p. 82.

2. Zweig, F., *Women's Life and Labour*, London: Victor Gallanz, 1952, p. 74.
3. Government of India, "International Trends," *Women in Employment*, Labour Bureau, Ministry of Labour and Employment, 1964, pp. 58-59.
4. Klein, Viola, *Britain's Married Women Workers*, London, Routledge and Kegan Paul, 1965, pp. 36-37.
5. Ranade and Ramchandran, p. 18.
6. Zweig, F., *op. cit.*, p. 74.
7. Leaflet, 11, "Why Do Women Work?" 1951, as quoted in Ray E. Barber *Marriage and the Family* New York, McGraw Hill, 1953, P. 348.
8. Kapoor, Promilla, *Marriage and the Working Woman In India*, Delhi: Vikas Publications, 1970. P. 395.
9. Promilla Kapoor, *op. cit.*, p. 396.
10. Durand, John D., "Married Women in Labour Force," *American Journal of Sociology*, 26 (November, 1946), pp. 217-74.

3

Working Women and Their Conditions of Work

Authors on industrial sociology have pointed out the importance of work conditions in the study of working force.[1] This consideration becomes still more important when a study is made of the working women. That is why in the present study, the relevant data have been brought together to throw some light on the work conditions of the respondents. First, we shall note the difficulties working women encounter in seeking employment and the facilities that are provided to them, their relation with the employers, and satisfaction with work. Next, their attitude to full-time or part-time work shall also be ascertained.

DIFFICULTIES IN GETTING JOB

When asked to enumerate the difficulties working women encountered in their effort to get employment, slightly lesser than one-half of them cold not recall any and a little more than one-half said that they did face difficulties in getting employment. Initial family opposition was considered to be the most formidable hurdle. In a Delhi study only 12.2% employed women faced difficulties.[2] The frequently mentioned difficulties are given in Table 3.1 according to rank order.

Most of the working women mentioned family criticism as one of the main obstacles. A majority of the working women engaged in petty trader (88.9%) stated lack of money as the main hurdle in starting business. A large section of the professionals and the skilled workers made mention of tough competition. Some of the respondents said that they did not know about the vacancies. Some of the low professionals stated the prevailing corruption in offices as the major difficulty in obtaining employment.

Working Women and Choice of Work

When asked to add if they got the employment of their choice, a large percentage of them (72.3%) replied in affirmative and only 23.7% said that they did not get the job of their linking. For instances some nurses reported that they wanted to become doctors, but low percentage of marks in qualifying examinations precluded the possibility of their getting admission in Medical College. Similarly, some teachers reported that they wanted to become nurses but the parents and the relatives did not approve of their choice. Many teachers expressed their desire to become lecturers, but tough competition and little job opportunities did not allow them the chance to be so. Most of the unskilled labourers were keen to become ward-ayhas in hospitals or peon in schools, but failed to get those jobs.

TABLE 3.1

Difficulties in Getting Job (201)

	Difficulties faced	*Rank Order*
1.	Family opposition	1
2.	Tough competition	2
3.	Ignorance about vacancies	3
4.	Less remuneration despite higher qualifications	4
5.	Corruption among higher authorities	5
6.	Lack of money to start work	6
7.	Difficulty in contracting people	7
8.	Lack of experience about doing things properly	8

Besides the N.C.C. instructor, larger section of skilled workers and the professionals could get those job which they wanted, the lowest percentage being that of the semi-skilled. As many as forty-six per cent of the semi-skilled workers said that they could not get the job they wanted. Most of them were uneducated and they wanted to become peons in schools.

Desire to Change Work

The whole question, however, took a significant turn as soon as they were asked "whether they are desirous of doing any other work but this?" In other words, whether they would leave present work and take up any other form of occupation if opportunities were provided.

Over one-half of the working women did not want any change in their occupation. Only less than half of them wanted a change. It may, however, be noted that besides those who did not get the job of their choice, some of those who got jobs of their choice also wanted a change. A large percentage of the semi-skilled (53.8%) expressed their desire for change. It may be noted that a sizable section of the semi-skilled did not get the job of their choice and so they wanted change. Some of them felt that their jobs were mainly seasonal and there was no security of service and also that they earned very little. One of the low professionals also reported that the male colleagues did not behave properly. A large section of the professionals (77.7%) did not want to change their job, and this percentage was the highest of all the working women employed in various other occupations. It may be because they were specialised hands and their services were secured and also that they earned more.

JOB PREFERENCE

When their preference about work in which they would like to be employed was ascertained, more than one-half of the working women preferred permanent jobs while one-third of them favoured such jobs as offered extensive opportunity for promotion. Only 7.7% of them mentioned such jobs as might provide more reward and salary.

Besides the N.C.C. instructor, the number of the semi skilled workers seeking permanent jobs was the largest as compared to that of the women of all other occupations, and the majority of the professionals favoured occupations with promotion opportunities. Higher salary was mostly preferred by the unskilled workers.

HOURS OF WORK

The question of hours of work in a particular employment is also an important aspect for consideration in an examination of the condition of employment. "Whether more or less be earned, wrote Charles Booth, "affects, no doubt, immediate comfort, whereas a working day unduly prolonged injures the whole life."[3]

Turning to the data of this study to see the length of time that working women put in for satisfying the demand of their work, we find from Table 3.2 that the average number of hours of work put in by working women is 6.295 per day.

TABLE 3.2
Working Hours (400)
In Per Cent

Hours of Work	*Per cent*
Upto 2 hours	00.8
2-4 hours	07.0
4-6 hours	25.5
6-8 hours	56.7
8-10 hours	05.2
10-12 hours	03.0
12-14 hours	00.8
14-16 hours	00.2
16-18 hours	00.8
Total	100.0
Mean working hours	6.295 per day

In addition to salary and hours of work which are undoubtedly the basic from of compensation for services rendered, the working population is expected to receive other facilities from their employers. These may be in the from of medical facilities, social security scheme or facilities for leave. It is of interest, therefore, to determine to what extent these facilities are available to working women.

MEDICAL FACILITIES

Approximately one-half of the working women (49.8%) said that medical facilities were provided to them but two-fifths of them said that they were not provided any. The question was not applicable to one-tenth of the working women. They were petty traders. Semi-skilled workers also did not get medical facilities. Less than half of the unskilled workers working in schools, offices and factories received medical facilities while more than half of those working as maid-servants or day-labourers did not get any. A majority of women employed in skilled occupations, low professions and professions mentioned that they were provided medical facilities and mostly in the from of medical reimbursement.

SOCIAL SECURITY

It is intended here to find out from the working women, the facilities they have been getting related to social security scheme.

Only 200 working women were covered by social security schemes. Pension, provident fund, insurance and bonus were the most frequently mentioned benefits.

LEAVE FACILITIES

Apart from having a few hours for rest and recreation everyday, workers in every field of occupation whether manual or desk job require a day of rest at the end of a stipulated number of working days which is in most cases one day in a week, and also an annual holiday with full pay. In a report of International Labour Office on holidays with pay, it is stated: "The Social importance of payment for rest days is such that the principle has been acknowledged in various recent constitutions as one of the workers' social rights. Together with the annual holiday with pay, a practice which. . . has become almost universal, it has done much to improve the workers' lot.[4]"

It is attempted here to see to what extent the working women enjoyed such privileges.

As many as 63.5% of working women have said that they could take casual leave if it was essential and fifty-three per cent of them reported that they were allowed to stay away from the work in the event of illness without fear of losing their salary. One-third of the working women mentioned that they could get maternity leave; 27.8% of them reported that they were allowed privilege leave and 25.5% of them said that they could get half day off (specially nurses and in some cases clerical worker). 11.3% of them said that they could even get study leave (doctors, lecturers, teachers and clerks). Only sixteen per cent of the working women said that they hardly could afford to be on leave without running the risk of losing the job itself leave aside the wages for that time.

FEELING OF FATIGUE

This question was asked because the aim was to try to reach an estimate of overtiredness, not of ordinary tiredness. Of course, every body, in any work whatsoever, feels tired at intervals. Table 3.3 represents the answers given by respondents.

TABLE 3.3

Feeling of Tiredness (388)*

(in Per cent)

Opinion	*Per Cent*
Never feel tired	23.8
Feel tired	76.2
Total	100.0

* The twelve working women reported that they did not participate in household duties. It means that they are performing only one job and not two jobs. Hence, this question is not applicable to them and as such distribution is given of 388 working women only.

On an analysis of answers, a little more than three-fourths of the working women felt overtired and slightly less than one-fourth said that they did not feel tired.

It is a matter of surprise that some women did not feel fatigued because of their work. When probed, they reported that they were so much accustomed to the way of life that they did not feel that they were really tired after work. Some of them reported that they felt tired when they did not do any work.

TABLE 3.4

Occupation and Tiredness (388)

(in Per cent)

Occupation	*Feel Tired*	*Do Not Feel Tired*
Petty trades	05.7	08.6
Unskilled work	42.0	25.8
Semi-skilled work	09.2	11.8
Skilled work	06.4	16.1
N.C.C. and armed forces	00.3	—
Clerical and law professions	30.2	28.0
Professions	06.2	09.7
Total	100.0	100.0

On the basis of occupation, as has been given in Table 3.4, it was found that among those who felt tired, the unskilled workers constituted the largest section and among those who mentioned that they were never tired, the largest percentage consisted of the low professionals (28%).

The break of data in terms of the age of children as presented in Table 3.5 shows that irrespective of the age of their children a large section of working women felt overtired and it might be seen that with the increase in the age of children of the working mothers, the percentage of those who felt overtired went on declining showing that working mothers with small children felt more tired which was quite natural. They depended on their mothers for all their needs.

TABLE 3.5

Age of Children and Tiredness (268)*

(in Per cent)

Age of Children	*Feel Tired*	*Don not Feel Tired*	*Total*
18 + years (33)	78.8	21.2	100.0
6 — 17 years (107)	80.4	19.6	100.0
5 years and below (128)	81.2	18.8	100.0

* There are eighty one unmarried and 319 married women (including widowed and separated) out of these fifty one do not have children. Hence, in this table data of only 268 working women are presented who have children.

EMPLOYERS' ATTITUDE TOWARDS WORKING WOMEN

It might be suggested that good relation between the employer and the employee is one of the chief factors of employee's efficiency, satisfaction and her decision to stay on in the job. Some employers treat their subordinates like robot to act according to their will and carry out their orders. This brings to a consideration of the nature of relationship between the employer and the employees. The working women were asked a question with regard to the relationship between them and their employers based on the kind of treatment they received, for, there was no doubt that the manner in which the employees were treated varied greatly from occupation to occupation.

A majority of the working women (54.5%) said that the employers were sympathetic towards them and (27.5%) of them pointed out that they were neither harsh nor lenient while only 7.8% of them said that the treatment of the employers was harsh. The question was not applicable in the case of 10.2% of the working women.

Except the working women belonging to the unskilled and semi-skilled occupations, and majority of working women felt that their employers were sympathetic. As many as 39.3% of the unskilled workers said that their employers were neither sympathetic nor harsh. 25.6% of the semi-skilled pointed out that the employers were very harsh, they cut their salaries on minor mistakes and paid very little to them. Their other main complaints were as follows: (a) not getting salary in time; (b) no leave even when required urgently; (c) more work and meager salary. The detailed distribution of responses is presented in Table 3.6.

TABLE 3.6

Occupation and Attitude of Employers (400)

(in Per cent)

Occupation	*Sympa-thetic*	*Neither Sympathetic Nor Harsh*	*Harsh*	*Not App-licable*	*Total*
Petty trades (125)	—	—	—	100.0	100.0
Unskilled work (158)	48.7	39.3	12.0	—	100.0
Semi-skilled work (39)	20.6	28.2	25.6	25.6	100.0
Skilled work (34)	67.7	32.3	-	—	100.0
N.C.C. and armed (1) force	100.0	—	—	—	100.0
Clerical and Low profession (116)	77.6	18.1	00.9	03.4	100.0
Profession (27)	70.4	18.5	03.7	07.4	100.0

SATISFACTION WITH WORK

It is understood that there are some tasks and occupations which are not very pleasant and socially satisfying and hence workers may not feel satisfied with them.

In order to gauge the extent of satisfaction or dissatisfaction, a question was, therefore, asked whether the working women themselves were satisfied with the nature of their work and with the conditions prevailing in it.

As expected, a larger percentage of the working women (67.3%) was satisfied with their work than of those who were not satisfied (32.7%). The percentage of the skilled workers and the professionals who reported satisfaction was the highest. Besides the N.C.C. instructor, the percentage of dissatisfied workers was the highest of the semi-skilled (61.9%), the lowest being that of the skilled workers (5.9%). It is surprising that the N.C.C. instructor found the job that she wanted yet she was not satisfied with the job, perhaps because her job was temporary.

Looking into the fact that most of the women said that they were tired after work, it was thought essential to ascertain the attitude whether they would prefer full-time job which might make them very tired or they would prefer part-time job.

ATTITUDE TOWARDS FULL-TIME/PART-TIME EMPLOYMENT

The working women were asked to indicate their preferences for full-time and part-time employment. Whether they preferred full-time occupation or part-time?

One of the working women was undecided (0.2%). She was a needy petty trader and wanted any job whether full-time or part-time. More than three-fourths of all the working women said they preferred full-time job (seventy-eight per cent) and only slightly more than one-fifth of them gave preference for part-time job (21.8%).

The main responses of those who preferred full time jobs, were:

(1) Time passes easily. Do not like to sit idle at home.
(2) Get more money.
(3) There is unnecessary botheration in part-time job.

Those favouring part-time jobs, their main responses were:

(1) Part-time job is better because one can devote time to the care of children and family.
(2) One gets sufficient time for rest and recreation.
(3) One gets extra time to utilise for higher studies.

TABLE 3.7

Occupation and Attitude Towards Full-time/Part-time Employment (400)

(in Per cent)

Occupation		*Full Time*	*Part-Time*	*Undeci-ded*	*Total*
Petty trades	(25)	52.0	44.0	4.0	100.0
Un-skilled work	(158)	91.2	8.8	—	100.0
Semi-skilled work	(39)	59.0	41.0	—	100.0
Skilled work	(34)	89.2	10.8	—	100.0
N.C.C. and armed forces	(1)	100.0	—	—	100.0
Clerical and low professions	(116)	74.0	26.0	—	100.0
Professions	(27)	71.5	28.4	—	100.0

When the data were broken up on the basis of occupations as shown in Table 3.7, it revealed that besides the N.C.C. instructor, a very large number of the unskilled workers (91.2%) preferred full-time job. Their percentage was the largest of all the working women, the smallest being that of petty traders (fifty-two per cent). Forty-four per cent of the petty traders preferred part-time jobs and their percentage was relatively higher than that of all the working women engaged in various other occupations, the lowest being that of the unskilled workers (8.8%). However, it may be noted that even among petty traders a large percentage of them (fifty-two per cent) wanted full-time job. A survey of Bombay and Delhi also indicated that a very large majority of women "did not want to take up part-time employment....[5]

It is an already known fact that although cash benefits are the chief aim of the working women of the job, they are not the only aims, for, a job means much more to her than that. It is closely integrated with her whole life and is likely to shape her attitude to her environment. Therefore, a summary of the condition of work would be incomplete without taking into account the working women's own feeling of satisfaction with her environment. With this in view, in the end, a section is added to examine the personal satisfaction of the working women.

PERSONAL SATISFACTION

The assessment of the satisfaction of any individual or group is a difficult problem. Both the theoretical and empirical criteria used to evaluate satisfaction are diverse. In recent years, however, some of the social scientists, have conducted studies dealing with the study of the level of satisfaction. In this section an attempt is made to compare the feelings of satisfaction in working women with those of non-working women. What is attempted here is a general assessment of significance of employment on working women's satisfaction with life. It is quite possible that one aspect of the life of an individual may be satisfactory but the same may not be the position in other aspects. It is also possible that the satisfaction in one area may influence the behaviour in the other area. It is very difficult to have a measure of general satisfaction. Having this in view, in this study, several items are included to indicate the level of satisfaction in the area of relationship which is considered to be important. The five items included are as follows:

1. Family income
2. Relationship to children
3. Relationship to husband
4. Relationship to family
5. Daily work.

Since a single dimension does not seem to be quite logical sociologically, these five items are given separate treatment and the composite has been used as an index rather than a scale.

The respondents were asked to indicate the degree of satisfaction or dissatisfaction in each of the areas. The responses were coded and weightage was given in the following order: Highly satisfied = 2, partly satisfied = 1, Dissatisfied = 0. On the basis of the scores, mean for each area was computed as presented in Table 3.8.

TABLE 3.8

Areas of Satisfaction (400)
Mean Satisfaction

Items	*Working Women Mean Satis-faction*	*Non-working Women Mean Satis-faction*	C.R.
Family income	1.950	2.405	7.583 **
Relations with children	2.832	2.890	1.49
Relation with husband	2.428	2.800	6.06 **
Relations with family	2.609	2.700	1.93
Daily work	2.627	2.800	4.285 **

**Statistically significant at .01 level.

(i) Satisfaction with Family Income

A glance at the table shows that non-working women were generally satisfied with their family income in comparison to the working women. It is quite likely also. A large number of working women reported that they worked because of economic pressures. Had they been satisfied with their family income, possibly most of them might not have gone to work outside the four-walls of their homes. This is contrary to the findings of Nye, who reported that no significant differences were found among employment categories with respect to satisfaction.[6] However, it is interesting to find that inspite of their employment working women were not satisfied with their family income. Meagre income might be the reason for this dissatisfaction.

(ii) Satisfaction with Children

In regard to satisfaction with children, there was no significant difference between the working and non-working mothers. This is in conformity with Nye who found no significant difference between working and non-working mothers as far as satisfaction with children is concerned.[7]

(iii) Marital Satisfaction

Significant difference is seen between the working and non-working wives in regard to satisfaction with their husbands.

The non-working wives were better satisfied than the working wives with their husbands. Similar findings have been reported by Nye[8] and Locke Mackepring.[9]

(iv) Satisfaction with Family

Both the working and the non-working women reported their high satisfaction with their families. But there was no significant difference between the two.

(v) Satisfaction with Daily Work

A significant difference was found between the working and the non-working women in regard to their satisfaction with daily work. Those who were not employed were better satisfied. The result of this study is contrary to the results of the study conducted by Nye who found that the employed women were more satisfied with their work than the non-employed women.[10]

A Satisfaction Index

We have analysed so far the satisfaction of the working and the non-working women in each of the five areas of life and it was found that except for relationship with children and family members, significant relationships were found in all the three areas. In two areas where the relationships were not found significant, the mean difference favoured somewhat the non-working women.

Though in three areas, association were found significant, yet to treat satisfaction as a single dimension was logically and statistically not satisfactory. It might serve the purpose of only a quasi-scale. Therefore, it was decided to compute total score by giving one point of reach item answered "generally" or "entirely satisfied." The distribution of satisfaction score is from a low score of zero to a high of five. Table 3.9 is designed to present this aspect.

TABLE 3.9

Working Women and Satisfaction Total Scores* (400)

(in Per Cent)

Satisfaction Scores	*Working Women*	*Non-Working Women*
0-1	17.75	06.50
2-3	52.25	30.75
4-5	30.00	62.75
Total	100.0	100.0

*The relationship is statistically significant.

To present a clear picture of an over-all satisfaction among the working women, the mean scores of satisfaction in all the five areas were worked out. On the basis of comparison of mean satisfaction of 2.808 for the working women with a mean of 3.688 for the non-working women, a critical ratio of 9.42 was obtained which is significant beyond .01 level. In general, total scores favoured the non-working women. In summary form, the findings about the satisfaction in each area are given in Table 3.10.

It has been the hope that women's employment would provide them more satisfaction because employment gave them independence and provided an opportunity for social contacts but this hope was belied in view of the results described in the Table 3.10. The non-working women were significantly more satisfied with their family income, relationship to husband and daily work. The non-significant differences in satisfaction with relation to children and family members also favoured the non-employed women. The total satisfaction score was also significant for the non-employed women. It is more than clear from the table that non-working women, on the whole, were more satisfied than the working women.

TABLE 3.10

Employment Status and Satisfaction

(in Per Cent)

Item: Satisfaction	*Working Women*	*Non-Working Women*	*Direction Favours*
Family			
Income	36.0	62.0	Employed<Non-Employed*
Relationship to children	59.3	7.3	Employed<Non-Employed
Relationship to husband	42.0	78.3	Employed<Non-Employed*
Relationship to Family	70.3	77.5	Employed<Non-Employed
Daily work	72.3	83.3	Employed<Non-Employed*

* Difference is statistically significant.

< = Less than.

CONCLUSIONS

Since work conditions have important bearing on the employment of women, a brief discussion of this aspect is made here. Most of the working women did not find any difficulty in securing a job. If there was any hurdle, it was the initial opposition by the family members. As they said, they were engaged in the same occupations which they wanted to join. A large number of the working women were satisfied with their present job and, by and large, they did not want any change. They preferred permanent jobs. These working women were devoting, on an average, 6.3 hours per day to their job. They were provided with various facilities such as medical facility, provident fund, insurance, pension and bonus. They also get without much difficulty "leave" due to them. A large number of the working women felt overtired because of the work they were expected to do. In most of the cases the employers of the working women had sympathetic attitude towards them. It is interesting to note that a large number of the working women showed their interest for full-time job. With regard to the satisfaction with family income relationships to children, husband and family members and daily work, it was found that a significantly larger number of working women than non-working women were not satisfied with family income, relationships to husband and daily work. There was no significant difference between the working and the non-working women in regard to satisfaction with their children and family. On the whole, the non-working women were significantly more satisfied than working women.

REFERENCES

1. Schneider, E.V., *Industrial Sociology*, New York, 1957, p. 339.
2. Ranade, S.N., *The Employed Women*, Part II, p. 13.
3. Booth, Charles, *Life and Labour of the People in London*, London, 1903, Vol. 5., p. 182.
4. I.L.O. Reports and Enquiries, "Holidays with Pay: Public Holidays and Weekly Rest Days," *International labour Review*, 60 (July 1949), p. 18.
5. Ranade, and Ramchandran, *op. cit.*, p. 44.
6. Nye, F. Ivan, "Personal Satisfaction," *The Employed Mother in America*, pp. 324-25.
7. *Ibid.*
8. *Ibid.*
9. Locke, Harvey J., and Mackeprang, Muriel, "Marital Adjustment of the Employed Wife," *American Journal of Sociology*, 54 (May, 1949), pp. 536-39.
10. Nye, F. Ivan, *op. cit.*, pp. 324-25.

4

Social Characteristics of Working Women

Social characteristics such as age, marital status, occupation, income, employer-employee relation, motivation and social background have been found to have significant influence on the employment structure. Many researchers, in their studies have tried to assess the significance of these variables.[1]

In India, the study of working women has been conducted mainly by economists with emphasis on occupation wage-structure, economic status, unemployment, under-employment, standing of living and indebtedness. Some casual references have been made to household features also.[2] A proper understanding of the working women is, however, not possible without a consideration of all the related factors. In this chapter, it is proposed to present a few of the basic social characteristics of the working women.

Age

The study of the working women necessitates an enquiry into their age distribution. For, age acquires a special significance as far as efficiency is concerned. It influences the capacity for work. The age of the working women ranges from a low fifteen to a high of seventy five years. For the purpose of analysis the different age groups have been classified into three broad categories, i.e., Young (below thirty years), Middle (thirty years and below fifty-five years) and Old (Fifty-five years and above).

The percentage of working women in various age groups shows an increasing trend reaching the maximum in middle age group after which it shows a falling trend. It may be seen that while 42.5% of the working women are young, a little more than one-half of the working women fall in middle age group (51.3%). As we go to higher age-group, the percentage of working women declines drastically. As a matter of fact a very small percentage of working women belongs to old age-group (5.7%). Age was not specified by 0.5% working women. A convenient summary index of age composition is the mean age. The mean age of the working women is 34.3 years. In Bombay and Delhi, most of the working women are of young age group (77.3%) and 81.9% respectively).[3] In Japan also, the vast majority of the working women are young under the age of twenty-five years.[4]

Religion

Religion is an important basis of social organisation in India. In this study there is not even a single working women who does not affiliate herself with one of the other religious category.

The two major religious groups Hindus and Muslims account for 81.8% and 8.2% respectively of all the working woman of this study. Hindus form the majority and Muslims the most substantial minority. Other religious groups such as Christians (6.7%), Sikhs (2.0%) and Jains (1.3%) form only insignificant minority. In Bombay, Christians form the majority of the working women (88.1%) and in Delhi 86.36%) are Hindus.[5]

Caste

Caste has become so significant in Indian social structure that a meaningful study is not possible without its being taken into account.[6]

The working women represent various castes. They belong to more than thirty-six different castes. The Brahmins constitute the single largest group among all the working women. For purpose of convenience, various castes were grouped into four main ordinal groups: (1) Upper, (2) Middle, (3) Lower and Scheduled Castes and Tribes, and (4) Others. Brahmins represent the highest caste as per he traditional caste system. They constitute the upper caste which accounts for fifteen per cent of all the working women, the middle castes for twenty-six per cent lower Scheduled Castes and Tribes for 43.2% and others fifty per cent. It appears that relatively large number of working women come from lower, Scheduled Castes and Tribes. A survey of working women in Delhi reports that Khatris formed the majority i.e. 53.6% and Brahmins only 10.9%.[7]

Marital Status

To determine the marital status of the working women, we attemnted to find out the number of those that were unmarried, married and widowed or separated at the time of enquiry.

It is found that more than a half of the working women are married (56.3%). Widowed and separated constitute 23.5%. Only 20.2% are unmarried.

This distribution is similar to the one given in a Survey Report of Government of India.[8] New Delhi and Bombay fifty-two per cent and forty-three per cent of working women respectively were unmarried.[9]

Nature of Family

The incidence of nuclear family was higher among working women of this study. Slightly more than half of the working women belonged to the nuclear family. They constituted 52.3% of all the working women; 43.2% come from joint-families and only 4.5% belong to single member families. The difference between the percentage of nuclear and joint families is not much.

Size of Family

The family size ranged from the extremes of a uni-member family to a family consisting of as many as seventeen members. Relatively larger percentage of the working women (44.7%) has medium-sized families, 35.3% large sized families and 15.5% small sized families. Only 4.5% of them belonged to single member family. The average size of the family of the working women was found to be of 5.8 persons per family which is slightly higher than the average size of Indian household which according to 1961 census is 4.16 per household.

Number of Dependents

The number of dependents in a working women's family ranged from 0 to 15. Ten per cent of working women did not have any dependent. This also included those women who were all alone in the family. The largest percentage of working women (42.3%) had 1-3 dependents. There was only one working women who had as many as fifteen dependents. The average number of dependents was 3.92 (Table 4.1).

TABLE 4.1

Working Women: Number of Dependents (400)

Number of Dependents	*Per cent*
No dependent	10.0
1-3	42.3
4-6	36.5
7 and more	11.2
Total	100.0
Mean dependents	3.92

Number of Earners

The number of earners in working women's families ranged from 1-8. A majority of them (71.3%) belonged to such families as had 2-3 earning members. In one working woman's family we found eight earning members whereas in the families of 16.7% working women there was only one earner, i.e., the respondent herself. The mean earners in working women's families were 2.3.

Region to which Working Women Belong

A little more than three-fourths of the working women belonged to Rajasthan (76.2%) whereas a little less than one-fourth were from outside Rajasthan (23.8%) of those who claim to be of Rajasthan only 16.1% belonged to rural Rajasthan whereas 83.9% belonged to urban areas of Rajasthan. Of those who were from regions outside Rajasthan only 1.2% were from rural areas whereas 96.8% from urban areas.

TABLE 4.2

Working Women: Number of Earners (400)

Number of Earners	*Per cent*
1	16.7
2-3	71.3
4-6	11.7
7 and more	00.3
Total	100.0
Mean Earners	2.3

Distribution by Locale

Having ascertained the region of the working women, we proceed to inspect by studying their local distribution how far they represented the city of Jodhpur.

We note that as many as 64.2% of working women belonged to Jodhpur and the remaining 35.8% were from outside Jodhpur, but they were residents of Rajasthan.

Out of the 196 working women belonging to Jodhpur, 96.8% were city born and only 3.2% were village born.

Distribution by locale indicates that the working women were mostly local and urban. As many as forty-eight per cent of the working women had been living in this city since their birth and fifty-two per cent of them for several years with a mean of 16.9 years.

Education

So far as formal education is concerned, slightly less than half of the working women were non-lettered (48%); 10.5% were educated up to junior basic or even less in some cases; 27% were under-graduates and 14.5% had received education upto graduate level and above. Of those who mentioned education upto graduate level and above, two reported that they were Ph.Ds, and some of those (37.4%) had been trained in education. For purposes of analysis, these educational categories have been grouped into three, (1) approximately one-half of the working women were *non-lettered;* (2) only one tenth of them were *low-educated;* and (3) slightly more than two fifths of them were *highly educated.*[10] In Delhi forty-four per cent of the working women studied upto matric and forty-two per cent were graduates. In Bombay fifty per cent studied upto matric and forty-four per cent were graduates.[11]

Occupation

The working women were employed in a wide variety of occupations, ranging from professions to relatively unskilled occupations as is evident from Table 4.3.

In this study, the percentage of working women engaged in unskilled occupations was the highest (39.55) lowest being that of petty-traders (6.2%). The distribution indicates that women did not generally work in more skilled or professional occupations but were employed in unskilled jobs such as day-labour, domestic servants, sweepers etc. This finding is in conformity with that of Pune.[12] But in Delhi fifty-nine per cent working women were engaged in teaching, fifteen per cent in clerical jobs, thirteen per cent in professional and technical jobs and thirteen in miscellaneous occupation; and in Bombay, thirty-seven per cent in teaching and related jobs, thirty-nine per cent in clerical and twelve per cent in professional and twelve per cent in miscellaneous occupations.[13]

TABLE 4.3

Working Women: Occupational Distribution (400)

Occupations	*Per cent*
Petty trades	06.2
Unskilled work	39.5
Semi-skilled work	09.8
Skilled work	08.5
N.C.C. and armed forces	00.2
Clerical and low professions	29.0
Professions	06.8
Total	100.0

Nature of Employment

As many as 82.8% of the women were employed full-time, and only 17.2% part-time. In Delhi and Bombay only nine per cent of the working women were working as part-time workers.[14]

Length of Service

The data presented in Table 4.4 regarding the length of service indicate a wide variation among the working women. Only one-third of the working women were in service for more than ten years and two-thirds, for about ten years or less. The average service period of the working women was 8.3 years. In Bombay study women were in their present job for an average period of 4.61 years and in Delhi only 27.84% of them were employed in their present job for a period of more than five years.[15]

Occupational Mobility

More than four-fifths of the working women (84.2%) reported no change in their occupations. They had been working throughout in the same occupation. The remaining 15.8% reported a change. In fact, there was only nominal occupational mobility. In Bombay study also 50.38% women were in their first job and the remaining 49.62% changed their jobs ranging upto six. In Delhi study 73.17% women had no previous employment experience, while 26.83% had the experience of working in two or more jobs.[16]

TABLE 4.4

Working Women: Length of Service (400)

Length of Service	*Per cent*
5 years and below	43.3
6 — 10 years	22.5
11 — 15 years	11.5
16 — 20 years	11.2
21 years and more	11.5
Total	100.0
Mean service period	8.3 years

Of those working women who reported change in their occupations, a larger percentage (68.2%) changed from one occupation to another, i.e., from one household work to another but these occupations were of the same status; 19.1% reported upward mobility, i.e., when they started work they joined those occupations which were readily available to them but later on they moved to comparatively better occupations. For example, one peon became a teacher, four teachers became lecturers. 12.7% of working women however, reported downward mobility. When such women started work, they found better occupations as lecturership, but these jobs were temporary and later on they had to leave them. Then they took up the job which was readily available to them, even if inferior. The lack of mobility might be explained in terms of the fact that most of the working women were unlettered and the job opportunity was not much. Besides, the women did not want to go elsewhere.

Income of Working Women

The distribution of the monthly income of the working women brings out the fact that the greatest proportion of them (45.2%) earned only up to Rs. 100/- per month; 32% earned between Rs. 101/- to 200/- and less than one per cent of them earned more than Rs. 700/- per month. On an average, the monthly earnings of a working women was Rs. 150.75. The average income of women workers was also low in Chandigarh.[17] In Delhi, only sixteen per cent earned less than Rs. 100/- per month, sixty eight per cent earned Rs. 101-300 per month, twelve per cent earned Rs. 301-400 and four per cent earned Rs. 401 and above. In Bombay to five per cent earned less than Rs. 100/-, 78% earned Rs. 101-300, seven per cent earned Rs. 301—400 and three per cent earned Rs. 401 and above.[18] A distinctive picture of the income distribution is given in Table 4.5.

Family Income

In addition to the individual income earned by working women, there were also earnings by other members of the household. The total of these two sources of income has been termed as the family income.

TABLE 4.5

Monthly Income of Working Women (400)

Income in Rupees	*Per cent*
1 — 100	45.2
101 — 200	32.0
201 — 300	13.5
301 — 400	02.2
401 — 500	03.0
501 — 600	01.5
601 — 700	01.5
701 — 800	00.3
801 — 900	00.5
901 — 1000	00.3
Total	100.0
Mean Income of Working women	Rs. 150.75 per month

Only two working women belonged to families where the average income of the earners went beyond Rs. 1900 00 per month. Half of the employed women 50.2%) came from families of low income groups.[19] Two fifths of the working women (40.5%) belonged to lower-middle income groups.[20] A small proportion of them 7.8%) came from upper-middle income groups and only 1.5% were from higher income group. The mean monthly income was Rs. 193.25. Delhi and Bombay studies also report that mostly working women belonged to lower income families.[21]

Working Women's Contribution to Family Income

The data regarding the income of the working women have further been analysed in terms of the contribution they actually make to family income. Table 4.6 provide a vivid description. Proportionate contribution by each working women suggested that more than seventy per cent of the working women contributed on an average fifty per cent or less per month, but on the other hand, 16.8% of the working women contributed more than ninety per cent o the family income. These working women were the only wage earners in their household. They were mostly widowed and the separated having no other bread winner in their families to support. Working women contributed, on an average, Rs. 45.3 per month to the total income of the family. Nearly one-third of the women interviewed in Delhi were earning upto sixty per cent of their families' total income, and their contribution did not help to raise the standard of living. In many cases it was a matter of keeping the wolf away from the door. Low income and high prices were responsible for this situation.[22]

TABLE 4.6

Working Women's Contribution in Household Income (400)

Share in per cent	*Per cent*
10 and below	08.0
11 — 20	13.2
21 — 30	15.2
31 — 40	18.2
41 — 50	17.5
51 — 60	07.0
61 — 70	02.3
71 — 80	01.0
81 — 90	00.8
91 — 100	16.8
Total	100.0
Mean Contribution	45.3 per cent

Each of the following aspects is not related ot other for a better picture to emerge.

Age and Education

Working women have been classified according to their age and level of education in Table 4.7.

TABLE 4.7

Working Women: Age and Education

Age Group		*Level of Education*			*Total*
		Non-lettered	*Low-educated*	*Highly educated*	
Young	(170)	25.2	11.1	63.7	100.0
Middle	(205)	61.3	10.7	28.0	100.0
Old	(23)	91.4	04.3	04.3	100.0
Age not specified	(2)	100.0	—	—	100.0

It appears that proportion of illiteracy was higher in old age group, which was quite natural. Free educational facilities are available to women to-day in Rajasthan which were not available to them in the past. This is evident from the proportion of young-age-group women in highly educated category which was much more than that of the working women of other age-groups.

Age and Occupation of Working Women

Table 4.8 has been designed to show the age and occupational distribution of working women.

TABLE 4.8

Working Women: Age and Occupation

	Occupational Categories							
Age Groups	*Petty-Trades*	*Un-skilled work*	*Semi-skilled work*	*Skilled work*	*N.C.C. and armed forces*	*Low Pro-fessions and cleri cal*	*Pro-fess-ions*	*Total*
Young (170)	04.7	18.8	08.2	09.4	0.6	51.2	07.1	100.0
Middle (205)	05.9	54.1	10.2	08.3	—	14.2	07.3	100.0
Old (23)	21.8	56.5	17.4	04.3	—	—	—	100.0
Age not specified (2)	—	100.0	—	—	—	—	—	100.0

One-half of the working women of young age group were engaged in teaching and clerical occupations, whereas only 14.2% of middle aged working women were engaged in these occupations and none of the old aged were found in these occupations because the age of retirement was fifty-five years and most of them were not so educated as to be in these jobs. One-half of the middle age working women were in unskilled occupations. As many as 56.5% of old aged working women were engaged in unskilled occupations. Only 18.8% of working women of young age group were found in unskilled occupations.

Caste and Age

Table 4.9 indicate that with the decline in caste status, there was an increase in the mean age of the working women. The working women of upper caste were the youngest of all the working women. This is because of the fact that upper caste women took no part in any out-door activities in the past and many observed purdah. They never left the house without purdah. Thus, the question of their serving outside did not arise.

Caste and Education

In a caste-ridden society we expect to find that the educational level of different caste-groups would be different and that educational level of caste-groups higher-in-order would be higher than that of caste-groups lower-in-order. These can be examined with reference to Table 4.10 in which working women are classified according to their castes and educational level.

TABLE 4.9

Working Women: Caste and Age (400)

Caste Groups	*Average Age of the Working Women*
Upper caste	29.3
Middle caste	30.3
Lower, Scheduled Castes and Tribe	30.6
Others	34.2

TABLE 4.10

Working Women: Caste and Education (400)

(in Per Cent)

Caste Group	*Education Groups*			*Total*
	Non-lettered	*Low educated*	*Highly educated*	
Upper (63)	07.9	11.1	81.0	100.0
Middle (104)	15.4	11.5	73.1	100.0
Lower and Scheduled Castes and Tribes (173)	83.8	11.6	04.6	100.0
Others (60)	4.3	05.0	51.7	100.0

The working women of the upper and middle caste groups were highly educated in comparison to those of lower, Scheduled Castes/Tribes and other castes. A large number of upper and middle-caste working women had received education above the High School level. The rate of illiteracy was very high in lower, Scheduled Castes/Tribes (83.8%), lowest being in the upper caste group (7.9%). It suggests that there was a sharp and significant difference in the educational standard of the working women belonging to upper, middle, lower and Scheduled Castes/Tribes and other castes.

Caste and Occupation

Recent studies have clearly shown that in communities which are stratified on the basis of caste-system, there tends to be a congruence between the social status of the caste-groups and the occupations followed by the members. We may, therefore, examine Table 4.11 whether occupational distribution follows order of caste status.

Describing the emergence of caste system Nesfield maintains that castes have emerged out of occupations and that they are related. In this study, caste and occupation seem to be distinctly related. Through the working women of upper and middle caste groups did not differ significantly in their occupation, yet they differed significantly from working women of lower, Scheduled Castes/Tribes. The latter were largely employed in unskilled occupations. They were either domestic servants, ayaas in hospitals or factory workers. Larger section of upper and middle castes working women were employed in prestigious occuaptions.

TABLE 4.11

Working Women: Caste and Occupation (400)

(in Per Cent)

Caste Groups	*Occupational Categories*							*Total*
	Petty trades	*Unski-lled-work*	*semi-skilled work*	*Skilled work*	*N.C.C. and armed forces*	*Clerical and low pro-fessions*	*Pro fessions*	
Upper (63)	—	07.9	04.8	04.8	01.6	66.6	14.3	100.0
Middle (104)	03.8	12.5	11.5	05.8	—	51.0	15.4	100.0
Lower and Scheduled Castes and Tribes (173)	10.4	72.3	09.2	01.7	—	51.0	0.06	100.0
Others (60)	05.0	25.0	13.3	36.6	—	18.4	01.7	100.0

Marital Status and Age

The percentage distribution shows that unmarried working women were clustered heavily in young age group (88.9%), whereas the clustering of married working women was in middle age group (59.6%). The number of the widowed and the separated was relatively more in the middle age group. The distribution has been given in Table 4.12.

TABLE 4.12

Working Women: Marital Status and Age (400)

(in Per Cent)

Marital Status	*Age Group*				*Total*
	Young	*Middle*	*Old*	*Age not specified*	
Unmarried (81)	88.9	11.1	—	—	100.0
Married (225)	37.3	59.6	02.2	00.9	100.0
Widowed and separated (94)	14.9	65.9	19.2	—	100.0

Marital Status and Education

There appeared to be a striking difference between married and unmarried working women's education. Whereas there was only one unmarried working woman who was non-lettered (she was a factory worker), there were slightly more than one half of the married working women who were non-lettered (53.8%).

About, three-fourth of the widowed and separated working women are non-lettered. Compared to the widowed, the separated and unmarried working women, the proportion of married working women with low education was slightly higher. On the whole, the unmarried working women are more educated than all others. The distribution details is given in Table 4.13.

TABLE 4.13

Working Women: Marital Status and Education (400)

(in Per Cent)

Marital Status Group	*Level of Education*			*Total*
	Non-lettered	*Low-educated*	*Highly Educated*	
Unmarried (81)	01.2	08.7	90.1	100.0
Married (225)	53.8	11.6	34.6	100.0
Widowed and Separated (94)	74.4	09.6	16.0	100.0

Marital Status and Number of Children

Slightly more than half of the married, the widowed and the separated working women had small number of children (1-3 children). One-third of married working women had medium number (4-6) of children, whereas only sixteen per cent of the widowed and the separated working women had medium number of children. The percentage of working women with larger number of children (7 and above) was more among the married than the widowed and the separated. Only one-tenth of married working women had no children whereas slightly more than one-fourth of the widowed and the separated working women did not have any child. Table 4.14 shows the detailed distribution.

TABLE 4.14

Working Women: Marital Status and Number of Children (319)*

(in Per Cent)

Marital Status	*Number of Children*				*Total*
	No. child	*1—3 children*	*4—6 children*	*7 and more children*	
Married (225)	10.7	52.0	34.2	03.1	100.0
Widowed and separated (94)	23.7	54.2	16.0	01.1	100.0

* 81 Unmarried women are not included.

Marital Status and Age of Children

The data clearly shows that more than half of the married working women had children of pre-school age and one-third of them had school age children. Even less than one-fourth of the widowed and the separated working women had children of pre-school age. The number of the widowed and the separated with school age children was somewhat higher than owners. Approximately one-third of the widowed and the separated working women had children of eighteen years or above, whereas only one-twentieth of all married working women with husbands had children of eighteen years or above. It reveals that women not only with children of school age but also of pre-school age entered the labour force in greater number. This finding is different from that of Nye and Hoffman who found that women with children of school age have entered the labour force in greater number than mothers of pre-school children.[23]

TABLE 4.15

Working Women: Marital Status and Age of Children (268*)

(in Per Cent)

Marital Status	Age of Children			Total
	+ 18 years	*6—17 years*	*5 years and below*	
Married (201)	05.5	38.3	56.2	100.0
Widowed and Separated (67)	32.8	44.8	22.4	100.0

* 81 Unmarried women and 51 those women who have no children, are not included.

TABLE 4.16

Working Women: Marital Status and Income Distribution (400)

(in Per Cent)

Marital Status	Income Groups			Total
	Lower	*Lower middle*	*Upper middle*	
Unmarried (81)	23.5	66.6	09.9	100.0
Married (225)	60.1	30.6	09.3	100.0
Widowed and separated (94)	74.4	25.6	—	100.0

Marital Status and Income of Working Women

About three-fourths of the widowed and the separated working women belonged to low income group with reference to their own income, whereas more than one-half of the married working women and even less than one-fourth of unmarried working women, belonged to this income group. More than half of the unmarried working women belonged to lower-middle income group whereas only three-tenths of married working women and only one-fourth of widowed and separated belonged to this. The percentage of unmarried and married who belong to upper-middle income group was almost equal (9.9% and 9.3% respectively). None of the working women earned so much as to place them into the upper income group.

Education and Occupation

The distribution of working women in terms of their education and occupations are given in Table 4.17.

TABLE 4.17

Working Women: Education and Occupation (400)

(in Per Cent)

Education Categories	*Occupational Categories*							*Total*
	Petty trades	*Unskilled work*	*Semi-skilled work*	*Skilled work*	*N.C.C. and armed forces*	*Low profesions and clerical*	*Professions*	
Non-lettered (192)	13.0	74.0	13.0	—	—	—	—	100.0
Low-educated (42)	—	38.2	26.2	07.1	—	28.5	—	100.0
Highly educated (166)	—	—	01.8	18.7	0.6	62.6	16.3	100.0

The education and occupation are also related. The highly educated women were engaged in professions such as Medicines, Teaching, Law etc. Those who were non-lettered or low educated were employed in unskilled work. This shows relation of occupation and education.

Since professional work like Medicines, Law, Teaching in Universities or Administration could not be taken up without higher education, it was natural that educated working women were found in such occupations and those who were not educated would go to such occupations where education was not a prerequisite.

Occupation and Income

It has generally been demonstrated in various studies that occupation is highly correlated with income derived from occupations. Table 4.18 also shows that occupation is correlated with income. Of those working women who were engaged in professions, 81.5% belonged to the upper-middle income group. Clearly the income range skewed on the lower side.

Conclusions

In order to present a comprehensive picture of the social characteristics, a detailed socio-economic enquiry into the conditions of working women was conducted. The average age of the working women was 34.3 years and they are clustered in the middle age-group. Only a small number of working women belonged told age group. Hindus formed the majority of the women in employment. Most of the working women came from low castes, Scheduled Castes/Tribes. But if each caste was taken separately, Brahmins constituted the single largest group. The married women were found in larger number in the working force. Majority of the employed women belonged to nuclear families and the size of their household was generally medium. Generally 1 to 3 persons depended on them and most of the working women belonged to the families where 2 to 3 persons earned. Mostly they were local and urban.

TABLE 4.18

Working Women: Occupation and Income (400)

(in Per Cent)

Occupation Groups	*Income Groups*				*Total*
	Lower	*Lower middle*	*Upper middle*	*Upper*	
Petty trades (25)	88.0	12.0	—	—	100.0
Unskilled work (158)	86.0	14.0	—	—	100.0
Semi-skilled work (39)	94.9	05.1	—	—	100.0
Skilled-work (34)	14.7	73.5	11.8	—	100.0
N.C.C. armed forces (1)	—	100.0	—	—	100.0
Clerical and low Professions (116)	19.8	77.6	2.6	—	100.0
Professions (27)	3.7	14.8	81.5	—	100.0

Nearly half of the women were non-lettered and engaged mostly in unskilled occupations. The overwhelming majority was full-time workers. On an average, they had been working for about 8.3 years mobility was only nominal. Earning of most of them was low and they generally belonged to lower or lower-middle income group families. The working women contributed a sizeable proportion of their earnings to family income. Those of young age were more educated and were in prestigious occupations. Upper caste working women were mostly young and those of lower, Scheduled Castes/Tribes were mostly old. Those who belonged to the upper and middle castes were highly educated and lower, Scheduled Castes/Tribes were generally non-lettered. Upper castes working women were engaged in prestigious occupations whereas lower, Scheduled Castes/Tribes were engaged in lower occupations. The unmarried working women were highly educated and even mothers of pre-school are children went to work. Earning of unmarried working women was more than that of others. Education and occupation seemed to be related. Those with high education were employed in prestigious occupations and with lower education in low occupations. The working women of prestigious occupation also earned more than those engaged in non-prestigious occuaptions.

REFERENCES

1. Miler, Freida S., "Women in the Labour Force," *The Annals of the American Academy of Political and Social Sciences,* 251 (1947), pp. 35-40; Kyrk, Hazel "Who Works and Why?" *Ibid.*, pp. 44-52 Hauser, P.M., "The Labour Force as Field of Interest of the Sociologists", *American Sociological Review,* 16 (1951), pp. 530-38; Baber, R.E. *Marriage and the Family,* New York : McGraw Hill, 1953, pp. 341-47.
2. Mukherji, R.K. *Indian Working Class,* Allahabad: Hindkitabs, 1945, p. 216; Thorner, Daneil, and Thorner A., *Land and Labour In India,* Bombay: Asia Publishing House, 1962, pp. 72-73.
3. Ranade, S.N., and Ramchandran, P., *women and Employment,* Bombay: Tata Institute of Social Science, 71 AS, 1970, p. 7 and p. 3.
4. Koyama, Takashi, *The Changing Social Position of Women in Japan,* UNESCO 1961, p. 109.
5. Ranade and Ramchandran, *op. cit.*
6. Mukherji, R.K., "Caste and Economic Structure in West Bengal in Present Times," in Saxena, R.N. (ed.,) *Sociology, Social Relations and Social Problems In India,* Bombay: Asia Publishing House, 1961, p. 157.
7. Ranade and Ramchandran, *op. cit.*, p. 4.
8. Government of India, *Economic and Social Status of Women Workers in India.* Labour Bureau, Ministry of Labour, Publication No. 15.
9. Ranade and Ramchandran, *op. cit.*, p. 19.
10. Grouped educational categories are: (1) Non-lettered 48%, (ii) Low educated (Junior basic and below) 10.5%, (iii) Highly educated (under graduates and above) 41.5%.
11. Ranade and Ramchandran, *op. cit.*, p. 19.
12. Sovani, Apte and Pendse, *Poona: A Resurvey,* 1956, Chapter 3.
13. Ranade and Ramchandran, *op. cit.*, p. 19.
14. *Ibid.*, p. 18.
15. *Ibid.*, p. 19 and p. 17.
16. *Ibid.*
17. D'Souza, Victor S., *Social Structure of a Planned City Chandigarh,* New Delhi: Orient Longmans Limited, 1968, p. 73.
18. Ranade and Ramchandran, *op. cit.*, p. 19.

19. Income categories included in various income groups are given below:

(i)	Lower	(upto Rs. 125)
(ii)	Lower-Middle	(Rs. 125-399)
(iii)	Upper-Middle	(Rs. 400-999)
(iv)	Upper	(Rs. 1000 and more)

20. Ranade and Ramchandran, pp. 13 and 38.
21. *Ibid.*
22. Ranade and Ramchandran, pp. 20.
23. Nye F. Ivan and Hoffman, Waldis, "The Socio-cultural Setting," *The Employed Mother in America*, Chicago: Rand McNally and Company 1963, p. 8.

5

Quality of Women's Working Life

"Quality of Life" the Concerned Expression

Nobody seems to know who coined the word 'quality of life' which has lately achieved a remarkable popularity among the academic communities of social scientists and more specially among work oriented organisations and their managements. The same term issued differently in different languages in the developed countries and more often the term is used in complaint made by representatives of the developing countries in the United Nations about living conditions in their homeland.

Szalai (1978) approached eminent researchers, personally and through correspondence who were participants of two symposia devoted to the discussion, on various aspects of quality of life at the Ninth World Congress of Sociology (1978) at Uppsala. The attempt produced some evidences that the expression first came into light in the late 1950s or early 1960s but not in scholarly context, rather in newspapers or general publications mostly in connection with problems of environmental pollution, the deterioration of urban living conditions and the like. Szalai also canned through 20 major encyclopaedias published uptil 1978 but he could not locate any mention or entry having quality of life as its subject or any direct or indirect reference. He then argued that the expression has basic orientation in day-to-day conversation questions. "how are your?" which proves capability of human beings to keep in evidence of life, the conditions of their existence and to form integral judgement about the life. Therefore, the age old and ubiquitous "how are you" type of questions have as their vaguely defined object, the expression of an interest in health, welfare and prosperity, in the goodness of life as the `quality of life' of the person addressed.

Quality of life acquired sociological importance and became a topic of social research which converge largely on people's welfare and well being, then living conditions, their style of life, their standard of living. A new branch of socio-economic investigation took a formal shape called "study of social indicator system" and were applied in the processes of socio-economic planning, public policy decision making and even in marketing research.

Blishen and Atkinson (1978) also observed growing international concern about quality of life but stated that there was no agreement on specifying meanings of the term which resulted in differences in defining statistical indicators. Largely, two types of indicators come into picture about quality of life. Objective indicators, such as, money and sub active indicators, such as financial status, living standard, job etc. The objective indicators define the quality of life in terms of goods though to constitute desired states of existence by Govt. agencies while the subject indicators conceptualise individuals to define themselves, the quality of their life as perceived by them.

Hankinss (1978) pointed out that research work has revealed that quality of life is not simply the sum of its component units; it is much more than the resultant of interaction of welter of herogeneous forces and factors. And since, in the course of this interaction,the raw variables registered during the interviews undergo a through transformation, their ultimate meaning and significance can be determined only if they are analysed as the component parts of life-quality, considered as a coherent and integral system. Like Blishen and Atkinson he also argued that objective variables are concerned with the comparison of immediate surveys or census data which may allow important and valid inferences to the quality of life of the population. However, the immediate comparison of subjective variables, such as, attitudes, aspirations, fears, frustrations and satisfactions or dissatisfactions need more careful and controlled observation and in fact with such indicators one can go beyond the surface registration of cross-cultural similarities and dissimilarities.

A number of researches pertaining to problems regarding socialisation and personality development have cleared the doubts that a strong and systematic relationship exist between the personalities of individuals and social structures that socialise and support them. General measures of socio-economic status have been shown powerfully to condition the attitudes the values of individuals, in particular, the degree of their authoritarianism (Lipset, 1960) their sense of personal efficiency, their satisfaction with their jobs and life situations (Inkels, 1960), and the values around which they socialise their children (Pearlin and Kohn, 1966). The nature of the jobs men hold, especially the job's substantive complexity as well as feelings powerlessness and self-estrangement (Kohn and Schooler, 1973 and Kohn, 1976).

In the late sixties and early seventies the behavioural scientists started looking at the concept as the subject assessment was their own responsibility. It was believed that in objective indicators the parametres show unchanged structural features whereas in the subject indicators there are fundamental differences about the way people arrive at the assessment of their well-being. With the argument certain models were developed to view 'quality of life' from a combination of factors which were statistical and psychological. Abrams, 1973; Hall, 1976 in Britain, Andrews and Withey, 1976; Campbell et. al, 1976 in U.S.A. and Blishen *et. al.*, 1975 in Canada.

Rezsohazy (1978) also defined quality of life by calling it as ways of life and considered it as life style as an overall behaviour resultant of occasions like occurring daily (as at work) or seasonally (as vocations) or irregularly (as sickness) or even at unique occasions (such as marriage).

Stone (1978) in his theoretical paper on "organic solidarity and life quality indicators" accepted the importance of psychological factors in the assessment of quality of life. An individual has to consider the question of everything in terms of satisfying or frustrating. Certain satisfying things may become dissatisfying or frustrating at a span of time and one time scheduling may disrupt others resulting into frustration.

Solomon *et al.* (1978) have pointed out that industrialisation has caused social and environmental disturbances. The declarations for improvement of quality of life of people as a national objective is easy to agree upon but there is little consensus on how the quality of life should be defined, measured and fostered? According to them, quality of life is, therefor,e both material satisfaction of vital needs and aspects of life such as personal development, self realisation and a balanced eco-system. They also believe that quality of life has objective and subjective components which define a unique way for improvement for different social groups, cultures and nations.

Many authors have defined human needs and proposed classification schemes (Bossel, 1976; Galtung, 1975; Hankiss, 1976; Jarett, 1976; Mallamann, 1977; Masini, 1975; Maslow, 1971; McHale *et al.*, 1977). All of these are attempts to determine the necessity and, if possible, independent needs in order to describe all possible human behaviours.

Verwayen (1978) has reported that the Organisation for Economic Cooperation and Development, Paris had initiated social Indicators Development Programme in some of the countries to measure quality of life on the assumption that similarities of well-being and methodological principles of these surveys will be constant for all the countries under study. The areas that have been selected for this intensive work were:

1. healthfulness of life,
2. measurement of learning,
3. employment,
4. quality of working life,
5. time and leisure,
6. income, wealth and material deprivation,
7. housing conditions,
8. quality of the natural environment,
9. measurement of victimisation,
10. inequality,
11. economic accessibility,
12. comprehensive survey,
13. methodological issues in data collection,
14. presentation of social indicators and statistics, and
15. applicability of selected social concerns and indicators to particular national contexts. Sixteen projects were initiated and results of these studies are yet to be published.

Similarly, a number of other studies have highlighted various factors of quality of life which include work as most important aspect. The work provides a number of social material and psychological satisfactions because it largely yield money, either in the form of wages/pay or profits in a business organisation. Work has the potential to motivate individuals in numerous ways, what seems to be more important is an individual's perception of his work and his working life. This directly indicates existence of two types of factors, one related to the conditions of work and the other as to how the individual is perceiving these conditions of work to obstacle or facilitate his work output. At individual level working life and feelings towards work conditions determine his work environment and any improvement to it will led to improvement in terms of total productivity.

Rise of QWL Movement

In the context of quality of life, researches have been done in abundance taking working life as one of the factors but, as an independent factor, quality of working life (QWL) acquired its importance very recently. The debate among scientists in various disciplines are putting forth their thoughts towards definition, measurement and effective utilisation of the concept in industrial settings.

The managers of the recent time have been confronted with various organisational problems, out of which the most crucial is labour problem because machines materials, and the energy to run the machines don't perceive their environment, only man or workers do perceive. A number of researches have helped in understanding the concept and other associated concepts which will be discussed to arrive at operational definition of the term for use in the present investigation.

Newly acquired economic maturity appears to be one of the causes of the increased concern for improving the quality of working life. In many societies he framework of problem awareness for evaluating work experience has changed. This new awareness is generally attributed to the hightened aspirations of workers with regard to their working life, aspirations which in turn have been affected by improving living standards and higher educational levels of the work force in general.

Many of the current, against traditional problems are not the result of deteriorating social and working conditions rather, a consequence of hightened worker expectations and aspirations. Moreover, a number of aspects traditionally considered to be important are gradually giving way to new concerns.

New problems affecting the QWL, fall in several categories. Some have surfaced as a result of new technological and social developments, other represent changing and accelerating emphases on long recognised problem situations and conditions and still others relate to certain aspects of previously uncontested conditions which only recently have aroused concern regarding their compatibility with an acceptable level of QWL.

Walton (1975) pointed out that even though attention tends to be focussed on a few cases of obvious improvements which are widely publicised, demands for changes are usually not restricted to one or two aspects of the QWL. In fact, the extent of issues related to the QWL. In fact,the extent of issues related to the QWL is as broad as the whole range of labour problems

Although opinions remain divided, there is some proof that unfulfilled needs and demands may led not only to worker dissatisfaction but also to alienation from work, low productivity and social instability.

Along with the individual differences in the perception of the QWL, there are also political, economic, social and cultural conditions which differ vastly among societies, they also result in widely varying degrees of problem consciousness and in different counter measures that have been devised in response to workers' needs that have recently emerged.

In the pst few years, quality of working life has emerged as a central issue not only in India but also in other developed nations. The growing concern is evident from the growing number of national and international conferences of managers, union leaders, government officials and behavioural scientists. Perhaps the major cause for much of the recent concern is the alarm expressed by many about what has been termed the QWL problem facing today's workers and organisations. Yet there is currently a great deal of uncertainty and disagreement about just how serious this problem is, how widespread it is or whether it exists at all. Some argue that the problem is very real and very serious. Others view it as little more than the normal and expected growing pains of industry especially as maturity. Finally, still others view the quality of work life problem as one largely created by the media and little more than a passing interest.

There are a few valid or conclusive data that speak directly to the existence, the seriousness or the scope of the quality of working life problem much less to its sources or its effect but the importance of the problem is perceived as serious by few due to following reasons:

1. Worker alienation and job dissatisfaction are increasing primarily a result of meaningless jobs and authoritarian superiors.
2. The productivity of workers and industry is declining while counter productive behaviours (such as, sabotage, strikes, absenteeism, union militancy or alcoholism at work) are increasing.
3. The confidence of the public in large institutions in general and big businesses in particular is eroding.

The surveys conducted earlier shows that the behaviours like absenteeism, turn-over, job satisfaction and productivity are partially influenced by quality of working life. The reason is that while all of these attitudes of behaviours are indeed influenced by QWL, each are influenced by other factors as well. The other factors are: individual's expectations and values as well as what happens at work, technology, skills as well as motivation, etc.

Quality of working life is both a good and on-going process for achieving it. As a goal, QWL is the commitment of any organisation to work improvement, the creation of more involving, satisfying and effective jobs and work environment for people at all levels of the organisation. As a process, QWL calls for efforts to realise this goal through the active involvement of people throughout the organisation. As a result of their involvement, people can make more meaningful contributions to the organisation, its objectives and its ability to cope with the changing demands of a changing environment and at the same time, experience greater feelings of satisfaction, pride in accomplishment and personal growth. Importantly, QWL brings together the needs and development of people with the goals and development of the organisation.

QWL is also a philosophy and a concept of management. The philosophy is broad, many facetted and varying somewhat in its specific form, one culture to the next or from one organisation to other within the same organisation. But the basic idea is same, a climate must been couraged in which the fundamental human dignity of all members of the organisation are recognised, not only because they are entitled to it but also because workers are the most critical assets to the organisation and its future.

In France, when the main employers' and workers' organisation decided in 1973 to launch inter-industry negotiations upon "working conditions," the issues to be discussed were classified under these headings: work organisation; organisation of working times payment by results; health and safety, and the role of supervisory staff.

All these considerations lead to the view that the concept of quality of working life should first be used in its broad sense in order to examine the total labour problems of each society. First, on the basis of past and present economic conditions of each nation, one can judge the areas in which meaningful improvements can realistically be made and at what level. Secondly, the socio-cultural background of society helps to define not only what goals should be selected but how they should be pursued.

In spite of the great variety of economic, social, cultural and political situations in industrial societies, there is a broadly shared conviction that coherent and multi-facetted national policies are needed for the improvement of working conditions and of the quality of life. There is no doubt that increased protection of the physical and social working environment, new working time arrangements, improved pay systems, new and imaginative ways of organising work, wider application of ergonomics, and increased participation of workers in decisions directly affecting their working life. All these can make a substantial contribution to eliminating outdated and harmful methods of work and help promoting the QWL.

The continuous rise in material living standards tended to fulfil workers' need to achieve on the one hand power and equity and on the other prosperity. The goal of these workers began to rise higher and also to develop in a variety of directions. The relaxation of social control made it possible for them to express overtly their needs and problems, and to pursue personal satisfaction more directly. This liberation entailed first a general elevation of the level of aspirations, from material to psychological and from immediate to long range.

The internal work environment within the organisation began to prove inadequate in the light of new worker values. Many of the previously accepted technical, organisational and social assumptions of organisations began to cause dysfunctional symptoms. This was not so much due to a modified work environment as to a change in worker expectations towards that environments. As a result, productivity in same cases declined.

Having experienced difficulties, managements began to take remedial measures. Improvements could be made in many areas, especially in work environment and conditions of work. Upon closer examination, a number of managements concluded that one of the most promising areas was work itself. This decision was also much in line with some of the latest theories and experiences. Thus, the new area of management focus came into existence as the quality of working life.

In India, context the QWL as a movement may be considered rising but, the concept is viewed in terms of western context, where there are wide variation in Indian and western culture. The set of industrial norms are quite different in both the civilisations and on top of this as compared to west, India's industrial growth is in developing stage. In India, in spite of efforts by the Government and the private sector, the unorganised sector is still existing which is as vast as the organised sector.

In India the concept of QWL is considered useful to improve working conditions only for higher level workers. Perhaps no significant attempt has been made to explore QWL of the workers at the lower level and specially, unorganised sector has remained untouched. This does not mean that workers in the unorganised sector do not have any perception of their life in the context of their work.

Some of the objective parameters have been studied and a little glance has been made by some of the labour market studies to curb the malpractices of bonded labour in India which does not seem to be totally eradicated but their status surveys have thrown light on their conditions of work.

After studying the QWL movement and interest of many social and behavioural scientists in it, it was realised that the concept should be applied for in-depth study of workers in the unorganised sector of industries.

Women are the most downtrodden in the world of work, over burdened with hard and arduous work in dual role playing situation, at place of work as well as at home while performing economic responsibility and domestic discourses. Women workers in the construction industry are being considered the lowest in the ladder of workers.

Quality of Working Life: Concept and Terms

The notion of quality of working life, as an English idiom is closely related to the quality of life concept. Both emerged relatively recently in the industrialised nations where English was the primary language. Parallel concepts and innovative moves towards life goals developed, however, almost simultaneously in several other industrial countries. Humanisation of work, for instance, is often used in a number of languages as a synonym for quality of working life. In France and other French speaking countries, the most useful expression is "improvement of working conditions," while in the socialist countries the established term is "workers protection." In Scandinavia, the central concepts are "working environment" and "democratisation of the work place." However, the English concept of "quality of working life" is broadly understood in all industrialised countries, even if it is sometimes barely used (Thorsrud, 1976). In the case of Japan, for instance, the concepts of *hatarakiqai* and *ikiqui* which gained impetus in usage around the same time, are surprisingly similar to those of quality of working life and quality of life respectively. These developments would appear to indicate that the majority of industrialised nations have undergone certain common experience during the past quarter of a century.

Sayeed and Sinha (1981) stated that from the time of Taylor (1911) researchers have over the years, dwelt upon the development of working conditions and other related aspects, falling within the realm of social sciences. Most of the work in the area of industrial and organisational psychology had one common feature or an ulterior goal, primarily aimed at improving quality of work and working life and enhancing employee motivation in order to increase organisational viability.

A variety of concepts have been used to map up the conditions of QWL. Earlier, it was called morale and later termed as human relations, organisational development and redesign of work system. Presently, many researchers are inclined to describe the industrial democracy as a measure of quality of working life. Whatever way we have attempted to understand it, the question still remains whether we have made any headway in this direction in terms of integrating relevant findings to result in a new area of enquiry?

Attempts at defining the concept of QWL has been made by many. Tylor's (1973) and Sprin's (1975) view point can be considered for an operational definition which describes QWL as "the degree of excellence in work and working conditions which contribute to the overall satisfaction of the individual and enhances individual as well as organisational effectiveness." Prominent among those who have contributed to the area are Herrick and Maccoby (1972), Heizel, Geodale, Jayner and Burke (1973), Cherns (1973, 1975), Davis and Cherns (1975), Emry and Thorsrud (1976), Macy and Mervis (1976), Graen, Cashman, Ginsburg and Schiemann (1977) and Miller (1977).

The work on QWL had begun in India a decade ago with differences in the social, cultural political and economic spheres. A major thrust in this area was a tough proposition. But social scientists have gradually weaned their way and the efforts of Ganguly (1976), Joseph (1978) De (1977, 1980), Mehta (1976) and Sinha (1977) are to be lauded. It is further interesting to note that most of the work in the Indian setting dealt with the QWL in a theoretical and descriptive framework or mostly in an action research context to bring about some desirable changes in the design of work system (De, 1980).

The psychological factors have been seen from the angle of labour problems by Delamotte and Takezawa (1974) in their report for International Labour Organisation on QWL. They defined QWL as a set of new labour problems and their counter measures which have quined recognition as important determinants of worker satisfaction and productivity in many societies during the period of their sustained economic growth.

Sashkin and Lengermann (1984) have taken a thread from Herzburg's two-factor theory and considered 'conditions' (C) and 'feeling' (F) towards these conditions as important determinants of QWL.

The QWL—C/F is the result of a ten-year research programme that is based on classical sociological analysis of the relation between work and workers in society. These approaches suggest that workers become alienated from their work when the work has little inherent meaning such as repetition of the same minute set of actions over and over or denies the worker control or power over this or her own actions. These conditions lead to subjective feelings of alienation that sociologists call "self-estrangement"—feelings of being cut off from one's own true working self (Blauner, 1964).

In 1970, several research projects were initiated to empirically examine the relations between alienating job conditions which we now refer to as "quality of work life conditions" and workers" self-estrangement which we call `quality of work life feelings.' These working results led to a series of studies involving computer operators, clerical workers, machine operators, and medical technologists (Kirsch and Lengermann, 1971; Maurer, 1972). This work continue in order to explore effects over time, however, the instrument that was developed during the process of research now has enough evidences of validity to be generally useful (Wilmoph, 1983).

Measurement of QWL

In view o the dearth of systematic work in the area of quality of working life the measurement of the same seemed to be a practical difficulty. Majority of the studies in this area are theoretically oriented, concerned with what QWL is or what are its dimensions that should be included in the measurement of QWL. Through the list of QWL dimensions to be considered for its measurement is quite exhaustive, with the exceptions of General Motor's Survey (as reported by Carlson, 1978). The QWL dimensions mentioned by other investigators are either speculative or arbitrarily selected. Apart from this most of the surveys have been conducted in the western countries.

Boisvert (1977) identified fifteen dimensions for measuring the QWL. On the other hand, Walker's (1975) quality of working life involved the task, the physical work environment and the social environment within the organisation, the administrative system of the enterprise and the relationship between life and the job. Similarly, Ghosh and Kalra (1982), Ganguli (1979), Joseph (1978), Carlson (1977) etc. Took different dimensions for their study of quality of working life. The important of all these studies àre by Carlson and Walton in American set-up and Sinha and Syeed in Indian set-up. Very little, however, has been done at the empirical level to relate QWL dimensions with various processes of the organisation.

Sashkin and Lengermann (1984) have taken a combination of two factors i.e. conditions of the work and the feelings aroused and the impression of the worker to each of the condition with emphasis on the productivity in an organisation. The conditions of work were measured by autonomy, work speed and routine, task related interaction, personal growth opportunity and work complexity. The feelings have been measured by asking certain questions about various activities of the work.

The dimensions taken by Sayeed and Sinha for the measurement of QWL were, economic benefits, physical working conditions, mental state, career orientation, advancement on merit, job stress, effect on personal life, union-management relations, self-respect, supervisory relations, apathy, confidence in management, meaningful development, control, influence and participation, employee commitment, general life satisfaction and organisational climate.

The studies on QWL have taken various dimensions and at this stage when the concept is in its early stages of development, many more researches need be conducted to exactly identify the dimensions of QWL.

The present investigation also has the same thought to explose various dimensions which are correlated with QWL and also the external factors affecting QWL. The importance of these factors are all the more necessary for the workers of the lowest order.

Changing Technology and QWL

We are living in a period of rapidly increasing wrenching social and technological change. Organisation and job structures are undergoing change in response to these developments and because of our increased knowledge of the behaviours of organisations and individuals. Industrial society is in transition from one historical era to another and the environmental characteristics of the emerging era will led to crisis and marine dislocation, unless there is some form of adaptation. The structures of most purposive organisations based as they are on concepts of the industrial era, are becoming increasingly disfunctional because they stand at the confluence of changes involving technology, social values, economic environment and the practices of management.

The emergence of the post industrial era is stimulated by an ever increasing rate of changes in technology. The latter contributes to changes in values, not only by evoking new social systems and roles for organisational members but by stimulating the rising level of expectations concerning material, social and personal needs. They changes in technology changes the attitudes, aspirations of major segments of society. The seeming ease with which new technology satisfies material needs, coupled with the society's provision of subsistance, lend support for its citizens has stimulated a growing concern on the part of groups and individuals about their relationship to work, its meaningfulness and its values are the concerns of QWL.

The high rate of change of technology has consequences for organisation and job structure. On the product side, frequent new developments are leading to the growth of shorter production runs with the resulting need for adaptability of organisation and workers to more changes. On the production side, there is the phenomenon of more sophisticated machines and simpler manual activities embedded within automated complex production processes. The advanced technology presents is with a number of opportunities to develop new and more humane organisational foorms and jobs leading to a high QWL. First, although it poses new problems, highly sophisticated technology possesses an unrecognised flexibility in relation to social systems. There exists an extensive array of configurations of the technology that within limits can be designed to suit the social systems needs.

The new technology increases the dependence of the organisation on individuals and groups and requires more individual commitment and autonomous responsibility in the work place. Their requirements for mutual dependence and independence provide opportunities to redress past deep-seated errors in social organisations and member's roles.

The introduction of technology in the unorganised sectors, specially in the construction industry has affected deployment of heavy equipment for which the workers require basic skills. The training opportunities are limited and if we see gender differences, women are considered out of place. The employment opportunities in agriculture fields are also replacing the women folk as they are unable to handle modern equipments. In this way, the immediate employment to women both in agriculture fields and construction industry are gradually reducing and so is the case with the work force participation rate. This factor would definitely be influencing change in perception of QWL by these workers. All attempts of enhancing the QWL have led to successful results, whatever may be the type of interventions.

Gain from Improve QWL

There are various elements which influence the individual's work experience. Therefore, it is certain that an improved QWL will affect these variables. As the perception of QWL differs from individual to individual so is the gain perceived in various terms. QWL programmes incorporate a number of critical elements including a commitment from top management—acknowledgement from both management and employees that a voluntary desire from both sides to co-operate is essential.

From the organisations, point of view the gain of QWL improvement is significant because there is:

- improved quality,
- increased output,
- reduced absenteeism,
- higher turnover,
- better labour management relation etc. and to employee; the gains are:
- job satisfaction
  - greater control over one's own job
  - recognition
  - increased self esteem

— a sense of accomplishment
— fewer mental health problem, improved physical and phychological health.

In short, we can say that a higher quality of working life can often lead to decreased absenteeism, and higher turn over, few accidents and higher quality and quantity of output of goods and services.

The most direct and immediate gain from an improved QWL is higher job satisfaction. These two phenomenon are so closely related that they are often assumed to be one and the same and people sometimes use to interchangibly. But the term job satisfaction refers to an individual's affective reactions or feelings, toward his job and the term QWL refers to the individual work experiences. Job satisfaction is determined largely by how well an individual's actual rewards and experiences on his job are compared his desired or expected rewards and experiences, it is based largely on job. Quality of work life is a broader concept than job satisfaction in the sense that it includes both the job content and job context.

Generally, the workers having high QWL experience high job satisfaction. Individuals whose important needs are being satisfied by their job related activity, invariably experts positive feelings about these jobs and hence, there is increase in individual productivity.

Individual productivity and quality of work lie are closely related, specially when productivity is defined in terms fo the individual's internal work standards. High productivity is both a cause and an effect of a high quality of work lite. The term productivity is much more than merely the quality of the individual's work output. It also includes such work behaviours as poor turnover, absenteeism, defiance of rules and authority, grievances, strikes, union activities sabotage, theft, accidents and specially the quality of work output. All of these behaviours have been shown to be directly influenced by the individual's job satisfaction, involvement or commitment and these attitudes are directly affected by the quality of the individual's work life. Although, QWL is not the only determinant of individual productivity, yet it is the most important determinant. So, in any attempt to improve productivity the other various factors, both inside and outside the organisation, must also be taken into account. A high QWL does not always or necessarily assure a high level of productivity but the poor QWL definitely discourages the productivity to some extent.

Improved quality of working life improves the organisational effectiveness on the whole. If the interests of workers and goals of the organisation are mutually supportive, improvement in the quality of work life will result in gains for both parties. As for example, improvement in job design will produce not only more intrinsically motivating and enriching tasks but also higher individual productivity. However, there are many areas where the interests of individuals are not clear and inevitable conflict with the goals (economic goals) of the organisations that employ them or with the interests of the other groups in the organisation. The worker's demand of more pay or greater security are in direct conflict with the profitability of most organisations and similarly, the demand of increase in power or autonomy of non-management workers because it will cause reduction in autonomy and authority of managers. If these cases significant benefits can be gained from improvement of QWL, which has an impact on the ability of inter-dependent individuals and groups to work together toward organisational goals, to communicate effectively with each other, to co-ordinate their activities and to resolve their conflicts.

The Quality of Women's Working Life

There is fundamental difference in female and male work roles which need extensive examination of he nature of these socially accepted sex-bound roles. Although, no society is a sex based division of labour, there is an extraordinary variety of sex typing of occupations across cultures suggesting that the sex typing is not based on unchangeable, genetic, physiological or psychological differences between the sexes but is and has been a social construct.

The industrialisation brought about a revolutionary change in the occupation expansion with varying degree of basic human input required from the workers. This gave impetus to misplacing women socially and in the labour market. The women are still considered inferior to men in terms of skill, pay, prestige and authority.

The female role has to face two conflicting situations in the world of work as responsibility at work place and at home as care taking mother, performing perfect domestic and social activities. This is common for all the societies, irrespective of occupational category.

The quality of working life of women has to undergo various stages in the life cycle. After being prepared to under-take work and coming out of the domestic situation, the marriage brings about numerous changes and extra responsibilities on the part of women workers. At times women have to withdraw themselves from the world of work due to their marriage.

Many studies have proved that like men, women are also motivated to work for money. Working women's income is of considerable economic importance even when it is additional to the husband's income which determines sufficiency or deprivation in the family.

The QWL of the women workers has so far not been assessed by any of the research study. In India, the efforts were not significant. The need is to undertake indifferent research works to study QWL of women workers.

Earlier Studies on QWL

Since quality of working life is a relatively new concept, most of the work in this area are on a theoretical-descriptive line concerned with how QWL should be defined and measured. However, a few empirical studies have been reported from India which tried to relate QWL to job satisfaction, work performance or managerial expectations or to some demographic variables.

In an attempt to study the relationship between job attitudes and QWL, Joseph (1978) collected data from 96 skilled and semi-skilled technicians in a public sector enterprise, following a questionnaire approach. Conceiving QWL as an evaluation process of one's life in the work context. Job attitudes operationalised in terms of work, pay, promotion, co-workers and supervision. The findings of the study indicated that

(a) attitudes towards the nature of work is clearly associated with QWL. The more one feels that his/her work is interesting, challenging and that it gives him/her a sense of achievement, the higher would be his/her perceived quality of working life;
(b) associates or co-workers have the potential to make QWL high or low, and
(c) attitude towards supervision and pay appear to be least associated with QWL even though supervision seems to be a general factor influencing other job aspects.

Singh and Maggu (1980), while studying the corporate quality of working life, operationalised QWL in terms of five dimensions and collected data from 251 managerial level employees representing 42 organisations. The results showed that QWL was considerably low across all the categories of respondents and across all the parameters of work system, perceived QWL being the poorest in the case of democratisation of work process. It was further observed that he variation in managerial hierarchy, income and experience do not significantly influence the perception of the QWL.

In another study, Ghosh and Kalra (1982) collected the importance ratings of 15 QWL factors from 70 managers in public and private sector organisations in their attempt to study how the different factors associated with the concept of QWL are influenced by variables like age, income, qualification, experience etc. The results of this study revealed significant perceptual differences only in relation t four factors; employee welfare, advancement base don merit, absence of under job stress and union-management relations. The enquiry further showed that 'employe welfare' was influenced by age and income, 'advancement' based on merit, was influenced by education and experience, absence of under job stress' was influenced by professional, non-professional categories and the perception of 'union-professional categorisation of respondents. However, "various QWL, factors are likely to be perceived differently by different groups."

In a more comprehensive study, Sayeed and Sinha (1981) examined the relationship between QWL and job satisfaction and performance taking data from 184 class III employees working in two organisations. For measuring QWL, they used the inventory developed by Sinha and Sayed (1980). For Job satisfaction, they used the same dimensions as used by Joseph for measuring job attitudes. And performance measures were obtained from worker's self and supervisor ratings. Overall, the results indicated that higher QWL leads to greater job satisfaction and better performance.

Emery (1976), Srivastava (1975) and McGregor (1960) in their studies stressed that the organisational structure played a significant role in developing human personality. All these studies have demonstrated beyond doubt that a bureaucratic culture severely inhibits human growth and that it is inadequate for inducing commitment to work. Friedlander and Newton studied the impact of organisational climate on the individual's job values and job satisfaction. They found organisational climate to be a significant determinant of individual job satisfaction. Lyon and Lvaucvich observed that the organisational climate had the most significant impact on self-actualisation a lesser impact on autonomy and only slight impact on esteem.

In spite of the awareness of these findings and many other researches which clearly high-light the role of the corporate culture and quality of working life in determining human behaviour. Kapoor has concluded that about 25 per cent of the work force is in the dissatified range, 30 per cent in the satisfied group and remaining 45 per cent in the neutral zone. In a survey of 2821 American managers, Tarnowieasi concludes that 70 per cent of the managers were satisfied with their present career. The same study reveals that within the preceeding five years nearly 50 per cent of the executives surveyed had either changed or seriously considered changing their line of work for more meaningful career. Based on the study of the middle level managers, from 500 organisations Tasrnowieaski further reported that the middle level managers were highly dissatisfied with the contemporary organisational work life.

According to Mehta (1976) work amenities including economic compensation, interpersonal support, autonomy on the job and respectful supervisory behaviours are important factors in work related satisfaction. Studies also suggest the importance of general life satisfaction in promoting work satisfaction and efficient functioning in work organisation (Mehta 1976). Repeated studies done by Mehta (1976) and Veccho (1980) on several categories of people including government officials, managers and supervisory staff show that perceived availability of influence and autonomy are the major source of satisfaction or dissatisfaction. Similarly, influence and autonomy were another important indictors of dissatisfaction at the work place is the employee's perception of lack of amenities such as general welfare amenities and inadequate economic compensation including inadequate salary. In several cases, non-availability of adequate water and canteen facilities, inadequate medicine and health care provided to be a major source of work related dissatisfaction (Mehta, 1976).

In developing countries, various kinds of developmental activities, following political and social freedom have led to very significant rise in the people's aspirations. Such rising aspirations are bound to effect the sense of life satisfaction among the workers. Similarly, socio-economic factors also play an important role in shaping attitudes towards work and related matters in the context of rising aspirations. For instance, studies identified economic factors like income, promotional opportunities, social security as important factors in employee's sense of life satisfaction. Factors like working hours and nature of job did not find same importance as salary, security and advancement (Ganguli 1976).

Another important finding in various studies is related to age of the employees. The young entrants to organisations and younger employees showed greater work related dissatisfaction. Such dissatisfaction tended to decrease with increasing age of the employee (Mehta 1976). Mehta also fund that older employees felt more satisfied with life related issues in comparison to the younger ones. Although, it is not clear why the older employees feel so. With the increase in age, they are expected to have greater family and social responsibility and therefore, greater concern for salary increments than younger ones. The dissatisfaction among the younger employees seems to be realistic to a certain extent because they have rising aspirations and expect more from the job than they actually get at the work place.

In another study Ahmed (1971), Ashraf (1975) find that lowly educated younger employees show greater sense of dissatisfaction with their life conditions. As a rule, lesser educated employees also get lower pay and lower benefits as compared to higher educated employees. Dissatisfaction due to economic factors is enhanced by rising aspirations. Such employees carry their disatisfaction with life conditions with them to their work and work place.

Singh (1982) in his study of quality of corporate work life found that perceived QWL was considerably poor in Indian industries and.perception did not change with the change in the managerial hierarchy. The findings of his study further revealed that the income did not significantly influence the perceived quality of work life.

In another important study, Mehra (1984) found the relationship of job involvement to background factors, perceived importance of needs and need satisfaction. Although, his study was not directly related to individual need fulfilment, yet individual's job involvement has its roots in the principles of need satisfaction and motivation. Job of an individual is of great importance and the individuals involvement in job depends on satisfaction f needs derived by individuals on the job. His study throws light on income and length of service having significant correlation with need fulfilment among other factors. The subjects with more income were found more satisfied with their needs and were more job involved. Level of education and place of birth did not make any difference to the need satisfaction and job involvement.

Livneh (1978) in his study on quality of work experience found that patterns of changes in work values, job reward are contingent on specific facet of work involved, rather than age being uniformly a significant determining factor. He also found that education has the most important relation t various work values followed by occupation.

George (1984) studied lower, middle and upper managerial workers to study QWL in Public Section Undertakings. Along with the background variables quality of life was correlated with QWL. The results indicated that high quality of life will have high quality of working life, older employees have lower QWL, no relationship existed between length of service and income with QWL.

Mishra (1985) studied quality of working life of managers and Research and Development personnel of two Public Sector Undertakings to find relationship between age, length of service, education, income and need fulfilment. The results indicated that age and length of service did not affect QWL perception. QWL was a function of income of the employees, the high income leads to high QWL, higher the educational level, higher was the QWL perception. QWL was significantly related to need fulfilment.

On the basis of the review of concerned literature and various methods and studies in the direction of concept clarification, following hypotheses were framed for testing. Seven null hypotheses have been framed because the supporting and parallel evidences are not available in the literature surveyed.

Hypothesis I— The difference in the level of QWL will have no relationship with background variables of the women construction workers.

Hypothesis II— The relationship of QWL with work related variables of women workers will not be significant.

Hypothesis III— The living condition variables will not have any significant relation with QWL.

Hypothesis IV— The general awareness of the respondents will have no relation with level of QWL.

Hypothesis V— The attitude towards education of the women construction workers will have no relationship with QWL.

Hypothesis VI— The performance level of the women construction workers will not be significantly related to QWL.

Hypothesis VII— The need fulfilment of the women construction workers will not be significantly related to QWL.

6

Women and Common Social Issues

The poor, rural, self-employed women usually belong to the so-called lower caste groups in the village. The caste system leads to a whole set of problems faced by these women. In fact, one of the major causes of their poverty-stricken, exploited and deprived situation is that they belong to the lower caste and hence, apparently, deserve no better. There are several dimensions to this basic factor of caste, which we shall describe in this section under social issues of poor, rural, self-employed women.

Untouchability exists in many villages of Ahmedabad district. The *harijans* suffer the most because of this practice. Their homes are always at the end of the village and away from the mainstream of activity. They are not allowed to fill water from the wells, or wash in the lake. The barbers do not attend to them, people will not buy their milk or *ghee*. They have to make their own arrangements for these services. In villages where untouchability is very strictly practised, there is a lot of resentment among the *harijans* about this fact. They call the upper castes condescending. The upper caste people still cleanse themselves with holy water after accidental contact with the *harijans*. Other forms of ritual purification are also practised. They will not drink water, tea or eat at the *harijans'* homes. Even when the study team went to the *harijans'* homes there was a lot of curiosity and enquiries were made about what we did there. If we had water or tea at their place, the message would reach the upper castes quite soon. We were even told by a muslim woman running a grocery stall in one village. 'You had tea at the *bhangivaas*. Now nobody else will offer you even a glass of water in this village.' But there are villages where the *harijans* do not feel so cut-off from the upper castes. They are not exactly welcomed with open arms, but the stigma of untouchability is not there. They are allowed to fill water and intermingle to some extent with the other castes. In the poorer villages, the difference between the castes appears to be less than that of the villages that are economically better off.

Apart from the *harijans* there are other castes who feel discriminated against, because they are of a lower caste although not untouchable. The *vagharis*, for instance, are not untouchables but they are not treated any better either. They are also very resentful. The lower castes are somehow seen as unworthy of living a decent life, of acquiring assets, or requiring assistance, of fairness. Even though they may not directly interfere in the power relations of the village, they do watch everything. They know that injustice is being done, that they are being deprived but are helpless. In one village, for instance, the *gauchar* land had been confiscated by some of the landlords, and was being tilled for farming. The poor people were having difficulties grazing their goats but were notable to stop the landlords from tilling the land. They knew that *gauchar* land belonged to everybody in the village. They knew that the landlords were doing wrong and they talked about it to anybody who would listen. Similarly, in another village, some *vagharis* had been forcibly deprived of their land, even though the land records showed that they owned the land. They had tilled the land for many years but still could not stop the powerful elements in the village from evicting them and claiming it as common land.

In Dehgam, many villages have piped water reaching all the homes in the village including those of the *bhangis.* They all have to pay a water tax of this facility. However, we came across cases where the flow of water to the *bhangi* residences was cut off after the first year or so, by installing more taps in the pipe-line at points before it reached the homes of the *bhangis.* These taps would constantly be left open so that only a trickle of water reached the *bhangis,* who nevertheless, had to pay tax regularly.

In other villages the lower castes were forcibly made to work as agricultural labourers, in the fields of the landed class, or beaten up and driven out of the village. The poor know that this is wrong but they are helpless and unable to correct the situation on their own.

The relations between the castes are often very strained even when there is no untouchability. The rates of agricultural labour, the facilities provided to the lower castes, the assistance extended to them to avail of the development schemes, the availability of raw materials for them, are the reasons for these strained relations. The upper castes generally believe that the government is providing too much aid, schemes and benefits for the lower castes and they are pampered, that they should not be given any special help from the upper castes. Out of this belief stems a lot of their behaviour towards the lower castes, apart from the centuries old exploitative relationship. The upper castes try and minimise the benefits made available to the lower castes so that the gap between them is not reduced because of these government schemes. The lower castes are aware of this. They say,

> If we had everything, would we be living like this. These land-owners think we have got everything, but who is giving us anything at all. The government is making schemes for us, but how can we get the benefit. We don't know how to read and write. We don't know how to fill forms and talk to big officials. The *sarpanch* and *talati* know that, but they don't want to help us. To get something passed we have to go so many times to the *taluka* office. We don't have money to go so often. We have to spend from our pocket for the fare and lose our earnings for that day. And then the officials there will also ask for money. If the *sarpanch* desires he can get these things done very quickly for us. But why will he do anything for us. He will only do the work of the rich.

The attitude of the *sarpanch* makes a lot of difference to the nature of relations between castes. If the *sarpanch* is willing to help everyone irrespective of caste, there is less tension in the village. The poor and the lower castes have some sense of psychological well-being in these villages. They feel more secure and assured that the *sarpanch* will help them if any misfortune be falls them. In villages where the *sarpanch* does not help all the castes, there is tension. In many villages the *sarpanch* takes sides and actively disallows development assistance to reach the lower castes. Here, the relations between the castes become increasingly strained.

Housing facilities, loans, subsidies, scholarships, old age and widowhood pensions, land allotment to landless families, roads, child-care programmes, electricity connections, and the use of *panchayat* lands, are some of the programmes in which the *sarpanch* plays a decisive role. He can facilitate or block the access of such programmes to the poor. The *sarpanch* and the *talati* usually know of the existence of these programmes and it is part of their duty to inform all the people concerned about these programmes. When officials of development agencies and programmes come to visit the village, they first meet the *sarpanch*. The poor are rarely at home in the day so they do not get a chance to meet the officials directly. Therefore, they can only find out about these programmes when they see others availing of the benefits in their own village or other villages. Very few have direct contact with the officials from whom they can find out details of these programmes.

They have, out of necessity, to depend on the *sarpanch* and *talati* for all the information regarding the existence of the schemes as well as details of the procedure. In many villages, the poor are intentionally excluded from this information. They are ignored by the *sarpanch* and *talati*. If the poor come to know of the schemes from other sources, and approach the *sarpanch* or *talati*, they are still ignored. Sometimes, for appearance's sake, the *sarpanch* and *talati* may go through the motions of helping them. They may even fill up the forms and then not let the forms move any further. In other cases, the *sarpanch* will tell the family concerned to go and get all the details themselves and then he will consider whether or not he will help them. Often, they are made to come again and again to remind the *sarpanch* about the pending forms. This is the situation in villages where the relations between the castes are strained and where the *sarpanch* does not want to help the lower castes. But in villages where the *sarpanch* is impartial, he himself calls the deserving families and helps them to get the benefits of specific schemes. In these villages, the poor have a protective umbrella as long as there is an impartial *sarpanch*.

The cases system has its concomitant division of occupations. There is quite a strong feeling among the women about what is their work and what is not. Thus, working with reeds is only *bhangi's* work, working with leather is only *chamar's* work, working with clay is only potter's work, growing vegetables is only *vaghari's* work, etc. Even if there is an opportunity to do work other than their hereditary occupation there is some resistance against. It. The uncertainties are too many and their capacity to absorb unanticipated losses, to make new investments, is very limited. Sticking to the caste-based occupation is a very convenient way of avoiding all such risks. But if the skills traditionally practised by other castes are taught in a training programme by some agency, they are willing to come and learn. Their own risk is minimal in such an arrangement. They usually get a stipend and have a buffer in the form of the training programme. There is group backing too because others also step out of the caste occupations defined by the caste they belong to. They can draw strength from being a group and deal with the social sanctions if they are imposed by the village in such instances.

The children of the poor also suffer. They learn the skills of their parents if they are interested. Otherwise, they grow up with no vocational skills as at all. Very few acquire other qualifications, so chances of getting work other than manual labour are very bleak. In such cases, the children grow up with a sense of inadequacy. Their poverty aggravates the social situation. In school, the children of the poor are discriminated against, and as adults are ill-equipped to earn a decent livelihood.

There is also a sense of doom among the poor. 'We are destined to do this work. We must have done some terrible things in our previous birth so we must suffer now. This is our fate. We are born poor, we will die poor. Who is going to listen to us.' These are some of the very common responses of the poor. This again is a symptom of helplessness and the inability to do much alone. They do not know how to improve the situation on their own. It does not mean that they do not want to improve their situation. If they see even a glimmer of hope they take it, 'Now that you have come to our village and are writing everything down, please do something for us. Nobody else in this village is going to do anything about us. You don't forget us after you have gone from here'. Such statements show the hope which gives them the strength to live. But they also experience disillusionment, 'So many people have come and written down and gone away. You people waste so much paper, but nothing happens afterwards. We have grown waste so much paper, but nothing happens afterwards. We have grown old doing the same work, but nothing has changed'. The realistic appraisal of their situation is obvious.

To meet the demands of survival they have become very immediacy-oriented in their whole outlook. The present and today alone matter. 'Who knows whether we will even be alive tomorrow' is their attitude at one level and, 'Our parents did not do anything for us. At least we should do something for our children otherwise they will also have to suffer like us,' is their attitude at another level. They find so many different ways of surviving, and this has made their approach to life contingency-oriented—prepared for most situations. They develop extreme mobility and are willing to go to work at very short notice. They are also willing to go anywhere to work, especially those who work as labourers. Their families, their belongings, are all adapted to an extremely mobile lifestyle. Wherever it is possible to earn an income is where their home is. They do not burden themselves with assets which will inhibit their movements, they learn to make do with a minimum of facilities, they can put up a shelter anywhere and pass their days. Their children are not sent to school so that they can remain mobile.

Those who live by making their own investments are a little less prone to extreme mobility. They make their base in one village and are only mobile when procuring or selling. Their mobility is of short spells and they do not shift their homes very easily. But those who earn from labour alone have long spells of mobility and are willing to shift homes for long periods.

This mobility makes them develop a contingency approach. They do not make commitments with a long term implication because they themselves do not know what will happen at any time. They do not know where they will be at a particular time. Their decision-making is therefore non-committal and temporal. Topicality is of prime importance to them.

7

Women and Common Economic Issues

An analysis of the detailed descriptions of the trade groups taken up for study, reveals certain common economic issues which predominate the lives of poor, self-employed women.

Low income is one of the basic issues for these women. They can barely eke out a living and are constantly worried about being able to make both ends meet. Even basic needs of food, clothing and shelter are not met from the money got from most of the trades. The nature of their work is such that there is an *inherent uncertainty* about the income they will earn in a particular time period. Being self-employed, they have learnt to live with this uncertainty. The number of days they will be able to find work, even in activities where they provide only labour, is not known to the women. Where they will get work, how much they will get paid, what will be the going rate, are all not known (as in agricultural labour, construction work, brickmaking, etc.) Whether they will be physically fit and therefore able to work when they find some, whether their family will be able to survive till some work is available, are serious doubts which are constantly preying on their minds. For those who invest their own funds and resources, the uncertainty is concerned with the prices they will be able to get for their products; what and how many raw materials they will be able to collect or get; how much they will be able to buy; how much they will be able to process; whether they will be able to sell they produce; and whether they will be able to recover their costs and earn something. The question of good health is of as much concern for own account workers as it is for those who provide labour (as in bamboo work, reed work, leather work, vegetable growing, etc.).

The *work opportunities* are restricted to their caste-based occupation or to physical, labour-intensive, unskilled work. Those who have been able to learn the caste-based occupation have an additional skill, other than physical labour. But many do not even know their caste-based occupation (such as, weaving). Women particularly, have little scope of getting work opportunities, other than unskilled labour. Even in caste-based occupations or family-based production units, the women do the unskilled and tiring labour work. The traditional division of labour is such that they do not get a chance to learn the whole work process (as in pottery, weaving and leather work). They can, therefore, earn a livelihood only from whatever skills they have. To the extent that a particular skill is viable in terms of demand

and supply, in terms of its earning capacity, it enables them to survive. If the skill becomes obsolete, they are pushed to the brink of starvation (as in weaving, and cotton-boll shelling). This scarcity of work opportunity is one of the main causes for the low incomes they draw.

Landlessness and *lack of assets* are problems for the poor. Very few families of the lower castes (who make up the majority of the poor) have land. The few that do own land have such meagre holdings that their families are unable to draw sustenance from the land alone. The land is rarely in the name of the women. Their ownership of assets is also very limited. Whatever capital, cattle, or property (housing), or equipment for production, is owned by the family, is in the name of the men normally. The asset base is also very minimal. It is more often than not handed down from their ancestors. If they had to purchase such assets today, it would be almost impossible for them to do so on their own. Only if they are able to get the benefit of some development programme would they be able to procure new assets (loans for equipment, cattle, housing facilities, land from the Land Ceiling Act).

The *status of women* in the village depends on whether they are daughters or daughters-in-law of that particular village. Traditionally, the daughter is not married off in the same village. The adult female population in a village is mostly of women who have come to the village after getting married—the daughters-in-law. It is very rare to find adult daughters in the female population of the village because girls are normally married off in their teens. Only in cases where daughters have been deserted by their husbands, or are widowed, have they come to stay at their parental home. Unmarried adult daughters are very rare. The activities in which adult women are involved are thus pursued mainly by the daughters-in-law. They are not allowed as much freedom as the daughters. They also have the additional roles of wife, mother, and homemaker to fulfil along with their role of worker. They are expected to contribute to the family income among the poor. If they do not have any income-generating skills, they are taught them. Educating (to pursue a trade) the daughter-in-law is seen as a permanent asset for the family. The daughters constitute the adolescent female population of the village.

Their *work skills* are *acquired* mainly from the family (parental or marital), neighbours, or friends. As such, they do not know where else to acquire new skills if the skills they have are not viable any more. They do not have easy access to training programmes, nor do they know of the existence of many such facilities. The women, particularly, are quite unaware of the avenues that may be open for acquiring new skills, even when they are willing to learn. Sewing machines and *charkha* spinning have come to symbolise the need of the women to acquire new skills, because they are the avenues which the women have seen and made use of in their own experience. Even if the women know of the new skills which can help them, they do not know the procedure followed at various levels, to get training facilities. They have perforce to operate through their husbands.

Those engaged in providing labour have to *maintain contact* with gang leaders or retain friendly relations with farmers and others who need work to be done. As there is no employer-employee relationship with any one person, they have to ensure that their work opportunities continue indefinitely. If they do not have stable contacts with those who need labour services, the women (along with the mean) have to go from site to site, or farm to farm, asking if their services are needed (as in migrant labour, construction work and brickmaking).

Similarly, those who are own account workers, have to maintain their contact with the sources of raw materials, funds, and equipment. They also have to maintain cordial relations with the purchasers of their products so that they market is ensured (as in bamboo work, pottery, reed work, leather work, weaving, vegetable growing, poultry and milk production).

Usually, however, these contacts are managed by the men, especially, when it involves people outside the village. Within the villages, the men relate to the men and the women to the women. With gangleaders, the women usually operate through their men. If these relationships are not maintained, the own account workers have to deal with even greater uncertainties as far as their income is concerned or, they have to find new sources for the inputs, or forego their trade altogether and find other work (as in reed work, leather work, vegetable growing, agricultural labour and construction work).

They *prefer the customers to come to them* to procure what they need (agricultural labour, construction work, pottery, leather work, milk products, bamboo work). This is a way of ensuring that they have the final say in the rates or prices quoted. If the customer comes to them, the customer is acknowledging his/her need for the goods or services. If such a situation does not arise, and they are desperate, they do go to the customers to sell their goods and services. This situation is perceived as a distress sale situation and is only resorted to in extremely dire situations. But when they have no choice, they are forced to take up this option. The customer has the final say in quoting the rates and prices in such cases (migrant labour, brickmaking, construction work, vegetable selling, reed work, bamboo work, pottery). The workers do not have much bargaining power when the staying power (to hold on to goods and services) is exhausted. They have to recover their investment and/or earn income to survive and thus, the compromise on the prices of their goods and the rates of their labour.

A low income for the women means a *low income for the whole family* because, very rarely, does the *income* come in the *hands of the women*. They are workers, beyond doubt, but they do not always control the income directly. In own account work they mainly work as one member of a family unit. In labour work, they have a greater opportunity to work in an individual capacity. Nevertheless, the income is seen as family income, even if it income for the basic needs of the family. When the money available to them is not enough to meet their basic needs, the family has to borrow funds.

Credit is not easily available to the poor in rural areas. Credit from private sources (money-lenders and others) is very strictly controlled. Only those who have material assets, such as, land and cattle, are considered creditworthy. The poor women, and especially those belonging to the lower castes, are not trusted in money matters. Most of them do not own land or other assets and it is, therefore, very, very difficult for them to get credit. They can borrow small amounts (Rs. 20 or Rs. 25) as advance payment on work on a personal basis. It has, however, to be repaid within a few days. Larger amounts are quite out of the question. If their relationship with the well-off is particularly good, they can borrow a couple of hundred rupees on personal surety. For most of the poor families, even amounts of a few hundred rupees are available only by pledging ornaments, utensils, or other such belongings. Loans are normally for a short duration of between three and six months only and the interest rates vary between Rs. 2 and Rs. 10 per cent month, for every hundred that is loaned. If the interest and principal are not repaid within the stipulated period, the articles pledged are sold. Because of these stringent terms the poor are very wary of borrowing on interest. As it is, they do not have any material assets, and if they do own something, they are reluctant to pledge it. The uncertainty of their income does not encourage them to pledge whatever little they may own. Only if they are very certain of being able to pay it back, do they borrow on interest. That, or they have to be very desperate indeed. They will then be reconciled to the possibility of having so sell off their ornaments. Pledging them is only a way of buying more time—if they are able to earn and repay the loan, the ornaments can be recovered. For the very desperate it is little short of a stalling mechanism. They condition of advancing money only for short durations is adhered to because of the inherent uncertainty of work and income in self-employment. Both lender and borrower are aware of it. In some cases, the loan is made for a period of a year but never more than that. The loans are also taken in kind—usually grains for consumption. These have to be repaid in kind—usually one and a half, or twice the quantity borrowed. The repayment is normally during harvest time. In other cases, the loan is in cash but the repayment and interest, in kind. All these negotiations are normally finalised between the men. The involvement of women is not encouraged.

Loans from banks are also available to rural people. Only in principle, however. The reason for initiating rural credit facilities through credit societies and nationalised banks, made available through development programmes, has been made in order to facilitate the flow of funds to the villagers. This laudable goal, however, does not actually reach the poor, particularly the women. The procedural requirements, the certifying and attestations necessary (from the *sarpanch* and *talati*), the need for surety, all of these make bank loans almost inaccessible to the poor. Even if they get the bank loans, the women are not given credit facilities. It is the privilege of men alone. The strained relationship between the lower and upper castes; the unwillingness of those with influence to let development agencies with the power elite of the villages; the ignorance of the poor people regarding schemes and procedures; all these ensure that the avenue of bank loans is effectively closed to the poor. Unless there is active intervention from women's organisations to divert bank facilities to women under the development programmes, the poor, rural women do not have access to them.

The transactions of poor, self-employed people (rural and urban, men and women) are usually *verbal*. This is because they deal with very few people, with people known within their reference system. The amounts involved are also small. The rural women are quite well versed with conducting verbal transactions as well as the safeguards to be respected in such dealings. Being illiterate is not a handicap in such transactions because reading and writing are not necessary. Nor is it necessary to know procedural details, to have contact with officials, or information about various programmes and schemes. But the development programmes, the schemes for assistance, the rules, the procedures, the sanctioning of assistance, the evidence required to establish genuineness, all require the poor, self-employed to be proficient in written transactions. Written authentication, written applications, written forms, written sanctions, written records and testimonials, are the basis for this assistance. The women are handicapped by this shift from verbal to written. As far as their own work-related transactions are concerned, they can still survive by verbal dealings. But their work opportunities, their prospects for improving their situation, have become inextricably linked with official development efforts (governmental and non-governmental). For this, they have to acquire proficiency in written transactions. The women (and even the men) have neither any direct information about the schemes and facilities available, nor do they know in detail the procedural formalities to be followed. They do not even have any clout with the power elite in the village or the various offices which would help them overcome their handicap. Not being literate, then, becomes a serious constraint. They can be cheated, they can be fooled, they can be short-changed.

This *general lack of awareness* of detailed procedures and formalities extends to other fields as well. Those engaged in providing labour do not always know the minimum rates which are applicable to them, they do not know of their rights regarding shelter, sanitation, child-care, leave, health, and accident compensation. Those who need their services are able to manipulate them and play upon their ignorance (as in migrant labour, construction work, digging mud, and agricultural labour).

Women work mainly as *members of the family unit* in own account work. They do not know all the stages of the work because the work of men and women is divided in such a way that women get to specialise only in activities requiring manual labour. The activities requiring dealings with the outside world, such as, procuring raw materials from the market, going to sell the products in the markets in town, are all handled by the men (as in weaving, bamboo work, vegetable growing and grocery stall keeping). The women are not able to get a sense of the market forces, they do not get an opportunity to acquire these skills. Even within the production process, quite often women cannot handle all the details independently (as in pottery, leather and bamboo work). The work of the women is viable only as a family unit and not independently as of individuals. Their sense of confidence, of being able to work individually, is, therefore, not very developed.

Raw material can be got from the collection, in exchange for a service, or, alternatively for cash (reed work, leather work, processing milk and bamboo work). Women are familiar with the social mechanisms of free collection and also of getting raw materials in exchange for a service. They can procure these raw materials even without the men. When the raw materials are owned by the family, of course, then, the women are comfortable.

But when it comes to buying raw materials (with cash) from the market then the women feel handicapped. Similarly, for the selling of finished goods, women only feel comfortable when they sell it retail in their own or neighbouring villages (as in vegetable growing). They do not, however, go in to town to sell wholesale. Their links with the larger markets are very minimal. Their illiteracy, and inability to count, is a great deterrent. Those who can count do go out of their own village. This is really a matter of getting exposed to the outside world. The men are also largely illiterate but have learnt, through experience, how to handle dealings (in a limited manner) in the larger markets.

The *shortage of raw materials* and the escalating prices, are yet another issue for the women. They feel increasingly the impact of the raw materials they need being used for the industrial manufacture of goods—bamboo, yarn, leather, straw, paddy husk. The supply/demand position of the raw materials affects the prices at which they are available and, quite often, they get priced out of the reach of the poor. There are no facilities available for the transport of raw materials and of finished goods. It can become uneconomical to pursue certain trades with only a small capital if the cost of raw materials and transportation goes too high. The poor are not always able to buy raw materials cheaply and get a reasonable price for the finished goods (bamboo work, weaving). Since their returns depend on the economical use of raw materials, the purchase price and sale price, they do not think several of the activities even worth an effort. Others, in the same activity, are able to earn least enough to subsist because they have been able to make a niche for themselves. All these efforts of locating cheap sources and good markets have to be made by the family on their own, without any assistance from anywhere. If they are able to establish contact, they are able to earn. Otherwise, they are left to their fate. The women's role in making these contacts is not very great. Women are also not very familiar with a accounting and costing methods.

Being exposed to only a very limited sphere of a large economy and having only one or two basic skills, they are *not able to monitor market changes,* product demand changes, and the nature of competition, which comes in from factory made goods or substitute products. Consequently, they are not able to make adjustments to their niche in the market, or even to consistently protect their earnings and income. They are not able to monitor and influence policy changes which have an impact on them (bamboo forests being leased to paper mills, podless cotton seeds being promoted, fodder for animals going to strawboard units).

The *skills* they have and the services they provide are *viable* only in a *subsistence economy* where the free collection and barter of goods and services is common. Products and by-products which were needed as inputs only in traditional skills are now in demand for other purposes as well (bamboo, leather, straw). There is a cash value available for by-products which did not have any such demand earlier (reeds, straw). *This changed profile of raw material consumption creates forces of commercialisation.* Even the original users of the raw materials, who used to get them free, now have to pay a cash price for them (clay, reeds). The selling price of their goods does not rise much and therefore, their trade becomes unviable because it cannot absorb the cash cost of raw materials. This interplay of commercial forces in a traditional, subsistence economy, affects the very survival of the poor. The women are worst affected because they do not even have access to the training and acquiring of new skills. There is a *continuous displacement of women* from trades which are being rendered unviable due to commercialisation, mechanisation, and competitive products coming into the market (weaving, pottery, tanning leather, reed work, bamboo work, making milk products). When new production processes are introduced in a particular trade the men get the opportunity to learn the new methods but the women get pushed out of work completely (leather tanning, weaving). Women are reduced to working as unskilled labour wherever work is available, if it is available.

Whenever work is available the *cash does not usually go to the women.* When men and women work together as labourers, the payment is more often than not made to the men. When women work as part of a family production unit, the cash goes to the person who goes to sell the products—which, more often than not, is the man (weaving, bamboo work, pottery). When women work alone, the cash does come to them (reed work, grocery stalls). Various forms of the *jajmani* system are still prevalent in the rural areas. Payment is often made either in kind, or a combination of cash and kind (pottery, agricultural labour, reed work). Payment made in grain certainly helps stave off starvation, but the present day economy demands cash transactions for very many purchases. Travelling to town, buying clothes, buying inputs for their trade, expenses for children's education, materials for housing, taxes, loan instalments, etc., all have to be paid in cash. They need, a source of cash income much as they might value payment in kind. They have to find sources of work which will earn them some cash (usually labour work).

If work opportunities are not available in their own village, they are *forced to migrate,* in search of work. Sometimes, the men alone migrate and women stay back in the village (agricultural labour). In other cases, the whole family migrates to wherever work is available (brickmaking, construction work, agricultural labour). The women have to bear the burnt of the problems migration brings in its wake. They have to learn to put up house in the open, in strange places, in the fields, on construction sites, on brick-kiln sites. They learn to make do with the bare minimum as well as accept an almost nomadic life style. Even facilities like water, sanitation, fuel and rations are managed with great difficulty and its is women who have to bear most of this burden.

Women have to *work very long hours* combining both income-generating and household work. They usually have a work day of fourteen or fifteen hours and in places where the infrastructural facilities are very few, their work day stretches up to seventeen or eighteen hours. Looking after children and the family is a constant worry for them. If they can avoid going out of the house to work they prefer it but with the work opportunities being so few they have little choice to go out looking for work. Of the fifteen trades taken up for study, ten are *home-based activities* (except agricultural labour, construction work, digging mud, brickmaking and vegetable growing). This shows the significance of home-based work for poor, rural women. It is one way in which they can combine their various roles (social and work) with relative ease. It is only when they are unable to earn a livelihood from a home-based activity that they go out for work. Even when they migrate in search of work, they are constantly on the look out for opportunities which will enable them to pursue a home-based activity. If they are able to work out some way by which to earn a livelihood by working at home, they stop migrating altogether.

The common pattern today is to *pursue two or three seasonal income-generating activities to maximise earnings.* The caste-based occupations are not pursued singly but rather interspersed with agricultural or other labour work. Some livestock is also tended side by side, such as, poultry, goats, or cattle. Seasonal work opportunities are fully availed of wherever they are available. The uncertainty of returns from a particular trade are dealt with to some extent by pursuing more than one activity. They spread out their risks and try to ensure some inflow of cash and as well as an income in kind, for the family. This is a survival strategy to manage every kind of contingency.

All the self-employed women have to make *their own provisions for meeting the exigencies and contingencies of life.* They are not entitled to any assistance if they are own account workers. If they are labourers they are entitled, in some cases, to certain facilities but rarely get them. Health is a major concern for them because their body is their main asset and they have to pay for their medicine, etc. They are able to earn a livelihood if their health does not desert them. The cost of dealing with occupational hazards is also borne by the workers themselves. Similarly, expenses for children's vocational education, housing, social occasions, are all met from their own resources.

Women in most trades do *not* have *representative organisations* to help them protect their interest. Very, very rarely are women enrolled as members even when representative organisations do exist, such as, those for brick workers and milk producers. Traditionally, many of the trades studied here, have had guides to protect the interests of workers (bamboo workers, weavers, leather workers, potters). These guilds have disintegrated today. Their link with the policy-making process is almost absent and consequently they are *unable to influence* the policies that are formulated. They are not able to counter policies made against them, either.

The raw materials and finished products have an *intricate rural-urban network.* Several raw materials are found only in the rural areas and the products are also consumed in only the villages (reed work, pottery). Other products are consumed primarily in the urban areas (brick work). Yet others are consumed in both the urban and rural areas (weaving, leather work). There are also products which use raw materials from other regions. The raw materials are sold in the urban areas and processed in the rural areas (bamboo work-*sirkis*). The finished products are consumed both in the urban and rural areas.

There is also a chain of rural to urban to rural connections for some raw materials. Cotton, for instance, is grown in the villages. The cotton-bolls are shelled in the villages and then the ginning is done in urban areas. The spinning is done in the textile mills and on *charkhas* (towns and villages). The yarn is used for mill production in the towns and for *khadi* and handloom in the villages. The cloth produced is used in the villages and towns.

This kind of network exists for other raw materials and finished goods too. Agricultural labour, for instance, is concentrated in the villages. But the produce of agriculture is consumed in both rural and urban areas. The inputs for agriculture—seeds, fertiliser and pesticides—are produced both in the urban and rural areas. Similarly, construction work sites are located in both urban and rural areas, even though the labour force is mainly from the rural areas. The facilities created— roads, dams—benefit both the rural and urban population, but not necessarily the poor families in either region. Brickmaking uses the labour and some of the raw materials of rural areas. Other inputs like broken coal and cinder are by-products of production units in urban areas. The bricks are consumed mainly in the urban areas and large construction activities like dams in the rural areas. Leather is a raw material of rural areas but the finished goods are used in the urban and rural areas. The bamboo products, cloth, reed work, pottery, milk products, and vegetables and used in both urban and rural areas. The raw materials are sometimes from other regions. Grocery stalls bring goods produced in the urban, to the rural areas and also redistribute rural products.

There is a greater variety of influences acting on the prices, at different stages in the chain, in such cases. The availability, prices, and supply-demand position fluctuate quite a lot and the rural women do not understand this network very well.

Similarly, they view other villages and the urban areas as a *large mass of inhabitation.* They try and keep abreast of what kinds of goods and services are available in various villages and towns (blacksmiths, carpenters, potters, weavers, tools, chemicals, bamboo, yarn, etc.). If they need a particular kind of facility, they usually make attempts to find out which village or town it is available in. The men are more informed than the women in these matters. But, through their men, the women do come to know something. Knowing what is available where, is helpful in making decisions about whether they can afford it, whether they can find other ways of obtaining it, etc. It provides a basis for reality orientation and an estimate of how much effort will be involved in obtaining the facility.

Being self-employed means that there is no age limit to the productive life. As long as they have strength in their bodies they can pursue their trade and work. In a poor family, the aged feel that they should also contribute to the household income. They are not able to be as active as the young but they do not wish to be a burden on the family, either. They also need to eat, and poverty often blunts the human relationships of the aged, even with their own family. They find their own ways of maintaining dignity and not being a burden. Less exhaustive activities like poultry, reed work, cotton-boll shelling, and milk production are pursued by the old. Their children may or may not live with them, but they still try and earn their keep. Often, they look after the infants in the family which enables the adults to go out for work. They may even accompany their children to the work sites and look after the children their. This kind of mutual help makes it easier for the old women to stay with their family.

The traditional system encourages self-employment for most people in the villages and urban areas. This point is also obvious from the negligible number of people who have regular salaried jobs with an established employer-employee relationship, in the villages. The forces of mechanisation and industrialisation, termed modernisation, are slowly changing the system. More and more work opportunities are being created. In fact the training programmes, the schemes, the development activities view the whole workforce to be in need of jobs. Hence, plans are formulated with the objective of providing jobs for people. The plan is to ensure that everyone has a job. The fact is, however, that most of the women (and men) are not seeking jobs—they are seeking work and income. The schemes and programmes which are started in the name of modernisation do not realise that they are shifting the trend from self-employment to other-employment. The people's aspirations are centred on self-employment and the schemes, therefore, constantly face the problems of low productivity, low integrity and a lack of work identity when they provide jobs. The same trade followed on the principles of self-employment has different dynamics in the same place (weaving, bamboo work).

Another *drawback with the development programmes is that they are worked out with the reality of the well-off people, in mind.* For instance, the bankable scheme for poultry is worked out on the basis of a poultry farm having several hundred birds. This is the way a well-off person would raise poultry. But the way the poor pursue the same activity is quite different. The poor economise on every front in order to maximise their return from a given investment. They can make poultry profitable even with an investment of less than Rs. 100. The poultry farm schemes worked out by the development agencies would be profitable only with the investment of several thousand rupees. Such schemes are totally beyond the capacity of the poor and it is not wonder that they are not accepted by the poor. The conclusions drawn by the development experts are, that the scheme is unsuccessful and it is, therefore, dropped. The fact, very often, is that the scheme itself is not suitable to the needs of the poor. There is a big gap in the designing of schemes and the way in which the poor engage in the work concerned. The economics would be minimal and within reach of the poor if the schemes were designed keeping in mind the way a poor family functions.

8

Women's Survival

In all societies, both women and men work. But not necessarily at the same tasks or to the same extent. Not only do the conditions of work change over time owing to a wide variety of reasons, but perceptions of what constitutes 'work' also vary between people and over time. The term work acquires new meanings with changes in the nature of work. In this chapter we shall explore the analytics of work and survival in order to cast the diverse empirical studies that follow within a meaningful explanatory context. We do this by arrogating for myself the privilege of an admittedly partial perspective, that is a feminist one for we do believe that this partial perspective is immensely more illuminating, enriching, meaningful, explanatory and empowering both for the researcher and for those researched upon than those perspectives that claim to be 'objective,' 'unbiased,' 'scientific,' 'value-free' or 'apolitical'.

Labour and gender constitute the main themes of this book. The chapters that follow pertain to issues relating to the urban labour market scenario, in particular to how women participate in them with differential impacts and outcomes, and how they ensure both their own and their household's survival. Moving between descriptions, delineations and analyses of the macro-structural aspects of Indian urban labour markets and some finely textured micro-level analyses based on ethnographic situations, participatory fieldwork and investigative snooping around to capture the hidden and invisible dimensions of the so-called 'informal sectors,' the thrust in each of these attempts has been to provide a gendered understanding of the functioning of the urban labour market. This entire work is based on the thesis that gender issues cannot be studied in isolation but need to be located within the overall structural context of an economy. Starting off with a scepticism about the relevance of the hitherto widely applied methodological approaches to the study of labour markets—the neoclassical and the classical Marxist— the exercises in the following chapters, quite wideranging in themselves, attempt at conceptualising patriarchy and gender, analyse the interaction of patriarchy and capitalism, postulate 'an articulated multistructural system as the defining feature of the urban economy, and provide some theoretical and empirical insights into the diversities of forms of production. The underlying view of much of this work is that work and reproduction are two very crucial and mutually impacting spheres in women's lives, and that an understanding of the multiple fields of force and power relations that enmesh women's lives has to ground its analysis in these two spheres.

GENDER IN THE PARADIGMS OF ECONOMICS

The fundamental principles of the neoclassical paradigm presupposes that the impersonal working of the market in a capitalist system brings about an efficient allocation of resources, and each individual, whether producer or consumer, seeks to maximise his/her profits or utility.[1] This assumption of the individual is premised on the universality of the 'rationality' of man. *Homo Oeconomicus—the* economic man—postulates a single notion of rationality. This rationality implies that persons are construed as 'individuals' who are self-seeking; they are maximisers and calculating agents. The Cartesian rationality of neoclassical economics does not recognise that 'individuals' are both historically and culturally constituted. As Godelier (1972) noted, 'this analysis proceeds from the existence of *abstract individuals* endowed with certain scales (whether transitive or intransitive) of subjective preferences and with a psychology, simple but "natural" that consists of a tendency to maximise their satisfactions.' He further noted that 'it is then assumed that these individuals, who are so many embodiments of a theoretical fetish, the eternal *Homo Oeconomicus,* live in a world where they cannot but compete with each other.'

Since individuals are differently placed, economies are differentiated and cultures, though interacting, are distinct; and although individuals, economies and cultures today are articulated with one another through a complexly expanding network of market relations, the uniform notion of 'rationality' as it operates in everyday life is still questionable: Very often individuals in households on the verge of subsistence find that their work and consumption do not maximise their utility but maximise the survival chances of the household as a whole. Equally, in communities that are still in a transition to a fully marketised system, certain forms of behaviour do not conform to the assumption of *Homo Oeconomicus.* For instance, money could be lent within a community, not for interest but to ensure a member's survival. More importantly, the identity of *Homo Oeconomicus* excludes gender, that is, it does not square with what men and women actually are. And by stating it so, we do not imply an essentialised understanding of 'man' and 'woman,' but with men and women as historically constituted, and socially and culturally constructed beings. In this construction, the division between men and women is not just a division but an asymmetry with men having more power and status. This aspect is not reckoned with at all in the neoclassical paradigm.

The Marxist paradigm (according primacy to productive forces and production relations in the analysis of economic structures and its underlying processes) challenges the concepts of neoclassical economics, such as value and price. While significant insights on the position and role of women in societies can be obtained from the works of Marx and Engels, starting from Engels *The Origin of the Family, Private Property and the State* through to *Capital,* the position of women—be it their substitution for men with technological change or their role in the reserve army or in the sphere of reproduction—has always been seen as the outcome of capitalism, and subsumed under an analysis of class relations. Gender relations, as one aspect of social relations, is not accorded an autonomous analytical position, and capitalist commodity relations assumes primacy over social relations. This is due to the main objective of explicating the capitalist mode of production. It is clear that had precapitalist modes and their transition been more thoroughly analysed, it would have been difficult to ignore kinship and gender relations as autonomous categories within social relations, as the burgeoning literature on the anthropology of gender now indicates. The point being made here is that though the processes of creation and recreation of class and gender relations takes place simultaneously and involves both material and ideological dimensions, it is necessary to distinguish them *analytically* while pointing out their concrete articulations, and the mechanisms by which this articulation takes place. In the empirical and theoretical insights provided in the works of Marx and Engels, we do not find this analytical distinction.

Marxist and socialist feminists have developed an integrated analysis in which class and gender formation, struggle and reformation are looked at simultaneously as a necessary step for the understanding of social reality, with some significant theoretical advances. There is no doubt that the basic Marxist paradigm has been more useful in incorporating gender analytically, though this exercise is far from complete, and despite all the difficulties faced with regard to the hairsplitting debates on the political implications often engaged in by dogmatic Marxists. What the foregoing indicates is that the major paradigms of social research do not incorporate 'gender' as an analytic category, as a category that is essential for the understanding of society in all its dimensions. It is hoped that this chapter, exploring the analytics of work and survival with the gender dimension being incorporated, as well as the succeeding empirical chapters, would provide new and additional insights on the problematic of gender which, despite all the fast growing literature in the field of 'women's studies' is still in need of fresh and bold thinking.

THE CULTURAL DISCOURSES ON WOMEN'S WORK

The terms work, labour, employment, job and trades are frequently used and, over the years, have come to acquire certain meanings. Cryptic semantic histories of some of these terms in the English context are found in Raymond William's *Keywords.* In Tamil also (which is my mother-tongue), there are a number of words to denote various 'activities'. If one examines the set of words for each of the categories 'work,' 'labour' and 'employment' in Tamil, it can be noted that there are common words in each of the sets, thus indicating that language use did not sharply differentiate these. Some words existed prior to the emergence of new activities and so, in the assignment of denotative words, there are probably instances of both an excess and a deficiency of 'significance' with the 'signifier' performing more or less, than what is supposed to be 'signified'. The words that are not common or present in the other sets often help to differentiate the context in which these words are used. 'Work' is more general and is often used in the sense of 'doing'. Labour carries with it connotations of 'effort,' *(uzhaippu),* and employment denotes occupation, work in offices and activities that are modern in nature. These linguistic practices have implications for cognising women's work. For instance, women's housework is always referred as 'work' *(velai)* and is not considered 'labour' *(uzhaippu)* which connotes 'effort', 'drudgery,' and so on. Further, those who are familiar with Tamil would realise that there are very few words relating to 'work' referring only to the feminine gender. Most words have masculine endings, and the few that are applicable to both are quite neutral. The lack of a vocabulary for women's work in Tamil is suggestive of the probable discursive silences surrounding much of women's activities. This feature may be present in other languages as well. The purpose of discussing this aspect is to sensitise the reader to language as an important component of ideological structures. It is necessary to understand the cultural and ideological underpinnings and the attitudes that result in these silences. To what extent does the lack of words lead to a lack of cognition of the varieties of women's work, and to what extent is the inability to cognise a consequence of linguistic lacunae? Also, is this deficiency prevalent only in instances of women's activities?

Even when cultural discourses do not silence women's activities, cultural translations often do. It has now acquired the status of a paradigmatic truth that in the production of anthropological knowledge, ethnographers (often male) carry their ethnocentric and patriarchal assumptions into their interpretive frameworks to understand other cultures.[2] The presence of an ethnographer is, however, not necessary to produce these misrecognitions and non-recognitions. The encoding of knowledge about society through bureaucratic instruments and the apparatuses of the modern state, a distinct product of a different culture that was sought to be transplanted in the other parts of the world, has also been important and influential in producing these problems of cultural translations.[3] We shall shortly examine some of these problems as well.

With the growth and expansion of markets for commodities and labour, the valuation of women's work in all its different aspects undergo changes as well. A new category of 'marketed' work (that is, work resulting in cash earnings) appears, and a society's perceptions of what work is worthy and prestigious also change. Women's identities are also thereby reconstituted. It is indeed very common today for a woman, who is a 'housewife', when asked as to whether she is working, to reply 'no'. Implicit in the answer is the assumption that what was implied meant wage work outside the home. It is only at the next stage of probing that she acknowledges her work in the house and, as the conversation proceeds further, one realises how overworked she actually is. Both the arithmetic and the semantics of women's work have been in the forefront of feminist concerns all over the world. In many of the developing countries in which women are predominantly engaged in agricultural activities, the scale of non-market activities is very large, making the reckoning of women's work that much more difficult. In India, debates surrounding women's work predate the emergence of a collective feminist consciousness on these issues. These concerns have been reflected in the discourses of the colonial state as a part of its project of enumerating and classifying people.

THE OFFICIAL DISCOURSES ON WOMEN'S WORK

The earliest of these debates is to be found in the first Population Census of 1870-71. At the request of the Registrar-General in England, Farr (who was responsible for the British

Census of 1861 and who had a general classification of occupations) was asked to modify his classification for use in the 1871 British Census. India also adopted Farr's classification in principle. Accordingly, there were six broad classes and each class had certain orders. Farr's original classification had the following classes: professional; domestic; commercial; agricultural; industrial; indefinite and non-productive. The domestic class had two orders—occupation in the family, and occupation in personal service. The first order included all women who had no occupation producing wages or fees (that is, the wives and daughters of the mass of the population). *This class was included by Farr from the idea that every person should be represented as having an occupation.*

The statistical committee which examined the modifications of Fan's classification in the context of India found this an anomaly. According to the committee:

> the great object of the 'occupation' tables is to show how the means of living is obtained by the people, how the waste of consumption is replaced and more than replaced by reproduction. So important is this fact that Dr. Farr heads his last 'nonproductive,' showing that other classes are supposed to be reproductive. But women and children in the family are consumers, not producers. Their comfort and support is largely the object for which men emerge in reproduction, that is, take an occupation. To enter the wives and daughters on par with the workers of the household is to confuse the object with the means employed in attaining it (India, Census, Report of the 1871 Census).

These views were so strongly felt that in no case was this order adopted in practice. In Bombay province it was dropped altogether. In the North-West and Central Provinces, all the children were returned under the occupation of the head of the household, grossly inflating figures in some of the occupations. In Madras Presidency (excluding Madras town), women were not included at all in the occupation tables.

The 1881 Census Report noted the following on female occupations.

> The occupation of females is a difficult subject to deal with. In every country females do much hard and necessary work which is not among the trades and is not strictly productive. A yet more numerous class of females do a certain, if not continuous, share in the total productive work, but a share which is combined with productive work, and this in such varying degree that it would be impossible to draw any line which should say (e.g.) this is primarily an 'agricultural labourer' and that is primarily 'a wife'. In India all women work; some merely at household drudgery but in the most numerous and important of all classes, 'the agricultural,' female labourers are an important part. But with the custom of early marriage, the mass of females of working age are primarily wives and whether they work in the fields or not, they have certainly to work at home. Some of these have been returned as 'agricultural'. Some as 'wives of specified occupations' and some merely as 'wives, which is regarded as an occupation' and some as 'unemployed' (India, Census, Report of the 1881 Census).

The report cautions that the returns of female occupations should be taken with reserve.

The 1891 Census omitted 'wives' from occupations. Also, instead of enumerating workers, it found out the 'means of subsistence' of the entire population, that is, either as workers or as dependents.

It is important to note that these 'official discourses' on women's work contained in the decennial censuses embrace a number of interesting issues. Colonialism brought about new forms of governance and new modes of intervening in society. Decennial censuses, initiated in most parts of the empire, were sooner or later governed by the necessities of these new forms of governance. The 'reasons of the state' which initiated the era of counting by the state led to the constitution of 'enumerated communities'. In the course of time, these 'communities' came to play an important role in the newly emerging modern polity. Thus, unlike in the earlier periods, it is to be noted that in the modern era, the definitionally constituted identities of groups and individuals becomes an object of political contestation. Law and statistics become important modalities for that. Occupational classification is one such instance of public discourse initiated by the modern state through which it seeks to define individuals and groups, and demarcate and shift the boundaries of the so-called public and private domains with a view to marking out spheres in which its legitimacy to intervene will become less and less questionable and more and more acceptable and will, over time, appear as something quite 'natural'.

It is interesting to note that this redefinition of the relation between the state and civil society occurs at a time when industrial capitalism and markets are growing. The state and markets are two pervasive institutions of the modern era of capitalism. It is by now well recognised that, in general, the growth of markets and exchange does bring about changes in the sexual division of labour, whether as a consequence of the expansion of the scale of production, technological changes or the, emergence of new lines of activities. Associated with it are changes in the valuation of work itself. With goods being exchanged on markets for cash incomes, activities that helped in acquiring such cash incomes come to acquire greater status than work that does not result in marketed output. A distinction between 'productive' and 'unproductive' work thus emerges. Much of women's work within households—cooking, nurturing and care services, and reproduction—comes to be devalued by this process.

The debate on census classification, as pointed out earlier, reveals a tension in the treatment of women's work as 'wives'. It was not merely the problem of rendering applicable in one context the classificatory schemes evolved in a vastly different context of a more capitalist and industrialised country, but there were also basic ideological positions to be adopted regarding women's work even in Britain. If everybody was to be represented as having an 'occupation,' which was Farr's idea, it was derived from the laissez-faire doctrines of classical liberalism which sought to remove traditional privileges and to open opportunities for all on the market principle.

The census was introduced in Great Britain in 1801, ten years after the first American census. Until 1831, the British census was primarily concerned with population size—there was very little interest in the activities of the population, and these activities were not differentiated on the basis of productivity. Fan's occupational classification of 1851, which was refined in 1861, was the first official attempt to categorise activities scientifically. Fan based his conception of 'productive work' on the view that population was 'living capital' and the unit of productive activity was the individual rather than the family. Until 1831, the census takers in Britain had recorded only family occupation. The individual occupations of adult male and female domestics were recorded along with the family occupation in 1831. From 1841, individual occupations alone were recorded for the entire population. By 1851, the census differentiated the work of the family members—wives 'and adult children in farming and small businesses assisting their husbands and fathers were recorded in their menfolk's occupational category. In the 1871 Census, these women were placed in the domestic class and were distinguished from other wives and daughters. Farr's view that domestic work was important to the nation, and that such labour should be placed among the productive classes along with paid work of a similar kind, met with opposition from the Scottish census officials. At the 1871 Scottish Census, they eliminated the domestic class and redistributed its members to show how many were dependent on each occupation.[4] Similarly, the classification of female relatives of farmers and small businessmen in a separate occupational category was modified in the 1881 Census. Women engaged in domestic duties and female relatives not reported as assisting were included among the 'persons without specified occupations' in the 'unoccupied class'. *All these were attempts to define women, who did not have paid jobs, as dependents.* Thus, even though Farr, who was influenced by laissez-faire liberalism, sought to represent women as legitimate workers inside and outside the home, there was an alternate school of thought which, basing itself partly on the Malthusian fears of population growth, sought a workers/dependents categorisation as it was also presumed to be more suitable to identify sectors or groups that suffer greater deprivation.

It also needs to be noted that the 'official' construction of the 'dependent woman' in England emerged at a time when capitalist development was drawing both men and women into employment in modem industries. The extent to which such a construction of women constrained them from participating on equal terms as men in the newly emerging labour markets for modern sector employment has been debated by feminists there. Desley Deacon argues that the alternate viewpoint to Farr sought precisely to effect such labour market closures in the Australian colonies that adopted which it this viewpoint in their census classification. Also, it should not be forgotten that such social constructions emerged at a time when is with a the modern liberal state was sought to be consolidated in England and extended to other parts of its empire. The modern state, which was interventionist in character, sought to redefine the private and public spheres in the newly constituted relationship between the relation state and society. The ideology of domesticity and the 'dependent woman' sought to give effect to this private—public dichotomisation by shaping the domain of privacy and the degree of permissible intervention in that private sphere. It also thereby tried to define the role of woman in the public sphere which, increasingly, was labour, sought to be seen as a male domain.

We have dealt in some detail with the British experience because the debates on the censuses in England, Wales and Scotland were of work refracted in the census debates in many of the British colonies. We have in the preceding paragraphs referred to some of the debates some to in the Indian and Australian censuses. In India, too, the statistical marketed committee at the 1871 Census explicitly noted that women and children in the family were only 'consumers' and not 'producers'. It built into its arguments the patriarchal ideology that men take up an occupation for the comfort and support of women and children in the family. The 1881 Census report is entangled in a, reveals bunch of contradictory statements on women's work. It recognises was not that all women in India work, some merely at household drudgery; text the that in the agricultural classes there are a large number of female labourers; that a mass of females of working age are *primarily* wives and, whether they work in fields or not, they have certainly to work at home. The 1891 Census tried to solve the problem by omitting 'wives' from occupations and adopting the worker/dependent categorisation, thus conferring on women a dependent status remove at a crucial stage in the development of modern economy.

The official construction of the 'dependent woman' in India followed the deindustrialisation process which, by 1871, was almost completed. Hand-spinning, in which millions of women were employed in their homes and which was done in conjunction with housework and/or agricultural work, was completely wiped away consequence. Labour in agriculture in many parts of the country was clearly undergoing transformations and, though customary forms of wage payments were still widely prevalent in agriculture wages in urban areas was clearly emerging as a market category. In many parts of the country wages and price series were sought to be constructed for the first time. Modern sector employment in the textile industry and in railway transport was also growing. All these set the stage for a widespread market economy in which the market, as an institution encompassing large regional and national territory, was clearly becoming entrenched.[5]

Earlier we had indicated how the modern state demarcated the public-private boundaries and the role it envisaged for women in the public domain. This ideological manipulation in the Indian context by the modern colonial state had its countervailing forces as well. The nationalist movement redefined the private—public dichotomy into the cultural and material one, in which the cultural and spiritual sanctity of India was to be defended inside the home by the women, and the material sphere was one in which both women and men participated and in which the forces of modernisation were allowed to play a role (Chatterjee, 1989). Women were, thus, ideologically freed to participate in the material life of the nation outside their home as well as to participate in the making of the nation through their involvement in the nationalist movement. Even though the vast millions of poor rural and urban women always worked, and many of them outside their home, the middle class nationalist movement, through its hegemonic position, sought to provide legitimacy for it. It is important to understand this phenomenon as it was this middle class, with a modern world-view, that appropriated state power at independence. An understanding of the ideological basis of patriarchy in the public sphere has to take into account the conjunctive effects of these two sets of forces as well.

The extent to which the ideological construction of the 'dependent woman' is likely to have affected labour market factors is examined below. The era of modern industrialisation needed trained and disciplined bodies. Optimisation of human energies led to the optimisation of capitalist profits and, therefore, 'industrial time' and 'work rhythm' had to be organised. Labour had to be given time to recuperate and reproduce energies, and yet be made to supply their energies on a continuous basis. While this was certainly an area of contestation and struggle between the workers and capitalists (as Marx and Engels have so wonderfully analysed), this field of contestation itself was defined by the requirements of modern industrialisation. Regulatory measures by the state emerged with the objective of optimising human energy production and energy use so as to sustain modern industrial production organised on capitalist lines. With the diffusion of capitalist forces and new forms of industrial organisation throughout the world, international organisations to initiate and advise such statutory regulations became necessary, and thus was founded the International Labour Organisation in 1919. The ideological assumptions on working class families figured in a major way in the formulation of statutory regulations as the family and the household was the site where energies could be recuperated and reproduced in both the short and long run. Since the reproduction of energies entailed costs, the extent to which such costs had to be borne by the capitalists was an issue of consideration leading to a series of regulatory norms on wage fixation. In the Indian context, debates surrounding the acts (such as the Minimum Wages Act, the Fair Wages Act, and the Equal Remuneration Act) expose the ideological assumptions about women's work and their role in the family.

The textile industry, which is one of the oldest and most important industries, employed a significant number of women in the early part of this century. This industry also initiated a number of issues regarding women's work and their role in the wage fixation debate. *The Report of the Textile Labour Inquiry Committee,* which deliberated on the *living wage standard* noted:

> The first is the number of earners per family to be allowed in our calculation, and the second is the question of supplementary earnings. The consideration of the first question is made easy by our adopting the *natural family* as the basis of our calculations. (The natural family refers to a family of four persons, that is, a man, his wife and two dependents who would ordinarily be children under 14.) In such a family, the question can refer only to the earnings of the wife; the dependents or children can obviously not be expected to earn anything. Should any allowance be made for the possible earnings of a wife? It has been argued that, *under a proper interpretation of the term living wage standard, a wife should be spared for the duties of the household and for looking after the children. She cannot be and should not be expected to supplement the earnings by extra paid work....* The conclusion we arrive at is that an adult male should be held to have to support the family without the help of any supplementary earner or any other source of income (Government of Bombay, 1941, pp. 78—80, emphasis added).[6]

Regarding the fixation of wages for women, the same committee noted that *'the standard of responsibilities for the calculations of a woman's wage is defined in a different manner from that of an adult male'* (Government of India, 1954, p. 21, emphasis added). Even though there were alternate views at the time, in the course of time this view came to be accepted as the standard justificatory one. The committee on Fair Wages (1954) in post-independence India also opined similarly when it noted:

> if minimum wages, and consequently fair wages, are to be calculated on the basis of the requirements of the worker and his family, there is every justification for rating the standard family at a lower number of consumption units in the case of a woman worker than in the case of a man, for she will not be expected to support at any rate her husband even though she may have other dependents and encumbrances. According to this line of reasoning, the wages of a woman worker should be based on two consumption units if those of a male worker are calculated on three (Government of India, 1954).

Thus it can easily be worked out how the ideological construction of the 'dependent woman' affected women's involvement in the labour market on equal terms with men. The modern state and the emerging capitalist forces sought to promote particular family and household forms, which were often at variance with the reality. The Committee on the Status of Women in India (1974) noted:

> An argument which is often raised in debates regarding Women's employment is that their employment deprives men of jobs that they need to support their families. It is assumed that all women who work are only supplementing the family income to ensure a higher standard of living. These theorists have never tried to investigate how many women who work are the sole or main earners in the family. The majority of working women whom we met were supporting either their parents and younger brothers and sisters or their own children (Government of India, 1974).

STRUCTURE, PROCESSES AND WOMEN'S LABOUR

In introducing the categories 'work' and the worker,' we had highlighted the role of the state, the market and the cultural context in which households function. We shall now elaborate on the roles and the changing contexts in which the forementioned three institutions operate, and their implications for women in their productive and reproductive roles.

The agency of nations and people in the choice of development trajectories are severely circumscribed by world historical processes. Post-colonial societies participated, though involuntarily and most often coercively, in the making of the capitalist world system. In this system they were integrated not only as unequal partners, but in an asymmetrical context of power that increasingly rendered almost all of them to a state of powerlessness in a world rapidly organising itself into a unipolar one in which Wall Street and Washington orchestrate states, markets and peoples in far-flung areas of the world. Capitalism, ushered in by way of European expansionism in the nineteenth century, unleashed the forces of modernisation which, on the one hand, was characterised by the rise of commercialisation and the growth of markets (in particular of labour markets), technological changes and the processes of urbanisation and, on the other, of the emergence of modern nation-states.

Charged with the responsibility of taking care of its citizens, these nation-states set goals and targets, initiated policies and worked out strategies to attain these goals. What the goals and the strategies were was determined most often through a political process that was not often and always a democratic one. From a given repertoire of goals and strategies, the choices effected often reflect and are guided by the class character of the state. Even though the state, as an autonomous entity, mediates and balances conflicting interests and demands, the will of the state is shaped by the will of the controlling interests of the state. Drawing inspiration from Keynesian macro-economic management and the experience of planning in the then Socialist Soviet Union, development theories and ideologies in the early post-colonial decades of the fifties and sixties envisaged a direct role for the state in alleviating the poverty of the vast millions even as the process of marketisation became widespread, and indigenous entrepreneurship even in the modern sectors began to develop.

Planning emerged in the context of a 'mixed economy' in which both the private and public sectors had clearly demarcated roles. Planning in the context of development was seen as not merely steering the economy on to projected growth paths but to have distributional roles as well. *Planning was conceived in a manner in which even while it was concerned with poverty and inequality, it did not curtail the growth of market forces.* Thus, even though planning was accompanied by measures to curb the concentration of economic power (be it industrial monopolies or the big landlords), it did not envisage fundamental changes in property relations, such as state ownership or the socialisation of all the means of production. Planning in a 'mixed economy' was, therefore, vastly different from socialist planning. Some of the markets were sought to be regulated, but the principles of such regulation—whether it was the pricing of public utilities, fixation of administered prices for crucial capital goods produced in the public sector or the dual pricing of basic commodities distributed through the public distribution system catering to the vast millions of the poor—were sought to be derived from the postulates of neoclassical economics.

Politically, planning was a method that reflected the collective consensus on desired outcomes, whether of the short run or the long run. State policies to achieve the targeted levels of growth rates, output, income and employment shaped and moulded specific policies in each sector, industry and activity.

While the conception of planning for development in 'mixed economy' situations was a strikingly modern and democratic experiment, the implementation was fraught with many difficulties. States underplayed the redistributional roles of planning, bureaucratic power grew in a manner that could not be restrained, pressure groups with conflicting aims sought to arrogate benefits for itself and/or whittle down or check the flow of benefits to intended groups, and targeted groups were often badly defined or poorly targeted.

Macro-processes of marketisation of both commodities and labour, technological changes and urbanisation in conjunction with macro-policies evolving out of the plan process with the goal of achieving a 'socialistic pattern of society' within a basically market economy impinge on the wide range of activities carried out in the economy. Figure 8.1 indicates how the system as a whole, and the interactions within it, can be conceived. Every activity, and here we refer to economic or productive activity, is embedded in a structural context which can be identified in terms of factors relating to technical-production and social-ideological aspects. The former relates to the bundle of rights and claims on the ownership, access and control of property and other resources, the division of labour, the use of technology and the organisation of production, and the nature of its links with the sphere of exchange. The latter refers to the social implications of particular work organisations which would include both the social aspects relating to the location of work, the social implications of the use of different types of labour, and the cultural meanings that particular activities are endowed with. Associated with each of these structural contexts are particular modes of appropriation of surplus value or *exploitation,* and particular forms of ideological manipulation of individuals, whether these are at a symbolic level (in terms of meaning-constitutive processes) or at a material level. We refer to these as modes of *domination.*

When macro-processes and macro-policies impinge on activities, they operate on these factors as well. The conditions that lead to the reproduction of one structural context and its changes are a matter of historical-empirical inquiry. No a priori specification of the importance of particular factors, forces or causes in one structural context to enable the reproduction and change of the structural context, and/or the likely directions of change, and/or the gender and class effects is either methodologically or realistically possible or desirable. The emphasis here, however, is that the structural context within which certain effects play themselves out needs to be examined both for analytical purposes and for appropriate policy measures. Some of the studies that follow do, however, contribute to an empirical understanding of these issues. In what follows we shall develop these ideas, taking account of the specificities and changes in order to unravel and lay bare the complexities in developing a gender-sensitive analytic of work and survival in the Indian context. Examining first some of the interactions between the three institutions—the state, markets and households—the analysis then focuses specifically on the role of planning in India and its effect on women workers in the so-called urban informal sector; the role of markets, keeping in view the recent efforts of integration with the global economy and the structural-adjustment process that has been initiated in the Indian economy since July 1991; and the household dynamics focusing on issues relating to women's labour and the relative deprivation of women in poverty households, once again specifically concentrating on the Indian scenario.

The State, Markets and Households as Interacting Institutions

The state, markets and households are the three significant institutions of any modern economy. All economic and political processes, forces, transactions and practices either emanate or impact on these. The operations of the state and markets, hitherto termed

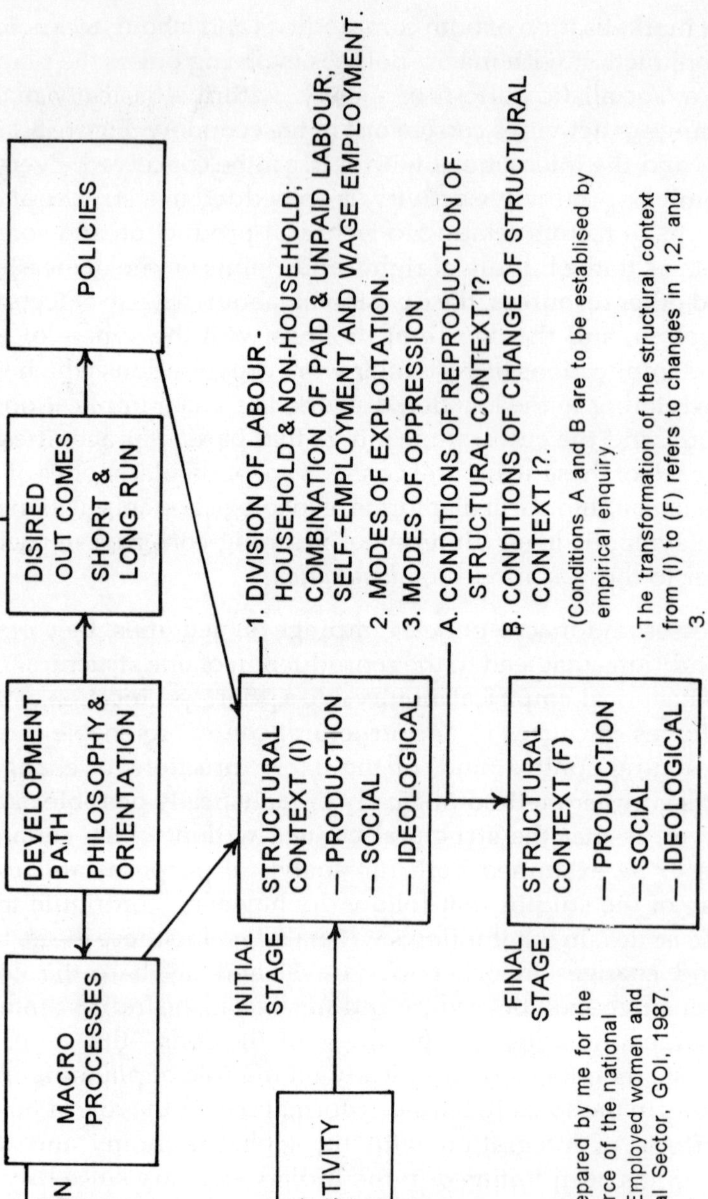

Note: This diagram was prepared by me for the macro policies taskforce of the national commission on Self-Employed women and women in the informal Sector, GOI, 1987.

Figure 8.1. Structure, Process and Activity (Landscape)

'macro-policies' and 'macro-processes,' are far too detailed and fine-tuned in complex modern economies and so defy any detailed specification. However, in the following pages we shall outline some of the substantive gender issues. What we delineate below are merely the broad contours of the nature of interaction between these institutions, even if it may appear a simple-minded exercise for political economists.

It is a widely held view that in modern economies, the state and markets are viewed as institutions that compete for 'economic space'. Economies where the role of the state is seen to be large are considered as those in which the sphere of the market forces is curtailed. While this may be true of capitalist and socialist economies, it should also be recognised that the modern state, its roles and functions greatly expanded with the growth of market forces, that is, with the growth and spread of capitalism on a world scale. Over time, the modern state came to be conceptualised as the sole source of all laws within its territory, that is, the political entity that has come to be defined as the 'nation'. Thus, what is defined as 'economic space' within a 'nation' in which the 'free and full' play of market forces can be seen to operate is, in fact, a space that is shaped and moulded by the laws of the state.

These laws encompass a very wide spectrum covering property, management of the economy with respect to investments, savings, employment and other macro-economic aggregates through monetary and fiscal policies and regulatory laws concerning the works and lives of its citizens often seeking legitimacy for such laws through the roles and goals assigned for the state by the respective constitutions.

Development planning evolved out of the understanding that the state was charged with the duty of taking care of all its citizens. Development planning is a rather recent aspect of governance by the modern state. Laws in the realm of development planning affect producing, trading and consuming units in the economy. However, not all laws have the same degree of justiciability—some are merely indicative and normative, and some are strictly enforceable (that is, in the nature of being prohibitive), with a wide range of flexibility in-between. In the next section, we examine the main shifts in thinking in Indian planning.

Not only do the laws arising out of this feature of governance shape the 'economic space,' they also define the nature of the market forces themselves. In a later section we shall examine the effects of the marketisation process, in general, and against the background of the current liberalisation trend in the Indian economy. It is a rather fundamental axiom in economics that market outcomes are determined by the strength of the initial endowments of its participants. The idea of development planning was meant to arrest the unfavourable outcomes of a vast majority who have been involuntarily drawn in as participants in the labour and commodity markets of developing economies. Through various measures that act on either, or both, the market factors of prices and quantities, and on the entitlements of its participants, development planning embodied in state policies attempts to influence the nature of the market forces.

Market forces, in turn, seek to mould, influence and shape state policies. However, it should be clear that market forces is a concept. Its influences are generated and regulated by the ideological crystallisation of market forces in the practices of various institutions in an economy. These are the institutions of production, exchange, trade and consumption. The stronger the participants in terms of their endowments, the greater the powers they seek to arrogate to tilt policy outcomes in their favour. And, by now, it is well known that with the integration of markets into the global circuits, there has developed correspondingly supra-national agencies that not only seek to restore the unhindered working of the free and full play of market forces at the global level, but are also on the side of the strongest participants in the international markets.

In any economy, households are numerous, differentiated and changing. They are not only differentiated in terms of their economic functions (such as consuming, producing or trading), but may be further differentiated in terms of their resource endowments. The extent to which households as a group can influence the state and the market, through political and economic processes, is greatly determined by their resource endowments which.-enable them to command further resources, goods and power, even though populist governments in national democracies may appear to appease the poorer households for political-electoral gains. The influence of households on market forces also depends on their resource endowments. Households that merely possess unskilled labour as a resource are, in fact, often the worst affected, along with the non-labour supplying households producing at subsistence levels. Much of the empirical analysis that follows refers to these households.

In this work, we examine some of the likely gender effects arising out of the functioning of these three institutions.

THE PLANNING PROCESS, INFORMAL SECTOR AND WOMEN

For a critical feminist perspective on how the planning process affected the lives of women, it is necessary to cast the analysis of Indian planning in three phases. The first phase may be termed the growth with redistribution phase, the second as the minimum needs and target-oriented plan phase, and the third phase as the one in which feminist and other critical perspectives have emerged. In the growth with redistribution phase, importance was given to achieving targeted growth rates, based on which sectoral planning and outlays were decided upon. Though redistributive measures (such as land reforms) were conceived, even though it was not integral to the plan as such, the overall philosophy of the plans was that the benefits of growth would trickle down to all classes; the redistribution strategies were not seen as integral to the growth strategies for attaining some measure of equity.

The Second Five Year Plan, based on the Mahalanobis plan model, gave a boost to industrialisation in the country and investment in the core capital-goods sector as well as encouraging the wage-goods sector. This was an important stage in the country's development as the Second Five Year Plan also decided on the nature of the industrialisation programme which was envisaged, as following the strategy of growth through import substitution rather than growth through export promotion. It also decided and allocated the roles for the public, and the private sectors, and the broad thrust of industrialisation based on the principle of balancing different and opposing forces. Thus, in the debates that were initiated even earlier (that is, both in the periods immediately preceding and following independence), of the choice between the Gandhian and the Nehruvian alternatives, the latter vision, encompassing the ideal of a modernising and industrialised society, triumphed. The Mahalanobis model was an attempt to translate this vision into policy. This strategy for growth ushered in the phase of modern industrial development. Even though encouragement and protection was given to both the modern small-scale sector and traditional small-scale activities, this policy orientation, along with macro-processes of marketisation, found the traditional sector losing ground to the modern sector. This orientation also crystallised the dualism between the traditional and modern sectors which, with the sluggish growth of employment in the modern sectors and with demographic and urbanisation pressures, very soon got transformed into the dualism of the organised and unorganised sectors or formal and informal sectors. Thus the unintended consequence of the Mahalanobis model was that it provided the intellectual and political legitimacy for a planning process that could ignore the vast unorganised or informal sectors of the economy. Since then, sectoral planning in India could never accommodate into its analytical framework the multiplicity of forms of production organisations and the variety of enterprises, and how these forms were articulated in a changing and dynamic context. Whereas the modern sectors were conceived at the activity levels as 'enterprises,' those of the traditional sectors were correspondingly conceived as 'persons' engaged in these activities. This conceptual distinction between enterprise and person has important ramifications in a plan framework.[7]

Policies and interventionist strategies aimed at enterprises are thought of in a vastly different manner from those aimed at individuals. Enterprises are seen as contributing to capital formation and growth while individuals are seen as a charge on the state and society, and also as enclosed within targeted groups as the weaker or vulnerable sections. Human capital formation and human resources development are rather late entrants in the jargon of planners. If sectoral planning for an articulated multi-structural system with variegated forms of production organisations had been properly conceived, other ideas and efforts (such as, regional planning, decentralisation and backward area industrialisation programmes), which now remain at the level of analytically ill conceived administrative programmes, could have yielded better results.

Be that as it may be, this lacuna in the growth strategy actually yielded very different interpretations in the heyday of informal sector debates in the late seventies. In the current period of liberalisation and structural adjustment, these issues are raised again in a different manner. These are that the informal sector is the outcome of excessive controls and state regulation as a consequence of planning; that the, informal sector is growth inducing in contrast to the Mahalanobis view that the capital-goods sector, through its backward and forward linkages, would be growth inducing; and that workers in the organised sector exploit those in the unorganised sector, completely obliterating the role of private monopoly capital, the articulation between the two sectors, and the role of trade unions in helping organised sector workers organise themselves and wage struggles, and conveying the misleading idea that if the organised sector workers did not exist, there would be no unorganised sector and no exploitation of that sector's workers by the other workers. However, the validity of the binary opposition, which clearly needed to be questioned, was done in a misleading manner.

The implications of this growth strategy was that most of the women were involved in activities that did not come directly within the ambit of planning. Also, as the traditional industries (which were generally household-based) began to lose to non-household manufacturing industries of the modern sector, women were adversely affected as many were engaged in traditional activities. This was a loss on numerous counts—of employment, traditional artisanal skills and their survival base itself. An examination of this process at the 'level of industry will probably reveal that these processes had, in fact, even earlier origins. We have already referred to the deindustrialisation phenomenon in the nineteenth century, but the modern growth strategy under planned development certainly exacerbated and, in some cases, hastened and intensified these processes.

Not only did these processes adversely affect women's activities and their survival base, but the Plans did not, reckon women as 'productive workers' either. From the First Plan onwards, women were targeted for welfare support. The Central Social Welfare Board, established in 1953, symbolised the welfare approach to women's problems. This welfare approach, combined with the community development approach, resulted in the promotion of Mahila Mandals, or women's clubs, in which the community developer was seen as a harmoniser of interests rather than as a stimulator of awareness (Government of India, 1988b). These Mahila Mandals became the site for women from the rural elite to promote their vision and ideals for rural women, which was completely at variance with the existential realities of the millions of poor rural and urban women.[8] The ideological hazards of such an approach for the women's movement has not been realistically assessed, though it is easy to concede that if political consensus was the basis for a planning that was catering to the elite rather than the poor masses, all efforts to generate that consensus were in order; and the Mahila Mandal strategy was just one, and perhaps perceived as not a significant one at that in evolving that consensus.[9]

By the end of the Fourth Plan period (1969-74), however, it became clear that growth effects do not trickle down to all classes. Indeed, evidence was forthcoming that the growth strategies (such as the green revolution) were, in fact, leading to greater agrarian differentiation and, consequently, increasing asset and income inequalities in rural and urban areas. Such processes threaten the basis of consensus which is a requisite for the planning process. Thus, renewed attempts were made to evolve, maintain and strengthen the basis of that consensus, resulting in a shift from the 'growth with redistribution' strategy to the 'minimum needs and target approach'.

The minimum needs approach to. planning was one way to make the state acknowledge its responsibility to provide the basic minimum needs for the poor. It was much more broad-based than mere quantitative estimates of target growth rates for sectors and of welfare services. The needs of the poor were identified in terms of life-sustaining inputs (such as employment, health and nutrition) as well as physical and social infrastructural support services (such as protected water supply, sanitation, roads, hospitals and schools). But there were basic problems in its conception as well. The needs and inputs were not identified against a backdrop of the macro-structural processes that are under way in the economy. Consequently, there was no understanding of why, in fact, these needs were not met hitherto, nor of how the processes were going to exacerbate the deficiency of these needs in the future as well. But this was a politically important step in focusing on the poverty groups in the country. However, even in this the needs of different women were not adequately represented. Social infrastructural inputs that were initially focused upon did not consider women's productive and reproductive roles in the diverse occupational contexts, or how their efficiency could be improved upon and their burden mitigated by the provision of such social infrastructural inputs. Once the focus on poverty groups became inevitable, the target approach to these groups followed. For planned interventions to reach the poor, it was necessary both to define and identify the poor. Even though women in poverty households suffered relatively greater deprivation, it was not considered possible to identify them, as most of the Plan schemes intending to enhance productive efficiency (such as income, employment, credit and training programmes) were targeted at households as the beneficiaries. Targeting households, rather than individual members, was itself derived from the conception of a patriarchal family in which women were either dependents or supplementary earners. Paradoxically, there was no difficulty in identifying women from these households as targets for family planning programmes.

Even though women were not specifically targeted, Plan schemes to empower the poor in their productive roles did cover many women from the poor households. These were in the nature of employment promotion schemes for wage and self-employment, credit assistance and training programmes. We shall critically examine some of these a little later. For the moment, let us recapitulate the point made earlier about the conceptual distinction between enterprises and persons. The target approach to poverty alleviation was greatly aided by this conceptual obfuscation. The schemes did not envisage the promotion of enterprises but that they were merely providing assistance to individuals who, for some reason which was not clearly articulated, became vulnerable. Levels of assistance were projected at such unrealistically low levels that the long-run viability and sustainability of enterprises were never taken into serious consideration. This resulted in low allocations for poverty alleviation programmes in the Plans, and its outlay vis-a-vis capital outlays in key sectors (such as power/energy or transport, or the defence sector) was seen as something negotiable and amenable to pruning and scaling down.

There is no denying the fact that the focus on poverty groups in the Plans actually contributed to the emergence of a critical consciousness among feminists as well as those who either speak on behalf of other marginalised groups, and/or are themselves marginalised in the mainstream development process. The current phase of Indian planning, in striking contrast with the earlier phases, has to be evolved and implemented within a set of critical perspectives on development strategies, an articulate body of activists and non-governmental grassroots organisations and the contending supporting and oppositional forces of the free market, liberalisation, and structural-adjustment advocates, the supporters drawing their support from US-led multilateral agencies. The pulls and pressures on the planning system are quite significant. In this critical phase of planning, focusing on gender issues has resulted in some significant perspectives on overall development.

Among those articulating the concerns of poor women are two schools of thought. One believes that the problem is one of integrating women in the development process. This has come to be known as the women-in-development (WID) approach. The second school is of the opinion that merely integrating women into development programmes is not enough and that it is, in the first place, necessary to probe why the marginalisation of women occurred at all. The latter school, therefore, does not perceive gender issues in isolation but is linked to the macro-structural processes in the economy. These two divergent perspectives came into conflict over the formulation of the National Perspective Plan for Women for 1988—2000 by the Government of India. Thirty-nine women's organisations expressed their concern over the orientation of the National Perspective Plan that was then on the anvil. They noted:

> A development plan for women which does not examine women's relationships with these types of macro-policies for national development in different sectors, in our view, runs the risk of becoming confined to welfare handouts, evading the major issue of women's participation as equal partners, decision-makers and agents of national development.[10]

They found that the holistic approach endorsed in the National Perspective Plan was no different from the minimum or basic needs approach as it did not link poverty and marginality among women to the macro-processes and macro-policies in the economy.

Earlier it was noted that the target approach to poverty gave rise to schemes to promote wage-employment and self-employment. The critique of these approaches to poverty alleviation actually resulted in a nuanced and subtle understanding of women's occupations and employment in the so-called informal sector among feminists in addition to what has hitherto been displayed in the many administrative approaches and literature. It was to translate these feminist understandings into accessible knowledge for the policy makers for the better conception and implementation of policies that the National Commission on Self-Employed Women and Women in the Informal Sector was constituted. Its report is probably the most authoritative account of women workers in the informal sector in the country so far (Government of India, 1988a).

By examining the operation of a variety of macro-policies (such as the technology policy, the licensing policy, the credit policy, the policy pertaining to training, marketing and raw materials in the context of macro-processes such as marketisation, urbanisation and technological changes, the commission identified the vulnerabilities and survival problems of women workers across a wide range of occupations and activities. It recommended an integrated and holistic approach to tackling the basic issues regarding women through planning. Such a strategy, according to the Commission, should aim at the following:

1. Ensuring them fuel, fodder and water to meet their basic requirements;
2. Strengthening their existing employment by providing appropriate support in the areas of skill, training, credit and marketing;
3. Protecting their employment in the sectors where it is declining due to technological advancement;
4. Creating new employment opportunities for them based on local markets for mass consumption goods;
5. Protecting women workers from casualisation and contractualisation, which lead to their exploitation;
6. Providing supportive services to women (like housing, toilets and child-care facilities);
7. Proper and effective implementation of industrial and protective legislations.

As can be easily surmised, this holistic approach is quite different in content and spirit from the minimum needs programme. To meet these objectives, the Commission recommended the formulation of macro-policies in various areas that are well integrated. It called for the formulation of an integrated strategy for the use of natural resources (like land, water and forests), taking into account the fuel, fodder and water requirements of the poor. It called for an integrated strategy for industrial development that would ensure the healthy and complementary growth of the large-scale sector, the small-scale sector and the traditional sector. The Commission also noted that industrial policy has to be meaningfully related to the policy pertaining to natural resources so that resource use is beneficial to poor women rather than deprive and exclude them of that use. It also called for a reformulation of the anti-poverty programmes in a manner that it supplements and complements the overall development process, and thereby shift the focus of these programmes from the target approach. So far we have highlighted the shifts in thinking in Indian planning. It-is evident that the recent critical thinking appears to be a very significant improvement over the earlier approaches. The extent to which these insights can actually be embodied in the Plans in the current environment of liberalisation and structural adjustment is a matter of concern to the sceptical critic. However, it cannot be denied that a certain amount of critical consciousness on these issues has been built up.

MARKETISATION, GLOBALISATION AND STRUCTURAL ADJUSTMENT—GENDER EFFECTS

We have already indicated, though not in detail, the likely effects of the marketisation process on poor women's lives. Here we shall elaborate on the marketisation process and the likely effects of the contemporary trends of globalisation and structural adjustment under way in the Indian economy. Neoclassical economic theory would have us believe that the operation of the invisible hand of the market would ensure, in most instances, an efficient and equitable market clearing equilibrium. Situations that did not result in such solutions were characterised as those in which indivisibilities, non-appropriability of benefits, and non-attributabilities of costs and benefits arising out of externalities render a divergence between the social marginal costs and returns from the private marginal costs and returns. While the nature of good was specified, the nature of the participants were, as indicated earlier, subsumed under 'abstract individuals' as rational agents.

There is also a great deal more to that incomplete Marshallian story of markets in different time periods. It does not recognise that many participants in the market, identified as the very short-run, usually dealing with perishable commodities, are those with very low initial resources. The inelasticity of supply, identified as a defining feature, has to reckon with the survival question of such producers as well. The isomorphic treatment of producers and consumers in neoclassical theory does not reckon that producers are consumers as well, and that their survival has to be ensured. Even though the analysis figures out resource constrained utility maximisation problems, such individual optimisers with unequal initial resource endowments are assumed to be similarly treated as actors on the market. Neoclassical and general equilibrium theory treats the market as a set of forces, though the metaphorical significance of the term finds itself inadequately incorporated in its analytics. Forces, as in 'armed forces,' carries associations with 'incursions or invasions' and 'defence'. And that is what, in fact, 'market forces' are. When survival is threatened, one has to defend oneself from such invasive forces. These invasive forces cannot be halted but could be slowed down and their evil effects, to some extent, can be mitigated. Notice Marx's statement in *Capital* (Vol. 1) in his analysis of primitive accumulation: 'Force is the midwife of every old society pregnant with a new one. It is itself an economic power (see Chap. XXXI 'Genesis of the Industrial Capitalist'. p. 703). Rosa Luxemburg (1951), in her analysis of the expansion of capitalism to precapitalist societies, also noted• that since precapitalist economies cannot be penetrated through simple market competition, there being no markets, there must be other forces such as 'force'. Notice the similarity of functions that 'force' in both the connotations is expected to play. Are individuals, communities and nations sufficiently empowered to defend themselves against the onslaught of such invasive forces on the powerless?

Despite the conception of 'market forces', neoclassical and general equilibrium theory has not been successful in treating the problem of survival analytically.[11] Markets in real life, however, are 'institutions' and, like all institutions, are embedded in socio-cultural contexts and governed by norms and rules. Actors participate in them and, in doing so, markets acquire a structure and individuals acquire an identity, and begin to see themselves as part of a set of new and changing social relations.

Initial resource endowment plays a significant role in differential market outcomes. For a vast number of people, and particularly for women, the involvement in the markets of both commodities and labour is both involuntary and disadvantageous. Economic history and economic anthropology are providing evidence from different culture areas of the differential gender as well as class effects of the marketisation process (Leacock and Safa, 1986). In India, there are innumerable regional, caste, class and community variations in the resource position and autonomy of women. Regional economies, differentiated on the basis of agrarian and industrial regimes, also indicate differing labour demand and supply conditions. The extent to which women are affected by both an intensification and extension of the market for commodities and labour is an outcome of the widely differing resource context as well.

In what follows, we shall examine some of the likely outcomes in the context of commodity, land and labour markets, with specific reference to the Indian situation, though with no implicit assumption that women across India are uniformly affected. The most significant aspect of the growth of commodity markets is that of agrarian commercialisation. Forced commercialisation, resulting from high rents and interest demands, impinges directly on cultivating households in terms of availability of food and seed stocks, shift from food to cash crop cultivation to meet rent and interest demands, an intensification of work hours by the members, lack of investment, and debt bondage which, in the course of time, turns them into dispossessed wage labourers. In this whole cruel process, women in the household play a very crucial role in thwarting or stalling the pace of the process of dispossession and proletarianisation. In most such situations (granting differences in local contexts), women are the last to enter wage labour from these households. Questions of household honour do play a role. Women enter wage labour only after exhausting all attempts at preventing complete dispossession. They eat less, work more, send their children to work both within and outside the home, mortgage their few possessions, engage in a myriad of survival activities, and so on.

Similarly, traditional non-agrarian activities were enmeshed in caste and family and kin relationships. Social relations (which earlier enabled productive and social activities) become constraining with the growth of market forces. With men moving out of traditional activities with the growth of wage labour, women in traditional production activities are left to burden under new constraints. This is true of many caste and kin-based production forms, such as craft and traditional artisanal activities.[12] Even in activities where women were formally engaged as home-based workers in family/household production forms, production for the market most often involves them in a new set of dependency relations. They become put-out workers working for merchant contractors who cater to large markets and are dependent for raw materials and obtain either piece-rate wages, or become engaged in sale and purchase transactions with merchant contractors that are not substantively different from piece-rated wage work.[13]

Further, with the expansion of markets, women in many traditional and subsistence production activities have been found to lose control over their income and earnings and/or have much less autonomy in what they do. While there are certainly a number of new wage earning activities for women which gives them control over cash earnings, autonomy and status (and we recognise that the tendency to 'invisiblise' women's work is much stronger in subsistence non-cash income activities), it does appear, on the whole, that when markets transform subsistence activities, the women who lose out in consequence are not the same as those who gain some advantage, be it in terms of employment, income or autonomy. With the growth of markets (in many of the coastal fishing regions, for instance), women in the traditional fishing economy had immediate and direct access to the fish catch of the male members of their households, and they were engaged in marketing it. Once traditional fishing gave way to large-scale-capitalist fishing (with mechanised trawlers for export and distant domestic markets), the village auction system was evolved in many parts. Here the village, as a collective, engages in the transaction with large capital to fix the price. Since, in any case, capital's might is much larger, this is the only way villagers can empower themselves. However, as a consequence, women lose out as they lose access to income directly. If they want to engage in the fish trade, they have no option but to engage in the auction system. Their very limited resource position renders them vulnerable participants in the market. But, with the growth of markets (both export and domestic), the fish processing industry has grown as well. In many of its activities, it employs predominantly young women workers. However, these women are different from the wives and daughters of traditional fishermen.

As markets expand and grow, men and women with a small resource base are increasingly alienated and become peripheral actors. In the course of time they lose out to become wage workers. In general, women's resource position is inferior to that of men. With the emergence of land markets, women in many parts who enjoyed usufruct rights—either of village common property for the collection of fuelwood and fodder, or the rights of cultivation in ancestral and familial (both natal and marital) property—soon lose out. Similarly, if income from certain lines of activities were still available to women, even in the changing context, it was in most instances because the task, having been defined as a woman's task by traditional practices, was still being done by them. But this has not always been true of wage activities. In wage activities, tasks performed by women are, in many instances, taken over by men when wages go up and/or also undergo changes in skill classification, the same task getting upgraded as skilled when done by men and classified as semi—or unskilled when done by women. Thus, changes in the market do play a significant role in changing work organisations and the division of labour. The expansion of the market renders necessary the scaling up of production activity, and in that reorganisation women completely lose out, either their employment itself or get relegated to the low-end tasks. Similarly, when markets contract, production activities are scaled down and women are again the first to lose out. Some of the later chapters explore why the market so persistently works against women.

With this background and understanding of the marketisation process and its effects on women, let us now examine the likely consequences of the current globalising efforts. It should be mentioned that the marketisation process that we have so far been analysing is indeed a global one, and has been so for over two centuries. In the evolution of world capitalism, the spread of markets (that is, the spread of trade and exchange in consequence of expanding commodity production that unleashed the process of proletarianisation in all parts of the world) has been taking place at different speeds with different dynamics in different parts of the world—better understood by the phrase 'combined and uneven' development of capitalism.[14] The literature on the 'articulation of modes of production' has been particularly useful in highlighting these different dynamics. The crucial methodological insight of the articulationist school is that transitional social formation is subject to a double history—on the one hand, the history of capital itself which, for the most part, is written outside such social formations and, on the other hand, the history of the transition specific to the modes of production which are articulated. While the resulting social formation reflects not only the dynamics of capitalism but also the dynamics of the precapitalist modes, it is constituted by their articulation. Feminist literature in the articulationist perspective has highlighted the profound changes in the sphere of production and exchange with associated changes in the sexual division of labour and women's autonomy.[15]

While the articulationists have developed the interaction between capitalist and pre-capitalist sectors more systematically, studies on the nature of imperialism focused both on the changing nature of capital in the centre and the changes it wrought in the peripheral areas of the world. Whereas the classical Marxist theory of imperialism (as exemplified in the works of Hilferding, Bukharin and Lenin) stressed the formation of monopolies on a national level and analysed the intensification of competition on a world scale between national groupings of capital, it did not deal adequately with those of the underdeveloped countries. It is those who followed Rosa Luxemburg's line of thin king (namely Paul Baran, Andre' Gunder Frank, Samir Amin and Wallerstein) who have concerned themselves both with the world system as a whole and its effects on the periphery. Differing from classical Marxist thinking, they accord primacy to relations of exchange rather than relations of production. Indeed, each one is different. Wallerstein defines the world system (and it does not have to necessarily cover the entire globe) as a unit with a single division of labour, multiple cultural systems and without a single central authority. For him, nation-states in the modern world are not closed systems and, therefore, cannot be analysed as such. The interaction of local and global processes in the constitution of anthropological subjects has received attention in contemporary Western anthropology.

Around these theoretical perspectives have emerged, in the last two decades, a large number of studies on world-market-oriented industrialisation and the associated strategies of multinational companies, of which redeployment and relocation of industrial units in the developing countries and sub-contracting strategies have been in the forefront of issues.[16] Recognising that there were indeed regional and national specificities in responses to this global trend of world-market-oriented industrialisation, many of these studies have focused on the MNC's preference for a particular type of worker, and their effect on the workers and society. Since MNC's have been known to prefer women workers in food processing, garments, electronics and pharmaceuticals, there is significant evidence today of the conditions and status of women workers in these sectors in Mexico and the countries of Latin America, Africa, and southeast and east Asia. The overriding conclusions have been that the preference of MNC's for these workers is because they are cheaper than the male workers in the region, and certainly cheaper than the workers in the advanced countries. Many studies have also highlighted the new forms of patriarchal control at the workplace that these MNC's have evolved, drawing and reconstructing from the values and cultural norms of these patriarchal societies. Thus, even though MNC's opened up avenues for the employment of women (and, in many instances, they were either first generation women workers in factories, or recent rural migrants into the urban centres, and these women do seem to enjoy apparently greater autonomy in their lives even if they contributed to the household income pool), it did not, in most situations, enable the women to overcome forms of patriarchal control. After all, in these lines of production MNC's needed swift assembly-line workers who were docile and submissive, and it is not unexpected that such new entrants would be subjected to capitalist discipline even more rigorously. Thus, 'young women find themselves in a dilemma. While increased autonomy within the household was achieved to some extent, they had to subject themselves to new forms of control. There is growing literature on how these women struggle to reconstitute their subjectivities either through continual social conformity or through sporadic acts of resistance in the new and different fields of power relations (Ong, 1987).

The south Asian response to world-market-oriented industrialisation has been remarkably different from other regions. India, in a sense, exemplifies the south Asian situation. Having a relatively complex industrial base, what we shall explore in the next chapter as a 'multistructural system'—traditional industries with a long history of craft production organised on the basis of family-kin, caste and village have coexisted with technologically advanced modern industrial sectors. As indicated earlier, the Indian industrialisation strategy has so far had an inward orientation. Its primary aim was production for the domestic sector based on import-substitution. The current globalising efforts which have arisen in part due to the pressures of multilateral agencies—such as the World Bank and the International Monetary Fund—seek to displace the earlier strategy. Recurring deficits on the balance of payments account, owing to a multiplicity of factors on both the import and export ends (reflecting in part both structural bottlenecks and the relatively halting growth of the economy) has forced India to rely increasingly on these agencies both to offset and redress short-term imbalances in balance of payments, as well as long-term development assistance.

This situation has occurred at a time when international arrangements (particularly the North-South one) are undergoing significant shifts. Since the eighties, and particularly since the mid-eighties, there has been a continuing net transfer of funds from the developing nations to the developed world. With commercial banks of the developed nations folding up assistance to the developing nations at the first signs of fatigue of the latter in debt servicing, multilateral agencies have been forced to undergo a change in their attitude as well. The development-aid mentality of the period of sixties has faded out; now assistance to the developing world is reckoned in commercial terms, and tested on the grounds of profitability and rates of return as all other investments.

As advanced capitalism gets deeper into its own crisis, it aggressively seeks to create and expand for itself newer and newer markets, making one wonder whether Rosa Luxemburg was really all that wrong! The potential markets that are now coming under easy accessibility for advanced capitalism are the countries of the former Soviet Union and the Eastern bloc. India and China represent a very vast market potential to be conquered by it which, in the course of time, would also seek to devour the African markets as well. In this neo-expansionist phase of advanced capitalism, the 'nation-state' mentality that is so deeply entrenched in post-colonial societies acts as a block retarding that expansion. Critiques of the globalisation strategy in these societies represent, in part, the anxieties of a decentring of the economies and cultures from the nation-state perspective, even while the inevitability and necessity of an increasingly interdependent world is being acknowledged.

Since July 1991, the Indian government, through a series of policy measures, hastened the integration of the Indian economy with the world market, a process that was undoubtedly started in the mid-eighties. It aims to drastically reduce the role of the state in the economy and also enlarge the role of market forces. With a view to promoting international competitiveness, the government announced several changes in the public sector policy, industrial licensing policy, foreign investment and foreign technology policy, and the policy regulating monopoly capital. These policy changes have been part of a structural adjustment package mooted by the IMF and the World Bank. Three key prices govern the macroeconomics of an IMF stabilisation programme—the price of foreign exchange, the price of credit and the price of labour. Correcting price distortions and getting 'prices right' is the motto of the stabilisation-adjustment programme. These are meant to affect pricing in the public sector, in particular, so that the essential characteristics of a 'public sector' can be whittled down and erased by the market forces in full play. The structural adjustment programme of the World Bank that seeks to complement the IMF stabilisation programme addresses 'economic efficiency' issues at the micro-economic level.

It is expected that MNC investment in India consequently will increase in the near future. Thus, export-oriented industries which have been female intensive in the use of labour are likely to expand in the future: In some lines of production (such as pharmaceuticals), MNCs may compete and push out domestic industries such that the overall net effect on female employment will be lower to that extent. Certainly, in an economy with a large and expanding unemployed labour force, additional employment is to be welcomed. But the experience with these industries has shown that the conditions of work leave much to be desired owing to increased sub-contracting relations and the tendency towards informalisation of labour relations.

Modernisation and technological upgradation that are sought to be brought about are likely to be both labour displacing and labour reorienting. An exit policy to facilitate the closure of loss making industries has been framed. As a part of its stabilisation and structural-adjustment programme, the IMF has promoted the idea of 'safety nets'. Though there is generally no agreement about what constitutes a 'safety net,' it is meant to provide a positive reinforcement for the process of change. It seeks to encourage individuals to accept the process of change, and provides opportunities for individual adaptation thereby generating a social consensus for the political decision of structural adjustment. It is generally recognised that stabilisation and structural adjustment do create social hardships in the short-run, which are expected to be compensated by long-term benefits, a claim that could as well be a dubious one. Among the identified social hardships in the initial stage are higher age-specific unemployment, the slow growth of formal sector employment, increased poverty in the rural areas and among the urban poor, reduced spending oh social programmes (particularly health care and education), lower real wages, reduced employment and increased redundancies among public sector employees as a result of reduced government expenditure and the privatisation of state-owned enterprises, lower standards of living among the poorer sections as a result of lower subsidies on basic commodities and food, the removal of price controls, and exchange rate, tariff and quota restrictions on imports, and a further aggravation thereof of the inflationary tendencies in the economy.

The structural adjustment process does not account for the fact that poor women enter the process on an unequal basis, as already deprived and marginal actors. Not only did the development process marginalise them (as all indicators of development-employment, health, literacy, nutrition, and so on, have so overwhelmingly indicated), but they have also had to bear, in that condition, a greater burden of the household survival.

The adjustment process spelled out so far in India does not incorporate explicit employment and safety-net policies. In the area of employment the only proposal is for the setting up of a National Renewal Fund. This is meant more as an 'unemployment' rather than an employment fund to provide severence benefits for retrenched organised sector employees (particularly from the public sector), and for some amount of retraining and reskilling. Not only are the vast millions of rural and urban informal sector workers not 'targeted' under this fund, but the expenditure under the existing poverty alleviation programmes are presently suffering a decline in real terms, with all the prospects of a decline in the near future in money terms as well. Macro-economic projections under different growth assumptions suggest that open unemployment, as a consequence of the adjustment programme; could range anywhere between 4 to 10 million persons additionally in the next few years (ILO-ARTEP, 1992). The behaviour of the labour market in the past has indicated that with high open unemployment there would be a tendency to withdraw from the labour force, particularly among women, so that invisible unemployment would also increase significantly. Disguised unemployment (implying both low productivity employment as well as sporadic employment) are also bound to increase these adverse employment effects, impacting more on the informal sectors of the economy. Reduced employment will affect women both directly and indirectly. Since a large number of men will be without jobs and in the older age groups and cannot be retrained, they are likely to compete with women for the low skilled and low paid jobs in the informal sector in which women predominate. There is also the possibility that with the new parameters for judging efficiency, women, even if they do not lose their jobs, will be forced to accept lower wages and/or undertake more strenuous jobs for the same pay.

The structural adjustment process also envisages increased allocations and efforts in the sectors of social-infrastructural inputs (such as health, education, nutrition and child services). Though stated, there is no assurance that expanded financial outlays for these sectors or an expanded 'safety net' covering all these aspects will be in operation soon. Although the idea of 'adjustment with a human face' has been promoted by some international agencies (Cornia and Stewart, 1987), such an agenda is not very different from the target approach and the basic needs approach that were examined earlier in the chapter. However, in order to effect better targeting, the Planning Commission has envisaged the formation of a national grid of voluntary organisations to play a role in monitoring these programmes. An official role for NGOs in the Plan process was initiated by the Janata government of V.P. Singh in 1989. While welcoming the idea of an enhanced role for NGOs, which can become operational and meaningful only with decentralisation and the devolution of power to local agencies (which is not likely to take place anyway), it is also necessary to be watchful so that they are not transformed into tools of the government to promote the vision and aspiration of some of the multilateral agencies.

How macro-processes and macro-policies impact on the lives of women can be meaningfully analysed only by examining household dynamics and politics. This will be done in the section that follows.

HOUSEHOLD DYNAMICS AND GENDER POLITICS

It is impossible to recapitulate, even briefly, the prodigious contributions from converging disciplines on family, kinship, household production and the organisation of production and reproduction activities.[17] Anthropological perspectives on gender have focused on the conceptual distinctions between family and household, explored the changing sexual division of labour and its implications for women's status, the constitution of women's identities, their roles and their desires, how meanings adhere to women's activities and how they change, how micro-processes at the family-household level link up with macro-processes in the economy and society and, above all, questioned the category of 'women,' the 'essentialness' of attributed qualities across cultures, the 'naturalness' of the domains of activities that seem to be universally relegated to them, and how ideologies of gender are constructed. Marxist-feminist literature on the household conceptualised it as a productive and reproductive unit, and analysed family-household reproduction at three levels (namely, the reproduction of labour power on a continuing and daily basis, biological reproduction and social reproduction). Socialist feminist analysis brought the underlying power relations within households explicitly into focus.

The focus of this analysis is restricted to examining household responses to macro-processes and macro-policies, and how gender politics within households change under the circumstances. Household responses are to be analysed in terms of the following: changes in household structure; changes in the work organisation within households; changes in access and control over resources, in particular changes in income pooling and sharing arrangements; changes in reproductive behaviour, and the combination and allocation of productive and reproductive tasks; changes in consumption patterns; changes in household survival strategies; and renegotiations of household relations in an attempt to refashion 'selves' and reconstitute subjectivities. White recognising that there are no prescriptive or a priori ways of reading a particular outcome as the consequence of a particular process or event, the possible directions of change are sought to be explained here.

While the family is a biological unit centred on kinship relations, the household is a social arrangement which could be both equivalent to the family or different, in terms of being both more or less than the family. The family-kinship unit derives its normative beliefs and sanctions from the cultural rules and legitimation practices in the symbolic and material realms. These govern relations between gender and across generations, and shape family ideologies ascribing roles and status to its members, and allocating work and resources (in particular, property). Its material and emotional basis builds expectations and promotes fulfilment among its members within its overall normative sanctions. Family ideologies, though not unchanging over a long period, are more resilient to change in the short run. So, at any time, family ideologies could be enabling or constraining to any of its members.

Yet individual identities are constituted in a complex manner, at time emphasising the collective aspect of existence and at times encouraging individuation, by participating in and through familial practices in everyday lives. Power relations—both those that are normatively sanctioned and the 'unsanctioned' ones as well—play a significant role in socialising its members. This primary socialisation is very important, and fulfils many societal requirements. The docility of nubile factory girls in export-oriented industries or the rebellious individuals instigating trouble leading to shop-floor struggles are, to a great extent, the outcome of such primary socialisation within families. The household, on the other hand, is a social-residential arrangement constituted either with all or some family members, and sometimes others outside of the family. Such household arrangements are responsive to economic situations in the short run as well.

In what follows we shall use the expression household to signify both these aspects together. The 'household is not a static or insulated unit. It is subjected to the pressures of ongoing societal change. The classification of households is indeed a complex sociological exercise.[18] Sociological literature in India has highlighted the changes in the family structure in response to urbanisation, modernisation and agrarian differentiation. Thus macro-processes affect the structure of households. From a joint family scenario, middle class urban households have moved to nuclear ones since the beginning of the century. The structure of households in rural India has also undergone tremendous changes as a result of agrarian differentiation and commercialisation. It should be noted that there are differences in rural household structures in the different culture-areas of the country, and differences among caste groups as well. Even though patri-virilocal marriages may be common in most parts, short-term residence practices are often quite varying (Palriwala, 1991). Thus, household structures are in a constant state of flux. Changes in household structures triggered off by agrarian differentiation also do not affect all classes of households in the same way. Whereas at one end of the peasant spectrum that is consolidating the gains, there may be a tendency to expand the structure, at the other dispossessing end there may be a tendency to disintegrate (Krishnaji, 1980). State intervention, in terms of defining and changing the rules for the acquisition of private property and inheritance, have also, played a role in changing household structures. These, changes affect women members of the household in terms of changes in the power and authority structures of the household, work allocation, and changes in duties and responsibilities to list a few.

There exists a close connection between the constantly changing productive and labour market structures and the dynamics of the household. Work organisations within households undergo changes. This refers to changes in the division of labour between household members for domestic work; changes in the sexual division of labour for production/ activities located within households (such as traditional manufacturing and artisanal activities), 'and home-based production under some putting-out arrangements; and changes in the former or in both to release members for wage work outside the home. Forced commercialisation and compulsive market involvement through inflation, technological change and other factors leads to an intensification of work, bringing about a, reorganisation. How the women members of a household are affected by such work intensification and work reorganisation is a matter of empirical inquiry. It is my expectation that given a patriarchal ideology and rigidity in altering arrangements with regard to domestic work (even though we recognise that in very poor households even the degree to which these can be manipulated are severely constrained), such work intensification is bound to be unfavourable to women. We shall further examine how the patriarchal assumptions of the male bread-winner being the provider and protector of the family affects the terms and conditions of women's labour supply in the context of segmented labour market structures. Gender politics in work organisations, both within the home and in work-sites outside the home (be it the fields, factories or offices), has been an area of considerable feminist thinking as many of the following chapters indicate. There is considerable evidence to believe that the interplay of class and gender relations that confronts the relations of wives and husbands within the household does determine and set limits to women's participation in other arenas as well, whether it be work outside the home, organising unions or participating in strikes or processions.

Access and control over resources (in particular, income pooling and sharing arrangements though guided by cultural sanctions and varying across classes) are' also subject to changes with the changes in economic and work situations, and is an arena of intense gender politics both overt and covert. In a patriarchal context, women's control over their resources and earnings are severely constrained, not to mention their control over the overall income pool. The proportion of income disclosed by male members, their contributions to the pool, and the quantum that they appropriate for themselves for personal use are all factors over which women do not have control. Given the fact that women bear a disproportionately greater burden 'of household survival in poor working class households, this lack of control exacerbates their burdens,[19] As the economic situation in the household worsens, women progressively lose whatever control they had over the resources, though the pressures of household survival also act as a countervailing force to curtail individual autonomy. Even here the forces of curtailment impinge first on women, and only thereafter on men.

It is not expected that poor working class households would be endowed with any significant assets, and marriage becomes the only chance in life for acquiring some. The widespread shift from bride-price to dowry among almost all caste groups and working-class households is a response to economic changes. A quickening pace of differentiation, brought about by the marketisation process, sets off aspirations at the higher and middle levels of society, and intensifies needs at the lower level, thereby making dowry a pervasive feature and a force of primitive accumulation that is enmeshed with the larger circuits of accumulation and the circuits of subsistence.[20] This affects a woman's life and prospects directly. The commodification of women's labour and sexuality in both contexts, rendering them more and more powerless, intensifies their vulnerability. Dowry is both a caûse and a consequence of asymmetrical power relations between the sexes within the family, and in society at large. The manifestations of household level gender politics on the dowry issue (such as domestic violence and bride-burning) are well-known and need no restatement here. A further understanding of how the sex/gender systems in society are enmeshed with the politico-economic systems is gained by considering the sphere of reproduction and the domain of reproductive politics. Reproductive behaviour and politics undergo changes with the overall changes in the society and economy.

By reproductive behaviour both the conditions of sexual life as well as the practice of child-bearing and child-rearing are implied. In patriarchal societies, poor women are subjected to multiple pressures on their sexual life. In many instances, sexual life is accompanied by domestic violence as well. The demands of drunken husbands for sexual services have to be complied with at all times. In addition, desertion and the 'other women' syndrome in poor working class households adds to a tension-ridden sexual life. Women's existence as sexual beings themselves and their rights go correspondingly unacknowledged. In such a situation, women's control over sexuality assumes importance. In many instances, children are wanted. The absence of any life-cycle social security system in the country has resulted in children being viewed as an asset, in the sense that poor households with minimal investment can hope to get returns after a few years as the incidence of child labour is quite high. However, children from such households also assert their independence and autonomy quite early, as the period of childhood is, compared to the middle and upper classes, correspondingly shorter. Families have to ensure the spacing of children in such a way that there is always at least one growing child with them, for both emotional and economic support. This is not to suggest that their emotional lives are governed by rationality, instrumentality and functionality, but *ex post facto* rationalisations indicate that their behaviour and expectations could be analysed in such a calculative frame. Often, owing to women's lack of control over sexuality, children turn up out 'of time, and are probably more numerous than what was expected or wanted.

The need of poor women for control over their sexuality coalesced with the state's interest in population control. It would be naive to equate the two, for their motivations are vastly different—control over one's own body is the opposite of the interventionist and invasive tendency of an external agency (like the state) to control women's bodies. With the rise of development discourses from the fifties and sixties, Malthusian fears translated themselves into these interventionist and invasive policies, and population control became a major aspect of the development agenda of many nation-states that were often pushed and jostled around by imperialist interests and those of international agencies to check population growth. Even in the Western nations, population debates have always been racist and anti-poor. The third world analogue also had the cold, war fears of the forces of communism enveloping the world owing to unchecked population growth and the consequential mass poverty.[21]

A curious enmeshing of the politics of reproduction at the household level with the politics of reproduction at the level of the nation-state seems to have taken place. This has resulted in two apparently contradictory rationalisations often coexisting in working class discourses. The understanding at the macro-level of the correlation between population growth and poverty coexists with the understanding at the micro-level that household poverty is not the consequence of family size but due to other factors (such as non-availability of employment, low wages, low education and skill levels, and a low asset base). This tension exists in part at other levels as well, for it is quite difficult to explain why there have been so few feminist analyses of reproductive politics in India even when the juggernaut of family planning programmes moves on.

As the economy tightens and as unemployment and poverty increase in the phase of structural adjustment, population control programmes are likely to gain additional momentum. Issues of reproduction are closely tied to issues of women's and children's health and nutrition, as high mortality rates among infants induce higher conception and birth rates. While social-infrastructural inputs are expected to increase in anticipation of the short-run negative effects of structural adjustment, it is both too premature and perhaps even optimistic to believe that in a situation that is already quite deplorable on these counts, there would not be a worsening of the situation once the adjustment process begins to unfold.

The planning of such social inputs has also to take into account the fact that, under a worsening economic situation, poorer households have perforce to intensify their work efforts, which is bound to affect the health of women and children negatively. Women combine both productive and reproductive roles, and the effects in one sphere impact on the other sphere as well. The ability to combine these two roles will be severely curtailed when survival strategies in the adjustment phase are likely to have little room for such rnanoeuvring.

Not only would the health of women and children be affected by additional workloads but there are likely to be direct and significant cuts in their food consumption as well. The structural-adjustment process aims to reduce all subsidies. Food subsidies form an important component of this. While a mass of critical opinion has already been formed within the country to prevent cuts in food subsidies or the dismantling of the public distribution system, it would be difficult to sustain this lobbying and political pressure through the democratic process for a long and sustained period. Even if food subsidies are not tampered with in the first year of the adjustment process, it is difficult to predict the outcome as years go by, for the adjustment process as envisaged is likely to extend over a time period ranging between six to ten years. Given the by now well established fact that women in poverty households suffer relatively greater deprivation and that the intra-household allocation of food is not in favour of women, it is expected that women (and consequently children, particularly female children) would suffer more from the withdrawal of food subsidies and the lower availability of food for such households.

Household consumption patterns are the most quickly amenable and responsive to economic changes in the short run. Casual labour households with erratic employment and daily earnings would testify to the frequency of such changes in their diet. Consumption patterns of poor rural households also undergo changes, as numerous studies have indicated. As the forces of marketisation begin to penetrate peasant agriculture, forced commercialisation often involves putting up more on the market and drawing down the balances for domestic consumption. Shifts in the cropping pattern have often involved a shift from coarse grains used predominantly for domestic consumption to finer cereals produced for the market, or a shift from a food crop to a non-food commercial crop. In all these cases, the amount available for domestic consumption gets drastically reduced. In the case of dairying, production for urban centred markets through the cooperative network has also reduced the availability of milk for domestic consumption in the poorer household, even if the dairy cattle were obtained through credit schemes of poverty alleviation programmes. The range of commodities now available on the market forces poorer households to obtain more and more cash incomes, and thus the tendency to encash everything leaving little or nothing for self-consumption. Coupled with inflationary tendencies, the problem gets compounded. In all situations of reduced food availability in poor households, women are adversely affected.

Household survival strategies (of which women are clearly the more adept and clever managers) also undergo changes as a response to macro-processes and macro-policies affecting households on various fronts. The combination of activities in a vector constituting a strategy are, themselves, subject to change. There are no detailed long-duration ethnographic studies of household survival that capture the variations within the vector constituting each strategy. However, it is my conjecture that as survival become more and more threatening, the activities that get substituted in the strategy vector are those that call for greater ingenuity, sacrifices and burdens from the women of the household. Methodological approaches to the study of 'gender and poverty' and 'gender and famine' need to consider this aspect as well. Despite the social rigidities that bind many women in various parts of the world, women's bodies, their energies for work, their multiple roles and activities and their needs are generally perceived to be immensely more flexible than the rigid needs and requirements of men. The essentialising of woman as 'accommodating' does not indicate that the 'accommodating' nature has been constructed through a complex field of power relations within the family, reflecting in part such power relations in the society at large, and how they get construed in the survival strategies of poor households.

This is not to suggest that there are no negotiations of household relations and that there are no attempts to refashion 'selves' and to reconstitute subjectivities, for that would be denying women their agency as social actors. In Chapters 6, 8 and 9 we shall examine instances of resistance, struggle and mobilisation that indicate such agency. Without dampening the enthusiasm and optimism for social change through mobilisation and solidarity, it is also necessary to recognise that not only is the agency of individual women circumscribed by the overarching relations of power, but that such power, in fact, constitutes their 'self as well. Power relations, unleashed by the forces of the state and the market, also refashion the 'self. Even though, in the Indian context, we do not expect the 'individual', as postulated in the Western liberal tradition, to emerge (for there is enough anthropological evidence to suggest that non-Western cultural 'selves' do not approximate to the bounded and autonomous 'selves' of the Anglo-Saxon tradition), the cultural 'self' of Indians, both women and men, seen as more relational, is likely to change as well. The challenge for the feminist movement in India in the years ahead would be to reconcile and balance these conflicting forces between the emergence of competitive 'selves,' and the associated changes in societal norms of virtue and morality, with the pull of solidarity politics of the feminist movement as conceived today.

CONCLUSION

This chapter explored what we refer to as the 'analytics' of work and survival. Such an exploration does not, in any way, constitute an overall analytical work and, indeed, we are quite sceptical if such an overarching single framework is at all possible or desirable. By 'analytics' we refer to the whole range of issues that one is likely to confront and that need to be problematised in exploring gender issues relating to work and survival. This chapter has merely laid bare the issues, and the context in which they evolve. It has brought to the centre-stage the interaction of the forces unleashed by the institutions of the state and the market, and the manner in which they impact on poor households and on the lives of women. It is recognised with appropriate historical, empirical and theoretical underpinnings that, in most instances, market forces have had a negative effect on the poor. It, therefore, gives rise to the possibility that my position could be mistaken for a 'neo-populist' criticism of the market. That, indeed, would be a mistaken conclusion for the analysis both in this chapter and in some of the following ones has attempted to highlight the inevitability of generalised commodity production, of the differentiation process both quickening and sharpening, and of the processes of proletarianisation and pauperisation becoming more widespread, avoiding at once any teleological notions or linearity assumptions regarding 'development,' 'progress' or 'stages of growth'. A positive interventionist role for the state in regulating market forces to assure the survival of the very poor has been argued to be a necessity in this context. The plea has, however, been for a gender sensitivity to poverty alleviation approaches. The examination of household dynamics and gender polities in consequence to the macro-processes and macro-policies is to be seen as a methodological attempt to incorporate into the analytics the interactions between what are generally regarded as the micro and the macro levels, for-such methodological tensions regarding the appropriate units of study has often led to the not-so-fruitful compartmentalisation of social science disciplines. Feminist understandings have always tried not to trivialise or trade-off the experiences of 'everyday lives' in order to secure 'epochal' understandings.

The remainder of this book provides empirical insights and theoretical arguments for many of the issues raised in this chapter. Such a multistructural system gives rise to the segmentation of the labour market, and we have drawn some analytical insights on the implications of such segmentation for female workers. This analysis clearly indicates that all dualistic classifications of the Indian economy are quite simple and misleading, a point that was vigorously argued earlier. Chapter 3 examines the characteristics and trends of the urban labour force in India using different rounds of employment and unemployment data of the National Sample Survey Organisation. Apart from indicating the size and composition of the labour force, the analysis helps to differentiate the labour force into useful empirical categories of self-employed and wage-earning, with the latter being further classified into regular wage earners and casual wage earners. These empirical categories are carried through in most of the other chapters as well. The analysis indicates both the long-term sectoral shifts as well as shifts in the status of the labour force, and examines the employment—unemployment nexus. All these are done keeping in view the specificity of the female labour force as well as the regional differences in their characteristics. Above all, it brings into sharp focus the fact that empirical categories, even though they may be very useful in describing and analysing the reality around us, often tend to obfuscate theoretically derived, a priori principles and features; and that one needs to differentiate between empirical categories and theoretical categories. The concluding section of this chapter can be tied up with the understandings on the multistructural system provided in Chapter 2, for it deals with the issue of the reproduction of such a 'multistructural' system. Howsoever preliminary and untheorised it may be, the analysis of the articulated 'multistructural' system suggests that it may be useful to conceive of two modes or circuits of production and circulation in the economy. One is the circuit of accumulation which is geared to the production of surplus value, and the other is the circuit geared to the production of subsistence and not oriented to the generation of surplus value.

The differentiation of the labour force in the multistructural context indicates the possibility that the Marxian notion of the 'reserve army of labour' may have secular implications as well. The specificity of the female labour force necessitated me to probe, as to what specific ways female labour satisfies the conditions for the different roles of the reserve army in a secular context. In all these chapters so far, there has been an overwhelming case for both conceptualising and analysing 'patriarchy' in conjunction with the forces of capitalism. Patriarchal ideology, as manifested in various societal practices, has to be incorporated into any analysis that seeks gender-specific explanations.

Evidence is drawn from across a range of industries and activities to explore the reasons for the demand for labour being women-specific, and suggest some ideas both on the nature of the industry, and the technology and organisation of production that may seem to account for such a demand. These ideas are pursued in far greater detail, which deals with the garment export industry in Madras city as a specific case-study. This survey-based empirical study classified production units on the basis of the nature of the labour process, and examined the implication of each for the type of labour used. It also examined the characteristics of the labour force in the industry, which was overwhelmingly female, and analysed the nature of the trade union movement in the industry. The study highlighted the practices of 'informalisation' through the processes of sub-contracting, and the dynamic elements in them that makes these practices vary according to the changing nature of the market.

Even though we have argued for a non-dualistic representation of the economy, we have quite often used the formal-informal sector division, more as a way of describing in terms that could be easily recognised, and not as categories that are necessarily analytically valid. Starting with an ethnographic profile of workers in the informal sector, emphasising their existential crises on multiple fronts occasioned by low wages, a low resource position, instability of livelihood options, and so on, we then engage in some reflections-On the nature of struggle for the women workers in that sector.

In an era of economic liberalisation clearing the way for market forces to operate in full sway, grassroots organisations are likely to be subjected to multiple pressures. Their strategies to empower poor women workers to confront both the invasive forces of the market and the state would probably need far greater determination and vigour.

NOTES

1. This section is based on Kalpagam (1986).
2. Annette Weiner's expose of Malinowski's inability to perceive women's production, exchange and wealth of the banana leaf cloth, even as he perceived and made famous the exchange among men of the Kula ring in the Trobriand Islands, is a classic example. See Weiner (1976).
3. The concept 'cultural translation' as used here, though somewhat similar to the way it is used in social anthropology, is still different. For the way it is used in social anthropology, see Asad (1986). Asad sensitises us to the problem of inequality of language in the project of cultural translation which is inevitably enmeshed in conditions of power—professional, national and international'. The encoding of knowledge through the project of governance, even if it does not seek to decipher and inscribe meaning and coherence in alien cultural discourses as the way an ethnographic enterprise does, nevertheless attempts to understand alien cultures through its own categories.
4. This section draws ideas from Deacon (1985).
5. Most books on the economic history of nineteenth century India would provide evidence on these aspects.
6. It should be emphasised that this was not the first time that wages in the Bombay textile industry were debated and contested. Wage debates have figured from the latter half of the nineteenth century. It was in response to one of these debates that the Bombay Labour Office was instituted by the government to scientifically examine, the issue of work and wages in the mills. One of the first surveys of Working Class Budgets was conducted by the office in 1922—23 to verify the conflicting views regarding workers' savings, remittances to homes in the villages and the extent of indebtedness.
7. See also Banerjee (1988).
8. For a detailed examination of this issue, see also Caplan (1985).
9. For a general understanding of the politics of consensus underlying the planning process, see Chatterjee and Sen (1988).

10. All India Democratic Women's Association, et al. (1988), Draft National Perspective Plan for Women AD 1988-2000:. A Perspective from the Women's Movement, mimeographed. New Delhi.
11. Koopmans, in fact, recognises the problems of survival of consumers in a competitive equilibrium at the analytical level. He notes that the most difficult problem in the specification of the Arrow-Debreu model is to make sure that each consumer can both survive and participate in the market, without anticipating in the postulates what specific prices will prevail in an equilibrium. He notes that 'most authors have ignored the analytical difficulty of a model that ensures the possibility of survival, blithely admitting any nonnegative rates of consumption as sustainable.' Further, while a stationary state interpretation Of the Arrow-Debreu model is useful in some instances, it does not admit of exchange in society, and Koopmans recognises that, in modern society, exchange is necessary for survival. He suggests several alternative directions for the 'survival problem' in the stationary state approach and he makes it clear that it will serve 'different purposes'. The three alternatives he proposes are interesting for their ideological implications. He notes:

    One 'hard-boiled' alternative would be to assume instantaneous elimination by starvation of those whose resources prove insufficient for survival, and to look for conditions ensuring the existence of an 'equilibrium' involving the survival of some consumers. An alternative *more realistic* for highly industrialised private enterprise societies would be to recognise the existence of income transfers through taxation and social insurance, and to look for conditions, including tax and benefit schedules, ensuring general survival in an equilibrium. Finally, either as a further alternative or in addition to the foregoing, one might find it possible to specify lower limits on the productivity of the various types of labour, expressed in terms of quantities of commodities rather than values, and to specify upper limits on quantitatively defined minima for subsistence, so as to ensure the possibility of survival of all consumers through the sale of their labor whenever other resources are insufficient (Koopmans. 1957).

    Let us grant that the Arrow-Debreu model is an entirely analytical exercise, and that outcomes under different assumptions are purely postulational in nature, and that postulational thinking does not aim at a realistic representation; the question then arises as to why Koopmans, in spelling out the three alternatives, shifts to a seemingly 'realistic' one in the second alternative. Are we then to surmise that, even if unstated, the other two alternatives (the first one being clearly the more outrageous) are 'realistic' for non-highly industrialised countries, by which is most certainly implied the developing countries'? Or, if those alternatives arc posed as unrealistic and left unstated, why shift to a realistic one when referring to the developed countries? Blinded by analytical rigour, one often fails to make visible the ideological underpinnings of these dominant discourses.

    For a better understanding of this issue of survival', see Koopmans (1957).
12. See, for instance, Krishnaraj (1992).
13. Sec Chapter 9, in this work, for such put-out organisations of work in diverse home-based occupations and the associated problems that women experience.
14. See the classic work by Wolf (1982).
15. See, for instance, Etienne and Leacock (1980), Meillassoux (1981) and Coquery-Vidrovitch (1975).
16. See the trendsetting work by Frobel, Heinrichs and Kreye (1980). Also see Mandel (1975).
17. Those interested may read Moore (1988).
18. For a sociological analysis of households see Shah (1973), Gray and Mearns (1989), and Saradamoni (1992).
19. Also see Standing (1991).
20. See Chapter 3 of this book for further details on these two circuits.
21. Also see Greer (1984).

9

Past Trends and Future Prospects for Women

Asia and Oceania is a region of many cultures and strategies for development which are reflected in the rich diversity of the lives of women. Asia is best understood as a region of subregions rather than as a simple entity. Fifty-five per cent of the world's population live in Asia (excluding Japan and including developing countries of Oceania): 13 per cent in East Asia (excluding Japan), 22 per cent in middle South Asia and the remaining 10 per cent in the combined subregions of eastern South Asia (and developing countries of Oceania) and western South Asia (excluding non-Arab countries). The reliability of data for female activity in Asia varies. "In Asian countries with large Muslim populations...women's agricultural contribution remains largely invisible... 'Invisible crop activities'...occupy almost as much of their time as 'visible ones'" (United Nations, 1986b, pp. 39-40).

In many countries of middle and western South Asia, which includes the Middle East or Arab countries, much of the work women do is "invisible" and, therefore, not reflected in statistics from government sources which provide the basis for these data. For these countries, the level of female economic activity is higher than the data indicate. Since governments are generally consistent over time in the degree to which they evaluate the work women do, these data provide for an assessment of trends in female participation—which is the central focus of this analysis. They demonstrate stagnation in eastern South Asia and Oceania, declines in middle South Asia, and increase in East Asia and Western South Asia.

Economic Activity, 1950-2000

Eastern South Asia and Oceania (Developing Countries)

Eighty-six million females or 33 per cent of the female population are projected to be economically active in the year 2000. Eighty-two million are women between the ages of 15 and 64. The remaining 4 million comprise the active population outside this age range, predominantly girls below the age of 15. This 82 million figure represents 49 per cent of women between the ages of 15 and 64 in eastern South Asia and Oceania. In 1950, 33 per cent of the female population and 52 per cent of women between the ages of 15 and 64 were estimated to be economically active. Over the next 25 years, these rates declined to 31 and 51 per cent respectively. During the Decade for Women, the crude activity rate increased slightly whereas the refined rate remained at 51 per cent, representing stagnation in the advancement of women during this period. Alternative I shows for the year 2000 a slight increase of the crude activity rates from the level reached in 1985 and a further decline in the refined activity rate, i.e. 49 per cent of the women aged 15-64 years.

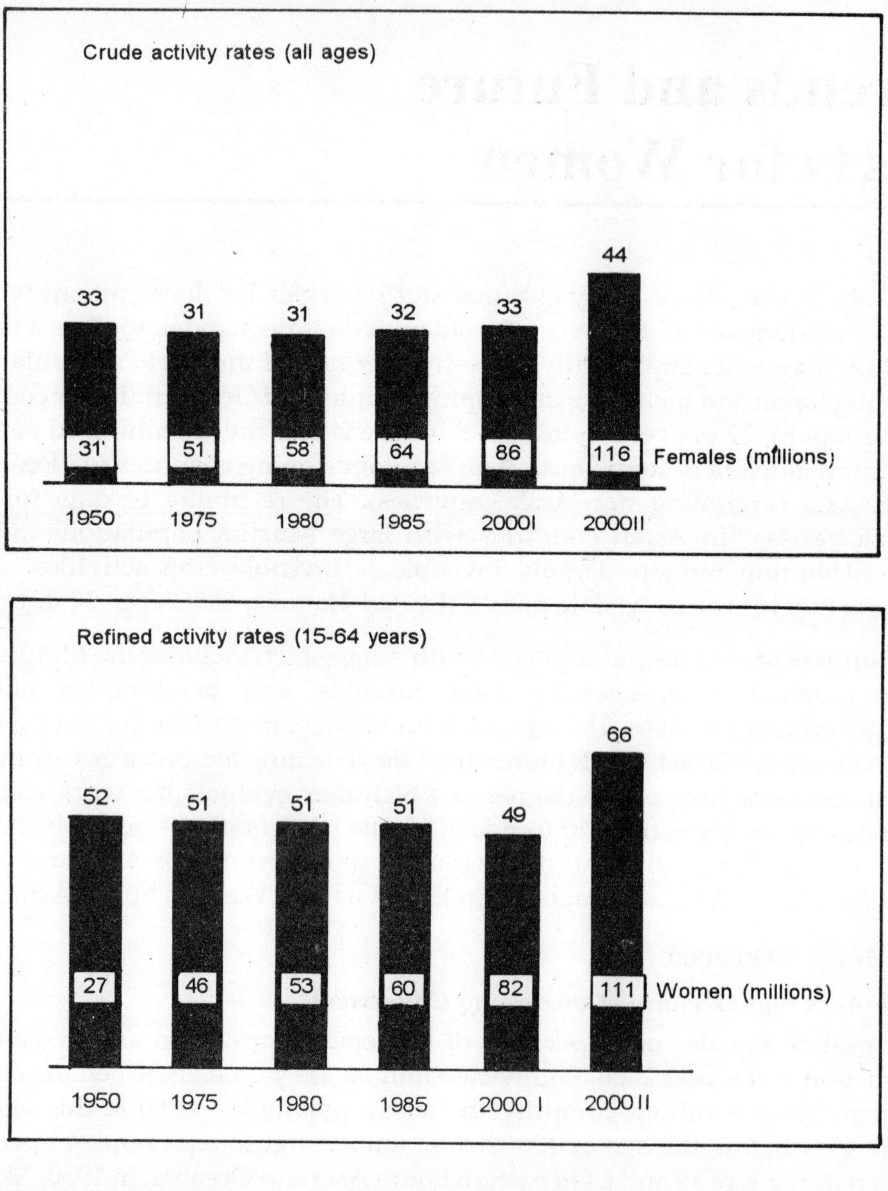

Source : As for chart 1.

Chart 9.1. Crude and refined female economic activity rates for eastern South Asia and Oceania (developing countries), 1950-2000 (in percentages)

In 1950, the women of this region represented 36 per cent of the total economically active population (see chart 9.2). During the next 25 years, they secured 41 per cent of the growth in economic activity. The result was an increase in the female share of the economically active population from 36 to 38 per cent. During the Decade, women benefited insufficiently from the growth to increase their share in the economically active population. Despite their 38 per cent share in 1985, they are projected to benefit from only 33 per cent of the growth during the next 15 years. The result is a projected decline in the female share of the economically active population from 38 to 36 per cent during the next 15 years. This decline assumes the annual creation of 4.3 million opportunities during the 1985-2000 period. Since only 2 million opportunities were created annually in eastern South Asia and Oceania during the 25 years preceding the United Nations Decade for Women, this projected decline represents a doubling of annual efforts to create gainful activities.

Almost a tripling of efforts is necessary if women and men are to have equal access to economic activity in 2025, as suggested by Alternative II projections. To meet this goal, 6.3 million opportunities need to be created annually, of which 54 per cent or 3.4 million should be made available to women. These intensive efforts would result in an increase in the female share of the economically active population from 38 per cent in 1985 to 43 per cent in the year 2000, resulting in 66 per cent or 111 million women being economically active (see chart 9.1).

Middle South Asia

According to Alternative I, 112 million females or 17 per cent of the female population are projected to be economically active in the year 2000 (see chart 9.3). Of these, 105 million will be women between the ages of 15 and 64. These active women comprise one-quarter of the female working-age population. The remaining 7 million will be predominantly girls below the age of 15 years.

In 1950, 58 million females were estimated to be economically active, representing one-quarter of the female population. Fifty million of these were women between the ages of 15 and 64. During the 25 years preceding the United Nations Decade for Women (1976-85), the proportion of economically active women declined from 38 to 31 per cent (see refined activity rates in chart 9.3). During the first half of the Decade their participation declined to 29 per cent and during the second half to 28 per cent. It is the continuation of this trend which accounts for the continued decline to 25 per cent during the next 15 years.

In 1950, women made up 28 per cent of the total economically active population (see chart 17). During the next 25 years, females secured only 19 per cent of the increase in economically active population, and therefore their share in the total declined to 25 per cent. A further decline of the share to 23 per cent was registered at the end of the Decade for Women. Alternative I assumes a continuation of this trend, and therefore the share of females will drop to 22 per cent at the end of the century.

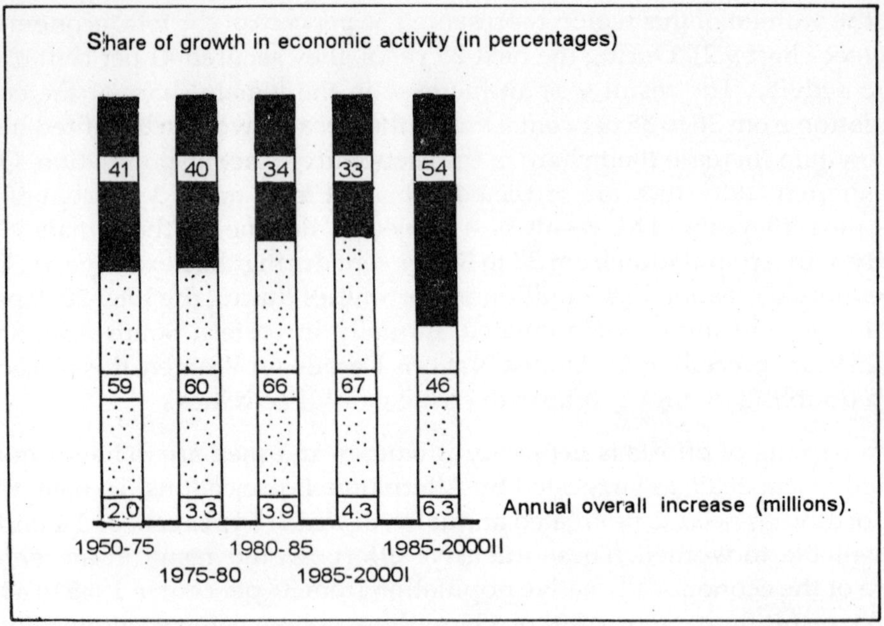

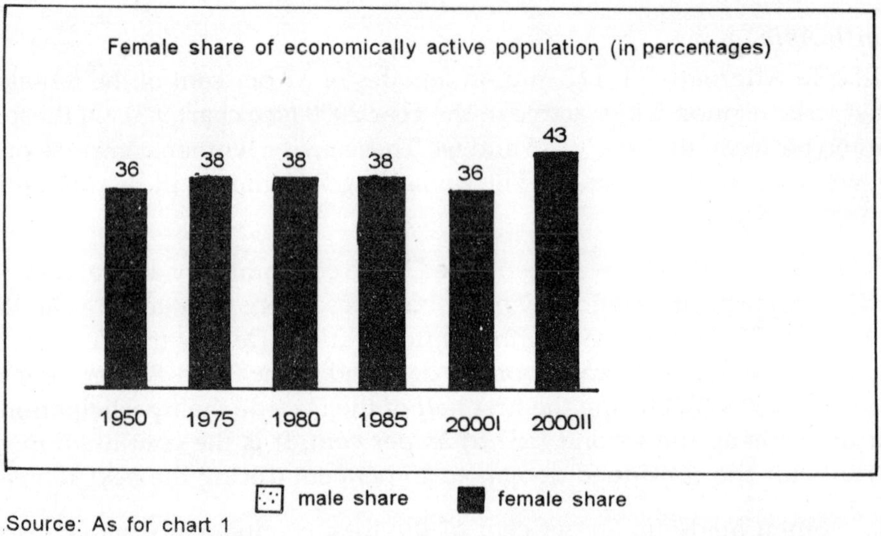

Source: As for chart 1

Chart 9.2. Female and male shares of growth in economic activity; and female share of total economically active population for eastern south Asia and Oceania (developing countries), 1950-2000

Intensified efforts are essential to reverse this downward spiral. A doubling of efforts to create economic opportunities during the next 15 years must be combined with a commitment to create opportunities for gainful activity for the women of middle South Asia. A departure from past trends embodied in Alternative II projections necessitates the annual creation of

17.4 rather than 9.3 million economic opportunities, along with a commitment to allocate 56 per cent of this growth to women. The result of these efforts would increase the female share to 36 per cent by the year 2000.

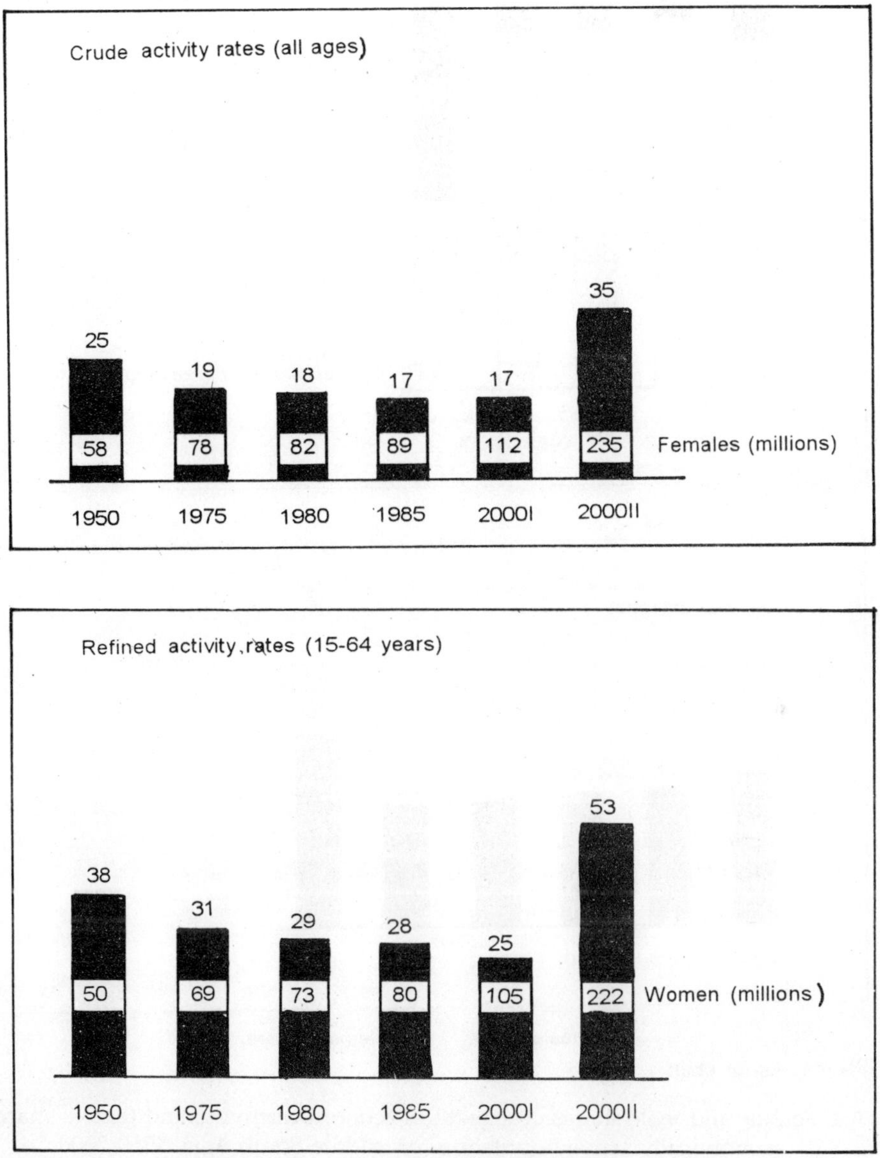

Source : As for chart 1.

Chart 9.3. Crude and refined female economic activity rates for middle South Asia, 1950-2000 (in percentages)

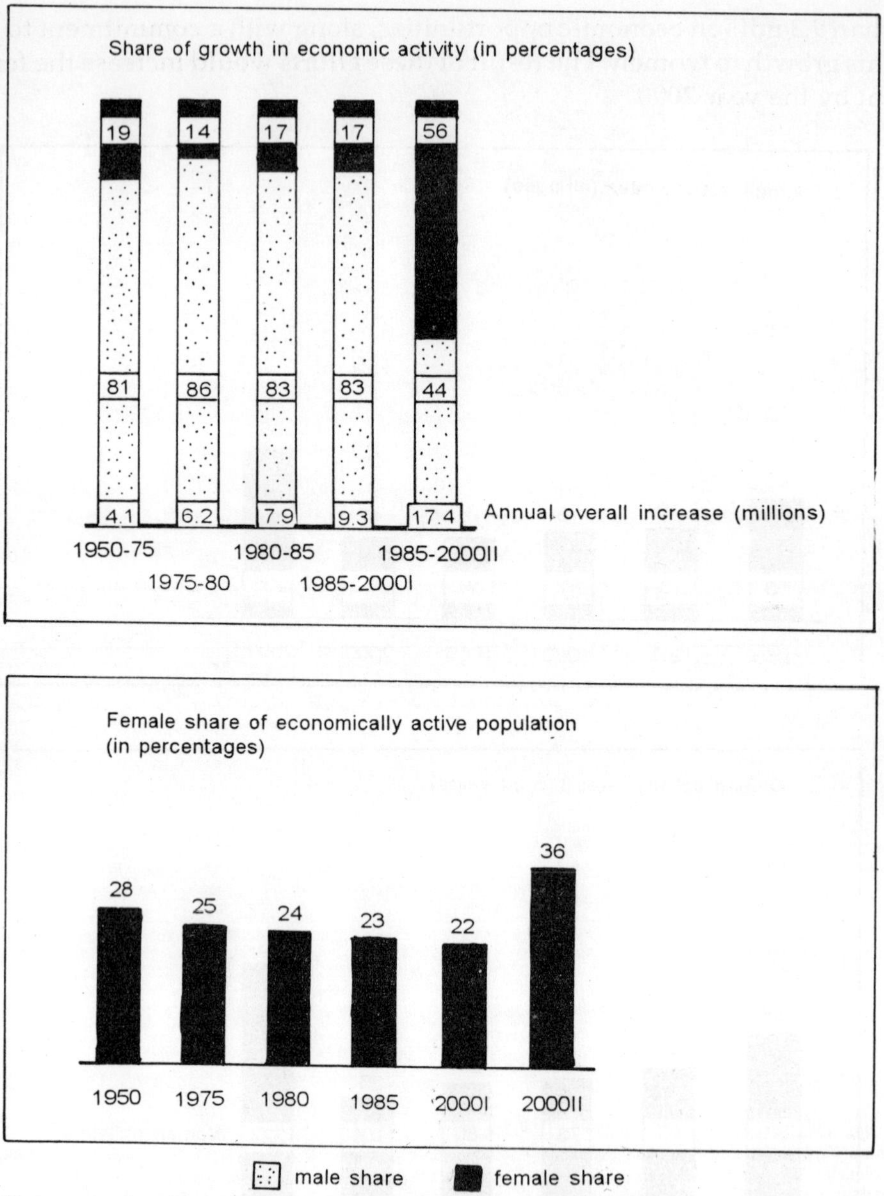

Source: As for chart 1.

Chart 9.4. Female and male shares of growth in economic activity; and female share of total economically active population for middle South Asia, 1950-2000

Western South Asia

About 1 per cent of the world's population lives in western South Asia. A major share of the female population in this region is classified as economically inactive, a fact which is the subject of criticism (United Nations, 1986b, p. 32). Data from national sources provide the basis for the estimates and projections which are available for our analysis. Alternative I projections for the year 2000 estimate that 4.9 million females, or 11 per cent of the female population, will be economically active. Most of them will be women between the ages of 15 and 64, 19 per cent of whom are projected to be economically active (see chart 9.5 for these crude and refined activity rates). This participation represents a small but steady and increasing trend in female economic activity. In 1950, 5 per cent of all women were economically active. By 1975 their participation had increased to 11 per cent and by the end of the United Nations Decade for Women it had increased to 15 per cent. If present trends continue, 19 per cent of women and 11 per cent of all females are projected to be economically active in 2000.

In 1950, women made up 6 per cent of the economically active population (chart 9.6). During the next 25-year period women secured an even greater share of the growth in economic activity—17 per cent. As a consequence, the female share of the economically active population increased to 11 per cent. This trend held during the United Nations Decade, the result of which was an increase to 14 per cent. If this slow but steady increase continues to 2000, women will benefit from 23 per cent of the growth in new opportunities, the result of which will be an increase in the female share of the economically active population to 18 per cent in 2000.

Extensive efforts in western South Asia are essential if women in this region are to have the resources necessary for economic independence and self-reliance. Alternative II projections suggest the necessity of a doubling of current efforts (see chart 9.6). In particular, in order for women and men to have an equal opportunity for economic activity by 2025, 1.2 million economic opportunities need to be created annually, 50 per cent of which should be made available to women. These efforts require the active participation of 10.5 million women or 43 per cent of the female population between the ages of 15 and 64 years.

East Asia (Developing Countries)

According to Alternative I, over 347 million females are projected to be economically active in the year 2000 in East Asia (excluding Japan), a figure which represents 53 per cent of the female population and over three-quarters of working-age women (see chart 9.7). These figures reflect a trend of increasing economic activity based on an initial high level of participation in 1950, when 46 per cent of all females, or 130 million, were economically active. The proportion of the total female population which was economically active had declined to 45 per cent by 1975. This decline was a result of an increase in the dependent or non-active part of the female population, particularly among the young. In fact, during the same period, the participation of women aged 15-64 increased from 68 to 72 per cent. An increase of both crude and refined activity rates has been reported during the United Nations Decade for Women.

In 1950, women made up 39 per cent of the economically active population. During the 1950-75 period, they benefited from a greater share of the growth in economic activity (48 per cent), which produced an increase in the female share of the economically active population to 42 per cent (see chart 9.8). The female share increased to 43 per cent during the first half of the Decade, but stagnated during the second half when women registered equivalent share of growth—43 per cent; and this share is likely to remain stable until the year 2000.

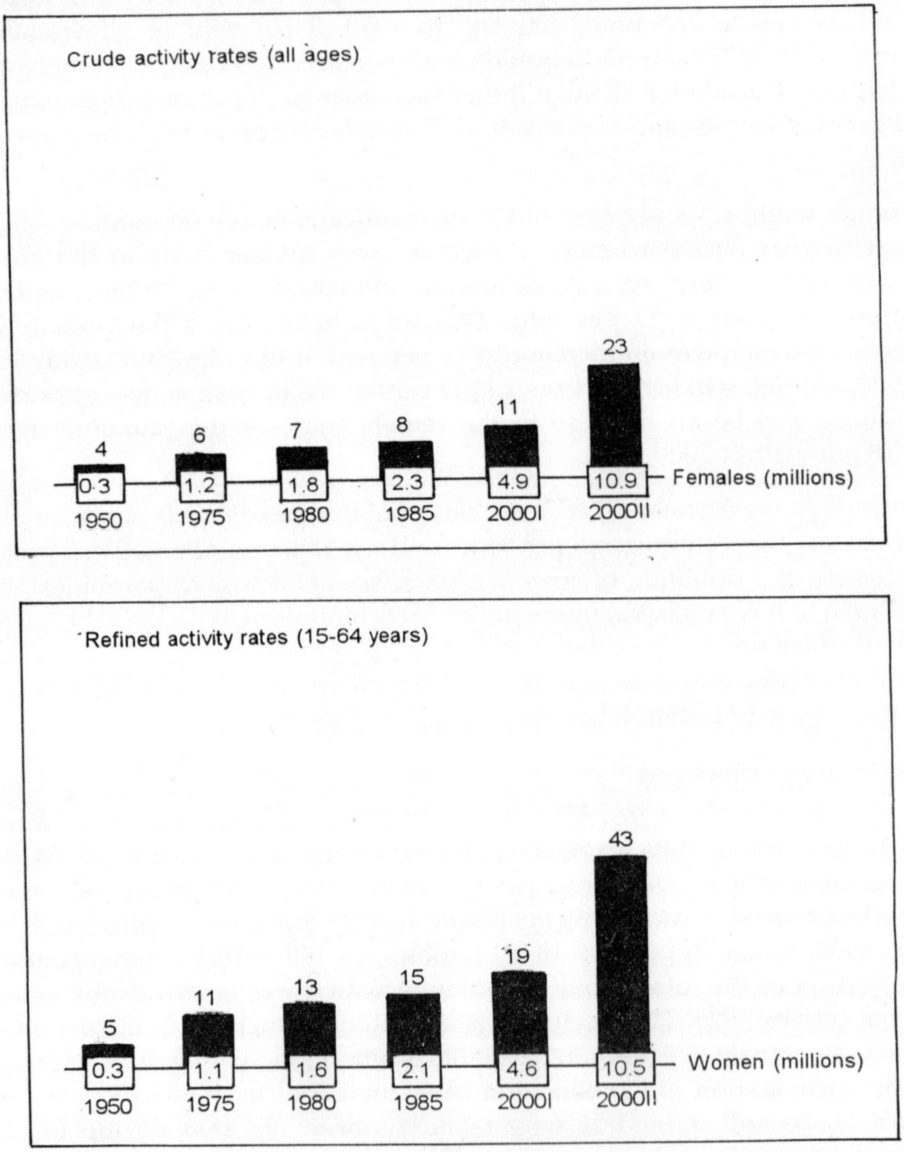

Source: As for chart 1.

Chart 9.5. Crude and refined female economic activity rates for western South Asia (excluding non-Arab countries), 1950-2000 (in percentages)

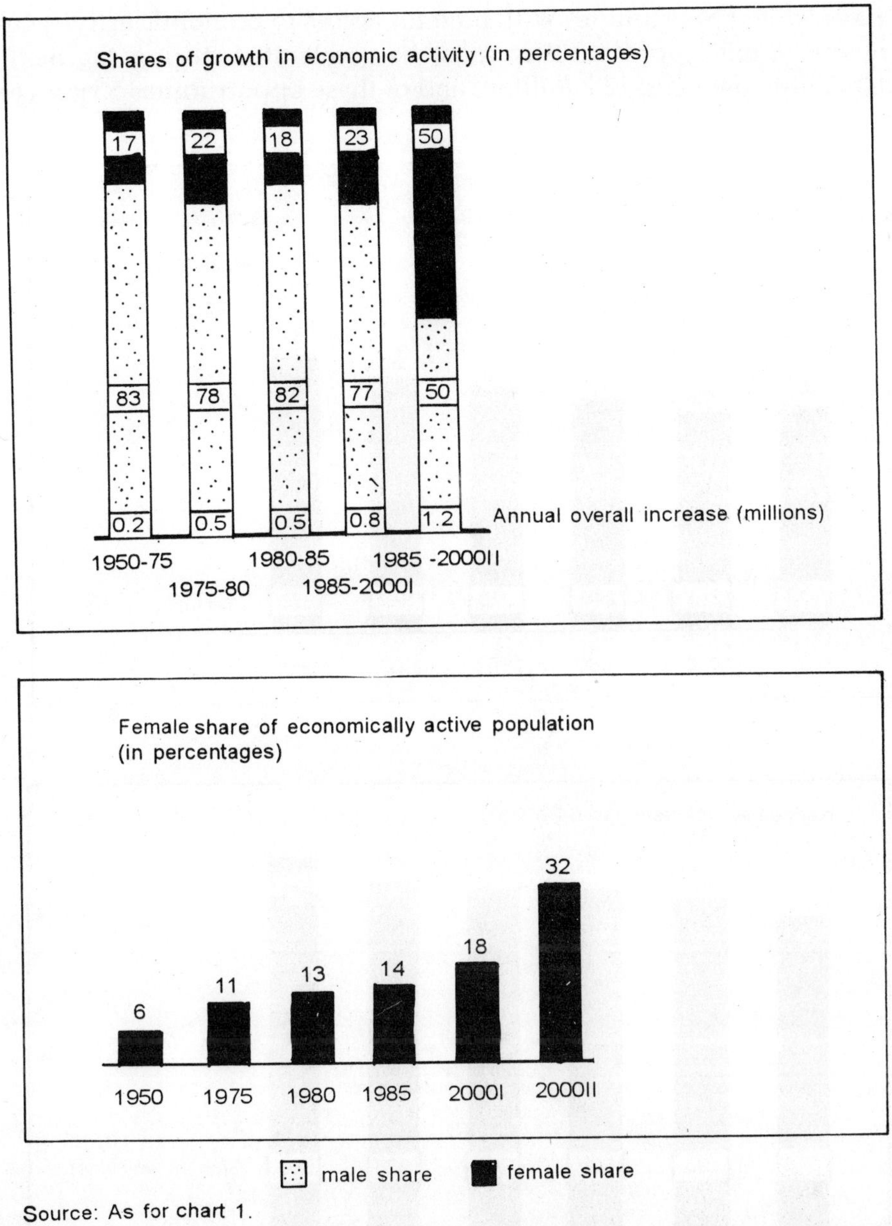

Source: As for chart 1.

Chart 9.6. Female and male shares of growth in economic activity, and female share of total economically active population for western South Asia (excluding non-Arab countries), 1950-2000

Alternative II projections produce a 45 per cent female share of the economically active population. This set of projections suggests the possibility of nearly 375 million economically active females in East Asia by the year 2000, a figure representing 57 per cent of the total female population (see chart 9.7). For Alternative II to become a reality, and for women in

East Asia to have equal opportunities with men for access to economic activity by 2025, the creation of new economic opportunities must be accelerated during the next 15 years. Instead of 10.3 million per year, 12.2 million, and of these opportunities 53 per cent, should be for women.

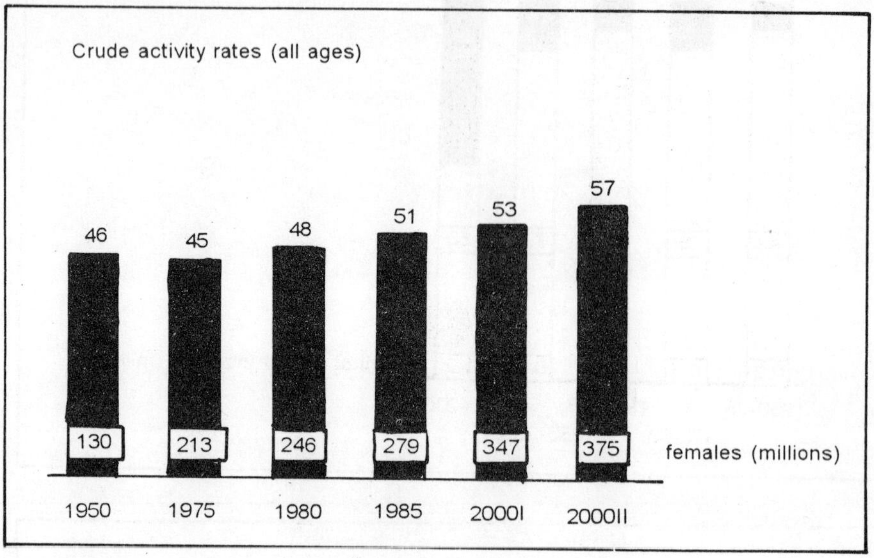

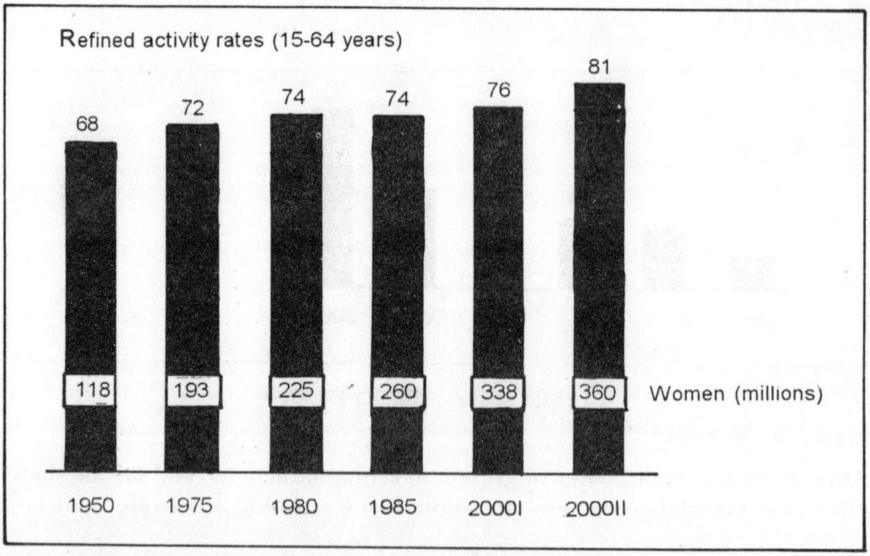

Source: As for chart 1.

Chart 9.7. Crude and refined female economic activity rates for East Asia (developing countries), 1950-2000 (in percentages)

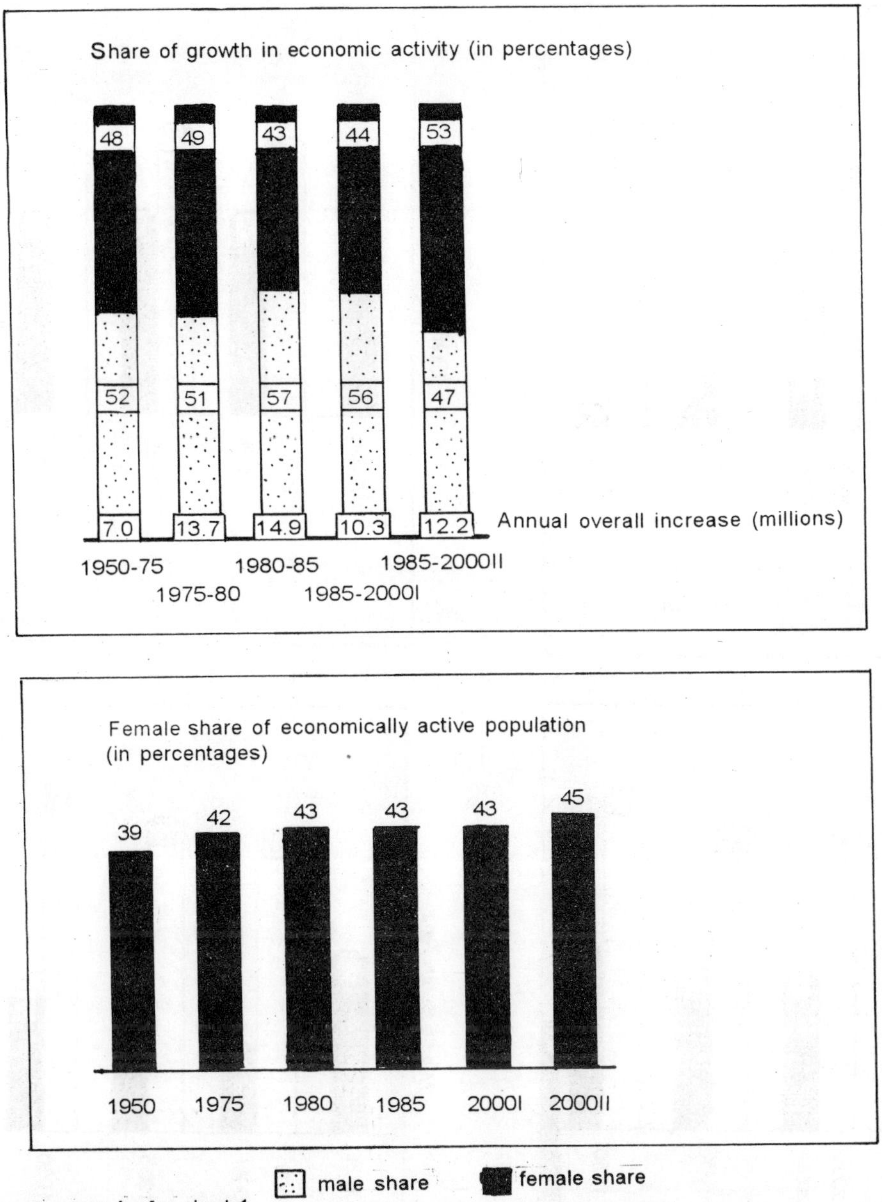

Source: As for chart 1

Chart 9.8. Female and male shares of growth in economic activity; and female share of total economically active population for East Asia (developing countries), 1950-2000

C. Gross Years of Working Life, 1950-2000

The information presented in chart 9.9 highlights the consequences of these varying levels and trends in economic activity in terms of increases and declines in the number of years women can expect to be economically active during the 1950-2000 period. The data

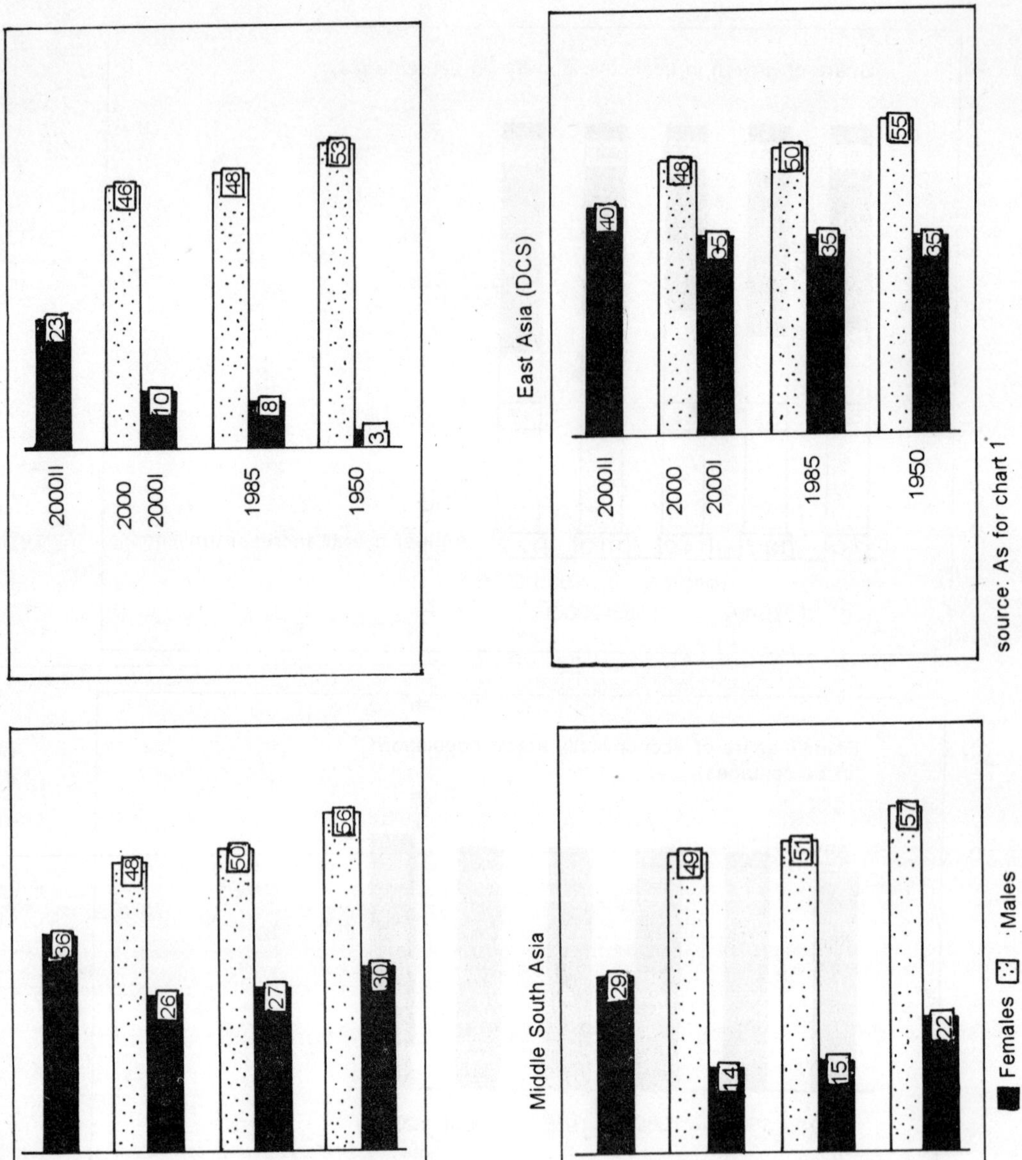

Chart 9.9. Gross years of working life for females and males in subregions of Asia, 1950-2000

also illustrate variations in gross years of working life for males and females, which reflect variations at the regional level and trends in male and female economic activity. As the figures for male working life show, there is comparatively little variation among the regions in the economic activity of the male population. Men have high levels of economic activity which are reflected in gross years of working the ranging from 53 to 57 years in 1950 to 48 to 51 years in 1985, and projections of 46 to 49 years for the year 2000. The trends in all regions are characterised by declines resulting from a variety of changes in the economic lives of men, in particular longer education, earlier retirement and increased coverage of workers in pension schemes. Patterns of working life for the female population vary uniformly with changes in economic activity during the 1950-2000 period. Declines are projected for middle south and eastern South Asia. Along with stability for Eastern Asia and Oceania and increases for western South Asia.

If present trends continue to 2000, the gross years of working life of women in eastern South Asia and Oceania will decline from 30 years in 1950 to 27 years in 1985 and to 26 years in 2000. In middle South Asia it will also continue its downward trend from 22 years in 1950 to 15 years in 1985 and to 14 years in 2000. In western South Asia it will increase, while in East Asia it will remain stable. Women were active for an average of three years in western South Asia in 1950 and for an average of eight years in 1985. In 2000, they are projected to be active for ten years. The corresponding figures for East Asia are 35, 35 and 35 years.

If greater efforts are to be made to advance women towards economic independence and self-reliance by providing them with the increased opportunities suggested by the Alternative II projections, some of these trends would be accelerated while others would be reversed. Instead of being economically active for 26 years, women in eastern and South Asia and Oceania could expect to be active for 36 years. Women in middle South Asia would experience an increase in economically active life from 14 to 29 years. Correspondingly, women in western South Asia would increase their economically active life from ten to 23 years. In East Asia, women could expect to be economically active for 40 years. In all regions, Alternative II projections provide the basis for growing similarity in the gross years of working life of men and women which would reflect an increasing trend towards equalising the opportunities between women and men for economic activity.

D. Economic Activity by Major Sector, 1950-2000

Eastern South Asia and Oceania (Developing Countries)

Projections for the beginning of the twenty-first century show that the majority of economically active males as well as females will be in the non-agricultural sectors of eastern South Asia: 53 per cent and 58 per cent, respectively. The information in chart 23 highlights the trends which explain these projections. In 1950, 79 per cent of women and 78 per cent of men were engaged in agriculture. The proportions in industry and services were 6 per cent and 15 per cent for females and 6 per cent and 16 per cent for males. During the 30 years between 1950 and 1980, both women and men moved out of agriculture into the non-agricultural sectors. Between 1950 and 1980, the proportion of females in agriculture

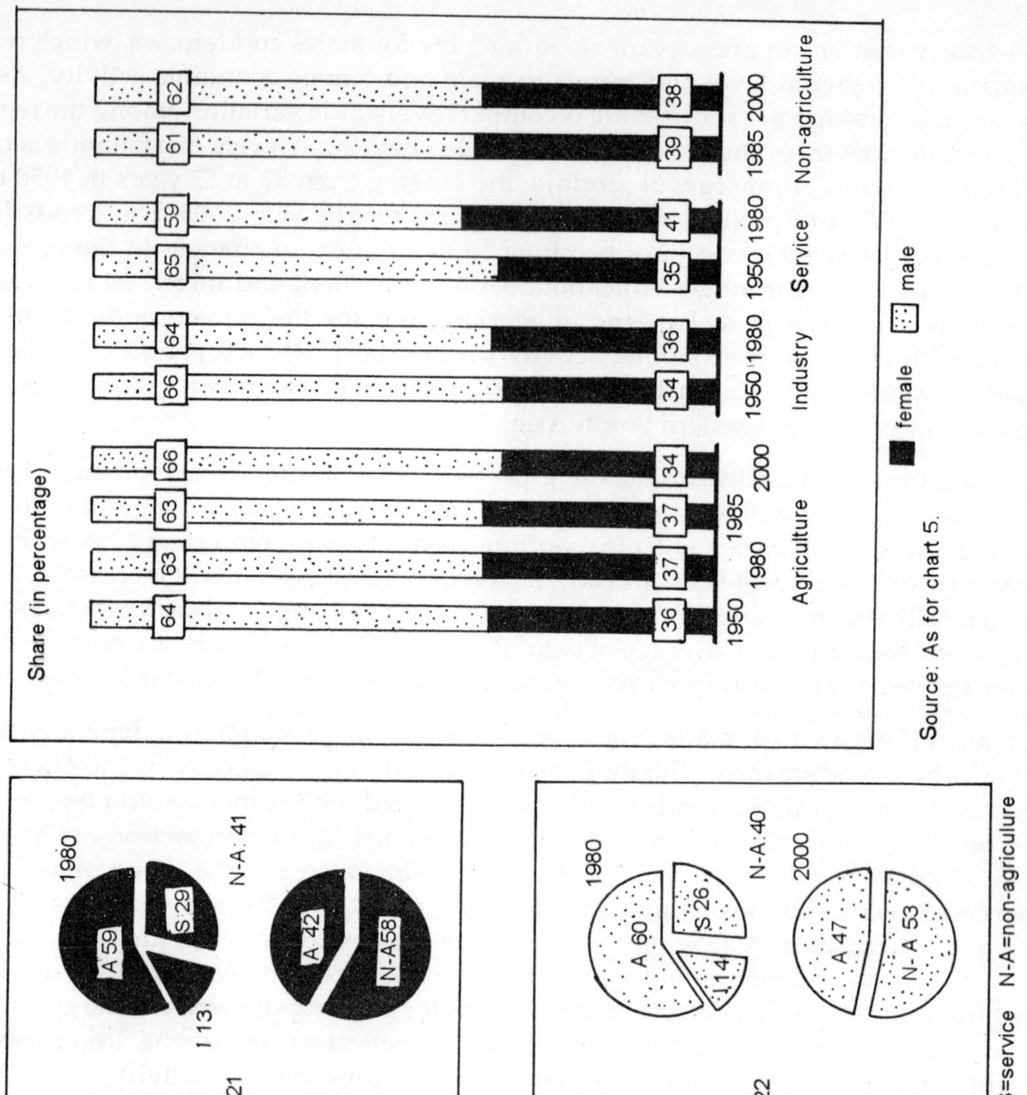

Chart 9.10. Distribution of economically active females and males among major sectors; and female and male shares of major sectors for eastern South Asia and Oceania (developing countries), 1950-2000

declined to 59 per cent. For males, it declined to 60 per cent. During the same period, the proportion of all economically active females in industry increased from 6 to 13 per cent, while that of males increased from 6 to 14 per cent. The female proportion in services increased from 15 to 29 per cent and the male concentration increased from 16 to 26 per cent.

Females and male shares make it possible to explore the female-male position in each sector. The chart shows that women make up approximately one-third of all sectors. The female share in agriculture is projected to decline slightly from 36 to 34 per cent during the second half or the twentieth century. During the 30 years between 1950 and 1980, the female share increased in both the industrial and services sectors. Projections for the year 2000, however, show a moderate decline from 39 to 38 per cent for the female share of the non-agricultural sectors. These data show that opportunities for activities for women need to be expanded in the three sectors, namely agriculture, industry and services, in conformity with Alternative II projections.

Middle South Asia

In 1950 (see chart 9.11), 89 per cent of all females were in the agricultural sector. This figure had declined to 77 per cent by 1980 and to 74 per cent by 1985 and is projected to decline to 64 per cent by the year 2000. The proportions of males in agriculture were the following: 74 per cent in 1950, 65 per cent in 1980, 64 per cent in 1985 and 59 per cent in 2000. Clearly, women are currently more concentrated in the agricultural sector than are men in middle South Asia. Male-female differences are also apparent for the non-agricultural sectors. First, more of the economically active males than economically active females are estimated to be in these sectors, e.g. 35 as compared to 23 per cent in 1980. Men, however, tend to be more concentrated in services while women are more evenly distributed between industry and services: of the economically active women in 1980, 11 per cent were in industry and 12 per cent were in services. Twenty-one per cent of economically active males were in services as compared with 14 per cent in industry.

The male and female shares take into account the number of economically active males and females in each sector. The female share of agriculture is projected to be 23 per cent at the end of the twentieth century. This figure is the result of a steady decline in the female share dating to 1950 when it was 31 per cent. During the same 50-year period, the male share is projected to increase from 69 to 77 per cent.

The female share of the non-agricultural sector is projected to increase from 18 per cent in 1975 to 19 per cent in 2000. Increases are estimated for the 30 years between 1950 and 1980 for the female share of both industry and services: it increased from 15 to 20 per cent in industry and from 13 to 15 per cent in services. Even so, in 1980 the male shares were 80 and 85 per cent, respectively.

These data suggest the importance of expanding economic opportunities for women in all sectors of the economy in middle South Asia. Since the male share of each sector is approximately 80 per cent, intensified efforts are essential to expand opportunities for women in all sectors, and in particular in the non-agricultural sectors.

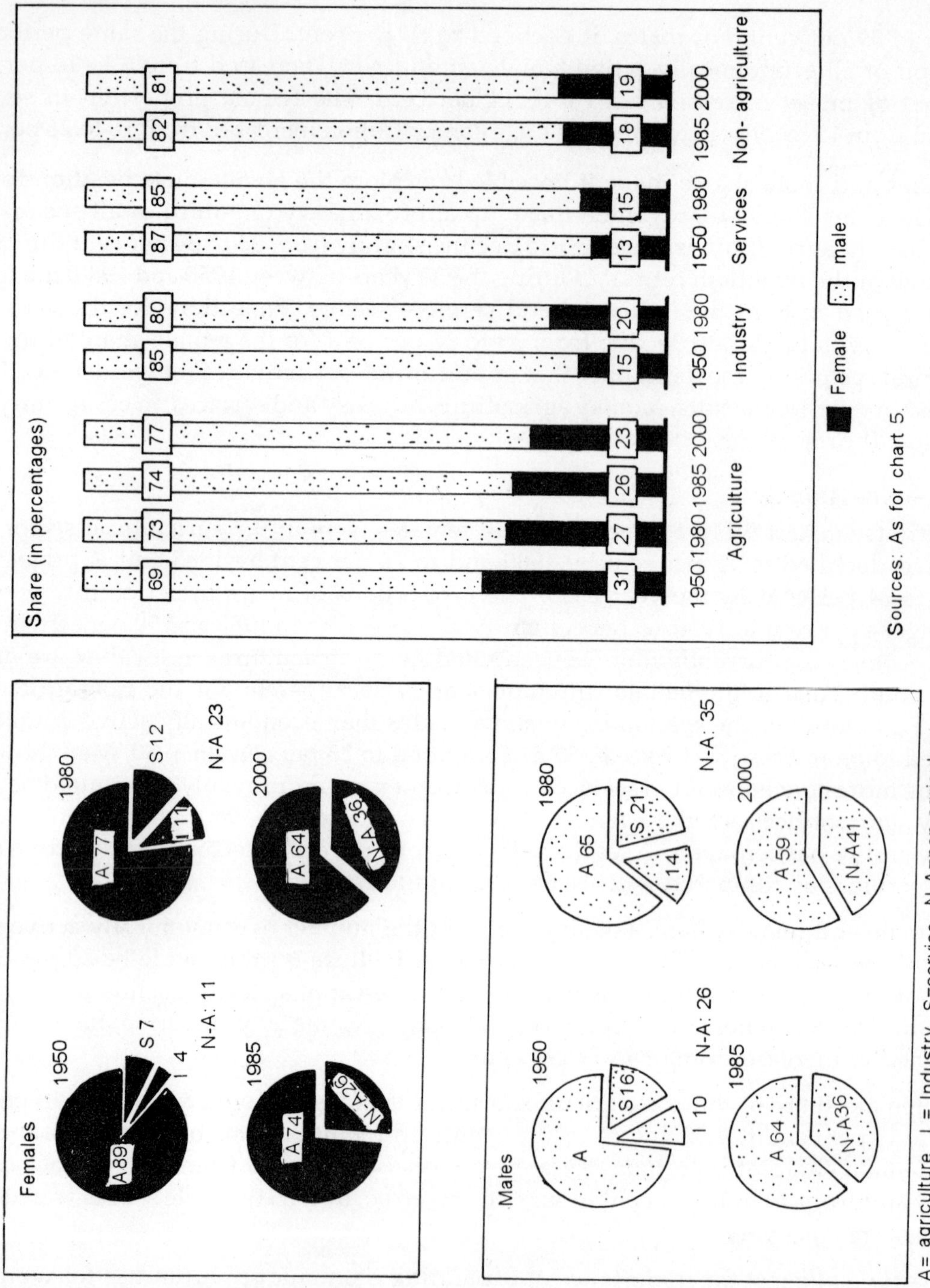

Chart 9.11. Distribution of economically active females and males among major sectors; and female and male shares of major sectors for middle South Asia, 1950-2000

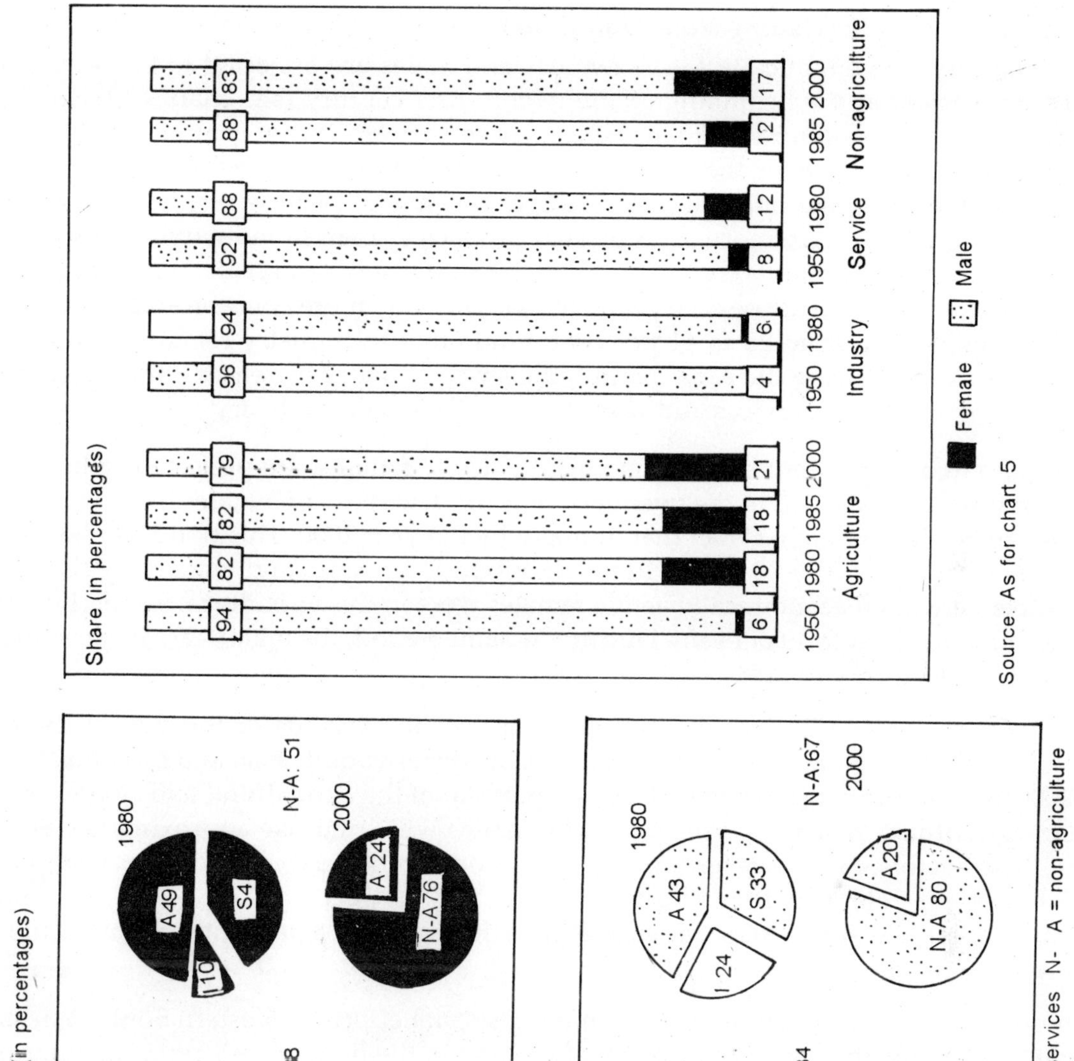

Chart 9.12. Distribution of economically active females and males among major sectors; and female and male shares of major sectors for western South Asia (excluding (non-Arab countries), 1950-2000

Western South Asia (Excluding Non-Arab Countries)

The majority of economically active females and males are projected to be in the non-agricultural sectors at the beginning of the twenty-first century (see chart 9.12). In 1950, women were more concentrated than men in these sectors: 38 per cent and 34 per cent respectively. By 1980, however, the situation had reversed. Now men were more concentrated than women in the non-agricultural sectors: 67 per cent and 51 per cent respectively. In 1950 both women and men were more concentrated in services than in industry: 28 per cent of economically active females were estimated to be in the services sector, while 9 per cent were in industry. During the next 30 years, females became more concentrated in services, their share increasing from 28 to 41 per cent, while that in industry remained about the same—10 per cent. During the same period, the share of males increased for both sectors, from 20 to 33 per cent in services and from 14 to 24 per cent in industry.

An estimated 24 per cent of all economically active females are projected to be in the agricultural sector at the end of the twentieth century. The share of females in agriculture is projected to be slightly higher than that of males by the year 2000. This trend can be traced to changes during the 1950-80 period in the distribution of males and females by sector. In 1950, 62 per cent of all economically active females were in the agricultural sector. By 1980, the share had declined to 49 per cent. During the same period, the male share in agriculture declined from 66 to 43 per cent.

An examination of the female and male shares of the various sectors reflect the low levels of economic activity recorded for females in western South Asia and Oceania. In the year 2000, women are projected to make up 21 per cent of the agricultural and 17 per cent of the non-agricultural sectors. Correspondingly, males will comprise approximately 80 per cent of these sectors. Estimates for the 1950-80 period for the services and industrial sector suggest an even greater female-male differential. In 1980, 94 per cent of the active population in industry were male and 6 per cent were female. In services, 88 per cent were male and 12 per cent were female.

These data suggest the importance of making special efforts in western South Asia and Oceania to examine the current real work of women in the light of new recommendations for economic activity, particularly those changes which expand the inclusion of unpaid family workers as economically active. Intensive efforts are also necessary to create opportunities for gainful activities in all sectors of the economy. Since between 80 and 90 per cent of those active in agriculture, industry and services are male, efforts need to be accelerated to create opportunities for women in all sectors of the economy.

East Asia (Developing Countries)

In the year 2000, the majority of economically active females and males are projected to be in the agricultural sector of the economic of East Asia (see chart 9.13). This projection in based on trends dating to 1950, when 91 per cent of all females and 85 per cent of males were in the agricultural sector. By 1980, these concentrations had been reduced to 77 and 69 per cent, respectively. During the same period, the female share in the non-agricultural sector

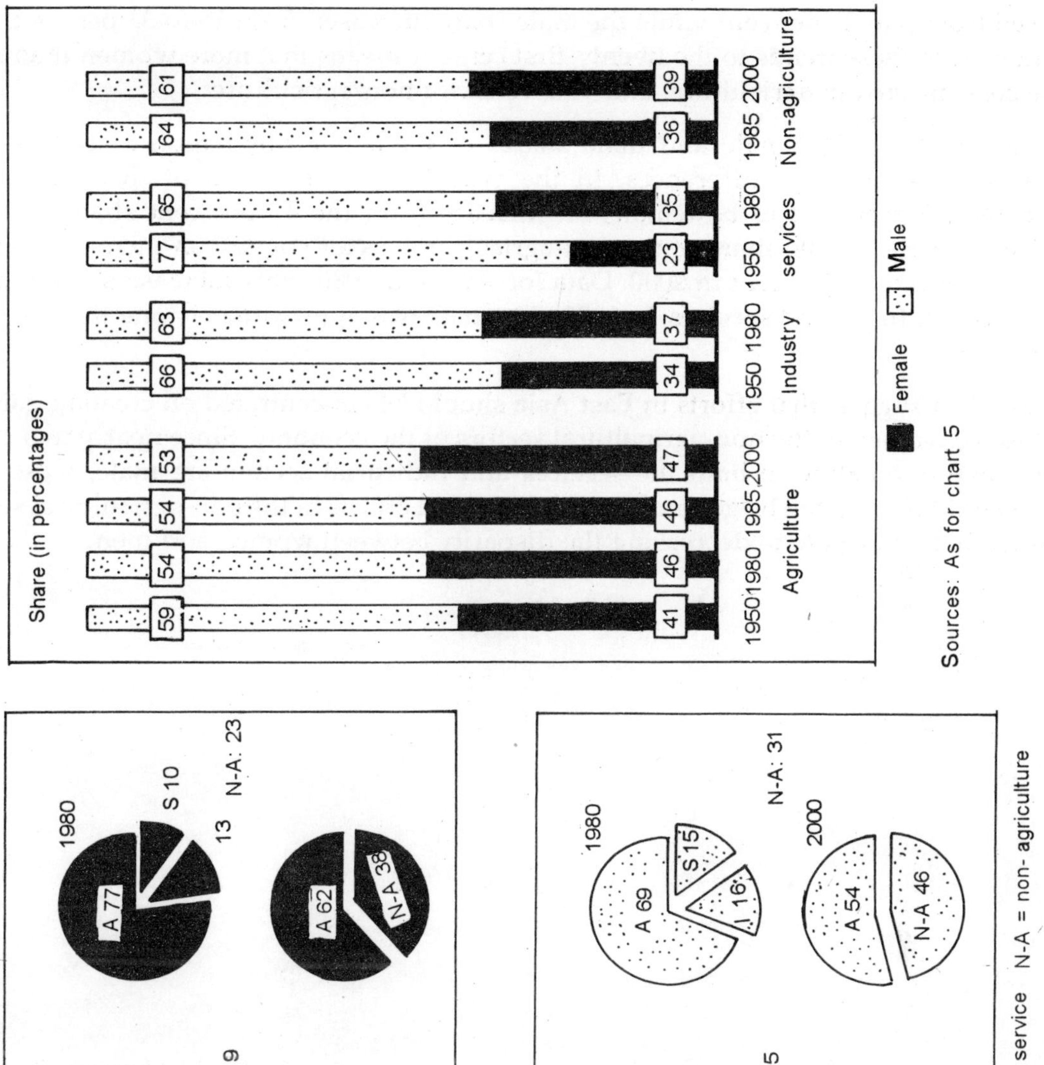

Chart 9.13. Distribution of economically active females and males among major sectors; and female and male shares of major sectors for East Asia (developing countries), 1950-2000

increased from 9 to 23 per cent while the male share increased from 15 to 31 per cent. The continuation of these trends to the twenty-first century means that more women than men will be concentrated in agriculture, and vice versa for non-agriculture.

An examination of female and male shares of the active population in each sector highlights some of these differences. In the year 2000, 47 per cent of those active in agriculture are projected to be female, an increase from the 41 per cent share in 1950. Projections for the female share of the non-agricultural sector suggest an increase from 36 per cent in 1985 to 39 per cent in 2000. Data for 1950 and 1980 show increase in the female share of both industry and services. In 1980, this share was approximately one-third of both sectors.

These data suggest that efforts in East Asia should be concentrated on creating gainful activities for women in the non-agricultural sectors of the economy. Since nearly two-third of the active population in both the services and industrial sectors are male, these two sectors should be targeted by governments. Intensified efforts in the non-agricultural sector would further contribute to decreasing the disparity between women and men.

10

Measuring the Economic Activity of Women: Limitations and Strengths of the Data

Ideally, an examination of women's work at the global level would evaluate differences by occupation and industry, age and marital status, hours and conditions of work, income, educational attainment and level of skill, geographical area, e.g. region and urban/rural residence, and so on. For the majority of the world's countries, however, these data are simply not available. At best, such detailed information from these countries is available for only a small group of women whose work does not reflect that of women in the country as a whole. More data are available from the industrialised countries. Even these, however, are frequently limited in their comparability across time and countries.

In an effort to avoid the biases inherent in analysis of data from predominantly industrialised countries which claim to reflect the characteristics of the diverse regions of Africa, Asia and Latin America, this analysis uses only those data which are available for female economic activity in developing as well as industrialised countries. The most extensive set currently available are the estimates and projections of economic activity prepared and recently revised by the ILO, covering practically all countries, territories and areas of the world (ILO, 1986a). This is the first analysis of these data for female economic activity. The major limitations are not attributable to the current methodology for making estimates and projections, though it is recognised that such methodology is constantly being improved. Instead, they may be traced to the basic information used to develop the estimates, mainly derived or assessed from national sources (population censuses, labour force surveys, etc.).

Limitations of data for female economic activity from national sources were recognised and acknowledge throughout the United Nations Decade for Women. The Plan of Action adopted in Mexico City gives high priority to the collection of adequate data and information about women. In 1975 governments agreed that information about the economic activities and conditions of women "... are essential in formulating policies and evaluating progress and in effecting attitudinal and basic social and economic change" (United Nations, 1975, para 161). Adequate information to evaluate the work women do is particularly essential. In the Strategies Document. United Nations members gave emphasis to the fact that "the lack of reliable data prevents the assessment of relative improvement in women's status in various sectors" (United Nations, 1986a, para. 351). Research is only beginning to reveal the rich diversity and magnitude of the economic contribution of the female population. Concurrent with the preparation of this book, the process is under way to improve the create measures to ensure that all the work women do is acknowledge for its contribution to society. Until these data are available, statistical analyses must make use of those which exist, taking into account, wherever possible, their known limitations.

Estimates and projections are only as accurate as the basic data used to develop them. Two types of information are used to develop those used here. The first and most basic are estimates of a country's population and its age structure, i.e. the portion of the total population in five-year age groups. Even this basic population information is not available for many countries. To aid policy-makers, the Population Division of the United Nations developed a set of estimates and projections by sex and age group for governments between 1950 and 2025 (United Nations, 1986c). In addition to being the most extensive estimates available, they are frequently updated to reflect new and valuable information. Despite continued efforts, they remain limited by assumptions about fertility, mortality and migration (Sehgal, 1986).

International agencies use these data as a basis for their estimates and projections. For example, the United Nations Educational, Scientific and Cultural Organisation (UNESCO) uses them to estimate literacy and enrolment in formal education; the ILO uses them to develop estimates of economic activity for the female and male populations; and the Food and agriculture Organisation of the United Nations (FAO) combines the use of these population data with ILO estimates of economic activity by major sector between 1950 and 1980 to produce estimates and projections for the participation of women and men in agricultural and non-agricultural activities for 1985 and 2000 (FAO, 1986).

These ILO and FAO estimates and projections provide the basic data for this analysis. Both sets of data are only as reliable as the information used to produce them, namely, the United Nations data which describe population by sex and age, and the census data from governments about the economic activity of the male and female populations. Activity rates for males are universally high and, as a consequence, errors in projection rates are unlikely to be significant (Sehgal, 1986). There is near universal agreement, however, about the limitations of information about female economic activity.

Throughout the United Nations Decade for Women (1976-85) and up to the present day, the inadequacies of these data are the subject of much discussion, the focus of which is on criticisms of the definition of economic activity as excluding the economic contributions of women and on the methods of data collection as contributing to the undercounting and/or misclassifying of the work women do. The discussion makes clear that the economic contributions of women are less likely then those of men to be encompassed by the definition and to be identified by current methods of data collection. In response, the definition was improved in 1982 at the Thirteenth International Conference of Labour Statisticians (ILO, 1983) and efforts are under way to minimise the bias in the collection of data (e.g. Anker, 1983; Anker *et al.*, 1987 and 1988; ILO, 1986a; and United Nations, 1984a and 1984b).

Data using the new definition and revised methods were not available for the development of the estimates and projections used here; this new definition will be employed by most countries for the first time for the 1990 census. The information on female and male economic activity which provides the basis of estimates and projections analysed here is derived from national population censuses or labour force sample surveys undertaken during the period 1945-84. As a consequence, it embodies most of the limitations which were the focus of criticisms during the United Nations Decade for Women.

Definition of Economic Activity: Employment and Unemployment

Economic activity is neither a measure of the work women do, nor is it a measure of the economic contribution of women. Data for economic activity reflect several definitions adopted by the international community during the last 30 years—

> We all think we understand the term "work" and yet this common word often means different things to different people. To some it means only wage-earning activities. To others it means all the activities whereby economic goods and services are produced and sold. But the concept of work may also over subsistence and domestic activities (Tomoda, 1985, p. 663).

It is, therefore, imperative for the international community to provide a common definition for the types of work encompassed within the concept of economic activity.

During its fourteenth session, in October 1966, the Statistics Commission of the United Nations adopted resolutions defining the scope and nature of statistics for economic activity which should be made available by each government. To be classified as economically active, a person must "...furnish the supply of labour for the production of economic goods and services during the time-reference period chosen for the investigation..." (ILO. 1976, p. 32).

Statistics for economic activity may reflect "current activity" for which the time-reference period is generally no longer than one week (ILO, 1976, p. 32) and which is usually referred to as "labour force activity", or it may reflect the much longer time frame of "usual activity":

> Where it is considered that classification on the basis of current activity over this brief period of time does not reflect year-round activities, particularly where there is a highly seasonal pattern of employment and regular periodic sample surveys are not held during the year, supplementary information on "usual" economic characteristics over a longer period may be collected (ILO, 1976, pp. 32-33).

To be classified as economically active, a person may be classified as either employed or as unemployed. Definitions for these two concepts were adopted during the Eighty International Conference of Labour Statisticians in 1954. Employed persons are those:

(a) at work; persons who performed some work for pay or profit during a specified brief period, either one week or one day;

(b) with a job but not at work; persons who, having already worked in their present job, were temporarily absent during the specified period because of illness or injury, industrial dispute, vacation of other leave of absence, absence without leave, or temporary disorganisation of work due to such reasons as bad weather or mechanical breakdown (ILO, 1976, p. 29).

Also included among the economically active population are the unemployed.[1] Unpaid family workers are to be included as employed persons and, therefore, as economically active only "...if they worked for at least one-third of the normal working time during the specified period" (ILO, 1976, p. 29).

Limitations of The Data: Criticisms During The United Nations Decade for Women

Data for economic activity do not differentiate among several factors which are important for the advancement of women, particularly with regard to the progress of women towards economic independence and self-reliance. As the definition implies, economic activity combines the employed with the unemployed populations. It combines seasonal activities for some countries with current or usual activity for others. It combines full-time with part-time activity. It combines the activity of a worker who is paid for one hour's work with the activity of an unpaid family worker who must work one-third time. Economic activity encompasses a wide range of possibilities for work and remuneration which have important implications for measuring women's activity.

The limitation which received the most attention during the United Nations Decade for women is the undercounting of female economic activity (Boulding et al., 1976; ILO, 1985, p. 203; ILO/INSTRAW, 1985). Current research highlights this limitation. It is widely accepted, for example, that women in secluded societies have low levels of economic activity. Data from middle and western South Asian and northern African countries substantiate this belief. Studies of secluded women in Muslim areas of Nigeria, however, reveal new information about female economic activity. Though clsssified as economically inactive, these secluded women are engaged in work appropriately classified as economically inactive. "Women participate actively in commodity production and in trade in spite of, and in fact partly because of, their seclusion, inasmuch as they are freed from considerable labour, e.g. in the fields..." (Pittin, 1984, p. 475).

It is generally believed that women in Latin American countries also have low levels of economic activity. Data from national sources support this belief. Current research, however, brings into question these official data. An examination of women in agriculture in three regions of Colombia and Peru, for example, suggests a gross underestimation of female unpaid family workers. "In sharp contrast of census data...women participate actively not only in field work and animal raising, but also in the processing and marketing of agricultural and animal produce. Moreover, women are also engaged as seasonal labour on plantations, haciendas and modern commercial farms producing for export" (Deere and Leon de Leal, 1982, p. v). The rate of female activity is found to be so high that "...the farming systems in the areas studied would be more accurately characterised as family rather than male farming systems as they had been previously" (Deere and Leon de Leal, 1982, p. v).

The criticism of underestimations extend to the continent of Africa where many national reports show low levels of economic activity for African women while current research suggests much higher levels: "...studies by anthropologists, sociologists and extension workers show that women contribute two-thirds of all hours spent in traditional African agriculture, and three-fifths of hours spent in marketing" (United Nations, *Women in Africa,* 1975, as cited in FAO, 1984, p. 2).

Much of this activity is carried out by unpaid family workers. The exclusion of their work from statistics on economic activity received a great deal of attention during the last ten years. "Unpaid family workers are found in all economic sectors in many countries but play a particularly important role in the agricultural sector of the developing countries "(ILO, 1985, p. 203). In fact the undercounting of the activities of unpaid family workers in agriculture has been a major thrust of criticism during the entire Decade:

> Women's work is especially underenumerated in agriculture. This is so despite the fact that in many developing countries, notably in Africa south of the Sahara, women constitute the predominant labour force in this sector. The paucity of statistical data on women's participation in agriculture is striking in view of the availability of qualitative data based on in-depth micro studies of women's roles in agriculture in several developing countries. These studies...point out that *the number of women working in agriculture may be double the number registered.* Women contribute as much as 80 per cent of the agricultural labour in such countries...(United Nations, 1986b, p. 15; emphasis added).

Data also vary arbitrarily from country to country with regard to the inclusion of many subsistence activities among economic activities. "A study on the statistical treatment of subsistence activities in 70 developing countries throughout the world showed 76 per cent of them included under this heading the imputed value of fishing 71 per cent forestry, 50 per cent handicrafts, 39 per cent food processing and 7 per cent water carrying" (Tomoda, 1985, p. 662).

Increasing attention is being directed at the informal sector as a source of economic activity for which statistics are not available or are difficult to collect. It is in this sector that major segments of both the male and female population in many countries conduct the activities which provide the resources for their survival and that of their families.

Women workers are underestimated in official statistics, largely because their work

> tends to be confined to sectors that escape registration, such as the informal labour sector, agriculture and trade...
>
> This is particularly true for petty traders, who may double as farmers or temporary service workers. The extent of underenumeration is more difficult to estimate for trade than for agriculture because there are no in-depth studies of trade along the lines of that conducted in agriculture. Moreover, trading belongs to the informal sector, which has historically been one of the most underenumerated for men as well as women.
>
> Women are also underenumerated in services, since many service occupations belong to the informal labour market (United Nations, 1986, p. 15).

This sector has proved to be a primary source of female employment. Moreover, there is a "...striking degree of gender segregation within the small-scale sector" (Scott, 1986, p. 317). Many are excluded "...because they are highly mobile, seasonal, illegal or culturally disapproved of" (United Nations 1984b, p. 43, para. 91).

Central to the criticism during the Decade is the proposal for a redefinition of economic activity which encompasses all the work women do, work which occupies so much time and energy that it is impossible for women to engage in those activities currently defined as economic:

> Consequently, one common criticism of the economic activity concept is that the work many women do, ostensibly outside the labour force, such as walking long distances in rural areas to fetch water, is of as much use-value as being economically active in the more conventional sense.... The need to spend a large part of the day in this kind of work...precludes labour force participation (Standing, 1976, p. 5).

Household work is a currently subject of debate (Goldschmidt-Clermont, 1982 and 1987; ILO, 1985, p. 203; ILO/INSTRAW, 1985):

> The current debate on the measurement of unpaid "economic activity" of women is basically centred around three issues: (a) the extent to which unpaid household work should be considered as "economic activity"; (b) how this "economic activity" should be identified and measured in surveys and censuses; and (c) what monetary value should be attached to the measurement of economic activity for statistical and other assessments (Mehran, 1983, p. 12).

Finally—

> A major limitation of this approach is that through treating the employed, unemployed and economically inactive as three clearly defined homogeneous groups, it is inappropriate for measuring the extent and incidence of labour underutilisation in developing countries when the problem is largely one of underemployment rather than open unemployment (Farooq, 1985, p. 19).

A proper classification of economic activity may reveal massive underemployment as well as well-hidden unemployment of women who would prefer jobs in the formal sector to unpaid family work in informal sector activities. For example—

> Industries which are very small often fall outside the present government structures and...are not counted in official statistics...This problem also masks female unemployment, as there is no way to identify how many rural women are seeking and unable to find income-generating activities (Lynch and Fahmy, 1984, p. 4).

The data for female economic activity are more limited than are those for male activity in terms of reliability and availability. The subsistence activities of men are undercounted, including those in agriculture. Male economic activity in the informal sector are also underenumerated. Currently, data for male economic actively, however, are more extensive and more reliable than they are for women. Several factors account for this differential:

> ...The evidence available shows the discrepancies between national census statistics and micro-studies are more extreme for the Latin American, Middle Eastern and North African regions. In these areas, two main factors are responsible for such discrepancies:
>
> (a) considerable underenumeration in the census of rural women who are economically active as unpaid family workers; and (b) the fact that livestock care, usually the domain of women, is rarely considered economic activity (United Nations, 1986b, p. 38).

Household data frequently disguise the work of women as housework, rather than as economic activity:

> The design of current censuses and household surveys in many countries tends to reflect preconceptions of households and families as consisting of nuclear marital units in which both spouses are present, and of women being married, mothers, occupied with domestic tasks and economically dependent on a male head of household (United Nations, 1984a, p. 5).

The focus on the household frequently assumes it to be a "homogeneous unit with undifferentiated interests "(Lynch and Fahmy, 1984, p. 14). Recent research points out the importance of collecting information about the activities of each member of the household. The economic activity of secluded women studied in Nigeria demonstrates the importance of collecting this data:

> Most pursue at least one and often a variety of trades or crafts, the proceeds of which are inalienably their own... So separate is a woman's trade from her role of wife and mother that husband is expected to pay for food prepared for sale by his wife, even if the purchase is meant to feed their family. Similarly a woman may purchase from her husband's farm produce needed for her trade (Pittin, 1984, p. 475).

Instruments for data collection limit the collection of comparable information because of the types of question they ask:

> The majority of Latin American censuses use only one question to establish activity or inactivity; some use two, others use as many as six, others do not ask any at all but still have this as a census category. When a question is asked, it generally takes the form of "What did you do in week X?" (giving the dates), or "Of the following activities, which do you engage in?" (a list of alternatives then being given)... Different countries list different activities...some start with those which define inactivity and others with those which define activity... In some cases the respondent is given a whole list of alternatives and has to select one (and only one), while in others the interviewer stops reading out when the respondent indicates participation in activity (Leon, 1984, p. 13).

The selection of only one activity is difficult for women and men engaged in multiple activities. "The fact that women are often engage in multiple activities of short duration poses problems of coding in labour force surveys, which normally record only primary and secondary activities" (Tomoda, 1985, p. 662).

In areas where cultural practices make it desirable for a woman to be a housewife or where either she or her husband, or both, perceive her housewife role as of prime importance, women will be classified as housewives, while their multiple activities are ignored:

> The designation of occupation is the most common form of indicating participation for census purposes...in many societies, women tend to regard their primary responsibility as home and family. Even if they are wage workers, but particularly in the case of unremunerated family workers, women consider housework to be their principal activity and, hence, occupation, irrespective of their participation in agricultural production (Deere, and Leon de Leal, 1982, p. 50).

Attitudes and values of the respondents and those collecting the data influence both the quality and quantity of data. "Much of women's work is hidden because of denial or lack of recognition" (Lynch and Fahmy, 1984, p. 4).

Persons responding to census and surveys and persons collecting data are usually male. Studies document the consistent under-reporting of female economic activity as associated with the attitudes and values of male respondents and males who administer census and surveys (Anker, 1983). In such cases they report something different from what they see. For example, "...men reported that the potato harvest was a male activity, yet their own observations during the harvest week indicated that as many women as men were participating in the harvest" (Deere and Leon de Leal, 1982, p. 5). Even women respondents may not provide an accurate assessment of their economic activities. In a Latin American study, only 46 per cent of the households economic activities. In a Latin American study, only 46 per cent of the households reported women as the primary or secondary person charged with crop production while "...the detailed agricultural labour accounting schematic indicated that a woman took part in agricultural field work in 86 per cent of the Cajamarcan peasant households" (Deere and Leon de Leal, 1982, p. 52).

Historical analysis of census questions in Nigeria documents changes in questions to elicit economic activity which, over time, resulted in a change in classification of many women from economically active to inactive housewives. Females and males were equally classified in 1931. By 1952, however, only one-tenth of women were classified in "meaningful occupational categories" and the debate about "...whether the duties of housewife were or were not the primary occupation" had begun. By 1963, "men were 'in' and women 'out'" (Pittin, 1984), that is, men were active and women were not. The matter is complicated by the fact that "...what a woman considers as housework is culturally sensitive. A peasant woman may consider housework to include not just daily maintenance chores such as cooking and washing clothes, but also animal care activities and looking after crops, particularly if the fields are but an extension of the household" (Deere and Leon de Leal, 1982, p. 50).

Changes in questions asked in the census of India between 1950 and 1970 produced a dramatic reduction in the classification of women as economically active (ILO, 1981). Questions included in a recent labour force sample survey in Egypt produced a dramatic increase in the counting of female economic activity (ILO, 1986b). Increases in many countries may be the result of improved techniques for data collection and an increased awareness of women's work as economic activity.

Limitations of data are not only attributable to the design of census, labour force and household surveys. They may also be traced to the process of data collection. Since both industrialised and developing countries experience seasonal variations in labour force participation, the time of year when the data are collected is an important factor. Studies suggest that most data collection occurs when seasonal participation is low, since respondents are more likely to be available and willing to take the time to answer questions. As a result, labour force participation of women is often underestimated. In many countries women are predominately seasonal workers, particularly in agriculture. A comparison of the results of FAO surveys conducted during peak seasons and ILO estimates based on national censuses for 82 countries highlights the importance of seasonal work for women workers and the resulting underenumeration of female activity. "For all 82 countries combined, the proportion of women in agricultural labour force increases from 30 to 42 per cent..." (Dixon, 1982, p. 557).

Also important are variations in the minimum number of hours of work necessary for classification as economically active. Prior to the 1982 change in definition, unpaid family workers must work one-third of the time-reference period, usually a week, to be classified as economically active. The classification of unpaid family workers, however, varies enormously:

> Countries such as Turkey and Thailand count almost all farm women as unpaid family helpers, resulting in an enumerated agricultural labour force that is half female. But if unpaid workers are excluded, women are reported as only 5 per cent of Turkish farm labour and about 20 per cent in Thailand. Other countries apply the

definition of economic activity selectively so that female (but not male) unpaid family labourers are excluded (Dixon, 1982, p. 542).

These examples demonstrate the importance of efforts on the part of governments to revise the methods of data collection to assess more accurately the work women do as economic activity. The data used here embody all these limitations. As the definition implies, these data measure only a portion of the work women do. At best, they provide conservative estimates of female economic activity. At worst, they provided gross underestimates.

Strengths of the Data: Assessing Past Trends and Prospects for the Future

As has been pointed out above, the major limitation of currently available data is their tendency, particularly for some of the developing countries, to underestimate female economic activity. To focus an analysis on levels of female activity, therefore, is to focus on the weakness, rather than the strength, of the data. The focus of this analysis is on the strength, rather than the weakness, of the data. This strength results from national statistics producing fairly consistent data for female economic activity. They may be underestimates, but they are generally consistent underestimates. Major changes which result from new techniques of data collection (e.g. the examples of India and Egypt discussed previously) are easily detected by those skilled in the evaluation of data for estimates and projections. This consistency on the part of the national statistics is responsible for the strength of these data—their ability to assess past trends and prospects for the future. *The focus of this analysis is not, therefore, on the level of female economic activity but rather on the direction and magnitude of change during the second half of the twentieth century.* These data provide for an assessment of changes in female economic activity during the 30 years preceding the United Nations Decade for Women: Equality, Development and Peace (1976-85) and for an assessment of changes during this historic Decade. And, finally, they provide the basis for projections for the year 2000.

In an effort to emphasis the fact that the future need not be a continuation of the past, this analysis incorporates two sets of projections for the year 2000. The first set, alternative I, assumes the continuation of past trends. For the purposes of this analysis a second set, Alternative II, provides a positive projection for the year 2000. This set was produced to highlight the fact the projections do not determine the future. People determine their future! Consequently, it is entirely within the power of policy-makers everywhere to make a departure from the past, and, during the next 15 years, make special efforts to accelerate the advancement of equality of opportunity between women and men. Such a departure was the purpose of the United Nations Decade for Women and these projections in fact suggest the magnitude of effort which may be necessary to implement the Nairobi Forward-Looking Strategies and the resolution on equal opportunities and equal treatment for men and women in employment, adopted by the International Labour Conference in 1985.

Alternative II projections assume the implementation of paragraph 78 of the Forward-Looking Strategies: "by the year 2000, all governments should have adequate and coherent national policies to abolish all obstacles to full and equal participation of women in all spheres of society". These projections suggest the enormous effort necessary to implement paragraph (g) of the ILO resolution, which refers to one of the priorities to be undertaken:

> policies aimed at achieving equality between men and women workers which should include the development and implementation of comprehensive programmes of positive action to end discrimination against women in employment and to counter the effects of past discrimination. These programmes should incorporate measures on education, training, vocational guidance, counselling and placement, equality legislation and the development of support services for workers with family responsibilities.

While it may be difficult for some countries and some regions to provide these increased opportunities, they are indicated here as a regional goal and, most importantly, as an alternative to the worsening prospects for women which, without special efforts on the part of policy-makers and governments throughout the world, threaten to become a reality during the next 15 years.

A set of projections is not available for a third scenario. It is recognised that, without continued and, in most regions, accelerated efforts, setbacks worse than those identified in Alternative I are likely during the next 15 years.

Since many national statistics currently underestimate female activity, the concerned governments can promote a combined strategy of providing increased opportunities for women with providing more reliable estimates of female activity.

Several trends are evaluated in this analysis. First, all trends are analysed for the 1950-85 period followed by a comparison of the two projections of the year 2000. Then these trends are analysed globally with a focus on developing and industrialised countries, followed by a separate analysis of trends for Africa, Asia, Latin America and the industrialised centrally planned and market economies. Where appropriate, subregional variations are also analysed.

The first data analysed focus on changes in economic activity of the female population. These trends are evaluated using two measures of economic activity, the crude and the refined rates. The crude activity rate measures the proportion of the total population which is classified as economically active. Rates for males and females are the proportions of the male and female populations which are classified as economically active. When used for the analysis of trends, crude activity rates are influenced by changes in the structure by age. Of particular concern are changes in the younger and older populations which are economically inactive. A growth in the proportion of the population which is over 64 will reduce the economic activity rate and, at the same time, disguise or mask actual changes in activity. The same is true for increase or decreases in the population for which economic activity is not characteristics, namely the very young. Of particular importance for this analysis are variations for older populations. Given that women generally live longer than men, there are variations in the size of the male and female populations comprising this age group which camouflage changes in female economic activity. The result is that the statistics which is assumed to measure economic activity may actually be measuring increases in the inactive population over 64 years.

The *refined activity rate* controls for variations in these factors. For the purpose of this analysis, refined rates measure the proportion of the 15-64 age group which is economically active. Since the refined rates exclude the bulk of the non-economically active population, namely the young and the old, these rates are higher than are crude rates for both males and females. It is important to note that the refined activity rates tend to approximate estimates of current research based on small samples which are most frequently studies of the economic activity of adult women, rather than that of the total female population. Since refined rates control variations in the size of the populations most likely to be economically inactive, they are more comparable across region and, therefore, are highlighted in this analysis. In an attempt to distinguish clearly between these two important measures, the crude and the refined rates of economic activity, the terms female and male will be used when referring to the crude rates, since they characterise economic activities of the total "female" and "male" populations. The terms "women" and "men" will be used when referring to the refined rates, which characterise economic activities of these working-age populations. These rates are developed conceptually and graphically in the context of the introductory discussion of male and female economic activity by age between 1950 and 1985 and between 1985 and the year 2000.

An analysis of these trends is supplemented by an assessment of the distribution between women and men of changes in economic activity during the 1950-75, 1975-80 and 1980-85 periods, and the consequences of this distribution for changes in the female share of the economically active population, i.e. the proportion of the total economically active population which is female. Potentials for the future are evaluated based on the continuation of these trends to the end of the twentieth century (Alternative I projections) and based on a departure from these trends (Alternative II projections). These projections indicate the number of economic opportunities which need to be created during the 15 years remaining in the twentieth century, and the proportion of these opportunities which need to be made available for women.

At the global level, data for female unemployment are analysed for selected countries, *i.e.*, for countries with national unemployment data for two years during the United Nations Decade for Women (1976-85). The female share of unemployment is compared to the female share of the economically active population to determine if women experience economic activity more as part of the unemployed than of the employed populations.

Manifestations of differences in male and female economic activity are differences in the number of years women and men can expect to be economically active. Trends in gross years of working live[2] are analysed for women and men between 1950 and 1985 and as projected for the end of the twentieth century by the two models. These life expectancies are examined in order to assess progress towards equality between women and men.

This analysis is further supplemented by an analysis of the economic activity by major sector—agriculture, industry and services.[3] Here again, trends are examined for the distribution of women and men in these three sectors. Taking into account the numbers of women and men in each sector, the female and male share of each sector is evaluated and recommendations for target sectors for the creation of economic opportunities for women are made to policy-makers in the regions.

NOTES

1. The unemployed are defined as persons in one of the following categories:
   (a) workers available for employment whose contract of employment has been terminated or temporarily suspended and who were without a job and seeking work for pay or profit;
   (b) persons who were available for work (except for minor illness) during the specified period and were seeking work for pay or profit, who were never previously employed or whose most recent status was other than that of employee (i.e. former employers, etc.) or who had been in retirement;
   (c) persons without a job and currently available for work who had made arrangements to start a new job at a date subsequent to the specified period;
   (d) persons on temporary or indefinite lay-off without pay (ILO, 1976, p. 29).

   Persons not to be included among the unemployed—hence, the economically active—population are:
   (a) persons intending to establish their own business or farm, but who had not yet arranged to do so, who were not seeking work for pay or profit;
   (b) former unpaid family workers not at work and not seeking work for pay or profit (ILO, 1976, p. 29).
2. Gross years of working life do not take mortality into account (United Nations, 1971, p. 38).
3. Agriculture comprises: farming, hunting; forestry and fishing—branch 1 of the ISIC (1968 revision). Industry comprises: mining and quarrying; manufacturing; electricity, gas and water, and construction—branches 2, 3, 4 and 5 of the ISIC (1968 revision). Services comprise: wholesale/retail trade; restaurants and hotels; transport, storage and communication; financing, insurance, real estate and business services; community, social and personal services—branches 6, 7, 8 and 9 of the ISIC (1968 revision).

11

Trends and Prospects for Women at the Global Level

The United Nations estimates that 4.8 million people inhabited the earth in 1985. Seventy-four per cent lived in the developing countries of Africa, Asia and Latin America and the Caribbean. The remaining 26 per cent lived in the industrialised market and centrally planned economies.

> Although throughout history and in many societies women have been sharing similar experiences, in developing countries, the problems of women, particularly those pertaining to their integration in the development process, are different from the problems women face in industrialised countries and are often a matter of survival (United Nations, 1986a, para. 104).

A global analysis which is insensitive to these differences between industrialised and developing countries is of little value for the formulation and implementation of strategies to provide all women with the resources essential for survival, for economic independence and self-reliance.

Differences between developing and industrialised countries are reflected in the quantity and quality of data. Fewer data of lower quality are available from developing than from industrialised countries. The data analysed here reflect these differences. Data from industrialised countries, particularly the market economies, frequently reflect part-time economic activity and a disproportionate proportion of women in unemployment. Those from developing countries frequently reflect high levels of female underemployment, female economic activity in seasonal work and, for many countries, particularly in North Africa, middle and western South Asia and Latin America and the Caribbean, the underenumeration of the economic contributions of women.

To the degree that these general limitations continue to be reflected in data available from national sources, these data identify changes in female participation in economic activity. They document increasing disparities between developing and industrialised countries in the prospects for equality between women and men in opportunities for such participation. This chapter provides an introduction to the statistical concepts and methods used in this analysis in the discussion of economic activity by age. Here, variations in activity by age assessed for females and males. Then begins the analysis for the period between 1950 and 2000, which is duplicated for all regions in the following chapters: the analysis of overall economic activity, gross economically active life expectancies and economic activity by sector. Finally, the implications of these findings for the underemployment and underutilisation of women are discussed.

Economic Activity by Age, 1950-2000

An introduction to statistical information is essential to an understanding of variations in economic activity between females and males and for comparisons for females in the regions. Graphs are presented for Africa (developing countries), excluding northern Africa; northern Africa; East Asia (developing countries); middle South Asia; Latin America and the Caribbean; industrialised market economies; North America; and the USSR. Each of these graphs contains two sets of lines, a set of four lines for females and a set of three lines for males. Each line documents for one time-period the variation in economic activity by age group ranging from 10-14 years to 65 years and over. Each point on the line represents the percentage of the population in that particular age group which is classified as economically active. The space under each line represents that portion of the female or male population which is economically active. The space above the line is the portion considered inactive. Sets of three lines for females and males are presented to document changes in activity by age between 1950 and 1985 and, assuming the continuation of present trends, between 1985 and 2000 (Alternative I). The fourth line for females represents the proportion of females in each age group which will be economically active by 2000 if women and men are to have equal access to economic activity by 2025 (Alternative II).

An examination of these graphs suggests little variation for male when compared to female economic activity. While the meaning of economic activity varies widely among males—representing high levels of part-time work or underemployment in many of the developing countries in contrast to full-time employment in the industrialised economies—the height and shape of the lines for males are similar by region. Between 1950 and 2000, the major change in economic activity for males is an increase in the proportion of older males who are no longer active, in particular the male population above 60 years. In 1950 a major portion of the male population over 60 was economically active in all regions. By 1985 this portion had declined and is projected to decline further by 2000 (Alternative I).

A comparison of these same graphs shows wide variation in female economic activity. This variation is reflected is reflected in both the height and shape of the lines in the graphs. Variation in height is indicative of differences in the proportion of the female population which is economically active, i.e., higher lines represent higher rates of economic activity. Lines representing female economic activity in northern Africa, middle South Asia and Latin America and the Caribbean, for example, are much lower than are those for East Asia and the USSR.

A closer examination of individual lines provides information about changes in economic activity by age. The lines for Latin America and the Caribbean, for example, suggest increases in female participation in economic activity. In 1950 approximately 20 per cent of females in the age groups between 20 and 59 years were active. In 1985 over 30 per cent were active. Projections assuming the continuation of these trends, Alternative I, suggest further increase during the next 15 years. The lines for middle South Asia, however, suggest opposite trends. In 1950 approximately 40 per cent of the females in the age groups between 20 and 59 years were economically active. By 1985 only 30 per cent were so classified. Alternative I projections suggest further declines between 1985 and 2000.

Lines for Alternative II projections for the year 2000 suggest how much the economic activity of females will have to increase during the next 15 years and, correspondingly, how many opportunities will have to be created if females and males are to have equal opportunity for economic activity within each age group by 2025. The lines labelled "II" on the graphs in Chart 11.1 introduce these special projections. Equality between females and males is possible only if females and males within the same age group have equal access to economic activity. These projections assume that this equality is possible by 2025 and, thus, provide estimates of progress necessary by the year 2000. An examination of the lines for Africa (excluding northern Africa) and for Latin America and the Caribbean serve to illustrate the meaning of these projections. The lines for 1950 and 1985 suggest declines in female economic activity in sub-Saharan Africa during this 35-year period. In 1950, between 60 and 70 per cent of females between the ages of 15 and 64 were economically active. By 1985, these figures had declined and a further decline is projected for 2000 when projections are based on the continuation of past trends. The line for the projections for Alternative II, however, is higher than that for 1950 suggesting the possibility of reversing this negative trend. Obviously, such a reversal with require an enormous effort, the magnitude of which will be discussed later in the analysis. Rather than suggesting a reversal, the line for Latin America and the Caribbean suggests not only a continuation but an acceleration of current trends.

An example of variations in the shape of the lines illustrates different patterns of economic activity for females and males by age groups. The lines for the USSR, for example, suggest that for 1950 the patterns for females and males were quite different. By 1985, however, the patterns were similar and are projected to remain so. The shape of the lines in Africa (excluding northern Africa) is also quite similar for females and males. The major difference is in the height of the lines, which indicates that fewer females than males in this region are economically active or classified as such. The overall shape for females and males, however, suggests little fluctuation in economic activity by age. A comparison of the lines for males and females in 1950 and 1985 for East Asia also suggests an increasing similarity in the pattern of male and female economic activity, which is projected to continue.

Graphs for northern Africa, Latin America and the Caribbean, the industrialised market economic and North America suggest that males and females in these countries have a different pattern of economic activity by age. For 1950, the lines suggest a pattern of economic activity for females whereby they become economically active at an early age, and then cease activity for a varying period of time, after which major portions of them resume economic activity. By 1985, the shape of these lines suggests less fluctuation and, in fact, a closer approximation among these regions and, hence, between females and males. This change suggests that increasingly females in all regions are remaining economically active, i.e. engage in economic activity on at least a part-time basis, or they are leaving for shorter periods before resuming activity. Similarity in the shape of lines suggests that, globally, child care and family responsibilities are playing decreasing role in influencing whether females are economically active. Alternative I projections for 2000 suggest a continuation of this general trend. Alternative II projections assume an acceleration of it.

The space under each line represents the proportion of the total female or male population which is classified as economically active. In graphic terms, this rate represents the proportion of the female or male population of all ages which is represented by the total space under the line (the economically active portion of the female or male population) divided by the total population of females or males represented by the entire graph (the combination of the economically active and inactive populations in all age groups).

When used as a basis of analyses over time, "global" activity rates are influenced by changes in the age structure of the population. Of particular are changes in the younger and older populations. Note the changes in the shape of the lines for the over 64 age group and variations among regions in the first point on the lines for the very young population.

Refined activity rates (see Chapter 2 for a definition) control for variations in these two age segments of the population. Graphically, a refined rate refers to that portion of the female or male population which is below a line between the points for the 15-19 and the 60-64 age groups divided by the populations of females, or males, represented in the entire graph with these age limits, i.e. the combination of economically active and inactive persons between the ages of 15 and 64 years.

Economic Activity, 1950-2000

Over 1,000 million females, or nearly a third of the third of the world's female population, are projected to be economically active in the year 2000. Over 700 million of them will be active in developing countries. The proportion of the total female population which will be economically active is projected to be lower in developing than in industrialised countries (see chart 2). A 30 cent crude activity rate is projected for developing countries in contrast to a 38 per cent rate for industrialised countries. Refined rates also reflect this differential. In the year 2000, nearly 60 per cent of the women between the ages of 15 and 64 will be economically active in the industrialised countries, in contrast to less than 50 per cent in the developing countries.

While part of this differential is attributable to a greater underenumeration of economic activity in developing than in industrialised countries, it is none the less true that historical trends have contributed to a widening of the many gaps between developing and industrialised countries which, in turn, is reflected in an increased differential in female activity rates

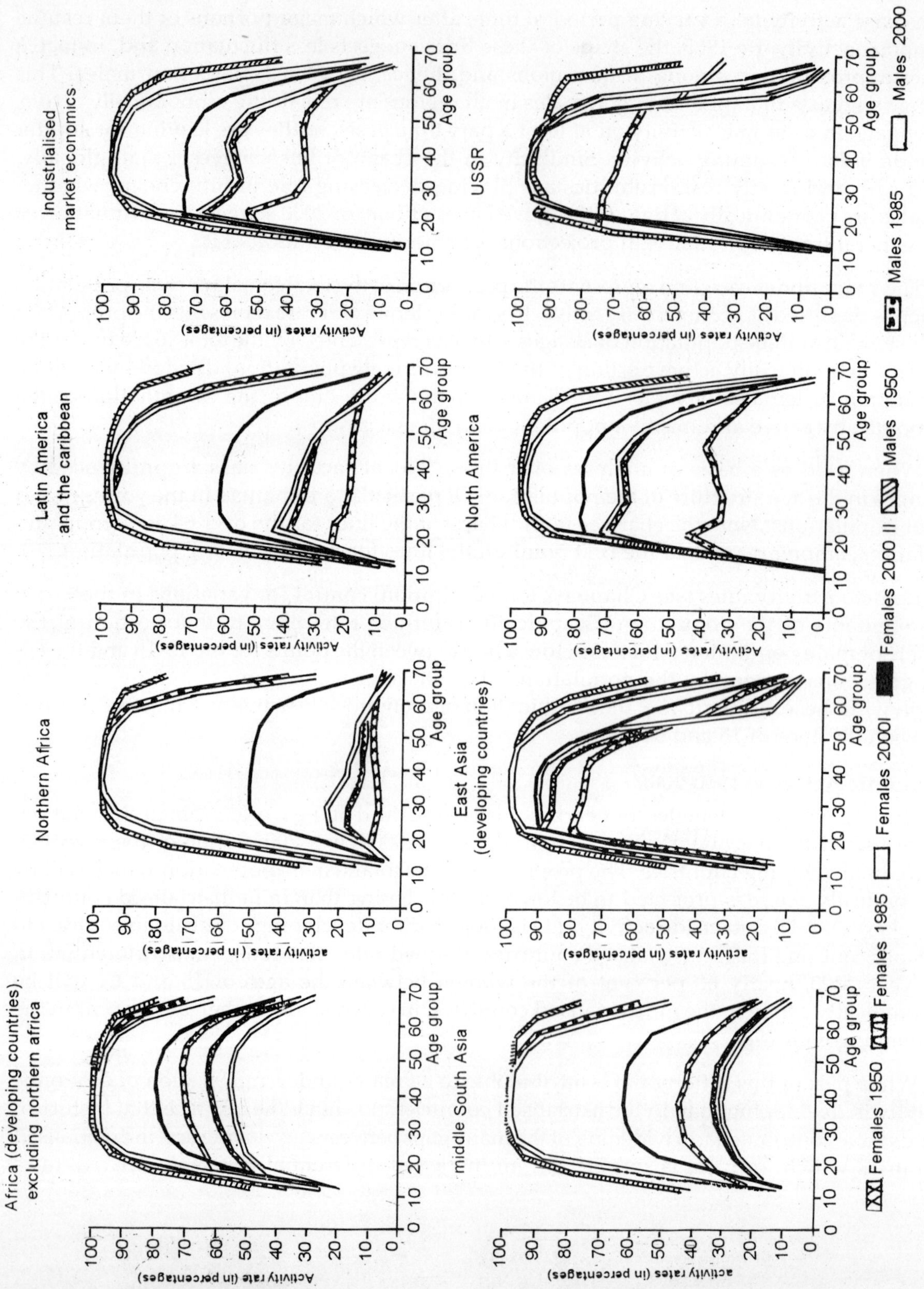

Africa (developing countries) excluding northern africa
Northern Africa
Latin America and the caribbean
Industrialised market economics
middle South Asia
East Asia (developing countries)
North America
USSR
Activity rate (in percentages)
activity rates (in percentages)
Activity rates (in percentages)
Age group
Females 1950
Females 1985
Females 2000I
Females 2000 II
Males 1950
Males 1985
Males 2000

Chart 11.1.

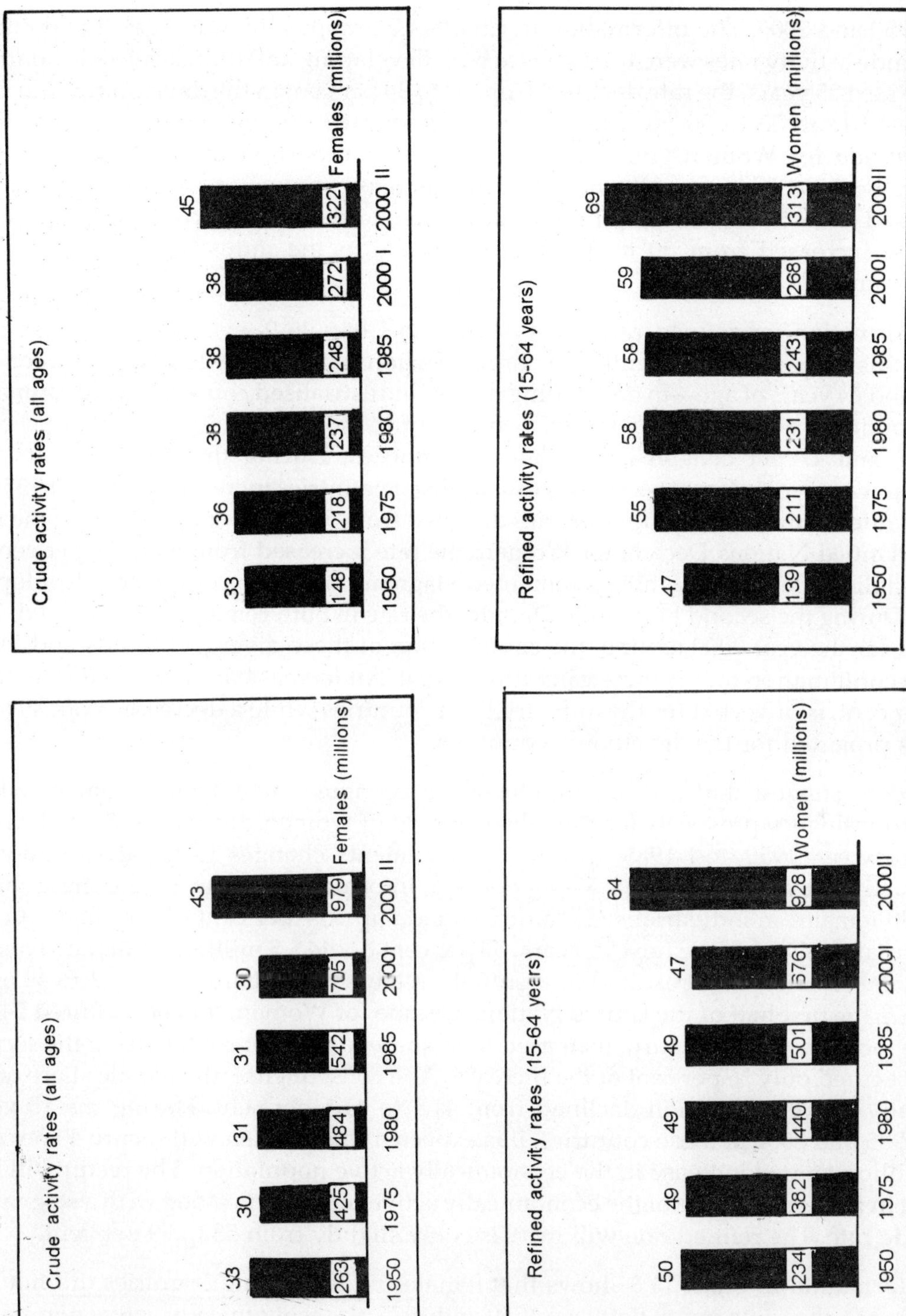

Source: As for chart 1.

Chart 11.2. Crude and refined female economic activity rates for developing and industrialised countries, 1950-2000 (in percentages)

between 1950 and 2000. The information in Chart 11.2 graphically illustrates this point. In 1950, the crude activity rates were the same for both developing and industrialised countries. During the next 25 years, the rate declined from 33 to 30 per cent in the developing countries and increased from 33 to 36 per cent in the industrialised countries. During the United Nations Decade for Women (1976-85), an increasing proportion of the world's female population became economically active. This increase, however, was greater in the industrialised than in the developing countries. In the developing countries, the crude activity rate increased from 30 to 31 per cent, while in the industrialised countries it increased from 36 to 38 per cent.

The information for refined rates, also shown in Chart 11.2, even more dramatically illustrates this increasing differential. A larger portion of women—females between the ages of 15 and 64 years of age—in developing than in industrialised countries were estimated to be economically active in 1950: the refined rate of economic activity was 50 per cent in developing and 47 per cent in industrialised countries. During the next 25 years this relationship was reversed as rates in the industrialised countries increased from 47 to 55 per cent, while rates in the developing countries declined from 50 to 49 per cent. During the first half of the Untied Nations Decade for Women, the rate increased from 55 to 58 per cent in the industrialised countries, while it remained stagnant at 49 per cent in the developing countries. During the second half of the Decade, the rate in both remained unchanged. ILO projections for the year 2000 assume the continuation of these divergent trends and, thus, project the continuation of this increasing differential. An increase in the refined rate, from 58 to 59 per cent, is projected for the industrialised countries while a decrease, from 49 to 47 per cent, is projected for the developing countries.

These data suggest that a dramatic change in economic activity for women, which threatens to influence prospects for the advancement of women during the next 15 years, occurred between 1950 and 1985. Chart 11.3 documents changes in the distribution of economic activity by sex during this 35-year period. Information for the female share shows that in 1950 females in industrialised countries made up 36.7 per cent of the economically active population. During the next 25 years, 53 per cent of the 5.3 million annual increase of the total were females. This resulted in a growth in the female share from 36.7 to 40.6 per cent. During the first half of the United Nations Decade for Women, females secured 54 per cent of the increase which, in turn, increased their share to 41.4 per cent. During the second half, they secured only 36 per cent of the increase. As a consequence, the female share of the economically active population declined from 41.4 to 41.1 per cent. During the 15 years between 1985 and 2000 in these countries, it is expected that women will secure 40 per cent of the 4 million annual increase in the economically active population. The result will be a stagnation in the female share of the economically active population along with a stagnation of the crude rate. The refined rate will increase only slightly from 58 to 59 per cent.

The information in Chart 11.3 shows that females in developing countries did not and will experience, the same trend. Between 1950 and 1975, the economically active population grew by 17.7 million per year. Females secured only 37 per cent of this growth, producing a

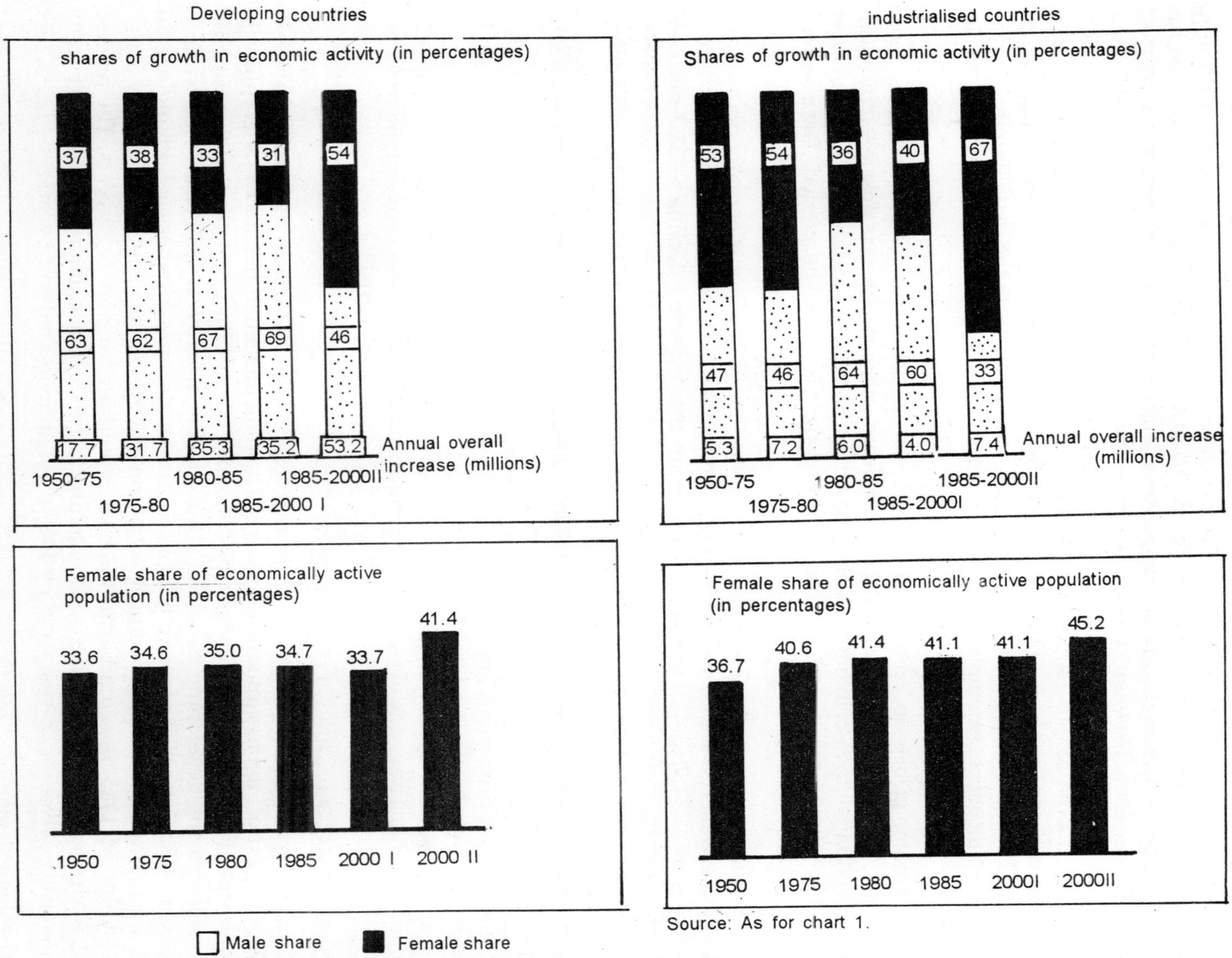

Source: As for chart 1.

Chart 11.3. Female and male shares of growth in economic activity; and female share of total economically active population for developing and industrialised countries, 1950-2000

slight increase in the female share of the economically active population during these 25 years from 33.6 to 34.6 per cent. During the first half of the United Nations Decade, 38 per cent of the growth was female, producing another slight increase in the female share, from 34.6 to 35.0 per cent. This gain was lost during the second half of the Decade as women secured only 33 per cent of the annual growth of the active population. Therefore, their share declined from 35.0 to 34.7 per cent. Females in developing countries are projected to receive an even smaller share of the 35.2 million annual increase of the economically active population during the next 15 years producing a further decline in the female share (i.e. 33.7 per cent). If this occurs, women in developing countries will have experienced practically no progress during this 50-year period.

With greater efforts to create more economic opportunities for women than those suggested by the projections during the next 15 years, major progress is possible in advancing women relative to men in both developing and industrialised countries. Only with these intensified efforts can the trend towards an increasing differential be averted. The progress, however, requires a doubling of efforts to create gainful activities for women.

The creation, in developing countries, of 53.5 rather than 35.2 million economic opportunities annually (see Alternative II) would increase the female share of the economically active population from 34.7 to 41.4 per cent, rather than the projected decline to 33.7 per cent. Intensified efforts would produce an increase in the crude activity rate from 31 to 43 per cent and in the refined rate from 49 to 64 per cent (see Chart 11.2). As the data in Chart 11.3 show, this improvement requires that females annually receive an additional 18.3 million new opportunities, bringing therefore the total annual new opportunities for females to 29.1 million.

Alternative II projections show that 322 million females will be economically active in the year 2000 in industrialised countries. The effort would require the annual creation of 7.4 rather than 4 million opportunities. This increase would bring up the female share to 45.2 per cent by 2000. The crude activity rate would increase from 38 per cent in 1985 to 45 per cent in 2000 and the refined rate from 58 to 69 per cent (see Chart 11.2).

D. Gross Years of Working Life, 1950-2000

Changes in economic activity for women correspond to changes in the number of years women can expect to be economically active. The data presented in Chart 11.4 graphically illustrate the consequences of changes in economic activity. The gross years of working life for women in the developing countries (DCs) declined between 1950 and 1985, while it increased in the industrialised countries, in contrast to declines for males in both regions. In 1950, a woman in a developing country could, on average, expect to be economically active for 27 years. By 1985, she could expect to have a working life of only 25 years. The reverse trend is characteristic of industrialised countries. In 1950, a woman could expect to be economically active for 25 years and by 1985 this had increased to 29 years.

The two alternatives for the year 2000 are dramatically different. If present trends continue, the number of years of working life that a woman can expect in the year 2000 will continue to decline to 23 years in developing countries, wand will stagnate at 29 years in the industrialised countries. If efforts to create gainful activities for women are intensified according to Alternative II projections, women can expect to be economically active on average for 34 years in developing and 35 years in industrialised countries. Such efforts would reduce the gap between the gross years of working life of females and males, as shown in Chart 11.4.

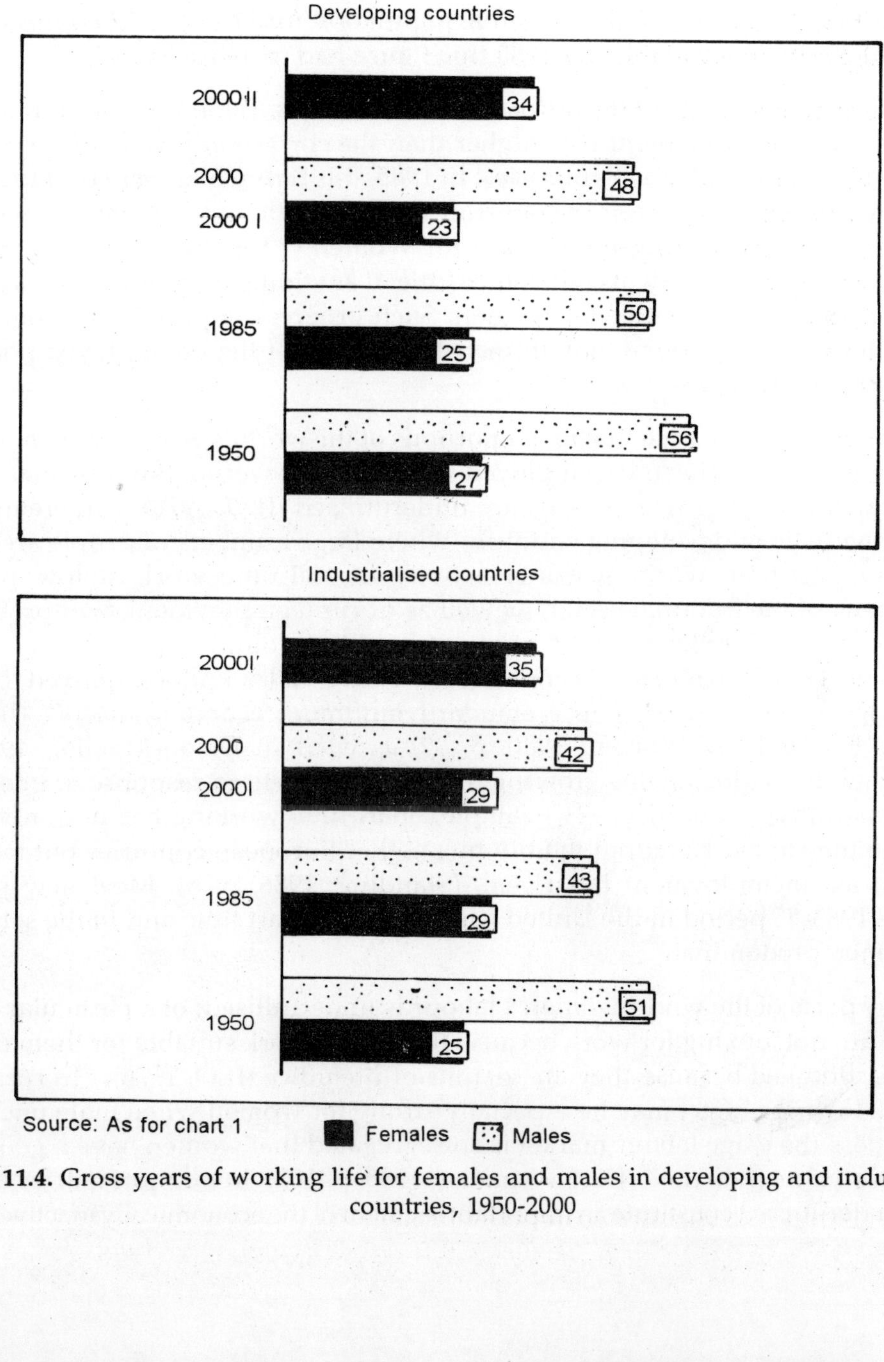

Source: As for chart 1

Chart 11.4. Gross years of working life for females and males in developing and industrialised countries, 1950-2000

E. Unemployment, Underemployment and Underutilisation

It is important that these new opportunities provide women with the resources to be economically independent and self-reliant. As pointed out earlier, the economically active population encompasses both the employed and unemployed populations. The data in table 11.1 show that during the United Nations Decade for Women (1976-85), females in many countries made up a greater share of the unemployed than of the economically active population. As regards developing countries, the share of females in unemployment in 1975 was higher than in the economically active population for 11 out of 22 countries for which official statistics were available. By 1985 this figure had increased to 14.

Data are available for 27 of the industrialised countries. Table 11.1 shows that in 1975 the female share of unemployment was higher than the corresponding share in economically active population in 18 of the 27 countries. In 1985, this figure had increased to 21. It should be noted that in several of these 18 countries the female share of unemployment increased rather than decreased during the Decade for Women (1976-85). While unemployment is considered economic activity, it contributes little, if anything, to progress towards economic independence and self-reliance for women. Such progress requires that women be given opportunities for employment, not an increasing share of the unemployed population, as the data in table 11.1 show.

It is also important to note that major portions of the world's women are underemployed and/or underutilised. The underemployed are those who would like additional work, who work for low incomes or whose skills are underutilised (ILO, 1976). Underemployment is most characteristic of developing countries where large numbers of people are engaged in involuntary part-time work, seasonal activity or full-time work at low pay. Further investigations of the informal sector, as well as of rural employment, will probably reveal high levels of underemployment. "A study of rural Java found 48 per cent of economically active females and 30 per cent of economically active males underemployed 'by reason of low earnings when compared to a standard minimum economic need'" (International Centre for Research on Women, 1980, p. 32, as cited in Dixon-Mueller, 1985, p. 112). Increasing evidence documents growing underemployment in response to unemployment in the industrialised countries. For example, "part-time working has not only been more common in the United Kingdom than in most other European countries but has increased substantial as unemployment has risen" (Standing, 1986, p. 6). Most new jobs created during the 1983-85 period in the United Kingdom were part time and in the services sector where women predominate.

In many parts of the world women's labour is underutilised; of a particular concern are those who are not looking for work because there is no work suitable for them or who have become discouraged because they are victims of prejudice (ILO, 1976). "In rural areas, the discouraged worker effect may be especially strong for women when male unemployment is high, unless the wage labour market is so segregated that women have a good chance of working even if men do not" (Dixon-Mueller, 1985, p. 107). In many countries those whose skills are underutilised constitute an important segment of the economically inactive population.

Excluding the women whose economic activity is not accurately counted, a major portion of economically inactive females are appropriately categorised as underutilised. Available data, however, provide only for the assessment of the economically active population. Of particular importance is activity by sector of the economy.

TABLE 11.1

Female Share in The Unemployment and Economically Active Populations for Selected Countries, 1975-85

Country	*1975*				*1985*			
	Unemployed population ('000)	*Female share (%)*		*Gap[1] between shares*	*Unemployed population ('000)*	*Female share (%)*		*Gap[1] between shares*
		Unemployed population	*Economically active population*			*Unemployed population*	*Economically active population*	
1	2	3	4	5	6	7	8	9
Developing countries								
Barbados	16.3[2]	57.1	43.3	13.8	21.2	59.4	47.2	12.2
Brazil	713.0[2]	28.3	24.4	3.9	2 533.0[5]	33.8	27.2	6.6
Chile	405.8[2]	35.2	24.8	10.4	551.9[6]	30.8	28.0	2.8
Costa Rica	41.6[2]	38.3	1.7	18.6	60.8	30.1	21.6	8.5
Ghana	30.5	21.5	41.9	20.4	23.5[5]	30.7	40.6	9.9
Guyana	2.0[3]	39.1	22.8	16.3	11.7[7]	38.1	24.8	13.3
India	8 918.0	11.9	28.5	16.6	24 861.0	17.0	26.2	9.2
Indonesia	157.2[3]	18.3	30.8	12.5	577.0[7]	25.4	31.3	5.9
Jamaica	211.0[2]	67.2	44.6	22.6	268.8	66.2	45.8	20.4
Korea, Rep. of	510.0	22.5	33.3	10.8	619.0	22.8	34.0	11.2
Mauritius	20.5	19.7	21.8	2.1	64.8	24.7	24.8	0.1
Panama	31.6	45.6	25.8	19.8	84.6	47.1	26.7	20.4
Philippines	581.0	38.2	32.8	5.4	1 316.0	51.1	32.1	19.0
Puerto Rico	149.0	25.5	28.3	2.8	211.0	26.1	29.4	3.3
Reunion	15.7	33.0	26.7	6.3	40.1[7]	39.6	33.2	6.4
Singapore	40.5[2]	40.4	30.7	9.7	49.8	36.0	33.4	2.6
Sudan	85.6[3]	13.4	20.0	6.6	48.8	25.2	20.8	4.4
Syrian Arab Republic	88.5	9.2	13.2	4.0	107.3[6]	25.5	16.0	9.5
Thailand	142.2[2]	38.5	47.1	8.6	917.5[5]	60.8	45.9	14.9
Trinidad and Tobago	58.6	37.5	27.8	9.7	72.8	36.3	29.7	6.6
Tunisia	64.5[4]	12.7	16.0	3.3	78.0[5]	17.6	23.0	5.4
Venezuela	233.8[2]	22.1	23.3	1.2	816.6	25.0	26.7	1.7

1	2	3	4	5	6	7	8	9
Industrialised countries								
Australia	302.5	50.4	34.4	16.0	571.2	39.0	37.8	1.2
Austria	55.5	54.1	39.6	14.5	139.5	39.6	40.2	0.6
Belgium	203.4	51.9	32.2	19.7	558.3	55.9	338	22.1
Canada	690.0	43.3	36.4	6.9	1 328.0	43.5	39.8	3.7
Cyprus	22.5	28.1	34.1	6.0	8.3	44.4	35.2	9.2
Denmark	125.6	31.9	40.0	8.1	199.5	55.6	44.2	11.4
Finland	92.0[2]	34.8	45.0	10.02	163.0	46.6	46.6	0
France	911.1	56.6	37.7	18.9	2 318.7[7]	53.8	39.6	14.2
Germany, Fed. Rep of	1 074.2	42.0	37.2	4.8	2 304.0	44.1	37.7	6.4
Greece	35.0	34.6	25.9	8.7	89.0	42.5	26.4	16.1
Ireland	96.2	19.5	27.5	8.0	230.6	26.2	28.9	2.7
Israel	35.1	48.4	31.8	16.6	98.5	41.4	33.5	7.9
Italy	1 226.0	54.6	30.1	24.5	2 471.0	57.4	31.7	25.7
Japan	1 000.0	34.0	38.3	4.3	1 560.0	40.4	37.8	2.6
Luxembourg	0.3	35.1	29.1	6.0	2.6	48.1	32.2	15.9
Malta	5.1	27.1	21.5	5.6	10.1	20.7	22.3	1.6
Netherlands	195.3	21.7	28.6	6.9	761.0	34.6	31.0	3.6
New Zealand	4.2	34.9	31.6	3.3	53.2	37.1	34.5	2.6
Norway	40.0	47.5	35.0	12.5	51.0	54.9	40.5	14.4
Portugal	177.5	44.8	30.9	13.9	397.0	56.9	36.3	20.6
Spain	623.4	24.3	21.7	2.6	2 934.0	36.1	24.1	12.0
Sweden	67.0	53.7	39.8	13.9	125.0	48.0	44.1	3.9
Switzerland	10.2	23.3	35.3	12.0	30.3	45.9	36.7	9.2
Turkey	116.8	11.4	36.5	25.1	934.6	16.4	34.0	17.6
United Kingdom	940.9	18.7	37.1	18.4	3 271.0	31.2	38.7	7.5
United States	7 929.0	44.0	39.1	4.9	8 312.0	45.6	41.5	4.1
Yugoslavia	540.1	50.7	37.1	13.6	1 039.6	55.7	38.4	17.3

1 The percentage point gap is italicised when the female share of the unemployed population exceeds that of the economically active population.

2 Figures for 1976.

3 Figures for 1978.

4 Figures for 1977.

5 Figures for 1982.

6 Figures for 1983.

7 Figures for 1984.

Source: ILO: *Year Book of Labour Statistics*, 1985 and 1986 (Geneva), table 9A; idem: *Economically active population, estimates and projections, 1950-2025* (Geneva, third edition, 1986).

F. Economic Activity by Major Sector, 1950-2000

Developing Countries

Projections for the year 2000 suggest that 57 per cent of females, but only 51 per cent of males, will be economically active in the agricultural sector of these countries (see Chart 11.5). Conversely, 43 per cent of females and 49 per cent of males will be economically active in the non-agricultural sectors of industry and services. These projections assume the continuation of past trends (FAO, 1986). In 1950, 87 per cent of economically active women were in the agricultural sector along with 78 per cent of men. By 1980 these figures had declined to 71 per cent and 63 per cent respectively. In 1980, 21 per cent of men were in services and 16 per cent were in industry, while 17 per cent of women were in services and 12 per cent in industry. In the year 2000, 64 per cent of all agricultural workers are projected to be male and the remaining 36 per cent female. This projection represents no change in the female share over the 1950 level of 36 per cent, but a decline from the 1980-85 estimates of 38 per cent.

Female economic activity in the sectors of industry and services are less likely to be underenumerated. Even so, much economic of this type takes place in the informal sector of developing countries, and it is quite likely that a good deal of it is not counted. The data which do exist, however, suggested the need for intensified efforts to expand opportunities for women in both of these sectors. In 1950, women made up approximately a quarter of both the industrial and services sectors of the developing countries. Thirty years later they comprised 28 per cent of those in industry and 31 per cent in services. If present trends continue, females will make up 31 per cent of the non-agricultural sector at the beginning of the twenty-first century.

The above trends show that an increased effort should be made in all sectors of developing countries to expand opportunities of work for women so that their share be more equal to the share of men in each in each of the three sectors concerned.

Industrialised countries

In 1950, 53 per cent of females and 65 per cent of males were in the non-agricultural sectors. Approximately one-third of both females and males were in the services sector. A greater proportion of the males were in industry (35 per cent) than were females (20 per cent). At the same time, females were more concentrated than males in the agricultural sector, 47 as compared to 35 per cent. During the next 30 years, agriculture declined significantly for both males and females. At the end of the first half of the United Nations Decade for Women (1976-85), only 16 per cent of females and 13 per cent of males were active in the agricultural sector, while more than 80 per cent of them were in the non-agricultural sectors. As opportunities in agriculture declined, females shifted their participation to the services sector and, to a lesser extent, to industry. During this 30-year period, the proportion of economically active females in services increased from 33 to 58 per cent. Their participation in industry increased from 20 to 26 per cent. Rather than being concentrated, men are evenly distributed between services and industry, 44 and 43 per cent respectively.

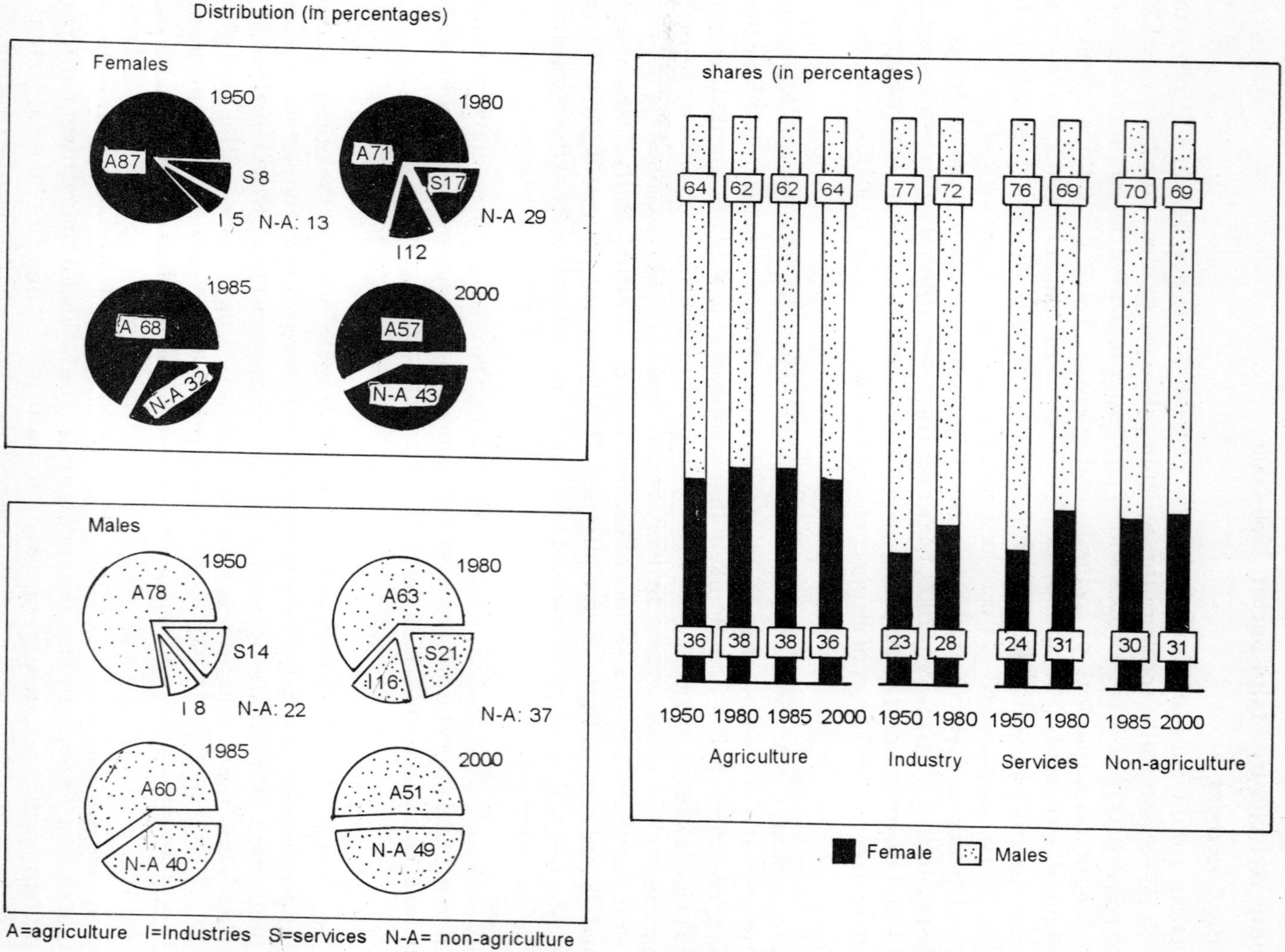

Chart 11.5. Distribution of economically active females and males among major sectors; and female and male shares of major sectors for developing countries, 1950-2000

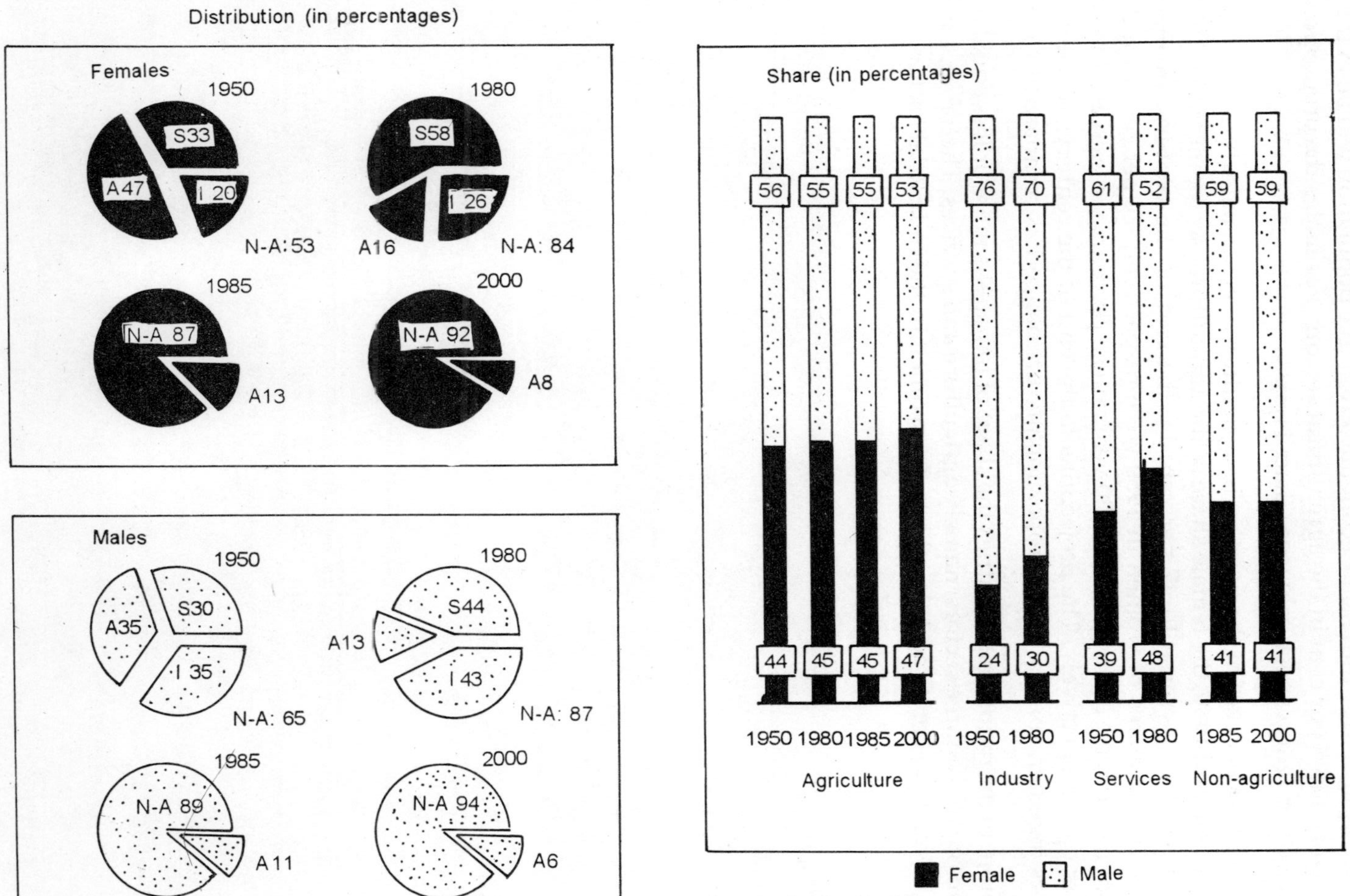

A=agriculture. I=Industry S=Services N-A = non=agriculture

Source: As for chart 5.

Chart 11.6. Distribution of economically active females and males among major sectors; and female and male shares of major sectors for industrialised countries, 1950-2000

In the year 2000, 92 per cent of the female economically active population will be in the non-agricultural sectors and 8 per cent in the agricultural sectors. For males the proportions are 94 per cent and 6 per cent respectively (see Chart 11.6).

In the year 1950, 44 per cent of those active in agriculture were female during the 30-year period between 1950 and 1980, the female share of the agricultural sector increased to 45 per cent and is expected to increase to 47 per cent by the end of the century. In the non-agricultural sector the shares of women in 1950 were respectively 24 per cent in industry and 39 per cent in services. During the next 30 years these percentages increased to 30 per cent and 48 per cent, respectively. The projections to the end of the century, available only for both sectors together, show a share proportionally unchanged as compared to 1980.

In conclusion, in the industrial countries the share of females is more or less equal to that of males in two out of the three sectors, namely agriculture and services. Therefore, a greater effort should be made to create additional jobs for women in the industrial sector.

12

Employment of Women—An Overview

As assessment of the trends in the magnitude and structure of employment (and unemployment) of women is beset with conceptual and measurement problems. Women are mostly engaged in household activities which are not considered "economic" and therefore, do not get counted as workers under conventional measures of employment. Market-oriented concepts of income and employment do not capture a large part of women's economic activities as these activities consist of production of goods and services for the use of their own households. Even women's work in the production of goods and services for the market often gets ignored because of its being intermitant and subsidiary to their non-market and "non-economic" household work. [Papola 1992]. Sample surveys of the National Sample Survey Organisation (NSSO) and Population Censuses have tried to devise ways to reduce underestimation of women's work and such attempts have to continue.

Comprehensive information on trends in the structure and levels of women employment is available from two sources, namely, the 1981 and 1991 population censuses and the quinquennial surveys on employment and unemployment of the National Sample Survey Organisation (NSSO) conducted from 1972-73.

The two censuses had broadly comparable concepts of workers, but during the 1991 census, additional probing questions were put to informants so as to identify workers among women so as to minimise underenumeration of women workers. Trends during the period 1981-91 revealed by the two censuses, therefore, need to be treated with caution. The three NSSO sample surveys conducted in 1977-78, 1983 and 1987-88 are based on comparable concepts and, therefore, enable an analysis of trends over the period 1987-88. These surveys also provide comprehensive information on the trends in the levels and structure of unemployment making uses of concepts designed to suit the specific features of a predominantly agricultural economy. Data on trends in employment in the organised sector of the economy are available from the Employment Market Information (EMI) programme of the Ministry of Labour (Directorate General of Employment and Training).

Extent of Participation of Women in Economic Activity

The Labour Force Participation Rate (LFPR), namely, the percentage of labour force to population, is a measure of the extent of participation in economic activity. These rates for women show that a majority of women, even in the working age groups, are outside the labour force. LFPR for women in the age group (15-59) is only 26.5% compared to 87.6% for men according to the NSSO 43rd Round (1987-88) survey on employment and unemployment. The rural-urban differential in the extent of women's participation in economic activity is substantial, LFPR for rural women being twice that of urban women (41.2% and 20.2%). On the other hand, LFPR for men is much higher in both rural and urban areas and not much different form each other (89% and 83.3% in rural and urban areas respectively). LFPRs for women in the age group 5+ are similarly quite low both in rural (29.3%) and urban areas (14.7%), the overall rate being 26%; and these are substantially lower than the corresponding rates for men. LFPR for women have also been stagnant over the eighties, according to the 38th and 43rd Round (1983 and 1987-88) NSSO surveys. The low level of participation rates for women has also meant a low and stagnant share of women in total workers (28.%) over this period.

Trends in Levels and Structure of Unemployment Among Women

The conventional and the most commonly used concepts of unemployment measure involuntary idleness but not 'invisible' unemployment and underemployment, which is a problem of a much larger magnitude in India. Involuntary idleness is measured in NSSO surveys of employment and unemployment using three concepts—Usual Principal Status (UPS), Current Weekly Status (CWS) and Current Daily Status (CDS). A person is considered unemployed on UPS basis if he/she was not working but was seeking or available for work for a relatively longer time during the reference year. A person is considered unemployed on CWS basis if he/she had not worked for even one hour during the reference week. Unemployment on CDS basis measures unemployment by aggregating unemployed days of all persons in the labour force during the reference week. UPS and CWS concepts estimate open unemployment, while the CDS concept, which is the most inclusive one, provides a measure of visible underemployment. An idea of invisible underemployment could be had by comparing these rates with poverty levels.

Incidence of unemployment is higher among women than among men, according to the 43rd Round (1987-88) survey of NSSO. The rates for women are estimated to have been 4.19% (of the labour force) on UPS basis, 4.92% on CWS basis and 7.61% on CDS basis (*see* Table 12.1). In absolute terms, unemployment is estimated to have been 3.61 million women, 3.99 million women and 2084 million women-days respectively during 1987-88. These respectively accounted for 31.%, 28% and 32% of total unemployment on the basis of each of the three concepts. The rates for different groups in different years estimated on the basis of the three concepts (*see* Table 12.1) show that underemployment is a much higher proportion of unemployment among women than among men. There is also a shift in the structure of unemployment from a state of widespread underemployment towards greater open unemployment. This trend is stronger in rural areas and in the case of women (Planning Commission 1992). Greater attention has, therefore, to be paid to creation of regular employment opportunities for women than to temporary, off season public works employment.

Incidence of unemployment among educated women is higher (27%) than that for men (10%). Among all the educated unemployed 27% are women. Incidence of unemployment among educated women has declined from 32% to 27%; and the share of women among all the educated unemployed has come down from 42% to 27% over the decade 1977-78 to 1987-88.

Trends in the Growth and Structure of Employment of Women

Overall women employment has grown at the average annual rate of 1.90% over the period 1977-78 to 1987-88 according to NSSO surveys. The rate of growth has been more or less the same (1.97%) as that of employment of men during the period and as a result, the share of women in total employment has remained at the level of 28% over the period. Women employment has grown much faster in urban areas (3.62%) than in rural areas (1.66%). The rate of growth of urban employment has been more or less the same for men (3.66%) and women but in rural areas women employment has grown faster than employment of men (1.48%). While the share of rural areas in total employment has declined from 82.% to 78.% the share of rural areas in total women employment declined less sharply from 89% to 87.%; and the share of rural women in total employment fell only slightly, from 24.9% to 24.2% (NSSO 1981-1990). Women employment thus continues to be predominantly rural.

Although the share of women in total employment has been stagnant at 28.%, and in agriculture at 32%, it has increased in construction (from 14% to 24%) and in finance, insurance and real estate (from 4.5% to 7.5%) and has declined in trade and commerce (14.%) to 13.%) during 1978-88. The average annual growth rate of employment of women has been higher than that of overall employment in agriculture (1.1% against 0.9), construction (16% against 10%), electricity gas and water supply (10% against 5%) and finance, insurance and business services (13% against 7.5%) (NSSO *ibid*). As the last two are small sectors in terms of employment shares, major gains in employment for women would appear to have occurred in sectors mostly offering insecure and unstable employment, namely, agriculture and construction.

Differential rates of growth of employment of women in different sectors have brought about some changes in the structure of women employment. The share of agriculture in women employment fell from 80% in 1977-78 to 75% in 1987-88 and the shares of each of the other sectors in women employment increased. Construction registered the most significant increases, from 0.93 to 3.33% but the shares of sectors like manufacturing, trade, transport and services in total women employment increased slightly. On the other hand, the share of agriculture in employment of men fell more sharply, from 67% to 59%; and that of construction increased less significantly, from 2.18 to 4.17% (NSSO *ibid*).

An analysis of trends in the structure of employment by category of employment, reveals a shift from self employment to casual work, with the proportion of regular wage/ salary earners remaining unchanged, but in the case of women workers, the shift is more towards regular wage/ salaried work 54.8% of women workers were self employed, 6.6% regular wage/salaried workers and 38.6% casual workers in 1977-78, while the corresponding proportions were 53%, 8% and 39% respectively in 1987-88. On the other hand, the share of the self employed in employed men declined from 58.% to 54%, and that of casual workers rose from 24% to 28% while the share of regular wage/salary earners remained at 18% during this period (Planning Commission 1992). Although a larger proportion of women workers are casual workers and a smaller proportion regular wage/salary earners than male workers, on the margin, women have been able to secure regular jobs better than men and avoid increase in the degree of casualisation.

Average annual rates of growth of overall employment as well as women employment are higher according to the 1981 and 1991 Census (2.4% and 3.4%) than those revealed by the 32nd and 43rd Round NSSO surveys (1.95% and 1.90%). The same is the case in some sectors, namely, agriculture, trade and commerce and 'other services' (other than transport etc.). Census rates of growth for overall and women employment are lower than NSSO rates in other sectors, namely, construction, mining and quarrying and transport, storage and communications. In all sectors except construction and trade and commerce, however, employment growth rates for females are higher than those for overall employment during the period 1981-91. The share of females in total employment has, therefore, risen from 20.3% in 1981 to 22.5% in 1991, though the share according to Census data is smaller than that revealed by NSSO surveys. Census data also reveal, like NSSO data, a slower shift away form agriculture in the structure of female employment (81.3% to 80.8%) than is the case with the structure of male employment (65.6% to 62.7%) (Registrar General, India 1993). The shift noticed from Census data is also much smaller than shown by NSSO data. The low growth of employment of females in construction and the fall in the share of construction in total female employment as well as in the share of females in construction employment during 1981 to 1991, is, however, contrary to the trends during 1977-78 to 1987-88 revealed by NSSO surveys. All these trends have to be examined in detail, taking note of the reasons mentioned earlier as also other relevant factors.

Work in the unorganised sector is the more predominant mode of employment of women than of men. The share of the organised sector even in overall employment is only 10%; but the share in the case of women employment is much less, only 3.2%. Employment of women in the annum) than that of employment of men 91.5% per annum); and as a result, the share of women in organised sector employment has increased from 12% in 1979 to 13.6% in 1989. Employment of women has grown relatively faster in certain subsecotrs of the organised sector, like financial services (8.8% per annum), transport, communications (6.8%), electricity, gas and water services (7.7%) and community services (4.6%). It registered an absolute decline in manufacturing and mining and grew slower than employment of men in agriculture and construction. Such deferential growth rates have led to changes in employment shares of women in different subsectors of the organised sector and in the structure of organised sector employment during the period 1979-89. Employment shares of women have risen fast in financial services (8% to 11%) and community services (16% to 20%); and the share has declined in manufacturing. In 1979, half of the women employed in the organised sector were in community services and a little over one-fifth in manufacturing;

and in 1989, the corresponding shares were 57% and 16% (Ministry of Labour-successive Annual and Quarterly Employment Reviews).

Public sector has been the main contributor to the growth of organised sector employment, with the public and private organised sector employment levels registering average annual growth rates of 2.35% and 0.36% respectively. Employment growth rates have been higher for women than men in both the public sector (4.8% against 2.1%) and the private sector (0.85% against 0.25%) (Ministry of Labour, *ibid.*).

Employment of Educated Women

Employment of educated women has grown faster (almost 10% per annum) than overall women employment and also faster than employment of the educated in general (7.5% per annum) during the period 1977-78 to 1987-88. The share of the educated in total women employment has consequently increased from 7.5% to 1.5% during this period, but the increase in the share of the educated in total women labour force has been sharper, from 19% to 33% (NSSO 1981, 1990).

Quality of Women's Employment

It has been seen that (i) women's employment is more predominantly rural than that of men's employment, (ii) the share of women workers has increased mostly in sectors offering only low paid, insecure and unstable employment (like agriculture and construction), (iii) the shift from agricultural to non-agricultural employment has been less marked and that to construction is more marked in the case of female workers than of male workers, and (iv) the proportion of casual workers among female works, though stagnant over the Eighties, is still higher than for male workers. These show that the quality of women's employment is not only relatively much lower than that of men but also that it has not improved over time.

Data on earnings of male and female workers from NSSO surveys on employment and unemployment confirm these trends. Notwithstanding the Equal Remuneration Act, average earnings of female workers continue to be less than those of male workers; and the disparity in earnings between male and female workers, regular or casual, has worsened over the Eighties in the agricultural sector except in rural public works. The disparity has reduced somewhat in the non-agricultural sector, and more sharply in urban sectors than in the non-farm rural sector. Further, the disparity between average daily earnings of male and female casual workers even in 1987-88 is greater that in the case of regular wage/salaried male and female workers (*see* Tables 12.2 and 12.3.)

Conclusions

To sum up,

(i) the level of participation, of women in economic activities is low; and this has meant a low and stagnant share of women in total workers (28%) over the years.

(ii) unemployment rates are higher for women than men.

(iii) visible underemployment is a much higher proportion among, women than among men.

(iv) The trend towards an increase in the incidence of open unemployment and a decline in that of (visible) underemployment, has been stronger in the case of women than in the case of men.

(v) Incidence of unemployment among educated women is much higher (27.%) than that for men (10%). A little over one-fourth of the educated unemployed in 1987-88 are women, though this share has come down from 42% to 27% in the Eighties.

(vi) Employment of women is more predominantly rural than of men.

(vii) Work in the unorganised sector is the more predominant mode of employment of women than men.

(viii) The share of women in overall employment has increased mostly in sectors offering only low paid, insecure and unstable employment; but here is also a trend towards an increase in some smaller sectors characterised by stable employment (namely, financial services and electricity).

(ix) The shift in the structure of employment from agricultural to non-agricultural employment has been less marked, and that to construction has been more marked, in the case of female than of male workers.

(x) There has been an increase in the stability of women's employment, in terms of proportion of regular wage/ salary earners among workers; the proportion has slightly declined in case of men. On the other hand, while proportion of casual workers has significantly increased in the case of males, it has remained unchanged in the case of female workers.

(xi) Women have been able to secure an increase in the organised, particularly public sector jobs much faster than men. A major part of this increase is accounted for by community services and financial services.

(xii) Average daily earnings of female workers continue to be less than that of male workers, the disparity being greater in the case of casual workers then regular wage/salaried workers. The disparity has worsened over the Eighties in the agricultural sector except in rural public works. It has reduced somewhat in the non-agricultural sector, and more sharply in urban sectors than in the non-farm rural sector.

(xiii) Quality of employment of women is, as seen from the foregoing, not only relatively much lower than that of men but also that it has not improved much over time. However, (viii), (x) and (xi) above indicate a trend towards some improvement.

TABLE 12.1

Incidence of Unemployment* by Sex, Residence and Status

Sector/Status/Sex			*1972-73*	*1977-78*	*1983*	*1987-88*
1			*2*	*3*	*4*	*5*
Rural	UPS	M	—	2.22	2.12	2.87
		F	—	5.52	1.41	3.52
		T	—	3.26	1.91	3.07
	CWS	M	3.02	3.57	3.72	4.16
		F	5.51	4.13	4.26	4.27
		T	3.86	3.74	3.88	4.19
	CDS	M	6.83	7.12	7.52	4.58
		F	11.22	9.18	8.98	6.91
		T	8.21	7.70	7.94	5.25
Urban	UPS	M	—	6.48	5.86	6.07
		F	—	17.76	6.90	8.77
		T	—	7.12	6.04	6.56
	CWS	M	5.96	7.12	6.69	6.71
		F	9.09	10.93	7.46	8.93
		T	6.53	7.86	6.81	7.12
	CDS	M	8.02	9.40	9.23	8.79
		F	13.67	14.55	10.99	12.00
		T	81.99	10.34	9.52	9.36
Total	UPS	M	—	3.07	3.02	3.60
		F	—	7.01	2.14	4.19
		T	—	4.23	2.77	3.77
	CWS	M	3.61	4.29	4.44	4.75
		F	5.87	4.97	4.70	4.92
		T	4.32	4.48	4.51	4.80
	CDS	M	7.07	7.59	7.93	5.54
		F	11.46	9.86	9.26	7.61
		T	8.35	8.18	8.28	6.09

* Unemployed as percentage of labour force.

UPS: Usual Principal Status.

CWS: Current Weekly Status.

CDS: Current Daily Status

M:Male F: Female T: Total

(—) Concept not in use in 1972-73.

Source: Eighth Five Year Plan (1992-97), Vol. I (Planning Commission).

TABLE 12.2

Average Wage/Salary Earnings (Rs.) Per Day of Regular Wage/Salaries Employees (1977-78 and 1987-88)

Group	Agricultural Sector		Non-Agricultural Sector		All Sectors	
	1977-78	1987-88	1977-78	1987-88	1977-78	1987-88
Rural						
M	3.56	14.58	10.14	34.90	7.19	30.14
F	3.71	10.65	7.28	26.28	5.97	21.56
F/M	1.04	0.73	0.72	0.75	0.83	0.72
Urban						
M	5.62	27.57	14.80	42.07	14.60	41.87
F	5.19	19.05	9.25	34.90	9.12	34.76
F/M	0.92	0.69	0.62	0.83	0.62	0.83
Total						
M	3.66	15.90	13.16	40.02	10.97	37.88
F	3.83	11.14	8.48	32.70	7.56	30.44
F/M	1.05	0.70	0.64	0.81	0.69	0.80

Source: 27th and 43rd Round Surveys of NSSO.

TABLE 12.3

Average Wage Earnings (Rs.) Per Day of Casual Wage Labour

Group	Public Works		Agricultural Operations		Non-Agricultural Operations	
	1977-78	1987-88	1977-78	1987-88	1977-78	1987-88
Rural						
M	4.39	12.62	3.73	11.09	5.12	15.48
F	2.12	9.31	2.58	7.32	2.74	8.86
F/M	0.48	0.74	0.69	0.66	0.54	0.57
Urban						
M	6.61	—	4.38	12.82	6.29	17.54
F	4.06	—	2.79	7.57	2.99	9.25
F/M	0.61	—	0.64	0.59	0.48	0.53
Total						
M	4.63	—	3.75	11.19	5.53	16.38
F	2.25	—	2.59	7.34	2.82	9.03
F/M	0.48	—	0.69	0.66	0.51	0.56

(—)Not available.

Source: 27th and 32nd Rounds of NSSO.

13

Women in Ready Made Garment Industry

The Ready Made Garment (RMG) industry had its origins in India during the Second World War, when such units were set up for mass production of military uniforms. The industry began growing fast, thanks to the shift in urban consumer tastes from custom-tailored garments to RMGs and introduction of export promotion schemes by Government in the Sixties. The rapid growth of the industry thereafter has been brought about by rising exports of RMG's. The performance of the industry on the export front, in terms of rates of export growth and increasing share of RMGs in total exports from India may be seen from the Table 13.1.

TABLE 13.1

Export of RMG's: 1960-61 to 1993-94

Year	*Value of Rs. Crores*	*Exports us $ Million*	*Av. Annual Gr. Rate (Compound) us $*	*Share in India's Exports*	*World Trade*
1	2	3	4	5	6*
1960-61	1	2		@	NA
1970-71	29	39	34.6	1.9	@
1980-81	550	696	33.4	8.2	1.8
1985-86	1067	872	4.6	9.8	2.3
1990-91	4012	2236	20.7	12.3	2.3
1991-92	5422	2199	(-)1.7	12.3	2.1
1992-93	6931	2393	8.8	12.9	NA
1992-93	(Ap-Dec)	1138	8.6	13.3	NA
1993-94	(Ap-Dec)	1216	6.9	11.7	NA

@ Negligible.

* Share in articles of apparel and clothing accessories (relates to calendar years)

Source: Economic Survey 1993-94.

The export sector dominates the RMG industry in as much as exports account for a sizeable proportion of the total apparel production in the country. The Northern Region accounts for 43% of the value of exports, with the Western and Southern Regions contributing 36% and 21% respectively. Among production centres, Delhi has a share of 41% of the exports and Bombay a share of 36%. 64% of the exports are cotton-based garments. 34% are synthetic/Man Made Fibres (MMF)-based and 1.7% are woollens. More than three fourths of the exported garments are based on cloth from the mill sector, a little over one-fifth from the knitwear sector and just 0.3% from the handloom sector (Ministry of Textiles: 1991; these figures relate to 1990).

Features of Industry

(a) General

The major source of information on the industry is the comprehensive survey conducted by the Textiles Committee during 1989-90. The Industry comprises, according to the survey, four types of units, namely domestic manufactures, manufacturer-exporters, fabricators and merchant-exporters/traders. This is facilitated by the flexibility of the garment manufacturing process—see the generalised flow sheet of garment manufacture at Fig. 13.1—which admits of decentralised production through parts of the process being formed out for job work. The industry is made up mostly of small and cottage size units, which account for 80% of the units, with medium and large units accounting for 14% and 6% respectively of the total number of units. (The size classification is based on the number of sewing machines in a unit large: 50+, medium: 21-49, small: 11-20 and cottage: <or = 10>. Domestic units are concentrated in regions like Calcutta, Delhi and Bombay; export units in Bombay, Delhi, Madras and Bangalore; fabricator units in Delhi, Calcutta and Bombay; and merchant-exporters/traders in Delhi, Calcutta, Bombay, Bangalore and Indore. The growth of RMG units is of recent origin, as can be judged from the fact that 42% of units had been set up between 1986 and 1989 and 30% during the period 1981-85.

About 86.7% of the 10.73 lakh machines in operation in the RMG industry are sewing/stitching machines. Specialised machines such as those which perform functions like embroidery, button-holing, stitching, fusing, zip attaching, bar tacking overlock and shade sorting account for another 7.2%. Processing machines (like thread trimming machines and trouser fusing machines), cutting machines and precutting machines account for 3.87%, 1.94% and 0.03% respectively. Most of the machines in the industry (70.49%) are in fabricator units. Domestic manufacturers and manufacturer-exporters account for 20.56% and 7.41% respectively of the machines. Merchant-exporters do not have much of a production of infrastructure, except perhaps for preparation of samples and their share of the machines in the industry is just 1.54%.

Only about 10% of the machines installed in the industry are imported, machines mostly form USA, Japan and (West) Germany. About three-fourths of such imported machines are with manufacturer-exporter (42.38%) and fabricators (32.60%). The merchant-exporter/traders account for 13.8% of the imported machines and the rest by domestic manufacturers.

FIGURE 13.1

Flow Sheet of Garment

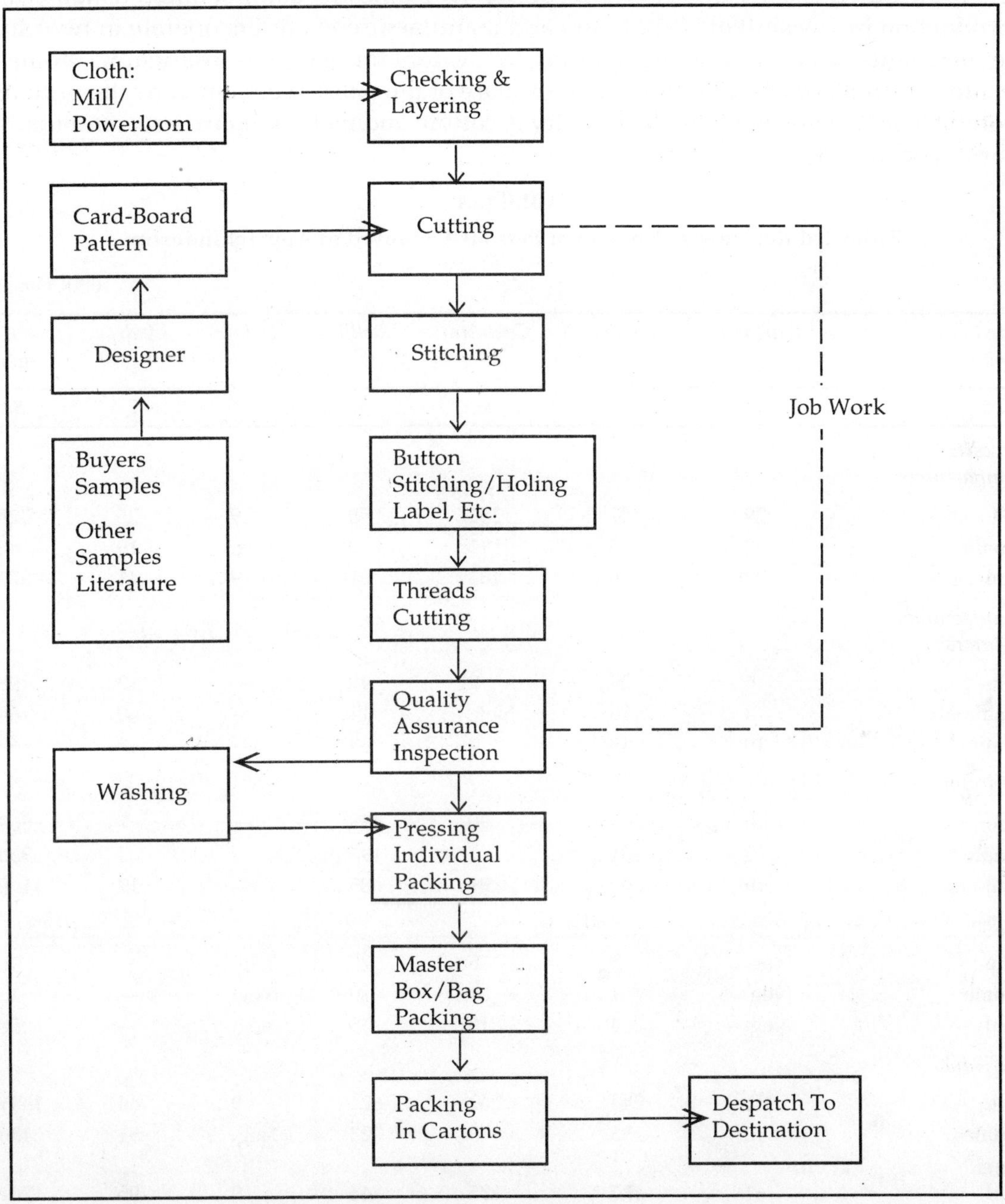

Source: Bombay Textile Research Association, In depth study of Indian Apparel Industry with special reference to steps to increase garment exports.

Domestic manufactures contributed to 48.26% of the estimated production of 1494 million garment pieces during 1988-89, while manufacturer-exporters and merchant exporters / traders contributed 17.07% and 34.67% respectively. Domestic manufacturers usually carry out production in one shift of 10-12 hours and manufacture-exporters operate in two shifts while merchant-exporters generally employ fabricators for garment production. Women's wear and children's wear account for a large share of the fabrics consumed by the industry. 39% of the fabrics consumed by the industry is cotton; and blended fabrics account for 37% of fabrics consumed.

TABLE 13.1

Estimated Regionwise Number of Persons Employed in Apparel Industry

(000' *Persons*)

Name of Region	*Bangalore*	*Bombay*	*Calcutta*	*Delhi*	*Indore*	*Madras*	*All India*
1	2	3	4	5	6	7	8
Domestic Manufacturers							
Male	29	51	152	58	9	25	324
Female	3	15	11	3	Neg.	16	48
Total	32	66	163	61	9	41	372
Manufacturers Exporters							
Male	6	29	2	49	—	12	98
Female	4	16	Neg.	14	—	30	64
Total	10	45	2	63	—	42	162
Fabricator							
Male	16	261	90	489	—	7	863
Female	3	101	1	196	—	5	306
Total	19	362	91	685	—	12	1169
Tradep							
Male	Neg.	3	18	25	Neg.	—	46
Female	Neg.	1	1	10	Neg.	—	12
Total	Neg.	4	19	35	Neg.	—	58
Sub Total							
Male	51	344	262	621	9	44	1331
Female	10	133	13	223	Neg.	51	430
Grand Total	61	477	275	844	9	95	1761

Source: 1991 *ibid.*

(b) Employment

A little less than two-thirds of the total estimated employment of 1.7 million in the industry (in the regions covered by the survey) is found in fabricating units (*see* Table 13.1). The shares of Manufacturer-Exporters and Merchant Exporters are 9% and 3.2% respectively while that of domestic units is 21%. A comparison with production shares and employment shares would appear to indicate wide differences in productivity levels between different categories of units. However, such a comparison is not valid and it seems likely that fabricator units take on a sizeable portion of the production load of not only merchant-exporters but also other categories of units.

The Delhi region contributes to a little less than half of the total estimated employment, the Bombay region a little over one-fourth and the Calcutta region a little less than one-sixth. The Madras and Bangalore regions together account for a little less than one-tenth. The share of piece-rated employment in the units surveyed is 54%. The share of piece-rated workers is 80% in fabricating units, 45% in domestic manufacturing units and 33% in manufacturer-export units. Merchant-Exporter units do not employ piece-rated workers. Supervisors, designers, cutters, stampers, sorters, stitching operators, pressmen, and trimmers are among piece-rated workers. Fabricating units employ a majority (77%) of these piece-rated workers. Bombay Delhi regions account for five-sixth of all piece-rated workers.

The functional profile of employment in the industry may be seen from Table 13.2.

TABLE 13.2

Employment in RMG Industry: Functional Profile (1988-89)

	Functional Designation	*Employment (000's)*	*Percentage*
1.	Managers/Managerial Personnel	47.37	2.69
2.	Supervisors	28.22	1.62
3.	Designers	5.14	0.29
4.	Markers/Graders	3.79	0.22
5.	Cutters	59.08	3.36
6.	Stitching Operators/Tailors	1403.92	79.70
7.	Pressmen	30.01	1.71
8.	Trimmers/Cleaners	19.94	1.14
9.	Packers	13.93	0.76
10.	Other Operational Workers	84.94	4.82
11.	Administrative Staff*	64.66	3.67
	Total	1761.00	100.00

* Includes marketing functions.
Source: (1991: Ministry of Textiles).

Stitching operators and tailors account for four-fifths of work force in the RMG industry. Manning norms revealed by the functional profile are:

(i) 30 stitching operators/tailors per Manager,
(ii) 50 stitching operators/tailors per Supervisor,
(iii) 272 stitching operators per Designer,
(iv) One Cutter/Marker/Grader feeds 22 stitching operators/tailors,
(v) One timer/clearer caters to the needs of 70 stitching operators/tailors,
(vi) One pressman/others handles the output of 16.5 stitching operators/tailors, and
(vii) One packer handles the output of 104 stitching operators/tailors.

(c) Employment of Women

One-fourth of the workforce are women. The share of women in total employment varies from 5% in the Calcutta region to 55% in the Madras region; and from 13% in domestic manufacturing units to 42% in manufacturer-exporter units. However, Delhi accounts for a little over half of the women employed in the industry. Delhi and Bombay together account for a substantial share (83%) of the women employed in the industry. Fabricating units contribute to a substantial share (71%) of total female employment in the industry (*See* Table 13.2).

Sex-wise employment pattern in different processes shows that pre-cutting processes involving cloth-spreading and pattern making are dominated by males; the stitching operation is largely shared by male and female workers; and specialised work involving processes like overlocking, embroidery and button holding and stitching are dominated by males. Since (a) a majority of workers in fabricating workers are piece-rated workers, (b) a substantial proportion of piece rated workers are in fabricating units, and (c) stitching operators are largely piece-rated workers, it is evident that a large proportion of women workers in the industry work on piece-rate basis.

(d) Employment in Subsidiary Activities

A large number of persons are employed in other ancillary and subsidiary and support activities like machine repair, supply of sewing threads, sewing needles, buttons, zippers, hooks, packing material and labels. About 200,000 people are estimated to be employed in these activities.

(e) Employment in the RMG Export Sector

Employment levels in the RMG Export Sector could be estimated by excluding domestic manufacturing units from consideration in Table 13.1. The export sector accounts for 79% of the total employment in the industry or 1.389 million (*see* Table 13.3). Overall employment as well as female employment in the RMG Export Sector is concentrated in Delhi and Bombay. While Calcutta accounts for about 8% of employment, Madras accounts for 9% of female employment. The share of females in employment is substantially high in Madras and quite low in Calcutta. The shares of Bombay and Delhi over around the overall share of 27.5% while that of Bangalore somewhat lower.

TABLE 13.3

Employment in RMG Export Sector

Region	*Employment (000's)*		*Share of Females percentage*
	Total	*Female*	
1	*2*	*3*	*4*
Bangalore	29 (2.1)	7 (1.8)	24.1
Bombay	411 (29.6)	118 (30.9)	28.7
Calcutta	112 (8.1)	2 (0.5)	1.8
Delhi	783 (56.4)	220 (57.6)	28.1
Indore		Negligible	
Madras	54 (3.9)	35 (9.2)	64.8
Total	1389 (100.0)	382 (100.0)	27.5

Source: Table 13.1.

(f) Functional Profile of Skilled Manpower in The RMG Export Sector

The functional profile of skilled manpower in the RMG Export Sector (that is, the profile of employees other than managers and administrative staff not concerned with production) may be seen Table 13.4. Skilled manpower in fabricator units constitute 88% of the skilled manpower in the export sector. Stitching operators account for 90% of the production personnel in fabricator units while it is only 60% in manufacturer-exporter units. The dominance of stitching operators in the (factory) workforce is seen in the entire export sector. The share of Fabricator units in the total number of stitching operators employed in the RMG Exports sector is as high as 92%.

(g) Manpower Requirements of Garment Exports Sector for 1995 and 2000

The Committee to Assess and Forecast Skilled Manpower Requirements upto the Year 2000 for the Garment Export Industry (1991) has, after examining available data on manpower employed in the industry, and forecasts made by different groups, projected the growth of manpower of various categories in the RMG Export Industry upto 1995 and 2000. It has assumed that (i) The "factory" workforce in RMG Export Sector would grow at an average annual rate of growth of 10% in both manufacturer-exporter units as well as fabricator units, and (ii) the functional profile will remain the same over the forecast period. The base year data utilised by the 1991 Committee was the data thrown up by the Textiles Committee Survey in view of its comprehensiveness of the survey and the fact that it was the latest data available. The 1991 Committee's estimates showed that production (factory) workforce of RMG Exports Sector would grow from 1.303 million in 1988-89 to 2.306 million in 1995 and further to 3.713 million in 2000. The number of stitch operators would rise from 1.131 million in 1988-89 to 2.001 million in 1995 and to 3.22 million in 2000. Detailed estimates may be seen in Table 13.4.

In the 1991 Committee's view an annual growth rate of 10% in the (factory) workforce along with simultaneous efforts to modernise and adopt better organisation and methods by the industry would enable achievement of an annual growth rate of 15% required in exports to realise the target of US $ 5 billion in 1995. The Committee has, therefore, emphasised the need to strengthen the information base of employment, manpower and production and productivity in the industry and on training facilities available for meeting the industry's needs and their inadequacies.

TABLE 13.4

Requirement of Skilled Manpower 1995 and 2000: RMG Exports Industry

Categories	*1988-1989*		*Total*	*1995*	*2000*
	Mfr. Exporter	*Fabricator*			
Prod. Asst./ Manager	1910 (1.3)	870 (—)	2780 (0.2)	4920	7920
Designer	1920 (1.2)	730 (—)	2650 (0.2)	4690	7550
Supervisor	7480 (4.9)	16960 (1.5)	24440 (1.9)	43260	69650
Marker and Grader	2670 (1.8)	720 (0.1)	3390 (0.3)	6000	9660
Cutter	6480 (4.3)	21670 (1.9)	28150 (2.2)	49825	80210
Stitch Operators	90450 (59.5)	1040155 (90.4)	1130605 (86.8)	2001170	3221880
Pressman	7250 (4.8)	9590 (0.8)	16840 (1.3)	29805	47990
Trimmers/ Cleaners	11180 (7.4)	6370 (0.6)	17550 (1.3)	31060	50000
Packing Man	6300 (4.1)	2800 (0.2)	9100 (0.7)	16105	25930
Any Others	16250 (10.7)	51300 (4.4)	67550 (5.2)	119565	192500
Total	151890 (100.0)	1151165 (100.0)	1303055 (100.0)	2506400	3713290

The above estimates of manpower requirements will, however, need to be reviewed in the light of trends since then and the new perspectives arising out of (a) the new economic policy of the Government, (b) the phasing out of the MFA over the period 1995-2005 following the Uruguway Round of Negotiations, and (c) free trade era beyond 2005.

(h) Training Facilities

The information base on the manpower and training aspects of the RMG industry is weak. Attempts made to bring together and analyse some data on these matters by (i) the techno-economic study commissioned by Apparel Export Promotion Council (AEPC) to set up the Apparel Training and Research Institute and carried out by Tata Consultancy Services (TCS) in 1988, (ii) then Working Group on Manpower Requirements in the Ready Made Garments Industry set up by the Planning Commission in 1989, (iii) the survey of RMG Industry carried out by the Textiles Committee (TC) for AEPC 1989-90, and (iv) the Report of the Committee to Assess and Forecast Skilled Manpower Requirements upto 2000 for the Garment Export Industry (1991) referred to earlier have only served to emphasise the urgent need to take up comprehensive studies and surveys in this area to strengthen and regularly update the information base.

Training facilities in apparel manufacturing and related technology are available at different levels. Courses offered vary widely in terms of duration, course content, emphasis and their nature. These institutions are government affiliated bodies, autonomous organisations, government institutions or private institutions, those offering long term courses leading to certificate, diploma, degree or even post-graduate degrees and other training institutions.

Vocational training institutes include small private institutions organising short term courses on sewing and tailoring and also those institutions which offer short term job-oriented courses which are recognised by the Directors of Vocational and Educational Training of various State Governments.

The Second category of courses cover a large spectrum of skills and expertise in operations/ processes of garment manufacture and related technology. One set among these consists of the certificate courses run by Industrial Training Institutes (ITI's) and the National and Regional Vocational Training Institutes for Women (NVTI and RVTI's), the recognition for such courses being provided by the National Council for Vocational Training (NCVT). The ITIs offer basic training in (i) cutting and tailoring, (ii) dress making, (iii) embroidery and needle work, (iv) knitting with hand machine, (v) calico printing, bleaching and dyeing while RVTIs and NVTI offer advanced skill training in (i) dress making, (ii) embroidery and needle work, and (iii) garment knitting. Another set of courses under the Apprenticeship Training relates to Designer and Master Cutter and Male Female and General Tailor leading to National Apprenticeship certificates. The fourth set of courses leading to a diploma or degree recognised by the All India Council of Technical Education (AICTE) provide intermediate level training in:

(i) Costume design,
(ii) Dress making,
(iii) Fashion technology,

(iv) Production technology,
(v) Knitting technology,
(vi) Garment technology,
(vii) Fashion coordination, and also
(viii) Technology and textile engineering.

The fifth set of courses provide managerial level training and these courses are run by the National Institute of Fashion Technology (NIFT) in:

(i) Fashion Designing
(ii) Apparel Manufacturing Technology
(iii) Garment Manufacturing Technology
(iv) Accessory Design
(v) Courses on other areas like Leather Garment, Knitted Apparel Design and Textile Design and Knitwear and
(vi) Continuing education programmes and workshops for the garment industry and consultancy services.

Information on training facilities available is not complete, especially in terms of output from the institutions. Patterns of utilisation are not also known. It is necessary to conduct a comprehensive study to collect information and also develop an upto date information system.

Productivity Levels and Skill Shortages

Available data on production and productivity in the industry is contradictory and not reliable, according to the 1991 Committee set up by the Ministry of Textiles. The Committee noted that the TCS in its study had assumed productivity in the industry as 6 pieces per worker-day, while the Working Group of the Planning Commission assumed productivity at 5 pieces/worker-day. According to the in-depth study of the Bombay Textile Research Association referred to earlier, *productivity per tailor* is about 10 to 15 shirts per day (compared to 25 to 30 in Hongkong, Japan and China).

The deliberations of the Working Group of the Planning Commission and the 1991 Committee of the Ministry of Textiles reveal that in the view of a majority of manufacturers there is a dearth of well trained pattern makers and cutters required for the industry. Further, in the context of the need to withstand competition from other developing countries, and increase exports to improve India's share of World trade in RMGs, through capturing untapped markets, especially in the post-GATT era and also improve unit value realisation, shortages of such skills may increase and become a bottleneck. Further, since tailors and stitching operators form the backbone of the industry, and since advances in technology have ushered in new types of machines, it is essential to upgrade the skills of such operational workers so as to enable them to handle new types of machines. Skills for handling operations like button-holding and button-stitching, spot-removing, fusing, finishing, pressing and packing with or without machines and gadgets/equipment have to be created and upgraded. Machine mechanics, machine motor electricians and quality controllers, are also needed in large numbers.

The 1991 Committee had made detailed recommendations on training and skill development for the industry both for raising its efficiency and enhancing the quality of its products and also in the context of the country's desire to benefit from the expanding potential of the international and domestic markets for RMG. These needed no repetition here. It is, however, necessary to note that many of these are still to be acted upon and to underline the need for speedy action being taken to implement them.

Finally, as suggested by the 1991 Committee it is necessary to launch scientific studies to assess productivity levels in the RMG industry and also comprehensive studies to collect data on (a) manpower available in the industry and its inadequacies *vis-a-vis* industry's needs, (b) training facilities available for meeting manpower/skill needs of the industry, and (c) gaps and inadequacies in the training offered *vis-a-vis* the requirements of the industry. Alongside, it is necessary to forget suitable links between the industry and the training system so that training is responsive to industry's changing needs.

RMG Industry—Prospects

About 80% of RMG exports form India are to the so called "quota" countries like USA, Germany,.France, Italy, Benelux, U.K., E.E.C. and Canada covered by Bilateral Agreements (BA) under the MFA and the rest to "non-quota' countries. As the quotas set by different countries have generally been over-fulfilled in recent years there is no scope for further increase in exports of those types of garments which are covered under BAs with quota countries. Increase in the value of exports has, therefore, to come through (i) exports of 'quota-free' types of garments such as night wear, rain wear, swim wear, winter clothing and industrial institutional clothing to quota countries. (ii) increased exports to non-quota countries, and (iii) enhanced unit value realisation of exports. It is also necessary to be ready to take advantage of the post-GATT era and the free trade regime that would come into being in 2005 after the MFA is withdrawn in phases over the ten-year period starting form 1995. This will call for the launching of an expansion and modernisation programme for the RMG industry in India. It would be useful if the following approaches are adopted for the purpose, by various agencies, reports, etc. (1994: Jaikumar; 1994: Satya Sundram; 1991: Ministry of Textiles; AEPC; Bombay Textiles Research Association):

(i) Modernisation of factories and upgradation of product standards to survive growing competition.

(ii) Improvement in labour productivity by upgradation of skills, creation of necessary additional skills, retraining of existing labour so that new technology and machinery could be utilised.

(iii) Diversification of exports into high range fabrics and garments including blended fabrics, standard shirts and trousers, winter garments, sports wear, night wear, rain wear and industry institutional garments, through greater R&D inputs, appropriate technology upgradation by importation, if need be of high speed and modern textile and garment manufacturing machinery.

(iv) Diversifying and upgrading the quality of the fabric base or import of fabrics of quality or supply of fabrics at international prices; and similar facility for accessories like buttons, zips, labels, etc., may be provided.

(v) Setting up a chain of fabric testing laboratories.

(vi) Setting up functional industrial estates.

(vii) Among the other suggestions made are Indian companies forging tie-ups with Market Leaders, further reduction in import duty on or duty-free import of machinery for manufacturing garments and extension of freight subsidy on RMG Export to Latin American countries to exports to all non-quota countries.

14

Women as a Reserve Army of Labour: A Reappraisal

The role of the industrial reserve army for capitalist accumulation under the capitalist mode of production is, by now, well known.[1] In this chapter, we shall examine the role of women in the industrial reserve army in the context of a labour surplus[2] multistructural system[3] with a variety of production forms differentiated on the basis of the extent of capitalist development. It is clear that such an examination implies that we emphasise the secular role of the industrial reserve army. Most studies of the role of women in the industrial reserve army concern only the cyclical aspect. An understanding of the secular role of women in the industrial reserve army is essentially an understanding of the process of female proletarianisation.

Marx and Engels' Vision

The following passages from the writings of Marx and Engels provide us with a glimpse of their ideas on female proletarianisation.

In *The Condition of the Working Class in England*, Engels noted:

> this report testifies to the gradual but sure introduction of the factory system into all branches of industry, recognisable especially by the employment of women and children.... In all directions machinery is being introduced and the last trace of the working-man's independence thus destroyed. In all directions the family is being dissolved by the labour of the wife and children, or inverted by the husband being thrown out of employment and made dependent upon them for bread; everywhere, inevitable machinery bestows upon the great capitalist command of the workers with it (1975, reprint: 497).

Marx noted in Capital (Vol. 1):

> Insofar as machinery dispenses with muscular power, it becomes a means of employing labourers of slight muscular strength, and those whose bodily development is incomplete but whose limbs are all the more supple. The labour of women and children, was therefore, the first thing sought for by capitalists who used machinery. That mighty

> substitute for labour and labourers was forthwith changed into a means for increasing the number of wage-labourers by enrolling, under the direct sway of capital, every member of the workman's family, without distinction of age or sex.... Machinery, by throwing every member of that family on to the labour market, spreads the value of man's labour power over his own family. It, thus, depreciates his labour power. To purchase the labour power of a family of four workers may, perhaps, cost more than it formerly did to purchase the labour power of the head of the family but, in return, four days' labour takes the place of one, and their price falls in proportion to the excess of the surplus labour of four over the surplus labour of one. In order that the family may live, four people must now not only labour but expend surplus labour for the capitalist. Thus we see that machinery, while augmenting the human material that forms the principal object of capital's exploiting power, at the same time raises the degree of exploitation (1977, reprint: 372, 373).

Elsewhere in the same volume Marx noted that 'by the excessive addition of women and children to the ranks of the workers, machinery at last breaks down the resistance which the male operatives in the manufacturing period continued to oppose to the despotism of capital' (1977, reprint: 379).

The views of Marx and Engels on the influence of machinery on different classes of society were far more perceptive than those of Ricardo (1975: 386) who also recognised that machinery affected the interests of different classes in society differently. For instance, Engels, in *The Condition of the Working Class in England*, noted:

> The bourgeoisie usually replies to this that improvements in machinery by decreasing cost of production supply finished goods at lower prices, and that these reduced prices cause such an increase in consumption that the unemployed operatives soon find full employment in newly founded factories. The bourgeoisie ignores the fact that it takes years for these results of the decrease in price to follow and for new factories... to be built. It is silent upon the point that every improvement in machinery throws the real work, the expenditure of force more and more upon the machine and so transforms the work of full-grown men into mere expansion which a feeble woman or even a child can do quite as well, and does for half or two-third wages; that therefore grown men are constantly more and more supplanted and not re-employed by the increase in manufacture, it conceals the fact that whole branches of industry fall away or are so changed that they must be learned afresh. It does not mention the fact that the process of improvement goes steadily on, and that as soon as the operative has succeeded in making himself at home in a new branch, if he actually does succeed in doing so, this too is taken from him, and with the last remnant of security which remained to him for winning his bread (1975, reprint: 430—31).
>
> The fact that improved machinery reduces wages has also been violently disputed by the bourgeoise as it is constantly reiterated by the working-men. The bourgeoisie insists that although the price of piece-work has been reduced, yet the total of wages

for the week's work has rather risen than fallen, and the condition of the operative rather improved than deteriorated. It is hard to get to the bottom of the matter, for the operatives usually dwell upon the price of piece-work. But it is certain that the weekly wage also has, in many branches of work, been reduced by the improvement of machinery (Engels, 1975 reprint: 431-32).

The worst situation is that of those workers who have to compete against a machine that is making its way. The price of the goods which they produce adapts itself to the price of the kindred product of the machine and as the latter works more cheaply, its human competitor has but the lowest wages. The same thing happens to every operative employed upon an old machine in competition with later improvements (Engels, 1975 reprint: 433).

Let us examine somewhat more closely the fact that machinery more and more supersedes the work of men. The human labour involved in both spinning and weaving consists chiefly in piecing broken threads, as the machine does all the rest. This work requires no muscular strength, but only flexibility of finger. Men are, therefore, not only not needed for it, but actually by reason of the great muscular development of the hand, less fit for it than women and children and are, therefore, naturally almost superseded by them. Hence the more the use of arms, the expenditure of strength can be transferred to steam or water power, the fewer men need be employed; and as women and children work more cheaply, and in these branches better than men, they take their places (Engels, 1975 reprint: 434—35).

The employment of women at once breaks up the family, for when the wife spends twelve or thirteen hours every day in the mill, and the husband works the same length of time there or elsewhere, what becomes of children? (Engels, 1975 reprint: 436).

In many cases the family is not wholly dissolved by the employment of the wife but turned upside down. The wife supports the family, the husband sits at home, tends the children, sweeps the room and cooks. This case happens very frequently: in Manchester alone, many hundred such men could be cited, condemned to domestic occupations. It is easy to imagine the wrath aroused among the working men by this reversal of relations within the family, while the other social conditions remain unchanged (Engels, 1975 reprint: 438).

Can anyone imagine a more insane state of things than that described in this letter? And yet this condition which unsexes the man and takes from the women all womanliness, without being able to bestow upon the man true womanliness, or the women true manliness—this condition which degrades, in the most shameful way, both sexes, and through them, humanity, is the last result of our much-praised civilisation, the final achievement of all the efforts and struggles of hundreds of generations to improve their own situation and that of their posterity. We must either despair of mankind, and its aims and efforts, when we see all our labour and toil result in such a mockery, or we must admit that human society has hitherto sought

> salvation in a false direction; we must admit that so total a reversal of the position of the sexes can have come to pass only because the sexes have been placed in a false position from the beginning. If the: reign of the wife over the husband, as inevitably brought about by the factory system, is inhuman, the pristine rule of the husband over the wife must have been inhuman too. If the wife cannot have her supremacy upon the fact that she supplies the greater part, nay the whole of the common possession, the necessary influence is that this community of possession is no true and rational one, since one member of the family boasts offensively of contributing the greater share. If the family of our present society is being thus dissolved, this dissolution merely shows that at bottom, the binding tie of this family was not family affection, but private interest lurking under the cloak of a pretended community of possessions (Engels, 1975 reprint: 439).

The foregoing passages contain the gist of the views of Marx and Engels on female proletarianisation. The three forms of relative surplus population, or the industrial reserve army, are the floating, the latent and the stagnant which, by exerting a downward pull on wage level, is one of the counteracting influences on the falling rate of profit in the Marxian scheme of capital accumulation. While, as mentioned before, the cyclical role of the industrial reserve army is well understood, an examination of the forms of relative surplus population indicates that Marx envisaged a secular aspect as well.

For instance, the floating reserve includes workers who are regularly discharged after a certain age (youth) from automatic factories where machinery enters as a factor or where only the modern division of labour is carried out, and that section of the working class in modern industry where the life expectancy being short calls for a rapid renewal of the generations of labourers. This floating reserve within the capitalist sector is a secular feature and independent of the booms and depressions of that capitalist sector.

The category of latent relative surplus population refers to the labouring population seeking employment in the capitalist sector consequent to the penetration of capitalism in the precapitalist sectors. While Marx only specifically refers to the agricultural sector, it appears to us to be valid for all precapitalist sectors.

The third category of the relative surplus population—the stagnant—forms a part of the active labour army but with extremely irregular employment. The chief form under which it occurs is domestic industry. It recruits itself constantly from the supernumerary forces of the modern sectors of industry and agriculture, and especially from those decaying branches of industry where handicraft is yielding to manufacture, and manufacture to machinery.

The last sediment of the relative surplus population dwells in the sphere of pauperism. This layer of society, according to Marx, consists of three categories—those able to work, orphans and pauper children and, third, those demoralised and ragged, and those unable to work.

Marx further noted that 'the greater the social wealth, the functioning capital, the extent and energy of its growth, and therefore, also the absolute mass of the proletariat and the productiveness of its labour, the greater is the industrial reserve army' (Marx, 1977 reprint: 603).

Summarising the issues so far, some views of female proletarianisation emerge from the works of Marx and Engels.

1. Factory production and the introduction of machinery draws women into production.
2. And, in so doing, substitutes female labour for male labour.
3. This substitution has repercussions on the family.
4. Machinery provides the capitalist greater control over the labour process.
5. The initial resistance to machinery by male labour is broken down by substituting it with female labour.
6. Machinery, by drawing all members of the family irrespective of age and sex, depreciates the value of male labour power.
7. Machinery, by transferring the expenditure of more and more motive power to the machine, transforms the work itself bringing about changes both in the labour used as well as wages. This transformation of work where the tools have been converted from being manual implements of man into implements of a mechanical apparatus enables the 'motive mechanism' to acquire an independent form 'entirely emancipated from the restraints of human strength. This enables the employment of labourers with 'slight muscular strength and those whose bodily development is incomplete but whose limbs are all the more supple'. Consequently, the labour of women and children was the first thing sought by capitalists who used machinery.
   Along with the tool, the skill of the workman in handling it passes over to the machine. The capabilities of the tools are emancipated from the restraints that are inseparable from human labour power. In the process, the division of labour gets altered. In place of the hierarchy of specialised workmen that characterises manufacture, there exists in the automatic factory a tendency to equalise and reduce to one and the same level every kind of work that has to be done by the minders of the machines; in the place of the artificially produced differentiations of the detail workmen step the natural differences of age and sex. This transformation of the work and the worker 'is generally referred to as 'deskilling'.
8. An examination of the process of proletarianisation cannot be conducted independently of an understanding of the secular aspects of the industrial reserve army.
9. While Marx's analysis of the forms of relative surplus population does not differentiate between any groups of labour, the following questions regarding female proletarianisation remain valid:
   (a) Within the floating reserve in the 'capitalist sector where machinery exists and the modern division of labour prevails, what is the incidence of women?

What are the sectors in which young women get constantly replaced after attaining a certain age and why? Is such a replacement of workers after youth more among women than men, and more in the female intensive sectors than others?

(b) In the latent reserve, does the rate of absorption of precapitalist sectors by capitalism differ between female-intensive and other precapitalist sectors of production? While households (as opposed to household production) are not viewed as production sectors, they do constitute a latent source of labour supply. What has been the impact of capitalism in augmenting labour supply and why does this process occur?

(c) In the stagnant form of relative surplus population, does capitalist domestic industry continue to remain resilient to transformation in the modern factory system and, if so, are these female-intensive? Why does this happen?

(d) It further needs to be noted as to what extent a sex-segregated employment is based in the laws of motion of capitalism which predict' that as women are taken up, they are converted in representative proportions into primary workers, such that even if they were initially disproportionately represented in cyclical unemployment, a secular homogenisation of labour begins to dominate their cyclical differentiation. Does capitalism, even if it destroyed the former precapitalist sex-segregated employment structure, give rise to new forms of sex-segregated employment structures, and why?

Any understanding of the process of female proletarianisation has to contend with these questions on the industrial reserve army as well as the substitutability effect and its implications mentioned in points 1-7.

We agree, as would all those following the method of Marx, that none of these questions can be answered a priori without examining the historical development and the dynamics of a particular social formation.

REVIEW OF ISSUES IN SOME RECENT LITERATURE

Studies on the labour process in recent times (see Humphries, 1983) have largely been initiated by the work of Harry Braverman (1974).[4] Without negating the major criticism of Braverman's work (namely, the fact that the analysis of the labour process is done independently of the analysis of class relations and state institutions or, in other words, from the organisation of the mode of production as a whole). I recognise that there are significant insights that can be gained from Braverman and others on the implications of the restructuring of the capitalist labour processes. For Braverman, the crucial determinant of change in the industrial reserve army is mechanisation and automation. Industries and labour processes subjected to mechanisation release masses of labour for exploitation in other generally less mechanised areas of capital accumulation. Conversely, in those industries in which mechanisation and automation have not developed on any significant scale, there is an increasing demand for labour. This, in turn, creates the tendency for capital to invest in methods of organisation of the labour process which utilises low wage labour. Braverman, thus, ties fluctuations in the demand for labour to his analysis of the expanding and declining sectors of the economy. However, what has not been tackled in Braverman's analysis are the implications on the gender division of labour consequent to the restructuring of the labour process. It is also not clear why certain categories of labour are low wage labour. If it is a question of skill differences/requirements, this raises the whole question of the concept of 'skill'. Skill can be conceptualised in three different ways. It can refer to complex competencies, involving both the conception and execution of a task, which are developed within a particular set of social relations of production; it can refer to control over the labour process; it can also refer to conventional definitions of occupational status. Does the use of 'low wage' labour in certain forms of production organisation imply that the labour process here is simplified? Or that particular labour has a marginal position in the labour process or low occupational status?

In certain production organisations, particular types of labour— women, children and migrants—are sought after as low wage labour, compared to other labour which could also be utilised. In the case of footloose and temporary migrants with a hold in precapitalist sectors, it is found that these precapitalist sectors provide a subsidy for low wage in the capitalist sectors (Beechey, 1982). I find the explanation for the low wage of women inadequate in Marx and Engels, and Braverman. It is my position that women as a 'low wage' category cannot be explained without introducing 'partriarchy' in the analysis, by which I mean the ideology of gender relations prevailing in society where man is deemed to be the provider and protector of the family, the concrete manifestation of this ideology being reflected in terms of control over resources and labour, among others. The value of female labour power gets discounted thereby. This particular gender ideology not only ensures a discounted rate of female labour power but also reproduces forms of dependence and subordination found within the family in the capitalist work environment. I conclude merely by noting that both in Marx and Braverman, the concept of the industrial reserve army is imprecisely specified both theoretically and empirically.

Feminist Marxist literature on female proletarianisation raises some of the following issues.

The existence of patriarchy within capitalist society is not merely a hangover from a preindustrial stage of capitalism or from precapitalist society, nor even of sexist attitudes and prejudices which can be purged, but is of fundamental economic, political and ideological importance to the capitalist mode of production (Wolpe, 1980). In this context, it was noted that while Marx's analysis of the general tendencies within capitalism provided a foundation for the analysis of female wage labour, it does not adequately analyse the relationship between the family and the organisation of capitalist production. The crucial way in which Veronica Beechey (1977) sees the relationship between the two emerging is through the contradictory tendencies within capitalism to which women are subjected. On the one hand, the tendency to draw married women into wage labour under the direct domination of capital (which has also given rise to the tendency for capital to produce more labour-saving devices for use in the house), and to produce some of the use values which were previously produced in the home within the system of capitalist commodity production. This tendency coexists with another tendency towards the maintenance of the family as a unit for the reproduction of labour power and of the woman's role as a domestic labourer within it, and attempts to lower the value of male labour power by producing use values which are necessary for the production and reproduction of labour power as a commodity, both on a day-to-day basis and on a generational basis. These contradictory tendencies, she notes, have been embodied in a number of ways of organising the labour process (such as the creation of flexible shifts and part-time work), which have enabled women to perform both forms of labour—domestic labour and wage labour.. It is her view that whether the woman labours as a domestic labourer outside the direct domination of capital, or as wage labourer under the direct domination of capital, the woman is vitally involved in capital's attempts to extract a high rate of surplus value, and to generate countertendencies to the tendency for the rate of profit to fall.

It was pointed out that Marx as well as Braverman do not recognise the reaction of the organised working class to changes or the restructuring of the labour process, and the implication of it for the gender division of labour in a patriarchal capitalist context. In other words, there are limits to the substitutability of one type of labour for another mentioned in the earlier section, limits drawn by political action rather than economic mechanisms.

Veronica Beechey (1977) argues that the specific position of women as a part of the industrial reserve army can be explained in terms of their labour power being paid for at a price below its value; their labour power having a lower value; and the existence of the family, and of women's dependency within the family, and the ideological assumptions which surround this, which enter into the determination of the value of female labour power. However, she restricts the use of the industrial reserve army concept to 'short, sharp shifts' in labour demand, in response to seasonal fluctuations or fluctuations in the business cycle. Long-term shifts in the structure of the working class and the introduction of female labour on a fairly long-term basis into particular branches of industry can more usefully be seen in terms of capital's attempts to employ forms of labour power which have a lower value, and in terms of the process of deskilling. If one recognises the secular aspect of the industrial reserve army, then Beechey's distinction between the two is essentially a distinction of the cyclical and the secular role of the industrial reserve army. Once again, I will say that much of this confusion exists simply because the concept is imprecisely specified both theoretically and empirically. Beechey is of the opinion that whenever women have a different value from that of male labour power, their distinctive position within production has to be understood with reference to the family and the role of women within it. I do not restrict it so narrowly, but say that it has to be understood in terms of the patriarchal ideology, as mentioned earlier.

Floya Anthias (1980), while agreeing with Beechey that the family/production nexus is crucial, warns that it would be a mistake to consider the family as 'presupposed' as it is inextricably bound, affecting and affected by the production process, although it is one of the conditions of existence of women's wage labour in capitalism. It is also her view that once the family is introduced, the analysis should be conducted at the level of social formation and not the mode of production as Beechey attempts to.

Anthias also considers Beechey's 'advantages' to capital of female labour different from the question concerning the reasons for women being drawn into production. According to Anthias, the issue is the reason why particular groups of human subjects, with certain characteristics, whether sex or race, fill a particular place in society and, specifically, in the labour process. Given this problematic, what is actually necessary, in her opinion, is a concrete analysis of the process by which women' have been drawn into employment and into various categories of employment.

Anthias also highlights some of the weaknesses in Beechey's argument of how female labour is advantageous to capital in three ways, in particular Beechey's argument that women can be paid less than the value of labour power, and her analogy of women with semi-proletarianised workers. While semi-proletarianised workers depend on another mode of production, in the case of women, according to Beechey, dependence is on the male wage. Anthias finds a circularity in Beechey's argument that women have got to be initially excluded from production within the capitalist mode in order to be constituted as economic dependents.

Anthias also points out that Marx's analysis of a reserve army was at a general and abstract level and did not refer to any particular group of people. She also finds the political implications of applying the concept of reserve army of labour to women unfortunate as it leads to a tendency to marginalise the importance of women's employment for advanced capitalism. Also, Beechey's emphasis on the dependence of women on male wage might lead to a strategy of 'payment for housework' (though Beechey, herself, has not said so) and the underestimation of the need for struggles along various other fronts, particularly on the ideological front.

While agreeing with Anthias on the issues raised, particularly the political ones, I do not think Beechey ever, had a narrow conception of struggles. Struggles on the ideological front are both against capitalism and patriarchy. Marilyn Power (1983) agrees with Floya Anthias (1980) that Marx's categories of the reserve army were general, and not intended to describe specific groups of people, and that in order to analyse the experience of specific groups (such as women), it is necessary to look at that experience in its concrete social formation. In the United States, she noted that the rapid and steady increase in the participation of married women in wage labour in the latter half of the twentieth century can be understood to be the result of the invasion of their traditional production for use and exchange in the home by capitalist production, and an increased demand for clerical and service workers in the capitalist sector. She noted that women were, thereby, freed into the latent reserve army and have been gradually incorporated into active wage labour as capitalism has expanded. This argument, she notes, had implications on the dynamic interaction between capitalism and patriarchy. The expansion of capitalist production by separating the work sphere from the home, and by incorporating women into the wage labour force, whittled away the economic and ideological basis of patriarchy. However, as there is no evidence that gender inequality (both within the labour force and the family) is decreasing, she notes that capitalism has not set the stage for the destruction of patriarchy, and that the oppression of women has become incorporated into the dynamics of capitalism in a complex and contradictory interaction.

Irene Bruegel (1979) seeks to defend the role of the reserve army in the face of two major challenges based on British experience from 1974—78, namely, the long-term trend towards women's increasing participation in the labour force, and the segregation of the labour force into men's and women's jobs. According to her, disposability is the crux in determining whether women constitute a reserve army. She sets out to discover whether women constitute a disproportionate section of the unemployed in times of crisis. There are two aspects to Bruegel's disposability model. First, the idea that women might cushion men from the full impact of recession could be taken to imply that women's employment opportunities, taken as a whole, deteriorate in times of recession. On the other hand, it can be taken to mean that an individual woman is more susceptible to redundancy and unemployment than a man in a corresponding situation. Bruegel argues that individual for individual, women are more susceptible to redundancy and unemployment, though this may not cushion men from the full impact of recessions. Also, the long-term shift towards women in the workforce through the expansion of the service and public sector have worked to cushion women from the full impact of the recessions. I find that Bruegel's analysis, though recognising the long-term shifts, has its primary focus on the cyclical aspect. I also note that, in Bruegel's work, there is no attempt at integrating the peculiar role of women in the industrial reserve army in the process of capital accumulation.

Based on the work of Connelly (1978) and Irene Bruegel (1979), Lynda Yanz and David Smith (1983) have criticised the simplistic assertion that women function as a reserve army of labour for capital without any proof or explanation. They are of the opinion that it is not wrong to describe women as playing a peculiar role in the reserve army at specific times and in specific places, though the concept as such is neither an adequate description nor explanation of women's subordinate status in the labour force. Based on the Canadian experience, they find that an increasing number of women, particularly married women, have joined the labour force in recent times in clerical and service type jobs. Though these are low-paying dead-end jobs, they are permanent and very few women are found to drop out. They, therefore, found that as women have been integrated into the labour force, the reserve army characteristic of disposability was not fulfilled. In their view, capitalism has a 'natural' tendency to extend women's employment opportunities because their labour power is available at a lower price, and this tendency forms the basis for a struggle around women's right to work, women's relation to the family and women's relation to men. The outcome of these struggles, in their opinion, was that women were available to capital in certain ways that correspond to the notion of women as a reserve army. And it is these struggles that were the key determinants in establishing women's relationship to the labour force, not women's role as a reserve army of labour.

We agree with Yanz and Smith that assertion is not explanation, but find their own analysis wanting. It is not clear why women's labour power is available at a lower price, or if this lower price and the struggles mentioned can be independent of a patriarchal gender ideology. We do not see the struggles as a determinant being distinctly separate from the reserve army role. We believe that the interaction between capitalism and patriarchy is a complex one which enables women as a group to play a peculiar role in the reserve army in terms of availability, disposability and cheapness.. While recognising that the reserve army is the, result of the process of capital accumulation (in particular, the increasing, organic composition of capital), the development of capitalism, while releasing or freeing labour in one sector, also increases the demand for labour in other sectors, I find capitalism's demand for labour to be type-specific. The implications of women-specific absorption and displacement, while part of the general absorption and displacement, cannot be analysed without introducing patriarchy, and without placing the specificity of female labour within a general model of capital accumulation.

Jane Humphries (1983) distinguishes clearly between the cyclical reserve army hypothesis and the secular reserve army hypothesis. She reviews the literature on this theme, including the critiques of the industrial reserve army hypothesis which suggest that occupational specialisation by sex introduces inflexibility in the labour market. In her view, the secular reserve army hypothesis cannot be analysed without an idea of the, views of Marx and Engels on female proletarianisation, which also includes the substitutability aspect. Using relevant data from the US, she explores how women constituted a latent reserve and the process of their assimilation into the labour force. She found that, in the US, conditions were ripe for the substitution of women workers with men. In her opinion, debates on the role of women in the industrial reserve army were not merely academic but had important political implications as well.

THE INDIAN SCENARIO

So far, we have characterised the Indian scene as a labour surplus multistructural one—multistructural in the sense that there exist even today, very different forms of production, ranging from artisanal production to modern manufacture, with different degrees of subsumption to capital. We also noted that these different structures do not exit in isolation but are interlinked and interact with one another. Given this multistructural system, the primary question is the experience of women in the labour force. I seek specifically to obtain an understanding of the process of female proletarianisation in a multistructural context. Using both macro evidence and the numerous micro studies on women and work, I seek to explore 'the eight issues raised earlier in the chapter. Except for certain sporadic evidence I have on the pre-independence period, my analysis will be confined largely to the contemporary situation in the non-agrarian spheres.

In the post-independence period, macro evidence on the manufacturing sector from the census data reveals a declining trend in the incidence of workers in the household sector, both male and female (though the magnitude of decline among females cannot be accurately stated), and an increase in the incidence of workers in the non-household manufacturing sector. Analysing the overall net employment effect of this structural shift in the manufacturing sector from household to non-household production, it was found that for the country as a whole, the net effect of employment among males was positive, while in the case of females it was negative. Clearly then, the growth of the non-household manufacturing sector is not accompanied by an absorption of women displaced from the household manufacturing sector (MIDS, 1988). This displacement takes place against the backdrop of an overall secular decline in female work participation (Mitra, 1980). Basing their analysis on occupational tables in the 1961 and 1971 Census, Asok Mitra *et al.* noted:

> Under those capital intensive industrial sectors that have limited employment-generating capacity, the scope for employment for male workers in India has been limited, but it has been even more constricted for female workers. Women workers are mostly employed in labour intensive occupations like tea, coffee, rubber and coconut plantations, carpet weaving, laundry, bidi making or making matches, coir making, construction work, pottery and kiln work and food processing activities. With growing emphasis on food crop production in each successive plan, there has not been any remarkable expansion in the employment generating capacity of the occupations mentioned above. On the other hand, with the increase in population and with unlimited supply of labour in the working ages there has been increasingly tough competition for employment between men and women in all sectors of the economy and, consequently, there is evidence of displacement of women workers from even those agricultural and household industrial activities which they were engaged in former decades (Mitra *et a!.*, 1980: 46).

This process, coupled with the fact of a very sluggish growth in the organised sector as a whole, and Of female employment in that sector in particular, has led to the emergence of the urban informal sector where women are largely concentrated and engaged in petty commodity production and trade. The urban informal sector constitutes a pool of stagnant labour reserve for the capitalist sectors of the economy. The formal capitalist sector uses a number of means for extracting surplus value from the informal sector through a set of linkages, the subcontracting production linkage being an important aspect (see Kalpagam, 1981; John Harriss, 1982; Acharya, 1983). Given the demographic pressure, a sluggish pace of industrialisation, and its accompanying capital intensiveness, this stagnant labour reserve is poised for growth rather than decline. The stagnancy refers to the likely assimilation in the capitalist labour force.

The latent reserve in the Indian context comprises those women in peasant agriculture and in other precapitalist non-agrarian activities as well as those who, due to continued unemployment and their inability to procure work, go out of the labour force. That women in peasant agriculture are getting rapidly proletarianised is evidenced from the remarkable growth in the agricultural labour force brought about by modernisation and the use of new technology in agriculture. While this is true of men too, the percentage increase in male agricultural labourers from 1961 to 1981 was from 13.73 per cent to 19.77 per cent, while in the case of women the increase was from 24.61 per cent to 45.57 per cent. That women tend to go out of the labour force when work is not available is evident from the fact that in the NSS 32nd round, the usual status labour force participation rate (both among rural and urban females) was lower than the current weekly status. This is also true for men. An exact quantification of the latent labour reserve is, however, not possible.

The floating labour reserve refers to that section of the labour force in the capitalist sector which, for one reason or another, is constantly renewed. All employment in capitalist sectors that are seasonal in nature or, say, age-specific, would constitute the floating reserve. No macro level indication of its quantum and trend is available or decipherable.

Given this overall macro picture, I shall examine specifically four issues from various micro studies. First, whether factory production and the introduction of machinery has drawn women, whether women have substituted men, and whether it has lowered the value of male labour power. Second, what have been the changes in the nature of the labour process, and its implications on the sex-typing of tasks. Third, to what extent do women satisfy the three criteria of availability, disposability and cheapness to capital and, fourth what is the role of a patriarchal ideology and the material forms of its manifestation to ensure the three criteria. The analysis will be done by broad industry groups.

Textiles and Garments

At present, it has been noted that the indiscriminate growth of the powerloom sector constitutes an opportunity for the handloom sector which is not only employment intensive, but also provides employment for women, particularly in the pre-weaving processes (lain, 1984). Thus, in this case new technology and new forms of production organisation constitute the displacement of women. Analysing all three sectors—handloom, powerloom and the mill sector—in Coimbatore, Isa Baud (1983, 1992) found that in the handloom sector, with a greater proportion of family labour in it than the other two sectors, the task division in the labour process is based on age, gender and family relationship, and was unfavourable to an equal division of labour between men and women and to women's social autonomy. The other two sectors (with their greater reliance on wage labour) appeared more favourable though, in the mill sector, there was increasing job segregation and a declining proportion of women to all workers. Pre-independence evidence on the mill sector in Bombay from Radha Kumar (1984) is very revealing.

In contrast to M.D. Morris' theory (1965) that the retrenchment of women from the mills from 1920 was due to the Maternity Benefit Act and the Act restricting women from working at night, Kumar (1984) found that it was the changes in the labour process brought about by mechanisation that were responsible for retrenchment. The introduction of the cheese-winding machine changed the winding process from one entailing some amount of hand labour to one using machines. The introduction of the universal winding machine simplified the winding and reeling process by compressing them into one, and reeling yarn into yanks for dyeing (which was a woman's task) became unnecessary. She also notes that, in the case of women, attempts at standardisation of wage rates actually led to a fall in wages. The rationalisation measures in the cotton mill industry adversely affected women. A large number of tasks in which women were employed before either ceased to employ women or ceased to exist as tasks. After 1926 there were no women waste pickers, as the task was taken over by machines; no women doffers in the frame department; no women cheese-winders as it was rationalised out of existence; no women reelers in the warping department; and no women washers in the bleaching department. After 1934 she notes that there were no women employed in the carding room as machine tenders, lap carriers or fly collectors. Nor were there any women handfolders left in the folding department. She also notes that the prevailing ideology defining the primary role of women as a 'reproducer' caused women's wage labour in the mills to be described as supplementary, which in fact it was not.

In the woollen industry, the growth of factory production sought to destroy the cottage industry in which women from poorer households were engaged in spinning. The handprinting industry is another case where women have been displaced due to mechanised printing (Jain, 1984).

The study of the lace makers of Narsapur by Maria Mies (1982) provides interesting insights. When lace making started in Narsapur around 1860, it was not with the intention of producing for exchange value. Christian missionaries had converted the Untouchable caste Malas and Madigas, who were formerly agricultural labourers. They taught this craft to the women of the converts so that they could overcome the social boycott they faced. At the turn of the century, lace export began on a 'regular commercial basis. Women of the fisherman caste, the Agnikulakshatriya, who had always worked outside the house selling fish, were engaged in lace work along with the Christians. In the course of time, due to the processes of agrarian differentiation, women of the agricultural caste, Kapu, who formerly belonged to tenant households, also joined in. When production on commercial lines started, the production process was reorganised along the classic putting-out system. Several women agents visited the artisans at regular intervals, gave them thread and the designs their customers ordered and, after some time, collected the finished articles. The artisans were paid piece-rate wages agreed upon. This system of production, Mies noted, was advantageous to the merchant-capitalists operating in this particular industry, characterised by the instability in export demand. As the labour force is simply 'sitting in their house,' the exporter does not run any risk when demand is slack. He simply gives less thread to a smaller number of women. And when he gets a number of orders, he has no problem sending his agents to more women who are just waiting to get work. These women thus, constitute a labour reserve, which is a mix of both the latent and the stagnant. On the political front, the scattered organisation of production and the isolation of producers from each other prevents labour from unionising, and gives the merchant-exporter greater control over labour.

The horizontal division of labour in the putting-out system was accompanied by an elaborate vertical division of labour. Some women would make small designs, others would make joining parts. All these parts and components would be collected by the agents and brought to where specially skilled women would join them together into lace goods.

With the rapid development of capitalist farming, brought about by the green revolution in the 1960s, the rich and middle peasants who had been able to accumulate, diverted a part to the lace business. Thus, a class of rich merchants from the Kamma, Kapu and other castes emerged. With this, the sex and caste composition of the agents changed. While, formerly, women functioned as agents, now the agents were Kapu men. These men now cover a larger number of villages on bicycles for the distribution and collection of lace. Men are also used for finishing work. Thus, with the growth of a new group of exporters, women have lost their access to the market sphere.

The organisation of the industry on a household basis, and the social definition of lace workers as 'housewives', has resulted in a situation where the industry is fully integrated in the world market system, but the relationship between the exporters and the producers—the women—has not been transformed into contractual wage labour relations, typical of factory work.

Studies on the garment export industry—Kalpagam (1981), Rukmini Rao and Sabha Hussain (1984), Knshnaraj (1.987) and Nirmala Banerjee (1984, 1991)—highlight the following aspects. The structure of the industry in the major centres of the country differs. In Madras, garment units are found in both, the factory and the non-factory sector. In the former, the scale of production is generally large such that they adopt some form of assembly line system (though the assembly line system itself varies with the scale of operation), while the non-factory sector consists of firms to which generally excess orders during peak times are subcontracted and where no form of assembly system prevails. In the assembly system, only women are employed on a time rate, whereas in the non-factory units men are also employed in production along with women in some units, and where generally every worker produces a whole garment on a piece-rate basis. The bulk of the women's workforce in the industry is young, below twenty-six years of age, with the non-factory sector having a greater concentration of young women workers. It was also found that the bulk of the women workers are first generation women workers in the family, and in a significant section, the male heads—either fathers or husbands— had some form of industrial employment. In this sense, one can say that women in industrial working class households constitute a latent reserve. With the development of new industries on capitalist lines, women from these households are the first to be absorbed in the workforce of these industries.

Fragmentation of production and the creation of small workplaces found in Madras was also noted in Delhi as mentioned in the study of Rukmini Rao and Sabha Hussain (1984) though in Delhi, put-out work was also prevalent. Again, young women were employed on the assembly line as in Madras, though in Delhi some companies employed them only on the condition that they resign on marriage, which is not the case in Madras. The Delhi study also highlights instances of managements promoting submissive ideology among the workers. It emphatically states:

> It is true that women fulfil many family responsibilities, and attempt to find work which is compatible with such responsibilities. Yet our study indicates that wherever

capital requires cheap labour in the form of women, it is able to draw them out and place them in different jobs. What is reproduced at their workplace is the ideology of women's secondary status (Rao and Hussain, 1984).

In Calcutta, as reported in Banerjee (1984, 1991), the garment industry is largely in the non-factory sector, with workers working from *bustis* as well. It was also found that production techniques were strictly an extension to the export market of the practices so far used for the domestic market, with no new elaborations. Sewing machines were not fitted with electrical motors, unlike the large firms in Madras. The garment industry, though labour intensive, had a low total labour cost compared to prices. The industry, thus, is constantly attempting to lower labour costs to make prices competitive in the export market. Women workers, on their part, are willing to accept low wage rates, thus providing the industry with cheap labour.

Oral discussions with researchers on the khadi industry reveals that with technological improvements in the *charkha*, productivity has increased manyfold, but it has also caused the substitution of women of different age groups. While, formerly, old women were employed, technological improvements have caused the *charkha* to be of greater weight such that greater muscular strength is required to rotate the wheel, and, consequently, only young women are now employed on these *charkhas*.

Food Industry

Paddy processing is one of the major industries that has shown a striking decrease in female employment over the decade, consequent to the growth of mills (Mukherjee, 1983). An analysis of the regional dimensions of such a change by Gita Sen (1983) has shown that in areas where commercialisation proceeded rapidly and where the marketed surplus of paddy was significant, paddy milling made greater inroads on female employment in hand-pounding. These areas also seemed to be the ones with a high incidence of women labourers in paddy cultivation. Clearly, in this case, capitalist production and exchange has caused a decrease in female employment.

The food processing industry in Kerala has the following characteristics, as revealed by Molly Mathew (n.d.). The fruit and vegetable processing industry is characterised by a low level of technology and unorganised employment. The fish processing industry is characterised by a tendency towards 'disorganisation'. In the initial stages of the industry, all the operations were done in the processing factories, and the industry as *a* whole was in the organised sector. The beginning of the 1970s marked a new era in the processing industry with the advent of small-scale shrimp-peeling sheds. With this development, the industry was divided into organised and unorganised sectors. The suppliers started peeling sheds on a home-scale basis employing local women on a piece-rate, and a large number of women were thrown out of the organised sector. Both these industries are seasonal, and the women workers are underemployed for part of the year. Also, in both, the demand for female labour is age-specific—a majority of the women are unmarried, below thirty years of age, and are asked to resign after marriage. This, again,, constitutes an instance of floating labour reserve. A similar situation also prevails in other seasonal food-processing industries, such as cashew processing for export in Tamil Nadu, where young unmarried girls are employed, and are fired after they reach a certain age or after marriage. The seasonality, and the consequent casualness of employment, permit such age-marital status specific demands for female labour.

In the prawn processing industry in Calcutta, Banerjee (1984) noted that women were involved in cleaning (which is an unskilled task) and grading (which requires skill). These two tasks together determine both the acceptability and the price of the product. However, women's wages formed only about one-sixth of the total value added to the cost of fresh prawns by processing till it left for export. The margin of returns on capital can be as much as *50* per cent of this value added. In this situation, she notes that wages are not low because the industry is keen to save on wages, nor can the industry's success be attributed to its low wage cost. The low level of wages is explained in terms of its opportunity cost. Regarding the sex-typing of tasks in the industry, she notes that so long as traditional tasks continue to be done by the same method and tools, modern industry does not alter the sex-wise division of tasks, which helps to keep traditionally inferior jobs at inferior wage levels, even though they may be crucial tasks for the success of the new industry.

Other Industries

The beedi industry of Allahabad has been studied by Zarina Bhatty (1981). This is essentially a household industry employing Muslim women of all ages. However, there are beedi factories where the method of production does not change, but workers are brought collectively wider one roof. Here, women home-workers can sometimes be treated as wage labourers or as petty commodity producers. Prior to the abolition of the contract system, they were all wage workers working for a piece-rate to a contractor under a putting-out system (a case of formal subsumption of capital). With the legislation abolishing the contract system in the beedi industry, there has been no change in the organisation of production, only all raw material distributed by the contractors to home-workers is deemed as 'sale' and all collection of beedi from the workers by the contractor is deemed 'purchase,' thereby beating the legislation. These home-workers constitute a stagnant labour reserve. The domestic production of beedis continues to survive alongside factory production because the patriarchal ideology of secluding Muslim women ensures a supply of such women willing to work at home at any wage rate.

The electric fan industry of West Bengal reveals certain significant features, as seen from Banerjee (1984). In the past, the fan industry used to employ women in significant numbers in several skilled jobs but, in recent times, these jobs have been taken over by men, and women are confined to crude unskilled jobs. According to Banerjee, this was true not only of big factory units but also of small workshops. Women were pushed out from tasks when a regulated wage structure increased the wages for those tasks and made it attractive for the male workers. Simultaneously, the supply of male workers for these tasks went up owing to the retrenchment of male workers in large units that had gone in for rationalisation.

What Can be Concluded?

The salient features of the micro studies that have been covered so far highlight the following facts.

1. The development of capitalism in the labour surplus multi-structural context of India and the introduction of machinery were, in many instances and contrary to what can be postulated from Marx and Engels, female labour-displacing. The kind of substitution of male labour by female labour, as expected by Marx and Engels, does not seem to have taken place. The development of capitalism in this context has also absorbed women in a number of new occupations.
2. Women do, in fact, constitute a cheap labour reserve, though the form of labour reserve differs based on the organisation of that industry. In this multistructural context, all three forms of reserve—latent, stagnant and floating—are prevalent and identifiable, and each aids, in a specific way, the process of capitalist development.
3. The tasks that women perform are generally unskilled, and there are instances where, through a change in the labour process or without any change, women have been pushed out from skilled to unskilled tasks.
4. Women are generally found to be engaged in tasks where only crude tools are used and no supplementary motive power is provided.
5. The process of 'informalisation' or 'disorganisation' of production units is done with a view to exploit the cheap labour that is available, female labour being an important constituent of it.
6. Export-oriented industries, where price competitiveness is necessary for a firm's survival and where instability is not infrequent, are not only seekers of cheap labour but also attempt to substitute machinery with labour.

These pointers do not adequately answer the set of issues we had started examining. The evidence we have on those issues is rather uncohesive in nature. This is to be expected as none of the studies explicitly focused on any of these issues.

Specifically, we find that while all the studies had indicated that women do constitute cheap labour, with the exception of Banerjee (1983) none of the studies had attempted an analysis of wage determination. Even here, the explanation is in a strictly conventional supply-demand framework. Though Banerjee (1983) recognises that women were specially vulnerable in the labour market, given the fact that they were relatively less prepared to enter the labour market and more desperate when they did and that the structure of wages reflect the social attitudes prevailing, there is very little analysis of the role of patriarchy in wage determination, and the concrete forms of its manifestation on both the supply and demand side, which imposes real constraints and compulsions on women, making them specially vulnerable.. The interaction of patriarchy and capitalism is a domain that needs closer scrutiny and wider elaboration.

Also, much more research needs to be undertaken on the changes in the labour process in particular industries, similar to the exercise undertaken by Banerjee (1985a) though with a greater and systematic focus on the implications of the changes in the labour process on the labour use patterns by sex and skills. In this context, a whole examination of the concept of 'skill,' and its implications on policy matters (such as 'minimum wages') appears to be an immediate need.

NOTES

1. For a clear and lucid account, see Sweezy (1970) and Marx, *Capital*, Vol. 1 (1977, reprint).
2. While we am aware that the reserve army principle holds true irrespective of the assumption on population growth, in concrete instances greater demographic pressure will have a greater depressing effect on wage rate.
3. An elaboration of the multistructural system will be found in Chapter 2.
4. Starting from Harry Braverman, others such as Andrew Friedman (1977), R.C. Edwards (1979). Maichel Burawoy (1985) and the Brighton Labour Process Group (1977) have focused on issues related to the labour process.

15

The View of Working Women Towards Existing Society

The women are supposed to keep their activities confined to the boundaries of the house. Though change is taking place in the traditional view, yet the "prison wall" have not so far been demolished.[1] To find women working outside their homes is, not a new phenomenon. Women have been participating in economic activities since times immemorial. It is believed that from post-Vedic period, however, women only of lower strata of society worked outside home. Seeking employment by women in plantations, mines started from the early years of the present century. Economic pressure seemed to have caused this situation.[2] A significant change took place after India became free in 1947. The Constitution of Independent India declared that there should be no discrimination against the employment of women. This created further opportunity for employment of women and an increase in their employment rate was seen more particularly among educated and upper caste women. This is a very significant development and is characteristic of Independent India.[3] There are many factors which are responsible for this change. Socio-economic emancipation had been greatest factor. The changes in the attitude of people are also important. Desai points out that "the real advance which has been made during this period is actually in the revolution that has been brought about in the outlook with regard to the conception of the status of women and her role in society. Now women is no longer looked upon as a child bearing machine and harlot in the home. She has acquired a new status and a new social structure".[4]

The employment of women has brought mixed reaction both from professional and lay persons. It is common knowledge that social changes evoke sometimes more negative than positive emotions. In regard to the employment of women, even social scientists for the most part, took a negative view. Psychologists gave negative comments. Lundberg and Farnham expressed a particular pessimistic evaluation.[5] Some sociologists also tended to lump the increased employment of women along with other trends, such as higher divorce rates, more crime and delinquency. Other such a Bossard took a strong negative position contending that such employment was gravely detrimental to children.[6] Many a people alert for a simple explanation of the numerous and complex social problems, speculated that the employment of women was the principal cause of current social problems. It was proposed that women should be forced out of employment. A very small number of sociologists such as Komarovsky and Lanclis favoured changes.

In the absence of sufficient empirical data, it is, however, difficult to say anything definitely about the reactions of society towards working women and vice-versa. Only recently there have been some serious efforts to examine empirically the attitude and related aspects about women's working. The enquiry described in following pages is designed to elicit the opinion of working women about some aspects of their life, their attitude towards work and related matters and also to assess the attitude of society towards them in terms of the perception of working women themselves.[7]

Recent History of Women's Work

During the first half of twentieth century, opportunities for Indian women to participate in economic activities increased at a much slower rate as compared to the rate of increase in female population. As a result in the case of women work force as percentage of the population decreased rapidly during the period 1911-1951.

Like the various other sections of a society, women derive their ideological and moral basis for their status and their institutionalised role from the religion.[8] Evidently, the various restrictions imposed on women and our notions about their proper role in the domestic and social spheres have been greatly influenced by the religious conceptions in regard to their fundamental characteristics, their assumed virtues and rites etc., which are substantiated by various legends and myths.[9] Buddhism and Jainism gave better freedom to women and due to the royal patronage, the religion received their teaching were promptly put into practice. The Bhakti movement and Nationalist movement, process of modernisation, impact of Western culture etc. have influenced to a great extent in bringing about changes in the social role of women. There is, however, a sharp difference of opinion about the changes taking place over years in the position of women in India. Some regard these changes as profound and pervasive. They point out to the changes introduced in their legal status, others maintain that the position of women has changed very little and that Indian society continues by and large to be a male dominated society.[10]

The present demand of the women for the provision of increasing opportunities outside home should at best be termed as a tertiary stage in the history of the women's emancipation, the shift over from the traditional role of the women subservient to menfolk to the neo-traditional phase, in which the women have been up in revolt against all types of exploitation reiterating their equality with men in all fields of rights and responsibilities ranging from education, employment, health, institutionalised welfare facilities, coupled with the participation of women at different levels of social and national activity. Then there is bound to emerge a highly developed society, based on harmonious relations allowing no exploitation, economic, intellectual or otherwise by eliminating all traditional taboos that have led to restricting the women's life to certain spheres only.[11]

Structure of Indian Society

Indian society is a fragmented society which never united its people on a common social platform and caused to differentiate people on the basis of their caste and class in particular and men and women in general. Such tradition is prevalent throughout the country and in all religions. Women are considered as secondary citizens, with no independence of any sort. Since centuries known and unknown, women were the target of social exploitation and subordination. Economic exploitation led to a more direct form of social oppression and women were made to pay a heavy price at the cost of their self dignity and independence. Male oriented and male dominated value system swayed the society throughout, while in subordination of women appeared in direct form in every walk of life. From gathering fire wood to cooking, from making daily purchase to looking after children, from searching for employment to undertaking different jobs. are the exclusive functions of rural women in particular and urban women in general. However, this may not be applicable to women belonging to upper economic strata of the society. Still in the existing society a majority of women have no control over their earnings and can't decide the manner in which it is spent. On the other side it is aptly remarked by someone that, "in any home, where financial compromises are to be made, it is the women who are 'compromised against. They are the first ones to be axed in any situation".[12] Thus, the influence of women is very little' on the family budget, debt and repayment.

The situation is significantly not different even in capitalist form of social relations. Although the character and nature of relations may differ to some extent, it still holds the feudal antecedents in the behaviour, particularly, in regard to the status of women.[13] The slave society and feudal society treated women as personal property of men and such value system continue to exist in a semi-feudal and semi-capitalistic system like ours. The family as a social institution upholds 'masculine superiority' and imposes such value system on the males since their childhood and they grow up inheriting the values to uphold them in future.

Marriage is another institution which has developed in the historical context representing discriminator' value system. There are no uniform laws governing the system of marriage and divorce and laws are generally seen against the-interests of Women. Child marriages, arranged marriages, lack of freedom to woman to choose her life partner, polygamy, bride price, dowry, traditional type of performing marriages requiring' huge expenditure, these are found as a general rule than exception.

Cultural Milieu

The role of women in the cultural development of a society is underestimated and underscored in India. The concerted efforts to make the language, literature, art, architecture, symbols, education, learning process etc. all male dominated and male oriented, indicate the negative value system and partisan attitude to perpetuate class - structure in the society. The usage, form, presentation and communication of these are highly anti-women in nature.

The caste-system, family marriage, child bearing, traditions, superstitions, beliefs, God fearing attitude, religious ceremonies and rituals developed during the course of history to perpetuate exploitation, have directly hit the position of women in society. The women were taught right from the cradle that the brain washing begins, and they were forced to uphold such slavish practices for ever in future. Each girl lives, waiting only for the time when she will go to her 'real' home (husband's home) and it is crucial for her survival to behave exactly as ordained, to be accepted there. There is just no going back.[14]

The history of the 35 years is clear enough. Why with the constitution-guaranteed equality of treatment and opportunities, with improved legal rights, with national policies to spread literacy, to improve health services, to carry on active propaganda against the cultural constraints against women—why, has the sex-ratio continue to decline, even after Independence? It is not just the sex ratio, there are' other demographic indicators to show the value of women in our society is going down.[15]

Do we need to reiterate that women in India, still after independence are 'very much the second sex? Without going into the history of women's inferior status, it is sufficient to say that "If one set of disabilities like — 'sati', 'child marriage', widowhood, female infanticide, 'purdah', unequal wages, no right in the family property has been removed by reforms and legislations others have taken their place. Independence has brought hopes, if not of an equal status, at least more opportunities in various spheres. The constitution promised her an equal treatment and series of progressive laws seemed able to translate the promise into reality. But these hopes have been fulfilled in small quarters of women but for common women, they are still far and distant. Where laws have existed, they have not been implemented. Women are yet too timid in demanding justice through law. When development has taken place, it has not benefited men and women equally and when women have gained, the gains have been confined to a small section of women, mainly of the urban middle class.

It can't be denied that opportunities for women have considerably widened at certain 'levels of Indian society and enabled women to achieve numerous advances in spheres which were never open to them before. But their development has remained severely restricted to a small coterie of upper class, primarily urban, privileged women. Their ability to participate on 'equal' terms with men in social and economic fields provides no clue to the' actual, desperate situation of the majority of women in India from the position that such women enjoy can be definitely misleading. We must grant that we have made some progress after in dependence. We have now family planning services, we have abortion services, though in the communication system there is tremendous gap, but still we have women committing suicide because they do hot know they can get a legal, proper, free abortion in certain hospitals in the country. We have also the Dowry Prohibition Act of 1961 which for all 'practical purposes has failed. 'The commercial use of women has increased, the incidence of rape has increased in urban areas. Prostitution has taken various forms in our society. In ever growing advertisements women have been made sex-object and sex-symbols.[17]

Women are discriminated, even not accepted in certain professions. When a company or firm is wanting to recruit an efficient professional it would undoubtedly prefer, a man to a woman so the discrimination goes on. The number of women in certain occupations like teachers and nurses has increased. However, they have been confined to those of stereotypes. When they go a little higher up as doctors or physicians, there again we limit them in gynaecology, obstetrics or paediatrics. They are not found in the sophisticated areas like heart transplant or heart surgery—why? The question is of employment. If a man and woman with equal qualifications apply, the man is preferred to woman for the job. The employer invariably would say, he has a family to support while the woman is single and 'she can be supported by her parents. So we have discrimination, subtle, invisible, latent. If this is true amongst professionals, then again one asks the question—what is wrong with our attitudes—mental, intellectual, social and political attitudes? Where to begin to change the picture? How can we bring women into the mainstream of-all the areas of our social and public life?

Perhaps it is not because 'he' has a family to support that the employer prefers him to the women. It is because the employers think that the woman will be giving most of her mind to the family and will not be concentrating on excellence in job. Excellence in job needs full concentration, full dedication which a woman in these circumstances just can't afford. The SNDT University, concerned with B.Sc., M.Sc., and Ph.D women scholars found that many of them on the one hand are not getting higher positions and they are occupying the intermediary positions, and that though the promotional possibilities are equal, in reality they are not so.

Another reason why the man is preferred to woman, is that it is taken for granted that he is the bread winner. Committee on Status of Women, on the contrary, while moving all over India found that the pattern in our society has changed. They found that often woman is the primary bread winner. A woman, even when her husband is working, very often does not get the money from him to run the house. Things have changed very fast and even in lower middle class where women were not going to work, now we find them working to support their parents. In circumstances when the women are deserted by their husbands, or husbands die or become invalid, the woman works to support the family. So, it is incorrect to say that man is the primary bread winner, and wife's income is secondary. No, it is not correct in today's economy. Committee, also observes the polygamy, in Manipur families, where women were the breadwinner. And reason for polygamy is that the woman is earner. She brought the money and husband sat at home. The more wives he had the more money he had. The Manipur women were asked by the Committee that why don't they revolt, leave their husbands as they are economically independent? They said, "where can we go?" The social condition is such that she can't think otherwise. Economic independence does not necessarily make her independent.

Women's education has been advocated by social thinkers and reformers in India. However, the advocacy has differed according to the understanding of the concept of 'education'. In the post-Independence period, education in the context of 'development' is recognised as an instrument of social change. Since the emphasis on promoting equality, education is seen as a means to bring about changes towards more equality. In the formal education, we observe a substantial step up in the enrolment of girls since 1951 in terms of statistics. Successive five year plans have laid big emphasis on universalisation of elementary education for girls, attracting them towards schools through various schemes. The progressive increase in the enrolment of girls in schools has been heartening in the post-independence period. However, the enrolment of girls at every level of education is much lower than that of boys. Also the rate of drop-outs among girls is so high that the later mingle into the ocean of illiterates. When you educate a man, you educate an individual; when you educate a woman you educate a family. Education is the only vehicle that can really make women aware of the happenings around them. No doubt, there is more awareness amongst women about their low status, than before. There is increasing activity by women and their organisations towards a woman's movement. Women have loudly taken up issues like dowry, rape, bride burning and have made some impact in the women's movement. However, the mass of women of India is still far from the action. What we need is a wide-based Women's movement suited to the needs of the common women. This will not happen unless they are organised in seeking change in their condition. This would be only possible as Pandit Jawahar Lal Nehru said, when women leave their 'long habit' of relying on others' goodwill rather than on their own efforts.[18]

To know the views of working women regarding the structure of society several questionnaires were given. To start with we asked them that "do you ever feel that it would have been better if you were not working?" In reply following result was obtained.

TABLE 15.1

Better to be a Working Woman or Not

Response	*No. of respondents*	*Percentage*
Yes	48	24
No	152	76
Total	200	100

24% of the total sample Indicated that they are not happy with being working women; 76% are satisfied with working women in this society. Here we can conclude that there is a tendency to go for a job rather than staying back at home among women.

While correlating this factor with the occupation, we got the confirmation to our conclusion that there is a tendency to seek a job.

Table 15.2 indicates that the women working as clerk, typist, steno do not want to continue with the work but are continuing because of financial support they are required to provide. The amount of pleasure and challenge derived from such jobs is comparatively less. Moreover, their jobs are more time consuming, routined, tiring and lack variety.

TABLE 15.2

Occupation and Tendency Towards Working/Seeking a Job

Occupation	*Better to work*	*Not to work*	*Total*
Teachers	77	10	87
Lecturers	15	6	21
Clerk, Stenotypist	20	28	48
Executives	30	4	34
Air-hostess	1	—	1
Architect	2	—	1
Research Asstt.	7		7
Total	152	48	200

Another aspect which has been analysed is whether these working women have any faith in the institution of marriage or with the economic independence they are losing faith in this institution. To ascertain this following questions were asked (1) Do you think marriage is a barrier in your career? (ii) Do you think that a girl who does not marry can lead a happy life?

Table 15.3 and Table 15.4 shows the following observations:

TABLE 15.3

Marriage as a Barrier

Response	*No. of respondents*	*Percentage*
Yes	27	13.5
No	173	86.5
Total	200	100.0

TABLE 15.4

Girl Who Does not Marry can Lead a Happy Life

Response	*No. of respondents*	*Percentage*
Yes	56	28
No	144	72
Total	200	100

Both the tables confirm that marriage is a respected institution in the views of working women. They have all faith in this institution. The other question which was asked to support was "Do you think after marriage you are more secure socially and can better concentrate upon your career?"

Table 15.5 indicates the result. 66% of the sample working women said that they are feeling better after marriage, or they are more secure. While 34% said they have not been able to concentrate upon their career because of added responsibilities. During the informal discussion with the sample working women it was revealed that some of them are working because of effective utilisation of their time, better prospects of marriage and better exposure to society. It was confirmed that being working women gives them confidence in their day to day interaction.

TABLE 15.5

Better Concentration After Marriage Upon Career and More Secure Socially

Response	*No-. of respondents*	*Percentage*
Yes	132	66
No	68	34
Total	200	100

Further to this the following questions were also asked to the working women. 'Whether they have any say in choosing their life-partner." Have the parents change their traditional way of choosing life-partners for their daughters? (Table 15.6).

TABLE 15.6

Choosing Life-Partner

Response	*No. of respondents*	*Percentage*
Own say final	61	30.5
Parent's say final	104	52.0
Mutual	35	17.5
Total	200	100.0

It is revealed from the above table that the traditional pattern is still predominant. It is the parents (52%) who have the final say in choosing the life-partner for their daughters. Even the mutual consultancy (17.5%) is very low. But the 30% who have said that they have the final say in this matter is quite amusing. It shows that change is taking place. With the economic independence they are free to choose the partner for themselves. But the traditional values are very strong and deep rooted. Woman, though, is economically independent and educated but she is forced to accept the partner for her life chosen by her parents and she is accepting it due to the strong social values and norms. She is still not confident and mature enough to deal this matter alone. But slight change which is observed during informal discussion is that they are asked whether they like the boy or not. But the norms and values are such that they are basically shy to accept the fact. If we look into the table 30.5% working women are of the opinion that they should have the final say while choosing the life-partner and 17.5% are of the opinion that final choice should have the approval of the parents. Putting both the figures together it comes to 48% i.e. nearly 50%. It can not be treated as a less percentage on any account. In a traditional society like ours if 50% working women feel like this, many more might be having such feelings but could not openly express just to honour the traditional values. However, during an informal discussion the sample respondents openly said that since they in the future will become family heads, they will first give better education to their daughters, get them settled in some service or business and then allow them to choose a life-partner of their choice.

The above explanation and fact revealed in course of informal discussion proves beyond doubts that modernisation has the direct bearing on the attitude of working women toward societal values.

When we enquired why society is not accepting a working woman with full respect and credibility. The general observation was, it is because of male domination (more than 50%) as shown in Table 15.7.

TABLE 15.7

Society not Accepting a Working Woman with Full Respect Why?

Response	No. of respondents	Percentage
Because of traditional values	38	19
Because of male domination	105	52.5
Because of male ego	25	12.5
Woman herself is responsible	26	13.0
Any other reason	6	3.0
Total	200	100.0

The major elements leading to male domination were—

(i) traditional values (19% of the respondents).
(ii) male ego (52.5% of the respondents).
(iii) lack of confidence in the woman for which she herself is responsible (13% of the respondents).

Related to the previous factor, we further asked that with the changing social system and social values, whether the status of working women has improved. We put the question, "Are you still struggling for gaining full respect you deserve or are comfortable with the present status you have acquired in this society?"

From the above response it is very clear that situation is more comfortable with working women. The response, however, confirms the view but during the informal discussion quite a large number of working women admitted that they have not got adequate recognition beside long hours of work they put in their office and the money they earn. Working married women said that their position is still worst as they have to do the household work, looking after the children, besides attending their office work. Most of the women were emphatic that they are not getting assistance from their husband or in-laws in the matter of household work.

TABLE 15.8

Response	*No. of respondents*	*Percentage*
Still struggling	55	22.5
Comfortable	145	77.5
Total	200	100.0

It is indeed ironical that despite so much talk on the equality of the women, the society is adopting double standards in the case of working women. Even the attitude of the same set of people is different in different situations. However, despite all this, there is a welcome shift in the attitude of people towards giving education to the women folk. This in turn is broadening the attitudes of women and they want to stand on their own legs.

The foregoing analysis proves beyond doubt that modernisation and employment have played a vital role in shaping the attitude of working women towards old social values. Now they are in a position to feel economically independent and if situation so warrants, they can take an independent view of every thing.

REFERENCES

1. Talwar, Usha, *Social Profile of Working Women*, Jodhpur, 1984, p. 1.
2. *Ibid.*
3. Sen Gupta, Padmini, "in trades and professions", *The Women of India*, Baig, Tara Ali (ed.), New Delhi, The Publications Division, Government of India, 1958, p. 236.
4. Desai, Neera, *Women in Modern India*, Bombay, Vora Publishers, 1957, p. 253.
5. Lundberg, Ferdinand, and Fartiham, Marynia F., *Modern Women: The Lost Sex*, New York, Harper, 1947 as quoted in the *Employed Mother*, p. 7.
6. Bossard, James, H.S., *The Sociology of Child Development*, New York, Harper, 1954, pp. 282-86.
7. Talwar, Usha, *op. cit.*, pp. 200-01.
8. Murli Manohar, K., *Socio-economic Status of Indian Women*, Seema Publications, Delhi, 1983, p. 5.
9. Gupta, A.R., *Women in Hindu Society*, Jyotsna Prakashan, 1976, p. 178.
10. Manohar Murli, K., *op. cit.*, pp. 21-25.
11. Gupta, A.R. *op. cit.*, p. 19.
12. *India Today;* Vol. V., No. 15, August 1-15, 1980, p. 132.
13. Murli Manohar, K., *op. cit.*, pp. 21-25.
14. *India Today Report*, *op. cit.*, p. 132.
15. Bhalla, Era, Women-Car law alone change their status, *Employment News*, September 29, 1983, p. 2.

16

Women's Economic Independence and Attitudinal Change Through Employment

In the early human societies of primitive communism, going back hundreds of thousands of years, when food was procured by gathering or hunting, there was full equality between men and women. Though little is known about the structure of those societies, it is likely that young were cared for by mainly women. Women were crucial in creating the basis of social collectivity itself. And woman dominated agricultural production.[1] The societies were frequently characterised by a kind of matriarchy in which the dominant chief was a woman, who carried out the function of dividing up the tribal land for cultivation. There is evidence for such matriarchal societies in India. It is likely that the Harappa civilisation was characterised by such matriarchal rule while matriarchal and matrilineal tribal societies were predominant at one time throughout the subcontinent and survived in south India upto quite recent times.[2]

However, with the increasing development of the productive forces and the intensification of class-exploitation male dominance was established and solidified. There were two main reasons for this : First men monopolised the plough. Second males came to monopolise the means of violence and warfare, possibly because they were the first to react to nature in a violent form.

Thus the period of the rise of early class society and the triumph of patriarchy nearly coincided, and women became an oppressed sex. Now the oppressed began to organise collectively and consciously. The newly formed working class began to fight, first for economic survival but with an increasing awareness that they had the power in their hands to change society and end exploitation itself. For women of all classes the need for equality and freedom extended into the family and into challenging male domination.[3]

A United Nation's study shows that women provide two-third of the world's labour, earn one tenth of the world's income and own only one hundredth of the world's property. This economic vulnerability leads ultimately to social inequality and long term exploitation.[4]

Women are often their own worst victims. The psychological attitudes that women pass down to each other, specifically that female are to be meek, docile and tolerant as against the courageous, aggressive nature of men is in actuality a subtle brain-washing. As women continue to play their cards the situation gradually deepens and bring into existence the 'super ego' in men and 'inferior ego' in women. In its worst expression the super ego extends to the male psychology that she can be bought along with its side repercussions of dowry, rape, prostitution, adultery and pornography. Psychologists asset that these negative social elements are the basic desire to insult and wound a women, i.e., the desire to exert one up manship or superiority over women. What is worse still is women's complacency or indifference results in a complete break-down in society. Instead of contributing to a healthier, stronger society, she establishes disparity, social friction and inequality. In effect she contributes to society's decline.[5]

Economic Independence

The basic and most fundamental flaw in women is their ineffectiveness in demanding a monetary remuneration for work done at home. Without their monetary remuneration, her legal status is reduced to a dependent. She is not a contributor to the gross national produced and by law she is living under the protection and provision of her husband. Women, for years have accepted this dependency only to realise too late that they have been robbed of their right to self-respect and dignity. It was only with the advent of the 'suffragette movement' that she was able to salvage her rights to employment, ownership and status.

Most women are still unaware of the subtle brain washing and deprivation to their own sex. When husbands become member of clubs, it does not occur to her that membership should be on both names. When the name plate is put on the door, she will not realise that her name should be added. When a couple prospers as a husband and wife team, she will not care to point out that property, car, etc. should be on joint names. In several cases she has a costly price to pay for her oversight. If any break or friction arises in the marriage she finds herself out on the road penniless, often unable even to claim rights to her children. When a marriage breaks, the convenient remark of the husband is 'get out of my house'. Is the house his own on the first place?[6]

In underdeveloped countries and among weaker sections of society the monetary repercussions are manifold and male domination almost complete. Fathers and husbands to perpetuate this exploitation ensure that their daughters are left completely uneducated. This gives her no choice and forces her to subserviency. Gradually even mothers come to believe in male might and ensure that their daughters are taught to believe in male superiority. Humanists and psychologists refer to this as one of the worst types of mental cruelty. The woman is deprived of her self-confidence, assertiveness, individuality and self-sufficiency. Ultimately, the whole of society feels the impact. A house divided against itself can't stand. There is a lowering of over-all efficiency and material standards with its resultant effect on morality and culture.

Either advertently or inadvertently, the law is more oriented to safeguard the interest of men. Whilst it makes certain provisions for women it does not allow to her the same status, dignity and self-respect as that given to men.

Views of Prominent Personalities on Women

While inaugurating the ministerial conference of the non-aligned and other developing countries, Prime Minister Rajiv Gandhi reiterated that role of women in developing countries was very crucial to the rate at which a country developed and in many ways was the indicator as to how well the country was developing. "We have now to fight the historical, the social and cultural backwardness that has been thrust upon women and male superiority which has become in a way a vested interest. Like all vested interests, it is damaging the society, these vested interests have to be removed from our political, administrative, legal and social establishment".

Ms Pulido Briceno (U.N. Coordinator)

Speaking during her official visit to the United Nations office at Vienna in April last year Ms Briceno said, "Women need to acquire management skills. Women must learn that having children is not a handicap to their careers but a responsibility. Men too have to learn these new attitudes. Efficiency and productivity are related to commitment, not to traditional roles and values".

Ms Maragathan Chandrasekhar

Minister for Social and Women's Welfare and chairman of the conference of non-aligned and developing countries for the role of women in development, while inaugurating the conference for the 'Role of Women in Development' Ms Chandrasekhar said, "I feel that one of the most important tasks before us is to inculcate the spirit of confidence and the desire amongst women to achieve their own potential. it is really tragic that women subjected to an unequal status for generations have come to accept this as their fate. Unless women take up their cause seriously and with a full realisation of their responsibilities, society is not likely to be helpful to them.

Justice Sujata Manohar

Discussing the status of women Justice Manohar says, "If women have to bring about improvement in their social status, they have to become more aware of their rights and become more vigilant in preventing violation of their rights. Only then can they preserve their existing rights and improve upon them".

Talking about discriminatory laws Justice Manohar stated that it was only in 1955 that the Hindu Marriage Act was enacted prohibiting bigamy, permitting divorce and radically transforming marital rights of Hindu women. For the first time Hindu women were granted the same marital rights as men. It was only after the enactment of the Hindu Succession Act, 1956 that a widow and daughter could inherit property in the same manner and in the same proportion as a son.

Though world leaders lay great emphasis on apartheid, racism and other discriminations, very seldom are the atrocities committed on women given equal limelight.

The United Nations Decade for the Advancament of Women has laid out some of the more important changes to be made in social as well as national strategies.

1. Women like men have a constitutional and moral right to employment and economic freedom. Any breach of this right, goes against the constitutional rights of women to work and earn a basic livelihood.
2. That men and women were jointly responsible for rearing and raising a family. Any breach of this rule was tantamount to discrimination and exploitation.
3. That house work be considered a valuable contribution to society and the gross national product and that the monetary figures be accordingly reflected in official statistical data. That monetary value of house work and rearing children be recognised, and due and appropriate compensation be made to women working in the home without dignity and monetary remuneration was tantamount to slavery.
4. Rigid punishment to be implemented in all aspects of degradation and humiliation to womanhood in the forms of rape, prostitution, dowry and obscenity.
5. Measures were to be taken to allow women equal opportunities for study and training, special programmes were to be undertaken to correct past imbalances in this field.
6. To ensure full participation of women in government and other agencies. And to take steps to ensure that women take active part in the decision making process.
7. The programme asserted that government should explicitly state their firm commitment to rectify legislative and customary discriminations against women held for centuries in the vested interests of men. Special emphasis was laid on right to work and earning a livelihood. All legislative provisions in the social, economic and political sphere and in the penal civil codes were to be examined and regulations discriminating against women were to be repeated.
8. Legislation for maternity leave was to be examined and appropriately implemented.
9. To mobilise women, particularly poor women in rural and urban areas.[7]

Shekar Kapoor (Actor) said that the root cause of this is economic factor. In past a man had to physically protect his family. The man was the stronger force. Now that has gone. A woman can be as equal a financial protector as a man, it is just that in the past few hundred years it has not happened, but it is bound to happen. Once a woman is as capable of earning the same kind of money and giving financial protection to the family. Then the women's status will become equal. But mother-hood is one aspect that can never be changed whether father-hood can become as warm, close and biologically necessary as motherhood. What do you do about motherhood? Baby's biological need of suckling? There is a whole gamut of touch and feel and this the father will never be able to provide.[8]

The term 'egalitarianism' refers in respect of the position of women in the society as well as in the family. It is easier to assess her position in the society from the availability of opportunities of participation in the social and productive activities as also a gainful employment. But her position in the family presents many difficulties in regard to such an assessment.

It is evidently a grave mistake to speak of women as a homogenous social class. It is undeniable that like men, all women can hardly be treated as having the same social and intellectual status. Further, the disabilities to which women have been exposed in the past, have not affected all women in the same way and to the same extent; nor did all inequalities apply to all women. For example, the lack of employment opportunities to women applied only to the middle class women, as the peasant's women were occupied in the agricultural activity along with the menfolk and the women of the higher classes had hardly any wish or necessity to take up employment.

It is also an admitted fact that the tradition restricted the women to home and this is enough to describe the women's former role in the pre-industrial society. This state of affairs has been rightly described by Voila Klein as under: "daughters were brought up to be decarous, modest and chaste and they were closely guarded and chaperoned so as not to stray from the path of virtue. Knowledge and initiative, intelligence and experience were discouraged. The education of ladies was aimed at producing accomplishments—a smattering of music, art and needle work as well as social manners".[9]

In the first decade after independence when India was seeking to re-establish an identity, every aspect of its life needed to be explored, considered and recognised. Some of the images that had been formed while it was a colony had to be effaced and more authentic one offered.[10]

Status if seen as a derivative, the result of a pattern of relationships between men and women—a pattern composed of images they have of themselves and each other—certainty can not be evaluated by quantifiable measures either. Status for one set of women may be in relation to what other women have—now or in the past; to others what men have thought men would respect. Status really lies in the eyes of beholder.

There is bound to be great deal of difference of opinion between societies, between generations as well as probably within them in what is preferred group of characteristics a woman should aspire for. It is doubtful whether the difference in this area can ever be finally resolved. It is a question of morals rather than facts. Imitating men is an unsatisfactory goal for women and such a tendency must be a reaction to a situation where women feel-ill-treated by men.[11]

With a few notable exceptions, Indian sociologists have not devoted much serious attention to the systematic study of the position of women in their own society. There is no dearth of discussion on what may be called the women's question in India. But in the absence of systematic studies, there often leads to opposite conclusions.

This is the situation that the large masses of Hindu women in particular and Indian women from other societies in general face today. Though there are regional variations in the norms governing women's work, a tradition upper class norm that of excluding women from labour outside the family—still remains a status symbol and is often emulated by many who want to enhance their social status.

The forces which have most affected adversely the role of women in the Indian economy are: the general decline of handicrafts; increasing pressure of population on agriculture; increase of poverty in the rural sector resulting in migration; development of modern industry with its increasing technological advance; the spread of education; and the increasing cost of living, particularly in urban areas.

Technological changes have similarly affected the employment of women in industries like cotton, textiles, plantation and mines. At the same time the decay of village industries has thrown more and more women on agriculture for their livelihood, increasing their numbers and percentage but reducing their levels of employment. On the other hand, the rising cost of living, education and social changes in the urban areas have led to the withdrawal of taboos that earlier affected women of the upper classes and have enabled some of them to enter new professions/occupations in the tertiary sector which were closed to them earlier.

Because of this differential impact of development, a macro-analysis of women's economic participation purely in quantitative terms is not enough. Thus any appraisal to women's economic roles has to be separated for specific segments differentiated by socio-economic and locational characteristics as well as by their degree of adjustment to the economic process. "The greatest difficulty in understanding the problems of women's participation", says the ICSSR report of the National Committee on Women, "has been caused by looking at women workers as a homogeneous group". This assumption has influenced the collection of data the laws, and the policies adopted to improve conditions of women workers and also the popularly held notions about women's participation in the economy.

The ratio of female to male workers has declined in all categories in the rural and most categories in the urban areas. The participation rates of men and women differ widely in all age-groups except the youngest (one to fourteen), the difference in urban areas being much higher than in rural areas. The distribution of women workers in the nine industrial categories adopted by the census shows their increasing dependence on agriculture and a decline in both the industrial and service sector.

Having found the census report not very useful, the National Committee on the Status of Women in India has for an accurate and more comprehensive assessment classified the whole lot of women workers in two broad categories according to the degree of organisation and nature of problems of their sector of employment, the unorganised and organised sectors.

The difference between those two is not functional, as between agriculture, industry and services, because the functions may be found in both sectors. The real difference between them lies in the organisation of productive relations, the degree of penetration of public control and regulation, and recognition by data collecting agencies and scientific investigators.

The status of women workers in India is, therefore, very unhealthy from the fact that 94 per cent of them are found in the unorganised sector, leaving only 6 per cent of them are found in the unorganised sector, leaving only 6 per cent in the organised sector. But for the sake of convenience we shall deal with the roles, rights and opportunities of that category of women's participation in the organised economy, which comprises only 6 per cent of working women.

The number of women employed in this sector increased from 1.37 million in 1962 to 2.14 million in 1973, an increase of 56.2 per cent. While this increase was faster than the total increase of employment in this sector, women's proportion in total employment remained practically constant at 11 per cent in this period. As we noted earlier, in spite of the fact that this sector has been steadily growing the women employment in it formed only 6 per cent of the total workers in 1971, 2.7 per cent being industry and 3.3 per cent in the services and professions.

Undoubtedly the number of women employed in the public sector increased by 110.4 per cent, but in the private sector the increase was only 29.9 per cent. The proportion of women in the public sector increased from 35 per cent to 47 per cent while their share in the private sector declined from 65 per cent to 52.8 per cent in this period. Public sector employment is mainly provided by state governments, local bodies and public undertakings. Their position in the Central Government is not very satisfactory.

A study (action plan), besides finding solutions to the problems affecting participation of women, will have to actively promote participation of women as as to bring about improvement in their economic and social status and a positive change in attitudes towards working women.[13] In this context analysis of the existing situation at the national level through an examination of published data indicates that the following guidelines will be meaningful: Increased participation of women in occupations where they can be more or less productive than men. Productive both in terms of jobs/skill requirement and of ability to manage a job along with household chores and fulfill her child-rearing responsibilities. The occupations indicated are largely those requiring either certain levels of professional vocational/technical training and skills requiring manual dexterity in handling the work or no formal education. The major occupations in which women are employed in significant numbers are nursing, medical and health technology, teaching, stenography, typing and punching, maids, sweepers and such other service workers; plantation forestry and mining labour, spinning, weaving, tobacco production. Some of these are occupations where women are perceived as more equally productive as some employment is a result of economic incidence.

Although total employment in factories has been increasing since 1947 steadily. Women's employment in this sector has decreased since 1964, their share being reduced from 11.43 per cent in 1951 to 9.1 per cent in 1971. The number of women employed in mines declined from 109,000 to 75,000 between 1951 and 1971. Whereas total employment increased from 549,000 to 630,000. The women's share of employment of declined from 21.1 per cent to 11.9 per cent a decline of 47.4 per cent the heaviest decline was in coalmins from 55,000 to 2,000. There was, however, a general decline in the employment of women in all categories in 1963. This was more marked among administrative, executive and managerial workers (from 5,000 to 1,000), and professional, technical and related workers (from 55,000 to 31,000). Some new professions like advertising, market research, hotel management and cottage industries employ women in management cadres. Best traditional industries have not yet accepted women at this level. While it is generally difficult to give an all correct profile of women in service and professions, a review of the available data indicates a change in the occupational pattern and two trends are clearly visible; concentration of women in teaching and medicine and recognition of certain low prestige jobs in the clerical services as particularly suited to women.

In 1967-68 the medical work force of 120,000 doctors included 1,2000 women, the new profession of social work has emerged since Independence, but in 1947, the year noticed the existence of two such schools, the Tata Institute of Social Sciences, Bombay, and the Delhi School of Social Work. There are now more than 20 such institutions. According to a study in 1968 there were 3,153 social work graduates whose number is estimated to have increased to 6,000 by 1971.

The sectorwise examination of women's employment trends indicates that major forces affecting women's employment stem from structural changes within the economy as a whole (from a traditional to a modern market economy, from a laissez faire to deliberate planned development, from unorganised to organised production, from unregulated to regulated relations of production or from labour to capital intensive technology, and from intensification of socio-economic inequalities.[14]

In succeeding pages now we discuss the empirical findings and the views expressed by the sample respondents. On the basis of our empirical findings, we have also tried to make some generalisations.

TABLE 16.1

Monthly Contribution

Contribution	*No. of respondent*	*Percentage*
Less than Rs. 500	80	40
Rs. 500 to Rs. 1,000	60	30
Rs. 1,000 to Rs. 1,500	30	15
Not giving the exact figure	30	15
Total	200	100

In regard to economic independence and their contribution to the family, we put several questions to the sample working women and wanted to know to what extent they are economically independent and what contribution they have a made for the development of their families. The first question we put to the sample working women was that "what financial contribution you make to your family per month?" In reply to our this question the reply of the 200 sample respondents are presented below (see Table 16.1).

It has been observed that 40% contribute less than Rs. 500 to their families. 30% contribute between Rs. 500 to Rs. 10,000; 15% contribute between Rs. 1000 to Rs. 1500 a month. It is worth mentioning that these respondents apart from their salaried job are engaged in some other activities to generate additional finances. Remaining 15% contribute 3/4 of their income every month to their family. Another issue closely connected to that we wanted to check up as to what amount they use to spent on themselves their response in regard to the personal expenditure varied between Rs. 100 to maximum Rs. 500. Two explanations can be given to this. First either they were evasive in their reply or they are really too involved in establishing the fact that they were too much concerned about all-round development of their families. Personal expenditure also varies with the position held by the women. Even though the difference is not very significant as woman's personal expenditure is still not very high. She is more concerned about the welfare of her family members rather spending more money on herself.

Another aspect that as to what amount of their salary they spend on development and education of their children? The response to this issue reflected their admission that either they live in joint family or under the total guardianship of their husband, in such a situation the question of spending on the development of education to their children hardly arise. It was further confirmed by them that it is the duty of the head of the family or the husband to look after the maintenance and educational facilities of the children. However, they admitted that sometimes they use to give pocket money to their children. They also admitted that they are consulted about the right place for the child's education and even at times their decision is respected.

TABLE 16.2
Monthly Saving

Saving	*No. of respondents*	*Percentage*
Rs. 100 to Rs. 200	100	50
Rs. 200 to Rs. 500	60	30
More than Rs. 500	40	20
Total	200	100

Sense of insecurity about the future is apparently visible among the women whether they are traditional or modernised. The sense of insecurity compel the women to think in terms of saving more in comparison to their male counterparts. Keeping this fact in view were put question before the sample working women as to what saving they make every month out of their earning? Table 16.2 shows the result.

Fifty per cent respondents told that they save between Rs. 100 to Rs. 200. 30% admitted that they save between Rs. 200 to Rs. 500 per month. But some over-enthusiastic (20%) respondents said that they save more than Rs. 500.

However, from the foregoing analysis it can be said that sense of economic independence has developed among the working women. They are alive to their family responsibilities and future apprehension of bad-days. This is reflected from the fact that either they contribute to their family income or they try to give better education to their children or save something for the future.

In regard to economic independence and their attitudinal change, we wanted to know that given the preference what type of job they would like to have. It is interested to note that as high as 85% of them stated that given the preference they would like to join teaching profession either in government schools or in colleges. Alternatively they would like to have some administrative job in government and in public undertaking according to their qualification. A negligible percentage of 15% preferred for the job of typist or a clerk. While making a deeper probe, we wanted to know as to why they will prefer teaching or administrative job. Giving explanation to our this query they said that in teaching profession there is little supervision in and greater independence as also little danger to their chastity and more job satisfaction. Similarly in administrative jobs there are enough facilities, little inconvenience and higher status. In regard to their low preference for typist or clerk's job, they had to state that their jobs are like double-edged sword. Moreover, it is a tangible job and there is no job-satisfaction or less job-satisfaction. They also find these jobs monotonous. In long term it leads to health hazard as either she will be always loaded with heap of files over her head or she has to sit throughout the day on her typewriter. Again it is interesting to note that a negligible percentage of sample respondents preferred for a job in private concern. It is because of the fact that sense of insecurity is always attached with private job. Even if an employee is employed on permanent basis, he or she can't feel secure for the job. This is more alarming in the case of female worker as she has always to dance at the tunes of her master. If she refuses to do so she can be discharged any moment. These are the reasons that the sample respondents preferred to enter into teaching or administrative jobs. Sense of job security in the government service may be the most vital reason for that.

It has often been reported by the researchers and working women themselves that sometimes they find it difficult to make adjustment between their household work and office work. As such as we wanted to know from the sample respondents as to whether they have faced such adjustment problems. The reply of our sample respondents is presented in Table 16.3.

The table 16.3 shows that as high as 88 per cent of sample respondents reported that they were quite comfortable with their both the responsibilities and the problem of adjustment hardly arise before them. Only negligible percentage reported that it was very difficult for them to discharge their both the responsibilities of a housewife and a working woman. They said that it becomes so difficult sometime for them that they are compelled to think in terms of quitting the job. But it was reported in a very small case as such it can be said that a comparatively high majority of sample respondents have brought changes in their attitude and tried to adjust in two environment i.e., environment of the house and environment of the office.

TABLE 16.3

Are You Feeling Comfortable with the Job and Household Work?

Reply	*No. of respondents*	*Percentage*
Comfortable	176	88
Uncomfortable	24	12
Total	200	100

Now we analyse some of the social characteristics of the sample working women, which may be responsible for the change in their attitude regarding economic independence and other factors.

In a large number of studies social characteristics such as age, marital status, occupation, income, employer-employee relation, motivation and social background have been found to have significant influence on the economic structure of the society. Here we discuss some of the basic social characteristics of the working women which are considered to be the related factors.

Education

As our sample includes the educated elite section of women in Delhi, we have noted that the level of education is high among them as shown in Table 16.4.

TABLE 16.4

Level of Education

Level of Education	*No. of respondents*	*Percentage*
Undergraduates	6	3
Graduates	62	31
Post-graduates	91	45.5
Professionals	41	20.5
Total	200	100.0

If we combine post-graduates and professionals, we find that 66% of the sample women are highly educated and are engaged in professions like teaching and administrative jobs. Now if we look into the occupation table we note that education and occupation have the direct impact on the attitudinal change of the working women as shown in Table 16.4.

As shown in Table 16.5 the occupation distribution verifies that most highly educated women even prefer teaching profession.

TABLE 16.5

Occupational Distribution of Working Women

Occupation	*No. of respondents*	*Percentage*
Teachers	87	43.5
Lecturers	21	10.5
Clerks—Typist, Steno	48	24.0
Executives	34	17.0
Air-hostess	1	.5
Architects	2	1.0
Research Assistants	7	3.5
Total	200	100.0

Marital Status

To determine the marital status of working women, we attempted to find out the number of those who were unmarried, married, widowed as per the following Table 4.6.

TABLE 4.6

Marital Status

Status	*No. of respondents*	*Percentage*
Married	157	78.5
Unmarried	43	21.5
Total	200	100.0

It is found that more than two-third of the working women are married (78.5%) i.e., almost 80% of the sample working women. Only 21.5% of the working women are unmarried. It is merely a chance that no widow or separated woman is there in the sample. This distribution is similar to the one given in a survey report of Government of India.[15]

Family Status

Data show almost half of the sample working women belong to the joint family and half to the nuclear family as shown in Table 16.7.

TABLE 16.7

Family Status

Status	*No. of respondents*	*Percentage*
Joint	100	50
Nuclear	100	50
Total	200	100

Number of Dependents

The number of dependents in a working woman's family ranged from 0 to 9. 40.5 per cent working women did not have any dependent. This also includes 21.5% of those unmarried women who are just working to pass their time and to make their career. The table further shows 20% of married women did not have any dependent and they live in nuclear family too. 34% of the working women have more than two dependents to support and 23.5 per cent have two to five and only 2 per cent have more than five dependents to support.

TABLE 16.8

Number of Dependents

No. of Dependents	*No. of respondents*	*Percentage*
None	81	40.5
Two to three	68	34.0
Two to five	47	23.5
More than five	4	2.0
Total	200	100.0

Size of the Family

After analysing the data it is evident that size of the family is decreasing. As Table 16.9 shows that only 2 per cent reported to have more than 2 issues.

TABLE 16.9

Size of Family

No. of Issues	*No. of respondents*	*Percentage*
None	56	28.0
One	37	18.5
Two	103	51.5
More than two	4	2.0
Total	200	100.0

28 per cent reported having no issue, this also includes the 21.5% of the unmarried sample working women. 18.5 per cent have only one child. This reveals that working women are more concerned about the size of the family as out of the percentage of 80 married women, 78% had one or two children.

Occupational Mobility

As regards the nature of employment as many as 82% of sample women reported that they were permanent and only 18% said that they were temporary. Data did not include part time employees. The data represented in Table 16.10 regarding the length of service indicate a wide variation among the working women.

TABLE 16.10

Length of Service

Length of Service	*No. of respondents*	*Percentage*
Less than 2 years	36	18.0
2 years to 5 years	49	24.5
5 years to 10 years	41	20.5
10 years to 20 years	46	23.0
More than 20 years	28	14.0
Total	200	100.0

From the above table we find that those working for more than 5 years are about 42.5 per cent which clearly indicates that working women have less mobility. It was revealed that during the course of interview most of them are concerned about having an office close to their residence, lesser transfer, lesser change of job and more time for attending their children. It was concluded that majority of them had taken up the job as a source of additional financial support rather than as a profession.

When respondents were asked about their change in occupation, 75.5% reported no change and only 24.5% reported that they had changed their job. These 24.5% when asked to explain this mobility gave several reasons for example some changed their job due to their marriage as they came in Delhi from outside. Some reported that (specially teachers) precious school was very far off. So they changed to their new one. Only a negligible percentage of women reported that after getting more education they competed for higher status jobs and got it. This shows that women still are not very keen on changing their occupation unless they are forced to do so because their job being subsidiary to their husband's job and also not that much concerned for career because of transfer hazards etc. and for responsibilities of family and children. It can be inferred that they could not get any other status jobs because they have choosen the jobs of their choice, i.e. teachers, lecturers and administrators. Besides women did not want to go elsewhere leaving their family and children.

After analysing the social characteristics of the working women in this chapter, our main objective is to correlate the following factors:

1. Has education brought any change in the attitude of the women?
2. Do they feel that their occupation is rightly suited to their education? i.e. the relation between education and occupation.
3. Are they struggling for more prestigious job suited to their education?
4. Is there are any relation between marital status and occupation?
5. Has any attitudinal change of working women visible in the up-bringing of their children.
6. To make an assessment of the impact of job on their family life beside their economic independence.
7. Psychological factor effecting their inter-personal relations.

It has been suggested earlier that as a consequence of their employment, working women may develop a somewhat different outlook in life as compared to the non-working women. As our sample does not include the data of non-working, this is just depending on open data available in other reports. Our objective is to find out how significant are these attitudinal changes. Here are some of the correlation highlighting these changes.

TABLE 16.11

Correlation of Education and Occupation

Profession	*Under Graduate*	*Graduate*	*Post-graduate + professionally trained*	*Total*
Teachers	2 (2.3%)	32 (34.7%)	53 (61.0%)	87 (100%)
Lecturers	—		21 (100.0%)	21 (100%)
Executives	—		34 (100.0%)	34 (100%)
Clerk-Typist, Steno	4 (8.3%)	38 (58.3%)	16 (33.4%)	48 (100%)
Air-hostess	—	1 (100.0%)	—	1 (100%)
Architect	—	1 (50.0%)	1 (50.0%)	2 (100%)
Research Assistant	—	—	7 (100,0%)	7 (100%)
Total	6 (3.0)	62 (31.0%)	132 (66.0%)	200 (100%)

This shows that 66% of the sample are post-graduate and professionally qualified and 71% of the sample are as teachers, lecturers and executives which are their choice as they themselves have mentioned. It is inferred that they could not get any other better status job because they have chosen the job of their choice, teaching and administration. The level of education in case of teaching profession and executive cadre is quite high.

TABLE 16.12

Occupation and Marital Status Correlation

Occupation	*Married*	*%*	*Unmarried*	*%*	*Total*
Teachers	77	(88.50%)	10	(11.50%)	87
Lecturers	18	(85.71%)	3	(14.29%)	21
Clerk-Steno, Typist	32	(66.66%)	16	(33.33%)	48
Executive	30	(88.23%)	4	(11.77%)	34
Air-Hostess	—	—	1	(100.0%)	1
Architect	—	—	2	(100.0%)	2
Research Assistant	—	—	7	(100.0%)	7
Total	157		43		200

Keeping occupation as a stable variable we have analysed the relation between occupation and marital status. It is evident from Table 16.12 that teaching and clerical jobs have been the major areas of employment, there is no definite correlation between the occupation and marital status except that unmarried ladies continued working even after marriage in teaching profession and executive cadre. During the personal interview also it was confirmed when unmarried respondents were asked "whether they continue working after marriage?" Most of them who were in teaching profession, executive cadre replied in affirmative.

Attitudinal Change

Table 16.13 confirmed the view that working ladies in teaching profession, research work did not find any difficulty to adjust their life-style after marriage as they were able to find sufficient time to attend their new requirements. Even though the data shows that the high cadre job ladies are also comfortable but they have also shown their more involvement in the job and their jobs are more demanding. So they face more problems due to their personality rather than office. This is again confirmed when we analyse the fact of adjustability after marriage.

Table 16.14 is supplementary to Table 16.13 and goes on pressing again that working ladies by and large have low degree of conflict. As regard their occupation particularly in teaching profession, we also perceive higher degree of adjustment certain in comparison to other profession in their life-style specially after marriage. In order to confirm the findings, question was asked whether their profession come in the way of their adjustment towards their family after marriage? The ladies in teaching and executive cadre find less difficulty in adjustment. As in teaching they have more time available to them for their family. In executive cadre maturity of mind and high salary both pay to this adjustment. Overall analyses shows the high degree of adjustability after marriage among working women.

TABLE 16.13

Occupational and Performance of Responsibilities Towards Job and Household Work, How they Feel?

Occupation	*Comfortable*	*%*	*Uncomfortable*	*%*	*Total*
Teachers	78	(89.7)	9	(10.3)	87
Lecturers	19	(90.1)	2	(9.9)	21
Clerk—Steno, Typist	41	(85.4)	7	(14.6)	48
Executive	30	(88.2)	4	(11.8)	34
Air-hostess	1	(100.0)	—	—	1
Architects	1	(50.0)	1	(50.0)	2
Research Assistant	6	(86.0)	1	(14.0)	7
Total	176	(88%)	24	(12%)	200

TABLE 16.14

Occupation and Degree of Adjustment After Marriage

Occupation	*Degree of adjustment*				*Total*
	High	*%*	*Low*	*%*	
Teachers	75	86	12	14	87
Lecturers	17	81	4	19	21
Clerk—Steno-Typist	41	85	7	15	48
Executives	31	91	3	9	1
Air-hostess	1	100			1
Architects	1	50	1	50	2
Research Assistant	6	89	1	11	7
Total	172	86	28	14	200

The sample survey indicates that 62% of the sample working women are satisfied with their occupations and 29% of them are getting sufficient encouragement from their life-partners. Occupational satisfaction is restricted to the self whereas encouragement by other family members is something else. It can be inferred that only about 30% of working ladies are feeling that they are getting encouragement to work from the elders of their families. As 88% of the sample shows that they all are feeling comfortable though they are in different professions. Even the profession-wise analysis indicates that 85 to 90% of the sample respondents are finding it comfortable. Whether they are encouraged or condemned by their husbands, today's women pursue their career to better their personality or make both ends meet. This was made clear by the sample women in course of informal talk. But is it a positive or a negative sign? Looking at the positive side that husbands are broadminded to recognise that money is vital and also that the burden of managing the house when shared equally, reduces the responsibility of only one person. They appreciate independence, recognise their wive's individuality and allow them to develop their creative talents. But its negative aspect is that women have to play two roles. Most men show their resentment when their wive's job interfers with their housework.[16]

TABLE 16.15

Occupation and Attitude of Husband Towards Wives' Working

Occupation	*Satis-fied*	*%*	*Not happy*	*%*	*Encou-raging*	*%*	*Unmar-ried*	*Total*
Teachers	56	(72.72)	2	(2.59)	19	(24.69)	10	77
Lecturers	12	(66.66)	0	—	6	(33.33)	3	18
Clerk—Steno typist	20	(62.50)	6	(18.75)	6	(18.75)	16	32
Executives	10	(33.33)	5	(16.66)	15	(50.00)	4	30
Air-hostess	—		—		—		1	1
Architect		—		—		2	2	
Research Assistant	—		—		—		7	7
Total	98	(62.42)	13	(8.28)	46	(29.30)	43	157

If we have a look on the explanations of preceding pages we find that economic independence has brought marked attitudinal change in the working women. However, the degree of change depends on the level of education, the profession they hold and the attitude of the family members towards them. Even then our study suggests that by and large employment has brought a sense of confidence among the working women and they are now in a position to think about their independent existence without depending on husband and other family members.

REFERENCES

1. Murali Manohar, K., Ed., *Women's Status and Development in India,* ed. by Gail Omvedt; *Draft Statement on Women's Liberation* Published by SOWSTUD and IIPA Local Branch, Warangal, pp. 222-244.
2. *Ibid,* p. 234.
3. *Ibid.*
4. Karanjia, T., Women today what needs changing, *Flair,* Vol. 3, No. 1, January 1986, pp. 48.51.
5. *Ibid.,* p. 49.
6. *Ibid.,* p. 48.
7. *Ibid.,* p. 50.
8. *Ibid.,* p. 51.

9. Gupta, A.R., *Women in Hindu Society*, Jyotsana Prakashan, Delhi, 1982, pp. 153-248.
10. Jain, Devaki, Ed., *Indian Women*, Publication Division, Govt. of India, 1975, pp. xi-xxii.
11. *Ibid.*, pp. xx-xxii.
12. Beteille, Andre, *Position of Women in India Society*, Publication Division, Government of India, 1975, pp. 61-68.
13. D'Souza, Alfred, ed., *Women in Contemporary India : Traditional Images and Changing Roles*, New Delhi, Manohar Book Service, 1975.
14. Devendra, Kiran, *Status and Position of Women in India*, Vikas Publishing House Pvt. Ltd., 1985, pp. 31-p5.
15. Government of India, *Economic and Social Status of Women Workers in India*, Labour Bureau, Ministry of Labour, Publication No. 15.
16. Krishnan, Padmini, What do husbands think of their working wives, *Beautiful Working Women*, A Ross Murarka Publication, Vol. 10, No. 7, March 1984, p. 38.

17

Micro Economic Policies and Their Impact on Women

India has embarked upon a course of restructuring its development policy framework since 1991. The roots of the new paradigm of growth can be traced to the eighties, but the balance of payments crisis of 1991 was the decisive turning point, pushing the economy into a trajectory different from the import substitution path that had so far been followed. The new macro economic policies consist of both stabilisation measures as well as the Structural Adjustment Programme (SAP), under the umbrella of liberalisation and greater reliance on market mechanisms.

An assessment of the impact is made difficulty by the fact that many of the policies, especially with respect to the SAP, are still unfolding and there is invariably a time lag in availability of data for analysis. At present, there is very little disaggregated data, gender-wise, available from the national statistical Agencies.

The complexity of assessment is further compounded, given the multiplicity of women's roles in any society. Woman is an economic producer, home manager, child bearer caretaker of children and the elderly. Women work longer hours, with fewer resources, for lower rewards. They face greater constraints and harsher choices in times of change.

There is an assumption that women's time and unpaid labour is infinitely elastic and that any additional requirement may be filed by women increasing their workload. This assumption arises essentially out of the disregard for the unpaid work which women do. The dominance of the market leads to undervaluing things not directly calculable in its term, household work being a prime example.

It is important to examine how women respond to the changes and whether they are able of utilies the opportunities offered by the new economic climate and cope with the negative fallout, if any.

As early as 1974, the Report of the Committee on the Status of Women, highlighted that the country's economic policies had tended to marginalise women. The majority of Indian women were and continue to be in the informal sector. Data indicates that women, have not made very major gains in terms of employment. A small stratum has been able to enter the organised sector. Estimates suggest that around two thirds of female causal labourers in rural areas continue to be below the poverty line.

One positive development, however, has been a gradual decline in under-employment even within the unorganised and informal sector. The critical role of public expenditure, primarily in rural areas through poverty eradication programmes, has been widely acknowledged. The State's commitment to providing social services has also played a vital role in improving the quality of life indicators.

Stabilisation refers to short term attempts to steady the economy in the face of sudden shocks of existing macro-economic imbalances, especially, in balance of payments. They are basically contradictionary in nature. Restrictive fiscal and monetary policies aim to squeeze overall demand within the system so as to reduce imbalances in the external balance of payments and overall budgetary deficit.

Measures that are to be implemented are cuts in the Government expenditure and there is an anticipation of the market playing a more significant role in resource allocation, on the premise that one reason for poor economic performance is distortion in resource allocation.

It has been projected by some researchers that the economic policies may lead to increase in un-employment, with women bearing a disproportionate share of the brunt. The anticipated reduction in services implies that women may also have to allocate more time to activities that were previously at least partially provided by the State. The burden of work may be intensified by inflation which it is feared may squeeze real incomes and push women to seek alternate ways of their supplementation.

As yet, however, data from the field is not available on these aspects. In order to be effective, it is important that analyses of the data should be sectoral, detailed, policy-related and highlight threats as well as opportunities vis-a-vis poor women.

Unlike the stabilisation programme which is of short duration, the Structural Adjustment Programme is a longer run process aimed at a fundamental restructuring of the economy. The package consists of policies to increase the outward orientation of the economy, reduce the role of the public sector, and liberalise various sectors to make them more responsive to the markets.

It is clear that there are many kinds of responses within the current development discourse to the new macro economic policies adopted by the Government. These are mostly derived from experiences in other countries. They are primarily interested in the deprived sections of society — poor women, their livelihoods, basic needs, rights, equity and justice. These responses are, simplistically put, either pro or anti change.

The supporters of the new macro economic policies have expressed the view that liberalisation, as expressed through deregulation, was sorely needed. They believe that these policies present a unique opportunity to restructure the economy and redefine the role of the State in ensuring poverty eradication and social justice.

Those opposed to the policies fear that they may led to jobless growth, curtailment of support systems and adverse impact of the negative fallout of globalisation. The gender concerns that are being voiced are basically two-fold. Firstly, whether in the period of stabilisation when costs have to be borne, poor women would benefit from social safety nets put in position by the Government, or not. Secondly, whether the benefits when they begin to materalise, would necessarily trickle down to poor women. Several studies have been taken up in these areas.

How the Structural Adjustment Programme would affect the income earning opportunities available to women has also been the subject of wide-spread concern. Various related issues have been highlighted. There may be, for example, expansion of employment opportunities for women in export oriented industries, expansion of private sector in the core sector,expansion of the service industry, cash cops cultivation and agri-business. Yet, the uncertainties imposed by inequalising market structures and the fact that women may increase their labour contribution with little effective control over cash income, may be detrimental to their long term interests.

Another possible area of increasing employment opportunities may be finance, banks and insurance sectors. These improvements in employment may however, be offset by relative decline in the traditional sectors—which employ women in large numbers — as they diminish in importance. In addition, there may be a reduction in public sector employment, given the constraints of expenditure.

The ripple effect of change is likely to be experienced in the informal sector, too. As self-employed women primarily deal in non-tradeable goods in the informal sector, the emphasis on tradeables may limit their opportunities. The combined effect may, therefore, depress their earnings.

Overall, the economic pressures may compel households to resort to various difficult survival strategies. The feminisation of 'work' that may be consequence of the policies may, therefore, throw up both challenges and opportunities. It must, however, be emphasised that empirical studies and detailed figures need to be analysed further before arriving at any pre-conceived or definitive conclusions about the direction and impact of policy changes.

India is also currently going through a period of trade liberalisation. This is likely to have a profound impact on the lives of its people who have for decades been operating under extensive levels of protectionism, with limited access to international markets. The World Trade Organisation (WHO) has been established to regulate and monitor the world trading system. Decisions at the Uruguay Round of GATT talks, resulted in agreements to reduce tarrifs, standardise rules and integrate previously non-GATT sectors—textiles, agriculture and services—into the world-wide trading system. This is likely to have a deep influence on India's structure of exports.

While there is a consensus that trade is important for national development and growth, it needs to be recognised that the debate is of particular importance to women.

Women constitute the majority of the workforce in modern export industries and Multi National Corporations (MNCs) based in Free Trade and Export Processing Zones (FTZs/ EPZs). Most economically active women operate in the informal sector, producing goods that are extremely sensitive to external competition. Women dominate in sectors such as agriculture, textiles and clothing which may henceforth be closely integrated with the global trading system.

Technological transformation of production processes, needed to meet international standards, may represent a threat to women with low levels of education and technological skills, Any changes that trade expansion beings to the natural environment or to the State's ability to service its citizens are also likely to have a direct impact on women. So far, not much attention has been paid to the gender differentiate impact of expanded trade. The gender dimension has been overlooked in trade policy making processes.

While analysing these trends, it is important to take into account their multiple facets. On the one hand, trade expansion may cause displacement, unemployment and hardship in some sectors. Those sectors likely to suffer most from international competition may therefore to be targetted for financial and technical assistance. On the other hand, many new income and employment opportunities will emerge. Here, efforts may be made to identify potential growth areas and women should be provided the necessary skills and contracts to take advantage of these openings.

For women's needs and concerns to be voiced, it is of fundamental importance that women are better represented in trade policy making bodies at all levels. It is necessary to produce gender disagregated data for all sectors, to enable a better assessment of gender specific impact of global changes. Advocacy and campaign activities also need to be developed for policy changes along these lines.

The Government is conscious of the efforts that are required to mitigate the possible negative impact of these policies, specially for vulnerable sections, including women. India is laying emphasis on a high rate of growth of the economy, combined with an employment oriented composition of growth, supplemented by special employment programmes. Substantial inputs are being provided in agriculture and infrastructure and it is expected to realise the target of full employment by 2002.

For effect management of the new macro economic policies, steps such as control of inflation, careful choice of areas of budget cuts, training, retaining and redeployment of the working people, labour protection and efficiency of social security systems have already been taken up. The tone has been set to concentrate greater Governmental efforts in the social sector and poverty eradication.

The National Renewal Fund and the Social Safety Net are already in place. Under the Social Safety Net, allocation have been increased for programmes relating to the development of women and children, such as the Integrated Chile Development Services Scheme, National Creche Fund and the National Credit Fund of Women.

The National Renewal Fund provides funds for compensation to employees affected by restructuring or closure of industrial units, assistance to cover the costs of retaining and redeployment of employees arising as a result of modernisation, technological upgradation and industrial restructuring. It supports employment generation schemes. A total of Rs. 2549.66 crores has been budgetted for it.

What is now required is to give macro-economic and development policies and distinct gender perspective, with the overarching objective that poor women do not become worse off in absolute terms and that better off women are not worse off than men, in comparable social groups. The indicators of well-being should include not only income, but total hours of work, health and nutritional status etc. It needs to be appreciated that the relationship between women, the market and the State is a complex one in which conscious efforts are required to achieve gender equity.

WOMEN'S CONTRIBUTION TO THE ECONOMY — FOCUS ON AGRICULTURE

The largest sector of India's economy agriculture contributes a little over 30 per cent of the GNP and accounts for 60% of the employment. Although the percentage of rural population has dropped from 82.7% in 1951 to 74.3% in 1991, the average farm size has also fallen from 2.1 to 1.8 hectares during this period due to the steady increase in population.

There has been an increase in the number of landless families and families with small or marginal holdings. Much planning in research, extension and land production strategies is needed to address these problems and one factor which has yet to be acknowledged is the role of women in agriculture.

Of the women workers, 34.55% are cultivators, 43.56% labour and 4.63% engaged in livestock, forestry, fisheries etc. Of the marginal workers, 47.91% are cultivators, 41.43% are agricultural labour and only 1.64% are engaged in livestock etc. The rest are in the non-agricultural sector. Thus agriculture continues to be a major filed for women's employment.

Nearly 63% of all economically active men are engaged in agriculture as compared to 78% of women. Almost 50% of rural female workers are classified as agricultural labourers and 3795 as cultivators. The corresponding figures for men is the reverse; 55 per cent cultivators and 24 per cent as agriculture labour.

Statistics do not, however, provide a complete picture of the work done by women, the hours of seasonal, part-time, unpaid labour, apart from household work. Interestingly, there is no word in Hindi, and perhaps other Indian languages, for women farmers, though feminine counter parts exists for all other traditional occupations.

Paradoxically women's contribution to agriculture as well as in food processing and marketing, however does not entitle them to be included as beneficiaries in major sponsored programmes in these sectors. This is due to a certain gender-blindness that permeates much of development thinking. Access to resources such as land, credit, appropriate technology and training has always been difficult for them.

Women's participation in agricultural extension, training and research is also minimal. They constitute a mere 0.59% of farm extension workers. Since almost all such workers are men, women's requirements for upgrading skills are often overlooked. Segregation also discourages contacts between women farmers and extension agents, who are mostly men.

It is now being accepted that development framework should cater to the needs and provide services to women who work longer and harder. In the tribal economy of Orissa, for example, women spend 105.4 days per year on shifting cultivation (Bogodo'), whereas men spend only 50.11 days in the same activity.

In the Himalayas, a research study found, a pair of bullocks works for 1,064 hours, a man for 1, 2, 2 hours and a woman for 3,485 hours in a year on a one-hectare farm. For a one hectare farm women average 640 hours for agricultural operations like weeding, 384 hours for irrigation, 650 hours for transporting organic manure, 557 hours for sowing and 984 hours for harvesting and threshing.

Women in the three main rice-growing States of Kerala, Tamil Nadu and West Bengal make crucial contributions to the entire process of cultivation. Outside ploughing, an exclusively male task, women have a predominant role in transplanting, weeding, manuring and fertilising, harvesting, threshing, winnowing, drying, staking and carrying the produce. More than two-thirds of the inputs are provided by women.

While a fuller understanding of women's status and role is imperative, an exact quantification is difficult, not only because of regional variations, but also on account of the different socio-economic contexts in which they work, historical differences, and the limited interpretation of the concept of 'worker' in Census Reports.

The incorporation of gender issues into the development agenda needs to recognise women's participation in farm labour at various levels — as farmers, producers of crops, protectors of livestock, and users of technology. They need to be seen as active agents in marketing, processing and storage of food and in innovative areas such as sericulture.

An attempt in this direction requires strengthening the agricultural base and augmenting of rural incomes. Major constraints may be identified, so that supportive measures can be suggested, like separate training, preferential membership in rural cooperatives, access to technology, credit and marketing and encouraging the formation of women's collectives for farming under programmes such as DWCRA. (See Box)

To achieve sustainability and equity, it is essential that agriculture be made more women-centered. If gender issues are to get primacy, an alternative analytical frame is essential. This thrust will have to be initiated, and carried forward until rural women are sufficiently motivated and empowered to avail of the benefits of the mainstream farm support systems.

As beginning and in order to ensure the usefulness and relevance of the research and extension programmes to women the following points are being considered by the Central Ministry of Agriculture:

- — Planning be based on accurate and appropriate data, which reflects the status and needs of women farmers;
- — Women's development be viewed as part of the development of the total community and investments identified as necessary to secure it, be provided;
- — Training for women, to begin with, be on the skills needed for securing awareness, motivation, employment, leadership and participation;
- — Group approaches, be evolved in research and extension efforts targetting women farmers to optimise their impact,
- — Imbalances in the workloads and working conditions be recognised,
- — Employing of more female agricultural extension workers be promoted so as to reach rural women more satisfactorily,
- — Educational and extension activities be enhanced to meet needs of women for increased managerial, organisational, entrepreneurial and decision making skills.

A gender sensitisation module for policy makers has also been developed by the National Institute of Rural Development, based on extensive research in crop production, dairying, fisheries, forestry and sericulture and has been found to be extremely useful. This is being very effectively and widely disseminated.

Government is also implementing special projects in Tamil Nadu, Karnataka, Orissa and Madhya Pradesh, Gujarat and Andhra Pradesh, adopting innovative strategies and approaches. The basic assumption of these remain as follows:

- — Improvement in the technical skills of women farmers with special focus on small and marginal farmers, would result in tangible increases in agricultural production, and
- — Increased agricultural production is the base for improving the quality of life of these families and bringing about their economic stability.

In Orissa, the focus is on training of women as village extension workers. In the four districts trained at "Gramsevak Taaleem Kendra," (Extension Training Centres) for a duration of 12 to 14 months.

The curriculum is the same as that for male village extension workers, but additional information on the operations, such as post-harvesting technology, vegetable cultivation etc. are given due recognition. This approach hold tremendous potential and promise.

Besides these special projects, a Central sector scheme of women in agriculture has been formulated under the Eighth Plan and is under implementation in seven selected States, namely Punjab, Haryana, Rajasthan, Himachal Pradesh, Uttar Pradesh, Kerala and Maharashtra on a pilot-basis covering one district each. Implemented at the district level, it envisages provision of a package of training and extension support through facilitators and link workers. Each facilitator constitutes 10 farm women groups, each groups consisting of 20 farm women.

Technical training programmes are conducted at the village level, and refresher training is provided later. Study tours and result demonstrations also form an integral part of the programme. The concept of self-help thrift groups has been introduced to enable women to plan their own activities.

The scheme of Farmers Training Centres was initiated in 1966-67 and there are 188 such Centres in the country. Training is provided in crop husbandry, horticulture, animal husbandry and allied subjects. This improves the knowledge base and makes women more receptive to new ideas propagated by the extension machinery. Half of the training courses are exclusively earmarked for women.

The Indian Council of Agricultural Research has established 183 Krishi Vigyan Kendras which provide need-based vocational training to practicing farmers, women farmers, rural youth, village artisans and landless labourers. It also plans to set up a National Research Centre with the following objectives:

— To create a comprehensive data base on all aspects of women in agriculture;
— To study their participation in agriculture and allied areas;
— To identify relevant available technologies;
— To generate women-specific technology by research networking;
— To test and verify women specific technology and provide guidance on the basis of field work for technology refinement;
— To offer advanced training courses for research and extension scientists in order to sensitise them to women's role in agriculture;
— To act as a resource centre and clearing house for women-specific technologies for the Departments of Agriculture, Animal Husbandry, Social Welfare, Fisheries, Cooperation, Rural Development etc.

The National Sericulture Project was initiated a decade ago. Within this programme too, there has been a growing realisation that the gender component must be strengthened. As women are involved in the most critical stages of production of rearing, any effort to improve the quality of cocoons will necessarily imply increasing their participation not only in production but also in decision making processes.

The Small Farmers Agri Business Consortium, a Government programme introduced in 12 States is mainly focussing on projects exclusively managed by rural women particularly in areas that are not agriculturally fertile. In West Bengal, in Midnapore, the members of the Zilla Parishad (District Council) are collaborating with the Bankura Women's Organisation and the Centre for Women's Development Studies (CWDS), Delhi in order to replicate a successful sericulture project in a region that has a similar eco-system. (See Box 1).

These initiatives have been supplemented by efforts of non-governmental organisations. National and regional Summits of women have been organised over the last few years where valuable exchange of ideas and experiences have taken place between researchers, policy planners and implementors on the one hand and agricultural workers and grassroots' women on the other hand. This has created a synergy which will pave the way for acknowledgement of women's contribution to the economy and its backbone—agriculture.

18

State Protection for Mothers and the Problems of Rearing Children

State Protection and Societal Care

The protection given by society for women to realise their new social roles includes a wide range of activities of an economic, social, judicial, moral-ethical and psychological nature, and is supported by educational work designed to affirm the authority and social equality of women. In order for the protection of society to be beneficial in practice, women themselves must be aware of the necessity of developing their personalities and playing a positive social role.

Bulgarian labour legislation provides special protection for pregnant women and mothers with regard to their labour participation. Thus, for instance, article 119, paragraph 1, of the Labour Code states: "Enterprises, administrations or organisations cannot refuse employment because of the pregnancy of a woman desiring to be employed."

Although pregnant women and mothers enjoy full rights, in accordance with the Constitution of the People's Republic of Bulgaria, this section of labour legislation is an additional guarantee of the right of pregnant women to work. The employing organisation is, moreover, obliged to treat pregnant women with special consideration. In addition, pregnant women, mothers with children under 8 months old and wives whose husbands are doing their regular military service enjoy special protection against dismissal in cases of changes in conditions of work (article 35 of the Labour Code). Even when an enterprise is shut down, a pregnant women cannot be dismissed but must be transferred to another appropriate job with the same remuneration.

One of the most significant achievements of the state social policy for the protection of mothers and the assistance of women is the legislation governing leave of absence for pregnancy or childbirth. In article 60 of the Labour Code, the leave of absence for pregnancy is designated in accordance with the number of children and is considerably greater than the 12 weeks established as mandatory minimum in the Maternity Protection Convention (Revised), 1952 (No. 103). The duration of leave (in calendar days) is as follows:

No. of children	Calendar days
For the first child	120
For the second child	150
For the third child	180
for the fourth and every subsequent child	120

While she is on leave of absence, because of pregnancy and childbirth, the working women receives financial compensation equal to 100 per cent of her gross labour remuneration. In addition, legislation in Bulgaria provides for additional leave of absence for mothers looking after a baby, as follows:

No. of children	Months
For the first child	6
For the second child	7
For the third child	8
For the fourth and every subsequent child	6

The financial compensation which a woman receives during the period of child-care leave corresponds to the minimum wage for the country, i.e., 100 lev (LW) per month (article 156, paragraph 3, of the Labour Code).

In addition, should a woman desire to go back to work before the expiration of the additional child-care leave, she will receive from the enterprise where she is working not only her regular salary but also an additional allocation equal to one-half of her monthly remuneration. This enables the mother to make use of the services of other people in caring for her baby and provides a chance for her not to lose her professional qualifications.

Mothers also have the right to paid leave of absence for breast-feeding until an infant is 8 months old. Should the need arise for breast-feeding after that age, the mother has the right to additional leave of one hour a day.

If a working woman prefers, or is obliged, to take care of her child herself until he or she is 3 years old, this additional leave is unpaid but is counted as length of service. The woman retains her position and the level of her qualifications (article 61 of the Labour Code). During this leave she receives LW10 as minimum help per month.

Should the mother want to take care of her child until the age of 6, she can make use of the special provisions which allow her to work at home. If the enterprise where the woman has been working is not in a position to provide such work, the woman has the right to sign a labour contract with another enterprise for the same type of work at home until the child is 6 years old. The enterprise in which the woman is permanently working is obliged to give her unpaid leave of absence for the entire period of her new labour contract. This legislation has the purpose of combining a woman's professional activity with her ability to take care of the child and to rear it until school age (Council of Ministers' Decree, No. 38, 7 July 1980).

Special leave of up to 60 days annually is available for taking care of a sick child until the age of 16 years. This leave can be taken by either he mother or father of the child. For children up to 7 years of age, the parents receive 100 per cent of their wages, and for older sick children this remuneration depends on the length of services of the parent.

In addition to the financial compensation which is paid to the mother for pregnancy and childbirth, the State pays a grant at the birth of a child. This is LW100 for the first child, LW250 for the second LW500 for the third and LW100 for the fourth and all subsequent children. Another form of help is the regular monthly family allowance. This is LW15 for the first child, LW25 for the second, LW45 for the third and LW15 for the fourth and for each subsequent child.

Bulgarian legislation treats motherhood as socially useful work and acknowledges it as length of service. Motherhood also entitles women who are not employed to acknowledgement for length of service: 12 months for the first child, 14 months for the second child, 18 months for the third child and 12 months for the fourth and each subsequent child.

Working women who have reared five or more children up to the age of 8 years have the right to retire after 15 years' service and on reaching 40 or 45 years of age, depending on the category of work they have been doing (article 4 of the Pensions Law).

Regulations concerning women in the labour force include special provisions for the safety and protection of female workers. In this respect, all the international labour Conventions for night work, shift work and labour safety have been observed. In addition to this, special standards have been laid down for working women in occupations which are not appropriate to the physical and psychological needs of women who are bringing up children. A special list has been drawn up of the types of work particularly harmful to health, and women have been banned from such work. A list has also been made of activities which girls under the age of 18 are not allowed to undertake. Compulsory transfer to more appropriate jobs (for health reasons) is provided for pregnant women form the time pregnancy has been confirmed (article 118 of the Labour Code). The woman retains her original position and can return to it after the pregnancy and the allocated leave of absence for pregnancy, childbirth and child care. Should the transfer to more appropriate work be linked with a decrease in remuneration, state social security pays the difference (article 155, paragraph "a," of the Labour Code).

There are special women's and children's consultation centres at health-care institutions where medicine and treatment are provided for mother and child. Health care in Bulgaria is free for all citizens, and for pregnant women, and children of up to 3 years of age, medicines are supplied free of charge at their homes. Pregnant women, and children, are regularly visited at home by specialised medical staff.

The participation of women in all spheres of production has made it essential that children's institutions be rapidly expanded. In the first two years (1976 and 1977) of the

Seventh Five Year Plan, children's nurseries providing accommodation for 12,805 children, and kindergartens for 33,342 children, were built. The total number of children reared and educated with the help of children's institutions is constantly growing. In 1977 alone, per ten thousand children up to 3 years old, 1,725 places, or three times as many as in 1960, were made available in nurseries. In the same year, 755 children per thousand aged 3-7 years were accommodated in kindergartens (Komitet na balgarskite zheni 1980, pp. 52-53).

There are numerous communal dormitories, boarding-houses and canteens for school and university students. In the school year 1978-79, 31.6 per cent of all students ate in student canteens. Although education is free, the State gives scholarships to both school and university students, the size of which depends on the income of the parents and the scholastic record of the student. Scholarships are given to all "excellent" students regardless of the income of their parents.

In the Decision of the Politbureau of the Central Committee of the Bulgarian Communist Party of 6 March 1973 (Reshenie na Politbyurouna Tsentralniya komitet na BKP, 1973, p. 48), it is stated that provision must be made for the "fuller realisation and proper co-ordination of the basic social functions of the woman as a citizen of socialist society: to bear and bring up children; to take part in social labour; and to take part in the nation's socio-political life and administration."

Special attention has also been drawn to women's participation in the socio-political life and administration of the country (Reshenie na Politbyurouna tsentralniya komitet na BKP, 1973, pp. 20-22):

The Politbureau of the Central Committee of the Bulgarian Communist Party deems that women's participation in socio-political affairs and in public administration should be raised to the level of their education, their political maturity and their devotion to work. The number of women top executives should be increased especially in the medium and top-level state and economic bodies.

The broader involvement of women in all spheres and at all levels of management is a major aim of social development. Educational work aimed at promoting the idea of the equal value of women and men with regard to managerial functions and qualities must, therefore, be carried out continuously.

Social protection has the purpose of removing the negative consequences and supporting the positive aspects of emancipation, as well as helping the woman adapt to new conditions and new roles in life. Society's protection is essential in order to shape social opinion and firmly establish the belief as to the equal social value of women, since actual equality of the sexes cannot be based on legislative acts and social reforms alone. It is necessary that a change should take place in traditional thinking, in the way of life and in people's awareness.

Women and the Problem of Child-rearing

The involvement of women in the process of bringing up children is closely linked with the nature of the reproductive behaviour of the family. The extension of the social sphere to the rearing of children in no way lessens the role and responsibility of the parents and family in this social process. No state or social institution can supplant the specific features of family education and the mother's role in the rearing of small children. In contemporary society, fatherhood also assumes new dimensions, and the father's responsibilities are expanding.

When it comes to housework, however, women remain largely responsible — the degree of sharing among men and women remains minimal. When women were asked who in the family carried out various household tasks, a traditional pattern emerged (table 18.1). These statements are confirmed by a 1976-77 time budget study of working women and men; housework was done mainly by the women while the men had considerably more time for cultural and leisure activities (Table 18.2).

A national study carried out in 1957[7] (Informatsionno-sotsiologichieski tsentar pri TsK na BKP, 1975) looked for a qualitative evaluation of the interaction between mother and father in the rearing of children, and also compared the opinions of men and women. Analysis of these results indicates that 21.5 per cent of the women believe that both parents should take an equal part in the rearing of children, whereas for men the relative percentage is 34.7 per cent. It may be surmised that men either overestimate their participation or do not participate as much as they think they should. The same differences are evident in the answer to the question, "Does the man regularly help in the rearing of the children?" Women give a positive answer in 38.7 per cent of the cases and men in 43.7 per cent of the cases. The stand that the father very rarely helps in the rearing of children is taken by 9.8 per cent of the women and 4.6 per cent of the men, and that the father in general does not participate by 4.2 per cent women and 0.9 per cent of men.

Regardless of the observed differences in the opinions of men and women, we can definitely state the Bulgarian men take a much more active part in the rearing of children than in household work. The majority of people are beginning to acquire new standards and are distancing themselves from the outdated view that men have no duties with regard to bringing up children.

Analysis of the sociological research (1980) shows several basic trends in the rearing of small children. Generally, all children are cared for during their first year by their mothers who are on paid leave of absence. Following this period, the child continues to be looked after either by the mother, the grandparents, relatives, children's institutions or a hired person. In families with a larger number of children, the older ones take care of the younger child. A detailed picture of the ways children are looked after at pre-school age is given in table 18.3. Obviously, old family traditions and present-day life-styles are combined. This is confirmed by the fact that a considerable number of children are still brought up by relatives.

Table 18.1

Responsibility for Household Work, according to Women Interviewed, in Bulgaria, in 1980 (Percentages)

Who in the family does the work?	*Generally the wife*	*Generally the husband*	*Both spouses*	*Others (grandfather, grandmother, other persons)*	*Not indicated*
Cooking	84.2	1.0	6.3	8.2	0.3
Washing dishes	81.2	1.0	8.4	9.1	0.3
Cleaning, sweeping, washing (floors, windows), dusting	74.9	1.2	16.1	7.5	0.3
Washing	92.2	0.8	4.0	2.7	0.3
Ironing	88.9	1.0	4.5	5.3	0.3
Shopping	33.0	12.8	42.6	11.3	0.3
Takes care of winter heating	3.9	78.0	9.7	8.1	0.3
Small repairs in the house	4.8	81.3	7.7	5.8	0.4

Source: Sociological Research, 1980.

In the Bulgarian family, the children occupy a specific place in the value system of the mother. Data form the present study indicate that 44.4 per cent of married women consider it correct, from a moral standpoint, that "marriage should be preserved for the sake of the children even if it is not successful."

Data also show that most of the women questioned link their best family memories with their children. For about 78 per cent of the women, the children are the basic binding force in the family. It is interesting to note that 17 per cent of mothers express the view that they consider it natural for them to take care of their children after they have grown up and have started to work, while 43.2 per cent are of the opinion that they must help their children even when they have a family of their own.

The research data provide the possibility of analysing the attitude of married couples concerning the right of society to exercise moral control within the family. Those who think that "society must intervene in family life if the behaviour of the parents endangers the education of the children" total 79.7 per cent. The same percentage believes that society should impose sanctions on, and change the behaviour of, those grown up children who do not help their parents.

TABLE 18.2

Average Daily Time Spent in Household Work and Cultural/Leisure Activities by Working Men and Women in Bulgaria, 1976-77 (Hours and Minutes)

Activity	*Men*	*Women*	*Difference women-men*
Household work			
Food preparation and cooking	09	1 h. 32	+ 1 h 23
Washing, ironing, mending clothes and shoes (at home)	03	47	+ 44
Cleaning of house and yard	12	54	+ 42
Work on the auxiliary plot	59	33	- 26
Purchasing of goods and services	13	17	+ 04
Other activities linked with the household	36	15	- 21
Care of the children	04	19	+ 15
Educating the children	04	05	+ 01
Total	2 h 20	4 h 42	+ 2 h 22
Cultural/leisure activities			
Watching television	1 h 07	46	- 21
Reading books	10	07	- 03
Reading magazines	01	01	0
Cinema	04	04	0
Going to circus, pop concerts and dancing	08	03	- 05
Listening to the radio	02	01	- 01
Other	01	01	0
Total	1 h 45	1 h 03	- 41

Source: Komitet za odinna sistema za sotsialna informatsiya, 1878.

TABLE 18.3

Responsibility for Children in the Family, according to Women Interviewed, in Bulgaria, in 1980 (Percentages)

Who looks after the children in the family?	*Up to 3 years of age*	*From 3 to 7 years of age*
The mother is on leave or is not working	48.3	16.5
Joint effort of the whole family	10.5	19.1
In children's establishments	13.1	35.0
By relatives of the family	25.9	24.2
By a hired woman	0.4	0.2
By other children	1.8	5.0
Total	100.0	100.0

Source: Sociological research, 1980.

The relationship between society and the family in the bringing up of children is also evident in the requirements which mothers ask from society. Women voice the opinion that society should help them in the rearing of children, in household work and in realisation of their professional life. The basic stands in this respect are as follows (with percentages of women in favour in parentheses):

— rearing of children up to the age of 3 years to be handled by the mother in the family environment, provided that society ensures 100 per cent labour remuneration for the mother for the entire period (about 79 per cent);
— various services to be expanded so that all labour-intensive activities in the daily life of the family are taken over by specialised state organisations (63.4 per cent);
— an increase in the number of establishments for public catering and the production of semi-cooked foods (21.3 per cent);
— inclusion of the all child aged 3-7 years in children's institutions, which should be daily or weekly depending on the nature of the mother's employment (75.5 per cent);
— An increase in the number of boarding and semi-boarding schools so that children of school age who wish to attend may do so (81 per cent);
— provision of lunch for all students (52.1 per cent);
— support of children to be completely taken over by society (56.7 per cent);
— increase of the monthly allowance for children (74.8 per cent).

In the research carried out, we also paid attention to women's views on the difficulties encountered in the rearing of children and their own professional development. As seen earlier, about 85 per cent of the women did not think children were a handicap to their professional development. The results indicate that Bulgarian women are finding ways and means of reconciling motherhood with their working life. Moreover, they also take an active part in the socio-political life of the country, thus fulfilling the same social roles as men.

The present accelerated rates of economic, cultural and social development result in increased and basically different requirements as to the rearing of children. A woman deprived of socio-political rights, economically dependent and without education and culture, can hardly be a good educator and cannot meet the contemporary requirements for the rearing of children. It is becoming increasingly clear to present-day women that they cannot be successful mothers if they remain confined to the household.

Conclusion

The link between demographic changes and the social roles of women involves very complex contemporary social processes which are conditioned by the overall economic and cultural development of society. Thus, the basic questions in the scientific analysis of demographic problems are the determination of a demographic optimum, the factors determining reproductive behaviour, the qualitative characteristics of the reproductive process and the creation of systems which regulate demographic behaviour.

The interaction between demographic changes and the social roles of women depends to a large degree on the value system of the individual. If children assume the highest level in the value system, motherhood will take first place and will determine the realisation of the woman in her two remaining social roles. Should work rank higher than children, the women will want to fulfil herself in her profession, but this does not mean that she cannot be a very good mother at the same time. This, however, is a matter of individual preference. It should not be forgotten that value systems are subject to change. The values which rank highest in the value system of a woman can differ throughout the life cycle, and influence behaviour accordingly.

The social roles of women and the long-range possibilities for the elevation of women in the social structure are closely linked with the nature of women's changing needs. Present-day women have a considerably richer range of needs than women of former times. Changes in their needs are the natural outcome of the economic, scientific, cultural and social progress of society and inevitably lead to changes in the values, interests and aims of the individual, to alterations in behaviour and to special activities. As the attitudes and value systems of the individual are modified, changes in social status and social role occur.

The development of a model of management of the demographic behaviour and social status of women on the basis of needs would be a significant contribution to this complex field. It is important to bear in mind two basic needs. On the one hand is the need for the overall development of the woman as a mother, worker and leader in social life; on the other hand is the need for the development of the woman herself. We could provisionally speak of "a need for emancipation" which triggers women's interest in new social roles and which, when met, ensures the all-round realisation of women and of their equal rights in society. Social status built on the reconciliation of women's three basic roles is absolutely essential for the development of personality.

At present, more than at any other time, researchers in the field of politics, sociology and economics need to use their imagination constructively in order to find ways and means of encouraging the full development of women's overall potential, form the reproduction of children and production of material goods on the one hand to the creation of cultural values and social structures on the other. Thus, it is essential that women are given legal, economic, social and moral protection throughout the entire period of transition form their traditional position as adjuncts of the daily life of the family and secondary members of society to their natural status as free individuals with equal rights. Human progress and the humanisation of society are closely linked with women's social roles and the improvement of their social status.

NOTES

1. This research was conducted by the Institute of Sociology in collaboration with the Committee for Unified Systems of Social Information, and was carried out on the basis of a to-state cluster sample with probability proportional to the size of the clusters. In the first stage, 300 polling sections were designated from the list preserved from the population census of 2 December 1975, and at the

second stage, ten married women between 18 and 40 years of age were chosen from each cluster. The overall size of the sample had been fixed at 3,000 married women within these age limits, but because of human error in some of the census cards, cards for only 2,959 women were processed.

2. Life expectancy at birth is defined as the average number of years a person would live from his or her birth, based on age—and sex-specific mortality rates, observed in a given calendar "year."
3. The educational stages in this and subsequent tables are explained as follows: initial: grades I-IV (ages 7-10); primary: grades V-VIII (ages 10-14); secondary: grades IX-XI (ages 14-18); special secondary: grades IX-XII (ages 14-19), but with vocational training; semi-higher: after XIth grade, three-year vocational training courses (technical, teacher-training, medical or others); higher (university): university education, the duration being five or six years depending on the subject.
4. Given the descending birth rate, the period 1951-67 can be divided into three parts: 1951-55, when the birth rate decreased by an annual average rate of 1.30 per cent; 1956-60, when the decrease was 2.24 per cent; and 1961-67, when it was 2.60 per cent.
5. In the sociological research (1980), the questions on reproductive behaviour were posed only to wives who were 40 years of age or less, since childbearing decreases sharply after age 40.
6. The correlation coefficient ranges within the limits of 0 to 1, with its size dependent on the degree of the factor influence, Generally, it is considered that coefficients under 0.100 indicate an unimportant influence; therefore such characteristics have not been taken into consideration in the analysis.
7. The 1975 survey was representative of the whole country for married, divorced and widowed women aged up to 35 years and men aged up to 40 years. The sample comprised 1,857 women and 1,814 men.

BIBLIOGRAPHY

Atanasov, A. 1972. *Realisatsiya na zhelanata razhdaemost na zaetite zheni v narodnoto stopanstvo v NRB* (Achievement of the desired birth rate of working women engaged in the national economy of the People's Republic of Bulgaria]. Sofia, Ministerstvo na saobshteniyata.

——. 1973, "Mnenieto na raboteshtite omazheni zheni v NRB za broya na detsata, koito zhelayat da imat" [The opinion of Bulgarian working married women about the desired number of children], in *Statistika* (Sofia), No. 5, pp. 42-58.

Dinkova, M. 1976 *Savremennoto balgarsko semeistvo* [The contemporary Bulgarian family]. Sofia, Izd. na OF.

Dobrianov, V. 1982, "Za konkreten in diferentsiran podhod kam problemite na reproduktivnoto povedenie" [About a concrete and differential approach to the problems of reproductive behavioural], in *Sotsiologicheski problemi* (Sofia), No. 4, pp. 13-16.

Donkov, K. 1979. "Osnovni chasti na demografskiya prekhod v Bulgaria [Basic stages of the demographic transition of Bulgaria], in *Statistika*, No. 2, pp. 18-29.

Ilieva, N. 1970. *Ikonomicheski i sotsialni problemi na trudovata zaetoṣt na zhenite v Bulgaria* [Economic and social problems of the labour integration of Bulgarian women]. Sofia, Nauka i izkustvo.

——. 1972. "Sotsiologicheski problemi na zhenata i izgrahdaneto na razvito sotsịalistichesko obshtestvo" [Sociological problems of women and the building up of the developed socialist society], in *Sotsiologicheski problemi*, No. 2, pp. 24-32.

Ilieva, N.; Oshavkova, V.; Varbanova, L. 1973. *Kvalifikatsiyata na rabotnichkite to promishlenosta i tekhnicheskiya progress* [The training of women workers in industry and technological progress]. Sofia, Partidat.

Komitet na balgarskite zheni [Committee of Bulgarian Women]. 1980, *Zhenata v. Narodna Republika Bulgaria* [The women in the People's Republic of Bulgaria]. Sofia, BAN.

Komitet za edinna sistema za sotsialna informatsiya [Committee for a Unified System of Social Information]. 1962-80. *Demografska i ikonomicheska kharakteristika na naselenieto v NRB* [Demographic and economic characteristic of the population in the People's Republic of Bulgaria]. Sofia. Volumes for years concerned.

——. 1978. *Byudzet na vremeto na naselenieto v NRB* [The time budget of the population of the People's Republic of Bulgaria]. Sofia.

——. 1981. *Statisticheski godishnik* [Statistical Yearbook]. Sofia.

Informatsionno-sotsiologicheski tsentar pri TsK na BKP [Informational and Sociological Centre at the Central Committee of the Bulgarian Communist Party]. 1975, *Efektat to politikata za izdigane rolyata na zhenata v NRB* [The policy effect on raising the role of women in the People's Republic of Bulgaria]. Sofia, Izchislitelen tsentar na TsK na BKP.

Kasabov, V. 1977. "Varkhu vaprosa za rezervite na razhdaemosta v Bulgaria" [On the problem of the birth rate in Bulgaria], in *Statistika,* No. 4, pp. 27-34.

Kyuranov, C. 1980. "Zhenata i truda [Women and labour], in *Zhenata dns* [Sofia), No. 2, pp. 4-5; No. 3, pp. 8-9.

Lyutov, A (ed.) 1974 *Zhenata — maika, truzhenichka, obshtestvenichka* [The woman—mother, worker and worker in society]. Sofia, Partizdat.

——. (ed.) 1977. *Zhenata, trud, bit* [The woman—her work and life]. Sofia, BAN.

Minkov, M. 1976. *Naselenie i osnovni sotsialni strukturi* [Population and basic social structures]. Sofia, BAN.

Naumov, N. 1981. *Brachnata plodovitost v NRB* [Marriage fertility in the People's Republic of Bulgaria]. Sofia, KESSI.

Reshenie na Politbyurouna Tsentralniya komitet na KBP to 6 mart 1973 [Central Committee of the Bulgarian Communist Party of 6 March 1973]. 1973. *Za izdigane rolyata na zhenata v izgrazhdaneto na razvito sotsialistichesko obshtestvo* [On enhancing the role of women in the developed socialist society]. Sofia.

Rusev, B. 1976. Nyakoi aspekti na plodovitosta na omazhenite zheni v parvi brak v NRB" [Some aspects of fertility of married women in their first marriage in the People's Republic of Bulgaria], in *Statistika,* No. 5, pp. 39-50.

Spasovska, L. 1976. *Rabotnicheskiyat bit* [The worker's mode of life]. Sofia, Partizdat. Stefanov, I. et al 1974. *Demografiya na Bulgaria* [Demography of Bulgaria]. Sofia, Nauka i izkustvo.

Sugareva, M. 1980. "Izsledvane vliyanieto na nyakoi sotsialno-ikonomicheski faktori varkhu razhdaemosta v NRB" [Investigation of the influence of some socio-economic factors on the birth rate in the People's Republic of Bulgaria], in *Ikonomicheska misal* (Sofia), No. 2, pp. 27-35.

Totev, A. Yu. 1980. "Demografsko-istoricheski ocherk na Bulgaria" [A demographic-historical essay on Bulgaria], in *Sotsiologicheski problemi,* No. 3, pp. 24-39.

Tsentralno statistichesko upravlenie [Central Board Statistics] 1976. *Prebroyavane na naselenieto. Rezultati of nablyudenieto za razhdaemosta na omazhenite, razvedenite i ovdovelite zheni na vazrast of 15 do 54 navarsheni godini kam dekemvri 1975 godina/reprezentativno izsledvane* [Population Census. Data from the survey of the fertility of married, divorced and widowed women aged 15-54 on 2 December 1975/sample survey]. Sofia.

—. Komitet na dvizhenieto na bulgarskite zheni, Nauchno-izsledovatelski institut op truda [Committee of the Movement of Bulgarian Women, Research Institute of Labour]. 1972. *Zhenite v ikonomicheskiya, sotsialen i kulturen zhivot i v semeistvoto* [Women in economic, social and cultural life and in the family]. Sofia, Darzhavno upravlenie za informatsiya.

Zhekova, V. 1976. "Plodovitosta na zhenite v NRB prez perioda 1965-1975 g" [Women's fertility in the People's Republic of Bulgaria 1965-1975], in *Statistika,* No. 2, pp. 39-47.

19

Working Women in Socialist Countries

Throughout history, the position of women has been crucial not only for social development, but also for the survival of society itself. In recent centuries, the changing role of women has been closely interrelated with other aspects of the development of society, such as industrialisation, urbanisation, demographic revolution,[1] etc. The most characteristics feature of developed countries for roughly the past two centuries has been the growth and change of all social structures. It is necessary to see changes in the position, status and roles of women in society, together with changes in the levels of fertility, etc., in the context of this complex global revolution, as the position of women is deeply rooted in other social processes and has relatively little autonomy.

The relationship between the status of women and fertility levels has been cogently expressed by a well-known demographer: "...Our past success at population replacement, throughout all of human history, has been conditional on the discriminatory treatment of women" (Ryder, 1979, p. 366). This relationship is, however, two-sided. It is difficult to answer even the simple question of whether women have fewer children than in the past as a consequence of their emancipation or whether they are emancipated because of fewer children. And yet the emancipation of women has often been mentioned in the past as an important cause of the decline in fertility levels, along with factors such as social mobility, rising standards of living, urbanisation, the rise of individuality, the curtailment of parental power, the decline of mortality (in particular that of infants), compulsory school attendance and changes in the economic importance of children to the family.

The decline in fertility levels during the past two centuries has been relatively well explained by the theory of demographic revolution. It is both a part and a consequence of the economic, social and socio-graphic changes which make up a global revolution. Changes in the position, status and roles of women are another aspect of this complex process.

The period of increased birth rates lasted in the Czech regions until 1951, and in Slovakia for five years longer. This period is also marked by the start of socialist development which, with the introduction of a new social policy and population measures, influenced people's lives in many ways.

Although the Workers' Health Insurance Act had provided maternity benefits to insured women since 1888, and various financial measures designed to help mothers and families had been introduced after the First World War, the most important social policy measures were not implemented until after 1948. Family allowances for all employed persons, covering all children and increasing for every additional child until the fifth, were introduced in 1948. The National Insurance Act No. 99/1948 Sb. stipulated a uniform adjustment of all maternity benefits. Maternity leave was extended to 18 weeks, with maternity benefits to be paid for this period according to the wage or salary and the length of employment. These measures were not expected to affect the level of fertility, as this was considered satisfactory after the Second World War. However, they benefited employed women and families with children, as did the post-war rationing of goods and clothing.

There was a renewed decline in the level of fertility, accompanied by a change in the age structure of mothers, in the 1950s. In the Czech regions, the proportion of children born to mothers under the age of 30 years was 65.6 per cent in 1947, 70.0 per cent in 1950 and 83.1 per cent in 1960, while in Slovakia the proportion rose from 61.9 per cent in 1947 to 67.6 per cent in 1956 and 72.2 per cent in 1962. The reduction in the average age of mothers was no longer sufficient to compensate for the generally decreasing trend. However, in Slovakia, due to the postponement of the end of the demographic revolution, the level of fertility in 1962 was approximately the same as in the Czech regions ten years earlier.

From 1958, the decrease in the birth rate was also affected by the new abortion law which permitted induced abortion on social grounds. It can be assumed that as a result of this law the number of higher-parity births and the birth rate as a whole declined slightly, but its adoption resulted in no marked step in the overall trend towards lower birth rates during that period. This suggests that, on the one hand, illegal abortions had been available before the adoption of the law and, on the other hand, the social causality of fertility development after the demographic revolution was so complex that the existence or non-existence of such legislation was of secondary importance. In 1953, rationing was abolished and a currency reform was carried out. Although family allowances were increased simultaneously, incomes per head began to increase faster in childless households or in families with one child than in larger ones.

From 1963 to 1972, both in the CSR and the SSR, the birth rate oscillated slightly, though on different levels for the two populations (table 19.1). After the low point in 1960, the fertility level rose slightly in the CSR until 1964, before falling again to reach the lowest post-war gross reproduction rate (GRR)[2] of 0.09 in 1968. Fertility in the SSR wavered only in 1963 and 1964, and to a much lesser degree. After 1968, the fertility level increased again in the CSR and the GRR reached a peak of 1.20 in 1974. A similar peak in the GRR occurred in the SSR in the same year at the level of 1.27, narrowing significantly the difference between the two parts of Czechoslovakia. Such an evolution has prompted a good deal of discussion. The population measures discussed in the following section no doubt had some effect but a closer analysis also demonstrates the limits of these effects.

TABLE 19.1

Crude Birth Rate (CBR)[1] and Gross Reproduction Rate (GRR)[1] in the CSR and the SSR, 1963-81

Year	*CSR*		*SSR*	
	CBR (per thousand)	*GRR*	*CBR (per thousand)*	*GRR*
1	2	3	4	5
1963	15.4	1.12	20.4	1.42
1964	15.9	1.13	21.1	1.41
1965	15.1	1.07	19.3	1.36
1966	14.4	0.98	18.5	1.30
1967	14.0	0.93	17.4	1.21
1968	13.9	0.90	17.0	1.16
1969	14.5	0.91	17.7	1.18
1970	15.1	0.94	17.8	1.17
1971	15.7	0.97	18.2	1.18
1972	16.6	1.02	19.1	1.21
1973	18.3	1.12	20.0	1.26
1974	19.4	1.20	20.8	1.27
1975	19.1	1.19	20.6	1.25
1976	18.5	1.16	20.8	1.24
1977	17.8	1.14	20.6	1.21
1978	17.5	1.13	20.5	1.21
1979	16.7	1.11	20.3	1.20
1980	14.9	1.00	19.1	1.13
1981	14.0[2]	0.97[2]	18.6[2]	1.12[2]

1. For an explanation of these indicators, see note 1 to Chapter 1.
2. Preliminary data.
Source: FSU, 1970c; 1975; 1977; 1981; 1982.

While the quantitative effect of the political and economic stabilisation after 1968 cannot be measured, it probably played a very significant role in the increase in fertility levels. In large part, however, the upward trend seems to have been due to a change in the timing of birth (i.e. births delayed from an earlier period or those originally planned for the future). Such an evaluation is based on an analysis of the population climate, on the birth order of children born, and on generational fertility trends.

Population Policy Measures

The downward trend in fertility levels at the end of the demographic revolution and in the following decades gradually led to an increase in attention to population-development issues. Further measures to benefit mothers and larger families were adopted, and for the first time these measures clearly supported fertility. In 1956, maternity leave benefits were amended; leave remained at 18 weeks, but maternity benefit was made the same for manual and white-collar workers: for employees with less than two years' prior employment, 75 per cent of their wage; for those with two to five years' employment, 80 per cent; and for all other employees, 90 per cent. In addition, all women workers and employees as well as economically inactive women were to receive a birth grant of 650 koruna (Kcs) i.e. approximately 60 per cent of the average monthly wage of women at that time). Price reductions after the currency reform provided further help for families with children. Moreover, with the price reduction of 1959, children's clothes and shoes were greatly reduced; this price subsidy was abolished as economically unjustifiable only in the 1980s.

By the middle of the 1960s, population and population measures had become an important political issue. The 11th Congress of the Communist Party of Czechoslovakia, held in 1958, called for an increase in the personal spending capability of families, especially those in the lower income brackets with several children. The 12th Party Congress in 1962 dealt with this problem in greater detail. In the resolution on the main lines for development, pre-school and out-of-school care for children was stressed, as well as school meals and the further establishment of nurseries and kindergartens. The following Congress held in 1966 spoke of further support for families and working women and the supply of nurseries, kindergartens and dwellings for young couples.

Since the school year 1960-61, pupils in general educational schools up to high school level have received all textbooks and educational supplies free of charge. In 1959, family allowances were raised once more for third and subsequent children. In 1964, a differential pensionable age for women was introduced, dependent on the number of children raised. At the same time, a special compensation allowance was introduced for women transferred to lower-paid jobs during pregnancy or motherhood.

Since 1964, rent reductions have been granted in state-owned dwellings according to the number of children in a family. Act 58 of the same year introduced a significant increase in welfare during pregnancy and motherhood: maternity leave was extended to 22 weeks. For the first time, preference was given to single mothers; their paid maternity leave was extended to 26 weeks, provided that they dependent on their own earnings.

Maternity leave and cash maternity benefits were also accorded to women who took into their care another woman's child for later adoption or because of the mother's death. The Act also affords women legal claim to further leave, up to the end of the child's first year. The employer is obliged to re-employ the mother after this period has elapsed, in the same capacity and under the same financial and legal conditions as before the birth.

Also in 1964, the co-operative farmers' social security scheme was improved: family allowances and birth grants were provided under the same conditions as for wage earners. Family allowances were increased again in 1968. Maternity leave was extended from 22 to 26 weeks and in 1970 the amended Labour Code increased unpaid maternity leave until the child reaches 2 years of age. On 1 July 1970, a so-called maternity allowance came into force, amounting to Kcs500 per month, to be paid to employed mothers, with at least two children, who decide to stay at home after their paid maternity leave has elapsed in order to look after their children until the youngest child has reached 1 year of age.

The 14th Congress of the Communist Party of Czechoslovakia, held in 1971, emphasised new population policy measures designed to increase family size and to support young married couples and families with young children. From 1 November 1971, the period of the maternal allowance increased to two years after the birth of the youngest child and was made universal for all mothers, including housewives. From 1 January 1973, allowances for second, third and fourth children were increased and credits were established for young married couples to furnish their households after the birth of children.

Apart from an increase in family allowances in connection with price regulations in 1982, there have been no other major changes in population policy. Contemporary population policy, which is made up of a series of social and economic measures, was formed gradually during the first stage of socialist development. It is aimed primarily at improving the economic situation of families with children and of young people after marriage and the birth of the first child, the living conditions of employed women, etc. Attention is also given to services available for families with children, to the working conditions of women, especially mothers, and to mother-and-child welfare.

The Influence of Population Policy Measures on Fertility Levels and Population Climate

The influence of the population policy measures can be seen both in the fertility levels and in change sin the population climate. The population climate may be divided into two components: the basic component, which changes very slowly and which is related to certain social norms as to the most suitable (ideal, planned, desirable) size of the family in a given population; and the secondary component, which concerns the most suitable timing or spacing of children. The secondary component, though it does not directly affect the total number of children desired, can have an important impact on the CBR and GRR over a period, by concentrating births into one year or by postponing them to a later date.

The first survey of the population climate was organised in Czechoslovakia in 1956 and several further surveys were carried out in the next 25 years. The number of desired children ranged from 2.1 to 2.4 in various years and was always considerably higher in the SSR. Apparently it was not affected by population policy measures. It can be concluded, therefore, that these measures influenced mainly the secondary component of the population climate which was not shown by the surveys (Pavlik, 1977).

The oscillating fertility levels after the demographic revolution may be illustrated by an analysis of birth intervals (Table 19.2). Parallel to falling proportions of childless families, there is a shortening of the interval between marriage and the birth of the first child, both in the CSR and the SSR. This is partly connected with increased proportions of premarital conceptions among first children. On the other hand, the intervals between the first and second child, and the second and third child have been increasing, hence the oscillation of period rates.

Table 19.3 shows clearly the main reason for the increase in the CBR around its peak in 1974; this increase was due primarily to first births, then to second births and much less to third births; higher parities did not significantly affect the increase. This was evident, in particular, in a fuller and perhaps even more rapid realisation of the number of children planned but was not influenced by changes in the planned family size. The data were also affected by the age structure of population. But in spite of this their meaning is clear. Furthermore, the available analysis of cohort fertility has shown that generations with completed childbearing after the demographic revolution differ little in terms of completed fertility (Lesny, 1978, pp. 106-116).

TABLE 19.2

Birth Intervals (in Years) and Percentage of Births Occurring Less Than Nine Months after Marriage (PC) in the CSR and the SSR in Selected Years, 1935-78

Year	*CSR*				*SSR*			
	1st child[1]	*PC*[2] *(%)*	*2nd child*	*3rd child*	*1st child*[1]	*PC*[2] *(%)*	*2nd child*	*3rd child*
1935	1.95	35.3	2.43	2.04	2.01	24.2	2.31	2.36
1950	1.44	41.5	2.66	2.76	1.60	25.2	2.74	2.78
1968	1.34	52.4	3.32	2.68	1.21	43.7	3.26	2.98
1973	1.34	50.5	3.47	2.82	1.19	42.2	3.10	3.13
1978	1.34	53.4	3.42	4.31	1.18	51.7	2.98	3.84

1. First interval counted from the date of marriage.
2. The percentage of births less than nine months after marriage (PC) shows an approximate level of pre-marital conceptions; it was calculated from the first parity data only.

Source: FSU, 1935; 1950a; 1968; 1973; 1978.

TABLE 19.3

Crude Birth Rate by Parity in the CSR and the SSR in Selected Years, 1960-78 (Per Thousand)

	Birth order									
	CSR					*SSR*				
	1	*2*	*3*	*4 or more*	*Total*	*1*	*2*	*3*	*4 or more*	*Total*
1960	5.8	4.4	1.7	1.4	13.3	7.0	6.0	3.9	5.2	22.1
1968	7.1	4.7	1.4	0.8	13.9	6.4	5.0	2.6	3.0	17.0
1974	8.1	8.0	2.4	0.9	19.4	8.1	7.0	3.2	2.5	20.8
1975	8.0	7.9	2.4	0.8	19.1	8.2	6.9	3.2	2.3	20.6
1978	7.2	7.1	2.4	0.8	17.5	8.2	7.1	3.2	2.0	20.5

Source: As for Table 19.2.

FEMALE LABOUR FORCE PARTICIPATION

The Increase in Women's Economic Activity

The economic and social development of Czechoslovakia continued under socialist conditions after the demographic revolution. Changes in the structure of the economically active population between 1961 and 1970 are given in Table 19.4. In particular, notice that the share of agriculture has continued to decrease and that the economic structure of the SSR is approaching that of the CSR.

The proportion of economically active women among all women of productive age (15-54 years) is very high: it reached 76.9 per cent in the CSR and 62.7 per cent in the SSR in 1970; comparable percentages for men were 86.4 and 83.7 (Statisticke a evidencni vyadavatesltvi tiskopisu (SEVT), 1975, p. 119). In spite of the high level of economic activity among women in 1961, the level increased even further in 1970 and 1980. The largest increase was in the 25.34 year age group (table 19.5), when women up to the age of 30 years are still in the most intensive childbearing period or have young children. In 1980, the proportion of economically active women was high among married women, although it was slightly higher in the CSR than in the SSR. The decrease in economic activity in the 15-19 year age group was due mainly to the higher attendance of girls at secondary schools and at universities.

TABLE 19.4

Structure of Total Economically Active Population by Branch of the Economy in the CSR and the SSR, 1961-70 (Percentages)

Branch of the economy	*CSR*		*SSR*	
	1961	*1970*	*1961*	*1970*
Agriculture and forestry	15.9	11.7	27.0	16.9
Industry	37.4	34.4	25.5	28.2
Construction	7.5	7.2	12.2	11.0
Transport and communications	5.7	5.9	7.2	7.2
Commerce	5.2	6.5	4.4	5.6
Others	13.0	14.8	11.3	14.2
Independent, economically inactive	15.3	19.5	12.4	16.9
Total	100.0	100.0	100.0	100.0

Source: SEVT, 1965; 1975.

There is no doubt that the increase in the level of women's economic activity in Czechoslovakia during the past two decades has been very striking. Women are becoming almost as important as men in the total labour force. However, there are only two periods in women's lives when their situation is fully comparable with that of men: before the first child is born and after the youngest child leaves school. During the period when women are pregnant or looking after small children, they represent a specific kind of labour force as their economic activity in conflict with their maternal duties.

The increase in the proportion of economically active women after 1961 can be explained by two contradictory factors: the fall in the fertility level in the 1960s and the population policy measures in the 1970s aimed at overcoming the conflict between maternal duties and economic activity (women on maternity leave are considered as economically active). It is not easy to say which factor was more important. Hard evidence is difficult to obtain and various results from sample surveys can be interpreted in different ways; they depend very much on the methodology of the survey (for example, the formulation of questions, the self-censorship of respondents, not weighting the various factors which affect the respondent).

TABLE 19.5

Economic Activity Rate of Women by Czechoslovakia, the CSR and the SSR by Age Group, 1961, 1970 and 1980

Year	*Age group*											
	15-19	*20-24*	*25-29*	*30-34*	*35-39*	*40-44*	*45-49*	*50-54*	*55-59*	*60-64*	*65-69*	*70 and over*
Czechoslovakia (all women)												
1961	54.6	68.2	57.4	59.1	65.4	67.7	66.0	59.4	42.4	29.7	13.7	3.5
1970	41.3	78.7	79.5	79.0	81.0	80.2	77.6	70.2	35.9	17.9	28.9	2.4
1980	29.8	83.4	90.7	92.0	92.8	91.7	88.1	79.9	40.8	21.5	12.2	5.0
Difference 1961-70	—13.3	10.5	22.1	19.9	15.6	12.5	11.6	10.8	—6.5	—11.8	15.2	—1.1
Difference 1970-80	—11.5	4.7	11.2	13.0	11.8	11.5	10.5	9.7	4.9	3.6	—16.7	2.6
CSR												
Married women:												
1961	67.7	63.3	58.8	62.5	69.7	72.5	70.9	64.1	46.8	34.7	—	—
1970	77.9	76.8	79.1	83.1	86.2	86.0	83.6	76.9	39.1	20.0	—	—
1980	82.7	89.1	91.2	93.1	94.4	94.2	91.5	84.0	40.9	20.9	11.4	5.0
Difference 1961-70	10.2	13.5	20.3	20.6	16.5	13.5	12.7	12.8	—7.7	—14.7	—	—
Difference 1970-80	4.8	12.3	12.1	10.0	8.2	8.2	7.9	7.1	1.8	0.9	—	—
All women (1980)	30.0	84.7	91.4	93.1	94.2	93.9	91.2	83.8	42.8	23.4	13.8	6.0
SSR												
Married women:												
1970	71.1	75.5	71.1	68.5	67.5	64.5	60.0	51.3	27.9	12.8	—	—
1980	75.1	85.8	88.8	89.4	89.3	87.2	81.8	71.2	35.1	16.0	7.0	3.0
Difference 1970-80	4.0	10.1	17.7	20.9	21.8	22.7	21.8	19.9	7.2	3.2	—	—
All women (1980)	29.5	81.3	89.5	89.7	89.4	87.1	87.1	71.2	36.2	16.6	7.7	3.0

— = not available.

Source: Bartova, 1977, p. 138; FSU, 1970b, analytical issue, p. 70; 1980.

The economic and social breakdown of economically active women in 1970 is presented in Table 19.6. Differences between the CSR and the SSR can also be seen here. The far higher proportion of women working in industry in the CSR explains the higher proportion of the socio-occupational group "workers" (i.e. production workers) in the CSR in comparison with the SSR. However, the gradual economic equalisation between the republics is clearly shown by the similar proportion of women working in commerce, transport and communications, and by women who are "employees" (i.e., white-collar workers).

TABLE 19.6

Breakdown of Economically Active Women in the CSR and the SSR by Branch of the Economy and Socio-Occupational Group, 1970

Branch of the economy/socio-occupational group	*CSR*		*SSR*	
	No. of women	%	*No. of women*	%
Branch of the economy				
Agriculture and forestry	341 649	14.93	164 610	19.96
Industry	888 188	38.82	269 363	32.66
Construction	67 818	2.96	29 528	3.58
Transport and communications	112 965	4.94	34 546	4.19
Commerce	315 914	13.81	111 776	13.55
Others	561 283	24.54	214 883	26.06
Total	2 287 820	100.00	824 706	100.00
Socio-occupational group				
Workers[1]	1 223 083	53.46	398 400	48.30
Employees[1]	763 558	33.37	285 245	34.59
Co-operative farmers	218 208	9.54	100 210	12.15
Other co-operative producers	69 168	3.02	18 368	2.23
Independent farmers	7 456	0.33	20 106	2.44
Others	6 347	0.28	2 377	0.29
Total	2 287 820	100.00	824 706	100.00

1 These two categories correspond roughly to those of production workers and white-collar workers.

Source: SEVT, 1975, pp. 332-333 and 335-336.

The age structure of economically active women is given in Table 19.7. As a result of previous changes in the national economy, the age structure of these women in the SSR is considerably younger than that of the CSR. This holds for all branches of the economy, apart from agriculture and forestry where both republics are very similar. In spite of the fact that apprentices are not considered as economically active, the youngest age structure is found in industry. More than 41 per cent of women economically active in industry in the CSR and more than 52 per cent in the SSR were under the age of 30 years in 1970; the corresponding figures for agriculture and forestry were below 19 per cent for both republics.

TABLE 19.7

Percentage Distribution of Economically Active Women by Branch of the Economy and Age Group in the CSR and the SSR, 1970

Branch of the economy	*Age group*											
	15-19	*20-24*	*25-29*	*30-34*	*35-39*	*40-44*	*45-49*	*50-54*	*55-59*	*60-64*	*65 & over*	*Total*
CSR												
Agriculture and forestry	2.9	7.7	7.9	8.1	10.4	13.8	1.4	10.1	10.4	7.2	5.2	100
Industry	12.3	16.6	12.3	10.1	11.1	12.4	12.5	6.5	3.8	1.5	0.9	100
Construction	5.0	16.4	15.5	13.2	12.2	12.4	12.1	6.2	4.1	1.8	1.1	100
Transport and communication	5.8	17.0	12.0	10.3	10.7	12.9	15.7	8.2	4.9	1.8	0.7	100
Commerce	8.6	16.6	11.4	8.9	10.4	12.6	13.8	7.6	5.7	2.7	1.7	100
Others	4.1	15.4	15.9	12.3	12.4	11.7	11.6	6.6	5.4	2.7	1.9	100
All branches	7.8	15.0	12.5	10.3	11.2	12.5	13.2	7.3	5.5	2.8	1.9	100
SSR												
Agriculture and forestry	4.7	6.5	7.7	9.4	12.6	15.3	17.7	9.8	8.9	4.9	2.5	100
Industry	17.6	21.4	13.4	11.1	11.0	10.4	8.9	3.6	1.8	0.6	0.2	100
Construction	8.3	22.2	16.0	13.5	12.5	10.5	9.0	4.0	2.6	0.9	0.5	100
Transport and communications	6.8	20.2	12.9	13.2	12.9	11.9	12.7	5.7	2.7	0.8	0.2	100
Commerce	10.8	19.7	12.8	11.2	12.0	12.3	11.5	5.2	3.1	1.0	0.4	100
Others	5.7	18.9	17.5	13.9	12.2	10.8	9.8	5.2	3.9	1.4	0.7	100
All branches	10.2	17.5	13.3	11.7	11.9	11.8	11.4	5.6	4.0	1.8	0.8	100

Source: SEVT, 1975, pp. 335-336.

The age structure of economically active women according to socio-occupational group can be seen in Table 19.8. The oldest age structure is characteristic for co-operative farmers and independent farmers. The latter group will obviously become even less important in the future; almost 46 per cent of women in this group in the CSR and 29 per cent in the SSR were aged 55 years of above (i.e. of pensionable age) in 1970, and represented only 0.33 per cent of women in the CSR and 2.44 per cent in the SSR. The age distribution of economically active women depends largely on the age distribution of the whole population; however, certain features already noted can be confirmed. The proportion of working women is often lower in the age group with the highest fertility, and when children are very small, than before and after, and this decline occurs more among workers than among employees and other groups. The small size of these differences suggests a rather quick return to work if the mother does not return immediately after maternity leave.

Data (FSU, 1981) which concern the labour force only and not census data for the total population are given in Table 19.9. As can be expected, the branches of the economy where the proportion of women is highest fall within the sphere of non-material activities—mainly in social care, health services and education, followed by commerce. The lowest share of women is in construction and in transport and communications. The differences between the CSR and SSR are rather small.

TABLE 19.8

Percentage Distribution of Economically Active Women by Socio-occupational Group and Age Group in the CSR and the SSR, 1970

Socio-occupational group	*Age group*											
	15-19	*20-24*	*25-29*	*30-34*	*35-39*	*40-44*	*45-49*	*50-54*	*55-59*	*60-64*	*65 & over*	*Total*
1	*2*	*3*	*4*	*5*	*6*	*7*	*8*	*9*	*10*	*11*	*12*	*13*
CSR												
Workers	11.1	14.5	10.6	9.0	10.5	12.6	13.5	7.6	5.7	3.0	1.9	100
Employees	4.3	18.5	17.3	13.4	12.8	11.8	11.5	5.6	3.3	1.0	0.5	100
Co-operative farmers	1.6	6.0	6.5	6.9	9.8	14.2	17.6	11.0	11.8	8.4	6.2	100
Other co-operative producers	8.9	14.1	11.7	9.8	11.4	13.7	13.3	7.4	5.4	2.6	1.7	100
Independent farmers	0.6	1.4	2.4	4.3	6.6	11.8	15.7	11.3	17.2	16.8	11.9	100
Others	9.7	19.9	13.1	8.0	7.2	10.1	9.7	5.3	4.9	3.9	8.2	100
All groups	7.8	15.0	12.5	10.3	11.2	12.5	13.2	7.3	5.5	2.8	1.9	100
SSR												
Workers	15.6	17.2	11.2	10.0	11.2	12.1	11.6	5.5	3.6	1.4	0.6	100
Employees	5.3	23.3	19.3	15.4	12.7	9.6	7.9	3.6	2.1	0.6	0.2	100
Co-operative farmers	3.4	5.3	6.7	8.8	12.5	16.1	19.5	11.0	9.5	4.8	2.4	100
Other co-operative producers	14.6	16.4	12.3	10.7	12.6	12.7	11.4	4.7	3.2	1.1	0.3	100
Independent farmers	1.5	3.0	5.4	8.1	11.8	14.5	17.0	9.7	12.8	10.4	5.8	100
Others	22.7	22.5	9.3	7.1	6.5	7.9	7.9	4.2	4.2	3.5	4.2	100
All groups	10.2	17.5	13.3	11.7	11.9	11.8	11.4	5.6	4.0	1.8	0.8	100

Source: SEVT, 1975, pp. 332-333.

Czechoslovakia is one of the few countries in which population policy measures have been extensive. This might explain why the level of economic activity during the whole productive life of women is so high and is still rising. Although economic activity has always been high among unmarried increase among married women (table 19.5). The increased proportion of women in the labour force has been a decisive factor in the increase in the total labour force in Czechoslovakia in the past decade.

Women's Attitudes Towards Labour Force Participation

The attitudes of women towards their economic activity can be characterised either objectively by their behaviour or by the opinions of women themselves. The most significant objective characteristic is the high economic activity rate and the relatively quick return to work after maternity leave. According to a'survey carried out on, 6,176 women in 1962 (Srb,

1967, pp. 246-247), about one-third of women returned to work immediately after maternity leave; the remainder asked for unpaid leave or ceased working. The situation changed dramatically after 1968 and 1971, when maternity leave was extended and the maternal allowance introduced. Although no similar survey has been carried out since 1962, the proportion of women staying at home after their maternity leave has been considerably reduced (Table 19.17 and 19.18). This indicates that the most urgent demands were largely met by the last population policy measures.

TABLE 19.9

Breakdown of the Economically Active Population and Percentage of Women by Branch of the Economy in the CSR and the SSR, 1980[1]

Branch of the economy	*CSR Economically active population*		*% of women in total*	*SSR Economically active population*		*% of women in total*
	No. of workers	*% of total*		*No. of workers*	*% of total*	
Material production	3 877 539	76.3	41.8	1 735 159	76.5	40.8
Agriculture and forestry	630 975	12.4	42.6	398 992	17.6	40.6
Industry	2 025 651	39.9	40.8	766 968	33.8	40.6
Construction	472 774	9.3	17.3	252 642	11.1	16.2
Transport and communications	191 382	3.8	24.5	85 165	3.8	25.7
Commerce	545 451	10.7	69.0	226 733	10.0	70.6
Others	11 306	0.2	54.9	4 659	0.2	58.5
Non-material activities	1 205 884	23.7	58.8	532 964	23.5	59.0
Transport and communications	150 258	2.9	33.9	61.913	2.7	27.9
Science and research	120 003	2.4	35.2	48 895	2.2	40.1
Education	262 161	5.2	72.3	142 252	6.3	71.4
Culture	88 087	1.7	50.3	28.194	1.2	53.9
Health services	203 818	4.0	79.0	95 683	4.2	77.4
Social care	30 511	0.6	86.8	10 424	0.5	86.3
Others	351 006	6.9	55.4	145 603	6.4	53.3
Total	5 083 423	100.0	45.8	2 268 123	100.0	44.7

1 As of 31 December.
Source: FSU, 1981, pp. 1967.

The kinds of reasons women gave in 1962 for not returning to work after their maternity leave were as follows. Almost one-half of these women mentioned the lack of creches; they did not have anybody who could take care of the child. About 30 per cent of women clearly did not want to return and in 20 per cent of cases the husband did not wish it. The other reasons were much less significant in terms of percentages; about 10 per cent of women mentioned illness of the child and about the same percentage incapacity to cope with work and household duties. Further reasons given were the lack of working opportunities (7 per cent), health problems (5 per cent) and many children (2 per cent).

TABLE 19.10

Answers to the Question: "Should the Woman Work Outside the Home?" in Czechoslovakia, 1979 (Percentages)

Answers	*CSR*	*SSR*	*Total*
She should always work	8	16	10
She should work, but stay at home when the children are small	70	58	67
She should not work outside the home; she should take care of the family and children	18	24	19
Don't know	4	2	4
Total	100	100	100

Source: Bauerova and Bartova, 1980, p. 11.

In another survey, carried out in 1977 (Srb, 1979, p. 308), women were asked what was of greatest help to a working mother. In the first place they gave the understanding of their colleagues (30-49 per cent; more in the SSR than in the CSR); next was more places in creches (21-40 per cent; more in the cities and in the CSR). Other reasons were mentioned by smaller proportions of women—more time for children, a better financial situation, better services, etc. A fertility survey carried out in Czechoslovakia in 1981 (Dvorak, Srb and Ales, 1983) by and large confirmed the previous results.

Problems of families and the position of women were the main topic of a survey which was carried out in Czechoslovakia in 1979 (Bauerova and Bartova, 1980, pp. 3, 11). A standard interview was held with 2,228 inhabitants of different ages, nationalities and socio-occupational groups. The question which is of most interest here was formulated as follows: "Should a woman work outside the home or should she stay in the household and take care of the children?" As can be seen from table 19.10 the attitudes of the population towards the economic activity of women were generally positive. It is worth mentioning that women more often than men answered that women should work outside the home in any case. Older people preferred that women should stay at home. Workers and employees preferred that women should work, while the agricultural population declared the opposite. People in small cities and with the lowest educational level were the most conservative.

But how long should the woman stay at home with small children? The limit that was given most frequently was 3 years of age of the child (about 40 per cent); when the child is old enough to go to nursery school, the mother can go to work. Only about 30 per cent of the people interviewed put the limit at 6 years of age. This survey also gave an interesting picture of the use of time in the family (see further in "Women's time use and division of labour in households", below).

THE EFFECT OF EDUCATION AND NUMBER OF CHILDREN ON WOMEN'S ECONOMIC ACTIVITY

Education

A significant increase in the number of female students at all educational levels has been characteristic of socialist development. Girls now form a definite majority at universities and at many kinds of high school (Table 19.11). An especially high proportion of girls attend gymnasia, which mainly prepare students for university-level education.

The increase in the educational level has also been significant among production workers. The proportion of skilled workers among all workers has risen considerably in recent generations, and the difference between the CSR and the SSR has practically disappeared among those below 30 years of age (Table 19.12). Although the same process has occurred among women workers, they are still significantly behind men in terms of skills. This should always be kept in mind if comparing, for instance, the level of wages.

The above is confirmed by the data shown in Table 19.13, which are based on the micro-census carried out in 1970; the total number of people included was 14,142. According to this micro-census, university-level education is still twice as frequent among men but all other levels, with the exception of apprenticeships, show a higher proportion of women. The vertical socio-occupational distribution indicates the high level of women's participation in professional activities. Men are slightly more frequent among higher professionals (leading positions, university teachers, scientific workers, physicians, etc.), but women predominate among middle-grade professionals (professionals in the central administration, teachers, nurses, etc.). Men are more frequent among technicians and skilled workers, but women predominate among other employees. Such a distribution, which will change only slowly in the future, raises the following question: what degree of equality between men and women will be reached in the future under socialist conditions given the different roles and duties of each sex in reproduction and in social life?

Number of Children and Women's Economic Activity

In studying the relationship between the level of economic activity, education and fertility, we should start with the objective finding that economically active women have fewer children than inactive women. In 1961, economically active women in Czechoslovakia had on average 1.72 children below 14 years of age, while economically inactive women had 2.03 children (Table 19.14). However, women with one or two children below the age of 14 (were more likely to be economically active than inactive; this proportion was reversed among women with more children.

TABLE 19.11

Total Students and Percentage Who are Female at Different Educational Levels in the CSR and the SSR, 1980-81

Educational level	*CSR*		*SSR*	
	Total no. of students	*% female*	*Total no. of students*	*% female*
University level				
Technical colleges	49 371	21.2	33 397	25.1
Universities	46 478	60.4	22 112	66.8
Schools of economics	10 875	49.4	11 741	59.8
Agricultural colleges	11 482	32.9	8 995	36.3
Art colleges	1 644	37.0	547	37.1
Gymnasia	92 870	62.0	54 868	61.0
Technical and commercial schools	221 199	58.3	110 135	62.8
Selected universities				
Charles University	21 927	55.4		
University of Bratislava			13 760	64.2
University in Brno	9 067	58.5		
Technical University in Prague	16 950	13.8		
Technical University in Bratislava			17 617	27.7
Technical University in Brnö	13 613	17.0		
University of Economics in Prague	10 875	49.4		
University of Economics in Bratislava			11 741	59.8

Source: FSU, 1981.

TABLE 19.12

Skilled Workers as a Percentage of all Production Workers by Age Group and Sex in the CSR and the SSR, 1970

Age group	*Men*		*Women*	
	CSR (%)	*SSR (%)*	*CSR (%)*	*SSR (%)*
20-24	70.1	70.3	46.8	44.9
25.29	65.6	68.7	39.5	31.5
30-34	61.6	65.1	23.3	22.4
35-39	57.3	60.2	17.7	17.2
40-44	55.0	51.1	18.6	15.9
45-49	51.2	42.7	17.4	14.2
50-54	48.6	37.5	16.9	12.5
55-59	47.7	31.8	12.9	9.6
60 and over	30.5	17.6	8.2	6.4
All age groups	57.7	53.6	24.2	23.3

Source: FSU, 1970b.

TABLE 19.13

Percentage Distribution of Economically Active Population by Sex, Socio-occupational Group and Educational Level in Czechoslovakia, 1970

Socio-occupational group	*Educational level*								
	University	*High school*	*Vocational school*	*Lower commercial school*	*Apprenticeship*	*Elementary school*		*Total*	*% of total, all groups*
						Complete	*Incomplete*		
Men									
Higher professionals	82.9	5.9	5.9	1.2	—	2.9	1.2	100	2.1
Middle professionals	20.8	30.5	10.4	11.3	7.1	17.1	2.8	100	13.7
Technicians	16.8	46.6	3.5	13.2	8.7	9.1	2.1	100	15.3
Other employees	0.7	5.4	2.3	5.1	40.1	30.8	15.5	100	18.5
Skilled workers	0.2	4.9	1.8	4.7	88.4			100	32.4
Unskilled workers	.	.	.	.	.	62.1	37.9	100	13.8
Agricultural workers	.	1.2	0.3	5.4	31.8	31.5	29.8	100	4.2
All groups	7.3	14.1	3.1	6.3	39.6	19.5	10.1	—	100.0
Women									
Higher professionals	71.2	10.6	15.2	1.5	.	1.5	.	100	1.1
Middle professionals	13.0	34.7	11.2	16.4	3.8	18.7	2.2	100	16.8
Technicians	3.5	60.7	4.8	10.7	5.3	13.9	1.1	100	9.7
Other employees	0.1	8.8	7.0	13.5	20.3	39.6	10.7	100	38.8
Skilled workers	.	5.3	1.7	8.3	84.7	.	.	100	9.5
Unskilled workers	.	.	.	.	.	75.8	24.2	100	20.1
Agricultural workers	.	0.8	0.8	4.8	9.3	43.5	40.8	100	4.0
All groups	3.3	15.8	5.4	10.0	17.4	37.0	11.1	—	100.0

. = nil or negligible.

— = not applicable.

Source: Charvat, Linhart and Vecernik, 1978, p. 108.

TABLE 19.14

Economic Activity Status of Married Women with Children by Number of Children Below 14 Years of Age in Czechoslovakia, 1961 (Percentages)

Economic activity status	*1*	*2*	*3*	*4*	*5 or more*	*Total*	*Avreage no. of children per married woman with children*
Economically active	61.9	53.2	45.8	40.5	31.9	55.1	1.72
Economically inactive	38.1	46.8	54.2	59.5	68.1	44.9	2.03

Source: SEVT, 1965, p. 79

The differential fertility evident at the period of transition has been maintained until very recently. The differences have remained not only between the CSR and the SSR, but also among various socio-occupational groups (table 19.15). The group of employees, which consists mainly of white-collar workers, had by far the lowest fertility level in 1970, while the highest number of children was still found among women in agriculture. (In the CSR in 1961, 42.4 per cent of women among workers were economically active, 50.2 per cent among employees and 52.4 per cent among co-operative farmers; the corresponding percentages for the SSR were 35.6, 49.4 and 45.3.)

TABLE 19.15

Fertility of Married Women by Socio-occupational Group in the CSR and the SSR, 1970

Socio-occupational group	*% female*	*% distribution of married women by no. of children*							*Average no. of children per woman*	
		0	*1*	*2*	*3*	*4*	*5 or more*	*Total*	*All women*	*Women with children*
CSR										
Workers in agriculture	3.8	9.1	16.5	30.1	20.5	10.9	12.9	100	2.64	2.90
Other workers	51.9	13.6	26.3	36.4	15.0	5.0	3.7	100	1.86	2.16
Co-operative farmers	10.9	6.6	14.8	36.2	23.7	10.3	8.4	100	2.49	2.67
Employees	28.6	17.5	35.2	37.0	8.2	1.6	0.5	100	1.44	1.74
Others	4.8	14.6	25.1	33.6	14.9	6.0	5.8	100	1.97	2.31
Total, all groups	100.0	13.8	27.2	36.2	14.2	4.9	3.7	100	1.84	2.14
SSR										
Workers in agriculture	4.1	6.5	12.6	23.9	21.3	13.7	22.0	100	3.22	3.45
Other workers	46.2	9.7	17.6	29.2	20.2	10.6	12.7	100	2.60	2.88
Co-operative farmers	14.7	5.9	14.2	29.2	22.2	13.0	15.5	100	2.89	3.07
Employees	24.0	13.2	27.0	37.2	15.0	4.8	2.8	100	1.82	2.10
Others	11.0	8.8	12.9	21.6	18.5	13.1	25.1	100	3.32	3.64
Total, all groups	100.0	9.7	18.7	30.1	19.1	10.0	12.4	100	2.56	2.83

Source: SEVT, 1975, p. 77.

The level of economic activity, both among married and unmarried women, has increased significantly since 1961. Data from Table 19.16 show the magnitude of this increase for married women; it rose by more than 20 percentage points among women below the age of 35 years with one or two children between 1961 and 1970, and only a little less among women with three or more children. As has been mentioned, the comparative significance of population policy measures and of the decrease in the fertility level cannot be measured from these data. Because of the fertility changes, a higher proportion women had children over 6 years of age in 1970 than in 1961, and most of these women would have gone to work anyway.

The extent to which the age of dependent children is important to the level of economic activity can be seen from tables 19.18 and 19.19. In general, the significance of the relationship between the number of dependent children and women's economic activity decreased between 1970 and 1980, particularly for women whose youngest child was under 6 years of age. In 1970, mothers of young children were more likely to be inactive the more children they had. In 1980, this trend had almost disappeared except for those with three or more children. The increase in the level of women's economic activity between 1970 and 1980 occurred in all groups but was most marked for mothers of young children. In 1980, women with children under 2 years old were benefiting from the 1970 measure which extended unpaid maternity leave until the child reaches this age. (In 1980, there were 265,763 women in the CSR and 114,027 women in the SSR on child-care leave, representing approximately 11 per cent of the active female labour force in each republic.) Since activity rates do not decline for mothers whose youngest child is 3-5 years of age, compared with those whose youngest child is 0-2 years of age, most women seem to return to work after the end of their maternity leave. It should be noted that the data concern only the CSR, where this process was the most pronounced.

TABLE 19.16

Economic Activity Rates of Married Women by Age Group and Number of Dependent Children in Czechoslovakia, 1961 and 1970 (Percentages)

No. of children	*Year*	*Age group*				
		Up to 25	*25.29*	*30.34*	*35.44*	*45.54*
1	2	3	4	6	7	8
1	1961	56.9	/65.6	68.5	72.8	68.8
	1970	73.6	85.9	89.2	87.8	82.5
	Difference, 1961-70	16.7	20.3	20.7	15.0	13.7
2	1961	38.7	49.2	60.2	70.8	70.0
	1970	59.6	73.7	83.7	87.0	82.3
	Difference, 1961-70	20.9	24.5	23.5	16.2	12.3
3 or more	1961	30.2	41.1	57.0	63.7	65.1
	1970	45.2	58.4	71.5	77.7	74.1
	Difference, 1961-70	15.0	17.3	14.5	14.0	9.0

Source: FSU, 1970b, analytical issue, p. 70.

TABLE 19.17

Economic Activity Rates of Married Women with Dependent Children by Age Group of Woman, Number of Children and Age of The Youngest Child in The CSR, 1970

No. of children	*Age group of women*	*No. of women*	*Economic activity rate (%)*				
			Age of the youngest child				*All ages*
			0-2	*3-5*	*6-14*	*15 and over*	
1	Up to 24	121 891	70.5	86.4	87.8	—	73.6
	25-29	99 071	77.2	89.6	91.6	—	85.9
	30-34	52 373	74.1	87.4	92.0	94.2	89.5
	35-44	153 553	67.1	78.9	87.2	90.2	87.8
	45 and over	124 441	38.5	48.3	74.5	75.3	74.3
	Total	551 592	71.8	86.4	85.4	81.5	80.9
2	Up to 24	29 593	57.4	73.8	83.6	—	59.6
	25-29	94 520	65.5	79.3	86.0	—	73.7
	30-34	107 074	68.7	82.1	89.2	90.1	83.7
	35-44	176 462	65.2	78.6	88.2	92.1	87.0
	45 and over	37 965	52.0	62.7	78.9	83.2	79.6
	Total	445 675	63.3	79.6	87.3	88.3	80.1
3 or more	Up to 24	2 367	43.6	62.0	91.3	—	45.2
	25-29	16 306	50.5	68.3	77.4	—	58.4
	30-34	35 718	55.6	72.3	83.7	85.7	71.5
	35-44	63 110	55.9	71.4	83.7	90.7	77.7
	45 and over	8 860	51.2	57.5	74.2	84.6	72.8
	Total	126 371	52.5	70.7	82.4	87.8	71.6
Total	Up to 24	153 851	66.6	84.1	87.4	—	69.8
	25-29	209 897	67.3	82.9	89.0	—	77.3
	30-34	195 165	65.0	80.4	89.3	93.7	82.5
	35-44	393 125	60.8	75.7	87.1	90.7	85.6
	45 and over	171 266	43.9	54.2	75.8	76.4	75.4
	Total	1 123 638	66.2	80.6	85.9	82.8	79.4

— = not applicable.

Source: FSU, 1970b, analytical issue, p. 245.

TABLE 19.18

Economic Activity Rates of Married Women with Dependent Children by Age Group of Woman, Number of Children and Age of the Youngest Child in the CSR, 1980

No. of children	*Age group of women*	*No. of women*	*Economic activity rate (%)*				
			Age of the youngest child				*All ages*
			0-2	*3-5*	*6-14*	*15 and over*	
1	Up to 24	103 481	86.8	90.4	93.7	—	87.4
	25-29	81 598	90.6	92.8	94.0	—	92.1
	30-34	56 090	90.2	92.1	95.1	95.4	93.8
	35-44	152 578	88.9	88.7	94.5	95.8	94.8
	45-54	101 257	86.1	82.8	87.5	91.2	90.0
	55 and over	8 792	40.3	33.5	36.2	46.8	43.9
	Total	503 796	87.7	90.8	91.9	89.7	89.9
2	Up to 24	61 411	91.1	87.7	91.7	—	90.6
	25-29	172 041	91.2	91.5	94.1	—	91.7
	30-34	204 918	91.8	93.0	95.8	95.4	94.3
	35-44	213 001	90.4	91.7	95.9	96.9	95.3
	45-54	25 849	84.1	79.8	88.4	93.8	90.6
	55 and over	1 638	63.0	63.9	55.1	60.6	59.3
	Total	678 858	91.1	91.8	95.3	95.2	93.3
3 or more	Up to 24	5 924	83.1	78.4	100.0	—	82.8
	25-29	35 803	85.1	83.5	88.7	—	84.8
	30-34	66 978	87.0	88.0	92.1	100.0	87.0
	35-44	65 280	86.0	87.8	92.6	96.3	90.3
	45-54	4 459	67.8	69.9	82.6	92.3	81.9
	55 and over	312	52.2	58.3	51.6	48.0	53.0
	Total	178 756	85.6	86.7	91.6	93.9	88.0
Total	Up to 24	170 816	88.2	89.3	93.6	—	88.4
	25-29	289 440	90.0	90.9	93.8	—	90.9
	30-34	327 986	89.8	91.6	95.2	95.4	93.0
	35-44	430 859	88.2	89.8	95.0	96.1	94.3
	45-44	430 859	88.2	89.8	95.0	96.1	94.3
	45-54	131 565	83.0	79.5	87.4	91.5	89.8
	55 and over	10 742	48.0	45.4	40.7	47.6	45.9
	Total	1 361 410	88.9	90.6	93.8	90.8	91.3

— = not applicable.

Source: FSU, 1980 (in preparation).

The interaction between economic activity educational level and number of dependent children in the CSR can be seen in Table 19.19. Here also one of the main findings is confirmed: economically active women have somewhat fewer children on average than inactive women, taking into account education and marital status. Women with the highest educational level have fewer children than other women, and non-married women (mostly divorced) also have fewer children than married women; however, the proportion of single women plays a particular role here.

TABLE 19.19

Number and Percentage Distribution of Women with Dependent Children by Economic Activity Status, Family Status, Educational Level and Number of Children in the CSR, 1970

Economic activity status/family status/ educational level children	*No. of women*	*No. of dependent children*					
		1	*2*	*3*	*4 or more*	*Total*	*Average no. of*
Economically active							
Married:							
University level	39 438	55.6	39.8	4.2	0.4	100.0	1.50
High school level	211 948	55.4	39.6	4.5	0.5	100.0	1.50
Others	872 252	47.2	39.7	10.4	2.7	100.0	1.70
Total	1 123 638	49.1	39.7	9.0	2.2	100.0	1.65
Not currently married:							
University level	3 823	74.8	22.8	2.2	0.2	100.0	1.23
High school level	18 437	74.8	22.2	2.7	0.3	100.0	1.29
Others	92 451	64.6	25.9	6.9	2.6	100.0	1.49
Total	114 711	66.6	25.2	6.1	2.1	100.0	1.45
Economically inactive							
Married:							
University level	2 370	53.2	38.4	6.3	2.1	100.0	1.58
High school level	34 760	50.4	40.8	7.3	1.5	100.0	1.61
Others	254 519	43.9	37.6	12.9	5.6	100.0	1.83
Total	291 649	44.8	38.0	12.1	5.1	100.0	1.80
Not currently married:							
University level	107	78.5	16.8	3.8	0.9	100.0	1.28
High school level	1 0252	75.2	18.1	5.7	1.0	100.0	1.33
Others	17 798	63.5	20.7	8.9	6.9	100.0	1.63
Total	18 925	64.2	20.5	8.7	6.6	100.0	1.61

Source: FSU, 1970b.

Data from Table 19.19 led us to conclude that the educational level of the woman undoubtedly affects the number of children, but the differences in the period since the demographic revolution have been small. An even higher uniformity of the population in this respect can be foreseen in the future.

WOMEN'S TIME USE AND DIVISION OF LABOUR IN HOUSEHOLDS

Such factors as economic activity, socio-occupational group, education, fertility level, etc., are objective conditions of social development which are inter-related. Many more factors may be defined, but they are less often documented statistically; in other words, only soft data on them is available. Such data include women's attitudes towards their participation in the labour force, already mentioned above, and women's time use and the division of labour in households.

With the increasing level of female economic activity, the situation of women in households has not changed substantially in spite of the fact that after the demographic revolution the number of children decreased, usually to one or two. Even under socialist development, many traditional features of the division of labour between men and women in families still persisted. As early as 1959-60, a survey was carried out which aimed to describe the daily routine of women in one factory (Srb, 1967, pp. 232-233). The average daily work of a woman in the household (i.e., not at the factory) was very time-consuming (5-5.5 hours, including 1 hour for shopping and 2-3 hours for the preparation of meals; the rest was devoted to other work such as washing, sewing and looking after the children).

The results of this survey did not answer the question of whether women had enough time to cope with all their duties. The rest time of women was dependent on the number of children. Women without children rested 7.2 hours on average, with one child 6.6 hours and with two or more children 6.2 hours. The greater the time spent on caring for the children, the less the woman rested. These results are rather striking, but it should be kept in mind that one factory is not a very representative example.

Another, survey was carried out in 1960; it covered 5,964 people from the whole of Czechoslovakia, 2,918 of whom were men and 3,046 women (Srb, 1967, pp. 238-241). The difference in time use was far greater between men and women than between various socio-occupational groups (Table 19.20). In particular, work in the household amounted to only a little less time than work outside the home (with the exception of women staying at home). Economically active women had a second shift at home and therefore had significantly less free time and rest time than men.

Twenty years later, a similar survey showed comparable results (Tables 19.22 and 19.23). Differences can be explained mainly by the division of time use into working days and days off in the latter survey. In addition, a more detailed classification of activities was used. The division of labour between men and women was much more pronounced than among men, women or various socio-occupational groups. The differences among workers, employees and members of the uniform agricultural co-operatives (UAC) were very small. As might be expected, women staying at home had the most different system of time use. However, they had almost as little free time as women workers and employees and they had even fewer days off. Apart from essential personal needs, they devoted a considerable amount of time to cooking, cleaning, sewing, shopping and caring for the children. The time they devoted to themselves was less than in all other groups.

TABLE 19.20

Average Daily Time Spent in Various Activities by Sex and Socio-occupational Group in Czechoslovakia, 1960-61

(Hours and Minutes)

Activity	*Men*			*Women*			
	Workers	*Emplo-yees*	*UAC*[1] *members*	*Workers*	*Employees*	*House-wives*	*UAC*[1] *members*
Work outside home inc. travel[2]	8 h 05	8 h 01	9 h 31	6 h 57	6 h 52	50	7 h 10
Housework	1 h 17	1 h 18	56	5 h 07	4 h 39	8 h 18	5 h 19
Other necessary activities	10 h 12	9 h 52	9 h 54	9 h 26	9 h 38	11 h 07	9 h 24
Sleep, meals, rest	9 h 08	8 h 49	9 h 07	8 h 18	8 h 18	9 h 17	8 h 30
Care of self	45	42	40	43	49	46	37
Care of children	19	21	07	25	31	1 h 04	17
Free time	4 h 26	4 h 49	3 h 39	2 h 30	2 h 51	3 h 45	2 h 07
Education	1 h 02	1 h 28	48	23	37	36	21
Public activities	35	42	36	11	17	15	13
Active entertainment	12	15	04	04	06	03	01
Walking, dancing, etc.	24	21	12	21	20	27	10
Passive entertainment	2 h 05	1 h 51	1 h 21	1 h 20	1 h 58	1 h 13	
Wasted time[3]	08	07	08	10	11	26	09
Total	24 h 00	24 h 00	24 h 00	24 h 00	24 h 00	24 h 00	24 h 00

1. Uniform agricultural co-operatives.
2. Average of seven weekdays.
3. E.g. waiting in queues, etc.
Source: Srb, 1967, p. 239.

The structure of women's time use according to number of dependent children is presented in Table 19.23. It is interesting that the amount of household did not depend greatly on the number of dependent children (this amount rose only among women staying at home and among employees). Time spent in care of children did not depend on their number either. Some results were rather surprising and suggest a certain heterogeneity in the sample. Why do workers with three children have more free time than workers with one or two children? Why do workers and employees with five or more children devote less time to their care than all other women? Do these women perhaps belong to the gypsy

(Romany) population or do older children help care for younger ones in these families? However, the main results correspond quite closely with the results of the previous survey.

TABLE 19.21

Average Time Spent in Various Activities on Working Days by Sex and Socio-occupational Group in Czechoslovakia, 1979-80

(Hours and Minutes)

Activity	*Men*			*Women*			
	Workers	*Employees*	*UAC members*	*Workers*	*Employees*	*UAC members*	*House wives*
Work outside home	9 h 37	9 h 20	10 h 17	8 h 28	8 h 26	8 h 30	57
Paid	8 h 58	8 h 55	9 h 04	8 h 08	8 h 17	7 h 29	04
On own account	28	13	1 h 01	16	06	58	45
Other[1]	11	12	12	04	03	03	08
Necessary activities	3 h 57	3 h 56	3 h 15	6 h 05	5 h 44	6 h 26	11 h 08
Travel to work	1 h 10	1 h 07	41	57	53	40	—
Cooking	09	09	07	1 h 24	1 h 06	1 h 55	3 h 07
Cleaning, home maintenance	28	24	25	33	30	37	1 h 09
Washing, sewing	01	01	01	34	30	40	1 h 28
Care of self	45	47	45	47	50	45	44
Care of children	09	11	06	20	24	19	2 h 10
Shopping	13	16	08	39	39	29	1 h 01
Eating meals	54	51	59	47	43	56	1 h 19
Other	08	10	03	04	09	05	10
Free time	3 h 20	3 h 31	3 h 03	2 h 17	2 h 34	2 h 03	3 h 48
Cultural events	04	03	01	02	05	.	01
Television	1 h 29	1 h 23	1 h 27	1 h 09	1 h 05	1 h 05	1 h 25
Reading	22	32	21	12	21	08	20
Gardening	05	06	04	03	03	04	06
Sport	04	05	01	01	02	.	01
Country walks	04	04	01	03	03	01	13
Meeting friends	13	12	08	11	12	09	22
Visiting restaurants	01	.	.	01	02	.	01
Passive rest	10	06	12	06	03	11	14
Other	48	1 h 00	48	29	38	25	1 h 05
Sleep	7 h 06	7 h 13	7 h 25	7 h 10	7 h 16	7 h 01	8 h 07
Total	24 h 00	24 h 00	24 h 00	24 h 00	24 h 00	24 h 00	24 h 00

. = nil or negligible.

1. Studying, etc.

Source: FSU, 1981, pp. 539-540.

TABLE 19.22

Average Time Spent in Various Activities on Days Off by Sex and Socio-occupational Group in Czechoslovakia, 1979-80 (Hours and Minutes)

Activity	*Men*			*Women*			
	Workers	*Emplo-yees*	*UAC members*	*Workers*	*Employees*	*-UAC members*	*House wives*
1	2	3	4	5	6	7	8
Work outside home	2 h 14	1 h 44	3 h 39	52	39	2 h 05	37
Paid	0 h 41	38	1 h 26	20	16	1 h 01	
On own account	0 h 56	33	1 h 38	23	11	1 h 01	29
Other[1]	0 h 37	33	35	09	12	03	08
Necessary activities	5 h 10	5 h 45	4 h 47	8 h 40	8 h 50	8 h 33	9 h 29
Travel to work	06	04	07	03	02	08	
Cooking	22	25	17	2 h 58	2 h 48	3 h 16	3 h 16
Cleaning, home maintenance	1 h 11	1 h 20	1 h 06	1 h 03	1 h 12	59	1 h 00
Washing, sewing	03	03	04	58	53	52	40
Care of self	54	57	50	53	57	46	48
Care of children	15	19	17	26	30	25	1 h 31
Shopping	11	15	04	19	17	16	19
Eating meals	1 h 30	1 h 34	1 h 29	1 h 29	1 h 30	1 h 25	1 h 27
Other	38	48	33	31	41	26	28
Free time	7 h 46	7 h 58	7 h 01	5 h 48	6 h 01	5 h 01	5 h 31
Cultural events	08	09	07	06	06	05	03
Television	2 h 50	2 h 39	2 h 46	2 h 17	2 h 06	1 h 54	2 h 09
Reading	32	42	25	19	31	13	18
Gardening	09	22	06	08	10	07	05
Sport	14	15	08	04	08	03	02
Country walks	33	39	19	26	39	12	24
Meeting friends	1 h 02	1 h 00	59	1 h 05	1 h 00	1 h 04	57
Visiting restaurants	35	17	38	09	08	02	04
Passive rest	27	21	23	18	13	23	20
Other	1 h 16	1 h 34	1 h 10	56	1 h 00	58	1 h 09
Sleep	8 h 50	8 h 33	8 h 33	8 h 40	8 h 30	8 h 21	8 h 23
Total	24 h 00	24 h 00	24 h 00	24 h 00	24 h 00	24 h 00	24 h 00

. = nil or negligible.

1. Studying, etc.

Source: As for table 19.21.

A recent survey (Bauerova and Bartova, 1980, pp. 3, 11) also confirmed that the greater part of the work in the household is done by the woman; only in younger families does the man participate more in work at home. In many of these families, a grandmother provides considerable help to an economically active woman. All the persons questioned evaluated the time, and the physical and psychological demands on women related to their care of household and family, as great or very great. The women worked at home 25.5 hours a week, the men 14.5 hours; however, the amount of time for women was lower and for men higher than in the previous survey. Older people, people with lower education and those living in the country did more work at home than the others. Men considered work at home as somewhat demanding. The higher participation of men in work at home shown in this recent survey indicates the more democratic character of the family, and it is usually related to other attitudes and ideas. The persons questioned were more likely to think that the care of children should be divided equally between the man and the woman and that both partners should participate equally in family decisions. Only 7 per cent of men did not participate in work at home at all.

TABLE 19.23

Percentage Distribution of Women's Time Use by Number of Dependent Children and Socio-occupational Group in Czechoslovakia, 1960-61

Socio-occupational group/ activity	*No. of dependent children*					
	0	*1*	*2*	*3*	*4*	*5 or more*
Workers						
Work outside home, including travel	30.4	30.6	29.6	27.9	26.9	33.1
Housework	21.3	20.2	22.2	22.1	22.0	20.6
Care of self	2.3	3.4	3.4	2.1	4.5	1.9
Meals, sleep, rest	35.6	34.5	33.5	35.3	36.2	33.6
Care of children	.	1.7	2.4	2.6	2.5	1.6
Free time	10.4	9.6	8.9	10.0	7.9	9.2
Total	100.0	100.0	100.0	100.0	100.0	100.0
Employees						
Work outside home, including travel	30.9	29.6	28.7	29.2	28.8	29.6
Housework	16.4	19.4	20.3	21.9	22.3	27.3
Care of self	3.9	3.2	3.4	2.6	2.6	1.8
Meals, sleep, rest	35.8	34.5	34.4	34.0	33.1	32.2
Care of children		2.8	2.7	2.4	2.7	1.8
Free time	13.0	10.5	10.5	9.9	10.5	7.3
Total	100.0	100.0	100.0	100.0	100.0	100.0
Housewives						
Work outside home, including travel	5.5	4.6	5.3	4.5	4.3	5.2
Housework	32.9	33.1	35.1	36.9	36.1	37.7
Care of self	3.8	3.5	2.7	2.3	4.8	2.2
Meals, sleep, rest	41.5	39.7	37.4	37.7	36.5	37.9
Care of children		4.2	5.6	5.6	6.6	5.1
Free time	16.3	14.9	13.9	13.0	11.7	11.9
Total	100.0	100.0	100.0	100.0	100.0	100.0

. = nil.

Source: Srb, 1967, p. 240.

This recent survey showed one interesting feature which should not be overlooked. With the increased participation of men in home activities, the participation of children seems to be decreasing; it is higher in traditional families than in modern ones where the father shares the family duties. This could have negative consequences in the future when a new generation starts to build its own families.

STANDARD OF LIVING OF FAMILIES WITH CHILDREN

Standard of living and especially its material components are closely related to other social factors. In one survey carried out in 1961 (Srb, 1967, pp. 242-245), 7,955 women were asked why they worked. The resulting data are given in table 19.24. Such results are not surprising and confirm with other surveys that financial reasons are by far the most important.

Such a conclusion can be made in spite of the significant increase in the standard of living in Czechoslovakia since the Second World War. According to selected indicators of increase in the standard of living (Table 19.25), real wages rose from 100 to 255.8 between 1937 and 1980. Other indicators also show a considerable increase. National income per head rose more than 5 times between 1948 and 1980, while the yearly income per person rose 3.6 times between 1953 and 1980. The number of children in nursery schools and in creches also rose very markedly, as did the number of cars and other consumer goods.

The differences in standard of living among various socio-occupational groups were very small, and they are still gradually decreasing.

TABLE 19.24

Reasons Why Women Work by Number of Children in Czechoslovakia, 1961 (Percentage)

Reason for work	*No. of children*				
	1	*2*	*3*	*4*	*5 or more*
Financial reasons	79.1	81.6	85.6	89.0	90.4
Importance of the work for society	23.2	24.0	23.9	22.9	20.7
Woman wants to be independent	36.1	26.3	16.5	18.0	9.1
Other reasons	4.9	4.6	5.1	4.9	4.8
(More than one reason was accepted.)					

Source: Srb, 1967, p. 243.

TABLE 19.25

Selected Indicators of Increases in the Standard of Living in Czechoslovakia Since 1937 (Index: 1937 = 100)

Year	*Average monthly wage in socialist sector*		*Index of*		*National income per person (Kcs)*	*Personal consump-tion person (Kcs)*	*Social consump-tion per per person (Kcs)*	*Annual income per person (Kcs)*	*Direct financial support to families with children (million Kcs)*	*No. of children*		*No. of persons*		
	Kcs	*Index*	*Cost of living*	*Real wages*						*In nursery schools*	*In creches*	*Per car*	*Per radio*	*Per TV set*
1937	(764)	100	100.0	100.0	—	4 523	—	—	—	104 615	1 286	166.7	14	—
1948	823	107.7	—	—	5 686	4 389	—	—	—	188 274	6 050	100.0	—	—
1953	1 097	143.6	134.4	112.8	8.556	5 044	—	6 297	—	219 324	33 357	90.9	5	304[2]
1960	1 365	178.7	109.3	163.7	12 892	7 954	2776[1]	8 866	—	285 863	41 307	55.5	4	16
1965	1 493	195.4	112.4	173.8	12 610	8 212	3 319	10 800	—	330 084	63 332	34.5	3	6
1970	1 937	253.5	121.9	208.0	19 564	10 943	5 408	15 792	10 071	377 762	65 992	17.2	2	4
1975	2 304	301.6	122.3	246.0	25 051	13 408	7 230	19 731	15 350	475 004	71 013	9.8	2	3
1980	2 642	345.8	135.2	255.8	29 593	15 306	8 900	23 180	19 620	694 720	88 014	6.7	2	3

— = not available or not applicable.

1. 1961.
2. 1955.

Source: Vyzkumny ustav socialne ekonomickych informaci, 1981, p. 190.

20

The Origins of Women at Work and the First Vocational Schools

WOMEN AND WORK IN THE PAST

Human beings are constantly in search of their roots, and their discoveries, which for a long time remained in the hands of scholars or were confined to museums, are now widely disseminated by means of books, the radio and, more especially, the cinema and television, so that many millions of our fellows-beings know how their distant ancestors lived in the age of the cave-dwellers and how some peoples, unaffected by the 'technological era', still live in the depths of the jungle or in inaccessible places.

We see, through these discoveries, that the women of those times—like many today—were, above all, a prey to their offspring; pregnant, they would have to hold or carry year-old babies on their backs, while other infants would be crawling on all fours or toddling to the entrance of the cave or the hut. They had great difficulty in coping with their successive pregnancies and the breast-feeding of the infants. In addition, they had to dry or cook meat or fish; scrape the skins of animals, tan them, cut them up and sew them together to make coverings and clothes or to use as barter for other goods. It was also the women who engaged in weaving, the making of clothes, basketwork, pottery and other forms of craft activity. And, of course, for the daily preparation of meals, their responsibilities included picking leaves and berries, drawing water, hewing wood and keeping the fire going.

During this time, the men were hunting, fishing or making war. They dealt with the building and roofing of the huts, the capture and breaking-in of animals, the cutting of tools; when they met in a glade to elect a chief, judge a culprit or decide upon attacking an enemy tribe, this was a completely male affair.

At various moments, under the influence of climatic change, the way of life evolved slowly; as populations migrated, so the growing of good crops developed, leading certain groups to settle on fixed sites; for other groups nomadism continued.

Among the sedentary populations, women's work was increased by the arduous tasks of the new agriculture.

And so, in the less-distant past, women's first occupations were related to their traditional activities, and the oldest of these were closely and directly related to life and death; midwifery, laying-out and mourning. The women who performed these tasks were frequently the oldest in the village; they were trained by their mothers and, in turn, trained their own daughters. But one also found washerwomen, spinners, weavers and many craftswomen engaged in pottery, basketwork, jewellery-making, etc.

Therefore, when one ponders on the survival—even in so called 'modernised countries— of stereotypes of the division of labour between men and women, one should never forget that these images have roots that are buried very deep inside each one of us, in an *unconscious* heritage, maintained and built up throughout the ages, and that the present profile of man and woman, which is the product of it, seemed a natural one to the generations that preceded us.

In the light of the varying circumstances of each country, and having regard to the differing tempo of the changes that have occurred, our starting-point will be the situation that has prevailed in the developed countries. We shall distinguish, within the same country, rural and urban areas; even then, the picture can only be incomplete, as would be that of a painter who has only a few colours at his disposal.

THE FIRST VOCATIONAL SCHOOLS

Most developed countries, and it was Great Britain that gave the signal, entered the industrial era in the nineteenth century. That is when the countryside, where people lived poorly, lost its population to the towns. In France, for example, the poorest regions such as Creuse and Limousin saw their young men leave for Paris where there was a need to construct dwellings, buildings, factories, works, mills, workshops and depots. These exiles from Creuse and Limousin thus became masons; they returned to the country in winter and left again for the capital the following spring with brothers or cousins who also went to work in the building trade. By training 'on the job', they learnt a trade.

Later, entire families settled on the outskirts of the towns, where deprived areas mushroomed. In the morning, the men went off to work while the women remained in the house with the children gradually the rapid extension of the industrial zones increased the demand for labour and so women were hired—girls, unmarried women, widows without children, women of 40 whose children were grown up. As these women had received no initial training, they were used as labourers while their brothers and husbands, who had been trained for several years, occupied the qualified positions and could aspire to become specialised workers and foremen by training on the job.

This scheme of things, transferable to all countries where industrialisation is in its initial stages, explains in part: why women, from the beginning of the industrial era, were not interested in work outside the home; why, when forced by the need to earn their living, they accepted the least-well-paid jobs that required no qualifications; and why they frequently preferred repetitive and exhausting home industry which resulted in such flagrant exploitation that a defender of the working classes such as Albert de Mun denounced the scandal about 1885.

This nascent industry highlighted the need, throughout Europe, for workers with training in mathematics, the basis of engineering. As early as 1794. France created the Conservatoire des Arts et Metiers Polytechniques, initially intended to preserve the prototypes of all machines invented.

Institutes or colleges opened everywhere to train captains of industry, production engineers for engineering, the textile industry and the chemical industry. All these types of training were none the less reserved for men.

The developing industrial and manufacturing structures were soon joined by commercial organisations that were to acquire considerable importance within a few years. This is what, in the language of experts in the world of work, is termed the 'tertiary sector'. Secretaries and accounts clerks—ledger clerks—soon abandoned the pen for the typewriter, and this resulted in the proliferation of commercial schools and private typing and accountancy courses Young men, but also girls, frequently enrolled for evening classes; very rapidly the profession of office employee became a female profession. In France, twelve *ecoles pratiques de commerce et d'industrie* opened in 1892, and two of these were for girls; in the same year, the city of Paris established fourteen vocational schools, eight of which were for girls.

Domestic science colleges had at least as much success as commercial colleges. They taught what was already considered as being the monopoly of women—the job of housewife, which they could better perform outside their own home as 'servants' and, in the hotel business, as chambermaids and linen maids.

The development of national or provincial vocational schools was not seen in the industrialised countries until the end of the First World War (1914-18). In 1925 there were six such schools in France for girls. Should one see in this trend one of the consequences of the First World War? Without question, since for four years, all the countries involved, lacking men who had been killed, were on active service or had become prisoners, called on women to carry on work in factories, offices, workshops, shops, fields and fishing ports. It was thus proved that women were capable of doing all the jobs that had hitherto been reserved for men.

WOMEN IN RURAL AREAS IN THE INDUSTRIALISED COUNTRIES

The rural areas of the industrialised countries differed very considerably according to their geographical, climatic and economic features. But, in spite of all these differences, one common feature persists: the peasant women of Sicily or Ireland, Spain or Romania, France or Germany remained the serfs of men for a long time, performing all the household tasks (maternal and domestic) and also taking on other duties, such as the work involved in the *metayage* system, the milking of cows and goats, poultry-raising, cultivation of the family vegetable plot, the tying-up of vines the harvesting of fruit and vegetables and their preservation: jam-making, salting and curing.

A single, if sizeable, exception to this situation described frequently in the literature of the period can be found in the United States of America, where he daughters and grand-daughters of the pioneers, who worked alongside their settler fathers and husbands from the beginnings of mass immigration, became, with the rapid mechanisation of agriculture, not only mistresses of the house in charge of a large staff but also women who 'held the reins', inaugurating a completely new form of participation by women in the affairs of their community.

The situation of peasant women in Europe—which has persisted up to the present in the poorest countries and regions, particularly in the mountains—gradually evolved in areas where large estates began to be broken up. Some of the wage-earning agricultural workers (male and female agricultural labourers and *metayers*) became farmers whose situation improved. Their wives were able to obtain assistance for the various farm and domestic tasks, and, as the standard of living of these increasingly large categories rose, their sons formed the first intakes for the middle-level agricultural schools (or practical schools) when they did not become pupils in the normal secondary schools. Their daughters were also able to attend secondary schools in the towns or, more often, rural domestic-science schools.

The sons of landowners had already benefited from the higher-level training provided by the agricultural colleges *(grandes ecoles)* that were established in the last quarter of the nineteenth century. But in the country, as in the town, women continued to be assigned the almost exclusive role of wife and mother. Here again, it was not until the First World War that they took over the running of the farms, with guidance from the older men who had escaped the call up because of their age.

With regard to craft activities, practically every village had its carpenter, clogmaker, weaver, smith, farrier, wheelwright, saddler, etc. The women stayed in the house, having no place beside their craftsmen husbands; sometimes, if they lived in the centre of the village, a few of them ran the only general store, combining a grocery, haberdashery, refreshment bar, tobacconist's and newspaper shop. In their youth they had attended—as did their daughters up until the war—convent or church schools to learn the rudiments of elementary education and homecraft, the emphasis being placed on needlework and dressmaking.

In this environment, as in the surrounding agricultural estates, the activity of women was traditionally, and for a long time, concerned with the house and children, who were usually very numerous in these families.

21

Work Participation of Women

The document of the World Bank on Gender and Poverty in India highlights the "Statistical Purdah" created by existing concepts and the methods of measuring labour participation which renders women's work invisible.

Defined in conventional terms, women make up one third of the labour force. When women, engaged in the collection of fuel and fodder, or in dairy, poultry or kitchen garden production for the family, are added, the female labour force participation rate increases to 51% from 39% (only 13% lesser than the male participation rate of 64%). More detailed statistical information is given in Tables 21.1 and 21.2.

This is further elaborated in the Document of the World Bank is follows:

"Conventional definitions of economic activity would suggest that most Indian women are "housewives" but as the definitions and methods of measurement become more precise this picture comes into better focus. According to the 1981 Census, only about 20% of the women in India were in the labour force; when the broader definitions of work and the more intensive survey methods of the National Sample Survey (NSS) are used, this percentage increases to around 39%. Yet even this figure is acknowledge to miss a significant portion of women's gainful economic activity in the subsistence sector."

Definition of 'Work'

The different definitions of 'work' become relevant for quantifying employment or unemployment.

Census Definition

The Census of India recognises production for own consumption in cultivation as economic activity. The term cultivation in the Census, covers only growing of certain crops such as cereals, millets, sugarcane etc. Growing of plantation crops, vegetables, flowers and other crops are not included under cultivation. Growing of such crops if done, exclusively for home consumption, is not considered as economic activity in the Census.

Processing of primary commodities for own consumption and own account production of fixed assets are also excluded from the purview of economic activity in the Census. In other worlds, with the exception of cultivation, the Census does not include the *non-market economic activities* as work. Consequently persons working for the household in non-market activities would not be 'workers'.

TABLE 21.1

The Quantum of Women's Work

Row	(A)	(B)
(1)	Labour Force Activity	Non-Labour Force Activity
% Total population Within/Outside Labour Force	49.14	50.86
% Male of Respective Category	66.12	36.96
% Female of Respective Category	33.88	63.04
% Total Male Population	63.55	36.35
% Total Female Population	34.18	65.82

(2)	Main Workers	Marginal Workers	Unemployed
% Total Pop. Within Labour Force	87.34	10.70	2.06
% Male of Respective Category	71.66	19.01	76.24
% Female of Respective Category	28.34	80.99	23.76
% Total Male Within Labour Force	94.55	3.08	2.37
% Total Female Within Labour force	72.97	25.59	1.44

(3)	Paid Labour Force	Market-oriented Labour Force	New Standard Labour Force

(4)	Work That Produces cash Income			Work That Produces Goods and Services for Self-Consumption and Sale			Work That Builds Human Capital		Non-Work	
(5)	Regular wage Salary	Casual Labour	Self-Employ-	Unpaid Family Labour	Expanded Domestic (Code 93)	Conventional Domestic (Code 92)	Education of Self (Code 91)	Age (Code 94, 95)	Rentiers (Code 96)	Others (Code 97, 98)
(5.1) % Total Population	6.95	13.79	17.42	10.46	5.81	12.33	18.46	13.26	0.37	1.14
% Total Male Population	11.72	16.05	26.72	8.29	0.49	0.42	22.82	11.80	0.46	1.23
% Total Female Population	2.00	11.43	7.72	12.71	13.90	24.76	11.35	14.79	0.29	1.05
(5.2) % Total Population Within/Outside labour force	14.32	28.36	35.82	21.50	11.30	24.02	35.92	25.81	0.73	2.22
% Male to Respective Activity Category	85.92	59.41	78.31	40.48	4.35	1.72	63.11	45.39	62.16	54.87
% Female to Respective Activity Category	14.08	40.59	21.69	59.52	95.65	98.28	36.08	54.61	37.84	4.07
(5.3) % Total Male Population Within/Outside Labour Force	18.66	25.57	42.56	13.21	1.33	1.12	61.33	31.07	1.22	3.30
% Total Female Population Within/ Outside Labour Force	5.91	33.76	22.79	37.54	17.16	37.43	21.02	22.36	0.44	1.59

a. Persons in wage or salary employment for which workers are paid in cash or kind.

b. Includes (a) plus activity on a family farm or in a family enterprise or business that sells some or all of its products.

c. Includes (a) and (b) plus all activities involving production of primary products and processing of primary products by the producer irrespective of whether goods and services are old. Unlike (b), this definition includes "all food 'production' and food 'processing' including animal tending and milking, threshing in the home compound, processing and preparing food for presentation and storage and unpaid gathering of food or fruit...whether or not market-related exchanges occurs" (Anker et al 1988:31).

d. This is a special category developed by the NSS in an attempt to capture a larger portion of women's non-monetised economic work. The definition of "Code 93" is as follows: "domestic activities combined with free collection of foods (vegetables, roots, firewood, cattle food, etc.), dairying, poultry and kitchen gardening for the family, tutoring of children, sewing tailoring or weaving for household use."

Source: National Sample Survey, 1983 round. See Technical Note for details.

NSSO Definition

The NSSO has defined 'work' or 'gainful activity' as the activity pursued for pay, profit or family gain or in other words, the activity which adds value to the "rational product." Normally, it is an activity which results in production of goods and services for exchange. However, all activities in the agricultural sector (Division '0' of the NIC) in which a part or whole of the agricultural production is used for own consumption and does not go for sale are also considered as gainful. In short, work is defined as any market activity and any non-market activity relating to the agricultural sector.

Both census and NSSO do not include attending to household chores as work or gainful activity.

The NSSO, therefore, introduced a new, additional code (code 93) in its occupational classifications for the 32nd round (1977/78). This new code allowed the survey respondent to distinguish between the performance of conventional 'domestic activities" (code 92) and domestic activities and also free collection of goods (vegetables, roots, firewood, fish, cowdung, cattle feed etc.), maintenance of kitchen gardens, orchards, etc., work in poultry or dairy, sewing, tailoring, weaving, etc., for household use, water collection and tutoring of children" (code 93)." The results are shown in Table 21.2.

TABLE 21.2

Work Participation Rate, 1983/84 (Conventional and Expanded Concepts)

Labour Force Concept	*Rural*		*Urban*	
	Male	*Female*	*Male*	*Female*
Conventional	63.22	38.74	57.71	17.31
Expanded/a	63.83	50.97	57.88	25.06

/a: Includes persons engaged in "Code 93" activities.

Source: Kalpagam, *Women in the Labour Force: An Analysis of NSS Data*, 1998.

This document has further established that it is necessary to goby the various micro-level studies that have captured women's work to find where the women work. A major part of the work is unpaid domestic work and is, therefore, considered as non-labour force activity-particularly domestic work. If domestic work is included in the concept of work participation, 55% of the female population above age 5 would get included. The statistical profile would then change as in Table 21.3.

TABLE 21.3

Alternative Calculations of Women's Occupational Distribution

	Conventional		*Expanded I*		*Expanded II*	
	Labour	*Non-Labour Force*	*Labour*	*Non-Labour Force*	*Labour*	*Non-Labour Force*
Domestic work	—	54.59	53.31	—	40.27	—
Agriculture	80.56	—	37.62	—	50.66	—
Non-Agr. Informal	14.75	—	6.88	—	6.88	—
Non-Agr. Formal	9	—	2.19	—	2.19	—

Notes: Expanded I: Uses a conventional definition of agricultural work which excludes agricultural activities classified by the NSSO under expanded domestic work (NSS Code 93), such as kitchen gardening, dairying, etc.

Expanded II: uses an extended definition of agricultural activities classified by the NSSO under expanded domestic work (NSS Code 93).

Source: Calculated from *Sarvekshana*, Vol. IX, No. 4, April 1986, Table 1.

Concept, Definitions and Measurement of 'Work' in Censuses and Other Surveys

Data on the economic activity of the people collected upto the 1951 census was based on 'income' and 'dependency' concepts. From the *1961 census* onwards, the concept of work measured in terms of time or the labour force concept has been followed. This is in accordance with the recommendations of International Labour Office (ILO) and is generally followed in most of the countries. The classification of population as 'workers' and 'non-workers' based on the concept of work was introduced in the 1961 census.

In the *1971 census* every person was asked what his 'main activity' was i.e. how he or she engaged himself mostly. On the basis of this question, the population was divided into two broad streams of main activity as *'workers'* and *'non-workers'*. The reference period adopted was one week prior to the date of enumeration in the case of regular work in trade. A person was a main worker. If he had participated in any such regular work on any one of the days during this reference period and this had been treated as his main activity.

In the case of seasonal workers, a person's main activity was ascertained with reference to such work in the last one year, even if the person was not economically active in the week prior to the enumeration.

With these changes in the concepts, the 1971 census registered a sharp decline in the work participation rate (WPR) defined as the percentage of workers among the total population, as compared to the 1961 census.

In the *1981 census,* the economic questions were formulated so as to first divided the population into:

(i) workers, those who had worked any time at all during the year preceding the census; and

(ii) non-workers those who had not worked at all during the year.

Having classified the population into these broad groups, an attempt was made to sub-divide those who had worked anytime into two groups.

(i) 'Main workers' i.e. those who had worked in some economic activity for the major part of the year i.e. for a period of six months (183 days) or more and

(ii) 'Marginal Workers' i.e. those who had worked for some time during the last year but not for the major part.

An attempt was also made to find out whether those who were non-workers or those who were marginal workers—were seeking or available for work.

Thus, a trichotomy of persons into mutually exclusive groups of *'main workers', 'marginal workers'* and *'non-workers'* was introduced in the *1981 census.* A uniform reference period of *'one year'* preceding the enumeration was adopted for recording activity status in the 1981 census, irrespective of whether the activity was 'seasonal' or 'regular'.

While formulating the economic questions in the *1991 census,* it was decided to adopt the same long reference period of 'one year' for both seasonal and regular activities besides continuing the concepts and definitions used in the 1981 census. Further it was also adopted *to incorporate the words 'including unpaid work on farm or in family enterprises' to the main question relating to the work—with a view to capture the unpaid contribution by women and children in their family farms and family enterprises.*

In order to capture women's work in the informal sector falling within the Census' definition of work, special efforts were made during the 1991 census by improving the economic questions in the household schedules and by training the enumerators for capturing the information. Wide publicity was given in the print and electronic media to sensitise the women respondent in the census enumeration. This paid of dividends in terms of increased female work participation rates.

The questions which are included in the Individual-Slip to elicit information on the economic characteristics of the population including the 'unpaid work' are given below:

Q. 14A. Did you work any time at all last year (Including unpaid work on farm or in family enterprises)?

Yes
No(H/ST/D/R/B/I/O)

(see below for full forms)

Q. 14B. If 'yes' in 14A, did you work for major part of last year? Yes/No

(*"Major Part"* means more than six months or 183 days. It is thus the concept of time which determines the economic activity status.)

Q. 15A. Main activity last year?

'Yes' in 14B (C/AL/HHI/OW)
'No' in 14B (H/ST/D/R/B/I/O)

(For those who said they worked for more than six months in the last year, the major activity is classified into four categories:)

For Workers:

Cultivators (C)
Agricultural Labourers (AL)
Workers in Household Industry (HHI)
Other Workers (OW)

For Non-Workers, the categories are as follows:

Household Duties (H)
Students (ST)
Dependents (D)
Retired Persons (R)
Beggars (B)
Inmates of Institutions (I)
Other Non-workers (O)

Q. 15A. (contd.) If (Household Industry Worker) or (Other Worker) in 15A—give the following details?

Name of Establishment
Nature of Industry, Trade of Service
Description of Work
Class of Worker

(*"Description of Work"* refers to occupation, irrespective of the type of industry, trade or profession. For example, the enumerator should take care to see that there are no vague entries like "Government Service". The details of work should be given, such as "peon", "tehsildar" or "Section officer". *"Class of Worker"* refers to the following four categories: employer, employee, single worker, family worker, (i.e. working without wages or salary in cash or kind).

Q. 15B. 'Yes' in 14B—Any other work anytime last year?
Yes (C/AL/HHI/OW/NO)

'No' in 14B—work done any time last year (C/AL/HHI/OW)

(Meant for workers: Any other work anytime last year. This will net secondary work. (For non-workers as defined in QA. 14B,): Work done any time last year. This will also give an idea of the extent of marginal work. The details of work will be recorded in the same manner as in the case of workers.)

Q. 16A. If 'No' in Q. 14A. Seeking/available for work Yes/No

(Meant for non-workers (as defined in Q. 14A. The objective is to measure the extent of open unemployment.)

Q. 16B.If 'Yes' in Q. 16A.: Have you ever worked before? Yes/No.

(Meant for unemployed persons)

In order to ensure that the economic activity of unpaid workers on farm or in family enterprise (women and children are the predominant constituents of this workforce) is properly enumerated in the 1991 Census, the instructions to census enumerators were expanded and emphasis was laid on the need to ask 'probing questions' regarding the work done at any time at all last year or any of the seasons in the reference period especially in the case of women. The concepts adopted in the 1991 census are described below to facilitate ready reference.

Work is defined as 'participation in any economically productive activity. Such participation may be physical or mental in nature. Work involves not only actual work but also effective supervision and direction of work. It also includes unpaid work on farm or in family enterprise.

Reference Period In all the questions except Question 16B, the reference period is one year preceding the date of enumeration. For Question 16B, the reference period is any time before the date of enumeration.

Main Workers are those who had worked for the major part of the year are termed as main workers. By major part of the year is meant 6 months (183 days) or more.

Marginal Workers are those who had not worked for the major part of the year, i.e., those who had worked for less than six months (183 days) in the year are termed as marginal workers.

Comparison with ILO's Concept

According to Resolution No. 1 of the 13th International Conference of Labour Statisticians 1982, the 'economically active population comprises persons of either sex, who furnish the supply of labour for the production of economic goods and services as defined by the United Nations systems of national accounts and balances, during a specified time reference period. According to these systems, production of economic goods and services includes all production and processing of primary products whether of the market, for barter or for own consumption, the production of all other goods and services for the market and, in the case of households which produce such goods and services of the market, the corresponding production for own consumption.

Thus according to this definition, economic activities can be market activities or non-market activities. Market activities are those in which one produces goods or services for pay or for profit. The non-market economic activities are:

— Production of primary commodities for own consumption.
— Processing of primary commodities for own consumption.
— Own account production of fixed assets.

The Census of India recognises production for own consumption in cultivation as economic activity. The term *Cultivation* in the Census, covers only growing of certain crops such as cereals, millets, sugar cane etc. Growing of plantation crops, vegetables, flowers and other crops are not included under cultivation. Growing of such crops if done, exclusively for home consumption, is not considered as economic activity in the Census. Processing of primary commodities for own consumption and own account production of fixed assets are also excluded from the purview of economic activity in the Census. In other words, with the exception of cultivation, the census does not include the non-market economic activities as work.

Comparison with the Concept of "Work" Adopted by NSSO

The NSSO has defined 'work' or 'gainful activity' as the activity pursued for pay, profit or family gain or in other works, the activity which adds value to the 'national products. Normally it is an activity which results in production of goods and services for exchange. However, all activities in the 'agricultural sector' (Section 0 of the NIC) in which a part or whole of the agricultural production is used for own consumption and does not go for sale are also considered as gainful. In short, work is defined as any market activity and any non-market activity relating to the agricultural sector.

As in the Census, attending to household chores does not constitute work or gainful activity in the NSSO. Further, both in the Census and in the NSS, beggars, prostitutes etc. are not considered as workers even though they may have some earnings.

The NSSO have adopted three different approach to measure employment and unemployment. The three approaches are:

— usual status approach with a reference period of 365 days preceding the date of survey.
— current weekly status approach with a reference period of seven days preceding the date of survey.
— current daily status approach with each day of the seven days preceding date of survey as the reference period. Strictly speaking, this approach attempts classification of person days and not persons.

Of the above approaches, the measurement of employment and unemployment based on the usual status approach is the one that can be broadly compared with the Census. The usual status approach has a reference period of one year. In this approach, the activity on which a person had spent relatively longer time of the preceding 365 days prior to the date of survey is considered to be the principal status of the person. Accordingly, a person's principal usual status is considered as working or employed, if he or she was engaged during the reference period of 365 days, in any one or more of the work activities. A person is considered as 'seeking or available for work' or 'unemployed', if he or she was not working but was either seeking or was available for work for a relatively longer period of the specified reference period. A person is considered as 'not in labour force,' if he or she was engaged for a relatively longer period in any one of the non-gainful activities. Within the two broad activities, 'working' and 'not in labour force,' the detailed activity category is determined on the basis of time spent criterion. A person categorised as 'worker' on the basis of his or her principal status is referred to as 'principal status worker'. A 'non-worker', who pursued some gainful activity in a subsidiary capacity is referred to as 'subsidiary status worker'. Principal status workers and subsidiary status workers together constitute 'all workers' according to the usual status classification of the NSSO.

As will be apparent from the foregoing description of the classification of workers by the NSSO according to the usual status approach, there is a subtle but important difference in the concept of 'work' adopted by the Census and NSSO, particularly in the case of non-market activities and also in the minimum period in the year for which a person should work to be labeled as employed. In view of the differences it is not proposed to compare the results of the NSSO's 43rd round with the provisional results of the 1991 census in this paper. When the final figures regarding persons seeking/available for work based on the 1991 census tabulation are brought out, a comparison of the labour force as per the 1991 Census and the NSS data could be attempted.

Estimates of Value Added to GDP if Women's Unpaid House-work were Included

The *World's Women—Trends and Statistics,* 1970-90—quotes the estimated value of the unpaid house work in India as 33 per cent of GDP in 1970. It also records 35 per cent in Pakistan in 1975; 11 per cent in Philippines in 1982; 23 per cent in Canada; 60 in Denmark; 81 in Finland in 1979; and 24 per cent in USA in 1980. The Indian estimate of 33 per cent made by Mukherjee, in his study on "Contribution to and use of social Product by Women" (1988) which appeared in ILO's Report on "Economic Evaluations of Unpaid Household

Work: Africa, Asia, Latin America and Oceania—Women, Work and Development-14 (1989)". The method followed by Mukherjee to estimate the value of house-wise' services, is as follows:

— No. of House Wives: 90 million (1981 census)

(multiplied by)

— Average Annual Contribution per worker to NDP: (Computation of CSO India, 1981)

(a) NDP per worker in agriculture : Rs. 1282
(b) NDP per worker in overall national : Rs. 1884

— Imputed value of Housewives services:

Rs. in million	*NDP*	*Percentage(*)*
(a) 115880	845190	33
(b) 169560	845190	49

* NDP 345, 190.

To conclude, unpaid work down by women at home and on the farm could push up net Domestic Product by 49% and only on the farm by 33%. Surely this is a very substantial value of women's work.

22

Patterns of Women's Labour

Each of the women interviewed as part of the study gave an account of her 'employment career', in which she described her moves in and out of the wage labour force and the nature of her experiences as an employee. In giving this account, the women also supplied information about the organisation and division of domestic labour within their family households, and about other networks of support upon which they had relied at various times. This chapter, in which the women interviewed are first introduced, describes the patterns of labour which they had adopted, and indicates some of the social factors by which these patterns were shaped. It also includes some material from the women's accounts of their motives, feelings, and attitudes with regard to changing jobs and to decisions to leave or re-enter the paid labour force. Where possible, we use the women's own words to illustrate my account, and in doing this, I hope to convey some sense of them as individuals. (The name used is fictitious in every case, with each woman being given a different pseudonym.) The chapter is concluded with the first of the three portraits, in the form of a 'coda'. In subsequent chapters I consider strategies for employment, looking both at characteristics of women's strategies for employment, looking both at characteristics of women's labour and aspects of the labour market, and at the social relations of household work.

The majority of the women (75 per cent) had followed in their employment careers a pattern which has been well documented by sociologists and recognised by policy makers as the conventional one for married women. Broadly, it consists of entry into the labour force as a full-time employee on leaving school or college, and continuing this formal participation in economic life through the period of courtship and marriage, leaving the labour force only when the birth of the first child is expected. There then follows a shorter or longer spell devoted exclusively to household responsibilities, and above all to child rearing which is followed by a return to participation in the formal labour market, sometimes as a full-time, but very frequently as a part-time employee. A significant minority of the women in the study (25 per cent) broke with this more conventional pattern: their employment careers are discussed in detail later in this chapter. The fact that most followed the 'dominant' pattern described above should not mislead us into thinking there is nothing to be said about them, however, and in the section which follows we present sociologically significant information about their employment careers.

THE DOMINANT PATTERN OF WOMEN'S EMPLOYMENT CAREERS

The First Phase: Employment Patterns before Birth of First child

Most of the forty-eight women in this group left school at an early opportunity with no formal qualifications and immediately entered employment, although a few passed some examinations or went on to some form of higher education *(Tables 22.1, 22.2, 22.3, and 22.4).* A quarter of those who entered the labour force on leaving school stayed in their first job until they left employment several years later when expecting their first child. Only two of these had any educational qualifications, and all but one gave up her job when expecting her first child. (In most cases this first pregnancy was unplanned.)

How did they feel about their fist jobs? Most claimed to have enjoyed them, although with the benefit of hindsight, some respondents were able to recognise the limitations of their jobs:

> *Heather (on clerical work):* 'I enjoyed it while I was there...looking back on it...it was completely unproductive with no room for initiative or anything like that.'

The majority had received some form of training in these initial jobs, with the exception of two factory workers (who had less positive memories of their jobs) and one of the clerical workers.

TABLE 22.1

Age of School Leaving—Dominant Pattern

School leaving	*No.*
Left at 15	28
Left at 16	14
Stayed beyond 16	6
All	48

TABLE 22.2

Destination on Leaving school—Dominant Pattern

Destination	*No.*
Employment	40
Secretarial college	6
Teacher training college	1
University	1
All	48

Three-quarters of the direct entrants to employment, however, changed their jobs at least once before leaving the labour market to raise children. *Table 22.5* indicates the reasons given by these thirty women for their job changes. I have categorised the reasons given for changing or leaving jobs as follows: *instrumental* (for better pay and/or benefits), *family* (in order to fulfil obligations to parents or husbands, or to care for dependent children), *dissatisfaction* (because dissatisfied with working conditions, treatment at work or nature of duties), *travel* (to obtain more conveniently situated work), *social* (because dissatisfied with social contacts at work), *sexual harassment* (to escape unwanted sexual attentions at work), *redundancy, education* (to obtain further education or training), and *health* (of the woman concerned).

TABLE 22.3

Formal Qualifications Before Entering Employment—Dominant Pattern

*Level of qualifications**	*No.*
No qualifications	31
Secretarial qualifications only	3
CSE grades only	1
One or more GCE 'O' level pass	10
One or more gce 'A' level pass	3
All	48

* Highest qualification obtained.

TABLE 22.4

First Occupations of direct Entrants to The Labour Force-Dominant Pattern

Occupation	*No.*
Clerical workers	14
Sales workers	10
Factory operatives	6
Hairdressing apprentices	3
Miscellaneous*	7
All occupations	40

* Miscellaneous = telephonist, waitress, children's nurse, dressmaker, window-dresser.

For many (seventeen of the thirty), changing their job had also involved changing their occupation. The case of Caroline, who began a hairdressing apprenticeship on leaving school, but was unhappy in her job and left, before completing her training, to become a sales assistant, illustrates this kind of job change. Those who changed jobs were mostly motivated by instrumental and family reasons, but other reasons were also important, as can be seen in Table 22.6 and 22.7 overleaf.

TABLE 22.5

Reasons for Job Changes*—All Direct entrants to The Labour Force

Reason for change	*No. of changes*	*No. of respondents*
1	2	3
Instrumental	21	13
Family	18	14
Dissatisfaction	8	7
Travel	7	7
Dismissal	6	2
Social	5	4
Sexual harassment	3	3
Redundancy	3	3
Don't know/miscellaneous	5	5
Total	76	30

* Taking the 'main' reason given; obviously changing jobs may be the result of a variety of complex casual factors.

As already suggested, eight of the forty-eight women did not enter the labour force directly on leaving school, but engaged in some form of further education. Did their experience differ in any other important ways from the rest? The most striking differ in any other important ways from the rest? The most striking difference is that none of these eight women moved from one type of work to another during their first phase of participation in the labour force. All but one, however, changed her job at least once over this period, during which time the eight women had between them a total of twenty-three jobs. The six who went to secretarial college all found employment in clerical and secretarial jobs, and Jenny, who went to teacher training college, worked as a teacher. Frances, who went to university, dropped out at the end of her first year, partly because she failed her examinations, and partly because she had married. Her two spells of employment following this, and prior to the birth of her first child, were both in sales jobs. Another important difference between this group and the other women who had changed their employment during the first employment phase, is that *family* reasons were overwhelmingly the ones given for their job changes (see Table 22.8). These related primarily to marriage and husbands' job changes, but parents' job changes and health also played a part. Instrumental reasons, the most important explanation of job changes for the other thirty women, played a very significant part in shaping the early employment patterns of those who had gone on to further or higher education.

The detailed information given above (Table 22.5, 22.6, 22.7 and 22.8) is summarised below in Table 22.9, which indicates the relative importance of the various reasons for changing jobs given by all those in the 'dominant' group who had two or more jobs during this first phase of their employment careers.

TABLE 22.6

Reasons for Job Changes—Direct Entrants to the Labour Force who had more than One Occupation

Reason for change	*No. of changes*	*No. of respondents*
Family	12	10
Instrumental	11	8
Dismissal	6	2
Dissatisfaction	5	4
Travel	4	4
Redundancy	2	2
Social	1	1
Sexual harassment	1	1
Education	1	1
Health	1	1
Don't know	1	1
Total	45	17

TABLE 22.7

Reasons for Job Changes, by Type of Work—Direct Entrants to the Labour Force who had Only One Occupation

	No. of Changes				
Reason for change	*Clerical workers*	*Sales workers*	*Factory workers*	*No. of all*	*Respondents*
Instrumental	7	3	0	10	5
Family	2	3	1	6	4
Social	3	1	0	4	3
Dissatisfaction	2	1	0	3	3
Travel	3	0	0	3	3
Sexual harassment	0	1	1	2	2
Redundancy	1	0	0	1	1
Don't know/ Miscellaneous	1	0	1	2	2
Total	19	9	3	31	13

TABLE 22.8

Reasons for Job Changes—Women who Engaged in Further or Higher Education

Reason for change	*No. of changes*	*No. of respondents*
Family	9	7
Dissatisfaction	2	2
Social	2	2
Redundancy	1	1
Instrumental	1	1
Total	15	7

TABLE 22.9

Reasons for Job Changes—All Those Who had More Than One Job

Reason for change	*No. of changes*	*No. of respondents*
Family	30	21
Instrumental	22	14
Dissatisfaction	10	9
Travel	7	7
Social	7	6
Dismissal	6	2
Redundancy	4	4
Sexual harassment	3	3
Don't know/miscellaneous	5	5
Total	94	37

Leaving the Labour Market to Raise Children

If the process by which women leave the labour market in order to raise children is to be understood, it is important to know to what extent, if at all, their departure from paid employment has been a consciously planned event. Women in the study were therefore asked to disclose whether the birth of their first child had been 'planned' or not. Twenty-three of the women in this group said their pregnancies had been planned, while twenty said they had been 'unplanned'. (The five women who did not give this information, or who claimed to have left the matter to 'chance' are not discussed in this section.)

All but four of those who had planned their pregnancies had conceived their first child at roughly the time they desired (The remainder all had some years to wait). On average, they had been in the labour force for about seven and a half years when they left to have their first baby. The plans which these women had made (often jointly with their husbands) frequently took into account such factors as a desire to have children whilst they were still relatively young, and a recognition that they were 'settled' as a couple.

> *Christine:* 'We had decided about then—we had our own house as soon as we got married, and we gradually sort of spent the four years...getting it all together...and we had decided that the time had come to start a family.

Some of the women had mixed feelings about giving up their jobs to start a family, recognising the passing of a relatively carefree phase of their lives, whilst others had looked forward to motherhood without reservations.

> *Tessa:* 'I was really pleased—I couldn't wait to leave work. I think it was—at that particular time—it was really what I wanted. I wanted the home and the family and I wasn't interested in going out to work or earning a living or anything.'

> *Elizabeth:* 'I was a little bit reluctant to leave [my employers], but, you know, it was just one of those things, I mean I wanted a family just as well, so I had to make the choice.'

Only Carol disclosed that at the time having a baby was more her husband's wish than her own.

> *Carol:* 'We got to the stage that I was doing supervision and my husband could see the point that if I didn't soon leave, I wouldn't want to leave at all. There were people [at work] that were saying "You could go a long way...there's a lot you could do.... 'And he could see the point that I wouldn't want to leave—I would turn into a career person. He said, "I think we ought to start a family."'

Whilst their pregnancies and withdrawal from the labour force were thus in some sense 'planned', the idea of also planning for a return to employment had clearly not occurred to most of them.

> *Teresa:* 'I didn't [think about it] at that time, no...I suppose I thought when my children were off hands I would go out to work.... But I didn't even think of it then.

Several had thought of returning to employment when their children started school or were old enough to look after themselves, and one or two seven said that they had definitely intended to seek a job at this stage. However, none had made any plans about how she would organise this. Nevertheless, the average length of time spent out of the labour force before the first return to paid work was just under three years, and almost a third had less than eighteen months out of employment.

There were four women whose first child was 'planned' but who had to wait a number of years before conceiving. By the time these women left the labour force to raise children, they had been members of it for, on average, almost eleven years. All had been very happy when, after what was often a rather distressing period in their lives, they finally became pregnant. Although one began doing seasonal farm work when her child was only a few months old, the other three all had a much longer break of between four and a half and six and a half years out of the labour force.

Twenty of the women in this group had a first child as the result of an unplanned pregnancy. The average age of these respondents on the birth of their first child was just under 20 years, and the average length of time spent as members of the labour force before the child was born was just over four years. Five of the women in this group disclosed that they had become pregnant before marrying, and of these, two did not marry until after the child was born.

Despite the fact that their pregnancies had been unplanned, the women in this group expressed views about having a first child and giving up their jobs which were very similar to those expressed by the women whose first pregnancies had been planned. Many accepted their situation quite happily, and most either expected to be out of the labour force for some years, or had no thought about any future return to work.

BARBARA: 'Well, I'd always wanted children.... I thought perhaps that eventually I might get another job, but I didn't intend to work when the children were small. It was a struggle, butt didn't intend to anyway...it was...just a matter of drifting along.'

Pru: 'No, I didn't...it was purely accidental—I was quite shocked—it always happened to somebody else...quite honestly, I was on cloud nine—I thought I would never have to go to work again in my life.'

The main difference between the women with unplanned pregnancies, and the women who had planned their first child was that a minority (four of the twenty) had experienced very negative feelings about their situation. In some cases the feelings stemmed from a sense of being unprepared to start on family life, in others from a reluctance to give up a job.

Margaret: 'I felt terrible. I felt I was too young to have a child really. I liked my job so much and I wasn't really very happy about having a baby at all.'

Jenny: 'Not very happy—we were living in a rented flat.., and it wasn't big enough to 'bring up a baby in...we wanted to own our own house.., it came a bit soon.... We didn't know what we were going to do...eventually, it got round that we could afford to buy a house.., and it just arose, really, that I was going to go back to work' (Jenny did not leave the labour force until the birth of her second child.)

Return to the Labour Force

By definition, the women whose employment careers had followed the 'dominant' pattern all moved from the first employment phase (described above) into a period outside the paid labour force. During the latter period, they were almost exclusively engaged in domestic labour,, principally the bearing and rearing of young children. In considering their subsequent return to the labour force, as mothers seeking employment, it becomes necessary to distinguish between three groups, each of which has a different set of experiences.

The first consists of women who have only one child. Their return to paid employment is a relatively straightforward affair often a once-and-for-all event. The return to paid work came sooner than many had originally anticipated, in most cases within three years. The initial return was usually prompted by either financial pressures or a perceived need for social contacts, or a combination of both.

For many of these women, some unanticipated aspect of their lives as young, mothers prompted an early return. Gail was separated from her husband when her child was about a year old, and decided then to return to full-time employment.

Gail: 'I decided that if I ever wanted to be as independent... I would have to go back to work and get some money together.'

Another young mother found to her surprise that she was not perfectly content with being at home all day with a small baby.

> *Shirley:* 'I don't like a lot of female company, so coffee mornings, tupperware parties—all of that—I just couldn't take, and basically that's the only thing you can do when you're at home with a baby...and nothing annoyed me more than somebody coming round and talking about how they washed their nappies, or something—it's just not me... I couldn't stand it...plus, I didn't like not being able to barn my own money.'

For others, the decision to take a paid job was prompted by both financial difficulties and a desire to escape the isolation of housework.

> *Alison:* 'Mainly it was the money—we needed the extra money—and I was bored to tears at home.., although I had my daughter, it seemed I'd never, ever seen anybody, I was indoors with my daughter all day.'

One of the women, however, was prompted to return to paid work after only six months out of the labour force because of financial circumstances alone.

> *Marion:* 'The only reason I've come back out again is because (my husband's] overtime was cut... I didn't have any choice...we were on a tight budget anyway, so there was really no question—either he had to get another job, or I did. And it seemed better that I should, because he already works six days, and for tax reasons as well...it was better that I did.'

About a third of these women took temporary or seasonal jobs at first, but once the return to permanent jobs had been made, job changes tended to be prompted by a variety of factors: instrumental family, redundancy, personal health, and dissatisfaction. Wendy's account provides several illustrations of why women may change their jobs. She explained her move in 1971 from a part-time job as a shop assistant, to a full-time one in the school meals service.

> *Wendy:* 'Well, we'd had a lot done to the house, and we'd used up any money we'd had, and really more than 2 a week was needed then—so someone said, "Try school meals", and at that time they were very short of staff and they were glad of anybody.'

Wendy stayed in the school meals service for eight years, accepting promotion to assistant cook during this time. Why did she eventually leave to become a full-time sales assistant?

> *Wendy:* 'Well, school meals is really going down...and down...and down. When I first went in, the meals were—they had the best of everything and skimp.... I know school meals have always had a bad name, but it's not a case of how the meals were cooked. I mean, a lot of care and a lot of pride was taken in the meals themselves, especially where we were...and I enjoyed it like that.., it was excellent, and the money was good...but then the money didn't alter, and I mean the conditions got worse...staff left...they were not replaced, and so your conditions were worse...equipment wasn't replaced...and the pride.— I mean to them it didn't matter any more — you made do and mend...and now instant things are coming in...and what really made me decide to get [another] job was I was in charge, and I think we were really short of staff, and

six came from...top level and walked into the kitchen, purely looking at how we were working, and not one single one spoke. They looked round the kitchen, noses in the air, and they were just standing there, and I thought "this is it, out!"—no way do you have to work under those conditions.'

Wendy's vivid description of her progressive disillusionment with this job demonstrates her active membership of the labour force. Pride in her work, the need for her skills to be recognised, unwillingness to put up with being treated as if she were a machine rather than a person, all suggest a commitment to her job which breaks with the more conventional image of female employees as very passive members of the labour force. This attitude was by no means uncharacteristic of the majority of my respondents.

Clare's account of her employment career illustrates the commitment felt by many of my respondents to both their families and their job responsibilities. She explained why she resigned her job as a sales assistant when she was finding it necessary to have frequent time off because of her daughter's health.

Clare: 'I worked from May until...December, then again (my daughter] started having trouble, and I gave my notice in and said it wasn't fair—although [the Staff Manageress] did say to me that they would be prepared for me to have time off whenever she was ill, but I didn't think it was fair to the other girls. I mean.., it wasn't a long-term illness, but it used to spring up overnight and she'd be really ill for three or four days, and then be OK again.... I just didn't think it was fair to the company or to the girls I worked with to have to cover me.'

For almost all of those with one child, the kind of employment obtained after the break for childcare was of lower status and less well paid than that held beforehand. The post-childrearing phase typically included agricultural, domestic and catering, and sales employment, while the pre-childrearing phase had typically included clerical and secretarial, and sales employment.

The experience of women with larger families was different in several important respects, and these women form the second and third categories in the discussion here. The second group consists of those who took paid jobs in between the births of at least two of their children (about two-thirds of those with two or more children). For them, the 'return' to employment was not a single event, but involved a series of moves in and out of the tabour market.

The majority of them had two children, while others had three or four. For most of those with two children, there had been only a short gap (of between eighteen months and three years) between the two births. However, in a few cases the gap was longer, either because the second child was unplanned, or because there was a child from each of two marriages. For the women with three or four children, the longest gap between births was normally that preceding the last child—which in several cases represented an unexpected, and initially unwanted, addition to the family. Nearly all the women took paid employment between the births of each of their children. Most commonly this work was agricultural labour ('field-work'), often of a seasonal and casual nature, or domestic and catering work. Factory jobs, and sales and clerical employment were also quite common. Most jobs were taken on a part-time or seasonal basis, and usually the first return to employment occurred within a year.

Overwhelmingly, the motivation for taking a job at this stage was the need to supplement the family's income. At this point in their lives, most of the women were married to men in relatively poorly paid or insecure occupations—construction workers, semi-skilled manual workers, tradesmen, drivers, etc. The few husbands who were in occupations with relatively good potential earning power (police officers, technicians, and a surveyor) were all at the outset of their careers, or in the process of moving into those jobs from less secure ones, and thus not earning high wages when their children were small. Most of the women were quite frank about their reasons for taking a paid job at this time.

> *Maria:* '[My son] must have been about three or four months...and then I went out to work again...it was a situation where we bought our own home, and financially he needed support, so I went out to work...a part-time job, to help towards the home.'

> *Cheryl:* 'I had an early morning job when I used to take my eldest one with me. That was cleaning in a pub.... She was about fourteen months.., we needed the money...my husband's wage was about £18 a week then (1968).'

Several women had been unsupported by a husband at this time, either because they were as yet unmarried, or because their marriages had broken down.

> *June:* 'I did a little cleaning job, which was three days a week...for about two hours, I suppose, every morning...and then from there I used to go on the strawberry fields. [My daughter was] about three, I would say.., she used to come with me.... At this time I was on my own.

Some acknowledged that for them there were other motivations besides purely instrumental ones:

> *Elizabeth:* 'She was ten months [when I went back to work] money got tight.., there wasn't that much to keep me occupied really, and she was a devil when she was a baby, so I was quite glad to leave her in some ways.'

For those women who had more than two children, the arrival of a third or final child sometimes disrupted what had been the mother's gradual return to full participation in the employed labour force. Dawn, for example, had only just returned to her career in hairdressing after a seven-year break, when she had to leave because of a third, unplanned, pregnancy. She has not since returned to this occupation, feeling that her skills have subsequently become 'rusty' and old-fashioned. Pat's fourth pregnancy and temporary withdrawal from paid work came just as she had established herself in a permanent part-time job as a hospital bed-maker, following a number of years when she had only been able to undertake evening or seasonal work because of her family's needs.

Thus for two-thirds of those with two or more children, raising a family had by no means meant a complete withdrawal from the employed labour force. Much of the employment discussed above will not, of course, have been included in any official statistics on employment, but it is no less real or important for that. It should, however, serve as a reminder of the need to exercise great caution in interpreting official data about women's paid employment. For these women, finding a way of supplementing the family's income, by selling some of their labour power for wages, was an important part of what they saw as their family responsibilities. Most were only too well aware that if they were not earning their families' standards of living would drop significantly and they might well sink into poverty.

The third category contains women who remained out of paid employment until they had completed their families, just over a third of those with two or more children. The majority of those in this category had been in employment for over four years when they left the labour force to raise children, and on average had spent about eight-and-a-half years out of the labour force looking after their families. As one would expect, the women with larger families tended to stay out of the labour force for longer than those with only two children.

When interviewed, all but two of the women were married and living with their first husband. In contrast to those in the second category, most of these women were married to men in white-collar occupations with relatively high earnings—technicians, managers, and administrators, for example. The fact that their husbands had been bringing home relatively good wages had obviously been important in enabling the women to stay out of the employed labour force whilst raising their young families, and in enabling them to adopt a particular ideology of family life.

> *Yvonne:* 'I believe that if you have children, then you should look after them, and I stopped at home until they went to school.'

I do not wish to suggest that economic considerations played no part in prompting these women's eventual return to employment. Indeed, for some, the need to earn an income was the decisive factor, placing them in a situation where they felt they had no choice but to get a job.

> *Tessa:* 'I didn't work at all until my second daughter was born. My first marriage had broken up actually when I was still only six months pregnant...and it was necessity rather than anything else. Social Security wasn't very much and my husband's whereabouts were unknown. I took a part-time job in a local estate agents...purely and simply because I needed the money.'

> *Sandra:* 'I (still] had two [pre-school children]...the youngest one and the one I foster... I got a bit fed up with being at home...actually it was a case of having to (get a job], because my husband was out of work at the time.'

Sandra's remark, made apparently only in passing, almost conceals the importance which male unemployment may have for prompting wives to seek work. She was not alone among my respondents in having this motivation.

Christine, on the other Wand, took paid employment outside the home for slightly different reasons.

> *Christine:* We were going through a very dodgy time, you know, marriage-wise, and I was trying to consider what to do...and I thought perhaps if I could get some sort of job, it would make me more financially independent; and help me decide what I would do.'

Others saw employment as a means of achieving a limited, but specific, material objective.

> *Yvonne:* 'I started in September because I wanted to get two bikes for Christmas for them...and I thought I'll just go out to work and earn the money to get that.., and I got a job in a hotel, and I stopped there for five years.'

Several women-first began earning money again without needing to leave their homes, and in a few cases, husbands were active in providing their wives with income-generating work at home.

> *Christine:* 'I used to work sometimes for my husband('s firm) on a casual basis, doing their typing at home—he used to bring it home—and that all started when [the youngest one] was born...instead of getting a temp. in they'd send it home to me.

It would be misleading,, however, to concentrate on financial motives for returning to employment to the exclusion of the other important factors. For a number of women, obtaining a job was a constructive means of escaping their social isolation at home and of defeating their sense of lost identity once their children began to grow older.

> *Teresa:* 'I felt I needed something at that time. I was really getting into a rut at home and I felt I needed to be out. The children were both at school, and I needed... I felt I needed something different, it was really getting me down, so I thought, well, I'd have to do something...and that's when we decided that we'd go for the Christmas period, it would be a break—which several friends had done.... I stayed on there two years.'

How did their first employment on returning to the labour force compare with the jobs they had held prior to having children? Of the seven who had been clerical or secretarial workers before having their children, only one obtained such work when she first took a job afterwards. The rest went into sales jobs, factory work, and other manual jobs. Two other women had jobs with specific skills in their first employment phase: Anne had been a telephonist, and Yvonne a dressmaker. Both re-entered the labour force as domestic workers. The two other women who became domestic workers at this stage had previously been employed in sales and in factory work. Thus for most, the break from employment resulted in a deterioration of their occupational status. Two women, however, were to find higher status occupations on their return to work. Tina, who had originally been a factory worker, found an opening in nursery nursing, while Frances decided to train to 'be a teacher. She explains how she finally reached this decision:

> *Frances:* 'I [had always] said that I wanted at some date, when we were in a suitable place, and knew far enough ahead etc., that I would hopefully go back and do some form of further education, but.., it's a very easy thing to put off unless you've got that extra bit of determination — and obviously [my husband's] leaving was the push I needed.'

The employment patterns of the women with two or more children are also of interest following their return to the labour force *and* the completion of their families. These patterns are best described in relation to the age of the youngest child, whether of pre-school, primary school, or secondary school age.

All but two of the nine women who still had a pre-school child when interviewed had returned to formal, regular employment, most working part—time: only two were in full—time jobs (one as a the other as a hospital domestic) and both of these women had previously done a spell of part-time work. Five of the seven women had been employed in domestic and catering work, and other employment undertaken included clerical and secretarial jobs, sales jobs, agricultural jobs, and childminding. Three of those in regular employment had been in clerical or secretarial jobs prior to having their families—however, when interviewed, only one had returned to using these skills, while the other two were engaged in domestic work.

Seven of the eight women with a youngest child at primary school were in regular, paid employment, while the eighth was a full-time student at a teacher training college. Four were working full-time, and three part-time, and all but one of the full-timers had previously been a part-time employee. Again, manual jobs had predominated in the post childbearing phase. Four of the seven were or had been engaged in domestic work, four in other manual work (in factories and warehouses), and two in agricultural work. However, when interviewed, the seven also included two sales workers, a clerical worker, and a telephonist. Like those with preschool children, many of these women had also been unable to return to their former skills, especially in office work.

About half of those with two or more children (eighteen of the thirty-five) had a youngest child at senior school. Some had children in their late teens, or older ones who had left home. When interviewed, half were employed part-time, and half full-time, and all but one of the full-timers had worked part-time at some previous stage. Their occupations were as shown in *Table 22.10,* although at an earlier stage (after completing their families) seven had done paid work of a seasonal or casual nature, and four had done some kind of home work. Of the eight who had some kind of job-specific skills prior to having their children (clerical, hairdressing, dressmaking, telephonist), four had not obtained work using these skills after completing their families, and a fifth had only done so after taking a TOPS course (Training Opportunities course, funded by the Manpower Services Commission.

TABLE 22.10

Occupations of Selected Respondent* at Time of Interview

Occupation	*No. part-time*	*No. full-time*	*All*
Sales	3	3	6
Domestic and catering	5	4	9
Clerical	1	2	3
All	9	9	18

* Respondents with a youngest child at senior school.

Although a few of the women with two or more children were unsure of their future plans, the vast majority of them fell into one or other of two categories: those who expected to stay in the job they were doing when interviewed until retirement, and who did not intend to seek or accept any promotion or greater responsibility; and those who intended to remain in paid work until retirement, but who also planned to seek promotion, further training, or simply a better job.

How did the women who planned no changes in their employment careers understand their future? Just over half were employed part-time, the rest full-time. A third were in jobs where they had some responsibility, a supervisory role, or recognised seniority over more junior colleagues, while the remainder were in the basic grade in their various occupations—primarily hospital domestics and sales assistants. Many felt that they were happy in their current job, and desired no further changes. Helen for example, a frill-time domestic supervisor in an NHS hospital, was quite clear that she did not want any further promotion. She enjoyed the close contact with staff which her job entailed and knew that any higher grade job would not have this characteristic. She expected to stay in her job 'until I retire'—a further seventeen years if she retired at 60. Nancy, also a domestic supervisor, had similar plans, but emphasised her lack of ambition in relation to her job.

> *Nancy:* '[Promotion] just sort of fell into my lap ... I've never been ambitious, to be quite honest with you, I mean, all I've lived for is my home and my children, but when you are here full-time, it's a long day, so you think...your opportunities are there, and I'm gonna take them m not one to keep changing my job—in my last job I was there eight years, I was made redundant, otherwise I expect I'd still be there I can't see me not working, quite frankly... I can't see that I'll ever be financially well enough [off]...to pack up work 'altogether.'

Teresa, a part-time deputy supervisor in a large retail store, also emphasised that her employment career had to fit into her family life.

> *Teresa:* 'I suppose really you can't be (promoted any further) because I am only a part-

timer.... I think as I am now it suits my family commitments very well... I wouldn't want full-time work ... I'd be quite happy to continue as I am until, I suppose, retirement age.... I think if you have good working conditions, you adapt to them...that would be my only thing, if problems like that arose.'

Those who had basic grade jobs, and who were happy to stay in them, made similar comments.

Dawn: 'I'm happy as I am...but, if they come and ask [if I'd like promotion]... I expect I'd say yes, I'd have a go at it.... I'd stay here, I should think [till retirement]—as I feel now, anyway.' (Dawn was a part-time sales assistant when interviewed.)

Mary would have been glad to have her experience as a part-time clerical assistant recognised by her employers, but was not ambitious in any other respects.

Mary: 'Because I'm part-time, my grades don't go up—I mean, I'm doing a more responsible job within the department, than when I came—but my grades don't go up.... I know it's perhaps silly, but it would be nice for them to say "You've done well, you're now a clerk grade whatever".... I can't really see myself changing...basically, I feel that while the children are at home, you need extra money...but then, the way the situation is now, I think perhaps you'll continue to need extra money... I'll be fully happy to stay where I am.

Another respondent; a part-time domestic, put it quite simply.

Olive: 'I suppose [I'll stay] until I retire...yes, I shall be working until then, yes. I don't think I'd like promotion or anything m quite happy as I am.'

All but two of the women who had no plans to alter their jobs were married women, living with their husbands. The exceptions were Maria, divorced and living with her parents and one of her two small children, and Pru, who lived with her two late-teenage sons and her 'boyfriend'. Maria was not too certain about her future:

Maria: 'I should think [I'll stay] until he goes to school—I can't see myself getting another job and changing it before then...and of course if anything comes of this supervisor [training] thing, then I would stay here and do it.'

Pru also anticipated possible changes in her personal life which might affect her employment career.

Pru: 'The possibilities [for promotion] could be there, but I don't particularly want it.... I don't want any hassles.... I just want... [to stay'] as I am, because it suits home life.... If I could afford to, I'd leave because I prefer to be at home...possibly if I got married again, and finances were different, then I would probably try and leave.'

Nevertheless, many of the women wanted promotion, further training, or a better job. In other words, they were seeking further integration into the labour force. They fall into two categories: those who were already working for employers who made training opportunities readily available, and in jobs where there was an established career structure; and those, mostly in domestic and catering jobs, who recognised that their current jobs held little prospect of improved working conditions or employment opportunities, and who sought a future change of occupation as a result. Tessa, a full-time telephonist, was amongst those to whom job advancement was already available.

> *Tessa:* 'I'm waiting for a vacancy to arise...because I sat an exam and a Board for promotion to Clerical Officer. I mean I could stay here *ad infinitum* and just do the same job, which I'm not really prepared to do...but I could go there as a clerical officer, and Then do another exam perhaps and become an Executive Officer or a Higher Clerical Officer...really. I would like to...it's more of a challenge, and you're using a bit more of—your brainpower.... I like this job very much, but it doesn't require a lot of initiative, as long as you're polite and tactful and know your procedures, it doesn't require an awful lot more from you.'

Heather, a supervisor in a retail store, had set her sights relatively high. She had returned to full-time paid employment once her two children were both at school.

> *Heather:* 'I shall stay here till I retire...that's twenty-five years.... [After I'd been here a while] I thought I'd like to make a career of it, I'd like to go into supervision, when I then did.... I was promoted quite quickly—I intend to go on further, too.'

Maureen, a full-time personal secretary employed by a large paper-making firm, also wanted more than 'just a job', as her discussion of future plans illustrates. She felt fairly confident of obtaining more rewarding work with her current employer.

> *Maureen:* 'I wouldn't mind staying with them (until I retire)... If I can alter my job slightly—[to one that's] a bit more interesting, a bit more involvement, then I wouldn't mind staying.'

Anne, like several other women, was currently in a 'dead-end' job at the bottom of the occupational status ladder, and hoped for better employment opportunities in the future.

> *Anne:* 'I only do what I do simply for the money, really, I don't really like the work, you know.... [I'll stay] really until I can find an alternative job that I liked...it's just a matter of if a job was available.... I should think two years would be the limit I'd stay here. It would be a different type of work altogether that I would look for. I'm going to night school in September.... I'm going to take biology—I'm very interested in nursing...that's probably what I will do.'

Pat worked full-time as a hospital domestic, and like Anne, hoped to gain access to employment in nursing at some future date.

Pat: 'I love working here.., but I can't say I like doing what I'm doing. Because it's all mechanical, and, well, you just don't need a brain.... So later on I would like to change... I thought about going as a nursing assistant.'

Although plans for the future might not be achieved, many of these women nevertheless bore little resemblance to the passive members of the labour force which women are so often taken to be. Those who lacked ambition for promotion mostly anticipated participation in the labour force until their retirement, and those who had become well integrated into their employment environment frequently demonstrated considerable determination to 'make something' of their jobs. Carol's and Cheryl's comments about their attitudes to future employment were illuminating. Both lacked the kind of aggressive career ambition which characterises the 'male' stereotype, but neither was willing to accept a definition of their work as passive and non-assertive.

Carol: 'I have been asked to do supervision, but up until now I've never had the confidence to do it But now I'm thinking about it, because my children are getting older and they're [shy] like me, and I want to show them that if you tell yourself you can do it, you can.... [I'll stay] probably until I retired quite like to, because they are a good firm as regards pensions. It would pay me to stay here... I'd be silly to leave really.'

Cheryl: 'I always take it stage by stage... I was an assistant and knew I could do better, and I'm aiming at supervision. When I'm doing supervision I will then contemplate whether I am capable of doing better. But I never sort of say "Oh, I want to be a Departmental Manager"—I would love to, but I've got to take it in stages to see whether I am capable—just increase it gradually come back with the intention of working till I retire.'

The Impact of Marital Breakdown

Fifteen of the forty-eight women whose employment careers had followed the 'dominant pattern' had experienced marital breakdown. Of these, nine had re-married following their divorce. All but two of the fifteen had at least one child when their first marriage ended, including in eight cases a child aged 5 years or younger. What effect, if any, did the break-up of their marriages have upon their employment patterns?

For Angela and Elizabeth, neither of whom had children, the break-up of their first marriage had little effect upon their employment careers. Angela continued working full-time as a secretary, and did not change her job. Elizabeth gave up her job as an audio-typist partly because she could not cope with facing her colleagues at work, and partly because she decided to move back to her parents' home in a different town. However, she only had a short break from employment before going back to work full-time as an office temp., and subsequently taking permanent secretarial employment.

For the eight women who had at least one child aged 5 years or under when their marriage broke down, the event either increased or prompted their participation in the paid labour force. Four had not been to paid employment: of these, two took part-time jobs, and one a full-time job when their marriages ended. The fourth began full-time training to become a teacher. Of those already doing paid jobs, two changed from part-time to full-time hours (but staved with the same employer), one continued in her full-time job, and the remaining one took on additional casual and part-time work.

The remaining five women (whose youngest children were of school age when their marriages ended) had all been in paid employment, three working part-time and two full-time. All remained with their employers, and one of the part-timers went on to full-time work, as she explained.

> *Pru:* 'I got promoted to a supervisor... I did that for about two and a half years...still 5 till 8.... Then, because of finances—I got divorced—I needed more money. I had to take demotion, to go on to the forty hours.'

Paula, a clerical worker and one of the full-timers, stayed full-time, and after her divorce went through (shortly before our interview) applied for promotion to a more senior position.

The evidence of these women suggests that the impact of marital breakdown upon employment careers is fairly straightforward. Existing participation in paid employment tends to be maintained, and is frequently increased from part-time to full-time. Where women have not been engaged in paid work, the break-up of their marriage may prompt them to seek employment Whilst instrumental motives are especially compelling at such a time, and the need to earn an income may appear to be paramount, women also recognise the social importance of their jobs at this stage, when self-esteem and confidence may be at a low ebb. The 'poverty trap' into which women who have access only to low-paid employment or supplementary benefit may fall is one of which such women are well aware. But they may still choose to be at work. One woman who worked part-time explained what had happened to her.

> *Brenda:* 'It wasn't enough to keep me and two children on... I was on Social Security, and I had a few bills that I had a job to pay, and I ended up borrowing off my parents and getting deeper into debt. In fact I went up to Social Security one day, and they turned round and said, "Well, you'd be better off not working."'
>
> *S.Y.: 'How did you feel about that?'*
>
> *Brenda:* 'Oh, I couldn't have given the job up, I had to have something to keep me going.. I thought it was terrible...if I hadn't worked, the actual cash in hand would have been £4 less than what I was getting by working—and bus fares and other expenses were costing more than £4.... If I did extra hours at work, Social Security stopped the extra that I'd earned, so I was no better off by doing any, and I did feel a bit trapped, but there was nothing I could do to get out of it. Even if I was working full-time, I couldn't have—well, at the time, I wouldn't have left the children alone, not for too long anyway, because they were upset as well, and I think they needed me as much as I needed them at the time.'

Brenda's account, which refers to 1976, expresses many of the tensions and ambiguities affecting an unsupported lone parent. She recognises the need for time with her children, but also knows that her job is an important source of social contacts for her, and helps her to structure what at first appears as a shattered lifestyle. She wants to support herself, by earning what she can, but is caught by a bureaucratic social security system which lacks the flexibility to accommodate her particular needs.

A Note on Redundancy and Unfair Dismissal

In discussing patterns of women's labour, it is important to note that whilst many job changes made by women are (in the broadest sense) voluntary—women resign their jobs for personal, family, or instrumental reasons—this is not invariably the case. For the women in my sample, redundancy and dismissal (including various types of what may constitute constructive—and therefore unfair—dismissal) were also features of their employment careers. Almost a third of the forty-eight women in this group had experienced redundancy. Shops or restaurants where they had been working closed down, industrial firms cut back on staff or relocated, small companies went into liquidation. Most accepted their experience of redundancy as simply a fact of an employee's life. Rarely did women mention any kind of resistance to redundancies, and where they did, actions had been unsuccessful. I do not wish to suggest that women in general do not, and have not, put up determined and effective resistance to attempts to deprive them of employment. There are, of course, numerous examples of such action, and the case of women workers at Lee Jeans in Greenock, Scotland, who occupied their factory when threatened with redundancy, provides a recent example (Ryan 1981). However, my respondents had not been involved in such struggles.

In the interviews, women were not questioned closely or routinely about sexual harassment at work—unwanted or intimidating sexual attentions in the workplace—and it is entirely possible that some women had experienced problems of this type, but did not disclose them to me. Nevertheless, three women described incidents leading to their resignation from a job which constituted clear sexual harassment. All had been in their teens at the time of the incident, two still unmarried, and one recently married. Sheila's interview illustrates the tendency for incidents of this type to go unobserved.

> *S.Y.: 'What happened to you when you left school—did you go straight into a job?'*
>
> *Sheila:* 'Yes, I worked at [the paper] Mill—my mother got me a job. The first job I had.., for four months—but it didn't work out.'
>
> *S.Y.: 'What were you actually doing there?'*
>
> *Sheila:* 'Making, well, no—sorting, paper.
>
> S.Y.: 'Why did you leave?'
>
> *Sheila:* 'I left there because—you know, they kept saying, "Oh, your Mum works here", and all this... I didn't like it...you know.'
>
> *S.Y.: 'So you think it was because of that you left, rather than because of the actual work?'*

Sheila: 'I liked the work.... It was the foreman I didn't like...where I worked...he was dirty.'

S.Y.: 'So it was the people that you didn't really get on with?'

Sheila: 'Well, this particular bloke. He used to touch all the young [girls]...when the young ones used to start, they used to start in the cutter house; you know—they was all like fifteen-year-old girls, and he used to—you know—be rude to them. So... I told me mother, and she more or less smacked him in the mouth, and that was one of the reasons I left, you know.'

Barbara's experience was not dissimilar.

S.Y.: 'What happened to you when you first left school?'.

Barbara: 'I went to work in the dispensary at [a large chemist's store]...it wasn't what I wanted to do, so I was there a matter of three or four months I suppose.... I didn't settle in the job.... I felt that everything I did was wrong because I just didn't like what I was doing.... I was shut away in a little cubicle...plus, I didn't like the manager that was there, he was a creep.... I wouldn't have found (the work) difficult if I hadn't had this creepy manager behind me, so I think he was mainly [why I left]...you didn't have a proper office, you were just standing in this cubicle thing where they did the prescriptions, and I mean he was one of these people who'd come and smack your bottom, sort of, and in those days, you didn't turn round and tell him like they would today...he was I think the main reason why I left.'

Brenda was more direct than the other two.

Brenda: 'I worked as a stock control clerk in a garage...up until I was married... I quite enjoyed it.'

S.Y.: 'You said you did that until you got married?'

Brenda: 'Until after I got married.'

S.Y.: 'Why did you leave the job?'

Brenda: 'The stores manager started getting a bit fresh...(laughs)

Thus in factory, shop, and office, these women had been subjected to intolerable pressure of an overtly sexual nature, from men in more senior positions than themselves; and this resulted in their resignation. The kinds of evidence now becoming available concerning sexual harassment[2] would seem to suggest that these three women may represent the tip of the iceberg. The optimism of Barbara's view, that 'nowadays' girls would not put up with the kind of treatment she left her job to escape in the early 1960s would appear to be unjustified by the emerging facts.

Several women disclosed that their employers had offered them an impossible choice about their working hours and conditions, which in effect constituted 'unfair' dismissal. One had been taken on to work evenings as a catering assistant, but later found her employer insisting that she work weekends also. As she had a young family at the time this left her with no choice but to resign her job. Another was forced to leave her job when her firm re-located about fifteen miles away. She was told she could travel daily to the new venue if she liked, and was prepared to work longer hours, but for a woman with both a pre-school and a school-age child, an extra burden of this kind was out of the question. A third woman, working part-time as a merchandiser; was faced with the choice of doubling her hours (to 40 hours per week) or giving up her job. Since full-time hours were impossible for her because of her family commitments, she too had no option but to lose the job.

It may be that one or more of these women would have had a case for unfair dismissal under subsequent legislation. However, it seems likely that they would not have brought a case, even if legally entitled and aware of their right to do so. One of the things employed mothers seek to avoid is 'hassle'. If they are to accommodate the demands of their families and go out to paid jobs; they must organise themselves in order to avoid spending time and effort in unnecessary ways (see subsequent chapters). Most of the women I interviewed lacked the extra energy and determination which would be required to bring legal action for unfair dismissal, regardless of their chances of success.

ALTERNATIVES: WOMEN WHO HAD NOT LEFT THE LABOUR MARKET

Six of the women interviewed had not left the labour market since joining it on completing their school or college education. When interviewed, most were in their late thirties, and all were living with their (first) husbands. Since their continuous commitment to employment breaks with the more common pattern of at least a short period at home with very young children, it is worth examining their experiences in some detail.

Three had left school at 15 with no academic qualifications, two had left at 17 with four or five 'O' levels, but had not gone on to further education, whilst one had left school at 16 with several 'O' levels and 'CSEs', and had subsequently attended secretarial college for a year.

When interviewed, most had been with their current employer for a number of years: three for over twenty years, one for thirteen years, one for five years, and one for just two and a half years. All were in white-collar jobs with established employers, five in clerical occupations (ranging from clerical assistant to accounts supervisor) and the sixth in an administrative grade which was considered to be an executive position. Three had jobs which involved supervising other staff, whilst a fourth had responsibilities which included interviewing members of the public in connection with their requirements for personal financial loans.

Interestingly, none of the six women was following an employment pattern set by her own mother. None of their mothers had been in permanent jobs whilst my respondents were children, and only two of these mothers had permanent occupations outside the home after her family had grown up.

For most, there had been a delay of some years between marriage and the birth of their first child. Two had a first child within three and a half years of marriage, but for two others there was a five-year gap, and in the remaining cases the periods were seven and twelve years. These longer than usual delays between marriage and the first child's birth were significant in explaining their employment patterns.

In three cases, the respondents had planned their families so that they could continue in employment without leaving their jobs.[3] This involved not merely ensuring that the baby was born at a convenient point, but also making arrangements for the child to be cared for once it was born, and in one case, changing her job to one with less responsibility. I shall describe each of these cases in turn.

Sara was born abroad but came to England in 1966 on marriage. Her husband has been in the nursing profession throughout their marriage, and at the time of the interview held a senior position. On arrival in England, Sara did manual work for a couple of years, before obtaining a job as a clerical assistant in a public sector company in 1968. She was subsequently promoted to clerical officer. Her first child was born three and a half years after she joined the company, and she took two months maternity leave.

> *Sara:* 'Well, we discussed it before we had children, and I've never liked the thought of staying at home, you know, I've always wanted children and wanted to work as well. So we discussed it then, you know, whether I would be able to do both. So we said, 'Well, we'll try—if we can't, then I'll pack up', you know. But as it is, we've managed.... He does his share of work, and I do my share.... We decided at first that my husband would go on night duty—we did that for a while.... He went to work at night when I got home, you know.... I found it ever so hard to leave a baby after four weeks, to come back — but it's one of those things—I had to come back'

She goes on to describe how these arrangements were subsequently modified.

> *Sara:* 'We did that for a while, night duties, and we found out we were Just saying 'Good morning', and, you know, going out the house. So, one of my sisters came, to go to college, so he went back on normal working, the shifts—you know, they do one week a morning, one week afternoons—and so my sister was studying at home and looked after the baby for a while, and then he went to do his normal work.... The second one, we did the same—and then my other sister came and we did the same thing—she went to college and helped us out during the day. When I had the third one, she decided she was going to get married, so I had to find a baby minder.... I used to take one to school, one to nursery...and then the other one to the minder, in the morning. But it was very hard, you know—I suppose if you want to do it, you do it.'

Geraldine left school at 15 with no qualifications and took a job as a punch operator. She worked her way up through various grades to a supervisory position, before marrying nine years later. After five years of marriage, she and her husband wanted to start a family.

Geraldine: 'Now a supervisor has a lot of week-end work, a lot of overtime, so I decided to switch to be a clerk, an ordinary clerk.... I found my childminder before I was pregnant.... I used to pop over before the baby arrived, she was the first one to know when I was actually pregnant.'

When the baby arrived, in 1976, she took seventeen weeks' maternity leave. She described her feelings about going back to work.

Geraldine: 'I didn't want to leave him—you don't. It's a terrible wrench. I would never advise anybody to do it—and it's hard, jolly hard, on you, because you're losing your sleep at night...of course you can't breast-feed if you're going back to work after six weeks; it's not fair on the baby, so I had to bottle-feed him.'

Both Geraldine and her husband come from large families, and have chosen to have no more than their one child.

Andrea also left school at 15 with no qualifications. Her father had recently died and she considered herself fortunate to have obtained a job as a telephonist. After about three and a half years she married, and at roughly the same time was promoted to a supervisory post which involved working shifts. Her first baby was born about five and a half years later, according to plan.

Andrea: 'I'd arranged that she would go to a nursery when I came here I was on shift work then, as a supervisor—we used to do different duties, like eight till four, and either my husband or myself used to take her to the nursery in the morning, and one of us used to collect her at night.'

S.Y.: 'And you never considered giving up work at that period?'

Andrea: 'No. I'd always enjoyed work too much.'

The birth of her child was difficult, and because of this she decided not to have any more children—as she put it: 'It's best to have one that's perfectly all right.'

The remaining three women had not planned their pregnancies in quite the same way. Valerie was married for twelve years before the first of her three children was born. After a short spell as a shop assistant on leaving school aged 15, Valerie joined most of her male relatives, who already worked for the same public sector company, as a clerical assistant.

Valerie: 'I think it was just pressure from Mum and Dad. You know, "You ought to get that good little job", and all the rest of it. So I applied.... It's sort of family-orientated really.'

She married a few years later and was subsequently promoted several times. Why had she sought promotions?

Valerie: 'I just felt—I mean, you sort of work here, you just get caught up in it...and, I think,

> well, if I'm out earning, working, I want job interest...so, it was the natural...course of events to some extent...rather than...an inbuilt desire as always wanting to achieve this.'

She described how she came to decide to remain at work when she eventually had her family.

> *Valerie:* 'It was just something at the time. We'd been married twelve years then, and you sort of acquire a lifestyle, and there was no way that we could continue doing the things we'd become accustomed to doing, if you like...and selfishly enough we weren't prepared to give that up. Although we'd wanted a family—had it been forthcoming, you know, in our early years of marriage, when we'd planned it, I would have left work like most mums do, you know, and had the children, and then come back to work But having worked all that time, I was too old to get up and start scratching around really, because—you know, it is hard when you suddenly come down to one wage, and such like...and so we just decided that, you know..., as it happened, my mum would look after them, and so it worked out like that.'

Valerie had three children, and took four months' maternity leave from her job at each birth.

Neither Sally nor Louise had planned to start their families when they did. Before her marriage, Sally was employed for six years in a variety of jobs. A routine clerical job which she left after about a year, mainly through boredom, six months abroad as an au-pair, and several more office jobs, including assistant to a buyer in a large mail order firm, and supervisor of fieldwork in the market research department of a large company, her last job before marriage. This, she felt, was 'probably the best job I've ever had— I was in charge of the interviewers around the country.' On marriage she moved to Kent and left her job. Although she tried to find the same kind of work there, she could find nothing like it, so after a couple of months out of employment she took a job as a shop assistant in a department store.

> *Sally:* 'I stuck it for two weeks—it was utterly boring—in many ways an absolute insult to anybody's intelligence, supervised by a woman who had no sort of intelligence either. The whole thing was a complete waste of time—utterly boring—I really was bored.'

Following this, she succeeded in obtaining part-time employment as a market research interviewer, and was doing this work when she first became pregnant. However, neither this nor her subsequent pregnancy (eighteen months later), nor having two small children, prevented her from continuing this part-time work. The hours (about 20 per week) were flexible—'you just sort of did it in your own time'—and it was possible to make arrangements for the children.

> *Sally:* 'I used to strap ['the children] in the back of the car...and there were quite a few friends who would have them for the odd hour or two—and sometimes, I would take them with me.

She continued in her market research work for about six years, at the same time running her own farm shop. Once her two children were at school, however, she took a full-time clerical job with a local engineering company. She explained why she made this change.

> *Sally:* 'Really because my [self-employed] husband took a [second] job in the evenings.., we did need the money—and he didn't used to get home until about half past eleven, really tired, and things got to the point where the children were both at school and realised that he just couldn't go *on* doing it And I came along here for the interview.... And I sort of took over the earnings, if you like. My husband had to take [the children] to school, and he had to pick them up and he had to make sure they were all right till I got home. That was the arrangement—if I go out to work, he'd have to accept that responsibility.'

She was still working in this clerical job when interviewed, but has subsequently, after about four years there, changed her employer, going first to work full-time as administrative co-ordinator in an advertising agency, and later, after three weeks out of employment following redundancy, taking a part-time clerical/cashier job with a building society (for 20 hours per week).

Louise went to secretarial college after leaving school and worked as a typist with a building society for six years before changing her job on marriage. She explained:

> *Louise:* 'I met [my husband] there.., and you can't work for the same company' so I had to leave...[also] we moved...to London, because he got promoted.'

She described how she came to take her next job.

Louise: It was easy because it was London...I could have had almost any job but the reason—it's stupid really—but the only reason I chose [the company] was that we'd got a flat nearby and it was the most accessible place to get to. And I could get home in the lunch hours and start—you know, newly married, I thought get home and get the vegetables ready, and all this rubbish [laughs]—that lasted for about three days, but that was the idea. I thought... I wouldn't be able to cope with running a house and going up to town... I wanted a nice local job.., it was very close to the flat, so I could nip home at lunchtime and do the shopping, that was why I chose the job.'

Louise's first child was born three and a half years after her marriage. At first she found her pregnancy hard to accept.

> *Louise:* 'I asked, you know, if it was possible to terminate and (the doctor] wasn't very agreeable—but looking back, I probably wouldn't have done it, it was just that—I went to him because I hadn't come on, and he told me that I was pregnant. It was a bit of a shock I did ask, but he—he lied in fact—he told me that I was sixteen weeks gone, and I wasn't, I was nowhere near that, I was about ten[5]...looking back [my husband] would never have agreed to it anyway...to me, having a baby meant staying at home

and washing nappies and things like that'

S.Y.: 'So you thought it was going to mean giving up work?'

Louise: 'End of my life, in fact—yes.'

Through discussing what she saw as her predicament with other people, Louise came to realise that having a child need not mean leaving her job.

> *Louise:* 'I thought about it before he was born. And weighed up lots of possibilities....I got talking to a girl who happened to take my place on maternity leave.., and she told me her child was at a childminder's.... She said, do you want me to put you in touch with this girl? And I went round to see her, and it was very clean, she was registered, obviously... I was happy with her and she was happy with me....he went there before, in fact, he was six months. They were short-staffed at the office, because it was holiday time.'

Louise felt confident that her decision to stay at work and take maternity leave had been the right one for her. She found the period at home with her young baby difficult.

> *Louise:* 'I was not really very happy—my husband used to come home at night, we didn't seem to have anything to talk about...my mum still can't understand it, because she scraped and saved to, you know, bring us...up, and she feels that if she could do it—and they had no money at all—she doesn't see why I shouldn't.'

Since returning to work from her maternity leave, Louise has moved from London to Kent (because her husband has been promoted in his job). When this happened she was able to obtain a transfer within her firm, and had three weeks' leave of absence at the time of removal. During this time, she was able to make arrangements with another registered childminder for her son. Louise would like to work part-time, but her employers have a full-time only policy, and as she has been unable to find suitable alternative employment, she has chosen to reduce her workload by employing domestic help at home for four hours per week

These six women, whose attachment to the labour force has been virtually unbroken since they joined it on leaving full-time education, all showed evidence of an active commitment to paid employment. They had relatively few employers and most were currently well-satisfied with their pay, working conditions and with the nature of their jobs. Most had been able to take advantage of opportunities for promotion, and all planned to remain in employment until retirement. All referred to some difficulties in combining full-time paid jobs with raising children, but with the support of either husbands and other relatives, paid help, or the cooperation of friends and employers, these had not proved insuperable, and none suggested that she regretted the decision to remain in employment The choices they made might not always be ones which other women would select, but many might benefit from a genuine opportunity to consider remaining in paid work as an option.

ALTERNATIVES: SOME EFFECTS OF INDIVIDUAL BIOGRAPHY

Whilst most of the women interviewed had employment careers which followed the 'dominant' pattern described at the start of this chapter, and a minority' chose to remain in paid work despite changes in their family' lives, a further minority had employment careers which were quite clearly affected by the special circumstances of their personal lives. None of these ten women had conformed to the norms currently governing family formation behaviour and the conduct of personal relationships. Thus for them the social processes of marriage and childbearing had differed in important ways from those experienced by the majority of my respondents.[6] Whilst marital breakdown has become a commonplace of contemporary relationships between the sexes, and had been experienced by well over a third of the women interviewed, frequent breakdown of personal relationships (whether marital or extra-marital), the bearing of children outside of stable unions, and the failure of women to marry, continue to constitute behaviour which breaks with normative expectations. These are the characteristics of the women in this group. Disrupted private lives can have important effects upon women's employment careers. Some women seek stable, full-time employment as a 'constant' in their otherwise changeable lives. This enables them to escape dependence on either the state or men for their economic well-being, and gives them a sense of maintaining control over their own lives. Others find that the personal insecurities of unstable and unsatisfying relationships, often complicated by ill-health (mental or physical) and unplanned pregnancies, keep them from permanent or full-time employment

In four of the ten cases, attachment to the labour force had been strengthened. These women were all living alone with a child or children, and were, in effect, employed full-time.

Mavis was in her late twenties, had never married, and had an 18-month-old son. She was living in a small council flat, and gave every appearance of coping well with organising her life and managing her responsibilities.

> *Mavis:* '[It's] not really [a strain]...because I've always sort of sailed through things, and sort of not worried. Well, I do worry a little bit, but it doesn't bother me what other people think... I do what I want to do, and I don't care what anybody says.

She had two paid jobs, working 40 hours per week for a food processing company, packing food, and 7 hours on Saturdays as a butcher's assistant. She had been doing this for nine months when I first met her, and was still doing so when contacted again a year later. In the week, her child went to a registered childminder; whom she paid £12.50 a week, and on Saturdays her neighbour looked after him. Her Saturday job was quite important to her, and she had worked for this employer. on.and off for eight years, going back there when the baby was 6 months old and she was living on supplementary benefit.

> *Mavis:* 'That was a great help...because, also, he said "You know you can help yourself off the counter, like." So, I mean, that was an even bigger help,, that was...things like butter and cheese, and your meat, and it did save me a lot.., and after...doing it

about three or four weeks, I didn't honestly know how I could have gone back to just being on Social Security alone—I couldn't—well, to think about it now, I don't know how I really did manage.

Three months later she took the full-time factory job, and although she was toying with the idea of working shorter hours, she was aware of all the factors she needs to, weigh up.

> *Mavis:* 'Well, you see, you can gain and you can lose—at the moment, I can't claim for FIS,[7] because I am earning too much—but in November, they all go up again, so I can claim for them again.' (FIS = Family Income Supplement)

Kate and Cathy were both in their mid-thirties. Kate had four children, aged between 6 and 14 years, all living with her. She had been married three times, divorced twice, and said she was 'estranged' from her third husband. Cathy had been married and divorced twice, to the same man, and had three children. At the time of the interview she lived alone with the youngest child, a 7-year-old, while the elder two lived with their father. Neither woman was financially supported by a former husband, and both worked as hospital domestics. Kate worked a 40-hour week and did regular overtime of about 15 hours. Cathy worked part-time as a supervisor, but usually worked a 42-hour week including overtime:

Kate's first marriage had lasted two years, her second for twelve. She had one child from her first marriage and three from the Second. Her third marriage was breaking down after only a couple of years, when we met She described her estranged husband's attitude to her job.

> *Kate:* 'He doesn't like 'the idea—because of the independence side of it I suppose.... I was earning my own wage...so it gave me almost equal rights to him...and he didn't like the idea from.

She was bitter about her past.

> *Kate:* 'I've always done everything myself, anything to do with the home, cooking, looking after the children, everything. I've always been the one ye even taken on the responsibilities of bills, always have done.... I don't feel at all happy about it, mainly because it should be a shared thing between husband and wife. I don't know if it's me, or if it's just the type of people I've married—it just doesn't work out that way.

Her early experience of employment was in clerical work, which she found boring, and as a supermarket cashier. While her children were young, she worked for about seven years as an agricultural worker (working about nine months in every twelve), before having to 'give this up because of an injury, and taking a job as a hospital domestic. She planned to stay in this job 'quite a few years, I hope. All the time I'm able to, I will.'

Cathy's early employment career was inauspicious. In the first two years after leaving school at 15, she worked as a supermarket shelf-filler and counter assistant, in two jobs as a waitress, and as a factory operative. She was made redundant from one of these jobs, sacked—'for being mouthy'—from a second, and left the others of her own accord. Before taking a fifth job as a trainee laundry worker, she also spent some time caring for her sick grandmother. Cathy's employment career was broken again before she completed her training, when she became pregnant and had her first child. She married for the first time nine months later, and did not return to paid work (this time as a 'casual' agricultural worker) until three and a half years after this, by which time she had a second child. She continued in this work for about six years, although in the meantime she divorced, and three years later re-married, her husband. She then had to stop work to have a third child, but returned to agricultural work again soon afterwards.

> *Cathy:* 'I done one season of potato picking-up, after I'd had her....I've always suffered with my back, and that last spell of picking up potatoes just about finished me. I'd just about had enough. And then I decided that I would see if I could get a job inside.... I knew that there was one going (at the hospital) and I applied for it, and got it.'

Cathy's husband had no objection to her taking a more secure job.

> *Cathy:* 'He thought it was good that I was working...because then he could cut me housekeeping down, you see.., no, it's the truth' He always told me to get to work anyway—I did as I was told.'

As this second marriage came to an end, things deteriorated further:

> *Cathy:* '[my wages] all went in the housekeeping... I mean, I kept them all, from last May—because he never gave me anything at all—I was having to keep him, 'n all.'

How long did Cathy plan to stay in her present job? 'Until they get rid of me, I should think'

Susan was in her mid-forties, and had been living alone with her three children for over twelve years. Prior to that, she had been twice married and divorced. Susan's employment career began when she was 15, with a period of clerical work which lasted six years. During this time she married for the first time, giving up the job when she was expecting her first child. In the next three or four years, before her marriage broke down, she had another child and engaged in periodic seasonal work on farms, taking her children with her. After her marriage ended, she took on various casual jobs, including part-time clerical work and washing cars, before forming a relationship with the man she was later to marry. At first she lived with him, unmarried, but when she was expecting his child, she succumbed to pressure from her family, and, against her better judgment, married him. A few years later she obtained a part-time clerical job in the firm where her husband worked. This lasted for two years, until the marriage began to break down and she felt compelled to leave. After her second divorce, Susan gradually became more fully integrated into the labour force. She worked for a while in the school meals service, and then moved to a full-time office job. Finally, she took the advice of her sister, who worked for a public sector employer.

> *Susan:* 'I applied for a job here—my sister is an Executive Officer here, and.., she'd

brought up her family on her own. She said you' needed to get into a secure job, because you want a pension—you'd got to think about, you know, bringing up your children on your own—and this obviously made sense.'

Susan had been in this job for ten years when we met. She had accepted modest promotions, and had become very involved in trade union work At the time of her interview she was branch secretary of her union, and was also actively involved in Labour party politics, thus making the kind of link between her working life and her private life which is characteristic of male trade unionists. As she put it: 'What I do for the trade union here fits in with what I do in my leisure time—it's hardly separated.'

She expected to stay with her employers.

> *Susan:* 'I hope until I retire...all the time I'm fit... I mean, I shall need a pension.... We have excellent conditions of service, and because the [employers] have always worked closely with the unions, we don't have the unfairness that you get where you don't have union representation...[we have] flexi-time...we have a good superannuation scheme, we've got a welfare officer, benevolent society—this sort of thing...it's very secure.'

In many respects, the four women described here conformed closely to the stereotype of a 'male' than of a 'female' employee. Working regular overtime, taking a second job, relying upon earnings as a sole means of support, and active involvement in trade union activities are all characteristics more commonly found among male than female employees. Of course these characteristics have nothing to do with biological sex. What these women's employment careers demonstrate is that where women find it necessary to think of themselves as breadwinners, and shoulder all responsibility for themselves and their families, they are likely also to follow what has often been thought of as a 'male' pattern of employment

Three other women in this group were in paid employment when interviewed, but were only marginally integrated into the labour force. All were living alone with their children, but were not economically self-supporting in the way the four, women already described were. Jackie was receiving supplementary benefit, as well as support from two men, her former husband and the father of her second child, while both Hilary and Jane were in receipt of Family Income Supplement as well as a small amount of maintenance from their former husbands. Jackie and Hilary were both employed part-time, while Jane worked a 40-hour week, and sometimes did 5 hours overtime as well. In what ways had their personal histories resulted in their marginal integration in the labour force?

Jackie's employment career had been severely disrupted by ill-health several mental breakdowns, anorexia nervosa, and alcoholism. During the first three years of her employment career, she had three different jobs in residential homes for the elderly and handicapped, working as a care or nursing assistant: She left two of these jobs on account of her health, and the third following her marriage (when she was 21). After her marriage she took a full-time college course and qualified as a medical secretary, subsequently finding employment as secretary to a hospital consultant. She left this job after a year when expecting her much wanted first child.

She had not anticipated returning to employment for some years, but an opportunity to work 6 hours per week in the evenings as secretary to a general practitioner came up, and she took the job. After, just two months she had to be' re-admitted to hospital. Subsequently her marriage broke down and after a short spell living alone with the baby she lost custody of the child to her husband, 'because of my drinking'.

> *Jackie:* 'When I got her back [four months later] I still wasn't working.., and I just lived here on my own with her for a while, and I didn't work until the following year, until I got sober.... I started that about nine months after I stopped drinking.'

Her next job was secretarial work for a charity on one day a week, and she was doing this when we met.

> *Jackie:* 'I don't claim my money from there—which is £6 per week—until my telephone bill comes in—so it's purely for the telephone.'

She explained that a telephone was vital to her because of her alcoholism. Shortly before we met, Jackie had a second child. She intends to stay on her own, and says that the baby's father now 'maintains him'.

Hilary, in her early thirties, with three children-aged between 8 and 14, was married for just two years, although she has subsequently lived with another man for about four years. After leaving school at 15, Hilary had a number of short-lived jobs, as a factory worker and as a cinema usherette, before joining her parents, both agricultural workers. As she put it 'I went on to the farm with Mum and Dad... I did quite a lot of farm work'

She stayed in this work until her first, unplanned, child was expected.

> *Hilary:* 'Well, it didn't upset my plans—because I never had any plans—I never plan things anyway, it's no good...it's just that I knew—this fella that I was going with—before I married him...it wouldn't work And I thought, you know, getting married, *it* might alter him...well, it didn't. And then, when I found that I was pregnant, I thought "Oh God, how are we going to manage?"...and this is what it was.'

Her husband was unemployed throughout the two years of their marriage. 'I was going to work to keep him.' After her marriage ended, and following a spell when she lived on supplementary benefit, she began living with the man who is the father of her second and third children, a self-employed builder and decorator. During the four years this relationship lasted, she was not in employment, and her involvement in a car accident meant that 'The very last year that he was with me, I couldn't walk.' Hilary felt that neither of the men with whom she had been involved had helped her to shoulder the responsibilities of raising a family: 'I've brought my three up on my own, really.... Really, I mean, because the two boys' father, we never used to hardly see him, anyway.'

When she had recovered *from* her accident, she took a part-time job as a hospital bed-maker.

> *Hilary:* 'I wanted to get out... I was just shut in, day after day, and I just couldn't take any more of it. It was either come to work or crack up in the end, I think.'[8]

With help from her family with childcare, she kept this part-time job for over eighteen months. However, 'The reason I didn't stay was...because of the children, you know the seven-week school holiday.' Her next return to employment was as a part-time hospital domestic, a job which she had held for over three years when interviewed, despite a long period of sick leave, and a period of working reduced hours so that she could visit her youngest child in hospital following his injury in a road accident. She was not at the time of the interview entirely satisfied with her situation at work.

> *Hilary:* 'I have been moved about, quite a bit, just lately...they shove me off somewhere else. I fell out quite a few times with [management].... If I could find another job tomorrow, I'd go to it.'

Hilary was not finding it easy to cope: her children were difficult to manage, and she has had to call upon social services for assistance.

> *Hilary:* 'My children get me down....you know, sometimes...they really do make me cry....to think that I'm trying as hard as I can, to keep that house going and keep it nice, and they just don't care.

In the light of her past history, Hilary's expectations about her employment future seemed rather unrealistic: she thought she would stay 'until I find something else—or I get married—then I won't have to go to work'

Jane was a divorcee in her mid-thirties, with three children aged between 11 and 15. She had been married only once, for about seven years, and did not do so until after her three children were born. She was divorced five years before we met. After leaving school at 15, Jane was employed for five years in a variety of different jobs before having her first child. She worked as a shop assistant, in two factories, and as a bus conductress. She left the shop for better pay, was made redundant from one of the factory jobs, and left the other following an argument with the foreman. She left the bus company because of her pregnancy. There then followed a period of five years during which she did no paid work and had three children. How did she feel about being a single mother?

> *Jane:* 'Dunno... I just had to shoulder the responsibility, as with all three of them...it just happened....so that was that...'

At first she lived with her parents, but towards the end of the five years married and went to live with her husband. Her return to employment was prompted by the loss of her fourth child soon afterwards.

> *Jane:* 'I was getting a bit depressed, you know, with losing the baby and that, and I was sterilised—I had a Caesarean and sterilisation at the same time—so I took a job—that's about it.'

She took full-time work as a hospital domestic, but left after a year.

> *Jane:* 'I started having problems with the old man...whilst I was in hospital, he was carrying on with this woman....'

After two years without employment she started working again, as a barmaid in a pub.

> *Jane:* 'I started there a couple of dinner times, and then did three or four a week...and then several evenings a week. And then we split up completely...the marriage had really broken down, and then,. obviously, you know, I needed extra money, because of being on my own with three kids, so I took a job here.'

This time her job was again as' a hospital domestic, working full-time. She had been in this job for four years when I interviewed her. Although previously her personal life had tended to limit her attachment to employment, she now recognised that she needed to continue earning a living. I asked how long she expected to stay in her job.

> *Jane:* 'Well, as long as possible.'
>
> *S.Y.: '[Until] you come to retire?'*
>
> *Jane:* 'What can I say?... There's not a lot you can say about it, is there? It's a job.... The chance is, I might have to be.'

For these women, then, participation in the labour force had been, reduced by the nature of their personal relations and health. Unlike the four women described earlier, Jackie, Hilary, and Jane had not used employment as a means of structuring uneven and disrupted personal lives, but found that their employment careers were limited and fragmented by them.

The remaining three women had personal histories which temporarily interrupted their employment careers.

Annette was gentle and softly spoken, a woman who looked younger than her 27 years. Although she was caring for two children aged 12 and 14, she had no natural children of her own and had never married. At the time of the interview she had been living for four years with Jim and his two children by his ex-wife. Jim's wife had 'walked out and left' the family some six months before Annette moved in. Annette worked full-time as a clerical assistant and had also taken on the role of mother to Jim's children, and wife to Jim. Her early employment career had been rather chequered. She left school at 15 and worked briefly in a factory, and then in a hairdresser's, finding both unsatisfactory. After this she took another factory job, this time wiring electrical goods. She stayed in this job for two and, a half years, before being made redundant After some weeks out of work, she obtained a job as an office junior.

> *Annette:* 'I learnt how to operate the switchboard, and went from being a junior to doing all the credit control and the wages.'

Meanwhile, she had applied for another clerical job.

> *Annette:* 'My sister worked there... I suppose that was really the reason I went there—plus it was more money.'

She was taken on, and stayed two years before starting to feel restless. She then gave in her notice, and took work for the summer at a holiday camp—'getting away from home for a couple of months'. Afterwards, she worked briefly as a barmaid, before obtaining clerical work again, in a small company. By the end of the year, however, she had been offered her old clerical job back, and this time she stayed for almost three years, only leaving after moving in with Jim. She was quite keen to stop working, and Jim was anxious for her to do so: 'He's a bit possessive and a bit selfish, and he just wanted me at home.' After three years out of employment, however, Annette was anxious to return to her old job:

> *Annette:* 'The frustrations of being at home all the time had set in by then... [he didn't want me to come to work at all—it was purely at my insistence—at which he is pleased now—but it did take quite a few months.'

She had been back a year when we met What were her plans for the future? She explained that she had decided not to have children of her own, but that was not all.

> *Annette:* '[I have] distant thoughts of having a little business of my own.., perhaps a little shop.... I think I like working better knowing that it's not something that I'm going to have to do for another forty years or whatever...if I wanted to give up, I can give up.'

Alice was a 40-year old divorcee. She had left her husband and three children five years previously to live with another man, but the relationship did not last. She then spent some time living with her father, and, since his death, with another man and, more recently, her elder son. Like many of the women interviewed, Alice had several jobs between leaving school and having her first child, and married during this period. She left employment to have her first baby, and during the next six years her second and third children were born. At this stage she engaged in seasonal agricultural work and took on evening jobs—as a factory operative and as a cleaner. After the birth of her third child, she gradually began working more hours per week, at first as a cleaner but later as a laboratory assistant (at the same place of employment). She worked in this last job for about four years, and eventually left her family to set up home with her employer. She explained that she had been, unhappy about her marriage and her husband's attitudes to her employment

> *Alice:* 'It seemed to me that he would want me to work all day and all night.., my

money always went straight in the house—it was expected to go in there—it was never mine.... That's where I wrong... I felt like a slave. He liked to have his drink, and I was working for him to have his beer. I would come home after working from ten till six...and he admitted he'd been up since half past four, but he'd been asleep all afternoon, and he hadn't bothered—he hadn't made the bed, he hadn't washed up, he hadn't done anything...and before that anyway—he was never capable of looking after me.'

When her new relationship failed, Alice had a breakdown. Afterwards, in her own words, 'I pulled myself together, and went to work.' The work was in a paper mill, 'cutting holes in paper' and she found it hard: 'It was bonus work...you had to do so much...you had to keep going.' After two years, during which time she was also caring for her dying father, she gave the job up and took work as a full-time hospital domestic instead. Two years later, at the time of the interview, she was still working full-time, often doing 11 hours overtime each week She had no plans to leave: 'I think I shall be working here—well. I just think I shall always be here.' Alice's affair, divorce, and nervous breakdown had not severely disrupted her employment career, but had created a hiatus in its development

Penny's employment career had been interrupted in a way similar to Alice's, although the change in her personal life which caused' the interruption was different. Like Alice's, Penny's employment career followed a typical pattern for about twenty years. She took employment, married, and left to have her first child. She then did seasonal framework before moving into full-time permanent employment in sales after her child started school. She continued working full-time, although changing from sales to domestic work when her son was in his early teens. When he was 18, however, she found she was expecting another, unplanned, child. I asked her how she had felt..

Penny: 'I don't really know. I wasn't overjoyed, I wasn't bitter I always wanted another child.'

Having the child meant giving up her job, but also coincided with the breakdown of her marriage.

Penny: 'It finished.... And then, the hard times hit.... I had two choices—either live on social security, and poverty, or come back to work, and get above—just a little bit above poverty.

She returned to her former job, again full-time, and was able to place her child in the workplace nursery. What of the future?

Penny: 'I don't think I shall change [my job]... I don't think I'd like promotion... I think I've come to a standstill in my life—I think I just like being as I am. I don't think I could take on any more responsibilities because I already have enough... I'll keep continuing as long as can. I've got quite a lot of years left to continue work, and I still hope I can fulfil the years.'

As with Alice' and Annette, Penny's employment career was temporarily interrupted by developments in her personal life. Having a child unexpectedly late in her life had a similar effect on her employment career as moving in to be 'mother' to an existing family had for Annette, or leaving a family to establish a new relations hip had for Alice.

I have tried to show here that 'distinctive' personal histories such as those described do not have any simple effect upon women's employment patterns, but may influence them in a variety of ways. Some women use employment to structure their lives, while others may find changes and disruption in their personal lives spreading to their employment careers.

In this chapter, I have presented detailed discussion of the patterns of labour adopted by the women interviewed. Although most followed variants on a pattern usually regarded as typical (employment—childrearing—employment), two minority groups whose experience differed in important ways also emerged. In the first, women did not leave the labour force at all, but used maternity leave, or made other arrangements, to enable them to continue in their jobs. The second group consisted of a number of women 'whose personal histories deviated significantly from current norms governing personal relationships and family formation; in some cases this deviation had the effect of reinforcing integration into the labour force, in others of restricting it. It is important not to ignore the significance of the two minority groups. The former suggests a commitment to participation in the labour force with which women who are also mothers are not usually 'credited', while the latter tells us that there is no simple effect on employment careers which can be attributed to deviation from social norms concerning interpersonal behaviour.

The women in the main group (the 'dominant' pattern) had all left the labour market at least once to raise a child or children, and had returned to it at some subsequent point; none the less there were significant variations within this pattern.

Between leaving school and leaving the labour force to have a first child, most of the women in the group held more than one job; in many cases, changing jobs, even at this initial stage in the employment career, meant changing from one type of work to another, although this changing of occupation was uncommon amongst those (few) women who engaged in further education after school.

In establishing how women came to leave the labour force when expecting a first child; it was noteworthy that about half of first pregnancies were unplanned. These women thus had little opportunity to plan seriously for a future combination of domestic labour 'and wage-earning. These 'unplanned' first pregnancies reflect the fact that most young working-class women view marriage and a (first) baby as inevitable steps in the transition to adulthood. These steps are not usually subjected to rational economic planning, and often a 'the sooner, the better' approach is adopted. Once they are taken the individual can then get on with organising her life around what are seen as its essential components husband and children. Such economically irrational behaviour (which contrasts clearly with the career-oriented approach characteristic of the middle class) can best be understood in terms of the constraints and restricted opportunities of working-class life. Even amongst those whose first child was planned, little thought had apparently been given to returning to employment in the future, although many women said that they had vague expectations about this at the time.

Most women were to return to paid work much more quickly than they had expected. The return to employment represented a new experience of work, and the next few years were mostly characterised by a succession of part-time, temporary, or seasonal jobs. Most were in low paid and insecure occupations, and many would have gone unrecorded in official statistics. For the minority of married women who had more than one child and who remained outside the labour force throughout the entire childbearing phase, the average length of time between leaving and returning to paid employment was about eight years. It was notable that these women tended to have stable marriages and relatively well-paid husbands. Most placed a high value on their mothering role, and many sought employment partly because of a sense of lost identity when their youngest child started school.

After returning to employment there was a tendency to engage in several part-time jobs over a period of some years before taking on full-time employment Some women chose to remain part-timers, whilst for others full-time work was an aim which could only be achieved when the youngest child reached a particular age. Almost without exception, the women intended to remain in employment until retirement For many this intention reflected the fact that they had finally found themselves an acceptable occupation, where they were treated with some respect, derived some enjoyment from their work or working environment, and were earning wages on which they had come to rely. An important minority of the women were more ambitious however, and they intended to seek-promotion, further training, or a higher grade occupation. Many of these were women who worked for employers offering training and a career structure to all able members of staff. They had been made aware of the contribution they could make at work, derived a sense of self-worth from this, and had gained the confidence to pursue a career. Others were not positively motivated in this way, but rather felt undervalued and discontented in their present jobs. They knew they could do more demanding work, and recognised that they would need to change their occupation if their skills and abilities were to be used.

The evidence from the analysis of employment careers suggests that women may not be such passive members of the labour force as has sometimes been claimed. They have an experience of paid work which is fragmented and variable, but they also return frequently to employment, and intend to stay. Indeed, many have relatively ambitious plans for the future, and desire to be further integrated into the labour force.

CODA: BARBARA'S STORY

Barbara is 35, has been married to Frank since she was 18, and has two sons, Mark aged 17 and Philip aged 14. Mark left school recently and is doing an apprenticeship. Slightly plump, Barbara has a kindly, almost matronly appearance, and punctuates her conversation with the phrase 'I've been very lucky.' Looking back, she says that if a girl 'had a life like mine she wouldn't have a lot to complain about', although she readily admits that 'we' have our ups and downs—but (that's) all part of life.'

Barbara's employment career has conformed to the traditional stereotype for married women: several years in full-time jobs between school and having children, then a complete break while her family were young, followed by a return to employment in part-time work This pattern of employment reflects the traditional role which Barbara plays within her family. As she says herself, 'I'm not a great women's libber.' Of central importance in Barbara's life have been her responsibilities with regard to 'running her home',, a phrase to which she returned frequently. She says proudly that she 'didn't start work *(sic)* until the children were both at school', and finds some contemporary attitudes towards raising children rather puzzling,

> 'I supposed I'm old-fashioned...if you're having a baby, then obviously my thought would be to stay at home and look after it—I wouldn't want to go and leave it...but if that is sort of what career women really want, then I don't understand it completely, but I would think...[the law is right to permit it].'

Although she has no wish to he at home all day now that her children are older, Barbara has always considered it important to plan her life around the demands of her husband and sons. She explained what having a job meant to her, and how she fitted it into her life.

> '[Having a job] makes me better-tempered in some ways... You're so small-minded when you're at home, you just live in your own little world.... If it suits people, I mean, it's entirely up to them of course...obviously we all come out for the money, but I mean it is the company and the outside attachments.., the friendships that you make as well.... Even if I was well off—obviously if you were filthy rich you'd probably have other things to entertain you—but... I would have to have an awful lot of money not to, I think....otherwise I think you get a little bit stale ye always been lucky ye been able to find work where I can fit it in with family life ye more organised my jobs round the family than the family round the jobs.'

It may be useful to indicate just how Barbara has been able to do this. After the birth of her first child in 1963 (she gave up her job as a shop assistant at the beginning of that year) she was at home full-time until September 1970 when Philip started school. Only once in these eight years did she consider taking a job: when Mark was just a few months old she started work as an assistant in a children's nursery, leaving the baby with her mother who lived nearby. She found the separation from her child too hard to bear, however, and after two days abandoned the job. The years at home with the children were not entirely dedicated to caring for the needs of her own household however:

> 'I used to look after an uncle...we lived close by.... I looked liter him for seven years...he had his own place...and I used to just go along and do his cleaning. When he got beyond looking after at home...they put him into hospital...and then he died.'

Barbara took this additional responsibility quite for granted. As she saw it, caring for an elderly relative was simply another aspect of a married woman's duties towards her family.

When both her sons had started school Barbara started to look for a part-time job. She faced some opposition from her husband, and her mother was not enthusiastic. However, she persuaded her husband to 'let' her take a job by offering it as a means of achieving a specific objective:

> 'I told [him], if he wanted a car.... It was really to get extras... I mean, if we went out anywhere, it was either buses or we had to walk, and we thought it would be nice.'

This tactic was apparently successful; in any case, Barbara obtained Frank's consent, and made enquiries at a local college, where she started work as a part-time catering assistant: 'helping in the kitchens, clearing tables, serving meals, that sort of thing'. Barbara's mother had reservations about the idea of her daughter taking a job. She had never had a paid job herself, although as Barbara explained, 'she used to do little bits of needlework and that...she was able to make herself the little bit extra.' Nevertheless, she was soon persuaded that the arrangement could do no serious harm, since she recognised the financial pressures on Barbara and her young family. (Frank has worked for the past fifteen years as a warehouseman in a retail store. Prior to this, he worked as a bread roundsman and as a milkman. None of these jobs is particularly well paid.) Indeed, Barbara acknowledged that her mother 'was prepared to help if she could', but added that 'I wouldn't have done it if I'd had to get her to look after the children a lot.' Rather she had 'helped out on odd occasions.'

The job at the college involved striking an individual bargain with management:[9] officially, working at the weekends 'was supposed to be compulsory'.

> 'When I went for the job, I said, "No, I can't take the job because you want weekends"—and he got me to work a couple of evenings [instead]...and I...used to have a young girl—she looked after the children for half an hour before my husband got home. She lived next door but one, and she just came in and looked after them.'

Later, this arrangement about weekend work was not allowed to stand, and, faced with what was for her an impossible choice, Barbara left the job in the following summer. Her comments about the incident are illuminating:

> 'They were insisting then that we work weekends—that was purely because some of them were being funny about it—and so they said, "You'll have to do weekends", and I said, "I can't do weekends because my husband's working every other Saturday." And I didn't feel it was fair to ask the family, so I gave that job up, and had the summer holidays off.'

This explanation reveals that there were other factors in the background influencing the choice which Barbara was forced to make. She had the summer holidays in prospect, and although she was not officially required to work during this time she knew she would be asked to do so (in connection with conferences at the college), and that she would have either to refuse, or to seek support from her mother. Her reluctance to call on her family for support was influenced by both her feeling that the children were essentially her own responsibility, and by her knowledge that her mother was already involved in helping her sister with childcare. Thus a variety of factors combined to produce her decision to resign the job.

As the summer holidays ended, Barbara started to look around for work again. She was experienced in shop work, but did not look in that area:

> 'I didn't think it was worth trying, because I knew I wouldn't get the school holidays... I had to sort of compromise...and I mean most shop work is Saturdays anyway.'

As the school term began again, she decided to try a different kind of work.

> 'I did two days as a crossing patrol person along by the school—but my nerves wouldn't let me do that. Oh dear, I couldn't put up with that. I did it for two days and I went home and cried my eyes out. I just said to my husband, "I just can't go up there and do it".... A policeman is supposed to stand with you the first week apparently, and he was with me for one day—plus the other lady had left to have a baby, and the thing said "Stop Children"—and the comments I used to get.... Anyway, my husband went up and saw the headmaster, and said, "It's no good, she can't do it". And I began to wonder what I was going to do then, I used to look at the papers on Friday morning...and then I saw this little job.'

This account reveals something of Barbara's relationship with her husband, as well as of the difficulties which undertaking a new and unfamiliar task can entail. The failure to provide Barbara with proper training and the vulnerability involved in performing a task in public, where there is no protection from the comments of passers-by, both contributed to her lack of confidence in a job which involves a serious responsibility for the safety of children. The involvement of her husband in communicating her decision to abandon the job Illustrates the dependent nature of her relationship with him. As we shall see, it is not a relationship in which she has no power, but it is one in which she defers to his authority and wishes, especially in matters which concern the world beyond their family household.

Her next job (whose significance for her is neatly summarised in her use of the adjective 'little') was a part-time office-cleaning job. She worked at this for three hours each morning, making a 15 hour week. This job did not conflict with any of her domestic responsibilities, but as she suggests below, in discussing why she left it after two years, it had other disadvantages.

> 'We Wanted to do improvements on the home which would mean taking up more on the mortgage.... It was only just three hours a morning, and it wasn't very well paid, and I looked for a part-time assistant job in the paper...and there was one [in] a wallpaper shop... I came for an interview...and they didn't want Saturday work... I used to work from 9 am till 1 pm—I was there about six years—and then I changed the

hours to suit myself, as gradually the family were growing up.'

Barbara was to stay in this latter job until she knew the shop was about to be closed down. It offered a good arrangement for her because she was able to have the children in the shop with her (when necessary) during their school holidays, and had some flexibility in the hours she worked. It also gave her the opportunity to work on her own initiative and to take on responsibilities of which she had no previous experience. Although she had worked in shops before having her family, she had worked then as a counter assistant, mainly in two small shops, a grocer's and a baker's. Barbara enjoyed the challenge which this job represented for her, but found eventually that it began to impose rather too much upon her home life. She contrasted it with the duties of her current job, as a sales assistant in the retail store where her husband works:

> 'I had a lot of responsibility in there—management relief when management was off, responsibility as far as ordering goes, plus I mean, the nature of the work is completely different...you really are serving customers there...here, it's just a matter of they come and take what they want and come through the tills.'

Had she preferred the more responsible job?

> 'Yes, in a vain way...but no, not really, because it was beginning to...interfere with home life...we didn't get the staff, and the only...action...was that I gave more hours, which I did...then the manager....was off five weeks sick...and I had to take over for five weeks full-time, and you just hadn't got any home life...I enjoyed it, as I say, from a vain way...if I-was single and hadn't got any other responsibilities, then fine...but this job does work much better.'

Despite this assessment, Barbara finds some aspects of her current job unrewarding, and misses the control over her job which she had previously:

> 'Sometimes you feel if you were just left alone you could get on with the job as you would like to—it's like everything else, there are so many rules and regulations, because of the conditions that they expect—it sometimes gets a bit much—but you understand why it is.'

As I have suggested above, Barbara prefers to fit her job around the duties of 'running her home', and chooses part-time work as her strategy for employment rather than the alternative of enlisting the support of her family or of the immediate household. I asked her about her husband's role in the work at home:

> 'He's always willing to help...when I've been doing it full-time, or something like that—washing-up, he's always been one to give a hand...if he knows I'm really pushed he will help me do the cleaning—but I'm a bit independent that way... I get the extra time off, and it's nice to get work done then, so we can share the time together.'

Barbara's 'independence' with regard to the home is a measure of the extent to which she sees this as 'her' domain. She is confident of her abilities to keep it running smoothly, and, unlike her dealings with the outside world, she sees this as a place where she manages and organises matters as of right. In addition, she enjoys her husband's company, as their decision to have the same weekends off work suggests. In general, Barbara does all the cleaning, washing, ironing, and cooking herself, and she has a clear routine, involving doing particular jobs on set days, and ensuring that tasks like ironing, for example, do not 'pile up'. She prepares her sons' lunch-boxes daily, and is willing to cook twice in an evening if it suits them to have meals at different times. In addition to these tasks, she also does sewing: 'I'm making men's pyjamas at the moment. That I usually fit in at weekends or on my days off.'

Barbara has given some thought to the changed social arrangements whereby increasing numbers of married women have taken on paid jobs. She is not entirely happy about this development:

> 'The thing is, these days, I think they've *got* to—this is the sad part about it.... If want...a home own...mortgages are so high...plus, they do take the wife's wages into consideration now, don't they? When we first started ours, they didn't—'in some ways it seemed cruel to us, but I mean if was a lot kinder because you can manage on one wage... I feel so sorry for them...they can't start a family when they want to, perhaps...we encourage our boys to save as much as they can, mainly with that thought.'

The child of older parents herself, Barbara is sure that having a family while young is the best arrangement:

> 'Had my mother been younger, we could have done different things... I was always told I'd led a sheltered life and... I feel it more *now*.... I look at different people and they've got a wider experience of things than I have... my parents were very sort of protective.'

In fact, Barbara's adolescence involved a very straight forward transition from dependence on her parents, and an acceptance of their authority 'I was the type who did what I was told. I mean, that's what I'd always been brought up to do, and I didn't rebel or anything'—to dependence on her husband and deference to him—'I was only 15 when I met my husband, I just (wanted to) leave school and...get married and have a baby.... I had no real ambitions to do anything.'

Her early experiences of employment tended only to reinforce her sense of herself as powerless and as needing the protection of her parents or a husband. Not only was she driven from her first job by the unwanted familiarities of her boss (see earlier in this chapter), but her second employer, a shopkeeper, also treated her with no respect: 'He made you look very small plenty of times.' Significantly, her departure from this job was at the prompting of her parents:

'They were putting on me rather a lot... I used to have to take a lot of writing work home, and the family thought it was getting a bit much.... He didn't really want me to leave—be made it very awkward and had me in tears, but... I wasn't staying.'

As Barbara's husband had worked for a large retail store which employs many married women on a part-lime basis throughout the past fifteen years, I was curious as to why she had not sought work there until so recently (she had been employed there for less thin a year when we met). She explained:

'I'd always said I wouldn't before. I think when I was younger, I was more possessive. I think we were both probably a bit possessive. I didn't think it would work... But then... one of the foremen suggested to me, "Why don't you apply in our place?"—and we'd always said we wouldn't, so I thought it over for a while, and eventually I said to my husband, "What do you think?"

In the end she decided to apply for the job, 'for the security really', her confidence that it would have this characteristic stemming from her husband's experience.

Barbara has had no hesitations about staying at home if either of her sons has been unwell or has needed her for any other reason. I asked her how she felt about doing this:

'It was just the natural thing to do. Luckily again, wherever I've worked, they've realised that the family came first.'

In Barbara's experience, the standard arrangements with her employers in such an event have been either that she loses pay for the hours not worked, or that she makes up the lost time. 'I've been lucky.... If I couldn't work certain hours, I could do it at some other time.'

Barbara's earnings represent a significant contribution to the family budget. When we met in early 1980, she was earning approximately £30 per week (basic), while her husband's basic wage was approximately £69 per week. Their weekly household income was thus about £100, subject to deductions for tax and national insurance, and supplemented by a small contribution from their elder son. Their wages 'all go into the same bank account'. I asked Barbara if they could manage without her earnings:

'At the moment we run two cars—my son is having one of them soon—so obviously the first thing to go would be *my* car. It would mainly be the family holidays and the car—we might perhaps go for a smaller car...and just sort of a normal cutback—sort of fizzy drinks and biscuits, all the little extras in that line...entertainment, probably—since I've been here we've been going out a little bit more.'

Barbara and Frank are buying their own home, so have a mortgage ('we don't have hardly anything to pay now') as well as the usual household bills to pay.. Barbara says they have 'most of what we need we've been doing the home up now for a couple of years', but the house is less well-equipped with domestic appliances than many homes. It contains a washing-machine (twin-tub) and a fridge-freezer, but lacks items—tumble drier, automatic washing machine, a large food freezer—which other women find valuable. In general, their standard of living is modest, but it is difficult to see how they could maintain this level without Barbara's contribution.

Barbara plans to remain in employment until she reaches retirement age. She thinks it likely she will stay with her present employer and she says she may seek a modest promotion (to Deputy Supervisor), when she has been in the job a little longer. She has no intention of working full-time in the job, however, a decision which in itself effectively bars her way to any further promotion. It seems probable that Barbara and Frank will now complete their employment careers in the service of their current employer. The firm has a reputation for its benevolence and has a paternalistic style which accords well with the ideological framework which supports the couple's domestic arrangements. It seems entirely plausible that they are both regarded by their employers as model employees, just as, conversely, they (if Barbara's views can be taken as representative of them both) look upon theirs as an exemplary employer.

23

Women in Agriculture Sector

Indicators of agricultural employment are different: their most common source are large sample surveys or complete national censuses of households or arm holdings. *Population censuses,* which count the stock of workers at one point in time, are less sensitive to the interplay of different amounts and types of market and non-market activities throughout the year than are repeated time-use surveys. In contrast, *labour force surveys* usually include questions on numbers of days working for wages or on the family holding, days unemployed, daily wage rates, and so on, which can often be analysed by season and according to the characteristics of the household or the geographical area. *Farm censuses* or surveys that take the *agricultural holding* rather than the household as the unit of analysis can reveal the extent to which hired or exchange workers of either sex are brought in to supplement domestic labour on the farm on a temporary or permanent basis, sometimes permitting comparison of total labour days contributed by each type of worker according to characteristics of the holding such as size or dominant cropping pattern. In this chapter we review indicators of labour force participation, employment status, and under—and unemployment from each of these sources to provide a perspective on measuring sex differences in agricultural employment at the national and subnational levels. The data are particularly useful for planners interested in analysing spatial and temporal variations in agricultural employment.

Labour Force Participation

International standards for classifying persons by labour force participation and occupation are difficult to apply to developing countries, where workers are more likely than those in developed countries to be self-employed rather than wage earners, to work seasonally rather than year-round, to be underemployed rather than formally unemployed, and to engage in a fluid or sporadic pattern of diverse and shifting economic activities (Durand, 1975; Standing, 1977; Mueller, 1978; Blacker, 1978, (1980).[1] Moreover, the boundary between domestic production for the household's own consumption and economic activity for sale or exchange is blurred in agrarian societies (Boserup, 1975; Boulding et al., 1976; Fong, 1980a), as we have seen. In deciding whether a person is to be classified as economically active or inactive, we are forcing a dichotomy on a continuum of time inputs and on a spectrum of activities.

In many cases the criteria for reckoning labour force participation — already somewhat inadequate—are selectively applied so that women or children who engage in the same amount of agricultural work as men are less likely to be counted as members of the labour force. Although this error can be corrected in the field with careful training of interviewers and with scrupulous attention to the way questions are worded, most traditional labour force statistics under-represent women, especially those who work without pay on the family holdings.

Why are Women Undernumerated?

Sex-selective underenumeration results from at least four tests applied to the determination of economic activity. First, according to the United Nations Statistical Commission definition of 1966, the economically active are "all persons of either sex who furnish the supply of labour for the production of economic goods and services" during the time-reference period chosen for the investigation (ILO, 1976, p. 32).[2] Although comprehensive in theory, in practice the definition was often rather narrowly applied on the assumption that production solely for household consumption (use value) did not constitute economic activity (Boulding, 1976, p.,. 318; Bneneria, 1982, p. 122). In 1982 the ILO explicitly described the content of "economic goods and services" to include

> .... *all* production and processing of *primary products,* whether for the market, for barter, or for own consumption; the production of *all other goods and services for the market*, and in the case of households which produce such goods and services for the market, the corresponding production for own consumption (ILO, 1983, p. 2; emphasis added).

Only the production of "other" (non-primary) goods and services solely for consumption in non-market-oriented households is excluded from this definition. For workers engaged in the production or processing of primary products (e.g., crops, livestock, poultry destined wholly for their own or their household's consumption, however, the 1982 definition explicitly recognises them as "employed" only if the production comprises "an important contribution to the total consumption of the household" (ILO, 1983, p. 3). This qualifying clause leaves some flexibility of interpretation by each country in its data collection procedures.

Second, up to 1982 the ILo recommended that unpaid family workers assisting in the operation of a business or farm be considered as employed only if they worked at least one-third of the "normal" working time during the specified reference period. No minimum was set for those who earn pay or profit, however: "As long as money is involved, the person is always classified as employed" (United Nations, 1958, p. 25). The minimum time criterion was removed in 1982.

The third potentially discriminatory criterion is the reference period itself. The common labour force approach that asks about *current* activity in the day or week proceeding the interview will miss those women (and children, and the aged) whose major contributions to agricultural production or processing are seasonal, unless the census or survey is conducted in the busy months.[3] A longer reference period such as a year or a complete agricultural cycle will catch a higher proportion of this group of farm workers.[4] The 1982 international standards distinguish between two categories of the economically active population: the "usually active population" measured with a one-year reference, and the "currently active population" (similar in concept to the labour force approach) with a short reference period such as one week or one day (ILO) 1983, p. 1).

Fourth, many censuses ask respondents only for their primary occupation or main activity. Because male interviewers and male and female respondents alike frequently consider many of the things women do as "housework" regardless of their intrinsic nature, tasks that for men are labelled economic activity may not be so for women. In her Chilean fieldwork, Garrett noted that "We were struck in interviewing women on large estates by the number of women who defined even planting and harvesting as homemaking rather than agricultural work" (Garrett, 1976, p. 35). Similar examples can be cited from other settings (e.g. Stoler, 1975 in Java; Deere, 1982 in Peru). Male farmers are sometimes reluctant to report that their wives and daughters are working, especially in conservative Muslim areas (ILO, 1969, p. 27; Youssef, 1977). Interviewers may also ignore women's work or be instructed to do so for some age categories: women living on farms are sometimes classified as economically inactive merely on the basis of their sex and relationship to other household members (Standing, 1977, p. 29). "Unless enumerators are explicitly instructed to ask about the possible economic activity of women in the household in the same way as about that of men, they may tend automatically to enter women as homemakers, particularly if the women are married...." (Blacker, 1980, pp. 71-72; see also Recchini de Lattes and Wainerman, 1982).

Discrepancies Among Data Sources

Sex differences in labour force participation rates based on censuses or national surveys are not strictly comparable across countries because different definitions and practices lead to varying degrees of underenumeration of women workers. Examples abound of discrepancies across countries and even within countries from one census or survey to the next (e.g. Boserup, 1975; Durand, 1975; Standing, 1978; Deere and Leon de Leal, 1982; Dixon, 1982b; Recchini de Lattes and Wainerman, 1982 among others).

Different modes of data collection also lead to different outcomes. In Egypt, for example, where the 1960 population census counted women as only 4 per cent of the agricultural labour force, a detailed rural labour record survey indicated that about one-quarter of all productive work in farm households (excluding housework) was done by women (ILO, 1969, p. 27). A national Demographic Survey of Bolivia in 1975 found age-specific rural participation rates for women (including non-agricultural employment) from 181 to 223 per cent higher than did the population census of 1976, whereas corresponding comparisons for men were from 95 to 100 per cent (Recchini de Lattes and Wainerman, 1982, p. 25). And in the State of Sao Paulo, Brazil, a 1970 household survey resulted in Female age-specific participation rates in agriculture from 233 to 475 per cent higher, depending on age, than the census (discrepancies were even larger when only unpaid family workers were considered), whereas the corresponding comparisons for men were 90 to 102 per cent (Recchini de Lattes and Wainerman, 1982, p. 21).[5] Apparently men's economic activity is counted whatever the process; in contrast, women's (and children's) depends heavily on particular definitions and practices.

National-level data obtained from population censuses, standardised estimates prepared by the ILO, and censuses of agricultural holdings conducted under the auspices of the Food and Agriculture Organisation (FAO). Countries selected for illustrative purposes with estimates from all three sources for comparable years provide good examples of some close fits (e.g., Cameroon, Malawi, Republic of Korea, Mexico) and some startling contradictions (Egypt, Iraq, Sri Lanka, Argentina, Brazil). The population censuses tend to count fewer men and women as members of the agricultural labour force than the other two sources, producing lower activity rates for all persons 10 years of age and over. The FAO censuses of agriculture count the most workers, with the additional number drawn disproportionately from the ranks of women. The female share of the agricultural labour force (percentage female) thus tends to be far higher in the agricultural censuses than in the other tow sources, presenting a significantly different national portrait of the sexual division of labour in farm production. Indeed, the standardised ILO estimates appear to underestimate the female share of the farm labour force by as much as 14 percentage points, averaging across 32 developing countries, when compared with censuses of agricultural holdings (Dixon, 1982b, p. 554).

Why do farm censuses find more workers -- especially women — than population censuses or standardised ILO figures? First, a person who performs *any* agricultural work on the holding during the specified time period, regardless of the number of hours worked or of payment, in usually counted. Second, agricultural work includes caring for livestock and poultry, working in kitchen gardens, and other farm activities performed close to home that might be classified as housework or subsistence production in more restrictive labour force definitions.[6] Third, agricultural censuses may be taken during the busy season more often than population censuses or labour force surveys. These practices make a significant difference in the resulting labour force data by including those who did some farm work, whether or not it was their only or primary occupation during the period.[7]

New Categories of Labour Force Participation

One solution to the dilemma of who to include in the labour force is to distinguish among different levels or types of economic activity. Anker (1983c, pp. 714-716) proposes four categories of participation: (1) the *paid labour force,* to include persons engaged in activities for which they are paid directly in cash or kind (i.e., "employees"); (2) the *market-oriented labour force* which also includes the self-employed (employers, own-account workers, unpaid family workers, and members of producer co-operatives) who produce for the market, with no minimum time specified; (3) the *new standard* (my term) *labour force,* to include those activities recommended by the ILO in 1982 such as livestock tending, preparation of meals for hired labourers, and crop processing for home consumption; and (4) the *extended labour force,* which also includes activities such as gathering fuel or water, making clothes for the family, and other home-produced substitutes for purchased inputs (by the standards of developed countries, that is). Housework and child care are not included, in order to maintain some variability for analytical purposes.

These labour force distinctions require a modified form of the time-use survey such as that included in Appendix F. By attaching numerical values to the rough time categories, and by combining categories of activities, survey respondents are defined as economically active or not according to each of the four criteria. They can also be classified as full-time (more than half the day) or part-time (less than half) workers in each category. The more restrictive the definition (full-time wage labour), the smaller will be the total labour force and the smaller (in most classes) the proportion female. In contrast, the highest activity rates for females, and the highest proportions female among the total, will appear in the "extended labour force," especially if it includes those working part but not all of the day.

Table 23.1 is an interesting example of how a modified time-use survey permits the differentiation of respondents according to type of labour force participation. Middle—and low-caste women in the Baroda (India) survey reveal higher activities except those requiring land or assets (cooking for hired labourers, caring for livestock and handicraft production). Almost all women in all castes collect water. According to these definitions, middle—and low-caste women are seven times as likely as high-caste women to be in the paid labour force, four times as likely to be in the market-oriented labour force, one and one-half times as likely to be in the (new standard) labour force, and equally as likely to be in the extended labour force if water fetching is included.

In a somewhat similar formulation, De Tray's analysis of economic activity among Malaysian children according to their sex, age, and ethnic group employs several definitions of labour force participation: (1) the labour force as traditionally measured; (2) "labour force activities plus time spent producting goods for home consumption"; and (3) "the sum of all productive activities including housework and child care," (De Tray, 1983, p. 443). De Tray finds that girls participate as frequently as boys in labour market activities according to the traditional labour force definition among all three ethnic groups — Malays, Chinese, and Indians — although boys work more hours on average if they do work. Expanding the definition of participation increases the activity rates and hours of girls more than of boys, as one would except.

In sum, if one considers the labour force survey as a special variant of the time-use survey, the categories and approach of the latter can be employed in the design of the former to include information on a wider range of productive activities than is normally included (Hoffman, 1981). The different rates obtained from the four definitions of labour force participation permit some interesting comparisons across and within groups and over time that do not suffer from the lack of comparability of most current published statistics. For some purposes, it is only the paid labour force that is of interest; for others, the planner will want a broader definition to include production for sale or exchange or even solely for home consumption.

TABLE 23.1

Percentage of Married Women Aged 25-50 Participating in Various Labour Force Activities by Caste, Baroda, India, 1981

Labour force activity	*Barias (Middle/low caste)*	*Patidars (High Caste)*
Individual Activities		
1. Agriculture for others	47.6	3.4
2. Agriculture for family	14.9	9.0
3. Cooking for hired labour	1.7	2.2
4. Processing food for Storage for family	7.1	1.1
5. Livestock care	32.5	46.6
6. Handicraft production	0.7	1.1
7. Non-agricultural wage or salary work	1.5	0.6
8. Family business, petty trading	2.0	0.6
9. Other cash earning	4.3	1.7
10. Gathering sticks	82.5	51.7
11. Fetching water	89.0	90.4
12. Making cow dung cakes	55.4	33.7
Labour Force Measures		
1. *Paid LF:* activities 1, 7 9 plus 5, 6, 10-12 if paid.	52.4	7.3
2. *Market-oriented LF:* paid LF plus activities 2, 8.	59.7	15.2
3. *(New standard) LF:* market-oriented LF plus activities 3-6.	74.9	53.4
4. *Extended LF:* new standard LF plus activities 10, 12.	91.1	69.1
5. *Extended LF:* also includes activity 11.	93.3	92.7

Source: Anker, 1983c, pp. 718-719.

For each category of worker, the researcher can calculate a variety of labour force measures such as crude activity rates (number of workers per 100 population of all ages); general or "standardised" rates (workers per 100 population aged 10 or 15 and over); age-specific rates (workers per 100 population in each age category); age-standardised or refined rates (a single rates based on a common age distribution); the sex ratio of workers (numbers of male workers per 100 females); and the female share of the labour force (females as a percentage of all workers), among other indicators (e.g. Durand, 19775, Appendix A; Boulding *et al.*, 1976). If the data are comparable, they can then be analysed internationally with countries grouped according to region, level or rate of development, or some other criterion of theoretical interest (cf. Boserup, 1975; Durand, 1975; Standing, 1978; Dixon, 1983).

Employment Status

Classifications in censuses or farm surveys by employment status reveal important differences between women and men in their conditions of agricultural work. As we would except, women occupy a particular niche within the farm labour force. Table 23.2 which summarises population census data from 52 developing countries, reveals that females are a far higher proportion of all unpaid family workers—an unweighted mean of 35 per cent—then of wage earners and salaried employees (13 per cent) or of self-employed cultivators (11 per cent). (The last includes both agricultural employers and own-account workers such as owner-cultivators or tenant-holders with no employees). This pattern typifies all but the sub-Saharan African region where women constitute a higher proportion of independent cultivators on average than of hired labourers. The aggregate data obscure important variations within regions which appear when country figures are examined separately, however, and ignore the considerable overlap among them.

Once again, the data are subject to considerable error. Factors affecting the decision to count a person as economically active also affect decisions about employment status. A more in inclusive definition of economic activity will almost inevitably result in a higher proportion of unpaid family workers and thus of women among the economically active population. One method of making the labour force data more comparable across countries is to remove unpaid family workers from the totals and recalculate the percentages female among remaining self-employed cultivators and wage labourers. The exclusion of unpaid family workers from the labour force as reported in Table 23.2 (third column) narrows the differences among regions in female shares of employment and reduces the overall proportion female from 20 to 12 per cent in the 52 countries. The adjustment effect is largest in sub-Saharan Africa and in Asia, and smallest in Latin America where women are typically a low proportion of the labour force among all categories of agricultural worker as reported in population censuses.

This correction is unsatisfactory, however, because there is considerable ambiguity on the borderline of self-employment and unpaid family labour. How much does one need to earn in order to be classified as an own-account worker, for example? A woman who occasionally sells or trades a small portion of what she or her family produces may be considered an own-account worker in a cultural context in which women commonly earn independent incomes, but an unpaid family helper in a context in which this is rare. The censuses of Malawi, Nepal and Tunisia classify almost all economically active farm women as self-employed whereas those of Gabon, Democratic Kampuchea, Thailand and Turkey classify almost all as unpaid family helpers. Does this distinction reflect real conditions of work or is it a statistical artifact resulting from emuneration methods and underlying assumptions about women's roles?

TABLE 23.2

Sex Composition of the Agricultural Labour Force by Employment Status: Regional Average, Around 1970. Population Censuses and Surveys

		Women as percentage of:									
Region	*Number of countries*	*total agricultural LF*				*self-employed*		*wage labourers*		*unpaid family workers*	
		incl. unpaid		*excl. unpaid*							
		Mean	*CRV*[a]	*Mean*	*CRV*[a]	*Mean*	*CRV*[a]	*Mean*	*CRV*[a]	*Mean*	*CRV*[a]
Sub-Saharan Africa	9	38.1	.41	24.6	.69	30.9	.59	7.2	.85	50.0	.48
North Africa, Middle East	11	16.1	.99	5.8	.97	4.0	1.09	12.1	1.02	41.1	.73
South, Southeast Asia	10	31.7	.42	18.5	48	13.1	.61	28.8	.45	49.4	.44
Central, South America	18	6.1	.90	4.4	.75	4.0	.85	4.8	.74	12.5	1.00
English, French Caribbean	4	26.8	.57	21.2	.46	15.2	.57	24.8	.47	44.2	.38
All countries	52	20.3	.86	12.2	.99	11.3	1.17	12.9	1.00	34.6	.76

a. The coefficient of relative variation, CRV, measures the size of the standard deviation relative to the mean for all countries within the region.

Source: Calculated from ILO, *Year Book of Labour Statistics* (Geneva, various years).

These conceptual problems confound the interpretation of changes in the employment status of workers as well as of cross-national differences. Researchers have noted disproportional shifts among women workers as compared to male workers: from independent cultivator status to unpaid family helper with the spread of cash cropping in sub-Saharan Africa (e.g., Boserup, 1970, p. 60); from independent cultivator to wage labour with increasing landlessness in India (Committee on the Status Women in India, 1974, pp. 162-164); and from permanent hacienda workers to wage-earning rural proletariat in Peru (Deere, 1982) or to unremunerated family helper in Chile (Garrett, 1976). Each has had to grapple with the question of whether the reported trends are illusory or real.[8]

FAO censuses of farm *holdings* classify workers in different employment categories than do population censuses. A holding "is all land which is used wholly or partly for agricultural production and is operated by one person (the holder), alone or with the assistance of others, without regard to title, size, or lacation" (FAO, 1971, p. 13). The Chilean farm censuses used by Garrett identify supervisory and administrative personnel; permanent, resident workers; other workers; and proprietors and unremunerated family members (1976, p. 15).

TABLE 23.3

Seasonal Fluctuation in Employment, Unemployment, and Wages Among Female and Male Casual Agricultural Labourers in Rural West Bengal, 1972-73

Quarter	*Female labourers*					*Male labourers*				
1972-73	*Casual*	*All*	*Unempl.*	*Casual farm wage*		*Casual*	*All*	*Unempl.*	*Casual farm wage*	
	farm empl. (days/wk)	*empl. (days/ wk)*	*(days/ wk)*	*Rupees/ week*	*Rupees/ week*	*farm empl. (days/wk)*	*empl. (days/ wk)*	*(days/ wk*	*Rupees/ week*	*Rupees/ week*
Oct.-Dec. (busy)	3.93 (93)	4.49 (92)	1.12	2.29	8.99	5.28 (100)	6.08 (100)	.53	2.76	14.59
Jan.-Mar. (slack)	2.21 (52)	3.23 (66)	2.50	2.09	4.62	4.12 (78)	5.15 (85)	1.47	2.46	10.16
Apr.-June (slack)	1.91 (45)	3.05 (63)	2.57	1.76	3.36	4.44 (84)	5.15 (85)	1.57	2.56	11.38
Jul.-Sept. (busy)	4.24 (100)	4.86 (100)	1.28	2.64	11.18	4.90 (73)	5.67 (93)	.86	3.11	15.23
Oct. 1972-' Sept. 1973	3.15	3.97	1.83	2.33	7.33	4.69	5.52	1.11	2.75	12.91

a. Casual agricultural labourers are those "usually active" in the daily wage market and belonging to a household with agricultural labour as the principal occupational. The data here related to workers 15-59 years of age. Figures in parentheses are percentages of the highest quarterly figures.

Source: Kalpana Bardhan, 1981, p. 38, analysed from the 27th Round of the National Sample Survey of Employment and Unemployment, India, 1972-73.

Underemployment may be *visible* (persons who work fewer months or weeks or shorter hours than they would wish) and *invisible* (those who work full-time at underpaid labour with low productivity) (Standing, 1978, pp. 38-50; Hauser 1977). The concepts of unemployment or labour underutilisation are difficult to apply to persons who work on their own or rented land, however, since normative standards are vague and the reasons underlying labour at less than full capacity are not easily understood (Connell and Lipton, 1977, p. 18).

Type of Unemployment

Open unemployment includes members of the labour force who are available for work, willing to work at prevailing wages and actively seeking employment. Respondents are generally asked a question such as, "In the past week/month/year did you take any active steps to find work?" If they reported talking to friends and/or relatives, going to an unemployment exchange or agency, contacting employers or labour unions, or making other inquiries, they could be classified as having been openly unemployed at some point during the reference period. In rural West Bengal, for example, female labourers were fund to be openly unemployed an average of 1.83 days per week over the year compared with 1.11 days for male labourers (K. Bardan, 1981, p. 38). Days unemployed averaged 1.12 per week for female labourers in the busy season (Oct.-Dec.) and 2.57 in the slack season (April-June), compared with 0.53 and 1.57 days, respectively, for males (Table 23.3).

In a slightly different formulation, a labour market survey of six villages in a semi-arid tropical region of southern India measures ex differences in the average daily *probability of finding wage employment*, that is, the number of days the person was successful in obtaining farm on non-farm work (excluding one's own holding) expressed as a proportion of the number of days in the period that he or she "tried" (Ryan, Ghodake, and Sarin, 1980, p. 368). Table 23.4 presents these sex differences by district and village. The average daily probability of women finding work ranges across villages from 0.49 to 0.91, and of men from 0.70 to 0.92. Men find work more easily than women in the two drought-prone villages of Sholapur district (predominantly food-grain producing) and in the cotton-growing village of Kanzara. Women find work more easily than men in one cotton-producing village and one with irrigated paddy. Unlike most, the table includes tests of the statistical relative variation reflecting seasonal fluctuation in employment opportunities.

Table 23.4 also includes measures of sex differences in labour force *participation rates* (measured here on a daily basis as the proportion of days in the period in which a person worked or attempted to find a job on the daily labour market in and around the village, excluding days worked on the persons' own holding); the average daily *wage rate;* and the average daily *"opportunity cost,"* which is simply the wage rate multiplied by the probability of employment, interpreted as wages lost by not working. A number of interesting conclusions can be drawn from the comparisons of means and of coefficients can be drawn from the comparisons of means and of coefficients of variations. The survey also analyses sex differences by size of landholding and by season in participation rates, the probability of employment, and returns to labour (Ryan et al., 1980, pp. 368-370). The authors conclude that the overall probabilities of involuntary (open) unemployment (1 minus the probability of employment), which can be converted to average daily rates of about 20 per cent for males and 26 per cent for females seeking work, are fax larger than those usually reported for rural India.[10] These new figures help to explain the incentive to migrate citywards even in the face of high urban unemployment.

Concealed unemployment (sometimes known as discouraged workers) includes persons formally defined as not in the labour to seek, work because of low expectations of success. A simple question as to whether the person is available for work even if not currently engaged in an active search would tap this phenomenon. The more restrictive the definition of formal unemployment—that is, the more rigid the requirement of an "active" search and the shorter the reference period for the search — the more likely it is that potential workers (particularly women) will be classified as economically inactive rather than active but unemployed.

TABLE 23.4

Average Participation Rates Employment Probability Opportunity Costs and Wage Rates (in Rupees) for Women and Men in Rural Daily Labour Markets Six Villages of Peninsular India, 1975-76

District/ village	*Participation[a] rates*		*Probability[b] of employment*		*Daily oppor-[c] tunity*		*Daily wage cost rates*	
Sex	*Mean*	*CV[d]*	*Man %*	*CV[d] (%)*	*Mean Rs.*	*CV[d] (%)*	*Mean Rs.*	*CV[d] (%)*
Mahbubnagar	(irrigated paddy)							
Aurepalle								
Male	0.07***	48	0.71***	23	1.77***	25	2.50***	33
female	0.27	61	0..69	20	1.03	26	1.49	16
Dokur								
Male	0.25***	14	0.76***	30	1.97***	35	2.59***	17
Female	0.61	10	0.82	20	1.58	30	1.93	15
Sholapur	drought-prone; food grains)							
Shirapur								
Male	0.38***	29	0.70***	12	1.80***	12	2.57***	13
Female	0.25	22	0.49	37	0.68	47	1.39	18
Kaiman								
Male	0.29***	19	0.92***	11	2.50***	31	2.72***	19
Female	0.22	17	0.77	18	1.08	28	1.40	14
Akola	(relatively assured rainfall; cotton)							
Male	0.48***	14	0.82***	12	2.05***	15	3.72***	11
Female	0.39	22	0.77	30	1.41	35	1.83	12
Kinkheca								
Male	0.30***	22	0.88***	12	2.52***	19	2.86***	11
Female	0.36	20	0.91	7	1.41	22	1.55	19

a. Proportion of days working or searching for work in daily labour market.
b. Number of days working as proportion of days working or searching or work.
c. Daily wage rates multiplied by probability of employment.
d. Coefficient of variation, the standard deviation for each group expressed as a percentage of the group mean.
** differences between males and females significant at .01 level.
*** Differences between males and females significant at .001 level.

Source: Ryan, Ghodake and Sarin, 1980, p. 368.

In rural areas, the discouraged worker effect may be especially strong for women where male unemployment is high, unless the wage labour market is so segregated that women have a good chance of working even if men do not. Where men and women compete for the same jobs, women may simply withdraw rather than search fruitlessly for work. This is of course a matter for empirical investigation. In a large sample survey of rural West Bengal, women in labouring households reduced their current labour force participations by a statistically significant amount high.[11] Rather than compensating for the unemployment of their menfolk with heightened intensity of activity, women in this setting tended to pull out of the labour market altogether.

TABLE 23.5

Number of Months Employed in the Labour Market During Past Year by Men and Women in Garcia Rovira and El Espinal, Columbia, 1978, and Cajamarca, Peru, 1976

Region	Percentage employed					Number of
	1 months	2-4 months	5—11 months	12 months	Total	workers
Garcia Rovira (non-capitalist)						
Women	6	47	18	29	100	(17)
Men	—	31	38	31	100	(29)
Total	2	37	30	30	100	(46)
El Espina (advanced capitalist)						
Women	29	27	16	29	100	(56)
Men	3	11	40	46	100	(236)
Total	8	14	36	42	100	(292)
Cajamarca (predominantly			(121-260 days)	(261 + days)		
Women	40	13	13	34	100	(15)
Men	30	26	13	31	100	(69)
Total	32	24	13	31	100	(84)

Source: Deere and Leon de Leal, 1982, p. 113.

Latent unemployment is one step further removed from general visibility. These are the people who say they would work if we were higher or working conditions. Rarely measured in survey one estimate of the extent of latent unemployment appears in P.K. Bardhan's analysis of results from the survey of rural West Bengal. Among housewives who said they were not employed, not actively seeking work, nor available for wage labour 25, per cent said they would be interested in employment if work could be brought for them to do in their homes (P. Bardhan, 1979, p. 179).

Although we normally think of latent unemployment as an unwillingness to work for prevailing wages in view of the opportunity cost in time, energy, and other activities foregone, a series of questions pinpointing the conditions under which persons not currently in the labour force *would* be willing or eager to work could have important policy implications in the design of income-generating programmes, especially for women. Nag et al. suggest such a series in their proposal for Indian village studies:

> Would main informant be willing to work outside the home or community and/or work for others? What kin of work would she be willing to take? Would she be qualified to do this work? Is this type of work available? What part of the day/year would she be willing to do this work? How much pay would she need to get?......
>
> What do others in the family (husband, mother-in-law, others) think about (the possibility of) main informant working for others or working away from home....? Why? Would (does) this prevent the main informant from doing this work? (Nag et al., 1982, p. 23).

Types of Unemployment

Whereas the concept of unemployment applies only to those in the wage labour market, underemployment can include self-employed cultivators, unpaid family helpers, and paid farm workers alike[12] In assessing the degree of unemployment or underemployment it is important to distinguish among seasonal, occasional, and chronic conditions. Seasonal cycles, for example, tend to produce alternating periods of underemployment and overemployment when measured by hours worked per day amount all three categories of the agricultural labour force — wage labourers, unpaid family workers, and the self-employed. But there is some ambiguity as to whether an agricultural *wage labourer* experiencing short periods out of work is unemployed or underemployed, since much depends on the time reference. If we refer to the daily labour market, a Ryan et al. do in their study of southern India (Table 23.4), then days of no work appear as unemployment. If we refer to the entire year, as in Deere and Leon de Leal's comparison of Colombia and Peru (Table 23.5), then lays or months of no work appear as *underemployment* with reference to the yearly standard.

In measuring sex differences in the degree of underemployment among those who are working, we can distinguish between visible and invisible underemployment. The former includes persons reporting shorter hours or fewer weeks of work than they would like (or than is considered the norm); the latter, persons labouring virtually full-time year-round but at productivity or earnings considerably below their capacity.

There are several ways of a measuring *visible underemployment.* The most direct is subjective: asking workers whether they would prefer to be working longer hours or more days. In rural Egypt, 21 per cent of male workers, 4 per cent of females, and 12 per cent of children interviewed in an ILO labour record survey said they wanted additional jobs (figures the ILO believes to be underestimates, since one-quarter did not answer the question (ILO, 1969, p. 59). And in rural West Bengal:

> .... nearly two-thirds of the women working as casual agricultural labourers were seeking and/or available for more employment inside the village. Some of them were currently employed fully, but most were severely underemployed and suffered sharper seasonal decline in wages and employment than any other group- of rural workers (K. Bardhan, 1981, p. 17).

A second method of measuring visible underemployment is to compare the number of hours per day or days per year worked by specific age and sex groups with a set of norms representing full employment. This procedure clearly requires more detailed data than a simple yes or no response to a question about wanting additional work. In one type of comparison, hours or days of labour "available" in a cultivator household are related to the total number of man-days, woman-days, and child days of labour required for a given size of farm, based on normative standards for particular crops, irrigation systems, levels of mechanisation, and so on. This is an indirect method of estimating underemployment in which household members are not asked how many hours or days they actually worked; instead, their labouring capacity is compared with labour requirements for the farm. Saab used this method to estimate that in Egypt in 1952, averaging over cropping patterns, farm sizes and seasons:

> ..... approximately 170 man-days and 130 woman-days per cultivated feddan were available against annual requirements of 55 man-days and 60 woman-days; ..... The already over-abundant manpower annually available per cultivated feddan would rise to 220 man-days and 170 woman-days: four times the normal needs of cultivation for men and 2.8 times for women (cited in ILO, 1969, p. 58).

The ILO challenges this high estimate of underemployment on several grounds, however, among them that farm operations other than field work (e.g. animal and poultry keeping, processing of farm products, record keeping, travelling to the fields, marketing, clearing canals, etc.) usually account for almost half of total farm labour required, and should be included in the standards set (ILO, 1969, p. 58; see also FAO 1978:33).

Another normative comparison relates the yearly number of hours and days of labour available in a household according to standards of full employment for each age and sex group to the amount of labour actually utilised, as measured by time-use surveys. But what constitutes full employment in an agrarian setting? The ILO survey of rural Egypt identified 301 days per year and eight hours daily for adult males, seven for adult females, and six for young persons of both sexes aged 12-15 not in school as a standard against which the actual labour contributions of individual household members to economic production were assessed.[13] (Labour availability of full-time students was counted only during vacations.) According to these criteria, underemployment among adult males averaged 7 per cent over the year (a balance of considerable over-employment during the busy seasons and under-employment during the slack seasons), 3 per cent among adult females, and 30 per cent among young people (ILO, 1969, pp. 60-63).[14] Again, the ILO believed the amount of visible underemployment among women to be underestimated.

In a slightly simpler analysis, if we assume 12 moths of work to be full employment, data collected on the number of months employed in the labour market in the past year can reveal the extent of underemployment. On three communities in Colombia and Peru about two-thirds of wage earners worked fewer than 12 months (deere and Leon de Leal, 1982, p. 143). In two communities there were no sex differences in the probability of working the full year; only in El Espinal (characterised as 'advanced capitalist") were men more likely than women to work the full year (Table 23.5).

Invisible or disguised underemployment refers to those persons whose working time is not abnormally reduced, but employment is inadequate in other respect such as poor skill utilisation or exceptionally low earnings (ILO, 1969, p. 64). The phenomenon may be captured indirectly by a question as to whether a worker wants to switch jobs. In rural West Bengal:

> ..... The proportion of working women who indicated their willingness to take up alternative paid employment, inside or outside the village, was large [two-third's] — almost as large as the proportion of male workers who responded similarly. Nearly two-thirds of them were from the poorest households. There, 42% of the working women were ready for regular alternative rural employment at wage rates fractionally higher than what they were currently getting (mostly as farm labourers) K. Bardhan, 1981, p. 19).

Many of these underemployed women had been trying for more than six months to find better work. Most would undoubtedly be classified as underemployed with respect to earnings as well as productivity. A study of rural Java found 48 per cent of economically active females and 30 per cent of economically active males underemployed "by reason of low earnings when compared to a standard of minimum economic need (International Center for Research on women, 1980, p. 32).

The concept of underemployment is especially difficult to apply to women of cultivator households with heavy domestic responsibilities and to children in school. Hansen (1969, p. 312) remarks that anything over one-third of normal work hours for Egyptian children should be considered "overemployment," since the labour detracts from time they should be spending in school. The issue for women in even more complicated: what is, or should be, a "normal' work day when they are simultaneously carrying the burden of housework and child care? Is a woman "underemployed" who labours in the fields only three or four hours a day, if the rest of the time is spent in domestic work? Is the "overemployed" if she labours seven or eight hours? What are the standards for time spent on housework—for the essentials without which the household could not function adequately? How many others in the household can or will share in the domestic work? The Egyptian study cited above subtracts one women-day for every five household members from the available female labour supply but notes that time spent on housework may not decrease significantly with a smaller household size (ILO, 1969, pp. 60-61). A survey of labour use among Tanzanian smallholders concludes that most domestic work cannot be viewed as a constraint to the female labour supply because it is usually performed outside of "normal" hours for field work, that is, at "potential leisure periods" (Kamuzora, 1980, p. 131). Yet women in this setting typically add three hours of food preparation during daylight hours to their five hours of agricultural labour, along with other domestic work and work done at night, while men add only a few minutes to their average five hours for farm work and one hour of non-agricultural labour. With two hours less of leisure time during daylight hours than men, are women underemployed, overemployed, or neither?

Most published statistics on agricultural labour force participation are misleading because of their tendency to under-report women's (and children's) activities. Yet accurate data are essential for economic planning. A misreading of trends over time or variations within or among countries in agricultural and non-agricultural employment can lead to serious errors in the identification of employment needs and resources. Rural works projects designed to alleviate seasonal unemployment, for example, depend on accurate targeting of those segments of the population most in need of work. If censuses or labour force surveys exclude substantial numbers of women from the labour force because of their restrictive definitions or cultural blindness to the realities of women's labour contributions and economic need, then measures intended to ameliorate seasonal or chronic poverty may meet with only limited success. Problems of misidentification can be at least partially resolved by more careful design of questionnaires and training of interviewers to sensitise them to their own cultural biases and those of their respondents.

At the heart of the confusion is the question of whether a woman who works unpaid on the family holdings is counted as a member of the labour force or not. The literature is replete with references to the statistical distortions caused by this dilemma (e.g., Boserup, 1975; Standing, 1978; Recchini de Lattes and Wainerman, 1982). The task of correcting the figures to reflect women's real contribution is complicated by inconsistencies in the nature and degree of bias across countries and over time. Women are especially likely to be undercounted in the farm labour force of Muslim countries in North Africa and the Middle East and in Latin America, where strong patriarchal ideologies colour the perception of the economic value of women's work. If women are underenumerated in the labour force, then unemployment are underemployment figures are also biased because they are based on risks experienced by this group.

A comparison of different approaches to the collection of labour force statistics, such as censuses of populations and of farm holdings, reveals sometimes striking disparities in the total courts of agricultural workers. These disparities tend to be relatively small for male workers and for paid workers of both sexes, with some important exceptions. For unpaid females, farm censuses sometimes identify as many as two to ten times the number of agricultural workers as do other sources. Although many of these additions to the labour force are seasonal workers, or women who labour on their holdings for only one or two hours a day, the farm censuses convey a very different image of the sexual division of labour than do most other national-level censuses or surveys.

One solution to the problem of inconsistency across data sources is to adopt new standard definitions that distinguish systematically among several types of economic activity, such as wage labour paid in cash or kind, market-oriented production, production and processing of primary goods inclusive for home consumption, and economic activity encomapssing a range of cost-saving household activities such as gathering food or fuel (Anker, 1982a). Simplified time-use surveys can be applied to the collection of labour force statistics that allow comparability across diverse settings without doing violation to local conditions. Distinctions such as these would end themselves to the analysis of different aspects of labour force participation of particular interest to planners.

Properly specified data on sex differences in labour force participation rates and in the employment status of agricultural workers provide essential information on trends and variations in the sex composition of the farm labour force, and on processes of sex-selective displacement and incorporation. Improved methods of enumerating the unemployed and underemployed would also more accurately reveal the differential effects of economic stress on women's and men's employment chances by class, ethnicity, and season.

NOTES

1. The discussion in this section is drawn from Dixon, 1982b.
2. Economically active persons are classified in the *Year Book of Labour Statistics* ILO, various years) by occupation and by industry according to the 1968 revision of the International Standard Classification of Industries and Occupations. Agriculture as an *industry* includes agricultural and livestock production and services; hunting, trapping and game propagation; forestry and logging; and fishing. Agricultural *occupations* include farm managers and supervisors; general and specialised farmers; agricultural and animal husbandry workers; forestry workers; and fishermen, hunters, and related workers (FAO, 1978, pp. 2-2 to 2-5). The total *numbers* economically active in the industry tend to be slightly higher than those in agricultural occupations, but the *percentage* of women in the labour force is virtually the same in all 61 countries for which recent comparisons are possible.
3. Whereas the gainful worker approach to economic activity inquires about a person's normal or usual occupation, with a reference period extending upto one year, the more common labour force approach stresses *current* activity in a specified brief period such as the day or week preceding the interview (ILO, 1976; Standing, 1987; FAO, 1978). The ILO (1976) recommends that the time-reference period should not be longer than one week except where it is considered that classification on the basis of current activity over this brief time period does not reflect year-round activities, particularly where there is a highly seasonal pattern of employment...." Freedman and Mueller (1977, p. 27) recommend a one-year reference period for the rural labour force because agricultural incomes and expenditures are usually reckoned on this basis. Fong (1980a, p. 30) recommends both: "the gainful worker approach to `catch' regular, including seasonal activities, and the labour force approach to record the entire span of activities, regardless of their frequency, of the preceding week" (see also FAO, 1978). The differences can be significant: in Peru the 1940 census counted women as 31 per cent of farm labour when the question was based on "usual" occupation in a specified week, which probably excluded a large number of seasonal workers (Durand, 1975, p. 241).
4. In many countries up to twice as many persons may work during planting or harvesting as in the slack season (FAO, 1971, p. 208), with higher proportions of women. According to the 1971 population census of Indonesia, women were 41 per cent of an agricultural labour force of 33 million who worked during the "last cropping season" but 34 per cent of the 26 million who worked during the "previous week" of the slack season (World Bank, 1980, p. 26).

5. About one-fifth of males aged between 20 and 64 in the State of Sao Paulo were employed in agriculture in 1970.
6. According to FAO guide-lines, agricultural work includes "feeding and caring for livestock and poultry; working in the fields; working in the market or kitchen gardens; planing farm work; supervising other agricultural workers; keeping farm records; taking farm products to market; bringing feed, fertilisers or other supplies from town to the holding; repairing fences, farm equipment, machinery, etc." (FAO, 1977, p. 45).
7. Agricultural censuses have not been conducted in all developing countries, however, and some do not include or tabulate questions on farm employment. In some countries farm workers are not conducted at all, are restricted to certain categories (e.g., members of holders households only in Lesotho 1970, Uganda 1963-64); are not classified by sex (e.g., hired workers in the Republic of Korea 1961, Pakistan 1971-73); are reported only as total man-days of labour in the past week (e.g., temporary hired workers in many countries); are restricted to certain types of holdings (e.g., "traditional sector only" in the Congo, the Central African Republic, Cameroon 1972-73; European holdings only in Namibia, South Africa Kenya 1960; farm households only, excluding estates and plantations, in Malaysia 1959-60); are classified in a general category of household and permanent hired workers together (e.g., Brunei, 1964).
8. In her analysis of changes in the structural conditions of employment on the Chilean haciendas of the Central Valley drawing on censuses of farm holdings in 1935, 1955, and 1965, Garrett (1976, pp. 12-99) includes an extensive discussion of changes between censuses in methods of classifying workers by employment status, as well as of differences in enumeration practices and results between censuses of agriculture and of population. Garrett concludes that the decline in the female share among permanent, resident workers on large farms is not a statistical artifact but may be due to sex-selective displacement of women due to mechanisation and to discriminatory hiring and firing practices (ibid., pp. 22-3).
9. Temporary workers work less than one-half but at least one-third of the normal work time; occasional workers less than one-third. Reported separately in the 1960 and 1970 rounds of farm censuses, these categories are combined in the 1980 rounds.
10. The unemployment rate as measured in this fashion ranged from 30 to 80 per cent for females and 20 to 50 per cent for males. Peak and slack labour periods differed substantially between males and females in four of the six villages because of sex specialisation by task and crop, according to a detailed summary of the timing of major agricultural operations in each village (Ryan et al. 1980, pp. 368, 372-273).
11. Pranab K. Bardhan presented these data, based on the 43rd round of the National Sample Survey for rural West Bengal, in a colloquium to the Graduate Group in Demography, University of California, Berkeley, May 1981.
12. Sabot (1977, p. 400), drawing on the early work of Joan Robinson in 1936, argues that "By definition, visible underemployment is a wage sector phenomenon only." This is because own-account workers, whether in non-farm or farm sectors, are "free" to work as many hours as they wish. In contrast, the ILO (1969) survey of labour in rural Egypt, discussed below, calculates underemployment among farmers by comparing hours of labour "available" with hours "demanded" by farms of a given size and cropping pattern. Household members with more hours available than demanded are counted as underemployed.
13. It is interesting to compare this Egyptian male standard of 2,400 hours per year (which comes close to the measured averages of 2,280 hours for men in cultivating households and 2,324 for men in farm labourer households reported in table 14) to the typical observations for African farmers of abut 1,500 hours per year in agriculture and for Asian farmers of approximately 3,000 hours (Kamuzora, 1980, p. 124).
14. The degree of underemployment of males did not differ markedly by landholding status. About one-half of adult male household members worked less than 95 per cent of the yearly norm of 2,400 hours in both landless or near-landless households (less than two feddans) and in households with two to five feddans, and about one-third worked 106 per cent of the standard or more (ILO, 1969, p. 63).

24

Women in 'Men's Jobs in Public, Political and Trade Union Life

Opening up 'Men's Jobs' to Women

In her work *Medieval Women*, Eileen Power wrote that in the Middle Ages there were as yet no occupations from which women were excluded.[1] There were women butchers, chancellors (in the courts), as well as metal-workers, cobblers, glovers, belt-makers, bag-makers, hatters, haberdashers, furriers, gilders, bookbinders, painters, silk-weavers, embroiderers, grocers, smiths and goldsmiths. Women were to the found, too, in other trades.

It seems high time that the expressions 'men's jobs' or 'women's jobs' ceased to be used and that distinctions should be drawn only between jobs in industry, crafts, agriculture, trade, the administration, services, etc. This would mean that the notion of sex is no longer relevant when describing an occupation, which should be open to all, men and women alike, according to their ability and vocation.

In the preceding sections we have described the measures taken in both school and out-of-school education, by way of vocational guidance and continuing training, to give girls and women equal opportunities to participate in the economic life and development of their country.

If, then, it is accepted that the problems connected with the employment of girls and women should not be regarded as specifically female but as part of an overall view of the role of human potential in a country's economy, the whole approach to devising ways and means of making up the leeway is radically altered.

In this connection, the International Seminar on the Opening-up to Women of Vocational Training and Jobs Traditionally Occupied by Men, organised by UNESCO and held in Frankfurt from 11—13 November 1980, gave rise to a wide-ranging debate.

The ILO representative who took part in the seminar made the following comment:

> The effects of sex division of the labour market coupled with lack of broad- based

training has played a negative role for women in employment, placing them at a severely disadvantaged position.

It gives them little chance of further training later, limits job mobility, career or personal development, and leaves them vulnerable at limes of technological change or confronts them with redundancy in a particular industry or occupation.[2]

This view sums up well the difficulties usually encountered by women in the world of work. But the increasing pace of change in our societies and particularly in the conception of the role of women gives us reason to hope and indeed to believe that the objectives and principles of action set forth in Unesco's *Second Medium- Term Plan (1984—1989)* can be fulfilled, since the aim, and this is applicable to girls as well as boys, is,

to improve, at all levels of education, the attitude of young people to productive work and socially useful activities; to provide a better preparation for working life, taking into account the evolution of the structure of employment, in particular by revising syllabuses with a view to encouraging job mobility and providing a technological or polytechnical grounding within the system of general education; to develop and improve technical and vocational education.[3]

Since these objectives are likely to lead to reforms in educational structures, at least in some countries, it will be interesting to assess any changes resulting from them in terms of equality between men and women in education, training and employment.

Men's jobs, women's jobs. How can the areas of employment found throughout the world be divided into female and male occupations when certain types of work always done by men in some countries are just as regularly done by women in others?

For instance, building and construction are the exclusive areas of men in many countries, except in India where it is quite natural for women to do this type of work. Conversely, in India, typing and secretarial jobs are done by men whereas in most other countries it is women who do this kind of office work: in Africa, it is fairly evenly divided and there are many men who type and do secretarial work.

Weaving, a specifically female preserve in Latin America and in some African countries, is a man's job in India, except in some textile firms which have come under the European influence or were founded by Europeans.

Whereas in the marketing and distribution sector there are many women in Western countries working as shop assistants, packers, labellers and sales personnel and, though less frequently, in personnel or shop management, in some African countries (Ghana, Guinea, Ivory Coast, Nigeria and Zaire), women practically monopolise the wholesale and retail trade. Organised on a corporate basis, their economic importance has given them the power and assurance to be able to play a role in the political life of their country.

Understandably in the past certain jobs that required great physical strength such as tree-felling or stone-quarrying emerged as typically male occupations and certain types of work that were reputed to be dirty or dangerous did not appeal to women, and yet there was a time in the textile manufacturing industry (wool, hemp and linen) in France and Great Britain when women were employed in steeping and twisting processes under the worst imaginable conditions (heat, damp, etc.).

Today, working conditions have changed in nearly all sectors of activity as a result of mechanisation and automation. Division of labour on grounds of physical strength has been rendered meaningless except in certain very rare cases.

This is exemplified by the experiments carried out after the Second World War in the European socialist countries and in the USSR; girls who trained for the same jobs as boys in co-educational vocational schools, at all levels, have now reached adulthood and work on an equal footing with men in every branch of industry and agriculture.

In the other industrialised countries and in the developing countries, even where some 'male' jobs are beginning to be opened up to women, equal representation of men and women as a matter of course is still far from reality.

At the Conference on Equality for Women, organised by the Commission of the European Communities in Manchester in May 1980, the Vice-President of the Commission stated that:

> [men] will have to learn not to regard the exercise of hitherto specifically male occupations by women as a threat and they will have to understand that jobs that have hitherto been done mainly by women are not by definition less valuable.[4]

Despite all the obstacles and obstructions, there are barriers that have fallen and some jobs previously reserved for men are now open to women. The situation varies a great deal from one country to another, as well as within a single country and from one occupation to another. However, there are not sufficient data for a comprehensive picture of all changes that have occured.

Before going on to some typical examples concerning certain occupations from which women have been barred, entering them by deep-rooted tradition, it may be of interest to note: (a) that no reference will be made to the European socialist countries and the USSR in connection with these new developments for the simple reason that in these countries the problem of equal access by women to male occupations has been virtually overcome or is being overcome for there is in fact no longer any distinction between male and female employment; (b) that there will be relatively few examples taken from the developing countries where the situation concerning women and work is not the same as in the developed, more industrialised countries; and (c) that the growth of unemployment jeopardises the equal right to work, proclaimed though it is the world over.

Some Facts

1. The International Metalworkers' Federation has made a study of female labour

in its sector. According to this study, the proportion of women working in the metals industry is between 20 and 25 per cent of all workers in the branches considered; the lowest percentage (16) was found in Belgium and Canada, and the highest (29) in the Republic of Korea and Austria.

In 1978, the Austrian Federal Ministry of Social Affairs requested the Austrian Institute for Research on Vocational Training to carry out a study with special reference to 120 apprentices training for jobs related to the metalworking industry. One of the conclusions of the study is of particular interest employers who claimed that recruiting women for men's jobs was more expensive than the usual type of recruitment ultimately admitted that they had been wrong.

In addition, the Vienna Chamber of Trades and the Metalworking, Mining and Energy Union have organised technical training courses for girls wishing to enter this male stronghold.

2. In the Belgium armed forces in 1981, a royal decree conferred equal responsibilities and rights on women embarking on a military career. A previous law in 1976 had specified that female military personnel in the army, air force and navy as well as those working for the medical corps would have the same rights and duties as their male counterparts. They were still barred from certain posts, however, and it is that restriction that has now been lifted. Since 1975, 640 Belgian women have been admitted to the military police force.

   In the French armed forces in 1972, there were 9,000 women in the army, and in 1981/82 some 14,100, including 743 officers (136 in the medical corps, 657 junior officers and 86 senior officers). One woman doctor has the rank of a general. She is the Inspector-General of the Air Force health service.

3. There are now countless women in national and municipal police forces throughout the world. The policewoman in uniform has become a familiar figure, an image which a large number of films has helped to popularise. They are a valuable asset to the police force, especially in vice squads and in dealing with women who have been attacked, raped or battered.

   In Italy, in 1981 there were 264 women in the Rome police force, a figure which will soon be brought up to 1,400. In Luxembourg, there are twenty women serving in the police force. In Iraq, there have been women working in the police force for several years now.

4. In civil aviation, there are as yet not many women pilots and flight captains, although there are a few in the United States, France and Belgium. The USSR sent the first woman cosmonaut into space.

5. In Rotterdam (Netherlands), the municipality would like to recruit women for the fire brigade but firemen have raised objections. According to their spokeman, the team spirit would be adversely affected by their presence, which would furthermore entail considerable expense for the installation of cloakrooms, showers and rest rooms. However, the local authorities have not yet had their last word. The firemen are probably forgetting that their work also involves activities

which would be altogether suitable for women, since apart from having to scale high ladders with their fire-fighting equipment, firemen carry out rescue work in cases of asphyxiation, suicide attempts, and so on, which women could do just as well.

6. On the railways and in other forms of public transport, in France, the public transport authorities[5] employ 25,000 women, some of whom are Metro and bus drivers. In Spain, the railway authority has begun to recruit women mechanics and train drivers; the recruitment of a further 1,000 women is now under way. In Sweden, women are currently being trained for jobs in the railways.

   Italian women are fighting for their rights. A young woman from Trieste wanted to become a naval officer; when her application for the entrance examination was rejected by the Livorno Naval Academy, she filed a complaint and the court decided in her favour, reproving those who obstructed free access by women to all forms of employment. Two years ago, the dockers of La Spezia threatened to strike in protest against the recruitment of three women who had qualified as crane operators; the three held out and were finally accepted. At a competitive examination to recruit dockers in Italy (2,543 candidates, including 40 women), two of the female candidates came in the first 200, with 29 and 27 points out of 30. They had both been out of work even though one of them had diplomas in foreign languages and the other in accountancy; they decided to do a 'man's job' rather than remain unemployed. Their admission brought protests from some of their male colleagues.

7. Developments in women's entry into male occupations in the Federal Republic of Germany are as follows:[6]

	1976		*1977*		*1978*	
Occupation	*Total*	*Girls*	*Total*	*Girls*	*Total*	*Girls*
Auto mechanics	77 284	84	80 373	114	88 633	208
General engineering	11 243	30	11 322	34	11 680	102
Electricity	50 702	57	46 533	63	48 614	105
Telecommunications engineering	11 011	123	10 305	187	12 011	255
Painting-varnishing	27 311	197	30 048	343	34 370	621
Carpentry	26 481	264	30 079	382	35 139	627

8. Women miners. There are 2,574 women registered as miners in Appalachia (United States).

   The new technologies are bound to cause upheavals in working conditions, as certain scientific and technological discoveries and inventions have done in the past; this will naturally bring about a change in people's attitudes and will help to ensure effective equality between men and women.

Women in Public, Political and Trade-Union Life

Unesco's *Second Medium- Term Plan (1984—1 989)* states that

> The difficulties women encounter in attaining positions of responsibility strongly emphasise the fact that equality is basically a political problem and that it is related to the balance of power. The participation, or rather non-participation, of women in political life is a fundamental part of the problems surrounding the status of women.[7]
>
> In many countries, women are still excluded, in practice, from high-ranking positions such as head of state, government, political party, military hierarchy or judicial authority.[8]
>
> Stress should accordingly be laid on the need to interest women in these matters to a greater extent. The role played by women's associations, past or present, in this connection should be borne in mind, especially where, faithful to a long tradition, they remain a hive of initiative and concertation.[9]

General observations. Since the right to vote and the right of association are among those to which, in democratic countries, every individual is entitled, it would be of interest to examine how, and to what extent, women have managed to exercise these rights and also to look at the extent to which a woman in a position of power—head of government, minister—may influence the policy of her country in order to abolish inequalities between the two sexes.

The participation of women in trade-union life as ordinary members or officials is very important for their individual development, for a trade union is also a meeting-place where a woman who is employed for the first time will lose a little of her shyness and self-effacing manner as she is urged to give her opinion and take part in discussions. She will have a fuller awareness of her personality and her responsibility for the defence of her rights and participation in trade-union action.

In order to gain a clearer picture of women in elected assemblies, it would be useful to discover their representation percentage in the various political parties.

In *Belgium,* in the legislative elections of November 1981, with 212 seats to be filled in the Chamber, 12 women were elected; they lost 4 seats in relation to the previous legislatures. In the Senate, there are 14 women among the 106 members elected on a national basis; of 50 senators elected by the provincial councils, only 5 are women.

It seems that through the 'preferential votes' procedure, the electoral system has enabled women to progress in the opinion of the electors; unfortunately, this development has not been reflected in their position in the party lists.

In *Denmark,* legislative elections were held in December 1981; there are 47 women in the Danish Parliament among the 179 members; this is the highest proportion registered in the ten EEC countries. Once again as a result of the voting system, the greater preference expressed for women was not reflected by an increased number of seats, as it is the men who decide about places on the lists.

In *Spain,* at present, 30 women sit in the two assemblies out of a total of 558 elected members (20 of 350 in Congress, and 10 of 208 in the Senate).

In *France,* the comparison between the number of women deputies and senators reveals a curious development over the years.

Between 1946 and 1968, their number continued to drop in the National Assembly—from 5.4 per cent to 1.4 per cent— and in the Senate from 3.6 per cent to 1.7 per cent. At present 28 women (out of 491 members) sit in the National Assembly and 9 women (out of 316) in the Senate.

And yet the political role of women has constantly developed, and their position within the political parties has been consolidated—but not, it seems, to the point of establishing a position for them on the lists of candidates which would offer them a level of representation commensurate with their actual political strength.

In *Ireland,* at present, there are 14 women among the 166 members of Parliament; this is the highest proportion ever reached in this country.

In *Italy,* there are 49 women among the 630 members of the Chamber of Deputies and 16 out of 322 members in the Senate.

In the *Federal Republic of Germany,* there are 51 women out of 520 members of Parliament.

In the *United Kingdom,* the proportion of women Members of Parliament is low; at present, only 25 of the 636 Members are women.

In the *European Parliament of the EEC,* women received greater support from the electorate at the 1979 European elections than in the national elections; 67 were elected among the 434 members of the European Parliament. Following the 1984 elections, the figure rose to 75.

In the *developing countries,* some of which have relatively young political and administrative structures, there are states where women occupy very important functions or positions in national political life. Unfortunately, there are no statistical data that would enable detailed information to be provided in this respect.

In order to enable women to play an active part in politics, certain political parties and countries are considering the introduction of a quota system that would fix a minimum number of places to be occupied by women.

Women in Government

Male politicians realised a long time ago that it was in their interest to give women a share in government, long before the latter had obtained the right to vote. In France, for example, three women were appointed secretaries of state in the Popular Front government of 1936. This was an innovation which was well received.

It should be pointed out that a number of very capable women are currently presiding over the destinies of their countries. Countless countries throughout the world now have women ministers, and not only in ministries concerned with social matters. They are no longer an exception and they exercise their responsibilities to the full. But their number still remains relatively small.

Women and Trade Unions

The basic function of a trade union is to defend the rights of its members and to monitor the application of the laws that protect them with regard to remuneration, working conditions, accident prevention, etc.

Under the collective bargaining system, it is hardly possible for an employer to talk to each of his employees. A delegation is therefore required consisting of one or several representatives of the co-operate body and/or of each of its constituent categories. It is the trade unions that assume this role of representing the workers.

Every worker therefore has a material interest in belonging to a trade union, as a means of defending his own interests; and he may also feel a moral obligation to express solidarity with his fellow workers. What is more, the experience of trade-union life is intellectually rewarding and provides opportunities for the development of the individual.

The position of women in the trade unions. Statistics are lacking for many countries, especially in Latin America and Africa, and where they do exist, relate only to an international federation and not those trade unions that are not affiliated to it.

A study provided by the European Trade Union Confederation (ETUC) provides a few percentages in relation to the total number of members. In six countries, the proportion of women in the trade unions affiliated to ETUC range from 40 to 30 percent; these are, in descending order, Denmark, Italy, France, the United Kingdom. Ireland and Belgium. Next are the Federal Republic of Germany and the Netherlands where the levels are between 20 and 11 per cent.

It must also be stated that women are far from being represented in proportion to their numbers within the governing bodies. Thus for the seventeen organisations that replied to the ETUC survey, five have slightly over 10 per cent of women among their executive officers, eight have fewer than 10 per cent and four have none.

Women are most strongly represented in Finland: 30 per cent on the Executive Committee.

The Trades Union Congress (TUC) in the United Kingdom provides more precise figures: there are 2,265,000 women among the 6,022,000 trade-union members, almost 38 per cent. The distribution of women within the governing bodies is as follows: permanent trade-union representatives, ninety women for a total of 1,636 seats; delegates to the TUC, sixty-six women for a total of 418 seats; and members of the executive bodies, forty women for a total of 316 seats.

It has been noted that the level of union membership for both men and women varies greatly with the category of worker.

Trade-union action on behalf of women. In general, the trade unions' commitment to women has been rather weak.

They did not really grasp the fact that there was a female employment problem for a considerable time. For some years now, however, their leaders have been establishing commissions for the study of female employment and placing questions relating to women on the agenda of their discussions. But no real action on any scale has been taken to tackle this issue which, in spite of its occasionally specific and circumstantial nature, has to do with the rights of workers as a whole. Nevertheless, this situation is changing, as a few specific example will show.

In British Columbia, Canada, the civil service union has inserted clauses in a collective agreement whereby female workers benefit in terms of maternity leave, resumption of employment with recognition of the period worked prior to the leave taken in order to bring up a child, and retraining courses to assist them in returning to their occupational activity.

In the *United Kingdom,* at TUC instigation, an equal-opportunity clause is to be inserted in all collective agreements, to the effect that equal opportunities in employment are established without regard to the sex, matrimonial status, beliefs, racial or ethnic origins of the worker.

DIFFICULTIES FACING WOMEN IN THE WORLD OF WORK AND THE NEED FOR ACTION TO ENSURE EQUALITY OF OPPORTUNITY AND TREATMENT

Unemployment among Women

Unesco's Second Medium-Term Plan (1984-1989) states that

> in a period of crisis, the image of women as 'job-stealers' re-emerges with all its force. Although it is as well-known fact that women are the first to suffer from unemployment, owing to their lower qualifications and more restricted geographical and occupational mobility, current economic difficulties have been instrumental in reviving the ideology of a 'woman's place is in the home', which is hardly likely to speed progress towards equal opportunity.[10]

Unemployment is a social evil that is currently affecting every country in the world; as it worsens, it is disrupting the world economy to a dangerous extent; its side-effects are a threat to social harmony and degrading fix individuals.

Reasons Why Women are Particularly Affected by Unemployment

The majority of women in paid occupations perform jobs that are subordinate and ill-paid, requiring few qualifications, and involving repetitive, routine tasks; anyone can replace them after a short briefing and an unemployed man is always ready to take such a place as a last resort.

Automation, which does away with such jobs, hits women particularly hard.

In some sectors, the proportion of part-time (usually half-time) employees is particularly high among women; when jobs are lost, this is the first category to be affected.

Temporary posts, often accepted by women, are not renewed in periods of unemployment.

There are many more women applicants than men for jobs when work resumes after a long interruption; women have a greater number of problems, which are of a more complex nature.

Exploitation of Women Workers

Part-time work and half-time work. In order to reconcile the demands of an occupation with the need to run a home many women, especially when they still have young children, prefer part- time or half-time employment, the conditions of which (pay, job security, etc.) are generally less favourable than those of full-time work.

Doing work at home. A number of women who are obliged to stay at home also do paid work at home. For them, it is a means of supplementing family income, but for many employers, it is a means of making large profits by exploiting a work-force that is plentiful, passive, poorly informed as to its rights and so scattered that any monitoring of the situation is difficult, if not impossible.

Home workers are mainly found in the poorest rural areas and on the outskirts of cities. Owing to their numbers and availability, they are one of the main reasons for the persistence of low wages for women factory workers employed in the same manufacturing sector—the clothing industry, especially the production of underwear, knitwear, cheap leather goods, etc.

In such industries, they account for between 70 and 90 per cent of the total female work-force of the specialised firms. Despite laws to protect them—of which they are mostly unaware—they have no job security, there is no restriction as to their work-load and they do not even enjoy the benefits of social security.

Steps should be taken rapidly in order to create, in rural areas and the outskirts of certain cities, such facilities—and in particular transport—as would enable at least some of these exploited women workers to travel to centres where they could find work offering better conditions.

Strategy of Action to Change the Status of Women

Stressing the danger that action taken on behalf of women may become too isolated, Unesco's *Second Medium- Term Plan (1984-1989)* states:

> The crippling restrictions that weigh on women are hardly likely to disappear so long as they are regarded as 'women's' problems and not as global problems of concern to society as a whole; so long as any action on behalf of women is not preceded by the

> launching of activities designed to inform the entire community and arouse its awareness.
>
> For the expected process of change must involve the whole of society. The achievement equality between the sexes does not merely mean enabling women to attain the same status as men in order to fit into a world fashioned according to the interests and dreams of men alone.[11]
>
> Before setting Out, in the conclusion to this work, all those measures that would make possible, encourage and accelerate such change, we shall examine several models of action that could be taken in this domain.

Model A

This model is provided by the United States, where a federal authority exists side by side with the various state authorities, making it constantly necessary to ensure a balance—particularly in policies concerning equality—between the federal government's approach and the capacity of the local authorities to carry out such policies and introduce innovations.

Title IX of the Education Amendments of 1972, adopted in the United States, lays down that:

> No person shall, on the basis of sex, be excluded from participation in, be denied the benefits of or be subjected to discrimination under any educational programme or activity receiving federal financial assistance.

The Office for Civil Rights (OCR), bringing together representatives of the Departments of Education, Health and Welfare, is responsible for enforcing Title IX and may use an effective sanction—withdrawal of federal government funds from any project that does not observe these legal provisions.

Application of the principle of equality has subsequently been strengthened by three legislative measures.

The Women's Educational Equity Act (WEEA). Enacted in 1974, its main aim is to encourage all state departments of education, by means of technical support, to set up or develop training workshops for personnel in the main school systems, including technical schools and courses.

Accordingly, 42 per cent of WEEA projects between 1974 and 1977 concerned educators (teachers, administrators and counsellors); 33 per cent were aimed at groups outside the school system (parents, women's groups and community associations), an innovation of great importance.

The remaining projects were directly concerned with the development of new curricula and textbooks or dealt with careers, careers guidance and vocational training from the standpoint of the principle of equality.

A range of target groups have benefited from grants and contracts designed to ensure application of the equal right of girls and women to education, factors such as race or ethnic group, age and socio-economic background being taken into account.

Six major groups of specific WEEA activity may be identified.

Development and evaluation of school curricula, textbooks and educational materials.

Pre-service and in-service training of educational personnel programmes and methods.

Research and development.

Counselling and guidance, including the preparation of non-discriminatory tests or questionnaires.

Development of educational activities for the benefit of women who are unemployed or underemployed.

Extension and improvement of programmes for women in vocational education, career guidance, physical education and educational administration.

Also worthy of note is the creation of the National Advisory Council on Women's Educational Programmes. The seventeen members of this council, men and women, are broadly representative of the general public, reflecting as they do different racial groups, ethnic minorities, age-groups and places of origin.

The Vocational Education Act (VEA). In existence since 1963, it was amended in 1976 in order to incorporate positive measures designed to enforce equality between the sexes in vocational training.

This was an important step forward in opening up to women forms of training in occupational fields hitherto reserved for men.

VEA undertakes a real pursuit of discriminatory practices in education, career guidance and the vocational training of girls and women in instances where the institutions or bodies which provide these services receive federal government funding.

An annual report must be presented to Congress by the Secretary of Education.

'Citizen-watchdog councils' have been established in each state, comprising members of both sexes and including, by obligation, women who are well informed about problems of sexual discrimination in relation to employment.

Nevertheless, the granting of federal aid is not automatic; it is subject to the submission of five-year and annual plans concerning the opening of programmes to both sexes, the elimination of sexual discrimination and stereotyping and action adopted to encourage young men and women to follow careers where they are traditionally in a minority. Other measures are envisaged with regard to adult women in situations where they require guidance or further guidance, further training or retraining.

The Comprehensive and Employment Training Act (CETA). Passed in 1978, it tackles the existence of the sex-stereotyping of jobs and requires employers and those responsible for training to organise vocational training courses for women in all sectors where they constitute less than 25 per cent of the total work-force.

Results achieved. As these were pilot schemes (two of them are presented in Chapter II of this work), the evaluation contracted by the United States Office of Education stresses all the peripheral requirements that determine the long-term success of such large- scale undertakings.

Indeed, obstacles persist with regard to the adjustment of women to the conditions of male employment (factory work, shift- work, managerial work, overtime, mobile work). They concern, first, the social measures providing for the care of children when they are not at school, and, second, the financial assistance which should be made available during training, further training or retraining courses for the least well off.

But more important than the need for social and economic measures to accompany these reforms is the lack of a general consensus on the role of men within the home and at work.

Model B

In contrast with Model A, we will now examine the case of countries where action is developing within a centralised framework; these examples are taken from the Scandinavian region and the socialist countries of Eastern Europe.

B—1. Sweden. Sweden has undertaken a long-term reconstruction of the school system and of educational and vocational guidance in order to effect a fundamental change in attitudes: abolishing the work/home antithesis and thus changing the traditional allocation of specific roles to men and women.

Sweden is simultaneously implementing positive discrimination programmes aimed at giving women access to training sectors leading to so-called 'male' branches of activity. This is a completely new conception of the criteria governing the roles of women and men. Sweden had already expressed this in 1968 in a statement to the United Nations to the effect that a decisive and durable improvement in the status of women could not be achieved by measures aimed at women alone; it was equally necessary to abolish the conditions that tended to assign certain privileges, obligations or rights to men.

There can, furthermore, be no decisive change in the distribution of functions and status as between the sexes if the duties of the male were to remain unaltered.

The allocation of roles sought by Sweden since 1968 can be represented in Figure 24.1.

The original approach relating to child protection, the role of parents, the family economy, relations between girls and boys and participation in work and leisure which follows from this diagram can be recognised immediately. In the succeeding years, the principle of equality has been incorporated to an increasing extent in all educational processes, from the nursery school to the university, including vocational training.

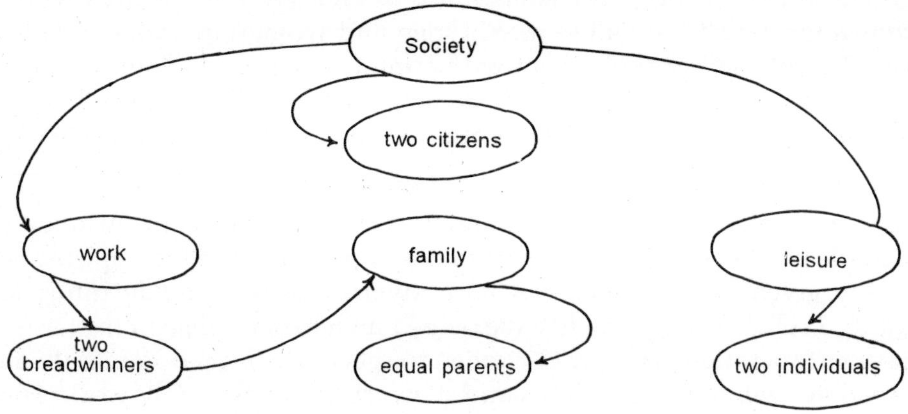

Fig. 24.1. Difficulties facing women in the world of work and the need for action

The Swedish model thus deserves to influence the education policies of the other industrialised countries that are still far from achieving this degree of integration of the principle of equal opportunity.

Nevertheless, the situation is far from being perfect. Admittedly, much real progress has been achieved, but Sweden has not yet arrived at genuine equality of opportunity for both sexes. Girls—even those who have received the same education as boys—still prefer the activities traditionally allocated to their sex. Women frequently look for part-time work, which reduces their chances of promotion and puts them first in line for redundancy during periods of economic crisis.

Nevertheless, it should be emphasised that the world of work has now joined the efforts undertaken in the education sector on behalf of women and to ensure a fairer sharing of domestic chores.

The pressure from trade unions and political parties has been decisive in this respect, hence the importance of the participation of women in those areas where their involvement at the level of decision-taking can only be beneficial to society as a whole.

There have been other initiatives along similar lines in the labour market to interest women in hitherto male professions. In the industrial sector, six counties have launched experimental programmes, two of which have already been mentioned (the Kristianstad County project and the Volvo works project at Koping).

These projects were incorporated in the selective measures prepared in 1970 by the Advisory Council on Equality between Men and Women. Working closely with the Prime Minister, this Council, since replaced by the *Jamstallhedskommitten* has been active in three areas: (a) in relation to local employment offices, requiring them to have staff specialising in the improvement of job prospects for women; (b) in relation to employers who receive a subsidy in return for which they must recruit men and women in sectors where they are absent or in a minority, and provide them with appropriate training; and (c) in relation to companies that receive state aid to establish new factories and contribute to regional development, the requirement being that women as well as men occupy at least 40 per cent of the new jobs created.

Development in the state sector. The National Telecommunications Administration is setting an example by encouraging the recruitment of personnel of the opposite sex to that dominant in any given sector. Brochures and advertisements provide information and create awareness. Probationary periods have helped men to specialise in the largely female telephone services (operation, sales) and women to specialise in predominantly male areas such as installation, maintenance of lines and networks, and assembly work. Forty-seven men and fifty-nine women took advantage of the initial trial period.

It was observed that while women appreciated their new working conditions, the men, with a few exceptions, were not happy with their new jobs—which they found monotonous, lacking in prospects and poorly paid—except as a provisional situation.

Other experiments are being conducted in the Swedish State Railways and in the Prison and Probation Administration.

In July 1980, Sweden promulgated a new Act on Equality between Men and Women in Working Life. This law makes provision for the banning of sex discrimination and required employers to take steps to promote equality.

Contrary to what is happening in the United States, the Swedish experiment, which is centralised and uniform throughout the country, has helped to produce a general consensus in favour of change in society with regard to equality between women and men.

B-2. The socialist countries. Here we see the alternative form of the egalitarian strategy in these highly centralised countries. Two points must be made: despite common features, there are appreciable differences from one country to the next; on the other hand, what distinguishes all of them from the United States and the Scandinavian countries is the absence of a systematic struggle against the stereotyping of women as being solely responsible for the home and children, in spite of the fact that they are generally working on a full-time basis.

The progressive family policy applied in most of the socialist countries of Eastern Europe was dealt with at length in the section on forms of assistance which governments may provide to working mothers. Hungary offers the best example in this respect, whether in terms of maternity leave and leave for bringing up children or the pre-school, school and out-of-school care services facilitating the supervision and protection of children during the absence of working mothers.

The measures to provide continuing education within the firm, the refresher and further training of 'returnees' and the arrangements facilitating retraining courses have also been mentioned; they are certainly necessary, useful and effective to the extent that all women who require these services could profit from them. But the amount of time which they are able to devote to this training depends upon the sharing of family responsibilities and chores between the married couple. Indeed, so long as women alone must shoulder these responsibilities and chores, they can only take part by extending their working day (work, family responsibilities, continuing education).

Nevertheless, there have been a number of changes since 1960: the percentage of women employed in activities of an intellectual nature has increased much more rapidly than the percentage involved in basic manual operations.

In the USSR in 1978,[12] of every 1,000 women of working age, 781 had, on average, received either higher or secondary education.

In the German Democratic Republic, the percentage of specialised women workers who had reached a comparable level rose from 28.9 per cent in 1961 to 47.8 per cent in 1978. In Poland the increase ranged from 27.9 per cent to 42.2 per cent between 1960 and 1978.

Whereas in the USSR the percentage of women engaged mainly in manual work stood at 46 per cent in 1970, in areas of intellectual work the advancement of women was appreciably more marked, the percentage increasing from 52 to 59 per cent.

In Hungary it was estimated in 1940 that 87 per cent of working women were employed in manual jobs while 13 per cent were engaged in intellectual work. In 1968 these figures had changed to 76 and 24 per cent respectively.

The number of women specialists with a high educational attainment is increasing everywhere. In Bulgaria, they were eight times as numerous in 1978 as in. 1956, their number having risen from 14,000 to 110,000.

In European socialist countries, about half the specialists are at present women. The number of women engineers in particular has increased to an impressive extent. In the USSR, women account for 35 percent of project engineers, over 45 per cent of technologists and 40 per cent of technicians.

In Bulgaria, women engineers represent one-third of the total number in this occupational category. The professions of teacher, economist and librarian have benefited especially from this increased number of women graduates. The medical profession, along with teaching, is particularly attractive to women, who achieve considerable success in these careers.

In Hungary the number of women doctors rose from 100 in 1952 to 11,300 in 1978; that year, they totalled 11,900 in Bulgaria and 640,000 in all fields of specialisation in the USSR (where their percentage figures have however recently fallen slightly from 75.8 per cent to 71.8 per cent).

The World Health Organisation (WHO), which provided this information (following a survey conducted between 1960 and 1970), says that women pharmacists are growing in number. In Poland, they account for 85 per cent and in Finland 90 per cent of the profession.

Among the many reasons that explain why men are leaving the medical sector, WHO includes the decline in prestige and earnings.

Women in these countries have also earned for themselves a high reputation as agronomists, zootechnicians and veterinary surgeons.

Generally speaking, the rapid rise of scientific and technological development in these countries has led to unprecedented economic and social progress. That women have contributed very largely to this can be seen from the number of female scientific workers in the USSR which rose from 59,000 in 1950 to over half a million (some 522,500) in 1978. By and large, they make up 40 per cent of the total scientific work-force including researchers and, more specifically, 14 per cent *of* holders *of* doctoral degrees in the sciences.

In Bulgaria, where the study of the sciences was at one time completely out of reach of women, they now account for more than one-third of workers in this field. In Hungary, there were nearly 10,000 high-level women scientists in 1978.

Born in Warsaw, Marie Curie, under the name of Sklodowska, paved the way for this progress, and it is now no longer rare to find women in fields of very high scientific ability, such as astronomy, nuclear fission, biology, genetics and many others.

The breakthrough by women in the European socialist countries in attaining the highest professional levels clearly shows that the war of the sexes' has no justification.

Progress in this direction should begin with the opening up to women of occupations other than those which they choose naturally. Admittedly, even in the USSR, women turn more towards traditionally feminine occupations such as textiles in which they are in the majority, since they are required to do forty hours of practical work in textiles during their introductory work activities at school; similarly, as they are required to take social service courses we find them, as adults, in the paramedical and health sectors where they represent 80 per cent of personnel.

The Soviet system for the further training of working women is based on a simple concept: when a worker has achieved perfect mastery over the type of work to which she is assigned, she can take a further training course in order to move up to a higher grade; she is then provided with all the facilities required for this second stage of learning. When she had completed all the stages in the process—while continuing to work—and has proved her ability at every stage, she can go on to the next level of training, thus moving up from post to post in the hierarchy of qualifications and corresponding jobs.

Admittedly many women stop at an intermediate level, but the most intelligent and tenacious—and those who are least encumbered with household obligations—will reach the very top of the ladder.

In concluding this description of the position of women in the economy of the European socialist countries, it can be said that there are still two weak points. First, there are many educated women who have perfect mastery over difficult techniques and abstract mathematical and physical laws, but they are not yet in charge of undertakings or major state bodies. Second, the fact that responsibilities in the home are not shared—or are inadequately shared—has not allowed women to benefit fully from the educational and training programmes open to them.

Model C

The Federal Republic of Germany offers us another model, that of a partly, centralised, partly decentralised system. There is no overall ministerial policy concerning women or measures aimed at changing the respective roles within the family, the school system or professional circles. However, girls are admitted to technical and vocational courses and boys can be trained in home economics. Nevertheless, owing to the shortage of qualified manpower, especially technicians, and male candidates for training in this category of employment, it has proved necessary to review the policy in this area. One of the solutions chosen has been the opening-up to women of branches of training and jobs which had traditionally been the preserve of men.

The Federal Institute for Vocational Training co-ordinates projects and organises the following: (a) consultations on the objectives and main areas covered by the projects; (b) regular working meetings between project directors, educational advisers, the Federal Institute, the Federal Ministry of Education and Science; (c) supervision of all projects; and (d) evaluation of results.

> *Common features of the pilot projects.* Projects generally stem from an economic need in a given region and/or specific problems within a firm. In all cases, there is close association between the professional circles and representatives of the Federal Ministry of Education and Science which may finance up to 75 per cent of the cost of an operation. Preliminary studies seek to determine the external and internal conditions on which the organisation by the firm in question of a training programme for young women depends, and to identify the industrial and technical sectors and the specific occupation within these sectors where young women will have a real possibility of employment after training.

In order to overcome obstacles that might subsequently prevent the extension of such experiments, an analysis of adverse or unfavourable factors affecting the incorporation of female workers in the industrial and technical branches concerned is undertaken throughout project implementation.

When groups are formed, an effort is made to ensure that they are mixed, small in number (15 to 20), and uniform in terms of basic educational levels.

Motivations are diverse: certain young women want to complete or change their field of training; others want to have a qualified occupation. Divorce, widowhood or merely the desire to be economically independent can also constitute adequate motivations. Women who are unemployed, who want to obtain a qualification, who are unmarried with dependent parents or children Or who need to return to working life are among those who could be interested in this type of project.

Choice of location for the pilot projects and the specialised skills taught. Choice of location is first of all geographical— states of the federation, cities; then by economic sectors—industries and industrial regions; lastly by structures—large, medium and small enterprises. Nineteen places, including large cities such as Berlin (West), Bonn, Bremen, Esslingen, Frankfurt. Frankfurt-Darmstadt, Hamburg, Hanover, Munich and Saarbrucken have received 700 trainees in close to 150 firms in various sectors (electrical and mechanical engineering; precision tool-making, metal cutting, auto mechanics, radio and television assembly; telecommunications, central heating and air-conditioning, etc.).

The length of the training courses held between 1978 and 1980, which were split up into stages, has varied: eighteen months for electrical-instrument fitters; thirty-six months for auto mechanics and gas and water fitters; and forty-two months for toolmakers and electrical fitters.

The first recorded results. It is still too early to make any definite assessment of the impact of these experiments, but it has already been observed that: (a) no serious problem has been reported during the training courses; (b) there were fewer drop-outs among the girls than the boys; (c) the performance of the girls was equal to that of the boys; (d) 90 per cent of the girls would have made the same choice again if required; (e) training personnel have generally assessed the girls very favourably; and (060 per cent of the girls had chosen their new career together with their parents.

But promises of employment at the level of the recently acquired qualification are not necessarily kept in all cases. In addition, regulations relating to female employment (working hours in particular) restrict access to certain industrial occupations and should therefore be amended.

Consequences of the experimental projects in the organisation of work. The revelation of certain contradictions between the political will to integrate women into the world of work and current regulations led the authorities concerned to study a number of problems from a fresh standpoint. This includes bringing legislation relative to female employment into line with the development of technology and the new training opportunities for women; introducing more flexible working hours for both men and women in different industrial sectors; re-examining conditions for part-time work with a view to extending it to workers of both sexes; and improving further training systems, particularly for women who have interrupted paid activity for family reasons, in order to provide them with better or new qualifications. In conclusion it must be pointed out that, in the first place, these pilot projects in the Federal Republic of Germany have provided the opportunity for effective collaboration between the

Federal and Lander Ministries of Labour and Education on the one hand and between the employers, trade unions and local authorities on the other. These projects are the expression of a genuine desire, justified by the need for qualified labour, to strengthen equality between men and women in vocational training and in employment, including access to occupations traditionally reserved for men. Furthermore, it is possible, with different means and in different contexts (United States, Sweden, socialist countries), to implement a policy of equality for men and women in education, training and employment, and to obtain encouraging results.

Legal Measures

It can be seen from an examination of various situations that, in most of the countries of the world which have proclaimed the principle of equality between men and women, there is no institutional framework, that is to say, a body of laws accompanied by measures to ensure their effective application; until the necessary effort has been made in real terms—and with an appropriate budgets—to enable the rural areas to reach the level of the urban areas, it will not be possible to achieve a de facto situation of equality—theoretically concerning both sexes but in fact affecting women more seriously—because of the difficulties of life in the rural zones.

Political declarations and laws. The former express intentions but without obligations, whereas the latter are binding. They express the political will of the government in concrete form and provide victums with the opportunity to lodge complaints, demand due treatment and compensation for harm suffered. Nevertheless, a law, however perfect, cannot be effective unless everyone knows about it and understands it, particularly those whom it seeks to protect.

Justification and scope of laws. Although in spirit certain specific laws have essentially the same aim, they cannot, however, disregard actual national situations—which differ from country to country— if they are to be effective. But taking account of these realities should not prevent the introduction of modifications and innovations in an appropriate manner.

The Democratisation of Laws

Admittedly, laws include niceties, are expressed in a language which is frequently specialised and sometimes allow of very finely shaded interpretations. Hut everyone is equally capable of understanding their spirit, utility and scope. The mass media can explain them simply and clearly in a language that everyone understands whenever this proves necessary.

Any law designed to combat discrimination in its various forms must include the education structures, from the nursery school to university, and the school and out-of-school aspects of career guidance and initial and in-service vocational training, and must guarantee respect for the dignity of woman and her physical and moral integrity, and protect her against the antagonism of every kind to which she may be exposed, including that originating in the mass media.

Legislation concerning female employment must be re-examined in accordance with the spirit of the ILO conventions and recommendations *inter alia* which seek to ensure equality of opportunity and treatment for women and men.

Social legislation must not only take account of the role of mothers by protecting maternity but encourage sharing of family duties by both parents while supporting and developing provisions for child care and making domestic chores less burdensome.

Placing issues concerning women in a global context. Advancing beyond the level reached by those countries which have established a 'ministry' or 'department for the status of women', states should establish a commission or higher councils whose task it would be to supervise the implementation of measures designed to ensure equality of opportunity within the overall context of the fully recognised interests of men and women, at both the individual and community levels, so as to ensure a better quality of life for all.

A Strategy of Action at the International Level

Awareness of the problem of inequality between women and men and of its adverse consequences for individuals, families, communities and countries has become universal, although major differences of emphasis and meaning still occasionally exist. Many associations and local, national and international organisations have studied this problem, concentrating on more important aspects in relation to the local, national or international context.

As regards inequality of opportunity in education, Unesco has, for its part, developed an extensive programme of action covering national and international studies, publications, meetings (congresses, seminars, consultative committees), experimental projects and the application of conventions and recommendations against discrimination in education on the basis of sex, race, etc.

Where educational action also involves vocational training, Unesco and ILO co-operate closely in joint operations to which each brings the knowledge and experience of its particular field of competence. The four meetings referred to in the Introduction to this work benefited from this close co-operation between Unesco and ILO.

The problem of inequality between women and men, in all its dimensions, is far from being overcome. But the knowledge and experience gained in this field should enable those countries which are determined to do so to devise and implement effective measures to tackle this problem, either in its entirety or in priority areas such as education, guidance, training and employment.

NOTES

1. Eileen Power, *Medieval Women.* Cambridge, Cambridge University Press, 1975.
2. A. G. Mitchell, *Summary' Records of Discussions. Annex IV:* Training of Women for Entry Into Non-traditional Occupations, p. 2, Paris, Unesco (International Seminar on the Opening-up to Women of Vocational Training and Jobs Traditionally Occupied by Men, Frankfurt, 1980) (Doc. ED. 80/ Conf. 708 (Cot. 2).

3. UNESCO, *op. cit.*, p. 126, para. 5064.
4. Address by Commissioner Henk Vredeling to the Conference on Equality for Women, Manchester, 28—30 May 1980.
5. Including the railways authority, the Societe Nationale des Chemins de Fer (SNCF).
6. *Women's Europe—Information Bulletin, Brussels,* Commission of the European Communities, General Information Office, 1981, 1982 and Supplement No. 7.
7. UNESCO, *op. cit.*, p. 279, para. 14016.
8. *Ibid.*, p. 280, para. 14017.
9. *Ibid.*, para. 14018.
10. UNESCO, *op. cit.*, p. 278, para. 14010.
11. UNESCO, *op. cit.*, p. 281. paras. 14028—9.
12. *Women's Participation in the Economic and Social Activities in the USSR and European and European Socialist Countries*, Geneva, International Labour Office, 1980, 22 pp. (distribution limited).

25

Women Workers in Unorganised Sector

A field enquiry is, of necessity, limited to a few selected aspects of a problem set in a fragment of the universe of discourse. This study is no exception, but before discussing the results of the enquiry in detail, a brief outline of the general problem and its recent history is presented here in an attempt to place the study in its proper perspective in time and space. This task is rather difficult in this particular case because the connotation of concepts like the informal sector or employment in this sector, have not yet been properly and clearly defined. As a result there are problems of measurement and comparability over regions and time. Studies on women face an added difficulty because until recently, the issue had attracted little attention from scholars, and therefore, disaggregated data for women alone is not always available.

The Character of the Unorganised Sector

Ever since attention was drawn to the widespread prevalence of informal or unorganised activities in the developing countries, studies of this phenomenon in numerous situations have been undertaken, often under the sponsorship of the International Labour Organisation. On the basis of the data obtained from such country-wide studies, several scholars have tried to make generalisations about the salient features of these groups of activities and workers. However, attempts to delineate the definitive characteristics of this sector, whether in terms of the character of the product or the technologies used (traditional or modern), the markets served (local or general) or the consumers of the product (poor or rich), have not been very successful because no such pattern appears to be universally valid. The exact combination of activities that actually exist in any one region at a given time, seem to be an outcome of the interaction of various factors such as the complexity of the economy, the actual extent and distribution of control of investment resources and the technological choices available to that economy. Since the configuration of such factors is almost always specific to each situation, what is true of one country at one time, fails to apply to another. All that can be said is that the sector usually consists of productive activities with loosely formed groups bound by diverse types of informal working contracts. It includes a section of the self-employed, wage earners, family producers as also the household workers.

While the concept 'unorganised sector' cannot be defined precisely, few would deny that in each of these countries there is distinct break in the economy separating the 'formal' activities from the other activities and it is possible to assign any activity or group of workers to either of the two sectors with a fair degree of general agreement. The division between the two sectors in each country is marked by a distinct change in the wages and working conditions enjoyed by the workers as they move from one sector to the other. This difference is sufficiently marked so as to warrant a qualitatively different treatment. For some reason, workers in the organised sector can bargain effectively with their employers while other workers in the country cannot. The bargaining strength of the former may be due to their superior skills, though generally it is greatly reinforced by the political militancy of their trade unions. Other workers are not capable of building up such bargaining strength and therefore continue to work under deplorable working conditions.

There are several reasons why the prevalence of such working conditions has become a matter of grave concern to social scientists and policy makers in India as elsewhere in the world. In India, as in most developing countries, small pockets of formal (officially recorded) activities were seen by the middle of the last century and this formalisation was concentrated mainly in the urban areas and often in organisations with a large-scale production for the farflung markets. Since this period, industries such as textiles, steel, tea, chemicals and engineering have flourished in several large-scale factory units following modern management styles and having trade unions of workers. The scope of such activities gradually increased and with it the difference between the organisation and working of the two sectors became clear.

However, this dichotomy was not as important in India at the time of Independence, as it is today, from the point of view of social justice. Workers in some occupations had well-organised and highly politicalised unions since the second decade of the twentieth century. However, till independence they had not won any significant economic concessions from the employers mainly because of the absence of political power in the hands of the Indian political parties. Therefore, the differences in the working conditions of the formal and the informal sectors were not so sharply marked, and the imbalance between the supplies of labour and the investible resources had not become so glaring. In India today, a fast growing labour force is confronted with a relatively slow growing and closely held stock of capital and the pressure of this uneven bargain is holding down the real wages in the free market, both in the rural and the urban areas. Trade unions with greater political importance have managed to maintain the actual earnings of their workers at a level at least above that required for a minimal living, but workers without such protection have lost steadily in the inflationary situation of the sixties and the seventies. Thus, the difference in the earnings and expectations of the two groups of workers has been steadily increasing.

In the absence of any systematic data about the working conditions in the informal sector of any region, it is difficult to give conclusive evidence about the extent of difference in the two sectors. The occupations and activities, as also the technologies used in each sector are not quite the same and it is not always possible to compare them. Nevertheless, the trends are unmistakable. For example, a study of the electrical fan industry in Calcutta showed that the average earnings per worker in the small units were less than those of the workers in the bigger units. Similarly, in the shoe industry the minimum salary of a worker in a registered large unit was over twice as much as that of any of the artisans working in the informal shoe industry. The same is true of the *biri* industry where a worker under the putting out system earns less than half the officially fixed minimum rates of pay for a *biri* factory worker. Apart from these differences in their earnings, the workers in the organised sector received other benefits such as paid holidays, medical or old age allowances and enjoyed a fairly high degree of job security. It is the absence of these very benefits that separates the lot of the workers of the unorganised sector from the rest.

The unorganised sector presents two knotty problems of social justice to policy markers. First, an increasingly large segment of the working population is being forced to live at the margin of survival. Second, given the availability of such cheap labour in the unorganised sector, employers are likely to divert more and more activities to such organisations. This would mean that the working class as a whole, will in future receive an ever declining share in the products of development. No popular government can afford to ignore these possibilities for long. The recent attempts at intervention by the state have, however, been rather confused and misdirected because very little is known about the production processes and working conditions in the informal sector. The need for more information has led policy makers, particularly the Central Ministry of Labour and the Planning Commission, to sponsor research in the field. The present study forms a part of the series of research studies of the unorganised sector that have been sponsored by the Unemployment Committee of the Planning Commission through the ICSSR for this purpose.

Employment in the Unorganised Sector. At the beginning of these explorations of the nature of the unorganised sector several public documents and records have attempted to delimit its bounds and to give rough estimates of its size both by the kind of activities involved and the areas where they exist.

TABLE 25.1

All India Work Force (1973)

	Organised sector		*Unorganised sector*		*Total*	
	Urban	*Rural*	*Urban*	*Rural*	*Urban*	*Rural*
Male	154.16	12.73	158.74	1258.97	312.90	1271.70
Female	15.30	6.05	56.40	700.25	71.70	706.30
Total	169.46	18.78	215.14	1959.22	384.60	1978.00

Based on Tables (4.1) and (4.16) of the *Draft Five Year Plan 1978-83*, Government of India, Planning Commission, New Delhi, 1978.

The employment figures in the organised sector are based on regular official records and are therefore, fairly accurate. The other figures are estimates based on nationwide sample surveys of employment and unemployment by the National Sample Survey authorities. In these surveys, the main problem is of definition of the term employment. Several alternatives defining this concept ranging from the most rigorous to the most permissive have been considered. At the rigorous end is the measure of the size of the work force by the daily status of each person—strictly on the basis of whether or not a person had worked on the day of the interview. A less rigorous alternative considered a person's weekly status, in other words, to include all those in the work force who had worked at least sometime during the previous week. A still more accommodating definition takes into account seasonal or part-time employment, or even a person's usual status whether he considers himself a regular worker or not.

These alternative specifications of the word 'employment' become necessary because of the amorphous character of the unorganised sector where the status of being employed does not, in itself, imply that a worker works for any standard number of hours a day or that he works regularly for a certain given number of days a year. Moreover, in the unorganised sector, employment does not necessarily mean that the worker gets a regular wage payment for the work. The work may take the form of unpaid family labour, or be a combination of manual labour and risk bearing ability as in the case of a self-employed person, or a contractual obligation for repayment of an outstanding loan as in the case of bonded labour. The payment may be in cash or in kind or a combination of the two, and it may be a regular time rate wage, a piece rate wage, a share in the family consumption, or merely a guarantee from the employers of a minimal living for a specific period.

Women Workers

Measurement of women's employment presents some additional problems. Even if the majority of women can be described as engaged in household tasks, the category 'housework' is very much an extended one for poor women. If a woman using her own labour produces from freely available materials certain kinds of goods and services which the family otherwise, would have had to purchase at a price in the market, then she has, in principle, earned that amount of real income for the family. Even if one ignores the alternative costs of services such as washing or cooking, there are several additional tasks that poor women perform for which the decision as to whether they are economic activities or not is really difficult. For example, rural women collect fuel and edible roots, greens and fruits from the forest. Urban women of Calcutta collect half burnt coals from rubbish heaps, make cakes from cowdung in the streets and use the combination as a fuel for cooking. In most areas and communities, women of artisan families participate in the family's production activities. They also look after the family's milch animals, poultry or vegetable plots—products which are partly sold in the market.

Women's economic tasks in India can thus be divided into three categories (a) as an entrepreneur, a self-employed worker or a wage earning employee producing goods and services for the market; (b) as a participant, in return for a share in the living, in the family' production activities whose products are, at least partially, meant for the market; and (c) as a contributor to the family's real income by processing some goods which are available free (at the expense of some labour in collection) in order to supplement or replace its market purchases. There is no uniform official policy as to whether or not all these three categories of tasks are to be taken into account for measuring women's employment. Nor is there any standard requirement about the number of days per year or hours per day a woman has to work on such tasks in order to be considered employed. This has led to frequent controversies about official estimates of women's employment. Controversies about measurement have obscured another equally important issue, a large part of women's work tends to fall in the second and third categories mentioned above. Changes over time have, if anything, reinforced this tendency. Work in the second category is slightly better than bonded labour—even if a particular person has some special aptitude or has acquired a skill with experience and age, there is no way that these extra qualifications can be rewarded at work by an increment or promotion. Work in the third category can only be an anachronism in present Indian society, where the supply of freely available goods is fast shrinking. The people still following this practice are doing so, not by choice, but only because they are the rejects of the market mechanism. Work in either of these categories does not give the woman any control over family's disposable income, including the share she has earned, and also denies her the status of a socially productive worker.

TABLE 25.2

The Number and Rate of Rural and Urban Sex-Wise Unemployment by Different Definitions—All India

(in millions)

		Female			*Male*		
		Number unemp-loyed	*Number in labour force*	*Unemp-loyment rates*	*Number unemp-loyed*	*Number in labour force*	*Unemp-loyment rates*
1		2	3	4	5	6	7
Rural	Usual status	0.34	70.97	0.48	1.49	128.66	1.16
	Weekly status	3.59	64.95	5.52	3.86	127.65	8.02
	Daily status	6.44	57.66	11.17	8.62	126.01	6.84
Urban	Usual status	0.46	7.64	6.05	1.57	32.86	4.79
	Weekly status	0.66	7.84	9.17	1.94	32.59	5.97
	Daily status	0.91	6.69	13.62	2.60	32.47	8.02

Based on Tables (5) and (3) of the *Survey on Employment and Unemployment*, National Sample Survey, 27th round, October 1972 to September 1973, Series 255/10.

For the purpose of this survey, the universe studied included all women who, at the time of listing and interview, were engaged in the delimited activities for a money return. This does not exclude the possibility that they also received some additional benefits in kind. To qualify as a worker in this investigation, there was no stipulation that a woman had to work at these jobs for a minimal number of days per year or hours per week because the intention was precisely to bring out the variations in the labour contracts that exist in the unorganised sector.

Sexual Discrimination. Even as an entrepreneur, the work experience of women is distinctly worse than that of men with equal qualifications. The available data clearly supports this contention. First, the overwhelming majority of women work in the unorganised sector even in urban areas. This is in sharp contrast to the experience of the male workers, whose numbers are almost evenly divided between the two sectors. It may be possible that the activities in which women form a significant section of the workers do not get organised. Second, for women, work is relatively less regular and steady.

TABLE 25.3

Weekly Earnings and Percentages of Working Days of Male and Female Labour Force—Urban All India 1972-1973

General-cum-technical education group	*Average weekly earnings*		*Female earnings as percentage of male earnings*	*Hours worked as percentage of total available work hours per week*		*Percentage figures of Column 5*
	Male	*Female*		*Male*	*Female*	
1	2	3	4	5	6	7
1. Illiterate	29.53	14.41	48.80	91.49	81.60	89.20
2. Illiterate with some technical training	59.75	27.21	45.54	99.69	66.67	66.88
3. Literate but below primary level or with primary education	68.30	19.17	28.07	92.20	80.13	86.91
4. Literate but below primary level or primary education and with some technical training	66.13	50.53	76.41	94.51	71.20	75.34
5. Middle education	47.12	33.91	71.96	89.16	69.54	77.99
6. Middle education with some technical training	67.41	50.18	74.44	85.84	69.75	81.26

Based on Tables (5) and (3) of the *Survey on Employment and Unemployment*. National Sample Survey, 27th round, October 1972 to September 1973, Series 255/10.

As the definition of the term employment becomes more rigorous the number of unemployed increase for both males and females. Unemployment figures are highest following the daily status concept where a person is unemployed even if only on the day of the interview. It is somewhat lower if a person is considered unemployed only if he has not worked on any day during the previous week. Unemployment is lowest, when confined only to people who are usually unemployed that is, those who have not found work for a fairly long period. As the table shows, the relative rates of unemployment are increasingly higher for women than for men as the definition of the term employment becomes more rigorous both in the rural and urban areas. Even when they are employed, women on an average, get less work per period of time and also a lower rate for the same work as compared to men holding the same qualifications.

Generally, for each category, the number of days per week for which women get employment is somewhat lower and the ratio of the weekly earnings of females to males is even lower, thus indicating that even for the days worked, women get a lower rate of payment.

Recent History of Women's Work. During the first half of the twentieth century, opportunities for Indian women to participate in economic activities increased at a much slower rate as compared to the rate of increase in female population. As a result, in the case of women, work force as percentage of the population (WFPR) decreased rapidly during the period between 1911 to 1951. In the 1961 and 1971 Census reports, the definitions of the term employment have been somewhat different but Mitra concluded that there was no marked change in the earlier trend of falling female WFPR.

TABLE 25.4

Female Workers as Percentage of the Total Female Population 1901-1971—All India

Year	*Female workers as percentage of total female population*	*Female workers as percentage of female population of working age (15-59 years)*
1901	31.70	53.60
1911	33.73	56.13
1921	32.67	54.96
1931	27.63	46.23
1951*	23.30	41.19
1961	27.96	51.74
1971	11.87	22.91
1971**	28.18	54.14

Based on census data as reproduced in Asok Mitra, *Literacy and Employment*, ICSSR, 1975, Table 18 p. 39.

* 1951 estimates use a somewhat rigorous definition of work and are therefore not strictly comparable.

** Alternative estimates for 1971 based on the data of the 27th round of NSS Employment and Unemployment, Series 255A, NSSO, 1976.

The decline in women's employment was a part of the general process of loss of industrial employment that affected the entire Indian population during the nineteenth and the early twentieth century. The once flourishing cottage industries in India suffered a severe set-back through the loss of both foreign and domestic markets because of stiff competition from British manufactured goods. The process was further accelerated in the early part of this century by competition from goods manufactured in Indian factories. The traditional textile industry of India was one of the worst affected by this process. Women textile workers suffered relatively more because the spinning yarn industry where they worked was almost entirely wiped out by competition from imported and mill-made yarn.

This process of shrinking industrial employment was further speeded up by the secular demise of the *yajamani* system during this period. The *yajamani* system was a traditional one whereby in each village, families belonging to particular service and trade castes such as barbers, blacksmiths and potters used to provide these services to the entire village in return for a traditionally fixed supply of grain or land from each family. As the pressure on land increased following an increase in population (especially agrarian population) and agriculture became more commercialised, this bargain became non-viable for the other residents of the village. As a result, the custom of maintaining entire castes by such occupation became obsolete and was replaced by isolated workers providing these services in return for monetary payment. A few economic historians have argued that the decline of court life in towns led to the disappearance of some of the finer arts and crafts existing there (Naquvi).

The decline of industries such as textiles and metal products, and of crude services rendered by potters and blacksmiths affected not only women but also men in large numbers. Surprisingly women's overall non-agricultural employment till 1961 never regained the absolute level it had reached in 1911, while for men, it only a meant a temporary set-back. After 1921, non-agricultural male employment rose both in absolute numbers and in proportion to total male employment. Of the non-agricultural jobs that women lost during the period 1911 to 1961, only eight per cent could be accounted for by specific female tasks becoming obsolete, and in the remaining 92 per cent cases, women were simply replaced by men in their past occupations. This was particularly seen in food processing and textiles industries and in construction. As a consequence of this loss of opportunities in non-agricultural occupations, more and more women workers joined the ranks of agricultural labourers if their communities permitted it.

Not only did women not retain their share in their traditional occupations, but they also took little part in the newly developing industries in India. During this period male employment in engineering, metallurgical and chemical industries increased. However, only two industries, textiles and food processing, accounted for the employment of three-fourths of the female manufacturing group both in 1911 and in 1961. The remaining female manufacturing group was employed in wood, rubber and ceramics industries. It may be added here that even in industries like textiles or food processing, over four-fifths of the female workers were confined to the household sector and the expansion in the factory sector of these industries meant little or no increase in women's employment opportunities. Another interesting fact was that though a few women had earlier gained entry into the factory sector of the textile industry, as soon as the factory sector wages and working conditions began to improve substantially after Independence, a majority of women workers lost their jobs in these factories in the name of rationalisation.

TABLE 25.5

Distribution of Non-agricultural Workers between Household and Non-household Occupations—1961

(in millions)

	Household industry			*Non-household industry*			*Total*		
	Persons	*Male*	*Female*	*Persons*	*Male*	*Female*	*Persons*	*Male*	*Female*
Rural	10.0	6.1	3.9	23.8	18.6	5.2	33.8	24.7	9.1
	(29.6)	(24.7)	(42.8)	(70.4)	(75.3)	(57.2)	(100.0)	(100.0)	(100.0)
Urban	2.1	1.3	0.8	21.7	19.4	2.3	23.4	20.7	3.1
	(8.9)	(6.3)	(25.8)	(91.1)	(93.7)	(74.2)	(100.0)	(100.0)	(100.0)
Total	12.1	7.4	4.7	45.5	38.0	7.5	57.6	45.4	12.0
	(21.0)	(16.3)	(38.5)	(79.0)	(83.7)	(61.5)	(100.0)	(100.0)	(100.0)

Based on A. Mitra, A.K. Shrimony and L.P. Pathak, *Household and Non-household Economic Activity*, Status of Women Series, ICSSR, 1979: 5.

Only 16 per cent of the men in non-agricultural occupations worked in the household sector, as compared to 38 per cent of the women who worked in that sector. Till 1961, the census reports did not give separate employment figures for urban and rural population. However, they did give the employment figures for the four major cities of India which reiterate the general conclusion that non-agricultural employment of women was falling very sharply throughout this period (see Table 25.10).

TABLE 25.6

The Percentage of Total Female Population in Different Occupations in 1911, 1931 and 1961 for Major Cities and All India

	Bombay			*Calcutta*			*Delhi*			*Madras*			*All India*		
All divisions	*1911*	*1931*	*1961*	*1911*	*1931*	*1961*	*1911*	*1931*	*1961*	*1911*	*1931*	*1961*	*1911*	*1931*	*1961*
Agriculture	0.56	0.21	0.30	0.12	0.05	N.S.	0.11	0.46	0.18	0.49	0.18	0.04	24.88	20.47	22.97
Manufacturing	11.47	4.76	2.42	1.06	0.95	0.54	5.12	1.39	0.57	2.15	1.04	0.91	3.45	2.27	2.36
Construction	0.25	0.05	0.28	0.36	0.40	0.04	0.12	0.55	0.22	0.52	0.24	0.21	0.23	0.20	0.11
Services*	0.36	4.84	5.76	9.62	5.78	5.46	3.70	3.39	3.41	7.25	35.31	5.18	3.66	3.57	1.34
Unspecified*	4.73	2.46	0.15	0.95	1.37	0.11	0.43	1.25	0.55	1.88	2.19	0.67	—	—	—
Total	26.24	12.36	8.81	12.51	8.37	6.09	9.46	7.05	4.46	12.07	38.92	6.33	33.75	29.83	27.91

* A small fraction of the unspecified jobs have also been included under services.

Based on J.N. Sinha, *Indian Working Force: Its Growth and Changing Composition*, Government of India, Ministry of Home Affairs, Office of the Registrar General, 1972, p. 123.

Female Employment and Urbanisation. The downward trend in female WFPR in urban areas in India was all the more remarkable because during this period, female migration to urban areas was exceptionally slow. The general pattern of Indian urbanisation between

1911 to 1961 can be summed up as follows (a) a growing concentration of population in the larger cities; (b) a lower and, for sometime, a falling sex ratio in towns, especially in large cities; and (c) a marked decline over time in work opportunities for women in the larger cities resulting in a clear trend showing that the larger the city, the lower the female WFPR. In view of these facts, the Committee of Experts on Unemployment Estimates concluded that if economic development meant greater urbanisation, it would lead to a fall in work participation rates, particularly in the case of women.

TABLE 25.7

Trends in Urbanisation and Urban Sex Ratios—All India, Large Cities and Calcutta Urban Agglomeration

	Urban India		*Urban areas with population of 1,00,000 and above*		*Calcutta urban agglomeration*	
Census Year	*Percentage of urban population to total Indian population*	*Sex ratio (females per 1000 males)*	*Percentage share in total urban population*	*Sex ratio (females per 1000 males)*	*Total popula-tion (in thous-*	*Sex ratio (females per 1000 males)*
1911	10.29	872	27.30	725	1718	536
1921	11.18	846	29.50	700	1851	515
1931	12.00	838	30.68	713	2106	504
1941	13.86	830	37.89	714	3578	495
1951	17.58	560	44.13	785	4589	604
1961	17.98	845	50.69	797	5737	650
1971	19.91	857	55.82	827	7031	698

Based on census of India 1971, General Population Tables, series I Part II A (i).

Recent Trends

Although the changed definitions of the terms worker and employment in the 1971 Census make it difficult to compare its results with those of the previous census reports, there is little reason to believe that the secular trends vis-a-vis women's work force participation have altered materially during the period following 1961. Subsequent to the 1971 Census, attempts were made to reconstruct the employment position in that year to make it comparable to the 1961 Census reports. On the basis of the results of these exercises the Planning Commission in its Draft Plan for 1978-83 claimed that for 1971, the female work force participation rates have not fallen any further from the 1961 level. However, a survey of employment and unemployment conducted in 1976-77 by the National Sample Survey Organisation seems to indicate that the 1971 WFPR for women may have been at par with the 1961 figures because the 1971 estimates included in the work force at least a section of the persons who gathered free materials strictly for the use of their own families. The 1961

Census definition on the other hand had specifically excluded them. The fact that even in 1976-77 over 20 per cent of the adult rural women of India had to depend on such work for helping their families reflects badly on India's planned economy.

Nevertheless, there are some minor but significant changes noticeable in the pattern of women's economic participation which may assume importance over the passage of time. For the first time, the proportion of agricultural and allied pursuits in the female work force did not increase but it actually registered a slight fall.

TABLE 25.8

Share of Agriculture and Allied Pursuits in Total Female Employment (1901-1971)

Year	*Percentage of female workers in agriculture and allied pursuits*
1901	67.01
1911	73.70
1921	74.63
1931	72.14
1951	78.45
1961	82.13
1971+	81.37

+ Based on rates cited by the National Sample Survey of Employment and Unemployment, 1972-73, 27th round, Series 255, NSSO, 1976.

The WFPR of urban women increased slightly from 11 per cent in 1961 to 14 per cent in 1971. This was seen in spite of the acceleration in the rate of urbanisation of women during this period. A contributing factor here was the fairly rapid increase in women's employment in the organised, mainly public, sector. Since such employment is largely concentrated in the larger cities, it would not be wrong to conclude that metropolitan cities are no longer as hostile to women's work as before. Nevertheless, as noted elsewhere, organised employment still accounts for less than 33 per cent of the urban female employment. Not all such changes need necessarily be indicative of an improvement in women's position. For instance, after a decline in its absolute level between 1961 and 1971, women's factory employment figures have recently registered an increase. In spite of this, women continue to lose their jobs in traditional areas like large-scale textile manufacturing and mines. They have not made any headway in the better paying metal or chemical industries and are mainly concentrated in poorly paid industries like food processing or tobacco. Further, women are gaining ground mainly in occupations where the majority of workers are women. Of the total non-agricultural women's employment in 1971, nearly 40 per cent were engaged in occupations where at least 70 per cent of the workers were women. Such high concentration of women in an occupation is usually indicative of very poor wages and working conditions.

The slight increase in the urban female work force is the outcome of not only an increase in the number of adult women in the work force but also of children and old people. In any society this is a bad omen reflecting a state of acute crisis in various sections of the population. It seems plausible that the increased work effort of women in the cities, at least partly reflects the increasing poverty in urban areas during the sixties.

TABLE 25.9

Age Group-wise Women's Labour Force Participation Rates 1961 and 1971

Age group in years	*Rural*		*Urban*	
	1961	*1971*	*1961*	*1971*
5-9	1.98	2.00	0.24	0.46
10-14	26.81	21.91	5.24	6.12
15-29	49.31	49.73	15.16	19.42
30-34	53.91	61.03	22.35	28.19
35-59	52.29	56.33	22.88	26.89
60+	24.41	21.86	11.50	12.42
Total	31.24	32.06	11.09	14.10

Based on the *Report of the Sub-group on Statistics on the Employment of Women,* Planning Commission, Employment and Manpower Division, 1978, p. 9.

Calcutta

Since Independence Calcutta and the State of West Bengal where the city is situated have witnessed a pattern of development which is somewhat distinct from that of the rest of the country. On the eve of independence, West Bengal was the most industrialised of the Indian states and the major share of the foreign industrial investment in India was located in this region, mainly around Calcutta's industrial belt. After Independence, the growth of new industrial investment in this region was somewhat slower as compared to the other industrialised regions of India. This was partly because a large part of the new investment funds of the region were used for buying out foreign interests in the existing industry. On the other hand its initial lead in the industrial field meant that public sector investments which aimed at a more balanced inter-regional growth tended to by-pass Calcutta and its surrounding areas. During the Second and Third Plans, there was considerable new private industrial investment in this region, but not at rates comparable with those of Bombay, Pune, Ahmedabad, Baroda or Delhi. Since then that channel has also dried up. All these factors have produced a situation where among the more advanced states of India, the growth of organised employment has been one of the slowest in West Bengal.

During the period 1947 to 1961, Calcutta received wave after wave of refugees from Bangladesh, so that by 1971 this immigration had increased the population by almost 18 to 20 lakhs. This number accounted for about 25 per cent of the total population of the Calcutta metropolitan district in 1971. Unlike the other migrants to Calcutta, these refugees came with their families. For these migrants there was no possibility of any source of rural income to supplement their earnings in the city. While it is true that the entire country is experiencing an imbalance between the supplies of capital and labour, the situation is particularly difficult in Calcutta with a large unwarranted increase in the labour force coupled with a stagnant investment picture.

The traditions of women's economic participation have been particularly weak in West Bengal in comparison with the rest of India. The table above indicates that for all censuses during the twentieth century, whatever the definition of the term worker, West Bengal female WFPR was always one of the lowest in the country. Table 25.11 indicates that even in 1961 the women workers in West Bengal were from the scheduled castes or tribes, and there was little or no tradition of women from the upper castes or class taking up economic activities. In spite of these facts it is worth nothing that the downward trend in women's WFPR in West Bengal between 1911 to 1961 was no less dramatic—it fell from 12.5 per cent to 6.1 per cent.

TABLE 25.10

Female Work Participation Rates in The Various States of India

State	*Female work participation rates in several censuses*					*1961 female work partici-pation rates*		*1971 female work partici-pation rates*	
	1911	*1921*	*1931*	*1951*	*1961*	*Rural*	*Urban*	*Rural*	*Urban*
Andhra Pradesh	41.58	37.53	30.30	21.42	41.33	46.00	18.81	51.07	23.04
Assam	40.05	36.70	34.88	31.18	30.95	32.58	9.98	9.95	6.01
Bihar	34.71	35.94	26.09	20.75	27.13	28.50	10.47	23.62	11.36
Bombay	36.74	32.74	29.72	31.84	34.61	42.40	12.16	45.67	17.85
Kerala	28.01	24.06	21.57	18.58	19.75	21.24	13.70	29.73	25.26
Madhya Pradesh	47.85	46.76	37.46	38.25	44.00	48.61	14.53	52.73	18.43
Madras	36.48	29.16	23.13	13.72	31.29	37.13	15.09	51.33*	19.77*
Mysore	26.14	24.12	25.32	98.25	32.02	36.79	14.98	49.74	19.32
Orissa	30.43	33.21	30.04	19.11	26.58	27.39	13.16	30.85	18.82
Punjab	11.94	9.20	12.67	17.51	14.20	16.51	4.77	32.23	15.43
Rajasthan	45.46	46.25	38.34	37.47	35.89	40.83	10.11	63.09	23.53
Uttar Pradesh	33.31	37.30	2.81	23.81	18.14	19.91	5.36	31.57	9.60
West Bengal	18.79	17.38	13.19	11.92	9.44	10.71	5.67	15.87	11.61

Based on Census of India 1961, Monograph No. 11, NSS No. 255A.
*Tamil Nadu

The strength of the social bias against female work in Bengal was highlighted by a Survey of Earners in the Calcutta Municipal Corporation area conducted by the NSSO in 1953. According to the findings only about five per cent of women in Calcutta formed a part of the work force and almost all of them were from the scheduled castes. A large majority were widows or deserted women, and were from outside Bengal, speaking languages other than Bengali. There was no tradition of caste Hindu Bengali women working unless under

TABLE 25.11

Crude Worker Rates (Workers Per 1000 Population) by Sex for Scheduled Castes, Scheduled Tribes and The Non-Scheduled Population in Different States of Rural and Urban India—1961 Census

State	*Female (Rural)*				*Female (Urban)*			
	All	*Scheduled castes*	*Scheduled tribes*	*Non-scheduled population*	*All*	*Scheduled castes*	*Scheduled tribes*	*Non-scheduled population*
1	2	3	4	5	6	7	8	9
India	31.42	35.86	52.47	28.20	11.09	21.07	31.58	9.87
Andhra Pradesh	46.00	59.13	57338	42.99	18.74	35.33	40.90	16.87
Assam	32.41	26.88	49.43	28.59	9.87	15.09	25.27	7.75
Bihar	28.49	41.16	56.65	22.44	10.40	24.08	29.14	8.28
Gujarat	34.15	38.07	50.12	30.16	9.24	19.24	27.94	8.01
Jammu and Kashmir	29.51	25.24	—	29.92	5.78	7.07	—	5.73
Kerala	20.88	43.91	40.61	18.22	13.00	32.82	31.82	11.92
Madhya Pradesh	48.60	53.04	58.18	43.86	14.50	28.24	40.40	12.42
Madras	37.11	47.23	49.91	34.27	14.95	28.43	33.94	13.35
Maharashtra	46.74	50.16	56.53	45.56	13.45	22.94	34.71	12.78
Mysore	36.79	45.03	47.27	35.28	14.87	25.17	29.37	13.71
Orissa	27.38	32.18	44.29	18.81	13.12	29.46	36.08	8.10
Punjab	16.50	14.55	693.42	17.00	4.70	10.89	—	3.86
Rajasthan	40.82	42.12	51.28	38.39	10.05	19.81	28.98	8.28
Uttar Pradesh	19.90	28.67	—	17.34	5.34	11.90	—	4.49
West Bengal	10.62	10.91	41.86	7.00	5.12	10.06	26.27	4.54
Nagaland	60.33	—	60.97	23.85	9.67	—	14.07	2.38
Delhi	21.98	23.48	—	21.52	4.46	9.99	—	3.73
Himachal Pradesh	57.74	58.80	60.95	56.83	11.90	21.42	27.08	9.43
Manipur	44.86	39.17	52.68	40.76	40.43	17.54	11.80	42.03
Pondicherry	22.96	46.41	—	17.55	11.20	37.27	—	10.11
Tripura	22.40	9.22	48.68	8.30	5.46	8.47	5.38	5.23
Nefa	17.21	—	31.95	13.40	—	—	—	—
Andaman and Nicobar Islands	22.42	—	51.60	6.30	5.07	—	—	5.07
Laccadwip Islands	51.68	—	51.62	54.43	—	—	—	—
Dadar and Nagar Haveli	57.94	54.39	61.02	28.83	—	—	—	—

Based on Census of India 1961, India Part IIA (ii), General Population Tables, Part V-A(i); Special Tables for Scheduled Castes, Part V-A(ii); Special Tables for Scheduled Tribes, as quoted by Reports of the Committee of Experts on Unemployment Estimates.

crisis. Nearly all these women were paid to work in personal services. A similar pattern was observed in the 1958 survey of Calcutta by S.N. Sen. There have been some marked changes in the last few years. A noticeable increase in women's participation in economic activities has been observed which is supported by available statistics. For urban West Bengal, Women's WFPR according to the 1961 Census was 5.12 per cent, and the NSSO in its 27th round Survey of Employment and Unemployment in 1972-73 gave an estimate of about 11 per cent. This increase of over 100 per cent is partly due to increased opportunities of work for women in the public sector and the professions, though it must be borne in mind that over 60 per cent of the women workers of Calcutta Metropolitan District in 1977 were in the unorganised sector.

TABLE 25.12

The Employment Situation of the Population in Age Group 15 to 59 Years in the Calcutta Metropolitan District 1977

(in thousands)

Age group 15-59 years	*Male*	*Female*	*Total*
Total population[1]	3201	2752	5953
Labour force[2]	2791	418	3209
Unemployed[2]	278	60	338
Employed[2]	2513	358	2871
(a) Organised sector[3]	1522	138	1650
(b) Unorganised sector	991	220	1211

1. Estimate of Calcutta Metropolitan District population in the age group 15-59 years based on projections of population on the basis of 1961 to 1971 Census trends with age distribution as in the 1971 Calcutta Metropolitan District Census reports.
2. Estimates of labour force and of the employed and unemployed based on the trends for urban West Bengal, *Survey of Employment and Unemployment*, 32nd round, NSSO.
3. Estimates of the organised sector employment are based on the Industrial Division of West Bengal's organised employment as given in *Economic Review 1978-79 Statistical Appendix*, Table No. 4.3, Government of West Bengal. Of this the share of the Calcutta Metropolitan District in the secondary and tertiary employment is as given for 1971 in *Calcutta Metropolitan District Facts and Figures*—CMDA, Table No. II. The sex-wise division of the organised sector employment is as per Annexure 3 of 'The Employment Trends in the Organised Sector 1976-77', *RBI Bulletin*, October 1978.

The figures given here cover the population between the age group over 15 years and below 60 years. There are children as well as old people working in Calcutta who would all fall in the unorganised sector. Thus, the latter's share, if anything, would be greater.

The brief review presented here cites some of the facts that establish the relevance of the study. The unorganised sector employs a large section of the work force even in the urban areas of India and especially in calcutta. Although it is difficult to estimate the contribution of this part of the urban economy to the national product, there are signs that its span of activities and products is increasing. If the difference between labour costs in the formal and informal sectors continues to increase as it has in recent years, then it is likely that more activities would be switched over to the informal sector. In a labour surplus situation this will ultimately weaken the position of the working class as a whole, because the areas where the labour can bargain collectively will remain restricted.

Women's work patterns have been more or less complementary to that of the other workers. In the past, in the labour markets where they had participated, their employment acted as a balancing factor adjusted to changes in the overall labour demand so that male employment suffered relatively less from such vissisitudes. Within the family, they were expected to supplement male labour and perform the more tedious and less killed jobs in return for a share in the family living. Their enterprise and labour contributed to the family's product and income without giving them an unambiguous claim to either. Recent trends show that in the urban areas, women's employment is increasing at a significant rate in an otherwise stagnant labour market. It is evident that women as a group, accept wage rates and working conditions inferior to those of other workers. These two facts taken together imply that women's employment is increasing at the cost of male employment and the relation between male and female employment is no longer complementary but competitive. Women in the urban economy are working largely outside their household occupations and their wages form an important part of the total family income. However, it remains to be seen whether or not this gives them an added status in the family.

WHO ARE THESE WOMEN?

One conclusion about the tradition of women's employment in India does not seem to be unwarranted on the basis of the facts outlined earlier. Women workers here have always formed a separate category in the labour market, concentrated in certain specific occupations and under particular types of organisations and working conditions. This category has shown wide variations from time to time in the size of the total employment vis-a-vis the population. Changes in the occupational structure of the group have often failed to match those warranted by the direction and speed of development in the economy as a whole. Not only have these changes lagged behind the general trend but have often been in a contrary direction. This tendency appears to have been more pronounced in the case of women in Calcutta. Although there have been some improvements in women's work force participation since the seventies, it has not led to a complete integration of women with the rest of the labour force. Even in 1972-73 not more than 15 per cent of the women in Calcutta were in the labour force and the majority of them were in the informal sector. On the whole, women's work experience at each level was distinctly inferior to that of men. This continued segregation of women workers could be partly explained in terms of their social backgrounds and characteristics which have been briefly reviewed in this chapter.

Personal Characteristics

Age. For working in the unorganised sector there is no upper or lower age limit for a worker. Therefore, age limit was not stipulated in drawing this sample. The sample showed a surprisingly wide distribution of ages ranging from below 15 years to 60 years and above.

The modal age of the workers was over 30 years though their distribution between age groups was about even with a gentle taper at the two ends. Children below 15 years formed seven per cent of the total sample. This figure was significantly higher than the figure reported in the 1961 Census—below two per cent among West Bengal urban women workers.

TABLE 25.13

Distribution of Sample Women by Education and Age Group

Age group in years	*Illiterate*	*Can only read*	*Can read and write*	*Primary educa-tion*	*Secondary education and above*	*Fre-quency*	*Cumu-lative fre-quency*
15	14(50.0)	—	7(25.0)	3(10.7)	28(100.0)	28	28
16-20	9(19.2	3(6.4)	4(8.5)	12(25.5)	19(40.4)	47(100.0)	75
21-25	25(46.3)	3(5.6)	1(1.9)	7(13.0)	18(33.3)	54(100.0)	129
26-30	46(66.6)	6(8.9)	8(11.9)	4(6.0)	3(4.5)	67(100.0)	196
31-35	32(53.3)	8(13.3)	9(15.0)	7(11.0)	4(6.6)	60(100.0)	256
36-45	78(78.8)	3(3.3)	6(6.6)	6(6.6)	6(6.6)	99(100.0)	355
46-60	31(78.5)	3(7.7)	2(5.1)	3(7.7)	—	39(100.0)	394
60+	6(100.0)	—	—	—	—	6(100.0)	400

Note: Figure in parentheses indicative row-wise percentages of total frequency.

Compared to the average educational level of all women in Calcutta of whom less than 40 per cent are illiterate, the overall educational records of women in the sample were very poor, possibly because they were from very poor backgrounds—women's education is closely correlated with the level of family income. The younger women fared somewhat better which confirms the general impression that educational opportunities for children are improving with the passage of time. But literacy level was very low among the child workers, thereby implying that even if opportunities for education were expanding, children from poor families who had to earn a living could not take advantage of them. On the whole, the low literacy level of this group probably worked as a barrier to their access to information about the labour market and tended to isolate them from other workers.

The education level of the head of the household had a significant influence on the education level of the respondents—higher the education level of the head of the household, the better the chances of a woman receiving higher education. Only 13 per cent of these women came from households where the head was less educated than themselves. On the whole, only about 32.5 per cent of the women could read and write, but in households where the head was educated, about 61 per cent of the women could read and write.

Language, Marital and Religious Status. The overwhelming majority of women in the sample were Bengali speaking. Only 15 women workers had come from outside the Bengali speaking areas. Of these two Oriya women spoke Bengali fairly fluently in addition to their own language. The others were from Hindi speaking areas except for one who was from Gujarat, but most of them understood Bengali.

TABLE 25.14

Civil Status and Religion

Religious status	*Married*	*Unmarried*	*Divorced deserted*	*Widowed*	*Total*
Hindus	170+(7)	79	8+(1)	95+(5)	352+(13)
Christians	1	—	—	—	1
Muslims	20+(1)	2	1	9+(1)	32+(2)
Total	191+(8)	81	9+(1)	104+(6)	385+(15)

Note: Figures in parentheses indicate the number of women from other than Bengali speaking groups.

The high percentage of married and unmarried Bengali women in this sample indicated that there had been a fairly radical change in the social attitudes of the people of Calcutta regarding female work force participation. As already indicated elsewhere, a study of female earners in Calcutta had shown that Bengali women constituted only about 33 per cent of the total female earners. This was observed even though these studies had considered female earners in all occupations, including the professions and the organised sector where the overwhelming majority is Bengali. It was striking to observe that in this sample where all these occupations had been excluded, married and unmarried Bengali women still constituted nearly 70 per cent of the total workers. Evidence relating to social conventions such as early marriages, and multiple and early child-bearing which tend to restrict women in their performance as workers is very significant.

Although marriage was a universal feature seen among all females above 25 years of age, there was a slight increase in the average age of marriage for women below 25 years. This improvement was confined to women with some level of education.

TABLE 25.15

Age group-wise Level of Education of the Unmarried and average Age at Childbirth and Number of Children of the Married

Age group in years	*Number of un-married workers*	*Unmarried with at least primary workers education*	*Average age of married children at birth of first child*	*Average number of per married worker*
15	28	10(38)	—	—
16-20	38	29(76)	16.1	2.1
21-25	14	11(79)	15.8	2.8
26-35	1	1(neg.)	16.5	3.75
36 and above	—	—	16.7	3.80

Note: Figures in parentheses indicate percentage to total married.

If a woman was to remain unmarried after the age of 16, it was expected that she be from a social class where women's education was an accepted value. The older a woman, the more important was her class in determining whether she remained unmarried or not. On the other hand in social groups where women's education was not an accepted feature, the age at marriage or at the birth of the first child as well as the average number of children was not significantly different for older and younger women. The younger women were still able to bear children and there was no apparent reason why their average number of children were much below that of the older group. In fact, the average age of 16 years of women in the sample at the birth of the first child was well below the average for all females of urban West Bengal for the period 1971 to 1975. There was a sharp difference vis-a-vis the conventions regarding marriage between women with and without educational achievements. This was not due to the fact that educated women were more emancipated on account of their higher education level, but because in some social groups, women's position was somewhat better and this was reflected both in their access to education and in the relaxation of the practice of early marriage.

Nevertheless, access to education did appear to help in the formation of maturer attitudes among women. Table 25.16 highlights the close correlation between higher levels of education and a positive response to family planning among married women of child-bearing ages. Among the better educated, the chief reason for not practising family planning was lack of easy access to facilities, while in the case of others it was because of religious or family taboos.

TABLE 25.16

Practice of Family Planning Among Married Women of Child-bearing Ages

Educational level planning	*Practise family practise*	*Do not*	*Total*
Illiterate	64(66)	33	97
Some education without formal qualifications	18(60)	12	30
Primary level	15(83)	3	18
Secondary level	13(81)	3	16
Total	110	51	161

Note: Figures in parentheses indicate percentages.

Family Income and Standard of Living

The per capita income of the families of these women was generally very low even when their contributions were added as is evident from the Table 25.17.

According to the official policy of the Government of India as stated in the fifth Five Year Plan all persons with a per capita monthly income of Rs. 22.50 at 1960-61 prices were considered to be living below the poverty line. Allowing for a rise in the cost of living since then, the poverty level of incomes in 1976-77 would be approximately rs. 65 for Calcutta city. By these standards, nearly 70 per cent of these women and their families in the sample could be regarded as poor. Moreover, the percentage of families living below the poverty line of Rs. 65 per capita per month is especially high for the two groups namely, child workers and married women with young children. In other words, these two groups were particularly desperate when they entered the labour market. Surprisingly, the widows and divorcees were better off than the others in terms of their mean and modal incomes. Unmarried women above 15 years of age generally belonged to higher social groups and their education levels were better. Married women had the support of their husband. Even then the per capita family incomes of both these groups were not comparable with that of the last group (See Table 25.17).

TABLE 25.17

Civil Status and Per Capita Monthly Family Income

Per capita monthly income group in rupees	*Civil Status*					*Total*	*Per cent*
	Unmarried		*Married*		*Widowed divorced*		
	Age 15 years and below	*Others*	*With children under five years*	*Others*			
0-45.0	16	16	66	21	42	161	40.25
	(75)	(62)	(82.5)	(69)			
45.1-65.0	5	17	28	31	29	110	27.50
65.1-105.0	5	15	16	12	29	87	21.75
105.1-145.0	1	4	3	8	11	27	6.75
145.1+	1	1	1	3	9	15	3.75
Total	28 (100)	53 (100)	114 (100)	759 (100)	120 (100)	400	100.00
Mean monthly income per capita in rupees	48.2	61.0	47.5	62.6	65.5		57.3

Note: Figures in parentheses are percentages to column-wise totals.

In spite of these interesting variations, the overall family income of these women was meagre compared to the liabilities of the family. Their main strategy of survival was to send out more and more workers (See Table 25.18). Nearly half of the families sent out not less than three workers. Among those to be sent out first were unqualified and illiterate women, followed by children and old people. The average income per earner was inversely related to the number of earners in the family, it can therefore be assumed that families sent out more workers not because of the abundance in skills but because the income of none of the workers was adequate.

TABLE 25.18

Average Monthly Earnings of Families by Number of Earners

No. of earners	Frequency and Mean Monthly Income of the Family					
	With at least one worker in the formal sector			*With no worker in the formal sector*		
Frequency in the family		*Mean monthly family income*	*Average income per earner*	*Frequency*	*Mean monthly family income*	*Average income per earner*
1	—	—	—	62	166.63	—
2	16	343.75	171.88	137	214.78	107.38
3	16	371.87	123.96	101	274.51	91.50
4	2	425.00	106.25	45	339.94	84.99
5	3	425.00	85.00	15	322.17	64.44
6 and above	—	—	—	3	408.83	68.14

The mean monthly income for the total sample households was Rs. 256.03.

The difference between the mean incomes of families with and without one worker in the formal sector was significant no matter how many workers there were. Less than ten per cent of the families (37) had one person working in the formal sector, and among these, even families with only two earners were better off than others with as many as five earners. It may be noted that none of these 37 families had more than one worker in the formal sector. In other words, having a relative working in the formal sector does not appear to make it any easier for other members of a family to get a similar job.

Incidentally, the findings indicate that secondary or even higher level of education was neither a necessary nor a sufficient condition for getting a job in the formal sector. Of the 37 formal sector workers in these families, only 22 had such qualifications, the rest were either illiterate or barely literate. As compared to this, in the other 263 families, there were more than 100 people (apart from the interviewed women themselves) who had such qualifications but were either unemployed or employed in the informal sector. Better education could have improved their chances of getting such a job but had not ensured it.

In spite of the large number of earners in the family, only one-fourth of these women lived in joint families. The remaining two thirds lived in nuclear families and the rest, a small minority, lived singly. The ratio of earners to family members was 49.6 to 100 in nuclear families as against 44.96 to 100 in joint families. This clear shows that nuclear families were sending out more children as workers, though not all these children were minors, but they were all still unmarried. This was another indication of the desperate situation of these families.

Although the survey was not necessarily confined to slum areas, the generally low income level of these families ensured that their housing standards would be about the poorest in the city. Of the entire sample population, only 36 families had two or more rooms. The others lived in one room with a small verandah or partially covered space for cooking. For all families which had only one room, the average number of persons per room was 5.18 a figure significantly higher than the average of 3.41 persons per room for Calcutta city as a whole in 1971.

Apart from being overcrowded, the housing structures were of a very poor quality. The residents there enjoyed very few of the urban civic services. Only 60 families lived in structures with *pucca* floors, walls and roof. Of these half the houses were in official slums. Another 107 families lived in houses which were completely made of *kuccha* material. There was no unambiguous information about the rest. In Calcutta, only the relatively better off segment of society enjoys the exclusively use of a tap or a sanitary latrine or a service privy. The exclusive enjoyment of such facilities was rarely experienced by the families in the sample. Although half the area of the city is sewered, this was generally not seen in areas where these families lived.

TABLE 25.19

Number of Families of Interviewees by the Type of Infrastructure They Enjoy

	Common tap shared with neighbours	*Exclusive tap on the pre-mise*	*Shared bustee tubewell or well*	*Street tap or tube-well*	*Total*
Connected to a sewerage system					
(a) Exclusive lavatory	—	2	—	—	2
(b) Common lavatory	36	—	—	—	36
Sanitary lavatory					
(a) Exclusive layatory	6	3	—	—	9
(b) Common lavatory	198	—	3	—	201
Kuccha service privy					
(a) Exclusive lavatory	1	—	—	—	1
(b) Common lavatory	38	—	7	13	58
Pucca service latrine					
(a) Exclusive lavatory	2	—	—	—	2
(b) Common lavatory	3	—	2	—	5
No facilities	33	—	1	52	86
Total	317	5	13	65	400

Social Background and Caste-wise Distribution

The population of Calcutta comprises of people born in the city, refugees who have migrated from Bangladesh after partition and those who have migrated either from other districts of West Bengal or from other states of India. The pattern of refugee migration differs from that of the other migrants quite significantly. According to earlier surveys, refugees coming to Calcutta generally travelled with their entire families; the heads of the refugee households were relatively better educated and, they were generally from urban or semi-urban centres and not from rural areas of East Bengal. Compared to this, the other migrants were often single adult males who had come in search of a job or in case of women, after marriage. They had migrated from rural areas either of West Bengal or of the other states and the two types of migrants were treated separately.

TABLE 25.20

Female Migration All India 1971* and Cause of Migration and Civil Status of Sample

Types of migrants	*Un-married*	*Married*	*Widowed/ divorced*	*Total*	*Per cent dis-tribution of sample migrant women*	*Per cent dis-tribution All India migrant women 1971*
Refugees	15	23	20	58	33.7	1.0
On marriage	—	7+(1)	3	10+(1)	6.4	12.4
On economic grounds						
(a) To join earning head	4	10+(4)	—	14+(4)	10.5	50.2
(b) Individually for work	10	15	13+(2)	38+(2)	23.2	7.0
(c) with family for work	4	18+(3)	16+(4)	38+(7)	26.2	29.4
Total	33	73+(8)	52+(6)	158+(14)	100.0	100.0

Note: Figures in parentheses indicate number of migrants from non-Bengali areas.

About 40 per cent of Indian women migrate at least once in their life time usually after marriage or to join the earning members of the family at their place of work. In this study, of the total sample population, 174 women that is, approximately 40 per cent were immigrants to the city. Of these one-third (58) migrated as refugees from East Bengal, 14 were from the other states of India and the rest from other districts of West Bengal—usually rural areas. This kind of migration was particularly important in Calcutta as compared to the rest of India.

At least 40 migrants had come individually to seek work in the city which was quite unusual compared to the All India pattern and more so because nearly all of them were Bengali speaking. Twenty-five of them were not destitutes or widows but had families. Six of them had children below five years of age whom they had left behind with the rest of the family. This was probably an entirely new development in India. The migration of ten young unmarried women alone to he city was also very unusual considering the traditions of this region.

A common factor underlying migration was the poverty of the family in their original place of residence and both single migrants as well as those moving in with their families had come to the city to look for work; though the difference in their expected incomes at home and in the city would probably be quite high, but that alone was not a sufficient cause for migration. In all these migrant non-refugee families the incidence of unemployment was very low as these migrant women revealed that the decision to migrate was taken only when there were definite prospects of sufficient work and initially, only those members with such prospects migrated to the city. The others joined later when their own prospects of work improved, this implied that if there were jobs only for women or girls, then they migrated alone. In case of women who had come to the city for economic reasons, a study of the occupation of the head of the household indicated that the majority were from agricultural households and of these, about two-thirds including 37 single migrants came from landless families. The other three came from homes where the head of the family was unemployed.

TABLE 25.21

Backgrounds of Migrants Coming to City on Grounds of Poverty

Occupation of the head of family before migration	*Frequency*
Cultivators	12
Sharecroppers	11
Agricultural labourers	51
In other occupations	18
Unemployed before migration	4
Data not available	7
Total	103

The caste-wise distribution of these women was not clear as they did not usually specify their caste. They were classified on the basis of their family names which sometimes indicated the upper castes and scheduled castes but a large majority of women were grouped into the middle castes because their actual castes could not be accurately identified.

Given that almost all the women in the sample belonged to very poor families, it was rather surprising that 12 per cent of them could be clearly identified as belonging to the upper castes. Only 32 women could be clearly identified as belonging to the scheduled castes. Surprisingly, the average family income of the upper caste women was not higher than the average for the entire group, though there was a slightly greater incidence of women belonging to families with one member working in the formal sector. Upper caste women did have an edge over the others in educational performance since nearly one-fourth of this group had received secondary education or more, and only one-fourth were totally illiterate. This meant that their average age at the time of marriage was somewhat higher. Without going into a debate about the close coincidence between class and caste, it appears that upper caste families had more liberal views about a woman's position.

TABLE 25.22

Caste-wise Distribution of Workers in the Sample

Social group	*Frequency*
Christians	2
Muslims	34
Hindus	
(a) Upper castes	54
(b) Middle castes	262
(c) Scheduled castes	32
(d) Unidentified	16
Total	400

Among the younger women, there was a sizeable group who had enjoyed some opportunity for education and faced less constraints in terms of early marriages and child-bearing. However, this liberalisation of traditional constraints was not universal nor was it progressive for all the young workers. Most of the child workers, that is, workers below the age of 15 years had been denied access to thee growing educational opportunities. The results point to some radical changes in the social traditions vis-a-vis women's economic activities. As compared to the situation revealed by earlier surveys, there was a much higher incidence of married and unmarried Bengali women as opposed to widows or divorcees in the work force. Another striking change was the significant number of women who migrated singly to the city for work, a phenomenon hitherto unknown in this region. The majority of workers were no longer from the scheduled castes or tribes and a significant proportion belonged to upper caste families.

Two types of processes account for these changes. On the one hand there could be a general social movement towards women's emancipation which would be reflected in a shift in women's attitudes towards self-reliance. On the other hand it could be that the growing poverty of their families had forced them to join the ranks of workers. Although one would like to believe that the first explanation is valid, the weight of the evidence favoured the second explanation. The family income of this group of women put the majority of them firmly below the official poverty line. Even for their meagre earnings, the families had to send out several, sometimes as many as five or six earners. The marginal contribution to the total income of a family from an additional workers usually declined as the number of earners increased indicating how unprepared these additional workers were for entering the labour force.

The poor dwellings and the lack of access to civic facilities in the majority of the cases lent support to the hypothesis that extreme poverty and desperation led to the changes described above. Surprisingly, though there was a significant percentage of women from upper castes or from social groups with more modern traditions, the poverty level was almost unvarying. The relatively better off families were those with at least one member working in the formal sector. However, there were only a few such families in the sample and of these few not one had more than one such worker. This does not augur well for ideas regarding mobility and connections between the formal and the informal sectors.

THE OCCUPATIONAL STRUCTURE

A casual acquaintance with the existing state of affairs in the informal sector indicates that there are fairly stable traditions about the division of workers between occupations. Apart from the division between sexes, there are long standing conventions in Calcutta about particular social groups undertaking specific tasks. For instance, the hand-*riksha*-pullers are usually Biharis, a large percentage of the tailors are either Hindu speaking Muslims or Hindu refugees from East Bengal, and the *biri* workers are usually Muslims. One does not know anything about the barriers which work to maintain these divisions nor how rigid they are in the context of the rapidly changing conditions of workers and residents. It has to be examined whether the barriers are raised mainly by social conventions or are based on more rational grounds such as the distribution of skills and access to training between workers. Nor is it clear whether these barriers are raised by employers who have definite preferences between groups of workers or by the which are not based on their respective working conditions alone. In other words, it remains to be seen whether the concentration of certain categories of workers in specific occupations is the result of differentials in the price offered by employers to these groups in specific occupations or in the demand price acceptable to each group in that kind of work.

In contrast to the impression that the informal sector is divided into several imperfectly competitive groups, a few authors have commented on the high degree of competition between workers in the informal sector which stems from the mobility of workers between occupations. According to them, the distinctive characteristics of the informal sector are the ease of entry of the new workers into these type of occupations and the non-formal methods of skill training available. In addition to these opportunities for accumulation of human capital in the form of skills and knowledge of markets and occupations, employment in the informal activities is also said to provide workers with opportunities for collecting some financial or physical capital for investing in small enterprises of their own.

In a low employment, labour surplus economy, it is not unexpected that there should exist a high degree of competition between workers. Nor is it unexpected that despite their desperation in search for employment, workers still accept certain conventional taboos about the type of work they do. This could be explained in terms of the high degree of ignorance and illiteracy which is characteristics of this group. Another widespread belief about the informal sector is that the employers in this sector are mainly small entrepreneurs who, either as self-employed workers or as petty producers, employ only a small number of workers. Therefore, it is believed that no one employer is in a position to influence the wage rates and there is no collusion between them. As a result, the market on the whole, is a competitive one where neither the workers nor the employers indulge in collective bargaining or use any kind of preemptive powers, instead they let the wage rates be determined by market forces alone. These hypotheses have not been adequately verified by studies in any region or period of the country so far. Nevertheless, they form the basis of several policy measures relating to this section of the economy.

In this study the occupational structure and its flexibility in the segment of Calcutta's informal sector and the process of organisation as well as wage determination in it has been analysed with a view to shed some light on these questions.

Occupational Structure

Although in the sample there were workers engaged in as many as 31 different occupations (See Appendix II), they have been divided into four (or five when relevant) broad categories for the purpose of analysis. These categories differ significantly from each other in terms of the contents of the jobs and the attitudes of the people working there.

1. The 912 Code Workers were domestic servants who did cleaning and washing. The occupation code of this category as per the Indian National Code 1971 is 912; but in Calcutta they are generally known as *jhee*. If a worker lives at home but works for one or more employers she is known as *thika jhee*. Less than one-fifth of this '912' category lived in an employer's house and worked exclusively for one family. The rest were *thika jhees* working for more than one employer.
2. Other Domestic Workers were domestic workers who had some special skills. This group included cooks, housekeepers, *ayahs* and nurses. They often combined one type of job with another. A few of them lived in the employer's house while the others lived either with their own families or in a women workers' boarding house. While most domestic workers worked on monthly contracts, a few worked as casual workers on daily wages.
3. Skilled Workers included workers in either manufacturing or service occupations and they had some degree of formal or non-formal training.
4. Other Unskilled Workers included workers who performed non-domestic tasks requiring no initiation or training.

Without going into the question whether the skills required in these categories were distinctly different or not, the grouping here was in harmony with the standard social attitudes towards such employment. Domestic service was an accepted 'woman's job', and the 1955-58 survey of Calcutta by Professor S.N. Sen showed that over 70 per cent of the women workers from a universe comparable to this sample were in domestic service. Among the domestic servants, workers of the second category belonged to a somewhat distinct group, for example, cooks were usually from the upper castes and midwives in urban areas were usually better educated. The two groups of domestic servants could be meaningfully separated.

The other two categories—skilled workers and unskilled workers, were not so clearly defined as they included many occupations which were new to women. However, there was an objective requirement of skill training for some of these occupations which made categorisation easier. The skilled worker category included conventional women's jobs such as embroidery, tailoring or *papad* making. Previously, workers in these traditional occupations came from certain specific groups. For example, embroidery was mainly done by Muslim women and *papad* making was confined to the Gujarati areas of the city. There had been some liberalisation of these conventions when women of different social groups entered these traditional occupations and irrespective of social groups, they ventured into novel activities. The unskilled jobs included both a number of standard women's occupations such as making cowdung cakes, paper bags or garlands and new jobs like cutting rubber tyres for cheap shoes and fixing plastic parts. For such jobs there was literally no skill training required and no period of apprenticeship.

The Existing Occupational Structure. The table below gives the distribution of the 400 workers by the major occupational category, they were employed in at least four categories at the time of the enquiry. In order to check the degree to which the sample was representative of the population, a random sub-sample of 200 workers was drawn from it. This provided two sub-samples of 200 each. For testing the major conclusions, results for the two sub-samples are given separately. The distribution between occupational categories was similar in the two sub-samples and in the population, and it was concluded that this sample was fairly representative of the population in Calcutta.

TABLE 25.23

Occupational Structure of the Two Sub-samples and the Total Sample

Occupational categories	*Sub-sample*	*Sub-sample*	*Total*
'912' code	71	72	143(35.75)
Other domestic workers	40	42	82(20.50)
Skilled workers	53	52	105(26.25)
Unskilled workers	36	34	70(17.5)
Total	200	200	400(100.0)

Domestic service was no longer the only avenue open to women as had been the case at the time of the previous survey in 1953. Even then, at the time of the survey, about 56 per cent of the women worked as domestic servants. The rest were engaged in a variety of tasks in manufacturing and the services. The most common skilled jobs were tailoring and embroidery and as many as 59 women were engaged full-time or part-time in these activities. Some of the other skilled occupations were *biri* making or leather work, electrical fitting or glass blowing (See Table 25.24).

Although the total number of non-domestic workers in the sample was only 175, they held 191 jobs between them because 16 workers were engaged in more than one non-domestic job. This practice was most common in East Calcutta where ten workers worked on two jobs simultaneously. They were mainly tailors who were frequently unable to find sufficient work to keep busy throughout the week and they sought other work like cutting and fitting plastic parts or electrical connections. Domestic workers also took up additional work like making paper bags or cowdung cakes for sale. Some of them were engaged in plastic or leather cutting, and sewing, and one even made toys.

TABLE 25.24

Frequency Distribution of Different Non-domestic Jobs by Area Code and Occupation Code

Area code	*Occupation code*						
	Tailoring 710 719	*Paper products 856*	*Electrical goods 769*	*Tobacco 842-849*	*Food processing 920-829*	*Others*	*Total*
South Calcutta I	12+(1)	4+(3)	1	—	2	15+(2)	34+(6)
South Central Calcutta II	2+(1)	1	1	—	1+(1)	10+(1)	15+(3)
Central Calcutta III	2+(1)	4+(1)	—	—	7	11+(2)	24+(4)
North calcutta IV	33+(1)	2+(1)	2	—	6	13+(6)	56+(8)
East Calcutta V	6	4+(1)	8	6	1	37	62+(1)
Total	55+(4)	15+(6)	12	6	17+(1)	86+(11)	191+(22)

The area-wise spread of workers over occupations highlighted some between domestic and non-domestic categories was quite different. The proportion of domestic workers to the total number of workers was much higher in South and South Central Calcutta. In Central and North Calcutta, the distribution of domestic and non-domestic occupations was almost even and in East Calcutta, the weightage was overwhelmingly in favour of non-domestic jobs. This pattern closely follows the distribution of activities in Calcutta. South and South Central Calcutta are mostly middle and upper middle class residential areas interspaced by huge *bustees* and some large industries. In these areas there are not many small workshops and industries (with the exception of a few engineering units) that are frequently seen in other parts of Calcutta. In East Calcutta especially, there are numerous workshops for producing an ever-changing range of products from divorce materials.

In South and South Central Calcutta therefore, the majority of workers were engaged in domestic service and there were relatively few non-domestic workers. The latter were confined to traditional activities like tailoring, making cowdung cakes or paper bags. A few were engaged in clay-modeling around the Kalighat area. In North Calcutta, there were two very large slums housing a sizeable population of East Bengal refugee tailors. Moreover, there was a huge industry of readymade garments which was earlier limited to family units with male tailors but had rapidly passed into the hands of large commercial operators who increasingly employed the services of women from these families for executing the orders. The population studied here included many such women. North and Central Calcutta, apart from being thickly populated residential settlements, also house traditional small industries such as *biri* rolling, printing, book binding, and food processing. At the time of this study, these occupations were being passed from male of female workers and the latter were largely represented in the sample. It was observed that in East Calcutta women ventured into an array of newly developing occupations, some of which were thrown open to women for the first time. The latter included pottery, glass blowing, paper products, garlands, as well as electrical fittings, plastic goods and rubber and leather products. Making cowdung cakes or paper bags was commonly observed in all areas. Since there was no skill or capital required for these tasks, the work could be done in their spare time and there was always a ready market for these products everywhere.

It would not be unwarranted to conclude that women were willing to participate in a wide variety of jobs and the particular occupational structure that existed in any region was largely determined by the availability of jobs. There was little to indicate that women themselves were reluctant to take up non-traditional jobs or that there were barriers to their entry into these fields. In fact, there is a possibility that women had taken over some of the standard male occupations during this period. It is important to note that where such a choice of alternative occupations was given to them, domestic jobs (which were available everywhere) definitely got a lower rating. It still remains to be seen why. In expanding their occupational variety, women had broken several of the more obvious traditional taboos, for example, caste Hindu women worked on leather garments and bags. A woman with a high school certificate used to grind *dal* for a sweet shop and at the same time tutor students as well.

Changes Over time. Changes in this occupational structure over the seven years covered by this study offer further evidence about these tendencies in this labour market. The table below gives the occupational category-wise break up of workers from their date of joining the job they held at the time of the interview. The total number of entries was 450 because this include 50 secondary jobs held by workers whose primary job was in another category. For each entry, the second figure is the frequency of secondary jobs in that category. Over time a clear trend emerged, more and more workers tended to opt for non-domestic jobs. The weightage of domestic workers, especially of the '912' code variety was much higher among workers who had worked before 1973. 1973 onwards, the pattern shifted in favour of non-domestic jobs and this was especially true in the case of secondary jobs. Before 1973 two-thirds of the secondary jobs entered were in non-domestic categories. Since 1973, this proportion increased to 84 per cent or even more, and jobs of the skilled variety were particularly rapidly increasing.

TABLE 25.25

Distribution of Workers by Type of Jobs and Year of Joining

Year of joining service	*'912'*	*Other domestic servants*	*Unskilled workers*	*Skilled workers*	*Total*
Before 1974	102+7	56+1	43+7	55+9	256+24
	(38.92)	(20.36)	(17.86)	(22.86)	(100.0)
Since 1973	41+3	26+1	27+7	50+15	144+26
	(25.88)	(15.88)	(20.0)	(38.24)	(100.0)
Total	143+10	72+2	70+14	105+24	400+50
	(34.0)	(18.44)	(18.66)	(28.66)	(100.0)

Note: Figures in parentheses are percentages of row-wise totals.

If non-domestic jobs were categorised by the type of product and the year of joining, it appeared that after 1973, the entrants overwhelmingly opted for jobs which were non-traditional. For example, though tailoring, food processing or tobacco still remained important jobs for women, the post-1972 jobs were largely concentrated around electrical fittings, plastic and rubber products, engineering and glass works. Therefore, even during this brief span of seven years there was a distinct shift in women's occupational pattern in this region. Not only did new workers enter into new occupations, but the older workers appeared to have acquired new skills and opted for different types of jobs, usually on a part-time basis though occasionally as a full-time occupation. Thus, the hypothesis that there was some scope for training in skills in the unorganised sector and of mobility from one type of job to another could be accepted. The question arises how did this shift in occupational structure come about? The most obvious explanation appears to be that the younger workers as compared to the older workers preferred non-domestic work.

TABLE 25.26

Distribution of Workers by Occupational Category and Age Group

Age group in years	*Skilled*	*Unskilled*	*'912'*	*Others*	*Total*
25	58(45.0)	29(22.5)	31(24.0)	11(8.5)	129(100.0)
26-35	33(26.0)	22(17.3)	49(38.6)	23(18.1)	127(100.0)
36-45	12(12.0)	17(17.0)	40(40.4)	30(30.3)	99(100.0)
46 and above	2(4.4)	2(4.4)	23(51.1)	18(40.0)	49(100.0)
Total	105(26.3)	70(17.5)	143(35.8)	82(20.5)	400(100.0)

33 per cent of the workers in 25 years or less age group, opted for domestic work as against 60 per cent in the age group 26-35 years or 70 per cent in the age group 36-45 years. In the oldest age group nearly 90 per cent were in domestic jobs. The variety in non-domestic jobs was a later development and therefore, it was not surprising that there was a lower incidence of such occupations among the older workers. However, for the younger workers the choice of domestic jobs was still open. Also, data regarding wage rates and working conditions shows that this was not on grounds of relative returns from such work. Wages and working conditions in domestic jobs were marginally better than in the other jobs. The likely explanation seemed to be that the younger women with their relatively better educational qualifications, had come from specific social groups where domestic service a priori got a lower rating. As further evidence in support of this hypothesis it may be mentioned that in the case of domestic workers, either they themselves were the heads of their families or the heads were unskilled workers in casual employment. On the other hand, in the case of skilled workers in more than half the families the heads were white-collar or skilled workers.

For a long time, domestic work had been the only employment open to women in Calcutta. The scale of employment was limited and workers came from a few specific groups. Even at the end of the study, it was observed that the backgrounds of women who engaged in domestic service had not changed materially, but the entire group of women workers expanded to include many new groups who opted for work other than domestic service.

Occupational Structure and the Traditions of Work. Additional evidence was available which lends support to this idea that in the later half of the period under consideration, a new group of workers had entered the labour market—a group having even weaker traditions of women's work. Each interviewee was asked whether her mother or mother-in-law had ever worked for money. Those who replied in the affirmative were said to have had a family traditional of women's work. Taking this as a criterion, women who joined work before and since 1973 appeared to fall into two distinct groups. 1973 onwards, women with a family tradition of work appeared to have opted for domestic service.

TABLE 25.27

Percentage of Workers with A Tradition of Work in Each Occupation Who Joined Before 1973 and Since 1973

Occupation	*Percentage of workers within each category with a tradition of work—workers who joined before 1973*	*Percentage of workers within each category with a tradition of work—workers who joined after 1973*
'912'	31.37	42.5
Other domestic workers	14.82	33.33
Skilled workers	20.34	17.39
Unskilled	39.53	34.62
Total	26.24	30.93

Background data regarding women's work force participation in West Bengal indicated that working women largely belonged to the lower social strata. On the basis of this information regarding work tradition, one could conclude that before 1973 when opportunities for non-domestic work were relatively scarce, women from all social groups, if forced to work, had to take up domestic jobs. Since then a wide range of jobs and avenues have opened for women and those with better backgrounds opted for non-domestic tasks. It was largely women from inferior social backgrounds who continued to man the domestic services. It is obvious that, given a choice, social taboo did work against women on the whole, with the exception of those belonging to specific social groups engaged in domestic service. It is not clear whether the new social groups who had entered the labour market during the mid-seventies would actually have done so had not the non-domestic jobs become available.

The Self-employed

Of the 400 workers, 34 skilled or unskilled workers were self-employed in the sense that they had their own business-selling the output (product directly to the consumers and had invested their own or borrowed capital in the business. Some of them were engaged in businesses ran by the family as a whole. A few also employed outside paid labour. It should be noted here that although 15 of these 34 self-employed workers had started their business after 1972, they had not been able to start making and selling any of the more sophisticated products such as electrical fittings, glass or pottery items. Although the self-employed were few in number, a definite pattern emerged from this group. There was a group of laundry workers who were *rajak* by caste, and had a family traditions of this business. There were, at the other end, a few very poor and desperate women (either widows or with unemployed husbands) who earned their living by making cowdung cakes, paper bags or darned old clothes—anything they could do without any initial investment or training. There was yet another group of women from families which once belonged to the *Bhadralok* group—women with some education and training, and with access to capital, and they either singly or with their families, attempted to manage their enterprise. They usually took up tailoring or food processing—work which had no social stigma attached to it. All these groups differed from the others in terms of their background and expectations from the business but not necessarily in terms of the level of success they attained or the rate of return they earned from their labour. Only the traditionally professional family workers like laundry workers did slightly better.

TABLE 15.28

The Self-Employed

Occupation	*Self-employed*	*In family businesses*	*Who employed outside workers*	*Who had invested capital*	*With education till at least primary level*
Tailoring	9	5	1	4	6
Paper product makers	6	3	—	3	2
Cowdung cake makers	7	—	—	1	—
Leather	1	1	1	1	—
Food processing	1	1	1	1	1
Service	5	5	3	5	—
Others	5	2	—	5	2
Total	34	17	6	20	11

It appears that self-employment was not increasing rapidly among these women. In South East, South Central or Central Calcutta, areas which are relatively more affluent, there were very few self-employed women apart from the laundry owners or the occasional paper bag makers. The rest were from North or East Calcutta, areas having a tradition of small enterprises, especially among the Hindu Bengalis. It is worth noting that the *rajaks* or laundry workers were all Hindi speaking Hindus. One Urdu speaking Muslim family had a packing box business. The others merely sold a few cowdung cakes. One enterprise making leather *chappals* was run by a scheduled caste Hindu family. The rest were Bengali speaking caste Hindus and a significant number were from the upper castes.

Secondary Jobs

A close study of the pattern of secondary jobs that these women engaged in provides an interesting sidelight. Over the years, there was a significant increase in the percentage of women holding more than one job. This could partly be due to the easy available of part-time work in this sector. Indeed, the extent to which workers experimented with new skills and occupations while maintaining their stake in their usual occupations showed that the employment contracts in this market were extremely flexible. This flexibility, no doubt, helped the workers who could find additional work to fit in with their existing commitments. It was particularly appealing to employers as it made the supply of labour continuously divisible. In the organised sector, such divisibility in labour supply through part-time or over-time work is generally available at a greater than proportionate rate. For these workers the additional work was only rarely at a higher marginal rate of payment, and they offered this flexibility in employment contracts as an attempt to attract prospective.

TABLE 25.29

Year-wise Number of Workers Working on More than One Job, their Share in the Job Intensity

Year	*Number of women working on more than one job*	*Percentage of total workers working in that year*	*Job intensity i.e. average jobs of each worker holding on more than one job*
1969-70	40	21	2.95
1970-71	48	20	3.40
1971-72	72	27	2.89
1972-73	86	30	2.85
1973-74	100	31	2.81
1974-75	125	34	2.87
1975-76	145	36	2.90

For women working in Calcutta's informal sector, opportunities for work had increased and also diversified fairly rapidly during the period covered by this study. In each of the different areas of Calcutta, they had gained access to a number of occupations which were determined by the general character of the region and the overall pattern of activities in that region rather than by any kind of sex-wise taboos on the part of the employer. There were some significant reversals as well-occupations like *biri* rolling or glass blowing which were previously male strongholds became accessible to women. The workers themselves, appeared to entertain some reservations about the choice of occupation. While these reservations could partly be explained in terms of the relative rates of return from different occupation for the qualifications required in each, it was also possible that depending on their social background, they could have observed certain taboos in their choices. An increasing number of new entrants to this labour market belonged to social groups which viewed domestic work as a less preferred alternative.

Entry into these occupations in the informal sector was accompanied by a considerable degree of mobility of workers between occupations. There were instances of workers learning new skills while in a job and taking up some new type of work. However, it still remains to be seen how valuable were these skills to the workers in terms of an increase in their income earning capacity. A survey confined to workers in the informal sector alone cannot throw any light on whether this skill formation or waiting period in the informal sector helps the worker to move into the formal sector or not. There is some information about a reversal in the process. In this study, there were several workers or other members of their families who had previously worked in the formal sector, but had lost their jobs and had moved into occupations in the informal sector.

There is significant evidence supporting the hypothesis that additional skill formation takes place in the informal sector, but it does not support the contention that workers accumulate any physical or financial capital as a result of this work. The few self-employed workers in this study had obtained their capital either from the formal sector activities of some members of the family or had inherited it—several women tailors had inherited sewing machines from their husbands or fathers. Other workers like those in food processing had bought the machines and paid for them from the retirement benefits of some family member. The laundry businesses were the only ones where families had built up their capital through generations of work. It should be remembered that except for the very rudimentary enterprises, the few workers who had made an effort in this direction were usually from higher social groups or had a background of such work experience.

The question of the degree of competition in this labour market is not easy to settle. The workers were not in any way practising collective bargaining. Each of them formed a small part of the total supply and they were constantly exposed to further competition from new workers because of the ease of entry and learning skills. This competition was further intensified by the fact that other workers could offer themselves for part-time or occasional work. Thus, a quick rise in the pressure of demand could be adjusted through the flexible employment contracts and gave no bargaining strength to the workers already in the labour market. Their lack of education and extreme poverty severely limited the mobility of these women between areas. In the sample, none of the workers who had originally migrated from outside the city had moved from one area zone to another within the city. All the workers with the exception of those who lived in the employer's house, worked at jobs located within walking distance from their homes because they could not afford to spend time and money on travelling to work. Moreover, if there were social groups where certain prejudices inhibited the choices of workers, then the position of these women was highly vulnerable to market forces.

Though the study provided no direct information about the employers, interviews with the workers highlighted several points. In case of domestic service, each employer was in search of only one or two part-time workers and there were numerous such employers in each area, but this did not put them on par with the employees. Each employer had a much higher degree of staying power and could in the short run, keep his demand elastic by temporarily substituting his own labour and skills for that of the worker. The worker on the other hand, had nothing but her labour power to fall back on and was at a greater disadvantage for withholding her supply. In case of manufacturing in the unorganised sector, the employer could be in the market using the labour of several employees, but by the very nature of the unorganised sector, he did not want to build up a regular, steady contractual relationship with any particular group of workers at any one place. Even if he had the same worker in his employ for several years, he was reluctant to enter into a lasting contract with the worker, and preferred to give the impression that at any time and price schedules, there were close substitutes available to him for the worker whose services he was using, and he was indifferent as to which worker actually worked for him. In this sector, the employer invested little on overhead of any kind—either in tools, buildings or amenities. Therefore, there were no constraints on the scale and technique of his operation even in the short run, except his finances and the market conditions for his inputs and output. As such, the employer had very little commitment to a particular production process or a particular group of workers. Although these were manufacturing activities, few of the employers were industrial capitalists. Many of these operations were financed through commercial capital with its usual requirement of a quick turnover and little long-term investment. The workers in the market had little choice about withholding their labour and were fully exposed to competition from new full-time or part-time workers; the employers on the other hand, even if without any collusion, were in a much better position to withhold their demand. The bargain in no sense could be conceived of as a between equals.

26

Women Workers at Home

The general expansion in women's work force participation noted earlier took place in spite of the consistently poor working conditions and the low wages that were offered for work in the informal sector in Calcutta. There was no noticeable improvement in this area over the period under consideration. Even those occupations which were relatively new to the region and to the workers there, offered no additional incentive to attract new workers. In other words, while the demand for this type of labour in the informal sector occupations has probably increased, it was apparently being matched at unchanged wage rates by fresh additions to the supply.

The clues derived from the records of actual events are seldom definite or substantial enough to enable one to establish the superiority of one explanation over other contending hypotheses. Therefore, one does not make an attempt to examine all possible explanations, only one was put forward—while jobs were being created, the labour supply schedule was also shifting because of other changes such as the falling real incomes of a number of families. These changes induced the families independently to send out more workers. Wage rates which had always been near subsistence level remained the same while increasing numbers entered the market to find jobs. Increase in the supply and demand for labour could both be independent and unevenly matched insofar as wage rates during this period went down in real terms. Here an attempt is made to examine how far the workers' work force participation decisions were influenced by the changes in their family income levels. Further, their earnings vis-a-vis the family income levels and the manner in which their contribution was utilised was also examined.

Family Incomes and Work Decisions

It has already been observed that the women in the sample came from very poor families where the average income per family was about Rs. 250 per month. Whatever the contribution of the women to the family income, it was nevertheless crucial for the survival of the family. Following this, it would be logical to argue that the decisions of these women regarding any particular work or the total quantum of work done would significantly depend on the relative levels of their family incomes and responsibilities.

While attempting to examine this hypothesis about the existence of a significant relation between the levels of family income and the quantum of work done, a difficulty arose—the available data showed only the actual ex-post amount of work done by workers at different levels of family income. This could not be used to formulate ex-ante aggregate supply schedules at different levels of family income because the existing position was the outcome of this as also of other determinants of supply and demand for such labour. There was a probability that not all the women in the group found as much work as they wanted, thus, the quantum to actual work done would appear to be less clastic in relation to changes in the family income than was the case.

In order to avoid this difficulty, one '912' category workers were considered. This was one category of work of which there was apparently no shortage at the going rates of wages. As the wage rates of later entrants to this occupational category were somewhat higher than the average for all such workers, there was reason to believe that demand was not a limiting factor. Another advantage observed in this labour market was the fact that the supply and demand for work was not in large indivisible units, it was fairly flexible and a worker could add or delete additional jobs to or from her existing work load. In other words, if necessary, she was free to take up or give up work for one of her several employers and thereby alter her work load.

Table 26.1 reveals that there was a fairly steady negative relation between the workers' hours of work (the quantum of work) and the levels of monthly per capita income of their families. Over 70 per cent of the group with very low incomes worked for nearly nine hours or more per day. Very few worked part-time or less than 30 hours a week. The position of workers from families earning over Rs. 20 per capita monthly income was quite different, the majority worked for a normal length of time and a significant percentage even worked part-time.

TABLE 26.1

Percentage Distribution of '912' Workers by Weekly Hours of Work and Per Capita Monthly Family Income without their Contribution

Per capita monthly family income in rupees	*Distribution of workers by weekly hours of work*			
	30	*31-60*	*61±*	*Total*
5.0	1.50	28.45	70.10	100.0
5.1-10.0	1.80	43.90	54.40	100.0
10.1-20.0	14.30	50.00	35.70	100.0
20.1-30.0	20.00	60.00	20.00	100.0
30.1 and above	—	—	—	—
Total	3.50	37.80	58.80	100.0

In the table 26.1 the family incomes of workers were considered without the contributions of these workers because with the addition of the workers' contribution there was a tendency for most per capita family incomes to cluster round the modal value. In other words, it appeared that the women worked chiefly to raise the level of per capita family income close to the standard value. If the level was particularly low without their contribution, they worked harder. If not, the opposite was true. In any case the level of family income appeared to be a major determinant of the quantum of work done by each worker. This was presumably true of workers in other comparable occupations.

Contribution to the Family Income

Given the fact that women worked in order to raise the level of the family income as compared to the norm, the question arises how important was their contribution towards this end? Was it marginal or vital? It was observed that in almost all these families the woman's contribution was vital. In nearly half the cases, the woman earned over 40 per cent of the total income. In over a quarter o the cases, the woman's contribution was over 60 per cent. Surprisingly, the percentage of those earning more than 40 per cent of the family income was as high as 39 per cent for workers of 15 years or below. For those between 16 and 25 years, it was only 34 per cent, this figure was significantly below that for the younger group, probably because the young workers of 15 years or less came to the labour market only when the family situation was really desperate. Of those between 26 and 50 years of age, over 50 per cent earned more than 40 per cent of the family income and nearly 20 per cent earned over 80 per cent of it. For the oldest age group, this percentage was even higher.

Among the women who earned over 60 per cent of the family income, 82 per cent were in domestic services, and a large number of this group were resident servants. This figure was much higher than the weightage of domestic service in the general sample population, probably because it was easier to earn a higher income in domestic service with the terms of appointment being flexible which allowed a person longer hours if necessary. The rates were somewhat better in some of the cases. Looking from another angle, it could be said that women went in for domestic service jobs when they were more desperate than the average.

Secondary or Supplementary Earners. One of the standard arguments for the casual attitude towards discrimination against women in economic activities is that women are viewed as secondary or supplementary earners within a family. In all household activity analysis, the economic activity of only the head of the household is considered primary and all other earners are considered secondary for the household. In this study, the generalisation that women's work is secondary was not wholly supported by the evidence obtained from the sample. There were several widows, divorcees and unmarried women who claimed that they were the head of their household. In addition to these, there were several married or unmarried women from households where the head was unemployed and the woman was the principal earner. A large majority of this group had several dependents—unemployed husbands, fathers, children and siblings. Of the 164 women, over 50 per cent were in the '912' occupational category as against only 36 per cent in the total sample. On the other hand, there were relatively few skilled workers. This could be explained in terms of the fact that the former type of work was relatively easy to get and was more steady. Skilled work on the other hand, was often in short supply and while supplementary earners could perhaps afford to wait for an opportunity to get skilled work, those on whom a family's living depended could not do so.

TABLE 26.2

Distribution of Occupation-wise Workers by Age and Share in Family Incomes

Percentage share in family income of the worker	*Age in years* 15	16-25	26-35	36-50	50+	*Total*
1	*2*	*3*	*4*	*5*	*6*	*7*
20.0						
'912' workers	1	1	7	5	2	16
Other domestic workers	—	2	1	5	2	10
Skilled workers	6	16	17	4	—	43
Unskilled workers	1	9	10	5	1	26
Total	8	28	35	19	5	95
20.1-40.0						
'912' workers	3	6	18	14	3	44
Other domestic workers	—	4	3	6	1	14
Skilled workers	3	17	8	3	—	31
Unskilled workers	1	13	4	7	—	25
Total	7	40	33	30	4	114
40.1-60.0						
'912' workers	6	8	9	11	3	37
Other domestic workers	—	1	4	12	3	20
Skilled workers	2	8	4	5	—	19
Unskilled workers	1	2	5	2	—	10
Total	9	19	22	30	6	86
60.1-80.0						
'912' workers	1	3	9	9	-	22
Other domestic workers	1	3	2	3	—	9
Skilled workers	—	3	3	1	—	7
Unskilled workers	—	1	—	2	—	3
Total	2	10	14	15		41
80.1						
'912' workers	1	1	8	10	4	24
Other domestic workers	1	1	9	14	4	29
Skilled workers	—	1	3	—	1	5
Unskilled workers	—	3	1	2	9	15
Total	2	6	21	26	18	73

Women's work is often dismissed as secondary in yet another way. Even when a woman earns a significant part of the family income, this amount is often used for purchasing non-essential commodities for the family. In other words, the wages raise the standard of living of the family above the basic minimum rather than ensure the basis minimum itself. This was not observed in the sample studied here. The earnings of the women in the sample were essential, not for ensuring extra comforts for the family, but for providing the bare necessities.

TABLE 26.3

Women Who were Formal or Informal Head of Household

Civil status	*Total number*	*'912' workers*	*Skilled workers*
Widows and divorcees from househods with no other head			
(a) with dependents	88	52	14
(b) without dependents	27	13	3
Married women from households with unemployed head			
(a) with dependents	27	14	2
(b) without dependents	5	3	1
Unmarried women from single member households	2	1	1
Unmarried women from households with unemployed head	15	2	6
Total	164	85	27
Percentage	(100.0)	(51.8)	(7.9)
Percentage in total sample population	41.00	35.75	26.25

TABLE 26.4

Number of Women with Families Possessing Basic Amenities in Each Occupation Group

Occupation group	Buys full ration	Owns a ratio/ clock/watch	Owns any two of the items	Owns all the items
'912' workers	69(42.0)	9(6.3)	6(4.2)	1(neg)
Other domestic workers	27(32.9)	8(9.8)	6(7.3)	—
Skilled workers	61(58.1)	18(17.1)	19(18.1)	12(11.4)
Unskilled workers	33(47.1)	21(30.0)	5(7.1)	3(4.3)
All	181(45.3)	56(14.0)	36(9.0)	16(4.0)

Note: Figures in parentheses are percentages of the row-wise total for each occupation.

It is clearly evident from the table above that woman's work had not been adequate to ensure even the basic necessities for the family. More than half the families were unable to buy a full supply of cereals, pulses, sugar, cooking oil and kerosene to which they were entitled under the rationing system. Very few were able to buy anything extra for the family. It was seen that even women who had worked for five or more year failed to accumulate reserves to buy durables. Not more than 22 women in this group possessed a radio set. Another ten owned a watch or a clock. Only ten families owned all these three commodities. It was observed that in this group of women who had worked for five or more years, the higher a woman's contribution to the family income, the less were the family's chances of obtaining any extras. In other words, since a woman's total earning capacity was severely limited in these occupations and in this labour market, a family which was largely dependent on a woman earner was on the border of subsistence. This state of affairs reflected adversely on the labour market employing women. It did not detract from the importance of a woman's work for the family' survival.

Apart from this information regarding the expenditure on essentials and luxuries, information about their life style was also elicited. An important factor to be considered here was the amount of help they received in executing their double load of housework and other wage work. As seen earlier, most of these women had very long working hours without the relief of occasional paid leave or a weekly holiday. In addition to the long working hours, these women had a particularly heavy load of housework. To begin with, all but two of the families had to fetch water from a well, a public tap or a tubewell. Most of the women collected cowdung to make cakes for fuel and also went over garbage heaps to find any bits of paper, wood or half-burnt coal which could be used as fuel. The only readymade foods available were bread and *muri* (parched rice). Most of these women had large families with more than one minor children.

To ease their heavy load of housework, only three could afford paid help, while the others could not even afford the most elementary labour and time-saving gadgets. Only 356 women offered information on this issue—30 per cent had a kerosene stove for cooking, while the others relied wholly on coal stoves which require a tremendous amount of effort to light and keep going. None of the families had any cooking gas facilities, and only eight owned a pressure cooker. Although electricity was available in most areas, the majority used an oil lamp for lighting. Less than ten per cent of the houses had electrical fittings, and the ones who did have electricity in the house used it very sparingly and used only low watt bulbs.

Among their other possessions, nearly a quarter possessed one or two costs. These cots were often *charpais* which the adults took out at night to sleep on the pavements. The extremely poor families were also aware of the hazards of malaria and a common and essential commodity in these areas was a mosquito-net. Over half the families possessed at least one net. Others had more than one net including a separate one for children. These few gods generally completed the list of their entire possessions, though some owned a chair or a small table, and usually a trunk and a clothes horse. The men in the family frequently had a shirt or a pair of trousers made of synthetic material, but rarely did the women or the children possess such relatively expensive things except when they were given old clothes by others.

Health and Education of Children

Another way of effectively utilising the income of these women could be for giving their children a better start in life which would include lowering the incidence of infant and child mortality. In the sample, the rate of child mortality was quite high. Nearly 13 per cent of all children born alive had died before the age of one and over a quarter of the children born alive had died before the age of one and over a quarter of the children had died before reaching five years of age. In this sample there was considerable improvement over time—children born since 1970 had a much higher life expectancy than those born between 1960 and 1970 and a still higher expectancy than those born before 1960. The current estimate (at the time of the study) of infant mortality for the whole of West Bengal was only 8.07 deaths for 100 live births within one year of birth and the figures obtained from this sample were consistently higher than this figure.

It may be significantly that among the children born since 1970, the mortality rates for infants and children of unskilled workers mothers were significantly higher than among the rest. This may be partly due to the differences in family incomes and partly to the differences in cultural backgrounds.

A striking feature observed in this connection was the high incidence of miscarriage among skilled workers. It may be possible that following 1970, a significant percentage of miscarriages could have been induced as part of the family planning drive, though to a certain extent, it could have been a result of the long hours these skilled workers spent working on their sewing machines throughout the year.

TABLE 26.5

Deaths Per 100 Live Births of Infants (One Year) and Children (Five Years) Born at Different Time Periods

Born	*Deaths per 100 live births of*	
	infants	*children*
Since 1970	8.40	13.49
Between 1960 and 1970	13.57	14.09
Before 1960	16.16	15.41
All	12.86	13.53

Even if women could do little to improve either their own or their children's health or their surroundings, they could use their income to provide the children better education. But in this direction too, they achieved little. The West Bengal Government records indicate that by 1975-76 for male children in the age group 6 to 11 years, entry into primary schools was nearly universal whereas for female children, it was over 60 per cent. In this study however, not even half the male children and only about one-third of the female children between 6 to 11 years of age attended primary school. Those who did manage to attend school showed a lower rate of dropouts as compared to the total West Bengal average of 33 per cent or more. Official records for West Bengal reveal that nearly half of all the boys and a quarter of all the girls in the 11 to 15 years age group were in secondary school. The comparable figures in the sample weer 20.5 per cent for boys and 17.5 per cent for girls. On the whole, 55 per cent of all the living children of these women were illiterate. The percentage of illiteracy among children in the 6 to 10 years age group in 1976-77 was not significantly lower. Apparently, these children had not been able to take much advantage of the expanding educational facilities in the region. Added to this was the disturbing fact that several women had been compelled to send their children who were below 15 years of age to work.

Table 26.6 does not include children who worked only part-time or occasionally. Nor did it include the vast platoon of female children who helped their mothers regularly in the latter's occupation and/or performed some household tasks like cooking or baby sitting. As mentioned before, a large number of these women coped with their heavy burden of work—both at home and outside, with assistance from their daughters.

TABLE 26.6

Minor Working Children of Interviewees by Their Ages

Age in years	*Male*	*Female*	*Total*
9	—	1	1
10	—	2	2
11	—	1	1
12	4	14	18
13	4	3	7
14	5	12	17
15	6	14	20
Total	19	47	66

Leisure Time Activities

With their limited income there was not much choice of entertainment open to these women. Though 40 per cent of them were literate, not more than 15 per cent read anything at all. Most of them owned no radio or transistor sets and only about 20 per cent ever listened to an occasional programme. Cinema was a very common form of entertainment, and over 75 per cent said that they managed to see a film occasionally. However, only the young unmarried girls had some leisure time and spare money to buy a film magazine or to see a film at least once a month. A common form of relaxation was a visit to one's relatives or to a religious place. The younger married women found it extremely difficult to find time for visiting their parents. Their '912' workers were the worst off in this respect because they did not get time off even during festivals.

To conclude one may say that the data indicated that women's decisions regarding the quantum of work they did in the labour marked depended not so much on the levels of wage rates as on their per capita family income. The poorer the family, the more the amount of work the women tried to undertake. Interestingly, there were substantial differences in the per capita family income levels exclusive of the earnings of these women workers, but inclusive of their earnings the per capita income in all worker families tended to cluster round the mean level. This mean level was in accordance with the prices prevailing at the time of the survey, very close to the margin of subsistence. It could be said that these workers' main motivation in seeking work was to raise the family per capita income level to a target level. This explains why these women put in extra work when marginal and average wage rates remained constant or even deteriorated. About 40 per cent of the women in the sample were the chief earners in the family and were the formal or informal head of their household. Regardless of the age group, over half the women earned more than 40 per cent of the family income and a quarter earned 60 per cent or more of it. Therefore, the tendency to regard women's work as secondary and less deserving of social consideration is not only unjust to them as workers but could seriously affect the welfare of their entire family.

This was all the more so because women in the unorganised occupations belonged to families on the brink of subsistence. There was a close link between on the brink of subsistence. There was a close link between women's decisions regarding the amount of work done and the shortfall in the family income for the basic requirements to ensure the survival of the family. In spite of the substantial percentage-wise contribution they made, the families were hardly able to afford a regular and adequate supply of the bare necessities. Few of them could afford to build up a stock of any durables. Even though they worked for unusually long hours outside the home, few of them could afford either paid help or buy any gadgets to reduce drudgery of housework. Nor could it be said that their work enabled them to give their children a significantly better life. They could not ensure for their children a higher than average life expectancy or education level or even a childhood free of economic pressures. Children were often found helping their mothers regularly in order to enable the latter to carry on with their work both at home and outside, and were also compelled to take up regular paid work themselves. These women carried on a continuous struggle for survival without the hope of offering better prospects to their children and without occasional relief through relaxation, entertainment or change.

WORKING WOMEN AND CHILDREN

WORKING WOMEN AND CHILDREN

Volume - 2

Working Women in India

Editor-in-Chief

C. P. RAI

LAXMI SHIKSHAN SANSTHAN
LUCKNOW

&

ANMOL PUBLICATIONS PVT. LTD.
NEW DELHI - 110 002 (INDIA)

ANMOL PUBLICATIONS PVT. LTD.
4374/4B, Ansari Road, Daryaganj
New Delhi - 110 002

Working Women and Children

First Edition, 2000
ISBN 81-261-0658-1 (Set)

PRINTED IN INDIA

Published by J.L. Kumar for Anmol Publications Pvt. Ltd., New Delhi -110 002 and Printed at Mehra Offset Press, Delhi.

CONTENTS

27

Problems of Urban Working Women—At Home

Our advancement in science and technology notwithstanding, the women remain backward and poverty stricken. The condition of women in India in general is considered to be very miserable. Women's problems are linked with her general living conditions in society.

The women perform many functions in the society and for the society. They produce children, mothers and wives. However they are largely excluded from high status occupations and from positions of power. They do cooking, mending, sewing, washing and many other odd jobs. But in terms of the rewards of prestige, wealth and power, women invariably come off worse.

The emergence of middle class women as working women is a recent phenomena; however the society has mostly remained a traditional one, leading to the women facing many problems. The problems of working women are multidimensional and differ from women to women. The problems are different for different sections of women such as rural and urban women, the educated and uneducated ones, single women and ones with family. Women in joint family, nuclear or extended family, of orthodox and modern family etc. again, have their own problems. Even the atmosphere in the place of work, attitudes of the fellow workers and the authority, age of the women, kind of work, timings of work, distance of work-place from the house etc. are important factors in the lives of working women.

Promilla Kapur in her study of hundreds of working women employed in various salaried jobs and professions, found that their problems are of three types: environmental, social and psychological. In each of them the problems emerge due to the stained situations at home and work place. In turn, they are due to two factors; one is the inner conflict due to dual commitment and concern, and the other is the practical difficulty of combing the dual commitment.[1]

Raka Sharan in her study found that the social degradation, economic subjugation and dependence of Indian women manifest in triple forms of exploitation—first, at the family level, secondly in working environment by their bosses or employers and finally by the political leaders, pressure groups and trade unions.[2]

Discrimination in the family is a major problem for women in Indian society. The example of the three girls who committed suicide in Chandigarh the day their brother was born, clearly pointed this out.[3]

Forgarty[4] and his associates in their study on the family, career and working life of qualified women in top jobs found five types of dilemmas:

(1) Dilemmas arising from sheer overload.
(2) Dilemmas from experiencing in one's environment strongly conflicting ideas and directions about what is considered right and proper in a given area of behaviour.
(3) Dilemmas caused by conflicts within oneself about whether one is being a good person (good human being, good wife and mother, good woman) in leading a certain type of existence.
(4) Dilemmas produced by conflicts in obligations, attachments, desires, and so on relative to one's network of relatives, friends and associates.
(5) Dilemmas due to the conflicts between roles that may be variable in their demands at different times, eg., the marital role demands in relation to the work demands of each partner at different points in the life cycle.

The Problems of Married Working Women

Women as a group, specially married women, have certainly become an important part of the work-force all over the world. The march of wives into the work-place is gradually changing the family, marriage and child-bearing practices. In other words the phenomenon of career-couples is having its impact on the institutions marriage, sex, children, life-style, and the dream of home. The double income does liberate both husband and wife from financial stringency and self-denial, but it creates more problems for working wives.

Dual Responsibility

The major problems for working wives arise out of the dual responsibilities of the working women—house work and the office work. Even though the employment of women is accepted, most of her in-laws and majority of the husbands have not accepted the changing life pattern. They are not prepared to share the responsibilities of the household and of looking after children. These duties are still considered to be exclusive of the wife. It is a common sight that the women get up early in the morning, prepare break-fast, cooks the lunch, dresses the children for school and goes to office. In the evening when she returns the house job is waiting for her. She prepares tea and serves the husband and children, attends pending work and prepares dinner. If it is a joint family the mother-in-law or the sister-in-laws feel that they work for the whole day in house when she is in the office. Now it is her turn to work. If she is with her husband or children, they feel that she is not doing enough work for the house. They criticise and abuse her. They even comment loud that she is not earning for them or she is not obliging them by working, that they also work a lot. At times her share of work is kept apart. Sometimes they remark that she has a change to go out in the name of work, while the other sisters-in-law are totally confined to home. They are jealous of her freedom and the status she enjoys. Even derogatory stories are fabricated to hurt her. If the husband is sensible and sympathetic and does share some work to help her he is blamed as a "henpacked" husband. The in-laws do not like his attitude and criticise him also. However, even such husbands are only a few.[5]

Krishna Chakraborty in her study, *the Conflicting Worlds of Working Mother* found that employed housewives all over the world have to face this problem of adjustment among their varied role expectations. They are required by their position to play a dual set of roles—one as home makers, wives and mothers, and the other as employees. Being simultaneously confronted with the dual demands of home and work, they are liable to face adjustment problems. At home, in addition to biological functions, there are other duties which they are expected to perform because of the prevailing cultural norms and values. These new circumstances and responsibilities, require a redefinition and reallocation of roles, duties and responsibilities, not merely for them but also for every member of the family. Unless and until it is achieved there is no chance of lessening the overload on working house-wives, and therefore, mitigating the severity of their problems. Whether it is out of their own choice or economic necessity that they have taken up employment outside, adjustment between their role obligations is not an easy task. It requires not only ability and goodwill but also physical endurance and psychological acceptance.[6]

Conflict between the Two Roles

In addition to the above described burdens on the women, the dual role also demands of her two different sets of values. Difficulties arise because often these two roles make a simultaneous demand on the person whose physical capacity, energy, endurance and time have definite limits. Often the fulfilment of these two roles requires qualities of different and diverse kinds—one requiring cooperation and self-negation and the other calling her competition and self-enhancement. Women's business functions require such qualities as efficiency, courage, determination, intelligence, sense of reality, responsibility and independence. In the professional sphere they are expected to act in 'business-like' manner, to be straight forward and non-sentimental. In addition to these characteristics, and partly in conflict with them, woman who is a wife also expected to be sweet and soft, sensitive and adaptable, gentle, unassertive, good-humoured, domesticated, yielding and in most cases, not too intelligent. Hence a kind of conflict arising from a lack of adjustment between two competing roles is likely to be faced by those persons who have to comply with dual obligations at a time. This problem would not arise if job and home were considered as two mutually exclusive fields of life. The typical woman is dedicated to her family. She may feel that one way of serving her family is by earning additional money. At the same time she might feel that her husband would prefer her staying at home, and rendering more domestic service, that and her children need her presence at home, and that her presence there would have prevented the emergence of some of their problems. She wonders whether the additional money—which she may earn by working outside and which might not be large after meeting additional expenses—is really worth and sacrifice. Often she is heard to make statements like a working woman cannot be outstanding both at home and in job, she had to make a choice or 'it is hard to stay happily married while working', or the 'quality of motherhood will suffer when the mother engages in a full-time job outside.' Further religious rituals and customary practices are expected to be preserved and perpetuated by the women. 'Despite her heavy work burden women, more than the men, are the loudwearies of the rituals. Thus the problem of adjustment of working women becomes more serious.[7]

Krishna Chakraborty[8] correctly hypothesize—(i) that the changes in the position and role of women is still thoroughly ambiguous; (ii) that the dual responsibilities of home and work are likely to create some difficulties for the incumbents in fulfilling the dual obligations, and expectations with equal competence and satisfaction, and (iii) that the persons performing the dual roles, therefore, are liable to experience a sort of strain and conflict between dual obligations seemingly incompatible.

That the two roles, the role of an employee and of a home-maker, are distinct and different by nature, and that there is wide possibility of role conflict and role strain being perceived by persons who want to reconcile them simultaneously, have been amply proved by sociologists and social psychologists. Myrdal and Kelien write. "The characteristic feminine, dilernma of today is usually summarised under the headings 'Career and family' ... Today the conflict has become 'internalised' and continues as a psychological problem which may assume many different variations and shades; and just because there is no longer an absolute 'either or' to be decided on at the beginning of adult life, the pull in two directions goes on practically throughout a women's life."

In fact carrying out almost all responsibilities single handedly the women are over-strained and get exhausted. The illusion of having new experience and variation from drudgery of the routine house-work soon fades away. All the aspirations are shattered. All these make a combined effect on her nature. They get irritated in trivial matters, get angry on children and husband. The home (family) which is expected to be better than paradise, get disturbed and thus happiness and peace vanish.

The ideas of multiple responsibilities also create problems for working women. On the one hand they want to be efficient workers and try hard to fulfil the job-duties and at the same time they also want to be good wives, good mothers and better home managers. She wants to maintain her status in the society and be respected by the other members of the family. Her sincerity towards all the responsibilities is itself a cause of trouble. After finishing the home-job she runs to the office. if she is late, she is in tension. The officer authority would blame her for insincerity. If she has to put on some overtime work, she is late at home and she is worried for the children coming from school.[9]

In some houses, of course, the working of women is appreciated. They are treated with great respect; her burdens and feelings are understood. Development of her personality and emergence into an enlightened status is encouraged. In such families working women have a comfortable position. They enjoy their work and aspire to do their best to be outstanding in their fields. But unfortunately this type of situation is found rarely.

Working Women and Children

Another type of problem experienced is the feeling of neglecting the children when the mother is working. The mothers often feel or made to feel that the children are not properly looked after, that they do not enjoy the facilities that the other children enjoy, that they have to let go many things, and that in addition they have to do some work at home to help the mother. When the mother is tired and gets angry, they feel that they are missing the mother's love and get disappointed. In this situation the working mother's experience, her psychological problems arising from inner conflict and a feeling of guilt, anxiety or tension are caused by the dual commitment and concern.

Control Over Income

Even though many women work, not many of them have any control over the income they earn. A great majority of them have to hand over their salary to their husbands or in-laws. They are not supposed to manage their own income. The amount is spent in the expenses of home. In some cases they are not given even the pocket money or the amount to buy things for their personal use. She has to demand and is given some money as a grace-granted to her. In short, the working women is always short of pocket money to use for herself despite having her own income. Thus employment still does not mean control over money or economic independence for the women.

The problem becomes worse when some persons feel that the women are working to satisfy their whims or as hobby. There are also instances when the men gradually withdraw themselves from leaving much of the responsibilities of running the house on themselves and pass them into the women. In the beginning the woman does not mind. But after some time she realises that the husband has thrown the whole burden on her and this creates strained relations.

Impact on Marital Relations

The whole drama of the life of an Indian woman is played around the husband and his relations. Even though a man is well educated and dressed in Western clothes, has a look of modernity and even advocates women's emancipation, in his relations with his wife he is still like traditional husband, with age old orthodox attitude towards his wife. He may be a staunch exponent of equality of women with that of men. But at home he enjoys domination over his wife, who has to meekly obey him without questioning. He is not able to accept his wife arguing the truth. He likes his wife's earning but it defiles his ego to accept her as his equal. He is not able to even accept the fact that his wife can efficiently handle the man's job at her office. He enjoys to see her as weak, docile and always dependent on him. The problem becomes more difficult when the earning of the woman is higher than the husband's or she is more able and efficient in her work. He tries to hide his feelings of inferiority complex, by manifesting it in actions that express exaggerated superiority over her.[10] This breeds very oppressive conditions for the woman, who is neither able to give up nor face this oppression day in and day out. Thus working women face a severe problem when their salary is more than that of her husband. Aware of the man's ego and the stereotyped notions of a woman being less than a man, women take extra care of their husband's feeling, never express their superiority and deliberately adopt a low self image and low posture. But the husbands are always conscious of the fact, and this aggeravates the oppression of women.[11]

Restrictions on Movement

The finding of Urmila Patel[12] show that in some cases the freedom of movement of the working women is also restricted. She is allowed only to go to the place of work. If she is late by half-an-hour, she is answerabled. She is not allowed to go elsewhere alone. If she wants to go, she is accompanied by younger sister-in-law or someone else. Some women express that if they have to work late in the office, they are misunderstood by their husbands or the in-laws. She is badly rebuked and a big fuss is made of it. Some women complain that even if they are physically unwell and badly exhausted and could not respond to the husband's sexual needs, they are not only misunderstood but are alleged to have illegitimate relations with some colleagues or the boss. They are inhumanly treated, tortured and even beaten. Women feel hurt by such humaliating actions of the husbands towards them especially when their integrity is questioned. There are examples where the husbands have illegitimate relations with other women and to hide their fault, they put on allegations on women and blame, so the latter may not question them.

Other Related Problems

There are other problems also. They are off-shoots of her being a worming woman. The working woman is left with little time for relaxation or entertainment or social life. Apart from leading to her own over work, burden and tension, she becomes the buff of social criticism. For the major part of the day, the woman is working in the office or the work place. After coming back she is busy with house work and her family. She has no time left to maintain relations with her neighbours, friends and relations. She is not able to visit them freely and spend time with them or join them in common programmes. She is not even able to go to their help when they need especially at the time of illness, marriages, deaths or other occasions. This is often mistaken for arrogance due to earning and the friends and relatives criticise her.[13]

The working woman has not time of her own. She needs rest. She wants to thin of her problems or plan her future. She wants to read and write. She wants to undertake activities of her own interest, say creative arts. At times, she desires to be on her own not disturbed by anybody. There is no time for her. She cannot afford to be moody.[14]

Again, to ease her job she has to depend more on domestic help and servants. She has to be generous to them to get work done. For that also she is criticised as extravagent. On the other side the servants very well know the difficulties the mistress and they exploit the situation. This also create problems for working women.

In all these worries the woman has no time left to look after her health. Still, she has to take care of her health and keep herself physically fit to work. She has to take to nourishing food and proper treatment when needed. Again due to hard work and over burdened by responsibilities, she gets into rapid ageing effects. The unending worries and tensions of modern life and the family also hastens the ageing process. She is criticised by her in-laws and the neighbours as an extravagent and fashionable lady. When she goes out of the house, well dressed she receives their criticism in crude words saying, 'dressed like a prostitute to attract males.[15]

In the Sphere of Food

One more situation that is an off-shoot of the hectic life of the working woman is the use of fast food. It does help her a lot to reduce her burden at home. But it is undoubtedly expensive and less nutrious. The family members and the older generations do not appreciate its use. They naturally prefer home-made dishes. Sometimes fast-food is below standard. So it affects the general health of the member of the family and may at times be a cause of food poisoning or some other disease in the long run.[16]

One New Way of Development and Modernity

Another note-worthy change we observe is that by working outside the four walls of the house, women are thrown in the open world. Every day they have new experiences and face new situations. Their mental horizons are widened, new aspirations aroused. Their ways of thinking is also changed. They want to give a new shape of their lives. They try to find new solutions to their problems. While the other members of the family are still having the same traditional outlook. The generation gap between the elders and the working women is increasing day by day. She is not able to cope with them though she wants to live with them. She hankers for the life of her thinking. This is a constant cause of increasing mental conflicts. If both the husband and wife are of a liberal outlook there is a free democratic family structure with the grab of autocracy fading away. The children grown up in this free atmosphere are able to develop their personalities. But when the grown up children take their own decisions and arrange their lives in their own way, the parents feel hurt. They feel, the grown up children now ignore them and do not recognise them. They comment that the latter do not take their advice or act according to it. They face the same problem which their elders used to face. They are happy to see the well developed and independent personality of the children but cannot throw away autocratic mentality inherited from the traditional culture and want to keep the children under their wing. It is a paradox which can never work. This also creates new conflicts and new problems.[17]

PROBLEMS OF SINGLE WORKING WOMEN

Women as a group, specially single, have certainly become an important part of the work-force not only in India but all over the world. Women in general have to face so many problems, due to various factors. But being a single woman, she has to face some special problems.

Problems of Getting Employment

Most of the women work to help heir families in their economic disparities. However, the general impression of the society is to the contrary. When they search for a job, they have to compete with male candidates. The women in general suffer from some of the assumptions and prejudices which the authorities particularly the male, have towards them. The management feels that women are not serious or efficient workers. They put in less work and come only to pass time. As soon as they get married, they will go away. Again even if they continue after marriage, they will demand leave a number of times for domestic reasons. Maternity, childcare, transfer of the bands, work demands of the husband and family with make them give up jobs, play traunt or become indifferent and efficient. For many such reasons the women candidates are not preferred. Some managements even think that the women may spoil the strict atmosphere of the office.[18] In fact this type of discrimination with young girls is nothing but a crime against entire women community.

Once they are selected, they are subjected to other types of oppression. The stares and the banters of the male colleagues, their typical curiosity and their uncivilised and unwarranted remarks, "She is charming and that is why she is selected" etc. are some of these oppressive ways. if the young women mix freely with them they are misunderstood. if they keep themselves confined to the work alone, they are labelled as arrogant. If the boss appreciates their work and they enjoy the confidence of the authorities, they are scandalised. They crack jokes at them and pass cheap remarks which in fact are unfair to the young women and hurt them.

Single Women and Status in the Family

In a study carried out by Arora, Bhattacharya and others on the unmarried working girls employed as typists, clerks, receptionists or telephone operators in Bombay, it was found that "with the majority of respondents their role of an earner in the family had not earned them a new freedom from parental control except perhaps in the area of marriage, nor were their status very much changed in the family with an exception of few where they got much more importance because fo their economic contribution towards the maintenance of family."[19] In fact being an employed member of the family her responsibility increases and the family expects something from her without changing her traditional status.

Problem of Getting Married

The marriage of the daughter has become an acute problem for the parents of working girl. There are persons who do not like earning wives. They think that earning wives would try to dominate them. Some feel that they cannot be good house wives, with their well developed personalities. It becomes a difficult job to find a proper match for them. Their expectations go higher and they want a husband who would try to understand theirs. If they do not get a man of their choice they prefer to remain unmarried. But in our traditional Hindu society the parents would force them to compromise. Sometimes the result is discontent, quarrels, restlessness, frustration and disintegration of the family thus the women have to play a terrible price for keeping their jobs suppressing all their emotions and dreams they shoulder the responsibilities of life.[20]

Problems of Parental Responsibility

There are families where the parents and other members of the family are totally dependent on the income of the young girls. They are mightly afraid of the girls getting married. They avoid settling the latter's marriages on one excuse or other. The young girls, emotionally attached with the parents, feel guilty in moving out and neglecting their responsibility to parents. The marriageable age passes away.[21] This cause a great frustration to unmarried girls.

An eminent social scientist had the same opinion, when she observed in Bombay on the unmarried women office workers, that their parents were not interested in their daughters getting married; they postponed the latter's marriages because, if the daughters got married, the parents would not get their daughter's earnings, and thus they would be at a great disadvantage. Such working girls feel most insecure and uncertain of their future and have no one, who is interested in finding a suitable match for them. It was also pointed out by this sociologist that the number of abortions amongst the office girls was increasing which created both social and emotional problems for them.[22]

Problem for Residence

A single woman, married, unmarried or widowed if alone, faces a problem of residence in India. Except in some of the big cities, there is no provision of working women's hostels. If it is there, it may not be well managed. In these hostels the working women are protected like children and these conditions restrict their freedom and ultimately hamper their wishes. While it is difficult to have a rented house in a limited income, the house owner looks at the single woman with suspicion and is not willing to rent it. Thus the unmarried women have many problems to face in housing.

Conclusion

Thus the working women, married or unmarried, belonging to middle class or lower middle class, face variety types of problems at the home level. Almost all of these problems are not of her own creation at all. Much of it is based on the continuing notions of the society, its patriarchal values as internalised by men and women, and their expectations of the women's contribution to home work. Some of the dilemmas of women are born out of the values they have inherited and which they find hard to shake off. Her duty for the children, and parents, her anxieties for the family stability and happiness etc. are borne out of the values and expectations built into her from childhood. The stability of the system of the family system, religious and caste system, of the society and State depend to a large extent on her playing this dominant role in the family up keep and children's up bringing. Hence, the dilemmas are not just her own dilemmas; they are society's and man's dilemmas which they had transferred to the women.

The responsibility of solving them, hence, should belong to the man and society, though the working woman often tends to believe herself to be responsible. A changed family relations based on a changed and egalitarian power relations within the family and between man and woman, is thus a need. Alternative arrangements, whenever necessary and possible, for child care during the early years and later, support services like creche, housing, etc. are needed if the working women have to be relieved of their avoidable stresses. Above all the men in general and male colleagues in the offices need to be educated on the equality and rights of women, their capabilities and contribution to productivity, rather than be treated as sex models and partners.

NOTES AND REFERENCES

1. Promila Kapur, *The Changing Status of the Working Women in India*, p. 62.
2. Raka Sharan, *Indian Women Workers*, p. 20.
3. *The Statesman*, (New Delhi), March 22, 1989.
4. Cited in Krishna Chakraborty, *The Conflicting Worlds of Working Mothers*, p. 51.
5. Urmila Patel, "Problems of Working Women in India" in T.M. Dake (ed.), *Women and Work in Indian Society*, pp. 216-17.
6. Krishna Chakraborty, n. 4, p. 46.
7. *Ibid.*, pp. 46-47.
8. *Ibid.*, p. 48.
9. Urmila Patel, no. 5, p. 218.
10. Chakraborty, n. 4, pp. 220-1.
11. *Ibid.*, pp. 22-4.
12. Urmila Patel, n. 5, p. 221.
13. *Ibid*, p. 222.
14. *Ibid.*
15. *Ibid.*, p. 223.
16. *Ibid.*, p. 224.
17. *Ibid.*, p. 224.
18. *Ibid.*, 225.
19. K.K. Arora, Bhattacharya and others, *Women and Career*, A group Project Report submitted to the Tata Institute of Social Sciences (Bombay) for Post-graduate Diploma in Social Services Administration with specialisation in Family and Child Welfare, 1963.
20. Urmila Patel, n. 5, p. 226.
21. *Ibid.*, pp. 226-27.
22. Promila Kapur, n. 1, p. 67.

28

Problems of Urban Working Women—At Work Place

The condition of working women in India as well as in the entire world in general is considered to be very distressing. Working women in general are subject to discrimination at various levels. The problems and difficulties of working women are multi-dimensional, varying from woman to woman at personal level, and section to section at general level and hence need to be analysed in depth. One may believe that there are two clear-cut sections—privileged and unprivileged among the urban working women. Women working in factories, mines, plantations or in electronics, garments or chemical units or banks, schools and hospitals appear to be the privileged sections among women.

However, the problems of working women at work places are multiple and differ from woman to woman according to the nature of the work and position. Ms. Aruna Broota, a phychologist of Delhi University, is categorical in stating that no girl is respected in the office if she is known to be a single woman. In fact, in India women are considered less of and individual than as an object of vice by men whether she is single or married. this is particularly true for the women who are working among the males. Working women of the present generation, in the opinion of Ms. Broota, are at the cross-roads. They are aware that they are being exploited and ill treated. Yet they consciously or unconsciously adopt their mother's roles of subservience to the male. So, women, in general, have to be taught to develop their self-confidence, as well as self-respect and not accept the apologetic and subservient role instilled in them since childhood.

Relationship with Colleagues

The efficiency of a working woman is always suspected. Especially in the upper class cadres, even though other qualifications are equal, men are preferred. the authorities are doubtful whether she would be able to handle male subordinates, take independent decisions, cope with crisis and manage her duties. Even though she has proved her efficiency, they think twice before promoting her. Even if she is given a chance, there is always a remark that she has been taken because she is a woman.[1]

The male co-workers in the office cannot mentally accept the superiority of the woman's work. They take extra pains to ridicule her. The male colleagues get together and pass comments. As the woman is brought up in a protected atmosphere in the family, she is not mentally prepared to face this kind of situation. She feels helpless and often breaks down. This further leads to the misconception that women workers are not fit for outside work.

Women as Managers

It is equally difficult a situation where the woman is a boss. The male subordinates do not like to accept the authority of a woman boss. If she demands work, efficiency and discipline, she is criticised as harsh and dictatorial. She is supposed to dominate only to hide her inefficiency and inferiority complex. If she is polite, mild and courteous, she would be labelled as inefficient, talkative and what not. In any way, they do not carry out her orders and instructions, neglect their duties and take advantage of her goodness. They try to harass her in many ways. In short they are not able to accept a woman as their head.

There is another problem; while working with men, a woman tends to develop close relations with any one of them owing to prolonged and constant association. This, in the case of a married woman, creates social and psychological problems and tensions in her relationships, while in the case of an unmarried girl, it can create all sorts of socio-psychological problems if she gets involved with a married man. Sengupta in her study (1964) points towards the emergence of similar problems. In this connection Rosenquiet observes, "certain social conditions, most of them connected with recent changes in economic life, provide an environment quite favourable to divorce. The arrangement of office work, as now generally found, may be mentioned as an example. The professional men of male office worker and his female secretary, stenographer, or assistant are likely to develop personal attachments which endanger the marriage tie. More especially, this is likely to be true of one of the partners in this business relationship, usually the woman, is unmarried."[2]

Even if the woman who is working in the office with men makes only good friends with them and has no intimate relations with any one of them, she is still liable to be suspected and often accused of having intimate relations with them. This often humiliates and annoys her a lot and creates frictions in her married life.[3]

Office and Family

There is another type of problem which arise when she has to work over-time to complete her work. In certain government jobs the woman employee also face transfers, she finds it difficult to go, having the family behind. If she is married she can not go leaving her husband and children. In such a situation generally she has to give up the job. If she is unmarried the parents would not permit her to go alone. If she is married and working, she has to leave the job if her in laws do not approve of her working or if she is married in some other place then also she has to resign. Again if she wants to work at a new place, it becomes difficult for her to find a new job. In some cases women have to leave the job when the children are too young and there is nobody in the family to look after them. By the time children are grown up, women are out of touch with the field and are not able to find work again. Unfortunately, in our country the system of part-time jobs have not developed yet.

Part-time jobs would have been more convenient to young married working women with children. But it has not been acceptable as they are poorly paid for and part-time jobs consume comparatively more time and require equally hard work from her.

Not Much Choice

Another notable problem for the woman worker is that they do not get jobs in the fields of their interest. They have to accept the work they get. But this problem is not confined only to women. Many male workers also have the same problem.

The professional women have their own problems. As she is professionally trained, she aspires to utilise her skills, to put up the best performance and to earn a proper income. But the in-laws do not accept her working. In this way many women doctors, engineers and technicians leave their profession after marriage or do work for limited hours for pleasure only. Even when they work the fellow professionals, especially the males have a negative attitude. Sometimes the work women get do not befit their qualifications. For example, it is often believed that teaching, medical practice etc. are the ones more suitable for women, and thereby they are forced to accept what is available and do not achieve the levels they are trained for.

The composition of staff at the work-place also create problems. Some traditional families in India, for example, would like their women to be posted exclusively in a girls college or school. These families are afraid that in a place where the majority is men, their women will be looked upon as sex objects. The liberal-minded families do not entertain such a baseless apprehension and do not stand in the way of their women working in a male-dominated office, or a boy's school, or a co-educational institution. Sex segregation in the offices and establishments is an unhealthy pattern either for the present or for the future. It is a negation of equality with men.[4]

Problem of Transport

The present transport system is far from satisfactory; generally women have to suffer the worst due to misconduct or eve-teasing by co-passengers. Sometimes they have to wait for hours on the bus-stop to board a bus. Even when the bus comes, due to it being over-crowded she is not able to catch it. Even in train the position is not good. At present there is only one ladies' compartment in local trains in cities like Bombay and Delhi, and that too, is often occupied by men. At the peak hours one can hardly entrain or detrain without difficulty. In some metro-cities there is a "ladies' special" during busy hours. But it is unsatisfactory and limited. So the authorities should provide for more than one ladies' compartment in local trains and more 'ladies' special' to solve problems of various type for the women workers.

Wage Discrimination

The issue of discrimination in wages throughout the world is a matter of vital importance. Mencher and Saradamoni noted that it was often taken for granted that women should be paid less than men for similar jobs. Throughout the world, women are concentrated in low paid job sectors according to an I.L.O. report. Apart from lower wave rates poor urban women were rarely given any access to training schemes and their promotional avenues were severely limited. At every level of work, they are paid lower wages, defeating the constitutional position of equal pay for equal work for both men and women.

There has been quite a few micro-studies that show that women workers in unorganised sector invariably get paid much less than men. G.D. Gambhir in his study on "Labour in Small-scale Industries in Madhya Pradesh with special reference to women and child labour in cotton ginning, bidi making and rice milling and shelloc manufacture" found that wages of unskilled women workers ranged between 65% to 75% that of the unskilled men-workers. Men coolies earn double that of women coolies. In Kerala, in cashew processing and coir industries women are paid less than men.[5] Women construction workers are paid uniformly lower wages than their male counterparts in spite of the fact that she is doing equally, if not more hard work in comparison to men. In fact women in the unorganised sector as well as the organised sector are discriminated directly or indirectly. One can take a look at the wages in the organised sectors.

Only 11 per cent of the country's female work-force is employed in the organised sector. The organised sector comprises units registered under the Factories Act of 1948 and covers those using power and employing ten or more workers, as well as units not using power but employing 20 or more workers. In addition the organised sector is governed by legislation such as the Minimum Wages Act, Labour Welfare Regulations, and Contract Labour (Regulation and Abolition) Act. Strictly speaking violations of those Acts can be challenged in a Court of Law.

In the organised sectors of the economy, people are selected for job-positions and their rate of emoluments are fixed primarily in relation to the nature of the jobs concerned. There could therefore, be theoretically no sex-based differences in wages in the organised sectors. It is, however, possible that some establishments try to separate some jobs carrying less pay and it may so happen that only females get recruited to such jobs. This may not "technically amount to sex-based discrimination", though "such categorisation of jobs' may also sometimes be done purposely."[6]

Even in the public sector, where employment has gone up substantially, a large proportion of women are shunted into low-paid jobs. Official agencies admit that no assessment has been done as to what extent the equal pay principle has resulted in the displacement of women workers. After examining different industries the National Committee on Status of Women in 1976 came to be conclusion that the principle of equal pay has not been seriously applied in most of industries which continue to maintain wage differentials by direct or indirect methods. Evidence for this is available in occupational wage surveys conducted by the Ministry of Labour, indicating differences in the minimum, maximum and average earnings of women in most of industries. Though the survey reported that employees evade this principle by not employing men and women for the same jobs in the same establishments, such differentials were found even within the same establishments in some cases. A more successful method for evading this principle is by restricting women to certain jobs and prescribing lower wage rates for them.[7] A study of 400 working women by Usha Talwar also reveals that lower pay for equal work is one of the most important issues faced by those working women.[8]

Wage discrimination is a problem all over the world, especially in the third world countries, where the process of industrialisation is still going on. A double standard on pay still plagues women workers everywhere according to ILO report.[9] The average earning of women compared with men in non-agricultural activities in 1981 ranged from 44.8 per cent in South Korea to 86.2% in Australia. In the manufacture sector alone, these ranged from 43.4% in Japan to 90% in Sweden. According to I.L.O. Year Book the gap between women's and men's wages widened slightly between 1977 and 1981 in 7 countries—Czechoslovakia, Denmark, West Germany, Japan, Luxemburg, the Netherlands and Britain. the earnings of women compared to men went down from 55.8% to 53.5% in Japan and from 71.9% to 69.5% in Britain.

On the contrary, there was some improvement in women's remuneration in six countries—Belgium, Cyprus, France, Ireland, Newzealand and Switzerland. The increase was highest in Ireland going up from 80.1% to 83.7%. However women working in the manufacturing sector in Japan experienced further erosion of their earning compared to those of men, as they dropped from 46.1% in 1977 to 43.4% in 1981.

In India the average earnings of women are highly depressed. The average earning of regular wage/salaried female employees is about three times higher than of the females casual labourers. If the men and women are working on the same post in Government's jobs, there is not so much discrimination. But in other institutions there is a disparity prevailing. There is another aspect of wage discrimination in India that is female workers "are exploited as a piece-rate worker doing manual labour for trader, middlemen, contractors and big companies in the corporate sector." "There is a variation in the wages for identical work and skills." "Self-employed workers accept wage rate which potently do not cover their cost. It is difficult to understand why and how the difference exists and why workers accept them."[10]

Thus the wage-discrimination is a universal phenomenon and it needs a world-wide awakening and revolutionary movement to wipe out the basic discrimination at various levels of the economy and for this not only women but also men have to come under one-banner and fight against it.

Issue of Health

Women anywhere in the world have to suffer rrom some in built disadvantages, compared to men, because of certain biological reasons. They have to put up with menstruation, pregnancy, child birth, lactation, child rearing and menopause and their various complications. Physically, they are less strong. they are also ore vulnerable to sexual aggression and abuse. The different cultural, social and economic situations in India have given different focus to these biological disadvantages of women. These situations also influence the way these biological disadvantages affect the health of the working women.

One may hence analyse the status and conditions of these working women in various industries. A study done by Shahnaz Anklesaria gives us a clear cut picture. She has pointed out the defects of Factory Act which seeks to ensure protection to millions of women covered by it. It applies to any premises where 10 or more workers are employed and where a manufacturing process is carried on with or without the aid of power. The Act is enforced by the State Governments through their factory inspectorates. It was amended in 1976 to include the three sections which deal specifically with health hazards that the workers face.[11]

The Act outlines the principal health risks to factory workers, which arise from dangerous gases, acids and dust, harmful bacteria and micro-organisms, compressed and rarefied atmosphere, improper lighting, extremes of temperature, humidity and excessive strain. But it is silent on the impact of all these on women workers. The repercussions on women can be slightly different from those on men because of the additional physical and psychological factors and can be complicated by pregnancy, maternity and gynaecological issues. Further environmental factors like, heat, humidity, repetitive work, toxic substances also affect women. They can adversely condition pregnancy, child birth, lactation, child rearing and menopause and their various complications.

The law prohibits women's employment in dangerous and heavy operations in organised sector. At the same time in unorganised sector, as head-loader, handcraft puller, construction workers, women work more than men—for longer hours and sometimes for less wages.

What the Factories Act does say is that women must be prohibited from employment in dangerous and heavy operations. No women worker should be asked to clean or lubricate or adjust any machinery while it is in motion, if her work exposes her to the risk of injury from any moving part. No woman workers should be employed for pressing cotton in any part of a factory in which a cotton opener is at work. There are also specified limits on the amount of weight a woman worker can carry. This is limited to 65 lbs for an adolescent and 30 for a child. The State governments can, therefore, restrict or prohibit the employment of women in any operation which may expose them to serious risk of physical injury.

It is well spread belief that the physical structure and maternal functions of women place her at a disadvantage. But practices do not follow this. women have never shirked hard labour; whether it is farming, planting, transplanting, winowing, weeding, harvesting, grinding, pounding, nothing holds them back. It is has been seen that work which is physically very strenuous is done not by men but by by women like head-loaders, handcraft pullers, construction workers etc. Any "disadvantage" that women's maternal functions may cause is largely man-made. So these responsibilities have to be seen as vital functions to perform for which a woman must be adequately compensated. Male refusal to take on specific home and child-care responsibilities has also placed a dual responsibility of home as well as office on working women. These responsibilities cause mental as well as physical problem which ultimately leads to health hazards.

Further instead of outlining the kind of health hazards in modern industry for women, the law merely lays emphasis on the negative stereo-types of working women which restrict her access to certain kind of work.

The Act also says that there should be separate toilets and sanitary, dressing rooms for women workers. It specifies the need for keeping both clean. Besides the obvious health reasons. what is not so well known is that modern industrial processes subject employees not only to dangerous dust and vapours, but a variety of diseases—breeding organisms that can be transmitted by fellow workers to one another. Hence the need for eliminating unhygenic contacts between workers. In study after study we come across the women workers' complaint of the absence or shortage of separate toilets at their work place. The fact is that the Factories Acts which are enforced by the factory inspectors, are not implemented. Thus in different industries women workers are suffering from innumerable difficulties and nothing has been done to alleviate them.

Both men and women can be working on the same jobs, but women can for a variety of reasons be affected more than their male-colleagues. A survey of the agate workers in Gujarat, revealed that lungs disease had affected 70.6% of women and 60.4% of the men. Pneumonia and T.B. affected 19.6% and 21.6% respectively of the women, compared to 17.9% and 12.9% of the males.[12]

Lack of Other Facilities

A study conducted by M. Vanamala[13] on Public Sectors in Andhra Pradesh shows that except the maternity benefits, the other facilities are poor and inadequate. Only about 20% of the women employees are provided with transport facilities, 16 per cent housing facilities and 38 per cent child care facilities. This indicated that the public enterprises miserably neglected the women in providing employment opportunities and adequate status.

In the present situation maternity leave is being revised and improved. The provision for unpaid "special leave" of varying length in excess of the statutory maternity leave as is practised in France, may be followed.

In fact health problem of under privileged working women are worst due to exploitation, oppression, denial of social and economic justice. Hunger, poor sanitation and housing, unhealthy source of drinking water, infesting of insects and parasites, lack of protection from various elements of nature, poor educational status and limited access to media of mass communication, are some of the major consequences of these conditions which affect the working pattern of the society. Under-nutrition and malnutrition are common phenomenon among the working women in India, particularly in the underprivileged section.

Thus, besides the patriarchal discrimination, women in India suffer due to exploitation and oppression by the privileged sections. Such exploitation is also closely linked with extensive health problems that prevail among the women belonging to the underprivileged class. Because of this, they also have less access even to community financial health institutions. The struggle for health of women should therefore be a struggle for social, economic and political emancipation of the underprivileged as a class. With a platform of equal rights and status of women, women and men will have to fight together to attain emancipation of the underprivileged.

NOTES & REFERENCES

1. Urmila Patel, "Problems of Working Women in India" in T.M. Dak (ed.), *Women and Work in Indian Society*, p. 228.
2. Promila Kapur, *The Changing Status of the Working Women in India*, p. 69.
3. *Ibid.*, p. 69.
4. Indra Chauhan, *Purdah to Profession*, p. 203.
5. K.P. Khanna and M. Mathew, *Women Workers in the Unorganised Sector of the Coir Industry in India*, ICSSR, 1979 (Unpublished thesis).
6. Geetanjali Dash, *Status of Women Workers in Industrial Area in India*, (Unpublished M. Phi. thesis). Delhi University, p. 50.
7. *A Synopsis of the Report of the National Committee on Status of Women in India*, p. 73.
8. Usha Talwar, *Social Profile of Working Women*, p. 51.
9. "Double Standardss of pay hit the women workers," *The Hindustan Times*, 7, 1983.
10. *Shranshakti*, New Delhi, 1983.
11. Geetanjali Dash, n. 6, p. 60.
12. Shahnaz Ankesaria, "Slow Death is their lot", *The Statesman*, January 4, 1984.
13. M. Vanamala, "Employment Status of Women in Andhra Pradesh State Public Enterprises" in K. Morali Manohar (ed.), *Women's Status and Development in India*, p. 87.

29

Women Commuters Working in the City

As the centre of a large metropolitan district, Calcutta daily attracts a large number of commuters for work of business. These include women working in offices or other professions. Apart from these white-collar workers, there is a regular multitude of women hawkers coming to the city to sell vegetables or rice. The office and professional workers usually reside within the Calcutta Metropolitan District itself while the hawkers, especially the rice sellers, often travel as much as 70 kilometres a day. Female construction workers are largely seasonal migrants to the city. In addition to these groups, there is a noticeable development in recent times of women commuting to work for unskilled low paid jobs in the unorganised sector. These women usually come from outside the metropolitan district travelling a considerable distance every day. Since these women had no residential address in the city, they could not be represented in the sample. Therefore, a special study was done of 24 women working in the occupations delimited for the entire study in the unorganised sector.

Background and Personal Characteristics

Nearly all these women workers commuted from 24 Parganas. Only one came from the Hoogly district. Two came from outside the metropolitan area. However, 16 of them came from urban or semi-urban areas and only eight were from rural areas. Nearly all of them came from within a circle of radius of approximately 35 miles from the city centre, the furthest points being Diamond Harboar in the south-east to Bashirhat in the north-east. The average distance travelled by each was about 17 miles and in some cases it was as low as 4.5 miles. They all used public transport—suburban trains or buses or a combination of the two. The time taken for the trip each way was never less than 40 minutes and sometimes even as long as two hours. The older skilled workers held a monthly pass for rail travel but the domestic servants and younger workers confessed that they often tried to avoid buying tickets. If all journeys were to be aid for, 18 of the workers would spend an average of 70 paise daily on travelling alone. For the others this daily expense would vary between 40 to 50 paise.

Of these women four were domestic servants in the '912' category. They all worked in South Calcutta and travelled by train every day.

TABLE 29.1

Types of Occupation and Nature of Jobs.

Occupation	Nature of job	Number
Ampoule makers	skilled	3
Bangle makers	skilled	3
Plastic or rubber workers	unskilled	3
Tailors and embroiders	skilled	4
Leather workers	skilled	6
Services	unskilled	1
Total		20

With the exception of two women, none of the women who commuted to work had engaged in this work before 1972. One had joined earlier in 1966 and worked as an embroiderer. The other was a tailor and had begun work in 1969. Of the 24 women, 19 had joined after 1974 and the domestic workers had started work in as late as 1975. The ones who joined later, were engaged in the newer types of occupations such as ampoule making, plastic products or leather goods. Commuting to work for this type of work was a fairly recent development.

All the women who commuted were Bengali speaking Hindus. The two women who had been working since the sixties were both above 30 years of age, but the others were much younger. There were two girls aged 13 and 14 years respectively, who had been working for a year. The average age of the all the workers was 22.5 years. With the exception of a 30 year old leather worker and a 25 year old domestic servant, all the women were literate. Five had left school after completing the primary level and seven had completed secondary education or more. Two of the domestic servants could also read and write.

TABLE 29.2

Age and Civil Status

		Civil status		
Age in years	*Unmarried*	*Married*	*Divorced*	*Widowed*
15 and below	2	—	—	—
16-20	8	2	—	—
21-25	1	4	2	—
26	—	3	1	1
Total	11	9	3	1

The relatively late age at marriage and the higher level of education indicated that the commuter workers were from a distinctly higher social background than the workers residing in the city itself. For instance, five were from upper caste families and 15 from the middle castes. Only four belonged to the scheduled castes and two of them were domestic servants.

The occupational pattern of the heads of household was distinctly superior. Two of them were agricultural labourers, and two were vegetable vendors and three were skilled factory workers (but only one worked in a registered factory). The rest were either unemployed or were in ill-paid white-collar jobs. The monthly family income was somewhat higher. The average was Rs. 276 as compared to Rs. 256.03 for the residents of the city. None of these families had more than three earners though usually there were only two earning members and the average monthly income per earner was relatively higher—Rs. 131 as compared to Rs. 100.76.

Conditions of Work

As commonly observed in the informal sector, all the women worked for long hours every day, the only exception being a child who worked for about seven hours a day.

TABLE 29.3

Distribution of Workers by Daily Hours of Work.

Daily hours	Frequency
8	3
9-10	13
10-12	8

The bangle makers worked for nine hours on a working day but were able to get work for only four days a week. Five of the skilled worker and one unskilled worker worked on a piece rate basis but their workshops were not open on Sundays. Two were on daily wages so that they were not paid for any holidays or when they were absent from work. The rest earned a fixed monthly salary with Sundays as holidays, and they all reported that occasional absence from work did not usually lead to a wage cut. Repeated absenteeism however, could cost them their jobs or at least a cut in their salaries. The domestic servants got on weekly holiday though they were not punished for occasional absence from work, and one was even given paid leave for a week when she was sick.

Apart from the advantage of paid holidays there were no other advantages the commuters enjoyed as compared to the residents. Their working hours were very long and they had to spend over an hour on travelling to and fro. There were no arrangements for sick leave or maternity leave, no annual holidays and no security of work. Although no one had been dismissed so far yet none of them were sure how long the work would continue. For instance, the workers engaged in tailoring since 1966 reported that on one occasion she had been sick and had not only received no wages for any of those days but had also temporarily lost her job and had to wait for a whole month before she could get it back.

Wages and Incomes

Piece rates for commuter workers were the same as those for regular residents who had joined during the same period. Hourly wage rates worked out somewhat better for the commuters. In the case of piece rate workers, several of these women appeared to be more efficient. For others, time rates meant fewer losses due to lack of work or occasional inattention. All these workers expressed their preference for jobs with monthly wages.

Domestic workers did better as compared to the others but the difference between them and the others was not so marked as in the case of resident workers. The differences in wage rates could be explained in terms of the relative age of the workers. Younger workers always received lower rates. All the skilled and unskilled workers who were below 20 years of age received an average hourly wage of only .41 and .24 respectively. Surprisingly, one worker below 20 years of age received better wages as compared to the rest and had been educated up to the secondary level. In this group, the workers with longer experience received a higher rate and a higher monthly income either through promotion to better paid work or by way of recognition as a senior worker. Thus, there was this definite advantage of working in a workshop rather than at home. With higher wage rates and less uncertainty about the daily earnings, the monthly incomes of these workers were significantly higher than those of the resident workers.

TABLE 29.4

Hourly Wage Rates and Distribution of Workers by Wage Rate Ranges

Rupees per hour	*Distribution of workers by wage rate ranges*		
	Skilled workers	*Unskilled workers*	*Domestic workers*
.30	1	1	—
.31 to .40	8	1	—
.41 to .50	3	1	2
.51 to .75	4	1	2
.76	1	—	—
	.50	.45	.59

While calculating these money incomes the value of benefits in kind have not been included because with such a small sample no average value could be assigned to the benefits received by each individual. The domestic workers appeared to be better off than the resident workers, but after covering their transport costs, the difference between the two was no longer remarkable. In the case of others, even after allowing for transport costs, their incomes were significantly higher although none of these workers had invested their own capital in the business.

The domestic workers had been introduced to the various jobs through relatives residing and working in the city. The bangle makers had connections with the trade through relatives, though a number of other workers had managed to get jobs by responding to advertisements pasted in places like the Sealdah station and the rest through other male or female workers in their locality. Being better educated, this group consisted of several fairly well-informed women who knew the ways of the city.

TABLE 29.5

Distribution of Workers by own Monthly Income Ranges and Occupation

Income in rupees	*Unskilled workers*	*Skilled workers*	*Domestic workers*
50	1	—	—
51-75	—	6	—
76-100	2	4	1
101-150	1	3	3
151-200	—	—	—
201-250	—	3	—
	4(95.0)	16(116.0)	4(119.0)

(Figures in parentheses give the average monthly income in rupees for each group).

Their Status and Views

In spite of their greater access to information, none of these workers belonged to any trade union. They were aware about these organisations but had not been approached by any such organisation. They pleaded that their long daily routine did not leave them enough time to look around for one. At home, the unmarried women were allowed to keep a certain percentage of their earnings for their personal use but at least 50 per cent or more of their income was handed over to the head of the household. The married workers were worse off because they had greater responsibilities (several had unemployed husbands) and they usually kept for themselves only the bare minimum needed for daily expenses. The widows or the divorcees were the chief or the only earners in the family. All the workers with the exception of the married workers wanted to save some money on their own and even the domestic servants had information about post office accounts. These women were away for long hours during the day, hence, they were not loaded with housework. The married women only managed to do some cooking in the morning and usually had somebody else to do the rest of the work. They were often entrusted with shopping since Calcutta had better shopping facilities than their own localities.

All the married women with the exception of the domestic servants practised family planning. These facilities were apparently readily available in the areas where they lived. Two of the domestic servants had been advised by their employers in this matter but they thought that it was still too early to do anything about it.

These women had a practical approach towards working. With the exception of very young girls, the rest of the workers had accepted the fact that they would always have to work and were on the look out for better opportunities. They expressed their willingness to undergo any training if necessary. The older women educated their daughters till the secondary level and were extremely eager to know about the training their daughter should be given. The domestic servants were willing to learn other kind of work and one of them even expressed that a friend would introduce her to the work of an hospital *ayah,* but none of these domestic servangs had really thought of training their children who were still too young to go to school.

The unmarried women frequently visited the cinema and read film magazines. They were avid listeners of radio programmes. The rest found little time or money for their own entertainment but a few expressed their interest in novels and stories.

The workers commuting to work and especially to non-domestic jobs were from a slightly better social background than their counterparts among the residents. Their caste composition, educational level and family income all point in this direction. This made it possible for them to get information about such jobs even when they lived far away. This does not explain why they took up these kinds of jobs. Although they were better paid than the resident workers, their work was harder since they had to cope with the additional problem of transport. It may be possible that women from this background were being compelled to take up such jobs because of the likelihood of falling living standards and lack of better jobs.

Although these jobs in the informal sector were without the protection of labour legislations and trade unions, the greater awareness of these women helped them to avoid the worst jobs in the informal sector. For example, piece rate work was less common and there were few opportunities for promotion. Occasionally, the workers received recognition for longer experience in a job.

At home, they appeared to get a better deal though this may be primarily because they just had no time at home. It was still accepted that a married woman would cook the morning meal even if she had to leave home at seven o'clock in the morning. Their greater contact with the outside world both through literacy and mobility increased their awareness of their rights as citizens and workers. In the society where they lived, their status as earners appeared to be somewhat better than that of their counterparts in the city since they had easy access to public services. On the whole, the problems of work in the information sector remain unaltered, but the commuters managed to do better chiefly because of their greater awareness of the world around.

30

Working Women—Attitude Towards Marriage and the Family Living

"Quest for food was a tough job for the early man. Sometimes he bad to go far away from his shelter in search of animal he hunted for his food. If, during his absence, the woman was taken away by someone else, there fighting ensued and bloodshed resulted. To avoid this, there arose the need for giving a social recognition to the union of man with woman."[1]

NECESSITY OF MARRIAGE

Such cohabitation of man and woman gradually transformed into the institution of marriage. Sexual instinct is there always since the origin of human species and like animals man also blindly followed his impulse of mating which is no more than mere copulation. Thus, the sexual urge also necessitated marriage. But with the advent of civilisation, there laid certain norms and customs for the marriage, and it made compulsory for security and social status.

Dr. Radhakrishnan observes that marriage is a must to fulfil the four great objectives of life—*Dharma, Artha, Kama* and *Moksha.* Marriage is necessary for woman as she cannot go to heaven unless her body was consecrated by the sacrament of marriage.[2] Das observes, "Man cannot make any progress if there be no woman standing by his side, ready to cooperate with him in all activities. Man's powers lie dormant so long as they are not touched by the spark of woman's love and affection".[3]

Marriage is most important of all *samskaras* and it was there in every society and it is regarded as necessary and desirable to all.[4] Scriptures regard marriage as sacrament and it is a religious necessity. Without wife, man cannot perform any religious functions. This is the reason why wife has been termed as 'Dharmapatni', i.e., a wife married for the fulfilment of sacred law. In the case of female too, marriage is a must, as it is the only sacrament allowed to her under the Hindu law out of ten sacraments.[5] *Mahabharata* also stresses the significance of marriage in a different way. A daughter of Kuni Garga practised seven penances for the whole of her life. She was, however, told by Narada that, as she. was unmarried, she could not go to heaven for all her austerities. Therefore, she induced "Sringavat" of the Galava family to marry her in exchange for half the merit she had earned by her lifelong austerities. She stayed with him as a wife for a day and only then door of heaven was opened to her.[6]

We can get all the material comforts without marriage, but the sexual union is usually sanctioned only through marriage.[7] The creator Brahma have divided his own body into two halves says Manu, "because male by one half and female by the other half, so divided, man and woman become a perfect person only when united again in wedlock. The wife is husband's *'ardhangi'*.[8] In this connection, we considered Lord Shiva as "Ardhanaree swarudu".

Goode says, "For a Hindu woman marriage was not an option but an obligation and for her parents a sacred duty, which stemmed partly from the belief that it was the only way to protect her from the dangers of her own security".[9] From ancient times marriage was considered as a ritual and a sacramental union. Marriage is an indispensable event of Hindu life and the person who is unmarried is considered unholy?[10] P.A. Sorokin says, "For a large majority of men and women, marriage is the most vital, the most intimate and the most complete unification of body, mind and spirit into one socially approved individual". In a good marriage, the individual egos of the partners merge. The joys and sorrows of one become the joys and sorrows of the other. All their values, aspirations and life experiences become fully shared. This mutual loyalty is unconditionally pledged until death do part them. The bond of marriage is truly sacred and indissoluble".[11]

Every society throughout the world in the past regarded marriage as important for the welfare of the society and for social order.[12] in the Vedic literature we find ample evidence that women too underwent the stage of *Brahmacharya* along with men.[13] Some persons refrained from marriage because of poor health and because they carried genetic defects which they did not . want to pass on to their children.[14] Marriage was made obligatory for girls in contemporary Persia. Matrimony, however, was not regarded there necessary for spiritual salvation of men.[15]

But, with the emancipation of women, the attitudes towards marriage have changed considerably and in addition, with the women's out of home employment underwent a marked, change in their attitudes. Once, marriage was considered as a traditional necessity. But now it has changed to the other aspects of life— economic, sexual and emotional satisfaction of the partners. The modern woman does not view marriage as a sole necessity but one among many aspect's of home, material comforts, good health and youthfulness." In the American society a new phenomenon of living together without marriage (*i.e.* cohabiting with each other following the norms of the marriage without its celebration) is in practice. During 1980, there were about 15,60,000 couples of this type in America.

Table 30.1 shows that 84.6 per cent of the respondents opine that marriage is necessary. Only 15.4 per cent opine that marriage is not indispensable in life. Medical women are less favourably inclined towards marriage than the other two categories of working women in the present study. Because of their professional degrees, they sometimes prefer to serve the society rather than to be married and settled in family life. The data were statistically cross-tabulated (Table 30.1, Chi-square = 11.8193; d.f. = 2; P.<0.05) and it was found significant that higher the position of the respondent, the lower her stress on marriage and lower the position of the respondents, the higher her stress on necessity of marriage. One of the respondents, a chief in the general hospital, asserted "Marriage is not absolutely necessary". From her school days she was crazy to become a doctor and to serve the needy. Hence, she has remained a spinster. She, says that she is happy than married doctors as she has no family troubles and is fully committed to her profession. With the economic independence the working women are adopting single life. Balse's[17] study of students and parents revealed that 26.50 per cent of students and 4.80 per cent of the parents did not view marriage as must. It infers that the educated community is less favourable towards the importance of marriage than the uneducated and older generations. As a reaction to their long subjugation and ill-treatment by men the women became hostile towards marriage. Hate's study reveals that nearly 50 per cent of unmarried educated girls declared their wish to remain unmarried.[18]

TABLE 30.1

Necessity of Marriage

Subjects	*Yes*	*No*	*Total*	*No reply*	*Grand total*
Office Staff	71 (93.4)	5 (6.6)	76 (100)	24	100
Teaching staff	87 (87)	13 (13)	100 (100)	0	100
Medical staff	68 (74.7)	23 (25.3)	91 (100)	9	100
Total	226 (84.6)	41 (15.4)	267 (100)	33	300

Chi-square = 11.8193; d.f. = 2; P. < 0.05

Figures in the parentheses give the percentages.

Traditionally, marriage was made necessary for the attainment of goal of life. But, with the development of education and modernisation of society, the educated women's, particularly working women's, perception of marriage has considerably changed.

Table 30.2 clearly shows that higher the position of the respondent, higher her option towards biological and social necessity of marriage and the lower the position of the respondent, higher her option towards traditional necessity of marriage. The data also were cross-tabulated statistically and it was found significant (Table 30.2, Chi-square = 45.4348, d.f. = 6; P. <0.05).

AGE FOR MARRIAGE

The customs of marriage of a girl differs from age to age, from period to period, from region to region, and also from culture to culture and it depends on the respective lawgivers of the respective periods. In ancient India, as soon as a female child was born, her parents used to name her future husband—a maternal uncle or someone else. Such is the anxiety of the parents in disposing off the 'Kanya'.

TABLE 30.2

Reasons to Get Married

	Reasons	*Office staff*	*Teaching staff*	*Medical staff*	*Total*	
(a)	Companionship and to share the happiness and sorrow	24 (27.3)	34 (38.6)	30 (34)	88 (100)	(32)
(b)	Biological and social necessity and status	24 (31.2)	12 (15.6)	41 (53.2)	77 (100)	(28)
(c)	To have family of her own, to get security and respect in the society	5 (22.7)	8 (36.4)	9 (40.9)	22 (100)	(8)
(d)	Traditional necessity and to have children	47 (53.4)	33 (37.5)	8 (9)	88 (100)	(32)
	Total	100	87	88	275	(100)
	No reply		13	12	25	
	Grand total	100	100	100	300	

Chi-square = *45.4348;* d.f = 6; P. <0.05.

Figures in the parentheses give the percentages.

Yagnavakya opines that parents of girl who do not arrange for her marriage before puberty "will be visited by the sin of the destruction of the foetus at every time of her menses". According to Marichi "A father who gives in marriage a girl of eight, goes to heaven, the giver of a girl of nine, to Vaikuntha, one who gives his daughter in marriage before she attains the age of ten, attains the heaven of *Brahma.* But, the father of a girl married after puberty goes to hell." Parasara observes "A father who fails to give away his daughter in marriage when she has reached the 12th year, her ancestors drink her menstrual flow every month. The father, the mother and the eldest brother of a maiden seeing her in her menstrual course, go to hell."[19]

"An added incentive to infant marriage is the ancient Hindu belief that the human husband of a girl was actually her fourth, when the pubic hairs began to appear, the God of Sowa was thought to enjoy the maiden first, when breasts grew, a gandharva and thirdly at menstruation the God of Agni. Hence, later law makers insisted that girls ought to be married before the celestials developed interest in them".[20]

The census report[21] of 1931 gave the figures who married under the age of *15,* as follows:

Age group	*Percentage of the married*
0 to 1	0.8
1 to 2	1.2
2 to 3	2.0
3 to 4	4.2
4 to 5	6.6
5 to 10	19.3
10 to 15	38.1

Virginity as the qualification for marriage was stressed in the earlier scriptures written before the foreign invasion. So, the real reasons for child marriage seem to be a rigid chastity imposed upon women.[22] According to Manu, a damsel must wait for three years though she be marriageable but after that time, she should be allowed to choose herself a bridegroom of equal caste and rank. Vasistha observes that the maiden should not permit her menstrual flow to go on for more than 36 months.[23] This implies that both Manu and Vasistha granted post-puberty marriages. *Dharmasastras* and *smritis* advocated marriage immediately after puberty. Any negligence on the part of father was considered in this regard as a sin. Daughter should not wait any more after three months of the first menstruation. *Smritikaras* like Gauthama and Baudhayana also supported the marriage immediately after the puberty.[24]

According to *Grihya Sutra*, the marriageable maiden is referred to as a *nagnika*, who is fit to be undressed in privacy by her husband for cohabitation and, therefore, as one who has attained perfect maturity.[25] Prabhu supports early marriage. Paul Popeno suggests "People should marry after they are physically mature, after they are emotionally mature and before they are intellectually mature". It is deemed to be early twenties.[26] During the Vedic period marriages used to take place at the age of 16 or 17 years.[27] According to Buddhist law, as soon as girls attain the age of 20, they had the privilege of getting independent choice of husband.[28]

Now the modern educated women are not in favour of early marriage. Attainment of education itself takes long time for them and dowry supplements the age at marriage. Hence, the educated working women of the present study were asked to tell their preferred age for marriage to allow the researcher to know tile level or change among them.

Looking at Table 30.3, we find that half of the sample is in favour of higher minimum age of marriage *i.e.* 17 years. 41.5 per cent of the sample are of the opinion that the proper age for maidens to marry is between 21.24 years. Again almost equal, *i.e.* 29:8 per cent and 27.1 per cent are at the age between 17-20 and 25-30 years respectively. It is a very modern trend to choose the age for marriage between 25-30 years. University and, professional courses lead them to the age of 24 to 25 years. Hence, they prefer higher age for marriage. It is found that the higher the age for marriage, the higher the success, and the lower the age for marriage .the lower the success in the marriage.[29]

TABLE 30.3

Preferred Age for Marriage

Subject	*17-20*	*21-24*	*25-30*	*Above 31*	*No limit*	*Total*	*No reply*	*Grand total*
Office staff	28 (32.6)	23 (26.7)	32 (37)	0	3 (3.5)	86 (100)	14	100
Teaching staff	24 (27.6)	39 (44.8)	23 (26.04)	1 (1.4)	0	87 (100)	13	100
Medical staff	27 (29.3)	48 (52.1)	17 (18.5)	0	0	92 (100)	8	100
Total	79 (29.8)	110 (41.5)	72 (27.1)	1 (0.4)	3 (1.3)	265 (100)	35	300

Chi-square—21.6927, d.f. = 4; P. <0.05.

Mean preferred age at marriage = 22.68.

Figures in the parentheses give the percentages.

Table 30.3 suggests that the women occupying higher positions prefer higher age for marriage. 68.6 per cent (41.5+ 27.1) of the respondents opined that the proper age for a woman to get married lies between 21 to 30 years. The mean preferred age for marriage is 22.68 years. It was reported in the local newspapers that one thousand child marriages were held in Meeward district of Rajasthan on April 26, 1982. In each village 50 marriages have been performed, which were supervised by the village heads only. "Aahutoy" is a famous festival day for child marriages. It was stated that due to more marriages, all the marriage parties could not get musical parties. So, they have completed the marriages with the common musical parties.

They were asked to state their actual age for marriage for comparing with the preferred age for marriage.

As per Table 30.3, 41.5 per cent of the working women preferred age of marriage to be between 21-24 years. 50.7 per cent of the working women (*vide* Table 30.4) were actually married at the ages between 21-24 years. It infers that they have married at the age which they preferred to be good. And 27.1 per cent preferred the ages between 25.30 years as good for marriage and the same per cent (27.1) have actually married at the preferred age. Hence, both the preferred age and the actual age for marriage are the same. It is also clear from the table that highly professional women got married at higher age. Our hypothesis is significant for Table 30.3 (Chi-square = 16.9935, d.f. = 6; P. <0.01). The mean actual age for marriage is 23.75 years. The preferred mean age at marriage (22.68 years) and the mean actual age (23.75 years) is somewhat very near to one another; difference of only one year is there between the preferred age and the actual age for marriage. Both the preferred and the actual age for marriage are far above than the Indian standard mean age of 17.2 years during 1971. This is very progressive trend in the educated working women community.

TABLE 30.4

Actual Age for Marriage

Subjects	*Below 20*	*21-24*	*25-30*	*Above 31*	*Total*	*Not applicable*	*No reply*	*Grand total*
Office staff	17 (24.6).	35 (50.7)	13 (18.8)	4 (5.8)	69 (100)	20	11	100
Teaching staff	16 (24.6)	23 (35.4)	24 (36.9)	2 (3)	65 (100)	20	15	100
Medical staff	9 (9.9)	56 (61.5)	24 (26.4)	2 (2.2)	91 (100)	9	0	100
Total	42 (18.7),	114 (50.7)	61 (27.1)	8 (3.5)	225 (100)	49	26	300

Chi-square = 16.9935; d.f. = 6; P. <0.01.

Mean age for marriage = 23.75.

Figures in the parentheses give the percentages.

They were also asked to answer the question whether the age difference must be there between the couple? 47.7 per cent agreed that the age should not be equal between the mates. 35.7 per cent feel they do not mind even if the partners are of equal age. And again of those preferring age difference between mates, 51 per cent opined that at least 5-10 years of difference must be there between the partners while 39.2 per cent opined that the age difference between the partners must be between 8 to 15 years.

It is a known fact that the age difference between the couples leads to marital harmony. 99 per cent of traditional as well as the modern parents prefer to get their daughters to marry persons of older age than their daughters. Kapur pointed out that Terman (1938) and Mowrer (1928) in their studies on marital harmony found, that "the age difference between the couples is not highly important factor affecting happiness. There is no evidence that the husband must be older than the wife for an effective adjustment".[30]

Smith states that age difference, however, makes little difference in the reported happiness of the couples. Terman (1938) found that those few cases in which the wives were considerably older than their husbands were the happiest of all groups.[31] Landis and Landis state that difference in age is not associated with happiness and unhappiness in marriage. However, Bernard's studies indicate that women were most satisfied with their husbands when their husbands were from one to five years older than themselves. The men tended to be most satisfied with their wives when they were zero to ten years older than their wives.[32] Kirpatrick also emphasises the same and says that age difference influences the marital adjustment.

To achieve marital harmony the age difference of at least 5 to 10 years between the couple is a must, in the Indian society, if not for western societies.

Some of the unmarried working women with thirty or more than thirty years age, do not find suitable mates of their choice in their castes or communities. They now prefer to be second wives or co-wives. If they get mates younger than them, they are getting married without hesitation.

MATE SELECTION

Once brides simply used to nod their heads to affirm their faith in their parents when they were informed of the selection of their future husbands. It was a custom to show respect towards the elders. Her choice was not at all given weight nor her say was taken into consideration. We can observe this procedure even today ;in the rural parts of India, avid some cases in urban areas where parents select the grooms without consulting the girls. She has to obey the decision of the elders ignoring her own desires and inclinations. Most of the marriages, in India, take place with the help of a friend, a relative or a negotiator.[33] Majority of the women think that arranged marriages have been, good for them, and they support this system as the best one for the marriage stability. The reasons given for continuing the practice of arranged marriage were that it is impossible for a girl to judge the life partner.[34] At least, the educated community has changed their attitude and outlook and they are now arranging a meeting between the prospective mates in the presence of the elders, just to exchange views. At times, brides are also asked to sing a song. Of course, this meeting alone may not prove enough for understanding each other fully. But in most cases, the brides have to forgo their own desires and inclinations for the sake of the selected husband. Klemer states the views of his respondents about their future husbands in mind "Today, the typical young husband is constantly compared to the best athletic manliness and the finest gentleman's manners. And the men will have all the resoluteness, decisiveness, intelligence, perception, good looks and wealth of the television hero. In addition, their men will naturally have all the desirable attributes of the girls' fathers".[35]

The women oriented towards modernity, are now opting for their mates themselves and due to their employment and economic independence the working women are very particular while selecting their life partners.

In the western countries, particularly in the United States, love oriented marriages are more, almost all marriages take place out of love. The parents of the boys and girls encourage them to date with the opposite sex. A young woman could be expected to call attention to herself, perhaps even to pretend that she is really in love and thus to attract a boy and get married.[36] On the other hand, a Hindu girl is brought up under the assumption that the goal of her life is to marry and settle in family life. It is actually equivalent to man's profession because it gives her security, subsistence and livelihoods In practice, most Indian marriages come to mean this Man can have free sex at home and also someone to look after his household, cooking, and bearing and rearing of Children, which for the women constitutes a whole-time profession. Soda-economically, she works on his will and lends him her body whenever he. needs, excepting the prohibited periods. In some cases, she herself may find pleasure in coitus with her husband, but mostly she is there for his satisfaction and pleasure. Having been brought up under these circumstances, girls in Hindu society generally prefer for arranged marriages.

But there were instances of brides selecting their mates in the ancient periods. The custom of *swayamwara* is a typical example where the bride would select her own choice merely by garlanding him. She either could choose a person who could prove his valour and wisdom or one belonged to a respectable family and had a good reputation of character, for example among the Kings, rulers and also some among the tribal communities.

Loving and being loved is not the only important condition for mate selection, but having money and high social status and success in her man's profession are more important factors for her. Though the educated working women admit that love is very necessary for a good marriage and for personal satisfaction, today love plays only a minor part in her choice of a life partner. She takes greater stock of the character, education, earning capacity and potentiality of her future husband. She thinks of security and of a comfortable future and chooses a mate with a cool and calm head and wide open eyes, rather than with a confused head, and vision blurred with sentimental and romantic love. Today, she would like to have a husband who could fulfil her material as well as emotional needs, though now the emphasis on the fulfilment of material needs has become much more pronounced than before.[37]

In Chesser's study, the English women expected their future husbands being affectionate, warm and understanding, to be much more important than, say, his being good looking and his having physical strength. Kapur, referring about working women, says, "They are likely to be more ready to fall in love with a partner who meets the objective, requirements—social status, office status, money, education, health and good character".[38] Thus, the working women are stressing their option on the capability of the would be-consort in providing material as well as social comforts.

Table 30.5 shows that 49.5 per cent of all the respondents wanted a partner to be understanding and adjustable person. 40.3 per cent of office staff expected their life mate to. be well educated and remuneratively employed as against 47.7 per cent of medical women who wanted their life mates to be equal to their status. Hence, we can infer that lower the position of the respondent, higher her preference for partner to be remuneratively employed and higher the position of the respondent, higher her preference for partner to be equal to her status. Data also were cross-tabulated and was found significant (Table 30.5, Chi-square = 59.9944; d.f. = 6; P. <0.05).

For Indian society, love is not suitable and many of love marriages end in failure. Due to lack of empathy between the couples, elder's blessings, social ostracism, economic problems, etc., these couples cannot pull on the life. Kadetotad says that love marriages are not really love marriages but they take place due to the best physical needs of the partners and also for coming close in an illicit manner.[39]

TABLE 30.5

Type of Partner Preferred

Subjects	*Under standing and adjust able*	*Well educated and remunera tively employed*	*Who has capacity to handle family matters*	*Equal to .my status*	*Total*	*No reply*	*Grand total*
Office staff	35 (52.2)	27 (40.3)	2 (2.9)	3 (4.5)	67 (100)	33	100
Teaching staff	25 (55.6)	13 (28.9)	6 (13.3)	1 (2.2)	45 (100)	55	100
Medical staff	43 (44.8)	12 (12.5)	1 (1.0)	40 (41.7)	96 (100)	4	100
Total	103 (49.5)	52 (25)	9 (4.3)	44 (21.2)	208 (100)	92	300

Chi-square = 59.9944; d.f. = 6; P. < 0.05.

Note: Figures in the parentheses give the percentages.

It is well known that love marriages as well as selection of mate by bride were practised in the Vedic period. The young nubile women were allowed to go freely and attend the functions and feasts while they would select their mates. Vatsyayana considers love marriage as the best form of marriage.[40] *Atharva Veda* tells that fathers not only gave the daughters a free and in the selection of their partners but also encouraged them to have a love marriage.[41]

TABLE 30.6

Preferred Type of Marriage

Subject	*Arranged marriage*	*Love marriage*	*Mutually consented marriage*	*Total*	*No reply*	*Grand total*
Office staff	63 (73.2)	4 (4.7)	19 (22)	86 (100)	14	100
Teaching staff	46 (56)	9 (10.9)	27 (32.9)	82 (100)	18	100
Medical staff	31 (38.3)	13 (16)	37 (45.7)	81 (100)	19	100
Total	140 (56.2)	26 (10.4)	83 (33.3)	249 (100)	51	300

Chi-square = 21.2690; d.f. = 4; P. <0.05.

Note: Figures in the parentheses give the percentages.

The working women of the present study have very favourable (54.8%) opinion towards love marriage but they discard them as unfeasible.

Table 30.6 clearly shows that higher the position of the respondent, the lower her preference towards arranged marriage and higher preference towards mutually consented marriage and lower the position of the respondent, the higher her preference towards arranged marriage and lower the preference towards mutually consented marriages. The data also were cross—tabulated statistically and it was found significant (Table 30.6, Chi-square = 21.2690; d.f. = 4; P. <0.05) to our hypothesis. And all the respondents were not in favour of love marriage even though 54.8 per cent (Table 30.8) of them were found favourable towards love marriage. How can we afford to make love? We have to earn for our living instead of love making.

INTERCASTE MARRIAGE

Traditionally, among the Hindus, marriage is possible within the framework of the caste system.[42] *Bhagvad Gita* sermonises us to be faithful to perform caste duties which take precedence over all other obligations and states further that perfection is only attained by a man who follows with devotion the duties of caste.[43] The preaching of the *Shastras* left their imprints on the minds of people and people used to follow the caste norms. We heard several times that some people were ex-communicated from their own castes for violating the caste while marrying. Manu too did not favour intercaste marriage. He suggested that twice born communities shall take a wife of the same caste as himself for a first marriage which is the only lawful marriage in his eyes, and he permits second marriage only when one is impelled by sexual urge and is unable to control himself."

During Vedic period intercaste marriages were allowed. Both *Anuloma* and *Pratiloma* marriages were prevalent during this period.[45] Karksivat and Vimala both belonged to Brahmin families, but they were married to Kshatriya girls. On the other hand, Saravati. i.e., daughter of a sage Angirasa, was married to King Avangi. The King Snanaya-Bhanayavya, i.e., brother-in-law of Karksivat, was married to a Brahmin. Even marriage of Yayati and Devayani was of the same type, i.e., Kshatriya male marrying a Brahmin.[46] *Anuloma* marriage, i.e., marriages of males of higher castes with females of lower caste, were not uncommon in societies down to the 8th century A.D. Even orthodox *Smritis* regarded them legal, though not commendable down to the 14th century A.D.[47]

There is great antagonism among the public towards intercaste marriages. In some castes, both the couples were expelled from the caste as well as their families. In some castes the couples were not allowed to take part in public gatherings and religious functions and when they violated that practice, they were punished. Yet, in some nomadic tribes, those who overtake the caste obligations at the time of marriage, are sometimes killed. There exists a practice of discussing these caste feuds in the village panchayats and the respondents are punished with the expulsion from caste and the village. These people are not allowed to show their faces daily as it contaminate the others.

Intercaste marriages were found to be undesirable when the cultural differences between the Brahmins and other castes had become so wide. Marriages between Brahmins and non-Brahmins first went out of vogue, when Brahmins made their own group endogamous. Other castes followed suit and intercaste marriages even of the *Anuloma* type, though permitted by *Smritis,* disappeared from society[48] in course of time. During Vedic period Brahmins were more or less non-vegetarians. Only during the times of Manu, they were changed to vegetarianism.

Special Marriage Act of 1872 legalised intercaste marriage, the Arya Samaja marriage validity act of 1933 which legalised inter-caste marriage among the Arya samajists in India, Hindu marriage disabilities removal act of 1946 which validated clan marriages, and validity act of 1949 which enacted marriages between Hindus, shall be deemed to be valid.[49]

Even the reluctance from the public, particularly from the older generation, is due to the strict adoption of the caste norms, illiteracy, caste heirarchy and rigid adherence to the cultural taboos, etc. Even the educated elite is unfavourable towards these marriages. We can observe easily the antagonism of the mass against these marriages. The author could observe this during his data collection when he approached the working women; people suggestively says, "go to her, she is so and so, she is love married, she was married out of her caste". These only suggested the aversion of the society to intercaste marriage.

But, with the advent of Independence, and the progress of education, the trend has changed to a large extent. But it is not up to mark. Even though the couple tend to marry outside their caste, their parents are. not in favour of them. We can find number of intercaste marriages in the educated community, particularly among educated working classes. But these marriages are happening in the society quite accidentally. Romantic involvement is one such powerful factor, When love reaches the climax, it is almost forced and compelled by the circumstances to get marriage rather to forget the affair between them. It is really a sanctity. We can observe easily that many marriages of this kind are in trouble due to the non-acceptance by the elders from both the sides. But it is not the case with all of them. A few cases involving young men and women are there who want to marry out of caste and some elders are also found who happily accept their daughter's/son's inclination towards marriage outside the caste. Our thanks are due for them always. But this trend is very restricted within the educated community only and it is not spreading towards the countryside. There is great correlation between the education and the intercaste marriage. We can find only a handful of the notable intercaste marriages among the public figures—Mrs. Indira Gandhi, Prime-Minister, Sri Sadiq Ali, Governor of Maharashtra and our Vice-President of India, Sri Hidayathullah, etc., have married outside their castes as well as religion.

Here, we can observe through Table 30.7 that lower the position of the respondent, lower is her willingness towards intercaste marriage and higher the position of the respondent, higher is her willingness towards marriage outside the caste. Our hypothesis is significant with the data (Table 30.7, Chi-square = 22.2840; d.f. = 2; $P.<0.05$).

TABLE 30.7

Views on Intercaste Marriage

Subjects	*Yes*	*No*	*Total*	*No reply*	*Grand total*
Office staff	35 (45.5)	42 (54.5)	77 (100)	23	100
Teaching staff	51 (60)	34 (40)	85 (100)	15	100
Medical staff	76 (80)	19 (20)	95 (100)	5	100
Total	162 (63)	95 (36.9)	257 (100)	43	300

Chi-square = 22.2840; d.f. = 2; P. <0.05.

Note: Figures in the parentheses give the percentages.

The study conducted by Promilla Kapur revealed that the educated working women are in favour of intercaste marriages or they do not mind for these intercaste marriages. The author of the present research topic could observe that backward caste women with higher education do not get suitable mates in their castes due to lack of improvement of education in their menfolk. Such people try ,to fall in love with some other caste people and get married. Generally, intercaste marriages are occasioned by virtue of romantic involvement.

The number of women who favoured intercaste·marriage pointed out that the couple must be financially self-sufficient as no support is likely to be given to them by their respective families.

LOVE MARRIAGE

"Love is very difficult to define, because, like electricity, love can be described by its results but it is hard to pin down exactly what it is".[50] Different scholars have different opinions towards love. It may be between mother and child, wife and husband, brother and sister, brother and brother and love may be between man and the animal and *vice versa.* The love between these differ from each other. Hence, attempting to define love is very difficult and complex.

Sociologist Joseph Folsom described the symptoms of 'Cardiac respiratory' love, in which being in love involved, "a deep sigh and feeling about the heart as if it had stopped, followed by palpitation or rapid beating and a feeling akin to fear".[51] Robert Bell defines conjugal love as a "strong emotion directed at the opposite sex and involving feeling of sexual attraction, tenderness and some commitment to the other's ego needs".[52] Kaphart states "it is sometimes said that the sexual embrace is the acme of love, but though it may be a more intense emotion and a more sexual experience than romantic love, sexual love is not romantic love"." No scholar could come to definite conclusion with regard to love. Freud gives the impression that love is a by-product of repressed sexual desire, but there are loves beyond sexual love. Smart and Szward[54] quoted Capallanes' definition "love is a certain inborn suffering derived from the right of and excessive meditation upon the beauty of the opposite sex which causes each one to wish above all things the embraces of the other and by common desire to carry out all of love's precepts in the other's embrace".

But the romantic love is different from the other one. Romantic love generally remains mixed with lust in nature. Without sexual instinct between male and female, love cannot exist deep into life. When an individual makes love at first sight, he/she will be feeling like seeing the beloved before him/her. They cannot live without seeing each other. It is very difficult for them to pull on their time without seeing the loved one. Capallanes pointed out that the very Latin word 'amor' of which 'love' is the English equivalent, comes from the word 'amos' meaning 'look' or 'capture'. Thus, the attachment aspect of love is contained in its name. The person who is held captive by love tries to attract a person by his allurements and exerts all his efforts to unite two different souls with an intangible bond.[55] Ira Reiss says that a progression to love begins with rapport (feeling at ease with the other person and being released and eager to talk about one's own self and learn about the other person). Rapport leads to intimate self-revelation, which in turn, leads to mutual dependency and finally to fulfilment of personal needs.

Love is very common in the West. Without love and romance, marriages do not take place in these countries. American society is very famous for love-oriented marriages and it sets example for others. Here, parents and elders encourage nubile daughters and sons to have courtship and dating with the opposite sex. Health and beauty will make a person more lovable to the opposite sex.[56] Love marriages are widely prevalent in Russian society also.[57] Love is institutionalised in the modern society and it is considered the necessary basis for marriage. To ensure that people fall in love with the right people, parents and others start to emphasise the importance of social homogamy and to arrange daily life in a way that will maximise contact with families of economic status and ethnic background through formal or informal desires, a pool of eligible mates is formed and from this, a proper match can be made. The dating pool is somewhat larger than the mate selection pool.[58]

Kadetotad[59] says, "love marriages are not really love marriages but they take place due to the best physical needs of the partners and also to come together in an illicit manner". Again, he says that love is temporary and the partners do not think of the factors which make a good marriage. The love marriages based on illogical and petty emotions of two young people may not endure longer.

In Indian society, our classical literature has ideolised sensuous and romantic love.[60] In the epic period, bride was allowed to choose her husband from amongst the men who were selected by her parents as worthy of their daughter. *Swavamvara* became popular. Arranged marriages were also had the consent of the daughter.[61] *Gandharva* marriages were in vogue in this period. *Vedas, Sutras and Smritis* have recognised romantic love marriages and *gandharva* marriage though not very popular was approved one of the forms of marriages.[62] *Abhignana Shakuntalam* endorsed *gandharva* union. The marriage of King Dushyantha and Sakuntala is of this type. Manu did not approve it. He regarded *gandharva vivaha* as being based on lust and. therefore, unworthy."

Authorities are not in agreement with the issue whether love marriages should be included within the category of approved marriages. The *Baudhayana Dharma Sutra* refers the approval of some of the thinkers of the love matches." Lord Krishna, God incarnate also eloped with Rukmini to protect her from forced marriage as she was in love with him. This also shows that love marriages were prevalent during epic period. In the Vedic period, instances are available where young men and women had opportunities to move freely which resulted in love marriage.

Vatsyayana considers this form of marriage as the best one which was discarded by other visionaries on moral and religious grounds.[65] The *Mahabharatha* includes *gandharva* marriage within the approved marriages. Manu seems to be indecisive in this regard. The same is the case with Narada. Vedic literature does not refer to parents controlling the marriages of their sons and daughters, though they might have played an important part in arranging and financing them. On the other hand, we have references of beautiful brides selecting their own husbands.[66]

Even in contemporary India, love affairs and simultaneous marriages are more. But, these marriages are held more due to the physical beauty of the sexes than empathetic love between them. These love affairs commonly happen and flourish at the educational institutions, particularly co-educational institutes and at the work places like hospitals and offices of public and private concerns. A college or university campus could be a place marking the beginning to friendship with opposite sex that may lead finally to the tie of marriage. We can observe easily the love affairs among the university students who are deemed to be in love. They always appear at the parks, gardens and the places of privacy, talking, laughing, discussing something and sometimes caressing each other as if they were in the other world. Those who are sexually impulsed and with the mistaken notions about love or two people who have no basis for companionable friendship may feel delighted in considering themselves to be in love and get married. Many such marriages do not last longer.[67] Even kissings, caressing and petting is somewhat common among those who have reached the peak of romantic attachment. If it is really love affair, indulging in the outward sexual activity is no harm. But in some cases, the love-birds go further—to have sexual coitus anticipating their marriage. If they fail to prolong their affair with love and affection after having sexual union, it costs the female partner too dearly. She will be the sufferer and man goes away freely. Somerville's study asserts that the basic components for heterosexual love are "trust, confidence, inspiration and shared valour, interests and activities". The subjects of Somerville agreed that these are the components of friendship. This suggests the general acceptance of the definition of heterosexual love, offered some decades ago but still found useful, as a combination of sexual attraction and friendship.[65]

Number of such love failures result in suicides and murders due to some conflicts or misunderstandings. While men generally separate sex and love, women incline to combine them.[69] Once men satisfy their urges, they try to keep away from them (females). If these vulnerable women press the males to get married, they simply hideout the things throwing the matter on the shoulders of parents. Sometimes the man doubts the female chastity and feels that female who easily gave her body to him can easily offer the same to others as well. With this, his male ego does not favour the continuation of his love affair. Therefore, he uses such females temporarily, while entering into permanent relationship with other woman of his choice.[70] Good number of love marriages fail after some time when the sexual enjoyment with the particular person gets satisfied, more so, in cases where sensuousness alone brings the couple together.[71]

In an award winning Telugu movie "Keerthi-Kantha-Kanakam" (Fame, Woman and Money) which was screened recently, the heroine was betrayed by a professional seducer. The hero of the movie is a medical student. He is a son of a wealthy public figure. The latter would preach lofty ideals which he himself did not follow. When, she approaches the hero with pregnancy, he refuses to admit that the pregnancy was due to him. She tries to go to court. To protect his son, and for the sake of his reputation the father of the hero keeps his anonymity and subjects her to abortion. And he too tries to take advantage to seduce her having known that she was already seduced by his own son. Finally, she kills both the criminals—son and the father. Such is the cannibalistic attitude towards women in the male-dominated society.

Pregnancies of this type are rampant now among the students as well as the working women. When the author approached the maternity hospital authorities, he learnt that they receive such cases daily in great numbers. Even the private medical practitioners and the nursing homes reported the author the same fact. Parents too consult doctors to get rid of the unwanted pregnancies of their daughters. However, these girls are also disposed in marriages to some other persons.

Parents' disagreement for love marriages is the other difficulty which the love-birds may have to face. Once the daughter reveal that she is in love with some one, and decided to get herself married with him, parents cannot cope up with the unexpected situation and get frustrated with shock. As a result, quarrels, suicides, etc., are common at that critical situation. Hence, the opinion were sought from the working women of the present study to assess their views on the love marriage.

It was assumed that the higher the position of the respondent, the higher would be her likeliness towards love marriage and lower the position of the respondent, the lower her likeliness towards love marriage. And the data were cross-tabulated statistically and it was found significant (Table 30.8, Chi-square = 7.8013; d.f. = 2; P. <0.05) as was hypothesised.

About one-third of the respondents did not respond to the question. These working women are suspected to have avoided to answer, because they might not have liked to express the personal views on love, and some may have already tasted the failure of the love or its banes and such cases might have skipped away from answering. Some subjects who were reportedly love-birds before marriage declined to answer.

TABLE 30.8

Views on Love Marriage

Subjects	*Yes*	*No*	*Total*	*No reply*	*Grand total*
Office staff	25 (50)	25 (50)	50 (100)	50	100
Teaching staff	30 (44.1)	38 (55.9)	68 (100)	32	100
Medical staff	59 (65.6)	31 (34.4)	90 (100)	10	100
Total	114 (54.8)	94 (45.2)	208 (69.3) (100)	92 (30.7)	300 (100)

Chi-square = 7.8013; d.f. = 2; P. <0.05.

Note: Figures in the parentheses give the percentages.

Those love-birds who were blessed with the married life face numerous problems and their success in marital harmony reportedly is less. A man who has sexual coitus with a female before marriage, does not feel satisfied with the same woman after marriage, due to lack of thrill and novelty. As a result, the gauge of marital harmony will be less and the couples will be always in frivolous conditions. Among such marriages there is greater chance of failure. Parents too do hot allow couples of this type to share company with their families. Economic troubles start when the love-birds do not obtain the blessings of their elders. Hence, there is every possibility to get failure of love marriages but for the earning women, it is possible to get success of these marriages due to their economic independence.

Kadetotad[72] says, that love marriages arc not suitable for Indian society because these marriages break the cultural traditions and customs of our caste and religion. So, the older generation does not like such partners. These marriages overtake the caste, sub-caste, and *gotra* (endogamy) relationships. So, the partners may not get the cooperation of the castes and kinship. The children of these couples may not get love, encouragement and cooperation of the fellow members of the society.

Hence, the respondents were asked 'whether love marriages are failures'. 47.3 per cent of the sample answered affirmatively and 31.7 per cent negated it. It seems those who favour love marriages also agree that most of them are failures. But they assert that it is due to the outdated parents and also the troublesome in-laws, who are unable to accept the new mates as it is prohibited by the traditional patterns. Some of the respondents agree that the failures are due to the lack of empathy and tolerance among the couples to face the new situation.

DOWRY

Dowry is one of the social evils of the Hindu society. Nobody, either poor or rich, can escape from its bite. If the parties understand its pros and cons clearly and implement it properly, dowry custom is not at all harmful. But it is misused by the society due to the avarice for wealth.

The word 'dowry' in the ordinary sense, means the property that a girl brings with her at the time of marriage. This is a generally accepted view. The Dowry Prohibition Act, 1961, however, describes 'dowry' as any property or valuable security given or agreed to be given either directly or indirectly—(a) by one party to a marriage to the other or *(b)* by the parents of either party to a marriage or by any other person, to either party to the marriage or to any person, during or before or after the marriage as consideration for the marriage of the said parties; but does not include dowry or 'mahr' in the case of persons for whom the Muslim personal law (Shariat) applies.

It is prevalent in the society since ancestral period and it is a universal phenomenon.[73] The bride and the groom need a new home after marriage Which either the girl's parents or the boy's parents can help establish by providing household articles. Even The scriptures speak of gifts at the time of marriage.[74] In the earlier periods, daughters were not given equal share in their father's property. They were given presents at their marriage ceremony almost equal to the property they ought to be given. They substituted these presents as pure affection and for the well-being of her future but not as equal right. It is only optional on the part of the bride's parents but not compulsory. In the ancient period the nubile females of Kajakthan of Russia used to walk on the streets with the gold hanging on their necks. The gold would contain the quantity which they can afford to pay as dowry. Males, thus would select their brides according to the sum of the gold they had in their necks." Kings and affluent people would provide even more wealtheir presents both at the time of marriage and at the time of bride's—departure to her parents-in-law's house. A respectable marriage required the payment of cattle and goats to the groom's father, found satisfactory by him is terms of quality and quantity before the bride takes up residence at her husband's home.[76] *Atharva Veda* refers to royal brides bringing with them the dowry of a hundred cows. Draupadi, Subhadra and Uttara also brought with them rich presents of horses, elephants and jewels at the time when they left their parents' home.[77] There is ample evidence that king of Vidarbha ministered handsome presents with his sister Iudumathi, at the time of her departure with her husband. These offerings can hardly be called dowries, for they were given voluntarily after, marriage out of pure affection. *Smritis* no doubt recommended the bride should be given in marriage along with valuable ornaments, but their number and price were left to the ability of the bride's father.[78] But the author strongly believes that the parents offer gifts to their daughters not only as pure affection but also seek to compensate for their loss of share in the father's property. *Rig Veda* also mentions about dowry.[79] Religious concept of marriage as a sacrifice also helped the adherence to this custom. Dowry was regarded as *Dakshina* attending the main gift of the girl, and to the extent it was offered willingly. Since the daughter is denied the right of inheritance, this custom got deep-rooted in the society.[80] A girl in a social set-up of Hindu Community must marry. Her separation from her parents at a particular age was, therefore, inevitable. This created a natural anxiety in parents to give some gifts to their daughter at the time of her marriage.[81]

Gradually the practice of offering rich presents at daughter's wedding transformed into a rigid custom, in course of time, due to inflation, high cost of living, price rise, joint family living. Hooja[82] observes that ethical and economic reasons were instrumental in making the custom of dowry rigid. Hence, dowry custom has proved to be a permanent liability to the girl's parents and asset to the groom's parents. Now, the boy's family naturally searches for the best suitable combination of beauty, wealth and status in their selections. Often the girl's parents have to borrow large sums of money with exorbitant rates of interest in order to meet dowry, but this is indispensable for the best of the daughter.[83] In addition, the groom who is well educated and lucratively employed, settles himself as an attractive son-in-law. He naturally acquires a high price in the marriage market.[84] Modernity is also contributing to the exorbitant rise, of dowry. The civilised people often crave for a higher standard of living with its attendant comforts and new types of recreation. Urbanism also seems to emphasise individuality arid privacy, which gives another incentive for being independent of the large family group.[85] Material comforts like, scooter, TV, refrigerator, etc., also demand more money. Furthermore, the young couple tend to part away from large family to lead sexually happy life, at least in the initial periods of marriage.

These are all the aspects which influence the demand of dowry at the time of marriage settlement. It is happening from the countryside to the capital—Delhi. Recently, due to the problems caused by these dowry demands, dowry deaths have become disturbingly frequent in the national capital. A cabinet minister in the Madhya Pradesh government was trapped in the dowry drama. The bride's father allegedly paid Rs. 20,000 in cash, apart from costly articles, clothes and jewellery to meet the dowry demands. The bride's party reportedly made VIP lodging and boarding arrangements for the groom's party as the minister also attended the wedding ceremony. Instead of the customary caparisoned horse, the groom allegedly demanded an open car, which the bride's father procured after much difficulty.

The ceremony started. When both stood up to exchange the traditional garlands, the groom was reported to have said that be would not accept the garland from the bride unless he was given a Bajaj scooter. The bride's helpless father placed his cap at the feet of the groom and begged for mercy.' He did the same to minister and other relatives of the groom. The bride's parents almost fainted. Then the bride showed rare courage by announcing that she would not marry the boy now, even if the demand for the scooter was withdrawn. Her courage enthused many young men and women present.

The mob assembled at the ceremony demanded the minister guilty of breaking the dowry law.[86]

Thus, the public figures like ministers also make things miserable.

The middle class and those who cannot afford to pay the dowry are the sufferers. At the time of marriage settlement these parents generally agree to pay large amounts, but after marriage, they fail to fulfil the commitment and keep dodging the matter. In such cases, if the in-laws are greedy natured the daughter-in-laws are in trouble. They have to face humiliation which finally leads to suicide. These types of attrocities have earned notoriety for Delhi and these incidents are being reported in the leading newspapers and magazines daily. In some cases, parents-in-lawn as well as the husbands do collude to kill them (daughters-in-law). During the preceding two or three years, there was never a day without dowry deaths in our country. Women's welfare organisations protested against these dowry deaths. But there is no end for them. Dowry custom has thus got deep-rooted in the society and we cannot eradicate this social evil by the ordinances. The in-laws and the grooms must realise that wife is not an article who comes along with dowry. They will have to realise that she is a life-long partner in happy as well as in crisis situations and she is friend and mother.

Of course, the working girl is financing the dowry. She works now to accumulate money for the dowry and to reduce the parents' burden.[87] The working girl is preferred but nobody cares to regard her salary as a perennial dowry. Her father is still forced to pay dowry at least at a lesser rate.

No doubt, a good number of families benefit from the prevalence of dowry. It provided an occasion for people to boost their self-esteem through feasts and displays of material objects, to help prevent the break-up of family property, to get better mates for daughters and to furnish their daughters with some kind of social and economic security.[88] Taking dowry custom as a boon, rich people dispose their black money to some extent. The author personally feels that there is no harm if the dowry system prevails in the society but it should not be too rude and barbarous and rigid. If the parents of the bride afford to pay, he should be allowed to pay but the grooms should not demand. Some marriages could riot be solemnised at the last moment to the inability of the bride's parents to secure the settled dowry. This only highlights human greed for money: in such cases, courageous brides sometimes refused to have such mates.

Dowry is most prevalent in upper caste and highly educated community.[89] With the development of education, the custom is also threatening to go deep into the society. If the intercaste and love marriages are encouraged, its menace can be curbed. If we can come back again to matriarchal families dowry system can be made to feel much less severe.

Table 30.9 shows, 80.5 per cent of the respondents are of negative opinion towards dowry system. Only 17.6 per cent are of positive opinion towards dowry. Out of the respondents stating unfavourable opinion shown, the office staff stands in the higher percentage and the rest two categories constitute lower percentage of respondents giving unfavourable views towards dowry custom than the other. This particular trend is due to the economic position of the respective respondents. Office staff gets lower income than the other two categories and hence, they cannot afford to pay dowry. As such, they are at higher percentage unfavourable towards dowry system. The other two categories of subjects are economically high placed than office staff and hence, they can somewhat afford to pay. As such they are at higher percentage unfavourable towards dowry. Here, the hypothesis is that the higher position respondents are favourable towards dowry, and the lower position respondents are unfavourable towards the dowry custom. It is significant that working women at lower level cannot afford to bear dowry, whereas the working women at higher level can afford to bear dowry.

TABLE 30.9

Opinion on Dowry System

Subject	*Favour-able*	*Un-favourable*	*In-different*	*Total*	*No reply*	*Grand total*
Office staff	7 (8.5)	75 (91.5)	0	82 (100)	18	100
Teaching staff	18 (20.7)	65 (74.7)	4 (4.6)	87 (100)	13	100
Medical staff	21 (22.6)	71 (76.3)	1 (1)	93 (100)	7	100
Total	46 (17.6)	211 (80.5)	5 (1.9)	262 (100)	38	300

Chi-square = 12.6087; d.f. = 4; $P. < 0.05$.
Note: Figures in the parentheses give the percentages.

It is surprising to note the public opinion on dowry as was gathered by the Ministry of Social Welfare, Government of Uttar Pradesh, in the year 1982. It was revealed that 60.4 per cent youth, both male and female, favoured dowry system. They viewed the custom as a necessary one. It was a baffling fact indeed to learn that in Meerut district even the local people favoured dowry system.[90]

A question was put 'do you like *kanyasulka*,,? Maximum 90 per cent of them were found opposed to this. A few percentage of respondents were, however, found favourable to *kanyasulka* as it enhances the position of the women.

THE POSITION OF WIDOW IN HINDU SOCIETY

From the dawn of Indian history, the fair sex is looked down upon within the society. The mere birth of a female child is regarded as unwelcome and ominons. The birth of a girl, grant it somewhere, here grant a boy—from middle ages down to present times, the birth of a girl has been looked upon with resignation.[91] This discrimination of the society towards the female is the cause for all the illtreatment towards her.

When woman dies man can marry again but the woman does not enjoy such liberty. What is wrong with the pathetic widowed lady? Her mere sight itself is inauspicious. She is debarred from all the pious activities—marriages, festivals and religious ceremonies. She is almost shackled in the house-hold tasks. She has to take the food only as the last member in the family. Her travails as a widow begins with her head tonsured and ornaments stripped off from her. Hence forward, she is entitled to wear no other clothes but a plain white saree without the adornment of even the border. She must sleep on the hardest surface, frequently a stone floor, eat but one meal a day, that too, not sumptuous, and keep a strict twenty-four hour fast twice a month, during which not even water might pass through her lips. Influenced by the lawgivers of the respective periods, child marriages prevailed in the society and child widows were the result of these marriages. The child widows, even virgins were looked down upon in the society. They were asked to self-immolate with their dead husbands on the funeral pyre. Angiras argued, that the only course the Hindu religion has prescribed for a widow is that of *Sati*. Haritha maintained that a wife can purify her husband from the deadliest of sins if she burns herself with his remains, the two will then reside in heaven happily for three and half crores of years. Parasara observes that just snake drags out from a hole by force, in the same manner the *sati* takes out her husband from hell and enjoys heavenly bliss with him for three and half crores of years. Even if the wife had led dissolute life, it would not matter— her immolation, even if not voluntary will ensure a permanent seat in heaven both to herself and to her husband.[92]

The widows were burnt along with their dead husbands even if they were not willing to die. In 1845, for instance, when Jawahar Singh (suspected of treachery to the nation) was killed, his wives, who refused to become *saris,* were dragged by the soldiers and consigned to the flames.[93] The *Smritis* like that of Ved Vyas recommend that a widow should become *sati,* otherwise she should tonsure her head. It is said that the braid of hair, if continued to be retained by the widow, would result in the husband being put in bondage throughout in the other world.[94] *Dharmasutra* and Buddhist texts do not refer *sati* w either of them. But the Vedic hymns refer to the remarriage of widows rather than their self-immolation.[95] Though widow burning was So widespread according to the Brahmincal religion, its origin is not rooted in the Vedas. But as per the primitive beliefs man Continue to feel the needs of the things which he had when he was living, including his wife after death.[96] In Egypt, we find even today that people prepare their graves with their favourite things but wife's immolation is not prevalent. In the Solomon and Fiji Islands, widows used to be killed after the husband's death.[97]

During the Vedic period, women were treated equal to the male and were given equal opportunities. The position of women deteriorated from the post-Vedic period. The position of women still downrated from the Sutra period that it was in this period that the Aryan husband acquired a non-Aryan wife in addition to the Aryan wife. This is why Dr. Altekar says 'the introduction of a non-Aryan wife into an Aryan household is the key to deterioration of the position of women that started at about 1000 B.C. and was marked in 500 years'. The non-Aryan wife was ignorant and did not enjoy the same religious status as the husband. There was confusion because the Aryan wife was admitted in the religious rituals to which the non-Aryan wife was not entitled. So, all women were made ineligible for Vedic studies by Aityayana in 200 B.C.[98]

During 19th century Raja Rammohan Ray was the main crusader to revolt against the barbaric custom—suttee, which would compel a widow to burn concomitant with her deceased husband. In 1818. He has launched crusade against this social evil. His coaxing induced Lord William Bentinck—the then Governor General of India—to declare suttee illegal on 4th December, 1829, as it was made a crime of culpable homecide punishable with fine imprisonment or both'? The orthodox Hindus petitioned against the regulation but Raja Rammohan Ray took a lead and organised the counter-petition which condemned the rite as "murders according to every *shastra* as well as the common sense of all nations". He even called upon all his friends to organise a vigilance group for detecting sati immolation in violation of government restrictions. On *sati* controversy Rammohan Roy wrote tracts in Bengali composed as a dialogue between "an advocate for, and an opponent of, the practice of burning widows alive". On November 15, 1830. be sailed for England in order to counteract the possible nullification of the act against suttee. During his stay in England, the first reform act was passed in 1832. He hailed the act as the charter of liberty, justice and victory over oppression, injustice and wrong. Even then, if the widows were willing to self-immolate, they were not prohibited by the law but the forced widow-burning was stopped. In the recent years news appeared in the Press that Rajput widows tried to burn themselves along with their deceased husbands but were prevented due to the timely alert of the police.

In prehistoric periods there prevailed a belief in several societies that the life and needs of the dead in the next world were more or less similar to those in this life. It, therefore, became a pious duty of surviving relatives to provide a dead person with all the things that he would need when alive. Especially when an important personage like a king, a noble man or a war-son died, as a custom, his usual paraphernalia should be sent with him. He could, of course, require his wife, horses and servants in the next world, and it would, therefore, be necessary and desirable to kill these all, and burn and bury them with him. Such a belief has given birth to the custom of burning and burying the wife also with the deceased husband. Man, however wielded supreme power in society almost everywhere and was not prepared to sanction a custom adverse to his own interest and comforts. It may, however, be pointed out that in *Ashanti,* King's sisters were allowed to marry handsome youth among commoners, but they were compelled to commit suicide on the death of their royal consorts.[99]

The census of 1881 recorded 80000 widows below the age of twenty. Out of 80,000 widows 60,000 were Brahmins. Today there are more than 23 millions of widows in India as per the 1981 census.

Hindu widows according to the Census of 1921[100]

Widows of ages upto 5	= 11892
5 to 10	= 85037
10 to 15	= 237147

Widows according to 1931 Census[101]

Age group	*No. of widows*
0-1	1515
1-2	1785
2-3	3485
3-4	9076
4-5	15018
5-10	105449
10-15	183998
15-20	514394
20-25	846959

The prevention of *sati* was in accordance with humanitarian principles but it left before the widow a miserable and inhuman existence, If she fails to face *sati* immolation she has to face the signs of griefs like first, physical symptoms; second, loss of contact with reality—inability to comprehend the loss, brooding over memories and changing to possessions a feeling that the dead man is still present, expecting him home with every turn of the key in the door and talking to him as if he were still alive; third, tendency to withdraw—to escape from everything—that recalls the loss, from sympathetic friends and relatives, from any interest in life at all; fourth, hostility against the doctors, against the fate, in turn against oneself.[102]

In addition, being economically dependent on the members of her husband's family, she is ill-treated, abused and sometimes blamed and cursed for any unhappy occasion in the family. She ought to work hard in the house and put up with all kinds of indignities and humiliations from the elders and at times even from the younger members of the family. And as if this was not sufficiently degrading, she was considered in auspicious. To see her in the morning and to face her while going on a journey or some mission was considered as a bad omen. Her presence on any auspicious occasion was considered to forbade calamity and frustrations. Consequently, she would keep herself away or at a distance even on the occasion of marriage of her own children. She was unreasonably expected to be chaste. Even if she was seduced by a man outside the family or more likely by her family members or otherwise, the man goes free and it is she who is condemned.[103]

Gradually, some reform-minded people supported remarriage of widows at least for young virgin widows. Preferably the marriage was solemnised with the brother of the deceased husband. The Aryans wanted more sons to fight, the non-Aryans and this may be one of the reasons as to why they discontinued the practice of widow burning.[104]

'Niyoga' or liverate was known in the Vedic period and was not uncommon. *Rig Veda* (X.110.2) may mean either Niyoga or widow remarriage. After the husband's death or

during his lifetime, the widow or the wife was asked to have a son or sons through Niyoga or with an appointed man. A son alone could offer funeral oblations to the ancestors, hence a sonless man's wife or widow used to resort to *Niyoga.*[105] When Ratna tried to catch the golden deer to fulfil the wish of his wife Sita, Maricha in the metamorphosed form of golden deer cries "Lakshmana, Lakshmana" in the Rama's tone to shudder Sita and keep away Lakshmana from her. As expected she gets panicky and asks Lakshmana to go and help Rama as he is in danger. But Lakshmana having known the might of Rama, tries to persuade Sita that the cry is not of Rama, but of demon Maricha. While Sita in the state of panic says "0 Lakshmana, you are planning to capture me after my husband's (Rama) death. It will not be possible for you: She says that she will die herself to avoid that situation". But this does not clearly state that Niyoga or liverate prevailed during that period, but it gives such opinion or clue.

The famous emperor Chandragupta Vikramaditya married his elder brother's wife after the death of her husband. Kumara Gupta, a son of this union, became an heir to the Gupta's empire.[106]

Baudhayana and Gauthama speak of *niyoga* but not remarriage. In the sacred scriptures we get very few instances of remarriage of widows, probably because the *niyoga* was getting popular at that time.[107]

The institution of *Niyoga* is not mentioned in the Vedic texts. In the *Rig Veda* we find the widow married to her brother-in-law. Gauthama says that the inheritance of sonless man should go to the sapindas, sagotras of those connected by descent from the same Sri or the wife. But the wife may also seek to raise issue to her dead husband. This clearly refers to *Niyoga.*[108]

Several heroes of *Mahabharatha* and *Puranas* were born of *niyoga.* If a woman would lose her husband during epic period, she married her brother-in-law.[109] Under the system of *niyoga,* if a woman's husband was dead or found incapable of procreating children, she was allowed to have conjugal relations with her brother-in-law or some other near relative, till she begets children. The brother-in-law of the woman was regarded as the most eligible person for this duty.[110] The marriage of Hamlet's mother Claudious and of Henry VIII with Katherine indicate an earlier custom of *Niyoga,* eventually developing into a regular remarriage with a brother-in-law.[111] Among the Jews, a widow becomes her husband's brother's wife without any ceremony, if he refuses to marry her, she would spit in his face. The Old Testament also declares that if a woman becomes a widow, her husband's brother shall go into her and take her as wife, and perform the duties of hushand.[112]

Gradually, widow remarriage outside *niyoga* used to he held. Baudhayana sanctions widow remarriage for virgin widow, "if after a damsel has been given away or even after the nuptial sacrifices have been offered, the husband dies, she who thus has left her father's house may be again wedded according to the rules applicable to second marriage provided the marriage has not been consummated".[113] Buddha preached equal rights and equal opportunities for both male and female. In this period widow was not looked down upon in the society. Widow remarriage prevailed freely in Buddhist period allowed to widowers as well.[114] Manu was against widow remarriage: He said if the widow be still virgin or one who has returned from her first husband after leaving him, she is worthy to perform, with her second husband or her first deserted husband, the nuptial ceremony. Hence, a widow who is not virgin is unworthy of the sacrament. He said that once a father has given his daughter in marriage, he cannot give her to another man again since, 'Kanyadan' cannot take place twice.[115]

Widow remarriage in the Ramayana period not only prevailed but it was sanctioned by the highest society. When King Ravana died, his widow queen Mandodari was given marriage to Ravana's younger brother Vibhishana by Rama. Mandodari is one of the memorable great women of India who are called "Pratahsmaramiya satees". When Vali died, his widow Tam was given marriage to Vali's younger brother Sugreva by Rama.[116]

Dharmasastras also permit widow remarriage.[117] Uloopi was a non-Aryan Widow married to Arjuna.[118] The marriage of widows prevailed during the periods of Manu, Vasistha and Kautilya.[119] It is argued by many that the marriage of widows was in vogue in the earlier *yugas,* but has been forbidden in the *Kaliyuga.*[120]

With the efforts of Iswarachandra Vidyasagar, widow remarriage was legalised on 7th December 1856. Sri Srichandra Vidhyasagar, son of Iswarachandra Vidyasagar, married a child widow Kalavathi on that day itself. To encourage widow remarriage in Bengal society, the then Lieutenant Governor of Bengal gave the newly married bridegroom a job of Deputy Magistrate for his courage and connection.[121]

Gandhiji once quoted, "just as winter clothes are useless and often harmful in summer, the customs and traditions of one era are useless and often harmful in other erus."[122] He has also generously supported the widow marriage. He asked the young men to marry young widows, thereby helping the cause of widow remarriage. He also asked men to control their lust and refuse to marry young girls of fifteen and sixteen. During his period many widows and many a youth vowed never to marry anyone but the widow.[123]

Smt. Lakshmibai Desai, the staunch advocate of widow remarriages, redicules those who oppose widow remarriage and says, "it is not possible for a widow to lead an austere life in the midst of worldly pleasures. The widow's guardians themselves have to be ascetics and lead an austere life if they want the young widow in the house to lead such a life".[124]

Firstly, out of 185 widows contacted by Mrs. Vatsala Mehta, 41 per cent did not favour the remarriage of widows. Mrs. Gunial Desai, on the other hand, found 89 of the widows she contacted (83.3% being child widows) favoured it. However, she found the middle class graduate women whom she also interviewed, to be more traditional minded. Of the 810 married women surveyed, 322 (nearly 40%) believed that widows, even child widows, should not think of remarriage. Among those who favoured remarriage, 60 per cent would permit it only for child widows. Secondly, whereas it was permitted, only in specific cases, when the widow is young, helpless and or childless, passionate, or needing protection against social scandal. It was not considered a normal right but a concession to same of the weaknesses to which the widow might be a victim because of her social position.[125]

Table 30.10 clearly shows that all the working women are in favour of widow remarriage. Out of the total sample, teaching staff are somewhat less favourable to widow remarriage. It was cross-tabulated satisfactorily and it was found dependent as all the working women agreed to widow remarriage (Table 30.10, Chi-square = 25.2547; d.f. = = 2; P. <0.05). And out of total sample 2.7 per cent of the working women are of widow remarried category. This in itself is a marked trend in the Indian context.

TABLE 30.10

Views on Widow Remarriage

Subject	*Yes*	*No*	*Total*	*No reply*	*Grand total*
Office staff	60 (70.&	25 (29.4)	85 (100)	IS	100
Teaching staff	35 (46)	41 (53.9)	76 (100)	24	100
Medical staff	80 (81.6)	18 (18.4)	98 (100)	2	100
Total	175 (67.6)	84 (32.4)	259 (100)	41	300

Chi-square = 25.2547; d.f. = 2; P. <0.05.

Note: Figures in the parentheses give the percentages.

DIVORCE

Marriage is a sacred bond between male and female and it is indissoluble institution. By marriage, the husband and wife are one person in law. That is, the very being of both is a legal existence. As a result, separateness of woman is suspended from the marriage.[126] God made them in the beginning as male and female, and said "for this reason a man shall leave his father and mother and be joined to his wife, and two shall become one, so they are no longer two but one. God has joined them together, let not man put as under".[127]

Hindu society does not allow divorce at any circumstance. For a Hindu, marriage is a *Samskara* and as such, it is a sacrament which could be broken only by death. According to the *Mahabharata*, 'a wife is given by God'. Hinduism regards marriage as a means of fulfilment of life, the true purpose of being a complete companionship in fighting the battle of life together. In our culture the sacramental and indissoluble character of marriage has always been emphasised.[128] Marriage, as an institution, is a device far the expression and development of love.[129]

The highest *Dharma* for a Hindu wife is *pativrata,* i.e., complete devotion and loyalty of a woman to her husband, alive or dead taking him to be her God and as her only means of ultimate salvation. Roman Catholics regard that marriage once established and consummated is indissoluble because it then falls under the jurisdiction of God and not within the control of any human agency.[130] If a husband is of bad character, or has gone abroad, for long, or is guilty of treason, or is dangerous to his wife, or has become an outcaste, or has lost virility, he may be abandoned by his wife".[131] Primitive societies had high rates of marital dissolution.[132] Kautilya approved divorce and thus said, "if the husband or the wife hated each other, divorce was to be granted. If a man apprehending danger from his wife, sued for divorce, he had to return her whatever presents he had".[133]

Manu granted the right to a husband to repudiate his wife for very trifling offences, but laid down the rule retained to this day that a Hindu wife can under no condition escape from marriage bond.[134] Jain[135] says that husband was ideally regarded as a deity to the wife and her life is only with her husband.

Hebrew husbands obtain divorce essentially by announcing "I divorce thee". They feel that divorce is a personal matter, neither church nor the State has authority to control it. This was followed not only by the Jews but also the Greeks and the Romans. Divorce was husband's prerogative among the patiarchal societies and barrenness and adultery on the part of female was the most common grounds.[136] *Dharmasutra* and *Smritis* also allowed divorce for a. wife when the husband is away for six years, impotent, outcaste, etc. Altekar[137] opined that divorce was permitted before the beginning of Christian era. In the Kuruvan tribes of India, if the wife wants to divorce her husband, she simply returns the rice which has been given to her by the groom, at the time of her marriage. There is a great demand for women of this kind who have divorced for seven times. Marrying this type of divorcee is regarded as a pious thing for the menfolk.[138]

Mervelle quotes "Marriage like God, is not dead. True marriage is always blissful after the honeymoon bloom wears away. But it can fulfil our most human needs, as nothing else can. I predict that the pendulum will swing back towards a deeper awareness of the advantage and good sense of strong, dedicated marriage".[139] Bhavabhuthi described the, ideal couple as "The dearest friend, the essence of all kinship, the fulfilment of all-desires, a veritable treasure, the very life itself—all there is a husband to the wife and *vice versa*".[140]

In the modern society, it has become quite easy for both the sexes to get divorce granted due to the slackening attitude of the State and the society towards divorce. In the United States due to liberation, liberal divorce laws, the changing public opinion towards divorce, etc., have contributed to the increase of fragility in the marriage relationship.[141] The rate of divorce in this country was five per 1000 population in 1976.[142]

Why the Incidence of divorces is increasing in this society? The development of education, opportunities for employment, demand for equal rights etc., are contributing to divorce. Many people believe that more marriages fail of late after women changed their roles by furthering their education, careers and demanding that the wife and husband have equal role in decision making, dealing with daily life tasks, etc.[143] A word can make wonders, hard word is like a pebble dropped in a pond, It disappears in a second, but leaves behind ripples of ill-will, bringing bitterness between the couples. Instead of harsh criticism one can look for the good qualities in one's partner.[144] If the egos of the partners hurt, there lies the trouble.

Couples with both sexual and financial dissatisfaction were found to have, the highest divorce rate.[145] Education also plays an important role in marital harmony. If the wives happened to be superior in education than their husbands, they were found to have low score of happiness, while the scores were much higher in cases where the husbands happened to be higher in education.[146] Lack of empathy between the couples also, leads to marital discords. Some couples do not understand each other empathetically. Such couples are at the risk of misunderstanding and ill will between them. These types of partners cannot cope up with each other at the time of frictions. They both stick to their word and cannot lessen their obstinacy. In such times there is every possibility of marital disharmony between the couples.

Especially the working women, with the newly acquired employment, want that their say must be given due consideration in the family affairs. Husbands sticking to traditional notions do not accept wives' demands, though the wife earns half of the family income. The other salient feature is that the Indian male still estimates the traditional woman as a housewife. Though the, men are highly educated and in prestigious positions, they are still traditional and even orthodox in their attitudes.[147] Troubles with in-laws are common as the working women do not obey or oblige the mother-in-laws superiority. With higher education followed by lucrative employment, these women do not bend their heads to the traditional minded and out-dated mothers-in-law, who do not equal with her in any aspect, except in experience. In such circumstances, these old women (in-laws) furiously create troubles between the couples and at times these troubles certainly lead to marital disharmony.

The age of marriage also influences the divorce rate. If the ages of the couples are, under twenty years, divorce rate is more and if the age of marriage is higher, the divorce rate lowers.[148] For the Indian couples, if the span of married life increases, the marital success also increases, whereas, in the United States, with the increase of married life the divorce rate also increases.[149]

Sexual dissatisfaction and impotency of the husband also lead to marital failure.[150] Due to lack of the sexual communication between the couples, the partners may end their lives in disharmony. Particularly the Indian wife cannot communicate to her husband the ways and means of enjoyment of sexual happiness of her choice.

As per Table 30.11, 35.8 per cent of subjects agreed that sexual dissatisfaction leads to marital failure, whereas 64.2 per cent have not agreed. Even among the three categories of subjects the change of opinion was markedly different. Hence, the data were cross-tabulated statistically and found significant (Table 30.11, Chi-square = 23.4019; d.f. = 2; P.<0.05). Views emerged that the lower the position of the respondent, the less she felt that sexual dissatisfaction leads to marital disharmony and that higher the position of the respondent, the more strong is her feeling that it leads to marital discords. We can also say otherwise, that lower positioned respondents feel in greater numbers that sexual dissatisfaction does not lead to marital failure and *vice versa*.

TABLE 30.11

Sexual Dissatisfaction Leads to Marital Failure

Subjects	*Yes*	*No*	*Total*	*Not appli cable*	*No reply*	*Grand total*
Office staff	0	15 (100)	15 (100)	20	65	100
Teaching staff	2 (9.5)	19 (90.5)	21 (100)	20	59	100
Medical staff	32 (54.2)	27 (45.8)	59 (100)	9	32	100
Total	34 (35.8)	61 (64.2)	95 (100)	49	156	300

Chi-square = 23.4019; d.f. = 2; P. <0.05.

Note: Figures in the parentheses give the percentages.

It is clearly evident from Table 30.12 that more respondents preferred, divorce in case the husband want to marry again in addition to existing wife. And next importance is given to unfaithfullness of the husband and the respondents emphasised that the important factor for divorce is impotency of the husband. Most of the Medical staff asserted that impotency constitutes a cause for divorce. The data also infer that the higher the position of the respondent, the greater is her preference for divorce for all the demerits mentioned in Table 30.12 and lower the position of the respondent, the lower is the intensity of her option for divorce for the above causes.

However, divorce is not advisable for Hindu women. Whatever may be the reasons for troubles between the partners, Hindu philosophy does not suggest divorce. The mere thought of divorce is inauspicious and unworthy for us. But most of the deserted women of the present sample informed the author that they prefer desertion rather than divorce, because they feel embarrassed to go to court and to stand in the box with a witness in the presence of audience. Hence, they feel it better to desert their husbands when they feel like. Out of the total sample, 2.3 per cent are of divorced, and 4.3 per cent are of deserted category.

PREMARITAL SEX

"Sex and life are coeval and inseparable. The sex instinct has always worked as a powerful motivation and propelling force in the dynamics of life. From the beginning of time, man has been feeling enthralled by its depth and intensity, its rage and ramifications and its might and mystery. But never before was it such a rage as today".[151]

TABLE 30.12

Options for Divorce

Options		*Office staff*	*Teaching staff*	*Medical staff*
If the husband is				
(a)	unfaithful to wife	31	35	40
(b)	drunkard and beats his wife	10	20	23
(c)	wishes to get married again	30	42	53
(d)	impotent	11	36	46
(e)	no reply	11	36	11
(f)	not applicable	20	20	9
	Total	100	100	100

Schofield states: "Sex in psychological terms is one of the basic drives motivating human behaviour". Ellis regards sex as "the central problem of life—sex lies at the root of life, and we can never learn to reverence life until we know how to understand sex".[152] Geddes writes "sex is an urge, an impulse, a drive, something we are born with. It manifests itself in the first months of infancy, sometimes even at birth. It lasts until death. It has peaks of urgency".[153]

In this connection, Arnold has observed: "Sexual interest, excitement and desire is a deep, basic biological urge which has been present in mankind since the dawn of time. Its expression and satisfaction have passed, through infinite variation, but its central presence has remained to give pleasure, joy, jealousy, hatred, and the continuation of a race".[154]

H.G. Wells has expressed the view that "for most of us, sex is a necessity, and a necessity not merely as something urgent that has to be got rid of by, for instance, incidental meretricious gratification, but as a source of energy, self-confidence and creative power".[155]

Hindus look upon sex as sacred. Vatsyayana has used the term *Kama-sex* as a synonym of love and his *Kama-sutra* is well known as a treatise on the art and rites of love rather than on the art and technique of sex. Vatsyayana calls it "science of love", and not "science of sex". though it deals with the theme of passionate love rather than the theme of romantic love. In this important sociological treatise, sex has been recognised as an essential part of the full and vigorous life.[156]

Sex has given more importance in human lives. But it was primarily permitted to the married person and within the marriage itself. The puritans put importance on chastity of both sexes. They believed that sex is strictly confined to marriage and should be practised only for procreation but not for pleasure. Anyone including in premarital and extramarital sex could be executed. But some societies allowed premarital sexual coitus for both the sexes.

In the primitive societies, premarital sexual coitus has been permitted.[157] A number of incidents in the lives of Gods and sages described in the *Mahabharata* and the records of the life histories of eminent epic personages clearly shown that virginity was not necessarily demanded of a girl.[158] In the age of *Rig Veda*, the life of a girl was gay. easy and free, she was allowed to mix with young men and premarital sex was tolerated. She could even choose her own husband. This is evident from her participation in the *Samana* festival. At the *Samana*, men and women of all sorts used to congregate.[159]

The following instance from the *Mahabharata* shows evidence to the premarital sexual coitus: Parasara says to Sathyavathi, the virgin daughter of Uparichera Vasu, "Darling, satisfy my desire". Satyavathi says "How can I do it here in the boat, for people from the shores may see us in that act". So Parasara created fog and under the cover of it he gratified his lust. He gave her a boon that despite this sexual union she could even remain a virgin.[160]

Virginity was considered a nuisance during the 16th century in India, if not afterwards, and prospective groom shuddered at the very idea of marrying a girl who has not been deflowered.[161]

Virginal purity was not at all prized. Among certain African tribes, a man hesitated to consume marriage if his bride was not deflowered by her former lover with his tacit and unenquiring competence.[162] Defloration was the duty of the state in Philippines. Special officers were appointed to deflower girls before marriage and they were highly paid for their labour. In New Caledome men were hired by their husbands to deflower their brides. The people of Burma employed white men for defloration.[163]

According to Nayar custom, when Nayar girls are ten or twelve years old or more, their mothers perform a marriage ceremony for them. But the bridegroom leaves the bride and goes away without touching her on account of her being not deflowered. Then the mother of the bride goes begging others to deflower her daughters but they hesitate to deflower, as an unclean thing to do.[164] Thus, they have to get their daughters deflowered before they go to nuptial bed. Even in pome African tribes, defloration ceremony is performed before marriage with the boy friend. In some tribes, female circumcision is practised at the age of eight or nine.

Reiss wrote: "I still feel that the evidence is not fully in, but the data that are coming in are so consistent in their findings of higher non-virginity rates at specified ages. I am now willing to assert that the changes predicted have occurred and that the actual premarital non-virginity rate is now close to 70 per cent in female".[165] All the authorities in this study, *viz.*, Terman, Kinsey, Burgess and Wallin, etc., have concluded that about 50 per cent of the women born in this century were not virgins at the time of their marriage.[166]

Murdock found premarital sex relationships to be fully approved in 65 societies, to be conditional in 43, to be disapproved in 6, and to be forbidden in 44. In some societies where complete premarital freedom is not sanctioned, intercourse with selected persons such as cross unions, who are potential marriage partners, is permitted. In some, about 70 per cent of the societies permits premarital relations. In most of the others, the taboo falls particularly upon female and seems to be prohibited to prevent pregnancies.[167] Leslie says that in some societies almost complete freedom of premarital sexual relationships between boys and girls was allowed and in some societies premarital chastity was a minority pattern.[168]

Despite strong resentment towards premarital sexual intercourse within the society, the rate of premarital coitus is increasing particularly in the Western societies. Among early Jews, the bride who was not virgin and the wife who was engaged in adultery was stoned and strangled, together with her lover.[169] Hindus use even today a white sari when marriage is to be consummated, in order to test the bride's virginity, if she fails to bleed, she may be or even ought to be non-virgin and is killed by her father or brother who acts as the guardian.[170] Even today Hindu society-does not permit premarital coitus.

But in the West particularly in United States, premarital coitus is rapidly increasing in both the sexes, particularly among college going youths. Recent studies at several colleges indicate the latest preference of about 80 per cent of college students to choose to live with an-unmarried partner if they were given the opportunity and could find the right partner.[171] Permissiveness with affection is becoming the dominant-sexual standard. Persons who hold this view, opine that premarital sexual coitus is acceptable for both men and women as long as the couple feel mutual affection.[172]

Smart and Szwed's study shows that females are not only more likely, to have premarital coitus than they were generation ago, they also appear to be having it with more partners. Non-virginity and the number of sex partners of a college girl seems to be related to her physical attraction. They found that 56 per cent of most attractive girls, 31 per cent of medium attractive and 27 per cent of the lesser attractive girls were non-virgins.[173]

Premarital coitus may help sexual adjustment in marriage. Women who experience orgasm in premarital sexual relations are more likely to experience orgasm through sexual act after marriage than women who have not had premarital relations. Moreover, premarital orgasmic women may be more capable of feeling orgasm than those who did not experience premarital premarital coitus.[174] It is common among middle class American women.[175]

But it is still taboo for Indian society. Indian maiden is praised in overseas countries only due to her premarital chastity. With the advent of western education and modernisation, the attitude of our women towards the premarital sexual coitus appears to have changed. Once, it was strongly believed that a girl should not go about with a man alone and should not make male friends, though mixing between boys and girls amidst elders was not prohibited.[176] But now they feel nothing wrong about moving with the boys and outing of the girls themselves in the company of each other. They even felt that they could also indulge in holding hands or casual kissing on the forehead, cheeks, hands, and on the lips, but at the same time their percentage was much less.[177] Kapur finds from her educated working women respondents these choices who have justified in having sexual relationship before marriage if there was sincere love between the partners or if they were engaged to be married or if they sincerely loved each other and planned to marry or even in cases where a woman was faithful to her lover and was not promiscuous.[178] Wide change was discernible only after ten years of gap between her two studies. Kapur's study of working women discloses that while attitudes towards mixing of sexes in groups, towards casual kissing and even petting have become more liberal, the attitude towards fornication are still conservative and traditional.[179]

From Fonseca's study of University students and non-students in India, over 60 per cent in both cases were found to disapprove of premarital sex relations. Among. them 14 per cent said that it was highly improper and immoral. Woman students and non-students expressed their views more emphatically. Some of the women in Fonseca's sample remarked, "Sex enters after marriage and there is no need to carry on any. experiment in this matter before the right time. Sex relations before marriage end up in frustration or neurosis for normal people" or, "No sex relations before marriage, I believe, it is suicidal for girls".[180]

Premarital coitus among the prospective mates is common in the West, but very rare in India. It is well known that in India the boy or girl who indulges in sex freely, rarely marries. Those who marry find that their married life is full of apprehensions, primarily due to man's inhibitions that he married a non-virgin, even though she might have lost virginity to the same person. He fears that a woman who agreed easily to sexual submission to him, could have done the same to others. In reverse, clever females with sexual experience often use it as a trap to secure husbands, mostly as blackmailing technique, after becoming pregnant. The male, as is well known, indulges in premarital sex with the idea of enjoying a pleasurable activity, without the least thought of getting involved permanently or emotionally. He promises love and even marriage merely to get the assent and response of the female. Those who cannot make false promises visit the brothels. But the females who indulged in sexual relations, get emotionally involved and hope that their submission would bring deep emotional involvement from the male. Unfortunately, man goes away marrying someone of their elders' choice. Only the female has to suffer humiliation and mental agony. But some females may succeed in getting themselves married with that male by showing the antidote of pregnancy. But the partners do not get happiness in their lives who have had coitus before marriage. There are. however, many happy marriages in which there is love, friendship, emotional attachment, and passion without coitus prior to marriage—between the two partners, Inhibition, guilt and oedipus complex are all responsible for unhappiness of the former kind of marriages.[181]

Despite all the vices with regard to premarital sexual indulgence some women try to have such activities and some others get trapped by the seducers. Hence, it was intended to ascertain whether the working women of the present study approve of female premarital sexual relations. Rampal says that in the Indian cities, premarital petting is common, and so is the premarital coitus, as well as homo-sexual relationships and masturbation. About 85 per cent of Indian city girls have some kind of petting experience before marriage, while 55 per cent of the city girls have homosexual experience and masturbation at one time or other, prior to marriage.[182]

During the pilot study, the researcher observed strong resentment among the respondents for facing the question. However, the question was included in the schedule to know the views of entire sample. As was expected, only *59.7* per cent have responded." But, out of the total respondents, 95.5. per cent are not in favour of premarital coitus and only 4.5 per cent are in favour of it. The data were also statistically cross tabulated and found not significant (Table 30.13, Chi-square = 1.8226; d.f. = 2; P.>0.05) as all the working women are not in favour of premarital sexual relations for women. It infers that there is no correlation between the position held by the respondents and their opinion on the pre marital relations for women. At the same time, they were again asked whether males should be allowed for premarital sexual activity, to contrast the same with the former.

TABLE 30.13

Views on Female Premarital Sex

Subject	*Yes*	*No*	*Total*	*No reply*	*Grand total*
Office staff	3 (5.7)	49 (94.2)	52 (100)	48	100
Teaching staff	4 (6.2)	61 (93.8)	65 (100)	35	100
Medical staff	1 (1.6)	61 (98.4)	62 (100)	38	100
Total	8 (4.5)	171 (95.5)	179 (59.7) (100)	121 (40.3)	300 (100)

Chi-square = 1.8226; d.f. = 2; P. > 0.05.

Note: Figures in the parentheses give the percentages.

When it comes to males (Table 30.14) 14.5 per cent agreed that males can have premarital sexual intercourse before marriage, whereas only 4.5 per cent approved of female indulgence in such relations. Our hypothesis is not significant statistically, as 85.5 per cent of the respondents are not in favour of premarital sexual relations for males too.

Balse[183] quoted Indian respondents' opinion with regard to premarital sex relations. 7.10 per cent of students and 2.10 per cent of parents of his study felt nothing wrong with the premarital relations. Maximum of 74.60 per cent and 89.10 per cent of students and parents respectively, felt premarital sexual relations to be wrong. And a margin of 11 per cent and

4 per cent of both categories okayed fornication only when the couple decided to get married. Hence, it is concluded that premarital sexual relations are not advisable as well as not suitable for the Indian society either for male or female. Sometimes these relations compel the female to resort to prostitution, and leads her to suicides and murders too. Abortions and venereal diseases are usually of common occurrence.

TABLE 30.14

Views on Male Premarital Sex

Subject	*Yes*	*No*	*Total*	*No reply*	*Grand total*
Office staff	6 (12)	44 (88)	50 (100)	50	100
Teaching staff •	5 (8.3)	55 (91.7)	60 (100)	40	100
Medical staff	13 (23.2)	43 (76.8)	56 (100)	44	100
Total	24 (14.5)	142 (85.5)	166 (55.3) (100)	134(44.7)	300 (100)

Chi-squarc = 5.5261; d.f; = 2; P. > 0.05.

Note: Figures in the parentheses give the percentages.

IMPORTANCE OF SEX IN MARRIED LIFE

Marriage without sex is meaningless. Actually marriage takes place for the fulfilment of carnal desires and to regulate sexual life in the society. If there is no importance of sex in marriage, the marriage would, not have existed. But it is necessary to discuss the extent of importance and the extent of satisfaction between the couples. It varies from society to society, from period to period and also from culture to culture. In general, almost all societies in all periods, stressed the importance of sex in marriage.

Sexual relations between the couples lead to the status of parenthood. Further, sexual satisfaction is regarded as an essential characteristic feature of a successful marriage. The pandits strongly believe that a woman who gets sexual gratification in her union with her husband will never be unfaithful to him: Sexual lapses on the part of the man are held as a sign of unsuccessful marriage.[184] Sexual dissatisfaction leads to feeling of exploitation, degradation, manipulation between the couples.[185] Sexual adjustment, no doubt, is a desired condition for marital success and the sex act has become the symbol of complete marital union.[186]

Kapadia says. "The importance of Hindu marriage is said to be *dharma*, *praja* (progeny) and *rati* (pleasure). Though sex is one of the functions of marriage, it is given third place, indicating thereby that it is the most desirable aim of marriage.[187] It may be in the third place, but without the sexual compatibility between the couples, the attainment of other objectives is very difficult. Without the physical satisfaction, partners may not get harmony in life and they cannot pull on their lives as a couple. Sexual incompatibility in married life is the right source of disappointment and frustration that can lead to deep resentment between the partners and ultimately to divorce.[188]

Physically sex drive is a slow process in female than male. With mere sight of a maiden, man gets aroused but the woman is not even if she comes across a man. She gets aroused only when the atmosphere is lustrous, when she is touched gently, kissed or fondled and/ or embraced. It takes some time for her to get initiated. Man, on the other hand, gets aroused easily and tries to advance towards her. There is a natural breakout on the male in that his ability to repeat ejaculation of sexual fluid within a short span of time depends upon the rapidity with which his glands can secrete the fluid and he can be resensitised to sexual stimulation. Since a woman's response is not dependent upon any such secretion and ejaculation, she may, in some cases, have a series of climaxes far surpassing the number of her husband's climaxes. This means that the most responsive women are more responsive than the most responsive men. Women's physiological capacity for sexual response infinitely surpasses that of men. But this is not the same as that of woman's response in individual acts of sexual intercourse. Man's response to intercourse is more rapid and spontaneous, woman's response is lower and less spontaneous. These two differences between the sexes—one rapidity of arousal and spontaneity of response, the other, capacity for repeated response—are often confessed.[189]

And it takes long time for woman to get orgasm. The rate of orgasm is low in women than in men. The orgasm may be different in kind as well. If the female feels orgasm, she is said to be satisfied fully with the sexual intercourse. Hence, sexual empathy should reach the couple for the harmony in life.

Man's sexual ability or desire reaches its peak at the age of 18 and thereafter declines, while woman's sexual interest and desire culminates when she is in her twenties and remains relatively stable. It helps some parents to know that experimentation among married partners in positions and techniques for intercourse.[190]

Beginning from Kinsey of late 1940s and early 1950s and continuing till 1960s, researchers have found relationship between sexual adjustment and total marital harmony. In Bruce and Thomson's study of young well educated couples, for example, mutuality or orgasm was found to he related to marital adjustment. In addition, Kinsey says that both sexual and marital adjustment tended to be better if the spouse was perceived to be sexually attractive, if sexual intercourse was by mutual desire, and if mates were willing and able to have intercourse as often as they wished.[191]

Higher the rate of frequency of sexual intercourse, the higher the sexual satisfaction among the couples, lower the rate of frequency of sexual coitus the lower the harmony rate. And those who get orgasm frequently get harmony in life at a higher rate.[192] The contemporary male says to himself you satisfy yourself and your sexual partner'. He has to make sure that he is a better lover at least in sexual union, if not others. He has to cope up with the sexually demanding woman. Something else is required in addition to the considerable amount of coping.[193]

The rate of frequency of intercourse is higher among housewives than among working women. Due to preoccupation of works, the working women have less time for the demands of marriage. Lack of domestic help physically and mentally exhausts, a working woman. As a result, she is often left with no energy for sex.[194] According to the studies of Khanna and Varghese, most Indian women are satisfied with sex, 36 per cent always, 58 per cent sometimes. It is also interesting to note that 38 per cent of women who are not satisfied sexually, continue their conjugal life, although adjustment is made more difficult.[195]

The findings of the Indian Study of Khanna and Varghese[196] of Housewives as well as Working Wives are as follows:

Subjects	*Attitude towards sex (%)*			
	Very frequently	*frequently*	*rarely*	*never*
Housewife	40.34	42.79	11.72.	5.15
Working wife	26.73	37.98	17.11	18.18

The rate of frequency, of sexual coitus is less among working wives than that among the housewives, as they are preoccupied with the dual role of office work and house work, whereas the housewives are burdened only with the housework and feel less tiresome than the working wives and hence, the frequency of sexual coitus among them is more.

How long does good sexual adjustment take? There is no rigid time schedule. Some partners whose expectations and attitudes synchronise easily and who understand and accept each other's feelings are relatively well-adjusted right from the time of their first adventure in sexual activity. For others, it can take weeks, months, or even years and in certain cases, the couples may not get satisfaction sexually at all. But such couples may not last longer in strengthening their marital harmony. In a study of 409 married couples. Landis and Landis reported that one-eighth of the couples needed many weeks, or months, but did reach an adjustment they considered satisfactory, within a year. However, one-tenth of the couple required an average of six years to work out the sexual adjustment in marriage and some of them required as long as twenty years.[197]

Hence, it is significant to know the opinion of the working women of the present study about the importance of sexual relations in the married life.

As was predicted. the difference of opinion with regard to importance of sex in married life is clearly visible in Table 30.15. Subjects being educated working women, it was assumed that these subjects would put more emphasis on sex in the married life. As such, totally 57.8 percent agree that sexual happiness in the marriage is a must. The data were also statistically cross tabulated and found significant (Table 30.15; Chi-square = 12.1059; d.f. = 2; P.<0.05) in that higher the position of the respondent, higher the emphasis on importance of sex in married life and lower the position of the respondent, lower the importance given to sexual pleasure in married life.

TABLE 30.15

Views on Importance of Sex in Married Life

Subjects	*Yes*	*No*	*Total*	*Not applicable*	*No reply*	*Grand total*
Office staff	15 (34.9)	28 (65.1)	43 (100)	20	37	100
Teaching staff	44 (66.7)	22 (33.3)	66 (100)	20	14	100
Medical staff	56 (62.2)	34 (37.8)	90 (100)	9	1	100
Total	115 (57.8)	84 (42.2)	199 (100)	49	52	300

Chi-square = 12,1059; d.f. = 2; P. < 0.05.

Note: Figures in the parentheses give the percentages.

Kapur's[198] study states that the working women showed increasing consciousness of their right to derive sexual gratification within marriage. And it was also found that most of those women whose husbands thought and believed that sex was one-sided affair to be indulged in at the will of the husband alone, reacted resentfully. They also resented the husbands who cared only for their own sexual satisfaction and did not consider it their obligation to see that the wife is in a proper frame of mind and body who also may be inclined to desire and enjoy it. Many of her respondents expressed deep concern that satisfactory sexual indulgence in marriage alone should lead to marital success.

If the couples fail to get sexual satisfaction, some of them may try to fulfil their urges through extramarital relations. The extramarital sexual coitus may be had through the neighbours, relatives, and friends, if she is a working woman, she may satisfy her sexual needs through her colleagues.[199] Mortan Hunt claims that almost every married person has the desire for an affair, at least once during his/her married life.[200] In United States, the middle class woman has right on par with her husband to engage herself in extramarital sex.[201] But this may not fully apply to the Indian society.

The prevalence of extramarital sexual relations is more in the United States of America. Communes, group marriages, swinging clubs, etc., prevailing in this society are the typical examples for extramarital relations. Why different types of institutions like communes, group marriages and swinging clubs are there? It is just for sexual satisfaction of the couples outside the marriage with or without knowing each other. Couples exchange the partners for one night or two, sometimes having sexual coitus with anyone other than the marriage partner, only with the mutual consent of the original couples. They simply want to enjoy with anybody they may like, and yet they remain as couples. Now, swinging clubs are rampant in the —American society, where different pairs of couples select one-common place—club, hotel or some other house—assemble there at pre-determined time, drink, smoke, exchange mates according to their taste and enjoy sex for that night or so. After that, the original couples go back to their residences. Why all these extramarital sexual-coitus? They are just for variety and for utmost sexual happiness of both the couples but not as a sign of resentment towards the mates. They enjoy this type of sexual satisfaction with the wholehearted consent of both the partners and willingly letting each to others.

John Cuber and Peggy Haroff found in their study of 437 upper middle class significant Americans that many of their respondents were involved in extramarital relationship either for one night's thrill, or, for some deeper emotional bond.[202] For, American male, many opportunities exist for an affair with the woman who works in his office or whom he meets in his suburban neighbourhood, while his own wife is working in somebody else's office. Sometimes, these relationships blossom into full-scale love affairs fulfilling needs of both partners that are not met in their marriage.[203] it is learnt that every working woman in America, at least once or twice, is exploited sexually by her colleagues or her employer during her service.

To fulfil the canons of hospitality, the primitive man willingly has lent his wife as a sex mate to his guest.[204] As the story of the *Mahabharata* goes, when Vichitra Virya dies, Satyavathi, the mother, asks Bhishma to raise sons to his brother's wives, Ambica and Ambalica. But he resents and Vyasa's services are requisitioned.[205] This infers that extramarital relations prevailed during the epic period also. But, Manu and Kautilya opposed this type of sexual relations for both husband and wife.[206]

Kapur's[207] study of working women at two stretches shows that they are not in favour of extramarital sexual coitus for married women under any circumstances: But after ten years, their views somewhat widened and they thought that a married woman would be justified, under certain' subjectively significant need satisfying conditions, to indulge in extramarital sex and might actually indulge in it.

In Kinsey report, a quarter of females experiencing extramarital coitus, had it in their forties. Between the ages of 26 and 50, one in six and one in ten, were having extramarital coitus. Middle aged and older women were given more to extramarital activity than younger ones.[208] Some females find extramarital coitus more satisfying than coitus with their husbands. Many women do it to acquire social status or, to oblige a respected friend. In some cases, it is reported as a retaliatory action against the spouse's extramarital activities. In some cases, it is for asserting one's independence and in some others, as a source of emotional satisfaction. In most cases of extramarital coitus, there were no difficulties involved as long as the spouse was ignorant of it. In some cases, husbands themselves encourage extramarital coitus of a wife, either with the genuine idea of ensuring satisfaction to their wives which they could not give themselves, or, from a desire to find an excuse for their own extramarital affairs. Some wives, with or without the husband's consent, indulge in such relations, just to earn money for living or for assisting her family financially. In most cases, wives of low paid husbands are of this type. In some cases, if both wife and husband happen to be employed and go for work on shift duties, or for one night or continuous night duties, there is every chance of the wife entering into illegal sexual relations with the neighbours or with others. Such women may do so for one night's thrill or just to earn. Reportedly there are number of such women who share bed with the VIPs at the guest houses or visit the sex wolves. There is also possibility to exploit his/her sexual urges when they happen to be alone in the family as, the other partner goes for night duty. Some neighbours may try to exploit the situation.

In some well-educated and well-placed groups, the husbands themselves encourage some kind of prostitution by their wives just to boost their position, income, prestige or status. Some husbands encourage their friends to have coitus with their wives as sadistic satisfaction. But cases of divorces and desertions proved that husbands sought divorce due to wives, extramarital coitus much more than wives seeking divorce on these grounds.[209] There are good number of families, where there is no familial harmony due to the inhibition or mistrust towards the partner's chastity, particularly the female partner. We can daily encounter the news items in the newspapers, magazines and journals, where wives or husbands are reported to be killed due to conjugal infidelity between the partners.

Some clever women of this class succeed in creating in their husbands a deep-rooted inferiority complex for their so-called sexual inadequacy by ridiculing or expressing disgust at his sexual performance after each coitus, subsequently taking advantage of it in extramarital coitus, which the husband might tolerate in view of his alleged inadequacy. This type of sexual infidelity is rampant among the educated and well-to-do families, where the wives built up with the comforts of her family always yearn for sexual happiness if the husband happens to be money-minded and always remains away from home due to the business trips and does not put much importance to sexual relations in the family.

Rampal[210] quoted a story happening at Dehli in which a foreign. educated man, later placed in extremely fortunate circumstances, was married to the daughter of a highly placed and extremely influential man. The bridegroom, who was sent abroad by the efforts of his father-in-law, came from a poor family and had not got over the inferiority before his in-laws' family. The girl took full advantage of her father's favours to her husband and began to have affairs with her paramore which came to the husband's notice. She became reckless day by day and started to invite her sexual partner to her house itself, in the presence of her husband. During summer, she used to go on a holiday sojourn at hilltop or other places with the lover, leaving the husband alone. In such a peculiar situation of one legal husband and other illicit lover that woman continued to live. Almost everyone knew in the circle of friends and relatives this peculiar type of relationship of hers. This case study clearly shows that the girl has neither inhibition in the matter nor any kind of regret, the husband has no anger or jealousy and the illegal sexual partner has in his - soul, no element of shame or humiliation. Each one of them has cordial relations with the other and they seem to stay together in her house though it appears to be most unnatural. Exception may not prove a rule, but it clearly indicates possibility. This case proves that some women can live happily with one husband and an extramarital sex partner, while there are husbands also who can compromise with this is society where male generally dominates.

Yet a very peculiar case was reported by Winn[211] in his book *Prostitutes* stating that some husbands in London allow Africans (Negros) to have sexual coitus with their wives just to satisfy their (wives') uncontrollable sexual impulses. That too, the coitus takes place at their husbands' presence. The husbands get satisfaction while their wives pick up with somebody at their residence in front of them. At the end they pay lump sum amount to the male used for the extramarital coitus. Thus, some husbands of London get their wives satisfied sexually and thereby they too feel happy. The author personally feels, this type of most peculiar and improper sexual coitus may not happen in India society.

Hence, it was intended to know the views of the working women of the present study, whether extramarital coitus should be allowed for male as well as the female.

As was expected (Table 30.16) the entire sample was found against female extramarital sexual relations. The data were also statistically cross-tabulated and found insignificant (Table 30.16; Chi-square = 4.4673; d.f. = 2; P. >0.05), as all the women (92.7%) were found against female extramarital coitus.

TABLE 30.16

Views on the Female Extramarital Sex

Subjects	*Yes*	*No*	*Total*	*Not applicable*	*No reply*	*Grand total*
Office staff	5 (10)	45 (90)	50. (100)	20.	30	100
Teaching staff	1 (1.6)	60 (98.4)	61 (100)	20	19	100
Medical staff	7 (10.6)	59 (89.4)	66 (100)	9	25	100
Total	13 (7.3)	164 (92.7)	177 (100)	49	74	300

Chi-square = 4.4673; d.f. = 2; P. > 0.05.

Note: Figures in the parentheses give the percentages.

Table 30.17 clearly shows that all the working women are opposed to the male extramarital coitus. The data were cross-tabulated statistically and found insignificant (Table 30.17; Chi-square = 2.9904; d.f. = 2; P. >0.05), as the greater percentage of the respondents were found against male extramarital coitus. Only 7.3 per cent (Table 30.16) of respondents approved of female extramarital coitus, whereas 24.5 per cent (Table- 3.17) of the same sample okayed extramarital relations for male. It is an unreasonable change in outlook among the women and this shows their servile attitude.

TABLE 30.17

Views on the Male Extramarital Sexual Coitus

Subjects	*Yes*	*No*	*Total*	*Not applicable*	*No reply*	*Grand Total*
Office staff	17 (24.6)	52 (75.4)	69 (100)	20	11	100
Teaching staff	11 (17.7)	51 (82.3)	62 (100)	20	18	100
Medical staff	19 (31.1)	42 (68.91	61 (100)	9	30	100
Total	47 (24.5)	145 (75.5)	192 (100)	49	59	300

Chi-square—2.9904; d.f. = = 2; P. -> 0.05.

Note: Figures in the parentheses give the percentages.

MARITAL HARMONY

Kapur observes that marital adjustment depends upon the conception of marriage and the standards of adjustment prevalent in a particular society at a particular time. Landis has used the term 'adjustment' to refer to the state of accommodation which is achieved in different areas where conflict may exist in marriage.[212] Locke and Williamson have defined marital adjustment as "the presence of such characteristics in a marriage as a tendency to avoid and resolve conflicts, a feeling of satisfaction with the marriage and with each other, the sharing of common interests and activities, and the fulfilling of the marital expectations of the husband dud wife".[213] Again, they have refined it as follows : "Marital adjustment is an adoption between husband and wife to the point where there is companionship, agreement on basic values, affectional intimacy, accommodation, euphoria, and certain other unidentical factors".[214] Kapur says, "Marital adjustment can be considered to be that state of accommodation in marital relationships and environment which is characterised by a tendency in spouses to resolve and solve conflicts and by an overall feeling of happiness and satisfaction with marriage and with one another".[215]

Various factors contribute to the marital harmony as well the marital failure. According to Stineft and Walters,[216] the following factors lead to marital success.

Pre-Marital Factors related to Marital Success

(a) Happiness out of parents' marriage, *(b)* personal happiness in childhood, *(c)* length of acquaintance, *(d)* age at marriage, *(e)* parental approval and *(f)* reason for marriage.

Post Marital Factors related to Marital Success

(a) Marital attitudes, *(b)* relationship with in-laws, *(c)* common interests, *(d)* cultural background, *(e)* desire for children, *(f)* relationship factor, (g) communication, *(h)* compatibility of role expectations, (*i*) personality characteristics, (*j*) occupation, (*k*) employment of the wife and (*l*) religious participation.

But, mainly two important factors affect the marital harmony— empathy and communication.

Empathy

It is an important factor because couples do not understand each other sincerely and there is lag between the attitudes and aspirations of the couples. If one of the couples does not know the other partner's needs and aspirations, he or she cannot fulfil that particular aspect. The essence of good marriage is respect for each other's personality combined with deep intimacy—physical, mental and spiritual which makes a serious love between man and woman, the most fructifying of all human experience.[212] Marriage counsellors Normal Lobsing and Maria Lasswell say that each partner wants the other to meet one or another need, and so the partners are mutually dependent. The more one partner depends upon the other for satisfaction of needs, the greater grows the dependency. Thus, according to this analysis, mental satisfaction depends largely on how well the partners can satisfy each other's needs. Satisfaction also depends upon opportunity that one partner presents to the other, to satisfy his and her own needs. It is important that each partner he made aware of the other's needs. Such analysis—finding out your needs and how much your partner needs them, or, how much you are frustrated by him or her in meeting your own—can yield a significant assessment of your marriage.[218] Successful marriages do not result if couples go into marriages with reservations. When the couple go through the marriage ceremony repeating the words "I take thee—for better, for worse, for richer, for poorer, in sickness and in health—until death... ", they are contracting for a lifetime of cooperation in all areas of living.[219]

In every marriage, the couples must harmonise their feelings about roles. A girl of potential accomplishment desirous of self-recognition, and the boy who feels that he must be the dominant, superior partner in the family, are likely to be an unhappy match, whether or not the wife ever holds a job outside the home. But an even-minded couple admiring each other's abilities and achievements and respecting each other, may have a chance of happiness, regardless of how they work out the division of labour and authority. Klemer and Smith cited one story: One young man was away from his new bride on a business trip. Each night he called his wife from the city where he was staying. One night she said to him, now lets try to save money, so that I can go with you on the next trip. Don't call me tomorrow night. All right'. The young man pleased with his wife's thrift and foresight, agreed, but when he called her two days later, she was angry. Why was she angry? He has not called her the night before.[220]

According to traditional norms of the society, a husband is expected to be the authoritarian figure whose will should always dominate in the domestic scene. The wife should regard him as her 'master' and should 'serve him faithfully'. The husband is superior, the wife is his subordinate.[221] A wife's roles and duties were prescribed specifically and she has to adhere to them strictly. In this connection, Indra says "She was to spend the whole day in considering matters entirely related to house and was particularly to be attentive to the needs and desires of her lord—always subordinating her own comforts to the convenience of his".[222] The wife's only concern in life was to see that all services needed by her husband were properly performed by her, the satisfaction of her husband being her sole joy in the life.[223] If the roles set out for the wife is not followed or violated, by her, the relationship invites tension and thereby troubles begin.

Communication

Communication problem between the couples is also a vital issue in fulfilling the marital harmony. Unless one partner speaks out his or her options and attitudes, the other cannot adjust to the feelings and desires of the former or latter. Say, for example, wife wants to gratify her sexual urge in certain pattern, of her choice, while the husband may be in the habit of enjoying it in some other pattern. If they do not communicate their respective ways of desiring sexual pleasure to each other, they cannot enjoy sexually. This sexual incompatibility between the couples may lead to marital frictions. The inhibited qualities and attitudes among the couples lead to incompatibility between them which may lead to marital failure.

Women who were once treated merely as sexual spittoons, receptacles for reproduction, are now insistent on matching her mate, not merely socially and intellectually, but sexually as well.[224] Traditional women used to obey all the commands of her husband, surrendering all her instincts and pleasures for the sake of her husband. But now, her modern counterpart wants to fulfil her yearning for pleasures at par with the husband. Sexual pleasure is no exception to this particularly educated women put more importance on sexual pleasure. Our data also support this, where in 57.8 per cent of the educated working women agreed that sexual gratification is must in married life. And again, 55.8 per cent of the same sample did not think that sexual happiness in the marriage is the only prerogative of the husband.

Blood, along with many other sociologists and economists, believe that money is the most common source of conflict between couples. It is the greatest source of friction, especially in the middle years of marriage.[225]

Age of couple at the time of marriage also plays an important factor in the marital frictions. If the age of the individual at the time of marriage is lower, higher the frictions in the married life and higher the age at marriage, lower the frictions in the married life. Higher the education of the couples, the higher the rate of marital harmony and lower the education of the couple, the lower the rate of harmony. Hence, data were obtained from the working women whether marital failure leads to divorce.

TABLE 30.18

Options on Divorce in the Event of Marital Disharmony

Subjects	*Yes*	*No*	*Total*	*Not applicable*	*No reply*	*Grand total*
Office staff	17 (26.9)	46 (73)	63 (100)	20	17	100
Teaching staff	47 (63.5)	27 (36.5)	74 (100)	20	6	100
Medical staff	72 (80.9)	17 (19.1)	89 (100)	9	2	100
Total	136 (60.2)	90 (39.8)	226 (100)	40	25	300

Chi-square = 45.2554: d.f. = 2; P. < 0.05.

Note: Figures in parentheses give the percentages.

As was expected, 60.2 per cent of the respondents agre that it is better to get divorced if the marital harmony is not achieved. The opinion given by the respondents markedly differ among the three categories of working women. The data (Table 30.18) show that the lower the position of the individual, lower the opinion that divorce is that remedy if marital harmony is not derived and the highter the positionof the individual, higher the opinion that divorce is the antidote for the maladjustment of marital harmony. The data were corss-tabulated statistically and found quite significant (Table 30.18, Chi-square = 45.2554; d.f. = 2; $P < 0.05$).

Considering all these things the subjects were asked to inform whether they were happy with their marital life. 96.7 per cent stated that they weere happy with their families and only 3.3 per cent responded in the negative.

RELATIONS WITH THE IN-LAWS

During the days of child marriages, the daughter-in-law would enter her in-laws' home in the subordinate role of a child. As an elder and head of the family, the mother-in-law had complete authority over her. In fact, it was the duty of mother-in-law to train the stranger, the ways and means of the household so as to enable her to take over the administration of the family in future. The daughter-in-law lost her individuality when she entered her husband's home and began to adopt herself to the traditions and customs of that family, both mundane and physical. She had to adjust herself to the mother-in-law, sister-in-law and other in-laws. She had to respect and obey all the elder members of their family, besides attending on the home duties such as cleaning, washing, drawing water, cooking, rearing children, tending cattle, nursing the sick and aged, etc.[226] But in the present society, the daughter-in-law is no more a child, particularly the educated working woman is not at all a child to obey and to be subservient to her mother-in-law. But she happens to be a woman of more self-confidence, knowledge and experience and views more sternly the mother-in-law's superiority. And these daughter-in-law are usually more educated than their mother-in-law. They have studied the theories of child-care, house-keeping and the behavioural patterns and they are now more aware of the society than the mother-in-law. All these pursuits deprive and nullify the mother-in-law's superior position, elderly personality and source of knowledge and tend to prone to the frictions between them, particularly if they happen to live in the same house. Now the young couples desire in more numbers to have a separate shelter when they are married.[227]

In such situations, the son is born between his inclinations towards calmer household and, on the other hand, duty and love towards his mother. When such situation arises, the relationship between mother and son weakens. It also enables the daughter-in-law to revolt successfully against in-laws' dominance, as her husband joins her frequently, with the passage of time.[228]

Most probably troubles come from mother-in-law's side. Having accustomed to work from childhood and with the completion of marital obligations, the old mother-in-law faces boring and unworthy situation in killing time. As is said, "An idle mind is a devil's workshop", the mother-in-law who roams here and there without any work, tries to find fault with the daughter-in-law who is fully involved in the family work. She tries to nag the daughter-in-law at every type of work. Thus, the troubles arise due to the unwelcome interference and nagging of the mother-in-law. The mother-in-law, who is authoritarian and meddlesome Lets displeased when the daughter-in-law is not good at cooking and obstructs her mother-in-law in having good relationship with the husband. Often, she treats her daughter-in-law as a captive, and in some cases, as a domestic servant. Fonseca quotes one of his subject's remarks: "I was hated, ill-treated, harassed, assaulted, beaten, etc. He (husband) was prohibited by his mother to stay with me". Again, his study states: "The mother-in-law dictated the husband in his marital rights and in one case she even refused to let the couple share the marriage bed. In some cases where the daughter-in-law is childless, she is reprimanded and ill-treated severely and in the case of daughter-in-law who has given birth to all female issues was beaten, scolded and nagged regularly. In some instances the daughter-in-law is even branded. The daughter-in-law here is an unhappy victim of ostracism, suspicion and superstition, and is considered at times as a harbinger of evil."[229]

The maiden sisters-in law also some times create frictions between mother-in-law and daughter-in- law. When daughter-in-law comes to new house, the brother may be generally very close to his wife in the tender years of marriage. At times, slight negligence may be meted to the sisters. In such instances, the sisters feel isolated and deprived of their brother's love and affection. As a result, they try to throw fault on the daughter-in-law. She is misunderstood to have captured and prevented their brother from keeping close contacts with his sisters. And sometimes, the nubile sisters-in-law, who are in their teens, happen to observe their brother and his wife enjoying sex and cannot resist their impulses and try to tease their sister-in-law as a sadistic sport. In this connection Fonseca rightly mentions that "sister-in-law shows mother-in-law syndrome. In her tendency she meddle to criticism, to backbite and gossip, to be dependent, to be possessive, to pamper and to intrude, the sister-in-law appears like a double doss of her demanding, escalating and meddle some mother-in-law whose reputation is, by now, well established.[230]

The widowed in-law sometimes creates troubles. As a reaction to her ill-fate or to keep her brother under her control, perhaps through an unconscious psychological reaction, often project her insecurity and want of love before her brother and is reluctant to relinquish control over his household and his personal affairs. She intends to mother him and he is likely to become a victim to her whims and wills.[231]

Sometimes the co-daughter-in-law also creates problems. When the other daughter-in-law is less-qualified or her husband is lower in position than the other, she often creates problems just out of jealously. Even the daughter-in-law herself may be responsible for family frictions. The educated daughter-in-law particularly educated working daughter-in-law, is very particular about mother-in-law's tiquctte and attitudes towards her. Having studied and economically being sound, she cannot oblige her uneducated and dependent mother-in-law, who can feel superior only as her husband's mother. As an educated person having familiarity with the society through her employment, she knows everything better than her mother-in-law. She refuses to be accommodative and (ends to be stubborn and disrespectable to her husband's parents and family members, turns quarrelsome and on several occasions resents the authority and dominance of the elders, particularly the nagging mother-in-law.

When she happens to be the only daughter of her parents, she cannot adjust to the new environment and sometimes is over dependent and seeks help and attention of her parents. In such circumstances, the disputes and discords between mother-in-law and the daughter-in-law will be more. In such complex occasions, it is difficult to pinpoint the exact cause, the person or the situation responsible for discord. In such cases, the embarrassed and puzzled husband is a silent spectator and is overwhelmed by two forces pulling towards opposite directions, namely, his household and wife. In that. the wife urges the husband to stay away from his parents and relatives. If not, in these crucial times, she stays with her husband and do the familial duties, but she wants her husband's assurance of kind treatment and a sympathetic dealing from the members of the house, and if this is not available, she could live separately with her husband. The cruelty meted out to her at times is so inhuman tbat she decides to live away from in-laws' family even deserting her huaband.[232]

Now the educated daughters-in-law are encouraging their husbands to part with their parents in :he initial years of marriage, to enjoy freely as a single family and to launch it. Even the parents of the bride also instigate their sons-in-law to put up separate family, so that they too can help the newly weds to put up a new family. Due to lack of empathy between the family members and failure to. pay the dowry of bride's parents, the relations between them exacerbate.

Fonseca quotes the remarks of his subjects: "In-law interference is an hindrance to happy life. Very often the poor husband does not know whether to take his wife's side or mother's. Often, human nature being what it is, the mother feels that she is deprived of her son's affection which could otherwise have been showred on her. This leads to dissatisfaction and quarrels". Again. Fouseca's respondent puts it as: "I have love for my mother who had to suffer in her old age. I will have equal love for my wife too. So, in the case of conflicts, there will not be good relations amongst us. But, as I am the only son, I will have to stay with my mother".[233]

But there are also families, which have had very good relations among the in-laws without any conflicts. In such families, the mother-in-law is considerate and sociable towards her in-laws. The present younger generation does not tolerate the domineering attitude of the elders. They like friendly and equalitarian attitude. If the elders behave accordingly, these daughter-in-laws are the most adjustable ones.

We sometimes find the daughter-in-law in rase with a pestle and with fatal results. Even mother-in-law also sometimes keeps away from home to escape the inhuman treatment meted to her by the daughter-in-law. Most probably the mother-in-law is troublesome and meddlesome, because she wants to retain the authority even after her children got married and she became grandma. Some daughters-in-law create problems for the mothers-in-law just by disobeying them. But the present educated daughters-in-law, particularly the working women, are clever in such situations. They try to prevent such things from the beginning itself, encouraging the husbands to put up separate dwelling. Being employed, they have to keep away from their homes.

Percentages of 116 Husbands and 160 Wives Reporting Various In-law Relationships, That were Causing Conflicts in Married life[235]

In-law	*Husband* %	*Wife* %	*Both* %
Mother-in-law	42	50	46.7
Sister-in-law	16	13	13.8
Father-in-law	15	11	12.3
Brother-in-law	3	6	5.0

But, such working women who have separate dwellings face difficulties to carry out the house work and office work without the help of the relatives in the family. Those who keep relatives with them may also have to face some adjustment problems. Yamini Gupta quotes her respondent's remarks: "We do all that we can, to make mother-in-law feel loved but, at the slightest provocation she threatens to go back to her home. She spoils and pampers our two children too much, but I am scared to say anything for this, she may take offence. How can we manage if she leaves? Both my husband and I have full time jobs and cannot afford to leave them (children) at any cost".[234]

It also clearly shows that the mother-in-law creates more trouble in the family than the other in-laws, because the woman-kind cannot adjust itself within its own sex. Various studies of Duval, Landis and Landis, Stinett and Walters state that the main person responsible in the in-law troubles is the meddlesome, interfering and nagging mother-in-law. Hence, it was intended to know the opinion of the working women of the present study whether they would approve of the mother-in-law's superiority or command over them.

TABLE 30.19

Do You Obey Mother-in-Law's Superiority or Command Over You

Subject	*Yes*	*No*	*Total*	*Not appli-cable*	*No reply*	*Grand total*
Office staff	59 (81.9)	13 (18)	72 (100)	20	8	100
Teaching staff	49 (67)	24 (32.9)	73 (100)	20	7	100
Medical staff	41 (51.3)	39 (48.7)	80 (100)	9	11	100
Total	149 (66.2)	76 (33.8)	225 (100)	49	26	300

Chi-square = 16.004; d.f. = 2; P. < 0.05.

Note: Figures in the parentheses give the percentages.

As the purview of the study is backward and poverty stricken area it was expected that these working women may not disobey the mother-in-law's superiority. As was hypothesised, the data correlate with the opinion, but the degree of obedience differs in each category of working women. The data were cross-tabulated and found significant (Table 30.19, Chi-square = 16.004; d.f. = 2; P. < 0.05) that the higher the position of the respondent, the lower she was prone to obey her mother-in-law and the lower the position of the respondent, the higher she was found prone to obey the superiority and command of the mother-in-law.

Regarding the other in-laws, 57 per cent of the working women like to be friendly and cordial towards them, on the other hand, 45.3 per cent of them like to revolt as a reaction to the in-law problems, whereas 54.7 per cent of them like to adjust. Again, those who are in the lower jobs are in favour of adjusting with the in-laws, than the women of higher jobs. It appears that the present day daughters-in-law are opposed to the authoritarian, irksome, inconsiderate and demanding type of mothers-in-law and the other quarrelsome. jealous, back nagging in-laws. They, want to be independent, self-domineering and do not like interference from the other members of the family.

FUNCTIONS OF THE COUPLE

Traditionally, wife is subordinate half of the couple. She has no right of decision making in any 'of the family matters and has no family responsibilities. She has to prepare food and nurture the infant and the rest of the duties remain vested in the hands of the husband. Her main duty is to attend the domestic tasks, to confine within the kitchen and to look after the home. Manu rightly calls her as the 'queen of the household'. Entertaining the visitors and guests, worshipping the family deity, etc., are the duties of wife. On the other hand, many duties and obligations—economic, social and educational—pertaining to the family, are on the shoulders of the husband.. He has to provide sustenance and shelter to his family members, education to the children and make them properly settle in life with marital and economic obligations fulfilled.

The moral demands of the married life, namely, faithfulness, loyalty, obedience and service, are made more on the wife than the husband. It is the wife who should be of one mind with the husband like a shadow, should be his companion in all good works and she always should remain cheerful and mindful of household duties.[236] *Yajur Veda* (14.2) says that wife should be like a sky and she should help achieving the desire, object, bravery and richness.[237]

TABLE 30.20

Being Earning Member do You Feel Against to Do the House Work

Subjects	*Yes*	*No*	*Total*	*No reply*	*Grand total*
Office staff	2 (6.5)	29 (93.5)	31 (100)	69	100
Teaching staff	12 (33.5)	24 (66.3)	36 (100)	64	100
Medical staff	70 (76.9)	21 (23)	91 (100)	9	100
Total	84 (53.2)	74 (46.8)	158 (100)	142	300

Chi-square = 53.4823; d.f. = 2; P. < 0.05.

Note: Figures in the parentheses give the percentages.

But times have changed with the advent of women's education and lucrative employment outside the house. Once the uneducated wife could not take any decision or take part in any family affairs, without the elders' blessings. Now the educated wife is very much involved in the family affairs, *i.e.*, taking decisions, advising the husband in times of need and educating the children, planning for the future, etc. Once the women were treated as chattels and were equalled with the scum. But the present-day educated women, particularly educated working woman, is very calculative and planning minded. As she is contributing to the family income, the husband treats her in a way different from that in the traditional society where he dominated everything in the family. He is in the dilemma whether to allow his educated and working wife's freedom and demands, or, to subjugate her. The changed situation has placed him in an ambiguous situation. But the modern woman is quite contrary to her counterpart, i.e., the traditional uneducated wife. She asserts her right as an earning member in all the matters affecting the family. Now-a-days the working wife does not consider all the family duties as her own responsibilities but of her husband as well. She demands her husband to share them. One of the respondents wanted the husband to do all the house works while the wife was working; they are not exclusively her duties, she asserted. She added that alone the wife was doing them when she was economically dependent on her husband. Hence, a question on this issue was asked to know the views of the working women of the present study.

As was expected, the data were found quite significant with the inference (Table 30.20; Chi-square = 53.4823; d.f. = 2; P. < 0.05) that the higher the position of the individual, the higher her resentment towards the household works and lower the position of the individual, the lower her opposition to do house works as an earning woman. A marked difference existed among the three categories of working women in their opinions against the house work. On the other hand, about half of the sample have abstained from answering. The author observes that they have deliberately avoided answering the question only to conceal their true feelings which causes embarrassment and also sometimes troubles. A teacher in a local girls school questioned the author during his data collection the wisdom of putting a question on family matters, as she felt it a taboo to divulge to others. She felt embarrassed to answer regarding the family affairs because some family frictions with the in-laws cannot be disclosed because it damages their family reputation, she pointed out.

TABLE 30.21

Views on the Proposed Sharing of Housework by the Husband

Subject	*Yes*	*No*	*Total*	*Not applicable*	*No reply*	*Grand total*
Office staff	35 (53.8)	30 (46.2)	65 (100)	20	15	100
Teaching staff	46 (63)	27 (36.9)	73 (100)	20	7	100
Medical staff	71 (85.5)	12 (14.5)	83 (100)	9	8	100
Total	152 (68.8)	69 (31.2)	221 (100)	49	30	300

Chi-square = 37.0116; d.f. = 2; p. < 0.05.

Note: Figures in the parentheses give the percentages.

Due to the double responsibility of house work and outdoor work, the working wives are at confusion whether to be assertive against the house work, as they are caught between the two. They are unable to adjust to the dual roles and they are constrained and compelled by the burden of work to feel that the husband also ought to share the household chores. The data (Table 30.21) signify that the higher the position of the individual, the more she feels that the husband should share the household duties and the lower the position of the individual, the less she feels that the housework should be shared by the husbands. This is due to economic potentiality of the wife. If the wife is of higher rank and earns more income for the family, she has every right and courage to ask her husband to share the housework, because, money is rated as of highest value in the society. Even the husband happily obeys the wife who is supporting the family with her salary.

TABLE 30.22

Do You Demand Your Husband to Share Household Work

Subject	*Yes*	*No*	*Total*	*Not applicable*	*No reply*	*Grand total*
Office staff	20 (31.3)	44 (68.7)	64 (100)	20	16	100
Teaching staff	24 (32.4)	50 (67.6)	74 (100)	20	6	100
Medical staff	49 (72).	19 (27.9)	68 (100)	9	23	100
Total	93 (45.1)	113 (54.9)	206 (100)	49	45	300

Chi-square = 29.7088; d.f. = 2; P. < 0.05.

Note: Figures in the parentheses give the percentages'

Indian women cannot press their husbands to share the house work as they were taught since childhood to be subservient to the male. And they are fed from infant stage with the misconception that they are the inferior sex and they have to obey the man as superior and dominant. Hence, the hypothesis signifies that the lower the position of the respondent, the higher she is opposed to demand of the husband to share housework even though she feels like, and the higher the position of the respondent, the higher she is prone to want her husband to share the housework. The data were also cross-tabulated statistically and found significant (Table 30.22; Chi-square = 29.7088 d.f. = 2; p. < 0.05). The husbands who have wives of high social status tend to give them equal importance in all aspects in the family as a respect to the social position held by their wives.

Working wives find less time to meet demands of the family, *i.e.*, serving the family members and other sundry work, because of her being away from the home for the day. Hence it was intended to ascertain the answer to the questions.

When it comes to the point of serving the family members, these working women, generally are in favour of it. If they fail to serve the family members due to their pre-occupation with the job, they will be nagged by the in-laws for every mistake and are liable to be called as women of loose character and made fuss out of it just to pull them to their track. To avoid these troubles and to be free from all these family feuds, these working women may be actuated to serve the family members though they are against it. They are in the whirl-wind of double role of housewife and the employee. 78.8 per cent of them are in favour of serving the family members. But the difference of the rate of willingness to serve also differs among the three categories of working women. The data were cross-tabulated statistically (Table 30.23 Chi-square = 27.1389; d.f. = 2 P. <:0.05) and found significant that the higher the position of the individual the lower her willingness and the lower the position of the respondent, the higher her willingness to serve the family members, though they are suffocated with the dual role.

TABLE 30.23

Views, as a Working Woman, on Serving the Family Members

Subject	*Yes*	*No*	*Total*	*Not appli-cable*	*No reply*	*Grand total*
Office staff	75 (93.8)	5 (6.2)	80 (100)	20	0	100
Teaching staff	66 (82.5)	14 (17.5)	80 (100)	20	0	100
Medical staff	52 (61.2)	33 (38.8)	85 (100)	9	6	100
Total	193 (78.8)	52 (21.2)	245 (100)	49	6	300

Chi-square = 27.1389; d.f. = 2; P. < 0.05.
Note: Figures in the parentheses give the percentages.

STRUCTURE OF THE FAMILY

At present only two types of families—joint and nuclear—are existing in the society. Extended family is now a rare phenomenon. Traditionally, joint family was considered to be a solace to the needy. Then, more labour was required for the cultivation. Aryans lived in joint families to fight with the non-Aryans. Then, joint family was felt to be the best form of family. Joint families were numerically more in villages. But these families have been affected by the impact of various forces 'stemming from economic progress and urbanisation. During this period, the technological age was her-aided in India. This upset the relatively stable traditional Indian society. Due to new types of economic and industrial organisation, wide communication, new kind of political organisation, and western type of education introduced in Indian schools, and new ideologies and way of life, large populations were brought to towns and cities.[238] With the industrialisation, the traditional family systems—joint and extended families—are breaking down.[239] Jyotirmayee Sarma observes that Bengali Hindu joint family usually consists of three generations of persons the male line with their wives and children living in same house, bowing common income and expenditure under the leadership one senior member.[240] We can observe from the *Mahabharata,* hostility between two sections of a large joint family—the Pandavas and Kouravas. Post-Vedic literature, scriptures and *Manusmriti* mention that agnatically joint and essentially patriarchal families prevailed in those periods)[241] Disorganisation of joint family took place due to industrialisation, mobility of the races from one place to another. Its pace speeded up with the employment of women in conventional and unconventional occupations.

The working women prefer their mates to be educated and lueratively employed. After their exposure to the urban life, these working families are not inclined to go to villages. Even the newly weds do not like to live in the joint families due to insufficient privacy to lead happy married life, at least during tender years. In addition, the bride's parents having offered dowry, do not like their sons-in-law to spend it on others. As a result, they encourage their sons-in-law to part away from their fathers' family. Particularly, today's brides encourage their husbands to have separate dwelling to enjoy sexually in the married life.

Even then, the joint families exist in the cities and towns due to the housing problem, particularly at populated areas. They neither afford to pay high rents, nor they have their own houses. Hence, joint family is the remedy for them to some extent. We can observe easily in the metropolitan centres and cosmopolitan places, more particularly at Bombay, Delhi, Calcutta, etc., the working families sheltered in the slums. They work in the air-conditioned offices facilitated with car, telephone, etc., but they live in the clustered joint families or in the slums. Having accustomed to city life, these working population do not go to village even after their retirement. Fifty per cent of rural as against 66 per cent and 75 per cent of urban and traditional groups respectively, suggested social security as the basis for their choice in favour of joint family living.[242]

Economic factors have probably been the main determinants for increasing family separations and the inability of the elders to lend support to the growing population has forced many sons to leave home to seek their livelihood in the growing cities.[243] The growing strength of husband-wife relationship in smaller family units definitely tends to weaken the affection between mother and son. It also. enables the daughter-in-law to revolt more successfully against her mother-in-law's control.[244] B.B. Shah, speaking about the 'youth and joint family', observed that the modern youths are fast changing and want to break away from the traditional ties of joint family.[245]

But, now the trend is towards the nuclear family. Leslie defines: "The term nuclear family refers simply to two adults of opposite sex, living in a socially approved sex relationship, and their own or adopted children. It is the family unit of mother, father and children".[246] Smart and Szwed observe: 'Father, mother and children make up a unit formed in all societies known as —the nuclear family. When this unit is called the conjugal family, it means that the husband-wife relationship is of primary importance. The nuclear family is established and regulated by marriage".[247]

After comparing 250 of the world's societies Murdock concluded that the nuclear family exists as a distinct and strongly functional group in every society and that it is universal because everywhere it performs four functions essential to human life—a sexual function, a reproductive function, an economic function and an educational or socialising function.[248] Many sociologists and anthropologists of the modern times have argued that the family type functionally adjustable to the modern, urban and industrial economy is the "nuclear family".[249] Hence, a question was put to our respondents to know their opinion on joint family;

Table 30.24 clearly shows the difference of opinion among the working women about the joint family. It appears that the higher the position of the respondent, the lower favourable her opinion towards the joint family and lower the position of the individual higher favourable in her opinion towards joint family. It was cross-tabulated statistically and found significant (Table 30.24, Chi-square = 8.1031 d.f. = 2: P. < 0.05).

TABLE 30.24

Opinion on the Joint Family

Subject	*Good*	*Bad*	*Total*	*No reply*	*Grand total*
Office staff	39 (63.9)	22 (36)	61 (100)	39	100
Teaching staff	31 (50.8)	30 (49.2)	61 (100)	39	100
Medical staff	30 (39.5)	46 (60.5)	76 (100)	24	100
Total	100 (50.5)	95 (49.5)	198 (100)	102	300

Chi-square = 8.1031; d.f. = 2; P. < 0.05.

Note: Figures in the parentheses give the percentages.

From Table 30.25 it appears clearly that the three categories of working women prefer nuclear family as the best form of family. The data were cross-tabulated statistically and found dependent (Table 30.25, Chi-square = 5.8018; d.f. 4; P. > 0.05), as all the staff members preferred nuclear family as the best choice.

It was also intended to know whether these working women are actually living in the families they like to live, for comparing them *per se*.

TABLE 30.25

Preferred Type of Family

Subject	*Nuclear family*	*Joint family*	*Extended family*	*Total reply*	*No total*	*Grand*
Office staff	48 (67.6)	21 (29.2)	2 (2.8)	71 (100)	29	100
Teaching staff	70 (82.4)	14 (16.5)	1 (1.6)	85 (100)	15	100
Medical staff	49 (69)	21 (19.6)	1 (1.4)	71 (100)	29	100
Total	167 (73.6)	56 (24.7)	4 (1.7)	227 (100)	73	300

Chi-square = 5.8018; d.f. = 4; P. > 0.05.

Note: Figures in the parentheses give the percentage.

Table 30.26 shows that the higher the position of the respondents, the more they are living in nuclear family and the lower the position of the respondents, the less they are living in nuclear family. The data, were cross-tabulated statistically and found significant (Table 30.26; Chi-square 25.4585; d.f. = 4; P. < 0.05). Those who prefer nuclear family (73.6%) are almost equally (73.4%) living in nuclear families. But, among the three categories of the working women the preferred family type differ from the actual family, because it may not be possible for all the women to have family of their choice due to the societal constraints.

TABLE 30.26

Actual Living Families

Subject	*Nuclear family*	*Joint family*	*Extended family*	*Total*	*No reply*	*Grand total*
Office staff	34 (58.6)	23 (39.7)	1 (1.7)	58 (100)	42	100
Teaching staff	47 (65.2)	22 (30.6)	3 (4.2)	72 (100)	28	100
Medical staff	73 (92.4)	6 (7.6)	0	79 (100)	21	100
Total	154 (73.4)	51 (24.4)	4 (1.9)	209 (100)	91	300

Chi-square = 25.4585; d.f. = 4; P. < 0.05.

Note: Figures in the parentheses give the percentages.

Nair[250] has compiled data of different studies with regard to broad family types.

Distribution of Percentage of Broad Family Types in Cities, Towns and Villages Reported in Different Studies

Location	*Broad family type*	
	Nuclear	*Non-nuclear*
Bombay	54.5	45.5
Delhi	48.9	51.5
Calcutta	57.8	42.2
Poona	69.0	31.0
Hubli	43.7	53.5
Mathura	61.0	39.0
Gokak town	28.7	71.3
Navasari town	53.3	46.7
Village near Navasari town	48.9	50.1
Other villages in Navasari taluk	38.8	62.2
Badapur	86.1	13.9

It clearly shows that more than halt of the families of the rural as well as the urban areas are nuclear, because the modern oriented people do not prefer to live in the clustered joint and extended families which has no privacy to socialite and always prevalent of troublesome atmosphere. They like free and easy type of family which promises calm atmosphere for studies as well as the. suitable environment, to nurture the children in the best manner.

Distribution of Family Type in The US Population, 1976[251]

Family type	*Distribution*
Nuclear family (with children)	44
Nuclear Dyad (without children)	15
Single parent	13
Reconstituted (remarried, nuclear presence of children)	15
Other traditional*	5
'Experimental' marriages and families	8

* E.P. Middle-aged or elderly couple, three generations, nuclear dyad, bilateral and extended kins.

Most of the present-day young couples prefer nuclear family dwelling. The working women of the present study also are in favour of nuclear family. In the cities like Bombay, Delhi and Calcutta, it is found that most of the joint families consist of working couples as they cannot afford to pay the exorbitant rents, whereas in the present study, the working couples may not feel it difficult to meet the rental expenditure because the respondents belong to semi-urban areas.

DECISION MAKING

Traditionally, woman is subordinate to man. She has to serve her husband and the family members. As river merges into sea losing its existence, she too loses her individuality as she is given marriage and she has to depend on her husband. She does not have any decision making power, even with regard to her own children's welfare.

But, the modern educated woman, on the other hand, wants her say to be implemented in the family affairs. Having studied economics, home education, psychology and nutrition, etc., the educated wife turns very particular when the question of policy making arises. She wants to involve herself in decisions, at least regarding children's education, shopping. budgeting and financial matters, especially the educated working woman' having supplemented the family with her salary is more particular and assertive with the family members to voice her say in the family affairs. Economic obligations play a very important role in the decision making in the family affairs. It is clear that an economic base is important in marriage, for, the higher the husband on the social scale, the greater is his authority in decision making in the family.[252] This is the case with the wife, too. Customarily, man was the earner and provider of the family, and the female was dependent on him. Hence, she was subordinate and could not make any individual decisions in the marital relationships. But, the educated working woman, on the other hand. earning for the family, has every right to take decisions with regard to her family for the future development. Moreover, she is educated and moderate, when compared with other in-laws.

The working wife plays very vital role in the policy making— decisions regarding children, purchases and living standards—than does the non-working wife. Holfman says that working wife makes fewer decisions about routine household matters than does the non-working wife and the husband of the working wife makes more. Blood and Wolfe observe that not only does the working wife have substantially more power than the non-working wife at all levels, but, that the more years the wife has worked since marriage, the more powers she has'. On the Other hand,. Middleton and Putney say that families in which wife works are significantly more patriarchal in decision than are those in which wife does not work.[253] The author of this research study strongly believes that the considerable years of working enhances the decision making power of the working wife. With the increase of married life span or after one or two children, *i.e.*, when the husband is in his forties, the decision making power of wife increases very rapidly. At that age, husband happily agrees with the wife's decision, and becomes completely dependent (affectionate dependent). Wives who have attained marital harmony in their lives tend to dominate husbands because these couples do not mind individuality. They feel they have merged their individualities. The husband who is in the forties (the age at which he cannot get a life partner again if he wants, in case he has troubles in the family), may automatically tends and attaches towards his wife more affectionally. In such a stage, the wife realises that she has captured her husband fully and that he cannot go beyond her control. She, from then onwards acts like older than him, advises and take decisions and sometimes commands him with affection and he too obliges as an affectionate partner but not as subordinate. But in the thirties he does not give much weight and cannot curb his male pride to his wife in any matters, having preconceived that he can get another woman if the wife does not obey him or otherwise. But, in the forties, he obeys his wife's affectionate dominance. In addition, if she is employed, she even dominates him more. If the wife takes and decision at bedtime, husband most probably obeys her decision. It is a general tendency or weakness of the male. At bed, she overtakes him and gets it done whatever her wishes might be. Women are also more calculative and very careful in taking decisions rather than the hasty decisions of the husbands. Constitutionally, women are of slow process and they take decisions very carefully and perfectly, as compared with males who are quick and imperfect.

On the similar lines, one interesting study by Robert Lewis reports that the wife's role in decision making reaches its zenith during the children's teenage years, and is at lowest ebb after giving birth and before the husband's retirement. This, of course, is consistent with the fact that the domestic role is crucial during the teenage years of children, while the husband's bread winning role in dominant after the child rearing role has been completed. It is, however, noteworthy that after delivery of an issue, wives want to make more decisions than they made during the preschool years, but could prefer to make fewer decisions than they made during the teenage years of off springs. A more equalitarian role in decisions, therefore, seems to be what they seek.[254]

The employed mothers take more decisions in matters of investment and budget control than the non-employed mothers. The other studies also reinforce that the mother who works tend to have more power in decision making in fiscal matters. This is one of the new emerging role systems among dual income families. It supports Wolfe's resource theory which states that power in the family is based upon the resources of a person as against the ideological theory which regards traditionally on the basis of power.[255]

TABLE 30.27

Do You Take Any Individual Decision in the Family Affairs?

Subject	*Yes*	*No*	*Total*	*Not applicable*	*No reply*	*Grand total*
Office staff	20 (26.7)	55 (73.3)	75 (100)	20	5	100
Teaching staff	28 (38.4)	45 (61.6)	73 (100)	20	7	100
Medical stuff	47 (61.8)	29 (38.2)	76 (100)	9	15	100
Total	95 (42.4)	129 (57.6)	224 (100)	49	27	300

Chi-square = 19.8521; d.f. = 2; P. < 0.05.

Figures in the parentheses give the percentages.

When wife is employed, the balance of power shifts. Studies of working women show that they often have more power than full housewives. Although non-working women tend to make everyday decisions about what to have for dinner, or whether to punish children, working women have more power in making decisions. The wife who brings home a pay packet, for example, has considerably more influence on decisions relating to spending the family income.[256]

The working women tend to take not only financial, budgetary, children's education and kitchen matters but also vital issues like their children's mate selection, fixation of dowry, future plans for the family's welfare, etc. Hence, the subjects were asked to answer the question (Table 30.27).

Most of the subjects of the present study are working to meet the gross economic necessity and to supplement the family income. But, yet, they are not fully sound in the financial position except a margin of subjects who have soundness in the family financial condition. Hence, it was expected that they may not be caking any individual decision in the family affairs. Only in the event of financial soundness, women can take individual decisions. Table 30.27 shows that 57 6 per cent of the total sample negated the query about taking decisions in the family matters. And 42.4 per cent of them seems to be taking decisions in the family matters. The data were cross-tabulated statistically and found significant (Table 30.27; Chi-square" = 19.8521; d.f. = 2: P. < 0.05). This implies that those in higher-ranks are in favour of taking decisions in the family affairs, while those in the lower ranks are not in favour of taking decisions in the family affairs.

The Main Decision-maker on Financial Matters in the Family[257]

	Men say %	*Women say* %
Husband	39	38
Wife	16	21
Both	42	39
Not sure	3	2

The working women say that they have no time to think after doing office and household work. Because they have to do all the house work—cooking, washing and cleaning, etc.—in the house and again have to attend the office work. How can they find time to think of decision making, they wondered. They say that they are somewhat relaxed only during Sundays and other holidays. They happily spend these days with children and prepare variety of dishes, etc. They cannot find time to think of decisions. That too, they are working for economic necessity and to supplement the family. Whereas, the medical staff, with high salaries and additional earnings with private practice, will be in financial soundness. They can employ servants for the housework. With the financial soundness one can have the opportunity to think with individualism while taking decisions in the family.

REFERENCES

1. Sur, A.K. *Sex and Marriage in India*, Allied Publishers, 1973, p. 2.
2. Kapur, Promilla, *Love, Marriage and Sex*. Vikas Publishing House, 1973.
3. Das, R.M., *Women in Manu and his Seven Commentaries*, Kanchana Publications, Varanasi, Agra, 1962, p. 38.
4. Das, R.M., *Women in Manu and his Seven Commentaries*, Kanchana Publications, Varanasi, Agra 1962.
5. Tribhuwan, Jyotsna. *Law relating to women in India*, Published by Mrs. Jyotsna Tribhuwan, Ahmedabad 1965, Mitra, S.M., *The Position of women in Indian life*, Neeraj Publishing House, 1881.

   Rao, Prakash, V.V. and Rao, Nandini V., *Marriage, the Family and Women in India*, Heritage Publishers, New Delhi, 1982.
6. Kapadia, K.M., *Marriage and Family in India*, Oxford University Press, 1966.

   Hate, C.A., *Changing Status of Women in Post-Independence India*, Allied Publishers, 1969.
7. Green, E.J., in association with Massay, R.F. and Massay, S.D., *Marriage, and Family: A Basic Self-instructional Guide*, McGraw Hill, 1977.
8. Kapadia, K.M., *Marriage and Family in India*, Oxford University Press, 1966, p. 232.
9. Kapur, Promilla, *Love, Marriage and Sex*, Vikas Publishing House, 1973, p. 85.
10. Kapadia, K.M., *Marriage and Family in India*, Oxford University Press, 1966.

    Ross, Aileen, D., *The Hindu Family in its Urban Setting*, Oxford University Press, 1961.
11. Streif, Grodon, F., *The Changing Family: Adoption and Diversity*, Addison Wiley Publishing Co., 1973, p. 14.
12. Burger, Ernest W., and Locke, Henry, J. and Thomas, Mary Margaret, *The Family*, Van Nostrand Reinhood Co., 1971.
13. Indra, M.A., *The Status of Women in Ancient India*, Minerva Bookshop, Anarkali, 1940.
14. Green, E.J. in association with Massay, R.F. and Massay, S.D., *Marriage and Family: A basic Self-Instructional Guide*, McGraw Hill, 1977.
15. Altekar, A.S., *The Position of Women in Hindu Civilisation: Prehistoric times to the present day*, Motilal Banarsidas, 1st ed., 1938.
16. Kapur, Promilla, *The Changing Status of Working Women in India*, Vikas Publishing House, 1974.
17. Balse, Mayah, *The Indian Female: Attitude Towards sex*, Chetana Publications, New Delhi, 1976.
18. Kapur, Promilla, *The Changing Status of Working Women in India*, Vikas Publishing House, 1974.
19. Thomas, P., *Indian Women Through the Ages*, Asia Publishing House. 1964, pp. 224-25.
20. *Ibid.*
21. Gandhi, *Women and Social Injustice*, Navjivan Publishing House, Ahmedabad, 1942, p. 42.
22. Jayal, Shakumbari, *The Status of Women in the Epics*, Motilal Banarsidas, 1966.
23. Indra, M.A., *The Status of Women in Ancient India*, Minerva Bookshop, Anarkali, 1940.
24. Apte, Usha M., *The Sacrament of Marriage in Hindu Society*, Ajantha Publication, Delhi, 1978.
25. Pradhu, Pandarinath H., *Hindu Social Organisation*, Popular Prakashan, Bombay, 1940.
26. *Ibid.*, p. 187.

27. Kapur, Promilla, *The Indian Family in the Change and Challenge of Seventies;* selected papers of the seminar organised by the life centre of The Indian Social Institute, New Delhi, Sterling Publishers, (P) Ltd., 1972.
28. Sur, A.K., *Sex and Marriage in India,* Allied Publishers, 1973.
29. Green, E.J., in association with Massay, R.F. and Massay, S.D., *Marriage and Family: A basic self-instructional guide;* McGraw Hill, 1977.
30. Kapur, Promilla, *Marriage and the Working Women in India,* Vikas Publishing House, 1970, p. 66.
31. Kapur, Promilla, *Marriage and the Working Women in India,* Vikas Publishing House, 1970.
32. *Ibid.*
33. Gupta, Giri Raj, *Family and Social Change in Modern India,* Vikas Publishing House, 1976.
34. Mehta, Rama, *The Western Educated Hindu Woman,* Asia Publishing House, 1970.
35. Klemer, Richard H., *Marriage and Family Relationships,* Harper and Row Publications, 1970, pp. 31-32.
36. Mervelle, Keith, *Marriage and Family Today,* Random House, New York, 1977.
37. Kapur, Promilla, *Love, Marriage and Sex,* Vikas Publishing House, 1973, p. 73.
38. Kapur, Promilla, *Love, Marriage and Sex,* Vikas Publishing House, 1973, p. 73.
39. Kadetotad, N.K., *Family and Marriage,* B.R. Publishing Corporation, Delhi, 1979.
40. Sinha, Raghuvir, *Family to Religion: A Theoretical Exposition of Basic Social Institutions,* National Publishing House, 1970.
41. *Ibid.*
42. Kapur, Promilla, *Changing Status of Working Women in India,* Vikas Publishing House, 1974, p. 13.
43. Kapur, Promilla, *Marriage and the Working Women in India,* Vikas Publishing House, 1970.
44. Das. R.M., *Women in Manu and his Seven Commentaries,* Kanchana Publications; Varanasi, Agra, 1962.
45. Shah, K.T., *Women's Role in Planned Economy,* Vora and Co., Publishers, Bombay, National Planning Committee Series, 1947.
46. Apte, Usha, M., *The Sacrament of Marriage in Hindu Society,* Ajantha Publication, Delhi, 1978.
47. Altekar, A.S., *The Position of Women in Hindu Civilisation: Prehistoric Times to the Present day,* Motilal Banarsidas, 1st ed., 1938.
48. *Ibid.*
49. Sinha, Raghuvir, A Critical Review of Family Research in India, *Indian Journal of Social Research,* Vol. XVII, No. 2, Aug 1981, p. 143.
50. Klemer, Richard, H., *Marriage and Family Relationships,* Harper and Row Publications, 1970, p. 57.
51. *Ibid.*
52. Klemer, Richard and Smith, Rebecca, F., *Klemer's Marriage and Family Relationships,* Harper and Raw Publishers, 1970.
53. Kaphart, William M., *The Family Society and the Individual,* Houghton Milfilin Co., Boston, 4th ed., 1974, p. 284.
54. Smart, Russel Cook and Szwed, Craig M., *Families: Developing Relationships,* McMillan, 1976.
55. *Ibid.*

56. *Ibid.*
57. Fisher, Weshley Andrew, *The Soviet Marriage and Market*, Praeger Publications, New Delhi, 1980.
58. Ross, Somerville M., *Introduction to Family Life and Sex Education*, Prentice Hall, 1972.
59. Kadetotad, N.K., *Family and Marriage*, B.R. Publishing Corporation, Delhi, 1979.
60. Kapur, Promilla, *Love, Marriage and Sex*, Vikas Publishing House, 1973.
61. *Ibid.*
62. Radhakrishnan, S., *Religion and Society*, George Allen and Unwin, 2nd ed., 1956.
63. Kapur, Promilla, *Love Marriage and Sex*, Vikas Publishing House, 1973.
64. Gore, M.S., *Urbanisation of Family Change*, Popular Prakashan, Bombay, 1968.
65. *Ibid.*
66. Altekar, A.S., *The Position of Women in Hindu Civilisation: Prehistoric Times to the Present Day*, Motilal Banarsidas, 1st ed., 1938.
67. Landis, Judson, T. and Landis, Mary G., *Building a Successful Marriage*, Prentice-Hall Inc., 4th ed., 1963.
68. Ross, Somerville, M., *Introduction to Family Life and Sex Education*, Prentice-Hall, 1972, p. 103.
69. Bouman, Henry A., *Marriage for Moderns*, McGraw Hill, 7th ed., 1974.
70. Rampal, S.N., *Indian Women and Sex*, Printon, New Delhi, 1978.
71. Hussain, Shaikh Akbar, *Marriage Customs among Muslims in India (A sociological study of the Shia* marriage customs), Sterling Publishers Ltd., New Delhi, 1976.
72. Kadetotad, N.K., *Family and Marriage*, B.R. Publishing Corporation, Delhi, 1979.
73. Hooja, S.L., *Dowry System in India: A Case Study*, Asian Press, 1969, p. 84.
74. *Ibid.*
75. *Andhra Jyothi*, 27 June, 1982, p. 111.
76. Burger, E.W. and Locke, H.J., and Thomas, M.M., Van Nostrand and Reinhood Co., 1971.
77. Hooja, S.L., *Dowry System in India: A Case Study*, Asia Press, 1969.
78. Altekar, A.S., *The Position of Women in Hindu Civilisation: Prehistoric times to the present day*, Motilal Banarsidas, 1st ed., 1938.
79. Apte, Usha, M., *The Sacrament of Marriage in Hindu Society*, Ajantha Publications (India), Delhi, 1978.
80. Hooja, S.L., *Dowry System in India: A Case Study*, Asia Press, 1969.
81. *Ibid.*
82. *Ibid.*
83. Mehta, 'Rama, *The Western Educated Hindu Women*, Asia Publishing House, 1970, p. 8.
84. Altekar, A.S., *The Position of Women in Hindu Civilisation: Prehistoric Times to the Present Day*, Motilal Banarsidas 1st ed., 1938.

    Sur, A.K. *Sex and Marriage in India*, Allied Publishers, 1973.
85. Ross, Aileen D., *The Hindu Family in its Urban Setting*, Oxford, University Press, 1961.
86. *Blitz*, August 21, 1982.
87. Dandiya, C.K., (ed.), *Women in Rajasthan;* University of Rajasthan, 1975.

88. Rao, Prakash V.V. and Rao, Nandini V., *Marriage, the Family and Women in India,* Heritage Publishers, New Delhi, 1982.
89. Sur, A.K., *Sex and Marriage in India,* Allied Publishers, 1973.
90. *Eenadu* (Telugu Daily), 29.4.1982.
91. Shirwadkar, Meena, *Image of Women in the Indo-Anglican Novel,* Sterling Publishers, 1979.
92. Thomas, P., *Indian Women Throughout the Ages,* Asia Publishing House, 1964, p. 231.
93. Thomas, P., *Indian Women Through the Ages,* Asia Publishing House, 1964.
94. Altekar, A.S., *The Position of Women in Hindu Civilisation: Prehistoric Times to the Present Days,* Motilal Banarsidas, 1st ed., 1938.
95. Sengupta, Nilakshi, *Evolution of Hindu Marriage,* Popular Prakashan, Bombay, 1965.
96. *Ibid.*
97. *Ibid.*
98. Mehta, Vatsala, *The Hindu Widow (with Special Reference to Gujarat),* Thesis submitted for the M.A. degree in Sociology, University of Bombay, 1956.
99. Alekar, A.S. , *The Position of Women in Hindu Civilisation: Prehistoric Times to the Present Days,* Motilal Banarsidas, 1st ed., 1938.
100. Unnithan, T.K.N., *Gandhi and Social Change,* Rawal Publications, Jaipur, 1979, p. 62.
101. Thomas, P., *Indian Women Through the Ages,* Asia Publishing House, 1964, p. 301.
102. Marris, Peter, *Widows and their Families,* Routledge and Kegan Paul, London, 1958.
103. Kapadia, K.M., *Marriage and Family in India,* Oxford University Press, 1966.
104. Mehta, *The Hindu Widow,* Thesis Submitted for M.A. degree in Sociology in Bombay University, 1956.
105. *Ibid.*
106. Altekar, A.S., *The Position of Women in Hindu Civilisation: Prehistoric times to the Present Days,* Motilal Banarsidas, 1st ed., 1938.
107. Sengupta, Nilakshi, *Revolution of Hindu Marriage,* Popular Prakashan, Bombay, 1965.
108. *Ibid.*
109. Altekar, A.S., *The Position of Women in Hindu Civilisation: Prehistoric Times to the Present Days,* Motilal Banarsidas, 1st ed., 1938.
110. *Ibid.*
111. *Ibid.*
112. *Ibid.*
113. Mehta, Vatsala, *The Hindu Widow,* Thesis submitted for M.A. degree in Sociology Bombay University, 1956.
114. *Ibid.*
115. *Ibid.*, pp. 99-100.
116. *Ibid.*
117. Altekar, A.S., *The position of Women in Hindu Civilisation: Prehistoric Times to the Present Days,* Motilal Banarsidas, 1st ed., 1938.
118. Jayal, Shakumbari, *The Status Women in the Epics,* Motilal Banarsidas, 1966.

119. Apte, Usha M., *The Sacrament of Marriage in Hindu Society,* Ajantha Publications (India), Delhi, 1978.

120. Poddar, Aravinda, *Marriage of Hindu Widows* (Iswarachandra Vidyasagar), K.P. Bagchi and Co., Calcutta, 1976.

121. Chakravarthy, Usha, *Condition of Bengali Women: Around the 2nd Half of the 19th Century,* Dr. (Mrs.) Usha Chakravarthy, 1963, pp. 19-20.

122. Mehta, Vatsala, *The Hindu Widow,* Thesis Submitted for M.A. degree in Sociology Bombay University, 1956, p. 61.

123. *Ibid.*

124. *Ibid.*, p. 461.

125. Kapadia, K.M., *Marriage and Family in India,* Oxford University Press, 1966.

126. Halem, Hynne Carol, *Divorce Reform,* The Free Press, New York, 1980.

127. *Ibid.*

128. Kapur, Promilla, *Marriage and the Working Women in India;* Vikas Publishing House, 1970, p. 84.

129. Kapur, Promilla, *Love, Marriage and Sex,* Vikas Publishing House, 1973.

130. Bowman, Henry, A., *Marriage for Moderns,* McGraw Hill, 7th ed., 1974.

131. Radhakrishnan, S., *Religion and Society;* George Allen and Unwin, 2nd ed., 1956, p. 181.

132. Goode, William J., *The Family,* Prentice-Hall India Ltd., 1965.

133. Altekar, A.S., *The Position of Women in Hindu Civilisation: Prehistoric Times to the Present Days,* Motilal Banarsidas, 1st ed., 1938, p. 85.

134. Das, S. *Purdah: The Status of Indian Women,* ESS Publications, New Delhi, 1979.

135. Jain, Devaki (ed.)., *Indian Women,* Publications Division, Ministry of Information and Broadcasting, Govt. of India, 1975.

136. Duberman, Lucile, *Marriage and Other Alternatives,* Preager Publishers, New York, 1974.

137. Altekar, A.S., *The Position of Women in Hindu Civilisation: Prehistoric Times to Present Days,* Motilal Banarsidas, 1st ed., 1938.

138. *Andhra Jyothi,* June 27, 1982.

139. Mervelle, Keith, *Marriage and Family Today,* Random House, New York, 1977, p. 19.

140. Carson, William F., *The Marriage Revolt,* Warner Laurie Ltd., London, 1915, p. 19.

141. Klemer, Richard H. and Smith, Rebeeca F., *Klemer's Marriage and Family Relationships,* Harper and Row Publications, 1970.

142. Leslie, Gerald. *The Family in Social Context,* Oxford University Press, 4th ed., 1979.

143. Gupta, Nirmal, *The Risk of Divorce in the American Society,* Vol. 9, Issue No. 203, May (first), *Woman's Era,* 1982.

144. Sethi, Raj Mohini, *Modernisation of Working Women in Developing Societies,* National Publishing House, 1976.

145. Reed, Angela, *The Challenge of Second Marriage,* Plume Press, Ward Lock, 1973.

Sethi, R., *Key to Happy Marriage,* Issue No. 202, April (second), *Woman's Era,* (1982).

146. Kapur, Promilla, *Marriage and the Working Women in India,* Vikas Publishing House, 1970.

147. Mehta, Rama, *Divorced Hindu Women,* Vikas Publishing House, 1975.

148. Smart, Russell Cook, and Szwed Craig, M., *Families; Developing Relationships,* Macmillan, 1976.
149. Duberman, Lucile, *Marriage and Other Alternatives,* Preager Publishers, New York, 1974.
150. Reed, Angela, *The challenge of Second Marriage,* Plume Press, Ward Lock, 1973.
151. Kapur, Promilla, *Love, Marriage and Sex,* Vikas Publishing House, 1973, p. 162.
152. *Ibid.,* p. 164.
153. *Ibid.,* p. 165.
154. *Ibid.*
155. *Ibid.,* p. 168.
156. *Ibid.,* p. 169.
157. Goode, William, J., *The Family,* Prentice-Hall India, 1965.
158. Kapadia, K.M., *Marriage and Family in India,* Oxford University Press, 1966, p. 140.
159. Sur, A.K., *Sex and Marriage in India,* Allied Publishers, 1973, p. 36.
160. *Ibid.,* p. 51.
161. Nair, P.T., *Marriage and Dowry in India,* Minerva (Associates) Publications, Calcutta, 1978.
162. *Ibid.,* p. 171.
163. *Ibid.,* p. 181.
164. *Ibid.*
165. Scanzoni, Letha and Scanzoni, John, *Men, Women and Change: A Sociology of Marriage and Family,* Mc Graw Hill, 1976, p. 58.
166. Terman, Lewis and Associates, *Psychological Factors in Marital Happiness,* New York, 1939.
167. Adams, B.N., *The family: A Sociological Interpretation,* Rand McNally College Publishing Co., 2nd ed., 1975.

     Bell, N.V. and Vogal, E.F., *A Modern Introduction to the Family,* The Free Press, 1968.

     Lesile, Gerald, *The Family in Social Context,* Oxford University Press, 4th ed., 1979.
168. *Ibid.*
169. Fullerton, G.P., *Survival in Marriage: Introduction to Family Interaction, Conflicts and Alternations,* Holt Rinehart and Winston, 1972.
170. Ardener, Shirley (ed.), *Defining Females: The Nature of Women in Society,* Croon Helm, London, 1978.
171. Marvelle, Keith, *Marriage and Family Today,* Random House, New York, 1977.
172. Smart, R.C. and Szwed, C.M., *Families, Developing Relationships,* Macmillan, 1976.
173. *Ibid.*
174. *Ibid.*
175. Thornes, Barbara and Collard, Jean, *Who Divorces,* Routledge Direct Editions, 1979.
176. Kapur, Promilla, *Love, Marriage and Sex,* Vikas Publishing House, 1973, p. 211.
177. *Ibid.,* p. 210.
178. *Ibid.,* p. 212.
179. *Ibid.*

180. *Ibid.*, p. 213.
181. Rampal, S.N., *Indian Women and Sex,* Printon, New Delhi, 1978.
182. *Ibid.*
183. Balse, Mayah, *The Indian Female: Attitude Towards Sex,* Chetna Publications, New Delhi, 1976.
184. Madan, T.N., *Family and Kinship: A Study of the Pandits of Rural Kashmir,* T.N., Madan, 1965.
185. Thornes, Barbara and Collard, Jean, *Who Divorces,* Routledge Direct Editions, 1979.
186. Fonseca, Mabel B., *Counselling for Marital Happiness,* Ph. D. Thesis submitted in the University of Bombay, 1965.
187. Kapadia, K.M., *Marriage and Family in India,* Oxford University Press, 1955, p. 159.
188. Klemer, Richard and Smith, Rebea F., *Klemer's Marriage and Family Relationships,* Harper and Row Publishers, 1970.
189. Bowman, Henry A., *Marriage for Moderns,* McGraw Hill, 7th ed., 1974.
190. Klemer, Richard and Smith, Rebea F., *Klemer's Marriage and Family Relationships,* Harper and Row Publishers, 1970.
191. Adams, Bert N., *The Family: A Sociological Interpretation,* Rand Mcwally College Publishing Co., 2nd ed. 1975.
192. Klemer, Richard, and Smith, Rebecca F., *Klemer's Marriage and Family Relationships,* Harper and Row Publishers, 1970.
193. Brenton, Myron, *The American male,* Coward-McCann, New York, 1966, p. 29.
194. Khanna, Girija and Varghese, Mariamma A., *Indian Women Today,* Vikas Publishing House, 1978.
195. *Ibid.*
196. *Ibid.*
197. Klemer, Richard H., *Marriage and Family Relationships,* Harper and Row Publisher, 1970.
198. Kapur, Promilla, *Marriage and the Working Women in India,* Vikas Publishing House, 1970.
199. Klemer, Richard H., *Marriage and Family Relationships,* Harper and Row Publishers, 1970.
200. *Ibid.*
201. Green, Ennet, *Personal relations: An Approach to Marriage and Family,* McGraw Hill Co., 1978.
202. Klemer, Richard H., *Marriage and Family Relationships,* Harper and Row Publishers, 1970.
203. *Ibid.*
204. Kapur, Promilla, *Marriage and the Working Women in India,* Vikas Publishing House, 1970.
205. Sur, A.K., *Sex and Marriage in India,* Allied Publishers, 1973.
206. Das, R.M., *Women in Manu and his Seven Commentaries,* Kanchana Publications, Varanasi, Agra, 1962.
207. Kapur, Promilla, *Marriage and the Working Women in India,* Vikas Publishing House, 1970.
208. Rampal, S.N., *Indian Women and Sex,* Printon, New Delhi, 1978.
209. *Ibid.*
210. *Ibid.*
211. Winn, Denise, *Prostitutes,* Hutchinson of London, 1974.
212. Kapur, Promilla, *The Marriage and the Working Women in the India,* Vikas Publishing House, 1970, p. 20.

213. *Ibid.*
214. *Ibid.*, p. 21.
215. *Ibid.*
216. Stinnet, Nick and Walters, James, *Relationships in Marriage and Family*, Macmillan Co. Inc., 1977, pp. 67-70.
217. Russel, Bertrand, *Marriage and Morals*, George Allen and Unwin, 3rd ed., London, 1976.
218. Green, Ennest, *Personal Relations: An Approach to Marriage and Family*, McGraw Hill Co., 1978.
219. Landis, J.T. and Landis, M.G., *Building a Successful Marriage*, Prentice-Hall Inc., 4th ed., 1963, pp. 4-5.
220. Klemer, Richard, and Smith, Rebecca, F., *Klemer's Marriage and Family Relationships*, Harper and Row Publishers, 1970, p. 51.
221. Kapur, Promilla, *Marriage and the Working Women in India*, Vikas Publishing House, 1970, p. 10.
222. *Ibid.*
223. Kapadia, K.M., *Marriage and Family in India*, Oxford University Press, 2nd ed., 1958.
224. *Eve's Weekly*, 6-12 February, 1982.
225. Blood, Robert, *Marriage*, Free Press, New York, 1962, p. 291.
226. Burger, James E.De (ed.), *Marriage Today: Problems, Issues and Alternations*, Schenseman Publishing Co., Inc., Massachusetts, 1977 and Rao, Prakash, V.V., Rao, Nandini V., *Marriage, the Family and Women in India*, Heritage Publications, New Delhi, 1982.
227. Burger, James E., De (ed.), *Marriage Today: Problems, Issues and Alternations*, Schenseman Publishing Co. Inc., Massachusetts, 1977.
228. *Ibid.*
229. Fonseca, Mabel B., *Counselling for Marital Happiness;* Ph.D. Thesis, submitted in the University of Bombay, 1965, pp. 124-25.
230. *Ibid.*
231. *Ibid.*
232. *Ibid.*, p. 120.
233. *Ibid.*, p. 260.
234. *Women's Era*, 1982.
235. Landish, J.T. and Landis, M.G., *Building a Successful Marriage*, Prentice-Hall Inc., 1973, p. 296.
236. Carson, William F., *The Marriage Revolt*, Warner Laurie Limited, London, 1915, p. 20.
237. Apte, Usha M., *The Sacrament of Marriage in Hindu Society*, Ajantha Publications (India), Delhi, 1978, p. 37.
238. Sahai, Indu. *Family Structure and the Partition*, Ethnographic and Folk Culture Society, U.P., Lucknow, 1973.
239. Goode, Williams J., *The Family*, Prentice-Hall, India, 1965.
240. Sinha, Raghuvir, *Social Change in Indian Society*, Concept Publishers, Delhi, 1978.
241. *Ibid.*
242. Gore, M.S., *Urbanisation and Family Change*, Popular Prakashan, Bombay, 1968, p. 122.
243. Ross, Aileen D., *The Hindu Family in its Urban Setting*, Oxford University Press, 1961.

244. *Ibid.*
245. Sinha, Raghuvir, *Social Change in Indian Society,* Concept Publishers, Delhi, 1978.
246. Leslie, Gerald, *The Family in Social Context.* Oxford University Press, 4th ed., 1979.
247. Smart, Russell Cook, and Szwed, Craig M., *Family: Developing Relationships,* Macmillan, 1976, p. 9.
248. Pasternek, Burton, *Introduction to Kinship and Social Organisation,* Prentice-Hall Inc., 1976.
249. *Ibid.*
250. Nair, P.T., *Marriage and Dowry in India,* Minerva (Associates) Publications, Calcutta, 1978.
251. Giele, Janet Zollinger, *Woman and the Future,* The Free Press, 1978. p. 153.
252. Drietzel, Hans Peter, *Family, Marriage and the Struggle of the Sexes,* Macmillan Co., New York, 1972, p. 133.
253. Adams, B.N., *The family: A Sociological Interpretation,* Rand McWally College Publishing Co., 2nd ed., 1975, p. 279.
254. *Ibid.,* p. 280.
255. Blood, Robert Jr. and Wolfe, D.M., *Husbands and Wives: The Dynamics of Married Living,* Free Press, New York, 1960.
256. Holfman, Lois and Nye, Ivan F., *Working Mothers,* Jossey-Bass, San Francisco, 1974.
257. Stinnet, Nick and Walters, James, *Relationship in Marriage and Family,* Macmillan Co. Inc., London, 1977, p. 169.

31

Working Women—Attitude Towards Education

There are evidences that the Vedic women were educated on par with the male. Some of the upper caste women were highly educated and they actively participated in intellectual discussions. One comes across references to woman sages like Gosha, Apala, Lopamudra, Indrani, Gargi and Maitreyi. During this period girls and boys were initiated into the Vedic studies by performing a rite of passage called *Upanayana* ceremony.[1] And epic period was also known for the ideal education of women. Gargi, the renowned philosopher of the time, launched an attack on Yagnavalkya, the newly assigned philosopher in the Kingdom of Janaka of Videha, with an admirable cool and confidence.[2] Epic heroines like Draupadi have been mentioned as 'Pandita' and 'Brahmavadina', Kunti's admonitions to the Pandavas show that she was well-instructed in mind and heart.[3]

But the post-Vedic period witnessed the deterioration of women's position. With the practice of child marriage, female education deteriorated considerably. Seclusion and *purdah* came to be widely practised and forms of proprietary and modesty have accelerated its pace.[4]

Literacy rates in India, 1891[8]

Province/Religion	*Male literacy*	*Female literacy*
1	2	3
Bengal	.108	.004
Bombay	.140	.010
Madras	.149	.010
Punjab	.074	.003
Hindus	.115	.004
Parsis	.777	.501
Christians	.347	.136
Indian as a whole	.110	.006

Again, during the 19th century, the importance of women's education gained ground due to the social reformers like Pandit Iśwara Chandra Vidyasagar, Raja Rammohan Ray, etc. Iswarchandra Vidyasagar alone was responsible for establishing about forty girls schools in Uttar Pradesh during the 19th century.[5] Towards the third quarter of the 19th century, there were 134 secondary schools and 1790 primary schools for girls in the whole country.[6] By the end of the 19th century, there were twelve colleges, forty-five training schools, 1467 secondary schools and 5628 primary schools for girls with a total enrolment of 4,44,700 students in the whole of India.[7] According to 1891 census the literacy rate in India was:

It shows that the female literacy rate was very low and particularly so among the Hindu women. During the 20th century, the pace of women's education gained momentum. Between 1910 and 1918, due to the gallant efforts of Gopala Krishna Gokhale, primary education was made compulsory in the country.

Girls under Instruction: 1921-22 to 1946-47[9]

Instruction	*1920-21*	*1931-32*	*1941-42*	*1946-47*
Primary school	10,87,131	19,44,070	3,123,643	2,715,230
Secondary school	124,954	196,170	410,333	442,503
Arts/Science colleges	1,207	20,685	11,778	16,284
Professional colleges	266	521	1,125	2,468
Professional schools	19,570	17,568	40,869	38,375

During 1946-47, there were 30 girls for every 100 boys.[10] According to 1971 Census, 39.5 per cent of males and 18.7 per cent of females were literates.[11] The Indian menfolk also realised the importance of female education. Industrial revolution, the employment of women outside the home, etc., have awakened the village people to educate their children, particularly females. Now the parents are encouraging their children for education in order to escape the dowry problem. The high cost of living and the inclination towards western life styles, the women are forced to have education. According to 1981 Census, 24.88 per cent was the female literacy rate in India. Rate of literacy in Andhra Pradesh is 29.94 per cent as per the 1981 Census. Out of this general figure, 39.13 per cent of males and 20.52 per cent of females were literates. Rayalaseema region (29.92%) stands second between andhra region (32.78%) and the Telangana (26.62%). With the Independence of India, equal rights were guaranteed for women through the legislation. Female education increased enormously. Even then, the female literacy is low when compared with male literacy. Of course, Indian literacy rate itself is low comparatively, than the developed countries. Due to the traditional dogma that a girl's place is in the home and she has nothing to learn from books, the female education could not be promoted.[12] Unemployment problem is also one of the causes for the low rate of female literacy in India.

However, in the post-Independence India, the importance of female education and its momentum gained precedence. It was realised that education for women is necessary to further the goals of democracy and equality. As a result, the portals of schools and colleges were thrown open to women, who, in ever-increasing numbers started availing themselves of the increased opportunities for education. When women strongly felt that they should not be confined to home, then they clamoured for formal education in order to be better equipped to share the responsibilities of the society by participating in all spheres of life equally with men.[13]

Hence, it is proposed here to study the level of change and attitude of the educated working women towards the education of women, for analysing the status of these women with the level of the positions they held.

TABLE 31.1

Aspiration for Higher Education

Subject	*Yes*	*No*	*Total*	*No reply*	*Grand total*
Office staff	45 (60)	30 (40)	75 (100)	25	100
Teaching staff	54 (61.3)	34 (38.7)	88 (100	12	100
Medical staff	43 (58.1)	31 (41.9)	74 (100)	26	100
Total	142 (59.9)	95 (40)	237 (100)	63	300

Chi-square = 0.1777: d.f. = 2; P. > 0.05.
Note: Figures in the parentheses give the percentages.

It is assumed that the higher professional respondents prefer higher level of education and lower professional respondents prefer lower level of education but the data do not correlate with the author's view. All the categories of working women aspired for higher education. The data were cross-tabulated statistically and not found significant (table 31.1; Chi-square = 0.1777; d.f. = 2; P. > 0.05), as all the working women were found inclined for higher education, whereas Sethi's[14] study of working women states that higher the level of modernity of an individual, greater the level of aspiration for further education.

Since the modern society lays more emphasis on equality of educational opportunities, it was assumed that the highly placed respondents will not discriminate between the education of men and women. In order to study as to what idea our respondents entertain about the extent of women's education in relation to man's a question was put, 'What is your idea about the extent of women's education'? It was hypothesised that the highly positioned respondents would prefer equal education for men and women and lower positioned women would opt for lower education for women than men.

TABLE 31.2

Attitude on the Extent of Women's Education

Subject	*More than men*	*As much as*	*Less than men*	*No limit*	*Total*	*No reply*	*Grand total*
Office staff	5 (5.8)	73 (84.9)	4 (4.6)	4 (4.6)	86 (100)	14	100
Teaching staff	3 (3.5)	60 (70.5)	13 (15.3)	9 (10.5)	85 (100)	15	100
Medical staff	2 (2.3)	13 (14.8)	4 (4.5)	69 (78.4)	88 (100)	12	100
Total	10 (3.9)	146 (56.4)	21 (8)	82 (31.7)	259 (100)	41	300

Chi-square = 144.51; d.f. = 6. P. < 0.05.

Note: Figures in the parentheses give the percentages.

Table 31.2 is not significant in that 84.9 per cent of office staff and 70.5 per cent of teaching staff are in favour of education on par with men and 78.4 per cent of medical women opine that there is no limit for acquiring education. It appears that all the working women of the sample are in favour of education on par with men. Sethi's[15] study does not tally with our data. According to her, higher the modernity of the individual, the more favourable is the opinion towards equal or more education for women as compared to men, and lower the level of modernity of an individual, the more unfavourable will be the opinion on equal education for men and women.

So far we discussed the respondents' opinion on the aspiration and extent of women's education on par with men. All the working women are aspiring for higher education and all the respondents wanted equal education with men. Hence, it is decided to study the preferred level of education.

The three categories of working women differed from one another while preferring minimum education for women. 35 per cent of office staff are not in favour of any education and 40.4 per cent of teaching staff preferring graduation as a minimum education for women and the medical staff opine that no limit should be there for education and women can study whatever and whichever course they like to study without reservation. Hence, we can assume that the lower the position of the respondent, the lower her preference for education and higher the position of the respondent, the higher her preference of education for women. The data were also significant statistically (Table 31.3; Chi-square = 108.0827; d.f. = 14; P. < 0.05).

TABLE 31.3

Preferred Level of Education

Subject	*PG*	*Graduate*	*Inter*	*School final*	*Professional*	*Technical*	*No limit/ No discrimination*	*None*	*Total*	*No reply*	*Grand total*
1	2	3	4	5	6	7	8	9	10	11	12
Office staff	8 (8)	38 (38)	8 (8)	1 (1)	2 (2)	2 (2)	6 (6)	35 (35)	100 (100)	0	100
Teaching staff	8 (8)	40 (40.4)	14 (14.1)	3 (3)	2 (2)	0 (0)	24 (24.2)	8 (8)	99 (100)	1	100
Medical staff	5 (5.1)	19 (19.6)	7 (7.2)	5 (5.1)	10 (10.3)	5 (5.1)	46 (47.4)	0	97 (100)	3	100
Total	21 (7)	97 (32.7)	29 (9.8)	9 (3)	14 (4.7)	7 (2.3)	76 (25.6)	43 (14.5)	296 (100)	4	300

Chi-square = 108.0827; d.f. = 14; P. < 0.05.

Note: Figures in the parentheses give the percentages.

TABLE 31.4

Attitude Towards Co-Education

Subject	*Favourable*	*Indifferent*	*Unfavourable*	*Total*	*No reply*	*Grand total*
Office staff	88 (92.6)	2 (2.1)	5 (5.3)	95 (100)	5	100
Teaching staff	79 (91.9)	3 (3.5)	4 (4.6)	86 (100)	14	100
Medical staff	69 (71.9)	10 (10.4)	17 (17.7)	96 (100)	4	100
Total	236 (85.2)	15 (5.4)	26 (9.4)	277 (100)	23	300

Chi-square = 20.8687; d.f. = 4; P. < 0.05.

Note: Figures in the parentheses give the percentages.

When the women are aspiring for equality with men in all respects, it is pertinent to study their attitude towards men. Hence, it was decided to know the working women's attitude towards co-education.

It is hypothesised, that higher the position of respondent, the higher her preference for co-education and lower the position of the respondent, the lower her preference for co-education. But this does not tally with the data, as all the working women were found favourable towards co-education. Sethi's[16] study states that the highly modern Indian working women have negative opinion towards co-education.

NOTES

1. Rao, Prakash, V.V. and Rao, Nandini, V., *Marriage, the Family and Women in India,* Heritage Publishers, New Delhi, 1982.
2. Altekar, A.S., *The Position of Women in Hindu Civilisation: Prehistoric times to the present days,* Motilal Banarsidas, 1st ed., 1938.
3. Jayal, Shakumbari, *The Status of Women in the Epics,* Motilal Banarsidas, 1966.
4. Kar, Meena Shirwardkar, *Image of Women in the Indo-Anglican Novel,* Sterling Publishers, 1979.
5. Mukharji, S.N., *History of Education in India (Modern period),* Acharya Book Depot, Baroda, 1966.
6. Soloman, Savithri, *A Study of Educated Ladies in Greater Bombay, in respect of utilisation of their talents in various walks of life on honorary basis,* (unpublished thesis submitted by Prof. Savithri Soloman, University of Bombay, 1978).
7. *Ibid.*
8. *Ibid.*
9. Mukharji, S.N., *History of Education in India (Modern period),* Acharya Book Depot, Baroda, 1966, p. 232.
10. Soloman, Savithri, *A Study of Educated Ladies in Greater Bombay, in respect of utilisation of their talents in various walks of life on honorary basis* (unpublished thesis submitted by Prof. Savithri Soloman, University, of Bombay, 1978).
11. *Ibid.*
12. Sethi, Raj Mohini, *Modernisation of Working Women in Developing Societies,* National Publishing House, 1976.
13. *Ibid.*
14. *Ibid.*
15. *Ibid.*
16. *Ibid.*

32

Women Solving Job and Family Conflicts

We love working and we love parenting. We feel have the best of both worlds and we want to enjoy them both to the fullest. But this is not always easy—or possible. The demands of one do not always dovetail with the other.

Working mothers often find it difficult to apply themselves to their careers with dedication and enthusiasm unless their number-one concern has been satisfactorily resolved: the problem of adequate care for their children while they are away at work. Today, over seven million preschool children are being cared for by others while their mothers work, and millions of older children require some sort of after-school supervision. It is this area of family/job conflict that we will explore first.

There is a basic amount of loving adult time that each child needs during his formative years if he is to grow up to be a competent, secure individual. There are no shortcuts. One individual alone doesn't have to fill this need, nor is the magic number two. It doesn't have to be just Mom and Dad and relatives. But *someone* has to provide consistent, stable, loving nurture.

After reading various case studies and interviewing a wide variety of parents who both work, we have come to the conclusion that families who are most successful at juggling parenting and outside-job responsibilities fall into three categories. They can be characterised by the following formulas that add up to 1—the number that represents the total amount of time necessary to meet the children's needs.

½ + ½ = 1. In this arrangement Mom and Dad share parenting equally. Both have full-time jobs, both limit those jobs so they do not impose on the family any more than necessary, and both take active responsibility for child-care and housekeeping matters. Additional help is hired when needed. Jan and we probably fall within this category.

3/4 + ¼ = 1. In this category, one parent takes, primary responsibility of the children and the home and only works part-time, or at a fairy flexible job that is close to home. The other parent has an extremely demanding job that requires long or irregular hours away from home. Babysitting services are used when necessary, and chores like weekly housecleaning are often hired out.

My friend Lorraine and her husband have this type of relationship. She is the chief prediatrician in an intensive-care nursery of a large hospital. The job is demanding, challenging, and time consuming. Her husband, an engineer, quit his demanding job with a large company to start his own "home-based" business so he could have flexible hours to get their four boys off to school, chauffeur them to their various lessons after school, and generally keep the family together during these critical child-rearing years. Now, instead of having to consult two work schedules to plan vacations and free weekends, they only need to consult Mom's calendar and they are free to take off. And having Mom home is a privilege—the kids enjoy surprising her by occasionally serving her breakfast in bed. Everyone has benefited. Her husband is even completing the building of a home computer—something he has wanted to do for years but never had time for.

This somewhat unequal method of sharing child-care responsibilities works well as long as each parent is happy and respects the other.

¼ + ¼ + ½ = 1. In this category, Mom and Dad rely on someone else to meet the majority of their children's needs. Usually both parents work at extremely demanding jobs that require long and irregular hours. A live-in relative or maid handles all the housekeeping and takes over the major responsibility for the children. When both parents have demanding jobs, however, it is impossible to have the same parental impact on the children. Successful child rearing can occur in these busy families if someone is available to love and care for the children, *and* if Mom and Dad let their children know that despite the demands of their jobs they love the children supremely and will spend quality time with them when they are all together. This usually means short surprise times during the week and on weekends, and fairly frequent vacations—at least more than two weeks in the summer. Some parents who fall into this category choose either not to work or to lighten their loads during the summer in order to spend more time with the children when they have summer vacation time. Scheduling time to be with the children is especially important for these families.

It is possible to be a successful parent and hold a demanding full-time job, but only if you can afford to pay for some of the services necessary to keep the family and home intact. Because single parents do not have the built-in support system of a spouse to help meet the time needs of their children, they usually opt for a less demanding job in order to provide the necessary flexibility to be home when they are really needed.

Actually, a single mother could fit into any one of these three categories, depending upon how much outside support is available or financially viable. Single mothers in the ½ + ½ category generally share the child-rearing responsibility equally with another working mother who has a slightly different schedule, or with a babysitter. Their jobs are usually regular and do not require too many after-hour appointments, overtime, or travel.

The 3/4 + ¼ category is the preferred arrangement of most single mothers who work only part-time or seasonally. Thy take on the major child-care and home responsibilities and rely on others for only a small portion of the time.

Single mothers who have highly demanding jobs must rely on someone else to take the major responsibility for child care—at least for preschool children. They may opt for a reversal of the $^3/_4$ + ¼ arrangement, utilising one additional full-time or live-in person to meet most of the household's needs. Or they may choose the ½ + ¼ + ¼ arrangement, relying on several people to share some of the chores, but giving the major responsibility for the children to one full-time or live-in housekeeper.

Taking *sole* responsibility for parenting (child care) while holding down a full-time job is like trying to light a candle with just half a match—it's a lot easier to get your fingers burned. And the chances of lighting the candle properly are just not as good. Sometimes it works—if it's a fairly easy candle to light or if the candle is older and has been lit before—but sometimes it does not. Some candles are just harder to light than others and require more time, and it's the same way with children. Some children are more difficult to rear and they simply require more time from one or a variety of caregivers.

Who Will Care for My Child?

The problem of finding someone to share the child-care responsibility must be faced and solved by each working mother. Sooner or later, you too may find yourself in a situation similar to the following:

You just got a new job and your boss has made it clear that you are to be there on time. Aunt Sue was to arrive at your house thirty minutes ago to take care of the baby. There is no one else around to babysit. If you don't leave for work right now, you'll be late. What should you do?

Government officials are visiting your office today. You've just begun introducing them to the operation when you receive a message that your child is very ill and must be taken home from school immediately. What should you do?

You love your job. It's a dream come true, but your third babysitter has just quit and you can't find adequate care for your children. What should you do?

In order to keep your job, you must take a class two nights a week. You've searched, but you can't find anyone to take care of the kids. What should you do?

You don't want to sacrifice your child's well-being for personal gain and satisfaction or even for financial stability. You want both. But the nitty-gritty reality is that *somebody has to take care of the children.* If you can't do it, how can you find someone who will give them the time, love and discipline they need to become competent individuals?

Finding the type of child care that is right for you and for your child is a difficult, time-consuming task. But unless you are completely satisfied with the substitute care you find for your child, you will never eliminate those nagging guilt feelings.

Available Child Care

The first decision you must make is what type of child care you prefer for your child. Here are some of the possibilities, with pros and cons for each.

Live-in maid or relative. Such a person can range from a full-time governess-housekeeper to a graduate student who will gladly exchange room and board to be a big sister or brother to your child. (Graduate students are particularly good for after-school and evening care but their class schedule must match your own needs).

A live-in helper is always there and available. This is especially convenient for working mothers with irregular and/or long hours. A live-in helper usually takes on more household responsibilities than a babysitter and provides the sort of stable and consistent care from one person that is especially good for small children. If child care is needed on a long-term basis, a live-in helper may become part of the family, making parents' departures less traumatic.

On the negative side, it may be difficult to find someone who shares your child-rearing philosophy and will get long with the children. If this person is handling house-work too, the children may not, in the long run, receive as much attention as the would from a person hired only to care for them. This care is expensive and one must have an extra room for living quarters. Finally, because a live-in helper is always available, parents may be tempted to spend longer hours away from their children and take short vacations without the children, instead of giving the children as much parental time and attention as possible.

Babysitter in your house. Home care is excellent for younger children who find it difficult to adjust to new situations. Babysitters are usually paid to watch, play with, and care for the children, should receive their sitter's full attention. With this arrangement working mothers can avoid the hassle of preparing diapers, bottles, toys, sweaters, changes of clothing, and everything else the child might need while he is away from home.

Regular daytime care—when teenagers aren't available—is more expensive than taking the child to someone else's house. People enjoy being in their own homes, so it is not always easy to find a person who is willing to come to your home. A high turnover rate can also be a problem since these individuals often find easier and more lucrative jobs elsewhere.

Family day-care "mothers." These are individuals who are licensed to care for a certain number of children in their own homes. Licensing ensures that certain safety and health standards are met. This type of care is easy to locate since a list of licensed homes is available through the licensing agency, which is usually the social-welfare office in your area. The children are in a home environment and usually have other children to interact with.

Problems may arise because family day-care "mothers" sometimes have very little if any, training for the job. Such care is not always stable and dependable. When a family day-care "mother" becomes ill, wants a day off, goes on vacation, there is no one else to care for your child. Also, in many states, if the "mother" becomes pregnant, regulations require a reduction in the number of children she can look after—and this could affect your child. Additionally, you have no control over the way a family daycare "mother" spends her day. She may do a beautiful job or she may spend most of her time watching television or reading magazines.

Nonlicensed home. Taking your child to a friend's or relative's home can be an excellent solution if the caregiver loves and disciplines the child as her own, and provides appropriate learning opportunities. Other children are often available for your child to interact with, and this type of care is usually flexible, which is important for mothers who work irregular hours.

You do not, however, have the assurance that health and safety factors are met if the home is not licensed. Care is not always available. Illness or other commitments may intervene, so you must have a back-up service. Training is not required, so the quality of the care may not meet your standards.

Exchanging child-care services. If mothers exchange service equally, no cost is involved. Because you are caring for each other's children, it is easier to discuss your philosophy and techniques of child rearing and compare notes on the children's behaviour. Depending on the caregiver, this arrangement might offer more flexibility.

Possible problems with this exchange include the following: One mother would abuse the privilege. It may be more difficult to make changes if you are not satisfied, because children other than your own are also involved. It may be difficult for your child to share you with other children. This is especially true with young children. Your child must spend twice as much time with other children as he would have to if you paid for child-care services. After a busy day at work, you may not feel like taking care of someone else's children. A back up service is needed in case the caregiver is ill or has a conflicting appointment.

Group care for children. Group care can be lumped into three broad categories: nursery schools (which are usually partial-day programmes); preschools (partial-day programmes which are usually connected to a school programme and may be more academically oriented than a nursery school); and child-care or day-care centers (full-day care and sometimes night care and after-school care).

On the plus side, care is always available on a regular schedule—which is great if the hours coincide with your work hours. Teachers have training and/or experience, and have no other responsibilities than to watch and teach the children. A wide variety of toys, play equipment, and learning activities are usually available. There is a planned curriculum and a regular schedule of activities. Centers must be licensed, so they should meet safety and health requirements. Government-funded programmes usually have a graduated fee scale to make such care available for everyone. If you care a single mother with a low salary, or are returning to school, this care might be very reasonable for you. Many centers have additional services, such as counseling, extended day care for older children, or bus service.

The problems are that group care may be more expensive than babysitting care; the centre may not be open when you need its service; the center may not take children on a flexible schedule if your job is irregular. Most centers are licensed to take children in a particular age group—usually two through six years of age. They may require the child to be toilet trained. Infant and toddler programmes are available in some communities, but without government funding they are very expensive. Keep in mind that the programme is only as good as the direetor and teachers. Some children (usually the younger ones) find it difficult to adjust to a group experience and may be happier in a home situation with fewer children. The larger the child care center, the more institutionalised the programme. It's difficult to find a "homey" atmosphere in a large center.

For mothers who are students or who are working part-time and only need child care for a small portion of the day, or during odd and irregular hours, the following types of arrangements might be beneficial.

Babysitting pool. Mothers sign up to take care of other children in exchange for irregular or part-time child care of their own. This is similar to exchanging child-care services, but it is handled on a larger scale. There is no cost involved if you exchange child care evenly. A large number of caregivers are available. This type of care can function as emergency back-up when you need extra services or your regular sitter is not available.

You must be willing to babysit other children. Since there are a large number of caregivers, your child may not have the consistency of one caregiver. Such care can be used only in limited ways, and it is not very practical for mothers who are working more than part-time. Also, someone has to keep the records. The bigger the babysitting pool, the more complicated the record keeping becomes.

Home play group. Usually four or five mothers with similar-aged children organise a morning or afternoon programme where all the children rotate to a different home each day or each week. The mother in charge becomes the teacher and plans learning activities for the children while the other mothers can enjoy a few hours of "free" time. Even though the children may rotate to different homes, the schedule of activities is usually similar. There is no extra charge involved in this type of care because each mother contributes the necessary supplies and time. The children are in a home setting with familiar caregivers. The children receive a nursery-school-type programme without cost to you. Mothers are involved in the child care, planning together what type of programme they want for their children, and are able to establish a group with friends who have similar interests and child-care problems.

Possible drawbacks are that a mother's working hours must coincide with the hours when care is available. The child is at a different house each day or each week depending on the schedule. It may be difficult to find a group of mothers who want to establish this type of care system and who hold similar child-rearing philosophies. The system breaks down when someone is sick, unless others are willing to substitute.

Parent cooperative nursery schools and day-care programmes. These programmes are owned and operated by the parents who participate. Most programmes are partial-day-programmes, or full-day programmes that cater to student families on college campuses. Participating parents must be involved a designated number of days in the teaching programme or they must volunteer to fulfill other needed services. A minimum fee is usually set to hire one teacher-director to keep the programme running smoothly.

The child has a nursery-school-type experience that is fairly inexpensive, as well as a consistent environment. The parents, fathers as well as mothers, are involved in the child's programme. The teacher is trained and will usually have in-service training sessions for the parents. Most parents find that a close community spirit develops in programmes where parents are working together the same goal—quality care for their children. They make good and lasting friendships.

In order to benefit from this type of care, you must have time to donate to the programme. The requirements for in-service training and the attendance at various organisational meetings may be too time consuming. Ultimately, the programme is only as good as the hired teacher-director, and even this can be undermined by irresponsible parents.

Qualifications of the Caregiver

After choosing the type of child-care service that best meets your needs, you must decide what type of person you want to influence and teach your child when you are away. The type of care you select is only as good as the person who will actually be caring for your child, whether it be your mother-in-law, a maid, a family day-care "Mother," a babysitter, or a teacher. For example, live-in-help may be ideal for your schedule, but if the only person you are bale to find is not the kind of person you want your child to grow up to be, then you should look at alternative types of care.

Parents continue to have the major influence on a child's life, but this influence may not be strong enough to combat the negative influence of a caregiver. The more time a child spends with another adult, the more he learns from that adult, the more he models that adult, and the more his life is influenced by that adult. This is especially true during the early years, but must be carefully considered even during the teenage years.

The effect on the child's self-concept must also be considered. Feelings of self-worth are influenced by the attitudes of those around us. Therefore, if a caregiver doesn't like your child (or doesn't like children in general), this attitude will be reflected in your child's feelings about himself. If the caregiver disciplines a child in a way that generates feelings of guilt or shame, this diminishes a child's self-concept. If the caregiver doesn't meet the child's need for love and attention, a young child often feels that he or she is at fault. This feeling can spread and the child may even erroneously reason that he is to blame for his parents' absence. He may believe that they leave him because they don't like him or enjoy being with him. Thus, his self-concept is further diminished.

Your success as a working mother is partially determined by your ability to find the "right" person to care for your could. As you make your selection, consider these essential qualifications of the ideal caregiver.

The caregiver should be supportive of the parents. Leslie, the mother of three small boys, was going through a very difficult period in her life. She was forced to keep a demanding full-time job because her husband did not have a regular job and was very irresponsible abut his family obligations. Leslie had searched for the right type of care for her children and finally found another mother of three who was willing to watch her boys for a reasonable rate.

Leslie promised to pick up her children before supper-time each evening. But she was not able to keep her promise on certain evenings when her husband took their only car and did not return on time. This, of course, infringed on the caregiver's family because they wanted to have supper alone. The caregiver would put the three little boys in another room and feed her own children. When the boys would cry, "We're hungry," the caregiver would say, "I'm sorry. Your mother promised to be here to pick you up before supper and if she really cared about you and loved you she would be here."

Such a seemingly innocent remark. But in reality this was much more painful to these little boys than a spanking would have been. When this was said every time Leslie was unable to pick up her children on time, it slowly destroyed the children's belie that their mother really loved and cared about them. And in their confusion of feelings they began to reason that if their mother, their very *own* mother, did not love and care for them, then they must not be very worthwhile little people.

Do not let this happen to your children. Be very careful to communicate with the caregiver so she can support you and help your children understand how much you love them even though you must be away from them part of the day. Your child's identity, his personhood, is all wrapped up in you. He is part of you and any words that demean you, demean that child too.

When in reviewing a prospective teacher or a long-term babysitter for your children, you might ask some of these revealing questions. "If we come home later than we promised, what would you tell my children?" "If you don't agree with the things we do and the way we spend my time, what would you say?" "If you don't like what I've told you to do or what I've asked you to see that the children do, what attitude would you exhibit in front of the children?" Of course, there is no guarantee that a person will follow through on his answers, but it is important to discuss your differences and the attitude that you would like the caregiver to display when she is with your children.

The undercurrent of a negative attitude can affect the caregiver's behaviour toward your children in subtle ways. Therefore, let the caregiver know that you expect her to discuss any disagreements or conflicts with you immediately. You want to have a chance to explain the reasons for your behaviour and clear the air. If your child is aware of a gulf between you and the caregiver, that can be very damaging. It's similar to a child's reaction when Mommy and

Daddy disagree. Because the child loves both, he dos not know which side to take. You want your children to know that you and the caregiver are in complete harmony. You may choose to act differently, but the principles behind your actions should be the same.

Establishing a harmonious rapport with someone takes time. If you want to have an understanding like this with your child's caregiver, it is essential to spend time with this person. Some mothers schedule a half-hour a day to discuss the day's routine, the activities the child enjoyed, any behaviour problems that occurred, and the interesting things the child said.

Thirty minutes a day is not necessarily the magic amount of time it takes to establish rapport. A five-minute talk when you collect the children, a telephone call during the day, or an occasional invitation for dinner might be sufficient. The important thing is to establish a regular channel for communication and evaluation.

When children are in a nursery school or day-care center, it is essential to exchange a friendly greeting with the teacher at the door each morning and evening. Linger for a moment, looking at your child's creative work or a new toy in the room, to give the teacher an opportunity to comment about the day. Closing time may be a busy time for the teacher, so if you have a question that requires more than a "yes" or "no" answer, you might want to just it down and ask the teacher to call you in the evening (after the kids are in bed), or set up an appointment to talk more leisurely.

Teachers, for the most part, want to share their day with you. Working mothers, however, are so busy that they often can't afford to linger too long. Teachers sometimes feel that parents really don't care what is going on in school. Therefore, don't wait for a teacher to tackle you; take the offensive and actively encourage good communication. He or she will be much more understanding and supportive of you.

The caregiver should be a master at combining love and discipline. Too often, babysitters allow the children to get away with murder. On the other extreme, they may dictate and punish the child into submission.

No mother should leave her child in someone else's care unless she is convinced that this person understands the age characteristics of children. A caregiver should also know how to require obedience in a firm but loving way, without resorting to harsh physical or psychological punishment.

When interviewing a prospective caregiver, don't be afraid to ask, "What would you do if Johnny stole a dollar from your purse or told you a lie or called you names?" Think of the worst situation possible. If you are satisfied that the answer is acceptable, you can probably assume that milder offenses will receive appropriate action.

Don't strip the caregiver of all authority. Disciplinary problems should be handled as they arise. A working mother wants to be granted with open arms, enthusiasm, and a recital of good things that the children have done—especially when the children can overhear. Negative tidings dampen the homecoming.

If a problem arose during the day that needs your attention, ask the caregiver to phone you. Then you will have time to brainstorm together on a combined strategy to cope with the problem. Don't allow the caregiver to criticise the child or discuss the problem in front of the family. No child (or adult) likes to have his faults talked about. But don't be indifferent to you children's problems. Problem behaviour is a sign that all is not well in the child's life. The sooner this is analysed and solved, the happier the child will be.

The caregiver should be open and willing to learn. It is difficult to work with anyone who thinks that she knows all the answers. A caregiver should be open to new suggestions and should not feel threatened when you disagree. She should be capable of making good decisions without having to ask you for detailed instructions. On the other hand, don't abdicate your responsibility as the mother and take a back seat when it comes to rearing your child.

The parent/caregiver relationship is most satisfying when there is mutual respect and an ability to talk things over on equal terms. If the parent seems to know it all, this often brings out the defensive nature of the caregiver. If the parent takes the position that the caregiver knows best, this, may create a superior attitude. When both are willing to consider the position of the other and learn from one another, the relationship will be a good one and the children will benefit.

To find out how your caregiver feels about certain child-rearing philosophies and disciplinary techniques, choose one or two good books that you have found helpful and ask the caregiver to read them. Then discuss the books when you have time for a lengthy chat. By taking time to task with each other in this manner you should both learn a great deal from the other.

The caregiver should be the kind of person you want your children to grow up to be. Because children are master imitators, you want them to spend time with someone who has personality traits that you will enjoy seeing exhibited in your children's behaviour. Look for a happy, enthusiastic, optimistic person who loves children. Next, look for evidence of orderliness, honesty, integrity, firmness to principle, and patience.

Because children have a way of bringing out the worst in some people, you will want to know how the caregiver deals with frustration and anger. Does she take it out on the children? Does she pout? Does she scream? Is she willing to explain her feelings to the children before they become so intense that they cannot be contained, controlled, or diverted into constructive activity? Is her speech a good model for your child to follow?

Don't be afraid to level with a prospective caregiver about the kind of example you want her to set for your children. Then ask her if she thinks she can live up to these expectations.

The caregiver should be willing to teach your child. A good caregiver should be willing to teach whenever the teachable moment occurs. If everyone is sunbathing outside and your child is busy watching a line of ants and asks, "Where are the ants going?" You don't want the caregiver to say, "I'm reading a book, don't bother me." Rather, you want her to put down the book, get up and say, "That's a good question. Let's follow them as far as we can." Your children should have every learning opportunity that they would have if you were home with them full time.

The teaching of values should not occur only when you are home. It is important that children know what other people consider right and wrong, valuable and good. Because this is such a sensitive area, you will probably want to choose a caregiver who shares your values and religious beliefs. If she doesn't, you will want her to understand your family values, and uphold those beliefs and principles when she is with your child.

The caregiver should be given specific guidelines. We recommend that a caregiver be given these three guiding principles by which to operate: (1) Place my child and his needs above everything else; (2) Treat my child as you would your own—with unconditional acceptable, reasonable firmness, and respect; and (3) Use your common sense.

Apart from these, remember to leave specific guidelines for the caregiver. For example you may request that she read to your child daily, or that she supervise at least one outdoor play experience each day. You may prefer that your child watch no daytime television; if so, the caregiver should know this. The caregiver needs to know when your child should have his meals, whether he is allowed to eat between meals and what he may have, whether you require that he brush his teeth after meals. She should know your views on discipline, on spanking, on having friends in to play, and she must be told precisely what to do in an emergency. (Be sure you leave signed permission for medical care to be administered to your child in your absence. This can be left with the caregiver or kept on file at the emergency room).

By spelling out your general and specific requirements in advance, you make the caregiver's job much easier and the possibility of satisfaction on her part—as well as yours and your child's—much greater.

A Suitable Environment

The third steps toward finding quality care for your child is to determine the kind of environment that will suit your child's needs if he is not in your home. For young children, this is what you should look for.

The environment should be as homelike as possible. Home is usefully a place where children are free to go inside or outside whenever they want. They want. Can play in little private corners without someone looking over their shoulders. Usually there is not a rigidly prescribed schedule of caryoning for ten minutes, stories for fifteen minutes, and puzzles for another ten minutes. People come and go; you get to watch the garbage man, greet the mailman, and answer the doorbell. There are usually curtains on the windows, pictures on the walls, a comfortable rocking chair, and carpets on the floors. Even if the facility does not look like a home, you want to make sure that the programme scheduling and the atmosphere feel more like a home than an institution.

It is naturally easier for a small center to be more homelike than a large center. In fact, centers that serve over sixty children find it more difficult to maintain a homelike quality of care. The more children there are, the more regimented the programme tends to become.

The environment should be healthy and safe. Licensing does not ensure that safety and health conditions will be completely met for your child, but it is a step in that direction. The room and yard should be clean, neat, and free of broken equipment, and there should be adequate and convenient toilet facilities for the children. Drinking water should be available both inside and out, and a nutritious, hot meal should be served. For naptime each child should have a cot and blanket of his own.

There should be a fenced yard with both sunlight and shady places to play. Grass, plants, and trees add to the aesthetic aspects of a facility. Because of the danger of environmental pollution, the home or center should not be too close to a busy street or freeway, nor should it be downwind from factory smoke.

Be sure to ask if emergency procedures have been carefully worked out in advance. Find out what the caregiver would do if your child was involved in an accident and needed medical attention. Ask if there is an isolation room for sick children so others are not infected.

The environment should be conducive for learning. Make sure there are adequate toys and games, trucks and tricycles, and outside play equipment. Are there books, records, and musical instruments that the children can handle?

The children should be introduced to a variety of learning and creative activities throughout the day. They should be free to choose what they would like to work with. When children are regimented into a nonflexible programme that is not responsive to their needs, learning is stifled.

Evaluating the Quality of Care

After you have chosen the type of programme, the caregiver, and the environment, continue to evaluate the quality of the care and your child's reaction to that care. If you have established certain guidelines for your caregiver, periodically check to see that these are maintained. This can be done in the following ways.

1. Observe your child with the caregiver.
2. Ask the caregiver how she handled certain problems. Be specific. Listen to more than the words., Your impressions are important. If you feel a caregiver is not really leveling with you, say, "we have a feeling there may be more to the story. Can you think of anything else that may have contributed to the problem?"
3. Question your child. "How are things going? What do you really like or dislike about your caregiver? What activities does she plan for your? What special things do you do together?" Your child may be your most accurate source of information. On the other hand, such information may be biased because of anger, retaliation, or self-justification. Avoid tattling behaviour. If your child

gives you a negative report, simply say, "I'll check it out." Don't say anything in front of the child that will lower his respect for the caregiver.

4. If you have real questions about the caregiver and her relationship with your children, drop in unexpectedly Have your neighbour observe or ask a friend to drop by and watch the situation for a while.
5. If you see a potential problem, solve it at that level. Don't let it grow out of proportion.

Some children have a difficult time adjusting to new situations. Even though the situation seems ideal to you, your child may not be happy with the care that you have arranged. To ease your child's adjustment, let him get to know the caregiver in your presence. Act confident and mater-of-fact about the decision that you have made. If your child perceives that you are hesitant abut the child-care arrangements and feel guilty about leaving him, he is more likely to put on a good crying show for you and give you plenty of reasons for staying. If you feel confident, that attitude will help your child to adjust to the new experience.

If you have chosen a group child-care programme or a home that is unfamiliar to your child, then it is important that you allow your child the time to develop trust in the new adult. Make sure he feels comfortable in the new environment before leaving him alone. During this time, do not make any attempt to push the child away from your. If a child feels pushed, the tendency is to hold on all the tighter. After an hour or so most children tire of sitting on Mommy's lap and will begin to look around the room. The teacher or caregiver should be friendly—but not overwhelmingly helpful. That may frighten the child.

During this get-acquainted period, don't suddenly disappear when your child seems involved in another activity. If possible, let your child make the decision about when you can leave. If he knows you won't leave until he think he can handle it, he is free to become acquainted with the other children and the environment without having to worry that you will disappear when his back is turned.

If your child is too young to make such a decision, then tell him frankly that you are leaving for a specific amount of time and will return. Then go without any hesitation; no looking back or peeking around the corner. Stay away long enough to give the teacher a chance to comfort your child and establish some rapport. When your return, that should be a sign that it is time to leave the center and go home.

Don't be surprised if your child breaks down in a flood of tears when your return, even though he may have been happy and contentedly playing while you were away. This is natural. He has experienced many emotions during your absence and the sight of a familiar person will release all these emotions at once.

Continue with the care you have selected long enough to give it a fair chance of working. But if your child is still unhappy after a month, reevaluate your choice and consider other alternatives that may more readily meet your child's needs.

Continue to evaluate. Remember that your child's needs will change as he grows, and the quality of care may also change over time. A situation that is ideal now may be less than satisfactory a year later. Don't be afraid, at this time, to reevaluate and determine whether better child-care arrangements can be made. Here are a few questions to help you evaluate and continue evaluating the child-care choice that you have made.

Type of care. Does this care meet the current needs of my child? Is it appropriate for his age? How long might we expect this care to be appropriate? Is this care the best for my own personal needs?

Caregiver. Are we convinced the caregiver is the best we can find for my child? Is the person specifically interested in my child? Has she established a rapport with my child? Is she able to discipline my child in a firm but loving manner? Does she support me? Is she willing to talk to me about my could's progress as well as the problems? Is she encouraging to my child-as well as to me? Were we convinced she can act wisely in case of an emergency?

Activities. Are the activities my child is participating in appropriate for his age? Is there adequate freedom within the environmental so he can make appropriate choices to work or play with materials on his own time schedule? Is he able to work at his own level of ability without any pressure to perform just like other children? Are there a variety of activities and materials available to encourage learning?

Environment. Is the environment wholesome, healthy, and safe? Is good food served regularly? Is there an adequate resting period that is encouraged but not forced upon the child? Are there adequate emergency procedures?

Child's feelings and reactions. Is my child happy and satisfied? Does my child talk positively about child care? Is he eager to go or accepting of the situation? Are there any signs in my child's behaviour that would indicate unhappiness: sleeplessness, excessive crying, regression to immature behaviour, excessive aggressiveness, destructiveness, listlessness, a tendency to withdraw, nervous habits—nail biting, twisting hair, etc.? Are the children he is with the type of children we would want my child to have as friends?

Even if your child-care arrangements pass the test and seem ideal, almost all preschoolers go through periods of not wanting to go—or of not wanting Mommy to leave. You must accept your child's feelings, but you don't necessarily have to give in to his wishes. Try to find out what the reason might be. Often, tensions in the home might trigger such a reaction, or you may be so busy that you have not spent enough time with your child. Sometimes a slight change in a routine, such as having Daddy drop him off at the babysitter's, or the promise of a special activity with Mommy after work, will be enough to satisfy your child. If his reluctant behaviour becomes habitual, reevaluate the child -care situation. There may be a problem that can be solved by talking to the teacher, or you may want to change your arrangements, temporarily or permanently. It is important to feel you have options available if you need them.

As you consider all the alternatives, don't be afraid to consider the advantages and disadvantages of quitting work or taking a leave of absence for a while until you can find the right child-care situation. We begin to feel uncomfortable and dissatisfied with our situations when we don't feel free to make decisions that affect our lives and those of our children.

Common Questions About Child Care

Here are some of the questions that we are frequently asked about child care.

1. How do you handle your own jealousy when your child seems to like the babysitter more than you?

Answer: Spend more time with your child. This is a sign that your have not spent enough quality time together with your child so your relationship has not continued to grow. Be thankful you have found a person your child enjoys so much. If the caregiver is supportive of you, you have nothing to worry about.

2. When hiring a regular babysitter to come to my home, how businesslike does this arrangement have to be?

Answer: You should have a written job description that includes specific housekeeping duties you might require. You should pay at least the minimum wage. Pay periods should be regular. Check with the local Social Security office about reporting earnings, making payments for Social Security insurance, and filing quarterly statements with the IRS. Benefits are usually given. Allow at least one day of sick leave a fear for every day of the week worked. Vacations should include holidays and a yearly two-week vacation for a full-time worker. You can pay on an hourly basis or a salaried basis. This agreement should be signed by you and the employee. You should agree to an evaluation in one month as well as a quarterly review. Let the sitter know that the arrangement will be terminated before a specified trial period is over if you do not feel things are going well. Ask for two or three weeks notice if the caregiver wishes to quit.

3. When are children old enough to stay by themselves?

Answer: This does not depend entirely on age. It depends on the maturity of the child, the length of time the child is left alone and the proximity of help should he need it. Certainly, a child should not be left without any type of supervision before seven years of age. An eight-or nine-year-old may be able to handle an hour or two occasionally. By ages ten to twelve a child usually has developed enough maturity to stay alone during the after-school hours until his parents arrive. Even during the teenage years most children need and desire some type of occasional supervision. Lonely children are prime targets for unwholesome experimentation and rebellion. Teenage pregnancy, drugs, alcohol, smoking, delinquency, and accidents are often the result of lack of adequate adult supervision.

4. What guidelines should we give my school-age children when we leave them alone?

Answer: Children should not be frightened about being home alone, but it is important to give them the following common-sense instructions:

Keep the doors locked, even if you only leave the house for a short time. Keep an extra key holder outside the house in case you lose your keys.

If someone comes to the door, don't open it unless you recognise both the name and the voice. Don't tell anyone that you are home alone. Politely ask them to come back later, or ask them to go next door if they need help.

Don't give your name when answering the phone. Don't tell a caller that your are alone. Take a message and tell the caller that your parents will return the call. If you receive a crank call, hang up immediately.

Don't entertain friends without first getting parental permission. If in doubt about the safety or sensibleness of an activity, ask your parents' approval first.

Be predictable. Be where your parents expect you to be at the time they expect.

Keep emergency phone numbers handy. Write down the procedure to follow in case of an emergency, such as fire, accident, or illness.

Keep the house neat and do what you can to prepare for your parents' arrival. For example: finish your chores and your homework: start dinner if you have your parents' approval; and think of something you can do to pleasantly surprise your parents.

At times, every working mother must rely on others to fill some of her child's needs. If you plan thoughtfully and choose the right person to share the child-care responsibility with you, your life as a working mother will be more satisfactory.

Minimising Job/Family Conflicts

Once the matter of child care has been successfully resolved, the remaining problems of the working mother become chiefly a question of philosophical and practical approach. The dual roles of parenting and working can be compatible and satisfying when you learn the secret to success: you must become indispensable to the job and dispensable to the family. Consider the following illustrations.

Crystal was a skilled secretary—no doubt about that, as she typed letter-perfect memos at 140 words per minute. But she worked mechanically. It was her job—nothing more. She did only when was necessary. When work was slow she pulled out her needlepoint. When work piled up and a crisis demanded overtime, she politely excused herself. "My job description says my hours are from eight to five," she told her boss. She was frequently late because of babysitting problems. When her child became ill, pediatrician appointments interfered with office hours. Crystal made no attempt to make up this time. When a mother-daughter day was planned at her daughter's school, Crystal asked her boss for time off. Her boss, a kind, understanding person, was clearly not happy about the request. He suggested that she look for another job that would allow her a more flexible work schedule.

Lenore was not as good a typist, but from her first four on the job her boss was aware of her enthusiasm for her work and her dedication. Lenore was a working mother with preschool and school-age children. Her family/job conflicts exceeded Crystal's. But when it came to the job, she was one hundred percent there, ready and willing to go the extra mile. When the volume of work piled up, she came in early and worked late. And her dedication paid off. She was liked, she was needed, and she was considered an indispensable; employee. Once her track record was established—and it didn't take long—Lenore did not hesitate to ask for small benefits. "I'd like to take the afternoon off. My son's class has a field trip and he wants me to go along. The statements have been mailed and your latest tape has been transcribed. I'll be happy to come in early tomorrow morning if anything comes up that needs immediate attention."

"Sure, take the afternoon off," her boss replied. "And don't worry about coming in early. You deserve a break."

Why did Crystal's boss and Lenore's boss respond as they did? What made the difference? It was indispensability. Lenore had become indispensable to the job. Her boss viewed her as a valuable asset to the business, one he did not want to lose. It was to his advantage and to the company's advantage to make the job as attractive as possible in order to keep employees like Lenore.

When an employer has a valuable employee, he is often willing to help that employee reduce family/job conflicts. Employers are aware that most working mothers will favour the family when conflicts arise. Indeed, if conflict cannot be resolved, many working mothers will either quit or opt for a less challenging job in order to meet their families' needs. But if an employee can prove that she is indispensable to the job, most employers are willing to make concessions to keep the employee happy and satisfied.

However, this is only one-half of the secret. The second half is to become dispensable to the family. If a working mother feels that her family cannot survive without her, she will always be torn between her home duties and her job responsibilities when conflicts arise. Let's see how Crystal and Lenore handled this part of their lives.

Although Crystal worked, she wasn't able to shake the age-old idea that a woman's place is at home, caring for her children full time. This drove her to overcompensate for the hours spent at her job by taking on many more home responsibilities than her husband, and by doing things for her children that they should have learned to do for themselves. She believed that a good mother should be able to care for her children without calling on her husband, friends, or relatives for help. When doctors' appointments had to be made or when her babysitter was ill, she felt that it was her responsibility to take the day off to care for her children. Consequently, her children and her husband grew increasingly dependent on her, and her, and this reinforced her belief that the whole family would fall apart if she weren't around. Her family also began to feel that she was shirking her responsibility if she wasn't home on time.

Lenore, on the other hand, viewed her relationship with her husband as a partnership. She had encouraged him to care for the children since birth, and she did not hesitate to call on friends and neighbours to help out in a pinch. So when she went to work she had confidence in a number of adults who could step in and care for the children when her job demanded extra time and effort. She was also willing to give this same support to her friends when she was available. Her children and husband valued her work, and they never felt deprived, because she was always with them for the really important times. She also encouraged her children to take over home responsibilities. She taught them to prepare simple foods, to wash and dry their clothes, to mend and sew on buttons. She prepared her family for her absence, and in this way she became dispensable to her family when her job demanded it.

Becoming Indispensable to the Job

Although very few of us are ever completely indispensable, it is certainly possible to become so valuable to your employer that he or she will be willing to make small concessions when necessary. How can you accomplish this? Obviously, ability is a number-one prerequisite, but it's not everything. You may lose your job to a less capable person because you lack four essential qualities that require no special training—only the right mental attitude. These qualities are responsibility, enthusiasm, loyalty, and cooperation. If you can bring these qualities to your work, you can become on extremely valuable employee. Just follow these guidelines.

Follow directions. Do what you are asked to do, but use common sense. If you see a more efficient way of handling some task, don't hesitate to discuss your idea with your boss.

Remember What you are told to do. If you are given a number of instructions at one time, write them down immediately. If you consistently return and interrupt your boss with a stream of questions, he'll find it easier to do the work himself or hire someone else.

Clarify the importance of various tasks and finish them in order of priority. If you can't meat a deadline, give your boss enough notice so he can devise a substitute plan. Don't wait until the last minute.

Keep your employer or supervisor appraised of your progress and accomplishments. Unless you are closely supervised, your boss may not be aware of your achievements, especially if they are the less than tangible kind. At first, this might seem like bragging, but if it is done with a proper attitude, it won't be interpreted that way.

Jill Frazier, a professor at a large university, learned this lesson the hard way. She met her class assignments and kept her office hours, but, other than that, she came and went as she pleased. She was dedicated to her job, and her students felt that she was a real friend and counselor. Jill spent all her extra time preparing teaching aids and devising programmed-learning materials that she hoped to publish. She balked at accepting committee assignments or joining departmental social activities because it took precious time away from her major interests—teaching and counseling. Her departmental chairman was too busy with his own research to observe her teaching skills and materials, or inquire about her effectiveness with students. He only notice the obvious—she did not attend departmental functions and she was not in the office eight hours a day!

Jill's promotion request was denied, primarily because her departmental chairman was unable to justify it. When Jill realised the problem, he made an appointment with her chairman to show him the programmed-learning materials she had been preparing and to explain her heavy involvement with the students. As a result she received her promotion and was officially appointed student adviser for the department. Since then Jill has kept a written record of her activities and periodically advises her chairman of her accomplishments. In turn, he is more supportive of her efforts.

Plan for emergencies. Realistically, emergencies will crop up from time to time. Prepare for these occasions in advance and devise a back-up plan that can be put into operation when you need time off. It's much easier to ask for time off when you can assure your boss that the work will be completed. Take work home if necessary, put in some extra time the next day, or ask another employee to help you out, and return the favour when he or she needs it. If you plan ahead, you won't feel guilty and your boss will appreciate your dependability.

Maintain an enthusiastic attitude. Put your heart, as well as your mind, into your work. A spirit of enthusiasm stimulates others to give their all to a job and creates a pleasant office atmosphere. No one likes to work with an individual who complains. When you're given an unpleasant task, do it as quickly and cheerfully as possible. Don't bring your personal problems to your job.

Be cooperative and willing to work with others to accomplish a task. Listen to other people's points of view and compromise when necessary. Stubborn, willful, and egocentric people do not make pleasant co-workers. If you're willing to work with others cheerfully, your boss will be appreciative.

Give your company or employer the same loyalty you give your family. If you discuss company "secrets," gossip about your boss or other employees behind their backs, or take advantage of company policies, your're not likely to keep your job.

Becoming Dispensable to the Family

Becoming dispensable to your family does not mean that you are no longer important to them. It simply means that your family can survive without disruption and pain when your job becomes particularly demanding. This is possible if you follow these guidelines.

Make sure your family knows that they are more important than your job. When children feel that something else holds first place in your life they will constantly strive for that valued position. They will test your love, argue, fight, complain, and resent whatever fills that number-one place. To alleviate these feelings, you must convince your children of their prime importance. This is only possible if you follow the second guideline.

Be with your family when it really counts. Every family has special times when togetherness is particularly important—meantimes, worship times, after-school times, bed-time, birthdays, holidays, special school activities, performance times, and so on. Select the priority times for your family and *be there!* It might entail some inconvenience—coming home for supper, for example, and then returning to work—but this will convince your family that they do indeed come first.

Include your family in your job. When family members feel excluded from a major and important part of your life, they tend to resent it. Be willing to share. Even if aspects of your job are confidential, you can still share the tensions and deadlines with your family. You can still say, "I'm facing an important deadline right now. We need your encouragement and support for the next three days and then we'll celebrate."

If possible, let your children help with small projects at work—alphabetising files, folding letters, or stapling papers. When I'm facing deadline on the preparation of a manuscript, my children enjoy pushing the button on the copy machine and collating the pages. At other times they can help by being good—and quiet—so we can concentrate. When they know that they are helping me with a project, they feel involved, and they also fee a sense of pride in having contributed in some small way.

Be willing to share your child-care and other home responsibilities. Contrary to a wisely held notion, the best mothers aren't necessarily those who handle all the child-care and home responsibilities alone. Quality and diversity can be compatible. This is certainly true when a father is encouraged to share these responsibilities. Relatives and friends can also make an important contribution.

Teach your children self-sufficiency. If you teach your children to handle various chores on their own, you'll be able to spend your free time with your children in enjoyable ways, rather than tying up that time in a constant round of necessary and routine activities. If your children can prepare simple meals, you won't feel guilty if the boss asks you to come in early or work overtime. You can feel confident that they can pack their own lunches, get themselves off to school on time, or prepare supper for the family.

Don't expect perfection from others. Many working parents who try to share child-care and home responsibilities with others expect perfection. This creates dissatisfaction for the parents and discouragement and frustration on the part of those who are trying to help. Working mothers, especially, must guard against this tendency and accept and appreciate whatever help they receive from others. When Junior washes a tub of clothing, don't criticise the amount of soap he used. Just say thanks, and casually mention that a half-cup will suffice the next time. When your daughter fixes supper and burns the beans, tell her you appreciate her hard work, and explain how easy it is for food to stick to the bottom of the pan and burn if it isn't stirred. Don't kill their willingness by expecting perfection.

Instead, encourage then to learn from their mistakes. It's the effort and the motives that count. With practice, their products and skills will improve.

Finding the Right Job for Your Family's Stage of Life

Mother's of infants, toddlers, and preschoolers often face particularly difficult family/job conflicts. Although older children still require parental time and attention, they are much more self-sufficient, and other people can fill many of their needs. But there is no magic solution that will turn dependent infants into less dependent schoolchildren. Therefore, becoming indispensable to your job and dispensable to your family may only be possible to a limited extent, depending on the job and the ages of your children. To minimise conflicts you must focus on the changes that can be made in your work situation.

Consider these questions: is your job the right one for this stage of your family life? Is it flexible? Is it demanding? How much overtime is required? Are the hours regular? Can your children visit your office occasionally? Is your job taxing and tension producing? Is it fulfilling? Can you make changes within your job or change jobs?

Martha, a pastor's wife who attended one of my seminars, had just moved into the area and had to choose one of three possible nursing jobs. Each job held different advantages. "If we didn't have school-age children, I'd take the teaching appointment at the junior college," she told me. "But it requires teaching night classes, and we just can't depend upon my husband to be home. Private nursing pays the best—but the hours aren't regular or dependable. So I've deceived on the 7 A.M. to-3 P.M. hospital nursing job. My husband can easily get the kids off to school and I'll be there when they get home. It's ideal for me now while my children are young."

"I'll bet you're glad you took nursing," we commented. "It seems to allow you a considerable amount of flexibility."

"Well, the interesting thing is, we didn't take nursing at first. We were an elementary-education major and taught for five years before we had children. We loved it. In fact, it's still my first love."

"Then why did you change?" We asked, confused over this apparent contradiction.

"It wasn't easy to change. We had three preschool children when we decided to go back and take nursing. We knew we needed to work to supplement the family income, and teaching took up too much of my time: seven hours at school and the constant preparation at home. We could never take my mind off my teaching responsibilities. In addition, the job was too similar to my role as a parent—nurturing, caring for, and teaching children. It was too much for me. We needed to do something different at work so we could return to my children with enthusiasm and energy. We enjoy my nursing work, but someday when the children are grown, we wouldn't be surprised if we went back into teaching."

Similar conversations with mothers across the country indicate that many of these women avoid family/job conflicts by seeking a job that fits their stage of family life. Since this period is a relatively short one, they can return to more demanding jobs as soon as their children are old enough to be more self-sufficient.

As you seek the type of work that will minimise job/family conflicts, follow these steps.

Set your priorities. What do you really want from a job—high wages, flexible hours, job security and satisfaction, an understanding and supportive boss, or a convenient location?

List all your number-one priorities on one sheet and rank them in the order of their importance. Use the list as a guide when you begin searching for a job or making changes in your current job.

For long-term job satisfaction, try to imagine what your priorities might be in five or ten year and add those item to your list. An ideal job should meet your current needs and offer the potential of meeting your future needs. But finding such a job is not easy. You may have to compromise on some of your future requirements and take a job that best fits your immediate priorities if you are interested in minimising family/job conflicts.

Investigate careers that seem to mesh with your stage of life. Seek advice from career counsellors or from the personnel departments of large organisations that offer a wide variety of job opportunities. Talk to people whose jobs or careers seem to present the least conflict. Consider the possibility of further education or training. For example, skilled typists often contract for work they can do at home, such as typing grant proposals, report, or invoices. Because of my advanced professional degree, we can teach on a flexible university schedule, rather than being tied down to classroom teaching in a day-care center or an elementary school.

Pace your career. Women who established themselves in a job or career before their children were born often face fewer frustrations when they return to work. But for many women this is impossible. Don't fall into the trap of feeling sorry for yourself, or feeling cheated because your children arrived before you had a chance to begin the career of your choice. Be realistic. You may have to give up some of your hops for job recognition and advancement for the first few years. Be patient and plan ahead for the time when your children will not need you as much as they do now.

If you decide to quit your job for a while or work part-time while your children are small, establish and maintain contacts with other people working in your chosen field. Keep abreast of changes, innovations, and problems. If you gave up teaching temporarily, only to discover that teaching jobs have become scarce, use your time at home to prepare for another job. Use this time creatively. Even if you're not working, you don't have to spend all your time with you children. Go back to school part-time, take some night courses, read books and professional journals, learn a new skill at home, write an article. Prepare yourself for your eventual return to work. Because our society still expects women to assume primary responsibility for child rearing, many employers will not question a resume with several blank or low-achievement years. And as roles become more flexible, this attitude may be extended to fathers as well.

The following stories illustrate how some working mothers have solved family/job conflicts by fitting their jobs to their family's stage of life.

Jeanette Peterson was a very popular junior-high-school teacher, but she accepted a job as the educational director for a local church. The job allowed her to plan and prepare curricular materials at home while she cared for her one-year-old. On weekends, she taught in the church programme while her husband cared for their baby.

After medical school and an internship, Janice Kline decided to work only two afternoons a week in a family-planning clinic until her children were in school. During the next three years, her husband, also a physician, cut down considerably on his practice in order to take over primary family responsibilities while Janice finished a hectic obstetrics-gynecology residency. Now, as the children approach high school and college, both Janice and her husband are doing exactly what they want to be doing in their careers.

Marilyn Cramer, a librarian, quit her job when her two girls were small. At first she devoted her talents to developing the church library. Now that both girls are in school, she has become the school librarian. Her girls enjoy going to school with Mommy, and they proudly announce, "that's my mommy," every time they pass the library door.

Kathy Lyn, a teacher, corrected her garage into a very lucrative home nursery school for her own children and other. Now that her children have graduated from nursery school she has sold the preschool equipment, turned the room into a game room, and returned to her teaching position.

Connie Blue loved her position as a receptionist in a dental office, but she is now selling Tupperware and Avon products. This allows her maximum flexibility in dovetailing her working hours with her husband's.

Lisa Miller enjoyed her position as chef for a large restaurant. But she took a year's leave of absence to care for her new baby and write the cookbook she had always wanted to write.

Mary Brown was a French major who had difficulty finding a job in the field. When her children were young, Mary volunteered for various types of hospital work, trying to decide what she would eventually like to do. When her youngest child began nursery school, she was ready to go back and take the chaplin's programme.

Betty Taylor was a literary agent who worked overtime for five years, making as many sales as possible. She was planning ahead. When her first child was born, she had enough money to go into "semiretirement" for a few years.

Charlene Casper was in the fast-changing field of electronics. She quit when her first child was three years old and she was expecting a second. To remain active in the field, she took small consulting jobs, read technical journals, and dabbled on the side in her own research project.

Stephanie Jones, an assembly-line worker, asked her supervisor if she could work at home on piecemeal work. She took a year's leave a absence from the company. Although she lost company benefits, she maintains a profitable relationship with the company and has gained valuable time for her children.

Whatever your position, if you feel overwhelmed by family/job conflicts, you can minimise these conflicts with planing and determination. Women are making changes. Women are accepting temporary set backs in their career aspirations. Women are pacing their careers to benefit their families. Don't be afraid to voice your priorities to your employer. Think creatively about the changes you could make in your current job. Carefully explain that these are temporary, a result of your current stage of family life. You may be surprised by the respect you will gain when you take such a stand.

Family/job conflicts are usually minimised when a job is highly satisfying; when its schedule matches your own; when it is close to home, child-care facilities, or school; and when the administrators or supervisors understand your family obligation. Finding such a job may not be easy, but it is worth the effort.

The Importance of a Supportive Family

Your success in minimising family/job conflicts will be determined in part by the support you receive from your family. The negative attitude of relatives, especially your parents, can undermine your effectiveness. Family members tend to blame all problems on the fact that your are working, and this attitude only increases guilt and makes it more difficult to find an acceptable solution. *Spouse support it crucial.* Major problems can develop if a husband does not appreciate his wife's need to get out of the house or if he expects his wife to assume full responsibility for the children and the house while working full time.

Every working mother needs help occasionally. When your husband responds to a desperate phone call with a cheerful, "Sure, I'll be glad to pick up the children, stop at the grocery store, and fix supper," conflicts won't develop. But what can you do when you don't have this type of support system? The answer is to develop it.

Many working mothers find it difficult to communicate their need for spouse support. The following list high lights some common causes of misunderstandings.

1. The wife feels that her husband disapproves of her job.
2. The husband feels that he is doing his fair share; the wife dos not agree.
3. The husband thinks things are find because the wife has never openly discussed her feelings.
4. One spouse feels that the other is taking advantage of him/her.
5. The husband feels that the wife is so absorbed in the job that he and the children are being neglected.

All of these problems can be solved by effective communication and compromise. The first step is to establish some ground rules for communication. Study the following rules with your spouse and start using them today.

Agree to talk. Silence is a subtle method of manipulation that can cause bitterness and increase conflict.

Agree not to get angry. Anger only clouds the issues and creates resentment. Words spoken in anger often become weapons. Conflict cannot be resolved when either spouse in angry.

Listen to your spouse's position respectfully. Don't make snap judgments or hasty statements of self-justification such as, "You're being overly sensitive," or "we can't help it if my boss called me in at the last minute." Thee statements cut off communication prematurely before the issue is clearly understood.

Clarify your spouse's position. "Are you saying that you feel we care more about the job than the family?"

Be honest and specific. Issues can only be solved when they are out in the open. Don't allow resentments to grow out of proportion and affect family relationships.

Be willing to compromise. Never say, "It's impossible!" Brainstorm for possible solutions, then go back and evaluate each one. List its pros and cons. Don't discard a possibility until you both agree that its impractical. Don't argue abotu these ideas! Accept a wise, practical solution whether or not you proposed that option. Don't keep score of who wins. Consider the final solution as a joint solution.

When you reach an agreement, set up a specific timetable for its implementation.

Evaluate your solution on a weekly basis. Don't be afraid to discard it if it's not working. Go back to the bargaining table and find another compromise.

Encourage your spouse to be supportive through praise and appreciation rather than criticism. People are much more likely to repeat behaviour patterns that win them praise and appreciation. This behaviour-modification technique works for grown-ups as well as children? But your praise must be sincere; don't use praise to manipulate or change your spouse, or to get what you want.

Criticism often hardens a person's determination to maintain the status quo. If something bothers you, wait until you and your spouse have the time for a quiet talk, and then follow the ground rules for effective communication. Don't lash out impulsively; it's too easy to lose your cool.

Don't allow your job to interfere with your family time. Leave your job worries at your place of employment. If you are preoccupied with business dealings and worries when you're with your family, you might as well be at work. In fact, children feel most rejected when a parent is physically available, but psychologically absent. Avoid this family/job conflict.

Devote your time at home to the family. Bring work home only when it is absolutely necessary. When your job cuts into time that your family formerly enjoyed together, resentments will surface. When you're too tired to play with your children or go out for an evening with your spouse, your job is interfering with your family.

Share benefits with your family. Let them see that your interest and enthusiasm for your job spill over into your life at home. List all the benefits that your job contributes to the family and start a subtle public-relations promotion campaign to make sure that your family realises these benefits too.

It is impossible to avoid all family/job conflicts, but they can be minimised by facing problems squarely and working on solutions. Be creative and flexible, and don't ever be ashamed to ask or help. Develop as many support systems as possible. You *can* have a career and be a good parent, too.

33

Feminist Perspectives on Struggles in The Informal Sector

Women's struggles in the informal sector are diverse, and exist at many levels. Primarily, we see struggles as being on both the ideological and material fronts. For a detailed description of the forms of struggle in the Indian context, it is necessary to identify the issues connected with the informal sector in general, and to gender- specific issues related to it.

The term informal sector has been so overused that to define it now might be considered redundant. For the purpose of this discussion, we shall recapitulate briefly what constitutes the informal sector. The informal sector here includes both the rural and the urban sections, and would encompass the categories of self-employed and wage workers in both manufacturing and service activities that are characterised by the following features—ease of entry, reliance on indigenous sources, family ownership of enterprises, small scale of operation, labour intensive and adapted technology, skills acquired outside the formal school system, and the unregulated and competitive market. Thus it would include workers in household production working directly or under some form of putting-out system, small workshops and factories (including informal labour in the formal sector), as well as those engaged in petty occupations and all other forms of casual labour in the rural and urban areas.

EVOLUTION OF THE INFORMAL SECTOR

There are divergent views on the evolution and role of the informal sector in third world countries, including India. Each of these views has strong ideological and political implications. Stated simply, the two views on the evolution of the informal sector are as follows. One group sees the evolution of this sector as arising largely out-of excessive controls in the formal sector, attributable to the policies of the government. In fact, one of the defining features is ease of entry,' implying thereby that entry in the formal sector is controlled.

The liberalisation strategies ini'iated in recent times at the instance of multilateral agencies seek to make the formal sector less controlled. This view also holds that controls in the formal sector are effected by the power of 'distributional coalitions,' of which the organised trade union movement is one. The recently announced exit policy for the industrial sector by the government is targeted to whittle down the power of this coalition. It sees these controls in the formal sector as growth retarding, while the informal sector is growth inducing. The growth inducing potential of the informal sector was also the original position of the ILO, after Keith Hart's study team visited Kenya in the early seventies. The original position of technocratic populism—namely, that government policies should be oriented to support this sector as it provides large employment potential, particularly under conditions of zero growth and stagnation in the formal sector of the economies—has, over the years, been contested by the Marxist and neo-Marxist schools, in particular what might be identified as the 'petty commodity production' group.[1] Before I spell out the logic, content and problems associated with this alternate view, it is necessary to note, at least very broadly, the powers that can be associated with the first view. For instance, in a study sponsored by USAID, Jerry Jenkins noted:

> The emergence of informal economies cannot be explained without reference to formal policies of governments. To the extent that the aspirations of the people are thwarted by the policies of the governments, the population of participants in informal economies will grow..... Third World governments with their growth retarding policies, in conjunction with Third World people and their irrepressible human spirit, are nonetheless creating incubators for free enterprise and institutional development that is predicated on performance rather than privilege (Jenkins, 1985).

The prescriptions of agencies such as the IMF and World Bank today to most of the third world countries including India, which is currently in the forefront of debate in the country, reflect this position. All that is being emphasised here is that the view that the informal sector is the outcome of government controls, and that it is an example of free market economy, should not be viewed as an isolated fact arising out of a different paradigmatic perspective but is to be seen as part of the ideological-political discourse on development, and one needs to be clear about who initiates and who promotes such a discourse.

The other school of thought on the informal sector, identified as petty commodity production,' sees the evolution of the informal sector as structural (that is, the outcome of an incomplete transition to capitalist development), and as the outcome of its articulation with extant precapitalist forms of production. The reasons for this incomplete transition vary according to contexts. In some cases it is factors internal to a particular society (such as the limited size of the home market) that narrows the base of industrialisation and hence of the formal sector, the existence of monopoly capital, the relative labour surplus, and so on. It is also recognised that while structural factors contribute to the evolution and perpetuation of the informal sector, it is further exacerbated by policy measures of the government. The other view within the political economy of the petty commodity debate contexts the evolution and continuation to the incorporation of third world economies into the world capitalist system in a dependent and subordinate position. While the existence of both these factors are undeniable, the intensity of each of these depend upon the specificities of each case, which also include the nature of the industrialisation strategy (namely, the inward or outward looking orientations of policy). The political implications of each of these reasonings are- clear. Both are for structural change as the only solution—one at the national level and the other at the global level.

The manner in which these structural changes can be effected (that is, the issues related to political practice) has been a matter of great contention. Of immediate relevance is the debate within the left movement of the role of the petty commodity sector or the petty bourgeoisie. This debate, both in India and abroad, is of recent origin and in analogous to the debate on the 'peasantry' drawing from the legacy of Chayanov. The revolutionary potential of this section has been the issue. It has been the practice of the organised left parties to give strategic importance in the non- agrarian sector to the industrial working class in the large factory sector—that is, the industrial proletariat. While recognising that the informal sector is not homogenous and contains sections of free wage labour, the strategic importance to one section of the working class has been criticised by many autonomous left groups, who see in this growing informal sector a large mass of organisable elements whose revolutionary consciousness can be enhanced through newer forms of political practice, even if their objective position within the structure of production does not lead to effective mobilisation through conventional forms of left political practice.

The crucial theoretical points made by the petty commodity school is that the petty commodity mode is in a dependent position with the dominant capitalist mode, the articulation of these two modes leads to newer forms of dominance and subordination, and the informal sector as a catch-all category is not homogenous. The differentiation within the informal sector is recognised to be of great theoretical and political importance. For instance, the category of household production encompasses both petty commodity producers and wage labour as part of capitalist domestic production, and household production as part of the earlier form of natural economy. Policies to support household production would crucially depend on understandings of these differentiations. The linkage between the formal and informal sectors, in particular the manner in which capital constantly and creatively finds ways of increasing surplus, in which process the so-called 'informal sector' plays a crucial role, has been the object of concern at both the theoretical and political levels.

All political groups have been concerned with the practical interests of workers, some more so than others. Wages and working conditions constitute the minimal elements of that concern. The exploitative use of the informal sector by capital in the formal sector has established the point beyond doubt that the piecemeal tinkering with issues will not yield results—in particular the totality of the structures of production have to be the object of political concern.

Since, at the level of political practice, this is not so, it has led to conflicts between different groups. There is a trading of charges between the organised left parties and the autonomous left groups, the former accusing the latter of introducing divisiveness in the working class, and the latter accusing the former that the genuine interests of the large mass of workers is not the concern of the organised left, and that it uses one section in an instrumental manner to gain political advantage. If one now brings into the picture the other elements working within the informal sector, (that is, what I call the free market elements), it is no surprise to us that the conflict becomes more intensified, and the dangers of divisiveness more real.

To me this appears as a crucial ideological struggle that we need to wage if successful grassroot experiments in mobilisation are not to be hijacked by any ideological school to suit its ends. The statement of this macro-ideological position is important for yet another reason, namely, that both in the attempts at organising and at evaluating women's struggles in the informal sector, one ought not to camouflage this fundamental dividing line. The restatement of this very obvious fact arises from my concern that there is a strong depoliticising trend in the women's movement, which itself is a politically motivated one. Attempts to thwart this trend will be successful only if one links up the gender concerns with macro-structural issues, and if one is constantly aware of the macro-ideological positions.

WOMEN'S ISSUES

We shall now explore the gender-specific issues related to work in the informal sector which are germane to the question of struggle and organisation. Broadly, these issues can be categorised as the general concentration of women in the informal sector, and the specific problems of women who are engaged in home-based production, self-employed women engaged in retail trade and services not based in homes, and those in wage employment in the casual wage sector in rural and urban areas, including casual and contract labour in the formal sectors of the economy. We use the three categories of home-based producers, self-employed and wage employed even though they remain a theoretical categories without further specification, for the simple reason that these terms have gained wide currency.

The concentration of women in informal sector occupations that are characterised by low wages, low capital intensiveness, low energy and the use of crude tools, for instance, should lead us to question the structural and ideological factors that have led to such a concentration. Some of the structural factors have been mentioned before. These largely relate to the lack of dynamism in these economies resulting in a bloating of the informal sector. The specificity of the use of female labour in this sector calls for an elaboration of the ideological dimension. Many of the women working in this sector do so not out of choice, and many of them have been working all through their lives. Yet, at the ideological level, they are enmeshed in a patriarchal ideology whereby the man is deemed to be the provider and protector of the family. Acceptance and adoption of this ideology confers status and power in a stratified context, and remains a bourgeois ideal for many. From the point of view of women's struggles, one needs to unravel the complexities at the structural and ideological levels, in particular the manifestations of patriarchy at the level of ideology and patriarchy at the level of societal practices, which simultaneously and paradoxically offer protection, as well as the worst forms of oppression and indignity.

These issues will be clarified at the broadest level in the following analysis of work in the informal sector. Considering first the problems of home-based production, the following issues have been highlighted in the movement, namely, the lack of recognition of home-based work as work, and the consequent invisibility of much of women's work, deplorable working conditions and the non-applicability of labour legislations. Further, the overall development impact on home-based production, leading in certain cases to the loss of employment and, in yet others, to newer forms of putting-out work, has been of considerable concern. Related to this is the concern for a proper differentiation of home-based production. In some instances, home-based producers are independent artisanal or petty commodity producers, and in others they are dependent on a merchant contractor or industrial capitalist directly, the degree of dependence varying so that, in some cases, home-based producers are merely wage workers on a put-out system working generally for piece-rate payments.

Depending on the extent of independence and dependence, home-based producers face problems relating to availability and access to markets, raw materials, credit, and so on, and are often caught in a complex web of exploitative relations and hierarchical structures with middlemen, merchants and moneylenders. In the case of women, given their restricted mobility and access due to various reasons, these factors are further intensified. Piece-rated workers face the problem not only of very low wages, but very often it is not even recognised that home-based production involves family labour of both women and children. Given the invisibility of their work, even under conditions of piece-rated work, women and children's labour often turn out to be in the nature of unpaid labour.

Arguments are often cited that home-based producers have the advantage of flexibility and autonomous control over their work, enabling them to combine this with their domestic chores and other reproductive tasks. Much of this is a myth. There is no denying the fact that, for some sections, there are cultural constraints on women's mobility which is extended even to their spheres of work, for yet others a bourgeois ideology of restraining women to their homes continues to prevail even after their objective conditions, in particular their immiserisation and proletarianisation, warrants a change in their values. For such women, there are not only new conflicts arising out of new pressures and obligations, but their work and earnings being so crucial to the household survival, are very often in a situation of what may be termed piece-rated wage slavery. Thus, the ideology of domesticity in conjunction with the constraints of survival, and patriarchal controls in the form of control over their labour, time and the labour processes, and control over their earnings and disbursement calls a bluff to the romanticised notion of home-based production as being most suited for women. In addition, owing to the overall development process in the economy, many of these women live and work under constant threat of losing their jobs with no viable alternatives, or are increasingly forced to cater to unstable markets, such as the export market for handicraft production..

NATURE OF STRUGGLES

The objective of highlighting these aspects of home-based production is to evolve a perspective on struggles in this sector. The struggles ought to be at the four different but overlapping levels, namely, the ideological, the legal, the macro and micro levels. Ideological struggles, i.e., the ideologies of domesticity and of patriarchy. One also needs to contest, at the same time, the romanticising of home-based production as being the ideal. Thus while, on the one hand, the 'ideal' notion is contested, at the same time it attempts to legitimate the work done as 'work' in the legal sense. This apparently paradoxical aspect of ideological struggle needs to be resuscitated at all other levels of struggle, namely, the legal, the macro and the micro levels. This fourfold categorisation might not be totally satisfactory but has been done merely to simplify. Legal struggle refers to struggles of a legalistic nature, like legitimating home-based workers for the applicability of labour legislations. Macro struggle relates to the contexting of each micro struggle within a macro perspective. For instance, one already knows that the stability or otherwise of home-based production depends crucially on macro trends and development processes in the economy. If technological change in a particular industry is likely to oust women home-based workers, one needs to evolve some perspectives on macro issues, along with the immediate micro concerns. The immediate victims and direct participants of micro struggles ought to develop a perspective on the macro issue. As is clear by now, micro struggles relate to the numerous immediate issues relevant to an occupation or industry and, in the case of women, to gender-specific issues of work.

Self-employed women workers in retail trade and services, like home-based producers, face problems such as access to credit and, raw materials and lack of infrastructure. Though they do not face the prospect of imminent loss of work, like home-based producers, many of them face the problem of keen competition for a limited market as well as very low returns. The cultural restrictions on women's mobility often forces them into a small scale of operation and a deprived position in the market. Space becomes a contested terrain among women and men traders, and the police and municipal authorities, with women turning out to be the losers. Despite the fact that most of them are 'survival entrepreneurs,' creatively adapting strategies for survival, which is largely the outcome of the macro problems facing the economy, their efforts for survival are hijacked by certain international agencies to promote their ideological position. The strengthening of these forces, no doubt, would contribute to a worsening of their situation. USAID and World Bank has called these women 'micro entreprenuers' and 'heralders of free society'. A very influential spokesman of this school says:

> It is women who are in the forefront of small business activity worldwide. Interviews suggest that through business they obtain a sense of self-worth and independence, which might not otherwise be available to them. When these business women have been organised by voluntary organisations in such countries as India and the Philippines, they have developed leadership and other skills of great value to their families and their communities. In the search for social and economic equity, it may well be these organised business women who will be the impetus for change (Berger, 1985).

This is an arena of important ideological struggle. This conflict is further heightened by the fact that government policies to promote self-employment for women have to be accepted on pragmatic grounds and rejected on ideological grounds. At the ideological level, one needs to note that self-employment (as envisaged in promotional policies as a petty commodity producer) is at a low level of business activity and, in a context of expanding capitalism, remains in a state of permanent vulnerability. Equally, the macrostructural factors in the economy causing a stagnant level for the organised sector is the concern and responsibility of the state, which cannot be diluted by such tinkering efforts. At the ideological level, one needs to further note the extent to which international agencies have been responsible in influencing national governments for promoting such policies. The countrywide debates following the budget of 1992 focused specifically on the role of multilateral agencies—the World Bank and the. IMF—in framing the national government's policies.

Self-employed workers, unlike some of the home-based workers and the workers in the casual wage sector, do not have an identifiable employer—employee relationship. The generation of class consciousness based on the use of this particular relationship, which is the strategy of most trade unions, is not possible here. Consequently, other kinds of relations need to be used to build this consciousness. This raises two crucial questions, namely, the existence and identification of these other relations, and the class position of the workers in this sector. According to traditional Marxist theory, this group would not constitute the proletariat and, strictly, some sections would be described as 'unproductive labour'. A majority of them though have the perception that they belong to the working class (proletariat), particularly when their economic position offers no scope for promoting themselves and their business to the scale of a small capitalist. At every available opportunity they might function with a petty bourgeois mentality and, in many instances, there is likely to be very little solidarity, as expressed by their class actions with the working class. With appropriate mobilisation, it is possible to make this section align with the working class. The important relation here appears to be the relationship of this sector with the state. In a context where the state can be characterised as a 'big bourgeois landlord' state, its relationship with the petty bourgeoisie is intrinsically an antagonistic one. It is this contradictory relation that provides the focus for mobilisation against the state. Viewed in this context, the mobilisation of self-employed women to counter police harassment or to act as a pressure group with the banks, and so on, can be seen as one aspect of mobilisation, against the state.

Wage employment in the casual wage sector includes a large section of women in activities such as construction and domestic service in urban areas and large number of women in rural areas employed as casual labour in agriculture. Whatever might be the issues at the material level, there can be no doubt that the most fundamental issue is the one of low wages and instability of employment. The dispersed location of their work sites makes mobilisation that much more difficult. Those who have had occasion to work with this section know that, very often, in the perceptions of those belonging to this sector itself, they are not in 'employment' but doing 'coolie work'. It is no wonder that this sector remains marginalised both in the impact of development efforts as well as the mobilisation activities of the more organised trade unions. Another relatively unknown category of workers in which women do constitute a significant number are contract labourers. Often living and working under sub-human conditions of bondage, even governments are guilty of the super-exploitation of contract workers. Organised trade unions are alleged to ignore this section generally. For the casual and contract workers in the organised sector, the immediate struggle is to get the trade unions to take up their interests. In a number of instances, the interests of the permanent workers are at variance with that of contract and casual workers. Constituting a cheaper labour reserve at all times, they are occasionally also roped in as scabs (workers who replace those belonging to striking trade unions). One aspect of the ideological struggle would be to overcome the perceptions of divisiveness between permanent workers and contract and casual labour.

In the foregoing, I have highlighted the problems of the different sections of workers in the informal sector, specifically referring to the problems of women workers and the different levels of struggle. In addition to the issues they face as workers, women in these different sectors of the informal sector face certain common problems as women. Most women work not out of choice but because of compulsions of survival. In addition to the long hours of work they put in for that purpose, they also bear the burden of all other domestic chores, child-rearing and cultural obligations. Given the dominant patriarchal ideology, the internal structure of even working class households (that is, the power and authority structure) is generally adverse to women, though there are differences even among women in terms of age, marital status and ritually defined position in the family. While the culturally defined sexual division of labour and its concomitant public and private domains provide some space for women for their autonomous exercise of power, the increasing crises of existence and the compulsions of survival have vastly eroded these spaces.

In the sphere of reproduction these women are forced more and more into having a large family, both to augment household income as well as a measure of social security in the absence of any state supported measures. This has not, only worsened their position economically in the short run, but has also further burdened women with reproductive tasks. Not only has familial violence on women been on the increase, but state encouraged oppressive family planning measures and the instrumental use of these women, both by international agencies and by multinational drug companies, has become a part of their daily routine. Such routinised imperialist assaults become, 'for women so oppressed, increasingly difficult to decipher given their involvement in survival struggles. An important aspect of the ideological struggle in this sphere would be to unravel these complex situations. While struggling to acquire greater control over their sexuality and fertility, they have to struggle simultaneously both at the material and ideological level against being used as instruments to serve other ends.

Yet another issue is the increasing crisis of existence, both in urban and rural areas, that affects this section of the population most severely. Lack of housing, water and sanitation, health care facilities and reduced accessibility to the public distribution system in urban areas, and the problems posed by the non-availability of fuel, water and fodder in rural areas have further eroded their real incomes apart from the decreases suffered on account of price increases. A study of the struggles of informal sector workers cannot, therefore, be restricted merely to economic issues on the work front alone.

PERSPECTIVES ON STRUGGLE

So far, by highlighting the objective conditions facing women informal sector workers, I have also demarcated certain arenas of struggle. In what follows, I shall discuss some of the perspectives on struggle, mobilisation and organisation of this section of women workers.

A broad conspectus on perspectives on struggle can only be arrived at after gaining sufficient knowledge and insight on various struggles conducted so far in different regions of the country. This literature, though growing, is still limited and more needs to be recorded. But, with what little knowledge we have so far, some issues can be raised.

Earlier, I had stated that struggles have to be conducted at different levels-ideological and material. Many struggles have been conducted on both fronts. At the material level, struggles are aimed at and have supported what, according to Maxine Molyneux (1986), may be termed 'strategic gender interests' and 'practical gender interests,' with the former emphasising the overall goal of gender equality and the latter addressing the immediate needs of women. At the ideological level, however, it appears that there are arenas of confusion—deliberate or based on insufficient understanding. The analysis of the different forms of struggle and of the perspectives of different organisations on mobilisation might help to clarify some issues.

Crucial to the debate is the existence of spontaneous struggle and the need for mobilisation. Even before the birth of the organised trade union movement, history is replete with examples of spontaneous struggles. These have been sporadic, and have been the outcome of excessive oppression. These spontaneous struggles can be individual or collective. At the individual level, they are manifested in resentment and rebellion. At the collective level, one needs to know more about how it can collectively emerge spontaneously, and whether there are organising and unifying elements internally. In other words, one needs to reflect more clearly on the aspect of spontaneity. At another level, one needs to understand both the efficacy and limitations of spontaneous struggle. To what extent do spontaneous struggles have an internal momentum to lead to a sustained movement? It is necessary to reflect on these issues before one glorifies spontaneity. The plea to reflect on 'spontaneity' does not necessarily imply an acceptance of party 'vanguardism'.

There is, no doubt, overwhelming support that there does exist scope as well as a rationale for mobilisation and organisation through external impetus. Here, again, there are divergent views. Some pose the role of organisations as one of promoting development. 'Struggle through or with development' has been the slogan along with others which exclusively emphasise struggle. Another issue is the link with other movements and struggles, in particular, the link with trade unions vis-a-vis the role of autonomous organisations. Increasingly, the power connotations implicit in external impetus are being questioned, and an alternative of 'empowerment through self activity' is being posed. In the following pages, I shall reflect on each of these issues.

Mobilisation strategies based on the logic of 'struggle through development' are of the view that the existing structural context provides for mobilisation through the use of certain existing instruments. These also strengthen the economic base and, to some extent, diminish the vulnerability of women. Thus, this strategy does not directly confront the elements of power but attempts to strengthen the powerless by bringing them to a state of preparedness. The successful experiments of SEWA and WWF can be viewed in this context. However, once the limits of radicalisation within the system are reached, struggle becomes inevitable. In this case, often development inputs are deliberately kept at levels that do not threaten the existing power base. While credit interventions (as in the case of SEWA, WWF and Annapurna) have made women realise their contradictory relationship with the state, other interventions completely remove women from these contradictions such that political consciousness achieved through confronting contradictions is completely absent. One of the most widespread and influential strategies is the promotion of so-called income- generating projects. Based on 'the incontestable argument of augmenting incomes, they often serve as a cap on worker militancy and social unrest. As a strategy for raising consciousness, by its very inception, it signifies retreat. Rather than confront the oppressive forces directly, it withdraws the oppressed from the scene completely, and does not increase their bargaining power. Even if the projects are successful, which often they are not, they do not offer the true solution of oppressive work conditions as it cannot be envisaged that these can be multiplied manyfold.

Another issue that needs to be debated is the relationship of these organisations with the trade union movement. This was briefly referred to earlier. Given the enormous scope of organisation in the context where large masses of workers are unorganised, the mere presence of certain autonomous organisations is also no proof that trade unions have not shown concern. A systematic documentation of the arenas where trade unions have organised and where they have not is an initial step. This ought to be followed by the outcomes of such organisation. This work is not aimed at providing a defence for the trade unions. Equally, one should be aware that external agencies are interested in positioning trade unions and these organisations in an antagonistic relationship. The dangers of succumbing to such viewpoints need to be clarified. The existence of these organisations ought not to be viewed both by those involved and others as alternatives to trade unions, but their' existence ought to provide a challenge to trade unions to break out of their conventional rigidities.

Some of these organisations are, no doubt, posed as alternative strategies. Conventional forms of organisation, both in trade unions, parties and other organisations, are viewed as the 'top- down' approach. It is deemed that this reinforces domination and hierarchy that exists in the world outside, the transformation of those structures being the fundamental objective of these organisations. Also, those organised ought to be able to shape their own destiny and not be puppets or the mere objects of others. This has led to an increasing acceptance of the strategy of 'empowerment through self-activity'. While the plea that the oppressed shape their own lives would evoke appeal from large progressive sections, and organisations pursuing this strategy need to be supported, two issues remain unanswered. First, the phrase 'empowerment through self-activity' has a striking resemblance with the language and phrases of some international agencies, and seems to be used increasingly by a wide cross-section of activists whose ideological positions appear to be very different. It is not clear what empowerment means or implies at the grassroots level. Does empowerment mean social transformation based on class, caste, gender and nationalist struggles? In other words, the question is empowerment for what? Different answers to this question would signify differing basic ideological positions. It is not for long that one can avoid the question: What are the possibilities and limits of ideological pluralism and how far can they facilitate or inhibit the achievement of certain practical short-term gender interests? Is there a way of choosing between differing tactics arising out of ideological pluralism to achieve certain strategic gender interests?

'The term 'self-activity', too, has a dangerous significance. Some international agencies, such as USAID and the World Bank, are pushing dangerously the strategy of a 'self-help programme,' the underlying philosophy of which is that the poor can help themselves. The translation of such an ideology into organisational practice would seem very similar to the strategy of 'empowerment through self-activity'. In the objective of democratising organisational practice, one should be clear that the need of the hour is one of clarity of issues. Consciousness-raising through self-activity ought to be able to bring the interrelationship of gender and macrostructural factors, of the linkages of micro struggles with macro struggles, and of the nuances of ideological struggle into much greater clarity that what exists. The limitedness of perceptions based on a limited worldview and life experiences cannot constitute a democratic solution, howsoever democratically it has been arrived at.

NOTE

1. See Henry Bernstein (1986) and the special issue 'Rethinking Petty Commodity Production', *Labour, Capital and Society* (April 1986).

34

Organising Around Credit: The Case of the Working Women's Forum

The women's movement in India had a new lease of life in the 1970s, after nearly two decades of lull after Independence.[1] However, it should be noted that the term women's movement is an abstraction. In reality, it comprises heterogeneous groups, some engaged in consistent and some in sporadic action—action itself ranging from a wide variety of militant struggles with a focus on structural change to welfare-oriented social service agencies that do not question the status quo. The period of the 1970s saw an increased participation of the urban masses, drawing particularly the educated middle class in the urban areas. The declaration of Emergency in 1976 was preceded by one of the most militant working class struggles in the post Independence period on a countrywide basis—namely, the railway strike exposing state brutality in its most powerful form. The post-Emergency political awakening in the country led to a re-examination of the true nature of democratic polity in the country. This manifested itself in the emergence of numerous civil liberties organisations and women's groups. The UN declaration of the decade of women strengthened these newly formed women's groups by providing both moral and material support as well as a rationale for their existence that could, in some instances, camouflage their own political origins.

In many instances, political awakening among a certain section was synonymous with a disillusionment with party politics. It was generally felt that political parties were deviating more and more from the grassroots, and the genuine needs and aspirations of the people found only inadequate expression in their political agenda. The leadership of the parties was not only estranged but contained very few from the oppressed sections of society, (such as women, poor or the depressed castes).

In the case of women, the disillusionment with party politics led to the formation of independent and autonomous women's groups, drawing, in some instances, women from political parties, and coopting others who would otherwise have been drawn closer to the parties. These independent and autonomous women's groups may be termed 'non-party political formations' and do not constitute a homogenous lot in respect to ideologies or strategies. Some of the groups are the outcome of dissatisfaction with the left parties' traditions and have a conscious class-based political and feminist approach with struggle as their focus, while others that are the outcome of non-left political and trade union practices have a developmental approach rather than struggle.

This developmental approach to the mobilisation of women and collective action has received a fillip from international agencies. Whatever perspective on development the agencies might have, there is no denying the fact that such developmental organisations have served the useful purpose of promoting consciousness among women during periods of what may be called 'normal levels of exploitation'. Unlike periods of intensified oppression (such as the Emergency, with consequent actions like the suppression of civil liberties when spontaneous collective actions emerge which, at times, lead to militant struggle), periods of 'normal levels of exploitation' have, by and large, been accepted and internalised by the masses as a 'way of life'. Politicisation and consciousness-raising during this 'normal' period serves the long-term strategic interest of creating a highly developed and emancipated consciousness among the masses. This provides the *raison d'etre* for development organisations with a focus on empowerment and consciousness raising. In what follows, I shall examine the experiences of one such organisation, recognised the world over as a very successful experiment.

The Working Women's Forum (WWF) in Madras city is a grassroots organisation, exclusively involved in mobilising poor working women. We have called this an experiment in collective action as it exhibits a case of such women coming together, mobilising their resources, and achieving their objectives with whatever methods are- suited best. These women have, not only provided the leadership, but are also the potential agents of social change. The primary objective of the Forum is to empower poor working women both in their productive and reproductive roles. Empowerment is understood as providing a sufficient degree of control and decision-making power, access to resources and raising the level of consciousness of both their class and gender status. Using credit as a point of entry, the WWF mobilises the 'micro entrepreneurs' in the urban informal sector, and the home-based producers in the rural areas of three southern states. It has now extended its activities to two cities in the northern state of Uttar Pradesh, and hopes to venture soon into another northern state—Bihar. The manner in which credit intervention is conceived transforms it from an end to a means of forming a collective. Neighbourhood collectives of women drawn together for credit purposes, also take up numerous other issues affecting their work and lives and become, over time, conscious participants in collective action.

The activities of the Forum can be listed under three broad groups: the credit programme, the family planning and health programme, and social conscientisation activities. When the President of the Forum and her allies decided in 1978 to break away from the women's front of the Congress party, which had by then split with the dominant Congress (I) party, they decided to form a women's organisation that would be apolitical (that is, non-party oriented and women-intensive). This was based on their conviction that grassroots development organisations, though no substitute for political parties or political solutions, could lead to political action. Thus, when the organisation was formed, they had to decide on the focus and the activities. Credit was theft identified as an instrument of mobilisation.

Credit Programme

The Forum has two channels of credit for women informal sector workers—through nationalised banks and through its own cooperative credit societies. Since its modest inception in Madras city in 1979 with about 800 members, the Forum's credit activities have grown both intensively and extensively in such a way that it now has a membership of nearly 200,000 and covers the following women workers: informal sector workers in Madras city; agricultural labourers and shandy (wholesale market) workers in Dindigul taluk, Madurai district, Tamil Nadu; fisher women in Adirampattinam, Thanjavur district, Tamil Nadu; Beedi workers in North Arcot district, Tamil Nadu; agarbatti workers in the slums of Bangalore city, Karnataka; lace makers of Narasapur, Andhra Pradesh; rural non-agricultural workers in Bidar district, Karnataka; silk weavers in Kancheepuram, Tamil Nadu; chickan embroidery workers in Lucknow, Uttar Pradesh; and night schools for migrant workers in Kanpur, Uttar Pradesh.

The objective of credit intervention is to relieve women engaged in subsistence occupations from the clutches of moneylenders and middle-men by providing them working capital at low rates of interest. Individually, it reduces the interest burden as well as provides women with a certain autonomy, access and control over resources, and enhances their contribution to household income.[2] These individual effects are the outcome of supplying cheap credit. The most striking impact, however, is the 'collective consciousness' and 'collective action' generated by the manner in which credit intervention is organised.

The core of the organisational structure consists of its members constituted into groups, with a group leader nominated from within. The group leaders of the neighbourhood loan groups report to the Forum's organisers (who are full-time employees on a monthly salary) on all matters relating to the Forum. The initiative for the formation of groups in a neighbourhood is obviously local. The entire credit intervention system revolves around the neighbourhood loan groups. Loans are not given to individuals but to groups, with group leaders providing the guarantee as well as the responsibility of collecting the dues. Thus, when an individual approaches the Forum for credit, she is asked to identify nine or ten others like her in similar occupations and in need of credit, and form a group. The neighbourhood loan groups provide both peer group support and peer group pressure.

Loans for groups are negotiated with nationalised banks under the Differential Rate of Interest Scheme, whereby loans carrying a 4 per cent rate of interest are given to weaker sections of society (weaker sections refers to those households with a low annual income, the limit of which was specified in 1985 as less than Rs. 3,000 per annum). Alternatively, the Forum has its own cooperative credit societies in all centres where, for a share of Rs 20, the members can obtain a loan ten times the value of the share. The initial capital base of these societies is met through grants. Here, too, loans are given only to groups. However, the rate of interest on loans from credit societies is high (13—15 per cent per annum).

TABLE 34.1

Working Women's Cooprative Society: Progress of Credit Programmes in Branches of Tamil Nadu and Others State (1981-91)

	Year of Starting	*No. of Members in WWF)1)*	*No. of Loans*	*Loan Amount Disbursed*	*Recovered*		*Default Groups*	*Recoverable Loan Outstanding*		*Bad debts*	
					Amount	*%*		*Amount*	*%*	*Amount*	*%*
Madras											
Central Madras											
South Madras	1981	52,786	31,186	16,026,376	15,235,135	96.58	292	309,387	1.93	238,854	1.49
North Madras											
Rural Tamil Nadu											
Adirampattinam	1985	19,013	16,857	5,615,600	5,410,296	96.34	163	199,599	3.56	5,705	0.10
Dindigul	1985	17,219	14,552	3,980,800	3,785,519	95.09	104	178,068	4.48	17,213	0.43
Velore	1984	14,849	16,101	5,555,800	5,210,919	93.79	246	271,081	4.88	73,800	1.33
Kancheepuram	1990	3,044	2,679	2,784,200	1,572,134	56.74	—	1,212,066	43.53	—	—
Karnataka											
Bangalore	1982	23,070	12,596	5,055,000	4,450,114	95.40	229	113,275	2.50	99,411	2.10
Bidar	1988	11,564	9,328	2,527,600	2,400,540	95.13	165	118,880	4.70	4,180	0.16
Andhra Pradesh											
West Godavari	1984	44,427	42,029	10,128,500	10,118,960	99.90	7	9,540	0.10	—	—
East Godavari	1984	8,097	7,665	2,092,045	2,090,686	—	—	1,359	—	—	—
Bhimavaram	1988	6,271	6,498	1,842,000	1,838,470	—	—	3,530	—	—	—
Total		200,340	159,491	55,607,921	52,116,773	92.90	1,206	2,416,785	6.60	439,163	0.50

There are different sets of people involved in the entire credit programme—members, groups and group leaders, organisers, Forum staff, staff of the cooperative credit societies and banking personnel. Relations between these different people determine, to a large extent, the success or failure of the credit programme. The fact that, in the last seven years, there has been a manifold increase in membership (see Table 34.1) confirms the strength and success of the group system. This is not in any way to brush aside the constant tensions and contradictions that surface everyday, most of which get resolved through the 'collective process'.

It is also the responsibility of the group leaders to cultivate among their members the spirit of the women's collective. Different leaders, depending on the extent to which they themselves are conscious, try to promote this in different ways. The most common is by interacting closely with members' families and listening to their problems in a concerned way. Quite often, group leaders have brought to the attention of organisers instances that they have encountered on such visits of desertion, dowry harassment, suffering at the hands of drunken husbands, wife beating, and the 'other woman' syndrome. Obviously, on these matters, there are no guidelines by the Forum on bow group leaders should achieve their goals, and this is largely left to their discretion, temperament and the situations in which they are placed.

In a slum clearance tenement in Madras city, I was witness to a massive confrontation between the members and group leaders. Members complained that group leaders very often threatened them that they would not get their loans if they did not attend the Forum meetings or participate in processions, and it is because of these threats that they attended. The group, leaders countered that there is a tendency to view the Forum as Only a loan giving agency, and that the ideology of the Forum and the spirit of the women's collective is not understood. Given the terms of reference of both groups, each group's arguments seemed valid. A younger member of the group intervened to say that this kind of problem would not come up if the Forum arranged more meetings in that area. Infrequent meetings have kept the members at a distance and without complete identification with the Forum's ideology.

The task of the organisers is to extend the activities of the Forum to other rural areas and urban slums, to screen the new groups formed, inform them of the rules and regulations of the Forum, assess their genuine credit needs by probing into the economics of their occupations, and to negotiate with the banks for loans and help the groups in repayment. Thus the organisers serve as a vital link between the groups and the Forum. All problems in the area are brought to the attention of the organiser who, in turn, brings it up for discussion at the meetings where all the other organisers and office bearers are present.

Clearly, the extent to which the organisers can understand and appreciate the work and lives of the members and their ability to maintain a good rapport with the groups determine the kind of results they can achieve. In this context, the socio-economic background of the organisers becomes important. A majority of the organisers come from working class households with prior occupational experience in the informal sector. A little over a quarter of the organisers have themselves not been engaged in any occupation, but the personal crises in their lives have cemented their solidarity with the working women. Personal crisis here could be a state of dependence forced on them by the death of a father or husband, desertion, inability to procure a marriage partner owing to excessive dowry demands, harassment due to the presence of 'the other woman' or alcoholism. Such crises do enable the woman to dovetail with the class-based oppression of other working women also.

The following case study is a hood illustration of this point. Sivagami, a young widow with two children, recalled that soon after her husband's death in an accident, she approached *amma* (meaning mother, and refers to the President of the WWF) for a job in the Forum. Married after her school final to a bank clerk, Sivagami had led a protected and cloistered life till then. She was emotionally and economically shattered when she went to work as an organiser among the fisherwomen of Adirampattinam, but she soon realised that there were people worse off than her, and now she moves around with confidence organising the fisherwomen.

Joining the Forum creates, in women like Sivagami and others, a new awakening, and they begin to perceive their .own specific oppression as one amongst a wide range in a class, caste and patriarchal society. However, as in the case of group leaders and members, here, too, there ate tensions and challenges. Bangalore city, with its two ethnic groups—Tamil migrants and the local Kannadigas—offers a striking example. Conflicts between these two ethnic groups have, in recent years, led to some major conflagarations. Thus, the Forum was stepping into troubled waters, as it is an organisation based in Tamil Nadu. It, naturally, attracted a number of Tamil organisers and members in the beginning and created suspicion among the Kannadigas. These suspicions were further exacerbated when the few Kannadigas who joined the Forum found that the sanction for their loans through the bank was getting delayed. Now the Forum has its own cooperative credit society in Bangalore.

We have traced in detail the nature of the relationship between the members, group leaders and organisers as they constitute the core solidarity group. The most noteworthy aspect is that most of them are drawn from poor working class households—households engaged in informal sector occupations. Apart from these, the staff of the cooperative credit societies and the Forum workers who are involved in the credit programme are generally women below 30 years of age with a school education and sometimes with a diploma in cooperative training. These women are generally from lower middle class households.

The Credit Programme in Different Areas

Table 34.1 illustrates the coverage of the credit programme under the credit scheme in all the centres. In each of these centres, the dominant occupation for which credit intervention is aimed at is different, and we shall, in each instance, examine the efficacy of such an intervention as a means of mobilisation and its effects on increasing the awareness of oppression faced by the women.

Madras City: Within the Municipal Corporation limits of the city, there were 107,553 women workers in 1981. About 30 per cent of them were engaged in informal sector activities, both as self- employed and as casual wage labourers in low paid, low working capital low skill and low absolute surplus generating subsistence occupations. These self-employed women workers can, in fact, be called micro entrepreneurs as they are clearly very innovative in devising adaptive strategies for survival. But, most often, even these survival strategies are severely constrained by the lack of working capital finance, very high interest payments, lack of markets, lack of space and lack of mobility..

The organisation first concentrated its activities in Madras city where a large number of women in the informal sector are engaged in petty trade such a vegetable and fruit vending, selling of snacks like *idli* and *vadais* in the urban slums or selling cut-piece (pre-cut) cloth and sarees. They approached this section of women to find out their foremost needs. These retail vendors felt that their low absolute returns each days were further diminished by interest payments on loans taken either on a daily or weekly interest basis to meet their working capital requirements. These survival enterprises are largely dependent on the extent and availability of working capital. The women suggested that if loans at a lower rate of interest were given to them to meet their business requirements, they could free themselves from the local moneylenders. Thus, they perceived themselves, to be in an immediate antagonistic relationship with the local moneylenders.

Till 1985, the Forum had identified and provided credit assistance to 79 different occupations in the urban informal sector, though cut-piece, vegetable and *idli* sales accounted for nearly half of all the loans provided. I give below an account of these occupations.

All the vegetable vendors have to go to the wholesale bazaar in the city in the morning. Their loan requirements , as observed, range from Rs 100—Rs 500. In one of the retail markets I visited in north Madras, a rental of Rs 2 in the forenoon and Rs 2 in the afternoon was collected. Because of the renovation of the market, they had to pay an advance of Rs 5,000 per shop as well as a daily rent of Rs 12. A large number of women vendors, whose scale of business is rather small and who cannot afford to pay the rental for the market space, are seated outside on the narrow streets leading to the market, spreading their wares on the side of the street. Apart from passing cycles and autorickshaws squashing a few tomatoes, they are constantly harassed by the police by the constant threat of eviction. With the Forum mobilising the women and through their constant pressure, in the opinion of the women there has been a perceptible decrease in the number of police cases registered in certain areas.

A few profiles of those who have benefited under the credit programme in Madras' city are revealing.

Sundari, a vegetable seller in Pattalam market, notes that prior to her joining the *sangam* and obtaining credit assistance she used to borrow on an interest rate of 10 per cent per month (120 per cent per annum) with payments to be made every day or weekly. This money was largely rolling cash for her business, which did not roll with a one shot injection of a stock amount owing to unexpected market or personal losses. So far she has borrowed five times from the *sangam* starting with Rs. 200 to the most recent Rs. 800. She has even repaid that, and is waiting for her next loan. Now Sundari does not take money from moneylenders on *thandal* but when contingencies arise (particularly during periods when loans are fully paid and the next one gets delayed), she pawns a few items to the pawn broker.

Lakshmi, her husband, their 17-year old son and 9-year old daughter were all engaged in making cardboard boxes for a jewellery shop. With an initial investment of Rs 100 they could make a profit of Rs 50 if the entire family worked for a full week. Earlier, they would take money from moneylenders but, with the Forum's loan coming, their survival constraint was eased. But that was only for a very short period before they were caught up in a severe trap. Recently, her husband was hospitalised for a month with a heart attack and he is still unable to work. It was not only the hospital expenses that burdened them, forcing them to borrow from moneylenders but, more severely, their entire occupation was affected. Her husband was the only one who knew the measurements and the way to cut the cardboard for the boxes. The rest of the family did only the sticking. Lakshmi is now thinking of setting up an *idli* stall. Hesitant to take up this new occupation, she is forced into such a venture as debts with moneylenders mount everyday. She is now dependent on the Forum for the initial capital.

Summing up the impact of the credit assistance programme in Madras city, in most areas women who were previously indebted to usurious moneylenders for their working capital requirements now seemed to be relieved of them. However, delays in procuring the next loan and other unforeseen business and personal contingencies sometimes force them back to the pawn brokers, though there has been a clear decrease in their involvement with *thandals.* Secondly, the loan amount had, in many cases, provided the initial capital for a business or helped in expanding their scale of operation. In some cases, it helped in clearing old debts and meeting other household expenses. Women also reported that they were now eating better. Apart from these direct benefits relating to their occupation and income, the women could also perceive an enhancement in their status. Earlier, most of them had never stepped into a nationalised bank and those who had gone narrated how they were treated by the officials. These unseemly women chewing *pan,* and most often stinking after a day's work in the vegetable market, would be a nuisance factor to the more elite bank customers. Now, when they walk into the bank, they are offered chairs to sit on. With the starting of the Working Women's Cooperative Credit Society, their realisation that it is their own bank has enormously increased their self-confidence.

Dindigul: In the Dindigul taluk of Madurai district, two groups of women have benefited from the credit assistance programme—women from landless agricultural labour households and women shandy workers.

Natchikonampatti is a small hamlet with sixty households, where most of the members are hired agricultural labourers. A variety of crops are grown—paddy, sugarcane, cholam, tomatoes, sunflower, chillies and cotton. However, women here have work for only about 60 days scattered over the year. This is a dry taluk, lacking well irrigation, where agriculture depends largely on rainfall. Agricultural wages in 1985 stood at a very low Rs 3 for women and Rs 6—Rs 8 for men. During the harvest they are paid in kind--3 measures of paddy, which amounts to 2 kilos of rice. For cutting sugarcane, the leaves of the cane are given as wages. Fodder for cattle is very scarce in this dry region and so the leaves, which elsewhere command no price, are a substitute for money wages. Similarly, for plucking cotton, the inferior rejected balls are given as wages.. None of the women were aware of the existing minimum wages law. Here women and men face the problem of both availability of work as well as low wages. Some households had availed of goat loans and some others had dairy cattle on a *varam saram* basis, (that is, the landlord would buy the cattle and the labourer would rear it, and milk would be shared on a 50—50 basis).

Prior to obtaining these dairy loans, women would take loans both for purposes of consumption and to meet unforeseen contingencies, both from moneylenders and landlords. Harassment from moneylenders is known. When these women took loans from the landlord, they had to send their child to the landlord's *pannai* (farm) to work until the debt was cleared.

In this context, the kind of credit intervention the Forum launched in collaboration with the women agricultural labourers was to provide them loans for obtaining dairy cattle. By negotiating with a local nationalised bank, the Forum was able to provide dairy loans for 251 members in the district, Of these, 228 members got loans for the first animal and 23 got a second loan (either for a second animal or to replace a dead one). Twenty-two of the 60 households in Nachikonampatti had obtained dairy loans. The Forum had also arranged for milk marketing through a depot in Dindigul.

Keeping dairy cattle and making a living out of it is not an easy affair. Firstly, only some of these households had any experience in rearing dairy cattle, and many women had to be-trained by the animal husbandry officers. Secondly, with the scarcity of fodder in a dry region and the lack of access to grazing land owing to privatisation and encroachment of all village commons by the landlords, feeding the cattle becomes a costly affair when both fodder and husk have to be bought. Invariably, the loans were fully repaid after the second calving.

The impact of these dairy loans on the work and lives of women has been manifold. The women who are -now engaged in looking after the cattle do not take up agricultural work at such low wages as before, causing some annoyance to landlords during times of peak labour demand. They are often known to remark, 'Your hands have now been strengthened. You won't come and work in our fields.' Thus the landlords are now forced to draw labour from other hamlets, a threat the landlords had used for years whenever the local workers asked for higher wages. Now they are forced to carry out this threat—not because the landlords are powerful but because their power has been whittled down. The bargaining power of the cattle recipient has obviously improved. Yet their income from agriculture has not significantly improved, nor has their nexus with the landlord been severed.

First, in a household with more than one adult woman (of whom only one person is engaged in looking after the cattle), the others do take up agricultural work. Secondly, during dry-milking periods, even those otherwise engaged in looking after cattle seek agricultural work. During the cotton picking season, all the women go to work as it has to be done at the dawn, after which they come back to look after the cattle. Thus the labour supply situation for the landlords, due to the existing nexus and availability of labour from other hamlets, is not altered significantly. However, for the women, agricultural wages have increased over time from a low Rs 1.25 to Rs 3.00 today. The women recalled that a year ago they refused to take up agricultural work if the wages were not increased. But their struggle, which was only in the nature of a small pressure group, did not succeed. Even if these small increments in wages were due to the presence of an alternative income-earning opportunity, they were still very much lower than the legally stipulated minimum wages. Thus, both on the wage front and of altering dominance—subordination relations at the village level, there is need for a major thrust by the Forum.

Shandy Loans: There are a number of women in and around Dindigul selling items such as flowers, fruits and vegetables, tamarind seeds, banana stalks, ropes and old iron pieces. For four days in a week they traverse up to 10 kilometres to the larger villages and towns where the shandies are held. On the remaining days they sell their wares on the streets, or door-to-door. For vending in the shandies a rent is collected. Most of the women moving from the village to different shandies are shelterless.

Kotturavarampatti, a hamlet in Dindigul taluk, has a large number of womenfolk employed as shandy workers. This extremely isolated hamlet, with no public transport facility, lies in a drought- prone village. Little agricultural work is available during the year. Dairy cattle, as alternative employment, does not appear to have much scope owing to the non-availability of fodder and water. Thus a number of survival mechanisms have been adopted. Bananas, banana leaves and banana stalks are bought by the village women from the landlords and, sold in the shandies. With a low agricultural wage of Rs 7 for men and Rs 5 for women per day coupled with the extreme irregularity of agricultural work, women did not even have the funds to procure these items. Most of them pawned whatever jewellery they had with the cooperative bank and obtained loans on interest rates of 10 per cent per annum. Those who could not avail of this option invariably pawned whatever household items they possessed to the moneylender. As the professional moneylenders were not present in the village, the better-off families performed the moneylending role.

The Forum, through its credit programme, gave loans to these shandy workers once they formed credit groups, and has eased their survival constraint to a significant extent.

While these are the direct effects, the indirect but articulated effects are striking. All the women are now confident about speaking up in meetings and articulating their problems. This has been made possible by the numerous discussion meetings organised by the *sangam*. Further, their isolation, caused by spatial immobility, appears to have totally broken down. Those who were able to visit large cities (like Madras and Madurai) and towns (like

Dindigul) recalled what a tremendous learning experience and exposure to the world it was. Particularly, though not surprisingly their disillusionment with the functioning of political parties as well as their total understanding of the power relationships in the system, the role of politicians, the bureaucracy, landlords and moneylenders have totally transformed their perception of their own selves. Whereas, earlier, their powerlessness was matched with ignorance and a positive acceptance of fate, now their understanding of their powerlessness is accompanied by a strong and articulated resentment. Hopelessness had given way to attempts, however weak or meagre, at achieving a greater solidarity among themselves.

Adirampattinam: In Adirampattinam and twelve nearby coastal villages in Thanjavur district, the WWF has formed credit groups of women involved in fish marketing. The role of women in fish marketing can be understood only in the overall context of the fishing economy of the region. The entire catch is auctioned off, and no individual can sell directly to the market or hand over his catch to his wife. The village auction system evolved out of a necessity to generate common village funds as well as to have a regulated market for fish where the village collective could have greater say. Village funds are generally used for the purposes the community decides on (such as temple functions/renovations or inter-village litigations). Women not only support and strengthen these community decisions directly and indirectly but, very often, draw a lot of their social and cultural sustenance from these activities as well.

On the economic front, however, the emergence of the auction system has been adverse for women. Whereas, earlier, men used to give their catch to the women in their household to sell (thus enabling women to obtain a cash income along with some degree of control), this has now passed on to the men completely. Deprived of this as well as the fact that if women wanted to sell fish they also have to buy it in the auction, for which they needed cash, women's involvement in the auction system became-both compulsive and difficult. Women were forced to take loans from moneylenders at usurious rates and under humiliating conditions. The Forum's credit intervention enabled the women engaged in fish marketing to carry on their occupation outside the hold of the moneylenders. Apart from the fish sellers, the Forum has also mobilised other women peripherally engaged in the fishing economy (such as basket makers, salt sellers and those selling food items near the fish landing spot).

In several villages in Adirampattinam, the women pointed out that through the credit assistance programme of the *sangam* they have now been able to relieve themselves from the clutches of the moneylenders to a great extent. Almost all of them also indicated that the loan amount was grossly insufficient. Whether or not they were prompted by their menfolk, all of them wanted loans to buy nets. All the women are very clear that it is only the ownership of the means of production that can give them greater economic power, and for fishing households a larger number of nets mean a larger catch. This is in spite of the fact that women realise that not all of the higher earnings got thereby are going to percolate down to the household.

As in the other centres, one of the indirect effects of the *sangam* of raising the class consciousness of these women through their credit scheme has been their holistic understanding of power relationships (namely, the conflicts between the launch operators and the traditional fishermen, between the boatowners and others among the traditional fishermen, of their compulsive involvement in the auction system, and of the other dominance—subordination relationships, such as caste, in which they are caught in a total state of powerlessness.

Vellore: Most of the women workers in the household industry in Vellore (numbering 4,422, according to the 1981 Census) are beedi workers, of whom a little less than 50-per cent have been brought within the fold of the Forum. Most of the women and a large number of the men are engaged in the piece-rate putting- out system of work, though there are beedi factories predominantly employing men. The put-out piece-rate system is a hybrid one, also involving a sale and purchase transaction. The beedi workers buy the *tendu* leaves and tobacco and sell the rolled beedis to the beedi *mandis* (merchant-cum-factory owners) at a rate that amounts to only piece-rate wages. Most often, the 'sale-purchase' transaction involves a loss to the workers because of the bad quality of raw materials or fraudulence in the quantity measure. In order to ensure for themselves the stipulated piece wages, the workers are forced to meet the deficit raw materials. Further, during the monsoon period, the beedi *'mandis'* do not give out work at all and the workers are forced into a consumption loan trap. It is here that the credit of the Forum plays an important role. The credit assistance programme of the Forum found an enthusiastic response with women beedi workers.

The effect in terms of raising consciousness is noteworthy. No doubt these women on the put-out system were, to an extent, already sensitised on class issues, given their formal subsumption under merchant capitalists. Though not formally members of any trade union, these women workers are sufficiently influenced by the activities of the trade unions in the beedi factories, employing predominantly men. At the times of struggle by the organised beedi workers, the put-out women workers were laid off, and also during lock-outs in the factories no work was put-out. However, successful wage struggles in the factories found the put-out piece-rates increase only marginally.

The Forum's activities, while sharpening the class consciousness that existed, carried the women to a new height of consciousness. For instance, the articulated resentment of a Muslim woman against the refusal of Muslim *mandi* owners to give raw materials to women, while giving them only to the men of households on the put-out system, was seen as a way of reinforcing their cultural subordination in the domain of work. The resentment of working women against the functioning of the bureaucracy after their ordeal in getting *patta* for their homestead land, against elite researchers and against postmen who would visit the low-lying shims only on dry sunny days, are instances of their consciousness with respect to their class and gender status vis-à-vis others in the totality of the society.

Bangalore: According to the 1981 Census, of the 13,007 women workers in household industry in the Bangalore urban agglomeration, 3,337 women had been covered under the credit programme of the Forum in *1985.* In a span of two years, this is a no small achievement in an environment of suspicion and hostility between the two ethnic groups—the Tamil migrants and the local Kannadigas.

The organisation of the *agarbatti* (scented incense sticks) industry is on similar lines as the beedi industry mentioned earlier. It is characterised by the coexistence of factory, workshop and put-out production. Most women on the put-out system were home-based producers, dependent upon the exploiting merchant capitalist for raw materials. The credit programme of the Forum, in effect, transformed them from dependent home-based workers status to independent home-based producers by enabling them to purchase raw materials and sell independently. Though the increase in income was only marginal and the survival struggle itself was not overcome, the women felt less harassed now than before. More importantly, with their own working capital, during the monsoon period when they stop work due to the peculiarity of this activity, they are left with a part of that capital to meet their consumption requirements.

While the earlier attempts at unionisation focused only on the factory-based agarbatti workers, the Forum made the first attempt, as pointed out by the women themselves, at bringing together the home-based workers. The attendant trials and tribulations of bringing together two ethnic groups that were mutually suspicious and hostile has been an enormous learning experience for the Forum. For the women themselves, where these bridges of communication have been built, it has brought about an enduring solidarity among the poor women as one oppressed group.

Narasapur: Narasapur is situated in West Godavari district in the southern state of Andhra Pradesh. This is an agriculturally prosperous and highly commercialised region. With the green revolution came the capitalist farmer replacing the precapitalist forms of sharecropping tenancy. The tenants are now agricultural labourers.

While men previously cultivated the land as sharecroppers, their women were confined to domestic chores. In the late nineteenth century, these women learnt the art of lace making which has now become a flourishing export trade for the state.[3]

The lace making industry is predominantly in the hands of merchant exporters. They employ contractors to go around various villages distributing reels of thread along with export orders to the women lace makers on a piece-rate payment of Rs 4 per reel of thread woven. Apart from these contractors, the lace makers who are quick at work and have additional members at home, and for whom the thread given by these contractors is insufficient, prefer to make lace on their own and sell it in the weekly Palakol shandies. However, not all the lace makers go to the shandies to sell. In most villages, tradeswomen have emerged.

The lace makers, under the capitalist agricultural regime, belong to the agricultural labour households. The obvious display of communist party flags in the region may represent a strong tendency to unionise the agricultural labourers, but has apparently bypassed this section of the working class—the women lace makers— perceiving the, lace making activity as the leisure-time work of the women. Consequently, the political parties have missed the misery of the women lace makers of Narasapur.

The Forum's intervention in the West and East Godavari districts has been threefold. First, through its credit assistance programme it provided scope for the women to be independent lace makers selling for shandies, or to combine contract work with independent work. Second, through the Commerce Ministry, it sought to procure export orders directly and began to distribute thread to women on its own at a rate of Rs 10 per reel. The quantitative jump from Rs 4 to Rs 10 which proved feasible under the Forum's assistance, laid bare the exploitation of the merchants. The lace makers perceived this so clearly that they forced the merchants/contractors to increase the piece-rate to Rs 6 or Rs 8 per reel. Third, the Forum, through its credit programme, actively encouraged the not-so-good lace-makers, largely selling to the shandies, to shift to other occupations (such as coir rope making).

The credit scheme, by attempting to transform the women into independent producers, has forced them into another set of problems—that of marketing in the shandies. The demonstration effect of higher piece-rates through direct export orders runs into difficulties because the orders are erratic, the organisational resources are small and so the activity cannot be expanded, and the supply of quality thread recently (referring to the time when fieldwork was done—March 1985) has been affected by a lock-out in the major thread unit.

In the case of occupational diversification, the Forum is constrained by limited resources. This does not enable the setting up of mechanised coir rope making units on a cooperative basis, which would pay the women Rs 5—Rs 10 a day. The activity, therefore, is done manually in their homes involving even the children of the family.

Bidar: Bidar district, in the north-eastern corner of Karnataka, is one of the most economically backward regions in the state. In order to promote rural non-farm employment opportunities in this dry region where agriculture is solely dependent on the rainfall, the Karnataka government in 1981 initiated the Bidar Integrated Rural Development project also known as the BIRD project, specifically with a view to improve the quality of life of rural women and children with a substantial resource allocation of nearly Rs 6 crore. Under this project, it sought to provide non-farm employment to women by assisting in both technology and credit through the village technology centres and rural cooperative banks. The local Mahila Mandals were involved in the credit scheme. Each Mahila Mandal was given Rs 5,000 and had about thirty or forty women members. Through this initial capital, loans from commercial banks were sought for the members as start-up finance for new economic activities.

By 1985 this scheme ran into a number of difficulties. Invariably, the presidents of the Mahila Mandals were high caste women belonging to the Lingayat and Okkaliga castes, and these women were reluctant to reach out to the low caste women of the Scheduled Castes, and Muslims. Thus the sections that most needed assistance were deprived of it. Many of the members, not having had prior experience in this kind of activity, found themselves flush with money but did not know how to go about starting an economic activity, despite the technology centres. The banks did not advise them either. Those who bought themselves dairy cattle with the loan found no veterinary care. The animals often became sick and they found themselves helpless. Under .these conditions the Karnataka government, on the advice of UNICEF, (which had invested nearly 90 lakh into this project), invited the WWF(I) to take up this section of the BIRD project, and requested them to start a cooperative society as part of their Karnataka society under which the agarbatti workers from the slums of Bangalore city were already organised. The Bidar branch of the WWF(I) has been functioning since January 1988. The Forum restructured the membership of the Mahila Mandals into group systems, and did away with high caste leadership. Harijan and Muslim women in the region now engage in a number of non-farm activities (like poultry rearing, blanket weaving and making caps). When the Forum started its operation in Bidar in 1988, it had a membership of 2,000 women. By mid-1990, membership reached 5,000. The Forum has been able to reach 92 villages in all the four taluks of the district. The example of Bidar again proves the strength of grassroots initiative vis-a-vis the top-down approach.[4]

Kancheepuram: This ancient temple town in southern India could justifiably compete with Patliputra (today known as Patna), acclaimed to be the oldest town in the country, for a share in that unique historicity. Silk weaving has been carried on here since ancient times. Today, even though the prized silk sarees of Kancheepuram sell for exorbitant prices, the lives of the weavers, as in other parts of the country, are a tale of woe. The government, as part of its policy of protecting and developing the handloom industry, offers assistance to the weavers through its cooperatives.

This scheme is not without its share of difficulties. First, it admits only weavers as its members and, therefore, only men become members. Even though women and children as household members are involved in the various activities of this industry, they cannot formally become members of weavers' cooperatives. 'Secondly, government cooperatives offer assistance in both cash and kind. Assistance in kind is in the form of supply of gold thread (or *zari*). Often the weavers, taking the assistance of the cooperative society, pledge the gold *zari* with moneylenders. They fritter away that money, and wait until the sale proceeds of the finished sarees are realised to purchase *zari* on their own. Thus, cooperative assistance is transformed into a consumption loan used solely by the men, rather than a productive one. As a consequence, the male weaver's contribution to household income is also correspondingly reduced, though the women of their households contribute to that productive activity. The ILO agreed to support the WWF in starting its own cooperative society for the women in the weaving households as an experimental measure. This support from the ILO was linked with the third phase of the family planning programme. Thus, this was conceived as a credit-cum-family planning scheme. The scheme sought to provide credit assistance to the tune of Rs 1,000—Rs 1,500 to each woman to help redeem the pledged *zari* from the moneylenders and enable them to do the weaving themselves. It also attempts to replace the widely prevalent child labour force in the industry. Reports from the field indicate that most children in weaving households do not attend school, and do not evince much interest in doing so either. These children appear to be quite confident and content with their earning potential. While the Forum is aware that its credit assistance may not be quite sufficient for each household, it is quite wary of increasing its assistance. The Forum's enquiries in the town have revealed that in bigger cooperatives where male weavers have access to larger loans, it has often enabled them to bond the services of a couple of children to themselves. This is done by the weavers lending out the money under the bondage contract. By giving assistance to women, the Forum hopes that child bondage can be restricted. It is also in the process of organising night classes for the children.

Lucknow: The cool and comfortable Lucknowi kurtas with chikan embroidery are very popular during the hot summer months in all parts of the country. For the many thousands of poor Muslim women engaged in embroidery work, it is a life of sweat, and toil. This is shocking but true. On most pieces of work the women net only 10 paisa. They want the piece-rate to be increased to 25 paisa. The Forum has started its credit assistance programme to this section of the workers, and its membership today is nearly 1,000. As in the case of Vellore, Bangalore and Narasapur, the Forum hopes that through its credit programme, it can provide visibility to these workers and thus enable the piece-rate wages to be pushed up. For the home-based workers, the Forum believes that increasing the piece-rate wage is more important than organising marketing. Many .organisations that help in marketing function more or less like the merchant-contractors themselves, and do not alter the exploitative relations. In all the areas where the Forum's credit intervention programme was aimed at home-based workers, wages have increased over the years.

Jamshedpur: In and around this steel city, where the TISCO plant is located, are large sections of Harijans, Adivasis, Rajputs and Muslims. Though not strictly employees of TISCO, the male members of many of the households are engaged in some activity relating to the industry. Adivasi men are often called in for some months in a year as coolie labour. While the steel industry provides large employment opportunities, it is the people from outside and not the local population that get these attractive jobs. A large number of Adivasis are engaged in bamboo work, Harijan women are involved in making cowdung cakes, Rajput women in selling bangles and flowers, and Muslim women in some kind of home- based work. Adivasi women spend six months here in the town seeking some kind of work. For the remaining period they go back to their villages. However, this is true only of the older Adivasi women. The younger women do not want to go back to their village for agricultural work for part of the year.

The Forum has conducted a pilot study to explore starting a credit programme for these sections of the women workers. The Adivasi women are already organised in a cooperative society, but do not get loans for working capital requirements to pursue their occupations. The TISCO community centres train women for batik, embroidery, tailoring and candle-making in addition to providing creche facilities. The Forum feels that through its credit programme it can reach out to the vast tribal settlements in the villages in that region. However, it is interested in organising the women into credit groups for productive activities for which the TISCO centres offer training, and only if TISCO undertakes the marketing or guarantees to buy all the output. This is the first time the Forum is negotiating with the private corporate sector, and it will be to its credit if it succeeds in this venture. For the moment, the pilot study team,' comprising of Forum workers from the southern states, have come back with exposure to working class lives in other parts of the country.

So far we have covered credit programmes in the different centres. Table 34.1 gives the overall progress of credit in the various centres. It is very clear that in almost all instances, the intervention has been of such a nature that the survival constraints are eased but not eradicated. Neighbourhood credit groups have turned out to be an effective way of establishing a women's collective with leadership from below, promoting local initiative and, above all, bringing closer the members to the non-members and the members to the group leaders and the organisers.

In its efforts towards mobilisation, progress is perceptible. But, at the level of consciousness, varying results are obtained across occupation groups. We shall reflect on this below. In occupations such as vending, where the women are self-employed, credit intervention is viewed as an end rather than a .means, whereas in occupations where women are on a put-out system or under some form of wage labour system, women perceive the intervention as a means of mobilisation. In the case of self-employed vendors, they perceived themselves as being in an immediate antagonistic relationship with the local moneylenders, and once the moneylenders were eliminated from the scene through the credit programme, they themselves begin to function with a merchant mentality, albeit on a small scale. Their occupational situation does not enable class consciousness to be developed beyond a point, though they gain in their understanding of the state machinery (such as the police and banks).

Some self-employment activities are contexted within a collective, such as fishing which is an activity of the village community with a unique intertwining of the sphere of production with socio-cultural spheres. In these contexts, despite the self-employment status with no identifiable employer—employee relationship, credit intervention appears to reinforce the already existing collective spirit with the added gender emphasis. If this perspective is kept in mind, the apparently contradictory statements of the fisherwomen, (namely, their grievance that with the introduction of the auction system, men who now have access to cash earnings give very little for the household, along with their request to the Forum to provide loans for nets which would be used only by the men) is easy to resolve.

In occupations with an identifiable employer-employee relationship, credit intervention sharpens their class consciousness and enables them to raise a number of issues in their work sphere (such as child bondage, implementation of factory laws, minimum wages act, and bonus issues). While transforming them, in some instances, from dependent to independent producers can be construed as similar to the case of self-employed vendors, it also exposes in the process the exploitative system constituted by the hierarchy of middlemen. Further, it does not completely eliminate the merchant or capitalist from the picture and, to that extent, the antagonistic elements are still retained.

These insights drawn from the experiences of the women, and gathered during the course of fieldwork and later interviews, is substantiated to a great extent by the actual evolution of the Forum itself. The Forum started in 1978 and concentrated its activities amongst the self-employed vendors in Madras city. As the Forum spread to other areas involving agricultural wage labour and home-based workers, the class character of the oppression of women took a sharper focus as the antagonistic elements in the sphere of production and circulation were clearly perceivable by the women themselves. With the sharpening of this focus, the Forum also realised that its original grassroots development character could not be sought to be achieved without it at the same time assuming the character of a trade union to protect the rights of its members and to ensure for them their subsistence. With that end in view, the Forum registered itself as the National Union of Working Women in March 1981 under the Trade Union Act.

Family Planning and Health Programmes

Earlier, we had noted that the objective of the Forum is to empower women both in their productive and reproductive roles. The relationship between the two roles is well recognised. Empowerment in the reproductive sphere essentially means that women be given the knowledge and accessibility to methods of birth control, personal hygiene, and health care institutions. Further, empowerment also means that women be given the confidence and strength, that it is their right, to decide and to promote 'informed consent' on all issues of reproduction.

With this objective in view, the Forum sought to adapt the state sponsored family planning programme into a women centred grassroots health care project. This was done by retaining both the grassroots and, neighbourhood concept, as under the credit programme. So far, the programme has been conducted in three phases, with funding from the ILO, UNFPA and the Government of India for the third phase. Tables 34.2 and 34.3 give details on the progress of the scheme. The Forum recruited health trainees from amongst the grassroots women themselves, and provided them with the necessary training with the help of outside experts. Each trainee had to cover 20 households a day for six days a week, such that every household got covered in a week. During these weekly trips to the households, the trainee had to win their confidence on all matters relating to health, advise eligible couples on contraceptive methods, immunisation for children, nutrition, and so on. They would also accompany them to hospital or the health centre, and provide post-operative care to women after sterilisation and childbirth. The method is personal, based entirely on building up confidence and trust, unlike the mechanical and indifferent approach of the state health machinery.

The impact of this programme has been at two levels—the recipient household level and the women, and the trainees and their relationship with the health delivery system. At the house- hold level, there has undoubtedly been a breaking down of inhibitions in discussing intimate/personal affairs and, to that extent, what is deemed to be a private domain becomes narrowed down. The women do recognise that it is their right, and that they would take decisions pertaining to family planning. Numerous instances were cited of the struggle within households the women had to wage, and the kind of support provided by the Forum. Correspondingly, a certain degree of sensitisation among the male members of the household also appears to have taken place. Clearly, women's empowerment has been achieved to a significant degree.

TABLE 34.2

Progress of the Health and Family Planning Programme (1980-49)

Details	*Madras*	*Vellore*	*Adiram-pattinam*	*Dindigul*
Total no. of slums and villages	319	39	46	64
Total no. of workers	480	45	45	46
Total no. of families	110,000	10,800	10,200	10,500
Total population to be covered	536,313	53,914	48,406	50,589
Total no. of eligible couples to be covered	89,548	9,112	8,503	8,496
Total no. of children under 5 years	79,147	8,307	6,305	7,013
Family Welfare & Child Health				
Total no. of permanent acceptors	45,446	3,654	2,957	3,757
Total no. of temporary acceptors	32,779	3,405	3,437	3,186
Total no. of family planning acceptors	78,225	7059	6,394	6,943
Total no. of children immunised	3,353	—	—	—
Total coverage in first phase (1980—83) (%)	98	—	—	—
Total coverage in second phase (1984—85) (%)	88	90	87	94
Total coverage in third phase (1986-89) (%)	82	77	73	80

Source: WWF(I).

Note: The percentage figures indicated against 'total coverage' in the three phases refer to the proportion of Family Planning Acceptors to the Total Number of Eligible Couples (expressed as percentages) in each of the three periods covered.

The lacuna that one perceives is the dual level of consciousness of the women. Most women insisted that they need to have control over sexuality and fertility, and many others felt That an additional child was, given the existing context, an income augmenting and survival guaranteeing mechanism. Women in fishing households indicated a strong preference for sons—a minimum of four sons to own a boat—irrespective of the total number of children they would need to achieve the norm of four grown-up sons. Very few women attributed their household poverty to the number of children; the most striking manifestation was their criticism against the Chief Minister's Noon Meal Scheme for all school children. They say that those who have borne the children also know how to feed them. Yet, at a macro level, the women have absorbed the rhetoric of the state that the country's poverty is solely due to its population size. This contradictory nature of consciousness is due to an incomplete understanding of how the politics of reproduction within households is enmeshed with the state politics of reproduction. To that extent, while the private domain has narrowed, it still has to move to a stage where the private becomes political.

TABLE 34.3

Working Women's Forum (India)/ILO/UNFPA/GOI: Progress Report of Comprehensive Family Welfare Programmes (January-December 1991)

Baseline Data: January 1991	*Madras*	*Kanchee-puram*	*Vellore*	*Dindigul*	*Adiram-pattinam*
Total no. of slums & villages	232	25	26	38	44
Total no. of workers	180	30	30	30	30
Total no. of families adopted for coverage of family planning methods	90,000	15,000	15,000	15,000	15,000
Total population	416,776	69,775	72,498	66,981	64,659
Total no. of eligible couples	72,903	11,848	11,128	11,209	11,408
Total no. of children under 5 years	53,102	8,790	9,350	7,213	7,532
Family planning methods adopted: January-December 1991					
No. of tubectomy cases performed	29,782	4,541	4,281	4,496	3,483
No. of vasectomy cases performed	667	123	61	61	374
Total no. of permanent acceptors	30,449	4,664	4,342	4,557	3,857
No. of loops inserted	8,035	229	272	397	253
No. of persons using Nirodh	2,876	345	530	425	827
No. of persons using oral pills	3,837	338	327	556	1,038
Total no. of temporary acceptors	14,748		1,129	1,378	2,118
Total no. of family planning acceptors	45,197	5,576	5,471	5,935	5,975

Source: WWF(I).

The constant tussles between the state health personnel at all levels and the Forum's health workers has, as in the case of the credit programme, sensitised the workers to the functioning of the bureaucracy.

At a conceptual level, the introduction of the family planning programme into its activities has reinforced the fact of a dual existence—a collective existence and an individual one—and how both these features can be used for mobilisation. In the work sphere, the collective existence assumes dominance. Here, we had noted earlier, a difference in the level of consciousness of women in occupations with an identifiable employer and those who were self-employed. Thus, credit as a means of mobilisation has a limited applicability, especially among the latter. The Forum has circumvented this limitation by using the individual existence of women as a means of mobilisation. Thus, the family planning programme brings together all women as individuals, and the differentiation noticed in their collective existence as defined by their work status gets camouflaged.

Social Conscientisation Activities

In the two sets of activities described earlier, I had mentioned the aspect of change in consciousness. Activities are undertaken by the Forum specifically as a part of social. conscientisation. These include inter-caste marriages and group activities like role-plays, group singing and dancing, and group-eating.

TABLE 34.4

Number of Inter-caste Marriages Conducted from 1978 to 1991

Year	*Number of Marriages*	*Marriages where either Bride or Groom is a Adi Dravida*	*Inter-caste Hindus*	*Hindus & Christians*	*Hindus & Muslims*	*Christians & Muslims*
1978	63	54	—	8	1	—
1979	91	45	45	1	—	—
1980	106	73	24.	5	4	—
1982	59	46	7	4	2	—
1985	101	58	9	30	4	—
1991	61	32	28	—	—	1
Total	481	308	113	48	11	1

Inter-caste marriages play a very important role in the activities of the Forum. Table 34.4 provides information on these marriages. Normally, inter-caste unions among poor working class couples are in the nature of live-in arrangements or common-law marriages. These arrangements make the couple extremely vulnerable at a social level. While there is no ostracism, except perhaps by the respective families, when fights occur between the slum households or in the neighbourhood, the opponents generally mention this aspect as a derogatory form of union. For the women these alliances are more insecure as, with societal pressure, men are known to desert such women even after the birth of children. By performing inter-caste marriages, the Forum registers these marriages under different sections of the Marriage Act.

Couples already living under such arrangements, or planning to do so, are identified in the urban slums and rural villages by the credit groups, group leaders, organisers and the: health workers.. From the cross-section of such couples that we interviewed, it was evident that they were often very poor casual labourers. Most of the women responded that when they realised their parents could not get them married because of economic reasons, they decided to find their own partners. The couples themselves .were very happy that such a grand social function was being organised. They felt that even if they had gone to the Registrar's Office, they could have got only a dozen or so of their friends, but now there were thousands and they felt very honoured. In the course of time, many of these women get to know about the Forum's other activities and some do join the credit groups.

Inter-caste marriages highlight another interesting aspect on mobilisation, namely, how the Forum intervenes to transform individual struggles against the social system into a collective struggle.

Issues in a Nutshell

The experiences of the Forum raise a number of issues.

The Forum uses the appurtenances of the existing system to raise the consciousness of women. Its use of the DRI (Differential Rate of Interest) loan scheme, of the family planning programme, and so on, serve as examples. This leaves it with two sets of difficulties. Often, it can be dismissed as an exercise within the system without really challenging it or attempting to change the status quo. When probed deeply, it is clear that what has been achieved in terms of raising consciousness cannot be belittled. The growing consciousness, in the course of time, will bring the Forum in conflict with the existing system. The system will then put pressure on the existing modes of operation of the Forum. The possibilities of radicalisation within the system as well as the limits to such radicalisation is an area of concern.

This takes us to the next issue of whether the experiences of the Forum are taking the collective to a critical juncture where it gains a certain autonomous momentum of its own. The success of a collective can, in the long run, be judged only by the extent to which it has gained an autonomous status.

The experiences of the Forum in organising the informal sector micro entrepreneurs and the home-based producers have effectively demonstrated that new forms of mobilisation and forms of struggle for this section of the working class are possible and under way. To that extent, it challenges the more conservative trade unions where forms of mobilisation and struggle are limited to factory gates, shop floors and wage issues.

At the experimental level, the formation of neighbourhood groups, promoting grassroots leadership, and using peer group support and pressure tactics, thus minimising alienation, are inputs that are not region or culture specific and, to that extent, the organisational structure, and the structure of leadership and decision-making are replicable.

NOTES

1. Field work was first conducted in March-April 1985. The update on the Forum's current activities are based on interviews with the Forum staff in Madras in April 1992.
2. For a quantitative analysis of these aspects, see Kalpagam (1985) and Naponen (1987). For a general account of urban poor households' income earning and pooling strategies in Madras city, see Chapter 7 in this volume. Also see Naponen (1991). For another experiment in organising around credit, see the work on Annapurna (Bombay) by Everett and Savara (1984).
3. For a more elaborate historical account, see Mies (1982).
4. For a further understanding on this read, Arunachalam (1991).

35

Informal Women Laborures in Indian States

Women Labour in Ancient India

Women labour and their exploitation was found since historical times in our country. Women were employed to work as wine servers and as spies to get the secret of the drunkards without arising any doubts in their minds. Some reference in ancient literary works (particularly dramas) partly prove the existence of Dasis (female slaves) in those days. For instance, in Kalidas's *Malavikagnimitra, Parivrajita* testifies to the existence of Female spies, in *Mrichahakutika* of Sudrak. (a drama of Gupta age) the character of Madarika bears testimony of the existence of female slaves. Women in ancient India were also engaged as Ganika. We find such Ganikas in Sudraka's *'Mrichchakutika'* and in Dandin's *'Dasa-Kumar-Charita.'*

The system of employing women as Deva-Dasis, which is still found in the South India temple, was widely prevalent in ancient India. References to the employment of such Deva-Dasis at the temple of Mahakal in Ujjayani are found in Kalidas's Meghadoot, such Dasis were also kept in temple of Sun God when Hiuen Tsant visited India.[2]

Women Labour in Present Times

However, with the march of civilisation, the impact of social changes and developmental efforts benefit the women much less than man. Social and religious reformers, enlightened public authorities, and women's organisations waged battles against the oppressive position of women through centuries. But scourges as illiteracy, ignorance, superstitution still persist in some parts of the country resulting in unorganised low-paid exploited women labourers. Through the centuries, women have been working for their families as long as sixteen hours or more right from day break till late into the night. They manage the household work on the farm, fetch water, look after the cattle, feed the children as well as the adults in the family, clothe and educate the children.[3]

In most rural households in India, th_ bulk of the energy consumed, specially in the domestic sector, comes from fire wood. In poor households this fuel is typically gathered by women and female children mainly from forest land and village common land. In recent years with depleting forest many of these households are facing a fuelwood crisis, the burden of which has fallen mainly on the women.

Women in Unorganised Sector

A high proportion of working women in India are employed in the unorganised sector mainly in agriculture, livestock, forestry, the percentage being 79 as per 1981 census. Working women are manifested in agricultural activities like land preparation, seed grading, sowing, dibbling, planting, irrigating, threshing, winnowing, storing crops, feeding cattle, looking after milch animal and poultry etc. The nature of works in agriculture which the women labourers perform exposes them to particular health hazards. In various states, especially in South India, rich transplanting is done primarily by women labourers. This increases their susceptibility to a number of ailments such as intestinal and parasitic infections, arthritis, rheumatic joints, leech bites etc.[4]

TABLE 35.1

Women Labour in Different Sectors

Industrial Categories		*Percentage distribution of female main workers*	
		1971	*1981*
	Primary Sector		
(i)	Cultivators	29.84	33.20
(ii)	Agricultural Labourers	50.86	45.18
(iii)	Livestock, forestry, fishing etc.	1.96	1.06
(iv)	Mining and quarrying	0.40	0.36
	Total	83.06	79.80
	Secondary Sector		
(v)	Manufacturing, Processing, servicing and repairs		
	(a) Household Industry	4.24	4.59
	(b) Other than Household Industry	2.77	3.55
(vi)	Construction	0.65	0.80
	Total	7.6	8.94
	Tertiary Sector		
(vii)	Trade and Commerce	1.78	2.04
(viii)	Transport, storage and communisation	0.47	0.38
(ix)	Other services	7.08	7.05
	Total	9.33	9.37
	Total main workers	100.00	100.00

Source: 1981 census (excludes Assam).

Table 35.1 reveals that the percentage of the women labourers in India in 1971 in the Primary, Secondary and tertiary sector were 83.06, 7.66 and 9.33 respectively and the corresponding percentage in 1981 are 79.80, 8.94 and 9.47. Thus, it is obvious that there has been shift of women labourers from the primary sector to the secondary and tertiary sector during period under study. Again, out of total working women in 1971, the unorganised sector alone employed 94 per cent which has gone up to 96 per cent during 1981 per cent which has gone up to 96 per cent during 1981 census. Thus, it is observed that work participation in the unorganised sector has been an increasing trend. Immobility of labour is the greatest impediment of women labour that keeps them confined to low paying, irregular and local avenues of employment in unorganised sector. Ignorance, tradition-bound attitudes, lack of skill, seasonal nature of employment, heavy physical work of difficult types, lack of job security, long hours of work, lack of minimum facilities at the work place, ill-treatment and bondage are some of the features of the employment of women in unorganised sector.[5] In the tribal districts of Orissa, because of deforestation, increased pressure on land, lack of irrigation and recurring drought conditions, tribal women have been migrating to outside their villages, district and state for periods ranging from 2 to 6 months for working in construction projects, brick-kilns and tea-estates.

A greater percentage of women are employed in the unorganised sector in our country. It is lamentable to note that there has been drastic decline in the proportion of women population to total population. It has decreased from 33.7 per cent in 1911 to 14 per cent in 1981, which can be seen from Table 35.2.

TABLE 35.2

Women Component in Total Working Force

Year	*Proportion of women population to total population*	*Percentage of women labourers to total population*	*Percentage of women labourers to total workers*
1911	49.1	33.7	34.5
1921	48.9	32.7	34.0
1931	48.9	27.6	31.2
1951	48.6	23.3	29.0
1961	48.5	28.0	31.5
1971	48.1	12.1	17.7
1981	48.3	14.0	16.5

Source: Government of India, Census reports.

It is apparent from the Table 35.3 that the ratio of women in unorganised sector has gone up during the decade 1971-81 from 94 per cent to 96 per cent. Thus, work participation in the unorganised sector has been on increasing phenomenon. Those unorganised has broad dimension like agriculture, animal husbandry, fisheries, home-based industries like handicrafts, handlooms, coir industry, agrabati industry, bidi industry, sericulture, construction industry and the like. A good deal of studies corroborate the fundamentally subordinate position of women in the unorganised (or which may also be termed as informal sector) sector and their easy exploitability. In this informal sector in India, millions of people earn living as the tailors, furniture makers, street vendors, taxi drivers are only a few members of this over-growing army of workers.[6]

TABLE 35.3

Women Workers in India, (1971 and 1981)

	1971	1981
Female population as per cent of total population	48.2	48.3
Work participation (in millions)	31	48
Working women as per cent of total women	12.13	14.44
Total women in unorganised sector (in million)	29	46.24
Women in unorganised sector as per cent of total working women	94.00	96.33
Women in agriculture as per cent of working women	82.61	81.23

Source: Women Labour Force Trend and Pattern of Employment, by Atmanand, *Khadi Gramodyog,* March, 1990, p. 248.

In the tribal areas women contribute to the working in a more significant way than in the non-tribal society. While the ratio between the male and female labourers in the general population of the country is 5:1, it is 3:1 among the tribal among the non-tribal women 11.9 per cent are labourers whereas their tribal sisters have 20.75 per cent as labourers. The comparative picture of the participation rate of the non-tribal in the different sectors of economy have been represented in Table 35.4.

Tribal economy being mainly confined to primary sector 90.6 per cent of the women labourers are engaged in agriculture, as cultivators or as labourers, 2.67 per cent in livestock, forestry, fishing, hunting etc., and 0.6 per cent in mining. In recent years, because of various factors like industrialisation, growth of road, transports facilities, provision of education, contact with outside world and social mobility-all combinedly resulted in increase participation of tribal women labourers for economic gain and development.[7]

In addition to those women formally included as workers in the Census of national surveys, more than a quarter of the rural women and more than half of all women are engaged in these unrecorded activities.[8]

TABLE 35.4

Participation Rate of Non-Tribal and Tribal Female Labourers in Different Sectors

Occupational categories	*Cultivation*	*Agricultural labourers*	*Mining*	*Livestock, forestry, fishing, hunting etc.*
		Primary Sector		
General women	29.8%	50.5%	0.4%	2.5%
Tribal women	42.7%	48.9%	0.6%	2.6%
		Secondary Sector		
	Household industry	Manufact-uring etc.	Construction	
General Women	4.3%	2.8%	0.7%	
Tribal women	1.3%	0.9%	0.3%	
		Tertiary Sector		
	Trade and commerce	Transport etc.	Other services	
General women	1.8%	0.5%	—	
Tribal Women	0.6%	0.2%	—	

Source: Challenges to the Fair Sex (pp. 72-73).

Women in Household Duties

TABLE 35.5

Percentage of Women Reported as doing Household Duties Who Participated in Specified Activities for Family Benefits

		% W. in activity out of those engaged in house work	
		Rural	*Urban*
1.	Free collection of fish, game	6.24	0.80
2.	Free collection of firewood, dung etc.	14.34	3.11
3.	Maintenance of Kitchen garden	4.70	1.35
4.	Work in household poultry	11.06	3.11
5.	Sewing, tailoring, weaving	3.77	6.65
6.	Tutoring children	0.48	2.19
7.	Bringing water-from other villages	1.35	—
8.	Anyone of these specified activities	21.78	12.33

Source: NSS 32nd Round.

Women Workers in Non-Agricultural Sector

TABLE 35.6

Employment Status of Female Workers in Non-Agricultural Household Units

Economic Activity	*Employment in own account*			*Employment in establishments using wage labour*		
	Total No. (00)	*Female*	*F%*	*Total No. (00)*	*Female*	*F%*
1. Mining, Quarrying	2353	49	(2.0)	807	101	12.5)
2. Manufacturing, Repair	22909	5512	(24.0)	73926	7249	(9.8)
3. Electricity, Gas, Water	21	1	(4.7)	2293	59	(2.6)
4. Construction	565	24	(3.6)	1588	268	(16.8)
5. Wholesale and Retail Trade	27618	2010	(7.2)	26421	1503	(5.6)
6. Restaurants and Hotels	2657	327	(12.3)	88.74	372	(4.2)
7. Transport	1759	33	(1.8)	7285	194	(2.6)
8. Storage, Ware-Housing	468	6	(1.2)	1816	115	(6.3)
9. Communication	5	—	—	2955	202	(6.8)
10. Financing, Insurance Real Estate and Business services	1157	23	(2.0)	10664	876	(8.2)
11. Community, Social and personal service	6173	803	(13.0)	63175	10221	(16.1)
12. Others	193	18	(9.3)	3898	270	(6.9)
	63664	8769	(13.7)	203602	21430	(10.5)

Source: Ec. Census 1980: Statement 6 (published in 1985).

The foregoing table which is the outcome of the economic census 1980 conducted by the Central Statistical Organisation has revealed that at all India level (excluding Assam) there were 1841 million enterprises engaged in different economic activities other than crop production and plantation with 53.58 million persons working in them. Of these, 92 per cent were non-agricultural and 73 per cent of them didn't use hired labour. In other words, they were family enterprises, informal or self-employed units. In recent years, adequate attention has been focussed for the development of informal sector, which employs greater percentage of women labour. In the wake of rapid industrialisation and mechanisation, women experience acute unemployment consequent upon the delay of traditional crafts and handloom sector. They are unable to face the new challenge and participate in the advanced modern industrialised sector due to lack of skill and technology which is obstructed by family obligations and conservative attitude of the people.

Male-Female Participation in India

The comparative position of men-women participation in India is represented in Table 35.7.

TABLE 35.7

Comparative Position of Male Female Participation (1973-83)

	Population (in million)			*Work participation rate percentage to total persons above 5 years*			*Work participating Population (million)*		*Annual average increase P.C.*
	1973	1978	1983	1973	1978	1983	1973	1983	
(1)	(2)	(3)	(4)	(5)	(6)	(7)	(8)	(9)	(10)
Female Rural Area	210.3	241.0	264.1	37.53	38.48	38.74	79.0	102.3	3.0
Male Rural Area	226.6	259.2	284.1	63.84	64.06	63.23	114.6	179.5	2.4
Female Urban Area	66.0	76.0	15.53	15.53	17.0	17.31	10.4	14.0	4.0
Male Urban Area	71.6	81.8	57.09	57.09	57.48	57.71	40.9	51.7	2.6

Source: NSS enquiries on Employment and Unemployment, thirty eight round, January to December. 1983.

The table reveals that the women labourers increased from around 90 million in 1973 to 117 million in 1983, (At a rate of 3 per cent average increase from 185 million to 231 million (At a rate of 2.4 per cent average increase per (annum). The women rural participation rate has also increased from 37.53 per cent to 38.74 per cent during 1973 to 1983. The participation rate of women in urban area is also higher compared to rural area during the period under review.

Work participation rates for main workers by age group, area and sex in India during 1971 and 1981 has been represented in Table 35.8.

TABLE 35.8

Work Participation Rates for Main Workers by Age Group, Area and Sex in India, 1971 and 1981)

Age Group	*Area*	*Male*		*Female*	
		1971	*1981*	*1971*	*1981*
(1)	(2)	(3)	(4)	(5)	(6)
All ages	All	52.61	51.62	12.06	13.99
	Rural	53.62	52.62	13.36	16.00
	Urban	48.80	48.54	6.65	7.28
0-14	All	6.65	5.46	2.63	2.95
	Rural	7.56	6.30	3.05	3.53
	Urban	2.75	2.46	0.82	0.88
15-19	All	55.32	51.15	15.78	18.48
	Rural	62.31	58.19	18.80	22.27
	Urban	28.32	31.54	5.51	6.16
20-24	All	81.43	76.91	18.12	20.32
	Rural	86.56	82.71	20.58	24.29
	Urban	67.49	63.35	9.54	6.25
25-29	All	94.27	91.08	20.01	22.52
	Rural	95.45	92.79	22.16	26.14
	Urban	90.54	86.78	11.63	12.17
30-39	All	97.12	96.22	21.70	25.31
	Rural	97.61	96.71	23.78	28.45
	Urban	95.45	94.93	13.11	15.14
40-49	All	97.08	96.81	22.6	25.97
	Rural	97.62	97.25	24.4	28.90
	Urban	95.15	95.49	14.5	15.34
50-59	All	94.03	19.43	90.64	21.56
	Rural	95.50	94.08	21.08	23.94
	Urban	87.85	86.86	12.71	12.42
60+	All	73.82	63.71	10.64	10.19
	Rural	77.52	67.59	11.49	11.29
	Urban	55.35	47.49	6.46	5.75

Note: The data for 1971 have been adjusted to exclude that relating to Assam for comparability with the 1981 Census data.

Source: Census of India 1981, Series-1, Paper-2 of 1983; Key population Statistics based on 5 per cent sample Data.

A study undertaken by the National Institute of Urban Affairs has brought to light certain important conclusions which are specified below.

In urban areas, nearly 40 per cent of self-employed women are employed in services, followed by 30 per cent in trade, 15 per cent in manufacturing, 8 per cent in construction and

5 per cent in Primary activities. Substantial number of such enterprises consisted of individual enterprises mostly engaged in small business like dairying, pottery making, selling dolls, goldsmithy, pan-bidi selling, fruits and vegetables selling, laundry, cane and bamboo products in which the family members do also participates and cooperate as workers.

A high percentage of the self-employed women work out-side the home (57 per cent) and only 43 per cent work within the home. Out of the outside women labourers over 60 per cent are either mobile or operate them on pavements making vulnerable to the vagaries of weather which spells irregularity in work and income.

Table 35.9 represents workforce concentration both in rural and urban sectors. The largest concentration of labour for both men and women labourers are manifested in agriculture and allied activity. Because of planned economic development programmes, there has been changes in the degree of occupational diversification and decline of labour in the agricultural sector. The rate of decline in the proportion of labourers in agriculture during the year 1973-83 is less in case of women labourers (from 90 per cent to 87 per cent) than for male labourers (from 83.2 per cent to 76.8 per cent).

TABLE 35.9

Occupational Conception of Work Force (1973-83)
(Per Capita Distribution of Workers Sex-wise for Rural and Urban India)

Occupational Sector	*Rural*				*Urban*			
	Male		*Female*		*Male*		*Female*	
	1973	1983	1973	1983	1973	1983	1973	1983
(1)	(2)	(3)	(4)	(5)	(6)	(7)	(8)	(9)
Agriculture and allied activity	83.23	67.80	89.67	86.73	10.71	10.25	32.75	28.65
Manufacturing	55.73	7.21	4.65	6.91	26.86	27.39	25.02	27.39
Construction	1.56	2.57	1.06	0.87	4.26	5.05	3.26	3.64
Trade	3.06	4.43	1.46	2.06	20.17	21.10	9.39	1.54
Transport and Communication	1.00	1.78	0.04	0.05	9.04	10.17	0.94	1.54
Social and Personal Service	4.65	5.90	7.81	3.02	24.00	21.30	26.66	26.36
Self-employment	65.90	60.64	64.68	62.21	30.25	40.67	48.40	46.50
Regular Work Force	12.06	10.27	4.08	3.10	50.69	44.58	27.89	26.23
Casual Wage Labour	22.04	28.83	31'.44	34.69	10.06	14.75	23.71	27.27

Source: Percentage distribution of all workers for males and females in rural and urban areas—NSSO, Journal, April, 1986, pp. 112-113.

In the urban sector, the proportion of women workforce is about three times the proportion of male workers in the agriculture and allied activities.

Syndrome of Women Labour in Rural India

There has been substantial documenting of empirical evidence of women's work and their roles in rural India.

"There are a large number of women who primarily derive their livelihood from working in agriculture either as 'Free' wage labourers, sometimes on a regular basis and after on a seasonal basis, or attached labourers being permanently bondaged to a particular landlord mostly alongwith their menfolk. These families possess no land of their own but sometimes may own a bullock or two or a female bullock to their credit. The income derived from these sources is nominal but women invariably spend a regular part of their time in rearing these animals. These women generally belong to illiterate scheduled caste, scheduled tribe and backward classes." Further, studies indicate that seasonal fluctuations in employment is higher in case of women in rural areas and women remain without gainfull employment of longer periods in the crop season.[10]

Table 35.10 reveals that agriculture is the dominant sector which employs more women than other sectors.

TABLE 35.10

All India Workforce in Unorganised Sectors in 1981

Sectors	*(Number in Millions)*		
	Male	*Female*	*Total*
Agriculture	114.1 (75%)	37.56 (25%)	151.7 (100%)
Manufacturing	16.8 (81%)	4.3 (19%)	21.1 (100%)
Services	22.4 (84%)	4.4 (16%)	26.8 (100%)
Total	153.4	46.2	199.6

Sources: Women labour force: Trend and pattern of employment by Atmanand, *Khadi Gramodyog*, Vol. XXXVI, No. 6, March, 1990.

"Almost 90 per cent rural landlords have expressed their preferential choices for those rural women labourers whose husbands and their fore-fathers have been landless labourers for generations. Migrated labourers are preferred the least for farm activities. This may be one of the reasons that the landless age-old traditional labourers could not come up from their stark poverty and could not get rid of the landlord's clutches. They get easy access to farm employment with the landlord-elites who in turn have been exploiting them for generations. The exploiter exploitee ties are, very much strong in India agriculture even today."[11]

"The scene may be different, the occupation different but the essentials of the story remain—be they cashew workers coir workers, fish graders, bidi workers or laee workers, cart pullers, or coolies, domestic servants—name any occupation, it is the same unvarying story of long hours of work, poorly remunerated with little prospect of upgrading. Women in the unorganised sector have in secure jobs, are kept on temporary or casual basis, with not even the barest of welfare facilities, under conditions that pose health hazards."[12]

Various socio-economic, cultural psychological handicap continue women to a position, deterrent to their development.

TABLE 35.11

Distribution of Workers in Rural Areas

	Main Workers			*Cultivators*			*Agricultural labourers*			*Household industries manufacturing, processing and repairs*			*Other works*		
	1961	1971	1981	1961	1971	1981	1961	1971	1981	1961	1971	1981	1961	1971	1981
Persons	45.11	34.01	34.76	27.11	17.47	17.76	8.71	10.61	10.39	2.27	1.11	1.07	6.52	4.82	5.54
Male	58.35	53.62	52.62	35.51	29.89	29.02	9.38	18.73	12.63	3.40	1.71	1.51	10.06	8.29	4.48
Female	31.40	13.36	16.00	18.41	4.40	5.93	8.01	7.33	8.03	2.12	0.47	0.61	2.86	1.16	1.43

Source: Census 1961 and 1981.

Women Labour in Tea Plantations

The tribal population of Bihar, Madhya Pradesh, Orissa has been recruited in the tea gardens of Assam and West Bengal. There was heavy emigration of labour to the tea gardens in the middle of 19th Century. Recruitment was on family basis on men cold not be expected to leave their families behind. In addition to their domestic works women used to take important responsibilities in their homes.

The Table 35.12 indicates the employment position of women labourers in tea plantation during 1981 and 1985.

TABLE 35.12

Employment of Women Labour in Tea Plantations

Year	*Employment in lakhs*	*Share in total percentage*
1981	3.66	45.37
1985	3.92	46.86

Sources: Labour Bureau.

Bonded Labour in Plantations

Women labour have been abused and exploited like other sectors and therefore, to ameliorate their conditions Plantation Labour Act has been enacted and (subsequently amendments made to the original Act of 1951) brought into force with effect from 26th January, 1982. The Act makes provision for accommodation to their resident workmen and their families in all plantations. The planters adopted various methods of roraecruiting labour from all labour surplus area of India and brought them to the plantations. They were bonded labour brought under strict terms and conditions. It was a type of forced migration or slave trade under which labourers were made to sign a contract to serve tea gardens of Assam from 3 to 5 years. After the expiry of the contracted period the labourers were supposedly free to return home or get themselves re-employed for a fresh term, but in practice it was impossible on the part of the recruited labour to return home. However, many of them deserted tea gardens even before the expiry of the contracted term due to inhuman behaviour and bad working conditions.

Socio-economic Conditions of Women Labour

A research study conducted by the Madurai Institute of Social Work to go into the problems and living conditions of women labourers in tea plantations of Kerala State. The study has manifested the followings.[13]

Some women labourers had been serving for more than 30 years and even were forced to engage their children in their work.

Most of the women were married in the age groups of 13 to 16 since early marriage relieved pressure on crowded families.[14] The average income of the labourers being low, indebtedness and poverty were the sequal. The women toiling hard in plantations hardly go leisure time for extra carricullar activities or recreational activities, as they were otherwise busy at plantations or homes.

Another article throws light on the conditions of women labourers in tea plantations of Assam reveals that most of women labourers belong to backward tribal belts. Studies show that unmarried women workers and old women are more committed in plantations than the middle aged women, obviously because the latter are tied down by household work, child care, seasonal paddy transplantation in rainy season and paddy drying and husking in the winter. Surveys show that the entire North Eastern India has as much as 60 per cent women workers and in the case of Assam state alone 45 per cent women are employed in tea plantations. Nearly 70 per cent of the total industrial force in Assam is employed in tea gardens and industries and 40 per cent of the state's total income is fetched by tea industry. Assam has the largest area of tea cultivation in the world. It contributes about 18 per cent of the world's total tea production."[15] Lack of education, poverty, backwardness, lack of consciousness, under-employment and other evils still haunt the women labourers in Assam tea plantations.

Wage Discrimination to Women Labourers

There is widespread age and income discrimination in the realm of employed women labour. Despite their non-stop work from early morning to dark in agriculture operations like transplanting rice, women labourers are generally paid less than 60 per cent of the male wage. The inequality of women is generally due to greater concentration of poverty, backwardness and low level of literacy and technical know-how. As per 1981 Census, only 24.8 per cent of women are literate with higher rate of dropout of females than males in the school. It has been studied that the women labourers in the unorganised sector suffer due to lack of education and about 33 per cent are illiterates and about 13.5 per cent are educated upto middle level.[16]

This low level of literacy coupled with other physical, psychological and cultural handicaps results in employment of women labourers in poverty paid primary sector. For women labourers minimum wages and statutory working hours are alien words. The women as agricultural labourers are discriminated in wage payment throughout the country even in operations such as transplanting and weeding which are women intensive operations.[17]

The wages paid to women labourers is determined not by economic criteria but is a result of the cultural attitudes and practices and power structure in a society.[18] Wage discrimination is due to the fact that there is a common accepted notions that men are more efficient than women and the income of a women is only a supplementary earning while men are considered as principal earners.[19]

TABLE 35.13

Average Wage Salary Learning of Both Rural Male and Female Per Day in 1983

(in Rupees)

Age group	*Male*	*Female*
Regular wage/salaries employees		
15-59	16.09	10.85
60 +	9.21	4.30
All ages	15.04	10.11
Casual wage labourers		
15-59	10.53	5-11
60 +	9.35	3.77
All ages	10.27	4.89

Sources: National sample survey organisation, 1987, pp. 337-338.

Women with lower level skills or no skills are exploited in their wage payments for monotonous and straineous work. Planners and policy makers generally remain insensitive to the position of women within the patriarchical power-structure in the family and unequal power relation between women and men in the community. Women put more hours of work than men and the earnings of men are invested mostly on menfolk on the terms of better food, clothing, health, education, leisure and recreation.[20]

The inequality in receiving ages between rural male and female (women labourers) can be perceived from Table 35.13.

In Orissa, labour force participation marginally increased from 31.22 per cent in 1971 to 32.75 per cent in 1981. Male workers participation rates were 55.32 per cent in 1971 and 54.38 per cent in 1981 and that of women labourers were 6.84 per cent in 1971 and 10.71 per cent in 1981. The proportion of women labourers in primary sector to total women labour increased from 74.43 per cent in 1971 to 80.26 per cent in 1981 while the proportions of women labourers engaged in secondary and tertiary sector declined during the period.[21]

Women Labour in Tamilnadu

Women Labour in Salt Industry:—A study has been made by Prof. Kamalraj regarding women labourers in salt industry of Tamilnadu state. He has remarked that in India out of 2,19,190 crores of land utilised for producing 70 million tonnes of salt in Tamilnadu salt is cultivated in 34,772 acres for producing 15 million tonnes.[22] Salt-industry being a labour intensive industry when salt is produced by solar evaporation technique 50 per cent of the cost in salt industry goes to the workers men, women and children. Men and women labourers perform the same type of work, except scapping of salt. Men workers are paid Rs. 11 and women workers Rs. 9 as daily wage.[23] The services of omen in the salt works are specially needed to supply drinking water for all the workers. Women have walk far off places for fetch pots of drinking water. Usually they carry the salt from the ridges to the plotform.'[24]

Women Labour in Beedi Industry:—A study made by Dr. Kanan and Ilango reveal about the health hazards of women labourers in Beedi Industries of Tiruchinapalli in Tamilnadu state.[25]

The Beedi workers are more prone to allergic bronchitis and sinus problems, it may be probably due to the dust of the tobacco leaves which induces allergy. The girls are malnourished, about 60 per cent of them are anaemi-coupled with abject poverty. They also suffer from diseases of ulterus and other gynaec problems and even cancer.

Women Labour in Paddy Processing Industries:—A study conducted by Dr. Sundari and Manimekhalai has brought to light that poverty illiteracy, ignorance, casual nature a employment, lack of skill to take up other work and absence of union have all resulted in the economic exploitation of women workers in the paddy processing units of Trichinapalli.[26] Ninety per cent of women workers live below the poverty line. Added to the low income, the high level of expenditure and lack assets and indebtedness further ruins the economic life of these women workers. More than 80 per cent of the sample workers have debt ranging from Rs. 800 to Rs. 1200.[27] In the absence of institutional facilities and lack of security, all loans have been borrowed from either professional moneylenders or neighbours at high rates of interest.

It is the economic compulsion more than any other factor which motivates women to seek employment in the paddy processing industries.

There is heavy concentration of widow workers in this industry. Women do not have regular employment and their unemployment losts about four to six months in a year. There is no job security and there is complete denial of welfare measures such as medical and maternity benefit, creche facilities etc.

Handloom Industry:—Dr. Sundari and Manimekhalai has also studied the problems of women workers in unorganised handloom industries in Vengamedu village of Tamilnadu state.[24]

Handloom is the unorganised sector charcterised with large number of women and child labourers alongwith male labourers who are engaged as a cheap source of labour power, the most common mode of wage payment is piece-rate wage under which the workers self-supervise their exploitation. The study reveals that 46 per cent of women workers were unmarried, 30 per cent were married and the rest were either widows or divorcees. Less than 50 per cent of the women workers were literate, 66 per cent of household income is spent for food items low income, high levels of expenditure, high rate of indebtedness are the characteristics of the women workers of this industry.[22]

Informal Women Labourers of Bangalore

An attempt has been made by Thippaiah, on the basis of interviews with informal sector units of Bangalore metropolitan area which explodes some important findings.[30] The study reveals that women labourers are suffering from poverty, unemployment, under employment, insecure employment, exploitation, harassment, etc., Women labourers are the most exploited group composed to their counterparts in rural areas. Most of the women labourers in the urban informal sector are migrant families at different points of time because of drought, employment and marriages and wage differentials between urban and rural sector. Most of such labourers are in the age group of 18 to 32 years, with low level of literacy and live in slums and shanty towns which are devoid of basic amenities. The wage employed women labourers are mostly skilled, semi-skilled, unskilled, casual and contract labourers in construction works, industrial and commercial enterprises.

The study reveals that the annual income of informal women labourers was 1507 in waste collection activity as against the average income of informal male labourers, Rs. 2632. The informal sector women labourers, are paid low wages and their wage are just around the subsistence level. Some women labourers were asked to work 10 to 12 hours a day in addition to household work.[31] Under insanitary and less healthier conditions women labourers toil hard in order to make reasonable retu..n. Proper medical facilities and safety measures are not provided for these women labourers who are in contact with hazardous materials such as Chemicals in dyeing or cement dust in construction work. Consequently, most of these workers are suffering from ill-health and physical disabilities. The informal women workers of Bangalore are deprived of any social security benefits and as a result, children and dependents face a good deal of problems.

Women Labour in Rajasthan

An action research programme with motivational cum-educational camp was initiated by National Labour Institute (NLI), New Delhi in 1984 at Metholi village in Bharatpur district of Rajasthan.[32]

The study has brought to light that the rate of growth of literacy among families in Rajasthan and particularly in the study area is significantly low. It demonstrates the neglect of women. The female literacy in Rajasthan in 11.42 per cent as per 1981 Census but in the rural areas it is only 5.46 per cent.[33] The situation of the scheduled castes and scheduled tribes is bad, in their case, practically the entire population in the rural area is illiterate. It was noticed that the few literate women in these villages belonged to the upper castes. None of the women of marginal or landless families were literate.

Participant's Socio-economic Profile

Most of the participants were married (87.2 per cent), 5.1 per cent were unmarried and 7.7 per cent were widows.[34] About 60 per cent of the participants did not possess any kind of agricultural land. Some of them did not have any land for house. The principal occupation of women labourers was agricultural labour-cum-household work. Eighty two per cent of women agricultural labourers were found indebted.[35] "Thus, they were young and middle aged, illiterate, married, agricultural labourers without much substantial work, with high incidence of indebtedness and no land to cultivate."[36]

Lack of Employment Opportunities

In the absence of land, lack of employment opportunities was also identified as a persistent problem among the female participants. As the village economy is primarily agrarian, the only employment available within the village economy is in agriculture. However, agricultural employment available to women is only for two months in a year. Women do not get any other form of employment within the village and they cannot seek employment outside.

Study by Dr. Chandhoke

Dr. Neeva Chandhoke one analyst points out that women are triply subordinated—as housewives and mothers to men, as female in sex—segregated jobs with discriminatory wages and as workers, they are excluded from the higher levels of management in private and government enterprises.[38]

The benefits of development have been mixed, benefitting men more than women, it has increased inequality of access to resources and opportunities. Development has little meaning if it continues the personal underdevelopment of women. There is a growing trend towards amelioration, but the concept of welfare improvement leads to little meaningful change. There will continue to be little change if women have to depend on men as decision-makers.[39]

Women Labour in Orissa

Orissa is predominantly agricultural state, with agriculture contributing nearly 69 per cent of State's income. The working population contribute 32.8 per cent of the total state population of which 75 per cent are farmers and agricultural labourers. Rural women in the state constitute 88.98 per cent of the total female population and about 94.98 per cent of the total female population and about 94.69 per cent of the female labour force.[39] Of the total female labourer force in the state 78.10 per cent are engaged in farm sector either as cultivators or as agricultural labourers. The literacy rate among females in rural areas of the state is 18.46 per cent as against 24.28 per cent for males.[40]

The study demonstrates that improvement of economic status associated with relatively large holdings, rural women do not prefer to go out for wage employment. They spend more time on their own farm, attend household activities or engage themselves in other activities such as dairy, poultry bee-keeping, etc., which are mostly done within their own premises.

Female in our society, specially in rural areas are subject to several socio-economic constraints and discriminations. The incidence of poverty, unemployment and illiteracy are high among women. The study has brought to light that their low participation as recorded by official agencies do not necessarily reflect their low economic contribution. The study concludes with suggestions like "as women labour contributes more in terms of time, output and income, they need a fair deal both in socio-economic planning and in decision-making. The wage for women security measures for women and legal protection should also be substantially expanded keeping in time with their role in the economy."[41]

Women Labour in Balasore

A study made in the district of Balasore—a coastal district of Orissa, unfolds that women engaged in income-generating activities feel that they are inferior to the male-folk, as they earn less wages and perform unskilled labour.[42] Women in this part of Orissa would prefer to remain undernourished and poor to undertake income-generating activities. Women play a wide variety of roles which are either preparatory or supportive to agriculture, animal husbandry, craft etc., but since most of their work is of informal nature devoid of wages, it does not satisfy employment criteria and hence not accounted for while estimating participation rates. It is seen that 60 per cent of the sample respondents work in farms like breaking clods of earth, manuring weeding,[43] transplanting, harvesting, threshing and winnowing, while only 15 per cent of the sample respondents work in income generating activities like rope and basket-making, pottery, goat-rearing, handloom weaving etc., and these activities bring money to them. Low participation of women are because of low level of education, unpleasant work experience. They do not work because they are over tired and over-burdened with household work. They are being harassed by government officials for sanction of loans, and in the identification list of beneficiaries.

Women Labour in Ganjam

Another study conducted in Ganjam district of Orissa pertaining to role of women in agricultural sector reveals that the tribal women are taking up the hard task of cultivation in contrast to the women of plain and coastal areas.[44] In tribal areas men share with women in all the operations except land preparation and irrigation. Knowledge and use of fertiliser is more widespread among the farm women in plain and coastal area and less in tribal areas. About 70 per cent of the respondents have reported about the application of fertiliser in their field. Use of chemical fertiliser in crops is considered to be harmful by the tribals. It is observed from the survey that in coastal and plain areas women have better knowledge about the use of high-yielding seeds, fertiliser and pesticides compared to tribal women. The rich and higher caste women do not work in the field but only supervise the work. There are different agro-climatic zones and consequently variations in agricultural practices and cropping pattern in the state of Orissa. Women population is about the same as that of males and they play a significant role in performing different agricultural activities.[45]

Women Labour in the Tribal District of Koraput

An attempt has been made in a study conducted in Koraput, one of the backward districts of Orissa to assess the contribution of women to the development of rural economy.[46] The study revealed that agriculture was the main occupation of the study area. The level of education among workers in the region under study was low. The position was still worse among women labourers. The women labourers do not have even access to new skills imparted through th extension an community development programmes.

In addition to agriculture, the female labourers were also found to be engaged in other economic activities like collection of minor forest products, construction of road and buildings, quarrying household industries etc. The low standard of living in the area makes it necessary for women folk to cooperate in other economic pursuits to some extent.[47]

It was revealed that the contribution of men workers in crop production is 60.80 per cent and that of women labourers 39.20 per cent.[48]

The authors conclude that "it is high time that an integrated approach was formulated for the over all development of women folk to enable them to participate in the socio-cultural and economic development of our country. The problem of women's development should constitute an important segment of planning process. Any further neglect in this important issue would stand in the way of economic development of the country.

The Indian Council of Social Science Research, New Delhi has made several studies in a wide range of occupations in the unorganised sector on women, focussing new lights on different respects of women.

Studies, which were conducted in various parts of the country reveals the 'auful conditions' of the women labourers in unorganised sector. It has been observed that a significant percentage of, the jobs in this sector are managed by women drawn from lower caste and lower class women. Ignorance, tradition bound attitudes, illiteracy, lack of skills, seasonal nature of employment, heavy physical work of different types, long hours of work with limited payment, discrimination in wage structures of men and women, lack of guarantee of minimum wage, lack of job security, lack of comprehensive legislation to cover these labourers in unorganised informal sector, lack of minimum facilities at the work-site, ill-treatment, migration and disintegration of families, bondage and alienation etc., are the characteristics of the employment of women in this sector.[49]

All this boils down to a conclusion that women labourers constitute an important segment of the total work-force in our country. More than 90 per cent of the working women are engaged as wage labourers in informal sector in our country. Compared with men, most of women labourers are in the grip of poverty, backwardness, landlessness, under-employment and destitution. They are also subject to various types of exploitation like economic, cultural, sexual, political, psychological etc.

Informal Construction Women Labourers

Available data demonstrate that construction is one of the largest sectors of economic activity, second largest to agriculture in underdeveloped countries. Construction sector provides most of the economic infra-structure for the manufacturing sector and infact, provides greater employment opportunities to a large number of unskilled labourers. The construction sector, generally developed on traditional production lines, is considered as an important spectrum of informal sector. The complexity of the construction operation necessitates a host of skills, carpenters, masses, concrete workers, unskilled labourers etc.

Employment of Women Labourers in Construction Sector

As revealed from 1981 census, there were about 222.5 lakh persons in the labour force in our country. The available figures reveal that about 50 per cent of construction workers really lived in urban settlements while a large segments of labour force work in their villages and construction project site.

As an employment generator, the role of construction sector is significant as revealed from the Table 35.14. It is noteworthy that in the informal sector, on the fringes of monetary benefits considerable proportion of labourers, including women labourers are employed.

Construction women workers are mostly exploited in the public works, development projects and relief works. To repeat, though the informal construction women labourers are hired on a casual basis (daily or piece-rate), many of them have a long career of years, mostly migrating to distant and far off places. They suffer from temporary and shifting nature of work and undergo enormous physical strain, toiling hard in all seasons. They are mostly exploited by the contractors and middlemen, suffer from insecurity of job and poorly paid. 'Frequent changes in their worksites and the uncertain nature of their work deprive them and their children of the basic needs like health, education and even such a common thing as a ration card. Accidents and death at worksites are common and they hardly get any compensation."[50] The frequency of accidents in the construction industry is on the increase.[51]

TABLE 35.14
Employment of Labour in Construction Sector in 1981

(in lakhs)

Labour force	*In rural areas*	*In urban areas*	*Total*
Total number of workers in the country	176.4	46.1	222.5
Workers in the construction sector (including dams, bridges, roads etc.)	1.5	1.6	3.1
Workers in the building (industry alone)	0.9	1.2	2.1

Source: Census 1981, Govt. of India.

Studies on Construction Women Labourers

The Committee on Status of Women (1975) initiated two important studies on women construction labourers, one in Patna (Bihar State) covering three major projects, and the other in Delhi, covering nine construction sites. Finding of these studies unfolds the conditions of women in the construction sector.

A study made by DK Lal Das highlights sex discrimination against female workers in unorganised construction sector of Andhra Pradesh.[52] The study observes that development has improved the standard of living but increased economic and social disparities. Women have been displaced from employment because of new technologies. Similar views have been expressed by the Report of the National Committee on Self-employment in Women as it remarked that technological changes have adversely affected the employment of women in Industries.

Prof. R.N. Mathur has studied the problems of construction women workers and especially the quality of life basing upon both primary and secondary sources. The study has highlighted various socio-economic aspects of Delhi. Women construction workers and has been illustrated through Census data and theoretical frameworks.

National Building Organisation sponsored five studies (1977-78) in Delhi, Ahmedabad, Poona, Madras, KAVAL (Kanpur, Agra, Varanasi and Allahabad Lucknow) and surveyed 3425 workers for reviewing the living conditions of both male and female labourers.[53] The findings of the study revealed that there was constant problems of instability and insecurity of employment for the workers. "The migration workers was because of unemployment at home, insufficient income and indebtedness, expectation of better prospects in the city was found as the main reason of migration to city. Ninty-six per cent workers in Delhi, 69 per cent in Ahmedabad, 78 per cent in Poona, 70 per cent in Madras and 59 per cent in KAVAL towns were migrants from rural to other urban areas. The proportion of women workers was 5.2 per cent in Delhi, 25.5 per cent in Ahmedabad, 19.8 per cent in Poona, 25.4 per cent in Madras and 2.3 per cent in KAVAL towns, and almost all of them were employed on unskilled jobs. The women workers generally remain unskilled inspite of their continuous employment in construction for a number of years. The contractors also find the employment of women labourers beneficial because they perform the same type of task as men and are sometimes paid wages at a lesser rate.

The earnings of the construction workers fluctuate on account of discontinuity of employment which generally occur due to rains, non-availability of building materials and change of sites. Ninety per cent of the skilled labourers were getting more than Rs. 200 per month where as the unskilled were getting less."[54]

Study on Socio Economic Conditions of Women Labourers in Building and Construction Industry

A recent study on socio-economic conditions of women labourers in building and construction industry has brought to light several important facts and findings. The study revealed that women labourers engaged in the unorganised segment suffer from disabilities and exploitation of much higher magnitude than those employed in the organised sector. Although the conditions of work in the unorganised sector are not satisfactory both for men and women, yet the problems confronted by the latter are generally more acute because they are more vulnerable to various forms of exploitation.

There is also absence of reliable statistical and other data relating to the working and socio-economic conditions of women labourers engaged in the unorganised sector.

Construction works being scattered over all parts of the country and resources for covering the entire country being limited, the study was confined to four metropolitan cities of Delhi, Bombay, Madras and Calcutta.

Selection of Sample Projects

Only those construction projects which belonged to government, semi-government and public sector agencies and were employing five or more women labourers at the time of the conduct of field study comprised the overall sampling frame for the study. In Calcutta City, where the proportion of women construction labourers was fund to be very low, only a few construction projects engaged five or more women labourers. Thus, the coverage of the study was virtually reduced to three metropolitan cities of Delhi, Madras and Bombay.

Selection of sample projects for the study was made from the list of construction works which were collected personally at the time of the conduct of field study from the various construction agencies like central and state public works Departments, City corporations and Development Authorities, the Housing Boards etc. In total, 29 work-sites in Delhi, 14 in Bombay and 13 in Madras city were covered for the study. The total women employment, 503, 155 and 167 respectively as on the dates of visit to the work-sites of the cities under study.

Characteristics of Women Employment

Although many types of building and construction activities, viz. construction of building roads, railway lines, sewerage, etc., were being undertaken by various construction agencies, women labourers were mainly engaged in the construction of buildings. In some cases, they were also engaged in road operations. Their employment in works like electrical installations, underground sewerage, rail works, etc., was either very low or quite negligible. This was so, as they were mainly engaged in carrying earth, mortar, bricks, etc., and these jobs mainly available in the construction of building. Though the Building and construction industry provides employment to all categories of workers, viz., highly skilled and skilled, semi-skilled and unskilled person, yet women constituted nearly 25.5 per cent of the total persons employed in the sampled construction projects covered in Delhi, 15.0 per cent in Bombay and 29.3 per cent in Madras and all of them were unskilled persons. No women workers engaged in any construction project studied in the three cities was engaged in skilled or semi-skilled occupations. Further, as high as 37.9 per cent of the unskilled labourers in Delhi, 22.0 per cent in Bombay and 51.2 per cent in Madras were women. The unskilled women labourers were mostly designated as "coolies,' whereas their male counter-parts were called as 'beldavs.' In some construction projects, male and female labourers were both categorised as `Mazdoors' or labourers.

A staggering 95 per cent of the unskilled labour engaged in various construction projects covered in Delhi were those who had migrated from the rural areas of other states like Rajasthan, Madhya Pradesh, Uttar Pradesh, Bihar etc. The states of Madhya Pradesh and Rajasthan taken together contributed slightly more than two-thirds of the total unskilled labour employed in various sampled construction projects. The interesting feature of migration from Rajasthan and Madhya Pradesh states was that generally both male and female members of a household migrated. However, in the case of Bihar State, mostly male members migrated to the construction sites and the female members generally stayed back in their villages.

Wages and Earnings

In the case of highly skilled, skilled and semi-skilled jobs in which only males were employed, not a single case could be detected where the wage Act was violated. It was only the skilled category that the prevailing wage rates actually being paid were labour than those remained under the minimum wage rates of the workers, particularly of women labourers, were in many cases below the minimum wages fixed under the Act.

The daily wages being paid to unskilled women labourers were less than the statutory wages in as many as nine of the 14 construction projects studied in Bombay and 5 of the 13 projects studied in Madras. In some cases, women workers' daily wages were even less than half or three-fourth of the minimum wages.

The women labourers were not entitled for any leave with wages and were paid only for the days they actually worked. The labourers were also not getting any social security benefit under any Act. They were not benefitted by the Employee's Provident Funds and Miscellaneous Provisions Act, 1952 even though some of them had been continuously employed at the same work-sites for long periods.

Working Conditions and Welfare Provisions

The work at the selected construction sites were carried on mostly during day time in a single shift. However, the work continued till late night when roofs of the building were to be laid. In such cases, women labourers also worked during night hours. There is at present no legislative provisions which could prevent women construction labourers from working during night hours.

Women labourers employed in the sampled construction projects were found carrying heavy loads of cement bags, mortar, bricks etc., which in some cases weighted more than 30 Kg. At present there is no legislative provision which would prevent the women construction labourers from carrying heavy loads. No women labourer at any selected work-site was found to have been provided with handgloves or any other protective equipment for handling the hard and rough building and construction materials. Thus, their hands and feet in most of the cases were fond in pitiable condition having many scratches. At present there is no legislation providing safety provision for the labourers engaged at the worksites. The employees had not made any special arrangements for providing drinking water to their workers. Whatever water was being used for construction purposes was also available to the labourers for drinking. Latrine provision was not there in most of the work-sites. Urinal facilities and washing facilities were also not available. The maternity Benefit Act is not applicable to the women labourers working at the construction sites. The living accommodation provided by the employers consisted of make-shift huts mostly without any ancillary facilities like Kitchen, Bath, etc. There were no drainage, sanitary, and ventilation facilities in these labour huts. No recreational amenities nor any canteen did exist at any of the construction sites. The working conditions of women labourers were worse than those of male workers. There is, infact, need of a separate comprehensive legislation for the workers engaged in the building and construction industry which may take into account all the peculiar characteristics of the Industry. There was widespread illiteracy among the women construction labourers. As many as 68 of the total 79 children of the women labourers in Delhi and 39 of the total 45 children in Bombay i.e., 86 and 86.6 per cent respectively were not attending schools. No male or female labourers engaged at the construction sites studied in the three cities was reported to be a member of any trade union. There was lack of consciousness among the women construction labourers as almost all the women labourers were not even aware of the beneficial provisions contained in the important labour Acts like the Minimum Wages Act, 1948, the Equal Remuneration Act, 1976, etc.

Dadan Construction Women Labourers

In the state of Orissa women labourers migrating to different parts of the country through contractors or Sardars known as dadan labourers. Several economic factors are responsible for such an exploitative dadan construction women labourers. Being landless and burdened with the heavy weight of maintaining a large Family, and being deprived of job opportunities, the labourers do not dare avoiding the offer that would bring them some income.[55] But it is deplorable to note that they are made to work pretty long hours in excess of the statutory workhours, not being provided with medical benefits, proper food and shelter. They are, quite often, not paid the wages that had been promised to them. In many cases, they are paid less than the agreed wages. Deprived of their wages, they are sometimes forced to board trains without the needed tickets and are cought and thrown into jails.[56]

Reports in the news papers reveals that each year about two lakhs of dadan labour of Orissa which also includes women labourers for construction industry, are going to the other states to seek employment. The recruitment of dadan labourers in Orissa is made mostly from the rural and tribal areas of Keonjhar, Mayurbhanj, Sambalpur, Sundargarh, Puri and Ganjam districts. However, it is not possible to estimate the exact size of the inter-state migration of workmen.[57]

According to 1981 Census, out of a total of 35 lakh construction workers, 10 per cent are women.[58] Although the construction labourers are covered under various Acts like the Minimum Wages Act, the Contract Labour Act and the interstate migrants Act, these laws are more observed in their breach than in their genuine enforcement.

Thus, a paramount feature of construction sector is its heavy dependence on migrant labour. This sector employs a large number of casual workers who are outside the purview of protective labour laws which apply to organised labour in other fields. The peculiar nature of employment in the construction sector has created enormous problems of construction labourers, specially, the unskilled and women labourers.

Therefore, it is imperative of safeguard the interests of women construction labourers by the effective enforcement of various labour laws, punishment for the violation of the same, upgrading the skills of such workers, welfare provisions and by organising them to fight against exploitation.

REFERENCES

1. Saran, K.M. *Labour in Ancient India*, Vora and Co. Publishers Pvt. Ltd., Bombay 1957, pp. 64-65.
2. *Ibid.*
3. Nair, G. Ravindran, Women Workers—The lingering Paradoyes' *Social Welfare*, May, 1988, p. 5.
4. Mencher, Joan and K Saradamani, Muddy feet and dirty hands; rice production and female agricultural labourers, *Economic and Political Weekly*, December, 25, 1983.
5. Kaptan, S.S., The income, wages and working conditions of women in the inorganised sector, *Social Welfare*, May, 1989, p. 29.

6. *The Indian Workers*, Jan. 8, 1990, p. 4.
7. Prasad, Sushama, Sahay, Economic and Physical Exploitation of tribal female labourers, p. 73, in Gupta J.L., *Challenges to the Fair Sex: Indian Women Problems, Plight and Progresses*, Delhi Giani Publ. House, 1988, XXIV p. 132.
8. Desai Neera, Maithreyi, Krishnaraj, *Women an Society in India*, Ajanta Publication, New Delhi, 1987, p. 84.
9. Dr. K. Murali Manohar, *Rural Women, Class Formation and Development*, Kakatiya University, Warangal (Andhra Pradesh).
10. Saikia, Anuva, Seasonal variation of female participation in farm work, *Kurukshetra*, Vol. XXXI, No. 19, July 1-15, 1983 p. 17.
11. Sunita and others, Rural Women labour: Differential treatment by land lord-elites, *Journal of Extension System*, 3(2) Dec., 1987, p. 80.
12. Desai Neera Maithreyi, Krishnaraj, *Women and Society in India, op. cit.*, p. 94.
13. Gupta, Vishwa Nath, Women labour in tea plantations, *Social Welfare*, Vol. XXXVII, No. 2, May 1990, p. 3.
14. *Ibid.*
15. Badruddin, Women Workers in Assam tea plantations, *Social Welfare*, Vl, XXXVII, No. 2, May 1990, p. 29.
16. Mathur, R.N., *Quality of Working Life of Women Construction workers.* Commonwealth Publishers, New Delhi, p. 45.
17. Sharma, Narayan Prasad (Dr.) Wage differentials for women agricultural labourers, *Yojana*, July 1-15, 1989, 33(12), p. 8.
18. Pushpa Sunder, Characteristics of Female Employment—Implications of research and policy. *Economic and Political Weekly*, May, 1981.
19. Rojas, Isabela. "Factors in womens' labour force participation' quoted in "Women Labour Force. Trend and Pattern of Employment" by Atmanand, *op. cit.*
20. Mathur, R.N., Quality of working life of women construction workers, *op. cit.*, p. 35-36.
21. Sahool, B. (Dr.), Changing pattern of women employment in Orissa—Problems and prospects *Vision*, Vol VIII, No. 384, January-June, 1989, p. 38.
22. Kamalraj, M., Women in Salt Industry, *Khadi Gramodyog*, Vol. XXXVI, No. 10, July 1990, p. 411.
23. *Ibid.*
24. *Ibid.*, p. 412.
25. Kannon Jayam (Dr.) and Ilango P., Health Hazards of women working in Beedi Industries, *Social Welfare*, Vol. XXXVI, No. 12, March, 1990, p. 10.
26. Sundari, S. (Dr.) and Marunekhalai, N.—Women Workers in the paddy processing Industries, *Social Welfare*, Vol. XXXVI, No. 10-11, January-February, 1990, p. 14.
27. *Ibid.*, p. 15.
28. Sundari, S. (Dr.) and Marinekalal, N. Problems of women workers in Handloom Industry at Vengamedu, *Khadi Gramodyog*, Vol. XXXV, No. 6, March, 1989, p. 286.
29. *Ibid.*, p. 2289.
30. P. Thippaiah, Women Workers in Urban unorganised sector, *Social Welfare*, Vol. XXXVI, No. 2, May, 1989, p. 21-22.
31. *Ibid.*

32. Jain, Mahaveer, *Metholi Revisited: An account of camp processes of Agricultural women workers*, National Labour Institute, New Delhi, November, 1985.
33. *Ibid.*, p. 10.
34. *Ibid.*, p. 10.
35. *Ibid.*, p. 11.
36. *Ibid.*, p. 11.
37. *Ibid.*, p. 18.
38. ILO, Geneva, *Women at Work* (1) 1984, p. 21.
39. (Dr.) Neera Chandhoke, *Development Process:* Heightening of oppression: A case study of sub-Saharan Africa.
40. Patnaik, S.C and Debi, Sailabala, An assessment of Womens' Economic Contribution to the Farm Sector: A micro level study, *Journal of Rural Development*, National Institute of Rural Development, Rajendranagar, Hyderabad, Vol. 5, July, 1986.
41. *Ibid.*
42. *Ibid.*
43. Rath, Shardha and Rath, Navneet, Attitude of Rural Women in Balasore towards Employment, *Social Welfare*, Vol XXXVII, No. 7, October, 1990.
44. *Ibid.*, p. 19.
45. Bhuyan, B.G. and S.K. Tripathy, Role of Women in Agriculture—A Study in Ganjam District of Orissa, *Journal of Rural Development*, Vol. 7 (4), pp. 445-452 (1988) NIRD, Hyderabad.
46. *Ibid.*
47. Mahapatra, P.C. (Dr.) and B Eswar Rao, Patnaik, How can we improve Socio-economic condition of women, *Yojana*, May, 16-31, 1988, p. 13 17.
48. *Ibid.*
49. *Ibid.*
50. Singh, Mohinder, Women and Development Process in India, *Khadi Gramodyog*, Vol. XXXV, No. 4, January, 1989, p. 200-201.
51. G. Ravindran Nair, Women Workers demand a better deal, *Yojana*, Vol. 34, No. 4, March, 1-15, 1990, p. 20.
52. *The Indian Worker*, March, 12 and 9, 1990, p. 4.
53. Das, D.K. Lal, Sex Discrimination against Female Workers in Unorganised Sector, *Indian Journal of Industrial Relations*, Vol. 2, No. 2, Oct. 1985, pp. 232-239.
54. Mathur, R.N., *Quality of working life of women construction workers, op. cit.*
55. *Ibid.*, p. 53
56. *Ibid.*
57. Tripathy, S.N. (Dr.), *Bonded Labourer in India*, Discovery Publishing House, New Delhi (1989), p. 78.
58. *Ibid.*
59. *Ibid.*, p. 79.
60. G. Ravindran Nair, *Women workers demand a better deal, op. cit.*

36

Living Conditions of Informal Women Workers

Consumer expenditure reflects the economic conditions of the people and is generally used as an index of level of living of the population of a particular geographical area and their social customs and habits. A higher consumption level indicates affluence and vice-versa. The provision of basic necessities such as food, reasonable condition of housing, clothing, education, health facilities and a minimum level of income is essential for maintaining a tolerable living standard for the citizens of a country. A welfare society is committed to provide these basic minima for its people..

It is for fulfilling this avowed objective, that our planners had originally planned in doubling the per capita income in every twenty-five years time. But this objective could not be achieved and the desired improvements in the level of consumption could not be brought about.

An attempt is made in this chapter to explain the consumption pattern of 125 households (consumption of informal women does not mean the consumption of the women in the family alone, but it includes the standard of living and pattern of consumption of all the family members). Since a predominant percentage of sample households belong to SC and ST, it can also be stated as the "consumption pattern of tribals of Phulbani." It is hoped that this study, besides presenting the level of living as reflected by the consumer expenditure of the tribals of the region, will reveal the weaknesses of family budget, the items where there is a need for increasing the expenditure and the items for which expenditure should be curtailed.

The data obtained by survey method, with the need of the household recollecting information from his memory. Inspite of all the efforts made to elicit information by careful interview, it would be wrong to assume that "lapse of memory" on the part of the respondents was fully overcome with regard to the minute details abut the expenditure incurred in various ways. Again it should be mentioned that many households (having marginal land) produce some paddy and vegetables which help a lot to them in their day-to-day consumption out of home grown produce has been evaluated at the present prices, of all items of consumption, the monetary value of the item as evaluated by the State Bureau of Economics and Statistics has been taken into account.

Since there are divergent income groups in the sample households, ranging from 400 to 20,000, it will not serve our purpose to take the whole to determine consumption pattern. So the total households are divided into two categories; income below 5,000, and income above 5,000, are analysed differently. Below, 5,000 income three are 94 households constituting 75.2 per cent of the sample.

TABLE 36.1

Percentage of Distribution of Consumption Expenditure on Food and Non-food Items Among the Sample Informal Households of Income Groups Below Rs. 5,000

(94 families)

Sl. No.	*Items of consumption*	*Percentage of Total Expenditure spent*	
		Sample survey of 94 families	*Sample survey of 1963 by planning and co-ordination department, Orissa*
(1)	(2)	(3)	(4)
1.	Food	68.92	79.49
2.	Clothing	9.60	0.46
3.	Fuel and Light	5.29	0.46
4.	Intoxicants	6.89	7.33
5.	Medicine	0.04	0.19
6.	Education	2.04	0.90
7.	Other Expenditures	7.22	1.77

Notes: 1. — Column 3 indicates the findings of the sample survey of 94 families.

2. — Column 4 indicates the findings of the sample survey 1963 conducted by the planning and co-ordination department, Govt. of Orissa among 671 tribal families to find out the living condition of the scheduled tribes in scheduled blocks of Orissa.

It can be seen from column three of Table 36.1 that the major item of expenditure is food which comprises 86.92 per cent of the total income. Expenditure on clothing is that next important item of the family which comprises 9.60 per cent of total income. The proportion of expenditure on intoxicants (i.e. drinking and smoking) occupies third important place and comprises of 6.89 per cent of the total expenditure. Percentage of expenditure on fuel, light and other expenses like festival and entertainment are more or less same and occupy respectively the next two places in the family budget. The proportion of expenditure on education is lower (2.04 per cent) and that of health is negligible and occupy least important place in the consumer's budget.

TABLE 36.2

Distribution of Per-Capita Consumer Expenditure Among the Sample (94) Households of Phulbani Town according to the Size of Income

Sl. No.	*Size of Income groups*	*Number of Households*	*Consumer expenditure per month (in Rs.)*
1.	below 1000	5	19.42
2.	1001 to 2000	9	26.66
3.	2001 to 3000	28	38.19
4.	3001 to 4000	36	50.97
5.	4001 to 5000	16	73.84

Disproportionately higher expenditure on food items than on the non-food items on the total consumer expenditure is a characteristic feature of the people of low income groups are gradually developing. If they will allocate the budget with proper foresight i.e. increasing expenditure on education of children and further reduce the expenditure on intoxicants, and last but not least adopt family planning, (because larger in number, greater the poverty and lower per capita expenditure) then their economic condition and standard of living will definitely increase over period.

31 householdsrs are there in the income groups 5,000 and above. These families lead the life of middle class-8 households belonging to higher middle class and rest 23 (mainly among the income groups 5,000-6,000) belong to the lower middle class. While listing the number of consumer durables it is found that all most all of 31 households possess a small house of their own, may be made up of mud/Kucha, brick and thatched or of khaparali/ Tiles/Asbestos roof. Some of them also possess radio, wrist watch bycycle etc. Per capita consumption expenditure of these 23 households is Rs. 86.95 approximately.

Comparatively higher middle income group, (exceeding an income of 10,000 per annum) 98 in the sample, maintain an average standard of living and possess consumer durables like T.V., Gas Cylinder Radio, Tape Recorder etc. Four of them also maintain two wheelers. They give sufficient attention towards the education of their children and so on.

Though only 21% families show a deficit in their current budget. 40% of the families reported indebtedness to varying amount, mostly of an amount larger than Rs. 1000/-, there is no lesser he income, greater is the proportion of food item and vice-versa.

A comparison between the findings of the sample survey in Orissa in 1963 with the present study indicates that there has been a fall in the percentage of expenditure on food to the total expenditure among the tribals in Orissa. However table 36.2 reveals that proportion of expenditure on food is increasing (per capita expenditure in increasing, food item occupying 68.92 per cent is also sure to increase) in case of higher income groups. Among the low income earners, the quantum of consumption increases with the increase in income only in case of those who have not been able to satisfy their desire for food and other necessaries. Thus a proportion of expenditure on food among the relatively low income group dos not indicate any economic development of tribals, over the period, rather it indicates the intensity of poverty among the people.

However, an insight into problem reveals that people in the area are developing slowly. Their expenditure on intoxicants has decreased relatively and interest towards education of children is increasing gradually. It is true that with an income of 3,000 to 4,000 it will be comparatively easy to maintain the family in rural areas than in towns. Thus decreasing expenditure on food items among the informal workers may be due to the fact that they have to incur mode expenditure on clothing, housing, education and again they have to afford for food at a higher rate in the town than in their native rural origin.

Thus comparing the consumption pattern of rural tribals in 1973 to that of migrant tribals in the town reveal that, they consistent relationship between family income levels and proportion of indebted families. Debt is incurred due to multifarious causes.

PERCENTAGE OF HOUSEHOLDS AND POVERTY LINE

As per the projections on the poverty line made in the sixth plan the monthly per capita consumption expenditure in the rural areas of India has been calculated at Rs. 75.71 in 1977-78[2] at current prices by the central statistical organisation. This figure is calculated on the basis of daily caloric intake of 2400 per person. Subsequently, on the basis of an assessment of several rounds of N.S.S. on household consumer expenditure, it has been observed that 50.52 per cent of rural population are below poverty line in 1977-78[3] By applying this criterion among the sample households it would be evident that (Table 36.2) 94 families constituting 75.2 per cent are below poverty line.

Thus the consumption pattern and standard of living of the informal workers indicate the limited impact of the plans on the well-being of the poor section of population and our inability to restructure the distribution of assets to provide productive employment for a growing workforce. After three and half decades of planned development a large section of our population has yet to share the benefits of progress.

Informal Women Workers and Household Management

In recent years there has been a growing concern, among economists in developed countries, in the activities, taking place at home, which perhaps indicates the conviction that work at home is in some sense productive and hence needs to be analysed in economic terms. Considerable work has been done on the economics of household behaviour facilitated by the development on the theoretical front of the new consumption theory of Becker (1965). The recognition that households are engage din production "for use" also led to increased effort to measure the value of home production and a near unanimous claim to include this value in national accounts. The available estimates by researchers (Summarised in Hawrylyshyn 1976) reveals that in countries such as the United States, the household sector contributes to over one third of the output produced in the market, which is not a negligible amount.

The implications of this view of domestic activities can be even more relevant and important for developing countries like India where a significant fraction of economic activity occurs within households. Yet these activities are regarded as unproductive and persons performing them do not figure in official statistics. For instance, the decennial census of India is an important source of information on the extent of economic activity in this country over the decades various items like "actual workers" "earners," "self supporting and earning dependents," "main activity worker" plus "having secondary work" "main workers" and "marginal workers" have been used to denote the economically active population. All these definition in one sense or other imply that a person is being regarded as "economically productive" only if he/she reports having worked at least some time in the reference period and by this criterion unpaid workers and persons engaged in domestic work are deemed unproductive and categorised as "non-workers." Since bulk of the unpaid/domestic work is performed by women, the census figures of women's work participation rate's is an inadequate indication of their true productive role. According to the 1981 census, about 55 per cent of the "non-workers" among women are engaged in house-work and they should be ideally considered in the enumeration of women's work.

Besides the issue of treating house work as productive, some economists in this country have argued in favour of computing the money value of house work and of its inclusion in national product. This is because commission of this sphere of activity leads to downward bias in G.N.P. statistics which can be substantial. The bias could be particularly severe for a country like India, where sizeable production in real terms occurs within households and is also time consuming in nature. In the industrially advanced countries, in contrast, house work does not require much time input. This is partly the result of mechanisation of some categories of housework and partly the emergence of specialised industries such as food processing as a result of which food preparation has become much less demanding in time. In view of this difference, we believe that the value of home production in India is likely to be much more compared to the developed countries.

Estimating the money value of household services has implications for other issues also. For instance, analysis of income distribution across households should take into account the value of domestic work since the goods and services that a family consumes consist in large measures of commodities produced at home. If this value of home production differs more or less between individual house holds than does their market income, then a measure of income distribution that considers only the latter is insufficient. Even in tax collection, imposing a tax on marked incomes but not on the income generated by house work results in narrowing the tax base and unequal treatment of people who may otherwise be equally placed. (Musgrave, 1956) Evaluating house-work in monetary terms has legal implications in the context of divorce settlements where it has been pointed out that account should be taken of the contributions "in the form of money, service, prudent management, earning for the home and family."[5]

Economic View Points

Economics of housework can be examined from micro and macro angles.

Micro economic analysis is a neo-classical tool. A household is taken as a consuming unit. It spends as a whole. An individual who takes decisions is synonymous with the entire household. That the household consists of individuals with their own preference is completely ignored. The theory treats the family as a black box with all its internal dynamics kept away from the theorists. Prof. Galbraith took off the lid from the box in order to examine the household role of men and women. He saw women as the administrator of consumption.

Nature of housework is influenced by incomes the man earns, when income is low, women spend most of the time in routine drudgery from coking to cleaning, from childcare to husband care and from storing to preserving, when income level rises sufficiently for house holds the lady of the house is supposed to oversee, coordinate and manage the activities of full time or part time servants. She takes on a managerial task which is not less arduous.[6] The only way left to society for inducing women to housework is to develop a system of palliartives in the form of social virtue in them. The expressions "the devoted wife," "the hard working, sincere and faithful wife," "Soft and gently lady," "the better half," are subtle social arrangements used to pursuade women to perform irksome tasks silently and uncrudingly.

In the micro analysis setting the following conclusions can be emphasised—

1. When a housewife tries to follow law of maximum satisfaction, she was to weld the different preferences of family members into a coherent whole. This task requires affection and understanding, knowledge and information about fashion, quality and price of goods etc. There is lack of appreciation of their work by men and society.
2. With the help of goods and services brought from the marketing and by devoting her time and energy to convert goods into eatables and services, she becomes the end all of many economic activities in society. Family equilibrium is obtained mostly all the cost of her, when she is in disequilibrium. Women become a subordinate class in their very homes.
3. The dividing line between the nurturing role of women and the working role of men, though vague, is very clear in feudal and capitalist societies. Domestic works consume a major share of women's time. Many attempts in this regard have been made to find out the extent of time devoted for the work in the domestic sector. The studies of 12 countries have shown that women allocated 22% of their time to formal work and 78% of total time in house work and related obligations.[7] Soviet women spend 40 hours a week during house work while men spend 15-20 hours[8] Women in the wall street employee's family spend 99.5[9] hours in a week for house work. It is also marked that women who work in the market place continue to allocate almost the same amount of time for house work like the women who stay at home full time. In U.S. the full time working married

women spend 25 hours a week on house work in 1975-76; where as it was only 13 hours a week on the part of men.[10] Married women who were part time workers in the market sector spend 33 hours a week in home related duties and full time house makers devoted 41 hours in a week.

It is estimated that National Income will increase by 25 per cent if contribution of women's house work is taken into account.' A survey of wall street employee's families shows that the imputed value of women's housework is Rs. 250.00[12] in a week. In 1979 Evenly Kaye calculated the same job to be worth about $700 a week and $35,000 a year.[13] It was estimated that if women in the U.S.A. were paid for their household work at the 1970 survey's rate, it would come to around 500-650 billion dollars per annum which is more than half of the G.N.P. Scoot has estimated the housewives housework to be $257 per week and $13,364 a year.[14] Clark in 1956 calculated the annual estimated value of housewives' housework at 1956 prices to be $494 per capita in U.K. in 1871 and $570 per capita in 1956[15]

Table 36.3 shows the value of women's unpaid work and time allocated for different types of housework by women in the wall street employe's family in 1979.

TABLE 36.3

Time Allocation and Money Value of Domestic Labour in Wall-Street Employee's Families

Sl. No.	*Type of work*	*Hours per week*	*Rate per hour*	*Value per week*
1.	Nurse maid	44.5	2.00	89.00
2.	Housekeeper	17.5	3.25	56.88
3.	Cook	13.1	3.25	42.58
4.	Dish-washer	6.2	2.00	12.40
5.	Laundres	5.9	2.50	14.75
6.	Food Surveyer	3.3	3.50	11.53
7.	Gardener	2.3	3.00	6.90
8.	Chauffeur	2.0	3.50	6.50
9.	Maintenance Man	1.7	3.00	5.10
10.	Seam stress	1.3	3.25	4.22
11.	Diatician	1.2	4.50	4.40
12.	Practical Nurse	0.6	3.75	2.25

Source: Lisa Leghorn and Katherine Parker *Women's Worth, Sexual Economics* and *the World of Women*, (London: Routledge and Kegan Paul, 1981).

The economic activities in which informal women workers of Phulbani participate, can be broadly classified into three groups: (1) Household works without direct economic benefits, (2) Agricultural and non-agricultural works in the family firm and (3) wage earning employment in the agricultural field the participation of women in almost negligible since 75% of them belong to the category of "no land" and "marginal land" group.

But it is found that women in the IFS are engaged in wage earning-employment. They go to market either to sell their vegetables, accompany their husbands to work in construction activities or to wash the cloths. In these works they devote 6-8 hours daily, and earn almost equal to their male partner. Added to these burden are that they have to engage in household activities daily for 6-8 hours (as seen from Table 36.4) comparing monetary value (in Table 36.3) with hours of work (Table 36.4), if the monetary value will be imputed, it is clear that contributor of women to the family will be greater than their husband. The tribal women of Phulbani are hard working and generally they bear greater burden of economic activities. Women share the work load, which should be generally done by men-folk, but not the otherway round. Thus after the wage earning hours, while men are engaged in enjoying drinks, (Salap juice, and other local drinks) the poor women are engaged in house works. An average women works 12-14 hours a day. Longer hours of works coupled with poverty, illiteracy and ignorance, repeated pregnancies and deliveries, poor nutrition, insanitary and crowded living account for the ill-health and low life expectancy of women.

TABLE 36.4

Average Hours Engaged in One Week in Various Household Activities by the Informal Women Workers in the Sample (125)

	Type of work	*Average Hours engaged in one week*
1.	Cleaning and washing	11.72
2.	Cooking	11.93
3.	Care of children	9.88
4.	Weaving	5.74
5.	Sewing and Kinitting	1.84
6.	Husking and Threshing	3.15
7.	Milking	3.33
8.	Kitchen gardening	2.27
9.	Flower gardening	2.00
10.	Rearing silk and work Muga and Endi	—
11.	Others	1.80
	Total	53.66
	Percentage of weekly hours engaged,	31.94
	Daily average hours engaged	7.67

When compared to household management of formal and informal women workers it is found that informal women workers are more efficient in managing home than that of formal workers. Since formal sector women workers have to devote a particular time, (10 A.M. to 4 P.M. generally) they find less time to devote for house work.

Value of Household Services: A Macro Exercise

Now let us turn our attention to the macro aspects of women's domestic work. It is possible to say that women's work is related to national economy in two ways. When she is tied to home, she is prone to spend more on devious consumer articles, durable and otherwise. With education and modern informal system, she is able to raise family consumption to higher level. Thus by maintaining consumption and demand she supports the productive apparatus of the economy. This is the Galbraithian thesis.

Marxists link women to the productive system through supply channel, women's womb is a factory for producing babies, procreation being a natural process, society gets children, the skill and motivation which she creates in them make them fit to join the labour force. The labour power so essential for an economic system is a major contribution of women. One can agree with the Marxists when they say that women create a surplus value that is appropriated by the dominant sex. Thus the reproduction of labour and production of utility to maintain a labour force are important economic activities rendered by women. These feminine activities give colour to macro-economic system.

Finally, it is enlightening to derive an estimate of the value of home production (household services) for the country as a whole. For this is required the data on time spent by women in household tasks which can be multiplied by the price of time (either the opportunity wage or the cost of hiring replacement workers to do the house work) to yield the estimate of the value of work at home. However, with the exception of a work by Mukerjee (1987),[16] and R. Malathy, we are not aware of any attempt in this direction for India. According to R. Malathy household works done by women in India yields a value that constitutes about 47 per cent of Net Domestic Product (NDP).[17] This is certainly not an insignificant amount. As pointed out earlier, these estimates are rather crude but certainly indicates that domestic work can't be brushed aside as uneconomic nor can it be overlooked on grounds of measurement difficulties.

REFERENCES

1. Govt. of Orissa, Planning and Co-ordination (Evaluation) Department.
   Living condition of Scheduled Tribes and Scheduled Castes and other backward classes in Orissa, 1963, Evaluation Study No. 10, O.G.P. 1965 Table No. 4.8, pp. 26-27.
2. G.S. Srinivasan and N. Kumar Swamy "Eradication of Poverty: Measures," *Khadi Gramodyog*, Vol. XXVIII, No. 12, Sept. 1982, p. 539, Table 1.
3. Govt. of India, Sixth Five Year Plan: 1980-85.
4. Hawralyshyn, A. "The value of Household Services: A survey of Empirical Estimates." *Review of Income and Wealth series* 22, No. 2, pp. 101-132.
5. Cited in Hawralyshyn (1976).

6. J.K. Galbraith, *Economics and the Public Purpose"* (Delhi, Vikas, 1974), p. 32.
7. J.R. Caparman (ed) *Economic Independence for Women* (London, Sage, 1976), p. 47.
8. Lisa Leghorn and Katherine Parker, *Women's Worth: Sexual Economics and the World of Women* (London: Routledge and Kegan Paul, 1981), p. 76.
9. *Ibid.*, p. 169.
10. June O'Neith: 'Earnings Differentials: Empirical evidence and causes" in G. Schemid and R. Weitzel (ed.) *Sex Discrimination and Equal opportunity* (New York: St. Martins Press 1984), p. 75.
11. G.K. Galbraith, p. 33.
12. Lisa Leghorn and Katherine Parker, *op. cit.*, p. 33.
13. Evelyn Kaye, "Worth of a mother? $35,000 says article "Bostone Globe" 24th, July 1975.
14. A.C. Scott "The Value of Housework: for love of money," *Ms. Magazine* in J.K. Galbraith, op. cit., p. 3.
15. Collin Clark, "The Economics of Housework, *Institute of Statistic Bulletin*, 20, May 1958, p. 209.
16. Mukerjee, M. (1987) "Contributions to and use of social product by women" in Jain, D, and Banerjee N. (eds.) *Women in Poverty: Tyranny of the Household Investigative Essays on Women's work.* pp. 258-274. (New Delhi, India, Shakti Books, A Division of Vikas Publishing House Pvt. Ltd.).
17. R. Malathy in his article *The Value of Household services of Women in India,* published in *Artha Vijnana,* March 1988, v. 30, No. 1.), p. 99.

37

Government Policy on Women Labourers

The Constitution of India promises to secure all its citizens, justice, liberty, equality and to promote fraternity among them all. To realise the goals the Constitution guarantees certain fundamental rights. Alongwith these, certain negative rights, prohibiting discrimination or denial of equal protection of law are also guaranteed. The Constitution recognised the unequal social position of women and a special clause empowers the state to make special provisions for women and children even in violation of the obligation not to discriminate among citizens.*

Article 1(1) and 16(2) of the Constitution grant the right of equal opportunities in regard to employment to men and women without any distinction. The Directive Principles of State Policy which has a bearing on this point is 39 (a).

Article 43 of the Constitution says, "The State shall endeavour to secure by suitable legislation or economic organisation or any otherway to all workers, agricultural, industrial or otherwise, work, a living wage, ensuring a decent standard of life, and full enjoyment of leisure and social, cultural opportunities.

Therefore, special laws have been enacted for the protection of women workers in factories, mines, and plantation, and to provide maternity relief to women workers in organised sector.

There is a plethora of laws for the protection of benefits of working women which regulate the hours of work, provide measures for safety and well-being of female labourers especially in organised sector. The unorganised sector has not been concerned effectively by any of these laws. The legislative measures are framed from time to time in order to ensure that women are not discriminated and exploited. These are the special marriage and Divorce Act, 1954 Suppression of Immoral Traffic in Women and Girls Act, 1956. Hindu Adoption and Maintenance Act, 1956, Hindu Succession Act, 1956, Maternity Benefit Act, 1961. The Dowry Prohibition Act, 1961, Indecent Representation of Women (Prohibition) Act, 1986. The Commission of Sati (Prevention) Act, 1987. All these legal measures and Acts

---

* Article 15(3), Constitution of India.

aimed at ameliorating the condition of women labourers and safeguarding women from the tyrannies of age-old social customs, superstitious values and exploitation.

Hindu Marriage Act, 1955

The Hindu Marriage Act applies to all the Hindus by religion which includes Vaishnavas, Lingayats and members of the Brahmo, Prarthana, Arya Samaj. It also applies to the Buddhists, Sikhs and Jains and to legitimate and illegitimate, children of parents who belong to the above religions and sects. All 'Hindu's who do not marry under the special Marriage Act are governed by this Act. Under Hindu Marriage Act the conditions for marriage are:

- — Either spouse should not have an earlier living spouse.
- — Should not have mental problem, mental illness.
- — Men should be 21 years complete and girls 18 years complete.
- — The parties are not within the degree of prohibited relationship, unless the custom or usage governing each of them permits a marriage between the two.
- — The parties should not be sapinda to each other unless the custom or usage governing them permits such marriage.

A Hindu cannot contract a second marriage with another till the first marriage is dissolved by divorce or decree. If this is done he/she can be prosecuted by law. A report given to the police by the near relative is entertained. If such a second marriage is proved he/she can be imprisoned and also find. Under the Act, certain types of marriages are void and fraudulent.

When the spouses find it difficult to continue to live with each other, either of the spouse can apply for divorce under the law.

For the dissolution of the marriage, the law has provided certain conditions only on which a decree for divorce can be granted by the court. However, the dissolution of a marriage can be applied for not before the expiry of one year of marriage or of passing of the decree of judicial separation unless permitted by the court under special circumstances. The grounds on which the dissolution of the marriage can be granted by the court are cruelty, adultery, unsoundness of mind, desertion, not being alive, suffering from disease and mutual consent.

The Special Marriage Act, 1954

The Act permits marriage of people from different religious faiths without changing their religion.

The Hindu Marriage Act, 1955 and the Special Marriage Act, 1954 were amended in 1976 to provide for the right of a girl to repudiate before attaining maturity, marrying as child whether the marriage has been consumated or not. Cruelty and desertion were added as grounds for divorce and mutual consent were recognised.

Hindu Succession Act, 1956

The act confers the rights of absolute ownership over property and the women can make 'will' leaving her share of property to the heirs. Section 10 of the Act provides for the property of an intestate being divided among the heirs in accordance with certain prescribed rules.

Hindu Adoption and Maintenance Act, 1956

Any Hindu man of sound mind can take a son or daughter in adoption provided that if he has a living wife and he gets the consent of his wife to do so, unless the wife has completely renounced the world, is of unsound mind and has ceased to be a Hindu.

A Hindu woman can take a child in adoption if she is unmarried or is a widow, her marriage has been dissolved, her husband has renounced the world, has changed his religion and he is declared to be of unsound mind.

Under Section 9, the consent of father and mother is necessary for giving the child in adoption unless (i) they or one of them is dead or (ii) the father or mother has completely and finally renounced the world or (iii) has ceased to be Hindu or (iv) has been declared by a court of competent jurisdiction to be of unsound mind.

The Child Marriage Restraint (Amendment) Act, 1976

The Act raises the age of marriage for girls from 15 to 18 years and boys 18 years to 21 years. The offences under this Act have been made cognizable.

The Factories Act, 1948, Mines Act, 1952 and Plantation Labour Act, 1951

These Acts prohibit the employment of women between 7 p.m. and 6. a.m. in factories, mines and plantations, regulate the working hours and contain provision for their safety and welfare. The Government is authorised to fix the maximum load that may be lifted by women and to open creches etc.

The Employees' State Insurance Act, 1948

The benefits provided under this Act include sickness benefit, maternity benefit, disablement benefit, dependent benefit, medical and funeral benefit.

The Maternity Benefits Act, 1961

This Act is applicable to every establishment, plantation, mine or factory and provides for payment of maternity benefit at the rate of average daily wage for the period of women's actual absence. It has been amended in April, 1976 to cover women, who do not fall within the purview of the Employees State Insurance Act, 1948. A proposal to further amend the Act is under consideration of the Labour Ministry.

The Factories (Amendment) Act, 1976

The Act provides for establishment of creches where 30 women are employed (including casual labourers or contact labourers) as against one for every 50 hitherto.

The Equal Remuneration Act, 1976

The Act provides for (a) the payment of equal remuneration to men and women workers and (b) prevention of discrimination on the ground of sex against women in the matter of employment and for matter connected therewith or indentical thereto. There is a proposal under consideration of Labour Ministry for amendment of the Act with a view to further liberalising its provisions in favour of women.

The Contract Labour (Regulation and Abolition) Act, 1978

The Act regulates the working conditions of contract labour (which includes women), payment of wages and provides for welfare facilities and creches for the children of working women engaged in construction work.

The Medical Termination of Pregnancy Act, 1971

The Act legalises induced abortion by qualified doctor on humanitarian and medical grounds. This is primarily a welfare measure to protect the health of women though it has also a family planing aspect. Women can now have induced abortion through qualified people. The service is free in public hospitals. All the documents are kept confidential. Before undergoing surgery, if the patient is a minor or of unsound mind, written consent of the guardian is necessary. Since the inception of the programme in April, 1972, 223 million terminations were done upto September, 1981.

The Dowry Prohibition Act, 1961

The Dowry Prohibition was first legislated in 1961. The Act was amended in 1984 to make the offence cognisable, to enhance the penalty both fine and imprisonment and to widen the scope of the Act to make it more effective. The Act was further amended in 1986 to make the penal provisions more effective and stringent. The minimum punishment for taking or abetting taking of dowry has been raised to 5 years and a fine of Rs. 15,000. The advertisements in newspapers, periodicals etc., offering a share of property as consideration for marriage is punishable. The amendment proposes appointment of Dowry Prohibition Officers by the State Governments. Offences under the Act have been made non-bailable. A new Offence of Dowry Death has been included in the Indian Penal Code consequential to the amendment in the Act.

The Suppression of Immoral Traffic in Women and Girls Act, 1956

The Suppression of Immoral Traffic Act prohibits trafficking in women and girls for purposes of prostitution as an organised means of living. The Act which was amended in 1978 was further amended in September, 1986 with the objective of making the penal provisions in the Act more stringent and effective. The amendment Act is retitled as "the Immoral Traffic (Prevention) Act, 1986" and the salient features are—widening the scope of the Act to cover all persons, whether male or female who are sexually exploited for commercial purposes; enhancement of the period of imprisonment where offences are committed against minors and children; appointment of Trafficking Police Officers, who will have the powers to investigate inter-state offences; prescribing punishment as laid down for rape under the Indian Penal Code or the seduction of victims of trafficking while in custody; interrogations of women and girls removed from the brothels to be held by women police officers or in their absence in the presence of women social workers and setting up of Special Courts for setting offences, which have inter-state ramifications.

Amendment to the Criminal Laws

The Indian Evidence Act, the Indian Penal Code and the Criminal Procedure Code were amended in 1983 to make the offence of rape and such crimes against women much more stringent and effective and also to make a new provision to the Indian Penal Code to make cruelty against women by the husband and other relations punishable. The onus of proof of innocence would rest on the accused of such offences.

Family Courts

An Act was passed in 1984 for the setting up of Family Courts in the country with a view to promoting reconciliation in, and securing speedy settlement of disputes relating to marriage and family affairs and for matters connected therewith.

Indecent Representation of Women (Prohibition) Act, 1986

The Indecent Representation of Women (Prohibition) Act, 1986 was passed in Parliament in December, 1986 with the objective of having separate legislation to effectively prohibit the indecent representation of women through advertisements, books, pamphlets etc. The indecent representation of women has been defined to mean the depiction of the figure of a women in such a way as to have the effect of being indecent or of being derogatory to women or is likely to deprive, corrupt or injure the public morality; to prohibit all advertisements; publications etc., which contain indecent representation of women in any form; to prohibit selling, distribution circulation of any books, pamphlets etc., containing indecent representation of women. Offences under this act are made punishable with imprisonment of either description for a term extending to two years and fine extending to two thousand rupees on first conviction.

The Commission of Sati (Prevention) Act, 1987

The Commission of Sati (Prevention) Act, 1987 was passed by the Parliament in December, 1987 to provide for more effective prevention of the commission of Sati and its glorification and matters connected therewith or incidental thereto. The Act defines Sati comprehensively to include not only the burning or burial alive of a wife widow with a deceased husband but also of a widow or women with the body of any other relative or any article associated with the husband or relative; anyone who abets the commitment of Sati by inducement, encouragement, participation in processions, preventing the widow from saving herself etc. would be punishable by the maximum penalty, i.e., death or imprisonment for life; the abetment of an attempt to commit Sati would be punishable with imprisonment for life; in the case of persons prosecuted under these offences, the burden of proof that he had not committed the offence shall be on him; those convicted for such offences shall be disqualified from inheriting the property of the persons committing Sati; persons convicted under such offences shall be disqualified under the Representation of People's Act, 1951 from the date of such conviction and shall continue to be disqualified for a further period of five years after release; glorification of Sati has been defined in details. The Act of glorification includes observance of ceremonies, collection of funds and construction of temples; punishment by imprisonment which may extend to seven years for the glorification of Sati has been prescribed; while the provisions of the Act necessarily have to be prospective, acts of glorification carried out in further would be covered; the propagation of the practice of the commission of sati or its glorification by a candidate or his agent shall be deemed a corrupt practice under the Representation of People's Act; powers have been specifically provided to the Collector/State Government that, if satisfied that in any temple or structure any ceremony is carried out with a view to prepetuating the multilated concept as dealt with in this Act, the state Government in the case of structures and the collector in other cases, can direct the removal of such temple or structure and the Collector can also seize, properties collected for the glorification of Sati.[1]

Women belonging to small farmers, landless labourers, lower middle classes' (lower petty bourgeoisie) and the industrial working class fall under the severe yoke of oppression than their counterparts. By far to this section of women sexests, sati and even dowry hardly matter for their very survival is at stake in this class-ridden and patriarchal society who are in majority.[2]

However, law has accorded special protection to the women ever since the time of Manu. This is because of their physical structure, social status and conditions of the Hindu Society. Most of the Hindu women are illiterate and ignorant of their legal rights and duties, economically dependent on men, socially backward, politically un-informed. Accordingly, the framers of the Indian penal code and the criminal procedure code provided special provisions for women, including Hindu women.[3]

Some important offences relating to women under Indian Penal Code (IPC) are listed here:[4]

TABLE 37.1

Offences Under the IPC Protecting Women

Sl. No.		*Name of the Offence*	*Section*	*Minimum period/ Maximum period*
1		2	3	4
1.	Obscene acts and songs in public place.	294		3 months or fine or both.
2.	Dowry Death.	304-B		7 years inprisonment/ Life imprisonment.
3.	Causing miscarriage without women's consent.	313		Life imprisonment or 10 years and fine.

1		2	3 4
4.	Simple hurt-wife beating	323	One year and also fine upto Rs. 10,000/- or both.
5.	Grievous hurt-wife beating.	323	7 years and also fine.
6.	Assult or criminal force to women with intent to outrage her modesty.	354	Imprisonment of two years or fine or both.
7.	Kidnapping.	363	7 years imprisonment and also fine.
8.	Kidnapping of a minor for begging.	365-A	10 years imprisonment and also fine.
9.	Kidnapping, abducting or inducing women to compel her marriage.	366	10 years imprisonment and also fine.
10.	Buying or disposing of any person as a slave	370	7 years imprisonment and also fine.
11.	Selling minor for purpose of prostitution.	372	10 years imprisonment and also fine.
12.	Buying minor for purpose of prostitution.	373	10 years imprisonment and also fine.
13.	Rape.	376	7 years imprisonment/ 10 years imprisonment and also fine.
14.	Sexual intercourse with one's wife living separately.	376-A	Imprisonment of two years and also fine.
15.	Intercourse by public servant with women in his custody.	376-B	Imprisonment of 5 years and also fine.
16.	Cohabitation caused by a man deceitfully inducing a belief of lawful marriage.	493	10 years and also fine.
17.	Adultery.	497	5 years or fine or both.
18.	Subjecting a women to cruelty.	509	3 years and also fine.

However, despite these legislative measures, the economic and physical exploitation of unorganised labour force in general and female labour force in particular, continue unabated. Central and State Governments though framed several rules and enacted legislations to combat the exploitative forces but the irony of the fact is that there has been a staggering gulf between the framing rules, enacting legislations and their effective implementation. The women labours and tribal women in particular, have been drawn into the unorganised labour force for about past three decades are in process of striking a balance between their economic problems, which force them to accept the drudgeries of unorganised labour employment, and the exploitative both economic and physical forces.[5] Women have always been the victims of aggressive male sexuality. Among bonded labour households it has been observed that women have to provide sexual favours to the landlords creditors to whom the household is indebted.[6] Further, it is pointed that the widespread use of sexual violence and exploitation is not the exclusive prerogative of men in the government, the police and the military. Women are raped at work, on the streets, in the fields, in their houses by men who are their employers, their neighbours, their relatives.[7]

Indeed, in one study (Gupta, 1985) relating to the Jaunsar-Bawar region of Uttar Pradesh, women from bonded labour households were routinely sent into prostitution to repay the debts incurred by the husbands, typically for subsistence. The brothel owner pays the husband an advance which the latter uses for debt payment, while the wife puts in several years as a prostitute.[8] Dr. G.K. Kamble has narrated causes where masters of bonded labour families as they have full control over family members and could compel their women for immoral acts. In certain regions, wife of a bonded labourer was mortgaged with the landlord to clear off debt. During mortgage period, the landlords could use her as a congubine. Such women were often ill-treated by the masters and forced to be the victims of brothel houses in urban areas. Sexual exploitation of migrant women is fairly common.[9]

Forms of abuse range from humiliation and economic blackmail to physical brutality. The wounds sear the mental and physical health of many victims for life. Yet those victims often refrain from seeking help because they fear further violence, lack economic security or wish to shield their personal lives from public scrutiny.[10]

A summery by the Family Planning Association of India show that 68 per cent of women admitted to some kind of sexual abuse by relatives or friends of the family. Women are commodities, objects of pleasure, objects to be used and discarded. Prostitutes, rape victims, victims of harassment in buses, in gardens, in factories and in offices, and even in temples.[11]

Thus, the forgoing analysis demonstrate that unless the various labour laws and Acts are made leak-proof, the unorganised labour, including the tribal female labourers in particular and women labour in general, would continue to be economically and physically exploited.

Development-oriented Measures

In recent years government has undertaken various policy measures for the development of women which have been enumerated below:

DWCRA

Women from nearly half the population of India, and it is they who raise children to muturity. As such it is in their hands that the future of our country rests. Development of Women and Children in Rural Areas Programme (DWCRA) therefore, has been planned to make women economically productive and confident members of society and equal partners with men in bettering the living conditions of families.[12]

Role of Gram Sevika

In the implementation process of DWCRA Gram Sevikas play the paramount role. Gram Sevika has been assisted by Mukhya Sevika and Project Office in a particular locality. To maintain the records of project implementation, to identify different ways of improving the capacity of women for income generation among the members of society etc., are the duties of the Gram Sevika. Gram Sevika helps women in analysing their socio-economic situation and assists them in finding solutions for their problems. Gram Sevika should also be in a position to give ideas, information and assistance regarding any possible income generation activities that women of a group can undertake. She can help them to get information from banks, District Rural Development Agency (DRDA) and other Government programmes and thereby, forms a link between women of group and outside agencies.

Women who come under the purview DWCRA programme are devided into various categories like those who follow the traditional occupations like weaving, basket making, daily wage earners, miscellaneous occupations like flower selling, fire wood selling and those who are absolutely unemployed. Besides trainign in income generating activities, organisation of women labourers, provision of easy and low interest based credit, learning of skills etc., are also provided with the women workers through the DWCRA.

Selection Criteria

Criteria for selecting an income generating activity under the programme are: (i) raw material required is available locally can be transported to the working place at reasonable cost. (ii) ready marketing facilities. (iii) Small investment (iv) simple skills that can be learnt quickly (v) those that can be pursued at home or in the village, (vi) short gestation period and (vii) easy availability of training facilities and other technical inputs. Training, monitoring and evaluation of the programme is ultimately the test of success and hence has to be given the priority consideration. Involvement of women in DWCRA programme is of great significance for effective and proper implementation of DWCRA programme. The training of DWCRA functionaries is arranged by the National Institutes of Rural Development, Hyderabad. The traditional skills of rural women are being supplemented by training imparted under Training of Rural youth for Self-employment (TRYSEM) programme.

Women and Education

The sixth five year plan (1980-85) remarked 'a low rate of literacy and low economic status stress the need for greater attention to the economic advancement of women." And that improvement in the socio-economic status of women would depend to a large extent on the social change in the values, attitudes and social structure prevailing in the country. Education has to be recognised as the basis on which health care of the children, the mother herself and the realisation that frequent pregnancies are a source of great danger to the women and her family can be safely built. Education enables women to be aware of their rights and responsibilities for the development of the nation as well as the region in which they live. Education adds to one's earning capacity, widens the scope of employment.

The National Perspective Plan for Women

The National Perspective Plan for Women (1988) has recommended the following measures for effective improvement of women at the grass roof level in the democratic institutions:

(i) Reservation should be made of 30 per cent seats at Panchayat to Zilla Parishad level and local municipal bodies for women. Whenever possible, higher representation of dalit/tribal women of weaker sections should be ensured.

(ii) Thirty per cent of executive heads of all bodies from village Panchayat to district level and a certain percentage of chief executive of panchayati Raj bodies at lower, middle and higher levels must be reserved for women.

(iii) A more effective step would be to declare a certain percentage of constituencies in the lower tier of Panchayati Raj as exclusively women's constituencies and all executive positions in a certain number of territorial jurisdiction reserved for women candidates.

Thus, the National Perspective Plan for Women aims at not only integrating women aims at not only integrating women into the mainstream if economic development but also ensuring equity and social justice for them.

An Evaluation

The position on women is closely associated with their economic standards which in turn, depends on opportunities for participation in economic activities. Development of women is considered as an index of society's stage of development and therefore, effective use of human resources of which women constitute an integral part is indispensable. "The opposition to increasing opportunities for women's participation in economic activities springs firstly from a conservative view regarding women's proper role in society. It also arises due to situations of chronic unemployment and under-development where the prospects of large-scale entry of women in the labour market is regarded as a potential cause of economic disorganisation. Technological changes have adversely affected the employment of women in industries as also noted by the Report of the National Committee on self-employment of women."[13] Because women's Traditional economic contribution to the survival of their families in being eroded by Technology as the control and profit of technologies flow largely to men.

The attitude of employers has also been rather lukewarm towards the employment of women on account of protective legislative enacted for women labourers. The enforcement of Equal pay principle for men and women, the increased financial burden to be incurred by the employers because of maintenance of creches, the payment of maternity benefits etc., appear to have adversely affected women's employment in organised sectors. In industrial organised sector, stumbling-blocks are created because of the limitation on hours of work, prohibition of women employment in night shifts and restrictions on load carrying etc.

So long as gender is an important indicator of economic, social and political roles, here will be a need for special policies targeted to rural women for education, trainign technology transfer and credit.[14] The inequality of women every where origionates to a very large extent from mass poverty and general backwardness of the majority of the population caused by under development. The causes of the inequalities between women and men are directly associated with a complex historical process. The inequality also derives from political, economic, social and cultural factors. It is obvious that poverty and under development have sharpened and continue to sharpen these inequalities which is strikingly apparent in the present world profile of women: while women represent half.

The Central Social Welfare Board (C.S.W.B.)

The CSWB extends financial assistance to voluntary organisations for setting up income generating units under the 'Socio-economic programme' by introducing technical and marketing support with focus on diversified occupation for women. Educational and vocational training courses are being organised by the aided agencies to improve their employment prospects and for rehabilitation of women in distress. In order to develop leadership qualities among rural women and to involve them in developmental activities, the Awareness Generation Project for Rural Women has been evolved. A National Plan of Action was formulated by the Ministry of social welfare which suggested a series of measures for the betterment of women including those unemployed.

A new scheme, namely, Women's Development Corporation would be taken up for promoting employment generating activities by supporting schemes for women groups and women from poorer section of society. A Women Development Planning and monitoring cell will be set up for collection of data and monitoring of plan programmes.[15]

National Commission of Women

The Planning Commission in 1990 has focussed its attention on women workforce in the unorganised sector where they are exploited, underemployed, paid low wages by middlemen and exploited by anti-social elements.[16] A national commission on women would set up to "monitor and accelerate the process of equal representation for women to enforce all legislation for women's rights including labour laws and to check discrimination in all spheres." The commission will also look into specific problems arising out of discrimination and atrocities against women, identity the constraints and recommend strategies for their removal.

Planned Measures

During the sixth plan, the government launched a good deal of schemes and programmes in order to ameliorate the working conditions of women. A special cell was established in 1976 to look after the employment of women and monitor the implementation of the Equal Remuneration Act. The Equal Remuneration Act was to provide for wages equal to those of men for work of similar nature. The Directorate General of Employment and Training (DGE and T) established three regional vocational trainign centres at Bombay, Bangalore and Trivandrum, and a National Vocational Training Institute at New Delhi, with the total absorbing capacity of 600 women trainees. Exclusively for women about 144 Industrial Training Institutes have been established in different states with the intake capacity of 11,200 women per annum by the end of sixth plan period. As an integral part of IRDP, the National Scheme of Training of Rural Youth for Self-Employment covered 3.27 lakh women during the plan period. It is aptly remarked that "added impetus was given to the training of women in instrumentation technology for repair and maintenance of electronic equipment in offices and hospitals. In certain areas of West Bengal, tribal women were trained in making blocks from stone chips, in bambo craft and rope making. Tribal women were also trained as rural health workers in Maharashtra. For creating increasing awareness of the role of women in development and the need for improvement of their status, various media units under the Ministry of Information and Broadcasting presented an appealing programme on social and economic problems and other related issues faced by women."[17]

Financial Allocations

An outlay of Rs, 2,487.47 crores (Rs. 1,250.81 crores central and Rs. 1,236.66 crores State share) was provided for the seventh plan for the National Rural Employment Programme. The total Central provision made 1985-86, 1986-87 and 1987-88 comes to Rs. 1,492.27 crores for implementation of NREP.[18] It has been reported that the employment generated during 1986-87 was 395.39 million mandays which has substantially exceeded the plan target of 290 million mandays per annum.[19] During this period the Government set up the women's Development corporations in all the states and Union Territories for providing better employment opportunities for women in order to enable them economically self-relient and independent. These corporations were entrusted with the responsibility of identifying women entrepreneurs, supply of credit through financial institutions, facilities of training through the institutions etc. Under the scheme of Development of women and Children in Rural Areas (DWCRA), 50 districts have been brought under this programme during 1986-87 and 1987-88.[20]

Syndrome of Observations

In spite of planned endeavours, enactment of Plethora of laws for the regulation of hours of work safety and welfare provisions for informal women labourers, their effective enforcement is far from satisfactory. In practice, wage discrimination continue unabated. "Many studies have indicated that the nature of economic development, agricultural mechanisation, commercialisation etc., have their adverse impact on women's employments. Women are treated as a source of cheap, unskilled secondary labour that can be hired to suit the requirements of the employer.[21] Conditions of 95 per cent of the working women in the fields, mines and construction sites cottage and household industries are even worse. They have to do monotonus strenous back-breaking work at very low wages, in unhealthy and inhuman working conditions without facilities, permanency of jobs, creches, maternity benefits and protection of unions."[22]

Despite equal turn over of work, discrimination and disparities and inbalances exist as an ever ending factor. The existing disparity has been, inter-alia, because of a combined complex factors like the absence of bargaining capacity of labourers, lack of special machinery to implement the relevant Acts, lack of extension of credit facilities and absence of strong unions.

A perusal of the foregoing paragraphs makes it obvious that women population of our country though constitute half of the total population, yet their socio-economic condition is distressing. They are exploited and their contribution is invisible in the planning process in the Surveys, studies and census reports. There is yet an effect national policy to emerge. New paradigms are to be evolved for mitigating their basic problems. The unorganised sector or what we call informal sector, has not been covered very effectively by adequate legislative provisions in ameliorating their socio-economic conditions.

REFERENCES

1. Salient features of laws relating to women *Social Welfare,* September, 1989.
2. Pathy, Suguna, Of women and society, *Frontier,* Oct. 28, 1989, p. 10.
3. Shastri, Madhu, 'Status of the special protective provisions of penal and criminal codes under the constitution of India" In Sushila Agrawal (Ed.) *"Status of Women."* Printwell Publishers, Jaipur, 198, pp. 23-24.
4. *Ibid.,* pp. 25-27.
5. Parsad, Dr. (MRS) Sushama Sahay, Economic and physical exploitation of tribal female labourers In Gupta, J.L. *Challenges to the Fair-Sex: Indian Women: Problems, Plights and Progress,* Gian. Publishing House, Delhi, 1988, p. 78.
6. Devi, Mahesweta and Ghos, Nirmal, *Bonded Labour in India* (In Hindi) Radhakrishna Publishers, New Delhi, 1981.
7. Ghadially, Rechana (Ed.), *Women in Indian Society—A Reader,* Sage Publications, New Delhi, 1988, p. 203.
8. Gupta, Jyoti., 'Himalayan Polyandry: bondage among women in Jaunswer-Bawar' pp. 258-281 in Ustsa Patnaik, and Manjari Dig-Waney (Ed.) *Chains of Servitude: Bondage and slavery in India,* Sangam Books India Pvt. Ltd., Madras, 1985.
9. Tripathy, S.N. (Dr.), *Bonded Labour in India,* Discovery Publishing House, New Delhi, 1989, p. 17.
10. *The Indian Worker,* Jan., 29 and February, 05, 1990, p. 15.
11. Bhasin, Kamla, Girl child or fish among crocodiles. *Kurukshetra,* Vol. XXXVIII No. 12, September, 1990, p. 31.
12. Roy Edmond, Development of Rural Women, *Orissa Review,* December, 1988, p. 32.
13. Joshi, Uma, Improving the Status of Rural Women, *Social Welfare,* Vol. XXXVI. No. 3-4, June-July, 1989, p. 14.

14. Rajuladevi, A.K., Technological Choice and their Impact on Eomen. *Kurukshetra*, Vol. XXXVI, No. 2, Nov. 1987, p. 7.
15. Sinha, Ajit Kumar, Improving the Lot of Rural Women. *Yojana*, Vol. 32, No. 9, May 16-31, 1988. p. 28.
16. Gupta Ashoka, Let men change their attitude *Kurukshetra* Vol. XXXVIII, No. 12, September, 1990, p. 11.
17. Seventh Five Year Plan, Government of India, New Delhi, Vol. II, pp. 323-326.
18. Singh, Mohinder, Women and Development Process in India, *Khadi Gramodyog*, Vol. XXXV, No. 4, January, 1989, p. 202.
19. *Ibid.*
20. *Ibid.*
21. Kaptan, S.S., The income, wages and working conditions of women workers in the unorganised sector. *Social Welfare*, May, 1989, p. 31.
22. *Ibid.*

38

Productivity and Returns to Labour

The activity-specific and time-use approaches to the division of labour can tell us how much women, men, and children participate in various aspects of agricultural production, processing, and marketing. But we learn little about the result of their efforts: the amount of work accomplished or its economic returns. In this section we explore several methods of measuring productivity and returns to labour. Productivity, defined as output per person-hour of labour, depends on the amount of human energy and skill applied to the task at hand (i.e., labour inputs), on non-labour inputs such as seeds, fertilisers, and tools, and on the management efficiency with which they are combined. Returns to labour refer here to economic benefits such as wages in cash or kind, income derived from the sale of goods or services, and the value of production for home consumption. Also crucial to the analysis of sex differences in work incentives is the question of control over returns to labour, that is, the extent to which workers can decide on the disposition of the income.

Sex Difference in Productivity

The simplest measure of labour inputs, hours or days worked, has been reviewed in the discussion of time use. For standardised units of inputs, time worked by each age and sex group in each activity can be converted to an index based on a common denominator, usually the average time contributed by males in their prime working years. Hours worked by women or children or the aged are then expressed in units such as "adult male equivalents" or "producer units" or "man-days" — a convenience that standardises the labour inputs by time but obscures the separate contributions of each group. In a Javanese village, the "directly productive" average work inputs of boys aged 15-19 were calculated to be 71 per cent and of girls 86 per cent of the average hours worked by all males aged 15 and over. On the sole basis of labour time, boys and girls in this illustration are worth 0.71 and 0.86 producer units (Nag *et al.*, 1980, p. 256).

Factors Affecting Productivity

People work at different intensities and efficiencies, depending among other things on their body height and weight, health, skills, the availability of social support systems, the organisation of the labour process, and the nature and urgency of the task which vary by season (Connell and Lipton, 1977, Mueller, 1982).[1] Whether efficiency makes a difference to output depends on the activity in question. Some tasks require little concentration for adequate performance (keeping a cow from straying into a neighbour's field, for example, which little children can do) while others require much larger investments of energy or skill.

TABLE 38.1

Labour Efficiency of Men, Women, and Boys Aged 12-18 in Farm Tasks, Korea, 1930: Farm Area Completed Per Hour[a]

Activity	*Men*	*Women*		*Boys*	
	Area	*Area*	*Ratio women/men*	*Area*	*Ratio boys/men*
Ploughing					
Paddy field with cattle	145	—	—	—	—
Paddy field without cattle	17	10	.59	10	.59
Other field with cattle	152	—	—	—	—
Other field without cattle	28	10	.36	11	.39
Transplanting					
Paddy field	23	12	.52	12	.52
Other field	25	15	.60	11	.44
Weeding					
Paddy field	34	17	.50	14	.41
Other field	33	14	.42	13	.39
Harvesting					
Paddy field	33	14	.42	15	.45
Other field	47	21	.45	20	.43

a The area measured is a *tsubo* of six feet square.

Source: Calculated from Lee (1936) in Mueller, 1976, p. 116.

Productivity in agriculture depends not only on labour efficiency but also on non-labour inputs such as tools, seed quality, or fertilisers, with limits set by environmental constraints. Because of the sex segregation of tasks on family farms and in wage labour, it is difficult to obtain "pure" measures of sex differences in labour efficiency. Where tasks are similar, women often work by while men appropriate the more advanced technology — the chemical fertilisers spread by machine rather than the organic ones spread by hand tools, the machine threshers over manual threshers, and so on (Boserup, 1970, p. 53; Deere and Leon de Leal, 1982, pp. 60-62). A simple substitution of tools may change the sex-typing of a task and widen the productivity gap. In Java, the adoption of the sickle for use by male harvesters displaced women who used the smaller *ani-ani* (bamboo knife which cuts stalks singly) (Stoler, 1977, p. 88). Thus it is not surprising to find rather larger productivity gaps by age and sex because labour efficiency disparities are compounded by differential access to labour-saving devices.

Labour efficiency per se can theoretically be measured by controling for non-labour inputs; we assess the output per hour of males and females or adults and children working under identical conditions. An early Korean study of 1,249 farms in 1930 measured the relative efficiency of men, women and boys aged 12-18 by the average area ploughed, transplanted, weeded, and harvested in an hour for paddy and other crops (Table 38.1). Techniques were presumably similar except that thee are no measure of the area ploughed by women or boys with cattle. Women in this comparison averaged about half the efficiency of men except for ploughing non-paddy fields without cattle, and slightly more than teenage boys in transplanting and weeding. In a more recent Indian Government study testing two types of potato-digging equipment in 1973-74, women were found to be over three times as efficient as men using the "spring time cultivator" and almost three times as efficient on the "potato digger elevator" as measured by *picking rate* per labourer (meters in row picked per minute) and hours taken for the same job (Agarwal, 1979, p. 16).

Direct comparisons such as these are rare, however. Most researchers rely on surrogate measures of labour efficiency, the most common being hourly or daily wages paid for the same tasks. A Bangladesh survey devised an indicator of "productivity per unit time" of male children of different ages compared with adult males from wages paid for harvesting, including a cash equivalent for meals (Cain, 1980, p. 244). According to this criterion, boys aged 7-9 were 00.68 as efficient as men aged 16 and over in amount harvested per day, boys 10-12 were 0.80 as efficient, and boys 13-15 were 0.94 as efficient. Reviewing evidence from Egypt, India, and Indonesia, Mueller (1976, pp. 116-118) concludes that "agricultural wage rates for women generally average about 60 per cent of the male rate and those for children about 50 per cent." But to reflect the concentration of women's and children's employment in the busy season when they are likely to work at greater intensity, Mueller raises her estimates of women's average productivity from 0.60 to 0.75 of an adult male equivalent, and of children from 0.50 to 0.60.

If wages are paid on a piecework basis, then deriving labour efficiency from wages is appropriate.[2] But in general, the assumption that unequal wage rates paid to women, men, and children reflect differences in labour efficiency rather than sex or age discrimination in the labour market is probably unwarranted. Indeed, government standards sometimes set lower legal minimum wages for women farm workers quite apart from any evidence of differential productivity, even in settings where farm employers recognise that women work harder than men do. Deriving productivity estimates from daily wage rates can also be risky where the normative day for women's farm labour is shorter than for men.

Measures of Sex Differences in Total Productivity

In viewing total productivity rather than just labour inputs, we find that output per person-hour is frequently expressed in "adult male equivalents," representing an amalgam of variant levels of productivity across individual males. Connell and Lipton note that productivity weighings by age and sex in most studies they reviewed appear to be based on guesses rather than hard evidence (1977, pp. 52-53). Observing that "women are more efficient than men at cotton-picking and less efficient on all other crops," for example an Indian study standardised women's productivity at 75 per cent of men's. (For a critique of this finding, see Agarwal, 1979, p. 15) A Malawi study rated adult males and hired labourers as 1.0, "other adults" and females as 0.7, children and "relations" as 0.3; and Guatemalan study rated females as 0.5 male equivalents, all without supporting documentation (Connell and Lipton, 1977). In addition to their potential for bias, *a priori* weightings of this type lose specificity by averaging productivity across tasks, crops, and seasons as well as across social categories of individuals. Other studies, reviewed in Minge-Kalman (1977), err in generalising productivity measures from one crop to the whole. Good crop-specific or operations—specific measures of sex differences in productivity would be helpful to planners in identifying areas in which interventions of technical assistance or other supports could raise the output of workers labouring under excessive constraints.

At another level of analysis, several interesting studies comparing the aggregate outputs of male-managed or jointly-managed farms with female-managed farms suggest that the disadvantages women face in their more restricted access to non-labour inputs are sometimes compensated by more intensive applications of labour or by greater skill or ingenuity. In a district of western Kenya characterised by heavy seasonal and long-term male outmigration, where 38 per cent of the farms were run by women on a day-to-day basis, output of maize among female-managed farms fell only slightly below that of male-managed farms (17.1 versus 17.8 200-pound bags per acre) in spite of significantly lower use of chemical fertilisers, hybrid plants, insecticides, and restricted access to extension services and loans (Moock, 1976) (see table 38.2). Although women farmers applied marginally higher labour inputs in hours per acre, the results of a regression analysis indicated that "these women were more technically efficient maize farmers than the men" in achieving significantly higher outputs at mean levels of input use (Moock, 1976, p. 833). The efficiency factor was isolated through regression techniques rather than through controlled observations.

In a related approach, Table 38.2 compares the output of staple tuber crops in male—and female-headed households for seven common garden types in a village in Papua New Guinea (Boyd, 1981). The key measure here is the output in *kilograms per producer unit* averaged within the two types of households, rather than *output per unit of land* as in the Kenyan example. Female-headed households produced significantly less forest sweet potato and significantly more grassland yam-taro and tilled sweet potato per producer unit than male-headed households, an outcome Boyd attributes to different gardening strategies resulting from the scarcity of male labour needed to clear and fence the forest gardens in the female-headed households. The table does not permit direct comparisons of productivity since the area planted in each type of crop is not controlled. The higher productivity of at least one type of gardening among female-headed households is implied, however, in Boyd's comment that:

These findings should not be interpreted as evidence that female-headed households tend to avoid making gardens in the forest. Like all Llakian households, they do make large forest yam-taro gardens. The averaged size of this type of garden for female-headed households is only one-half that for male-headed households (.43 and .086 hectares, respectively), but the average percentage contribution of forest yam-taro gardens to the total amount of tubers produced is just over 15 per cent for both groups (1981, p. 84).

Net Productivity: The Value of Labour

The ongoing debate among demographers about the economic value of children in peasant agriculture and its relation to reproductive goals has led to an important modification of productivity estimates. Researchers attempt to estimate the age at which children become net economic assets by subtracting from the value attached to their labour time the value of food or of total household resources they consume at each age. Again, estimates of differences across age-sex groups in food consumption are often based more on educated guesses than on hard evidence. Some studies measure consumption by average minimum daily caloric requirements for a given age and sex category with no indication as to whether consumption actually meets this level or not (e.g., Cain, 1980, p. 244). Others include household cost-accountings of food, clothing and medical care consumed by each person as observed or reported to interviewers (e.g., Evenson et al., 1980, p. 342).

TABLE 38.2

Comparison of Tuber Production for Male-headed and Female-headed Households by Garden Type among the Ilakia Awa, Papua New Guinea, 1972

Garden types	*Measures of household production*				
	(1)	*(2)*	*(3)*	*(4)*	*(5)*
	Tuber output (kg.)	*Output/ producer (kg. / prod. unit*	*Output/ consumer (kg./cons. unit)*	*Output/total consumer (kg./human + pig cons. unit)*	*Percentage of total tuber output*
1	2	3	4	5	6
Forest yam-taro					
Male-headed mean	385	178	149	109	15.5
Female-headed mean	192	155	183	145	15.2
F-ratio	16.5	0.9	1.6	3.0	0.0
Significance	< 0.001	n.s.	n.s.	n.s.	n.s.
Forest sweet potato					
Male-headed mean	946	434	345	255	31.6
Female-headed mean	135	135	169	116	8.3
F-ratio	13,8	6.6	2.3	3.4	10.3
Significance	<0.0001,	< 0.05	n.s.	n.s.	< 0.01

1	2	3	4	5	6
Irrigated forest taro					
Male-headed mean	30	14	10	7	0.9
Female-headed mean	0	0	0	0	0.0
F-ratio	2.5	2.4	2.3	2.3	2.5
Significance	n.s.	n.s.	n.s.	n.s.	n.s.
Grassland yam-taro					
Male-headed mean	671	306	258	190	26.4
Female-headed mean	561	506	819	433	39.1
F-ratio	1.3	8.2	16.4	20.7	8.3
Significance	n.s.	< 0.01	<0.001	<0.001	< 0.01
Tilled grassland sweet Potato					
Male-headed mean	398	178	142	106	14.9
Female-headed mean	369	318	385	299	27.9
F-ratio	0.1	9.2	24.7	27.9	11.2
Significance	n.s.	< 0.01	<0.001	< 0.001	< 0.01
Untilled grassland sweet potato					
Male-headed mean	57	22	16	12	2.0
Female-headed mean	20	20	25	14	0.9
F-ratio	0.6	0.0	0.2	0.0	0.4
Significance	n.s.	n.s.	n.s.	n.s.	n.s.
Irrigated grassland taro					
Male-headed mean	246	111	78	62	8.7
Female-headed mean	122	110	131	85	8.7
F-ratio	2.1	0.0	1.5	0.5	0.0
Significance	n.s.	n.s.	n.s.	n.s.	n.s.

Source: Boyd, 1981, p. 85.

A range of "consumption units" appearing in the literature is indicated in Table 38.3. Mueller deliberately chose low consumption estimates for children to challenge the argument that children in peasant agriculture become net producers at an early age (Muller, 1976). The United Nations and Epstein models in the table represent middle-range estimates, whereas the high Cabanero scales are based on actual consumption of food, clothing, and medical care reported in the Philippines Laguna household survey. The treatment of sex differences in consumption is interesting: Muller's low estimate differentiates male and female consumption levels only past 15 years of age but the medium estimate past five years of age; the United Nations estimate differentiates only at 10-14 years of age; Epstein differentiates only past 15 years of age; while the Philippines findings show increasingly wide disparities beginning from near identical consumption under 5 years of age to only 75 per cent for adult females, the lowest figure of all the models. Again, one must assume that these weightings are not based on hard evidence of actual differences in consumption patterns, with the exception of the Philippines data.

TABLE 38.3

Consumption Units Scales from Various Sources, by Age and Sex

Sex and age	Mueller low est.[a]	Mueller med. est.[b]	United Nations[c]	Epstein model[c]	Cabanero Philippines[e]
Males					
0-4	0.12	0.32	0.45	0.50 (1-4)	0.68
5-9	0.26	0.52	0.65	0.70	0.72
10-12	0.44	0.82	0.85	0.83	0.78
15-19	0.84	1.00	1.00	1.00	0.91
20+	1.00 (20-54)	1.00 (20-54)	1.00	1.00	1.00
Females					
0-4	0.12	0.32	0.45	0.50 (1-4)	0.66
5-9	0.26	0.48	0.65	0.70	0.69
10-14	0.44	0.68	0.75	0.83	0.72
15-19	0.68	0.80	1.00	0.83	0.68
20+	0.80 (20-54)	0.80 (20-54)	1.00	0.83	0.75

a "Low-consumption profile" in Mueller (1976, p,. 107) based on assumptions of minimal consumption by children. At age 55-59, males = .90, females .72; at 60-64, males = .80, females *.64; at 65 and over, males = .70, females .56.

b "Medium-consumption profile," with same assumptions for older ages.

c Based on unidentified sample and survey data, cited in Mueller, 1976, p. 105.

d Estimated by Epstein and cited in Mueller, 1976, p. 105.

e Calculated from Cabanero (1977) in evenson *et al.*, 1980, p. 342. Data Refer to average annual expenditures on food, clothing, and medical care by age and sex.

How are these consumption units translated into estimates of net productivity? Testing several different combinations, Mueller develops an aggregate model based on assumptions of medium consumption (Table 38.3) and "standard" production with a gross reproduction rate of 3.0 (average of six children born per couple) (1976, p. 127). Expressing the production and consumption of males and females of different age groups according to standardised adult male-equivalent units, each is weighted by the proportion of the total population in each age group to arrive at an aggregate estimate of the net deficit or surplus contributed by each age and sex category. In this model males consume more than they produce in standard units until 15 years of age and then produce more than they consume to 54 years of age, at which time the levels balance out. Females consume more than they produce at all ages with the greatest current deficit at 5-9 years of age. It should be emphasised that no value has been placed on household production and maintenance, only on market-oriented labour.

In a different formulation, Cain's analysis of the value of children in a Bangladeshi village begins with the average daily caloric *consumption requirements* for males of different ages (females were excluded because of lack of good productivity estimates). The total production of each age group (productivity units multiplied by time-input units) is expressed as "calories produced," and caloric consumption is subtracted from production to arrive at an "average daily product net of consumption" for each age group. Cumulation of these averages over the years reveals that the economic deficit incurred by male children, which peaks at 10 years of age, reverses to a cumulated surplus by 16 years of age and then escalates rapidly after that (1980, p. 244). In contrast with Mueller, Cain concludes that "male children may become net (current) producers as early as age 12, and compensate for their own cumulative consumption by age 15, and compensate for their own and one sister's cumulative consumption by age 22" (Cain, 1980, p. 218).

Because the potential for significant measurement error (apparent already in the calculation of age and sex differentials in gross productivity) is undoubtedly compounded by consumption estimates, net productivity figures must be treated with caution. The debate over the value of children is by no means resolved, in part because of disagreements over measurement techniques and in part because variations across diverse farm settings in the amount to directly productive work that children (and adults) do make generalisations hazardous. Calculations of net productivity can be helpful in narrowly defined work settings such as Food-for-work schemes in Bangladesh where the adequacy of prevailing wage rates (units of wheat paid per unit of earth moved) is assessed by comparing *calorie requirements* of each age-sex group employed on the scheme according to hours worked, energy expended, and other nutritional needs (e.g., pregnancy or breastfeeding) with *calories produced* in wages (Chen and Ghuznavi, 1977). In settings where the range, timing, and intensity of daily and seasonal activities vary more broadly, however aggregated estimates of net productivity are likely to be of limited use to agricultural or employment planners.

Returns to Labour

For each unit of time spent in a given productive activity, returns to labour can be contrasted by age, sex and other characteristics such as class, caste, crop, or season. This review will avoid the controversial issue of how to measure the value of housework even though labels such as "enabling production" (Cain, 1980, p. 221) and "expenditure-saving production." (Farouk, 1980, p. 171) clearly signify its monetary nature. This issue has been thoroughly addressed by Evenson *et. al.*, 1980, pp. 335-336; Gronau, 1980, pp. 65-66; International Center for Research on Women, 1980, pp. 12-15; Goldschmidt-Clermont, 1982, among others. Instead, we consider the economic returns to *directly productive agricultural activities:*

both those with exchange value—wage labour, tenancy or sharecropping, reciprocal labour, and agricultural production for sale—and those intended for household consumption.

TABLE 38.4

Ratio of Female to Male Wages, Minimum and Maximum Agricultural Rates, Selected Settings and Dates, India.

Location and activity	*Wage rates* Min.	Max.	*Location and activity*	*Wage rates* Min.	Max.
Agricultural labourers[a] (1970-71)			*Agricultural labourers* (cont'd)		
Bihar			*Uttar Pradesh*		
Sowers	.78	.67	Sowers	.95	.72
Weeders	.80	.82	Weeders	.99	.71
Reaper	.79	.64	Reaper	.92	.88
Haryana			*Plantation Workers* (1963-65)		
Weeders	.56	.62	*Tea Plantations*		
Reaper	.65	.56			
			Pluckers	.61	.73
Madhya Pradesh			Labourers	.89	.52
			Supervisors	.91	.90
Sowers	.74	.70			
Weeders	.84	.84	*Coffee Plantations*		
Reapers	.88	.89	Maistry/Kangani	.90	.79
Punjab			Labourers	.76	.75
Weeders	n.a.	.68	*Rubber Plantations*		
Tamil Nadu			Field Workers	.75	.75
			Tappers	.87	.90
Sowers	.59	.62			
Weeders	1.00	.64			
Reapers	.61	.77			

a Standardised to correct for shorter work days for women than men. It is not specified whether these are legal or actual wage rates.

Source: Compiled from *Committee on the Status of Women in India*, 1974, pp. 165-6, 195.

Economic returns to labour depend not only on productivity but also on the price at which the commodity or service can be sold. In the case of work for wages, returns are ascertained by counting income in cash, kind (meals, clothing, a share of the output) and other benefits. For exchange or festive labour we need to value the food, drink, or reciprocal services provided as payment. Valuing farm production in a family enterprise involves measuring and pricing total output net of non-labour inputs and wage payments for produce that is sold or consumed by the household.

Wages

Women's wages are lower than men's in most but not all agricultural settings (Boserup, 1970, pp. 73-75; Mueller, 1976, pp. 115-117). In the Indian examples in table 38.4 women's daily wage range from 52 to 100 per cent of men's , with an unweighted mean across all examples of 76 per cent and a standard deviation of 12.7. The female/male ratio is slightly lower for agricultural labourers than for plantation workers (75 versus 79 per cent) and slightly lower at maximum rather than minimum pay scales (73 versus 80 per cent). Children's wages in agricultural labour (not shown here) average 59 per cent of men's wages.

Although the daily earnings in this comparison have been standardised to control for the shorter average working day of women, one cannot tell whether the remaining differentials reflect sex specialisation in tasks of different productivity, sex differences in performance of the same task, or discriminatory wage structures.

In other formulations, it is difficult to decipher whether gender disparities in total daily or weekly wages reflect fewer hours of women's work, lower rates per hour, or less productive piecework. According to the 1964/65 Egyptian rural employment survey, for example, women's daily wages for farm labour in six provinces average from 52 to 68 per cent of men's wages, and children's from 44 to 56 per cent — a fairly stable ratio despite strong differences among villages and provinces in the absolute level of pay scales (ILO, 1969, p. 70). Figure 38.1 reveals the average number of working hours per eight-day period throughout the year for men, women, and children, and their average daily wages in each eight-day period expressed as an index with 100 as the yearly base. Women's daily earnings average 69 per cent of men's (11.9 piastres year-round) and children's 49 per cent of men's (8.6 piastres). Strong seasonal fluctuations in daily wages for women and children correspond to fluctuations in hours worked per week, suggesting that this reserve of workers floods the agricultural labour market in response to higher wages at times of peak demand. But if the average working day is also longer during the busy season, then shifts in hourly earnings are less pronounced. The daily wage gap by gender narrows in the busy season when women earn 86 per cent of what men earn, perhaps in part because women work longer hours per day, or because the increased demand for labour raises their wage rate more than men's. The gap widens in the slack season when women earn only 61 per cent of what men earn.

Hart's useful analysis of seasonal changes in patterns of household labour allocation by class in Java does distinguish between hours worked and wages per hour (1980, p. 211). The upper half off Table 38.5 indicates that women in the peak month earn from 64 to 79 per cent of what men earn per hour depending on landholding status, while in the slack season they earn only 35 to 50 per cent. Although women in large and small landholding households add proportionally to their hours of wage work in the peak month more than men do, landless women add proportionally fewer hours than their menfolk because they are already labouring at a relatively high capacity even in the slack month. A number of other interesting comparisons by sex and class can be drawn from Hart's table. For example, hourly farm wages for females do not differ significantly by class but they do for males, producing a wider sex gap in returns to labour among the larger landholding households than among the landless.

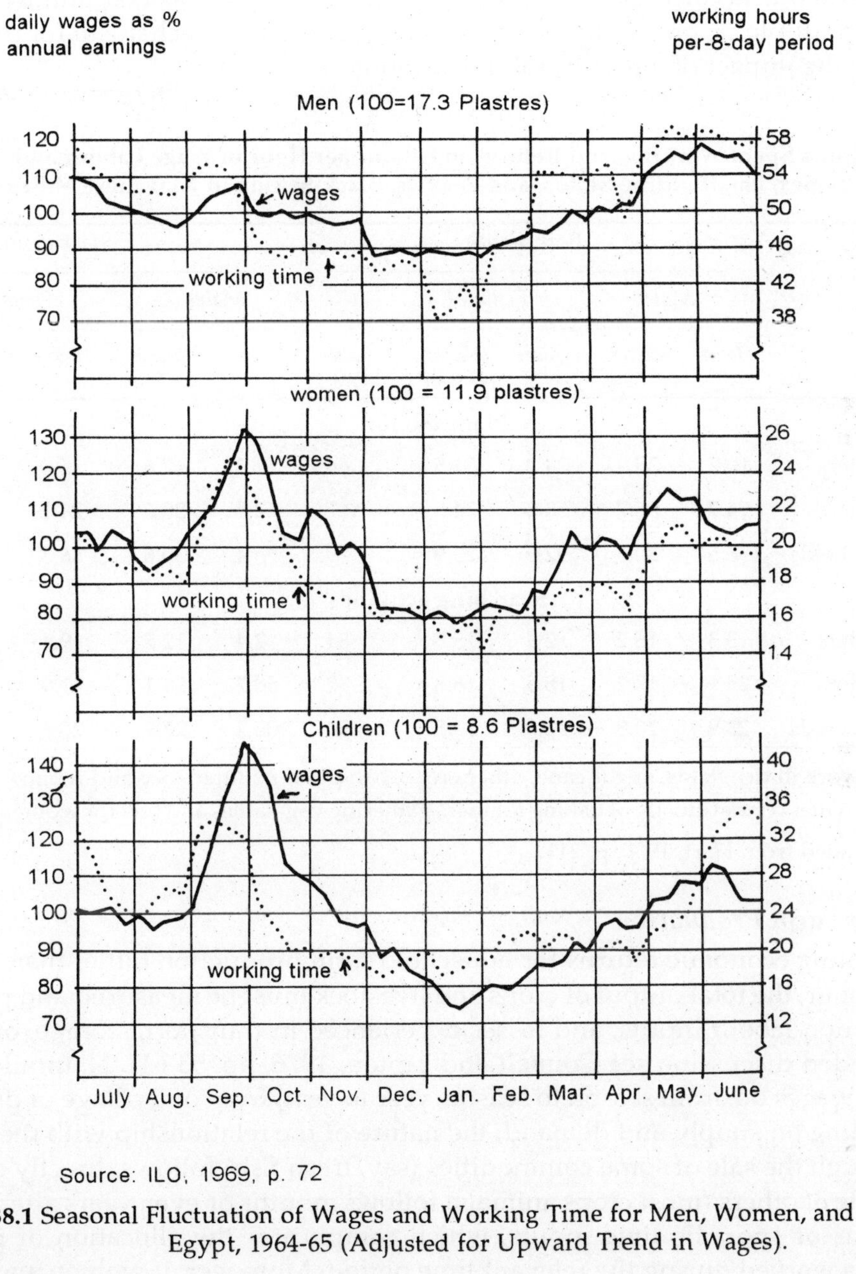

Figure 38.1 Seasonal Fluctuation of Wages and Working Time for Men, Women, and Children Egypt, 1964-65 (Adjusted for Upward Trend in Wages).

Source: ILO, 1969, p. 72.

This type of data presentation is particularly helpful to our understanding of the dynamics of household response to seasonal changes in employment opportunities as they differ by gender and class. The analysis could be extended to incorporate gender contracts in returns to labour according to activity, crop, or factors such as community patterns of irrigation or multiple cropping, among other distinctions, as a mechanism for planning and for assessing the impact of agricultural innovations.

TABLE 38.5

Average Hours Spent Working, and Returns to Labour per Hour in Wage Labour and Searching Activities by Sex, Landholding Status, and Peak vs. Slack Season in a Javanese Village, 1975-76

Landholding	*Peak month*					*Slack month*				
	Males		*Females*			*Males*		*Females*		
	Hours	*Rupees per hour*	*Hours*	*Rupees per hour*	*Ratio F/M*	*Hours*	*Rupees per hour*	*Hours*	*Ratio per hour*	*Ratio F/M*
				Wage labour[a]						
Large landholders	10.7	38.2	24.2	24.5	.64	7.3	47.6	5.0	16.6	.35
Small landholders	94.7	36.7	53.8	24.6	.67	62.8	38.6	24.2	15.6	.40
Landless households	156.5	30.3	92.6	23.9	.79	75.4	30.6	86.5	15.2	.50
				Searching activities[b]						
Large landholders	3.3	18.2	2.9	15.3	.84	2.4	12.7	9.4	11.9	.94
Small landholders	25.9	17.2	18.9	16.8	.97	56.7	34.1	11.9	14.6	.43
Landless households	23.9	20.8	16.0	10.5	.50	103.2	27.9	26.6	11.2	.40

a Includes work in rice fields, sugar cane, other crops, fish pond maintenance and repair.

b Search activities consist mostly of fishing for men, gathering vegetables and fuel for women and children.

Source: Calculated from Hart, 1980, p. 211.

The Value of Farm Production

In calculating economic returns for household farm production rather than for wage or exchange labour, the total output of crops and livestock must be measured and priced net of wages paid, non-labour inputs, and losses experienced in transport, storage, or marketing (for an extended discussion see Connell and Lipton, 1976, pp. 53-61). Naturally the prices will vary, as wages do, from season to season, year to year, from one village or district to the nest, depending on supply and demand, the nature of the relationship with the buyer, and so on. Although the sale of some commodities (say, fresh fish) follows directly on the work effort, the sale of others (most crops animals) follows months or even years after a sequence of continuous or sporadic time inputs, which complicates the allocation of proceeds to person-hours worked during the relevant time period. Moreover, if women and men work interchangeably on a crop, or if women do the weeding and harvesting and men the planting and irrigation, then it is especially difficult to calculate sex differences in returns to labour on family farm production.

In these cases of mixed inputs, the simplest procedure is to take the total number of hours worked by females on farm production as a proportion of total hours of family labour expended and multiply this by the net value of farm production. This will reveal the total value to be attributed to females, but will not reveal gender (or age) differences in returns to labour because everyone's hours are assumed to be equally productive. If sex-typing of activities steers women into more labour-intensive operations, or if women are less productive than men in the same operations because of differences in labour or non-labour inputs, then hours input will overestimate their relative contribution. One could of course eight hours by a productivity factor for different age and sex groups and then calculate differential returns to labour, but such weightings are problematic, as we have already seen.

TABLE 38.6

Contribution (in Rupees) to Total Income of Sample Households by Male and Female Adults and Children Aged 1-14, Eight Villages in Nepal, Mid-1970s

Activity	*Adults 15 +*		*Children 10-14*		*Total*
	Male	*Female*	*Male*	*Female*	
Animal husbandry	69 115 (47.0)[a]	50 069 (34.0)	12 440 (8.4)	15 590 (10.6)	147 218 (100.0)
Agriculture	458 271 (45.8)	490 197 (49.0)	18 615 (1.9)	33 728 (3.4)	1 000 811 (100.1)
Hunting and gathering	40 589 (43.7)	42 289 (48.9)	1 793 (1.9)	5 211 (5.6)	92 882 (100.1)
Manufacturing	15 698 (43.0)	19 899 (54.6)	332 (0.9)	536 (3.6)	36 465 (100.1)
Food processing	30 054 (10.8)	236 878 84.8)	2 544 (0.9)	10 092 (3.6)	279 568 (100.1)
Profit from trading	58 902 (60.3)	38 932 (39.7)	—	—	96 503 (100.0)
Wage and salary	154 902 (77.0)	42 932 (21.3)	1 385 (0.7)	1 925 (1.0)	201 144 (100.0)
Total household income	826 853 (44.6)	923 547 (49.8)	37 109 (2.0)	67 082 (3.6)	1 854 591 (100.0)

a> Percentage of total contribution.

Source: Acharya and Bennett, 1982, p. 63.

An additional problem arises in deciding which activities are to be included in the time-use calculations. If we concentrate on those directly associated with farm production, then women's proportional contribution to total output will average lower (in most cases) than if we include hours spent on processing crops for home consumption or on supporting tasks such as carrying water or collecting fuel. If the full range of home maintenance and reproductive tasks is also included then average female hours will usually outnumber male hours, and their proportional contribution will reach its peak.

In cases where males and females do specialise in specific crops, animals, or poultry, value obtained is more easily attributed to the producer as the products are sold or valued at market prices when consumed by the household. Hart uses this technique in Table 38.5 for calculating returns to labour for "searching activities" in Java — for men mainly fishing, for women and children gathering wild vegetables and fuel for consumption or sale. prices are attached to outputs according to seasonal markets, and returns to labour directly ascribed to hours invested by search person. The pattern of sex and class differences in this comparison is less clear than for wage labour, with the widest sexual disparity in economic returns to searching activities appearing among the landless and the narrowest among larger landholders.

Women's Contribution to Household Incomes

Once returns to labour are calculated for each category of household member, their contribution to total household income can be evaluated. A household budget survey of Beti farmers in southern Cameroon concluded that:

> the home-produced portion of food consumption amounted to about 45 per cent of total household income. Allowing for the fact that men do some kinds of work in the food provision system, one can conclude that up to 40 per cent of real family income was provided by women's subsistence work in 1964 (Guyer, 1980, p. 10).

Women's cash activities in trade and other areas such as wage work in the cocoa crop contribute additional income in the Cameroon study.

In eight villages in Nepal, female adults contributed one-half of the household income from agriculture and from hunting and gathering and one-third of the income from animal husbandry, with girls of 10-14 years of age contributing additional amounts (see table 38.6). In this study, household income generated by activities other than wage and salary work was apportioned to individuals according to their labour time in that activity as a percentage of total labour time required. Note that although men contributed the lion's share of incomes from trading, wages, and salaries, women's contributions in other activities — especially food processing — resulted in a larger share of total household income accruing from women than from men. Girls produced more income than boys in all areas, including wage and salary work.

Calculations such as these of the relative contribution males and females to household incomes in landowning or farm labour households by class and by season can reveal patterns of importance to planners. Guyer's review of West African studies, for example, concludes that:

> Women's incomes in rural areas of West Africa are generally much less seasonal than men's. Women earn small amounts at regular intervals, and therefore tend to be responsible for the small, regular purchases. Consequently the daily level of nutrition and standard of living may depend more heavily on the women's than the men's incomes (Guyer, 1980, p. 6).

According to Guyer, seasonal fluctuations in men's incomes are likely to have more effect on lump sum expenditures such as housing, school fees, and brideprices than on the provision of daily necessities. Since women and men specialise in different types of expenditures, "Patterns of consumption for the `household' as a unit reflect the proportional contribution of the men and the women to total expenditures, and not simply the absolute level of pooled income" (Guyer, 1980, p. 6).

Control Over the Returns to Labour

Calculations of economic returns to labour are based on the assumption that they accrue directly to individuals investing their time: output per person is valued and reported as a ratio of input time. Parallel calculations of returns to labour for the collective work contribution of the household as a unit are relatively easy to perform. But if we recognise that particular household members may differ considerably in their incentive to contribute labour depending not only on social norms regarding hat is expected of them but also on the basis of their anticipated material rewards, then we need to compare the returns of women and men, adults and children, or other categories of interest. How do we do this if they are not directly compensated? How do we deal with the typical case of the "unpaid family helper" who contributes labour but does not receive a specified share of the earnings?

In an attempt to deal with this dilemma, Burfisher and Horenstein (1982, p. 29) apportion the returns deriving from crop production among the Tiv in western Nigeria according to the portion of each crop that women and men "control." To control a crop refers here not to the amount of labour contributed, but "control over the disposition of, and income from, a crop in order to meet obligations."

In the semi-subsistence Tiv economy much of what is produced is consumed on the farm. But the household economy is not an undifferentiated unit; rather, husbands and wives are responsible for different sets of expenditures, and goods and services as well as cash may be exchanged among household members according to quite specific agreements. A husband may pay his wife for her labour on "his" mallet with a share of the crop which she then markets for her own income, for instance, or a wife may loan her husband money and charge interest:

> The division [of income within the household] reflects the value of the proportion of each crop over which each sex has control. This control stems from the disposition of the crop between home consumption and sale, and the use of the crop or income from it to meet obligations toward household support. In the case of yams, for example, women are estimated to control 80 per cent of the yam crop and to give 20 per cent to

men for men's use in entertaining and ceremonies. Women thus earn 80 per cent of the value of the yam crop while men earn 20 per cent, but women's and men's returns per day of labour input into the crop can differ because of their different labour roles (Burfisher and Horenstein, 1982, pp. 11-12).

Income for each crop is calculated from expected crop yields per hectare under traditional and improved cultivation methods valued at "farm-gate" market prices net the cost of seeds, fertilisers, and insecticides, Both marketed and home-consumed portions of the crop are included. The incomes from each crop are then allocated to women and men according to the proportion that each controls. The researchers estimate that returns from sorghum, maize, and cowpeas are totally controlled by women; those from yams 80 per cent by women, from cassava 75 per cent, from sesame 40 per cent, from water-melon 25 per cent, and from millet and rice 20 per cent. No crop is entirely controlled by men. (These portions are not based on individual or household data but on a "community portrait" of district patterns drawn from. ethnographies and project documents). Finally, the crop-specific incomes apportioned to women and men as a group are divided by the total number of man or woman-days of labour invested in each crop to obtain an average measure of the returns to labour by crop for each sex (see table 38.1 for the proportions of total labour contributed by women and men).

Table 38.7 presents a summary of projected *changes* in labour requirements for communities included in the district-wide scheme and in net returns per person-day for women and men resulting from the adoption of improved cultivation techniques for each group. Through this format we are able to compare the projected cost or savings in additional labour invested by each sex and the benefits accruing to each from their efforts. Both men and women are projected to benefit from improved rice cultivation techniques, with declines of at least 20 per cent in labour inputs and increases of at least one-third in returns per person-day. Other scenarios are less promising; e.g. The additional labour required for cowpeas will be only half repaid by increases in net returns for men and not repaid at all for women, a situation which provides little incentive to innovate on this crop. Men stand to lose in relative terms if they adopt improved methods on sesame, women to gain; women stand to lose on late maize, men to break even. The data have value for planners as a means of identifying areas of promise, potential resistance, and labour bottlenecks (especially when analysed by season) in the introduction of new techniques of crop production.

Control over returns to labour could be ascertained at the household level with a carefully constructed series of questions on the disposition of household incomes. This requires not only time-use data but a complete listing of all incomes earned in cash or kind by all household members according to their source, e.g. sale of produce, trade, wage work, etc. Focusing on returns from agricultural activities, we need to identify earnings paid directly to the worker in cash or kind from labouring for others; earnings deriving from the sale or exchange of crops, livestock, and poultry produce by the household; and "expenditure-saving" income from the portion of farm production consumed by the household. The value of farm production marketed or retained must then be apportioned to individual workers according to their relative labour inputs, perhaps weighted by a productivity factor, perhaps separately for each crop or animal type. Once apportioned, we have a measure of the percentage contribution of each household member to total household income from each source.

TABLE 38.7

Projected Changes in Labour Inputs and Net Returns to Labour Among Tiv Farmers of Central Nigeria as a Result of Agricultural Project Interventions, by Sex and Crop

Crop	*Percentage increase or decrease in:*			
	female		*male*	
	labour input	*net return per person day*	*labour input*	*net return per person day*
Yams	+ 25	+ 33	+ 17	+ 42
Millett	- 12	0	- 13	0
Sorghum	+2	+ 13	+ 6	0
Cassava	- 1	+ 12	+ 2	+ 9
Early maize	+ 4	+ 39	+ 9	0
Late maize	+ 43	+ 45	+ 44	0
Rice	- 20	+33	- 23	+40
Sesame	+61	+ 9	+ 10	+ 61
Watermelon	+ 27	+ 13	+ 18	+ 21
Cowpeas	+ 238	+ 122	+ 280	0
Total	+ 17	+ 31	+ 6	+ 28

Source: Burfisher and Horenstein, 1982, p. 30.

The question then becomes one of identifying patterns of control over earnings. What portion of the income does each worker receive or retain for discretionary use and what portion is turned over to a general household fund? With regard to the latter, what role does each person play in deciding on its disposition, e.g. between immediate consumption and savings or among competing consumption needs? A household member "controls" his or her personal fund plus the portion of the household fund reflecting the agree of participation in decision-making.

According to this model, a young man who turns his entire wages as an agricultural labourer over to his father and no say in how they are distributed has zero control over the returns to his own labour, and zero control over total household earning if he dos not participate in decisions about the general fund. A woman who sells her yam crop and retins all of the earnings has total control over her own returns to labour from this source, and many have some control over the earnings of other household members if she decides in part how they are to be spent. A woman who raises sheep or goats for sale but depends on her husband to market them is in a more complicated position. If he returns the cash to her with no questions asked, she retains 100 per cent control. If he keeps it for himself and she has no say as to how he spends it, she has zero control. If he keeps 20 per cent, gives her 20 per cent, and the remaining 60 per cent goes toward household expenses in which the distribution of decision-making responsibility averages about 25 per cent hers and 75 per cent his, then she controls 0.20 + (0.60) = 35 per cent of the returns to her labour from this source and her husband controls 65 per cent. Of course if her husband also contributed labour then the percentages would have to be adjusted accordingly. And her control over other household earnings again depends on the extent of her participation in decisions about how they are spent.

Sharma identifies several "family styles of budgeting" distinguished by caste and class in two communities of northern India (Sharma, 1980, pp. 105-112; see also Deere and Leon de Leal, 1982, pp. 100-101 for similar analysis in Peru). The extent of women's control over earnings depends on the number of earners in the family, the total household income, the share allocated to individual learners, and the type of expenses for which earners are responsible. Law-caste labouring households revealed greater individual autonomy over earnings, but room for discretion was limited because of shared poverty. Sharma concludes that control over household resources has at least two separate dimensions:

> (a) the absolute size of the household's income (does the family have enough money for the question of choice and decision making to be important?) and (b) the demarcation of responsibilities for expenditure of different kinds (what is the range of a woman's responsibility relative to that of her husband or other members of the household?) (Sharma, 1980, p. 112).

Although these household patterns of control over returns to labour are not quantified, they suggest an approach to measurement that could be fruitfully pursued. Nag et al. suggest similar formulations in their proposal for Indian village studies (1982, p. 125).

> If any woman in the household earned anything in cash or kind during the last year, what happened to it? Was all or part of it given to the husband or someone else? To whom? If all or part of it was spent by the woman herself, how was the money spent? Was it necessary to take permission of the husband or someone else for spending this money?
>
> Who usually decides how much money to spend on various items of regular household expenditure ... and also on occasional expenditures such as rituals, ... travel, purchase of land, purchase of house, purchase of consumer durables, etc.? If men usually make final decisions, how much do they consult women (especially the main informant)? What are the items of expenditure in which women have relatively greater control? Has there been any change in this respect in the recent past? (*ibid.*, pp. 25-26).

The issue of control over returns to labour is not entirely academic because it can affect the motivation of workers to engage in different types of income-generating activities. Village women in Bangladesh will sometimes choose activities they can perform in secret in order to maintain control over their earnings:

> For example, one woman stocked rice in another woman's house as her husband would not know she had it. Another woman had a neighbour raise a goat for her so her husband would not know about it. Another woman secretly sold rice from her own store [supply]. Yet another woman has opened a *pan* business with her young son and has told him to keep their earnings secret from the husband. Most women say that they hide their savings in holes in the bamboo, in the roof or under piles of cloth (Abdullah and Zeidenstein 1982, p. 47).

Women in many settings perceive marketing as a major bottleneck: unless they can sell their produce directly or by using children as intermediaries (Schildkrout, 1982) they lose control over the income (e.g. Sharma 1980, p. 105; Abdullah and Zeidenstein, 1982, p. 47) and production may drop (Apthorpe, 1971, p. 73). Muntemba's survey of farm households in the central and southern provinces of Zambia:

> ... indicated that men uniformly and consistently returned only a small proportion of [jointly produced] agricultural income to their wives, in amounts varying between one-tenth and one-quarter of the total income. Men insisted that they bought household goods, paid children's school fees, and reinvested some of the money in agriculture, all of which were joint marital financial responsibilities. Women argued that they could not do their share [of family support obligations such as food and clothing] because of the meager portion their husbands gave them (Muntemba, 1982, p. 97).

Summary

Measures of sex differences in agricultural productivity and returns to labour analysed by class, season, and other criteria such as household composition can reveal significant inequities in output and benefits per unit of labour time invested. These inequities must be viewed in the context of the structural distribution of production assets and employment opportunities for a fuller understanding of their potential resolution. The unequal distribution of resources *across* households, compounded by the sexual division of labour *within* households, produces a situation in which women — especially those in asset-poor households — are frequently relegated to activities with the lowest productivity and returns.

Several major methodological problems permeate most research that includes measures of sex differences in labour productivity. Because males and females (as well as adults and children, workers in landholding and landless households, and other social categories of workers) generally specialise in different types of agricultural activities, and because higher status males tend to appropriate advanced non-labour inputs such as chemical fertilisers, high-yielding seed varieties, and mechanical equipment, gender differences in *Total productivity* reflect the confounding of labour and non-labour inputs as well as the confounding of gender and class.

Direct measures of the *labour efficiency* of females and males under controlled conditions are rare. The few studies that do attempt to limit comparisons to identical operations on the same crop with the same equipment sometimes find that women are more productive workers than men. Comparisons of the farm output of female-managed farms with male—or jointly-managed farms sometimes find that the former have higher output per unit of non-labour input (although the absolute levels of the latter are lower), suggesting that women are more efficient labourers or more skilled managers of inputs than are men under certain conditions. Nevertheless, the literature is pervaded with indicators weighting female labour hours as a fraction of "male equivalent units," averaging across crops and activities on the basis of scanty evidence and misleading assumptions. The use of wage rates as proxies for productivity differentials is especially unwarranted, given the discrimination factor that is built into most wage labour markets.

Difficulties are compounded when gender and age differences in consumption patterns are added to productivity estimates to derive measures of the net value of labour in peasant agriculture. Once again, consumption estimates are frequently based on assumptions about how much food and other household resources are allocated to given family members rather than on concrete evidence. The use of international standards of minimum daily caloric *requirements* for males and females of different ages and activity levels is misleading in several ways: not only does it obscure important variations in requirements among population subgroups, but it also fails to reflect significant surplus or deficits in the *actual* food consumption of individuals and groups. Thus, estimates of the net value of labour can be biased on both the production and consumption sides of the equation. It is hardly surprising that the controversy about the value of male and female children in agricultural production remains unresolved.

Returns to labour are measured by wages or salaries received, income earned in cash or kind and assessments of the value of farm production that is sold, exchanged, or consumed domestically. Although wages in cash or kind are easy to apportion to individuals in this area, the value of farm production is more difficult to apportion to individual workers. The simplest method, allocating to each household member the total value of income from crop or livestock production in direct proportion to his or her labour contribution to the total (based on home-use data), assumes that each worker is equally productive. Returns to labour from this method would be identical for everyone. But more sophisticated measures that weight labour contributions by a productivity factor acquire all of the problems inherent in the previous discussion.

Attaching a value to the agricultural inputs of each household member permits calculations of the relative contribution of each person, or category of persons, to the total household income. Incorporated in these calculations, as in the returns to labour mentioned above, are questions of what range of activities to include under crop or livestock production. Is time spent on activities such as preparing meals for field hands, or processing and storing crops for home consumption, to be included as part of the total farm labour input? The larger the "net," and the more activities that are included, the larger will be the share of women's (and children's) labour, and thus, the larger their contribution to household incomes based on these sources.

Similar issue arise in calculating indicators of *control* over income. How much of the value of each person's labour does she or he control? What portion of the value is a personal fund over which the worker has total discretion, or a common household fund over which the worker may have little if any control? The methodological problem here derives from asking about how decisions are made about household expenditures, and who "owns" the income or produce from different activities. Nevertheless, findings of this type can be extremely useful in assessing the actual or potential impact of agricultural interventions that alter labour requirements or returns to labour of men and women, or that alter the pattern or control over this income so that some workers perceive that they stand to lose from new modes of operation whereas others stand to gain.

In sum, although measures of sex differences in productivity and returns to labour are inherently difficult to collect and interpret, careful observations under controlled conditions in specific settings can contribute interesting and useful data for planing and evaluating development projects. But they make sense only in the context of inter—and intra-familial stratification of the distribution of production assets and employment opportunities.

NOTES

1. Each of these factors, if measured separately, may affect female labour efficiency adversely in comparison with male labour, with some important exceptions depending on the sex specialisation of the activity in question. Mueller (1982) emphasises the problem of lack of support systems for women workers that constrain their productivity, particularly problems of child-care, the double burden of household and farm work (apparent in time-use surveys), and the high prevalence of female-headed households in many settings. Seasonality of female labour may raise women's *average* productivity since women (and children and the aged) are more likely to be drawn into farm work at times of peak activity when time pressures and potential labour bottlenecks require more intense effort as well as more time than during the slack season (Mueller, 1976, p. 117). For a measure of urgency of tasks as it affects the length of the working day in Malawi, see Farrington, 1975, pp. 72-74.
2. Piecework rates rarely differentiate among types of worker. But in the Food-for-Work earth-moving schemes in Bangladesh, higher piecework rates were recommended for female workers on the grounds that because women and average were able to carry less earth than men in a given day, they would have to be paid at a slightly higher rate in order to earn sufficient food for their daily requirements (Chen and Ghuznavi, 1977).

39

Women Labour in Agricultural Occupation

Rightly Asok Mitra points out:

> In reality, however, there are extraordinarily few areas or circumstances where women's 'economic' contribution could be dismissed as merely supplementary or optional or dispensable. But this myth has been very successfully practised increasingly over the ages in protean forms to keep women under-subjection politically, economically and socially...[1]

National development should mean the process of social transformation in a manner where efficient use is made of human resources and the largest possible number of families obtain an improvement in their standard of living. In such a transformation then, 'people', and not profits must be the 'central social value'. Unfortunately in India half of the force of the people, i.e., woman folk remain in utter negligence and is left far behind in the race of social recognition and economic independence. The lot of women is still worst in rural areas where majority of them are the victims of double exploitation both as a house-wife in the family and as an agricultural labour in the field. In Bihar agricultural economy, where women labour take a heavy share of agricultural work, often their input being even greater than that of male members, the conditions of female agricultural labour in comparison to their male counterpart is still worst.

In Bihar, women are mostly employed as casual agricultural worker. They are hardly kept as attached labour for agricultural work. An woman labour of attached nature does the household work or serves as a maid-servant, and therefore, cannot be taken as agricultural labour. In the agricultural labour market there are two types of people who offer, themselves, one is those who do not cultivate any land, either owned or leased in and the other is those who cultivate some land but have to supplement their income by hiring, themselves, out as wage labourers. The role and condition of the women workers in this field, particularly in Bihar is less known. These women labourers contribute to the family earning. They are compelled to seek work in their villages itself in both peak and off seasons. During the off-seasons, they work at a still lower wage. There are certain social and domestic reasons which prevent women workers from going outside their villages to seek work for themselves. The main reason is this that the occupational status of an women worker is linked to that of her husband or father particularly so in the rural areas. This decision, almost a voluntary one, on the part of women agricultural workers to remain in their villages seeking occasional employment available within short distance, "spring from their family responsibilities and socio-psychological reluctance to move out of the familiar habitat..."[2]

An attempt has been made in the present chapter to discuss various dimensions of the major problems related to the condition of women agricultural labour in Bihar, viz., the problem of employment, the wage differentials, their living and working condition, their economic exploitation and lastly their abject poverty. The analysis of employment, unemployment and underemployment of women agricultural labour in Bihar is based on Rural Labour Enquiry I, 1974-75, Labour Bureau, Chandigarh. Unfortunately such data base is not available on different dimensions of poverty, living and working conditions of women agricultural labour in Bihar. Consequently the discussion of these aspects of the condition of women agricultural labour has been discussed with the help of some references available tin these context only. However, to fill up this gap of data is field survey has been conducted to study and to collect data on various aspects of socio-economic conditions of women agricultural labour. With the help of the primary data collected through field survey the aspects like poverty, living and working conditions, etc., have been duly focussed with the support of appropriate primary data in Chapter 3.

EMPLOYMENT PATTERN

As pointed out earlier, in Bihar, women agricultural labourers mostly work as casual labourers. The percentage of attached women labourers would be nil. It is true that male agricultural labourers have a preference to work on casual contact basis. The reason for male labourers' preference to work on casual basis rather than as attached labour, notwithstanding the security of employment, is attributed to unfavourable conditions of work. Due to this unfavourable conditions of work, and certain social and domestic reasons attached women agricultural laborers are generally not found. The occupational status of an women worker is linked to that of her husband or father particularly so in the rural areas.

If we take "the norm of 250 working days in a year as that of full employment,"[3] we find that casual women agricultural labourers worked for quite less than this period.

Table 39.1 shows the level of employment of women agricultural labour in general and also belonging to Scheduled Caste and Scheduled Tribe groups in Bihar in two different years, i.e., 1964-65 and 1974-75. Employment data related to these two years with the difference of a decade have been taken just to show the change if there is any employment opportunities of women agricultural labour in Bihar. Employment data presented in the Table 39.1 has two break-ups i.e., "wage-employment" and "self-employment". Similarly, women agricultural labour have two groups, i.e., "with land" and "without land". As indicated in Table 39.1 the levels of employment of women agricultural labour in general and also in case of Scheduled Caste and Scheduled Tribes is quite low in comparison to the level of employment of men and children. Taking the norm of 250 working days in a year as full employment, the wage employment in case of women agricultural labour is generally sometimes more or sometimes less than 30 per cent of the full employment norm, i.e., 125 working days. Even adding self-employment days with their wage employment days the total working days of women agricultural labour turn out to be far less than full employment norm. This is true to women agricultural labour in general and also to their Scheduled Castes and Scheduled Tribes groups. Table 39.1 evidents a clear cut decline in employment opportunities of all types of agricultural labour during the decade 1964-65—1974-75 but the decline is much more pronounced in case of wage employment of women agricultural labour when compared to their self-employment. Further, the level of self-employment of women agricultural labour "with land" is naturally higher than "without land" in cases of all types of women agricultural labourers. In comparison to women agricultural labour in general and of Scheduled Castes group, the level of employment in case of tribal women agricultural labour is higher showing thereby more hardy nature and greater participation of tribal women in agricultural activities.

TABLE 39.1

Level of Employment of Women Agricultural Labour in Bihar during the Years 1964-65 and 1974-75

Items/Types of labourers	*Wage-Employment*				*Self-Employment*	
	1964-65	*1974-75*			*1964-65*	*1974-75*
		With land	*Without land*	*All*		*With land*
1	2	3	4	5	6	7
Men	222 (89.87)	214 (88.42)	187 (96.89)	204 (91.07)	25 (10.12)	28 (11.57)
Women	134 (87.01)	125 (79.11)	115 (90.55)	121 (83.44)	20 (12.98)	33 (20.88)
Children	203 (91.44)	132 (65.67)	139 (86.33)	135 (72.58)	19 (8.55)	69 (34.32)
Scheduled Caste						
Men	232 (93.92)	222 (92.11)	174 (95.08)	199 (92.99)	15 (6.07)	19 (7.88)
Women	138 (89.61)	122 (81.87)	114 (91.93)	118 (86.76)	16 (10.38)	27 (18.12)
Children	196 (94.23)	142 (79.32)	132 (94.96)	137 (86.16)	12 (5.76)	37 (20.67)
Scheduled Tribes						
Men	224 (94.94)	222 (77.08)	234 (100.00)	224 (80.28)	17 (7.05)	66 (22.91)
Women	157 (85.32)	133 (73.07)	173 (93.01)	140 (76.92)	27 (14.67)	49 (26.92)
Children	296 (87.83)	113 (50.67)	104 (100.00)	112 (54.36)	41 (12.16)	110 (49.32)

Items/Types of labourers	*Self-Employment*		*Total*			
	1974-75		*1964-65*	*1974-75*		
	Without land	*All*		*With land*	*Without land*	*All*
1	*8*	*9*	*10*	*11*	*12*	*13*
Men	6	20	247	242	193	224
	(3.10)	(8.92)	(100.00)	(100.00)	(100.00)	(100.00)
Women	12	24	154	158	127	145
	(9.44)	(16.55)	(100.00)	(100.00)	(100.00)	(100.00)
Children	22	51	222	201	161	186
	(13.66)	(27.41)	(100.00)	(100.00)	(100.00)	(100.00)
Scheduled Castes						
Men	9	15	247	241	183	214
	(4.91)	(7.00)	(100.00)	(100.00)	(100.00)	(100.00)
Women	10	18	154	149	124	136
	(8.06)	(13.23)	(100.00)	(100.00)	(100.00)	(100.00)
Children	7	22	208	179	139	159
	(5.03)	(13.83)	(100.00)	(100.00)	(100.00)	(100.00)
Scheduled Tribes						
Men	—	55	241	288	234	279
		(19.71)	(100.00)	(100.00)	(100.00)	(100.00)
Women	13	42	184	182	186	182
	(6.98)	(23.07)	(100.00)	(100.00)	(100.00)	(100.00)
Children	—	94	337	223	104	206
		(45.63)	(100.00)	(100.00)	(100.00)	(100.00)

Notes: Figures in the parentheses in Cols. 2 and 6 show the percentage of Col. 10 and in Cols. 3 to 5 as well as in Cols. 7 to 9 show the percentages of Cols. 11, 12 and 13 respectively.

Source: Rural Labour Enquiry I, 1974-75, Final Report on Employment and Unemployment of Rural Labour Household, Part I, Labour Bureau, Ministry of Labour, Government of India, Chandigarh, pp. 308-13.

Table 39.2 presents an inter-State comparison of the average annual days of wage employment of women agricultural labourers. States have been arranged under the heads of the appropriate zones. In this table also wage employment data has been shown for the same two different years as in Table 39.1, i.e., 1964-65 and 1974-75. As indicated in Table 39.2, except Uttar Pradesh and Manipur, Bihar has lowest average annual days of wage-employment (133 days) available to women agricultural labour. The declining trend in the level of employment of women agricultural labour during 1964-65 to 1974-75 is also observed in Table 39.2 in almost all states of male agricultural labour in comparison to female agricultural labour is also confirmed in all states as shown in Appendix-I.

The above interpretation of Tables 39.1 and 39.2 amply supports the view that the phenomena of unemployment, under-employment and disguised unemployment is considerably larger amongst female casual workers than among their male counterparts.

The problem of unemployment among women agricultural labourers can be analysed and discussed further with the help of Tables 39.3, 39.4 and 39.5.

Table 39.3 shows the level of unemployment among different groups of women agricultural labourers in Bihar in the years 1964-65 and 1974-75. This table also shows unemployment causes due to different reasons in these two years. Table 39.4 and 39.5 also provide the same informations.about unemployment of women agricultural labour but at inter-state level and for the year 1964-65 only.

As indicated in Table 1.3 women agricultural labourers of all groups remain unemployed (as in the years 1964-65 and 1974-75) in the range of 133 days to 162 days due to want of work. Except tribal women agricultural labour, an increase in the level of unemployment during the decade 1964-65 to 1974-75 can be marked in cases of women agricultural labour of all the groups. Table also confirms comparatively lower level of unemployment among women labour in other than agricultural occupations.

TABLE 39.2

Average Annual Days of Wage-Employment of Usually Occupied Women Belonging to Agricultural Labour Household

Zones/States	*Agricultural labourers*		*Non-agricultural labourers*		*Other occupations*		*All occupations*	
	1964-65	*1974-75*	*1964-65*	*1974-75*	*1964-65*	*1974-75*	*1964-65*	*1974-75*
1	2	3	4	5	6	7	8	9
Central Zone	144	137	174	136	14	19	130	125
Uttar Pradesh	114	128	140	114	4	17	97	109
Madhya Pradesh	169	146	208	187	90	46	168	145
Eastern Zone	158	132	222	165	22	60	148	128
Bihar	133	121	140	121	17	86	121	119
Orissa	174	126	217	118	51	43	169	124
West Bengal	247	157	263	206	17	39	232	145
Assam	249	277	139	193	313	—	235	274
Manipur	39	231	—	—	—	182	31	226
Tripura	156	212	—	135	—	75	156	200
Maghalaya	—	200	—	208	—	—	—	188
Southern Zone	136	135	211	160	14	14	134	132
Andhra Pradesh	118	148	245	219	25	43	117	148
Tamil Nadu	149	126	201	204	13	9	148	124
Kerala	157	114	205	126	6	4	152	106
Pondicherry	—	123	—	365	—	61	—	124
Western Zone	205	188	205	228	30	33	200	185
Gujarat	247	177	320	236	52	—	245	176
Maharashtra	193	195	221	216	22	56	189	192
Karnataka	203	183	166	225	33	14	195	178
Goa, Daman and Diu	—	124	—	365	—	—	—	150

1	*2*	*3*	*4*	*5*	*6*	*7*	*8*	*9*
Northern Zone	172	172	204	224	14	17	155	127
Rajasthan	161	171	152	236	—	124	142	170
Punjab	176			239	12		103	
Haryana	184	158	223	57	30	—	167	117
Jammu and Kashmir	365	194	—	46	—	3	91	46
Himachal Pradesh	—	147	—	—	—	—	—	114
Delhi	277	—	261	—	—	—	278	—
All India	160	149	206	173	19	30	153	143

Source: Rural Labour Enquiry I, 1974-75, Final Report on Employment and Unemployment of Rural Labour Household, Part I, Labour Bureau, Ministry of Labour, Government of India, Chandigarh, p. 125.

TABLE 39.3

Level of Unemployment of Women Labour in Bihar

Items/Types of Occupation		*Due to want of work*		*Due to other reasons*		*Total*	
		1964-65	*1974-75*	*1964-65*	*1974-75*	*1964-65*	*1974-75*
1		*2*	*3*	*4*	*5*	*6*	*7*
Agricultural labourers		103	155	18	33	121	188
		(85.12)	(82.44)	(14.87)	(17.55)	(100.00)	(100.00)
Non-agricultural labourers		56	101	24	11	80	112
		(70.00)	(90.17)	(30.00)	(9.82)	(100.00)	(100.00)
Other occupations		21	118	6	52	27	170
		(77.77)	(69.41)	(22.22)	(30.58)	(100.00)	(100.00)
All occupations		95	152	16	33	111	185
		(85.58)	(82.16)	(14.41)	(17.83)	(100.00)	(100.00)
Agricultural labourers	SC	144	162	19	25	163	187
		(88.34)	(86.63)	(11.65)	(13.36)	(100.00)	(100.00)
	ST	157	114	—	51	157	165
		(100.00)	(69.09)	—	(30.90)	(100.00)	(100.00)
Non-agricultural labourers	SC	49	129	—	24	49	153
		(100.00)	(84.31)		(15.68)	(100.00)	(100.00)
	ST	—	—	—	—	—	—
Other occupations	SC	15	102	6	26	21	128
		(71.42)	(79.68)	(28.57)	(20.31)	(100.00)	(100.00)
	ST	—	46	—	52	—	98
			(46.93)		(53.06)		(100.00)
All occupations	SC	134	159	18	25	152	184
		(88.15)	(86.41)	(11.84)	(13.58)	(100.00)	(100.00)
	ST	158	107	—	50	158	157
		(100.00)	(68.15)		(31.84)	(100.00)	(100.00)

(Figures in parentheses show the percentages)

Source: Rural Labour Enquiry I, 1974-75, Final Report on Employment and Unemployment of Rural Labour Household, Part I, Labour Bureau, Ministry of Labour, Government of India, Chandigarh, pp. 212-17.

TABLE 39.4

Unemployment of Male and Female Agricultural Labourers, 1964-65

Zones/States	Number of Days *Unemployed during the year*		*Total No. of Days Employment was wanted*		*Proportion of Unemployed Days to Total No. of Days Employment was wanted*	
	Male	*Female*	*Male*	*Female*	*Male*	*Female*
1	*2*	*3*	*4*	*5*	*6*	*7*
Central	32	90	306	270 (88.4)	10.46	33.33
Uttar Pradesh	35	108	312	264 (84.62)	11.22	40.91
Madhya Pradesh	27	75	300	273 (91.00)	9.00	27.47
Eastern Zone	53	99	330	276 (83.64)	16.06	35.87
Bihar	70	103	317	257 (81.07)	22.08	40.08
West Bengal	37	73	350	322 (92.00)	10.57	22.67
Orissa	40	105	332	310 (93.37)	12.48	33.87
Assam	17	43	324	298 (91.98)	5.25	14.43
Southern Zone	66	125	301	272 (90.37)	21.92	45.96
Andhra Pradesh	16	99	271	231 (85.27)	5.90	42.86
Tamil Nadu	106	155	332	313 (94.28)	31.93	49.52
Kerala	106	120	304	285 (93.75)	34.87	42.11
Western Zone	38	62	321	281 (87.54)	11.84	22.06
Gujarat	44	82	336	332 (98.81)	13.09	24.70
Maharashtra	32	44	315	255 (80.95)	10.16	17.25
Mysore	44	8	317	224 (70.66)	13.88	3.57
Northern Zone	32	71	329	271 (82.37)	9.73	26.20
Rajasthan	41	81	308	280 (90.91)	13.31	28.83
Punjab	27	59	339	259 (76.40)	7.96	22.78
All India	48	96	315	274 (86.98)	15.24	35.04

Notes: 1. In formation tabulated here related to men and women agricultural labourers in agricultura labour households in agricultural and non-agricultural employment.

2. It needs to be stressed that the information regarding unemployment (in Col. 4) relates only tc those days when work could not be had though it was wanted. Table 39.5 gives fuller informatior on unemployment for this as well as other reasons. Still there is an element of understatemen in this column because it does not take account of the days men and women were occupied ir unclassified work.

3. Number of days unemployed during the year in Col. 2 stand for the days employment wa wanted in addition to the days for which men or women had paid employment or were in self employment.

Source: Rural Labour Enquiry, 1964-65, Final Reports Labour Bureau (1975).

TABLE 39.5

Number of Days of Unemployment of Agricultural Labourers Classified According to Reasons

Zones/States	Due to want of work		Due to other reasons		Unclassified		Days unaccounted		Total	
	Male	Female	Male	Female	Male	Female	Male	Female	Male	Female
1	2	3	4	5	6	7	8	9	10	11
Central Zone	32	90	20	23	20	49	19	23	91	185
Uttar Pradesh	35	108	22	23	16	39	15	39	88	209
Madhya Pradesh	27	75	16	23	26	51	24	18	93	167
Eastern Zone	53	99	12	17	7	18	17	54	89	188
Bihar	70	103	15	18	7	13	26	77	118	211
West Bengal	37	73	8	22	3	11	4	10	52	116
Orissa	40	105	7	9	10	37	16	9	73	160
Assam	17	43	22	45	19	16	—	9	58	113
Southern Zone	66	125	18	27	7	23	39	43	130	218
Andhra Pradesh	16	99	7	27	7	34	79	73	109	233
Tamil Nadu	106	155	20	25	7	11	6	16	139	207
Kerala	106	120	38	37	4	21	18	22	166	200
Western Zone	38	62	12	25	19	49	14	10	83	146
Gujarat	44	82	3	11	9	16	9	6	70	115
Maharashtra	32	44	10	28	22	70	18	12	82	154
Mysore	44	8	17	27	19	31	12	83	92	149
Northern Zone	32	71	17	35	7	13	12	46	68	165
Rajasthan	41	81	39	52	11	17	8	16	99	166
Punjab	27	59	8	12	5	7	13	87	53	165
All India	48	96	15	24	12	33	23	34	98	187

Notes: 1. Information in this table related to agricultural labourers in agricultural labour households.

2. "Days unaccounted" in Col. 5 are arrived at by subtracting from 365, the total of Cols. 2, 3 and 4 in the Table of Cols. 2 and 3 Table 39.3. This has introduced an element of overstatement which however is unavoidable because state-wise figures are not available for days of unclassified work which for all-India are placed at 6 for men and 2 for women agricultural labourers in agricultural labour households.

Source: Rural Labour Enquiry, 1964-65, Final Report, Labour Bureau (1975).

Further, Table 39.4 also reveals some very important findings on unemployment among women agricultural labour in different states of India including Bihar. Table 39.4 confirms that level of unemployment of female agricultural labour is higher than male agricultural labour in all states. Table 39.4 also shows the proportion of unemployed days to total number of days employment was wanted. This proportion in case of female agricultural labour can be observed very high (in the range of 40 per cent to 50 per cent) in states like U.P., Bihar (Eastern zone), Andhra Pradesh, Tamil Nadu and Kerala (Southern zone). In Bihar this proportion is as high as 40.08 per cent.

Table 39.5 shows number of days of employment of male and female agricultural labourers according to reason at inter-state level. Uniformly in all the states maximum days of unemployment have been reported due to want of work.

The analysis of employment/unemployment in agriculture has still an important dimension, i.e., seasonal variations in employment.

The agricultural labourers in Bihar are employed in the field in different crop seasons and in different months. This employment pattern varies in different operations in a particular season. North Bihar has three distinct crop seasons, each of 121 days. The principal *agahani* crops are the winter rice crop and sugarcane. The principal *Bhadai* crops are early rice, maize, whereas *rabi* crops are wheat, barley and arhar. Both the males and females are employed in different agricultural operations. Pre-sowing operations are exclusively carried out by male labourers. Female labourers help in manuring the fields. Child labour is not employed in this operation. In sowing and transplanting operations during kharif season almost equal number of male and female labourers are employed. During *rabi* and summer seasons the percentage of women labourers in employment decreases owing to the fact that transplantation operation is not performed during these two seasons. Children are rarely employed in sowing operations. In inter-culturing females are employed for more number of days than males. Irrigation operation is mainly done by male casual labourers. No child labour is employed in this operation. In harvesting almost equal number of males and females are employed in all the three seasons. The main inferences that can be drawn are: (a) In pre-sowing, transplanting and irrigation operations, it is the male labourers who are generally employed; (b) for inter-culture operation females are preferred; and (c) harvesting is performed equally by males and females.

A report of the study of 95 household of landless agricultural labourers in Purnea says:

> During summer season a male casual labourer was employed for 121 days out of a total of 122 days, while a female casual labourer was employed for 77 days only. In *kharif* season, on an average, a male casual labourer was employed for 122 days and a female labourer was employed for 199 days. Similarly during *rabi* season a male casual worker worked on an average for 104 days while a female worker was employed for 93 days only.[4]

Thus, from experience in day to day life it can be said about the female agricultural labourers in Bihar that there is no 'employment pattern' as such in the real sense of the term. These workers have no choice or preference. They associate themselves, particularly with the landless workers in farm operations who make themselves available whenever asked for by their employer, or whenever they get the opportunity.

Low labour utilisation and seasonal unemployment are a manifestation of rural poverty where individuals are forced to take on extremely low productive jobs which do not always ensure minimum subsistence. The basic problems that affect women's roles and opportunities for employment in this sector, spring from their helpless dependence caused by lack of adequate employment opportunities, limited skills and illiteracy, restricted mobility and lack of autonomous status. The occupational status of an woman worker is linked to that of her husband or father particularly so in the rural areas. The abject poverty of these workers is the result of their lack of control over adequate productive resources. The effect of possession of marginal land or landlessness, persistent gap between income and consumption, lack of continuous employment and low social position is further enhanced by near perpetual indebtedness. The cumulative effect of all these factors is that the worker is deprived of all bargaining power and occupational and geographical mobility. The totality of their problem results in increasing pauperisation and abject poverty.

THE WAGE STRUCTURE

The wage structure in agriculture is somewhat different than that of industry. The main difference between them lies in the fact that industrial wages are completely monetised in contrast to agricultural wages which are paid more in kind than in cash particularly in Bihar.

Another difference is the irregularity of payment of agrarian wages. In industry wages may be paid daily, weekly, fortnightly or even monthly. In agriculture, the casual labourers whether male or female get their wages sometimes daily or by-weekly and sometimes even weekly.

Wage differentials in agriculture—both inter-regional and intra-regional or between men, women and children are more apparent than in the industry. But inter-regional comparisons of wage levels is not easy due to difference in mode of payment and commodity-wise variations in price levels in different regions. In view of these characteristics, the wage structure in agriculture widely differs both in space and time.

The wages are not uniform for all farm operations. A male labourer may receive a little more a day at the time of harvesting but at the same time he may get less in other farm operations or in lean or slack season. In case of female workers, however, the maximum wage rate a day may be given to them at the time of transplantation of paddy. A study conducted nearly a decade ago of the landless agricultural labourers of Purnea district in North Bihar reveals that the average daily wage of a casual male labourer engaged in farm operations was Rs. 2.33 in 1970-71 as compared to 1.85 in 1969-70. The female labourers received 10 paise less in 1970 while they were getting 21 paise less in 1969. This area being agriculturally prosperous the study revealed some interesting features. Here women labourers earned relatively more than their counterparts in other parts of the country due to unique cropping pattern of this area. Paddy and jute are the principal crops of this area and both of these crops employ maximum female labour. In fact, there are certain operations like transplanting and harvesting of paddy and inter-culture of jute that are done mainly by women labourers.

The wages are paid generally in the rural areas of Bihar despite expanding monetisation in the rural areas. Kind wages are very common in farm operations. The study further reveals that the wage rate for transplantation work was 2 to 2½ seers of paddy with lunch. For harvesting a labourer got one in 16 bundles of harvested crop. They also got a few kilogrammes of corn in the form of *"Lodha Bichchia, Mutha, Antia"*, etc. Wages in kind are paid mostly in terms of inferior corn except during the peak season. For lunch, the labourers usually get bread prepared with barley flour or *Satu* prepared from *Khesari*, maize or barley. Wages are paid according to "small weights" or *"Katcha seer"*. The kind wage system protects the real wages of labourers from falling even when the consumers price index of labourers goes up in the area.[5]

Female agricultural labour, who look ragged, worn out and totally hopeless are also the victims of wage discriminations. The most important reasons for the low rates of wages, particularly for women labour in agriculture are the unorganised nature of farm labour, the case with which hired labour can be substituted by family labour, the seasonal nature of the demand for labour and the traditional classification of some jobs as the monopoly of women. Apart from the differentials in wages for the same jobs, discrimination against women is strengthened by having lower rates for the jobs traditionally done by women, viz., sowing, weeding, transplanting, winnowing, threshing and harvesting, as against ploughing normally done by men only. The other factor that contributes to the low wages of women is the practice of identifying work day as equivalent of 7-9 hours. "Women reporting even half an hour late because of domestic responsibilities are paid wages for half a day only".[6] The decline of village and cottage industries and the consequent loss of alternative employment as well as skills has resulted in occupational immobility a disability for women.

WAGE DISCRIMINATION

The other reasons of wage discrimination as explained by the National Commission on Labour, lay in the poverty and illiteracy of agricultural labour, the casual nature of their employment and their ignorance of the law, all of which apply particularly to the women. Because of these handicaps, agricultural labour as a whole and women in particular are not able to employ methods now common to industrial labour to improve their bargaining power. There are considerable disparities in wages between men and women depending upon the region, between crops and the bargaining power of labour. Apart from the differentials in wages for the same jobs, discrimination against women is strengthened by having lower rates for the jobs traditionally by women, viz., sowing, weeding transplanting, winnowing, threshing and harvesting, as against ploughing normally done by men only.

As per the Minimum Wages Act, 1948 (2nd Schedule) minimum wages are to be fixed by State Government for agricultural labour and the rates are to be reviewed periodically at intervals not exceeding five years. There are still some states which have not brought large areas of agricultural employment within the ambit of the Act. The machinery for the fixation and enforcement of minimum wages is not uniform. The National Commission on Labour had criticised the inadequate implementation of the Act.

In earlier times, the regional variations in wage rates were probably influenced by cultural variations in attitudes to women's work. In recent years, however, this situation has changed. As observed by the National Commission on Labour, 'the fixation of statutory minimum wages by the Government has tended to narrow the gap between wages of men and women". The Commission, however, noted the continuation of wage differentials larger sectors where women are employed, viz., agriculture and small industries, evidence shows that in fixing wages rates some State Government have not been free from discrimination against women". Table 39.6 indicates the difference in maximum and minimum wages of men and women for the same agricultural operations in selected states.

Table 39.6 shows the maximum and minimum ranges of wages for main agricultural operations sowing, weeding and reaping paid to men, women and children in different states of India including Bihar. Table 39.6 indicates a great gap in the level and range of wages paid to men and women in these states. Comparatively the phenomena of very low level of women wages is prevalent in different degree in all states. So far operation-wise difference in wages is concerned, this difference is not uniformly pronounced in all states, but comparatively wages paid for reaping and sowing are higher than that of weeding in almost all states. As indicated in Table 39.6, the general wage level paid to all types of agricultural labourers (men, women and children) are comparatively lower in Bihar and Madhya Pradesh particularly in comparison to Punjab, Haryana and Tamil Nadu.

TABLE 39.6

Agricultural Wages in Different States

		Maximum	*Maximum*
1	2	3	4
		1. Bihar State 1970 (for 11 months)	
Sowers			
	Men	44.05	15.95
	Women	29.50	12.50
	Children	19.25	10.53
Weeders			
	Men	41.30	16.12
	Women	33.76	12.90
	Children	21.00	10.25
Reapers			
	Men	67.00	18.75
	Women	38.95 (10 months)	13.50 (10 months)
	Children	19.31 (9 months)	8.50 (9 months)
		2. Haryana 1971 (9 months)	
Sowers			
	Men	72.20	47.00
	Women	2.50 (1 month)	—
	Children	—	—
Weeders			
	Men	64.00	43.50
	Women	39.60	24.50
	Children	15.00 (6 months)	3.00 (1 month)

1	2	3	4
Reapers			
	Men	74.80 (8 months)	30.50 (6 months)
	Women	31.50 (6 months)	10.00 (3 months)
	Children	16.50 (4 months)	8.50 (3 months)
		3. Madhya Pradesh 1971	
Sowers			
	Men (11 months)	44.75	15.25
	Women	31.25	9.25 (9 months)
	Children	23.00 (10 months)	7.75 (9 months)
Weeders			
	Men (12 months)	36.50	12.50
	Women	30.50	10.50
	Children	23.75	7.70
Reapers			
	Men (10 months)	35.00	10.50 (9 months)
	Women	31.25	9.25 (9 months)
	Children	23.75	5.75 (9 months)
		4. Punjab 1971 (12 months)	
Sowers			
	Men	95.00	63.75
	Women	—	—
	Children	—	—
Weeders			
	Men	95.00	64.00
	Women	37.50 (7 months)	—
	Children	—	—
Reapers			
	Men	78.25 (10 months)	44.00 (8 months)
	Women		—
	Children	—	—
		5. Tamil Nadu 1971 (12 months)	
Sowers			
	Men	48.25	23.00
	Women	30.00	12.96
	Children	24.25	12.49
Weeders			
	Men	42.00	12.00
	Women	27.00	12.00
	Children	24.25	10.07
Reapers			
	Men	58.00	24.23
	Women	44.80	14.82
	Children	44.28	16.01
		6. Uttar Pradesh (12 months) 1971	
Sowers			
	Men	66.56	11.27 (11 months)
	Women	47.70	9.75 (10 months)
	Children	17.50 (8 months)	5.50 (7 months)

1	2	3	4
Weeders			
	Men	60.00	11.23
	Women	42.80	10.16 (11 months)
	Children	30.20	6.00 (9 months)
Reapers			
	Men	52.60	8.87 (9 months)
	Women	42.85 (11 months)	8.07 (9 months)
	Children	29.20 (5 months)	7.50 (8 months)

Source: Directorate of Economics and Statistics, Ministry of Agriculture, Government of India.

Table 39.7 shows operation-wise wage level (per day) of women agricultural labour prevailing in different districts of Bihar. An overall comparison of women agricultural wages at inter-district and inter-regional levels on the basis of Table 39.7 clearly indicates comparatively lower level of women agricultural wages in the districts of Chotanagpur plateau. Generally higher level of women agricultural wages for various operations can be observed in the districts of South Bihar. The average figures at regional levels also confirm the above findings.

Further, as revealed from the table, there is not much difference in the level of women agricultural wages in the districts of the same region except a few exceptional cases of comparatively high wages in Patna, Aurangabad in South Bihar, Hazaribag in South Bihar (may be due to the impact of greater urbanisation in Patna and industrial impact in Hazaribag district) and comparatively low wages in Sitamarhi, Purnea and Katihar districts of North Bihar (these are agriculturally very backward and traditional districts with greater exploitation of agricultural labour in general and women agricultural labour in particular. Even at regional levels the difference in women agricultural wages is minor. Thus, throughout state the lot of women agricultural labour is uniformity bad in Bihar.

TABLE 39.7

Level of Average Wages of Women Agricultural Labour in Different Operations of Farming in Different Districts of Bihar (1978-79)

Districts	*Sower*	*Weeder*	*Reaper and Harvester*	*Other agricultural operation*	*Herdman*	*General wage level*
1	2	3	4	5	6	7
Patna	6.30	6.30	6.96	—	—	6.52
Nalanda	—	—	—	—	—	—
Gaya	4.47	3.70	4.05	2.62	2.77	3.52
Aurangabad	7.50	7.50	7.00	7.08	—	7.24
Munger	—	—	—	—	—	—
Bhagalpur	—	—	—	—	—	—

Rohtas	5.08	5.00	—	6.48	—	5.52
Nawada	5.00	5.00	5.00	5.00	4.00	4.80
South Bihar	5.67	5.50	5.75	5.29	3.28	5.52
East Champaran	5.00	5.43	8.00	5.62	—	6.01
Muzaffarpur	—	—	—	—	—	—
Sitamarhi	2.67	2.50	—	—	—	2.58
Vaishali	3.80	3.79	4.75	4.72	—	4.26
Madhubani	5.25	5.31	—	—	—	5.28
Darbhanga	5.00	5.00	7.38	4.83	—	5.55
Samastipur	5.00	5.00	—	5.21	—	5.07
Siwan	—	—	3.83	—	—	3.83
Saran	—	—	—	—	—	—
Saharsa	6.50	5.76	5.87	6.08	—	5.64
Purnea	2.78	2.78	—	3.50	—	3.02
Katihar	2.62	2.45	—	2.45	—	2.51
Begusarai	5.50	5.50	—	5.10	—	5.37
North Bihar	4.41	4.35	5.96	4.69	—	4.47
Santhal Pargana	4.00	4.00	4.00	4.00	4.00	4.00
Giridih	4.42	4.74	2.26	4.80	1.78	3.60
Hazaribagh	6.32	6.00	—	6.50	5.45	6.08
Ranchi	—	—	5.00	—	—	5.00
Palamu	4.00	4.00	—	—	—	4.00
Dhanbad	4.50	5.00	4.50	—	—	4.67
Singhbhum	5.20	5.26	5.38	4.80	—	5.16
Chotanagpur	4.75	4.83	4.23	5.02	3.74	4.64
Bihar as a whole	4.81	4376	5.32	4.99	3.66	4.75

Source: Directorate of Economics and Statistics, Ministry of Agriculture, Government of India, 1981.

So far agricultural operation-wise difference in wages of women labour is concerned in Table 39.7 does not show any wages for ploughing, as ploughing is not done by women in Bihar. Wages paid for sowing and reaping are comparatively higher (though the difference is very minor everywhere) than that of weeding in the districts of North Bihar and South Bihar). This trend, however, is not marked in Chotanagpur plateau (wages for weeding being higher in this region) may be due to the impact of industrial employment opportunities available during the season of weeding in most of the districts of this region.

POVERTY

In case of agricultural labour low labour utilisation and seasonal unemployment are a manifestation of rural poverty where individuals are forced to take on low productivity jobs which do not always ensure minimum subsistence. The female landless agricultural labourers from an important but weak segment of Bihar's rural population. As discussed in the previous section, they are faced with the problems of unemployment and under-employment.

This is all due to their helpless dependence caused by lack of adequate employment opportunities, limited skills and illiteracy, restricted mobility and lack of autonomous status. The estimates of poverty, measured on the basis of consumption-expenditure have attempted to calculate the number of persons below subsistence level. The effect of possession of marginal land or landlessness, a persistent gap between income and consumption, lack of continuous employment and low social position have brought these labourers near perpetual indebtedness. The cumulative effect of all these factors is that the worker is deprived of all bargaining power. The totality of this problem results in increasing pauperisation and abject poverty. The impact of the price increase of consumption goods, particularly of foodgrains cannot be ignored. The consumer prices, in fact, have risen more for the poor than for the rich.

The difficulty with the analysis of poverty of women agricultural labour as such is the utter absence of data on poverty specifically related to women agricultural labour because generally the concept of poverty is related to the households. In other words the level of poverty of a household is generally applicable to all the persons belonging to that household. In the present anti-poverty programmes also it is household which is taken as the unit of the programme and not the person. Therefore, in absence of specific poverty data related to women agricultural labour at least in Bihar the different aspects of poverty discussed in the present section refer to the available data on poverty of general nature. This fact is also supported by the Report of the Committee on the Status of Women in India (1974):

> It is difficult to estimate the proportion and number of women affected by this increase in poverty as data regarding this is not available. But the higher level of unemployment and underemployment among women leads us to conclude that their proportion below the poverty line is likely to be higher than men. The physical evidence of increasing destitution among women in recent years has been reported from various quarters. Unfortunately, however, no reliable data are available for estimating the size of this group.[7]

In order to have a background of incidence of poverty in Bihar to discuss the poverty of women agricultural labour in that perspective an inter-state comparison of per capita income and percentage of population below poverty line during 1979-80 have been shown in Table 39.8. As indicated in Table 39.8 Bihar has the lowest per capita income (Rs. 773) and has as large as 57.49 per cent of population below poverty line. Bihar witness the heaviest incidence of poverty next to Orissa and Madhya Pradesh. The lot of women—a neglect section of society can be imagined very well in the background of the incidence of poverty just now in the economy of Bihar.

To relate the problem of women's poverty with their deteriorating employment prospect in recent past one may cite the economic implications of the British exploitations in India. The domestic industries were the biggest traditional source of women's employment outside agriculture during the British period, but today agriculture continues to receive the burden of the surplus labour force both of male and female. Therefore, the interrelated problems of poverty, unemployment and underemployment affect the economy as a whole because the overwhelming mass of women workers, both by primary and secondary activity, are to be found in this sphere. The special disabilities that characterise the rights and opportunities for women's economic participations are more predominant in the unorganised sector and will required special attention and remedial measures.

TABLE 39.8

Per Capita Income at Current Prices and Percentage of Population Below Poverty Line in States (1979-80)

Sl. No.	*States*	*Per capita income (Rs.)*	*Percentage of population below poverty line*
1	2	3	4
1.	Andhra Pradesh	1176	42.18
2.	Assam	960	51.10
3.	Bihar	773	57.49
4.	Gujarat	1632	35.04
5.	Haryana (1978-79)	1600	24.84
6.	Himachal Pradesh	1317	27.23
7.	Jammu and Kashmir	1145	34.06
8.	Karnataka	1267	48.34
9.	Kerala	1091	46.95
10.	Madhya Pradesh	828	57.73
11.	Maharasthra	1903	47.71
12.	Manipur	822	29.71
13.	Meghalaya	N.A.	48.03
14.	Nagaland	N.A.	4.11
15.	Orissa	931	66.40
16.	Punjab	2278	15.13
17.	Rajasthan	913	33.16
18.	Sikkim	N.A.	N.A.
19.	Tamil Nadu	1350	52.12
20.	Tripura	861	59.73
21.	Uttar Pradesh	981	50.09
22.	West Bengal	1330	52.54

Source: Statistical Outline of India, 1982, Economic Survey, 1981-82.

LIVING AND WORKING CONDITION

The living and working conditions of female agricultural labourers in Bihar are the worst in the real sense of the term. They are weak as a class; they are unorganised and socially and economically vulnerable. They come chiefly from the poor landless and socially depressed class. They work only to supplement their income. This inadequacy of their earnings mostly account for their low standard of living. There is no standard at all. Their small wages attest to the inhumane margin of subsistence on the part of the women agricultural labourers. The overall standard of living of these labourers is highly deplorable. If we examine their food and clothing, their accommodation and household, their health and physique and above all their social habits and norms, we would be face to face with death in life. They spend a large amount of their meagre income on cereals and their average intake of cereals is not satisfactory. Even the poor quality cereals are not adequately available to these female workers. In order to deep, themselves, alive they depend more on sweet potatoes and wild roots. The daily menu cards of these workers include the water boiled rice or rice with a little salt and chillies or onions or a little vegetable. The only luxury they can afford from their meagre income is a little meat once or twice a year. These ill-fed female workers feel really blessed if they get two or three *sarees* in a year. This is only dress of the most of the women workers. They do not know how to wear any undergarments or foot-wear. It is of course a pitiable site to see them semi-naked in the winter season.

Like their food and clothing, their utensils and household bore a striking testimony to their abnormally low standard of living. A bed of straw with tattered jute, a few rags, a small pot and aluminium plate, a *lota* can invariably be seen in every household. If there are a few more persons it means an inclusion of a few more rags and some utensils for other members of the family.

As for the accommodation they have erected one *Jhuggi* made of bamboos, hay and straw. One *Jhuggi* for one family with an opening one-side is the lot of the female workers. This only room with earthen and uneven floors often serve as their kitchen. In fact none of these female workers had the adequate accommodation and the necessary privacy. To the agricultural labourers of both the sexes a latrine is unthinkable. They have to ease, themselves out in the surrounding fields. As for drinking water they depend on tubewells or wells. Most of them are seen taking bath in the dirty pools. The absence of sanitation and proper water supply make the villages, a veritable breeding ground of all sorts of diseases and a source of epidemics. As pointed out at the very beginning of this section, there is non-availability of data related to the living and working conditions of women agricultural labour particularly in Bihar that is why the above description of the different aspects of living and working conditions could not be duly supported by the appropriate data. However, the deteriorating living condition of rural people in Bihar can be shown with the help of the data presented in Table 39.9.

Table 39.9 Shows the percentage of rural people below the minimum level of living in different states including Bihar. These percentages are shown for the two years, i.e., 1960-61 and 1967-68 just to show the trend in the level of living during the period mentioned in the table. Table 39.9 clearly shows a very significant rise in the percentage of rural people below the minimum level of living in the states like Assam, Bihar, Gujarat, Madhya Pradesh, Uttar Pradesh etc. It is Bihar where this deterioration appears to be of the most serious nature.

With this much of deterioration in the level of living of the rural people of Bihar the deterioration in the living condition of women agricultural labour—the most neglected members of the agrarian community needs no explanation.

EXPLOITATION

The weaker sections of the rural population particularly the women are the worst victims of exploitation. The decline of traditional handicraft and cottage industries and the disappearance of many of these industries has led to a loss of skills as a result of which the majority of women workers in the agricultural sector today do not possess any skills other than the traditional agricultural ones. Women among the landless labourers in the villages of Bihar are reduced to utter destitution in the absence of employment in agriculture and their lack of skills in other fields. Therefore, whenever they are employed in any work as unskilled labourers they are given the lowest rate of wages. Their exploitation is multicornered. The vulnerability of the woman becomes still greater when her husband has been reduced to the status of bonded labour. According to the 1981 Census in the State of Bihar, there are 1,948,950 female agricultural labourers. Overwhelming majority of them are landless and come from socially depressed communities. They do not have any social status and economic position. Their representation in non-agricultural occupations is negligible. The degree of poverty and the higher participation rate among women in these sections of the population give the large land owning families and upper hand since attached agricultural labour generally comes from these sections and wage differentials discriminating not only between men and women but between the non-scheduled and scheduled workers in general is widely prevalent. The National Commission on Labour had expressed its concern at this state of affairs:

> Our concern is all the greater, since those who suffer more, even among women as a group, are ignorant, unskilled and semi-skilled workers coming from communities which convention recognise as belonging to the lower social strata and for protecting whom Article 46 of the Constitution is presumably intended. In a way women belonging to these communities are intend to be double protected: (a) because they are the weaker section'; and (b) because of the comparatively unfortunate communities to which they belong; and it is here that the protection is the least.[8]

The introduction of modern method of cultivation is also a dangerous trend for women agricultural labourers. This directly affects their participation in agriculture. The traditional pattern had ensured a high participation by women. But the introduction of modern methods of cultivation is resulting in a gradual displacement of women from their traditional position in the community. The process of shrinking women's activities might lead to a disastrous end. This is all due to the government agricultural extension workers' apathy to the women agricultural labourers who teach new methods to the men only. It would appear that the Government agents, influenced by their own biases or experience, are perhaps unconsciously precipitating changes in the participation pattern of these communities, which will affect the economic position of the women workers in the long run. It is clear that

TABLE 39.9

Percentage of Rural People below the Minimum Level of Living in Different States

Sl. No.	*States*	*1960-61*	*1967-68*
1.	Andhra Pradesh	47	38—51 (44)
2	Assam*	14	32—52
3.	Bihar*	38+	61—71
4.	Gujarat*	25—37	48+
5.	Haryana	—	29+
6.	Jammu and Kashmir*	8	21+
7.	Kerala*	42+	67—
8.	Madhya Pradesh	36—47	61
9.	Maharashtra	40+	56—
10.	Mysore*	34—	57—
11.	Orissa	56+	64+
12.	Punjab*	13	33+
13.	Rajasthan	33—	37
14.	Tamil Nadu	46—61 (51)	61—
15.	Uttar Pradesh*	39—	60—
16.	West Bengal	22—42	74+
	All India	38	53

* in Col. 1 indicates the states in which there has been a very significant rise in the percentage of rural people below the minimum level.

Note: These estimates are based on Cols. 3 and 5 Table 3 and NSS Data on percentage distribution of persons by rural monthly per capita expenditure groups at current prices for Rounds 16 and 22. Since the NSS expenditure groups are discrete, one cannot always read off an exact figure from the tabulated data. In the table (+) after a figure indicates that the actual estimate is slightly (by less than 3 percentage points) above it; similarly (—) indicates a slightly lower figure. When the actual estimate is significantly different from the upper and lower terminal values of the relevant expenditure groups, we have given a whole range of percentage. We could have used linear interpolation to give an approximate estimate for the cases in which we have given a whole range. But except for the cases of Andhra Pradesh and Tamil Nadu, even without any interpolation, the direction of change in the percentage of rural people below the minimum is pretty clear. In the case of Andhra Pradesh and Tamil Nadu, we have provided figures (arrived on the basis of linear interpolation) in brackets in the table to indicate the approximate direction of change. Punjab in the table includes Haryana in 1960-61, but not in 1967-68. It is being assumed that prices moved at similar rates in Punjab and Haryana for 1967-68.

Source: *Economic and Political Weekly*, Annual Number, February 1973, p. 262-A.

the main source of exploitation of female agricultural workers are rooted in their landlessness, lack of organisation, and inequality of status. The gradual commercialisation and modernisation of the economy, particularly in the unorganised sector where an overwhelming majority of workers are women and the efforts made by Government to replace traditional by modern institutions of credit and marketing, to stabilise ownership of land, and to maintain minimum wages, have by no means succeeded in organising the production relations to control the degree of exploitation of the weaker section. Nor have the Government solved the problems of low productivity, poverty unemployment and under-employment. The Census basically measures the level of employment of men and tends to ignore the inter-changeable roles of women as housewives and gainful workers.

Women folk as a whole and agricultural workers in particular face several kinds of exploitation. Many of them are unpaid family workers, both in family enterprises, and in wage employment where their contribution to the family earnings as helpers of the men earners in not always realised, or admitted. These unpaid family workers are predominantly women and children. Most of them fulfil dual roles by engaging in economic and household activity. More than half of the women who enter the labour force before the age of fifteen are unpaid family workers, as compared to one-third of the men in the same category. Gandhiji said that "Women is the companion of man gifted with equal mental capacities. She has the right to participate in the minutest details of the activities of man, and she has the same right of freedom and liberty as he... By sheer force of a vicious custom, even the most ignorant and worthless men have been enjoying a superiority over women which they do not deserve and ought not to have."[9] It has been argued that political equality is meaningless in a country where the mass of the population suffers from poverty, continuous threat of starvation, illiteracy, lack of health, and inequality of class, status and power. It is more so in the case of women who suffer from another dimension of inequality, namely, the weight of traditional attitudes that regard them as physically, intellectually and socially inferior to them.

The findings of the two studies of women construction workers—one of Patna[10] (covering 3 major projects), and the other in Delhi[11] (covering 9 construction sites) speak itself of the kind of exploitation that they suffer. "40 per cent of the Delhi respondents and 8.7 per cent of the Bihar respondents were 15 years of age"[12] employed as unskilled labourers for carrying earth, mortar or bricks, crushing bricks, all hard and strenuous work. 23.37 per cent of the Delhi group had continued working till the last day during pregnancy and 40.14 per cent till the 8th or 9th month.[13] This indicates that the provisions of the Contract Labour Act guaranteeing maternity leave have not been applied in the case of these women. Absence of a minimum health protection during pregnancy as well as continuous mal-nutrition has resulted in high infant mortality:

> 645 children had been born to these women but at the time of the survey only 389 of them were alive. For the Bihar group, out of 233 children born to these women 67 are dead, 29 of these died before reaching the age of 1 year,.. The Bihar study also reveals that the majority of the women continue to work even when they are ill rather than go without food for themselves and their dependents. Of the Delhi group, 30 who had suffered from some illness lasting more than 1 week, had received treatment in government dispensaries ann hospitals and 22 had been compelled to discontinue work for periods ranging from 4 days to 6 months. They did not receive any wages

during such absence. The other 8 continued to work during illness.[14]

The Bihar Government has also made regulations for controlling the terms and conditions of employment of the labour force employed by the contractors. "But it appears that most of these regulations are more honoured in the breach than in compliance."[15] The Delhi study reports further that though in most cases women earned as much as their husbands but they did not enjoy quality of status within the family. In this regard *Women in India:* Country Paper observes:

> Even when woman's income sustains the household, she is considered as a supplementary earner. This is in contrast to the many research findings which highlight the crucial role women play in their family's economy and well-being. The implications of this on women's status are far-reaching. Women are willing to take up any job to support the family. Without women's wages, many families would live below the subsistence level. The majority of women contribute up to 50 per cent of the family income. Yet, familial attitudes and social norms have relegated women to the status of supplementary earners.[16]

The status of women would improve if the existing gap between the laws relating to women, their property rights, guardianship rights and personal rights and their implementation is narrowed by educating women on the legal provisions relating to them, activising legal aid, particularly in the rural areas.

On the basis of the facts mentioned in this chapter regarding the problems with which women agricultural labourers are faced with, to sum up, this can be said that in Bihar agriculture, women are mostly employed as casual agricultural worker and hardly have the status of cultivators. They contribute to the family earning. They are compelled to seek work in their villages itself in both the peak and off seasons at a still lower wage. Most of them are landless workers and have a very low level of employment opportunity. The phenomena of unemployment, under employment and disguised unemployment is considerably prevalent amongst female casual agricultural workers than among their male counterparts. Female labourers in Bihar agriculture remain unemployed nearly for 133 days to 162 days for want to work. During *rabi* and summer seasons their employment position is still worst owing to the fact that transplantation operation is not performed during these two seasons.

So far the wages of women agriculture labour is concerned the differences in their wages are observed at many levels, viz., differences in wage between men and women agricultural labour difference in wages at operational levels and also difference in wages at regional level. The wage discrimination, i.e., the analysis of comparatively low wages of women agriculture labour than that of men confirms the discrimination more or less in almost all states including Bihar. So far operation-wise difference in wages is concerned, this difference is not uniformly pronounced in all states, but comparatively wages paid for reaping and sowing are higher than that of weeding in almost all states. The general wage level paid to all types of agricultural labourers (men, women and children) are comparatively low in Bihar and Madhya Pradesh in comparison to Punjab, Haryana and Tamil Nadu.

Though much intensive analysis of the levels of living, poverty and exploitation of women agricultural labour has not been done in this chapter due to the absence of secondary data on these aspects, some of the broader observations in these contexts discuss in the present chapter are the following:

Low labour utilisation, seasonal unemployment, landlessness and to a great extent their immobility are the causes of their poverty. This is further highlighted due to their helpless dependence caused by lack of adequate employment opportunities, limited skills and illiteracy.

With low wages and virtually at the bottom of the pyramid in status, with no scope for any improvement either in wages or the living and working condition the female agricultural labourers in Bihar are the worst in the real sense of the term. As regards the kind of work opportunities open to women working in the organised sector, very often the choice is made for them in the sense that they go for the type of work their parents or relatives are involved in.

They spend a large amount of their meagre income on cereals and yet their average intake of cereals is very poor. Women agricultural workers are the worst victims of exploitation. Wage differential is always maintained in their case. They do not have any social status and economic position.

However, it has already been pointed out that on such aspects as poverty and living condition of women agricultural labour in this chapter there is an awful paucity of quantitative data. To fill up this gap a field survey has been conducted to focus on these aspects and a detailed analysis of these aspects based on primary data is made in the next chapter.

While discussing the level of poverty, living and working condition and exploitation of women agricultural labour in Bihar in the previous chapter, the problem of non-availability of macro-level data on these aspects was confronted with on account of non-availability of these data and a gap in the analysis was felt. In the present chapter, an attempt has been made to fill up the gap of macro-level data with the micro-level data collected through a field survey.

The analysis of the present chapter is based on primary data related to various aspects of poverty, living and working conditions of women agricultural labour in North Bihar. A pilot study of 100 women agricultural labourers has been undertaken particularly in North Bihar because it provides a typical agrarian setting and is found appropriate for the study. In North Bihar also the district of West Champaran has been choosen just to compare and contrast the socio-economic problems of women agricultural labourers in two different settings, i.e., Tharu and non-Tharu settings in West Champaran. As Tharu population exists only in West Champaran so apparently there was no choice than to undertake the study in West Champaran. The case study of Tharu women agricultural labour vis-a-vis non-Tharu women agricultural labour was preferred due to basic differences in culture, creed, socio-economic adjustment and above all in overall perception of life. It was found interesting to study the status, the role and the mode of interaction in various socio-economic perspectives of women agricultural labourers in an women dominated system of Tharus on the one hand and non-Tharu family system with women's subordination on the other.

This chapter has its own analytical importance in the sense, it covers a very crucial dimension of the study which could not be covered by the official statistics available in Bihar.

For the socio-economic studies focussing on the problems and prospects of a neglected section of the agrarian community like women, it is the environment, the agro-economic situations, the institutional arrangements and the cross-currents of cultural forces and the family system which prepare a background for the analysis. It is with this view that a socio-economic profile of West Champaran district has been presented before analysing the phenomena at the sample level. After providing a socio-economic background of West Champaran district a specific section has been devoted to focus on Tharus—on the various aspects of their socio-economic life. This description of Tharus may help in understanding the typical emerging facts related to Tharu women agricultural labour in the subsequent analysis of this chapter. Finally, with a methodological note of the survey the various findings of the study on Tharu and non-Tharu women agricultural labourers in West Champaran district have been analysed and interpreted.

THE BACKGROUND—AGRO-ECONOMIC FEATURES

BRIEF HISTORY OF THE DISTRICT*

The district of Paschimi Champaran was created in the year 1972 as a result of reorganisation of the districts in the State. It was carved out of the old Champaran district. It was formerly a sub-division of Champaran District known as Bettiah Sub-division. It consists of 16 developed blocks. The district is bounded in the north by the hilly region of Nepal, on the south by Gopalganj district, on the west by Deoria district of Uttar Pradesh and on the east by Purbi Champaran district.

The District Gazetteer mentions Champaran as a corruption of Champa-arayan, i.e., the forest of Champa trees, a designation which is popularly believed to date back to the time when the district was a vast forest uninhabited except by solitary ascetics. The whole district is dotted with places held in religious esteem as the traditional abodes of Hindu *rishis,* such as, Valmiki, in whose hermitage Sita, the banished spouse of Lord Rama, is said to have taken shelter.

After the decline of the Videha empire, the district formed part of the Vrijjian oligarchical republic with its capital at Vaishali. The Lichchhavis were the most prominent of the clans which constituted the Vrijjian confederation. Ajatshatru the emperor of Magadh succeeded in subduing the Lichchhavis and occupying their capital at Vaishali. He extended his sovereignty over the present district of Paschimi Champaran which continued under the Mauryan rule for the next hundred years. Archaeological evidences pointing to the influence of the Sunga and Kanva culture have been found in the district.

* *District Gazetteer,* Champaran and District Census Handbook, 1971 and 1981.

The district thereafter formed part of the Kushan empire and later came under the Gupta empire though not much is known about the material culture of the district in that age. Along with Tirhut, the district was possibly annexed by Harsha during whose reign Hiuen Tsang, the famous Chinese pilgrim, visited India. The history of the district during the medieval period and the British period is linked with the history of Bettiah Raj.

The later history of the district is intimately connected with indigo plantation. Britain used to get supplies of indigo from her American colonies but this ceased after the War of Independence in 1776 as a result of which the colonies became free. This forced the British to fall back upon India for supplies of indigo. Many factories were set up by the Europeans in the indigo-producing areas of Bengal and Bihar. The Bettiah and Ramnagar gave leases of land to them for indigo cultivation on rather easy terms.

In the struggle for freedom the district played an important role and was among the outstanding districts in the state in regard to national movement.

Natural Division

The district consists of a few distinct tracts. The southern portion of the district is a flat alluvial plain but towards the north-west the surface is more undulating and rises gradually near the Nepal frontier. From the north-western corner a range of low hills extends in a south-easterly direction for a distance of some 32 Kms. Between this range and the Sumeshwar range which extends along the whole of the northern frontier lies the Dun valley. The northern portion is composed of old alluvium, and contains much lowland admirably suited for rice but unfit for the cultivation of *rabi* crops. It is a greatly rice-producing area traversed by a number of streams flowing south-wards.

The Gandak is the most important river of the district. It rises in the central mountain basin of Nepal known as Sapt-Gandaki from the seven streams which unite to form this river. After flowing for about 50 Kms. beyond the Indian border, the river descends to the plains at Tribeni, at its confluence with the Sonaha and the Panchnad. Being snow-fed, the Gandak is a torrential stream until it leaves the hills, after which it becomes wider and less turbulent. It is navigable up to Tribeni, timber being the chief product transported by river.

The Sikrahna is the second largest river in the district. It originates in the Chautarwa Chaur and flows in south-easterly direction through the central portion of the district till it turns south at Lakhaura, north of Motihari. The souther portion of the river is known as Burhi Gandak.

Climatic Conditions

The climate of the district of Paschimi Champaran is cooler and damper than the adjoining districts. The Terai area, comprising mainly Ramnagar, Bagaha and Narkatiaganj is unhealthy. Except in these tracts the climate is rather healthy in all other areas. Winter begins in November and lasts till February, followed by the hot summer months when the maximum temperature reaches up to 43°C. Rains set in during the latter part of June. The district receives some winter rain also.

Rainfall

The rainfall is heavier than most of the districts and is especially heavy in the submontane tract, partly owing to the heavy showers which fall when cyclonic storms break up on reaching the hills and partly because the monsoon is stronger towards the west over the parts of the district just under the hills. The normal annual rainfall in the district is about 56.

DEMOGRAPHIC FEATURES

Table 39.10 provides demographic features and other detailed information related to population of West Champaran district in the background of related informations on Bihar State as a whole. As shown in the Table 39.10 the total population of Paschimi Champaran district is 2.82 per cent (1,972,610) of the total population of Bihar State (69,914,734). Table also shows rural-urban differentials in population. As indicated in the table in both rural and urban areas of Paschimi Champaran and also in Bihar as a whole the percentage of female population is comparatively low (ranging between 45 per cent to 49 per cent) than male population (50 per cent to 55 per cent. The decennial population growth rate (1971-81) is +24.06 per cent in the state of Bihar and +24.30 per cent in the district of Paschimi Champaran.

TABLE 39.10

Population Statistics—At a Glance of Paschimi Champaran District

		Bihar State	*Paschimi Champaran District*
1	*2*	*3*	*4*
Population			
Total	Persons	69,914,734	1,972,610 (2.82%)
	Males	35,930,560 (51.39%)	1,032,033 (52.32%)
	Females	33,984,174 (48.61%)	940,577 (47.68%)
Rural	Persons	61,195,744	1,828,062
	Males	31,170,556 (50.83%)	954,582 (52.21%)
	Females	30,025,188	873,480
Urban	Persons	8,718,990	144,548
	Males	4,760,004 (54.59%)	77,451 (53.58%)
	Females	3,958,986 (45.41%)	67,097 (46.42%0
Decennial Population Growth Rate			

1	2	3	4
	1971-1981	+24.06	+24.30
Area (Sq. Kms.)		173,877,00	5,228.00
Density of Population (Per sq. km.)		402	377
Sex Ratio (Number of Females per 1000, Males		946	911
Literacy Rate	Persons	26.20	18.79
	Males	38.11	27.76
	Females	13.62	8.94
Percentage of Scheduled	Persons	14.51	14.74
Castes Population to	Males	14.36	14.47
Total Population	Females	14.67	15.04
Percentage of Scheduled Tribes	Persons	8.31	1.36
Population to Total	Males	8.11	1.34
Population	Females	8.52	1.38
Number of Occupied Residential Houses		9,891,123	300,967
Number of Villages	Total	79,208	1,505
	Inhabited	67,546	1.363
	Uninhabited	10,302	133
Constituents of Towns		1,360	9
Number of Towns		220	4

Source: Paschimi Champaran District Census Hand-Book, 1981.

As regards the literacy rate, it is 26.20 per cent in Bihar and 18.7 per cent in the district of Paschimi Champaran. It is 38.11 per cent in the case of males in Bihar while it is 27.76 per cent in the case of males in the district of Paschimi Champaran what is most disturbing is comparatively very low female literacy rate i.e., 13.62 per cent and 8.94 per cent in Bihar and in Paschimi Champaran respectively.

Further, while percentage of females belonging to Scheduled Caste and Scheduled Tribe in Bihar is 14.67 per cent and 8.52 per cent, in case of West Champaran these figures are 15.04 per cent and 1.38 per and respectively.

Table 39.11 shows the distribution of main workers as cultivators, agricultural labourers, household industry and other workers in Paschimi Champaran district (1971-81). While the percentage of male cultivators is 38.82 per cent, the percentage of female cultivator turn out to be as less as 7.39 per cent only in 1971. Census 1981 shows a definite in the percentage of both male and female cultivators, i.e., 41.38 per cent and 11.76 per cent respectively. On the other hand, the number of male agricultural labourers has decreased from 48.42 per cent in

1971 to 44.94 per cent in 1981. In case of female agricultural labourers also a decline from 88.69 per cent in 1971 to 83.00 per cent in 1981 is observed. But no substantial rise in the number of workers in household industries is seen in both the years. It is 1.89 per cent in the case of male and 1.28 per cent in case of female in 1971 and 1.94 per cent in case of male and 1.28 per cent in the case of female in the year 1981.

TABLE 39.11

Distribution of Main Workers by Cultivators, Agricultural Labourers, Household Industry and Other Workers in Paschimi Champaran District (1971-81)

		1971	*1981*
1	2	3	4
Cultivators	Male	38.82	41.38
	Female	7.39	11.76
Agricultural Labourers	Male	48.42	44.94
	Female	88.69	83.00
Household Industry	Male	1.89	1.94
	Female	1.28	1.49
Other Workers	Male	10.87	11.74
	Female	2.64	3.75

Note: Percentage of main workers in Agricultural, Household Industry and other workers to total workers in Paschimi Champaran.

Source: Census of India 1981, India, Workers and Non-Workers, Provisional Population, p. 92.

Agriculture

Paschimi Champaran ranks predominantly as an agricultural district in the *Mithila* plain. In the past, the agricultural economy was very colourful and varied. Even during the scarcity year of 1873, more than a century ago, the rice at Bagaha was sold "at nine seers a rupee".[1] Apart from the natural causes, the agricultural economy dwindled down due to prolonged negligence of land by the East India Company and their agents who forcibly introduced *Dadan* (advance payments) for indigo plantation and to achieve their colonial interests.

Truly, agriculture supports most of the food requirements and provides employment to the overwhelming proportion of the rural population. The success or failure of the main crops is interlinked with the geographical conditions of the area concerned. Out of the total 5.6 lakh hectares[2] of geographical area of the district, 3.3 lakh hectares are devoted to agricultural persuits.

Eighty-two thousand hectares of lands are under forests and 3,88,000 hectares of lands are put under variety of crops. Of all the crops, rice dominates (3,12,714 hectares) following by wheat (43,066 hectares), sugarcane (55,949) hectares) and other crops including vegetables and fruits. Besides, oil seeds, jute, tobacco are also grown in small proportions. Indigo and poppy cultivation are completely died out.

The per capital availability of land declined from 0.36 hectares in 1951 to 0.03 hectares in 1961 and 1971 and to 0.24 hectares in 1981, considerably lower than the State average (0.37 hectares). The per capita agricultural holding is 0.20 hectares as compared to 0.17 hectares for the State of Bihar. There are altogether four main agricultural seasons, viz., *Bhadai* (September-October), *Agahani* (November-December), *rabi* (March-April) and *Garma* (July-August). Owing to improvement in methods and agricultural financing facility, supply of good seeds, manures and fertilisers, protection of livestocks, better irrigational facilities, the very face of Paschimi Champaran is gradually changing. Moreover with the implementation of the Bihar Land Reforms Act (1950), and the *Bhoodan Andolan* (Movement, 1954), the agrarian problems have been reduced. Under the Five Year Plan programmes, a number of Development Blocks/*Anchals*, have been instituted all over the district for betterment and advancement of agrarian conditions of the rural people.

General Landuse

The land, one of the natural resources, provides facility for cultivation, grazing, orchards, habitation, transport line, factory sites, etc. For the current understanding of the use of the lands it is necessary to study the same with the following figures for the year 1977-78.[3]

TABLE 39.12

Landuse Pattern of Paschimi Champaran (1977-78)

Broad heads under land	*Area in hectares ('000)*	*Percentage of the total area*
1. **Land not Available for Cultivation**	152	31.40
(i) Forest	82	16.94
(ii) Land put to non-agricultural uses	50	10.33
(iii) Barren/Ushar etc.	20	4.13
2. **Cultivable Waste Land**	57	11.78
(i) Land under miscellaneous trees and groves	10	2.07
(ii) Other fallow land	8	1.66
(iii) Current fallow	34	7.02
(iv) Permanent pasture and other grazing land	2	0.41
(v) Cultivable wastes	3	0.62
3. **Area Sown**	388	80.16
(i) Net sown area	275	56.82
(ii) Double cropped area	113	23.35

It has already been mentioned that nearly 82,000 hectares of land are under forest. Recently the local authorities have implemented various schemes such as, Vana Mahotsava (Tree Plantation), conservation of forests and wild life sanctuaries.

Land not available for cultivation may be grouped into: (a) non-agricultural use, (b) barren, *ushar* and uncultivable land. The former accounts for 50,000 hectares (10.33 per cent) whereas the latter covers 20,000 hectares (4.13 per cent of the total area of the district (Table 39.12).

It has been observed that his type of land covers "a wide range of *usher*" including all lands under human habitations, factories, communication or under water. Such land is bound to increase in view of the extent of growing industrialisation and the growth of population and the gradual expansion of the cultural landscape.

Other uncultivable lands include permanent pastures, land under miscellaneous trees and groves, other fallow, current fallow, grazing grounds and culturable wastes. The percentage of pastures is high in the Madhubani and Mainatar blocks. The Terai also shows the high percentage of pasture lands. The cultural waste lands, however, accounts for 57,000 hectares of which Sidhaw, Bagaha, Mainatar, ramnagar, Gaunaha and Sikta blocks share considerable proportion of waste lands.[4]

TABLE 39.13

Cropping Pattern in West Champaran District

Name of the crops	*% area under crops*
1	2
Rice	34.00
Maize	15.88
Wheat	25.02
Barley	0.77
Gram	1.35
Arhar	5.28
Masoor	—
Foodgrains	82.31
Sugarcane	10.49
Potato	2.15
Sweet Potato	5.03
Commercial Crops	17.68
All Crops	100.00

Source: An unpublished Report—Economic Analysis of Rural Structure of North Bihar (An ICSSR Projects by Dr. S.P. Sinha, 1976), p. 79.

It will not be out of place to record about the acreage of land under different seasonal crops. Out of 3,88,000 hectares of cropped land, the Agahani crop (1,52,000 hectares) shares the highest proportion, followed by Rabi (1,08,000 hectares), Bhadai (1,01,000 hectares), Garma (18,000 hectares) and orchards (9,000 hectares). It may be noted that more than half of the cropped lands are irrigated. To cope with the pressure of population of the district, the introduction of multi-cropping, with an aid of irrigation and other infrastructure, is possible the only panacia to tackle the situation.

Table 39.13 shows the cropping pattern in West Champaran district. As indicated in the Table 39.13 foodgrains cover 82.31 per cent of the total cropped area whereas commercial crops over only 17.68 per cent of the total cropped area. Thus, the cropping pattern of the district is dominated by foodgrains. Further, in foodgrains rice emerges as the most prominant crop covering 34 per cent of the total cropped area alone. Next to rice it is wheat followed by maize covering 25.02 per cent and 15.88 per cent respectively. Pulses cover very negligible area. Among commercial crops the major crop is sugarcane covering 10.49 per cent of the total cropped area followed by sweet potato (5.03%).

Irrigation

Paschimi Champaran is one of the major agricultural districts in the North Bihar plain. The vagaries of monsoon often play *havoc* with the agricultural practices. Irrigation is, therefore, an urgent need of the district. Considering the configuration of the area, natural drainage system, distribution of rainfall, water-table, quality of soil, etc., the agricultural crops of the area require an artificial supply of water. The northern part of the district which is composed of *Bangar* soil needs irrigation in particular. The different kinds of irrigational schemes have been executed recently by the State Government. Out of 3.3 lakhs hectares of gross cropped area 90 thousand hectares of land were irrigated in 1971. The Gandak Project—a symbol of international co-operation between Nepal and India, is one of the largest, River Valley Projects of Bihar. This will enable to irrigate about 3.08 lakh hectares of land. The construction of the Gandak Barrage at Valmikinagar started as early as 1964 with the following schemes: (a) the construction of 734.84 Km. long barrage, (b) excavation of eastern (248 Km.) and western canals (192 Km.), and (c) hydro-electric power station at Nepal.

The Tribeni Canal, total length being 148.8 Km. takes off from the Gandak river at Bhainsalotan, near the Tribeni village in the Sidhaw block. The canal was opened for irrigation at a cost of Rs. 75 lakhs on the 7th June 1909 as a famine relief measure after the great Bengal famine (1896). This canal has proved to be of great value to this district, specially during the drought years. The extension of this canal has increased the total area under its command to 1.65 lakh hectares of land. With the completion of all expansion and extension projects, this canal is expected to cover more irrigated lands. With the commissioning of the Tirhut Canal, vast area lying in the Gandak-Sikrahana *Doab*, are now irrigated. This is a revolutionary step by the State authority for improving agricultural condition.

Apart from the canal irrigation, a number of electric tubewells (299 including pump sets), medium and minor irrigation schemes have also been sanctioned by the State Government. One of the striking features of irrigation is the limited use of wells (5,537). From the irrigation point of view, the worst affected areas are the northern part of the *Duns* and *Tharughat* where Government extending tubewell irrigation facility to the local people for their betterment.

Tenancy

The District Gazetteer describes the land revenue administration of the district as the one owned mainly by a few big proprietors, with a small number of petty revenue-free properties, and with few subordinate tenures. The greater part of the property was held by three states, viz., the Bettiah Raj, the Madhuban Estate and the Ramnagar Raj. Petty proprietors were fairly numerous in Madhuban, Dhaka and Kesaria, but everywhere else the Bettiah Raj and a few big Zamindars predominated.

There were only three very small Government estates under direct management. Of the three, two estates were originally Government camping grounds being unconditional gifts from the Madhuban Estate. These camping grounds, which were adjacent, were found to have been cultivated by tenants who paid no rent. They were consequently brought on the revenue roll and rent was collected by the collectorate staff. A large number of the tenures found in the district were held by concerns, whose business was previously the cultivation and manufacture of indigo. Of the *bakasht* area a large proportion had been settled with tenants. In addition since indigo the area directly cultivated by *mukarraridas* and *thikadars* had decreased, as they found it more advantageous to settle the outlying bakasht lands with tenants rather than cultivate these directly.

Mines and Minerals

The Dun and Sumeshwar hills in the extreme north are formed of ill-compacted sand stone, by the bare stony beds of the water courses down which the streams rush with considerable force in the rains. There are beds of *Kankar* in parts of the district and saltpetre is found almost everywhere.

Industrialisation

The proportion of persons dependent for their living on industries is small. The District has no important manufacturing towns. The manufacture of indigo, which has formerly the principal industry of the district, has now come to an end. The manufacture of sugar is the only remaining industry of any importance in the district. Besides there are a few rice-mills working in the district.

THE THARUS—SOCIO-ECONOMIC STATUS

The Tharus of West Champaran, and aboriginal tribe, made scattered settlements in the border areas of India adjoining Nepal. The Tharus now number about 90,000[5] in parts of Bagaha, Ramnagar, Sikarpur and Mainatar police stations of West Champaran district. All these areas are contiguous to Nepal Terai. They live in an area extending over 800 Square miles on the Northern border, bounded on the North-East and West by Nepal and on the

South by the Tribeni Canal. This area is known as Tharuhat.

The physical features of the Tharus are mongoloid. The women are more comely and energetic than the men. The women look much more intelligent. The Tharus are very fond of meat and fish. They tend cows, but never milch them. Fond of drinking, they often brew their own liquour from State cooked rice. Their craze for liquor has ruined many families. The language they speak is more or less Bhojpuri Hindi.

The Tharu women do not observe *purdah*. The present day Tharu girl of higher income group has taken more quickly to modern make-up and dress. The influence of the modernised Nepalese girls are quite apparent on the Tharus. They are fond of songs and dancing, but no Tharu women have been known to stage a communal public dance like the Adivasi women of Chotanagpur. They are artistic in temperament and have a good idea of colour and pattern scheme for their knitting, sewing and household work. They are good house-wives and home-proud.

Superior Status of Tharu Women

Till a decade or two back, a Tharu women would hesitate to partake of any food that has been eaten by any male member of her family. She would not even allow a male to enter into her kitchen. There is no doubt, that this complex is now liquidating itself but even today there are some ladies who observe these taboos. This taboo is very much contrary to the usual set up of a Hindu family life and suggests the higher caste complex in the women. Thus, the Tharu women have a dominant position in the society. They form 90 per cent of the crowd in markets and fairs. The women move about freely, and even smoke and drink in the Bazar. Fishing is feminine occupation and outdoor activity such as marketing produce, buying and selling, and business negotiations are also done by women. The women fish and hunt. They are expert painters and decorators; the paint pictures and scenes depicting fights and warriors on horseback.

Sub-Caste of Tharus and their Caste-Status

The closer analysis of the Tharus as a tribe shows that there are sub-castes with occupational nomenculture. A sub-caste of the Tharus, namely, Gaurihara was originally incharge of the maintenance of the cows, the word 'Gau' being a Hindu version of 'cow'. Similarly, another sub-caste 'Diswas', served as the scavengers, the word 'Disa' being the local term for night-soil. Originally divided amongst 60 to 70 sub-caste known as 'Gaurihara', Rautar, Bantar, Khausia, Diswa, etc., it is now difficult for many of them to disclose a complete list of the sub-castes. There is not much of watertightness amidst these sub-castes like their counterparts in the more orthodox Hindu community. It is significant that there is no care of caste-hierarchy among the Tharus.

Social and Family Organisation

In spite of the impact of the modern trends the Tharus have still their traditional head of the village known as *Gumasta*. The *Gumasta* is elected, but once elected, the office becomes hereditary unless a particular incumbent is considered misfit. An unsuccessful *gumasta* can also be removed by the villagers. The *gumasta* with the help of the influential members of the village would settle the family disputes of the Tharus and impose fine upon the defaulting persons. This fine is pooled, kept in custody and utilised for social purposes. The Tharus are not quarrelsome by nature and seldom use strong language. Their petty quarrels are often decided by the *Gumastas.*

Joint family system is still the rule. Every joint family has a Master *(malik)* and a Mistress *(malkin)* of the house. Usually the son succeeds the father and takes up the family responsibility. It is remarkable that the servants of a well-to-do Tharu family like ploughmen or herdsmen live as members of the family. They eat along with the other members of the family in the same dining groom and share the common food.

Social System

The Tharus have still a few indigenous customs and manners. Whenever a Tharu comes from outside he touches the hands of all the persons present by going round. They marry in their own clan or *gotra* and exchange of boys and girls with two families is a common form of marriage. This often leads to a disparity of age of the bride and the bridgeroom. Child marriage is common. The marriage negotiations among Tharus normally start from the bridegroom's side. The custom will also underline the superiority-complex of the Tharu women. The economic status of the bridgeroom is carefully appraised before a marriage is fixed.

Polygamy is prevalent to a limited extent. Widow marriage is quite common but marrying a brother's wife is a taboo. There is no recognised system of divorce but usually this is brought about by the girl's refusal to live with her husband and she is married to another man of the same clan and the husband has to pay a fine for being a misfit for the girl. The society and the families of the Tharus are comparatively free from a large number of taboos and this has led to remarkable resilience which has kept up the solidarity of the Tharu society. A Tharu woman has her social status and civil rights according to tradition and custom.

Economic Condition

The economic condition of the average Tharu is quite unsatisfactory. Nearly 20 per cent of the Tharus have some land and the rest are landless labourers. They have been too much exploited by the non-Tharu businessmen and moneylenders. The simplicity and the improvident habits of the Tharus have been fully exploited by the *mahajans* and the incidence of indebtedness of the Tharus is very high. Many of the Tharuhat areas are still without proper communication. During the harvesting season when the crops are being gathered, a large number of itinerary shopkeepers open their shope within Tharuhat and sell cheap trinkets and other attractive articles which take away most of their money. They are not very hard working and have not taken to any technical avocation.

THE SOCIO-ECONOMIC CONDITION OF THARU AND NON-THARU WOMEN AGRICULTURAL LABOUR IN WEST CHAMPARAN—A CASE STUDY

For a comparative study of socio-economic conditions and for an economic analysis of the level of employment, wages and exploitations of women agricultural labour of Tharu and non-Tharu areas of West Champaran district a field survey was conducted. The details of the methodological considerations adopted in the survey are the following:

The Sample Design

For this comparative study, naturally the two samples, one from the Tharu population and another from non-Tharu population were to be taken out. Tharu population is spread within one Block of the West Champaran district, i.e., Bagaha I. Therefore, Tharu sample was taken from Bagaha I Block. So far non-Tharu sample is concerned, it was preferred to take non-Tharu sample also from an adjacent Block with non-Tharu population so that for the comparison both the samples have a common socio-economic and agrarian setting. Bagaha II was found an appropriate Block for taking out non-Tharu sample.

Sample in both the Block was drawn using the technique of multi-staged random sampling. At the first stage one village from each Block, i.e., Tharhi from Bagaha I (Tharu) and Malpurva from Bagaha II Block (non-Tharu) was selected randomly. Further, a list of households having women agricultural labour was prepared for both the selected villages. At the second stage of sampling 50 households from each village were selected by simple random sampling method. Finally, women agricultural labourers in these two samples of the 10 per cent households (about 50 women agricultural labourers from each sample) were taken as respondents for the field survey. Thus, a total sample of 100 respondents were interviewed with the help of a well-constructed questionnaires with open ended, closed ended and attitudinal questions. After filling up the questionnaires the data were duly processed and a detailed tally processed and a detailed tally sheet was made out on the basis of their tally sheet. Finally different cross-section tables were constructed to test the various hypotheses related to socio-economic conditions and problems of women agricultural labourers.

The findings of the survey the discussed below with the help of the appropriate cross-section tables constructed on the basis of the data collected during survey.

Socio-economic Characteristics of the Sample

Before analysing and interpreting the major findings of the survey related to the levels of employment, income, living conditions, poverty etc., it seems proper to discuss first the socio-economic characteristics of the sample under study. Though socio-economic conditions, agro-economic situations and cultural setting of the West Champaran have been discussed in detail as a background of the study, here, only those socio-economic characteristics are discussed which are directly related with the sample as such and have great relevance in interpreting other findings of the survey.

Age Structure

Table 39.14 shows the distribution of respondents of both Tharu and non-Tharu samples in different age groups (15-25 years, 25-35 years and 35 years and above).

TABLE 39.14

The Age Structure

Age Groups/ Sample	*15 to 25 years*	*25 to 35 years*	*35 years and above*	*Total*
Tharu sample	10	17	23	50
	(20.00)	(34.00)	(46.00)	(100.00)
Non-Tharu sample	4	14	32	50
	(8.00)	(28.00)	(64.00)	(100.00)
Total sample	14	31	55	100

Note: Figures in parentheses show percentage.

As indicated in Table 39.14 maximum number of women agricultural labourers both in Tharu (46 per cent) and non-Tharu (64 per cent) samples come in the age group of 35 years and above. The minimum number of women agricultural labour come from 15 to 25 years of age group, i.e., 20 per cent in the Tharu and 8 per cent in non-Tharu samples. It may be due to the tendency of avoiding to send young girls to the field due to social taboo. As this taboo is much more strong in non-Tharu society, therefore, in the case as less as 8 per cent go to the field. In the age group of 25-35 years the number of women agricultural labour is almost same, i.e., 17 in Tharu sample and 14 in non-Tharu sample.

Nature of Family

Table 39.15 shows the nature and pattern of family prevalent in Tharu and non-Tharu society under study.

TABLE 39.15

Age Structure

Nature of Family/ Sample	*Single*	*Joint*	*Total*
1	2	3	4
Tharu sample	29	21	50
	(58.00)	(42.00)	(100.00)
Non-Tharu sample	34	16	50
	(68.00)	(32.00)	(100.00)
Total	63	37	100

Note: Figures in parentheses show percentage.

Table 39.15 shows the percentage of households in the two samples having single and joint nature of family. The concept of 'single' family is that of unit family consisting of husband, wife and children whereas a joint family consists of father, mother, brothers sisters and cousins also. There is a general tendency of breaking joint family in the modern society. The tendency is duly confirmed with 58 per cent of the households in Tharu sample and 68 per cent in non-Tharu sample having single or unit family. However, the norm and value of joint family is much maintained in Tharu society with 42 per cent of households still having joint family system.

Caste Structure

Caste system has its great importance and implications in the traditional society of Bihar. Caste is an important variable to explain the different socio-economic aspects of agrarian community. In the sample under present study, the Tharu sample represents a typical agrarian community with no particular caste consideration as is usually prevalent in Bihar. Of course, this has its own stratification in the society but entirely on different line which has no comparison with the case system in general in Bihar.

TABLE 39.16

The Caste Structure

Caste Group/ Non-Tharu Sample	*Upper Backward*	*Lower Backward*	*Scheduled Caste*	*Other Caste*	*Total*
Non-Tharu Sample	4 (8.00)	33 (66.00)	6 (12.00)	7 (14.00)	50 (100.00)

Note: Figures in parentheses show percentage.

Table 39.16 therefore, does not reflect any caste classification in case of Tharu sample. The caste groups mentioned in table for non-Tharu sample are "upper backward", "lower backward", "Scheduled Caste" and others (For details of the castes in different groups please see Appendix-III). As indicated in the Table 39.16 as many as 66 per cent of the total women agricultural labour come lower backward groups which is but natural, because castes in lower backward group constitute weaker section of the society and women in these castes have no option than to earn their livelihood along with their male members. Like upper castes, these castes do not have any social inhibition or taboo in permitting their house-wives for activities and employment in the field. The Table 39.16 shows only 12 per cent of the women agricultural labour coming from Scheduled Caste group which may be due to smaller number of households in this group in the village under study. Only 8 per cent of the women agricultural labour coming from upper backward group is an indication of their better socio-economic conditions in the village under study.

Marital Status

As indicated earlier, while discussing age structure, it is pointed out that there is a tendency not to send young girls, particularly unmarried girls, for employment in the fields.

This is very much evident from Table 39.17 which also shows marital status of women agricultural labour under study.

TABLE 39.17

The Marital Status

Marital Status/ Sample	*Married*	*Widow*	*Total*
Tharu sample	38	12	50
	(76.00)	(24.00)	(100.00)
Non-Tharu sample	39	11	50
	(78.00)	(22.00)	(100.00)
Total	77	23	100

Note: Figures in parentheses show percentage.

As indicated in Table 39.17 women agricultural labourers both in Tharu and non-Tharu samples are either married or widow. None of the women agricultural labour was found unmarried in the sample under study. As shown in Table 39.17, out of 50 women agricultural labourers in each of the Tharu and non-Tharu samples 29 (78 per cent) were found married and 11 (22 per cent) widow in non-Tharu sample whereas 38 (76 per cent) were found married and 12 (24 per cent) widow in Tharu sample. Thus, marital status of women agricultural labourers in both the samples is almost similar.

Land Ownership Pattern

While discussing socio-economic characteristics of the sample it seems essential to know as to what percentage of women agricultural labour come from the families having land base and what percentage from the landless. Because whether caste indicates the social status it is land which acts as an indicator of economic status in the rural areas.

As indicated in Table 39.18, 62 per cent of the total agricultural labour in Tharu sample and 66 per cent in non-Tharu sample come from landless households. Even the households of the women agricultural labourers having land, in fact, have very little land. This is confirmed by the fact that all such households in both the samples have land less than ' acre except one in the case of non-Tharu sample which has land between 1 to 2 acres. This table goes to confirm that it is the state of landlessness which compel women in the rural areas to come-out in the fields and to earn their livelihood. As pointed out above whatever little land base they have, is quite insufficient for their subsistence.

Occupation Pattern

In spite of some land base with some of the households under study, not a single women turned out to be a cultivator in the sample under study. This conveys the utter subordination of women as housewife inside the family and as agricultural labourer in the field. This is trure to both Tharu and non-Tharu samples. However, in Tharu sample as per Tharu culture, women have dominance but only in the process of decision-making. In the provisions of the rules, it is again the male proprietorship which works. That is why in Tharu sample, in spite of the dominance of women at all levels and for all practical purposes, it is male members who have been reported as cultivators. So far occupational diversity of agricultural labourers is concerned, women agricultural labour in Tharu area have a parallel opportunity to work as labourers in "stone breaking" and "head-load carriage work". They get some employment opportunity as labourers in forest industry also. But in this respect the case of women agricultural labourers in non-Tharu area is harder. Women agricultural labourers in non-Tharu areas have hardly any off-farm employment opportunity. So far spatial immobility of women agricultural labourers for employment is concerned uniformly all the women agricultural labourers in both Tharu and non-Tharu areas did not show any preference to move outside village for seeking employment. In comparison to male agricultural labourers, it is immobility on the part of women agricultural labourers which makes their lot more limited and poor.

TABLE 39.18

The Land Ownership Pattern

Land Ownership Group/ Sample	*Without land*	*Less than 1 acres*	*1—2 acres*	*Total*
Tharu sample	31	19	—	50
	(62.00)	(38.00)	—	(100.00)
Non-Tharu sample	33	16	1	50
	(66.00)	(32.00)	(2.00)	(100.00)
Total sample	81	18	1	100

Note: Figures in parentheses show percentage.

Employment and Wages

For the casual labour class the most important indicator of their economic condition and well-being are the level of employment opportunities they have and the level of wages they get as their remuneration. Table 39.19 shows the availability of employment in mandays and the level of wages in Rupees per manday for both male and female agricultural labourers in the areas under study.

TABLE 39.19

Level of Wages and Employment

Employment Groups/ Sample	*Wage level (in Rs.)*		*Below 100 days a year*	*100-150 days*	*150-200 days*	*200-250 days*	*250-300 days*	*Total*
	M	*F*						
Tharu sample	10	5	—	1	3	20	26	50
				(2.00)	(6.00)	(40.00)	(52.00)	(100.00)
Non-Tharu sample	8	4	—	—	6	44	—	50
					(12.00)	(88.00)		(100.00)
Total	18	9	—	1	9	64	26	100

Note: Figures in parentheses show percentage.

Table 39.19 clearly shows Tharu women agricultural labourers having employment for larger number of days than non-Tharu women agricultural labourers. As indicated in the table, 52 per cent of Tharu women agricultural labour get employment between 250 to 300 days in a year (almost fully employed* throughout the year), 40 per cent of the rest get employment between 200 to 250 days and only 8 per cent are such who get employment between 100 to 200 days. Whereas in case of non-Tharu sample not a single agricultural labour reported getting employment for more than 250 days a year, 88 per cent reported availability of employment between 200 to 250 days and 12 per cent getting employment between 100 to 200 days only. This greater employment opportunity in the case of Tharu women agricultural labour is, as pointed out earlier, due to parallel off-farm employment opportunities like stone breaking, head-load carriage and wood cutting in forest industry. These types of employment opportunities for women agricultural labour are completely absent in non-Tharu village under study leading to the non-availability of employment to them particularly during lean seasons of the years.

As further indicated in Table 39.19, there is a wage differential between men and women agricultural labourers in both Tharu and non-Tharu villages under study. While in Tharu villages male agricultural labourers get Rs. 10 per day as wage, women agricultural labourers get Rs. 5 per day only. In non-Tharu village the prevailing wage rate for men in Rs. 8 per day and for women Rs. 4 per day. Thus, in both the villages women get just 50 per cent what men get as wage. This is a glaring example of acute exploitation and worst lot of women agricultural labourers in the area under study. Analysis of Table 39.6 does not show such a wide difference between the wages of men and women agricultural labour in case of Bihar in any other state.

So far wage level to men and women agricultural labourers in general is concerned as shown in Table 39.19 in Tharu area wage level is somewhat higher than non-Tharu area though the difference is not very considerable.

Level of Income and Expenditure

The levels of income and expenditure are the direct indicators of the economic condition and standard of living of any class or person. The present section is devoted to the analysis of the levels of income and expenditure of women agricultural labourers of both Tharu and non-Tharu areas under study. For the purpose two sets of data are used—one set of data shows the level of income and expenditure at family level (Table 39.20 and 39.21), and another set of data shows the individual income level of women agricultural labourers from both agricultural and non-agricultural sources (Table 39.22, 39.23 and 39.24). As poverty is a concept to be generally analysed at household level, therefore, the poverty dimension with the help of income-expenditure data has been analysed at household level with the held of the tables, as mentioned earlier, i.e., Tables 39.20 and 39.21. Further, to show the ratio of

* Any person working 8 hours a day for 273 days of the year is regarded as employed on a standard person-year basis. In the area under study generally men and women agricultural labourers are in practice of working for 9 to 10 hours a day in the field.

agricultural and non-agricultural income of the individual women agricultural worker with a view to focus on their income avenues inside and outside agriculture, the individual data is used as per Tables 39.22, 39.23 and 39.24.

Poverty Dimension

The modern approach of poverty analysis is based on the concept of "poverty line". Poverty line is drawn from different criteria viz., income, expenditure and calorie intake. The most common method of drawing poverty line is based on income criteria. The concept of poverty line is very much used by the Planning Commission also to locate population below poverty line. During Sixth Five Year Plan, Rs. 3500 per annum at the then prices was used as a criteria of drawing poverty line. During Seventh Five Year Plan, in view of the price rise, the level of poverty line has been raised from Rs. 3500 to Rs. 4800 per annum.

Table 39.20 shows the distribution of households under different income groups both in Tharu and non-Tharu areas. As indicated in the table 39.20 taking Rs. 3500 per annum as the criteria of poverty line, 24 per cent of the households in Tharu sample and 44 per cent of households in non-Tharu sample turn out to be below poverty line. Further, taking Seventh Plan criteria of Rs. 4800 per annum at current prices as the limit of poverty line as many as 72 per cent and 76 per cent respectively of women agricultural labourers may be called below poverty line approximately as their income limit is Rs. 5000 just Rs. 200 per annum more than the Seventh Plan poverty line criteria, i.e., Rs. 4800 per annum. This shows that there is excessive poverty among women agricultural labour in the backward area under study of the backward state of Bihar. This is further confirmed by the fact that the Bihar state level percentage of population below poverty line is (57.49) somewhat lesser than the respective figures given above for the Tharu and non-tharu areas under study.

THE RATIO OF AGRICULTURAL AND NON-AGRICULTURAL INCOME

As pointed out earlier, the very purpose of discussing the ratio of agricultural and non-agricultural income is to focus on the avenues of the off-farm employment of women agricultural labour in the areas under study.

TABLE 39.20

Level of Income

Income Groups/ Sample	*Upto 2500*	*2500-3500*	*3500-5000*	*5000-7500*	*7500-10000*	*10000 and above*	*Total*
Tharu sample	5	7	24	11	2	1	50
	(10.00)	(14.00)	(48.00)	(22.00)	(4.00)	(2.00)	(100.00)
Non-Tharu sample	4	18	16	12	—	—	50
	(8.00)	(36.00)	(32.00)	(24.00)			(100.00)
Total Sample	9	25	40	23	2	1	100

Note: Figures in parentheses show percentage.

Table 39.21 shows the number and percentage of households having non-agricultural income and the ratios of their non-agricultural income to agricultural income. As indicated in the table as many as 56 per cent of households in Tharu area have women workers getting off-farm employment whereas only 6 per cent of households in non-Tharu samples have women workers with the opportunity of off-farm employment. While discussing occupational pattern earlier, it has already been pointed out that in Tharu area employment opportunities like stone breaking, head load carriage and wood cutting in forest are very much available for women and workers whereas women workers in non-Tharu area under study are completely deprived of such avenues. These 3 non-Tharu agricultural labourers who have reported non-agricultural income do domestic services in the houses of their landlords.

TABLE 39.21

Level of Non-Agricultural Income as Percentage of Agricultural Income

Non-agricultural Income Groups/ sample	*No. of households having non-agricultural income*	*Non-agricultural Income as percentage of agricultural income*	
		5 to 15%	*15 to 25%*
Tharu sample	23 (56.00)	7 (30.43)	16 (69.56)
Non-Tharu sample	3 (6.00)	2 (66.66)	1 (33.33)
Total sample	26	9	17

Note: Figures in parentheses show percentage.

Table 39.21 clearly shows that in non-Tharu area and even in Tharu area where 56 per cent of the women agricultural labourers have income from stone breaking, head load carriage, etc. The ratio of non-agricultural income to their agricultural income is not high. Both in Tharu and non-Tharu samples none of the women agricultural labourers have non-agricultural income beyond the limit of 25 per cent of their agricultural income. In other words the maximum ratio of non-agricultural income to agricultural income is 25: 1000. Table 39.21 shows that almost 70 per cent of women agricultural labourers having non-agricultural income have their non-agricultural income as 15 to 25 per cent of their agricultural income. Out of 3 non-Tharu women agricultural labourers only one earns non-agricultural income as 15 to 25 per cent of their agricultural income. The rest of the two have non-agricultural income 5 to 15 per cent of their agricultural income.

Level of Expenditure

The concept of expenditure used here consists of only the items of consumption, viz., food, clothes, etc., (as shown in Table 39.23) just to forms on the standard of living of women agricultural labourers in the areas under study. The class interval used in different farm expenditure groups is similar to that of income groups (in Table 39.20) to show the relation between the ranges of income and expenditure of women agricultural labourers. A comparison of Table 39.20, i.e., income structure and Table 39.22, i.e., expenditure structure clearly shows that the number of households of a particular income group more or less coincide with the number of the same expenditure group. For example, while the percentage of households in income groups upto 2500, 2500 upto 3500, 3500 upto 5000, 5000 upto 7500, 7500 to 10,000 and 10,000 and above are 10, 14, 48, 22, 4, 2 percentages respectively, in expenditure groups also the percentage of households in these groups are almost the same as 10, 14,46, 24, 4 and 2 percentages respectively. In case of non-Tharu sample also, almost the same pattern can be observed. This shows that what is earned by these women agricultural labourers is just sufficient for their subsistence, having no margin in savings or capital formation at all.

TABLE 39.22

Level of Expenditure

Expenditure Groups/Sample	*Upto 2500*	*2500-3500*	*3500-5000*	*5000-7500*	*7500-10000*	*10000 and above*	*Total*
Tharu sample	5	7	23	12	2	1	50
	(10.00)	(14.00)	(46.00)	(24.00)	(4.00)	(2.00)	(100.00)
Non-Tharu sample	2	19	17	11	1	—	50
	(4.00)	(38.00)	(34.00)	(22.00)	(2.00)		(100.00)
Total sample	7	26	46	23	3	1	100

Table 39.23 shows the percentage of total expenditure spent on different items of consumption. As indicated in the table as much as 80 per cent of the total expenditure of Tharu women agricultural and 83.37 per cent of non-Tharu women agricultural labour is spent on food alone. This further confirms women agricultural labour under study creeping at the core of subsistence. Next to food, 13.21 per cent in Tharu area and 8.24 per cent in non-Tharu area is spent on clothes. Expenditure on the items like fuel, tea, *Bidi*, todday, cosmetics is quite negligible ranging between 1 per cent to 3 per cent of the total expenditure. Thus, this consumption pattern reflected in Table 39.23 presents a very pitiable picture of the lot, the poor agricultural labourers have in the areas under study.

TABLE 39.23

Pattern of Expenditure

(In Percentages)

Items/Sample	*Food*	*Fuel*	*Tea, Bidi and Toddy*	*Clothes*	*Domestic instruments*	*Cosmetics*	*Fair and Picture*	*Total*
Tharu	79.08	1.63	1.91	13.21	2.80	1.74	0.98	100.00
Non-Tharu	83.37	1.30	1.69	8.24	3.18	1.52	0.67	100.00

Level of Indebtedness

The above analysis shows that the earnings of the households of women agricultural labourers is just sufficient for bare subsistence but they have to meet several social obligations such as marriage, *Shradha* and treatment during illness (as Table 39.23 does not show any expenditure on medicine and treatment). Naturally, to meet these obligations they have to go to the shelter of moneylenders for debt.

Table 39.24 shows the number of households under debt and also the level of indebtedness. As indicated in the table only 26 per cent of the households in Tharu sample and 12 per cent in non-Tharu sample area such who are without debt and the rest in both the sample have the burden of debt. Table 39.24 further shows that a few households in Tharu area have debt upto the limit of Rs. 2500 only (68 per cent debt below Rs. 1000 and 6 per cent between Rs. 1000 to 2500). In non-Tharu sample of the level of indebtedness appears to be still far higher, with the limit of debt upto Rs. 5000 and even above. In non-Tharu sample when 36 per cent of the households have debt below Rs. 1000, 52 per cent between Rs. 1000 to 5000 and the rest of the 12 per cent having debt of Rs. 5000 and above. When asked about the purpose and source of the debt uniformly all respondents reported marriage, *shradha* and medical treatment as the main purpose of debt and village moneylender as the sole source of debt. For the debt they have to pay exorbitant rate of interest, i.e., around 25 per cent in all cases. The above analysis of the level of indebtedness clearly shows comparatively less burden of debt prevailing in case of Tharu area may be due to their better earnings from off-from employment and less expensive social customs.

THE LIVING AND WORKING CONDITION

In addition to the level of income and expenditure the living condition of a household can also be reflected by the assets they possess in the name of property. The landownership pattern (land being the most important asset) has already been discussed in detail in earlier section. Next to land the other common assets which agricultural labour class can possess are simple agricultural equipment like *Khurpi, Kudal* etc., cow, ox and in the name of other assets radio and cycle.

TABLE 39.24

Level of Indebtedness

Debt Groups/ Sample	*Without debt*	*Below 1000*	*1000-2500*	*2500-5000*	*5000 and above*	*Total*
Tharu sample	13	34	3	—	—	50
	(26.00)	(68.00)	(6.00)			
Non-Tharu sample	6	12	21	5	6	50
	(12.00)	(24.00)	(42.00)	(10.00)	(12.00)	
Total	19	46	24	5	6	100

Note: Figures in parentheses show percentage.

Table 39.25 shows the asset of property structure of women agricultural labour households with land and without land in Tharu and non-Tharu areas under study. As indicated in the Table the asset position of households with land in both the areas is better than those of without land. While 47.36 per cent, 94.73 per cent, 36.84 per cent and 52.63 per cent of households with land possess cow, ox, ratio and cycle respectively in Tharu area, the percentage of households possessing these assets in this area are 16.12 per cent, 16.12 per cent, 9.67 per cent and 19.35 per cent respectively. In non-tharu area also most the same pattern of asset ownership between the households with and without land exists with the difference that in non-Tharu area the assets like radio and cycle are found very less (no radio with any of the household without land). So far, agricultural equipment is concerned, cent per cent of the women agricultural labourers possessed some agricultural equipments, except non-Tharu women agricultural labour without land (only 39.39) per cent of them possess their own agricultural equipment). Table 39.25 further shows that where most of the women agricultural labour without land (80.64 per cent in Tharu and 61.53 per cent in non-Tharu area) possess agricultural equipments worth below Rs. 100. On the other hand, most of the women agricultural labourers with land (89.47 per cent in Tharu and 82.35 per cent in non-Tharu area) possess agricultural equipments of the value between Rs. 100 to 500. This is but natural because agriculture labourers without land need generally simple agricultural equipments like *Khurpi, Kudal*, etc., having price below Rs. 100. But these who have land must be needing at least wooden plough and other equipments having price in the range of Rs. 100 to 500. Overall the asset position in Tharu area is better may be due to the additional income from off-farm employment.

Working Condition

The working condition of women agricultural labour in the area under study in general is not very good. They work in the field for nearly 8 to 10 hours a day. For that they get a lower wage rate in comparison to their male counterpart for the same farm operation. The implementation of minimum wages is least effective in this area and under-employment is a chronic malady among the women agricultural labourers in the area under study. These landless wage-earners cannot afford to remain unemployed and that in order to survive they take up any work however, low the remuneration or productivity. The totality of this problem results in increasing pauperisation and abject poverty. The absence of village and cottage industries and the consequent loss of alternative employment as well as skills has resulted in occupational immobility.

The women agricultural wage-earners in the area under study (particularly in non-Tharu area) are doubly exploited. They are exploited in the field by their employers and get further exploited at the household level by their housekeepers). They work in the field for nearly 8 to 10 hours a day to supplement the family's meagre income and then they attend to their household or domestic chores. By doing jobs that are hard and underpaid, neither the society nor the employer value their working status. In spite of working and contributory to the family's income, women do not gain any status either in the family or in the society.

TABLE 39.25

Asset Structure

Asset structure/ Sample		*No. of households*	*Cow*	*Ox*	*Cycle*	*Radio*	*Agricultural Equipment*		
							No. of house-holds having agricultural equipment	*The value of Agri-cultural equipment*	
								Below Rs. 100	*Rs. 100-Rs. 500*
Without Land	Tharu	31 (100.00)	5 (16.12)	5 (16.12)	6 (9.67)	3 (19.35)	31 (100.00)	25 (80.64)	6 (19.35)
	Non-Tharu	33 (100.00)	8 (24.24)	3 (9.09)	2 (6.06)	—	13 (39.39)	8 (61.53)	5 (38.46)
Below than 1 Acre	Tharu	19 (100.00)	9 (47.36)	18 (94.73)	10 (52.63)	7 (36.84)	19 (100.00)	2 (10.52)	17 (89.47)
	Non-Tharu	17 (100.00)	15 (88.23)	6 (35.29)	6 (35.29)	2 (11.76)	17 (100.00)	3 (17.64)	14 (82.35)
Total		100	37	32	24	12	100	38	42

Note: Figures in parentheses show percentage.

The women agricultural wage-earner's contribution and commitment to the family is far greater than that of the men, judging by whatever standards. Whether it is in terms of commitment towards the children or of wage contribution, the women seen to shoulder a greater sense of responsibility. If one were to judge the commitment of these women to the family by the proportion of their wage or daily earnings which they take back home and compare it with what their husbands contributed, women's commitment is clearly larger than men's.

In the non-Tharu area under study, some of the women reported their husbands' addiction to alcoholic drinks and narcotics resulting at times to physical assault on them. Wages earned by them is never their. It goes into the pockets of their husbands, and they can seldom do anything of their choice with their own earning. This sort of exploitation is quite rare among the Tharu. The non-Tharu women respondents reported that though they earned and made a substantial contribution to the family's income, they did not enjoy equality of status within the family. They further reported that they had to show due deference to the male members of the family and took their meals only after the male members of the family had eaten. But this was not the lot of Tharu women. They enjoyed respectability and equality of status within the family.

With a view to know the attitudes of women agricultural labourers to some of the open facts related to their status, exploitation, adjustment and interaction some attitudinal questions were framed and were put in the questionnaire to know their pattern of reaction in terms of agreement, disagreement and no response. Their reactions in these terms are interpreted below with the attitudinal questions as sub-headings.

(a) In A Backward Society the Only Fate of An Women is Her Social and Economic Exploitation

90 per cent women agricultural labourers of Tharu area showed their positive reaction and 10 per cent of them showed their inability to make any comment. In the non-Tharu area under study cent per cent expressed their agreement in favour of the statement. This confirms their common notion about their exploitation.

(b) Had There Been No Compulsion on the Economic Front for Going Outside Come for Livelihood it would have Better to Look After the Household Affairs

80 per cent of the Tharu women agricultural labourers and the rest 20 per cent agreed to it. Just the opposite is the case with non-Tharu women because cent per cent of them were in agreement to this question. This wide difference in response is on account of difference in the attitude of women in two different cultural set ups. For the Tharu women, laborious by temperament, extrovert by nature and with a position of dominance in the family system with no *purdha*, it is but natural to respond negatively to this statement. Working in the field, for them is no compulsion but a way of life. Whereas, physically weak and generally introvert by nature, with a training of becoming a sincere housewife, i.e., mistress within the walls, the non-tharu women agricultural labourers' agreement to the question endorses their perception of life in which working outside is a compulsion which one has to do out of purely economic motivation and necessity.

(c) By Wage Earning and the Contribution of the Wage to the Family the Importance, Position and the Control of An Women Increases in the Family

In response to this statement 100 per cent Tharu women seemed to be in agreement while in the case of non-Tharu women only 28 per cent of them showed their agreement to it and rest 72 per cent were in total disagreement. This shows that the Tharu society is quite unlike the traditional orthodox non-Tharu society. The sense of devotion to husband and service to the entire family is deeply rooted in the instinct of women. It is this instinct which is very much reflected and pronounced in the disagreement of non-Tharu women agricultural labour to this statement.

(d) The Women Agricultural Labourers Very Often are the Victims of Double Exploitation

In response to this statement cent per cent Tharu women replied that on the family level they did not suffer any exploitation but in the field cent per cent of them were the victims of wage discrimination. On the other hand, 100 per cent of the non-Tharu women said that they faced exploitation in the field in the form of wage discrimination and some of them reported lack of due recognition and appreciation to their earnings and services they rendered to the family.

The broader findings of the analysis made in the present chapter are summarised below. The analysis of social characteristics of the sample suggest the following salient features related to age structure, nature and type of the joint family, casts structure and marital status.

Regarding the age structure this has been found that no agricultural labour was below 15 years of age. The maximum number of women agricultural labourers both in Tharu (46 per cent) and (64 per cent) in the non-Tharu were in the age groups of 35 years and above. The minimum number of them come from 15 to 25 years of age group, i.e., 20 per cent in the Tharu and 8 per cent in non-Tharu sample.

Regarding the nature of family this has been observed that the joint family system is gradually breaking. This fact gets a further confirmation with 58 per cent of the households in Tharu sample and 68 per cent in non-Tharu sample having single or unit family.

The caste structure in Tharu society is a typical one when compared to the caste structure of non-Tharu. The Tharus belong to a agrarian community with no particular caste consideration. In the non-Tharu sample 66 per cent of the total women agricultural labourers come from the lower backward group. They form the weaker section of the society and without any land base they earn their livelihood by working in the field.

So far the marital status of the women agricultural labourers under study is concerned, no agriculture labour was found unmarried in both the samples. Either they were married or widow.

Further, the broader findings related to the economic characteristics of the sample are the following:

So far land base of women agricultural labour in the area under study is concerned 62 per cent of the total agricultural labourers in Tharu sample and 66 per cent in non-Tharu sample come from landless households, and those who have, it is very little. Thus, it is a compulsion on the part of the women agricultural labourers to work in the field and earn their livelihood.

In spite of some land base with some of the households under study not a single women turned out to be a cultivator.

So far, occupational diversity of agricultural labourers is concerned women agricultural labour in Tharu area have a parallel opportunity in off-farm employment. Natural circumstances have deprived women agricultural labourers of non-Tharu are of this employment opportunity.

The women agricultural labourers in both the areas under study did not show any preference to move outside village for seeking employment. In comparison to male agricultural labourers it is immobility on the part of women agricultural labourers which makes their lot more limited and poor.

The analysis of the level of employment indicated that the Tharu women agricultural labourers were employed for larger number of days in comparison to the non-Tharu women agricultural labourers. 52 per cent of Tharu women agricultural labourers get employment between 250 to 300 days in a year (almost fully employed throughout the year). 40 per cent of them got employment between 200 to 250 days and only 8 per cent of them were such who got employment between 100 to 200 day. But not a single non-Tharu women agricultural labour reported getting employment for more than 250 days a year. 88 per cent of them reported the availability of employment between 200 to 250 days and the rest got employment between 100 to 200 days only. The Tharu agricultural labourers remain employed for larger number of days because of their off-farm employment opportunity. This off-farm employment opportunity is not available in non-Tharu area under study, therefore, they remain idle or without wage-earning especially during the lean seasons of the year.

In the areas under study the wage structure shows a differential in wage between men and women agriculture labourers. In the Tharu area male agricultural labourers get Rs. 10 per day as wage, the women agricultural labourers get only Rs. 5, just the half of the male wage. In non-Tharu village under study, the prevailing wage for men is Rs. 8 per day and for women it is again Rs. 4, just the half, per day.

The major findings of the level of income and poverty may be summarised in terms of the percentage of respondents below poverty line. Taking Rs. 3500 per annum as criteria of poverty line 24 per cent of the households in Tharu sample and 44 per cent households in non-Tharu sample turn out to be below poverty line. Further, taking Seventh Plan criteria of Rs. 4800 per annum at current prices as the limit of poverty line as many as 72 per cent and 76 per cent women agricultural labourers respectively may be said to be below poverty line approximately, as their income limit is Rs. 5,000, just Rs. 200 per annum more than the Seventh Plan poverty line criteria, i.e., Rs. 4800 per annum. This shows that there is excessive poverty among women agricultural labour in the backward area under study of the backward state of Bihar.

So far non-agricultural income of women agricultural labour under study is concerned as many as 56 per cent of the households in Tharu area have women workers getting off-farm employment whereas only 6 per cent of the households in non-Tharu sample have women workers with off-farm employment opportunity. Both in Tharu and non-Tharu samples none of the women agriculture labourers have non-agricultural income beyond the limit of 25 per cent of their agricultural income.

A comparative analysis of income and expenditure of women agricultural labour under study suggests that what is earned by them is just sufficient for their subsistence having no margin of savings or capital formation at all. Further, as much as 80 per cent of the total expenditure of Tharu women agriculture labour and 83.37 per cent of non-Tharu women agriculture labour is spent on food alone. This further conforms women agricultural labour under study creeping at the core of subsistence.

The analysis of the level of indebtedness shows that only 26 per cent of the households in Tharu sample and 12 per cent in non-Tharu sample are without debt and the rest in both the samples have the burden of debt. When asked about the prupose and source of the debt, marriage, *Shradha* and medical treatment, they said, was the purpose of debt village moneylenders was the sole source. They paid exorbitant rate of interest, i.e., around 25 per cent in all cases. But Tharu women were comparatively less burdened by debt.

Considering agricultural equipment and also the cow, ox, radio and cycle as the assets of women agricultural labourers in both the areas, it was quite better in Tharu area might be due to the additional income from off-farm employment.

So far, working condition of women agricultural labour is concerned, this is far from being satisfactory. They work in the field for nearly 8 to 10 hours a day and the implementation of minimum wages is least effective. Unemployment and under-employment are the chronic maladies with them. These women agricultural labourers face double exploitation—exploitation in the field by their employers and exploitation at the household level by their house keepers.

Overall, the findings of the present chapter based on primary data collected through field survey in West Champaran the facts evolved out of whatever limited secondary data available on the aspects like living and working condition, poverty and exploitation of women agricultural labourers in Chapter 2. In addition to what was discussed in Chapter 2 about these aspects, the present chapter with its Tharu sample under study presents various dimensions of the conditions and problems of (Tharu) women agricultural labourers in entirely different socio-cultural setting. Unfortunately, not much has been said and discussed about the problems and conditions of women agricultural labour in Tharu belt of West Champaran district which still remain an explored field for the social scientists. The comparison and contrast presented in this chapter between socio-economic conditions of women agricultural labour in Tharu and non-Tharu agrarian communities are in a way a preface to the further research which is needed to look into their problems in a more detailed manner.

NOTES & REFERENCES

1. Mitra, Asok, *The Status of Women—Shifts in Occupational Participation 1961-71*, ICSSR, New Delhi, 1980.
2. *Towards Equality*, Report of the Committee on the Status of Women in India, Ministry of Education and Social Welfare, December 1974, p. 167.
3. A person employed in industry or Government office, etc., enjoys 52 Sundays and nearly 63 other holidays. Thus, normal working days comes to 250 in a year.
4. *Income, Saving and Investment of Landless Agricultural Labourers in an Agriculturally Prosperous Area: (A Study of Purnea District, Bihar, 1970-71)*, Agro Economic Research Centre, University of Allahabad, 1973, p. 26.
5. See *Income, Saving and Investment of Landless Agricultural Labourers in an Agriculturally Prosperous Area (A Study of Purnea District, Bihar, 1970-71)*, Agro-Economic Research Centre, Allahabad.

6. *Status of Women in India*, Country Paper, Ministry of Social and Women's Welfare, New Delhi, April 1985, p. 30.
5. *Bihar Information*, Republic Day Number, 1982, p. 5.
7. *Towards Equality*, Report of the Committee on the Status of Women in India, *op. cit.*
8. *Towards Equality*, Report of the Committee on the Status of Women in India, Ministry of Education and Social Welfare, December 1974, p. 168.
9. Gandhi, M.K., *Young India*, 26-2-1918.
10. Conducted by the Department of Labour and Social Welfare, Patna University under the supervision of Professor G.P. Sinha.
11. Conducted by the Delhi School of Social Work under the supervision of Professor S.N. Ranade.
12. *Towards Equality*, Report of the Committees on the Status of Women in India, Ministry of Education and Social Welfare, December 1974, p. 172.
13. *Ibid.*, p. 173.
14. *Ibid.*, p. 173.
15. *Ibid.*, p. 173.
16. *Women in India*, Country Paper, Ministry of Social and Women's Welfare, New Delhi, April 1985, p. 63.
17. *Bihar District Gazetteer*, Champaran, 1960, p. 324.
18. Booklet on West Champaran Industrial Centres (Hindi) 1978, p. 3.
19. *Bihar Statistical Hand Book*, Directorate of Statistics and Evaluation, Government of Bihar, 1978, pp. 32.33.
20. Based on Landuse Plate, *National Atlas of India*, 1978.
21. *Bihar Information*, Republic Day, November, 1982, p. 5.

40

Women Agricultural Labours

Introduction

Female agricultural labourers form the single largest category of workers among Indian working women. In absolute terms there were about sixteen million female agricultural labourers in 1971.[1] They comprised one-third of the total agricultural labour force. An agricultural labourer is a person who works on another person's land. Without exercising any supervision or direction in cultivation, for wages in money, kind or share of produce. She has no right or lease or contract on land on which she works.[2] On the other hand, persons who work on farms, held by them in ownership or on lease, are classified as cultivators. Thus, while the former are wage-employed, the latter are self-employed.

According to 1971 Census figures, the number of female cultivators has been declining while the number of female agricultural workers has been increasing. While in 1951 female cultivators comprised 45 per cent of the female labour force and agricultural labourers 31 per cent, the respective figures in 1971 were 30 per cent and 51 per cent.[3] These statistics understate women's economic contribution among cultivator families. Nevertheless, as Brita: Brandtzaeg notes.

> This overall trend in women's role in agriculture, a shift from cultivator to labourer status, can only be explained by loss of land for subsistence cultivation and inadequate growth of productive employment opportunities on family farms which leads to withdrawal of women from active cultivation.[4]

While only every fourth male rural worker is an agricultural labour, one out of every two female rural workers is engaged as agricultural labourer. Combining the fact that work participation of women in rural India is almost one-fourth that of men (the 1971 Census showed that male and female work participation rates were 53.55 and 14.55 respectively) with the distribution of male and female workers among various major occupational categories, the broad picture that emerges is summarised in the following table:[5]

Thus while every third agricultural labourer in India is a woman, only one in eight workers in other categories taken together is a woman. One would therefore be justified in saying that knowing about women agricultural labourers is a substantial part of the knowing about the Indian working woman particularly in rural India. At least, no picture of the

Indian working women can be drawn without including therein the woman agricultural labourer.

Number of Female Workers for Every 1000 Male Workers in Three Occupational Groups (1971)

Agricultural Labourers	Cultivators	Others Workers
511	141	187

History and Current Trends in Agricultural Labour

In earlier times in India landless families existed practically as slaves to landlords.[6] While this situation has gone on changing with the times, most agricultural labourers have remained bound to landlords through ties of custom, debt, and force. Payment for their services was usually in kind. More recently the increased commercialisation of agriculture and monetisation of the economy have resulted in the transformation of agricultural labour into wage employment. Cultivators hiring agricultural labourers by the day have for the most part replaced long-term agreements between persons with rights in the land and landless labourers. Instead of whole families working for a landlord, individuals are hired. Agricultural labour is seasonal work with long periods of unemployment and underemployment during the year. Although the landless were certainly oppressed by the earlier ties of dependence on landlords, there was some chance of aid when times were hard. Today, operating in the cash nexus, labourers eat only when they can find work.

Several recent trends in India result in a surplus of agricultural labourers for the work available.[7] There is a growing number of agricultural labourers because of the population growth and because people enter this field when tenancies are lost and depressions in other industries occur. There is also a decrease in the work available for agricultural labourers because of the increased use of farm machinery and a change in outlook among landowners. As they develop the perspective of capitalist farmers, they want to use as little hired labour as possible in order to maximise profits. It should be remembered, of course, that both in terms of historical development and in terms of current trends the regional variations concerning agricultural labourers are immense, and a clear picture will not emerge until numerous local studies are undertaken.

There are few existing mechanisms to protect agricultural labourers from growing impoverishment. Although the State Governments have set (varying) minimum wage levels far agricultural labour, these rates fall below minimum consumption needs (with the exception of the Punjab); and a study found only 2 per cent of the workers were aware of these wage rates.[8] The same study showed that only 1 per cent of the agricultural labourers were members of unions. Where the left political parties have organised agricultural labour unions, as in some parts of Kerala, Joan Mencher writes, "The fact is that the union activity has primarily served to help workers from sinking to lower and lower levels of poverty and starvation."[9]

A Statistical Perspective on Female Agricultural Labour

Practically, all women agricultural labourers are drawn from the agricultural labour households. The proportion was as high as 97 per cent in 1963-64.[10] The average size of agricultural labour households was 4.5 persons. A 1974-75 survey revealed that the proportion of agricultural households holding no land is as high as 53 per cent.[11] Also a substantial proportion of the agricultural labourers belong to the socially disadvantaged castes, often referred to in India as scheduled castes or Harijans. Though the scheduled castes comprise only 15 per cent of the country's population, they account for one-third of the agricultural labourers, male and female.[12] Literacy is very low, if not altogether non-existent, among the agricultural labourers, but its absence is particularly marked among women, 95 per cent of whom were classified as illiterate in the 1971 Census. The corresponding figure for men was 80 per cent.[13]

The average number of days that women agricultural labourers get employment in a year is 138 days as compared to 193 days for men. The incidence of unemployment is almost twice as high for female agricultural labourers as for male agricultural labourers. According to the 1974-75 survey, women are unemployed for 124 days in a year as against men's 76 days of unemployment due to want of work. The position of both male as well as female agricultural labourers seems to have deteriorated in this regard between 1964-65 and 1974-75. Earlier, while men were unemployed due to want of work for 48 days, women were unemployed for 96 days.[14] Not only is the average female agricultural labourer relatively worse off in regard to the days of work but also the wage she receives. In 1974-75, the average daily earning of women worked out to 30 per cent below that of men from agricultural operations.[15] The employment and wage differentials between men and women are embedded in the job segregation by sex that characterises most agricultural labour work. The principal reason behind the relatively greater incidence of unemployment for women compared to men appears to be that men have a distinct edge over women in agricultural operations, other than transplanting and weeding, in terms of employment opportunities. Only in weeding, however, do female agricultural labourers get work for significantly greater number of days than male agricultural laborers.

Regional variation in the nature and use of agricultural labour is quite extensive. While agricultural labour households comprised approximately 20 per cent of all rural households in 1964-65, their concentration was greater in the Southern and Western States.[16] The percentage of landless labourers is higher in the Norther, Southern and Western States and lower in the Central and Eastern States. Female labour force participation rates (LFPR) vary greatly among agricultural labour households (with a high of 78 per cent in Andhra and a low of 18 per cent in West Bengal in 1961). The rates follow the general female LFPRs which are highest in the Southern and Western States and lowest in the Eastern and Northern States. In all regions men were employed for more days than women. Men obtained more then 200 days of work in thirteen of the fourteen states and women did in only four states (1964-65). Both men and women were employed for the most days in the Northern and

Western States and the least in the Souther States. Regional variation is shaped by many factors—history, culture, level of development, etc.—and needs to be studied further.

A study conducted in 1974-75 concluded that more economically developed villages were associated with a decline in the LFPR of women (including agricultural labourers) and an increase in the wage differentials between men and women workers relative to the less developed villages.[17] Men migrated to the developed areas in search of jobs and displaced the women. Modernisation has also meant a decline in employment opportunities for the children of agricultural labourers. Many of these children now attend school. In Kerala, inspite of reduction in family size,[18] unemployment is on the increase. Increased literacy and lowered birth rates have gone alongside increased poverty among agricultural labourers.

Statistics, however, never tell the whole story, certainly not for a country so large and diverse as India. What follows is the life story of a woman agricultural worker from Kerala belonging to a major scheduled caste in that State and engaged in the cultivation of rice, the country's principal agricultural crop. Neither she nor her husband holds any land. It is hoped that this life-story will add fresh to the bare bones provided above by averages and give to the reader a glimpse of the living reality.

A PROFILE

My name is Kalyani.* We are thirty-five years old. We live in a small settlement on the outskirts of the city of Trivandrum with my husband and five children, three boys and two girls. By caste, we are *Pulaya,* a major scheduled caste of Kerala. We are first and foremost an agricultural labourer though we go for other work too when there is no work to be done in the paddy fields.

Parents

Both my parents were agricultural labourers and so were my grand parents. My parents lived in a village some twenty kilometres south of Trivandrum. We were four children in all, all girls. We are the third one of the four girls born to my parents. We were all born in their hut. My mother never went to a hospital for her confinements. We lost my father when we were nine years old. He was fifty years of age. My mother died four years thereafter. Luckily, my eldest sister was married by then. Since there was no one else to look after us, all the three of us moved to our sister's hut. Her husband was a coconut plucker and also a caretaker to a big landlord.

Marriage

My brother-in-law took a fancy to my second sister also and took her too as his wife. Also

* Though a real life story, the names given in this profile are not real. The story had to be fictionalised to this extent to protect the family identity. The story has been pieced together on the basis of interviews and observations extending over a period of almost two years as part of the research on *The Economic Profile of Working Women in Kerala,* a project financed partially by the Indian Council of Social Science Research, New Delhi.

under those circumstances, this appeared to be the best solution. When we were sixteen years of age, they found a *Pulaya* boy, who was from the same village, for me to marry. Though his parents were Christians, the difference in our faiths did not seem to matter. His parents did not insist on my getting converted or our having a church wedding. Ours was a very simple wedding. All that we got was a new set of clothes. There was no exchange of dowry. The sister after me was also married off when she was 16 or 17.

Migration to the City

Soon my elder sisters and their husband decided to move close to Trivandrum city and we decided to move along with them. We felt that work opportunities would then be greater for us. Meanwhile, my brother-in-law fell seriously ill and died; thereafter my two sisters did not want to live together any longer. My eldest sister had evidently developed a soft corner for her husband's brother and wanted him to move in with her. We heard that some people were squatting on some government waste land on the slopes of a steep hill outside of Trivandrum city. All of us decided to move there. We had to clear the land and put up our huts. My three sisters could squat next to each other and we found a piece of land a little distance away from them in the same settlement. Thus we were all within easy reach of each other. This way we could help each other in time of need and yet be independent. We could always depend on my sisters for baby-sitting. Also, if and when, one of us was short of any item of food or clothing we could borrow it from the other. In times of sickness in the family, it was good to know that there were one's own kith and kin close by.

Within years my second sister became a T.B. patient and had to give up working in the paddy fields. Instead, she had to earn her livelihood collecting medicinal herbs and lemon grass. When she was in the hospital we sisters took care of her only daughter in turns. Now that the girl is in her early teens, she is able to help her mother.

Size of Family

Except for my first two children, a boy and a girl, who were delivered at home in the village, the other four were born to me after our move to the settlement. These four, three boys and one girl, were delivered by me at a nearby hospital. One of these boys died when he was six years old.

We know that we have a rather large family, larger than we can feed and clothe properly. Social workers have visited me several times to persuade me to undergo sterilisation. Once we agreed to go to the hospital with them along with three others from the settlement but we gave them the slip out of food. We are scared of the operation and its after effects. What will we do if we develop septic condition? We may not be able to work as well thereafter. My husband too is afraid that if he undergoes operation he would not be able to do the hard work his job demands.

Husband's Work

My husband, who too was an agricultural labourer when we got married, has become a loader of trucks since our move to the city. This work is better paying. But loading granite stones can be strenuous and dangerous. Also he is away from the house for long hours. He leaves home around half past seven in the morning and is rarely back before eight o'clock in the evening unless there is a breakdown in the truck. Usually he is able to give me five rupees out of the twelve to thirteen rupees he makes on a working day. He has to spend a great deal on eating out. Luckily, unlike other men in his type of job he does not drink. However, since the money he gives me is neither regular nor enough for the seven of us to be fed and clothed, we have to go out to work.

Work in the Paddy Fields

We work in the paddy fields whenever work is available there. Paddy is raised here twice a year. The two crops are timed with the monsoons. One season starts from May and ends in September while the other commences in September and lasts till February. Thus for three months, between February to May, there is no work in the paddy fields. Even for the nine months of the year covered by the two paddy crops, women are not involved in all stages of paddy cultivation. In this part of Trivandrum district we, scheduled caste women, are kept out of certain operations that other women can take up.

My main job, or for that matter that of all women from my caste, is that of transplanting paddy. The raising of the nursery is done by men. We come into the picture only when the seedlings are ready to be transplanted. This job is more or less left to women from my caste. The reasons for this are simple. It is a very messy and back-breaking job. One has to stand in mud and slush for hours together in rain or sun. It is particularly hurting to move backwards while stooping. Once can easily catch cold, being exposed for long hours in such damp surroundings. Moreover, women from higher castes do not possess the skills to transplant. The success of a paddy crop depends on how well it is transplanted.

During transplanting time, there is a great demand for women workers. Transplanting in all the fields has to take place within a short period. But any one woman can get work for not more than 21 days during a season.

After transplanting, there is a month's gap before we get called to do weeding. The crop has to mature a little. But weeding does not last long. Nor does it require the same number of hands as transplanting. Where ten women are needed to transplant, only one is needed to weed. These days, even this ratio is coming down with the use of weed killers.

We work for more or less the same landlords every year. They know my work and we know that we can get the job with them. Usually, they would send world to my hut asking that we should come to such and such a field on the following day for transplanting. In a couple of cases not only do they call me but they also entrust to me the responsibility of calling other women. This way some times we can oblige my friends or relatives. Usually, however, there is such a great demand for women that even tribal women come down from the nearby hills to help with transplanting. They are hard working and easy to manage. Supervising and calling others to join me do not entitle me to any extra money. It only confers on me some prestige as a trusted worker.

A Transplanting Day

We are, the first to get up in my house. Usually we wake up around five o'clock and go down the hill to use some corner behind the bushes for toilet purposes. The bush area in the settlement has been divided into male and female zones. So we do not have to worry about running into any men. Still, we prefer to use the early dark hours of the morning to finish off with this daily routine. It takes me about half an hour to get back to my hut. We go to the nearby municipal tap, which is ten minutes walk from my hut, to fetch two pitchers of clean water for all of us to have a wash. We brush my teeth with some rice husk powder using my fingers. We wash my hands and face near one of the two banana trees in our yard. Only then do we take *pan* (folded betel leaf coated on the inside with a layer of lime and containing bits of arecanut and tobacco). We are addicted to chewing *pans* with tobacco and cannot do without them. Also, we feel *pans* have kept my toothache off. After we comb my hair, we change my clothes to go down to the tea shop. My 12-year old daughter, Nirmala, is already up and about and takes charge of the house before we are ready to leave for work.

We go to a small tea shop run by a Nair upper caste woman to have my breakfast. There we buy myself a hot cup of tea and a preparation of steamed rice powder with coconut and green chillies served with steamed whole green gram and fried *papadoms* (crispies made cut of lentil powder). There are proper tables and benches to sit on. We women sit on one side and men sit on the other side of the same room. The tea shop is visited mostly by working men and women. The breakfast costs me around 75 paise. It costs me more if my eldest son, Niren, decides to follow me to the tea shop. He does not like to eat *kanji*, the left-over rice gruel, with his brothers and sisters. We cannot scold him in front of my friends and send him home to a cold left-over meal when we are myself eating a hot meal. The reason we have to eat out on a working day is that we require a proper meal to put in the kind of physical work my job requires.

We must present myself at seven o'clock for work. We go straight to the nursery where we are usually joined by other women. The number of women in the group depends on the size of the paddy field to be transplanted.

Before we start work we must make some adjustments to my dress. We fold up my *lungi*, the warp-around skirt, to the knee level and tie around my head the cloth that we otherwise throw over my shoulders, to protect is from sun and rain. It also protects my hair from getting dirty. We must then tuck my stock of *pans* into my *lungi* at the waist.

Standing in the nursery in ankle deep water, we must bend down to pull out the rice saplings. We use both my hands, one to pull out the saplings and the other to hold them. If the nursery is well watered the seedlings come out easily. Every two minutes we pull out enough to make a bundle. Before We tie up the bundle we must free the saplings of all the mud and slush. So we dig in my right heel to raise my toe at an angle to beat the roots. More often, we carry with me a coconut frond stem, stand it up in the mud and beat the roots on it. One ties up the bundle after weeding out grass and other stray plants. The first half of the morning is spent in this operation, pulling out seedlings and bundling them up.

When the break comes around 11 o'clock, we would have worked already for four homes and made about 100 bundles. These bundles are kept in a line near the nursery bund. Our break lasts about one hour. All of us go to the nearby coffee shop. During transplanting time, coffee shops serve coffee brewed with ginger which is supposed to keep off colds. We also take some lentil doughnuts but avoid rice meals. We cannot digest a rice meal on a transplanting day. On other working days, we buy myself a full plate of rice and vegetables for lunch.

Transplanting starts around mid-day. We hold the bundle to be transplanted in one hand and transplant with the other hand, all the time bending forward. One plants three or four saplings at a time. The idea is that it least one of these will take root. Once we have transplanted all the saplings in my hundred bundles, my day's work is done.

We might take longer to transplant if the nursery is not well watered, if there are too many weeds or if the field to be transplanted is hard. If, however, the field is well puddled we can finish my work at 4 O'clock.

Actually, we quite like a transplanting day. We work usually in a group. Talking to each other and passerby, our time passes fast without feeling the strain. But we have to chew my *pan* every half hour to keep me going. It wards off my hunger, and also keeps off my toothaches. If by any chance we exhaust my supply of *pans,* we request one of the passersby to buy me a few more.

Once my work is over, we collect my wages in cash. The current daily wage is nine rupees. Usually, the landlord is there personally to pay the money or else he entrusts the job to the man who combines supervision of transplanting with head-load carrying of bundles from the nursery.

Exclusion from Certain Operations

While we try to get as much work as possible during the transplanting season, going from one field to another, it is simply impossible for anyone to be employed for more than the number of days the season lasts. As we said before, we also get quite a few days' work each season to do weeding. Being a woman, we have no access to harvesting which is an altogether male operation is this part of the country. My additional handicap is that we are a *Pulaya* woman. So we are not asked to do threshing and winnowing. The upper caste women who undertake threshing and winnowing do not like to share their *kanji,* rice gruel, with women of my caste.

Daily Shopping

My children know that if we have gone for transplanting, we would be back home around 5 o'clock and if we have gone to work elsewhere it would be around 6 O'clock. My second daughter who is about ten years old waits for me at the road junction near the squatter settlement where there is a small wayside market. She carries with her a small basket for rice and groceries and two bottles, one for kerosene and the other for coconut oil.

While there are a few regular tea, cigarette and grocery shops on either side of the road, the way-side market consists of ten or twelve women fish and vegetable vendors. Once in a while, a few women join in selling mud-puts and pans and other basic durables. We can find here almost all the items that we need to make the evening meal, the major meal in our house. We buy fish, vegetables and the groceries particularly rice, oil and kerosene. The total amount we spend daily works out to be about seven to eight rupees. We have to buy enough to last us not only for the evening but also for the following morning and noon when only children eat at home. Only when my husband and we do not have any work, do we eat at home in the morning and at noon.

Her Evening Bath

After we get back home we go down to the little spring at the foothill to have a bath and to wash my clothes. Though it is a natural spring, to get clean water, one must scoop out a few buckets of standing water. With no proper embankment, all the mud gets washed into it when it rains. We bathe with my working clothes on and then wash them with soap. We apply the same laundry soap to wash off the dirt and sweat from my body.

The Evening Meal

Once we get back to the hut after my bath, we must take over the cooking from Nirmala who would have started the fire, and put the rice to boil. We clean the fish and grind the spices. We do all this with the light from a small kerosene lamp as my kitchen is very dark. The evening meal is my family's major meal of the day. We cook a large quantity of rice so that not only is it enough for the evening but also part is left for the following morning for the children's breakfast. First we feed the younger children, then my husband and the eldest son, Niren. My daughter Nirmala, and we eat the last.

My husband usually gets back home by eight O'clock, that is just in time for the meal. Still, it is never certain when he will get back. We never eat before feeding him. Once he comes, we have to fetch water for him to bathe. He bathes in the yard, as it is too dark to go down the hill. If he could bathe near the public water tap it would have been easier but he is not supposed to do that. Some time back, some men from the settlement bathed there and the municipal authorities closed the tap. We were put to a great deal of hardship for six months. Now everyone is very much more careful.

Our house runs smoothly if both of us have work but such luck comes our way only for very short spells. It is largely because we get work very intermittently. Also, my husband has to spend a substantial part of this wage on eating out so that what he can spare for the family is by itself never adequate.

Crises in Life

My real problem is when some crisis comes. In the past few years, we had to face two major crises. The first crisis came when my husband got really sick because of some internal bleeding in the stomach. Though he had to be hospitalised for a short spell, he could not go to work for several months. There was a short period when even we could not go to work because we had to be with him. On days we did go out to work, my meager income could not provide for the house as well as for the expenses on him in the hospital, over and above the free meals and medicines.

It was then that we were forced to pawn off our ration card for one hundred rupees. This meant that we could not buy rice at the controlled price. Nor could we earn the four to five rupees we were making every month by selling my sugar entitlement to the grocery shop.[19] We knew that we would be a net loser and the family would be hard pressed for all the time to come but we needed the money desperately to buy medicine that the hospital would not provide free and to run my household.

Once my husband started going for work regularly, things looked brighter. Just when things started looking up, the second crisis struck us. The monsoon came with such fury that before we could do anything our roof was ripped off and our mud walls collapsed. Many other huts in our neighbourhood, including my sisters', were also damaged. But the damage to out hut was probably the worst and that too when we were perhaps the least prepared for it.

A friend of mine in the settlement, whose husband sometimes works for the same truck as my husband, was generous enough to allows us to double up with them temporarily. We were anxious to get back to our hut as early as possible. We had some differences with my husband on this. He felt that first the children and we both should have a new set of clothes. We all had gone without any new clothes for a whole year, when he was sick. But we felt that our top priority should be the hut. If we stayed too long with our friends we were bound to get into some quarrel with them. So we decided to plead for another one hundred rupees with the family with whom we had pawned my ration card. Of course, this means that we shall never be able to get back my ration card now. Repaying two hundred rupees is not going to be easy.

Children and their Schooling

Niren, my eldest child, who is about 16, left school because he was not interested in studies. He found school boring but has not found work. He wants to work like his father for the trucks as a loader. Though he is too young right now for that sort of work he should become independent one day. My immediate hope is that my daughter, Nirmala, will start working soon. She has been to school for a few years but we withdrew her when we needed some one to look after the house and the children when we were away at work. My ten-year old second daughter can start looking after the house, collect twigs and mind the kitchen when we both are out at work.

We never sent the second girl to school as she did not have proper clothes to wear. She was the only girl of her age who was not going to school in our settlement. But we are not worried. Of what use is a little bit of schooling? We shall never be able to keep her long in school. If things look up, we plan to keep the two younger boys in school and hope that they will do better than their brother.

The Perspective

We doubt if my own personal work situation will improve significantly. We do not get more than 60-65 days of work in the paddy fields. Being a woman and that too from a scheduled caste, we do not expect that we can do better than that. But we are always looking for work elsewhere be it in construction or for the prick kun. These jobs involve mostly head-load transportation of materials. Failing such work, we go out collecting medicinal herbs instead of sitting at home doing nothing. Living from day to day, not knowing what the next day has to offer, we never like to think of the future.

NOTES

1. Committee on the Status of Women in India (CSWI), *Towards Equality*, New Delhi: Government of India, Ministry of Education and Social Welfare, 1975, pp. 162-163.
2. See *Census of India 1971*, Series—9, Kerala, Part II—B (i), Economic Tables, 1975, Appendix I, Instructions to enumerators for filling up the economic questions of the individual slip, pp. 217-220.
3. CSWI, p. 163.
4. Brita Brandtzaeg, "Women, Food and Technology," *Economic and Political Weekly*, Vol. XIV, No. 47, Nov. 24, 1979, p. 1921.
5. *Census of India 1971*, Series 1: India, Papers of 1972, Economic Characteristics of Population (Selected Tables).
6. For a discussion of the evolution of the rural class system in one region of India (Tamilnadu), see Kathleen Gough, "Modes of Production in Southern India," *Economic and Political Weekly*, Vol. XV, Nos. 5-7, annual Number 1980, pp. 337-364. For a discussion of the historical evolution of agricultural labour in an area of Western India, see Jan Breman, *Patronage and Exploitation; Changing Agrarian Relations in South Gujarat, India*. Berkeley: University of California Press, 1974.
7. Joan Mencher, "The Lessons and Non Lessons of Kerala: Agricultural Labourers and Poverty," *Economic and Political Weekly*, Vol. XV, Nos. 41-43, October 1989, p. 1787.
8. *Indian Labour Journal*, May 1980, quoted in "Sham of Minimum Wages," *Economic and Political Weekly*, Vol. XV, Nos. 24 and 25, June 14-21, 1980, pp. 1044-1045.
9. Mencher, p. 1787.
10. See Labour Bureau (India), *Rural Labour Enquiry* 1963-65, *Final Report*, 1975, p. 121.
11. See Labour Bureau (India), *Rural Labour Enquiry* 1974-75, *Summary report*, 1978, pp. 22-23.
12. See Labour Bureau (India), *Rural Labour Enquiry* 1974-75, *Summary Report*, 1978, pp. 22-23.
13. See *Census of India 1971*, Series—1, India, Paper 3 of 1972, Economic characteristics of population (Selected Tables), pp. 78-79.
14. See Labour Bureau (India), *Rural Labour Enquiry* 1974-75, *Summary Report*, 1978, pp. 29-30.
15. See Labour Bureau (India), *Rural Labour Enquiry* 1974-75, *Summary Report*, 1978, pp. 48-49.
16. The statistics on regional variation in this section are drawn from the *Rural Labour Enquiry* 1963-65 as cited in Leela Gulati, "Unemployment Among Female Agricultural Labourers," *Economic and Political Weekly*, Vol. XI, No. 13, Review of Agriculture, March 27, 1976, pp. A31-A39. The following states are in each regional zone: Central—Uttar Pradesh, Madhya Pradesh; Eastern—Bihar, West Bengal, Orissa, Assam; Southern—Andhra, Tamil Nadu, Kerala; Western—Gujarat, Maharashtra, Maysore; Northern—Punjab, Rajasthan.
17. S.D. Sawant and Rita Dewan, "Rural Female Labour and Economic Development," *Economic and Political Weekly*, Vol. XIV, No. 26, June 30, 1979, pp. 1091-1099.
18. Mencher, p. 1785.
19. See Leela Gulati, "Rationing in a Semi-urban Community: Case Study of a Squatter Habitat," *Economic and Political Weekly*. XII, No. 12, March 19, 1977, for a description of the rationing system prevailing in Kerala.

41

Women Sweepers

Introduction*

The scavenging profession in India is strictly circumscribed by concepts of purity and pollution. As untouchables (officially classified as the Scheduled Castes) scavengers and sweepers are at the very bottom of the Hindu frame of reference. Divided into subcastes, their traditional work in rural India consisted of removing human excreta and refuse, often in basket-loads carried on their hands, and cleaning village roads. Despite adaptations, the basic nature of the job has not changed. Though the flush system is increasingly replacing the dry latrine, sweepers are needed to keep the sanitation system of India's cities and towns going. As no other caste will perform such defiling yet essential tasks, men and women of these castes retain a virtual monopoly over their traditional occupation.

It is an occupation in which both sexes participate. At the same time, job mobility chances for men are substantially greater than for women. Looking at data from studies conducted over the past twenty-five years, it becomes clear that the position of the female sweeper has changed little. Again, within the occupation as well, women tend to do the more defiling, arduous and less paid tasks. A 1952 study in Madhya Pradesh found that twice as many women as men were sweeping roads; men got promoted to supervisory posts, became watchmen, or were trained for driving refuse trucks, while women remained scavengers.[1] Male Bhangis in Bhiwani and Mathura are increasingly becoming labourers, rickshaw pullers and tonga drivers. Of those in the profession, most were in government employment, while their womenfolk remained in private scavenging jobs. Unpublished data collected for a sample study in the rural and urban areas of post-green Revolution Haryana showed that more than a third of Balmiki men had left the profession for better paid higher status jobs. Only two women had left the traditional occupation, to become agricultural labourers.[2]

Working Conditions

In 1977, we conducted a small study in a West Delhi Tenement colony among 80 Balmiki

---

* This is a revised version of a paper presented at the 10th International Congress of Anthropological and Ethnological Sciences, New Delhi, December 10-16, 1978.

women, a sub-caste of the scavenging Bhangi caste of North India. The aim was to determine male-female patterns of mobility and authority structures. Traditionally the Balmikis claim descent from Valmiki, the author of the *Ramayana:* this was substantiated in the Census of 1881. Delhi's Balmikis, most of whom are migrants from the neighbouring state of Uttar Pradesh, live dispersed throughout the city, living in slums and tenement colonies.

The migrant agricultural labourer or small farmer in India often has to leave behind his wife when he moves to the city; on the other hand, in North India the scavenger or construction worker brings his wife with him because he is sure of employment for her. Statistics on migration indicate that when the female participation rate is high in occupations which can be profitably continued in the urban milieu, there is a greater degree of equality in the sex (migration) ratio.[3] Further evidence shows that in essential, caste-bound occupations such as scavenging and laundering, women are invaluable participants in the system. In her study of slums, Singh found that washing of clothes was done only by women of the Dhobi caste, while ironing was shared between the men and women. Similarly, though the Delhi Municipal Corporation reserves 75 per cent of scavenging jobs for men and 25 per cent for women, the ratio is almost 50:50. A senior official commented that with more men moving out of the traditional caste occupation, the Corporation—the largest employer of scavengers in Delhi-had to engage women in excess of the stipulated quota. While male Balmikis still dominate the profession, the official felt it was significant that an increasing number were attracted by jobs in shops, commercial establishments and factories. On the other hand, this was rarely the case with women.

One of the most pressing problems for lower-class migrants is finding living accommodation in the city. Though the colony in which we did my field work was specially built for Municipal Corporation sweepers, at the time of interview, it was peopled mainly by illegal occupants. Shortage of urban living space means that migrants take shelter wherever they can. In the present situation relatives and co-villagers of the original tenants arrived several years ago in search of jobs. Even after the death or moving away of the rightful occupants they stayed on, resisting all attempts at eviction. This soon led to overcrowding, insanitary conditions and illegal constructions. In the colony under study only about half the families who had someone employed with the Corporation were legal tenants. The rest were illegal occupants.

Most of the women interviewed were between 21 and 35 years of age, and 60 per cent had migrated to the city, primarily at marriage. Half the sample had started working between the ages of 10 and 15 years, and late employment was the exception rather than the rule. The average number of children was 5.3, and the nuclear family appeared to be the dominant norm. Poverty was the chief reason which took Balmiki women out to work. All were in the traditional caste occupation, and a few said that they washed clothes in addition to their duties of cleaning latrines and throwing away garbage. Though some complained of the dirty nature of their work, no respondent spoke of a likelihood of leaving the profession. A fear of untouchability and a lack of training for any other occupation inhibited women from thinking of a change.

While the older sweepers appeared more resigned to caste discrimination, some of the younger women were assertive in their reactions. A typical example was Kamla, who had been put to sweeping by her mother at the age of 11 years. At the time of interview she was cleaning five homes, as well as looking after her four children between the ages of twelve and five. She accepted that she would have to work for many years to come; but she felt humiliated at being treated as an untouchable:

> "Who says that there is no untouchability? There is plenty of it. Even after all these years we are not allowed to go anywhere near the kitchen. We work for Baniyas who are very fussy. There is one relative of theirs—she says she is a school teacher—she lifts up her sari if she has to pass me. When she does that we feel like throwing acid on her face. Don't we have hearts and bodies just like you all? I'm sure your shudder to clean your baby's behind. What about us—foraging for generations in excreta and muck and carrying dung on our heads? It was only a man called Mahatma Gandhi who tried to change things for us; nobody else has done anything ever since. We life with the same stench with which we started."

While a third of the husbands of those interviewed were in non-scavenging jobs, women sweepers appeared more concerned with getting ahead within the profession. There was a substantial difference in the job requirements, remuneration and perquisites of women working in the municipal corporation, government institutions and hospitals, and those employed in private homes. Those working for the Municipal Corporation, its schools, government dispensaries and hospitals enjoyed in addition to a higher salary, maternity and other paid leave, uniform, and security of tenure. Hospital and school sweepers had to clean latrines, while the main function of Corporation sweepers was to sweep public roads.

In contrast, private sweepers often worked in several homes and were not entitled to any fringe benefits. Many complained of being tried after climbing several flights of stairs during the day and carrying garbage tins to and from the refuse heap. Maternity leave was unknown; it was common for most women in private service to work almost to the day their child was born, as well as provide substitutes—often a kinswoman—for their period of absence. The incumbent's salary during childbirth and subsequent isolation was claimed by the substitute. It was not surprising that 70 per cent of the present sample who were in private employment aspired for government or quasi-government employment, rather than a movement out of the profession.

In addition to harder working conditions, private sweepers were paid much less; sixty per cent of the present sample said that they earned less than Rs. 100 a month. Four women said that for working in about thirty houses they earned Rs. 50. This works out to Rs. 1.66 a month per house, or 0.05 paise a day for cleaning a latrine and throwing away garbage. The degree of exploitation is evident, where a minimum bus fare costs 0.30 paise and a cup of tea, 0.25 paise at a wayside stall. While there is no sex-based wage discrimination in public employment, no respondent had a husband who earned as little as these four women. Nor is mobility into permanent and better jobs easy; only five of the present respondents said that they had been taken into the Corporation after many years of private employment. Three admitted that the influence of kinsmen employed in the Corporation was instrumental in their being absorbed. Two widows had filled their husbands' posts.

Profiles

Disparities in life-style are vividly brought out if we look at the histories of Bimla and Rajbatti. Bimla, private sweeper, lived with her husband and four children in a one-room mud-walled tenement, while Bimla, her husband Hari and the youngest daughter of four months slept on a string cot, the other three children slept on the floor. The wooden front door was the only source of ventilation; a few gleaming cooking vessels were stacked in a corner near the bucket-stove. While children's clothes lay on the cot and a broken chair, a well-used suitcase contained two term winter quilts and Hari's woolen uniforms. An open drain abutted on the entrance, and we often saw the younger children defecating into it. In summer, the family slept out of doors, as did most other residents of the colony.

Bimla's father had retired as a senior sweeper in the railways and lived with his wife and other five children in old Delhi. Though the three sons had been to school, all the daughters were illiterate. Bimla was married to Hari, a *farash*[4] in a government office at the age of 14 years. A couple of years later, her first child, a daughter, was born and subsequently three more children followed in quick succession. After the last child, she insisted on having a tubectomy operation. Though Hari earned Rs. 395 a month, Bimla felt that she should work because she wanted a better life for her children. Besides, Hari had taken to hard drinking soon after the birth of the third child.

A slim twenty-six-year-old with sharp features against a dark complexion, Bimla worked in fifteen houses and earned seventy-five rupees a month. It was a twenty-minutes walk to the colony where she worked. She left at ten in the morning and was back home by two in the afternoon. In the evenings, she spread out a piece of jute matting on the pavement parallel to the main road running past the colony and sold vegetables which Hari had brought at the retail market earlier in the day. During the two years that we observed her, Bimla's life underwent certain major changes. When we spoke to her first, she had a matter-of-fact approach to life:

> "In our community there is no choice for a woman with regard to working: we don't ask questions. At the age of ten we are handed a broom. It's true that my parents did not put me to work before we were married, but we used to wander around with my mother and occasionally help. We never went to school—my father said that it was a waste of time. But we don't agree. My three older children are all in primary school, though the elder girl helps me with the cooking and cleaning.
>
> We do the day's cooking before we leave for work. My husband's duty hours are such that he is back by 10 a.m. and then goes back again at 4. p.m. He sometimes does the cooking. Usually he buys the rations and the kerosene oil. We have to take the baby with me. What is the option? We only own a bicycle, though in my father's house we

were used to radio. We do not even have a water line. We have to pay something monthly to our neighbour Rani for taking water from her tap. They made it clear to us that they are doing us a great favour, and others may be willing to pay more. But because we are neighbours, Rani is prepared to give the water to us rather than to anyone else. The world is a cruel place. People don't even give water to other free of charge.

For the birth of the first two children, we went to my *maike* (mother's house). My husband made arrangements for someone to relieve me at my place of work a month in advance each time. But this was no longer possible when the third child was on the way. We worked till the day on which my last two children were born. We nearly lost my job, because though my husband used to stand-in, he was very erratic. This was mainly because he thought it demeaning to clean latrines. On the last two occasions we had to stay at home for forty days because we had got so weak. When we joined work, we started taking the baby with me and nursing it whenever it cried. In winter and in the height of summer it was not easy: The baby used to cry the minute we took her out of this room. She used to get ill every month. Anyway, now we have had enough of children. We had myself operated after the last child was born. Most of my employers address me as 'jamadarni.[5] There is no personal relationship. We clean the latrines, throw away the garbage, sweep the stairs and driveways. We are not supposed to sweep any of the other rooms, though sometimes when the servant who does that is absent, we are asked to stand-in. We get very tried, carrying dustbins and bending over the stairs fifteen times in the day. We get a cup of tea in three houses, but no gifts at festival time. One lady gave my baby some old clothes when she was born.

We give my salary to my husband. He then hands me a sum of money with which to buy the daily vegetables. He buys clothes for children and for me. But lately, he has started drinking and abusing me. We don't know the reason for this. He rarely used to beat the children. Now he thinks nothing of raising his hand."

When we saw Bimla again after some months, she had lost weight and was untidily dressed. Earlier, she had been particular about her clothes. Her neighbour told me in a whisper that her husband had become a drunkard and used to beat her up regularly. His excuse was that she had illicit relations with a man who used to buy vegetables from her. Bimla had a different story to tell:

"My husband thinks that one can do business with a sour look on one's face. Just because we smile at my customers, he thinks that we are behaving badly. Some months ago, my sari had accidentally slipped off my shoulder, at a time when one of my regular customers was buying vegetables from me. Hari saw me talking to this *chaprasi*.[6] Since then, he is convinced that we have been having an affair with him. Though my neighbours have tried to explain to him that this is not the case, he gets drunk and beats me up regularly.

He has also stopped giving me any money for the household. How can we manage on

Rs. 75? So now we have taught my little daughter of two years to get money out of his pocket. She climbs on to his stomach when he is asleep, and puts her hand into his pocket. The following morning he misses the money and starts shouting. But when we shout back and ask whether he expects us to starve, he keeps quiet. It is only when he is drunk that he gets violent.

Apart from drinking, there is something else he has started. His parents owned a plot of land in his village, which he has inherited. He applied for a house-building advance loan a couple of years ago. The loan came through about eight months ago, and he takes casual leave every few weeks and goes to the village. He says that he is building a house. Two months ago, a relative of his visited me and said that he was building a house; but he had also started living with his dead brother's widow, a woman with married children. When we accused him of this, he beat me up and said 'Does a respectable man misbehave with his *bhabhi?*[7] She is like a mother to me.' But we know he is lying. He does things with her because she is supervising the construction of his house. He even brought her to my home last month. We lost my temper and slapped her face. Hari was enraged and hit me with a big stone. See, you can see the scar on my face."

Bimla's life is a striking example of the unequal status of the Balmiki women at work and in the home; her husband had left the profession and had joined the ranks of the ubiquitous government servant. When his wife was unable to go to work, he was reluctant to stand-in because it meant cleaning latrines. His work consisted mainly of dusting office rooms and furniture. In his own words. "We have hardly any work to do. Who bothers in a government office?" On the other hand, Bimla had to combine domestic chores with an arduous day's work. Leave was known and Bimla complained that her salary had been cut twice when she had been absent for a couple of days because of a child's illness.

At home, when it came to suspicion over extramarital relations, Bimla's husband beat her up regularly, Though she too had her doubts about her husband's fidelity, Bimla had no way of getting even with Hari. In addition, his frequent bouts of drunkenness and consequent refusal to support the family meant that Bimla had to look for more employment. There was substantial disparity between the social position of husband and wife.

In contrast, Rajbatti, a Corporation sweeper, had the same employment status as her husband who worked in a government school. Out of their combined earnings they had built an additional rook above the original tenement allotted to Rajbatti. The walls were freshly white-washed and a light bulb hung outside the front door where her son had recently put up a pained name plate. At forty, Rajbatti had nineteen years of permanent service behind her. The youngest of her six children was studying in class V, and the second son was a motor car mechanic. The total family income was about Rs. 800 a month. At the time of interview, Rajbatti's family owned two cycles, a radio and a sewing machine. Her eldest daughter who had taken classes in sewing, made small garments for people in the colony. Ram Swarup, Rajbatti's husband and her children shared in domestic chores. Rajbatti's working hours were longer than those of her husband. She commented:

"We were married at the age of twelve years, but did not go to my husband's home till we were fifteen. After a month of fusing over me, my mother-in-law told me, `New, daughter, like all of us, you must take up a job.' We started working in a few private homes until my eldest son was born. After his birth, they did not force me to go back to work. But when he was two years old, my father-in-law, a Corporation sweeper, asked me whether we would like to try for a Municipal job. My husband was already employed in a Corporation school. We said that we didn't mind. We went through some kind of interview, and was quite surprised when we got the job. In the beginning, it was difficult. We had to help my mother-in-law with the coking when we came back from my 6 a.m. to 10 a.m. shift. Then once we started having children every year, we wanted to give up my job. Everyone thought we were mad. No one gives up a permanent government job. Besides we used to get three months' paid maternity leave each time. So we decided to stay on. As we lived with my husband's family, looking after the children was never a major problem.

Now that it is all behind me, we are very glad we did not leave. It is true that we are out of the house for over eight hours in the day, but compared with women in private service, we are very fortunate. In the early mornings we sweep the roads, along with men sweepers. We have been given brooms with long handles so that we don't have to bend. We get home by 11 a.m., in time to see to the mid-day meal which my elder daughter has already prepared. We leave at 1.30 p.m. and am back home by 6.30 p.m. in the evening. In the second shift we clean the rooms of the local Corporation office as well as the bathrooms.

My work is little different from that of my husband, We are entitled to the same benefits and earn about the same salary. It is because we decided to stick on to my job that we were able to educate our children. After we retire, we shall get a person. Had we left my job, we would have been hard up. Besides, there is so much more demanded in private service. My neighbour, Santi, is expecting her third child. Poor thing, she is only eighteen years old. Though the baby is due in a few days' time, she is still working. Her employers have told her that if she cannot provide a suitable substitute she will lose her job. We have never faced any such problem.

None of my children are sweepers; it is true that the eldest boy is unemployed. But though he could easily get a sweeper's job, we want him to try for at least a *chaprasi's* post. Next year, we hope to buy some land in my husband's village. We look after the family finances. My husband and children hand over their earnings to me after retaining a certain amount for their own expenses. My old man gets drunk once in a while, particularly at festivals. We know my son smokes, and he certainly likes good clothes; but as he is contributing to the family funds, why should we grudge him his luxuries? My husband makes all the major decisions about how we should spend our money. Though we earn as much as he does, we do not expect to boss over him on financial matters. At one time, he was briefly out of a job. Even then, he was all-in-all; after all he is my lord and master."

The contrasting situations of Bimla and Rajbatti are examples of the internal stratification system within the scavenging profession. But though Rajbatti was more privileged than Bimla, her chances of a movement out of the profession were far less than for a man. A third of the husbands of women in the sample were in non-traditional jobs. In addition, a majority of those who were in the profession were in higher-status government or Corporation employment. Seventeen husbands were drivers, peons, night watchmen and mechanics, while seven were labourers. Two were office clerks.

Problems of Balmiki Women Today

Talking to Corporation officials in Delhi revealed that the number of Balmiki women seeking jobs did not seem to be decreasing. In addition to their own limited aspirations, most women in the present sample said that husbands would resist the attempts of wives to move out of the occupation. A case system which gives Balmikis a job monopoly is fully exploited by the community; assured of a secure income from the female members of the family, the menfolk often take time off to learn a trade, or look around for better jobs. Nine women—more than 10 per cent of the present sample—supported unemployed husbands or those who earned less than themselves. Another three women whose husbands were drivers and mechanics said that they had been the main provides while their husbands had been under training.

Boserup has pointed out that though more urban men are joining the modern sector, women persist with traditional occupations. This is corroborated by 1961 Census data on Delhi Balmikis which shows that while a quarter of the scavengers were women, only one woman out of thirty was likely to be in trade and commerce or manufacturing.[8] A lack of training opportunities, large families and hindered physical mobility are important factors which keep Balmiki women in the occupation. In addition it is advantageous for men to have wives in easily obtainable jobs which require no outlay or training. Again, when women provide the cushioning between starvation and subsistence, men are set free to seek their fortunes in other occupations.

Taking a linear view, Boserup points out that the female's displacement through mechanisation and industrialisation means more than a loss of income; her position in the market and the home steadily deteriorates. Without adequate training facilities, women continue in traditional occupations. Ultimately, however, with the progress of the modern economic system, it is possible that they will be pushed out of the productive sphere altogether. Industrialisation introduces the "polarisation and hierarohisation of men's and women's work roles" which affects relationships within the family. Boserup further adds that in societies where there are legal provisions for divorce, separation and maintenance, and employed divorcee or widow will be treated better by her male relatives because she can support herself.[9] The overall cross-cultural impression therefore appears to be that irrespective of class position, and employed woman has substantially more status than one who does not have a job.

Domestic Circumstances

Balmiki women perform a vital function in the city's life. If they chose to stay away from work, civic amenities would be substantially affected. Consequently, monopoly over a caste-bound occupation gives them an important bargaining position at their place of work. Using a few variables such as control over income, domestic workload, free-time activities and decision-making, we shall see whether the position of the Balmiki women in the home is affected by her being employed. Though Balmiki women did not question the need to work, a majority specified that the initial decision was taken by someone else. While a third said that their husbands had decided that they should work, 15 per cent of the women indicated that mother-in-law had taken the initiative. Most of those who had been employed before they were married said that their mothers had sent them out to work.

Three-fourths of those whose husbands were the heads of house-holds said that all salaries earned were deposited with the women. It was culturally accepted that husbands should retain a certain amount for buying *bidis*, cigarettes, drink and clothes. On the other hand, no woman said that she kept apart some money to spend on herself. Fieldwork showed that women kept family earnings with them because it was convenient. Husbands appeared unwilling to take the responsibility of deciding how to make ends meet on a shoe-string budget. Nearly all the women said that they had to give accounts of the broad categories of expenditure to their husbands. All major financial decisions such as taking a loan, buying a bicycle or a radio were taken by the men.

Most Balmiki women in the sample combined the arduous task of scavenging with a full load of domestic duties. Men rarely participated in the daily routine of housework and child raring activities. The only major functions they appeared to perform were fetching fuel for the family hearth, occasionally queing up for rations, or taking a sick child to the dispensary. Almost half the sample said that they managed the housework single-handed, and this included twelve women who were out of their homes for over eight hours in the day. For the rest, helpers consisted of female kin or in-laws. If sons helped, they did so only until the age of about their peers while their sisters minded younger children or helped with the housework.

A third of sample scoffed at my question on free time. Outings to the cinema, distant market places and fairs were unknown, except during the festival season in October and November. Gossiping at the doorstep while the evening *chapattis* were being made appeared to be the most common from of relaxation. On the other hand, it was expected that men would have their drinking sprees, buy new clothes and go to the cinema. While we had not asked any specific questions on alcoholism, we were told by the local social worker that both drunkenness and wife-beating were common. Bimla's life was a case in point. Only three women—one whose husband was a clerk, and two others whose husbands were away from home often—aid that they went out and bought clothes for themselves and their children. For the rest, they had to depend on the largesse of their husbands, relatives or employers.

A Balmiki woman's earning ability led neither to economic independence, nor change in the traditional structure of male-female relationships within the family. An earning wife had no right to spend her alary on herself; all earning went into the common kitty for running the home. A man, on the other hand, invariably kept back some money for his personal expenses Again, wife beating continued to be a common offence. Those subjected to such excesses were pointed out to me with a certain degree of vicarious shame and included a middle-aged woman who supported her unemployed husband. Women took day-to-day decisions on what to cook or indicated when rations and kerosene oil were needed; on major issues, men decided where a woman should work, whether a loan should be taken or if a visit to the natal village was due. The expenses of travelling meant that women rarely visited their natal homes many of which were in rural Uttar Pradesh. Even when women managed to get away for a family wedding or for Diwali, their husbands or father-in-law had the final say on the length their stay.

Though Balmiki women are indispensable to Delhi's civic life, their men often decide the circumstances under which they shall go to work. An important feature of Balmiki economic organisation is the system of "buying up" houses among private employees. By paying a certain sum of money to a Balmiki who is about to leave the area in which he or she has been working, another Balmiki "buys" up the right to clean in a fixed number of houses which constitutes the beat. No other sweeper can enter the area to work, nor can employers terminate the services of the incumbent and hope to get a replacement. Normally, a Balmiki who wishes to dispose of this right negotiates with kinsmen and friends. There is usually no difficulty in finding person who are interested in bargaining. While a widowed women will usually do the talking herself, a married woman's chief negotiator is her husband or a male in-law. In case the seller is a woman, transactions may be carried on directly by the woman, through in cases where there is difficulty in reaching an accord, menfolk may step in. When the seller is a man and the buyer a woman, or vice versa, men often take a major role in deciding the sum. Sometimes, a show of muscle power clinches the issue. While in all-male transactions women do not play any role, men usually had a decisive say in determining the area and number of houses in which their wives should work.

Other studies have shown that high-caste women play an important role in marriage negotiations.[10] While we had not asked specific questions on the role of women in this sphere, observations indicated that that men were instrumental in initiating discussions. Wives may have been asked their opinion, but except in the case of widows or some older women, they were rarely given a formal role in talks. Field work in Taiwan and tribal Africa indicated that wives often exercised substantial covert influence either by withholding sexual service or organising themselves with other women in informal groups.[11] Though this was not an area that we had investigated, the incidence of wife-beating provided ample testimony of male reactions to recalcitrant or obstinate wives. A Balmiki woman may occasionally cook bodly, neglect her children or sham illness. Such expression of fratration can rarely be sustained over a long period of time and are no indications of wife's power.

Public Private Power

We can now draw some distinctions between power in the public and private domains. Balmiki women occupy a pivotal position in Delhi's civic life. The threat of a strike causes intense consternation among public authorities, as does a high rate of absenteeism. At work, sweeper women interact freely with male colleagues and employers. On buses, or walking along the roads to work, they spar loudly with men in the profession or other acquaintances. But public roles and behaviour patterns rarely affect male-female relations with the family unit. The Balmiki woman's power in Delhi city is not carried over to the home. One of the chief reasons for a female's lack of familial status is the absence of control over the product of labour, which in this case is the Balmiki woman's salary. This factor is also what often distinguishes an upper-middle-class working woman from a working-class of lower-middle-class employed Indian woman. The ability to decide how one's earnings are to be spent gives a woman a bargaining position within the family. While Balmiki women may have administered the family earnings, they did not have the liberty either theoretically or actually to isolate their salary from the rest of the income, or plan how to use it. When the majority of families lived at the subsistence level all income went to provide food and shelter for the family. In addition, an unemployed husband expected his wife to provide him with food and money.

Not only do mot Indian working women have little authority in deciding how to spend their salaries, but also their work is rarely socially valued. Among middle-class professions the dominantly female occupations of nursing and teaching are accorded a low social status. Though women perform vital functions in agriculture, men own land and capital in most parts of India, and take all the major decisions. Women's income is regarded only as "contribution towards the salt," while the man's income is essential for the staple crop.[12] This attitude is reinforced when men go to the cities, and start earning more in non-traditional occupations. It was the duty of the Balmiki wife to work; an unemployed woman was regarded as a liability. While a man's desire to move away from a demeaning occupation was legitimate, a Balmiki woman who thought of leaving the profession was duly chastised.

Impact of Development

A working-class woman's position within the family is rarely enhanced by virtue of her being employed. She combines the roles of an additional earner with that of unpaid domestic help. A woman who stays at home may be shunned by her family or ostracised by the community. She avoids the dual roles of working long hours and cooking, cleaning and tending to children.[13] In terms of physical fatigue, an unemployed woman has a distinct advantage over her employed neighbour. However, in a situation where women rarely have a choice in the matter, such observations are, by and large, pointless. What they do establish, however, is that unless attitudes towards women change, a shift, for instance, in the nature of work, from the traditional to the modern economy will rarely affect status. A woman's work is economically productive; it has to be socially valued as well. Further, without rights over their products and an independent identity, women will continue to be governed by male authority structures. For example, a *dhobi* (washer caste) woman who becomes a seamstress will have to depend on her husband's network for a loan to set up a shop; it would not be unreasonable than to expect the husband to have a decisive say in how her earnings are to be spent.

The argument is not against the absorption of women in the modern economy; it is only to point out that though a woman's work may become less onerous, it may be some time before her status within the family and society undergoes a commensurate change.

There appears to be a universal dilemma facing industrialised as well as industrialising nations. The change in the means of production becomes primarily a source of power and authority; a rationalisation of values does not always keep pace with changed life-styles. Srinivas has commented on the ambivalence in the minds of those castes exposed to urbanisation and Westernisation.[14] In other words, in a highly industrialised system old prejudices and active discrimination still persist; modernisation *per se* does not lead to a change in value systems. Both men and women who are caught up in the process of development face certain problems. A man's mobility and limited domestic participation make the solution of these problems easier; a woman on the other hand has to make far greater adjustments in her style of life. A semi-skilled job in a factory may mean a substantial change in the working conditions of a Balmiki woman. At the same time, for the migrant peasant woman who was economically productive at her own time and pace in the village, the shift to an urban milieu may result is considerable anomie.

In a caste-based occupational system like India, the process of modernisation has to contend with certain unique factors. As we have seen, important among these is the continued retention of women in traditional jobs. This case study of Balmiki women shows that most women in the agricultural economy, as well as those in low-status service occupations, are subjected to cumulative inequality. *Together* with their menfolk, they rank at the bottom of the caste hierarchy; *in relation* to their menfolk, they occupy inferior positions socially as well as occupationally. The more arduous as well as defiling tasks are performed by women. The immediate developmental problem then is not of women being pushed out of the economic system because of mechanisation, but that of remaining behind in low status, strenuous occupations. Singh found that slum women in urban India have far fewer occupational choices than their menfolk. Most of them were employed in menial jobs. So long as the country's size and ecology serve to slow down the universal mechanisation of agriculture and civic facilities, low-caste women will continue to find jobs in essential occupations. On the other hand, their men will be progressively involved in "passing" in caste society by changing their names, learning a trade and dressing in the latest style. The status of women is thus further depressed in relation to their mobile menfolk. Working-class women in a modernising face a loss of status not so much because of unemployment but in relation to their upwardly mobile menfolk. It is likely that when men move into more prestigious jobs, attitudes towards their wives may become more arbitrary. Some men prefer to take their wives out of paid employment, as at certain levels the fact that one's wife can sit at home is a sign of high status. There are also other reactions; the wives of two clerks in the sample were full of shame and self-recrimination. They felt that it was humiliating for their husbands to have wives in a demeaning occupation like scavenging.

Empirical evidence amply substantiates the developmental theorists' point of view that *men are the chief beneficiaries of the modern economy.* However, country to established notions, there is no imminent threat of unemployment for the bulk of rural women and those in certain caste-based occupations. In fact, modernisation is helped by the continuation of women in traditional jobs which releases men for the new technology. In India where certain caste groups have control over some low-status occupations, it is not unusual for men to restrict female employment to traditional jobs. A change from one kind of occupation to another often involves some measure of uncertainty. For working-class men in particular, the risk of an unknown future is more worth taking when they are assured financial support from their women-folk than when both partners are on the job market or the wife does not work. We may generalise then that the increasing participation of Indian men at certain levels of the economy is facilitated by wives in traditional employment.

Education as a Means to Upward Mobility

What do such trends tell us about the future of social change among the underprivileged in India? Will things be different for the next generation of Balmikis? At independence in 1947 the newly elected representatives of the people were well aware of the need to help backward groups. Working on the premise that education helps social and occupational mobility, mass literacy drives and school expansion were stressed. In addition to free tuition and text-book aid, a certain percentage of seats were reserved in educational institutions for the Scheduled Castes and Scheduled Tribes. It was hoped that such positive discrimination would help a child overcome his background. But thirty years of experience have shown that education by and large reinforces the social system; the higher castes monopolise access to education. Yet, the discriminatory policy has not been a total failure. There is a growing elite among the Scheduled Castes whose success is due largely to being able to stay on in the educational system. It would be interesting then, to see how an illiterate group of the urban poor views education as a means of providing a better future for their children.

To start with, only three women were aware of the existence of freeships and reserved places for their children in school. As there was a distinct bias in favour of educating boys rather than girls, separate questions were asked on sex distribution of education. On the whole, it appeared that younger mothers were more optimistic and enthusiastic than those whose children had been exposed to the educational system. Fifteen mothers specified that their sons had dropped out of school and five had no sons. Of the dropouts, seven were employed as sweepers, mechanics and drivers while the rest were employed. Two sons had finished school and two were college students. All except one of the remaining 56 women wanted their sons to finish school. This desire for schooling, however, had to contend with two harsh facts of life: first of all, the respondents were not sure whether they would be able to se their children through school. This apprehension was based not only on the lack of ability to bear the expenses but also on the economic opportunity cost argument. Beyond a certain age it did not pay to have children going to school when they could either work in the home or outside and help supplement the family income; secondly, many respondents said that discrimination and prejudice in school worked against their children.

We were an observer to a protracted argument which developed between Mayavati, a Corporation sweeper, and a male colleague of hers. We were talking to Mayavati as she smoked a *bidi* after a day's work. Her responses were spirited and lengthy, When we came to the question of education, her co-worker, who had so far been puffing away pensively at his *bidi,* interrupted and said that in education lay the path to salvation. mayavati looked hard at him, took her *bidi* out of her mouth and hawked noisily into the nearby drain. She made it clear that she did not agree with Natho. All her four children were in school, but she felt that they were wasting their time. Attacking Natho directly she asked him what his "Class X pass" son had achieved five years after leaving school. Besides what about untouchability? She answered herself:

> "What do these schools teach anyway? Of what use is it to our children? Today they want books, tomorrow pencils and day after tomorrow something else. And in government schools it is all supposed to be free.
>
> The other day we happened to pass by the boys' school. We saw my ten-year old son playing marbles in the dust. We shouted out, 'Ohe Ramu, it is your free period?' He shook his head and said no. Some teacher was standing by and we heard her tell another one, 'Oh these Bhangis, they expect us to teach their dirty children.' We kept quiet and did not say anything but walked on. When Ramu came home we asked him what he did in school. He said. 'This and that, sometimes studies when Bahenji feels like it.' So, that's what school means for our children"

Natho did not make any comment during Mayavatis' monologue. When she stopped and looked questioningly at him, he asked her that if she felt so negatively about education, why did she continue to send her children to school. Mayavati paused for a bit, and shrugging her shoulders said, if they left school, "they would be on the streets." There were no jobs for them; yet she would resist their taking to the traditional occupation. School was a way of keeping children occupied temporarily.

Mayavati's comments were indicative of the general attitude towards schooling for boys. Its benefits as a way of keeping children out of mischief were far greater than its role in occupational mobility. Most mothers felt that it would have been more useful if their sons were able to have access to some from of job-oriented training rather than waste their time in schools. If most mothers were somewhat motivated to keep their sons in schools far fewer were so inclined for their daughters. This discrepancy in attitude towards education of boys and girls is borne out by other slum studies. Desai and Pillai[15] found that illiteracy was three times higher among slum women than among the men. In her recent study of slum dwellers, Singh observed that while "parents tended to have unrealistic educational and employment aspirations for their sons' They did "not consider education very important for their daughters."[16]

From the present sample, while ten did not respond or did not have daughters, thirty-six out of seventy—a little over fifty per cent — said that their daughters had not gone beyond the first few classes in school. Of these eleven had got married before they were fifteen and another six were employed as sweeper girls in early adolescence. Thirteen mothers out of the thirty-six specified that they positively did not want their daughters to be educated as they would anyway be married and employed as sweepers.

Phoolbatti, the mother of three daughters who had put her eldest daughter to work as a sweeper after five years of schooling exemlified the reasoning of many Balmiki mothers with daughters:

> "Nearly all our girls go to work as sweepers. Why should we waste time and money on sending a daughter to school where she will learn nothing of use? What does the Hindi alphabet mean to her? Will it help her to get any other kind of jobs? So why not put her to work so that when she is married she will know something of our work as well as be able to light the stove?
>
> We repeat, why waste time in sending my daughters to school? Do they learn anything here? Anyway, they will be married soon and their mother-in-law will put them to cleaning latrines somewhere. If they go to school they will get big ideas and then be beaten up by their husbands or abused by their mothers-in-law."

Of the mothers who were sending their daughters to school, most were pessimistic about the use of education. Its role in job mobility was wholly discounted.

Further, the opportunity-cost argument was more applicable to girls of the school-going age tan to boys. This was in keeping with the role image of Balmiki women as maintained by the community. Six mothers admitted that their sons were in school while their female siblings had been taken out of the educational system and put to work as sweepers. Close questioning of these mothers showed that they did not feel that they had done anything unusual or unfair. School was a waste of time in a situation of extreme poverty; if daughters could help either by looking after younger children and thereby releasing mothers for extra work, or worked themselves, the family unit stood to gain more.

Out of the entire sample there were only four girls in class VIII and above, and, significantly, two of them were the daughters of clerks. In general the attitude was one of skepticism towards of clerks. In general the attitude was one of skepticism towards the benefits from formal schooling. Education was regarded more as a liability than an asset for adolescent girls. Thus, while there was some motivation for keeping sons in schools, it was non-existent for girls. With a third of fathers mobile out of the traditional occupation, sons had more chances than their female siblings of moving out of the system. Similarly, despite criticism of the educational system it was significant that Balmiki girls were in schools in greater numbers than their mothers. While ultimately the years in schooling were regarded as wasted, as girls made their way to their scavenging and their *susrals*,[17] for the sociologist they have joined the ranks of the educationally mobile. For instance, though mothers were scornful of schools several admitted on closer questioning that being able to read and write would enable a girl to correspond with her *maike* (mother) after her marriage. To many who had been confined to a life of daudgery and exploitation it was important to be able to convey to one's natal home the situation after marriage.

We find them that modernisation has not helped the status of the urban poor woman. On the other hand, by keeping the hearth going, she helps her husband to move ahead. The present analysis of attitudes towards education shows that even for the next generation, Balmiki women tend to react positively more often a son's schooling. For a daughter, school is a waste of time. In other words, conventional notions of the female role are so well internalised that women can visualise little change in the status of their daughters. In light of the empirical evidence examined so far it is difficult to be anything but pessimistic about the future of the poor women in India's cities. Nor is it possible to advise panaceas or solutions. Employment, we find, is not a variable which determines the power and status of the bulk of Indian working women. This may be true of men as well; but, the chances of a man in the city being able to lead a better life are far greater than the chances of a woman in a similar position.

NOTES

1. Samuel Jayakar, *Rural Sweepers in the City* (Mysore, 1952), p. 26.
2. Figures provided by M.S. Ashraf on the basis of work done for P.C. Agarwal and M.S. Ashraf, *Equality through Privilege* (New Delhi, 1976).
3. Andrea M. Singh and Alfred de Souza, *The Position of Women in Migrant Bastis in Delhi* (New Delhi, 1976), p. 55.
4. *Farash* is a category of persons employed in Government departments for dusting and cleaning office premises but not floors, baths and latrines.
5. *Jamadarni* is the Hindi word of sweeperwoman.
6. *Chaprasi* is the Hindi term for peon.
7. *Bhabhi* is an elder brother's wife.
8. Government of India, *Census of India, 1961* (Delhi, 1966), p. 422.
9. Esther Boserup, *Women's Role in Economic Development* (Chicago, 1970), pp. 139-140; 1976, xii.
10. Veena Das, "Indian Women: Work, Power and Status," in B.R. Nanda, (ed.), *Indian Women* (New Delhi, 1976), pp. 132-139.
11. See Louise Lamphere, "Strategies, Cooperation and Conflict among Women in Domestic Groups," in Michelle Zimbalist Rosaldo and Louise Lamphere, (eds.), *Women, Culture and Society* (Stanford, 1974); and Margery Wolf, "Chinese Women Old Skills in a New Context," in Rosaldo and Lamphere, *Women Culture and Society.*
12. Veena Das, *Indian Women's Work, Power and Status*, p. 193.
13. T.N. Madan, "The Hindu Woman at Home," p. 72.
14. M.N. Srinivas, *Caste in Modern India* (Bombay, 1970), p. 95. Books initiated by the Women's Movement in the USA talk of similar problems in the attitude towards women See for instance, Martha Bhall and Barbara Reagan, *Women and the Workplace* (Chicago, 1976) and Rosaldo and Lamphere, *Women, Culture and Society.* P. Altbach and G. Kelly went further in stating that a system of internal colonialism in the USA affects blacks, women and the working-class alike: *Education and Colonialism* (New York, 1978), p. 25.
15. A.R. Desai and S.D. Pillai, *Profile of an Indian Slum* (Bombay, 1972).
16. Andrea M. Singh, *Slum and Pavement Dwellers in the Major Cities of India* (New Delhi, 1976, mimeo.), p. 74.
17. *Susral* is the Hindi term for conjugal home.

42

Women Street Vendors

On a Friday evening in a resettlement colony outside of Delhi, the weekly market is in full swing. The streets are lined with vendors selling their goods. Some hang their wares up on strings between poles. Saris, bars, shawls, and pajamas fly out from the strings like many-coloured films. Some hawkers sit behind low tables where they display columns of glittering plastic and glass bangles. Some sit on the ground with their goods on a cloth in front of them. Their spice merchants catch the Meanderer's eye with their mounds of vermillion pepper, golden turmeric and deep brown cinnamon. The fruit and vegetable sellers also display their goods on pieces of material that they spread in front of them. They arrange the squash or mangoes in symmetrical towers. Most of the vendors are men, but here and there are older women whose high voices advertising their goods mingle with the deeper male tones. These women blend in with the scene, but they are more unusual than they appear. They have each made a decision to seek outside employment, and this sets them apart from the majority of the women in their community.

When the market is over and the vendors return to their houses, the lay-out of the resettlement area can be seen more clearly. It is organised into blocks of houses and densely settled. The resettlement areas of Delhi are the properties on which the government has settled migrant workers and their families. These migrant families came to Delhi and set up their houses on public land. The government rented a plot of land to each household when they first moved the people. The migrants built their own houses. In this resettlement area there are about fifty thousand people. In 1976-77, we studied a group of women who had lived in this resettlement area for sixteen years.[1] Most of them had migrated from Rajasthan and lived in the same slum before being moved to this government colony. Neighbours in the slum area were placed next door to each other in the resettlement area. After we left, a colleague, Jane M. Coe, continued to send me information for two years.[2] By the time she left, many families had said good-bye to sons and husbands who had migrated to Iran. The area had the characteristics of both a community where people had been together for twenty-five years, and a migrant settlement where new families came from Rajasthan and men left to work in the new land of plenty, Iran.

We came to study working women in this community, especially those who sought employment outside their homes. We were interested in their contributions to their families' incomes and how the women's work affected their families' daily lives. Were they better off because they had another source of income or were too many household tasks left undone when the women went out for work? However, we were unprepared for the strong social constraints in the community against women going out for work. We discovered that we first had to learn what these social constraints were and what conditions enabled a woman to free herself from these constraints. We discovered that there are times in a women's life when she is less constraints to stay within her own house. One of these times is when she is a full-fledged member of her husband's family, which occurs after she has been married, had *gauna* (the ceremony accompanying the consummation of marriage), produced children and seen them grow beyond infancy. Another time is when she is a mother-in-law and her daughter-in-law has had a baby. Of the ten female vendors who will be discussed in this chapter, eight fall into the category of a married women with at least one child past infancy or a mother-in-law with a daughter-in-law who has had a child. One woman, whom we call Savitri, has an exceptional family history which is given later in the chapter. The other woman is pregnant with her first child but has worked for two years selling fruit. We did not get enough information about her to explain her case. She was reluctant to talk with me.

Before discussing the vendors, we will explain the research methods used and then the social constraints on women working at jobs outside of their residential area. The discussion of constraints gives a picture of the life of a woman in Laxmipuri to some extent.

Research Methods

My research was done in three parts: (1) a demographic survey in which all residents in a block of 344 houses were asked a few questions, (2) a pre-study in which we tested questions to se if they were meaningful to the people in the community, and (3) a scientific random sample. The pre-study was done in the first four months of the fieldwork and differed from the random sample in several important ways. First, there was no standardisation of questions asked during interviews. Secondly, my research assistant and we talked only with people who were eager to talk with us. After discovering the meaningful questions, we made up a questionnaire schedule. The questions were asked of one member of a household whose number was selected from a chart of random numbers. Fifty-eight random sample interviews were made represents fiftyeight households. Some of the interviews are not fully completed because the person was reluctant to answer a question or the person and one section of the questionnaire too difficult to answer. The result was the sometimes less than fifty-eight responses are tabulated for a certain question. The interviews were done in Hindi mainly by a research assistant who translated the questions we asked.[3] By the end of the study we could ask part of the questionnaire in Hindi myself.

A computer was used to find the frequencies of jobs, castes, and places of origin. The job most frequently held by women was construction worker. The next most frequently held job was hawker, usually a seller of fruit and/or vegetables. Since construction workers are dealt with in another chapter, the hawkers are discussed here. The castes represented by the majority of the people are Khatik, Raigur, Koli, and Raj Barari.[4] These castes are called scheduled castes which means they appeared on a government schedule of depressed castes receiving or worthy of receiving special privileges. They are considered low on the Indian social hierarchy. Seventyeight per cent of the people in this particular block are from Rajasthan. The name of the resettlement areas and the names of the women discussed have been changed to protect their privacy.

Social Constraints against Working Women

Before describing what enabled the hawkers to go out for work, it is necessary to understand the social stigma attached to the working woman. In this area, which we will call Laxmipuri, these social pressures were both expressed as the community's standards and observed in the customs. These lower class people feel the same kinds of social pressures that middle and upper class people in India from the same regions feel. Many Indians do not recognise this. For example, middle class Indians asked me to find them servants to work in their homes and were surprised when we told them that young women from Laxmipuri were not allowed to go out to work at such jobs.

The social standards expressed by the Rajasthani migrants were concerned with the role of a woman and her physical mobility outside of her home. The traditional role for a woman is defined in terms of responsibilities and rights within her home. The mature married woman who has joined her husband (had *gauna*) has all the responsibilities of the house: preparing food, cleaning the house, washing the clothes, and caring for the children. All these activities should be done within the house or just outside it. In return for these responsibilities a woman is the right to be supported by her husband and in-laws. A girl's responsibilities between the ages of six and *gauna* are to help her mother and learn how to perform domestic tasks well so that when she goes to her in-laws she will be ready to do all duties expected of a married woman. A mother-in-law's responsibilities are to manage the household activities, delegating many to her daughter-in-law.

A woman also provides the next generation for the family she marries into. This is both a right and a responsibility. He children belong to her husband's family, and having children makes her a full-fledged family member. If she dies her children will stay with her husband's family. If her husband dies after she has had children, she will remain with her husband's family. However, if she does not have children and her husband dies, she will return to her parents. In one case in Laxmipuri a woman's husband had died one month after she had married him. She was not pregnant and the bond was dissolved; she returned to her parents who were optimistic about marrying her again. A woman must insure the purity of the genealogical line as well as provide insurance for her husband and herself in their old age. She must not give the slightest suspicion that the children might have been conceived with a man other than her husband. One way a family insures that their children are their own is by confining their daughters-in-law to the house. This eliminates others from any opportunity to take advantage of the daughter-in-law and does not give the daughter-in-law a chance to form any other liaison. A young, unmarried girls is gradually prepared for this responsibility of restricted mobility by her family, who must increasingly pull in the boundaries of where she may go as she grows from a young girl to an adolescent. A Laxmipuri family must guard their adolescent daughters carefully for their own sake also, since any suspicion that she may have formed a liaison with a body would destroy her chances for marriage. The chances of her sisters and brothers would also be affected by her behaviour. An adolescent girl avoids going any place alone and often avoids going out even in chaperoned situations. There is considerable anxiety about the safety and reputation of daughters, which is one reason why daughters are married very young in Laxmipuri, often before the onset of menses.

Once a young girl is married also continues to live with her own parents until *gauna*, but she must behave differently. When she meets someone from her husband a village or area of residence, she must cover her face. After *gauna* a mother-in-law bears the responsibility for her daughter-in-law's travel outside of the house. If she sends her daughters-in-law out to shop instead of going herself or asking one of the men to shop, she may be considered lax in supervision and inviting trouble. In one household where there were three daughter-in-law—the oldest with three children all past infancy—none were allowed out of the house to shop for anything. The only way one of them could go out was to visit the temple in the same block.

There are many customs that activate the idea that a woman should remain within her house, not expose herself to the outside world, and not interact with it. There is the custom where a woman must cover her face with her veil or sari any time a male of her husband's age or older comes into her presence. This is true for all male members of a woman's caste who live in her husband's village or by extension, the area where her husband lives in the city. Laxmipuri is treated like a village for this custom. The custom is strongest closest to one's house. For instance, a woman of the most numerous caste sitting inside the front room of her house will often cover her face upon hearing the approaching steps of a man who would pass in front of her house. It is likely that the man is of her caste; he could be her husband's age or older, and he might be glancing inside. Outside of the block of residence the custom would be less strict because a woman visiting a relative or going for rations would not know if the men she was passing were the same caste or not. When women take buses outside of Laxmipuri, they do not cover their faces unless they meet someone they know. This custom does not apply for the men a women knows from her natal village or area of residence. Another custom that prevents normal interaction with other people applies to daughter-in-law. This is the custom whereby a daughter-in-law does not speak to anyone when she is in the presence of her mother-in-law or any older in-laws except a sister-in-law. We observed this custom often when we went inside to interview a household and found a mother-in-law and daughter-in-law. We might start by talking with the older woman but then ask the daughter-in-law her name and age. She usually would not answer. People said, and we observed, that when the daughter-in-law has had a child, this custom is not so strict. Gradually, in most households, as the daughter-in-law gets older and produces more children, she speaks to her mother-in-law and other in-laws, but it some families the custom persists indefinitely. The purpose of these two customs is that the woman who marries into a village can show respect and deference towards the village elders. But the custom effectively functions to limit a woman's discourse and interaction and to isolate her.

Another custom which limits a woman's freedom of movement is the stated preference to marry a daughter to a distant place or village so that she will make the break with her own family and become a part of her in-law's family. When this does happen, the woman has less chance to visit her natal home because someone must accompany her when she goes and because of the increased expense of travelling a long distance. A woman is most mobile in her natal village, and if this village or area is nearby and the imaginary boundaries between her residence and her husband's are blurred, her mobility is greatly increased.

A woman considers all the men of her own caste who live in the same village or same area as brothers or cousins in the sense that they are not possible marriage or sexual partners. These boys do not have the same responsibilities towards her that her real brothers and cousins do, but she does not fear them. She may talk with them and need not cover her face in their presence. Often all the boys of the girl's caste that she meets daily are related to her in some way. The boys of other castes in the same residential area are also not possible marriage or sexual partners and are not feared. But the adolescent girl maintains a social and physical distance between herself and the boys of different castes.

Outside the area where she lives, a woman is in a general state of fear. This seems to be partly because of the woman's vulnerability, since the consequences of any accident are so extreme, and partly fear of the unknown. One women described the problem of educating daughters beyond the 6th standard in her Rajasthan village. The school only went up to the 6th standard and after that the girls had to board a bus and go four kilometres to the nest town to the school. A bus was provided for girls, but the families were still afraid to send their daughters out of their own village. Another example of this fear concerns a sewing school in a nearby resettlement area. The school was well-organised with a guaranteed marketing programme for goods made, but it was a ten minute walk from the block of residence, This sufficiently inhibited many women from participating. In contrast, when a sewing class was set up in the block where the women lived, it was over-subscribed. For women to go out of "the village" was a big step.

We conclusion, the ideas and customs of the people of Laxmipuri are formidable constraints to be overcome if a woman chooses to look for work outside her home and area.

Streetsellers' Decision to Work

In spite of these ideas and customs, women do go out for work. The vendors are the second largest group of women workers in the block. Of the ten women who responded that they were hawkers, seven sell vegetables, two sell fruit, and one sells readymade *pakoras* (vegetables, sliced and fried in gram batter).[5] Most of these women said they made the decision to go to work themselves. Four women said they decided to go to work because they were short of money and one woman said she had too much idle time on her hands and wanted to buy more things for her children. Three women changed from construction work to selling because the work was less physically taxing.

Help and Hindrance from In-laws and Natal Families

After the woman has decided to work because of her understanding of her family's economic need or her desire to improve the family's standard of living, she must consider how her family will feel about her going out. Freedom from family disapproval is essential. Who is likely to disapprove? A woman's in-laws may disapprove; her husband may disapprove; and finally, her own natal family may disapprove. It is significant that among the ten women who produce and sell *pakoras,* only one of them lives with in-laws. She lives in a large extended family, but her in-laws do not disapprove of her working. In fact, she feels compelled by them to work. She is the middle daughter-in-law of three daughters-in-law, but she is the only working woman in the family. Her in-laws are quite old and her sister-in-law can take care of her children and do the domestic work of the household. In two cases the mother-in-law shifts her residence between her sons and their families. In the first case, a woman we will call Santara did not sell fruit until her mother-in-law was disabled. Her mother-in-law had been selling fruit from door to door ever since Santara came to join her husband. One evening on the way home from work when she was waiting for the bus, the bus sped into the stopping place and ran over her foot. She had to have her foot amputated. Santara took up the work of selling fruit to replace the income lost from her mother-in-law's job. Another woman who sells vegetables has a mother-in-law who travels between three sons all living in the same area. She does not interfere in the lives of her son's families. If a woman's in-laws are sick or very poor, she may expect less financial support and less disapproval of the idea of her working. The case of Savitri shows how neither her in-laws nor her natal family disapproved of her working. In fact, support from Savitri's own parents was the enabling factor in her going out for work., Savitri worked with her mother as a vegetable seller in Laxmipuri before she was married. She was married to a man in a Rajasthani village at fifteen and went to join him one year later. Her in-laws were very poor and very old and had only a few goats. Savitri and her husband tried to make a living by selling the milk from the goats, but most people who liked goat milk had a goat. Savitri and her husband could not make a subsistence wage. When she visited her parents in laxmipuri they told her to come back to the city with her husband and she could become a vegetable seller since she knew the job already. Savitri talked to her in-laws and they agreed that she and their son should leave the village and return to Laxmipuri. Savitri and her husband rent a room from Savitri's sister and go to the same vegetable market that Savitri went to with her mother. After a while Savitri and her husband were able to purchase a cart and sell their vegetables in the back streets of Laxmipuri from their cart. Now they are able to sent money back to the village to Savitri's in-laws. Because she had strategies available to her from her urban background, Savitri was able to help out her in-laws, her new family.

If a woman's husband disapproves of her working outside the home, she will not usually go out. Among those women who sell vegetables and fruit, there are no cases where the husband disapproves of the wife's outside employment. In three cases one is Savitri's, the husband and wife work together. They go to the vegetable markets to buy the vegetables together; they bring them home and clean them together; and they sell them together. In another case, the woman gets the vegetables from the market and her husband often joins her to help sell the vegetables in the evening market after he has come home from work.

In more cases a woman's natal family is helpful and supportive when she decides she wants to go out for work. There is the case of Savitri which is unusual, but if the woman lives close to her own parents, it is not unusual for them to help her find a job. Sometimes a woman will leave her children off at her mother's house while she works, if her mother lives nearby. In the case of the woman who sells *pakoras,* her married daughter comes back to her natal home every day to help her mother. The daughter milks her mother's buffalo and prepares her father's food also. Sometimes the daughter helps her mother prepare the *pakora* flour.

Occasionally, however, a woman's family will object to her getting a job. This was the case with Gisoda's daughter, Keesha. Although Gisoda herself is a whitewasher and a full-time worker, she educated Keesha up to eighth standard and felt Keesha was not above such jobs as construction work, whitewashing, and vegetable selling. Gisoda spent a great deal of money on Keesha's marriage and is still paying back the debt because she married her to a man who had completed the 12th standard. Gisoda felt very proud of Keesha's educational achievement and her marriage to an educated man. But Keesha's husband was unable to find a job, and he and Keesha lived on his widowed mother's wages as a vegetable seller. The mother was very resentful that her son and Keesha would sit at home while she was working. She wanted Keesha to work with her and felt her son should look harder for a job. Keesha felt she should not work as a vegetable seller, and the dispute was serious enough for her to go home to her parents. The supported her in her attitude about her own work and she stayed with her parents for a full year before there was a reconciliation between the two families. Keesha was assured she would not be forced to work selling vegetables, and she returned with her husband. But the situation was still the same and the case ended tragically. Keesha's mother-in-law's abuse of the couple because chronic, and the husband and wife decided to end their lives together and set their clothes on fire. The mother-in-law and neighbours found them and were able to save the man, but Keesha died of the burns later in the hospital. She was considered a martyr in Laxmipuri because she was able to convince the police who visited her in the hospital that she had a cooking accident, and thus she did not bring shame on her in-laws and their community. There are many factors which led to this difficult situations; the fast that more education sometimes makes the available jobs seem unappropriate; the fact that a mother-in-law usually does not want or allow a young daughter-in-law to go out of the house at all, to say nothing of going out to work; the fact that a daughter-in-law should do what her mother-in-law tells her, and finally the fact that Keesha's parents supported the idea that she was too educated to be a vegetable seller.

Different Types of Hawkers

There are several types of hawkers in Laxmipuri. The luckiest own their own shops in

Laxmipuri market or in another establish market. Other men and women have carts which they push, going from house to house in a set area. Still others may carry baskets on their heads or on bicycles. Of course, more vegetables can be displayed in a store than on a cart; more can be carried on a cart than in a basket. Savitri and her husband have a cart and a bicycle. If they do not sell their vegetables in Laxmipuri, they can go further with the bicycle. Another type of hawker has a permanent place along one of the main streets to sell his or her goods. Before the evening market they go to their places and spread a cloth down on the ground. Then they display their vegetables or fruit.

The vendors in Laxmipuri buy their vegetables and fruit to sell in one of two places. Either they go to the fields surrounding Laxmipuri and pick the vegetables themselves and pay for them, or they go to an early morning market about ten minutes away by bus. Usually groups of four to six women go together at 6 a.m. on the bus. They walk to the bus together and sit together. When they arrive at the market, it is in full swing. The vegetable market is a bustling place where the women spend two to four hours selecting and bargaining for vegetables. They usually have established relationships with several retailers who depend on their business. The women seem to linger over the market and genuinely enjoy each other's company. In fact, the market is more than a place to buy and sell. When we visited it, there were priests, travelling entertainers, and a partially mad, market, "clown" who could predict the future. Many different kinds of people mixed together. A make-shift tea shop was set up for those who wanted tea. The women from Laxmipuri sat and relaxed together after they had made their purchases. They even ate fruit, which is something we had seldom seen women do in their own hones in Laxmipuri. Then the vegetable sellers come home by bus or *tonga* (horse and cart). A few come home by bicycle. A bus costs extra for the loads of vegetables, about Rs. 2 for four bundles, and a *tonga* costs Re. 1 per bundle. When the women reach home they usually rest for a bit and then attend to housework. Later in the afternoon thy sort and wash their vegetables and then carry them to their places in the market. The market is in the evening, so that the people returning from work can purchase vegetables. Those who push a cart or carry vegetables on their heads may go straight for the early morning market and ell their vegetables in other areas of Delhi. Most vegetable sellers do have a broken-up day which makes fitting in housework and childcare easier. However, many work six or seven days a week. Customers count on them either coming to their door or being at a certain spot in the market. The most successful vegetable sellers make between 10 to 15 rupees a day and the less successful earn five to eight rupees. The initial cost of purchasing the vegetables in the early market is thirty to one-hundred rupees. It is possible to buy the vegetables from day to day on short term credit.

The women who sell vegetables and fruit contribute twenty to one hundred percent of their family incomes. Those who contribute one hundred percent work with their husbands. Table 42.1 shows the amount each hawker makes and the percentage this is of the family's income. This information is unavailable of the two fruit sellers and one vegetable seller. The husband and wife team who make the most money also work the longest hours. Reesum and her husband go to the vegetable market and buy their vegetables together. Then she goes by bus with a basket of vegetables in one direction, and he goes by bicycle with another basketful in another direction. They do not come home in the middle of the day. Their days are long, from five a.m. until four or five p.m. Most of the other vegetable and fruit sellers have an eight or nine hour day. The spend five hours getting their vegetables and three or four hours selling them.

The woman who makes *pakoras* has a different daily schedule. Her work does not start until about three O'clock in the afternoon. Then she begins cutting up vegetables and mixing the batter. She has a cart on which she carries her kerosene burner and vegetables. About four or five O'clock she pushes her cart to a designated place, which she has paid for in advance. Then she heats the mustard oil and starts the work and sell her *pakora*. She knows she could make more money selling vegetables, but she likes this job. She is proud of her delicious *pakora*. "People come to Laxmipuri just to buy my *pakora*," she says. Nevertheless, she works because she cannot count on her husband giving her money each day. Sometimes he spends his daily wages as a mason on drinking.

TABLE 42.1

Income of Hawkers

Job	*Rupees Per Month Income*	*Percentage of Family Income*
Pakora Seller	60-90	25
Vegetable Seller	150	20
Vegetable Seller	125	68
Vegetable Seller	250-300	100
Vegetable Seller	200	100
Vegetable Seller	100	30
Vegetable Seller	75	20

Hawkers' Opinions of their Jobs

When asked what were the advantages of selling vegetables, one woman replied, "There are advantages to selling vegetables over doing construction work, but neither job is a real position. We would like a real position that has some security with it. This is just a job." It would be difficult for the hawkers of Laxmipuri to find "positions" because none of them have been to school. Compared with other jobs available to them the hawkers know the advantage of selling.

The women compare vegetable and fruit selling with construction work, and find it less strenuous. They like being their own boss. They feel they can stay close enough to their homes to be "incharge." But they acknowledge that there is a greater risk involved in vegetable selling and some days they do not make any money. There are also certain skills involved in selling products. A woman must know how to calculate and she should be fairly quick at it. She must be outgoing enough to bargain, promote her goods, and establish relationships with customers. Knowing the market and when to buy what vegetables is another important skill. A woman must also have some equipment—a scale and weights. This costs about Rs. 50. She also needs money to make her initial purchase of vegetables.

Shared Domestic Responsibilities

Most of the women vendors have help with the household and childcare responsibilities. Several helpers have already been mentioned. Savitri's mother takes care of her daughter. The *pakora* maker's daughter, Uma, does her mother's chores when she is out selling snacks. Santara's mother's-in-law's former job. There are a few other cases of helping relatives that need to be mentioned. One of the vegetable sellers has a son and daughter-in-law living in a separate house nearby. The daughter-in-law living in a separate house nearby. The daughter in-law cooks the evening meal for her and brings the food to her house. Another vegetable seller's sister, married and living nearby, takes care of her child when she sells vegetables. The vendor who is the middle daughter-in-law says all the daughters-in-law share the household responsibilities.

Do the husbands and sons help out with the domestic tasks? The male relatives of this group of women do not help out as much as the male relatives of construction workers. This may be because there are other available female relatives, or because the vendors themselves have the middle portion of the day to cook and clean. The hawkers are also not as exhausted when they return form their work as are construction workers. However, the days when the husbands do not go to work, they often help out. basanti, the woman whose husband helps her in the evenings, works more days in a month than her husband. He is often seen sitting at home with his two younger daughters. The men in this community are expected to perform certain household tasks. Most men wash their own and their children's clothes. The men also do most of the shopping for clothes and vegetables. In the case of the vegetable vendors, the women take their supper vegetables form their selling stock. The women get the rations of rice and flour themselves, but, on the occasions when the family eats meat, the men purchase the meat. It is not unusual to see men helping their wives by cutting up vegetables for the evening meal. The men are willing to lend a helping hand.

The women of Laxmipuri keep the family money. The husband hands his salary to his wife or his mother, whoever is in charge. The man may keep some money for himself for transportation or tea and cigarettes. The women do not consider that keeping their family cash gives them much control over household expenses. There is so little money to control, they complain.

Work and Self-Image

The women were asked what difference working made to them. There of them answered that their jobs gave them a ready source of money every day. The *pakora* seller said that her job made her less dependent on her husband. When her husband came home drunk and without his wages, she was miserable, but she knew that there was the money from her *pakora* selling. The two fruit sellers said they and their families ate better food when they were selling fruit. Santara said her children got fruit every day when she was selling. She had stopped for six months to have a baby. She will go back to work soon and let her mother-in-law take care of her child. Then her children will have fresh fruit again.

In the random sample interview the women were asked the question "Who am I?" This was the final question the schedule and if the interview was unfinished, it was not asked. This is the case with two of the five random sample hawkers. In the pre-study, the *pakora* seller, and two vegetable sellers were asked the question. In total, there are six answers. Of those women asked, all of them could respond. This was not the case in the random sample, where four women could not understand the question, and several other answers are not comprehensible. The vendors, however, answered easily. Savitri responded that she was a human being, the equal of any other human being. The difference between her and other (we wondered if she was talking about me) was that she could not afford luxuries nor follow her own interests. She was poor so her poverty dictated what she would do. Another young vegetable seller answered that she was a person and a very good person. Basanti responded, "we are Koli" (her caste). The *pakora* seller said that she was a knowledgeable women who could tell me whatever we wanted to know about Laxmipuri. The vendor, who is the middle daughter-in-law, responded that she was an unfortunate person who had to work. She said what happened to her depended solely on luck. And the final answer form a vegetable seller: "We are my husband's helper. We must give him a hand with the family's income." The answers seem too various to make an analysis at this point.

The Hawkers' Aspirations for their Children

There is more consistency among the responses of the women to the two questions: "What are your hopes for your sons?" And "What are your hopes for your daughters?" Than for the previous question" Who am I?" There are eight responses and two women who did not answer these questions. Two of the eight said that they hoped their sons would feed them when hey are old. They did not put their hopes in their daughters because they would go to live with their in-laws. Another women said she hoped her children would grow up, marry, and be rich. Savitri gave a similar answer for her future sons (she has one two-year-old daughter). For her daughter and future daughters, she hoped they would get a good education. Then, she explained, if there is a problem of poverty in their in-law's house, they will be able to get good jobs and help out. Of course, that is exactly what happened in Savitri's life. Other women in the community now recognise that women may have to help out earning wages. Santara also mentioned that she would try to educate all her children (two sons and two daughters) so that they could all get good jobs, if that was necessary. Education seemed to be the key word in the answers to this question. But the purpose of the education was not always to enable the son or daughter to get a good job. One women hoped to educate her son so he would be respected and her daughter so she could write her letter after she went to her in-laws. In the answers to this question in the random sample as a whole, this was an often repeated reason for educating daughters. The mothers and fathers want to keep in contact with their married daughters. They also want their daughters to be able to communicate a difficult situation so they can come and get them.

Santara and Uma, the married daughter of the *pakora*-maker, said that daughters should be educated so that they could marry and educated man. Santara explained that if the parents want to marry their daughter to an educated man, the man's family will expect a higher dowry form an uneducated girl than form an educated girl. Uma said that families preferred educated daughters-in-law now. An educated daughter-in-law could pick up new skills more easily and would be less likely to be exploited by salespersons in the market. Both Uma and Santara hoped they could educate their daughters. Their ideas represented a new outlook toward the role of the married woman. To these two women, there were other considerations than solely a woman's ability to produce children and support them. Daughters are also seen by some people as possible helpers. The traditional attitude was the one expressed earlier that daughters go to their in-laws and their parents cannot expect any help form them. But Uma, not surprisingly, said she places more hope in her daughters than her sons. Sons can grow up and forget their parents; daughters will always remember their mothers and fathers.

None of the vendors stated that they hoped their sons or daughters would be fruit or vegetable sellers. Although they recognise selling has advantages for them, they want better jobs for their children. They hope their children will have secure positions or office jobs. Basanti sees her job as allowing her son to continue in school a little longer. Other boys might be expected to work, but with her income from selling vegetables, she hopes her son would be freed from the necessity of giving up schooling early to get a job.

Conclusions

Female vendors in Laxmipuri represent a group of women who are able to make the most of the situation in which they find themselves. Although they go against the accepted ideal that a woman should stay in her house, they are not insensitive to the community's standards. These women work at the stages in their lives when there are fewer household responsibilities, and they use the money to improve their family's standard of living. The vendors take advantage of opportunities that are found in the urban environment. Gradually, the role of the working woman, especially the women who is aware and considerate of the community's attitudes, will become an acceptable role.

NOTES

1. The study was made possible by a grant of Sabbatical Leave form the Arlington Country School Board.
2. Jane M. Coe sent me much information form 1978 until 1979. Some of that information has gone into the preparation of this chapter.
3. My research assistant was Promilla Yadav. We are indebted to her for her skills in translating and in making friends with the people of Laxmipuri. Without her, this research would have bene impossible.
4. The word "caste" is used in this paper as a translation of the Hindi word *"jati."*
5. Five women are form the pre-study and five are form the random sample. We used, all the vendors that we had in the random sample and then chose five from the pre-study so that there would be an equal number form both sources.

43

Women Construction Workers

As you approach Old Delhi on the Ring Road from New Delhi you come upon a narrow strip of land on one side of the road. Along it are strung a row of *jhuggies* or huts extending for about a thousand feet, most of them belonging to construction workers. A *jhuggie* is a square hut built of brick or rubble walls with a canvas stretched across the top for a roof. Sometimes thatch or even a piece of corrugated iron forms the roof of a better *jhuggie*. Many *jhuggie* walls are covered with mud or plaster; a few are even whitewashed. A family of four typically lives in a *jhuggie* of about 80-1000 square feet. Few extended families have survived the migration from the village to Delhi. There is little furniture in the huts—perhaps a *charpoy* for the father and one or two children to sleep on. In one corner of the hut are a few tin pans for eating and cooking. Outside the doorless entrance are a few stones where the fire is laid for cooking. If you travel along Ring Road at sunset the air is dense with the pungent smoke of four hundred cow-dung fires on which the evening meal is being cooked. The smoke hangs low over Delhi morning and evening, adding to a feeling of environmental deterioration and decreasing visibility.

This construction working community is populated largely (70 per cent) by immigrants from Rajasthan, as can be seen from the very full skirts and heavy silver anklets—often a woman's total wealth—worn by the women. The squatter colony is overcrowded, has an inadequate water supply, lacks communal baths or latrines, medial services and schools. Inhabitants rise at 5:30 to walk to one of five handpumps to wash. Water from the pumps is not potable, and there is no other water supply nearby. None of the huts has electricity; the Municipal Corporation has provided sixteen general lights for the colony. Needless to say there are not garbage disposal facilities.

Workers leave their *jhuggies* at 7:00 or shortly after, to walk to work, usually two to three miles away. Mothers take their small children with them to work, as there is no relative with whom to leave them in the colony. Work begins at 8:00 in the morning and ends at 5:00, with an hour for lunch. They then retrace their steps home, draw water, lay a fire, and cook the evening meal. Five stalls in the settlement sell general provisions and also function as social centers and tea shops. The evening meal consists of *roti* and vegetables / *dal*. They go to sleep at dark, exhausted. There are no lights, and in any case most do not read.

Residents live in the colony 3.5 years on the average. Two-thirds of the working population is employed in unskilled construction work, 7.5 per cent as skilled masons, 19 per cent in government service, and the remaining 7.5 per cent is self-employed. Nearly all adult women living here are illiterate. Some children are able to attend the new Mobile Creches at the worksite. About 40 per cent of the parents have sent one of the children to a municipal school at one time, and most hope their children will be able to enter a school through the Mobile Creche. If the children do not remain in school longer than three years, however, they may still fall into the class of functional illiterates. These are the urban slum dwellers from whom the construction workers are recruited in the Delhi area.

Similar colonies exist in Bombay and other large cities. Workers in Bombay and Delhi are more fortunate than in other cities to have some worksites supplied with Mobile Creches, the achievement of a small number of persistent social workers.[1]

Recruitment, Working Conditions and Wages

In terms of employment, the building industry is one of the largest in India, employing millions of workers. The total investment in the industry is made up of (1) the input of materials, (2) the input of labour of all types, and (3) the overhead costs. However, the industry relies essentially on unskilled labour; the use of mass production technology is practically absent. The industry is suitable to Indian conditions as it is primarily labour-intensive. Except in the urban areas, even machinery such as concrete mixers, power-cranes, reinforced concrete structures or pre-fabricated structures are not available. The employers have no real incentive for introducing better techniques as they are afraid of raising costs. The labourers, therefore, suffer from locational immobility as well. While construction work is considered unskilled, it is back-breaking. Workers cut soil, carry cement, stones, bricks, mortar, and water on their heads, crush bricks, and mix concrete.

According to the 1971 census there were 204,000 women construction workers in India (down from 290,000 in 1951); women comprised 10 per cent of the rural and 9 per cent of the urban workers in construction.[2] There is great regional variation in the proportion of construction workers who are female. Harijans or scheduled caste members make up the majority of construction workers in India. Among Harijans, the proportion of women construction workers is highest in the Western States and lowest in the Northern states.[3] Women in this field are drawn primarily from the rural poor and suffer discrimination on the basis of class, caste, and sex.

The methods and means by which labour is brought into various industries such as the building industry are not always straight forward and direct. Therefore, the labour often find himself/herself in a disadvantageous position. Language, caste, and class barriers inhibit direct communication between employer and worker. As ordinary villagers looking for jobs are not conversant with the intricacies of the employment process, a number of intermediaries or jobbers—known variously as *sardar, mistry, mukaddam, chowdhury, jamadar,* etc. —reap a substantial part of the benefit actually due to the workers. The jobbers understand the problems of the workers as they are able to communicate with them in their own language. Therefore they enjoy the confidence of the workers. When a group of workers are new to an environment, they look upon these jobbers as custodians of their interests and rights. Often the jobber thus becomes the supervisor or the labour contractor. Since the employers rarely want to take the trouble of dealing with the workers directly, the jobbers help in the day-to-day administration as well; for example, in granting leave or in providing substitute labour whenever needed. In return jobbers claim a share from the daily earnings of the workers. This is known as *peshgi* and involves (a) the *jamadar's* commission, and (b) interest on any loan which the labourer may have taken when he was looking for a job. Incidents have been reported in which the intermediaries secure unjust dismissals of workers and extract from them fresh commissions by providing them with reinstatements.

India has progressive labour laws on the books. They are not enforced; most laws do not even cover the vast majority of Indian workers, those in the "unorganised" sector. As contract or casual labour, women construction workers are part of the unorganised sector. A 1971 law (Abolition of Contract Labour Act) sought to eliminate the practice of contract labour and provide some benefits such as maternity leave to women labourers in this field. It, however, is often violated. In some states construction workers are covered by minimum wage law; in other states they are not. These laws are not adequately enforced.

The government itself is a culprit in this regard. Many construction projects-buildings, roads, bridges, railway lines, etc.—are in the public sector. The government is the largest employer in construction contractors solicit the services of labour contractors for supplying labour in order to complete the work on time. Because the construction contracts are short-term, based on tenders, scattered at different places, and because. The work is temporary, contractors cannot possibly maintain labourers on a permanent basis. Moreover, construction labour being casual and migratory, it cannot be organised on a permanent basis. Government regulations provide for amenities such as creches, sanitary services, and holidays as well as specified maximum hours and minimum wage rats for workers in construction projects of the Central Public Works Department. These conditions are not met.

In some cases construction workers are attached to a labour contractor on a long-term basis and work whenever he sends them. Often construction workers are migrant labour. Contractors bring whole families from depressed areas to work on large-scale projects in other districts or states. The practice of using migrant labour depresses the local wage rates. In other cases construction workers are hired on a daily basis and have no security of employment whatsoever.

There are ways—legal, illegal, and non-legal—through which employers circumvent labour laws; employees do not realise the potential of labour laws, which otherwise would help the workers. In this pattern, women employees are the most affected for reasons of ignorance and lack of organised strength. They have neither the support of militant unions nor the wherewithal to fight in courts. They are also handicapped in this regard because of both domestic obligations and the economic imperative of earning wages. The denial of equality in work and wages and the deprivation of basic amenities and minimum standards are particularly blatant in the case of women workers.

Despite the fact that women carry as much load men do, contractors pay them at a lower rate. While a man is paid typically Rs. 7-8 per day in the late 1970s, women are paid the rate of Rs. 4.50-5 per day. Women are paid less on the grounds that they work on small jobs which do not require the specialised skills of the bricklayer or cement mixer. The following was the wage schedule in road construction and the building industry in certain states for the year 1969-70.[4]

		Daily Wage Rates	
State	*Year*	*Men*	*Women*
Kerala	1969	2.69	2.00
Madhya Pradesh	1970	2.50	2.15
Himachal Pradesh	1970	2.50	2.20
West Bengal	1970	3.00	2.00
Tamilnadu	1970	1.80	1.50

Wages have risen since these rates were established, but the male/female differentials remain.

Worse still, labour contractors receive a payment in bulk at a flat rate from the construction contractors or the government contractors, for the total number of labourers supplied. Labour contractors get the signature or thumbprint of these illiterate labourers in the register book, though often paying them less than the fixed rate. The possibility of payment at the fixed minimum daily wage of Rs. 7 or Rs. 4.50 does not even arise. Thus not only is the provision of the Abolition of Contract Labour Law not observed, but the recruits are subject to exploitation by contractors.

According to the Model Rules of the Central Public Works Department of the Government of India there should be at least two huts with the *ayahs* (attendants) for children where there are more than fifty women working on a site. It is nevertheless rare to find such facilities. Canteens for workers are not always provided, so the women either have to take their meals with them for themselves and their families, if they are at the same site, or buy cheap food from the *cha-wallahs* (roadside tea shops). The contractors have no obligation to provide the workers with adequate housing, so small *jhuggies* or squatter settlements become the homes of these people. They live in dirt, squalor and constant want. Washing, bathing, and other daily hygienic needs have to be done in unfiltered filthy water, often in scant supply.

The desultory state of labour organisation and mobilisation has its effects on the problems of earnings in the construction industry. Increased wages and improvement of facilities are rigorously resisted by employers with much stronger bargaining power than employees. The wage rates in the building industry are conspicuously low, and the "sweating" of labour is still prevalent. The transitory nature of both work and workers in this industry prevents workers from forcing the issue with the authorities. Unfortunately the Minimum Wages Act of 1948 is not uniformly applicable to all workers, as they do not fulfill the requisite qualifications throughout the country. The rates and qualifications vary from state to state. Since these workers are not unionised, they have little recourse.

Women construction workers are special targets for wage discrimination. The Indian Constitution, in the Directive Principles of State Policy, has recommended equal pay for equal work. This Article (39D) of the Constitution—equal pay for equal work—is only a policy statement at present. It requires legislative sanction from all states and only when incorporated in the Minimum Wages Act will it take effect.

In this industry, to reiterate, women workers are in a disadvantageous position. In recent years, a steady decline in employment of women seems to be the trend, because of mechanisation and rationalisation. But many women are employed enlarge river valley projects or on large construction sites, like that of the Metro-politan Tube Railway of Calcutta. However, they mainly carry loads on their heads. They are employed by the contractors, who are under no obligation to provide these women with adequate shelter or other facilities. They are often found at sites with their children, as there are no creches or any other places where children can be left. They are not provided with any maternity or sickness benefits because they are essentially seasonal labour. Very often they are even denied accident benefits as well. These women workers are ignorant as well of the rights to which they are entitled; hence the status quo persists. For who among them, for example, would know of the ILO Convention of Equal Remuneration for Equal Work? They are almost mostly unskilled, illiterate, and have no capacity to improve their condition. The extreme elasticity of supply of female labour is another factor which keeps their wages from becoming equal to that of their male counterparts.

Demographic Characteristics

Based on three surveys of women construction workers (in Delhi, Bihar and Andhra Pradesh) a picture (not necessarily representative) emerges of these women and their social context.[5] Harijans and tribals are the largest groups represented, although they comprise only 15 per cent and 5 per cent of the Indian population respectively. Ninety-six per cent of the Delhi construction workers are Harijan migrant labourers from Rajasthan; Harijans and tribals together comprised 90 per cent of the Bihar sample and 67 per cent of the Andhra sample. As construction work is extremely physically taxing, most of the women are young (average age 25) having joined the workforce before they reached their teens. Almost all are illiterate. The Harijan women in Delhi and Bihar were married early and their marriages were arranged. The tribal women in Bihar tend to marry later. In Andhra the local (as opposed to migrant) women workers are mostly unmarried, as their parents depend on their earnings, and it is difficult for poor families with meager dowries to find husbands for their daughters.

Most of the women work to the day of delivery and resume work three to four weeks after the birth of a child, as they cannot afford not to work. Infant mortality is high and access to medical facilities is minimal. The women often take their small children to the construction sites, as no creches are provided. Few of the children of these women go to school and most work if there is any work available.

For most of the women, construction work does not provide a steady income throughout the year. For example, little work is available during the monsoon when many of the women must seek work as agricultural workers or as casual labour in other industries. Most of the women are in debt and they may pay between 25 to 160 per cent in interest a year. Contract workers tend to be in debt to their contractors and for that reason are not allowed to leave. Although many of these women are the major income earners in their families, they face the double burden of wage work and housework and defer to husbands or in-laws in terms of household decision making. Most of their income is spent on food for the family while their husbands' earnings are often spent on liquor. Approximately 30 per cent of the Andhra women reported that their husbands beat them when they were drunk. According to the researchers, "The [Andhra] women for the most part agreed that they were born to be subservient to man."[6]

A more in-depth view of the life of a woman construction workers is provided by the following profile.

Surabala, a Bengali Construction Worker

Little Swarna had to crawl out of the hole which they now call home; it is not even a hut like the one where they had once lived in their village of Swargahata in the Midnapore District of West Bengal. But both mother and child are resigned to their fate. Dusk was falling as Surabala took her daughter Swarna with her to the "coolie lines" of the workers employed by the Tube Railway Authorities in Calcutta. Rows of tarpaulin, precariously balanced on rickety poles over small square areas of space partitioned off between families by torn *bora* or gunny sacks form the huts where squatters live. They have been living here for nearly three years now, just off Chowringhee Road and Park Street, the most fashionable, sophisticated part of the city. Prior to coming here they were working on the same project at Belgatchia, further north, and have been shifted to this new site by the contractor under whose employment they work. About 112 families—men, women, and children—live here working at this site. Women are earning Rs. 3.50 per day, while men get Rs. 4, primarily for carrying loads from one place to another. They live and work under the same conditions year after year.

Surabala says that the only work assigned to them is carrying earth, mortar, or bricks or crushing bricks, and the work is much more strenuous than in any other industry. She gets up when the cock crows and feeds the family breakfast of tea and *chappatis* prepared the night before. Before she can go to work she cooks rice and *dal* (lentils) for the family for the day. The women work three-hours shifts, sometimes as many as three shifts per day, depending on the work at the site. The short stay at one place and frequent movement from one site to another make it difficult for them to have a settled life. They seem to have lost interest in their households. Meager utensils are scattered here and there, and all they have to sleep on are either *charpoys* (string cots) on gunny sacks. There are not even proper ovens to cook on. They are too poor to buy coal. Children gather firewood scraps to light the fire to cook a scanty meal of rice and *dal* for the family once a day when the women are at home. The age of these women is surprisingly low. Most of them are between twenty-six and thirty. When asked about their youth they smiled and said, "How would one be able to carry load up and down if they are too old?" In most cases the work life of these women comes to an end when they are about forty. Most of them already have three or four children, having been married young. They hạve their children with them most of the time. "Who else would look after them?" The children while away their time doing nothing. None of them can read or write, and none have any will to learn. They are often sick from malnutrition and hunger, without any medial help. There are no toilets, so the air around is foul with order; the children have no idea of cleanliness or hygiene.

In West Bengal, construction workers generally come from the Kaibartas. Surabala is a Mahato. Both are lower-caste groups. Some of them are of Santhal (tribal) origin also. Even when they were living in their own home in the village they had to live segregated from the upper castes. We asked Surabala why they came away. Most of them originally had been peasant-farmers working either in the paddy fields or cultivating jute. "They thought they would be able to earn a better living in the city," she says. "Don't they want to go back?" We asked. "A number of us go back during the harvesting season when there is work to do in the fields, for there also we work as day labourers. None of us own any land., At other times there is no work in our native place and if we stay there we would have to go hungry." So they flock to the city. Most of them, that say to taken up this job out of poverty, and of their own accord. Surabala had to earn a living somehow after her husband's death to feed herself and her four children. A few of them have been persuaded by their husbands. A small percentage of women were forced out of their homes, either by landlords or by parents in-low upon being widowed. Nearly all felt that they would have to continue as day-wage labourers, but would like to change for a job where the strain would be less. Wages are paid on a weekly basis by the *jamadar* (labour supervisor) and occasionally deductions are made from the salary in payment for firewood or for guarding the *jhuggies* when they are out for work. There is also no specific system for sharing their earnings, they say. There are no holidays, so if they do not work, they do not earn. None of them owns land, but none seem badly in debt as is usually the case with day-labourers in the villages. Neither has any accumulation of savings been possible. Surabala says that some women get preferential treatment on the job, "may be because of their looks." She says women in the city don't pay as much attention to *pujas* (worship) as they did in the village. *Pujas* in the village are observed especially at harvest time and during the monsoon, but in the city women forget these customs, Surabala relates.

We found a woman in the same compound in an advanced state of pregnancy. She was still continuing her work but would shortly go home to her parents, she told me shyly. She looked about twenty-six or -seven, was the mother of three, expecting her fourth. Asked her whether she had heard about family planning, she nodded in the affirmative and looked furtively towards her husband. "Where did you hear about it?" We queried. "From the Block Development Office at her village," was the answer. But we had a feeling that she hardly realised what it meant.

We found that three considerations were working behind employing women labourers in this industry. Firstly, they were cheaper, since many come to the city with their husbands, and they were also readily available. Secondly, being naturally docile in nature, they were less troublesome, and thirdly, men were reluctant to do the job which they were doing ungrudgingly.

The women in general appear to be conservative in outlook. They themselves are women and are working; they are happier to have a boy child than a girl. Surabala hopes her son can get into some other occupation, or if he stays in construction that he can learn a craft. She hopes her daughter Swarna will marry, settle down, and have a home of her own.

In spite of the back-breaking jobs of these women, their husbands or other menfolk staying with the family do not share the household chores. The men, in their free time, sit around, chat, smoke *biri* (indigenous cigarettes), or chew *pan* (betel leaves) while the women cook. Daughters too young to work on the job stay home looking after younger children, fetching water, and cleaning utensils. These women have traditional ideas about marriage, and they feel that dowry is an essential part in such an arrangement. This is one of the main causes of their indebtedness, but it is accepted as natural. These women appear to be used to their way of life, perhaps because they see no way to change it for the better.

NOTES

1. This portrait is drawn from *Ekalavya, the Mobile Creches Annual,* 1977, Bombay: Tata, 1977, pp. 57-63.
2. Committee on the Status of Women in India (CSWI), *Towards Equality,* New Delhi: Ministry of Education and Social Welfare, 1975, pp. 155, 172.
3. *Census of India 1961,* Part V-A, Statewise, cited in Harshad R. Trivedi, *Scheduled Caste Women: Studies in Exploitation,* Delhi: Concept Publishing Company, 1976, pp. 206-207.
4. Labour Bureau, Government of India, *Women in Industry,* New Delhi, 1970.
5. CSWI, pp. 172-173; K. Murali Manohar, *et al,* "Labour: Women Construction Workers of Warangal," *Economic and Political Weekly,* Vol. XVI, No. 4, January, 24, 1981, pp. 97-99.
6. Manohar, p. 99.

44

Women in Garment-Making

This project has made a beginning through organising 27 girls in a small, poor and isolated village of Chattisgarh, Madhya Pradesh, with an initial investment of Rs. 15,000. Though it is still to break even, if has managed to overcome many odds including the absence of even the basic concept of sewing among the tribal workers. Attempts to revive and organise the local weavers to produce consistent designs and standardised sizes have not proved very successful but the effort goes on.

Asha Handicrafts, Training-cum-Production Centre was born on November 26, 1975, in the small village of Chattisgarh, Jagdeeshpur, about 100 miles from Rajpur, Madhya Pradesh.

The Idea

For a period of over 15 years before this concerned individuals had discussed and prayed about the unemployment among the women, girls, men and youth of the community. But none felt they had any answer to the problem which continued to grow. Then a group of community leaders came to me (we were living in the community) and said, "You just have to do something about what is happening to our girls. Some work must be found for them." This led to a discussion of possibilities but nothing was decided.

The next day, the Project Director of TELARC (The Economic Life and Relief Committee) returned three sewing machines he had borrowed from the local high school for a men's tailoring class which had not worked out. Later an influential, well-educated and talented woman of the community said she was willing to conduct a sewing class for the girls if one could be arranged.

Finally, when the Director of the Mennonite Central Committee (MCC) visited Jagdeeshpur that week and heard about the happening of the previous four days, he said, "Well, we think MCC can give you an initial grant of Rs. 15,00 to start the project." Thus, exactly one week after the first visit of the concerned group, Asha Handicrafts Training-cum-Production Centre, Jagdeeshpur, began sewing in our home.

The Project

Our first order was to make 36 flannel blouses to be distributed to windows supported by the local church. But our primary task was to build meaning into the world "handicrafts" by displaying and discussing samples. Most of the teaching was done through studying these garments and handicrafted items brought in from outside. This has proved invaluable to the project even though quite a bit of finance is tied up in these sample items. It has taught us the price of goods in the market, the standard sizing for ready-made clothes, how to finish seems for the Indian market and similar aspects of the business.

A small "store" was also set up where orders for clothing can be given and where finished articles are displayed. This was the very first "ready-made clothing store" that most of the girls had ever seen. The whole concept was a new one particularly as ours is the only place within a 100-mile radius of which we are aware, where sales are made on a cash basis. All business in the area operate by giving goods on credit and collecting as they can at the end of the month. Nevertheless we can hardly expect an income of more than Rs. 2,000 from this shop.

Some effort has been made to work with the local weavers who are traditional in the area. Garments are made out of their handloom cloth where possible and Asha's speciality is handloom gingham for housecoats. Traditional designs have been used in place-mats, tea-cosies, tray cloths, bedcovers and table cloths. These have been popular items.

A stock of materials has been built up so that the expense of the 115 mile trip to the wholesale market will not have to be made too often. Eight sewing machines have been purchased as well as two large steel cupboards, a washing machine and ironing equipment.

The Finance

By the end of our first year 1,162 garments and other handicrafted items were produced with a cash income of Rs. 14,580.07 (excluding grants) and an average monthly income of Rs. 1,122. The income for 1977 our second year, was Rs. 25,484.66 and expenses were Rs. 60,646.20. In 1978 our income climbed to Rs. 41,592.86 and our expenses were Rs. 57,936.07.

Besides, three orders for 2000 garments for flood victims were received from the Lutheran World Relief through MCC, Calcutta, and the invoice for this shipment alone was Rs. 11,550. MCC, Calcutta, has been the funding group for our project. In three years they have given us grants for over Rs. 80,000.

The Workers

During the first year there was myself as project manager one supervisor-teacher, Ukia Sona, who kept the financial records and 18 girls working in the project. On Asha's second birthday a second supervisor-teacher, Manorama Walter, was employed. We felt that organising by departments would be a smart way to go, as we had a vision of many departments in the years to come. Ms. Sona became the supervisor for Asha Garments and Ms. Walter for Asha Nursery Craft, which sewed for new-born infants upto the age of 4. Ms. Walter also wrote out all the income receipts while Ms. Sona took the responsibility for the stock room. During our second and third years we could employ only 27 girls due to production being limited by our marketing problem.

The Problems

The weaving department finds it extremely difficult to have the weaver fill our orders because he has no resources to stock thread and we must buy the colours that he has already on hand. He also finds it difficult to produce according to our specifications. For example, since white thread is cheaper than coloured, he often tries to work in a white border rather than the coloured one that we ordered. It will take a large investment of capital to make the weaving section of Asha a successful reality but the potential for development is there.

Our biggest problem is marketing. During these three years, the production has come up to a working standard and emphasis now has to be put on the marketing aspects. Our only marketing method besides our local "store" is through going out to various places and holding "exhibition-cum-sales." This takes a lot of time, expense and effort.

The Satisfaction

What is happening in the community and to the girls? This is the most exciting part of the project. The girls have gained a real sense of self-worth and they are proud of their newly acquired skills in sewing, cutting and embroidery. The income they earn has permitted most of them to purchase the very first Sari they have ever been able to buy. They are dressing better and cleaner and so are the children of the community. We are trying to emphasise good quality and practicality rather than just "shine and glitter" with no wearing capacity. Through comparing our costs and prices they are learning how expensive it is to buy clothing from a store five miles away on credit.

A more formal course is being considered, following or adapting the syllabus from the Usha Sewing School. But because our original aim was to give employment to girls rather than just training, we have as yet not adopted a formal school-like course or syllabus.

Several other aspects of women's development are under consideration such as teaching, gardening, (the growing of vegetables) and cooking (the making of cakes and snack-foods). But because of a lack of personnel at the leadership level these new avenues are being held in abeyance.

Till now, no one but the two supervisors of the project can understand the work involved—how to buy, how to keep stock registers, how to set up useful and simple book-keeping, how to make patterns, how to sew with needles and on machines, how to mark ready-made items, how to display in a sale-room. But more than anything else, working on the project together has given each person involved a deep sense of hope and satisfaction at having made a beginning.

45

Women in Tailoring Job

[This urban project in Lucknow, U.P., has two significant aspects. Firstly, the organisers asked the women themselves to choose their income generating activity. The women not only did this but also stated their eagerness to study beyond functional literacy. Secondly, the project, though still dependent on fund-raising, has no marketing problem as it does order work almost exclusively. Detailed breakdowns on expenses of all garments have been worked out so that tenders can be submitted at competitive rates with some margin of profit.]

In May 1975 the Administrators of the nine Asian Women's Christian Colleges in Asia met and decided to establish an Asian Women's Institute. Accordingly all the colleges established a Centre for Women's Studies and the Isabella Thoburn College (ITC), Lucknow, U.P. started its Centre for Women's Studies and Development (CWSD) on September 1, 1975.

Seeing the importance of raising the socio-economic status of women in the weaker sections of society and thereby assisting them to be self-reliant, earning and useful members of the family and the community, the Centre set up two projects, the ITC Tailoring Training-cum Production Centre in February 1976 and the ITC-CSIR Rural Development Project (See Case: Nutrient-Mixing).

Training

A meeting of women was arranged in four different areas of the city's slums where literacy classes for adult women were already being run. A majority of the 120 women said they were eager to learn tailoring and sewing so that they could earn from stitching garments. They were also eager to study further after having attended the six-month literacy course.

CWSD made the necessary arrangements and purchased (and borrowed) sewing machines, tailoring equipment and other requirements. I.T. College provided the furniture. The response was good and soon there were 30 women and girls who registered. The registration fees was fixed at Rs. 3 and the monthly fees at Re. 1.

On May 1, 1977, a diploma course in tailoring and sewing was started as this was an expressed need of those women and girls who had studied upto Std. V or more. The teacher takes the class for two hours daily and is paid Rs. 100 per month. Six students sat for the examination a year later and passed well. The second batch of student took their examination in November, 1978.

Order Work

Three months after training, the women and girls were ready to do some order work. Arrangements were made to get orders for making uniforms (see Table 45.1) for school children, Lucknow University's Medical College and I.T College. Earning so soon was a great incentive for the students and many more started coming for training. Side by side literacy classes were run both for the women and their children.

TABLE 45.1

Income-Expenditure on Uniforms Stitched

Item	*Credit*	*Debit*			*Balance*
	Stitching Charges	*Wages*	*Thread*	*Cutting*	*Profit*
Pyjama	Rs. 1.25	.70p	.15p	.15p	.25p
Sweepers' Coat	Rs. 2.25	1.50p	.25p	.15p	.35p
Sweepers' Apron	Rs. 1.25	.75p	.25p	.15p	.10p
Dai Apron	Rs. 1.25	.75p	.25p	.15p	.10p
Coat and Pant	Rs. 5.50	3.50p	.50p	.10p	1.40p
Bush Shirt and Pant	Rs. 5.25	3.50p	.50p	.50p	.75p

Since only order work is done and for this material is given by the party concerned there is no investment as such. In place of marketing we submit tenders for stitching uniforms. As our main concern is that the women should earn we keep our rates reasonable and the margin of profit low. This profit covers our nominal expenses on contingencies like thread, electricity, servicing of sewing machines and the hire of a fan and a part time sweeperess.

Problems

But there are problems. Payments are not made in time by the Medical College so the women have to wait for their wages. Besides, material for stitching garments is sometimes not given on time and the women are left without work.

To overcome this, we are providing the women with embroidery work (see Table 45.2) so that they can still earn at the rate of Re. 1 per cross-stitch motif while awaiting the uniform material. Some private order work for stitching clothes is also taken on a small scale during this waiting period.

The main beneficiaries are the women and girls belonging to the poor Muslim families residing in the area and nearby mohallas. Being a Muslim area the attendance drops at the time of Muslim festivals and religious customs like Ramzan and Id. In the last few years riots have twice taken place here and due to curfew the students were not able to attend the Centre. When this happens the women earn less as the output of uniforms goes down.

TABLE 45.2

Expenditure-income-profit on 10 Embroidered Guest Towels

Cost of material—2.40 metres double width—Rs. 17.30 per metre		*Rs. 31.30	
Wages for embroidering @ Re. 1 each		Rs. 10.00	
Thread		Rs. 2.50	
Celophane bag @ 5p each .50			
Washing charges @ 5p each		.50	
Miscellaneous		.20	
	Expenditure	Rs. 44.00	
Sales price of 10 towels	Rs. 5 each	Rs. 50.00	
Expenditure		Rs. 44.00	
	Profit	Rs. 6.00	on 10 towels.

* As a strip of material is left over from which tea napkins are made the amount for the material has been reduced by Rs. 10.22p. (Rs. 41.52-31.30).

Management

This centre is run under the direction of Executive Director of the Centre for Women's Studies and Development. The teacher in charge of the Centre sees to both the training and production work. The other teacher responsible for the diploma course also helps with the production work when required. The collection of payment is done by the typist in the CWSD office and the assistant to the Executive Director regularly checks the work, accounts and everyday functioning.

This work is financed by the Isabella Thoburn College, Lucknow. Funds have been received by the Centre for Women's Studies and Development for the purchases of sewing machines, tailoring equipment and furniture for the Tailoring Centre. The students of I.T. College have also raised funds for this Centre.

Achievement

The college students are being conscientised to the needs of others and at the same time poor women who have missed the opportunities are being provided with education, vocational training and earning facilities through socio-economic schemes. Many are earning from stitching garments, and most of the women are able to sew all the clothes for the family thereby saving on tailoring charges. Besides, several of the girls who have been trained have married and moved on through the help of their earnings and new skills. Unfortunately, in India there are very few. This Centre is helping to fill the need.

The outlook of these women has changed. They are respected more at home as they are helping to augment the family income. After the women have been at our Centre for sometime we have observed the change in their expression, their eyes look brighter because they feel that they are playing a more useful role at home and in the community.

46

Women in Nutrient—Mixing

[The organisers of this project are running it on a "no loss" basis and have successfully motivated other institutions and agencies to collaborate not only in the income generating activity but also in other development work by supplying funds and raw materials and also through providing services. More significantly, however, this rural project is involving its workers (all women) at the supervisory level and in the marketing aspects of the enterprise, thus encouraging and strengthening them to eventually carry on the work themselves.]

As the Executive Director of the Centre for Women's Studies and Development (CWSD) of the Isabella Thoburn College (ITC), Lucknow, U.P., we first learnt of the needs of Kanchenpur Matiari village 12 km away from the Pradhan and Lekhpal. Later at a meeting the women themselves spoke out. They were eager to do something which would help them to earn. They wanted to learn how to tailor and sew. They wanted better health care.

CWSD decided to adopt village Kanchenpur Matiari and on December 16, 1975 the ITC-CSIR Rural Development Project was started with a Centre for health care and other rural development work, followed by training classes in tailoring and sewing. The village has a population of 2,986 the majority of whom live in acute poverty. Fifteen per cent have small holdings of land, 15 per cent work in Lucknow as Class IV employees (mostly peons in offices), and the rest are labourers earning from Rs. 50 to Rs. 100 per month on a daily wage basis.

Mixing 'Swasthyahar'

Our most successful effort so far is the production of 'Swasthyahar", a high protein multimix nutrient, made by the women in the village and given to those in our nutrition scheme. The equipment for the production of "Swasthyahar" was purchased through UNICEF.

As this is a good nutrient and the beneficiaries have gained weight and are looking healthier, this product is now being marketed outside. Orders have been received from a school, a psychiatric centre and a social welfare organisation so the production of this product has been stepped up. The women are paid 70 paise per kilo and the product is sold at Rs. 5 per kilo (See Table 46.1).

TABLE 46.1

Details of "Swasthyahar" Production Per 10 kg

Particulars	*Debit*	*Credit*	*Balance*
Income from 10 kg of "Swasthyahar" sold at Rs. 5 per kilo.		Rs. 50.00	
Expenditure on purchase of inigredients for "Swasthyahar" and other expenses.			
1. 4 kg wheat	Rs. 6.00		
2. 2 kg channa dal	Rs. 6.80		
3. 2 kg soya been	Rs. 7.60		
4. 2 kg ground nut	Rs. 12.00		
5. Grinding charges @ 80p per kilo	Rs. 8.00		
6. Celophane bag for packing	0.10p		
Total	Rs. 40.50p	Rs. 50.00	Rs. 9.50p

Profit of Rs. 9.50 on every 10 kg. of "Swasthyahar" helps towards supervision charges and overhead expenses.

Weaving Bamboo

The traditional art of the village was weaving bamboo or thread hand fans and table mats. To encourage this art, arrangements were made to provide the raw material which the village women were unable to afford. This work was soon started and the goods marketed.

Unfortunately, the hand fans and table mats take a long time to make and the labour cost becomes high making these items expensive. The only people who are then interested are foreigners who regard the works as "art". Indians are not prepared to pay Rs. 8 for a small mat or fan, or Rs. 12 for a larger size. We are making a limit number which we are able to sell.

Grinding Spices

The women were eager to earn through the grinding of spices. The equipment was purchased and this scheme has just been launched on a larger scale. Four women are doing this work and the numbers will be increased with the demand. The women are paid at the rate of 80 paise per kilo.

Teaching Troubles

We have only recently gone into production and are having our teething troubles. The village woman trained by us and now in charge of the nutrition scheme supervises the production of "Swasthyahar" and the teacher in charge supervises the grinding of the spices.

We encourage the women to sell our products and give them a commission of 10% but there is need for marketing courses to be held for these women which will help them in their selling technique.

We only make a marginal profit to help us in running the project on a "no loss"' basis. Keeping our prices reasonable-less than the market rate—helps us to sell our products quite easily. Yet we prefer to do order work as this is less of a marketing problem.

Another problem is the lack of sufficient accommodation for our production units so we will have to restrict our expansion. We are on the look-out for more space. Besides, the women are unable to work full-time and come whenever convenient so sometimes we have difficulty in supplying large quantities at one time. However, we will soon have four regular workers which will lessen this problem.

Witnessing Progress

In the three years of its functioning the Centre has witnessed great progress. The work is being done mostly by the older women of the village who are happy to earn and be able to augment the family income even though the amount is not much, between Rs. 25 and Rs. 50 per month. In due course as the order work increases the women will earn more.

These women have become more outgoing. They assert themselves. They speak out more easily in public. They perform dramas on special occasions with ITC students and staff in the audience. They take on responsibilities as the project centre with the goal of carrying on the development work on their own. Progress through continuing education and vocational training is self-evident. The youth participate in workshops and seminars in the city.

However, Kanchenpur Matiari is only one small village within a network of ten villages. Our work at Kanchenpur Matiari has more or less levelled off, and unless this village influences the surrounding villages in the same network, we feel that we will have reached a rut because we will be doing routine work, the same things over and over again. Though continuity is necessary, yet if we fail to widen our project area, we will have ceased to be truly effective in helping to make lasting changes in the situation of the women and in motivating them to become agents of still further change.

We have successfully motivated other agencies to collaborate through service, supplies or cash. Now we are eager to discover the viability of other socio-economic schemes in rural areas which will be beneficial to the villagers.

47

The Perspective on Self-Employment

There are basically two ways of earning a livelihood in an economy. Either you work for yourself or you work for somebody else. When you work for yourself to produce goods and/or services which are used for self-consumption, or sold for a price, or bartered for other goods and/or services, then you are self-employed. If you work for somebody else and sell your labour or skills as an employees, then you are other-employed.

To understand the issues which face people in their struggle for existence, it is important to look at the structure of the economy in terms of the means of the livelihood of people. A historical process analysis helps us understand how the two basic ways of earning a livelihood, self-employment and other employment, have interacted with each other in the process of transforming the economy to its present day reality. Such a process analysis has been attempted below.

Work in Traditional Societies

In traditional societies, most of the work is done on a subsistence level where each family has to provide its basic needs from its own resources, i.e., food, clothing and shelter. Most of the work is also done by manual labour. Very few people work for others in an employer-employee relationship, but some work is done for the community, such as, trading, artisanship, health services and priestly services. These services are not provided in an employer-employee relationship but in a patron-client relationship.

The production and work relations in a subsistence economy are centred around the individual or family unit owning its own resources for survival. The hours of work, the kind of work done, the income or output derived from the work, all of these depend on the choice of each individual unit or enterprise. Since most of the community owns its production resources, it is self-employed. The emphasis is on direct producer-consumer and buyer-seller relationships.

Transactions of small size, few transactions with known people, face-to-face dealings, mutual trust, personal references, verbal vouching for each other to enforce the terms of a transaction between two people and accountability to known people, are the processes which sustain subsistence economics. Customary laws are enforced by the communities to maintain their own social order. the communities themselves are small in size.

Natural calamities like fires, floods, famines and epidemics lead to the destruction of resources of some or all of the people. Fighting and warring between communities lead to the resources of individuals being confiscated or plundered. The administrative policies of the head of the community lead to the resources of individuals being confiscated. These processes establish groups of individuals who do not have their own means of production or the resources to meet their own basic needs. They are compelled to work for others who do own resources. This is the reason for the emergence of a people who survive by labouring for others.

Commercialisation

These processes are reinforced by the forces of commercialisation. As subsistence communities become larger, more and more geographical areas are covered under a common administration and the formation of kingdoms, countries and nations starts. As the means of communication improve, distant areas become more accessible and trade and commerce flourish. Commercially oriented work slowly starts taking over subsistence-oriented work. The concentration of resources in the hands of a few people starts, and many who own resources are deprived of them. The processes of exploitation start as the stakes for commercial activities get higher and higher. Competition for survival starts. The interests of the people are not ensured in such a situation. The subsistence economy becomes a subsistence-cum-commercial economy. The emphasis of work relationships is still on self-employment and the modes of production are still predominantly manual.

With the same resources it becomes possible to exercise control over larger geographical areas and over a greater number of people. Large volumes of work, large outputs, large markets and large accounts become possible. Slowly, dealings on a large-scale become more attractive to people. Large-scale necessarily means dealing with more people, unknown people, and people from distant places.

From Verbal to Written Dealings

Largeness paves the way for written dealings because it is humanly impossible to keep mental and physical track of all the transactions conducted. Face-to-face dealings are replaced with impersonal dealings. It is also not in the interests of any one to trust unknown people. Written dealings are necessary to substantiate the actual occurrence of transactions between unknown people. It is a way of ensuring that commitments are honoured; it is something to fall back on when there are disagreements, disputes of differences, on the details of a transaction. The concept of documented evidence emerges from written transactions. In transactions with unknown people both sides operate with a sense of distrust. Hence, written dealings are necessary to protect both parties against this distrust. With unknown people, verbal vouching has no credibility. The accountability to known people also loses credibility because both parties, since they do not know each other, will not be able to trust the judgements of each other's people or community. Therefore, a third party not known to either side, becomes more acceptable.

Accountability to unknown people and common administration of large geographical areas leads to written laws. Written dealings are necessary as evidence for the implementation of written laws and accountability to unknown third persons. Similarly, large state administrations resort to written dealings for maintaining records. Customary laws get replaced by written laws and constitutions. The fear of dealing with unknown people and strangers dissolves when people have the backing of written transactions which are legal tender.

The Industrial Revolution and the Written World

With the Industrial Revolution the modes of production shift from work being done by hand to work being done by machines; from work being done in individual homes to work being done in factories and offices. Mass production leads to greater outputs, bigger and bigger units and cheap goods displace the individually owned means of production in a subsistence economy. Subsistence families, own account workers, self-employed people who are displaced by mechanisation and industrialisation, are forced to work for somebody else. Centralisation of decision-making and concentration of resources increase rapidly in the hands of a few owners and explitation becomes rampant. The emphasis of production work relations in the economy shifts from self-employment for the majority and self-employment for some. The formation of large organisations is encouraged. An age of very large sizes and transactions with very large numbers of people is ushered in due to the development of very sophisticated technologies. The modes of work, the volumes of work, the size of units, and the large numbers of people involved, all reinforce the system of written dealings. The formation of nations and modern governments also creates more opportunities for other-employment. The modern labour movement starts as a response to rampant exploitation of employees and the role of the State/Government is influenced to protect those in other-employment. Rules, regulations, and labour laws get formulated in written form. The employer-employee relationship also gets integrated within the system of written dealings.

In the highly industralised countries, the process of industrialisation has continued for over 200 years and slowly included most of the working population into a regular, employer-employee relationship. This form of work and of earning a livelihood has become the norm. The rules, regulations, policies, legislations and regulations of the employer-employee relationship create a world of other-employment and also ensure that the interests of almost the whole working population are taken care of. Trade unions develop to protect the interests of employees. A share of the profits of the goods and services which employees have helped to produce and demanded and made available in the form of various employee facilities, such as, provident funds, gratuities, allowances, housing, health facilities, medical facilities, child-care facilities, maternal protection facilities, educational facilities and training skills, among others. The implementation of the labour laws which are written make written dealings between employers and employees imperative. Over a period of time, the world of other-employment has developed its own characteristics of written dealings, impersonal dealings and dealings with unknown people. This is the world of formal systems of work.

The formal systems of work have gone hand-in-hand with creating employer-employee relationships for the majority of the working population. Ownership of resources in order to earn one's livelihood is not seen as desirable for the majority of the population. Selling labour to somebody else for wages or salaries is instilled as a value and has slowly become the most preferred way of earning a livelihood. This choice is reinforced by making available a lot of additional benefits and incentives to those who work as employees. Motivation and involvement in work are sought to be maintained by employers by providing ever-increasing incentives to employees. The formal system of work gets equated with organised industry, organised labour and organised services, and these become more and more significant in the economy.

The Indian Economy

Even by countries such as India, which started large-scale industrialisation only fifty years ago, the highly industrialised countries have been adopted as models for development. Large scale industrialisation and enterprises of a large size are recent phenomena in these countries. Attaining independence, nationhood, and starting industrialisation on a large scale have happened at about the same time in India. A written constitution and written laws, enforceable for the whole population, have come into existence only since Independence. The labour movement, the trade union models, the laws, rules and regulations enforcing the employer-employee relationship, the role of the State/Government in protecting the interests of the employees, have all been modelled on the highly industrialised countries. A subsistence economy (agricultural and tribal) which was only partly commercialised has now been super-imposed on by a industrial economy. The economy is still largely agricultural and tribal, but from subsistence it has been catapulted into a commercial economy because of industrialisation. The concentration of resources has made the large majority of subsistence individuals resourceless and has forced them to work for others. But the economy as a whole is not industrialised and everybody does not have regular, salaried employment. The labour movement has developed but caters mainly to industrial labour. New technologies are constantly coming into existence and continuously displacing more and more of the subsistence-oriented people and forcing them to become labourers. In fact, modernisation has succeeded in shifting a number of people from self-employment to other-employment. But in spite of the present extent of industrialisation, only 11 per cent[1] of the working population is engaged in regular jobs with a recognised employer-employee relationship, the protection of the law, and the benefits of employee facilities, i.e., the world of other-employment and written dealings. The process of large sizes, industrialisation and written dealings covers only a small section of the total population. All workers who need protective policies can get them only if they become recognised employees. This is the present situation of the working population in India.

The rest of the population is also working—they have to fend for themselves and earn a livelihood in whatever way they can. They are self-employed. Some of these people have become integrated into the world of written dealings and are also well-off. However, the vast majority of these self-employed people are poor. they are the sufferers of the processes of commercialisation, industrialisation, the concentration of resources, and written dealings. Their world is still one of verbal dealings, of small sizes, of face-to-face dealings with small numbers of people. But they are being forced to deal with the world of written transactions. Their illiteracy, their ignorance of the written world, of written laws, procedures, rules and regulations, is a major handicap. They do not know how to get things done in the written world and they end up exploited, helpless, inadequate, diffident and dependent.

The Working Population in India

A graphic representation of the reality of the working population in India, due to this whole historical process, can be shown if the total working population is represented by a circle and is divided into high income, middle income, and low income groups. The approximate proportion of the working population in these three income groups would be as follows.

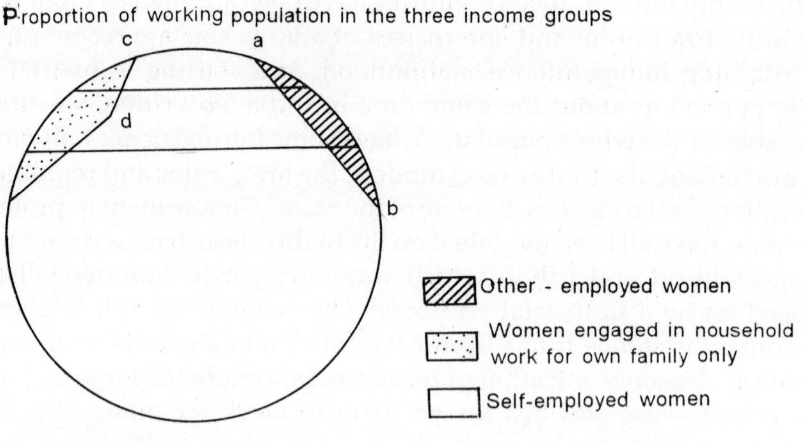

Fig. 47.1. Proportion of Working Population in the Three Income Groups.

Of this working population, 11 per cent are in other-employment—regular employees recognised by the law—which is represented by the small section cut off by chord ab in the circle below.

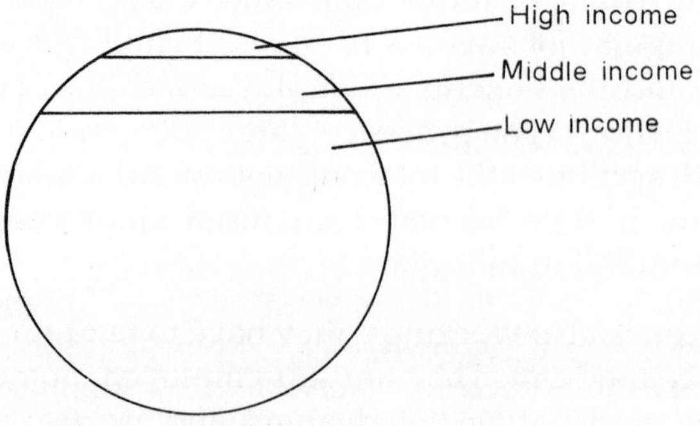

Fig. 47.2. Division of Working Population between Other and Self-employment.

People in other-employment fall across all the three income groups. The remaining population earns its livelihood by finding their own self-created niche in the economy and fending for itself. it is self-employed. The self-employed people also fall across all three income groups.

People in other-employment from the high and middle income groups include managers, officers, administrators, professionals, such as, doctors, lawyers, teachers, architects, engineers and accountants, holding jobs. The low income other-employed include factory workers, peons, clerks etc.

Self-employed people from the high and middle income groups include manufacturers and industrialists, entrepreneurs, consultants, professionals, traders, dealers, various contractors, big farmers, etc.

Self-employed people in the low income group includes small producers engaged in land-based, livestock-based, and manufacturing-based activities; vendors engaged in vending and the trade of essential commodities, such as, food, cloth, garments, shoes and household utility items; providers of services, such as, cleaning, transportation, washing, cooking; and manual labour, such as, farm labour, construction labour, contract labour and casual labour.

The low income, self-employed group comprises the majority of the working population of India.

Within this overall picture of the general population, it is also necessary to look specifically at the work of women in the economy. Of the population of working women in India, only 6 or 7 per cent are other employed[2] and 93 or 94 per cent earn their livelihood by their own means—they are self-employed. For women workers the graphic representation would look as shown in Fig. 47.3.

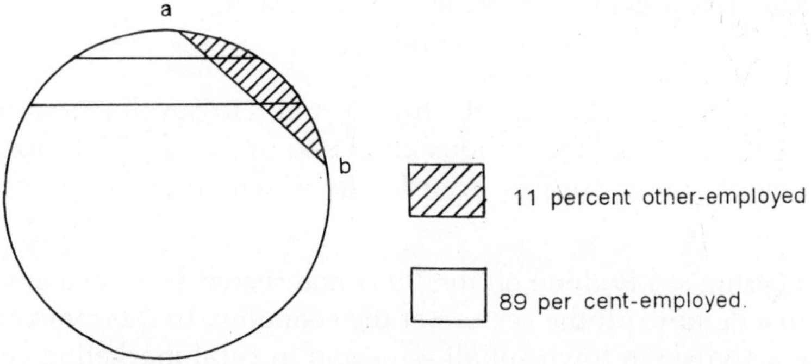

Fig. 47.3. Representation of Female Working Population.

If the total female working population in India is represented by a circle then the three horizontal sections represent the three income groups—high, middle and low—as approximate proportions of the total population. Women in salaried jobs, with an established employer-employee relationship, constitute 6 or 7 per cent of the population as indicated by chord ab in the circle, and are spread over the three income groups. Women who are involved only in unpaid household work for their own families are an additional category in this classification as compared to the picture for men. This group is represented by line cde in the circle. In the high income group, most women do not do their own household work but get it done by others. Women in the low income group cannot afford not to earn some income. So very few of them do only household work for their own families. Women from the middle income group are largely the ones who do only household work for their families.

All the remaining women are involved in some economic activity or other and are also spread across the three income groups. They are self-employed. Here too, as in the picture for the general population, the largest group is of the poor, self-employed women. This is the majority of the population of working women in India.

It is this large majority of the population (men, women and children) which is now called the 'informal sector' by the standards set by the industrialised countries. This sphere of work is seen as a discovery.

The Informal Sector

The term 'informal sector' has been increasingly used to refer to large numbers of people who are fending for themselves in order to earn a livelihood. The most commonly used definition, based on the ILO Kenya study report of 1972, lists a set of characteristics of the 'informal sector':

1. Ease of entry
2. Reliance on indigenous resources.
3. Family ownership of enterprise.
4. Small scale of operation.
5. Labour intensive and adapated technology.
6. Skills acquired outside the formal school system.
7. Unregulated and competitive markets.

This definition has, in a way, become the turning point in development work in attempts to understand the economies of the various countries of the world. Since the 1972 study, there have been several other studies in order to systematise the understanding of the 'informal sector'.

The ILO's pioneering study done on the 'informal sector' in Kenya envisaged the term 'informal sector' to extend to all the sectors of the economy. In their view it covered small scale non-farming activities in towns of all sizes and in rural marketing centres (p. 223). It could also be applied equally well to the agricultural sector. Although this is the general view of the study, when it comes down to specifics, we find that the characteristics of the informal sector, as defined by the ILO study, refer more to small scale enterprises than to farming or other allied activities. If the Kenya study were to be strictly followed, the focus of informal sector studies would become small enterprises which exist mainly in the urban areas.

This, in fact, is what has happened. Studies conducted subsequent to the Kenya study, both by the ILO and by others, have adopted the ILOS definition and concentrated on understanding the informal sector in the urban areas only. Thus, over time the term 'informal sector' has become synonymous with the 'urban informal sector'.

Some of the descriptive definitions which have been put forth to explain the informal sector are listed here.

Joshi and Joshi's book *Surplus Labour and the City*[4] is a concrete application of the informal sector concept to the city of Bombay. They do not collect any primary data but rely on secondary sources, such as, the Census, Directorate of Employment and National Sample Survey. The consequence of this is that the 'formal sector' becomes primary in their conceptualisation and the 'informal sector' is studied empiricallhy from the point of view of the 'formal sector'. As the authors emphasise in the book, 'The standard procedure in empirical work is to estimate the size of the urban informal sector by calculating it as a residual of those engaged in economic activity in urban area, excluding those who can be identified as working in the "Formal Sector" (op. cit.). They use the terms 'organised' and 'unorganised' to connote the formal and informal sectors respectively, in their analysis. To measure the number of workers in the informal sector they rely only on the size of the estblishment or enterprise.

> The family of criteria discussed above cannot easily be used for empirical investigation. We think however, that of these criteria, the size of establishment is a good and workable one for distinguished between the sectors in practice. Most establishments employing large number of workers have organised sector characteristics, most establishments employing small numbers of workers do not. The next question concerns the employment size which would serve as a useful dividing line. Since the Directorate of Employment and Training collects data on the organised sector, defined as all public sector establishments with more than 25 employees, this is certainly a convenient dividing line to use and we decided to use it.
>
> [They explain the heterogeneity of the informal sector as] "The Informal Sector" comprises a wide range of modes of production. Own account workers, unpaid family workers, household industries, `home workers', domestic servants, employees of small unregulated establishments, casual wage labour employed on a day-to-day basis by ephemeral employers or firmly established ones including Formal Sector enterprises. The kinds of production industries in which these workers are engaged are also multifarious. (*op. cit.*).

Dipak Mazumdar's paper 'Urban Informal Sector'[5] emphasises the wages and working conditions in order to differentiate between the formal and informal sector.

> The basic distinction between the two sectors turns on the idea that employment in the formal sector is in some sense or senses protected so that the wage level and working conditions in the sector are not available in general, to the job seekers in the

> market unless they manage to cross the barrier of entry somehow. (He describes the informal sector as) Thus it (informal sector) can be expected to act as a buffer between employment and unemployment. Some job seekers who are unable to find regular employment in the formal sector may for short or long periods participate in the informal sector rather than be wholly unemployed. In this view, a substantial part of the workers found in the informal sector will be the 'secondary workers' i.e. those who are not the main earners in the household.
>
> To look at it another way a disproportionately large proportion of females as well as those outside the prime working age group (say under 25 and above 50) will be found in the informal sector employment, if they are employed at all. Similarly migrants would be disproportionately represented in the informal sector.

Jan Breman in his article, 'A Dualistic Labour System ?[6] is critical of the concept of the dualistic division of the economy into the formal and informal.

> In my opinion, the informal sector cannot be demarcated as a separate economic compartment and/or labour situation. Any attempt to do so will give rise to numerous inconsistencies and difficulties, such as will be shown by even a discussion of social background, size and composition. Moreover by interpreting the relationship to the formal sector in a dualistic framework and in focusing on the mutually exclusive characteristics, we lost sight of the unity and totality of the productive system (p. 18).

He goes on further to explain how he views the economic system based on his research in a district town and its rural surroundings in South Gujarat (India).

> The results of this research show that it is fairly easy to find two extreme categories that oppose each other. On the one hand, those who earn their daily bread with the aid of poorly paid, unskilled intermittent work, which due to the considerable physical work involved, is considered of low standing; and on the other, those in permanent employment, for which formal education or trained skills required—jobs with a fairly high and often regular wage which ensures security and social respectability to the worker. However, these profiles are seen most clearly at the extremes of the two poles of the labour force. As the distance between the extremes lessens, similarities in recruitment, working conditions, and bargaining procedures gradually outdo the differences between various categories of labour, in this respect. In other words, gradations rather than watertight divisions. To split the employment systems into two sectors is, therefore, to adopt an approach which is over rigid and too little differentiated. (p. 1905).

Jan Breman tries to overcome the rigidity by postulating a fragmented labour market barring entry due to trade particularism, even within the informal sector.

S.V. Sethuraman in his book *The Urban Informal Sector in Developing Countries : Employment, Poverty and Environment*[7] begins with the premise that urbanisation is a process which is gaining more and more momentum, in both absolute and relative terms, in the developing countries of the world. The urban labour force is increasing much faster than the work opportunities in the formal sector. 'Under the circumstances the surplus population of the labour force has been forced to generate its own mean of employment and hence of survival' (p. 8). These people constitute the urban informal sector. He tries to clarify the term 'informal sector' by focusing on the choice of unit which would help to classify an activity as being formal or informal.

> Perhaps the distinguishing feature of the informal sector enterprises is that they made their appearance, not so much in response to investment opportunities as in the neo-classifical sense, but out of necessity to create one's own employment. Thus the accent was on employment generation and not in seeking suitable investment opportunities for th sake of realising a return on investment. The individuals/enterpreneurs associated with the informal sector enterprises are not capitalists in the classical sense of the term, seeking investment outlets. Since many of them are migrants to urban areas in search of employment and since few possess substantial capital, education or skills, the key characteristics of the informal sector would seem to be that the enterprises emerged in spite of the lack of necessary skills.

He goes on to give a definition of the informal sector as 'It consists of small scale units engaged in the production and distribution of goods and services with the primary objective of generating employment and income to their participants notwithstanding the constraints on capital. both physical and human, and know-how' (p. 17). He identifies the mode of production, the mode of organisation, and the scale of operation as the three basic criteria for classifying a unit of production as part of the informal sector. 'The search for the informal sector enterprises was thus confined to the following: all enterprises with 10 persons or less and engaged in manufacturing, construction, transport, trade and service sectors.' The selection is further refined by ...

> whether the enterprise is legal or not ? Works on an irregular basis ? Located in temporary structures ? Uses electrical power ? Depends on formal credit institutions? Relies on formal distribution networks ? Most workers have fewer than 6 years of schooling ? Needless to add, these ar but a few suggested criteria, and we could think of a number of other similar ones. the rationale behind the choice was simply that most of them can be applied without asking questions, just by visual observation of the enterprises. The essence of this additional measure was to include enterprises even though they had more than 10 persons provided they satisfied at least one of the suggested criteria of informality. (p. 22).

Fred Fluitman in *Training for Work in the Informal Sector*[8] sums up the present state of the work on the informal sector quite realistically as 'Today, following more than a decade of spadework by academics and by researchers in international agencies, notably the ILO, policy makers in developing countries and labour market analysts among others, increasingly recognize the existence of an informal sector, somehow separate from the traditional rural economy and the modern or formal sector.' He elaborates further.

> Terminology has occasionally given rise to confusion and debate. Alternative labels have been proposed to highlight particular aspects or special concerns or to narrow the field; the micro enterprise, the unstructured, the unregistered sector, the hidden or the people's economy, etc. Moreover, different units of analysis have been adopted in informal sector surveys—the enterprise, the household, the individual workers. It has admittedly proven difficult if not impossible, to move from a general notion to a precise and widely accepted definition of the informal sector: a definition which applies to all countries, all sorts of economic activities and all stages of development; a definition which draws a clear line between the formal and the informal sector.

The theoretical work on the informal sector has assumed this sector to be a transitional state of the economy. It is visualised that the workforce in the informal sector will be absorbed into the formal sector in the due course of time.

Informal and Formal Systems of Work

However, the basic limitation of all these and other definitions is that they convey the message that the informal sector has been discovered for the first time. This implication of a discovery may be acceptable according to the norms of the industrialised countries about what is work and who is a worker, but by the tradition of the developing countries the 'informal sector' has been the predominant mode of functioning for centuries.

The formal sector is of very recent origin in the developing countries. However, it has become central to their economy due to the adaptation of models of structuring the economy on the lines of the industrialised countries. The informal sector is not a discovery, it has always been there, and these people are finding it more and more difficult to earn a livelihood today.

It is more pertinent to use the phrases 'informal system of work' and 'formal system of work' instead of 'informal sector' and 'formal sector' to explain the reality of the economies of the developing countries. Informal systems of work are essentially based on verbal transactions as opposed to formal systems of work where written transactions predominate. the more the aspects of an individual's work and life are dependent on written transactions for validity, the more that individual is likely to belong to a formal system of work. The more the aspects of an individual work and life are based on verbal transactions for validity, the more that individual is likely to belong to an informal system of work. Viewed in this way the economies of developing countries have been functioning in informal systems of work for centuries. This is the way of work the majority of the population is familiar with and this is the basis on which the economy is structured.

The poor population, which is the majority of the population in developing countries, has been variously referred to as informal sector, unorganised sector, working poor, marginal, peripheral, third sector, lower circuit, residual, illegal, black economy, hidden economy and people's economy, in the literature on development. They are used interchangeably even though they mean different things.

Of all these terms, the terms 'informal' and 'unorganised' are the two most critical ones when formulating a conceptual framework to explain the reality of the poor population in developing countries. They refer to different processes altogether, in an economy, even though they have been used interchangeably. Whereas the informal-formal continuum of a system of work is indicative of the extent of verbal-written transactions, the organised-unorganised continuum is a function of the extent of collective action of for common goals by a group of people.

When these two terms are juxtaposed, the working population can be viewed as organised and formal, organised and informal, unorganised and formal or, finally, unorganised and informal. Any set of people can protect their interests only by organising. this is even more true for the poor in any economy. Because the terms 'unorganised' and 'informal' are used interchangeable, the real understanding of informal systems of work has been blurred. The relative importance of workers already organised has been over-estimated and the ways of organising workers in the informal systems of work have not been understood properly.

How does a group of people get organised ? How does it protect its interests after organising ? What are the pressures on an organised group to become formal ? How does an organised group stay informal or combine informal ? How does an organised group stay informal or combine informal and formal aspects ? A more appropriate under-standing of these questions emerges from the concept of an informal system of work and a formal system of work as explained here. Defining the term 'informal sector' per se then, does not assume criticality. The more pertinent question is—how does a section of the population—the poor—live, work and earn its livelihood ? Understanding the systems of work they are engaged in, then becomes more important.

The Structure of the Economy

The conceptual framework for explaining the reality of the poor population has to take into account the state of the economy, its ability to generate work and income for all, its structure and institutional framework. An economy which can provide work for the majority of the population in an employer-employee relationship with the protection of the law and with all the supportive legislation is different from an economy which can provide such work only for a minority of its population. In the world today, only the highly industrialised countries are able to provide regular jobs for the majority of their population. India is the tenth most industrialised country in the world, and yet only 11 per cent of the working population has an established employer-employee work relationship as recognised by the law. The scope of the economy to provide such work for greater numbers is very limited. The situation is the same for the majority of the countries of the world. The global economy as a whole is also not able to generate work of this kind in proportion with the need for work.

As the previous Director General of the ILO, Mr. Francis Blanchard, has written in *Training for Work in the Informal Sector*[9],

It would be unrealistic to insist that a solution lies in integrating all workers into the formal sector. The formal sector in many developing countries is simply too small to absorb more than a fraction of labour forces entrants even in the most favourable economy conditions. Indeed work in the informal sector undoubtedly relieves poverty and its valuable contribution to meeting basic needs should not be underestimated. We must take care not to smother it with regulations. It would be more pertinent to look for other ways to protect its workers, most of whom are self-employed or apprentices, against exploitation; to help them to set up additional small enterprises and co-operatives, to provide them with training, credit and other support required to diversify production and to improve their productivity and income.

Informal sector workers, whether they are in rural or in urban areas, self-employed or employees, must to a large extent help themselves in overcoming their difficulties. This will not be feasible unless they get together to defend their interests. Existing workers' and employers' associations should strive to meet the needs of their workers in the informal sector more effectively, by appropriate adjustment of their objectives and structures. In addition, or as an alternative, new forms of organisation and participation should be explored.

In short, we believe that it is of vital importance for the ILO to extend its concern to the entire world of labour, including the hundreds of millions of men and women in the fringe of, or outside, the organised, industrial, formal sector.

The structure of the economies of developing countries has to be understood in the context of informal systems of work and self-employment for the majority of the population.

Informal Systems of Work and Self-employment

Everyone has to live, has to survive, has to earn a livelihood whether it is a situation of poverty or a situation of plenty. Every individual can be seen as an instrument in the hands of somebody else or as a self-propelled entity able to make life options himself/herself. Work is also then, the most integral part of everyone's life. How work is viewed, how options are visualised for each individual, how sustained interest and involvement in work is sought to be achieved for everyone, how the potential of each person is to be brought out and best utilised, are important considerations which determine the structuring of an economy. Cultural and social systems also evolve accordingly and the total ethos of a society is developed.

Informal systems of work prevalent in India and other developing countries have been traditionally structured around generating self-employment for the majority of the population. A positive social and cultural value has been attached to ownership of one's resources in order to earn a livelihood. Selling only one's physical and manual labour and working for somebody else as an employee has been seen, culturally, as the least preferred way of earning a livelihood. The economy has been structured in such a way that the majority of the population is in a buyer-seller relationship. A sense of involvement in work; maintaining high motivation; developing accountability and responsibility to do one's work well; linking productivity and work performance to income; developing a sense of identity and belonging through the primary social system of family and kinship; are all sought to be achieved by reinforcing self-employment for the majority through buyer-seller relationships. Informal systems of work and self-employment for the majority have therefore gone hand-in-hand. Representative organisations of all occupations and activities have been established in the form of trade and artisan guilds to enable people to protect their work and social interests, to deal with conflicting situations, to set norms and standards of work, to ensure quality, to negotiate and bargain with other guilds and with the State and finally, to participate in public policy formulation. Representativeness has been ensured for every group by being organised around work and occupations. Hence, a highly organised economy developed on the basis of informal systems of work.

In the historical process of transformation, eleborated in this chapter, the development of formal systems of work has been described. The creation of a large majority of poor, self-employed workers in the economy as part of this process has also been explained. How can collective strength be created for this majority of people ?

Collective Strength through Representative Forums

All these self-employed workers (both men and women) also have to protect their interests. What would be a representative forum for self-employed workers to protect their interests? In India, guilds have been the forum for establishing representativeness for various occupational groups to protect their interests and to participate in policy formulation. This form of representativeness has, however, been undergoing a transformation. In the process of industrialisation, the group of workers with an established employer-employee relationship have become more and more organised along the lines of the trade unions developed in industrialised countries. They have been able to bargain and negotiate for more and more economic strength for their members even though they constitute a minority of the workforce. The majority of the workforce, which is self-employed, has remained outside the fold of the representative forums a called trade unions. This process of exclusion of the majority of the workers has continued to such an extent that the whole labour movement itself has become confined to those workers who have an established employer-employee relationship, and only these people are called 'workers'. The labour movement, the labour laws and policies, the national and international labour organisations, address themselves to the needs of those workers who have an established employer-employee relationship. What happens to the majority of the workforce then ? Are they to remain excluded ? Will they be able to tilt the direction of the labour laws and the policy framework in their favour ? Will they be able to command the respect due to the majority of the workforce in a democracy ?

This is possible only if the reality of the self-employed workers is taken seriously by the policy-makers, when the future envisaged for all these workers is seen within the perspective of strengthening self-employment in its own right instead of replacing it with employer-employee relationships. This is possible only by establishing representative forums of self-employed workers to protect their interest. Today there are very, very few representative forums for the self-employed workers because they have not been organised as workers. The traditional representativeness of the self-employed workers in the form of trade and artisan guilds has been destroyed for the poor, and it has not been replaced by other forums. The rich self-employed have been able to adapt the guild form of representative forums into the present day variations of trade and industry associations and federations, chambers of commerce, professional councils, etc. They are able to protect their interests through these forums as also to influence policy formulations to suit their needs. But these constitute only a minority in terms of the total number of self-employed people. the vast majority of self-employed workers have yet to establish their representative forums to truly protect their interests. Because their organisations as workers have been destroyed, they are presently *unorganised as workers*. But socially they are still highly organised, along caste, religious, and linguistic lines.

Representative Forum for Self-employed Workers

How can we build representative forums for self-employed workers ? The experiences of who many grass-roots organisations, working with different occupational groups of the self-employed, have shown that organising workers is the only way to strengthen the position of these workers in the overall socio-economic political context. Organising the self-employed workers is different from organising workers with an established employer-employee relationship. The conventional trade unions have experience in organising workers with an established employer-employee relationship. Their basis of organising is collective bargaining and wage negotiations with the employers. This basis of organising can be of very limited value for self-employed workers because there is no established employer-employee relationship and hence, no one employer with whom to bargain for improvement. The State and public policy are the main forces which determine the fate of the self-employed in any economy. So, the focus of bargaining shifts from one employer to public policy. The direction, nature, and implementation of public policies and the responsibility of the State, affect the overall economic situation of a country. The economic atmosphere becomes either conducive to, or antagonistic to, the survival and strengthening of the self-employed. The representative forums of the self-employed therefore have essentially to bargain with the State for public policies favourable to their members so that their niches in the economy can move from strength to strength. The representative forums themselves provide a variety of services to members to set a precedent for the State in initiating appropriate policies and alternate systems benefiting self-employed workers. This function becomes all the more vital in the face of adverse economic policies and deprivation for a large majority of the population.

However, the established organisations of workers, i.e., the conventional trade unions, do not understand this form of representativeness or bargaining. Trade unions of self-employed workers are very rare. The few that do exist are establishing pioneering precedents in the world of work and the labour movement. But in fact they are really showing the way for adapting the traditional form of representativeness for self-employed workers (the trade and artisan guilds) in the present day world of work and labour. The trade unions of self-employed workers are the modern day versions of the traditional guilds. Other contemporary methods of organising people, such as, co-operatives, societies, trusts and associations, can also perform the same function of representativeness for the self-employed. However, these forms are not yet seen in the perspective of trade unions, the labour movement, and the world of work.

When we consider the plight of self-employed women workers, the situation becomes even more complex. Women are not even perceived as workers, even though they may be spending most of their time in doing some work for an income either of cash and/or kind. Hence, it is very difficult to organise self-employed women workers and bring them into the mainstream of the world of work. But it is essential for this process to be promoted in a big way if the plight of the majority of working women is to be improved. The social status of women, the invisibility of women's work, the exploitation of women as women and as workers, the fact of being self-employed in an economic environment not conductive to promoting self-employment for the average person, are the major forces which have to be influenced to affect the overall situation of women.

This study is a step in the direction of understanding the reality of poor, rural self-employed women, and to plan interventions for organising and improving their life situations.

REFERENCES

1. Planning Commission Statistics, Census of India figures.
2. *Towards Equality,*' Report of the Committee on the Status of Women in India, 1974.
3. *Employment, Incomes and Inequality,*' ILO Report on Kenya, Genava, 1972.
4. H. Joshi and B. Joshi, *Surplus Labour and the City—A Study of Bombay,* Delhi, O.U.P., 1976.
5. Dipak Mazumdar, 'Urban Informal Sector,' *World Bank Staff Working Paper* No. 22, July, 1975.
6. Jan Breman 'A Dualistic Labour System ? A Critique of the "Informal Sector" Concept,' *Economic and Political Weekly,* 11 December 1976.
7. S.V. Sethuraman, *The Urban Informal Sector in Developing Countries: Employment, Poverty and Environment,* Geneva, ILO, 1981 (pp. 8, 17, 22).
8. Fluitman Fred (ed.) *Training for Work in the Informal Section,* Geneva, ILO, 1989 (pp. xiii-xiv).
9. *Op. cit.* (pp. ix-x).

48

Strategies for Women's Employment

I turn now to the arrangements which women negotiate with members of their families, and others, to free themselves from certain of the childcare and household duties normally assigned to women in contemporary British society, in order to take up paid employment. In addition, I present data on the personal adjustments which women must frequently make as individuals in order to combine unpaid domestic labour with wage labour. In the discussion below, I have grouped these strategies for employment' under three main heading—'household,' 'family,' and 'personal.'

HOUSEHOLD STRATEGIES

Most of the women interviewed for this study were, or had been, able to enlist some practical support from other members of their households (principally husbands and children), either on a regular basis, enabling them to combine childcare and household duties with paid employment, or as a means of coping with crises (e.g. sick children) or periodic difficulties (e.g. supervising younger children during school holidays).

Role Played by Husbands

All but two of the respondents were or had been, married; however, when interviewed only three-quarters of them were living with their husbands (and in nine of these forty-eight cases this was a second husband). The remaining women were mostly living alone with their children, although three were co-habiting and one was living with her parents. There was thus a substantial minority within the sample for whom the sharing of domestics tasks and childcare with husbands was currently impossible. When it is remembered that some of the women currently living with their husbands had spent time living alone with their children in the past, it can be seen that the sharing of domestic tasks with husbands is not even a theoretical possibility for many women, at least periodically. In fact about a third of all the women reported that they had at some time been living with their children but without a husband. This was usually after marital breakdown, although in a few cases the women concerned were single mothers. For some this arrangement was temporary, perhaps lasting just a couple of years between the breakdown of one relationship and the formation of another; for others it was virtually permanent, lasting for a decade or more. I draw particular attention to this phenomenon no order to stress that the sharing of childcare and domestic responsibilities between spouses is a strategy for employment which is not available to all mothers at all times. I need hardly add that, as I demonstrate below, there will also be cases where the husband is (theoretically) available, but the strategy is not. In some families husbands (and occasionally wives) continue to put up much resistance to the idea of male participation in the tasks of domestic labour.

What did my respondents have to say about the role played by husbands in the work at home? I think it important here to distinguish between the tasks associated with the care of children, and the aspects of domestic labour popularly referred to as 'housework'—cleaning, cooking, washing. Where young children are concerned, their care is a 24-hour job, although of course this dos not mean 24-hour labour for the person caring for the child. Some of the caring for children can be done while one is asleep, or watching television, or performing almost any household task. It consists of 'being at hand,' and ready to respond to the infant's sometimes unpredictable needs. Other aspects of childcare, of course, involve labour of a kind which can be physically exhausting; attending to the bodily needs of infants, keeping them in clean clothes, and playing with them or watching over them while they play. These are all tasks which those who care for children will confirm are often hard work indeed.

About half of my respondents reported that their husbands took (or had taken) a part in caring for their children. Frequently, the husband's willingness to do this—sometimes under protest—was the key factor in enabling a respondent to take a paid job. Husbands might care for their children on Saturdays, while their wives worked as sales assistants for example; or in the evenings, so that women could work an evening shift in a factory or take a part-time job as a hospital domestic. They might be willing to 'keep an eye on' the children first thing in the morning so that their wives could go out to clean offices or pubs. Whilst some of these husbands were no doubt relieving their wives of some of the *labour* of childcare, in many cases they were merely undertaking to 'be at hand'. For example, wives might find their husbands prepared to stay in from 5.00 to 8.00 each evening while they went out to work, but still themselves have to perform the labour of childcare. Lynne's husband was of this kind:

> Lynne: 'He likes more or less everything to be done as he gets home—apart from he washes up.... but I have to do the baby, get him ready for bed and that.'

Ruth's experience had been similar. When her children were very young she worked in the evenings, as a barmaid, and as a tupperware demonstrator.

> Ruth: 'My husband would do a lot of things, but — I think he has changed one nappy, because, as he says, he doesn't think that's a man's job, which I suppose is fair enough. So even when I went out [to work] you see, the children had to be changed and virtually ready for bed, or in bed preferably, before I actually went out.'

Some husbands were willing to take on some of the labour of childcare—but they were most definitely in the minority. Sara, who had never left the labour market, despite having three children, had a husband who was prepared to share this work with her. His occupation (nurse) had made him more familiar with the tasks of caring than are many men. Sara feels they are both able to work full-time, only because they have a high level of co-operation at home.

> Sara: 'He does everything when he's there—like looking after the baby, changing nappies, everything.... when he's on morning [shift], on the way in he will take the children to school, and he'll pick them up.... There's nothing that he will say — "Oh, that's not my job."

Such husbands, according to my respondents, were few and far between. More common was the response given by Yvonne.

> Yvonne: 'Well, he hasn't sort of given much time to the children, or to the house. He doesn't do a lot really.

Doreen made a telling point when she contrasted her husband's willingness to participate in household tasks with his attitude to childcare.

> Doreen: 'Caring for the children?.... When they were very small he was frightened of them — when it came to changing nappies — and things like that — he just didn't, at all ... He did what I call the easy side of caring for the children — making sure they'd their pocket money and so on — I tended to look after the children more, where he helped with the house.'

The 'easy side' of childcare certainly seemed to be all most husbands had been prepared to undertake. Being 'at hand' when the children were small, and being willing to take on some of the organisational tasks associated with older children, was all most women seemed to expect of their husbands.

> Heather: 'He does a lot with the children, which I'm thankful for. He will mend the bikes and run round buying things for them, sorting things out. You know, if Steven wants football bots or something, *he*'ll do it... this sort of thing, which relieves me..... At Christmas he has most of the school holiday off, of course he has to organise the children then... Which I think has been very good for him, because when the children were babies I felt totally responsible, especially for Steven, because he was still working his way up. I did everything for Steven, and I think now, looking back, we both agree that I shouldn't have done, it took away some of the joy from him, just because I thought it was my duty to do it. So I think he's reaping the benefits now — we lived a little bit in isolated compartments before.'

Husbands, then, had frequently been crucial in enabling women to take on employment (especially part-time jobs), but had only rarely been prepared to perform the more laborious tasks of childcare. In all but a few cases, the husband's role in caring for children was specifically related to the fact of the wife's employment. A small minority of husbands were willing to supervise children during school holidays, and an even smaller group would take time off work to care for a sick child.

What had been the extent of the husband's participation in the tasks of housework? About half of the women reported that their husbands played a significant role in the performance of domestic and household duties apart from childcare. This usually meant that their husbands would do washing up, and perhaps some preparation of meals, or household cleaning. A third of the women felt their husbands made (or had made) a really important contribution to the general tasks of housework. Such men were described as 'very helpful,' or 'sharing.' The nature of their participation varied between a willingness to do anything their wives requested, to genuine sharing of duties, and more independent activity.

> Elizabeth: 'He used to have Tuesday off.... so he used to do the house right through for me from to bottom — you know, the hoovering and dusting and everything.... when I was full-time.'

> Angela: 'We share everything ... [he does] washing up, cooking, hoovering, polishing bathing Jane, making beds.

Some women explained that their husbands carried out certain tasks on a regular basis. Of the women currently living with a husband, two-thirds had husbands who regularly did washing up, and about half husbands who would do some meal preparation (occasionally preparing entire meals but more frequently just preparing vegetables, or heating up meals previously prepared by the wife). Just over a third had husbands who did some household cleaning. A few husbands (six out of forty-eight) did the weekly shopping (alone), while a mere three would regularly make beds. Of all the women interviewed, only one said her husband would sometimes wash clothes, and none reported that her husband was willing to do ironing. Meryl's husband was more than usually active in performing household duties.

> Meryl: '[He does] half easily ... he often does the shopping — I don't think my first husband knew what a shop looked like from the inside — he takes care of the money, which is lovely because I've done that for years and it's wearing.... he does cleaning in the house, and so on ... he cooks meals — curries and spaghettis — but I do most of it ... washing I suppose I mainly do — [today] I pegged one lot out and there was some more and I said, "I'll call in on the way back from the dentist and do it," and he said, "Oh, I'll do it" — which he would.'

Several explanations were given for the more limited participation by husbands which was more common. Some husbands were (or were perceived by their wives to be) incompetent at performing such tasks. Feminists may suspect a male conspiracy of 'studied incompetence,' but it was clear that the process sometimes developed with the collusion of wives.

> Beth: 'I prefer to do the washing, because they always seem to shrink it — I don't

> know why, but they always do. Shopping, again, I'm very fussy and I like to see what meat they're farming off.... He got me some steak once—I'll always remember, 2 lbs of chuck steak—and when he brought it home, I wouldn't even give it to the dog.... I took it back — oh, I was angry..... and cooking — no, no-one can .... I prefer to do my own cooking, thank you.'

Other men were reluctant to undertake tasks which they identified as 'a woman's job,' and several women reported their husbands' refusal to do any domestic task which was publicly visible.

> Helen: 'The only thing he won't do is hang the washing on the line.... "I don't want women looking at me hanging the washing out." ... If anybody comes to the door, if he's wiping up he'll put the towel down and go and sit down.' *(laughs)*

A minority of the women were, or had been, married to men who took no part at all in household duties., Carol's apparent approval of the arrangements in her home was thrown into question by her unguarded remark 'Ah, sore pint actually.'

> Carol: 'Although I believe we should share — I am earning virtually as much as what he's earning — it is my duty as a wife to clean, polish, see the children are OK .... and I wouldn't want him to go to work and say "I had to do the washing because my wife's doing full-time work." If I could not manage to do full-time work and run my home, I wouldn't do it. [When] he knew I wanted to come back ... He said "if the housework starts to go, you've had your chips."

It is important in attempting to understand the sexual division of domestic labour to recognise it as part of a domestic bargain between spouses (see below). This means that a husband's attitude to his wife's employment (and earnings) is highly significant. I asked the women how they thought their husbands felt about having a wife with a paid job. Many husbands were apparently happy about their wives' employment because they appreciated the importance of their earnings in either enabling the family to make ends met, or having a higher standard of living.

> Lucy: 'Really, he's all for it, because otherwise we just couldn't manage.... or there would be a lot of things which we would definitely be without if I wasn't working.'
>
> Geraldine: 'He likes it — it gives him a bit extra to play with, doesn't it?'

While sometimes the extra income was seen as beneficial for the while family, in many cases it was made clear that the husband saw his wife's earnings as bringing a direct material benefit to him.

Cathy made this point mere clearly than any of the other women: 'He thought it was good.... because then he could cut my housekeeping down, you see.'

A further quite common response was that husbands were willing to tolerate their wives' employment, on condition that the women did not allow standard of domestic labour and childcare to 'slip.'

> Ruth: 'He said all the time that I can keep the house clean and tidy, keep the children nice, as long as I've got time for the children, then I can keep the job. But, he says, once one or the other starts going—don't get me wrong, he doesn't expect me to do the painting and this, that and the other — but he does expect the house to look nice and tidy ... once I start slipping on that, then I can start thinking about giving up.'

Similarly, some husbands disliked their wives having paid jobs because it meant they had to participate in domestic work.

> Shirley: 'He wasn't particularly keen about it being full-time.... he had to do more of the things at home.'

Although some of those who reported such an attitude were quietly critical of their husbands, many accepted that men had a right to make such demands of their wives and to exercise their authority in this way. Some made it quite explicit that they had sought their husband's *permission* before taking employment.

> Nancy: 'He said, "Well, you can to go work, provided you do something with it" ..... So what we've done with it is we've literally ploughed it into our home.'

A small group of women reported considerable resentment on their husbands' part. These men either disliked the idea of their wives earning money, and felt that men ought to be the family breadwinners, or were hostile to their wives having jobs because they saw the arrangement as a challenge to their authority.

> Linda: 'He doesn't like me working ..... he thinks he earns enough to support us .... a bit of pride there, I think.'

> Pru: 'He didn't like it — he didn't like it because that way it would give me a certain independence, and I wouldn't be, you know, the woman stuck at home.'

It would be inaccurate to leave the impression that all husbands either opposed their wives' employment, or liked it only for the additional income. Some women claimed that their husbands were content to see them go out to work, because they knew it made them happier. No surprisingly, such husbands were mostly amongst those with the highest participation in household tasks.

> Margery: 'He'd rather I be out at work, because he knows that I'll get really bored and fed up at home.'

> Wanda: 'It relieves the tension in the house.... I think he likes me going out — I don't get so miserable being indoors all day.'

Finally, it should be noted that a small number of women were married to men who took it quite for granted that they should be in employment.

> Rachel: 'He feels it's essential.... It makes me a person .... in his eyes, people who don't work are sponging on society.'

> Valerie: 'He likes me working — he wouldn't have it any other way. His attitude is "I've got to work till I get my pension, why shouldn't you?"'

Interestingly, these two women could expect very little assistance from their husbands with domestic tasks.

Of course, some women reported a variety of responses from their husbands, and ones which changed over time. Many of the husbands who were initially hostile to the idea of their wives having a job came to favour the arrangement as time passed, usually when they became aware of the advantages of additional income, or on finding that they could gradually escape involvement in domestic tasks.

> Pat: 'He wasn't keen .... he wasn't keen on me coming back out full-time..... Now, we're managing to buy a house and all different things, he's quite agreeable.'

> Geraldine: 'He started off doing the housework and cooking meals — and having my meal ready when I got home — but of course now David has got older and things have got easier he tends to leave it to me. He used to do shopping as well at one time.'

In my view, none of the couples so far described resembled the 'symmetrical family' anticipated by Young and Willmott (1973). There was, however, some scant evidence of marital egalitarianism. In a tiny minority of cases, women claimed that in their marriage, everything was shared, and that their employment was part of an agreed arrangement.

> Tina: 'We always do things together — he's never said to me "Don't go to work" ... We've never looked upon it as yours and my job. I think he's that sort of man — he doesn't look upon me as being the head cook and bottle-washer. A lot of wives are looked on like that, aren't they?'

Despite this however, the overwhelming impression of the marital bargaining over the question of wives' employment, was that husbands held the balance of power. This came as no surprise, but the evidence was quite clear; In general, wives sought husbands' permission, or at last approval, in taking a job. They got it, especially if husbands were to be involved in domestic tasks (that is, usually when full-time work was involved), only when the material reward in the form of the wife's wages could be seen to be of benefit to the family, and in some cases to the husband himself, or when the husband recognised that a more contented wife would be a pleasanter companion, and one better able to make his home, to borrow Lasch's compelling phrase, 'a haven in a heartless world.'

Children as Source of Support

When interviewed, forty of my sixty-four respondents had at least one child aged ten years or older living with them. Although there was no prompting about the role of children in the interviews, just over half of these women mentioned the part played by their children in carrying out domestic duties. It was clear from their comments, however, that in most of the families children performed only very few duties. Most frequently mentioned were: making their own beds, keeping their own rooms clean and tidy, washing up, hoovering, and preparing vegetables, or sometimes meals. A few women had children, mainly daughters, who would undertake washing ironing or shopping, while two had an elder daughter who would take care of a younger child after school hours. (Of course in most families there was not a large enough gap between the births of children for this arrangement to be possible).

A few explained that they paid their daughters to help at home.

> Doreen: 'My daughter's been old enough — and now the second one ..... it's been a paid job with them to cook our evening meal..... This is the benefit of the children getting older now.'

This practice could also reveal an interesting sexual division of child labour.

> Annette: 'Usually, Saturday mornings, Jill (aged twelve) and I will do the housework between us — we've got a thing going..... Young Kevin (aged fourteen) goes out and does the car-washing, by which he earns himself extra money. Jill isn't old enough, but wants to earn extra money — she has her pocket money — she takes the dog for walks, you know..... I think she does the brass and silver for that as well.... things like washing up don't count. I usually do the washing up, but occasionally I'll say "Oh, come and do the washing up for me," and they'll do that. But apart from that, like I say, she does housework — household chores, polishing, floors, you know, dusting, hoovering on a Saturday. We quite often do it between us and I pay her 35 p an hour, which has got quite a bit of fun with her. She writes it down and she has it in bulk when it's three or four pounds.

Indeed, daughters were more often relied upon for support than sons. Annette's comments, and the following extract, provide illustrations of this.

> Dawn: '[My daughter] does all her own ironing — she does do some of my ironing — I mean, she doesn't have a lot of time, she's at college. She goes out the house 8 o'clock and she doesn't get in till 6. [Also], she's got a week-end job.... my youngest, if I say to him go up the shops or something, he does. The boys make their own beds—I do stress that.'

In only a very few cases, however, did women rely at all heavily upon their children for support or assistance with domestic responsibilities. Kate, who lived alone with her four children, was one of the few women who had made a specific bargain with a daughter in connection with the sharing of household duties. She explained to me how she had talked matters over with her daughter (aged 14) before taking a full-time job:

> Kate: 'My eldest daughter.... she's always been — very sensible, very adult. I said "Shall we try it?" Actually it was her that pushed me into getting out of the house... and she said that she could manage—because she'd always learnt to cook, she wanted to do it on her own. And I said "Well, we'll see how it goes and if it doesn't work, then I'll take a part-time job" ..... she does the cooking and any light washing .... she cooks the meal, and she'll make cakes—anything that's going.... She's been doing it on her own since she was nine — she's done very well.

Kate's arrangement was exceptional, however. Many women expected very little from their children, often suggesting that they felt it unfair to ask them to participate in household chores.

> Paula: 'I don't ask [my son] to do very much because I have one of these complex things.... I go to work because chose to go to work ... I shouldn't put my chores on to them when they've got their school work.'

In a few cases, women expected assistance from their children, but stressed that this was because it was 'good for' children to help, rather than specifically because it would lighten their load as a working mother. As Rachel explained: 'He does do those chores, not because I need him to, but I feel he should do.'

In summary, then, it was evident that, in many households, children were not expected to play any significant part in domestic duties. However, a few women made statements which offered a challenge to the prevailing ideology concerning the sexual division of domestic labour.

> Margaret: '[My son] does cooking, and tries to do a bit of cleaning..... I think the mother should teach her son as much as she should her daughter.

In most families, though, the status quo in this respect was under no serious threat, and indeed was in many cases being systematically reinforced and reproduced.

Other Household Members

Three of the women's households included a parent or parents. Wanda had her father, and Andrea her mother, living in the family home. Both of these women were married and living with their husbands. In neither case did the parent make any really significant contribution to the domestic duties: Andrea's mother usually prepared vegetables for the evening meal, and Wanda explained that her father kept his own room tidy, often did the washing up,, and sometimes did the hoovering. Neither parent required any special nursing or other care. In Wanda's case, the arrangement was temporary, while her father waited for a council flat, and in Andrea's her mother was a permanent member of the household, but lived a relatively independent existence in a 'granny flat' linked to the family home.

Maria, a divorced woman, had lived with her parents and one of her two children since the breakdown of her marriage. All three adults in the household were in full-time employment, and Maria made it clear that she found the arrangement both convenient and beneficial. She and her mother shared the domestic chores between them, which lightened the load for them both.

> Maria: 'I have very, very smashing parents..... I don't pay them nothing ..... I'm not that extravagant being at home .... only a meal in the evening. My Mum cooks for Dad, and she gets an extra meal for me and the child..... She does the shopping as well .... I'm off [work] this afternoon — I'll go home, if there's any washing to do, I'll do it, general tidying up.... then I pick up Mum from work .... and start the cooking so it makes it easier on [her] ..... when she has her days off, she looks after my boy — I don't bring him in the nursery then, she has him at home.'

Three women in the sample were living with men who were not their husbands. They included Annette and Alice (discussed in Chapter 3) and also Pru. Pru had lived alone with her sons for three years following the breakdown of her marriage, and the present arrangement had existed for less than two years. She said that in her household 'everybody mucks, inn now,' and that both her sons and her 'boyfriend' gave her money. Nevertheless, she did all the main tasks—cooking, washing, cleaning—while the men simply helped out with washing up and odd jobs.

When women take on paid jobs, then, some sharing of domestic tasks with household members often develops. Certain duties may be off-loaded on to husbands, children, and occasionally other adults, but for the most part women themselves continue to take the responsibility for, and indeed to perform most of the labour of childcare and household work. Amongst the women interviewed, there was considerable variation in the role played by husbands (from making no contribution to, in a very few cases, taking an almost equal share), but children and other household members rarely did more than assist in minor ways. Husbands were often crucial, however, in enabling wives to take part-time jobs when there were young children at home. As shown below, women often have to adopt strategies other than sharing work with household members in order to combine employment with the domestic responsibilities assigned to them. In almost every case, these strategies involve women and not men.

FAMILY STRATEGIES

We use the term 'family strategies' to describe those arrangements enabling women to combine paid employment and domestic labour which involve kin who are not members of the household. As expected, female kin were the most important extra-household source of support for most respondents, in addition to or as an alternative to support from household members. However, a minority of my respondents had no access to this strategy for employment. A few women lived at a considerable distance from their kin while others had no kin, or no contact with them, because of death, estrangement, or simple lack of kin (e.g. no brothers or sisters). In addition, women whose kin were themselves in full-time employment (especially mothers and mother-in-law) usually found that they were denied access to this strategy.

Nevertheless approximately two-thirds of the women had been able to rely on family members outside the household for support. In many cases they lived in or near their place of birth, sometimes having parents or other relatives living in the same or the next street. This situation permitted frequent contact with kin. With a few exceptions, arrangements with kin were exclusively to do with childcare: caring for pre-school children while the respondent and her husband (when she had one) were at work, looking after children between the end of the school day and their parents' return from work, and taking care of children during school holidays, or when they were ill. Except in a very few cases, where respondents' fathers were involved, the support provided came from female kin: principally mothers and mothers-in-law, but also sisters, sisters-in-law, aunts, and grandmothers. Of those who reported family support, about half had, or had once had, regular arrangements whereby kin cared for their pre-school children throughout the time they were at work. This arrangement was especially popular as a means of enabling women to take part-time employment, although in a few cases women received such support when in a full-time job. A few women had arranged for kin to care for their school-age children after school hours, Family support was also important in enabling women to overcome the problems associated with school holidays and children's illnesses. Some women had relatives living at some distance who cared for children a holiday times, either by inviting them to stay, or by coming to look after them. Locally-based relatives were of course particularly important in helping out when children were sick.

Arrangements made with kin were often specific to a particular job, and usually had to be modified as children grew older. Sometimes they were temporary arrangements, used by mothers while they undertook seasonal work, or perhaps to cover the period between finding a job, and finding a suitable childminder. Inevitably, family strategies were also vulnerable to the vagaries of personal relationships.

> Maria: 'My mother-in-law used to look after them ... Of course, as soon as marriage broke off, she didn't want to know any more, so then I had to find my own. That is when I asked them for a place in the nursery here.'

Only four women reported assistance from their kin with aspects of domestic labour other than childcare. Anne had a younger unmarried sister who come to her home and prepared the evening meal on the days when Anne was employed. Valerie had paid her mother to come to her home and care for her children, from when they were small babies. After they reached school age, her mother continued to come to the house as before, but now did housework and washing etc. as well as looking after the children when they came home from school. Because of her full-time job, Pru's mother had not in the past been able to assist her daughter with childcare but, now that she was retired, Pru explained, she 'comes down every week to do my ironing for me.' Heather's is perhaps one of the most interesting cases of kin being involved in a strategy enabling both the respondent and her husband to take full-time paid employment. When interviewed, Heather was working as a supervisor in a retail store, having joined the company some three and a half years previously when her husband Paul was temporarily out of work. She described her attitude to paid employment at that time (when her children were aged 10 and 8).

> Heather: 'It was something I was looking for, but at that time I was still thinking of [a job with" school holidays that was the thing that was holding me back..... I could take this job because it was over the Christmas period, and Paul would be there. And then having found that I could manage it, and my mother-in-law offering support, then I took the plunge and said, "Yes, I'll go into a job that hasn't got school holidays. I recognise the fact that there will be some days when the children are poorly and I've got to work, but with my mother-in-law's support, then I can do it.,"'

In fact, support from both her own parents and her parents-in-law was such that she fairly quickly took on additional responsibilities at work.

> Heather: 'They look after the children when I'm not there my mother and mother-in-law are in the house by the time the children come home. They cook the evening meal. Both fathers come over and eat the evening meal with us, and then they go home about 7.30 after we've eaten.'

Later she explained how she felt about these arrangements:

> Heather: 'My job is important to me. The children I feel are quite adequately looked after and they're growing up in a loving community—well, group, family unit—with grandparents, myself and Paul. I like it. It's good for me and I think it's good for them.'

In general, the support of kin, especially other women, was clearly crucial in enabling many respondents to undertake paid employment. It is noteworthy that without exception, respondents saw it as their own responsibility (rather than a responsibility which they shared with their husbands) to make suitable arrangements for the care of children. This point was further underlined in connection with the commercial childcare arrangements which are discussed below. In a few of the cases where mothers provided substantial support, women reported considerably hostility to these arrangements from other members of their families.

> Valerie: 'My brothers and their wives — two of them in particular—took tremendous exception, so much so that they stopped speaking to my mother for four years because they objected so strongly to her looking after my children. They thought that I should leave work, etc.... for four years my eldest brother didn't talk to his mother .... they weren't directly involved... nobody was asking them to do anything, and they never have done.'

PERSONAL STRATEGIES

By 'personal strategies' we understand all those strategies for employment adopted by individual respondents which did not involve the assistance or active co-operation of members of their households or their kin. Women have recourse to a variety of such strategies, and included in the discussion here are commercial and *ad hoc* arrangements (principally in connection with the care of children); part-time employment and home working as 'solutions' for women who find standard full-time employment impractical; and the personally demanding strategy of engaging in long hours of labour, both paid and unpaid, which is a strategy adopted by, or sometimes forced upon, many employed mothers.

Commercial and *ad hoc* Arrangements

Most of our respondents had at some time made use of non-family sources of support, either on a regular, commercial basis, or in the form of *ad hoc* arrangements with neighbours or friends in times of difficulty. As I have suggested above, obtaining such support was usually considered to be the responsibility of women themselves rather than their husbands. However, just as women tended to seek the permission or approval of their husbands in obtaining jobs, so they might find that they needed their husbands' consent to specific arrangements of this type. Maureen, for example, described how her husband checked out the 'suitability' of the childminder she intended to use. She first heard of the minder through another employee at her evening washing-up job.

> Maureen: 'I got in touch with this lady who said..... she had a vacancy ... my husband went round first—I told him about it..... he went round and saw [her], and spoke to her, and saw the set-up, and he said "Yes, you'll have to go round yourself, it looks OK."'

Two-thirds (forty-two) of the women had turned to persons or agencies outside their families at some time during their working lives. Sixteen had paid childminders to care for their children for some or all of the time they were out at work, usually when children were of pre-school age, but including a few children who went to childminders during the school holidays. Children of seventeen of my respondents attended, or had attended, nursery schools or day nurseries. Eight of these women had had access to nurseries provided by their employers while they were engaged in agricultural work or hospital work Registered childminders and employer-provided day nurseries are relatively cheap ways of obtaining care for small children. In 1981 the childminding rate for full-time care for one child was £12.50 per week and in early 1981 the hospital day nursery used by six of the respondents was charging £1.40 per day. Childminders were highly valued by most of the women who had used them. In particular, their flexible attitude to the care of children, and their provision of 'family' rather than 'institutional' care was considered important. Many childminders were prepared to care for sick children, or to take children early in the morning and keep them into the evening when required. This kind of flexibility can be crucial to women who are sometimes trying hard to keep their jobs in difficult circumstances. Many childminders were also prepared to give children extra meals, to wash babies' clothes and nappies, and to take older children to and from school, or care for them during the holidays. The experiences reported by respondents, and in some cases witnessed by me in visiting childminders, did not seem to bear out some of the more sweeping criticisms which are sometimes made of them. This experience may well have been a typical (and consisted only of registered childminders) but it may be useful in offering a limited corrective to some of the harsher generalisations which have been made. Many of the women had found their childminders through personal recommendations.

> Ruth: 'A girl that used to live opposite me, her daughter used to go to Jane, and she had just mentioned...."If you do go back to work, I would get in touch with Jane, because in actual fact she is a terrific"—as I have found out since, obviously—but she said, "She is a terrific childminder, you know, if you don't just want to leave your child with anybody" ..... which I — well, once again, my husband wouldn't let me.....[It works] very, very well.... she also has my little boy during the school holidays..... [My daughter] is starting school [soon] .... and then they are quite welcome to go back there during their holidays, which is nice because it means then that I can carry on, you know, as per normal.'

Half of the women who used non-family sources of support (twenty) had neighbours or friends to whom they could turn, either on a regular basis or in an emergency such as children's illness, while fifteen women had at times been able to take employment only because they had a regular arrangement with a friend or neighbour who provided childcare for all or part of the time they were at work. In some cases neighbours cared for children after school, or perhaps looked after toddlers while their mothers were out at work. Sometimes neighbours or friends could be relied upon to take children to and from school or 'keep an eye on' older children who were thought to need a little supervision from a distance at holiday times or after school. Without exception, those giving such support were female—usually other married women, but occasionally the teenage daughters or respondents' friends or neighbours. Respondents usually paid for regular assistance of this kind, but not for occasional help.

All of these supportive strategies were put into effect outside the respondents' homes. However, a small minority of the women paid other women to come to work *in* their homes. Although such labour can usually be obtained relatively cheaply, women who are themselves low paid cannot normally afford to make such arrangements. For most of the women interviewed, paying for non-family domestic labour within the household had never been thought feasible or seriously considered as an option, and only three women had paid strangers to come to their homes to perform some kind of domestic labour. Doreen and her husband ran a shop whilst their children were still young, and during this time Doreen paid a woman to 'come in to clean the house and so on.' This relieved her of some chores, enabling her to work in the shop instead., Rachel started a full-time job shortly after moving to a new areas, and needed someone to supervise her 9-year-old son after school.

> Rachel: 'I paid a lady to look after my son, and old pensioner..... I put an advertisement in the local newsagents.... I didn't want her to do any housework, I just wanted her to be there.'

Louise had tried to cope with her full-time job and domestic responsibilities after her son was born, which worked well while she and her husband lived in a small flat. However, when they moved into a larger house, this became difficult. After weighing up various possibilities, she decided to employ domestic help.

> Louise: 'I looked around for a part-time job, you see—that was the idea.... but there wasn't anything ... [now] I have a lady in two days a week.... it was either that or a dishwasher, and I haven't got room for a dishwasher, so I have a lady come in, and she does the ironing on Tuesdays and on a Friday she hoovers through and does the bathroom and the kitchen.... [my husband] was a bit against it, because he thought we could do it, between us, but we tried it for a couple of weeks and I think he realised just how much it does involve, and in the end he sort of knuckled down to my way of thinking, and I advertised in the shop window.... she comes two mornings a week, for two hours .... I pay her £5.60 a week.'

With a husband in a managerial job, and herself bringing home between £70 and £80 per week, incurring such expenditure (in addition to childminding fees) was no problem for Louise. This would not have been the case for most of the other women in the study, however, especially those single parents who were perhaps most in need of extra help. Paying other women to work in one's own home was a 'last resort' strategy, to be adopted if other strategies were unavailable or did not work, but one which was not especially popular, even with the minority who could afford it.

Part-Time Working and Home Working as a 'Solution'

The majority of the women interviewed had found in part-time employment and/or home working a way of combining paid employment with family responsibilities. I have already detailed the extent of such employment in the previous chapter, and discussed it as an important component in women's varied experience of employment. In the present context, I consider these two types of paid work as strategies for employment, and look at the ways in which women find it practical and convenient to work for money in these ways.

Regardless of why a woman with children wants a paid job, once she has made this decision, she will need to develop a strategy enabling her to bring her intention to reality. For women with young children (those not yet old enough to be left alone at home), the central issue is inevitably their care. Where those strategies already discussed are not available, or not felt to be appropriate or complete solutions to the difficulty, women often choose to take employment on a part-time basis. When such employment is combined with the care of school-age children, it frequently removes the need to involved others in their care, except perhaps in cases of illness or at holiday times. A high proportion of the women interviewed had found part-time employment the only arrangement which they could manage while they had young children at school. This was especially true of women who lacked female relatives who were willing and available to look after their children. In some cases, employers had introduced special conditions of work, as well as special working hours, in order to attract married women.

> Doreen: 'I managed to get a "Mum's shift" in a factory, which was marvellous, because if the children were ill you just rang up and said "I'm not coming in," and it was accepted. I worked 9.15 till 3, so you could get the children to school, get to work, and you could leave in time to go and fetch them.'

Other women chose to combine part-time work with caring for pre-school children, some working at their jobs when their husbands could be at home to look after the children, others leaving their children with relatives or childminders.

> Lucy: 'I started back again when the baby was about two or three months old. My husband was then at home during the day because he works evenings ... so I took a little job for a couple of hours in the morning while he was there ... it was housework, cleaning.'

For some, the decision to adopt the strategy of part-time employment involved their recognition that the tasks of domestic labour fell overwhelmingly to them. Women who felt themselves solely responsible for the care of their children and the running of their homes, and who did not receive substantial assistance from other family members, sometimes stressed that a part-time job was all they could cope with.

> Brenda: 'The number of hours [is fine] ... I have been doing more lately, because of holidays and everything else, and I do find that gets me down a bit ... that it is a bit too much.'

An examination of the total workload of women who choose a part-time job as a strategy for employment, reveals that this is no easy option. The hours of domestic labour when added to the hours of paid work constitute a demanding full-time set of responsibilities. Linda's case was typical. When interviewed she was married and lived with her husband and there sons, aged 18, 16, and 14. She had a part-time job as a sales assistant, working 17 hours per week basic (mornings only), which in practice often rose to 24 hours per week (including some afternoons). She outlined a typical day's duties.

Linda's Day

6.30 a.m. get up
- cook breakfast for the family
- prepare sandwiches for husband and three sons
- make the beds
- dust, put the sweeper through
- tidy bathroom
- check sons are ready to leave for school/college

8.15 a.m. leave house, driven into town by husband

8.30 a.m. arrive in town, do any shopping required, as have time to kill before work

- 9.30 a.m. being work
  1.30 p.m. lunch (at work)
  2.30 p.m. arrive home

'I usually do some washing if I'm at home in the afternoon.... and just clean a room or turn out a cupboard... (if I work any afternoons).... I don't usually sit down until about half-past nine, because I like to keep things—you know, as far as possible — up to date. I like cooking, you see, and the boys like... cakes, so it's always cooking cakes.... I prepare the meals at night and leave them if I'm working.'

Whilst it was common for women to move from part-time employment into a full-time job, some, under pressure of domestic work, found in necessary to make the opposite transition. Lorna had worked full-time in a factory while her son was at nursery school.

> Lorna: 'I was really concerned about him going to school because I felt that I had to be there when he got home. I mean, 5 is no age to say "Here's a key, get in." I left that job, and went to a firm that would let me have school hours and fit in the time that I wanted .... another horrible job.'

Elizabeth went back to full-time work when her first baby was almost a year old, but after several months there were problems.

> "Elizabeth: `I had to go from full-time to part-time..... there was just too much pressure on me, you know.... I went to the doctor's and he said, "I really think you should do less work." I asked them if I could do part-time work — luckily they said yes.'

In discussing' who does homework,' in the context of her study of homeworkers in West Yorkshire, Allen has pointed to the inadequacies of those '*ad hoc* explainations. [which] are based on characteristics of the homeworkers' family situations.' In particular, she notes some 'homeworkers combined homeworking with outside employment' (Allen 1982: 80-1). Whilst I have used the term here to cover a broader range of home-based activities than did Allen (including childminders and self-employed shop-workers), my findings lend further support to her argument. My sample, too, included women who combined homeworking with part-time employment. June, for example, worked as a part-time caretaker in a community centre in addition to being a full-time childminder. There is indeed no simple link between onerous family responsibilities (several small children, sick or elderly relatives, etc.) and homeworking. Nevertheless, such conditions in the home frequently do apply, and must be seen as *part* of the explanation for the phenomenon. Several women had worked for money at home at times when they were confined to their homes by young children.

> Heather: 'I did typing at home... I'd fit that in probably when the baby was asleep... I then had a student for a little while, I've done that about three times now... and I did childminding — [my daughter] was about 4.... I had a little boy from 8 O'clock till 6 at night.'

To illustrate the complexity of the homeworking phenomenon, however, it is worth quoting the case of Maureen, whose employers themselves changed her conditions of work.

> Maureen: 'I got a job tying in a small office..... 9.30 till 1.30..... After a couple of months there the lease was running out on the premises and they approached three of us that were doing it and asked if we'd be interested in doing it at home. Well, just before I left that job, before the lease ran out, I found out I was having [a baby]—there were two of us pregnant, as it happened—so we didn't let on, we came home, to our respective homes, and carried on with the typing.... I typed all the time I was pregnant, I got a friend to cover me for a month, while I was in hospital and two weeks after.... and then I carried on and typed up until the baby was nearly one. And then.... we both had a letter saying that they were re-organising, and they set up another office in [another town].

Thus Maureen's spell of homeworking coincided with caring for a young baby, but the opportunity arouse for reasons quite unconnected with this fact. Since her period of homeworking was followed by over six months when she did not seek paid work (she waited until she felt her child was old enough to go to a childminder, at 18 months), it seems likely that she would have withdrawn from the paid labour market when she had her baby had this coincidentally (and temporarily) convenient circumstance not arisen.

For most of the women, then, part-time employment or homeworking was, or had once been, a means of organising their lives to enable them to undertake paid work and carry out the tasks of domestic labour. Often it had to be combined with other strategies — enlisting the support of friends or relatives, paying for childcare, or negotiating with husbands about how domestic responsibilities should be shared, for example. It is crucial that this part-time employment and homeworking strategy should be seen as the useful *partial* solution which many of my respondents found it to be , rather than as a panacea for all mothers who either need or wish to be employed.

Long Hours of Work

It was immediately evident from the details given in the interviews that some respondents had been unable to resolve the problem of having two main areas of responsibility, home and family, and job, by seeking part-time work or homework, by the sharing of domestic duties with husbands or children, or by seeking support from either their families or outsiders. Although such strategies enabled some to be 'working mothers' with little difficulty, others, although not necessarily denied access to the strategies, found themselves working very long hours in order to keep everything running smoothly. Because it is women with long weekly hours in paid employment who find domestic responsibilities such a difficult additional burden, I shall confine my discussion here to the forty women who were employed for at least 30 hours per week when interviewed.

Each respondent was asked to describe her daily routine on days when she went to work. By adding together her hours in paid employment and the hours she spent doing domestic duties and caring for children during the rest of the day, it was possible to calculate how many hours the women spent working each day. Including travelling to work time (40 minutes on average) the average was about 11 hours work each day. Almost a third worked 12 hours or more, with one woman working 14 hours—the longest working day.

What kinds of tasks were they performing? Most of the women rose early, some very early. Eighty per cent got up before 7,00 a.m., and almost half before 6.30 a.m. One women frequently rose as early as 4.45 a.m. and eleven between 5.00 and 6.00 a.m. Only three rose after 7.30 a.m. tasks done in the morning before leaving for 'work' typically included getting the family's breakfast, making beds, preparing sandwiches and flasks for husbands and/or children, dressing children, tidying up, washing up, putting washing machines on, or pegging wishing out, and dusting. A small minority chose to leave home in the mornings without performing any such tasks, but in all of these cases their children were teenagers or older. Several women appeared to have almost a day's work to do before they left home in the morning.

> Ruth: 'I usually get up about 6.15, followed by the children if they hear me about. I will tidy through... I would get their breakfast, may husband's, tidy through the kitchen, take his breakfast up, fill his flask—which is about as far as I go as regards getting his dinner ready, then by the time that I have either washed or bathed the children.... I dress the 4-years-old, I then dress myself. I then take my husband to work (takes 15 minutes) ... just generally finish picking up what the children have had, make sure they've cleaned their teeth, brush their hairs. We leave the house about 8.15. I take Jane to the childminder's.'
>
> Carol: 'I get up, I get the breakfast, my breakfast and his breakfast, I wash up—oh, and I do his sandwiches and his flask — I clear away, wish up. Then I clear the fireplaces out, I hoover the lounge, the hall and the stairs.... If I have a very early start, like quarter to five, I will do either washing or ironing. Then I always call the girls at quarter past seven. I get their breakfast, then I'm up there making their beds, and I make our beds as well. Then I come down, I wash up. Then I go and get dressed ... I take the girls down to catch their bus on the way to work.'

About half of those who had a full hour's break at midday said that during this period they regularly did chores such as shopping, going to the bank, paying bills, and in a few cases visiting elderly relatives. Several women who lived near their place of employment went home to do chores, such as preparing the evening meal or cleaning up, which had not been done before leaving in the morning.

The working day by no means ended when they left their employment. Even in the minority of cases where women had other family members who cooked an evening meal, there were many chores waiting for them. These might typically include preparing the evening meal, serving it up, washing up, ironing, washing clothes, bathing children, preparing meals for the next day, cleaning, and shopping (usually once a week).

Despite their heavy workload, a few of the women (usually those with older children) found time to go to evening classes, sing in choirs, go dancing or run Girl guide companies or Cub packs. Some women stressed that they would work longer hours on evenings when their husbands were out. Two examples can illustrate how a mother who is employed full-time may spend her evening.

> MAVIS *(employed 47 hours per week):* '[I] leave work quarter to 5.... collect Colin [aged 1] from childminder ... come in, change him, get him ready for bed, and cook my tea ... and then ironing, any tidying up that I haven't done .... I usually stop doing anything at 9 o'clock. .... If I haven't done it, it doesn't get done.'

> Shirley *(employed 40 hours per week):* 'Come in at 6, by which time [my husband's] in and got the tea on the go, Brian [aged 2] is in ... Spend some time with Brian, get him ready for bed..... wash up, generally clear up .... probably put the hoover round, put Brian to bed, sit down (about 8 o'clock).'

Tina explained that she 'always' worked on evenings when her husband was not at home. This reflected a concern (which she shared with some of the other women) to get chores' out of the way' while men were not around. For some this seemed to be part of a sense that it was 'offensive' to men to have women performing domestic tasks around them.

> Carol: 'I did my biggest wash Tuesday night, because he wasn't there, and I got that all dry yesterday.... I got it all finished before he came home ... I try and do it so that I'm not always working when the family are there, I try and work it so that if he is away on that particular day and I have got something to do the next day, I bring it forward, so that—I didn't want him to sort of come home.... and me over the washing machine. And me not having time to listen to him.'

For most of the women, says 'off,' whether at weekends or during the week, were days spent 'catching up' on household chores.

> Tina: 'I usually do all my cleaning on my day off, I find that I can manage to get through the house. It's a full day's work.'

> Gail: 'The weekend is usually spent doing the jobs that you don't have time to do during the week.'

Nor surprisingly, most of the women found that they tended to get tired. However, the majority did not regard this as a problem, and simply accepted it as a fact of life.

> Mavis: 'I do tend to get tired. I keep going till I finish, I sort of go to bed and flake out and that's it till the morning.'

> Carol: 'I do get tired, but I know that I mustn't stop until I've finished, because if I sit down as soon as I've cooked the meal, I have to really wrench myself to get back up again.'

Along with several others, Nancy responded to my questions about tiredness by indicating that this was a matter which caused her some anxiety. Interestingly, she was not at all sure whether she was right to worry about it or not.

> Nancy: 'Well, funny you should say that ... up till now, *no*, but the last six months, when I've had my periods, I seem to be tried all the time — and I feel old, you know? It's never hit me before — I suppose it's me age, it must be — but to be quite honest with you, I've thought about going up the doctor's with it.... and then I've thought, well, perhaps I'm burning the candle at both ends, and don't know. Are you expected to be tired at my age — you know? .... I put it down to the fact that ... you can't go home like your husband does and sit down and have a meal put in front of you, that's what I think ... and that's why I haven't been nowhere. ... The last six months, I am beginning to think. ... I feel like a zombie sometimes, and you think, "What's it all about?"—You don't seem to have time for the little things what matter.' (*Nancy is aged 38*).

One or two women seemed to be anxious about any tiredness only because they felt the need to conceal it from their husbands. This concern served to illustrate the fact that they could not expect additional help with domestic chores from their husbands, even if they revealed to them that they were overworked.

> Ruth: 'I get the days when I know that I've worked hard. My husband might turn round an say I'm beginning to look tried — but then, once again, I've got to be a bit careful, because if I did start to look tired every night, then it would just be a case of "You pack up work," and that would be it.'

Thus many women adopted the strategy of themselves performing long daily hours of labour. This strategy was often combined with others, but in some cases it was overwhelmingly the most important one. Carol had a full-time job as a sales assistant, and was training to become a supervisor (a position which she has subsequently obtained). She receives little help from her husband and daughters, and has no other relatives who could provide her with regular support. She can afford few modern appliances in her home, and is unwilling to change her standards of household care. What option has she left but to perform herself the often onerous tasks of domestic labour, in the early mornings, in the evenings, and at weekends? Her own labour is the only factor over which she feels she can (legitimately) exercise control. Her case is more extreme than most others, but illustrates well the situation of many mothers who have full-time paid jobs.

Labour-saving Domestic Appliances and Standards of Household Care

In the course of the interviews, details were collected about respondents' access to 'labour-saving domestic appliances,' which (allegedly) lighten the burden of domestic duties. *Table 18* shows the women's access to such domestic appliances and compares this with the ownership of these goods in the general population, as shown by the General Household Survey.

Whilst washing machines, vacuum cleaners, and refrigerators were seen by most women as basic essentials which were required in every home, some of he less commonly held items were seen as aids to working mothers which they wanted but were only able to afford because they were in paid employment.

> Margaret: 'I wouldn't have had them if I wasn't working — well, I would have had a washing machine, but I doubt very much whether we'd have had a dishwasher, because I wouldn't really have needed one, and we wouldn't have been able to afford one. I've had a dishwasher since I've been working full-time.'

This tendency amongst the respondents to purchase additioanl household items using their own wages may partly explain the discrepancy between my figures, and those produced from the General Household Survey.

TABLE 48.1

Ownership of Selected Domestic Appliances

appliance	*my respondents* %	*general household survey (1981)* %
vacuum cleaner	98	94
refrigerator	100	93
deep freezer	76	49
washing machine	96	78
tumble drier	35	23
dishwasher	11	4

(Source of GHS figures: OPCS Monitor Ref. GHS/81/1 1st June 1982).

A minority of the respondents disclosed that although they had certain of the appliances in their homes, they rarely used them. This was particularly true a automatic ovens (a number of women said they did not know how to work them, or did not trust their reliability), but was also sometimes a result of financial pressure.

> Susan: 'Frankly I've cut down on using my [automatic] washing machine in the last couple of years because of the electricity. I find electricity bills and gas bills a bit crucifying. I tend to soak a lot of my washing in Ariel in the bath, now, and in the summer I do hand washing — it's an economy I have made.'

Some of the women who lacked items which others regarded as basic essentials had found themselves in this position as a result of arrangements which had accompanied the breakdown of their marriages.

> Cathy: 'He wouldn't let me have [the washing machine] ... I had a tumble-drier and I had an automatic washing machine. And I had a fridge-freezer.... I know this is probably going to sound a bit far-fetched, but I know this is what happened. He

promised the two eldest ones everything ... so that they would stay with him... and he said that he wouldn't fight of the youngest one, if I agreed to be re-housed.... and I couldn't bear the thought of not having my little one.... so I just went along with everything he wanted .... and that was that, you know.'

Thus most, but not all, of the women interviewed were able to make use of modern domestic appliances. Many believed that possessing such items reduced their workload in the home. But there were some who, for one reason or another, had no access to even those items regarded as basic, and the domestic workload of these women, especially with regard to washing and cleaning, must have been heavy indeed.

Of course one strategy theoretically available to women who need to find a way of coping with the duties of a paid job and the tasks of domestic labour is the straightforward reduction of the latter, this might best be described as the strategy of lowering standards of household care. This has a certain 'common-sense' appeal, and is one which has been advocated by popular writers on 'coping with a double life' (e.g. Conran 1977). Its crucial weakness is that it neglects the ideological basis of ideas about acceptable standards of household care, and the function which these perform in a capitalist society whose members ('consumers') must constantly be reminded of the need to improve material conditions of life. Very frequently this 'improvement' involves additional work for those members of society (in his case women) who are assigned such tasks. Despite his pressure, which militates against any significant reduction in domestic labour, several of the women acknowledged that, since taking paid employment, they had adopted different standards of household care.

Heather: 'I think most women can cope with doing what housework they have to do, they perhaps have to let their standards drop a little, or not do things as often as they used to do them when they were at home all the time — it's picking out the priorities..... like , my oven doesn't get cleaned as often, or the windows don't get cleaned as often — we can all live quite happily in that situation.'

Lorna: [if I was at home] it would be much cleaner—and I wouldn't feel so guilty.'

Others, however, were quick to point out that having full-time employment did not mean that they took 'short-cuts' or neglected what they saw as 'their' responsibilities. Shirley's comments endorse my earlier remarks about the ideological basis of attitudes to domestic labour.

Shirley: 'I'm not one of those working mums who dives in from work and chucks everything in the [washing] machine and hopes to Christ it's all right—the only thing I put in there is nappies, sheets, towels — and everything else I wash by hand.

One women emphasised the fact that there were always household tasks to be done, and that because of this, women would 'make time' (that is, would deny themselves the alternative activities in which they could engage) to do them.

Brenda: 'I think when you're out to work, you've only got a limited amount of time to do everything, so you're going to get through it anyway—no matter what labour-saving devices you've got, you've still got to get through it.'

The ambiguous nature of the women's attitudes to housework is consistent with the findings of other researchers (e.g. Gavron 1968; Oakley 1974b). Many women stressed that they did not enjoy doing household chores, and did no more than was strictly 'necessary,' but at the same time they were mostly anxious to stress that their homes ran smoothly, and were not places where the comfort and convenience of husbands and children were put at risk. This ambiguity can only be understood when the social relations of household work are examined as part of the contradictory structures of a society which is both patriarchal and capitalistic.

SOME THEORETICAL IMPLICATIONS

In considering the theoretical implications of my analysis, I want to make some observations about the ambiguous nature of the contemporary family household. It seems clear that negotiations about the sexual division of labour, both within the household and in terms of income-generating activities, are not currently resolved without conflict between the sexes. These negotiations refer principally to the role of female labour—should it be exchanged for wages or not?—and its implications for the role of male labour in the household. In such negotiations women typically start from a position of relative powerlessness, men from a position of relative powerfulness. This is entirely to be expected in patriarchal families where marriage involves the state-sanctioned economic dependence of women on men.

I wish to argue, however, that a pure model of patriarchy is inadequate to explain the nature of intra-familial negotiations concerning how female labour is exercised. In particular, it fails to explain variation between different family households, and variation within the same households over time. I want to suggest that ambiguity over the issue of female labour can be partially understood by the incorporation of a model of the 'maximisation of household economic interests' into the model of patriarchy. My contention is that within family households negotiations about female labour may be resolved either on the basis of tradition (patriarchy) or on the basis of rationality (maximisation of economic interests), or both. Where one or the other is clearly dominant, negotiations will tend to consensus; where both models have equal or similar importance for household members in explaining their social world, negotiations will tend to conflict. The reaching of consensus, of course, does not necessarily imply that the spouses share an objectively equal situation. My point is illustrated in Figure 48.1.

The following examples may demonstrate my argument. Heather works as a full-time supervisor in a large retail store. Her husband is a quantity surveyor. They have two children aged 13 and 10. Conflict within the household about Heather's full-time employment is apparently minimal:

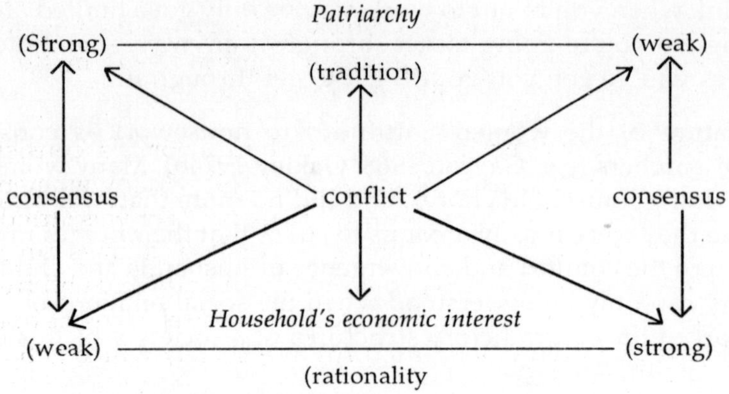

Figure 48.1 Model of negotiations about female labour within family households

> Heather: 'He was very pleased for me to come here. When I came here actually he was redundant, so that was my initial step in coming here. He was there to look after the children. I liked it so much that I wanted to come back, and my mother-in-law offered to help.... There has been the odd occasion when he's sort of laughed and said "Ooh, you know, I wish you were here to make me a cup of coffee when I pop in," but he knows how disinterested with life I was without a job, and .... of course, we've got another full income coming in, which, I mean, helps us to enjoy a lot more in life.'

Here, I would suggest, the couple operate with a weak model of patriarchy and a strong model of the maximisation of the household's economic interests. The family enjoys a relatively high standard of living, and the couple have a relatively egalitarian relationship.

By contrast, Christine, who works 28 hours per week as a clerical assistant, spoke of her husband's ambiguous attitude to her employment.

> Christine: 'I don't think he likes me working — but I think he likes the money it brings in — that's about the top and bottom of it.... He doesn't like the fact that you don't spend quite so much time doing the housework and, you know, making everything look fantastic. And although he says half-heartedly he'll help out with the children when they're on holiday and things like that, it always materialises in some way that he can't for some reason.... and I think just basically he doesn't really like it.'

Here the situation is clearly one where conflict predominates. This is a household where both patriarchal values (Christine's husband would like a subservient wife performing domestic labour at home) and rational economic values (he appreciates the extra income his wife brings in) co-exist, although neither is overwhelmingly powerful. The result, I would argue, is semi-perm. ıent conflict, and indeed, Christine made numerous references to the instability of her marriage.

My respondents do not include non-employed mothers, and because of this I use a hypothetical example of a family household operating with a strong model of patriarchy and a weak model of economic rationality. Such a family would include a father employed full-time and a non-employed mother who worked only on an unpaid basis in the home, even after her children were at school. This arrangement is unlikely to be in the household's economic interests, but would conform to a husband-dominant, wife-subordinate model consistent with patriarchy. I would contend that many such family households, apparently content with their lower standard of living and their 'traditional' arrangements, exist without extensive conflict.

It is important to bear in mind that the relative strength of the two models is likely to change over time within a single family household. Thus the household's interest in maximising income may be paramount prior to the birth of children, and during this phase the young couple are likely to be in agreement about the importance of both spouses engaging in paid work. With the presence of young children this factor may decline, and there may be resurgence of the patriarchal model in which women care for their children at home on a full-time basis. As children grow older and start school the position will again be subject to change. As already suggested, the conflict between couples which frequently precedes the wife taking paid employment is often reduced as the husband becomes aware of the advantages to the household (and perhaps principally to himself) of a second income. Patriarchy then recedes in the face of economic rationality. Of course many households are characterised by almost perpetual conflict over the sexual division of labour. Here there may either be a failure to reach one or other of the 'consensus' models I have suggested, or, most importantly, external factors (such as long-term unemployment or low male wages) may intervene, forcing the members of the family household to adapt in ways which they might otherwise find unacceptable (so for instance a wife might seek work only because the family cannot manage on the husband's low wages).

It seems possible that the conflict within the family household which is generated by the ideologies of patriarchy and capitalism may sometimes be sufficiently intense to provoke the breakdown of the marital relationship. This would certainly be one possible means of resolving the conflict. Whilst the precise elaboration of the process of conflict resolution in the household is beyond the scope of the present study (which did not collect systematic data about marital breakdown), it would appear to be a topic on which future research might usefully focus.

In the present context of changing labour market conditions, involving not only rising rates of unemployment but also changes in the structure of the labour market, it is as yet unclear whether the problems confronting capitalist societies will be attacked by a rejection of patriarchal ideology (a tactic used in the two world wars when women were called upon by the state to labour in industry, and nursery facilities were made available as an alternative to domestic childcare), or by a reinforcement of it (again, a tactic which has been used in the past to contend with unemployment). Historically, the ideologies of capitalism and patriarchy can be shown to have been both mutually competitive and mutually supportive. Clearly, the precise nature of the relation between the power of capital and the power of patriarchy requires further detailed elaboration: this, too, must be an urgent task for feminist analysis.

I will now consider briefly those strategies which involve accommodations between persons other than the two spouses, and used by single parents. It might be suggested that the various strategies available to women fall into two categories: a *private* category, including all those strategies which involve negotiations between individuals and within families, and a *public* category, where outside institutions such as the state and employers are involved. State and commercial childcare, and part-time employment, would then be seen as in the public category. It might indeed be argued that policy-makers and the state should concentrate exclusively on the latter, leaving personal and private arrangements to the individuals concerned. Many of my respondents said such things to me themselves.

However, I would like to suggest that to see the issue in this way is to pose a substantially false dichotomy. Although the 'private' strategies are indeed private in the sense that they are developed and put into effect within individual families and individual households, they are only so in this limited sense. It can equally be argued that they are not genuinely private because in every family where a mother wants or needs to take employment recourse must be made to such strategies.

This raises the issue of how far these 'private' strategies can or should be incorporated into public policy. As Novarra (1980) and others have demonstrated, the word of paid employment in advanced industrial societies remains oriented towards the male employee, for whom employment, rightly or wrongly, is taken to be a (if not the) central life interest. Although a few concessions have been made to women (part-time work and flexi-time are examples) it is still substantially true that if women wish to participate in the labour market, they must adapt to, and fit in with, the current requirements of most paid work, its routinisation and standard organisation of working time—requirements which are designed primarily to serve the interests of capital. In the general run of things, a woman who is a mother will have to make greater personal adjustments to fit in with these requirements than will most men, or indeed most childless women.

In 1984 women are faced not only with coping with the inconvenient way in which paid work is organised (and so relying, as I have indicated above, on a wide variety of alternative sources of primarily female labour to care for children) but also with seriously insufficient employment opportunities. In such a climate it is not realistic to expect campaigns for 24-hour state childcare, however broadly-based or well-conducted, to bear fruit. Many families are currently being forced into poverty, with all this means for women, because of the way labour and its rewards are organised. In any case, access to wage labour has never meant access to emancipation or equality for women, despite Engels' famous phrase—'the first condition for the libe ation of the wife is to bring the whole females sex back into public industry' (Engels 1972: 137-38). I return to these points in the final chapter, which contains my concluding remarks and some observations about the study's implications for social policy.

Coda: Lynne's Story

Lynne is 25 years old, has four children, and has been married since she was 19 to David, a self-employed carpenter and jointer. Her first child, Craig, aged 7, was born two years before her marriage (and is not David's child), and she has subsequently had twins, Darren and Mandy, now aged 4, and more recently another son, Jason, aged 1.

Despite her onerous family responsibilities, Lynne has spent only short periods of the nine years since she left school away from employment. When we met , she was working part-time in the evenings as a hospital domestic, but, as I describe below, she has undertaken a range of different jobs in the past. She has clear plans about her future in employment, and expects to be able to develop a career in nursing.

Lynne was born in Canada, but moved to England with her family soon after leaving school. Her mother is a trained nurse and her father a draughtsman. Because of the family's imminent emigration, Lynne took a part-time job serving take-away means for the few months between leaving school and going abroad. On arrival in England, she found full-time work as a sales assistant in a large chain store. She recalled that 'it was ... quite a nice company to work for,' but stayed in the job for only about seven months, as she became pregnant shortly after her arrival in England. The pregnancy was unplanned, but did not seriously disrupt Lynne's life as her family supported her, enabling her to cope with premature motherhood (she was just 17 years old when Craig was born). Her experience illustrates how, with a supportive family network, an unplanned teenage pregnancy can be accommodated with the minimum of drama. Lynne's recollections of her feelings at the time display none of the sense of panic or disaster which was evident in the accounts of some of the other women in this study who had had similar experiences.

> 'I was quite excited about it, you know—of course you are... but you don't realise what the work entails.'

Lynne continued to live with her parents after the baby was born, and before Craig was a year old she found (with her mother's help) part-time employment as a nursing assistant in a local hospital.

> '[I took the job] to help my parents.... my mother... because she worked at the [hospital] ... she managed to get me a job there, part-time, and it helped of course with the costs of the baby and everything.'

The arrangements necessary to enable Lynne to leave Craig for this but, as her comments reveal, he has only played a limited part in performing duties at home.

> 'He washes up every evening... but ... it would be a bit much to ask him to come home and do a load more ... he's never really been very domesticated.... He would do things if I asked.'

Indeed, it is clear that David has tolerated Lynne's employment only because of the financial pressure on the family.

> 'He didn't like [me having a job] at first .... but he doesn't mind now .... We've got used to it... you know, having to do it... It's not so much in this job, but previous jobs, I should say — this job's not so bad. But, you know, he likes more or less everything to be done as he gets home ... but I have to do the baby, get him ready for bed, and that... it was previous jobs more than this, that he didn't really like.

The couple's instrumental approach to employment (about which, of course, they have little choice, with a family of four children to provide for) means that they spend very little time together. David, who is self-employed, works 'every day — he's very busy,' and this includes weekends. In the evenings, he arrives home from work just half an hour before Lynne has to leave for hers. As Lynne said, 'I usually manage to sit and eat my dinner with him.... then by the time we've finished.... it's time for me to come out to work.' She gets home from her job a little before 9.00 p.m., and will be up again next morning just after 7.00 a.m. At present her earnings are being saved in a building society, with the specific objective of buying the council house in which they now live. They live from week to week on David's earnings, and on the support which they get from the state in the form of Child Benefit. The couple have domestic appliances such as an automatic washing machine, refrigerator, and vacuum cleaner in their home, but live an essentially frugal life, as they spend next to nothing on entertainment, do not have family holidays, and do not run a car.

At present, both Lynne and David are reasonably happy with their arrangements, both at home, and for employment. They are maximising their household income (the cost of childcare for three pre-school children would be prohibitive), and at the same time organising domestic work in a traditional (patriarchal) way, such that Lynne takes prime responsibility for the children, and does all the housework, washing and cooking. Further, they currently have a common objective in view (buying their home), which helps to promote consensus between a couple who are able to spend very little time together. It seems possible, however, that the future may hold conflict for the couple, as well as a continuation of their very hard-working lifestyle. Tentatively, I want to suggest that Lynne's clear ambition to undertake nursing training — 'I will change my job.... [when] I feel I can do my training — indicates that she intends to seek satisfactions other than instrumental ones from employment. She wishes to develop a career for herself beyond the domestic sphere; to do this she may require David's more active support at home. His present unwillingness to undertake domestic tasks (if unchanged) would represent a serious obstacle to Lynne's plans; and her career aims may pose a threat to his view of their marital relationship. Lynne's is a case where much depends on the respective power of two competing ideological frameworks. It may be possible for the couple to avoid conflict if a rational and economic model is adopted, at the expense of a traditional and patriarchal one. But, if attempts are made to sustain both, then continuing consensus between Lynne and David appears unlikely. The conflict, if it were to emerge, would then be over the issue of Lynne's labour, and how it should appropriately be performed.

49

Women's Involvement in Food Processing and Related Activities

Food processing industry is a very significant manufacturing sector in the country. It ranks 5th in its contribution to value addition and tops the list in terms of employment, (constituting 16.7% of the country's industrial labour numbering 1.2 million persons). 19% of the total manufacturing units in India are in the food processing sector. The conuntration of women's employment in the manufacturing industry is in food processing.

Food processing industry in India comprises three groups viz. Primary Food Processing Industry, Unorganised and Cottage Sector Industry and Processed Food Industry.

(i) *Primary Food Processing Industry Comprises—*

Rice Hullers	—	79,000
Flour Chakkis (Grinders)	—	2,66,000
Dal Mills	—	10,000
Oil Mills	—	2,20,000

(ii) *Unorganised and Cottage Sector Industries—*

Bakeries	—	55,000
Pasta goods Units	—	5,000
Traditional food units	—	15,000
Poha making units	—	2,000
Fruits, vegetables and species processing units	—	5,000

(iii) *Processed food Industries-*

Manufacturing units	—	18,000

The trend of growth in the primary processing sector shows a large increase in hullers, roller flour mills, oil expellers, solvent extradition units. Exports have been largely in the marine products sector, spice products, meat and poultry products.

The trend in the secondary and tertiary sectors of food processing have shown significant growth of fruit and vegetable processing, comprising jams, juice, pulp, beverages and tomato products. While exports of fruits and vegetable products have stabilised, the domestic sale has nearly doubled between 1982-85. This suggests a vast scope for further expansion.

Bakery products have increased very significantly in a decade registering a rather sharp increase from five lakh tonnes to 10 lakh tonnes. Other areas of noticeable growth are the sugar confectionery industry, moulded chocolates, soft drinks, malted milk food etc.

The technology in food production in India has been developed with intensive R and D work in the Central Food Technological Research Institute (CFTRI). With a growing population and a large agricultural base the potential for expanding the food processing industry seems to be immense. Government of India has established a separate Department for Food Processing in recent years to concentrate on the food processing industry in the country.

The small scale food processing units in the country use technologies which are largely outdated. A great deal of modernisation is necessary for improving and increasing production.

In the food processing sector, technology development has been quite slow. There is need for dissemination of information on modern technologies and techniques available in the National laboratories as well as other R and D organisations.

Poor quality of agricultural production (fruit and vegetables), packaging, marketing and high incidence of taxation are other major constraints of the industry.

Food processing in the informal sector is performed by women, largely as self-employed persons using their traditional skills. The National Commission on Self-employed Women and Women in the Informal Sector (June, 1988) have given the profiles of masala grinders, chilli grinders, spice processors, papad rollers, vegetable and food vendors etc. These profiles present a very gloomy picture of poverty and struggle for survival.

The intensity of women's activities in the market is closely related to example, in many parts of North India women are not involved in selling food, vegetables or fruits as they do not go out of their homes. In South India, on the other hand, women are largely engaged in these activities.

Most of women's enterprise in the informal sector, particularly in the food cycle, is an activity for a market within a small radius. They are confined within the village boundary where the market is very limited. Those on the periphery of urban areas reach the markets only on a retail scale. Often they become a small link, either at the supplying or selling end, for the longer chain of middlemen who control the various transactions in the trade (particularly in the case of vegetables and fruits).

The cultivation of greens has been taken over by women around large cities (e.g. as in the case of Tamilnadu). The land is taken on lease and greens are cultivated, and taken to the markets and sold by the women. Though, on a very small scale, women seem to be doing very well. They are very competitive in the market.

One of the major self-employed activities is food vending, as cooking is a natural skill with which women are endowed. Besides, it is a low capital intensive venture with quick turnover. In many market areas they prepare food for a limited clientele and specialise on snacks, breakfast, tea, lunch etc. When the scale of business enlarges, if often shifts to men.

The need for technology inputs from the household to the industrial level is beyond doubt. There do not seem to be any dearth of technology. The more closely one looks at the array of technologies the more aware one becomes of the intensive work going on in the Technical Institutions, Universities, Voluntary Organisations and by dedicated individuals. Almost every cereal, pulse, vegetable, fruit, seed leaf has been studied and analysed.

It would be most important to document all the technology that has been stabilised for different category of users.

Simple cost effective technologies for dehydration and preservation of chilli, ginger, okra, bittergourd, fish, green papaya, green mango, cabbage, seasonal fruits and vegetables are available. These are mostly traditional practices in different regions upgraded by scientific inputs that may ensure better quality or compress time. The UPASI had successfully taken up mushroom growing in their centre and were interested in initiating the poor women in mushroom growing activity with all the infrastructure support for providing the raw material as well as marketing.

The CFTRI were willing to share their technology on mini dal mils which women could operate for processing pulses. On further discussion with the Director of Marketing, Maharashtra, he felt it would be most feasible to market processed, packed pulses in the 'Apna Bazars' (Super Markets) if the women could be organised to take up this work on a decentralised basis and the Directorate of Marketing and Inspection of the Government of India would agree to bring it under 'Agmark' labelling.

Another very feasible proposition that has emerged is the preparation of weaning foods, using malted cereals etc. Already a networking of women's groups producing grounds spices, weaning foods with centres under the Integrated Child Development Scheme (ICDS) and noon-meal scheme has been done in Tamil Nadu with great benefit to the women's groups and the feeding centres. Similar networking can be done throughout the country where ICDS programme or noon meal programmes are implemented. A definite policy to bring in decentralised region specific production would be necessary. The Home Science Colleges the agricultural Unviersities, other non-Government organisations would have to be used as catalysts to accelerate this activity through proper technology transfer, training and re-training and quality control. Employment generation programmes of the various Government and associated agencies would be linked to this activity, so that employment becomes sustained and markets become secure.

Food processing would continue to be an important sector for employment of women even at higher technology levels if women are accessed to the technologies.

50

Women in Tertiary Sector and Entrepreneurship

Women in Tertiary Sector

In 1991 there were 6.96 million female main workers in the services sector (Trade and Commerce, Transport, storage and communications and other services) in the country (excluding Jammu and Kashmir). Of these 2.63 millions were rural females and 4.33 million urban females.

Within the services sector, industry-wise, females were pre-dominantly engaged in category "Other services" both in rural and urban areas. In this industry division 5.32 millions were engaged, 1.97 million in rural areas and 3.34 in urban areas. Female main workers in the services sector in 1991 census are shown in Table 50.1.

TABLE 50.1

Female Main Workers in Services Sector—India 1991*

	*Female Main Wokers**		
	Total	*Rural*	*Urban*
Trade and Commerce	1,433,612	606,955	826,657
Transport, Storage and communications	207,620	45,151	161,469
Other Services	5,316,428	1,974,851	3,341,577
Total services sector (tertiary)	6,957,660	2,627,957	4,329,703
All Sectors	64,273,909	55,995,971	8,277,938

Source: Census of India 1991, Series-I, India, Paper-2 of 1992, Final 'Population Total Brief Analysis of Primary Census abstract.

*Excluding Jammu and Kashmir.

The female main wokers in the service sector in the country (excluding Assam and Jammu and Kashmir) increased from 4.19 millions in 1981 to 6.82 millions in 1991 registering an increase of 63%. In the Other Services Division alone the increase from 1981 was 2 millions, i.e. 67%. Female main workers in the services sector and their proportion to the total in all sectors for 1981 and 1991 are shown in Table 50.2.

TABLE 50.2

Female Main Workers in Services (Tertiary) Sector — 1981 and 1991

	Female Main Workers (thousands)*		
	1981	*1991*	*% Increase*
Trade and Commerce	916 (2.0%)	1420 (2.3%)	55.0
Transport, storage and communications.	164 (0.4%)	204 (0.3%)	24.0
Other services	3,110 (6.9%)	5,196 (8.3%)	67.1
Total Services Sector	4.190 (9.3%)	6,820 (10.8%)	62.7
All Sectors	44,806	62,922	

Source: Census of India 1991, Series-I, India, Paper-2 of 1992, Final Population Totals: Brief Analysis of Primary Census abstract.

* Excluding Jammu and Kashmir and Assam.

Female main workers in the services sector constituted 10.8% of all female main workers in 1991 as compared to 9.3% in 1981. The share of "Other Services" Division alone increased to 8.3% in 1991 from 6.94% in 1981. However, share of 10.8% of the services sector for female main workers was much lower than its share of 23.3% for male main workers. The share of Trade and Commerce Division was particularly much lower (2.3% for female against 9% for males).

In the organised sector women employment in the services sector was 2.65 millions in 1993 (end of March constituting 66% of women employment in all sectors. In this sector women's share of employment was 16%. Community, personal and social services division claimed most of the employment viz. 2.27 millions. Female employment in the organised services sector registered an increase of 2.2% in 1993 over 1992 (2.59 millions).

In the organised services sector women employment was pre-dominantly in the public Sector, 2.14 millions and only 0.51 millions in the private sector in 1993. The increase in public sector employment over 1992 was 1.9%, whereas in private sector it was 3.7%. Women employment in the organised services sector can be seen in Table 50.3

TABLE 50.3

Women Employment in the Organised Sector

(In thousands)

Industry Division/ Sector	*1992 (31st March)* Public Sector	Private Sector	Total Sector	*1993 (31st March)* Public Sector	Private	Total
Wholesale, retail business and hotels and restaurants	14.0	21.8	35.8 (0.9%)	11.6	23.5	35.1 (0.8%)
Transport, storage and Communications	145.0	3.6	148.5 (3.8%)	145.9	3.9	149.8 (4%)
Finance Insurance, real estate and business services	152.3	29.1	181.4 (4.6%)	159.2	32.3	191.5 (5%)
Community, personal and social services	1785.2	439.6	2224.8 (56.9%)	1819.8	452.5	2272.3 (56%)
Services Sector	2096.5	494.1	2590.5 (66.3%)	2136.5	512.2	2648.7 (65.8%)
All sectors	2428.7	1479.3	3908.0	2476.7	1549.7	4026.4

Women Employment by Branch of Public Sector

Of the 2.19 million women employment in public sector in 1989, 1.00 million constituting 45.6 per cent (nearly half) were employed in State Government. Women employment in central government was 0.20 million (9.3%). Quasi Central Government and Quasi State Government employment of women was 0.28 and 0.16 million, forming 12.7 per cent and 7.6 per cent respectively. Local bodies claimed 0.54 million, a quarter of the public sector employment of women. Women employment in different branches of public sector are shown in Table 50.4 for 1987, 1988, and 1989.

Between 1987 and 1989, women employment under Central and State Governments grew on an average by 4.3 and 5.5 per cent per year, respectively. Women employment in Quasi State Government Organisations grew faster by 6.8 per cent per year in this period. Growth of women employment in Quasi-Central Government Organisations was low at 2.2 per cent per year and in local bodies it was 1.9 per cent.

Women in Central Government Services

Due to inadequate data on women in Services, discussion on the subject is limited only to women in Central Government. Women's employment under Central Government and their share in the total Central Government has been rising gradually from 1961 onwards. In 1990 there were 2.83 lakh women employees under Central Government forming 7.51% as shown in Table 50.5

TABLE 50.4

Women Employment in Different Branches of Public Sector, 1987, 1988 and 1989

Branches of Public Sector	Women employment *('000) (as on 31st March)* 1987	1988	1989	*Average Annual % Increase during 1987-89*
Central Government	186.5	198.5	202.8 (9.3)	4.3
State Government	898.9	953.0	999.5 (45.6)	5.5
Central Government (Quasi)	267.0	273.5	278.9 (12.7)	2.2
State Government (Quasi)	145.1	151.4	165.4 (7.6)	6.8
Local Bodies	522.6	525.9	542.6 (24.8)	1.9
Total Public Sector	2020.1	2102.3	2189.2 (100.0)	4.1

Source: Employment Review, 1987-88 and 1988-89, Directorate General of Employment and Training, Ministry of Labour.

Note: Figures in parentheres indicate percentages to total.

TABLE 50.5

Women in Central Government

(Figures in Lakhs)

Year	*No of regular employees in Central Government*			
	Total	*Men*	*Women*	*%age of women to total*
1971	26.99	26.32	0.67	2.50
1981	35.07	32.83	1.24	3.64
1990	37.74	34.91	2.83	7.50

Note: Census for 1979 and 1985 to 1987 have been skipped.

Source: Census of Central Government Employees 1971 to 1990, DGE&T.

Distribution of Women in Various Ministries

Women employment with this population to total employment in the Central Government and in major employing Ministries / Department for 1989 and 1990 are shown in t he table below. It can be seen that women employment in the Communications Ministry and 'other' Ministries is more than 10%.

TABLE 50.6

Distribution of Women Employees Under Various Ministries—1989 and 1990

S. No.	*Ministry*	*Women Employment*			
		1989		*1990*	
		Number	*%age share*	*Number*	*%age share*
1.	Communications	69136	10.62	77768	11.93
2.	Railways	53192	3.29	61788	3.78
3.	Defence (Civilian)	33002	6.09	36412	8.71
4.	'Other' Ministries	91828	9.89	107412	11.56
	Total	247158	6.60	283380	7.51

Source: Census of Central Government Employees (as on 31st March, 1990), Directorate General of Employment and Training, Ministry of Labour.

TABLE 50.7

Representation of Women in Selected Services (1985-87)

Year	*Total*	*Men*	*Women*	*%age of women to total*
1985	16055	15180	875	5.4
1986	16667	15736	931	5.6
1987	16987	15993	994	5.8

Source: Women in India—A Statistical Profile, 1988, Department of Women and Child Development, New Delhi.

Employment of Women in Central Government, as could be seen in Table 50.5, has been increasing steadily from year to year. The progress of 3.64 in 1981 to 7.50 per cent in 1990 is a definite reflection of change in the attitudes of women to come forward to take part in various fields of development. Among the total central government employees, only 3.3 per cent constitute the gazetted officers while rest are non-gazetted ones. This indicates women gazetted employees are still a minority. But still the growing attendance of women in government jobs is commendable.

Participation of women in the administration of the Government, although limited at present, is slowly increasing as women and public have become conscious of their rights and abilities. At the senior management level in the Government of India, representation of women has increased although marginally from 931 (5.6%) in 1986 to 994 (5.8%) in 1987.

Women in Decision Making in Government

For the purpose of reviewing the position with regard to women in decision making in the Government, we may consider the number of women in the three top services of IAS, IPS, IDS as these categories generally occupy the positions of senior management levels in the administration of the Government. The following data reveal the situation on the subject during 1985 and 1992.

TABLE 50.8

Representation of Women in Selected All India Services During 1985 and 1992

Sl. No.	*Services*	*Number of Personnel in position as on 1st Jan.*					
		1985			*1992*		
		Total	*Males*	*Females*	*Total*	*Males*	*Females*
1.	Indian Administrative Service	4284	3973	311 (7.3%)	4928	4498	430 (8.7%)
2.	Indian Police Service	2343	2325	18 (0.8%)	2825	2773	52 (1.8%)
3.	Indian Foreign Service	535	485	50 (9.3%)	721	658	83 (8.7%)

Source: (i) Women in India—A Statistical Profile, 1988, Department of Women and Child Development, New Delhi.
(ii) IAS Civil List—1994, Department of Personnel, Government of India, New Delhi.
(iii) IPS Civil List—1994, Ministry of Home Affairs, Government of India, New Delhi.

The above data on the 3 selected service of top administration indicate that the representation of women has improved during 1985 to 1992 which is quite encouraging. With the increased governmental efforts to recruit more women in the civil services, it is quite possible for more women to come up the serve as key executives and decision makers in the Government. Recognising the dual role and responsibility of women employees, Government of India extends special concession/relaxations to its employees, as listed in the Appendix III.

In assessing the position of women in the Service Sector as a whole it can be concluded that opportunities for employment in public service have been greater than in the private sector, as indicated by the larger numbers in the Public Sector. However, between 1992-93, the number of additional employment in the tertiary sector as a whole has been greater in the private sector than in the public sector.

A point strongly made by researchers on the women's employment situation is that the concentration of women's employment is greater in the lower echelons which tapers sharply as the pyramid rises. It may take many more years for this picture to change and would come about, only with determined efforts both on the part of women job seekers, and organisations employing them. They would have to climb up faster to the higher rungs of the Ladder.

The other sentiments that come from women workers is a feeling of gender discrimination in getting opportunities to handle certain kinds of jobs. Job satisfaction, employer recognition are areas meriting more attention.

Women and Entrepreneurship

A positive approach has been developing in recent years to induct women entrepreneurs into business. As yet the numbers may be a small proportion of the total number of entrepreneurs in all kinds of business, but the trend is a rising one.

The 1991 census has shown a significant increase in the category of 'cultivators' for women, while men have declined in this category. This is a positive sign of women taking over management.

At the level of tiny enterprises under self employment, the plethora of new incentives in the nature of credit under Rural and Urban programmes have encouraged women, to both get into business and also expand their petty business. The organised banking sector has slowly started opening up to women and giving them a package of training for Enterpreneurship as also credit to get into new business. The Integrated Rural Development Programme has provided for 40% of the assistance to be given to women beneficiaries. A large proportion of this assistance goes to diary enterprises which are the best for women with their linkages, and the predominance is understandable. Other handicraft, handloom and artisan sector activities as also marketing are taken up by women. The emerging strength of the self-employed in the tiny sector is the range of thrift and credit groups through non-government agencies from funds channeled both from Government and International or bilateral agencies. A large number of agro-based and food processing enterprises are coming up with the access to credit.

The fast growing sector in the economy is the Small Scale Industry Sector. Very special efforts have been made by the financing Institutions to develop women entrepreneurs through promotional measures.

The Industrial Development Bank of India has been conducting Special Enterpreneurship development programmes (EDP) through which Training is given to women, assistance is given for project preparation apart from follow-up and escort services—to solve teething problems. Substantial number of women entreprenuers have benefitted from these programmes and are shaping into successful entrepreneurs.

The National Equity fund set up under the IDBI offers financial assistance to the extent of 15% of the project cost as Equity Support on a service charge of 1%.

The promoter's contribution is expected to be at least 10%, the balance amount would be available as loan. The initial advance of 15% of the cost of the project is expected to be repaid in 10 years after a moratorium of 3 years. In order to facilitate easy access to all resources, a one window Approach has been adopted through the State financial corporations to tie up working capital and investment funds required for the enterprise.

The new race of women entrepreneurs are emerging in substantial numbers and would give a strong support for the growing economy. The limitation of data availability pre-empts any detailed discussion or analysis on this subject.

Epilogue

The empowerment of women is anchored on their economic status in the society. This status emerges with capacity building facilitated by education, skill, knowledge and information. The changing economic environment throws up new economic opportunities as well as new challenges which have to be pragmatically faced. Rapid changes compressed within short time periods demand greater propensity to absorb such changes. Adjustment becomes more difficult.

In order to draw up any meaningful strategy that can create enabling environments and reduce pain and penury would have to be based on sound analysis of the situations. Such analyses would require a great deal of data and specific information on the direction of the changes.

The data clearly showed the emergence of women very significantly as an economic resource. The larger numbers of women entering the labour markets, greater than ever before, during the last decade has given them a greater share of the unemployment while increasing their share in employment. It is most significant to notice that employment of women has trebled just during the last decade from 31.3 million in 1981 to 89.8 million in 1991, while during the same period employment of men increased only by a little over 50 per cent from 149.2 million to 224.4 million.

This substantial increase of women workers over the last decade, captured in the census has also been reflected in the doubling of women's employment in the organised sector and increasing their share from 11 to 14% in that sector, and near trebling in the unorganised sector raising their share from 19.6% to 28.58% between 1981 and 1991. It has also been noticed that the significant increases of women's employment have been in the primary and tertiary sectors.

These varying rates of increases of women's employment in the organised and unorganised sectors have lowered the proportion of women's employment in the organised sector. These trends are indicative of the impacts of the various income generation efforts made by the Government with their various target oriented programmes to generate more employment and specific quotas for women in those programmes—significantly the poverty alleviation programmes. The other significant factor is the larger proportion of educated women coming into services in the public and private sectors.

The concern now for the future is that the entry of women into the labour markets is going to be in even greater magnitude than before, owing to their improving education status, greater awareness, and increasing economic necessities.

On the demand side for labour, the agriculture sector, which is the major employer in the country has reached a saturation point. It is already inelastic to increasing production and, therefore, the scope for massive job increases is very limited. The sector on the other hand needs a new quality of labour with more technological inputs to increase productivity. Women and men remaining in the sector would need intensive measures for improving their skills to increase productivity in agriculture.

The new area that holds the greatest job potential are the post-harvest and agro-processing sectors to which substantial proportions of job seekers would have to shift. The infrastructure of training and skill development would have to concentrate on this to quickly equip the new entrants, as also help others to make appropriate job shifts.

The emerging areas of off-farm activities need a great deal of attention both for greater value addition and new employment. This is not to ignore new areas of horticulture and floriculture that would keep reasonable number of jobs on the farms. The shift from cereal crop cultivation to other category of crops is apparent.

The major concern in the country today is the impact of the structural reforms on existing employment and a fear as to whether it would render unskilled women workers superfluous and also reduce opportunities for others—or push them into more informal sector employment. The quality of employment is a real concern, particularly with decorporatisation. This has been experienced even in the traditional industries like cashew, coir etc. in the past.

Considering that employment in the organised sector has only hovered around 10-11% and the social security measures were not available to the workers in the informal sector, processes started for introducing better working conditions for the persons in the informal sector needs to be accelerated. Health and life insurance facilities need to be intensified to cover the large numbers in the unorganised sectors; better enforcement of minimum wages, provision of support services like child care, and other infrastructure facilities need special attention. Innovative measures for reaching these services to workers and particularly women workers, has to be devised by the community.

From the point of view of a rapid economic growth, harnessing the human resource with appropriate human capital investment assumes priority over all others. Both formal and non-formal training, specially relevant to the market has to be organised to give the right direction to the labour. Vocational guidance has to be systematically planned and organised.

Not only Government, but industry would have to take the lead to create the right kind of manpower, that the productive processes at different levels of technology demand.

The directions that have emerged in recent years to create an enabling environment have been discussed in the foregoing chapters of this book. May be the directions have been set, the pace has to be quickened to reach the new heights, and the vision cleared for greater focus.

Appendices

APPENDIX-I

Gender Sensitization of 1991 Census-Publicity Poster

APPENDIX-II

LIST OF MAJOR PROCESSES/PRODUCTS

(With Effect from 01.04.1990)

Central Food Technological Research Institute, Mysore-570013

Process Code		*Process/Product*	*Released By*
Animal Product			
AAP	003	Chicken: Dressing line and products	NRDC
AAP	006	Chitosan	NRDC
AAP	009	Corned beef	CFTRI
AAP	012	Egg albumen flakes	NRDC
AAP	015	Egg powder	CFTRI
AAP	018	Fish meal and oil	NRDC
AAP	021	Fish products: Thermal processed	NRDC
AAP	024	Meat gravy: Concentrate	CFTRI
AAP	027	Shark fin rays	CFTRI
AAP	030	Shrimp: canning of	NRDC
AAP	033	Shrimp: Freeze drying of	CFTRI
Beverage Products			
ABP	036	Coffee concentrate	CFTRI
ABP	09	Coffee beverage: Carbonated (incl. Coffee concentrate)	CFTRI
ABP	042	Coffee/Tea whitener	NRDC
ABP	045	Flavour blend: Cola	NRDC
ABP	048	Flavour blend: Organe and lime/lemon	NRDC
ABP	051	Flavour tea	CFTRI
ABP	054	Instant tea	CFTRI
ABP	057	Lactic beverage: Cereal based	CFTRI
ABP	060	Liquid fruits (clarified fruit juice-Banana, grapes, guava, cashew)	CFTRI
ABP	063	Malted beverage	NRDC
ABP	066	Toned milk: with vegetable protein	CFTRI

Disinfestation Processes

ADP	068	Cockroach Trap: Design and Bait formulation	CFTRI
ADP	069	Durobase formulation	NRDC
ADP	072	Durofume: Process and Formulation	NRDC
ADP	075	Lindane and by-products	NRDC
ADP	078	Methyl bromide	NRDC
ADP	081	Minifume tablets	NRDC
ADP	084	Pest-proof emulsion	NRDC
ADP	085	Pheromone Traps: for T. castaneum	CFTRI

Equipment and Machinery

AEM	087	Citrus juice extractor	NRDC
AEM	090	Double effect evaporator	NRDC
AEM	093	Hot air drier: Cabinet/tunnel type of Arecanut, Cardamom Cashew kernel, Desiccated coconut, Raisins	CFTRI
AEM	096	Maize mill system	CFTRI
AEM	099	Mini grain mill	CFTRI
AEM	102	Mini rice mill	CFTRI
AEM	105	Mini wheat mill	CFTRI
AEM	108	Modern dhal mill system	NRDC
AEM	111	Parboiling plant: Paddy	CFTRI
AEM	114	Rice bran stabilising systems	NRDC
AEM	115	Roller flaker	CFTRI
AEM	117	Single effect evaporator: 1000 kg/500 kg evaporation/hr	CFTRI

Fruit and Vegetable Products

AFV	120	Fruit bars: Mango, Banana,	NRDC
AFV	123	Fruit Cereal: Mango, Apple, Banana	CFTRI
AFV	126	Fruit juice concentrate/paste Mango, Pineapple, Apple, Orange, Tomato	CFTRI
AFV	129	Fruit juice powder: Mango, Banana, Guava, Tomato	CFTRI

AFV	132	Fruits/vegetables dehydration: Grapes, Banana, Onion, Potato, Peas	CFTRI
AFV	135	Instant pickles: Mango, Lime	NRDC
AFV	138	Jam: continuous production	NRDC
AFV	141	Papain: Crude, IP, BPC, Concentrate	NRDC
AFV	144	Pectin: from pectinous materials	NRDC
AFV	147	Strained Babyfoods: wet or dry Fruit, Vegetable, Meat, Egg	CFTRI
Cereal Product			
ACP	150	Biscuit formulations: Cocoa, Cocoa cream, Nutro, High protein	CFTRI CFTRI
ACP	153	Cereal flakes: Rice	CFTRI
ACP	154	Cereal flakes: Jowar	CFTRI
ACP	156	Instant Tradition Foods: [Each] Bisi bele bhath, Puliogre, [All] Sambar, Rasam, Pongal, Urd Bhath, Imli-Poha	CFTRI CFTRI
ACP	159	Ready mix: Snacks and sweets [Each Idli, Vada, Dosa, Chakli, [All] Jamoon, Jilebi, Cake, Maddur Vada, Pakoda	CFTRI CFTRI
Microbial and Fermentation Products			
AMF	162	Alcohol Banana, Cashew apple, Mahua flowers, Grapes	CFTRI
AMF	165	Alcohol: Tapioca (cassava)	NRDC
AMF	268	Baker's yeast	NRDC
AMF	171	Food enzymes: [Each] Fungal Amylase, Amyloglucosidase Pectinase [All]	CFTRI CFTRI
Plantation and Spice Products			
APS	174	Annatto dye: preparations	NRDC
APS	177	Citrus oils: deterpenation	NRDC
APS	180	Cocoa products: Cocoa mass, Cocoa butter, Cocoa powder	NRDC
APS	183	Compounded asafoetida	NRDC
APS	184	Coriander dhal 'Supari'	CFTRI

APS	186	Food colours: Natural	NRDC
APS	189	Garlic powder	NRDC
APS	192	Kokum: Concentrate and Powder	NRDC
APS	195	Mustard powder	NRDC
APS	198	Pepper: White and dehydrated Green	NRDC
APS	199	Plant growth Promoter:	CFTRI
APS	201	Spice oils: Pepper, Ginger, Cardamom	NRDC
APS	204	Spice oleoresins: Pepper, Ginger,	NRDC
APS	207	Tamarind: Concentrate and Powder	NRDC
Protein and Speciality Foods			
APE	213	Infant food: High protein and /or optimised 12% protein	NRDC
APF	214	Infant food: Lactose-free (Milk based)	CFTRI
APF	215	Mustard/Rape seed-integrated processing	CFTRI
APF	216	Protein isolate: Groundnut, Soya	NRDC
APF	219	Sesame: Dehulling	NRDC
APF	220	Sunflower seed-beneficiation	CFTRI
APF	222	Weaning food: roller dried	NRDC
Animal Products			
AAP	225	Animal food: formulations Cattle, Poultry	CFTRI
AAP	228	Bacon and Ham: Preparation	CFTRI
AAP	231	Bactopeptone: from fish waste	CFTRI
AAP	234	Chicken products: Sticks, Curried, Tandoori, Kabab	CFTRI
AAP	237	Egg: Extension of shelf-life-Egg washing and Egg coating	NRDC
AAP	240	Fish pickles	CFTRI
AAP	243	Fish Products: Freezing	CFTRI
AAP	246	Fish waste silage	CFTRI
AAP	249	Mackerel: Salt curing, drying	CFTRI

AAP	252	Meat soup cube	CFTRI
AAP	255	Meat tenderisation	CFTRI
AAP	258	Mutton: conditioning of	CFTRI
AAP	261	Sausage casings: Natural	CFTRI
AAP	264	Sausage: Preparation-Meat/Fish/Chicken/Pork	CFTRI
Beverage Products			
ABP	267	Ginger cocktail	CFTRI
ABP	270	Groundnut milk/curd	CFTRI
ABP	273	Honey beverage: bottling	CFTRI
ABP	276	Orange comminuted: Beverage base	CFTRI
ABP	279	Pan supari nectar	CFTRI
ABP	282	Sugarcane juice beverage: bottling	CFTRI
Cereal Products			
ACP	285	Curing of new paddy	CFTRI
ACP	288	Maize based preparations	CFTRI
ACP	291	Parboiling of paddy: Dry heat or Hot soak method	CFTRI
ACP	294	Paushtik atta	CFTRI
ACP	297	Refined millet flour	CFTRI
Confectionary and Convenience Foods			
ACC	300	Baking powder	CFTRI
ACC	303	Biscuit production: Salt and Sweet	CFTRI
ACC	306	Bread: production	CFTRI
ACC	309	Bread: production	CFTRI
ACC	309	Jamun: canning of	CFTRI
ACC	312	Rasogolla: canning of	CFTRI
ACC	315	Rasogolla: Soy based	CFTRI
Equipment and Machinery			
AEM	318	Air classsifier	CFTRI
AEM	321	Heat scaler: Continuous	CFTRI
AEM	324	Leaf cup machine	CFTRI

AEM	327	Paddy crack detector	CFTRI
AEM	330	Papad press (Hand or Pedal operated)	CFTRI
AEM	333	Pest proofing machine	CFTRI
AEM	336	Simple Pulse Dehusking machine: (hard operated or mechanised)	CFTRI
AEM	339	Strip lacquering machine	CFTRI
AEM	342	Triple roller extractor	CFTRI
AEM	345	Vegetable slicer	CFTRI
AEM	348	Vinegar generator	CFTRI
AEM	351	Volumetric filler	CFTRI

Fruit and Vegetable Products

AFV	354	Anti fungal paste	CFTRI
AFV	357	Curried vegetables: Canning of	CFTRI
AFV	360	Fruit Jams and Jellies: preparation	CFTRI
AFV	363	Fruit Preserves and Candies: Preparation	CFTRI
AFV	366	Fruit syrups and squashes: Preparation	CFTRI
AFV	369	Fruit toffees	CFTRI
AFV	372	Fruits and vegetables: canning of	CFTRI
AFV	375	Fruits and vegetables: refrigeration and freezing	CFTRI
AFV	378	Litchi products: Squash and canned	CFTRI
AFV	381	Mango ripening: Accelerated process	CFTRI
AFV	384	Muskmelon seeds: Dehulling	CFTRI
AFV	387	Mushroom culture	CFTRI
AFV	390	Pickles and chutneys: preparation	CFTRI
AFV	393	Pineapple: Osmo-air dried	CFTRI
AFV	396	Potato products: Flour, Flat dry chips	CFTRI
AFV	397	Potato Wafers/Chips: direct process	CFTRI
AFV	398	Potato Slices/Wafers:	CFTRI

		dehydrated and chips	
AFV	399	Tomato products: preparation (including ketchup concentrate from tomato paste)	CFTRI
AFV	402	Wax emulsion: formulation and use	NRDC
Microbial and Fermentation Technology			
AMF	405	Aflatoxin decontamination	CFTRI
AMF	408	Vinegar generation: Natural (incl. generator design) from Jaggery, Toddy, Pineapple waste	
Plantation and Spice Products			
APS	411	Cardamom: fixation of green colour	CFTRI
APS	414	Cherry coffee: monsooning	CFTRI
APS	423	Desiccated coconut	CFTRI
APS	426	Ginger: dehydration/bleaching	CFTRI
APS	429	Red chillies: dryin of (incl. dipsol formulation)	
APS	432	Red chillies: fractionation	CFTRI
APS	435	Turmeric: curing and polishing	CFTRI
APS	438	Wnlnut: processing	CFTRI
Protein and Speciality Foods			
APF	441	Balahar	CFTRI
APF	444	Composite protein food	CFTRI
APF	447	Groundnut flour: Edible	CFTRI
APF	450	Leaf protein: Concentrate	CFTRI
APF	453	Malted weaning food	CFTRI
APF	456	Multipurpose food	CFTRI
APF	459	Soya flour: Edible	CFTRI

APPENDIX-III

CONCESSIONS AND RELAXATIONS FOR WOMEN EMPLOYEES IN GOVERNMENT SERVICE

The Constitutional rights and privileges aimed at the upliftment of women become meaningful if these are translated into Government policies which enable women to come out of their hitherto enforced status of being left behind by the intermissions of certain upheavals in our history. It is this consciousness and concern which has been the guiding fore of some of the Government orders specially relating to employment of women in Govt. and some special provisions facilitating their dual role as mother/wife and a full-time employee.

(1) *Age relaxation for widows and women separated from their husbands for appointment in Groups C and D posts:*

For purpose of appointment to Groups C and D posts under the Central Government filled through direct recruitment the upper age limit in the case of widows, divorced women and women judicially separated from their husbands who are not remarried is relaxed upto the age of 35 years (upto 40 years for members of Scheduled Castes/Scheduled Tribes) by invoking the provisions in the relevant recruitment rules. There shall be no relaxation of educational qualifications or method of recruitment.

[Department of Personnel and Administrative Reforms O.M. No. 25012/13/79-Estt. (D) dated 19.1.1980]

(2) *Exemption from requirement of educational qualifications in respect of widows of deceased Government servants appointed on compassionate grounds to post of peons:*

The widows of deceased Government servants appointed as peons on compassionate grounds are exempted from requirements of the educational qualifications as laid down in the Ministry of Home Affairs O.M. No. 13/1/51-NGS dated 16.11.1951.

[Department of Personnel and Administrative Reforms O.M. No. 49019/6/80-Estt. (C) Dated 19.10.1982]

(3) *Initial appointment of women candidates in a State of pregnancy and declared as temporarily medically unfit:*

The Department of Personnel and Administrative Reforms O.M. No. 14034/5/75-Estt. (D) dated 19.7.1976 had provided that a women candidate who, as a result of tests is found to be pregnant of twelve weeks standing or over should be declared temporarily unfit and her appointment held in abeyance until the confinement was over. She was required to get herself re-examined for a fitness certificate six weeks after the date of confinement.

It has not been decided that it shall no longer be necessary to declare a women candidate as "temporarily unfit" if she is found to be pregnant during the medical examination before appointment against posts which do not prescribe any elaborate training i.e. they can be appointed straight-away on the job. However, where pregnant women are to be appointed against posts carrying hazardous nature of duties e.g. in Police Organisation etc. and they have to complete a period of training as a condition of service, the existing instructions laid down in the O.M. dated 19.7.1976 will continue to apply.

[Department of Personnel and Administrative Reforms O.M. No. 14034/4/84-Estt. (D) Dated 13.2.1985]

(4) *Representation of women members on various Committee/Boards concerned with Selection:*

The working group of the National Committee on the International Women's Year at its second meeting held during August, 1975 made the following recommendations:

"The various bodies which are concerned with the selection of candidates are generally composed of men. There are instances to show that there is discrimination against women which is a part of the prevailing attitude. The removal of such an attitude will take some time. Meanwhile, however, it seems necessary that women members should be appointed to the various bodies concerned with Selection."

After carefully considering the above recommendation it has been decided that while it may not be possible to ensure that various bodies/boards concerned with selection of candidates should always have a women representative on them, care should be taken by the appointing authorities to ensure that there is no discrimination against women candidates on grounds of sex, in the matter of selections made by such bodies/boards.

[Department of Personnel and Administrative Reforms O.M. No. 35021/5/74-Estt. (C) dated 17.12.1975].

The matter has been further considered and it has been decided that the Ministries/ Departments etc. should endeavour to nominate, to the extent possible, a lady officer on the Selection Boards/Committees concerned with selection of candidates for various posts/ services under them. In cases where a good number of lady candidates are expected to appear, no effort should be spared in finding a lady officer for inclusion in the Selection Board/Committee. In the event of such an officer not being available in the Ministry/ Department itself there is no objection to nominating a lady officer from any other office at the same station.

[Department of Personnel and Training O.M. No. 35021/1/85-Estt. (C) dated 8.11.1985].

(5) *Posting of husband and wife at same station:*

To enable women to continue with their jobs as also to lead a normal family life and to ensure the education and welfare of their children, the Department of Personnel and Training has issued an O.M. No. 28034/7/86-Estt. (A) dated the 3rd April, 1986 impressing upon the administrative authorities to post husband and wife at the same station as far as possible. A portion of this O.M. is reproduced below:

> "The question of formulation of policy regarding the posting at the same place of husband and wife who are in Government service or in the service of Public Sector Undertakings has been raised in Parliament and other forums on several occasions. Government's position has been that requests of Government servants and employees of Public Sector Undertakings for posting at the same station usually receive sympathetic consideration, and that each is decided on merits, keeping in view the administrative requirements."

The Government of India have given the utmost importance to the enhancement of women's status in all sectors and all walks of life. Strategies and policies are being formulated and implemented by different Ministries of the Central Government to achieve this end. It is also considered necessary to have a policy which can enable women employed under the Government and the Public Sector Undertakings to discharge their responsibilities as wife/mother on the one hand, and productive workers on the other, more effectively. It is the policy of the Government that as far as possible and within the constraints of administrative feasibility, the husband and wife should be posted at the same station to enable them to lead a normal family life and to ensure the education and welfare of their children.

(6) *Recruitment of women candidates to Central Civil Services/Posts-No. Discrimination:*

Recently a few instances came to the notice of the Government where the advertisements for filling up of vacancies in certain categories of posts contained a stipulation that women were not eligible for the post and the reasons given by the organisation was that plant for which the posts were advertised was located at some distance from the city and operated in shifts for extended hours and women candidates might not be able t reach the place of work and return there from at odd hours by the public transport. This was not considered proper and it was impressed upon the Ministries/Departments that whatever may be the reasons, this apart from being reminiscent of underestimating the potential and women is clearly violative of Article 16 of the Constitution according to which no citizen shall on the grounds only of sex be ineligible for, or discriminated against in respect of any employment or office under the State. The proper course of action where some difficulty is envisaged in the matter of availability of public transport of any other difficulties for that matter would be to remove those difficulties by providing necessary facilities rather than excluding women candidates from recruitment.

[O.M. No. 14034/10/86-Estt. (D) dated 5.6.1986].

It was also reiterated that the above instructions contained in O.M. No. 14034/10/86-Estt. (D) dated the 5th June, 1986 should be followed scrupulously and any action amounting to violation of the instructions dated the 5th June, 1986 will be adversely commented upon in their confidential reports.

[Department of Personnel and Training's O.M. No. 14034/10/86-Estt. (D) dated 12.8.86].

(7) *Maternity Benefits:*

The grant of maternity leave and the payment of cash benefits are included in all the Acts namely Factories Act, 1948 Mines Act 1952 and Bidi and Cigar Workers (Conditions of Employment) Act, 1966. In order to bring uniformity in scope, qualifying conditions and rates of benefits, the Maternity Benefits Act 1961, was passed which applies to factories, mines and plantation except those factories or establishments which are covered by the Employees State Insurance Scheme.

The Central Government employees are, by and large, governed by the Central Civil Service (Leave) Rules, 1972 and under these rules the female Government employees are at present entitled to maternity leave for a period of 90 days from the date of its commencement. During such period she shall be paid leave salary equal to the pay drawn immediately before proceeding on leave.

Maternity Leave is also admissible in cases of miscarriage including abortion subject to the condition that—

(a) the leave does not exceed six weeks; and,
(b) the application for the leave is supported by a medical certificate as required under the rules.

Abortion induced under the Medical Termination of Pregnancy Act, 1971 is also considered as a case of abortion for the purpose of grant of maternity leave under the Central Civil Services (Leave) Rules, 1972.

Maternity leave may be combined with leave of any kind. Any leave including commuted leave for a period not exceeding sixty days applied for in continuation of maternity leave may also be granted without production of medical certificate. Leave in further continuation of 90 days plus 60 days is also admissible on production of medical certificate for the illness of the female Government servant or for the illness of the newly born baby to the effect that the condition of the ailing baby warrants mother's personal attention and that her presence by the baby's side is absolutely necessary.

Source: Women Employees in Government, Monograh No. 3086, Department of Personnel and Training, Government of India, New Delhi. pp. 6-12.

APPENDIX-IV

SPECIAL COMPONENTS FOR WOMEN UNDER RURAL DEVELOPMENT PROGRAMMES

Development of rural areas is not possible without the development of women who from almost half of the total population. In order to bring them into the mainstream of development, almost all the programmes carried out by this Ministry are distinguished from other Welfare Schemes and have special components for women, as it was felt that unless their economic status is raised, no tangible improvement in their status can be brought about.

The Constitution (73rd Amendment) Act, 1992 envisages important role for women in the new Panchayati Raj set up. Now not only the Panchayati Raj Institutions would always be there is the position, it will also have at least one third women members. And this reservation of one third for women is not confined to seats in panchayats but would also apply to the offices of chairpersons of panchayats at various levels. All these would not only afford greater opportunity to women to participate in the public affairs, it would also require greater amount of the training to those members so as to enable them to discharge their responsibilities more professionally and successfully. Accordingly, the Ministry of Rural Development is giving emphasis on conducting training and awareness generation programmes on Panchayati Raj for women.

The Ministry of Rural Development have several schemes for providing better opportunities to the women in rural India. Forty per cent of the total assistance under IRDP and 40 per cent of trainees under TRYSEM are reserved for women. Thirty per cent of the employment opportunities under JRY have also been reserved for women. Under the IAY, priority is given to widows and unmarried women in allotment of houses. In all cases, houses are allotted in the name of women members of the household or in the joint names of husband and wife. Training is being given to enable them to play an active role in using handpumps for supply of drinking water.

Priority in Loans

Under the Integrated Rural Development Programme (IRDP) which aims at helping poor people with annual income up to Rs. 11,000 or less, 40 per cent of the total assistance is reserved for women. Under IRDP assistance is given to the rural poor through Government subsidy and bank credit to help them set up their own business enterprises in manufacturing, weaving, food processing and many other village based industries or agricultural activities and services. Consumption loans up to Rs. 1,000 are also provided by the District Rural Development Agencies and are aimed at protecting the poor people from exploitation by money lenders. Coverage of women has been consistently rising under IRDP from merely 10 per cent of total beneficiaries in 1985-86 to almost 34 per cent in 1993-94. Over 8,54,000 women were assisted under the Integrated Rural Development Programme during 1993-94 and over 3,30,000 women were assisted during 1994-95 up to November 1994.

Under the scheme for training of Rural Youth for Self-Employment (TRYSEM), 40 per cent of the trainees must be women. (TRYSEM), 40 per cent of the trainees must be women. TRYSEM training is given through Industrial Training Institutes or master craftspersons. It has helped many rural women set up their own enterprises with IRDP assistance after the training. Over 14.22 lakhs women have been covered under TRYSEM since inception of the programme. This includes about 45 thousand women who were imparted training under TRYSEM during 1994-95 up to November 1994.

DWCRA Programme

Under this scheme poor village women are organised in groups of 10 to 15 for taking up economic activities suited to their skills, aptitude and local conditions. All the districts have been covered under DWCRA. Every DWCRA group is assisted through IRDP subsidy and loan, TRYSEM training and a revolving fund.

Through the strategy of group formation, this programme aims to improve women's access to basic services like health, education, child care, nutrition, water and sanitation.

The revolving fund has been increased from Rs. 15,000 to Rs. 25,000 in the case of DWCRA groups which have been established and wish to diversify. Emphasis is now being laid on recognising occupational groups such as women bonded labourers, quarry workers, firewood gatherers as DWCRA groups. Thrift and Credit activities also are not an important part of DWCRA group activities. As many as 86,774 groups of women have been formed with membership of over 14.96 lakh women since inception of the programme in 1982-83. During 1994-95 up to November 94 over 17,900 groups were formed benefiting 3.12 lakhs women.

Special Provisions

Under the Indira Awaas Yojana (IAY) there is a provision of giving houses free of cost to the poorest of the rural poor. Under IAY, priority is given to widows and unmarried women. IAY houses, in all cases are allotted in the names of the women members of the household or in the joint names of husband and wife.

Under the Jawahar Rozgar Yojana (JRY), 30 per cent of the employment opportunities are reserved for women. JRY aims at providing additional gainful employment for the rural unemployed and underemployed. This is done by taking up works as per the basic requirements of the local population. Of the total employment generated during the last five years the share of women has been 1,035.93 million mandays which was 24.19 per cent of the total employment generation. During the current year, the share of women in the employment generation so far has been about 25 per cent.

The revised Central Rural Sanitation Programme (CRSP) provides for construction of sanitary latrines for rural households. This essential step towards clean living also ensures privacy to women. Separate bathing and washing places are also provided for women.

Up to 10 per cent of the annual funds can be utilised to provide public latrines in selected villages during the plan period, where the panchayats/charitable trusts/NGOs offer to construct and maintain village complexes exclusively for use by women.

Training is being given to enable women play an active role in using and maintaining handpumps for supply of drinking water. They are also represented in village level committees and are actively involved in selection of sites for handpumps and other sources.

The Council for Advancement of People's Action and Rural Technology (CAPART) provides funds to voluntary agencies working or rural women's welfare. CAPART also works to promote rural technology that makes work easier and quicker for women in their household and outdoor activities. So far over 1,300 DWCRA projects have been assisted by the CAPART since inception. A sum of Rs. 16.95 crores has been released by the CAPART to voluntary agencies for implementation of DWCRA projects.

Share of Women in Employment Generated under Poverty Alleviation Programmes in Rural Areas

Year	*Total Number of families assisted under self-employment programmes (IRDP+TRYSEM)* (Million Families)*	*Percent share of women*	*Total No. of mandays generated under wage employment programmes (NREP + RLEGP + JRY)** (Million Families)*	*Percent share of women*
1985-86	3.2	11.52	564.0	9.67
1986-87	3.9	16.61	701.5	15.47
1987-88	4.4	20.77	674.9	18.05
1988-89	4.0	24.53	691.5	29.75
1989-90	3.6	27.00	864.4	22.04
1990-91	3.1	32.29	873.8	24.64
1991-92	2.8	35.20	809.2	24.01
1992-93	2.3	35.22	782.1	24.78
1993-94	2.8	35.44	1023.7	23.31

Source: Department of Rural Employment and Poverty Alleviation, Ministry of Rural Areas and Employment, New Delhi.

* IRDP: Integrated Rural Development Programme

TRYSEM: Training of Rural Youth for Self-Employment

** NREP: National Rural Employment Programme (during 1985-89)

RLEGP: Rural Landless Employment Guarantee Programme (during 1985-89)

JRY: Jawahar Rozgar Yojana (since 1989-90)

Quality control through grading and marking of agricultural products is of great benefit to the consumers. The quality certification scheme 'Agmark' has resulted in increased quality awareness among the consumers. Consumer organisations with women representatives have been empowered to inspect Agmark products and draw samples for testing.

The States have been asked to issue joint pattas where ceiling surplus land is distributed to landless poor families. This will significantly improved women's access to land.

Share of women in employment generated under Rural development poverty alleviation programmes is given in the table on last page.

APPENDIX-V

TRADITIONAL AND NON-TRADITIONAL TRADES ADOPTED UNDER VARIOUS EMPLOYMENT-CUM-TRAINING PROGRAMMES

I. MINISTRY OF LABOUR

A. Vocational Training Programmes of Women at National Vocational Training Institute (NVTI) and Regional Vocational Training Institute (RVTIs)

(a) Basic Skills

1. Dress making
2. Hair and Skin Care
3. Secretarial Practice
4. Instrument Mechanic
5. Electronics
6. Computer Training
7. Architectural Draughtmanship
8. Desk Top Publishing
9. Cane and Bamboo Work

(b) Advanced Skills

1. Dress Making
2. Embroidery and Needle Crart
3. Secretarial Practice
4. T.V. Set Repairs and Servicing
5. Hair and Skin Care
6. Business Service
7. Architectural Assistant

(c) Instructional Skills

1. Instructor (General/POT)

B. Engineering and Non-Engineering Trades for Admission Under CTIs/ITIs: Engineering Trades

1. Welder (Gas and Electric)
2. Moulder
3. Mechanic (Diesel)
4. Plumber
5. Mason (Building Construction)
6. Upholsterer
7. Machanic Tractor

22. Turner
23. Machinist
24. Mechanic
25. Electrician
26. Instrument Mechanic
27. Elecroplater
28. Mech. (Radio and T.V.)

8. Sheet Metal Worker
9. Forger and Heat Treater
10. Carpenter
11. Pump Mechanic
12. Phototype Setter and Desktop Publishing Operator
13. Plastic Processing Operator
14. Desktop Publishing
15 Data Operation and Computer Software
16. Pattern Maker
17. Painter General Scheme
18. Wireman
19. Mechanic (Motor Vehicle)
20. Mechanic Agricultural Mechiner
21. Fitter
29. Wireless Mechanic-cum-Operator
30. Tool and Die Maker
31. Tool and Die Maker (Dies and Moulds)
32. Refrigeration and Air Conditioning Mechanic
33. Machinist (Grinder)
34. Millwright/Maintenance Mechanic
35. Draughtsman (Mechanical)
36. Draughtsman (Civil)
37. Surveyor
38. Electronic Mechanic (Chemical Plant)
39. Attendant Operator
40. Attendant Operator
41. Laboratory Asst. (Chemical Plant)

Non-Engineering Trades

1. Hand Weaving of Newar, Tape Durries and Carpets
2. Cutting and Tailoring
3. Embroidery and Needle Work
4. Book Binder
5. Cane Willow and Bamboo Worker
7. Weaving Fancy and Furnishing Fabrics
8. Weaving and Woolen Fabrics
12. Dress Making
13. Knitting with Machine
14. Baker and Confectioner
15. Preservation of Fruits and Vegetables
16. Photographer
17. Bleaching, Dyeing and Calico Printing
18. Hand Compositor
19. Stenography (English)

9. Manufacture of footwear
10. Leather Goods Maker
11. Letter Press Machine Minder (Platen and Cylinder)
20. Secretarial Practice
21. Stenography (Hindi)
22. Hair and Skin Care

II. DEPARTMENT OF WOMEN AND CHILD DEVELOPMENT

Traditional Trades

A. Support to Training-Cum-Employment Programme (STEP)

1. Agriculture
2. Small Animal Husbandry
3. Dairying Industries
4. Handlooms
5. Handicrafts
6. Sericulture
7. Khadi and Village
8. Social Forestry

Non Traditional Trades

B. Socio-economic Programmes (SEP)

1. Small Industrial Units
2. Handlooms and Handicrafts
3. Dairy Unit
4. Piggery
5. Sheep and Goat rearing
6. Poultry
7. Bakery

C. Setting up of Employment and Income Generating Training-Cum-Employment-Cum-Production Units (NORAD)

This scheme covers the following trades

1. Soft-toys Making
2. Socks Knitting
3. Readymade Garments
4. Coir Products
5. Turkey Towels (Handlooms)
6. Shawl Weaving
7. Typing and Shorthand
12. Dyeing
13. Printing
14. Weaving
15. Computer Training
16. Terrocotta Ceramic Jewellery
17. Embroidery
18. Electronics

8. Secretarial Courte
9. Leather Garment
10. Screen Printing
11. Bakery
19. Watch assembly
20. Radio-Repair
21. Beautician Course

D. Condensed Courses of Education and Vocational Training (CCE and VT)

III. MINISTRY OF RURAL AREA AND EMPLOYMENT

A. Training of Rural Youth for Self-Employment (TRYSEM)

Some of the common trades under TRYSEM are:

1. Tailoring
2. Embroidery
3. Typing
4. Stenography
5. Computer Operation
6. Radio and T.V. Repair
7. Animal Husbandry
8. Weaving
9. Carpentry
10. Leather work
11. Wood craft
12. Mushroom cultivation
13. Polishing
14. Metal craft
15. Sericulture
16. Electronics

B. Development of Women and Children in Rural Areas (DWCRA)

A list of some income generating activities is given below:

1. Adda leaf making
2. Agarbatti making
3. Bakery
4. Bamboo basket making
5. Bangle basket making
6. Basket making
7. Bed making
8. Bee keeping
9. Beedi making
10. Book binding
11. Brick klin
12. Brooms vending
13. Brush making
14. Goat rearing
15. Gobar stove unit
16. Granitejelly making
17. Gunny bag making
18. Iron boxes
19. Rope making
20. Ruling and printing
21. Salt vending
22. Sericulture unit
23. Sheep rearing
24. Soap making

25. Stone cutting
26. Supari units
27. Candle making
28. Canteen
29. Carpet weaving
30. Chalk making
31. Chappal making
32. Clay rearing unit
33. Plastic works
34. Poultry
35. Popcorn
36. Pottery
37. Printing and dying
38. Quilt making
39. Readymade garments
40. Rice vending
41. Coal making
42. Coconut vending
43. Cut pices centre
44. Dairy
45. Dhobhighat
46. Duckery
47. Embroidery
48. Envelope making
49. Firewood selling
50. Fishery
51. Fish net making
52. Food processing
53. Fruit vending
54. Garland vending
55. Juggery vending
56. Khadi spinning
57. Knitting
58. Lace making
59. Leaf plate making
60. Leather work
61. Lime works
62. Mat making
63. Masla powder making
64. Match making
65. Milch cattle
66. Narwar making
67. Oil extraction
68. Paddy pounding
69. Palm leaf mat making
70. Papad making
71. Paper bag making
72. Piggery
73. Pickles making
74. Tailoring
75. Tiles making unit
76. Toy making unit
77. Tooth powder making
78. Tumeric unit
79. Vegetable growing
80. Weaving
81. Wig making

APPENDIX-VI

CONSTITUTIONAL PROVISIONS FOR WOMEN

The preamble to the Constitution of India resolves to secure to all its citizens:

JUSTICE, Social Economic and political,

LIBERTY of thought, expression, belief, faith and worship;

EQUALITY of status and of opportunity; and to promote among them all.

FRATERNITY assuring the dignity of the individual and the unit and integrity of the Nation.

To attain these national objectives, the Constitution guarantees certain Fundamental Rights to all its citizens. Again the Directive Principles of State Policy enunciated in the Constitution embody the major policy goals of Welfare State. They concretize together with the Fundamental Rights, the vision of a new India socio-political order. While the Fundamental Rights are justiciable and enforceable in courts of Law, the Directive Principles are non-justiciable and non-enforceable in Courts. But the Directive Principles are:

> "nevertheless Fundamental in the governance of the country" and the State is charged with a duty "to (Article 37 of the Constitution).

2. It will be noticed that while the Constitution guarantees certain fundamental rights and freedom such as freedom of speech, protection of life and personal liberty, that may be termed positive rights, there are certain indirect rights such as prohibition of discrimination or denial of equal protection.

3. Indian women are the beneficiaries of these rights in the same manner as Indian men. Article 14 ensures that the State shall not deny to any person equality before the law or the equal protection of the laws within the territory of India. Again Article 15 prohibits discrimination against any citizen on grounds only a religion, race, caste, sex, place of birth, or any of them. However, Article 15(3) empowers the State to make any "special provision for women and children," even in violation of the fundamental obligation of non-discrimination among citizens, inter-alia of sex. This provision has enabled the State to make special provisions for women, particularly in the field of labour legislation like the Factories Act, the Mines Act, etc. These special provisions in favour of women need not be restricted to measure which are beneficial in the strict sense. Thus, it would support a provision like that in Section 497 of the Indian Penal Code which says that in an offence of adultry, though the man is punishable for adultry, the women is not permissible as an abettor (Yusuf *vs.* State of Bombay AIR 1954 S.C. 321). Restrictions upon the right of alienation of women have similarly been upheld (Kaur Vs. Jaggar, AIR 1961 Punj. 489). Similarly reservation of seats

for women in local bodies or educational institutions has been held to be valid in view of the provisions of Article 15(3) Dattarya *vs.* State of Bombay, AIR 1953 Bom. 311 and Sagar Vs. State, AIR 1968 AP 1967).

4. Article 16(1) guarantees that "there shall be equality of opportunity for all citizens in matters relating to employment or appointment to any office under the State." Again Article 16(2) guarantees that "no citizen shall, on grounds only of religion, race, caste, sex, descent, place of birth, residence or any of them, be ineligible for, or discriminated against in respect of, any employment or office under the State." This obligation not to discriminate in matters relating to employment or appointment to any office under the State has thus ensured a significant position and status for Indian women.

5. Coming to the Directive Principles of State Policy, some of them concern women indirectly or by necessary implication. There are a few others which are specific to women. The ones which concern women directly ad have a special bearing on their status are—

— Article 39(a) which directs the State of frame its policy for ensuring that the citizens, men and women equally have the right to an adequate means of livelihood;

— Article 39(d) which directs the State of ensure that there is equal pay for equal work for both men and women.

— Article 39(e) which directs the State to ensure that the health and strength of workers, men and women, and the tender age of children are not abused and that citizens are not forced by economic necessity to enter avocations unsuited to their age or strength; and

— Article 42 which directs the State to make provision for ensuring just and humane conditions of work and maternity relief.

Thus the Fundamental Rights and the Directive Principles are the instruments for attaining our national objective of Justice, Liberty and Equality. By adopting the principle of adult franchise, it seeks to establish a democratic republic by giving the adult population direct or indirect share in the Government. The special attention given to the needs of the women to enable them to enjoy and exercise their constitutional equality of status, along with other special provisions aimed at their participative role in society make the Indian Constitution a "social' document embodying the objectives of a social revolution. It is clear that the Constitution contemplates attainment of an entirely new social order where all citizens are given equal opportunities and no discrimination takes place on the basis of race, religion creed or sex.

Source: Women Employees in Government, Monograph No. 3-86, Department of Personnel and Training, Government of India, New Delhi, pp. 3-5.

APPENDIX-VII

LEGISLATIVE MEASURES

To safeguards the various constitutional rights, the State has enacted the following women-specific and women-related legislations to protect women against social discrimination, violence and atrocities and also to prevent social evils like child marriages, dowry, rape practice of Sati, etc. *The Equal Remuneration Act of 1976* provides for equal pay to men and women for equal work. *The Hindu Marriage Act of 1955* amended in 1976 provides the right for a girl to repudiate a child marriage before attaining maturity whether the marriage has been consummated or not. *The Immoral Traffic (Prevention) Act of* 1956 as amended and renamed in 1986 makes the sexual exploitation of male or female, a cognizable offence. An amendment brought in 1984 to the *Dowry Prohibition Act of 1961* made women's subjection to cruelty a cognizable offence. The second amendment brought in 1986 makes the husband or in-laws punishable, if a woman commits suicide within 7 years of her marriage and it has been proved that she has been subjected to cruelty. Also, a new criminal offence of *'Dowry Death* has been in corporated in the Indian Penal Code. *The Child Marriage Restraint Act of 1976* raises the age for marriage of a girl to 18 years from 15 years and that of a boy to 21 years and makes offences under this act are cognizable. *The Factories Act of 1948* (amended upto 1976) provides for establishment of a creche where 30 women are employed (including casual and contract labourers). *The Medical Termination of Pregnancy Act of 1971* legalises abortion by qualified professional on humanitarian or medical grounds. Amendments to *Criminal Law 1983* provides for a punishment of 7 years in ordinary cases of rape and 10 years for custodial rape cases. The maximum punishment may go upto life imprisonment. A new enactment of *Indecent Representation of Women (Prohibition) Act of 1986* and the *Commission of Sati (Prevention) Act, 1987* have also been passed to protect the dignity of women and prevent violence against them as well as their exploitation.

Policies Advocating Women's Concerns

In addition to the women-specific and women-related policies enunciated in various plan documents, the Government has also been creating a policy enabling environment in which women's concerns can be reflected, articulated and redressed by the Government, the Voluntary Sector and the Corporate World. As part of this effort, many policy instruments have been brought forth, over the years, leading to Action Plans and programmes in several spheres. Some of the important policy-guiding documents include—*The National Plan of Action for Women* adopted in 1976 became a guiding document for the development of women till 1988 when a *National Perspective Plan for Women* was formulated. *The National Perspective Plan for women (1988-200)* drafted by a Core-Group of experts is more or less a long-term policy document advocating a holistic approach for the development of women. *Sharam Shạkti—the Report of the National Commission on Self-employed Women and Women in Informal Sector (1988)* examines the entire gamut of issues facing women in he unorganised sector and makes a number of recommendations for he betterment of women in the

Informal Sector relating to employment, occupational hazards, Legislative protection, training and skill development, entrepreneurship development, marketing and credit etc.

1. Women and Employment in Kent, 1961-1977[1]

During the 1960s and 1970s the number of employees in employment in the county of Kent increased by approximately 54,000, reaching 508,392 in 1977. Almost all of this increase was the result of more women in employment.

There were also important shifts in the relative importance of the main industrial sectors. In the county as a whole, the *primary* sector's share of all employees in employment dropped from 9.4 per cent in 1961 to 4.6 per cent in 1977. The *construction* sector also lost a small part of its share in the county's employment, the percentage dropping from 6.6 to 5.7 per cent over the same period. The *manufacturing* sector witnessed a growth in its relative importance during the 1960s, but lost this during the 1970s: it accounted for 26.8 per cent of employees in employment in 1961, 30.3 per cent in 1971 and 26.7 per cent in 1977. The *service* sector contrasted with the other sectors, as would be expected from experience in Britain as a whole, showing a steady increase, from 57.0 per cent in 1961 to 63.0 per cent in 1977.

In Kent, women were markedly less well represented than men in both the *manufacturing* and *construction* sectors. In 1961, 18 per cent of female workers were employed in manufacturing, compared with 31.6 per cent of male workers; in 1976 the figures were 17.9 and 33.8 respectively. The construction sector employed a mere 0.7 per cent of female workers in 1961, and only 1.1 per cent and 9.6 per cent. The *primary* sector contained 9.2 per cent of all male workers and 9.8 per cent of all female workers in 1961, and by 1976 the percentages were 5.0 and 4.1 respectively. Throughout the period, the overwhelming majority of female workers were employed in the *service* sector. This contained 71.4 per cent of employed women in 1961 and 76.9 per cent in 1976. Although it was also the largest employer of male labour, men's concentration here was less marked than women's: 48.7 per cent in 1961 and 51.5 per cent in 1976.

More detailed figures (referring to the three Employment Office Areas, Canterbury, Maidstone, and Hence Bay/Whitstable) are available from the Annual Census of Employment, and these offer a picture of the relative importance of the various sectors in the areas from which respondents were drawn for the present study.

Absolute numbers of total female workers employed increased in all three areas between 1961 and 1976. In Canterbury the increase was 3,530 (37.4 per cent0, in Herne Bay/Whitstable 1,060 (34.7 per cent) and in Maidstone 7,959 (34.5 per cent). These figures are all well above the percentage increase in females employed in Kent as a whole, which was 25.2.

The percentages of female workers employed in the *primary* sector fell markedly during the period, although Herne Bay/Whitstable in any case started in 1961 from a low base, with only 3.9 per cent (122) of its female workers so employed. This dropped to 0.95 per cent (40) in 1976. In Canterbury, female employment in this sector (as a percentage of all female employment) dropped from 15.7 per cent (1,478) to 4.4 per cent (576) and in Maidstone from 19.5 per cent (4,498) to 5.8 per cent (1,804).

The *construction* sector had little importance as an employer of female labour throughout the period, although in all three areas a slight percentage increase is recorded. In canterbury, where this sector was most important as an employer of women, it employed 0.8 per cent (75) of the female workforce in 1961, and 1.2 per cent (151) in 1976. In Maidstone the corresponding figures were 0.4 per cent (97) and 1.1 per cent (337), and in Whitstable/Herne Bay 0.7 per cent (22) and 0.9 per cent (37).

The relative importance of the *manufacturing* sector for female employment presents a more varied picture if the three areas are compared. Only in Canterbury did the importance of the sector for women remain fairly constant: 7.3 per cent (693) of women in this area worked in the manufacturing sector in 1961, 8.2 per cent (960) in 1971, and 7.1 per cent in 1976 (928). In Herne Bay/Whitstable manufacturing industry became much more important for women's manufacturing industry became much more important for women's employment between 1961 and 1971, but this position was not fully maintained: 9.6 per cent (299) of the area's women worker were so employed in 1961, 30.5 per cent (1,114) in 1971 and 21.1 per cent (882) in 1976. In Maidstone, the period began wit a relatively high concentration of women in this sector, 23.7 per cent (5,470) in 1961, but this percentage gradually declined, dropping to 21.8 per cent (5,905) in 1971 and 16.2 per cent (5,032) in 1976. It will be noted that the absolute number of women so employed was not subject to great variation.

TABLE 1

Female and Male Employment in the Service Sector 1961-1976 (As a Percentage of All Female and All Male Employment)

	1961		*1971*		*1976*	
Area	*female %(no.)*	*male %(no.)*	*female %(no.)*	*male %(no.)*	*female %(no.)*	*male*
Kent	71.4 (119,282)	48.7 (140,075)	72.7 (135,431)	49.3 140,948)	76.9 (160,897)	51.5 (149,670)
Canterbury	76.2 (7,186)	61.1 (8,008)	85.3 (9,922)	71.1 (10,308)	87.2 (11,307)	70.9 (11,147)
Herne Bay/ Whitstable	85.7 (2,655)	60.6 (1,959)	66.3 (2,422)	49.0 (2,175)	77.0 (3,219)	48.4 (2,112)
Maidstone	56.4 (13,014)	43.8 (16,258)	69.0 (18,679)	48.3 (20,832)	76.9 (23,865)	57.5 (26,200)

In all three areas, the period began and ended with a high concentration of women workers in the *service* sector. In Canterbury and Maidstone this concentration became more marked as the period progressed, while in Herne Bay/Whitstable the percentage of women employed in this sector dropped between 1961 and 1971, but began to rise again between 1971 and 1976. Table 1 gives the detailed figures, both for female and male employment.

Detailed figures about the occupations of employed women in Kent are not readily available for the whole of our period. However, the 1971 (10 per cent) Sample Census yields data for that one year which may be of interest. The percentages in Table 2 have been calculated from the actual numbers made available to me by Kent County Council. I have included only those occupations in which substantial numbers of women were employed.

Some interesting features can be noted. In all four areas, these occupational groups contained substantial percentages both of all women employees and of married women employees. In the most extreme case, over one third of all employed women in Maidstone were engaged as clerical workers. It is clear that women in these areas of Kent were highly concentrated in a small number of occupations.

Comparison of the percentages for married women with those for all women reveals that there was a greater tendency for the former to be employed in sales occupations (in very case the figure for married women was higher than that for all women), and the same was generally true of 'service, sports and recreation workers,' with the single exception of Whitstale. Conversely, there was a tendency for married women to be under-represented in clerical occupations (again with the exception of Whitstale). This under-representation of married women was also fund in the fourth occupational order, 'professional, technical workers, artists,' although Maidstone and Herne Bay both show very little variation between all women and married women.

TABLE 2

Women's Employment in Selected Areas of Kent, by Marital Status and Selected Occupational Orders, 1971, in Percentages

Occupational order	*Maidstone*		*Caterbury*		*Herne Bay*		*Whitstable*	
	f	*mf*	*f*	*mf*	*f*	*mf*	*f*	*mf*
XXI Clerical workers	33.5	29.9	29.8	24.3	18.4	16.2	26.5	29.0
XXII sales workers	13.4	13.7	17.3	18.4	24.2	25.3	11.0	13.3
XXIII service, sports and recreation workers	22.8	26.6	25.0	27.3	26.7	30.5	29.8	29.0
XXV professional technical workers, artists	14.6	14.7	16.4	12.3	13.5	13.6	9.2	7.2
sum	84.3	84.9	88.5	82.3	82.8	85.6	76.5	78.5

* f - all females; mf = married females.

This general picture is not at odds with the information obtained from individuals in the empirical study. For example, it was frequently the case that women who had worked in clerical occupations before marriage and raising children later turned to other types of work.

As is well known, official data on women's unemployment paints a seriously inadequate picture of the true situation as regards the numbers of women seeking paid work. In 1981, the General Household Survey estimated that 41 per cent of employed married women, and 16 per cent of unemployed non-married women (compared with just 6 per cent of men) were not registered as unemployed. This means that large numbers of married women in particular are excluded from official statistics about both numbers of unemployed women, and rates of female unemployment. It should be noted that the 1981 situation represents the continuation of a marked trend towards registration by unemployed women: in 1975, 70 per cent, and in 1977 53 per cent of unemployed married women did not register. The phasing out of the option for married women to pay reduced National Insurance contributions (since April 1978) has no doubt been partly responsible for this change, a Sinfield (1981) has pointed out. The General Household Survey has also shown that many more women would seek work if good child care facilities were available Indeed, the inadequacies of official data concerning women's unemployment are so severe as to make them virtually useless. This situation has been further exacerbated by recent changes in the method of compiling the figures which now exclude those not claiming benefit. In addition, unemployment rates, broken down by sex and age for local ares, are not publicly available except in specific contexts.[2]

In the face of this inadequate data, it has seemed inappropriate (not to say foolhardy) to attempt a discussion here of trends in women's unemployment in the local labour markets with which the present study is concerned. It is only considered reliable to suggest that in Britain as a whole the decades 1961-81 witnessed a shift from low rates of female unemployment in the 1960s to rapidly accelerating rates in the late 1970s and early 1980s. Others have conclude that:

> 'Many more women are now out of work and their unemployment is lasting longer.... The rapid increase in the numbers of women out of work has been one of the most dramatic changes in unemployment during the last decade.'

(Sinfield 1981:83)

2. Data Collection Details

Standard from the Personal Details

Personal Details (No.—)

1. Name: ....
2. Date of birth: ....

3. Marital status: . . . .
(Show Card: Married, widowed, single, divorced, separated)
4. Have you been married more than once? . . . .
5. How many children do you have? . . . .
6. What are their ages? . . . .
7. Sex of children? . . . .
8. Do all of your children live at home with you? . . . .
9. Are all of these your natural children? (or are an of them adopted, fostered or your husband's children,for example) . . . .
. . . .
10. How many people besides yourself and your children live in your home?...................
Date of Interview . . . .

Outline Interview Schedule

Can you tell me what your job is at present?

What duties does that involved.

How many hours a week do you normally work? Days each week?

Do you ever work extra hours?

When did you first start working for this employer?

Have you been working there continuously since that time?

Have your changed your job or been promoted while you've been there?

If no: Do you think there is any chance of that happening, if you wanted it?

All: How do you feel about that?

If yes to promotion): Would you like to be promoted further?
Why is that?

How would you describe the pay you get in your job?
(show Card 1: excellent; good; fair; poor, very poor).

How easy or difficult do you think it would be to find a similar job in this area with better pay?

(show card 2: very easy; quite easy; quite hard; very hard; don't know).

Apart from your pay, are there any other benefits which go with your job?

What do you particularly *like* about your job and working there?

What do you particularly *dislike* about your job and working there?

How long do you think you will go on working for your present employer?

If you left your job, for any reason, do you think it would be possible to find another job at the moment?

Confirm details of family living at home:

husband, children (if any old enough, have they left school, are they working, do they contribute to family income?),

grandparents (their role in the home: are they above to help with domestic duties—care of children, cooking, cleaning etc., or do they add to mother's duties?), any others.

Do you have any other relatives who live at all near to you whom you see at all often?

Do any of your relatives need your help because they are ill or in from or for any other reason? What kind of help? How much of your time does this take up?

Your parents:

Has your mother ever had a paid job?

What was her occupation?

Did she go ou. to work when your were a child?

What is/was your father's job?

How do you think your parents feel about you having a job at the moment?

Your husband (if any):

Does your husband have a job?

What is his occupation?

Has he always done that job?

How do you think your husband feels about you having this job?

Your marriage:

How old were you when you left school?

When did you get married?

How old were you when your (first) child was born?

(as appropriate, ask about dates of divorce, re-marriage, husband's death, etc.).

Leaving school, first job and subsequent jobs confirm date of leaving school, and age at that time.

Did you obtain any qualifications at school? Details.

What happened to you when you first left school? (e.g. job, college, unemployed).

Did anyone help you or give you advice about what to do when you left school?

Did anyone help you or give your advice about what to do when you left school?

Could you describe your first job? — What you did, what the pay was like, what the people you worked with were like, etc.

Was there anything you particularly liked about that job?

Was there anything you particularly disliked about it?

How did you get the job—advert, job centre, school, parents, etc.?

How long did you stay in that job?

Why did you leave? Probe fully.

For all jobs up to first childbirth gain details of:

nature of work,
how job was obtained,
what liked/disliked about job,
length of time in job,
why left job.

First pregnancy Did you deliberately plan to start your family at that time?

(*if yes,* why did you choose that time?
if no, how did you feel when you found you were pregnant?)

Did you think at all about how starting a family was going to affect your working life in the future?

At that time, did you would return to employment again?

When did you expect that to be?

Going back to work after a break for childbearing What was the first job you did after your child was born?

When did you start the job?

When had you first started to think about coming out to work again?

Why did you want to work again?

How did your family feel about it? (husband, parents, etc.).

What special arrangements did you have to make so that you would be free to come out to work?

Did any of this prove to be a real problem?

To what extent does your husband share in the domestic duties (both running the home and looking after the children)?

Could you give me some examples of the things he does at home?

Ask about any subsequent pregnancies, etc.

Have you ever had to have time off work because of your child(ren)? (illness, breakdown of childcare arrangements, etc.).

How did you feel about doing that?

What was your employer's reaction? (check whether paid, took holiday, given unpaid leave, etc.).

Did you consider making any other arrangements? (e.g. asking friends or relatives to help, your husband staying home, etc.).

Make sure respondent has described all her employment.

Ask of she has ever done any paid work at home.

Use of earnings. I don't want to ask you detailed questions about money, but I would like you to tell me about the kind of things you spend your earnings on — first of all.

Do you think of the money *you* earn as part of the family budget, or as your own independent income?

Which of these things do you spend you own earning on?

(Show Card 3: personal things for yourself (e.g. clothes, makeup, hobbies, etc.); things for your children (clothes, toys, treats, school things); family holidays; car; improving your home (furnishing decorating, domestic appliances, etc.); the normal day-to-day running of your home (food bills, general household goods); entertainment; other items).

If you didn't have to spend less on or go without?

Using the card: could you tell me which group your own take-home pay comes into?

(Show Card 4: weekly pay (after tax, etc., but not including overtime):

A. less than £ 12 per week; B. over £12 but less than £20 per week; C. over £20 but less than £28 per week; D. over £28 but less than £36 per week; E. over £36 but less than £44 per week; F. over £44 but less than £52 per week; G. over £52 but less than £60 per week; H. over £60 but less than £70 per week; I. over £70 but less than £80 per week; J. over £80 but less than £90 per week; K. over £90 but less than £100 per week; L. over £100 per week).

Labour saving devices Some people think the availability of labour-saving devices has made it easier for women with families to go out to work—could you tell me which of the following things you have in your home?

washing machine—automatic; vacuum cleaner; refrigerator; freezer; spindrier; tumble drier; dishwasher; automatic oven (one which times itself); anything else which you think saves time or effort?

Do you think having these things is important in enabling you to cope with having both home and work responsibilities?

Typical Day I'd like you to describe to me a day's work and duties (choose a day when you go out to work) starting from when you get up, through the day until you either sit down and relax or go to bed at the end of the day.

Fatigue/illness Do you think that being a working mother has any effect on your health? What about tiredness?

Attitudes Looking back over your life so far, and the way you have combined being a mother with also having a paid job, do you think this is something which you would like your own daughter to experience in the same way as you have?

If you would like anything to be different for her, what would it be?

Imagine that for some reason you become unemployed (it doesn't matter why) and you are looking for another job. Which of the following, if any, would you look for, and which would be the most important?

(Show Card 5: 1. Work which you have done before; 2. good. pay and benefits; 3. suitable hours for your needs; 4. good holidays; 5. promotion prospects; 6. pleasant people to work with; 7. Interesting and/or demanding work; 8. something quite different from anything you've done before; 9. a job where you could acquire new or different skills).

Is there anything you would look for which isn't on the Card?

How far are you prepared to travel to work?

Unemployment Have you ever registered as unemployed when you have been looking for work?

Do you think you would gain any advantage by doing so?

Do you pay full NI contribution, or the special reduced rate for married women?

Career development Have you ever had to change your own plans for working in order to fit in with you husband's job/career?

If *yes*, how did you feel about that?

Would you be willing to do so (again)?

Statement *Either*

'More and more families nowadays seem to find it necessary to have both husband and wife earning in order to maintain an acceptable standard of living'.

or

'It is increasingly difficult to maintain an acceptable standard of living if there is only one wage coming into the family.'

Do you think the statement is true or false?

Why do you think that should be the case?

How do you feel about it?

Choosing again If you could start again right from when you left school, and you had opportunities for training or education which perhaps you didn't have at the time, do you think you would still do the same, or is there anything else you would like to have done?

Dual responsibilities Do you think there are any ways in which life could be made easier for women who have responsibilities both at home for their families, and at work?

Trade unions Do you belong to a trade union?

Have you ever belonged to (any other) trade union?

if yes to either:

Has anyone ever approached you at work (in any of your jobs) and asked you to join a trade union?

Why did you choose not to join?

Are there any circumstances in which you think you would join a TU?

Does anyone else in your family belong to a TU?

Whether a TU member or not:

What purpose, if any, do you think the TU serves where you work?

What about any other companies in which you have worked?)

Equal Opportunities Legislation During the 1970s there were a number of changes in the law concerning the employment of women—the Equal Pay Act, the Sex Discrimination Act, end the Employment Protection Act, which introduced the clause about maternity leave rights. [Explain] Do you think any of these changes in the law have affected you personally? If yes, in what way?

Do you think they have affected other women?

Do you think it was a good or a bad idea to change the law in the way these acts did:

The Equal Pay Act

The Sex Discrimination Act

Maternity leave

Why do you think that?

Would you be willing to be contacted again, if I wanted to check any details at home, or at work?

(*if yes,* obtain address and telephone number).

Postal Questionnaire

Name . . . .

Employer . . . .

in 1980/1 . . . .

in 1981/2 ....

Occupation

in 1980/1 ....

in 1981/2 ....

Hours Worked Per Week (Normal hours)

in 1980/1 ....

in 1981/2 ....

Periods Out of Employment

Have you had any periods away from work or out of work since you were interviewed in 1980? (Don't include holidays or your own temporary sickness).

Yes/No (delete as applicable)

If Yes, please give details (e.g. how long, reasons, etc.).

....

....

Marital Status

in 1980/1 ....

in 1981/2 ....

Persons Living With You at Home

in 1980/1 ....

in 1981/2 ....

Home

Have you moved house since you were interviewed in 1980/1?

Yes/No (delete as applicable)

If Yes, please give you new address and/or telephone number: ....

....

Thank you very much for your help. The information you have given above is needed for the concluding stages of the research. It will be treated as confidential.

SAMPLE CHRONOLOGY

Respondent Number 26

date	*personal/family events*	*employment, etc.*
1	2	3
Feb. 1942	born Surrey	(Saturdays: shop assistant in Woolworth's before leaving school)

1	2	3
July 1985	left school, went to college	(temp. In London during summer holidays)
Summer 1960	left college	1. typist for London insurance company
Mid 1961		2. secretary to one of the export managers in a London export-import company
1964	married	3. moved to Yorkshire with husband; worked as secretary in building firm (35 hrs pw)
August 1968	husband's employment involved move to Kent	left job 3 because of move; also, expecting first child (three months pregnant) claimed unemployment benefit for three months
(May 1969	birth of first child	
(May 1973	birth of second child	4. Started doing typing at home for husband's company intermittently, holidays etc.
September 1974	first child started school	
1975/76	wanting to start a job, so started second child with childminder one day per week	
February 1976	second child with childminder, experiencing marital difficulties	5. took morning job sorting magazines and newspapers in wholesale newsagents
June/July 1976		gave up job 5 because not enjoying it
October/ November 1976		6. secretarial work in small electronics company—at first 9.30—1.00, later from before 9 till 3.30
end July 1978	finding job 6 too much	left job
end August 1978		7. started part-time job as secretary (local authority) on two-year project, 9.00-2.30 (25 hrs pw)

1	*2*	*3*
September 1978 end July 1980	second child started school	end of project so job 7 finished
summer 1980		(tempted for one week for employer 6)
September 1980		8started clerical job—pricing and ordering goods in wholesale chemist's warehouse (28 hrs. pw)

3. RESPONDENT'S JOB AGE, AND FAMILY SITUATION AT TIME OF INTERVIEW

Name	*Current job*	*Age*	*No. of Children"*	*marital Status*
Alice	hospital domestic	39	3	divorced (c-hab)
Alison	hospital domestic	29	1	divorced
Andrea	telecomms. officer	40	1	married
Angela	administrative clerk	36	1	married (*2nd*)
Anne kitchen assistant		35	2	married
Annette	clerical assistant	27	**	single (co-hab)
Barbara	sales assistant	35	2	married
Beth	kitchen assistant	43	1	married
Brenda	catering assistant	38	2	married (*2nd*)
Carol	sales assistant	33	2	married
Caroline	deputy supervisor (sales)	33	2	married (*2nd*)
Cathy	domestic supervisor	34	3	divorced (*twice*)
Cheryl	sales assistant	36	2	married
Christine	pricing clerk	38	2	married
Clare	sales assistant	39	1	married
Dawn	sales assistant	41	3	married
Doreen	clerical officer	43	4 (1 died)	married

Elizabeth	n/a	30	2	married (*2nd*)
Frances	(student teacher)	32	2	separated
Gail	assistant manager (building society)	30	1	married (*2nd*)
Geraldine	computer clerk	35	1	married
Heather	supervisor (sales)	32	2	married
Helen	domestic supervisor	43	3	married
Hilary	hospital domestic	32	3	divorced
Jackie	secretary	28	2	divorced
Jane	hospital domestic	35	4 (1 died)	divorced
Jenny	supply teacher	27	2	married
June	caretaker and childminder	36	3 (1 died)	married (*2nd*)
Kate	hospital domestic	34	4	separated (*3rd*)
Linda	sales assistant	42	2	married
Lorna	supervisor (sales)	33	1	married
Louise	secretary and clerical assistant	28	1	married
Lucy	sales assistant	38	3	married
Lynne	hospital domestic	25	4	married
Margaret	sales assistant	34	1	married
Margery	sales assistant	29	1	married
Maria	hospital domestic	29	3 (1 died)	divorced
Marion	domestic supervisor	25	1	married
Mary	clerical assistant	39	2	married
Maureen	secretary	31	2	married
Mavis	food packer/butcher's assistant	28	1	single
Meryl	telecomms. officer	32	1	married (*2nd*)
Nancy	domestic supervisor	38	2	married
Olive	hospital domestic	43	3	married
Pat	hospital domestic	35	4	divorced (*co-hab*)

Paula	clerical officer	38	3 (1 died)	divorced
Penny	hospital domestic	42	2	divorced
Pru	hospital domestic	37	2	divorced (*co-hab*)
Rachel	word processor operator	41	1	married
Ruth	cost clerk	32	2	married
Sally	clerical officer	34	2	married
Sandra	hospital domestic	38	3	married
Sara	clerical officer	37	3	married
Sheila	hospital domestic	39	2	married
Shirley	sales assistant	25	1	married
Susan	clerical officer	44	3	divorced (*twice*)
Teresa	deputy supervisor (sales)	44	2	married
Tessa	telephonist	32	2	married (*2nd*)
Tina	catering supervisor	41	3	married
Tracey	kitchen assistant	35	2	separated
Valerie	accounts supervisor	39	3	married
Wanda	driver and car-washer	28	2 (1 adopted)	married
Wendy	sales assistant	37	1	married (*2nd*)
Yvonne	hospital domestic	33	2	married

* all ages

** no natural children, cares for her co-habitant's two children.

NOTES

1. The nature of these tasks has varied historically. See e.g. Oakley (1981) who discusses this point in her chapter on 'Domestic Work.'
2. Baines (1970) estimated that over half a million women and juveniles were employed in textile factories in the United Kingdom in 1856.
   Pinchbeck (1983) demonstrates that girls aged under 20 were strongly represented among female textile employees.
3. Turner (1962) refers to the 'unfair... disproportion between the wages paid to male and female domestic servants' (p. 28). His evidence is confirmed elsewhere by McBride (1976) ('male servants' wages were almost double those of females' (p. 50) and by Horn (1975) whose account includes a detailed appendix on 'Domestic Servant Wage Rates.'
4. The omissions and inadequacies of official employment data are well known. Seasonal workers, part-timers paid 'cash-in-hand,' and home.